W9-BJD-383

Psychology

A Framework for Everyday Thinking

Psychology

A Framework for Everyday Thinking

Scott O. Lilienfeld
Emory University

Steven Jay Lynn
Binghamton University

Laura L. Namy
Emory University

Nancy J. Woolf
University of California at Los Angeles

Allyn and Bacon

Boston • Columbus • Indianapolis • New York • San Francisco • Upper Saddle River
Amsterdam • Cape Town • Dubai • London • Madrid • Milan • Munich • Paris • Montreal • Toronto
Delhi • Mexico City • Sao Paulo • Sydney • Hong Kong • Seoul • Singapore • Taipei • Tokyo

Editorial Director: Leah Jewell
Editor in Chief: Jessica Mosher
Executive Editor: Stephen Frail
Series Editorial Assistant: Kerri Hart-Morris
Director of Development: Sharon Geary
Senior Development Editor: Julie Swasey
Associate Editor: Kara Kikel
Senior Media Editor: Paul DeLuca
Director of Marketing: Brandy Dawson
Executive Marketing Manager: Jeanette Koskinas

Market Development Manager: Maureen Prado Roberts
Production Supervisor: Karen Mason
Cover Designer: John Christiana
Cover Administrator: Kristina Mose-Libon
Production Service: Nesbitt Graphics, Inc.
Manufacturing Buyer: JoAnne Sweeney
Electronic Composition: Nesbitt Graphics, Inc.
Interior Design: Dorling Kindersley, Nesbitt Graphics, Inc.
Photo Research: Katharine S. Cebik

Copyright © 2010 Pearson Education, Inc., publishing as Allyn & Bacon, 75 Arlington Street, Suite 300, Boston, MA 02116.

All rights reserved. Manufactured in the United States of America. This publication is protected by Copyright, and permission should be obtained from the publisher prior to any prohibited reproduction, storage in a retrieval system, or transmission in any form or by any means, electronic, mechanical, photocopying, recording, or likewise. To obtain permission(s) to use material from this work, please submit a written request to Pearson Higher Education, Rights and Contracts Department, 501 Boylston Street, Suite 900, Boston, MA 02116, or fax your request to 617-671-3447. Many of the designations by manufacturers and sellers to distinguish their products are claimed as trademarks. Where those designations appear in this book, and the publisher was aware of a trademark claim, the designations have been printed in initial caps or all caps.

Between the time website information is gathered and then published, it is not unusual for some sites to have closed. Also, the transcription of URLs can result in typographical errors. The publisher would appreciate notification where these errors occur so that they may be corrected in subsequent editions.

While the author and Publisher of this publication have made every attempt to locate the copyright owners of material that appeared on the World Wide Web, they were not always successful. The Publisher welcomes information about copyright owners for uncredited text and photos included in this book. It may be sent to the Permissions Department at the address shown on this page.

Library of Congress Cataloging-in-Publication Data
Psychology : a framework for everyday thinking / Scott O. Lilienfeld . . . [et al.].
　　p. cm.
　ISBN 0-205-65048-1
　1.　Psychology.　I. Lilienfeld, Scott O.
　BF121.P7623 2009
　150--dc22

2009018782

Printed in the United States of America

10　9　8　7　6　5　4　3　2　1　　　[CIN]　13　12　11　10　09

Text and photo credits are on page CR-1, which constitutes a continuation of the copyright page.

Allyn & Bacon
is an imprint of

ISBN-10:　　　0-205-65048-1
www.pearsonhighered.com　　ISBN-13:　978-0-205-65048-4

We dedicate this book to Barry Lane Beyerstein (1947–2007), great scholar and valued friend.

My deepest gratitude to David Lykken, Paul Meehl, Tom Bouchard, Auke Tellegen, and my other graduate mentors for an invaluable gift that I will always cherish: scientific thinking.

—Scott Lilienfeld

To Fern Pritikin Lynn, my heart and my soul.

—Steven Jay Lynn

To my guys: Stanny and the Rodent.

—Laura Namy

To Larry, Lawson, and Ashley.

—Nancy Woolf

Brief Contents

Contents

CHAPTER 5

Learning 150

CHAPTER 6

Memory 186

CHAPTER 13

Psychological Disorders 452

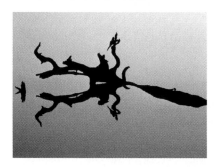

CHAPTER 14

Psychological and Biological Treatments 488

MEET THE
AUTHORS

SCOTT O. LILIENFELD received his B.A. in Psychology from Cornell University in 1982 and his Ph.D. in Clinical Psychology from the University of Minnesota in 1990. He completed his clinical internship at Western Psychiatric Institute and Clinic in Pittsburgh, Pennsylvania, from 1986 to 1987. He was Assistant Professor in the Department of Psychology at SUNY Albany from 1990 to 1994 and now is Professor of Psychology at Emory University. He recently was appointed a Fellow of the Association of Psychological Science and was the recipient of the 1998 David Shakow Award from Division 12 (Clinical Psychology) of the American Psychological Association for Early Career Contributions to Clinical Psychology. Dr. Lilienfeld is a past president of the Society for a Science of Clinical Psychology within Division 12. He is the founder and editor of the *Scientific Review of Mental Health Practice,* Associate Editor of *Applied and Preventive Psychology,* and a regular columnist for *Scientific American Mind* magazine. He has authored or coauthored six books and over 200 journal articles and chapters. Dr. Lilienfeld has also been a participant in Emory University's "Great Teachers" lecturer series, as well as the Distinguished Speaker for the Psi Chi Honor Society at the American Psychological Association and Midwestern Psychological Association conventions.

STEVEN JAY LYNN received his B.A. in Psychology from the University of Michigan and his Ph.D. in Clinical Psychology from Indiana University. He completed an NIMH Postdoctoral Fellowship at Lafayette Clinic, Detroit, Michigan, in 1976 and is now Professor of Psychology at Binghamton University (SUNY), where he is the director of the Psychological Clinic. Dr. Lynn is a fellow of numerous professional organizations, including the American Psychological Association and the American Psychological Society, and he was the recipient of the Chancellor's Award of the State University of New York for Scholarship and Creative Activities. Dr. Lynn has authored or edited 17 books and authored more than 230 journal articles and chapters. Dr. Lynn has served as the editor of a book series for the American Psychological Association, and he has served on 11 editorial boards, including the *Journal of Abnormal Psychology.* Dr. Lynn's research has been supported by the National Institute of Mental Health and the Ohio Department of Mental Health.

LAURA L. NAMY received her B.A. in Philosophy and Psychology from Indiana University in 1993 and her doctorate in Cognitive Psychology at Northwestern University in 1998. She is now Associate Professor of Psychology and Core Faculty in Linguistics at Emory University. Dr. Namy is the editor of the *Journal of Cognition and Development* and serves as the treasurer of the Cognitive Development Society. At Emory, she is Director of the joint major in psychology and linguistics, Director of the Emory Child Study Center, and Associate Director of the Center for Mind, Brain, and Culture. Her research focuses on the origins and development of verbal and nonverbal symbol use in young children, sound symbolism in natural language, and the role of comparison in conceptual development.

NANCY J. WOOLF received her B.S. in Psychobiology at UCLA in 1978 and her Ph.D. in Neuroscience at UCLA School of Medicine in 1983. She is Adjunct Professor in the Department of Psychology at UCLA. Her specialization is behavioral neuroscience, and her research spans the organization of acetylcholine systems, neural plasticity, memory, neural degeneration, Alzheimer's disease, and consciousness. In 1990 she won the Colby Prize from the Sigma Kappa Foundation, awarded for her achievements in scientific research in Alzheimer disease. In 2002 she received the Academic Advancement Program Faculty Recognition Award. She also received a Distinguished Teaching Award from the Psychology Department at UCLA in 2008. Dr. Woolf is currently on the editorial boards of *Science and Consciousness Review* and *Journal of Nanoneuroscience.*

Preface

"What are infants' earliest memories?" "Does watching violence on TV really teach children to become violent?" "Is human intelligence related to brain size?" "Is it dangerous to wake up sleepwalkers?" "Do genes contribute to obesity?" "Is the polygraph test really a 'lie detector'?" "Should we trust most self-help books?"

Every day, our students encounter a host of questions that challenge their understanding of themselves and others. Whether it's from the Internet, television programs, radio call-in shows, movies, self-help books, or advice from friends, our students' daily lives are a steady stream of information—and often misinformation—about intelligence testing, parenting, romantic relationships, mental illness, drug abuse, psychotherapy, and a host of other topics.

Without a framework for evaluating evidence, making sense of these contradictory findings can be a bewildering task for anyone. It's no surprise that the untrained student can find claims regarding memory- and mood-enhancing drugs, the overprescription of stimulants, the effectiveness of Prozac, and the genetic bases of psychiatric disorders, to name only a few examples, to be difficult to evaluate. Moreover, it is hard for those who haven't been taught how to think scientifically to avoid becoming captivated by extraordinary psychological claims that lie on the fringes of scientific knowledge, such as extrasensory perception, subliminal persuasion, astrology, alien abductions, lie-detector testing, hypnosis, handwriting analysis, and inkblot tests, among many others. Yet without a guide for distinguishing good from bad evidence, our students are left to their own devices when it comes to evaluating these claims.

As a result of the media's often misleading coverage, most of our students hold misconceptions regarding many everyday psychological claims, often making it difficult for them to evaluate genuine psychological knowledge. For example, because many students mistakenly believe that memory operates like a tape or video recorder, they may find it difficult to accept findings that some recovered memories of child abuse are false. And because the popular psychology industry rarely provides them with tools for evaluating both ordinary and extraordinary claims about everyday life, most students have a difficult time sorting out what's true from what's not.

A Framework for Applying Scientific Thinking to Everyday Life

Our goal with this text, therefore, is to empower readers to apply scientific thinking to the psychology of their everyday lives. By applying scientific thinking—thinking that helps protect us against our tendencies to make mistakes—we can better evaluate claims about both laboratory research and daily life. By encouraging students to evaluate the bases for claims, they can begin to understand how to think rather than merely what to think. Facts and figures are essential starting points, but they're not enough. We also need skills for evaluating evidence and it's precisely these skills that we teach in this text. In this way, we hope to empower students to develop a more critical eye in understanding the psychological world around them and their place in it.

THE FRAMEWORK IN ACTION

THINKING SCIENTIFICALLY

In Chapter 1, we introduce readers to six key scientific thinking principles that we bring up repeatedly in later chapters. We denote each principle in the margin with a colored "flag" whenever this principle appears in the text. In this way, we repeatedly reinforce these scientific thinking principles in readers' minds as key skills for evaluating claims in scientific research and in everyday life. These "6 Flags of Scientific Thinking" provide a framework for lifelong learning of psychology.

The **Six Flags of Scientific Thinking** represent the six key scientific thinking principles highlighted throughout the text. Each principle is accompanied by a brief question that reminds students of the key issues to consider when evaluating a claim.

What Scientific Thinking Principle Should We Use?	When Might We Use It?	How Do We Use It?
RULING OUT RIVAL HYPOTHESES Have important alternative explanations for the findings been excluded?	You're reading the newspaper and come across the headline: "Study shows depressed people who receive a new medication improve more than equally depressed people who receive nothing."	The results of the study could be due to the fact that people who received the medication expected to improve.
CORRELATION vs. CAUSATION Can we be sure that A causes B?	A finding shows that people eat more ice cream on days when many crimes are committed, and concludes eating ice cream causes crime.	Eating ice cream (A) might not cause crime (B). Both could be due to a third factor (C), such as higher temperatures.
FALSIFIABILITY Can the claim be disproved?	A self-help book claims that all human beings have an invisible energy field surrounding them that influences their moods and well-being.	We can't design a study to disprove this claim.
REPLICABILITY Can the results be duplicated in other studies?	A magazine article highlights a study that shows people who practice meditation score 50 points higher on an intelligence test than those who don't.	We should be skeptical if no other scientific studies have reported the same findings.
EXTRAORDINARY CLAIMS is the evidence as convincing as the claim?	You come across a website that claims that a monster, like Bigfoot, has been living in the American Northwest for decades without being discovered by researchers.	This extraordinary claim requires more rigorous evidence than the claim that people remember more words from the beginning than from the end of a list.
OCCAM'S RAZOR Does a simpler explanation fit the data just as well?	Your friend, who has poor vision, claims that he spotted a UFO while attending a Frisbee tournament.	Is it more likely that your friend's report is due to a simpler explanation—his mistaking a Frisbee for a UFO—than to alien visitation?

FOCUS ON POPULAR PSYCHOLOGY

Throughout the text, we intersperse examples from popular ("pop") psychology so that students can acquire experience in distinguishing fact from fiction in the media, on the Internet, and in conversations with friends. We also provide scientific thinking tools for evaluating a variety of pop psychology claims.

Sprinkled throughout the margins of each chapter we offer several **Factoids**, which present interesting and surprising facts, and **Fictoids**, which present widely held beliefs that are false or unsupported. In both cases, students will find their conceptions and misconceptions of psychology challenged and their perspectives of psychology broadened. These features also underscore a crucial point: Psychology can be fun!

Fact-OID

Some people experience a phenomenon called "jamais vu," French for "never seen," which is essentially the opposite of déjà vu. In jamais vu, the person reports feeling as though a previously familiar experience suddenly seems unfamiliar. Jamais vu is sometimes seen in neurological disorders, such as amnesia (see Chapter 6) and epilepsy (Brown, 2004a, b).

Fict-OID

MYTH: Consuming ice cream or other cold substances too quickly causes pain in our brains.

REALITY: "Brain freeze," as it's sometimes called, doesn't affect the brain at all. It's produced by a constriction of blood vessels in the roof of our mouths in response to intense cold temperatures, followed by an expansion of these blood vessels, producing pain that is felt as a headache.

EMPHASIS ON CORRECTING MISCONCEPTIONS

More broadly, throughout the text we sprinkle a variety of misconceptions often held by introductory psychology students. Equally important, we use many of these misconceptions as starting points for discussions of genuine scientific knowledge. We also present pieces of psychological knowledge that violate common sense, but that are true.

Each chapter contains a MythConceptions box focusing in depth on a widespread psychological misconception. In this way, students will come to recognize that their commonsense intuitions about the psychological world are not always correct and that scientific methods are needed to separate accurate from inaccurate claims.

Popular psychology tells us that twins sometimes develop their own language. Is this fact or fiction?

myth CONCEPTIONS — DO TWINS HAVE THEIR OWN LANGUAGE?

The idea of being a twin has a certain appeal and allure. Twins share their mothers womb, potty train together, and go through school at the same time. It's only natural to expect there to be a special bond between twins. One commonly held belief is that twins invent their own secret language, one only they can understand. This phenomenon is known as **cryptophasia.**

As fascinating as this notion is, the truth is less exotic. Cases of apparent cryptophasia among twins turn out to be a result of phonological impairment and other types of language delays (Bishop & Bishop, 1998; Dodd & McEvoy, 1994) that are more prevalent among twins than among singletons (children born one at a time). Twin pairs who've supposedly developed a secret language are simply attempting to use their native language but with poor articulation and significant pronunciation errors. These difficulties are serious enough to render their speech largely incomprehensible. Because twin pairs tend to make similar kinds of phonological errors, their speech is more understandable to each other than it is to their parents or nonrelated children (Dodd & McEvoy, 1994; Thorpe et al., 2001).

There *are* interesting, but rare, cases of children inventing their own communication systems. One example is deaf children of hearing parents who sometimes invent their own signs when not being instructed in sign language. This phenomenon is called

APPLICATIONS TO EVERYDAY LIFE

In keeping with the text's scientific thinking theme, we emphasize the application of scientific thinking skills to claims that students encounter in everyday life.

WHAT DO *you* THINK?

You are an intake nurse at an emergency room serving a diverse population, and you routinely ask patients to estimate their pain on a ten-point scale as a way of evaluating the urgency of their medical problems. What factors should you consider when judging the severity of a patient's case?

Located in every major section, What Do YOU Think? feature boxes provide opportunities for students to apply knowledge of the chapter content to a variety of real-world situations. These feature questions can also be used to stimulate class discussion.

INTEGRATED CULTURAL CONTENT

Wherever possible, we highlight noteworthy research findings bearing on cultural and ethnic differences. By doing so, students should come to understand that many psychological principles have boundary conditions and that much of scientific psychology focuses on differences as much as commonalities.

In the end, we hope that students will emerge with the "psychological smarts," or open-minded skepticism, needed to distinguish psychological misinformation from psychological information. We'll consistently urge students to keep an open mind to new claims, but to insist on evidence. Indeed, our overarching motto is that of space scientist James Oberg (sometimes referred to as "Oberg's dictum"): *Keeping an open mind is a virtue, just so long as it is not so open that our brains fall out.*

A Focus on Meaningful Pedagogy: Helping Students Succeed in Psychology

Our goal of applying scientific thinking to the psychology of everyday life is reflected in the text's pedagogical plan. Each aspect of this plan was developed organically within the context of the text, the end-of-chapter review, our online MyPsychLab resource, and the print and media supplements to ensure its effectiveness, value, and conceptual application. And, most important, these features were designed to help students achieve a mastery of the subject and succeed in the course.

HOW DOES THE FRAMEWORK HELP STUDENTS TO IDENTIFY THE KEY CONCEPTS IN PSYCHOLOGY?

Preview Questions highlight some of the common questions that students have about psychology and direct them to sections of the text where the answer is located. Together with the **Chapter Outline,** they also serve to preview the key topics that will be discussed. Each chapter is organized around numbered **Learning Objectives,** which are also highlighted in the narrative as they are introduced. The end-of-chapter summary and assessment material is also organized around these objectives.

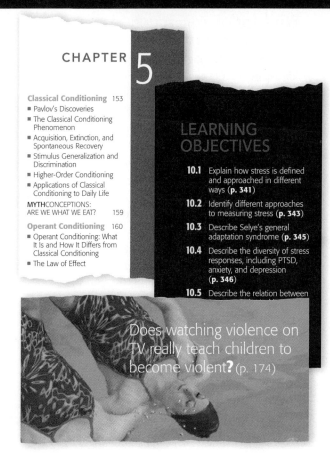

CHAPTER 5

LEARNING OBJECTIVES

10.1 Explain how stress is defined and approached in different ways (**p. 341**)

10.2 Identify different approaches to measuring stress (**p. 343**)

10.3 Describe Selye's general adaptation syndrome (**p. 345**)

10.4 Describe the diversity of stress responses, including PTSD, anxiety, and depression (**p. 346**)

10.5 Describe the relation between

Does watching violence on TV really teach children to become violent? (p. 174)

HOW DOES THE FRAMEWORK HELP GUIDE STUDENTS' UNDERSTANDING OF CONCEPTS?

We have designed the **Art as an Integrative Learning Tool** to enhance understanding and promote learning. In keeping with the text's theme on how we can be fooled from time to time, each chapter opens with a piece of photographic artwork depicting an illusion, reminding readers that their minds sometimes deceive them. Our anatomical art is color-coded across each brain image when possible to orient students at both the micro and macro levels as they move throughout the text and forge connections among concepts. Other art has been developed and highlighted specifically to capture psychological concepts in a clear and engaging manner to aid in student comprehension. Students' understanding of important terminology is enhanced with our on-page **Glossary.**

GLOSSARY

semantic memory
our knowledge of facts about the world

episodic memory
recollection of events in our lives

explicit memory
memories we recall intentionally and of which we have conscious awareness

implicit memory
memories we don't deliberately remember or reflect on consciously

procedural memory
memory for how to do things, including motor skills and habits

priming
our ability to identify a stimulus more easily or more quickly after we've encountered similar stimuli

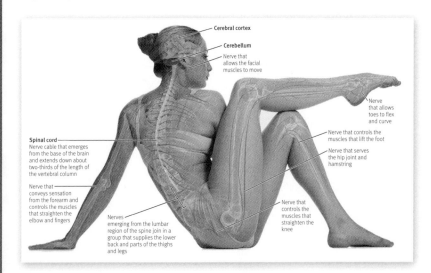

Cerebral cortex

Cerebellum

Nerve that allows the facial muscles to move

Nerve that allows toes to flex and curve

Nerve that controls the muscles that lift the foot

Nerve that serves the hip joint and hamstring

Spinal cord
Nerve cable that emerges from the base of the brain and extends down about two-thirds of the length of the vertebral column

Nerve that conveys sensation from the forearm and controls the muscles that straighten the elbow and fingers

Nerve that controls the muscles that straighten the knee

Nerves emerging from the lumbar region of the spine join in a group that supplies the lower back and parts of the thighs and legs

HOW DOES THE FRAMEWORK HELP STUDENTS TO REINFORCE WHAT THEY'VE LEARNED?

At the end of each major topic heading, we provide a true-or-false **Quiz** review of selected material to further reinforce concept comprehension and advance students' ability to distinguish psychological fact from fiction. In addition, a **MyPsychLab** video screenshot and quiz question allows students to take advantage of this superior online study tool to further their understanding of the section materials.

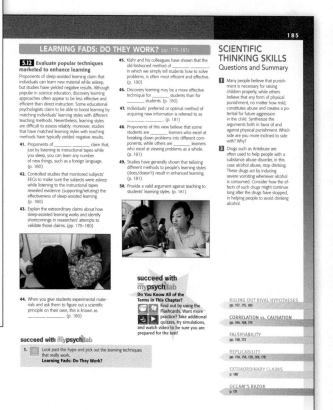

HOW DOES THE FRAMEWORK HELP STUDENTS SYNTHESIZE INFORMATION AND ASSESS THEIR KNOWLEDGE?

Once students finish reading the chapter, they can review what they've learned in **Your Complete Review System**. Organized by major sections and tied to the learning objectives, each review includes a summary, quiz questions, visual activities, and a **Succeed with MyPsychLab** section. The **Scientific Thinking Skills** section summarizes the scientific thinking principles covered in the chapter and includes two essay questions related to these skills.

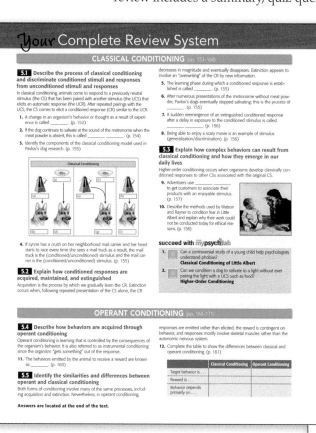

SUPPLEMENTS ▶ Putting Scientific Thinking to the Test: Innovative and Integrated Supplements

Psychology: A Framework for Everyday Thinking is accompanied by a collection of teaching and learning supplements designed to reinforce the scientific thinking skills from the text. These supplements "put scientific thinking to the test" by reinforcing our framework for evaluating claims and assessing students' ability to think scientifically in a variety of psychological and real-world situations. Instructor supplements are available to qualified instructors. Please contact your local Pearson representative for details.

The **Instructor's Resource DVD (ISBN 0-205-76851-2)** includes every instructional aid an introductory psychology professor needs to manage the classroom. The DVD contains electronic versions of all of the text supplements, including the Instructor's Manual, Test Bank, PowerPoint lecture presentation and art files, and interactive PowerPoints.

The **Instructor's Manual (ISBN 0-205-75718-9)** authored by Shani Harris Peterson (Spelman College) gives you unparalleled access to a huge selection of classroom-proven assets. First-time instructors will appreciate the detailed introduction to teaching the introductory psychology course, with suggestions for preparing for the course, sample syllabi, and current trends and strategies for successful teaching. Each chapter offers integrated teaching outlines to help instructors seamlessly incorporate all the ancillary materials for this book into their lectures. Instructors will also find an extensive bank of lecture launchers, handouts, activities, crossword puzzles, suggestions for integrating third-party videos and web resources, and cross-references to transparencies and the hundreds of multimedia and video assets found in the MyPsychLab course.

The **Test Bank (ISBN 0-205-75719-7),** authored by Judith Wightman (Kirkwood Community College) and Frank Provenzano (Greenville Technical College), contains, for each chapter, 200 multiple-choice questions, including additional applied questions, some of which address myths or factoids from the text and others from the MyPsychLab pretests, along with 25 fill-in-the-blank questions. Each of these questions has an answer justification with page reference, a difficulty rating (easy/medium/difficult), and skill type (conceptual/factual/applied). A number of test item questions also include item analysis data based upon actual student performance on test items administered by their instructors. In addition, these questions have all been correlated to the text's learning objectives. In the APA Correlation Guide we also offer a list of how these questions connect to the APA Learning Goals and Outcomes, enabling instructors to assess students' knowledge of specific skill types. Essay questions and short-answer questions, which deal specifically with scientific thinking skills, have also been included along with sample answers for each. A midterm and a final exam offer instructors a way to test students on their cumulative knowledge of the text.

The **Pearson MyTest (http://www.pearsonmytest.com) Computerized Test Bank,** a powerful assessment generation program that helps instructors easily create and print quizzes and exams. Questions and tests can be authored online, allowing instructors ultimate flexibility and the ability to efficiently manage assessments anytime, anywhere. Instructors can easily access existing questions, edit, and create and store using simple drag and drop and Word-like controls. Data on each question provides information on difficulty level and page number. In addition, each question maps to the text's major section and learning objective. For more information go to www.PearsonMyTest.com.

We are pleased to offer a unique and comprehensive collection of PowerPoint presentations for use in your classroom. The PowerPoints are available for download at the Instructor's Resource Center (www.pearsoned.com/IRC) or on the Instructor's Resource DVD. **A PowerPoint lecture presentation** by Fred W. Whitford (Montana State University) highlights major topics from the chapter, pairing them with select art images. To assist in delivering the lectures, additional examples and explanations from the Instructor's Manual appear in the "notes" section. **A condensed "Student" version of the PowerPoints** that can serve as handouts to students is available as well. A **PowerPoint collection of the complete art files** from the text allows customized lectures with any of the figures from the text. Finally, Pearson has developed a set of **interactive Power-Points** (available only on the Instructor's Resource DVD) with embedded animations, videos, and activities, authored by Derek Borman at Mesa Community College. Many of the slides include layered art, allowing instructors the ability to highlight specific aspects of a figure, such as identifying each part of the brain.

For instructors using **Clicker student response systems** in their classroom, we offer a collection of text-specific lecture questions for each chapter of the book. These questions can be used to evaluate students' knowledge of material or to enhance classroom discussions. Many of the clicker questions address specific critical thinking skills from the textbook.

PEARSON mypsych lab . . . Save Time. Improve Results. Put scientific thinking to the test.

Across the country, from small community colleges to large public universities, a trend is emerging: introductory psychology enrollments are increasing and available resources can't keep pace: in some instances, they are even decreasing. The result is instructor time stretched to its limit like never before. At the same time continual feedback is an important component to successful student progress. The APA strongly recommends student self-assessment tools and the use of embedded questions and assignments (see http://www.apa.org/ed/eval_strategies.html for more information). In response to these demands Pearson's MyPsychLab (MPL) offers students useful and engaging self-assessment tools, and instructors flexibility in assessing and tracking student progress.

WHAT IS mypsych lab?

MyPsychLab is a learning and assessment tool that enables instructors to assess student performance and adapt course content—without investing additional time or resources. Kimberley Duff (Cerritos College) is the managing editor for *Psychology: A Framework for Everyday Thinking MyPsychLab* and through her own experience teaching online, Kimberly knows the benefits and the challenges instructors face. Working closely with the text authors, she has developed a compelling on-line experience which reinforces the themes of the text. Students benefit from an easy-to-use site on which they can test themselves on key content, track their progress, and utilize individually tailored study plans. Instructors benefit from an easy-to-use resource which encourages independent

learning and helps ensure students are getting the reinforcement needed to master key concepts and the scientific thinking framework for everyday life.

 INCLUDES:

- An interactive eBook that allows students to highlight text and instructors to post their own notes for students to read.

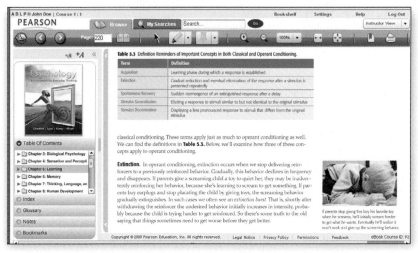

- Customized student Study Plans dynamically generated when students complete the available practice quizzes. Practice quizzes include questions specifically designed to assess students understanding of and ability to use the scientific thinking questions.

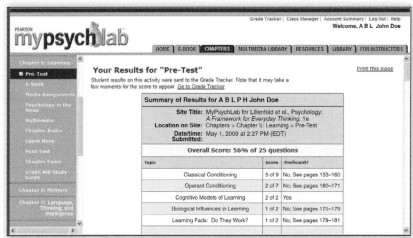

- An interactive timeline tool that presents the history of psychology

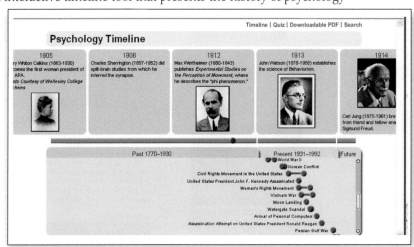

- Interactive mobile-ready flash cards of the key terms from the text—students can build their own stacks, print the cards, or export their flashcards to their cell phone.

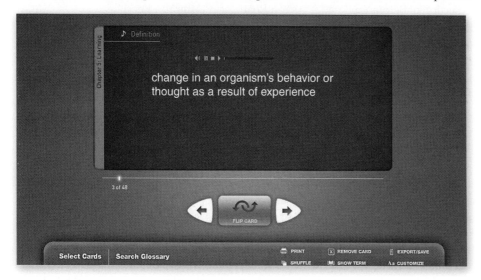

- A Multimedia Library with links to over 200 video clips, animations, and podcasts. Included within each chapter are specific key concepts paired with scientific thinking activities.

- Within each chapter, a **Psychology in the News** activity presents students with a real news story and then asks students to use the six scientific thinking questions to think critically about the claims introduced in the story.

- Audio podcasts present a hot topic in the field of psychology and utilize the scientific thinking framework to critically evaluate the issues.

- A Gradebook for instructors, and the availability of full course management capabilities for instructors teaching online or hybrid courses.

- **Unlimited use of Pearson's Research Navigator**™ —the easiest way for students to start a research assignment. Complete with extensive help on the research process and four exclusive databases of credible and reliable source material, including the EBSCO Academic Journal and Abstract Database, the *New York Times* Search by Subject Archive, "Best of the Web" Link Library, and *Financial Times* Article Archive and Company Financial, Research Navigator helps students quickly and efficiently make the most of their research time.

ASSESSMENT AND ABILITY TO ADAPT

MyPsychLab is designed with instructor flexibility in mind—you decide the extent of integration into your course—from independent self-assessment for students, to total course management. By transferring faculty members' most time-consuming tasks—content delivery, student assessment, and grading—to automated tools, MyPsychLab enables faculty to spend more quality time with students. For sample syllabi with ideas on incorporating MPL, see the Instructor's Manual as well as on-line at www.mypsychlab.com.

Instructors are provided with the results of the diagnostic tests—by students as well as an aggregate report of their class.

For more information on MyPsychLab go to www.mypsychlab.com

The **Study Guide (ISBN 0-205-75717-0),** authored by Annette Kujawski Taylor (University of San Diego), is filled with review material, in-depth activities, and self-assessments.

Special sections devoted to study skills, concept mapping, and the evaluation of websites appear at the start of the guide. Each chapter of the Study Guide is organized into three main sections: "Before You Read," "As You Read," and "After You Read."

The "Before You Read" section includes a brief chapter overview and a list of the numbered learning objectives and key terms (with page references).

The "As You Read" section features a variety of hands-on activities including Practice Activities, which are tied to the numbered learning objectives; Concept Map Activities; Myth or Reality sections, which ask students to evaluate examples of common myths and realities; Putting Your Scientific Thinking Skills to the Test sections that allow students to apply their scientific thinking skills to real-world problems; and activities related to MyPsychLab.

The "After You Read" section, which offers students a chance to assess their understanding of the chapter, includes two chapter practice tests, each with 20 multiple-choice questions. Students are encouraged to predict what percentage of questions they will answer correctly before they take the test and then compare their prediction to their final results. A complete answer key with page references is also provided.

APA CORRELATION GUIDE

This detailed correlation guide, which appears in the Instructor's Manual, shows how the learning outcomes in the text and the test bank questions correspond to the APA Learning Goals and Outcomes.

Additional Supplements for Your Introductory Psychology Course:

TRANSPARENCIES FOR INTRODUCTORY PSYCHOLOGY (ISBNS: 0-13-192699-3 AND 0-205-39862-6)

This set of approximately 200 revised, full-color acetates will enhance classroom lecture and discussion. It includes images from our major introductory psychology texts.

PEARSON TEACHING FILMS: INTRODUCTORY PSYCHOLOGY, INSTRUCTOR'S LIBRARY (ISBN: 0-13-175432-7)

This five-disk DVD series includes 82 segments covering all of the major topics in introductory psychology. All of the segments have been selected from ABC News, Films for Humanities & Sciences, Pearson Education's own assets, and ScienCentral.

PEARSON TEACHING FILMS: INTRODUCTORY PSYCHOLOGY, INSTRUCTOR'S LIBRARY ©2008 UPDATE (ISBN: 0-205-65280-8)

This update to the five-disk DVD series offers a fresh new set of video to illustrate key points and enhance your lectures. In particular, this DVD offers some new segments addressing science versus pseudoscience!

INSIGHTS INTO PSYCHOLOGY I, II, AND III (ISBNS: 0-205-46624-9, 0-205-40290-9, 0-205-47299-0)

These video programs include two or three short clips per topic, covering such topics as animal research, parapsychology, health and stress, Alzheimer's disease, bilingual education, genetics and IQ, and much more. A Video Guide containing critical thinking questions accompanies each video—also available on DVD.

Accessing All Resources:

For a list of all student resources available with *Psychology: A Framework for Everyday Thinking,* go to www.mypearsonstore.com, enter the text ISBN (0-205-65048-1) and check out the "Everything That Goes with It" section under the book cover.

For access to all instructor supplements for _Psychology: A Framework for Every-day Thinking_ go to http://pearsonhighered.com/irc and follow the directions to register (or log in if you already have a Pearson user name and password).

Once you have registered and your status as an instructor is verified, you will be e-mailed a login name and password. Use your login name and password to access the catalogue. Click on the "online catalogue" link, click on "psychology" followed by "introductory psychology" and then the Lilienfeld/Lynn/Namy/Woolf, _Psychology: A Framework for Everyday Thinking_ text. Under the description of each supplement is a link that allows you to download and save the supplement to your desktop.

For technical support for any of your Pearson products, you and your students can contact http://247.pearsoned.com.

Acknowledgments

For the four authors, writing this book has been a great deal of work, but it's also been a labor of love. When we began this undertaking—about five years ago—we as authors could never have imagined the number of committed, selfless, and enthusiastic colleagues in the psychology community who would join us on this path to making our textbook a reality. During the long months of writing and revising, the feedback and support from fellow instructors, researchers, and students helped keep our energy high and our minds sharp. We stand in awe of their love of the discipline and the enthusiasm and imagination each of these individuals brings to the psychology classroom every day. This text is the culmination of their ongoing support from first to final draft, and we are forever grateful to them.

In addition, the authors would like to extend our heartfelt gratitude and sincere thanks to a host of people on the Pearson team. We consider ourselves remarkably fortunate to have worked with such an uncommonly dedicated, talented, and genuinely kind group of people. Needless to say, this project was a monumental team effort, and every member of the team played an invaluable role in its inception. Particular thanks go to our original Editor-in-Chief Susan Hartman for her exceptional professionalism, generosity, support, and grace under pressure, not to mention her undying commitment to the project. We also owe special thanks to Jessica Mosher, Editor-in-Chief, and Stephen Frail, Executive Editor, for the enthusiasm, creativity, and support they brought to the project; Karen Mason, our truly exceptional production manager, for her astonishingly high-quality work and wonderful attitude; Sharon Geary, Director of Development, and Julie Swasey, our developmental editor, for their invaluable assistance in polishing our prose and sharpening our ideas; and to Jeanette Koskinas, Executive Marketing Manager, for her energy, creativity, and contagious enthusiasm.

Warm thanks also go to many, many others, especially April Walsh and Mark Mykytiuk, art coordination; Katharine Cebik, photo research; Timothy Nicholls and Julie Brown, permissions research; Stuart Jackman, design concept; Richard Czapnik, DK, original design; Jerilyn Bockorick, Nesbitt Graphics, design modifications; John McCullough, page design; Kerri Hart-Morris and Mary Lombard, assistance on all matters editorial; Margaret Pinette, copy-editing; Susan McNally and Paul Fennessy, full-service vendor coordination; Kara Kikel and Angela Pickard, supplements managing and hiring; Paul DeLuca, coordination of MyPsych-Lab; Maureen Prado Roberts, market development; and John Christiana and Kristina Mose-Libon, cover design. Special thanks go to Lisa Hamlett for her profound dedication and invaluable help with references; to Susan Daut for her terrific assistance with chapter cross-referencing; and to Sheila Rotter for her administrative help.

A FINAL WORD & THANKS

Steven Lynn extends his deepest appreciation to Fern Pritikin Lynn for her discerning editorial assistance, and to Jessica Lynn for her helpful comments and insights concerning preliminary versions of the manuscript. Laura Namy thanks her "Diva" pals, Lynne Nygaard and Robyn Fivush, for their unrelenting support during this process.

Thanks also go to Barry Beyerstein, whose early efforts were invaluable; Kelly May, for encouraging us to undertake this project and providing us with early support for it; Judy Hauck, for developmental editing guidance in the early phases of the project; Tunisa Williams at Kinkos and Jack Murray at Emory for technical support; Robyn Fivush, chair of psychology at Emory, for encouragement and assistance; and Susan Himes for helpful advice. Last but by no means least, we thank the countless others who helped in small but significant ways in bringing this text to fruition.

OUR SUPPLEMENTS TEAM

We have assembled a team of talented instructors who share our belief in the importance of scientific thinking and a scientific approach to psychology to develop a unique and comprehensive supplements package. We'd like to thank all of the instructors who contributed to the creation of our excellent teaching and learning materials:

David Alfano, Community College of Rhode Island
Megan Bradley, Frostburg State University
Kimberley Duff, Cerritos College
Lisa Farwell, Santa Monica College
Amy Hackney-Hansen, Georgia Southern University
Mei Jiang, Texas A&M University, Commerce
Brian Johnson, University of Tennessee at Martin
Patricia Kowalski, University of San Diego
Shani Harris Peterson, Spelman College
Frank Provenzano, Greenville Technical College
Jennifer Sage, University of California at San Diego
Heidi Shaw, Yakima Valley Community College
Valerie Smith, Collin County Community College
James Stringham, University of Georgia
Annette Kujawski Taylor, University of San Diego
April Thames, Alliant International University
Fred W. Whitford, Montana State University
Judith Wightman, Kirkwood Community College
Keith Williams, Richard Stockton College of New Jersey
Adena Young, Texas A&M University, Commerce

OUR REVIEW PANEL

We are indebted to the members of our Review Panel who evaluated chapters and provided expert analysis on critical topic areas. Others served on an advisory council, participated in focus groups, conducted usability studies, ran class testing of chapters, and attended our faculty forums for the text. Their input proved invaluable to us, and we thank them for it.

Alabama

Susan Anderson, University of South Alabama
Charles Brown, University of South Alabama
Michael Clayton, Jacksonville State University
Samuel Jones, Jefferson State Community College
David Payne, Wallace Community College
Chan Roark, Troy University
Christopher Robinson, University of Alabama—Birmingham
Royce Simpson, Spring Hill College

Arizona

Karina R. Horowitz, Glendale Community College
Kam Majer, Glendale Community College
Gregory Privitera, Glendale Community College
Linda Ruehlman, Arizona State University

Arkansas

James Becker, Pulaski Technical College
Yousef Fahoum, University of Arkansas—Little Rock
Caleb W. Lack, Arkansas Tech University
Travis Langley, Henderson State University
David A. Schroeder, University of Arkansas
Karen Yanowitz, Arkansas State University

California

Mark Akiyama, Diablo Valley College
David E. Campbell, Humboldt State University
G. William Domhoff, University of California—Santa Cruz
Kimberley Duff, Cerritos College
Debra L. Golden, Grossmont College
Steven Isonio, Golden West College
Margaret Lynch, San Francisco State University
Jan Mendoza, Golden West College
Michelle Pilati, Rio Hondo Community College
Amira Rezec, Saddleback College
Heidi Riggio, California State University—Los Angeles
Scott Roesch, San Diego State University
Catherine Sandhofer, University of California—Los Angeles
Kathleen Taylor, Sierra College
Inger Thompson, Glendale Community College
Dean Yoshizumi, Sierra College

Colorado

Pamela Ansburg, Metropolitan State College of Denver
Mark Basham, Regis University
Stefanie M. Bell, Pikes Peak Community College
Layton Seth Curl, Metropolitan State College of Denver
Linda Lockwood, Metropolitan State College of Denver
Peggy Norwood, Red Rocks Community College
Laura Sherrick, Front Range Community College—Westminster

Connecticut

Marlene Adelman, Norwalk Community College
Nathan Brody, Wesleyan University
Luis A. Cordon, Eastern Connecticut State University
Carlotta Ocampo, Trinity College
Amy Van Buren, Sacred Heart University

Delaware

Jack Barnhardt, Wesley College
Carrie Veronica Smith, University of Delaware

Florida

Glen Bradley, Pensacola Junior College
Kathleen Bey, Palm Beach Community College
Job Clement, Daytona Beach Community College
Peter Gram, Pensacola Junior College
Vicki Gier, University of South Florida
R. J. Grisham, Indian River Community College
Gregory Harris, Polk Community College
James Jakubow, Florida Atlantic University
Glenn Musgrove, Broward College—Central
Corrie J. Rakvin, Santa Fe College
Jermaine Robertson, Florida A&M University
Teresa Stalvey, North Florida Community College
Richard W. Townsend, Miami-Dade College—Kendall
Barbara VanHorn, Indian River Community College

Georgia

Deb Briihl, Valdosta State University
Richard Catrambone, Georgia Institute of Technology
Gregory M. Corso, Georgia Institute of Technology
Mirari Elcoro, Armstrong Atlantic State University
Janet Frick, University of Georgia
Mark Griffin, Georgia Perimeter College—Dunwoody
Amy Hackney-Hansen, Georgia Southern University
Michael P. Hoff, Dalton State College
Katherine Kipp, Gainesville State College
William McIntosh, Georgia Southern University
Corinne McNamara, Kennesaw State University
Shani Harris Peterson, Spelman College
Alan Pope, University of West Georgia
Julie Anne Resh, Georgia Perimeter College—Dunwoody
Nicole E. Rossi, Augusta State University
Suzann Shepard, Middle Georgia College
Robert Barry Stennett, Gainesville State College
James Stringham, University of Georgia

Hawaii

Howard Markowitz, Hawaii Pacific University
Tanya Renner, Kapi'olani Community College

Idaho

Richard Cluff, Brigham Young University—Idaho
Tera Letzring, Idaho State University
Steven E. Meier, University of Idaho
Randy Simonson, College of Southern Idaho
Shannon M. Welch, University of Idaho

Illinois

Lorelei A. Carvajal, Triton Community College
Steven Dworkin, Western Illinois University
Michael G. Dudley, Southern Illinois University—Edwardsville
Joseph R. Ferrari, DePaul University
Allen Huffcutt, Bradley University

Mary Johannesen-Schmidt, Oakton Community College
James Johnson, Illinois State University
Chad Keller, Lewis and Clark Community College
Margaret Nauta, Illinois State University
Cindy Nordstrom, Southern Illinois University—Edwardsville
John Skowronski, Northern Illinois University
Suzanne Valentine-French, College of Lake County
Jeffrey Wagman, Illinois State University

Indiana
Brad Brubaker, Indiana State University
Cynthia O'Dell, Indiana University Northwest

Iowa
Jennifer Bellingtier, Hawkeye Community College
Susan R. Burns, Morningside College
David Devonis, Graceland University
William Dragon, Cornell College
Doug Gentile, Iowa State University
Jennifer Grossheim, University of Northern Iowa
James D. Rodgers, Hawkeye Community College
Judith A. Wightman, Kirkwood Community College

Kansas
Mary Coplen, Hutchinson Community College
Tammy Hutcheson, Garden City Community College
John Sanders, Garden City Community College

Kentucky
Joseph Bilotta, Western Kentucky University
Eric L. Bruns, Campbellsville University
Lynn Haller, Morehead State University
Paul M. Kasenow, Henderson Community College
Sherry Rager, Hopkinsville Community College
Thomas W. Williams, Western Kentucky University

Louisiana
Gary J. Greguras, Louisiana State University
Matthew I. Isaak, University of Louisiana—Lafayette
Mike Majors, Delgado Community College
Jack Palmer, University of Louisiana at Monroe

Maine
Michelle Rivera, University of Maine

Maryland
Megan Bradley, Frostburg State University
Thomas Capo, University of Maryland
Cynthia Koenig, St. Mary's College of Maryland
Ann McKim, Goucher College

Massachusetts
Louis E. Banderet, Northeastern University
John Bickford, University of Massachusetts—Amherst
Daneen Deptula, Fitchburg State College

Trina C. Kershaw, University of Massachusetts—Dartmouth
Amy Shapiro, University of Massachusetts—Dartmouth

Michigan
Renee Babcock, Central Michigan University
David Baskind, Delta College
Joseph M. Fitzgerald, Wayne State University
Linda A. Jackson, Michigan State University
Mary B. Lewis, Oakland University
Paulina Multhaupt, Macomb Community College

Minnesota
Thomas Brothen, University of Minnesota
Kevin J. Filter, Minnesota State University—Mankato
Randy Gordon, University of Minnesota—Duluth
Brenda E. Koneczny, Lake Superior College
Joe Melcher, St. Cloud State University
Daren Protolipac, St. Cloud State University

Mississippi
Tammy D. Barry, University of Southern Mississippi
David Echevarria, University of Southern Mississippi
Linda Fayard, Mississippi Gulf Coast Community College
David Marcus, University of Southern Mississippi
Jeanette Murphey, Meridian Community College
Bonnie Nicholson, University of Southern Mississippi

Missouri
Michele Y. Breault, Truman State University
Jay Brown, Southwest Missouri State University
Carla Edwards, Northwest Missouri State University
Matthew Fanetti, Missouri State University
Donald Fischer, Missouri State University
Rebecca Hendrix, Northwest Missouri State University
Chris Mazurek, Columbia College
Kathleen McDermott, Washington University in St. Louis
Melinda Russell-Stamp, Northwest Missouri State University
Julie Tietz, Cottey College
April Michele Williams, Missouri State University

Nebraska
Jean Mandernach, University of Nebraska at Kearney
Keith Matthews, Northeast Community College

Nevada
Diana Anson, College of Southern Nevada
Paul Herrle, College of Southern Nevada

New Jersey
Fred Bonato, St. Peter's College
Bruce J. Diamond, William Paterson University
Christine Floether, Centenary College

Christine Harrington, Middlesex County College
Elissa Koplik, Bloomfield College
Lillian McMaster, Hudson County Community College
Elaine Olaoye, Brookdale Community College
John Ruscio, The College of New Jersey
Jakob Steinberg, Fairleigh Dickinson University
Keith Williams, Richard Stockton College of New Jersey

New Mexico

Jennifer G. Coleman, Western New Mexico College
Kathryn Demitrakis, Central New Mexico Community College
Richard M. Gorman, Central New Mexico Community College
Michael Hillard, Albuquerque Tech Vocational Institute
James R. Johnson, Central New Mexico Community College
Ron Salazar, San Juan College
Paul Vonnahme, New Mexico State University

New York

William D. Bowie, State University of New York—Broome
Jennifer Cina, Barnard College
Dale Doty, Monroe Community College
Robert Dushay, Morrisville State College
Melvyn King, State University of New York–Cortland
George Meyer, Suffolk County Community College
Laurence Nolan, Wagner College
Caroline Olko, Nassau Community College
Tibor Palfai, Syracuse University
Celia Reaves, Monroe Community College
Dennis T. Regan, Cornell University
Tracy L. Stenger, State University of New York—Fredonia
Jennifer Yanowitz, Utica College
Garry Zaslow, Nassau Community College

North Carolina

Trey Asbury, Campbell University
Elizabeth Denny, University of North Carolina at Pembroke
Rebecca Hester, Western Carolina University
Michael J. Kane, University of North Carolina—Greensboro
Mark O'DeKirk, Meredith College
Amy Overman, Elon University
Courtney Rocheleau, Appalachian State University
Keith Whitfield, Duke University

North Dakota

Jeff Weatherly, University of North Dakota

Ohio

Lorry Cology, Owens Community College
Anastasia Dimitropoulos, Case Western Reserve University

David R. Entwistle, Malone College
Stephen Flora, Youngstown State University
Joseph P. Green, Ohio State University—Lima
Traci Haynes, Columbus State Community College
Lance Jones, Bowling Green State University
Kathie Judge, Cleveland State University
Robin Lightner, University of Cincinnati
Elaine McLeskey, Belmont Technical College
Barbara Oswald, University of Cincinnati
Mark Rittman, Cuyahoga Community College
Wayne Shebilske, Wright State University
Vivian Smith, Lakeland Community College
Keith Syrja, Owens Community College
John Ward, Miami University
Colin William, Columbus State Community College

Oklahoma

Laura Gruntmeir, Redlands Community College
Kevin M.P. Woller, Rogers State University

Oregon

Susan L. O'Donnell, George Fox University
Deana Julka, University of Portland

Pennsylvania

Robert Brill, Moravian College
Mark Cloud, Lock Haven University
Gayle L Brosnan-Watters, Slippery Rock University
Perri B. Druen, York College of Pennsylvania
William F. Ford, Bucks County Community College
Carie Forden, Clarion University
Audrey M. Ervin, Delaware County Community College
Robert Hensley, Mansfield University
Cynthia Lausberg, University of Pittsburgh
Robin Musselman, Lehigh Carbon Community College
Gregory Page, University of Pittsburgh at Bradford
Barbara Radigan, Community College of Allegheny County
Mark Rivardo, Saint Vincent College
Janis Wilson Seeley, Luzerne County Community College
Adrian Tomer, Shippensburg University

Rhode Island

David Alfano, Community College of Rhode Island

South Carolina

Holly Beard, Midlands Technical College
Dr. Tharon Howard, Clemson University
Laura May, University of South Carolina Aiken
Lloyd R. Pilkington, Midlands Technical College
Frank J. Provenzano, Greenville Technical College
Elizabeth Purcell, Greenville Technical College
Kathy Weatherford, Trident Technical College

South Dakota
Brady J. Phelps, South Dakota State University

Tennessee
Gina Andrews, Volunteer State Community College
Andrea D. Clements, East Tennessee State University
Vicki Dretchen, Volunteer State Community College
Brian Johnson, University of Tennessee at Martin
Angelina MacKewn, University of Tennessee at Martin

Texas
Saundra Boyd, Houston Community College
Michael C. Boyle, Sam Houston State University
Maria Bravo, Central Texas College
Veda Brown, Prairie View A&M University
Jane Cirillo, Houston Community College—Southeast
Wanda Clark, South Plains College
Larry Cohn, University of Texas, El Paso
Perry Collins, Wayland Baptist University
Verne Cox, University of Texas—Arlington
Celeste Favela, El Paso Community College
Daniel J. Fox, Sam Houston State University
Jerry Green, Tarrant County College—Northwest
Erin Hardin, Texas Tech University
Bert Hayslip, Jr., University of North Texas
Nancy Woods Hernandez, Howard College
Lisette Hodges, Lamar State College—Orange
Joanne Hsu, Houston Community College—Town and Country
Linda Jones, Blinn College
Jerwen Jou, University of Texas—Pan American
Shirin Khosropour, Austin Community College
Irv Lichtman, Houston Community College
Don Lucas, Northwest Vista College
Ken Luke, Tyler Junior College
Jason Moses, El Paso Community College
Jane Ogden, East Texas Baptist University
Wendy Ann Olson, Texas A&M University
Keith Pannell, El Paso Community College
Julie Penley, El Paso Community College
Darla Rocha, San Jacinto College
Lilian M. Romero, San Jacinto College—Central Campus
Tamara Rowatt, Baylor University
Wade C. Rowatt, Baylor University
Valerie T. Smith, Collin County Community College
Jeanne Spaulding, Houston Community College—Town and Country
Susan Spooner, McLennan Community College

Melissa B. Weston, El Centro College
Victoria Van Wie, Lone Star College—Cy-Fair
John Wiebe, University of Texas, El Paso
Sharon Wiederstein, Blinn College, Bryan
Andrea Zabel, Midland College

Utah
Aaron Ashley, Weber State University
Scott C. Bates, Utah State University
Joseph Horvat, Weber State University

Vermont
Michael Zvolensky, University of Vermont

Virginia
Robin Eliason, Piedmont Virginia Community College
Jeff D. Green, Virginia Commonwealth University
Alicia Grodsky, Northern Virginia Community College
Kelly G. Lambert, Randolph-Macon College
Natalie Lawrence, James Madison University
Cynthia Lofaso, Central Virginia Community College
Mary Ann Schmitt, North Virginia Community College—Manassas
Stuart Tousman, Jefferson College of Health Sciences

Washington
Kathryn Becker-Blease, University of Washington—Vancouver
Pamela Costa, Tacoma Community College
Susan D. Lonborg, Central Washington University
Thomas J. Mount, Yakima Valley Community College
Heidi Shaw, Yakima Valley Community College
Kurt Stellwagen, Eastern Washington University
Bill Williams, Eastern Washington University
John W. Wright, Washington State University

West Virginia
Tammy McClain, West Liberty State College

Wisconsin
Sylvia Beyer, University of Wisconsin—Parkside
Tracie Blumentritt, University of Wisconsin—LaCrosse
Kathleen Kavanagh, Milwaukee Area Technical College
Dawn Delaney, Madison Area Technical College
Regan Gurung, University of Wisconsin—Green Bay
Jeffrey B. Henriques, University of Wisconsin—Madison

Psychology

A Framework for Everyday Thinking

Psychology and Scientific Thinking

Is psychology mostly just common sense? (p. 6)

Should we trust most self-help books? (p. 12)

Is psychology really
a science? (p. 8)

Are claims that can't be proven
wrong scientific? (p. 21)

Are all clinical
psychologists
psychotherapists? (p. 31)

LEARNING OBJECTIVES

TEST OF POPULAR PSYCHOLOGY KNOWLEDGE

1 Most people use only about 10 percent of their brain capacity. TRUE FALSE

2 Newborn babies are virtually blind and deaf. TRUE FALSE

3 Hypnosis enhances the accuracy of our memories. TRUE FALSE

4 All people with dyslexia see words backward (like *tac* instead of *cat*). TRUE FALSE

5 In general, it's better to express anger than to hold it in. TRUE FALSE

6 The lie-detector (polygraph) test is 90 to 95 percent accurate at detecting falsehoods. TRUE FALSE

7 People tend to be romantically attracted to individuals who are opposite to them in personality and attitudes. TRUE FALSE

8 The more people present at an emergency, the more likely it is that at least one of them will help. TRUE FALSE

9 People with schizophrenia have more than one personality. TRUE FALSE

10 All effective psychotherapies require clients to get to the root of their problems in childhood. TRUE FALSE

For most of you reading this text, this is your first psychology course. But it's a safe bet you believe you've learned an awful lot about psychology already. Pause for a moment and ask yourself: "Where have I learned what I know about psychology?"

If you're like most beginning psychology students, you've learned much of what you know about psychology from watching television programs and movies, listening to radio call-in shows, reading self-help books and popular magazines, surfing the Internet, and talking to friends. In short, most of your psychology knowledge probably derives from the popular psychology industry: a sprawling network of everyday sources of information about human behavior.

Take a moment to review the 10 test questions listed above. Most students taking their first psychology course assume they know the answers to most of them. That's hardly surprising, as they've become part of popular psychology lore. Many people are surprised to learn that the answers to *all* of these 10 statements are false! This little exercise illustrates a take-home message we'll emphasize throughout the text: *Although common sense can be enormously useful for some purposes, it's sometimes completely wrong.* This can be especially true in psychology.

What Is Psychology?
Common versus Uncommon Sense

William James (1842–1910), often regarded as the founder of American psychology, once described psychology as a "nasty little subject." As James noted, psychology is difficult to study, and simple explanations are few and far between. In reading this textbook, prepare to find many of your preconceptions about psychology challenged; to learn new ways of thinking about the causes of your everyday thoughts, feelings, and actions; and to apply these ways of thinking to evaluating psychological claims in your daily life.

PSYCHOLOGY AND LEVELS OF EXPLANATION

The first question often posed in introductory psychology textbooks could hardly seem simpler: "What is psychology?" Although psychologists disagree about many things, they agree on one thing: Psychology isn't easy to define (Henriques, 2004). For the purposes of this text, we'll simply refer to **psychology** as the scientific study of the mind, brain, and behavior. As we'll soon discover, most modern psychologists view "mind" and "brain" as different ways of describing the same phenomenon. Whatever their superficial differences, scientific psychologists are united by a commitment to understanding the causes of human actions—and those of animals.

Psychology is a discipline that spans many **levels of explanation.** We can think of levels of explanation as rungs on a ladder, with the lower rungs tied most closely to biological influences and the higher rungs tied most closely to social influences (Ilardi & Feldman, 2001). The levels of explanation in psychology stretch all the way from molecules to brain structures to thoughts, feelings, and emotions, and to social and cultural influences, with many levels in between (Cacioppo, Berntson, Sheridan, et al., 2000) (see **Figure 1.1**).

We'll cover all of these levels of explanation in coming chapters. When doing so, we'll keep one crucial guideline in mind: *We can't understand psychology by focusing on only one level of explanation.* That's because each level tells us something different, and we gain new knowledge from each vantage point. Some psychologists believe that biological factors—like the actions of the brain and its billions of nerve cells—are most critical for understanding the causes of behavior. Others believe that social factors—like parenting practices, peer influences, and culture—are most critical for understanding the causes of behavior (Meehl, 1972). In this text, we'll steer away from these two extremes because both biological and social factors are essential for a complete understanding of psychology (Kendler, 2005).

WHAT MAKES PSYCHOLOGY CHALLENGING—AND FASCINATING

A host of challenges make psychology complicated; it's precisely these challenges that also make psychology fascinating, because each challenge contributes to scientific mysteries that psychologists have yet to solve. Here, we'll briefly touch on three challenges that we'll be revisiting throughout the textbook.

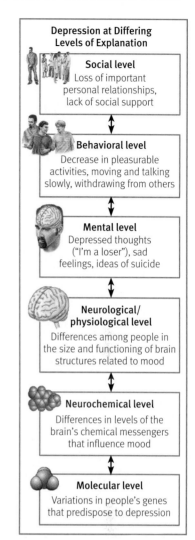

Figure 1.1 Levels of Explanation in Depression. We can view psychological phenomena, in this case the disorder of depression, at multiple levels of explanation, with lower levels being more biological and higher levels being more social. Each level provides us with unique information and offers us a distinctive view of the phenomenon at hand. (*Source:* Adapted from Ilardi, Rand, & Karwoski, 2007)

GLOSSARY

psychology
the scientific study of the mind, brain, and behavior

levels of explanation
rungs on a ladder of explanation, with lower levels tied most closely to biological influences and higher levels tied most closely to social influences

In a study by Chua, Boland, and Nisbett (2005), European Americans tend to focus more on the central details of photographs, like the tiger itself (left), whereas Asian Americans tend to focus more on the peripheral details, like the rocks and leaves surrounding the tiger (right).

First, human behavior is difficult to predict, in part because almost all actions are **multiply determined,** that is, produced by many factors. That's why we need to be profoundly skeptical of **single-variable explanations** of behavior, which are widespread in popular psychology. We may be tempted to explain complex human behaviors, like violence, in terms of a single causal factor, like either poverty or genes, but we'd almost surely be wrong because such behaviors are due to the interplay of an enormous array of factors.

Second, people differ from each other in thinking, emotion, personality, and behavior. These **individual differences** help to explain why we each respond in different ways to the same objective situation, such as an insulting comment from a boss (Harkness & Lilienfeld, 1997; Lubinksi, 2000). Individual differences make psychology challenging because they make it difficult to come up with explanations of behavior that apply to everyone.

Third, people's behavior is often shaped by culture. Cultural differences, like individual differences, place limits on the generalizations that psychologists can draw about human nature. For example, Richard Nisbett and his colleagues have found that Europeans tend to focus on central features of a photograph, whereas Chinese tend to focus on peripheral or incidental features of a photograph (Chua, Boland, & Nisbett, 2005; see photos above).

WHY WE CAN'T ALWAYS TRUST OUR COMMON SENSE

To understand why others act as they do, most of us rely on our common sense—our gut intuitions about how the social world works. As we've already discovered, however, our intuitive understanding of ourselves and the world is frequently mistaken (Cacioppo, 2004; van Hecke, 2007). In fact, as the quiz at the start of this chapter showed us, sometimes our commonsensical understanding of psychology isn't merely incorrect but entirely backward. **[LEARNING OBJECTIVE 1.1]** For example, although many people believe the old adage "There's safety in numbers," psychological research actually shows that the more people present at an emergency, the *less* likely it is that at least one of them will help (Darley & Latané, 1968a; Latané & Nida, 1981; see Chapter 11).

Here's another illustration of why we can't always trust our common sense. Read the following well-known proverbs, most of which deal with human behavior, and ask yourself whether you agree with them:

GLOSSARY

multiply determined
caused by many factors

single-variable explanations
explanations that try to account for complex behaviors in terms of only a single cause

individual differences
variations among people in their thinking, emotion, and behavior

(1) Birds of a feather flock together.

(2) Absence makes the heart grow fonder.

(3) Better safe than sorry.

(4) Two heads are better than one.

(5) Actions speak louder than words.

(6) Opposites attract.

(7) Out of sight, out of mind.

(8) Nothing ventured, nothing gained.

(9) Too many cooks spoil the broth.

(10) The pen is mightier than the sword.

These proverbs all ring true, don't they? Yet each of these proverbs contradicts the proverb across from it! So our common sense can lead us to believe two things that can't both be true simultaneously or at least that are largely at odds with each other. Strangely enough, in most cases we never notice the contradictions until other people, like the authors of an introductory psychology textbook, point them out to us.

Naive Realism. We trust our common sense largely because we're prone to **naive realism:** the belief that we see the world precisely as it is (Ross & Ward, 1996). We assume that "seeing is believing" and trust our intuitive perceptions of the world and ourselves. In daily life, naive realism often serves us well. If we're driving down a one-lane road and see a tractor trailer barreling toward us at 85 miles per hour, it's a wise idea to get out of the way. Much of the time, we *should* trust our perceptions.

Yet appearances can sometimes be deceiving. The earth *seems* flat. The sun *seems* to revolve around the earth (see **Figure 1.2** for another example of deceptive appearances). Yet in both cases, our intuitions are wrong. Similarly, naive realism can trip us up when it comes to evaluating ourselves and others. Our common sense assures us that people who don't share our political views are biased but that we're objective. Yet psychological research demonstrates that we all tend to evaluate political issues in a biased fashion (Pronin, Gilovich, & Ross, 2004). So our tendencies toward naive realism can lead us to draw incorrect conclusions about human nature. In many cases, "believing is seeing" rather than the reverse: Our beliefs shape our perceptions of the world (Gilovich, 1991).

Marriages like that of Mary Matalin, a prominent conservative political strategist, and James Carville, a prominent liberal political strategist, may contribute to the commonsense belief that opposites attract. Yet psychological research shows that such marriages are marked exceptions: People are generally drawn to others who are similar to them in beliefs and values.

Figure 1.2 Naive Realism Can Fool Us.
Even though our perceptions are often accurate, we can't always trust them to provide us with an error-free picture of the world. In this case, take a look at *Shepard's tables,* courtesy of psychologist Roger Shepard. Believe it or not, the tops of these tables are identical in size: one can be directly superimposed on top of the other (get out a ruler if you don't believe us!).
(*Source:* Shepard, 1990)

GLOSSARY

naive realism
belief that we see the world precisely as it is

When Our Common Sense Is Right. That's not to say that our common sense is always wrong. Our intuition comes in handy in many situations and sometimes guides us to the truth (Gigerenzer, 2007; Gladwell, 2005; Myers, 2002). For example, our snap (5-second) judgments about whether someone we've just watched on a videotape is trustworthy or untrustworthy tend to be right more often than would be expected by chance (Fowler, Lilienfeld, & Patrick, 2009). Common sense can also be a helpful guide for generating hypotheses that scientists can later test in rigorous investigations (Redding, 1998). Moreover, some everyday psychological notions are indeed correct. For example, most people believe that happy employees tend to be more productive on the job than unhappy employees, and research shows that they're right (Kluger & Tikochinsky, 2001).

But to think scientifically, we must learn when to trust our common sense and when not to. Doing so will help us become more informed consumers of popular psychology and make better real-world decisions. One of our major goals in this text is to provide you with thinking tools for making this crucial distinction. These thinking tools can help you to better evaluate psychological claims in everyday life.

PSYCHOLOGY AS A SCIENCE

A few years ago, one of our academic colleagues was advising a psychology major about his career plans. Out of curiosity, he asked the student, "So why did you decide to go into psychology?" He responded, "Well, I took a lot of science courses and realized I didn't like science, so I picked psychology instead."

We're going to try to persuade you that the student was wrong—not about selecting a psychology major, but about psychology not being a science. A central theme of this text is that modern psychology, or at least hefty chunks of it, are scientific. But what does the word *science* really mean, anyway?

Most students think that *science* is just a word for all of that really complicated stuff they learn in their biology, chemistry, and physics classes. But science isn't a body of knowledge. Instead, it's an *approach* to evidence (Bunge, 1998). Specifically, science is a toolbox of skills designed to prevent us from fooling ourselves.

Science as a Safeguard against Bias: Protecting Us from Ourselves. The best scientists are aware of their biases or at least aware they have them. **[LEARNING OBJECTIVE 1.2]** This principle applies to all scientists, including psychological scientists—those who study mind, brain, and behavior. In particular, the best scientists realize that they *want* their pet theories to turn out to be correct. After all, they've invested months or even years in designing and running a study to test a theory, sometimes a theory they've developed. If the results of the study are negative, they'll often be bitterly disappointed. They also know that because of this deep personal investment, they may bias the results unintentionally to make them turn out the way they want. Scientists are prone to self-deception, just like the rest of us. There are several traps into which scientists can fall unless they're careful: We'll discuss two of the most crucial next.

Confirmation Bias. To protect themselves against bias, good scientists adopt procedural safeguards against errors, especially errors that could work in their favor (see Chapter 2). In other words, science is a set of tools for overcoming **confirmation bias:** the tendency to seek out evidence that supports our beliefs and neglect or distort evidence that contradicts them (Nickerson, 1998; Risen & Gilovich, 2007). We can sum up confirmation bias in five words: *Seek and ye shall find.*

Fict-OID

MYTH: Physicists and other "hard" scientists are more skeptical about most extraordinary claims, like extrasensory perception, than psychologists are.

REALITY: Academic psychologists are more skeptical of many controversial claims than their colleagues in more traditional sciences are. For example, psychologists are considerably less likely to believe that extrasensory perception is an established scientific fact than physicists, chemists, and biologists are (Wagner & Monnet, 1979).

GLOSSARY

confirmation bias
tendency to seek out evidence that supports our hypotheses and neglect or distort evidence that contradicts them

Because of confirmation bias, our preconceptions often lead us to focus on evidence that supports our beliefs, resulting in psychological tunnel vision. One of the simplest demonstrations of confirmation bias comes from research on the *Wason selection task* (Wason, 1966), an example of which we can find in **Figure 1.3.** You'll see four cards, each of which has a number on one side and a letter on the other. Your task is to determine whether the following hypothesis is correct: *All cards that have a vowel on one side have an odd number on the other.* To test this hypothesis, you need to select *two* cards to turn over. Which two will you pick? Decide on your two cards before reading on.

Most people pick the cards showing E and 5. If you selected E, you were right, so give yourself one point there. But if you selected 5, you've fallen prey to confirmation bias, although you'd be in good company because most people make this mistake. Although 5 *seems* to be a correct choice, it can only confirm the hypothesis, not disconfirm it. Think of it this way: If there's a vowel on the other side of the 5 card, that doesn't rule out the possibility that the 4 card also has a vowel on the other side, which would disconfirm the hypothesis. So the 4 card is actually the other card to turn over, as that's the only other card that could disconfirm the hypothesis.

Confirmation bias wouldn't be especially interesting if it were limited to cards with numbers and letters. What makes confirmation bias so important is that it extends to many areas of our daily lives (Nickerson, 1998). For example, research shows that confirmation bias affects how we evaluate candidates for political office—including those on both the left and right sides of the political spectrum. If we agree with a candidate's political views, we quickly forgive her for contradicting herself, but if we disagree with a candidate's views, we criticize her as a "flip-flopper" (Tavris & Aronson, 2007; Westen, Kilts, Blagov, et al., 2006).

Although we'll be encountering a variety of biases in this text, we can think of confirmation bias as the "mother of all biases." That's because it's the bias that can most easily fool us into seeing what we want to see. For that reason, it's also the most crucial bias that psychologists need to counteract. What distinguishes psychological scientists from nonscientists is that the former adopt systematic safeguards to protect against confirmation bias, whereas the latter don't. We'll learn about these safeguards in Chapter 2.

WHAT DO *you* THINK?

Your neighbor travels several times a month on business and swears that she always seems to be flying out of the farthest gate from the terminal. How might you use confirmation bias to explain her perception of the pattern of flights she's on?

Belief Perseverance: It's My Story, and I'm Sticking to It. Confirmation bias can predispose us to another shortcoming to which we're all prone: **belief perseverance.** Belief perseverance refers to the tendency to stick to our initial beliefs even when evidence contradicts them. In everyday language, belief perseverance is the "don't confuse me with the facts" effect. Because none of us wants to believe we're wrong, we're usually reluctant to give up our cherished notions.

Recognizing That We Might Be Wrong. Good psychological scientists are keenly aware that they might be mistaken (Sagan, 1995). In fact, initial scientific conclusions are

Here are four cards. Each of them has a letter on one side and a number on the other side. Two of these cards are shown with the letter side up, and two with the number side up.

E   C   5   4

Indicate which of these cards you have to turn over in order to determine whether the following claim is true:

If a card has a vowel on one side, then it has an odd number on the other side.

Figure 1.3 Diagram of Wason Selection Task. In the Wason selection task, you must pick two cards to test the hypothesis that all cards that have a vowel on one side have an odd number on the other. Which two will you select?

Arthur Darbishire (1879–1915), a British geneticist and mathematician. Darbishire's favorite saying was that the attitude of the scientist should be "one of continual, unceasing, and active distrust of oneself."

GLOSSARY

belief perseverance
tendency to stick to our initial beliefs even when evidence contradicts them

Most of us believe that we evaluate political information objectively. Yet psychological research suggests that when our favorite presidential candidates contradict themselves, we quickly forgive them and explain away the inconsistency. But when candidates we don't like contradict themselves, we criticize them as hypocritical (Westen et al., 2006).

often wrong or at least partly off base. Medical findings are prime examples. Breast self-exams reduce the risk of breast cancer; oops, no, they don't. Drinking a little red wine now and then is good for you; no, actually, it's bad for you. And on and on it goes. It's no wonder that many people just throw up their hands and give up reading medical reports altogether. Scientific knowledge is almost always tentative and potentially open to revision. The fact that science is a process of continually revising and updating findings lends it strength as a method of inquiry. But it means that we usually acquire knowledge slowly and in small bits and pieces.

myth CONCEPTIONS: WHAT IS A SCIENTIFIC THEORY?

Few terms in science have generated more confusion than the deceptively simple term *theory*. Some of this confusion has contributed to serious misunderstandings about how science works. We'll first examine what a scientific theory is, and then address two widespread misconceptions about what a scientific theory *isn't*.

A **scientific theory** is an explanation for a large number of findings in the natural world, including the psychological world. A scientific theory offers an account that ties multiple findings together into one pretty package.

But good scientific theories do more than account for existing data. They generate predictions regarding new data we haven't observed. For a theory to be scientific, it must be capable of generating novel predictions that researchers can test. Scientists call a testable prediction a **hypothesis.** In other words, theories are general explanations, whereas hypotheses are specific predictions derived from these explanations (Bolles, 1962; Meehl, 1967).

MISCONCEPTION 1: A theory explains one specific event.
The first misunderstanding is that a theory is a specific explanation for an event. The popular media get this distinction wrong much of the time. For example, we'll often hear television reporters say something like, "The most likely theory for the robbery at the downtown bank is that it was committed by two former bank employees who dressed up as armed guards." But this isn't a "theory" of the robbery. For one thing, it attempts to explain only one event rather than a variety of diverse observations. In addition, it doesn't generate testable predictions. In contrast, *forensic psychologists*—those who study the causes and treatment of criminal behavior—have constructed theories about robberies that attempt to explain why certain people steal and to forecast when people are most likely to steal (Katz, 1988).

MISCONCEPTION 2: A theory is just an educated guess.
A second myth is that a scientific theory is merely a guess about how the world works. People will often dismiss a theoretical explanation on these grounds, arguing that it's "just a theory."

This phrase mistakenly implies that some explanations about the natural world are "more than theories." In fact, *all* general scientific explanations about how the world works are theories. A few theories are extremely well supported by multiple lines of evidence; for example, the Big Bang theory in astronomy, which proposes that the universe began in a gigantic explosion about 14 billion years ago, helps scientists to explain a diverse array of observations. They include the findings that (a) galaxies are rushing away from each other at remarkable speeds, (b) the universe exhibits a background radiation suggestive of the remnants of a tremendous explosion, and (c) powerful telescopes reveal that the oldest galaxies originated about 14 billion years ago, right around the time pre-

GLOSSARY

scientific theory
explanation for a large number of findings in the natural world

hypothesis
testable prediction derived from a scientific theory

dicted by the Big Bang theory. Like all scientific theories, the Big Bang theory can never be "proved" because it's always conceivable that a better explanation might come along one day. Nevertheless, because this theory is consistent with many differing lines of evidence, the overwhelming majority of scientists accepts it as a good explanation. Darwinian evolution, the Big Bang, and other well-established theories aren't guesses about how the world works, because they've been substantiated over and over again by independent investigators. In contrast, many other scientific theories are only moderately well supported, and still others are questionable or entirely discredited. Not all theories are created equal.

So, when we hear that a scientific explanation is "just a theory," we should remember that theories aren't just guesses. Some theories have survived repeated efforts to refute them and are well-confirmed models of how the world works.

> This textbook contains material on evolution. Evolution is a theory, not a fact, regarding the origin of living things. This material should be approached with an open mind, studied carefully, and critically considered.
>
> *Approved by*
> *Cobb County Board of Education*
> *Thursday, March 28, 2002*

Some creationists have argued that evolution is "just a theory." Cobb County, Georgia, briefly required high school biology textbooks to carry this sticker (Pinker, 2002).

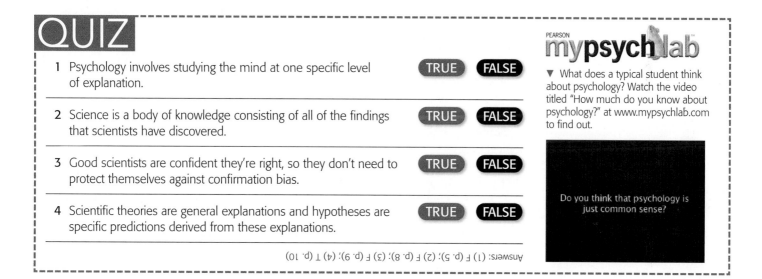

QUIZ

1. Psychology involves studying the mind at one specific level of explanation.   **TRUE**   **FALSE**

2. Science is a body of knowledge consisting of all of the findings that scientists have discovered.   **TRUE**   **FALSE**

3. Good scientists are confident they're right, so they don't need to protect themselves against confirmation bias.   **TRUE**   **FALSE**

4. Scientific theories are general explanations and hypotheses are specific predictions derived from these explanations.   **TRUE**   **FALSE**

Answers: (1) F (p. 5); (2) F (p. 8); (3) F (p. 9); (4) T (p. 10)

PEARSON
mypsychlab

▼ What does a typical student think about psychology? Watch the video titled "How much do you know about psychology?" at www.mypsychlab.com to find out.

Do you think that psychology is just common sense?

Psychological Pseudoscience: Imposters of Science

Of course, you might have enrolled in this course to understand yourself, your friends, or a boyfriend or girlfriend. If so, you might well be thinking, "But I don't want to become a scientist. In fact, I'm not even interested in research. I just want to understand people."

Actually, we're not trying to persuade you to become a scientist (although we'll be delighted if you do). Instead, our goal is to persuade you to *think scientifically:* to become aware of your biases and to take advantage of the tools of the scientific method to try to overcome them. As we'll discover in Chapter 2, the scientific method is a toolbox of skills that helps to protect us from being fooled. By acquiring these skills, you'll become better at making educated choices in your everyday life, such as what weight loss plan to choose, what psychotherapy to recommend to a friend, or even what potential romantic partner is a better long-term bet. You'll also learn how to avoid being tricked by bogus claims. Not everyone needs to become a scientist, but just about everyone can learn to think like one.

THE AMAZING GROWTH OF POPULAR PSYCHOLOGY

In most major bookstores, the self-help section is larger than the psychology section. Although studies show that many self-help books can be helpful, only a small fraction of them have ever been tested in scientific studies.

Distinguishing real from bogus claims is crucial, because the popular psychology industry is huge and growing rapidly. On the positive side, this fact means that the American public has unprecedented access to psychological knowledge. On the negative side, the remarkable growth of popular psychology has led not only to an information explosion but to a *misinformation explosion* because there's scant quality control over what this industry produces.

For example, about 3,500 self-help books are published every year (Arkowitz & Lilienfeld, 2006). Some of these books are effective for treating depression, anxiety, and other psychological problems, but about 95 percent of all self-help books remain untested (Gould & Clum, 1993; Gregory, Canning, Lee, et al., 2004; Rosen, 1993).

Coinciding with the rapid expansion of the popular psychology industry is the enormous growth of treatments and products that claim to cure almost every imaginable psychological ailment. There are well over 500 "brands" of psychotherapy (Eisner, 2000), with new ones being added every year. Fortunately, as we'll learn in Chapter 14, research shows that some of these treatments are clearly helpful for a host of psychological problems. Yet the substantial majority of psychotherapies remain untested, so we don't know whether they help. Some may even be harmful (Lilienfeld, 2007).

Some self-help books base their recommendations on solid research about psychological problems and their treatment. We can often find excellent articles in the *New York Times, Scientific American Mind,* and *Discover* magazines and other media outlets that present high-quality information regarding the science of psychology. In addition, hundreds of websites provide remarkably helpful information and advice concerning a host of psychological topics, like memory, personality testing, and psychological disorders and their treatment (see **Table 1.1**). Yet some self-help books may actually make people worse (Rosen, 1993), so we need to be armed with accurate knowledge to evaluate them.

Table 1.1 Some Trustworthy Websites for Scientific Psychology.

Organization / URL	
American Psychological Association *www.apa.org*	Society for Research in Child Development *www.srcd.org*
Association for Psychological Science *www.psychologicalscience.org*	Society for Personality and Social Psychology *www.spsp.org*
Canadian Psychological Association *www.cpa.ca*	Society for Research in Psychopathology *www.psychopathology.org*
American Psychiatric Association *www.psych.org*	Society for a Science of Clinical Psychology *www.bsos.umd.edu/sscp/*
Society for General Psychology *www.apa.org/divisions/div1/div1homepage.html*	Scientific Review of Mental Health Practice *www.srmhp.org*
Association for Behavioral and Cognitive Therapies *www.aabt.org*	Center for Evidence-Based Mental Health *http://cebmh.warne.ox.ac.uk/cebmh*
Psychonomic Society *www.psychonomic.org*	Empirically Supported Treatments for Psychological Disorders *www.apa.org/divisions/div12/rev_est*
Association for Behavior Analysis, Intl. *www.abainternational.org*	National Institute of Mental Health *www.nimh.nih.gov*

WHAT IS PSEUDOSCIENCE?

These facts highlight a crucial point: We need to distinguish claims that are genuinely scientific from those that are merely imposters of science. An imposter of science is **pseudoscience:** a set of claims that *seem* scientific but aren't. In particular, *pseudoscience lacks the safeguards against confirmation bias and belief perseverance that characterize science.* **[LEARNING OBJECTIVE 1.3]**

Pseudoscientific and other questionable beliefs are widespread. Consider the following findings from a large recent survey of the American public (Musella, 2005):

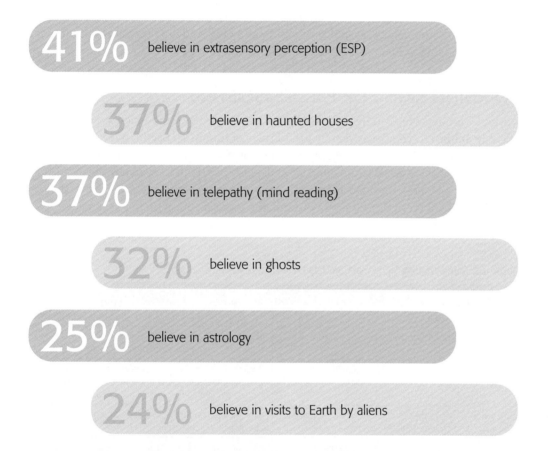

41% believe in extrasensory perception (ESP)

37% believe in haunted houses

37% believe in telepathy (mind reading)

32% believe in ghosts

25% believe in astrology

24% believe in visits to Earth by aliens

21% believe in communication with the dead

21% believe in witches

(Source: Musella, 2005)

The fact that many Americans *entertain* the possibility of such beliefs isn't by itself worrisome, because a certain amount of open-mindedness is essential for scientific thinking. Instead, what's troubling is that many Americans appear convinced that such claims are correct even though the scientific evidence for them is either weak, as in the case of extrasensory perseption (ESP), or essentially nonexistent.

GLOSSARY

pseudoscience
set of claims that seems scientific but isn't

As we'll discover throughout this text, many popular psychology claims are pseudo-scientific. These include many assertions regarding astrology, ESP, out-of-body experiences, polygraph ("lie-detector") testing, recovered memories of child abuse, the analysis of handwriting to infer people's personality traits, multiple personality disorder, and some questionable psychotherapies. That's not to say that all of these claims are entirely false. In fact, at least a few of them possess a core of truth. Still others might be shown to be true in future research. Yet, as we'll soon see, the proponents of these claims don't typically "play by the rules" of the game of science.

The difference between science and pseudoscience isn't always clear-cut. Some psychological products and treatments are based mostly on science but partly on pseudoscience, and vice versa. Still, we can pinpoint a number of helpful distinctions between science and pseudoscience, even if the boundaries between them become fuzzy around the edges (Leahey & Leahey, 1983; Lindeman, 1998).

WARNING SIGNS OF PSEUDOSCIENCE

Several warning signs can help us distinguish science from pseudoscience; we've listed them in **Table 1.2.** They're extremely useful rules of thumb, so useful in fact that we'll draw on many of them in later chapters to help us become more informed consumers of psychological claims. We can—and should—also use them in everyday life. None of these signs is by itself proof positive that a set of claims is pseudoscientific. Nevertheless, the more of these signs that are present, the more skeptical of these claims we should become.

Table 1.2 Some Warning Signs That Can Help Us Recognize Pseudoscience.

Sign of Pseudoscience	Example
Exaggerated claims	Three simple steps will change your love life forever!
Overreliance on anecdotes	This woman practiced yoga daily for three weeks and hasn't had a day of depression since.
Absence of connectivity to other research	Amazing new innovations in research have shown that eye massage results in reading speeds 10 times faster than average!
Lack of review by other scholars (called *peer review*) or replication by independent labs	Fifty studies conducted by the company all show overwhelming success!
Lack of self-correction when contrary evidence is published	Although some scientists say that we use almost all our brains, we've found a way to harness additional brain power previously undiscovered.
Meaningless "psychobabble" that uses fancy scientific-sounding terms that don't make sense	Sine-wave filtered auditory stimulation is carefully designed to encourage maximal orbitofrontal dendritic development.
Talk of "proof" instead of "evidence"	Our new program is proven to reduce social anxiety by at least 50 percent!

"HOWEVER, IT'S EXCELLENT PSEUDOSCIENCE."

(© ScienceCartoonsPlus.com)

WHY ARE WE DRAWN TO PSEUDOSCIENCE?

There are a host of reasons why we're all drawn to pseudoscientific beliefs. As the old saying goes, "hope springs eternal": We believe because we want to believe. Many pseudoscientific claims, such as astrology, may give us comfort because they seem to offer us a sense of control over an often unpredictable world (Shermer, 2002).

But perhaps the central reason for the popularity of pseudoscience stems from the way our brains work. *Our brains are predisposed to make order out of disorder and find sense in nonsense.* This tendency is generally adaptive, as it helps us to simplify the often bewildering world in which we live (Alcock, 1995; Pinker, 1997). Without it, we'd be constantly overwhelmed by endless streams of information we don't have the time or ability to process. Yet this adaptive tendency can sometimes lead us astray because it can lead us to perceive meaningful patterns even when they're not there (Shermer, 2002).

Our tendency to seek out patterns sometimes goes too far, leading us to experience **apophenia:** perceiving meaningful connections among unrelated and even random phenomena (Carroll, 2003). We all fall victim to apophenia from time to time. If we think of a friend with whom we haven't spoken in a few months and then immediately afterward receive a phone call from her, we may jump to the conclusion that this striking co-occurrence of events stems from ESP. Of course, it's *possible* that it does.

But it's also entirely possible, if not likely, that these two events happened at about the same time by chance alone. For a moment, think of the number of times one of your old friends comes to mind, and then think of the number of phone calls you receive each month. You'll realize that the laws of probability make it likely that at least once over the next few years, you'll be thinking of an old friend at about the same time she calls.

Our minds work in such a way that we often detect patterns in unrelated events, such as thinking of an old friend and then receiving a telephone call from that friend.

WHAT DO *you* THINK?

You are cleaning out your filing cabinet one day and come across some old photos of a former boyfriend or girlfriend you haven't talked to or thought about in years. Later that day, that person texts you unexpectedly. How would you explain this coincidence?

Another manifestation of apophenia is our tendency to detect eerie coincidences between persons or events. To take one example, consider the uncanny similarities between Abraham Lincoln and John F. Kennedy, the two most prominent American presidents who were the victims of assassination, listed in **Table 1.3** (on page 16).

Pretty amazing stuff, isn't it? So extraordinary, in fact, that some writers have argued that Lincoln and Kennedy are somehow linked by supernatural forces (Leavy, 1992).

In actuality, coincidences are everywhere: They're surprisingly easy to detect if we just make the effort to look for them. Because of apophenia, we may attribute paranormal significance to coincidences that are probably due to chance. Moreover, we often fall victim to confirmation bias and neglect to consider evidence that *doesn't* support our hypothesis. Because we typically find coincidences to be far more interesting than noncoincidences, we tend to forget that Lincoln was a Republican whereas Kennedy was a Democrat, that Lincoln was shot in Washington, DC, whereas Kennedy was shot in Dallas, and that Lincoln had a beard, but Kennedy didn't.

Recall that scientific thinking is designed to counteract confirmation bias. To do so, we must seek out evidence that contradicts our ideas rather than merely confirms them.

METAPHYSICAL CLAIMS: THE BOUNDARIES OF SCIENCE

It's essential to distinguish pseudoscientific claims from **metaphysical claims:** assertions about the world that we can't test (Popper, 1965). Metaphysical claims include assertions about the existence of God, the soul, and the afterlife. These claims differ from pseudoscientific claims in that we could never test them using scientific meth-

GLOSSARY

apophenia
tendency to perceive meaningful connections among unrelated phenomena

metaphysical claims
assertions about the world that are not testable

Table 1.3 Some Eerie Commonalities between Abraham Lincoln and John F. Kennedy.

Abraham Lincoln	John F. Kennedy
Was elected to Congress in 1846	Was elected to Congress in 1946
Was elected President in 1860	Was elected President in 1960
The name "Lincoln" contains seven letters	The name "Kennedy" contains seven letters
Was assassinated on a Friday	Was assassinated on a Friday
Lincoln's secretary, named Kennedy, warned him not to go to the theater, where he was shot	Kennedy's secretary, named Lincoln, warned him not to go to Dallas, where he was shot
Lincoln's wife was sitting beside him when he was shot	Kennedy's wife was sitting beside him when he was shot
John Wilkes Booth (Lincoln's assassin) was born in 1839	Lee Harvey Oswald (Kennedy's assassin) was born in 1939
Was succeeded by a president named Johnson	Was succeeded by a president named Johnson
Andrew Johnson, who succeeded Lincoln, was born in 1808	Lyndon Johnson, who succeeded Kennedy, was born in 1908
Booth fled from a theater to a warehouse	Oswald fled from a warehouse to a theater
Booth was killed before his trial	Oswald was killed before his trial

ods. (How could we design a scientific test to conclusively demonstrate or disprove the existence of God?).

This point doesn't mean that metaphysical claims are wrong, let alone unimportant. To the contrary, many thoughtful scholars would contend that questions concerning the existence of God are even more significant and profound than scientific questions. Moreover, regardless of our beliefs about religion, we all need to treat these questions with the profound respect they deserve. But it's crucial to understand that there are certain questions about the world that science can—and can't—answer. Science has its limits. So it needs to respect the boundaries of religion and other metaphysical domains. Testable claims fall within the province of science; untestable claims don't.

THE DANGERS OF PSEUDOSCIENCE: WHY SHOULD WE CARE?

Up to this point, we've been making a big deal about pseudoscience. But why should we care about it? After all, isn't a great deal of pseudoscience, like astrology, pretty harmless? In fact, pseudoscience can be dangerous, even deadly. This point applies to a variety of questionable claims that we come across in everyday life. There are three major reasons why we should all be concerned about pseudoscience. **[LEARNING OBJECTIVE 1.4]**

- **Opportunity Cost: What We Give Up.** Pseudoscientific treatments for mental disorders can lead people to forgo opportunities to seek effective treatments. As a consequence, even treatments that are themselves harmless can cause harm indirectly by causing people to forfeit the chance to obtain a treatment that works.

- **Direct Harm.** Pseudoscientific treatments sometimes do dreadful harm to those who receive them, causing psychological or physical damage—occasionally even death.

- **An Inability to Think Scientifically as Citizens.** As we'll see later, scientific thinking skills aren't just important for evaluating psychological claims—we use them in all parts of life. In our increasingly complex scientific and technological society, we all need scientific thinking skills to reach educated decisions about global warming, genetic engineering, stem cell research, novel medical treatments, and parenting and teaching practices.

The take-home message is clear: Pseudoscience matters. That's what makes scientific thinking so critical: Although far from foolproof, it's our best safeguard against human error.

Candace Newmaker was a tragic victim of a pseudoscientific treatment called rebirthing therapy. She died of suffocation at age 10 after her therapists wrapped her in a flannel blanket and squeezed her to simulate birth contractions.

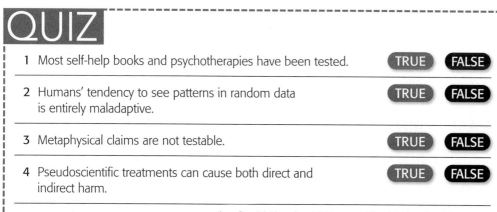

QUIZ

1	Most self-help books and psychotherapies have been tested.	TRUE	FALSE
2	Humans' tendency to see patterns in random data is entirely maladaptive.	TRUE	FALSE
3	Metaphysical claims are not testable.	TRUE	FALSE
4	Pseudoscientific treatments can cause both direct and indirect harm.	TRUE	FALSE

Answers: (1) F (p. 12); (2) F (pp. 14–15); (3) T (p. 15); (4) T (p. 17)

PEARSON
mypsychlab

▼ Can people talk to the dead? Watch the video titled "Cold reading: Talking to popular heaven medium James Van Pragh" at www.mypsychlab.com to learn how psychologists can explain the pseudoscience of psychics.

Scientific Thinking: Distinguishing Fact from Fiction

Given that the world of popular psychology is chock-full of remarkable claims, how can we distinguish psychological fact from psychological fiction?

SCIENTIFIC SKEPTICISM

The approach we'll emphasize throughout this text is **scientific skepticism.** To many people, the term *skepticism* implies closed-mindedness, but nothing could be further

GLOSSARY

scientific skepticism
approach of evaluating all claims with an open mind but insisting on persuasive evidence before accepting them

"... and, as you go out into the world, I predict that you will, gradually and imperceptibly, forget all you ever learned at this university."

You'll probably forget many of the things you'll learn in college. But you'll be able to use the approach of scientific skepticism throughout your life to evaluate claims. (© Science CartoonsPlus.com)

from the truth. The term *skepticism* actually derives from the Greek word *skeptikos,* which means "to consider carefully" (Shermer, 2002). The scientific skeptic evaluates all claims with an open mind but insists on persuasive evidence before accepting them. **[LEARNING OBJECTIVE 1.5]**

As astronomer Carl Sagan (1995) noted, to be a scientific skeptic, we must adopt two attitudes that may seem contradictory but aren't: first, a willingness to keep an open mind to all claims and, second, a willingness to accept these claims only after researchers have subjected them to careful scientific tests. Scientific skeptics are willing to change their minds when confronted with evidence that challenges their preconceptions. At the same time, they change their minds only when this evidence is persuasive. The motto of the scientific skeptic is the Missouri principle, which we'll find on many Missouri state license plates: "Show me" (Dawes, 1994).

Another key feature of scientific skepticism is an unwillingness to accept claims on the basis of authority alone. Scientific skeptics evaluate claims on their own merits and refuse to accept them until they meet a high standard of evidence. Of course, in everyday life we're often forced to accept the word of authorities simply because we don't possess the expertise, time, or resources to evaluate every claim on our own. Most of us are willing to accept the claim that our local governments keep our drinking water safe without conducting our own chemical tests. While reading this chapter, you're also placing trust in us—the authors, that is—to provide you with accurate information about psychology. Still, this doesn't mean you should blindly accept everything we've written hook, line, and sinker. Consider what we've written with an open mind but evaluate it skeptically. If you disagree with something we've written, be sure to get a second opinion by asking your instructor.

BASIC PRINCIPLES OF SCIENTIFIC THINKING

The hallmark of scientific skepticism is **critical thinking.** Many students misunderstand the word *critical* in *critical thinking,* assuming incorrectly that it entails a tendency to attack all claims. In fact, critical thinking is a set of skills for evaluating all claims in an open-minded and careful fashion. We can also think of critical thinking in psychology as *scientific thinking,* as it's the form of thinking that allows us to evaluate scientific claims, not only in the laboratory but in everyday life as well (Willingham, 2007).

Just as important, scientific thinking is a set of skills for overcoming our own biases, especially confirmation bias, which as we've learned can blind us to evidence we'd prefer to ignore (Alcock, 1995). In particular, in this text we'll be emphasizing *six* principles of scientific thinking (Bartz, 2002; Lett, 1990). We should bear these six principles in mind when evaluating all psychological claims, including claims in the media, self-help books, the Internet, your introductory psychology course, and, yes, even this textbook.

These six scientific thinking principles are so crucial that we'll indicate each of them with a different-colored flag that you'll see throughout the text. Whenever one of these scientific thinking principles arises in our discussion, we'll display that flag in the margin to remind you of the principle that goes along with it (see **Figure 1.4**). **[LEARNING OBJECTIVE 1.6]**

Scientific Thinking Principle #1: *Ruling Out Rival Hypotheses.* Most psychological findings we'll hear about on television or read about on the Internet lend themselves to multiple explanations. Yet, more often than not, the media report only one explanation. We shouldn't automatically assume it's correct. Instead, we should ask ourselves: Is this the only good explanation for this finding? Have we ruled out all important competing explanations (Platt, 1964)?

GLOSSARY

critical thinking
set of skills for evaluating all claims in an open-minded and careful fashion

Six Principles of Scientific Thinking

These six flags of scientific thinking, introduced on page 18 and used throughout
the text, will help you evaluate claims in research and everyday life.

What Scientific Thinking Principle Should We Use?	When Might We Use It?	How Do We Use It?
RULING OUT RIVAL HYPOTHESES Have important alternative explanations for the findings been excluded?	You're reading the newspaper and come across the headline: "Study shows depressed people who receive a new medication improve more than equally depressed people who receive nothing."	The results of the study could be due to the fact that people who received the medication expected to improve.
CORRELATION vs. CAUSATION Can we be sure that A causes B?	A finding shows that people eat more ice cream on days when many crimes are committed, and concludes eating ice cream causes crime.	Eating ice cream (A) might not cause crime (B). Both could be due to a third factor (C), such as higher temperatures. 
FALSIFIABILITY Can the claim be disproved?	A self-help book claims that all human beings have an invisible energy field surrounding them that influences their moods and well-being.	We can't design a study to disprove this claim. 
REPLICABILITY Can the results be duplicated in other studies?	A magazine article highlights a study that shows people who practice meditation score 50 points higher on an intelligence test than those who don't.	We should be skeptical if no other scientific studies have reported the same findings. 
EXTRAORDINARY CLAIMS Is the evidence as convincing as the claim?	You come across a website that claims that a monster, like Bigfoot, has been living in the American Northwest for decades without being discovered by researchers.	This extraordinary claim requires more rigorous evidence than the claim that people remember more words from the beginning than from the end of a list. 
OCCAM'S RAZOR Does a simpler explanation fit the data just as well?	Your friend, who has poor vision, claims that he spotted a UFO while attending a Frisbee tournament.	Is it more likely that your friend's report is due to a simpler explanation—his mistaking a Frisbee for a UFO—than to alien visitation? 

Some Warning Signs of Pseudoscientific Claims

These warning signs, which are discussed on page 14, will help you distinguish scientific from pseudoscientific claims so that you can become a more informed consumer.

Sign of Pseudoscience	Explanation	Example
Exaggerated claims	Pseudoscience tends to promise remarkable or dramatic cures, but rarely delivers the goods. Remember — extraordinary claims require extraordinary evidence.	
Overreliance on anecdotes	Pseudoscience tends to rely heavily on anecdotal evidence ("I know a person who" assertions). Anecdotes have three major limitations: they don't tell us anything about cause and effect, they don't tell us how representative the cases are, and they are difficult to verify.	
Absence of connectivity to other research	Most sciences are cumulative: new findings build on or "connect up with" previous findings. In contrast, pseudoscience neglects previous research and purports to create grand new ideas.	
Lack of review by other scholars (called peer review) or replication by independent labs	Most pseudoscience bypasses peer review and relies on anecdotes or conducts informal research that's never submitted to scientific journals. Many of these research studies are conducted "in-house" so there is no way to evaluate if they were conducted properly.	
Lack of self-correction when contrary evidence is published	Unlike science, in which incorrect claims tend to be weeded out eventually, in pseudoscience, incorrect claims never seem to go away because their proponents cling to them stubbornly despite contrary evidence.	
Meaningless "psychobabble" that uses fancy scientific-sounding terms that don't make sense	Pseudoscience attempts to lure consumers into accepting claims by peppering their advertising with technical terms that are devoid of meaning.	
Talk of "proof" instead of "evidence"	Scientific knowledge is rarely, if ever, conclusive. In contrast, pseudoscience tends to promise products or treatments that have been "proven" effective.	

What Scientific Thinking Principle Should We Use?	When Might We Use It?	How Do We Use It?
RULING OUT RIVAL HYPOTHESES Have important alternative explanations for the findings been excluded?	You're reading the newspaper and come across the headline: "Study shows depressed people who receive a new medication improve more than equally depressed people who receive nothing."	The results of the study could be due to the fact that people who received the medication expected to improve. 
CORRELATION vs. CAUSATION Can we be sure that A causes B?	A finding shows that people eat more ice cream on days when many crimes are committed, and concludes eating ice cream causes crime.	Eating ice cream (A) might not cause crime (B). Both could be due to a third factor (C), such as higher temperatures. 
FALSIFIABILITY Can the claim be disproved?	A self-help book claims that all human beings have an invisible energy field surrounding them that influences their moods and well-being.	We can't design a study to disprove this claim. 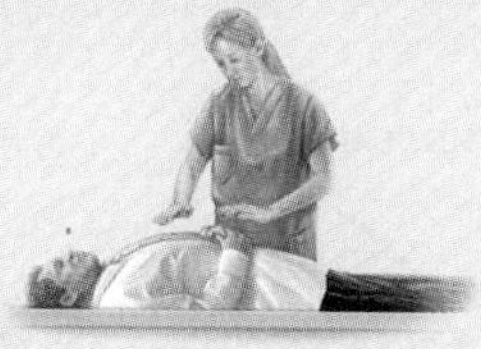
REPLICABILITY Can the results be duplicated in other studies?	A magazine article highlights a study that shows people who practice meditation score 50 points higher on an intelligence test than those who don't.	We should be skeptical if no other scientific studies have reported the same findings. 
EXTRAORDINARY CLAIMS Is the evidence as convincing as the claim?	You come across a website that claims that a monster, like Bigfoot, has been living in the American Northwest for decades without being discovered by researchers.	This extraordinary claim requires more rigorous evidence than the claim that people remember more words from the beginning than from the end of a list. 
OCCAM'S RAZOR Does a simpler explanation fit the data just as well?	Your friend, who has poor vision, claims that he spotted a UFO while attending a Frisbee tournament.	Is it more likely that your friend's report is due to a simpler explanation—his mistaking a Frisbee for a UFO—than to alien visitation? 

Figure 1.4 The Six Flags of Scientific Thinking That Are Used throughout This Textbook.

Let's take a popular treatment for anxiety disorders, eye movement desensitization and reprocessing (EMDR; see also Chapter 14). Introduced by Francine Shapiro (1989), EMDR asks clients to track the therapist's back-and-forth finger movements with their eyes while imagining distressing memories that are the source of their anxiety, such as the memory of seeing someone being killed. Proponents of EMDR have consistently maintained that it's far more effective and efficient than other treatments for anxiety disorders. Some have claimed that these eye movements somehow synchronize the brain's two hemispheres or stimulate brain mechanisms that speed up the processing of emotional memories.

Yet there's a problem. A slew of well-controlled studies show that the eye movements of EMDR don't contribute to its effectiveness. EMDR works just as well when people stare straight ahead at an immobile dot while thinking about the source of their anxiety (Davidson & Parker, 2001; Lohr, Tolin, & Lilienfeld, 1998). Most EMDR advocates neglected to consider a rival explanation for EMDR's success: EMDR asks patients to expose themselves to anxiety-provoking imagery. Researchers and therapists alike have long known that prolonged exposure itself can be therapeutic (Lohr, Hooke, Gist, et al., 2003; see Chapter 14). By not excluding the rival hypothesis that EMDR's effectiveness stemmed from exposure rather than eye movements, EMDR advocates made claims that ran well ahead of the data.

The bottom line: Whenever we evaluate a psychological claim, we should ask ourselves whether we've excluded other plausible explanations for it.

RULING OUT RIVAL HYPOTHESES
Have important alternative explanations for the findings been excluded?

THE FAMILY CIRCUS By Bil Keane

"I wish they didn't turn on that seatbelt sign so much! Every time they do, it gets bumpy."

Correlation isn't always causation. (Family Circus © Bil Keane, Inc. King Features Syndicate)

Scientific Thinking Principle #2: *Correlation Isn't Causation.* Perhaps the most common mistake psychology students make when interpreting studies is to conclude that when two things are associated with each other—or what psychologists call "correlated" with each other—one thing must cause the other. This point leads us to one of the most crucial principles in this book (get your highlighters out for this one): *Correlational designs don't permit causal inferences,* or, putting it less formally, *correlation isn't causation.* When we mistakenly conclude that a correlation means causation, we've committed the **correlation–causation fallacy.** This conclusion is a fallacy because the fact that two variables are correlated doesn't necessarily mean that one causes the other (also see Chapter 2). Incidentally, a **variable** is anything that can *vary,* like height, IQ, or extraversion. Let's see why correlation isn't causation.

If we start with two variables, A and B, that are correlated, there are three major explanations for this correlation.

(1) A → B. It's possible that variable A causes variable B.

(2) B → A. It's possible that variable B causes variable A.

So far, so good. But many people forget that there's also a third possibility, namely, that:

(3) C ↗ A ↘ B

In this third scenario, there's a third variable, C, that causes *both* A and B. This scenario is known as the third variable problem. The reason it's a "problem" is it can lead us to conclude mistakenly that A and B are causally related to each other when they're not. For example, researchers found that teenagers who listen to music with lots of sexual lyrics have sexual intercourse considerably more often than teenagers who listen to music with tamer lyrics (Martino et al., 2006). Listening to sexual lyrics is *correlated* with sexual behavior. One newspaper summarized the findings of this study with an attention-grabbing headline: "Sexual lyrics prompt teens to have sex" (Tanner, 2006). Like

GLOSSARY

correlation–causation fallacy
error of assuming that because one thing is associated with another, it must cause the other

variable
anything that can vary

many headlines, this one went well beyond the data. It's indeed possible that music with sexual lyrics (A) causes sexual behavior (B). But it's also possible that sexual behavior (B) causes teens to listen to music with sexual lyrics (A), or that a third variable, like impulsivity (C), both causes teens to listen to music with sexual lyrics *and* engage in sexual behavior. Given the data reported by the authors, there's no way to know. *Correlation isn't causation.* This point is so crucial that we'll come back to it and discuss it in more depth in Chapter 2.

The bottom line: We should remember that a correlation between two things doesn't demonstrate a causal connection between them.

Scientific Thinking Principle #3: *Falsifiability.*
Philosopher of science Sir Karl Popper (1965) observed that for a claim to be meaningful, it must be **falsifiable,** that is, capable of being disproved. Some students misunderstand this point, confusing the question of whether a theory is *falsifiable* with whether it's *false.* The principle of falsifiability doesn't mean that a theory must be false to be meaningful. Instead, it means that for a theory to be meaningful, it *could* be proven wrong if there were certain types of evidence against it. For a claim to be falsifiable, its proponent must state clearly *in advance,* not after the fact, which findings would count as evidence for and against the claim.

A key implication of the falsifiability principle is that a theory that explains everything—that is, a theory that can account for every conceivable outcome—in effect explains nothing. That's because a good scientific theory must predict only certain outcomes, but not others. If a friend told you he was a master "psychic sports forecaster" and predicted with great confidence that, "Tomorrow, all of the major league baseball teams that are playing a game will either win or lose," you'd probably start laughing. By predicting every potential outcome, your friend hasn't really predicted anything.

If as a psychic sports forecaster, your friend instead predicted, "The New York Yankees and New York Mets will both win tomorrow by three runs, but the Boston Red Sox and Los Angeles Dodgers will lose by one run," this prediction could be either correct or incorrect. There is a possibility he'll be wrong—the prediction is falsifiable.

The bottom line: Whenever we evaluate a psychological claim, we should ask ourselves whether one could in principle disprove it or whether it's consistent with any conceivable body of evidence.

CORRELATION vs. **CAUSATION**
Can we be sure that A causes B?

Some television shows, like *Medium,* feature "psychic detectives," people with supposed extrasensory powers who can help police to locate missing people. Yet psychic detectives' predictions are typically so vague—"I see a body near water," "The body is near a wooded area"—that they're virtually impossible to falsify.

FALSIFIABILITY
Can the claim be disproved?

WHAT DO *you* THINK?

You are giving a guest presentation in a nearby high school about the scientific method, and the students are having difficulty understanding the idea of falsifiability. To help them, you ask them to identify which of the following claims are falsifiable, and which are not falsifiable. (1) Republicans have higher IQs than Democrats. (2) Psychotherapy is effective. (3) All people are surrounded by invisible, undetectable auras. (4) Your introductory psychology teacher was once Cleopatra in a previous life. What would you tell them?

Scientific Thinking Principle #4: *Replicability.*
Barely a week goes by that we don't hear about another stunning psychological finding on the evening news: "Researchers at Cupcake State University detect a new gene linked to excessive shopping"; "Investigators at the University of Antarctica at Igloo report that alcoholism is associated with a heightened risk of murdering one's spouse"; "Nobel Prize–winning

GLOSSARY

falsifiable
capable of being disproved

ESP researchers often ask subjects to predict the outcomes of random events. Yet ESP findings have proven difficult to replicate.

professor at Cucumber State College isolates brain area responsible for the enjoyment of popcorn." One major problem with these conclusions, in addition to the fact that the news media often tell us nothing about the design of the studies on which they're based, is that the findings often haven't been replicated. **Replicability** means that a study's findings can be duplicated consistently. If they can't be duplicated, it increases the odds that the original findings were due to chance. *We shouldn't place too much stock in a psychological finding until it's been replicated.*

We should bear in mind that the media are far more likely to report initial positive findings than failures to replicate. The initial findings may be especially fascinating or sensational, whereas replication failures are often disappointing.

It's especially important that investigators other than the original researchers replicate the results because this increases our confidence in them. If I tell you that I've created a recipe for the world's most delicious veal parmigiana, but it turns out that every other chef who follows my recipe ends up with a meal that tastes like an old piece of cardboard, you'd be justifiably skeptical of my claim. Maybe I flat out lied about my recipe. Or perhaps I wasn't actually following the recipe very closely and was instead tossing in ingredients that weren't even in the recipe. Or perhaps I'm such an extraordinary chef that nobody else can come close to duplicating my miraculous culinary feats. In any case, you'd have every right to doubt my recipe until someone else replicated it. The same goes for psychological research.

The literature on ESP offers an excellent example of why replicability is so essential (see Chapter 4). Every once in a blue moon, a researcher reports a striking new finding that seemingly confirms the existence of ESP. Yet time and again, independent researchers haven't been able to replicate these tantalizing results (Gilovich, 1991; Hyman, 1989; Lilienfeld, 1999c).

The bottom line: Whenever we evaluate a psychological claim, we should ask ourselves whether independent investigators have replicated the findings that support this claim; otherwise, the findings might be a one-time-only fluke.

REPLICABILITY

Can the results be duplicated in other studies?

Scientific Thinking Principle #5: *Extraordinary Claims Require Extraordinary Evidence.* (Throughout the book, we'll be abbreviating this principle as "Extraordinary Claims.") This principle was proposed in slightly different terms by eighteenth-century Scottish philosopher David Hume (Sagan, 1995; Truzzi, 1978). According to Hume, the more a claim contradicts what we already know, the more persuasive the evidence for this claim must be before we should accept it.

For example, a handful of researchers believe that every night hundreds or even thousands of Americans are being lifted magically out of their beds, brought aboard flying saucers, and experimented on by aliens, only to be returned safely to their beds hours later (Clancy, 2005). According to some alien abduction advocates, aliens are extracting semen from human males to impregnate female aliens in an effort to create a race of alien–human hybrids.

Of course, alien abduction proponents *might* be right, and we shouldn't dismiss their claims out of hand. But their claims are pretty darned extraordinary, especially because they imply that tens of thousands of invading flying saucers from other solar systems have inexplicably managed to escape detection by astronomers, not to mention air traffic controllers and radar operators. Alien abduction proponents have been unable to provide even a shred of concrete evidence that supposed abductees have actually encountered extraterrestrials—say, a convincing photograph of an alien, a tiny piece of a metal probe inserted by an alien, or even a strand of hair or shred of skin from an authentic alien. Thus far, all that alien abduction proponents have to show for their claims

According to a few researchers, tens of thousands of Americans have been abducted by aliens and brought aboard spaceships to be experimented on. Could it really be happening, and how would we know?

GLOSSARY

replicability
when a study's findings are able to be duplicated, ideally by independent investigators

are the self-reports of supposed abductees. Extraordinary claims, but decidedly ordinary evidence.

The bottom line: Whenever we evaluate a psychological claim, we should ask ourselves whether this claim runs counter to many things we know already and, if it does, whether the evidence is as extraordinary as the claim.

EXTRAORDINARY CLAIMS
Is the evidence as convincing as the claim?

Scientific Thinking Principle #6: *Occam's Razor.*

Occam's Razor, named after fourteenth-century British philosopher and monk Sir William of Occam, is also called the "principle of parsimony" (*parsimony* means logical simplicity). According to Occam's Razor, if two explanations account equally well for a phenomenon, we should generally select the more parsimonious one. Good researchers use Occam's Razor to "shave off" needlessly complicated explanations to arrive at the simplest explanation that does a good job of accounting for the evidence. Scientists of a romantic persuasion refer to Occam's Razor as the principle of KISS: Keep it simple, stupid. Occam's Razor is only a guideline, not a hard-and-fast rule (Uttal, 2003). Every once in a while the best explanation for a phenomenon is the most complex, not the simplest. But Occam's Razor is a helpful rule of thumb, as it's right far more often than wrong.

During the late 1970s and 1980s, hundreds of mysterious designs, called crop circles, began appearing in wheat fields in England. Most of these designs were remarkably intricate. How on Earth (pun intended) can we explain these designs? Many believers in the paranormal concluded that these designs originated not on Earth but on distant planets. The crop circles, they concluded, are proof positive of alien visitations to our world.

The crop circle excitement came crashing down in 1991, when two British men, David Bower and Doug Chorley, confessed to creating the crop circles as a barroom prank intended to poke fun at uncritical believers in extraterrestrials. They even demonstrated on camera how they used wooden planks and rope to stomp through tall fields of wheat and craft the complex designs. Occam's Razor reminds us that when confronted with two explanations that fit the evidence equally well, we should generally select the simpler one—in this case, human pranksters.

The bottom line: Whenever we evaluate a psychological claim, we should ask ourselves whether the explanation offered is the simplest explanation that accounts for the data or whether simpler explanations can account for the data equally well.

There are two explanations for crop circles, one supernatural and the other natural. Which should we believe?

OCCAM'S RAZOR
Does a simpler explanation fit the data just as well?

QUIZ

1. Scientific skepticism requires a willingness to keep an open mind to all claims. **TRUE** **FALSE**

2. When evaluating a psychological claim, we should consider other plausible explanations for it. **TRUE** **FALSE**

3. The fact that two things are related doesn't mean that one directly influences the other. **TRUE** **FALSE**

4. Falsifiability means that a theory must be false to be meaningful. **TRUE** **FALSE**

5. When psychological findings are replicated, it's especially important that the replications be conducted by the same team of investigators. **TRUE** **FALSE**

PEARSON
mypsychlab

▼ Can you think yourself wealthy or think yourself to good grades? Watch the video titled "The Secret" at www.mypsychlab.com to find out what scientists say about the power of thought.

Answers: (1) T (p. 18); (2) T (p. 18); (3) T (p. 20); (4) F (p. 21); (5) F (p. 22).

Wilhelm Wundt (*right*) in the world's first psychology laboratory. Wundt is generally credited with launching psychology as a laboratory science in 1879.

Psychology's Past and Present: What a Long, Strange Trip It's Been

How did psychology emerge as a discipline, and has it always been plagued by pseudoscience? The scientific approach to the study of the mind and behavior emerged slowly, and the field's initial attempts displayed many of the weaknesses that pseudoscientific approaches possess today. Informal attempts to study and explain how our minds work have been around for thousands of years. But psychology as a science has existed for only about 130 years, and many of those years were spent refining techniques to develop research methods that were free from bias. Throughout its history, psychology has struggled with many of the same challenges that we face today when reasoning about psychological research. So, it's important to understand how psychology evolved as a scientific discipline—that is, a discipline that relies on systematic research methods to avoid being fooled.

We'll start our journey with a capsule summary of psychology's bumpy road from nonscience to science (a timeline of significant events in the evolution of scientific psychology can be seen in **Figure 1.5**).

For many centuries, the field of psychology was difficult to distinguish from philosophy. Most academic psychologists held positions in departments of philosophy (psychology departments didn't even exist back then) and didn't conduct experimental research. Instead, they mostly sat and contemplated the human mind from their armchairs. In essence, they relied on common sense.

Yet beginning in the late 1800s, the landscape of psychology changed dramatically. In 1879, Wilhelm Wundt (1832–1920) developed the first full-fledged psychological laboratory in Leipzig, Germany. Most of Wundt's investigations and those of his students focused on basic questions concerning our mental experiences: How different must two colors be for us to tell them apart? How long does it take us to react to a sound? What thoughts come to mind when we solve a math problem? Wundt used a combination of experimental methods, including reaction time equipment, and a technique called **introspection,** which required trained observers to carefully reflect and report on their mental experiences. In many respects, the pioneering work of Wundt marked the beginnings of psychology as a science. Soon, psychologists elsewhere around the world followed Wundt's bold lead and opened laboratories in departments of psychology.

THE GREAT THEORETICAL FRAMEWORKS OF PSYCHOLOGY

Almost since its inception, psychological science has confronted a thorny question: What unifying theoretical perspective best explains behavior?

Five major theoretical perspectives—structuralism, functionalism, behaviorism, psychoanalysis, and cognitivism—have played pivotal roles in shaping contemporary psychological thought. **[LEARNING OBJECTIVE 1.7]** Many beginning psychology students understandably ask, "Which of these perspectives is the right one?" As it turns out, the answer isn't entirely clear. Each theoretical viewpoint has something valuable to contribute to scientific psychology, but each has its limitations (see **Table 1.4** on page 26). As we wind our way through these five frameworks, we'll discover that psychology's view of what constitutes a scientific approach to behavior has changed over time. Indeed, it continues to change even today.

GLOSSARY

introspection
method by which trained observers carefully reflect and report on their mental experiences

1649: René Descartes writes about the mind–body problem

Late 1700s: Frans Anton Mesmer discovers principles of hypnosis

Early 1800s: Due to efforts of Franz Joseph Gall and Joseph Spurzheim, phrenology becomes immensely popular in Europe and the United States

1850: Gustav Fechner experiences crucial insight linking physical changes in the external world to subjective changes in perception; leads to establishment of psychophysics

1859: Charles Darwin writes *Origin of Species*

1875: William James creates small psychological laboratory at Harvard University

1879: Wilhelm Wundt creates world's first formal psychological laboratory, launching psychology as an experimental science

1881: Wundt establishes first psychology journal

1883: J. Stanley Hall, one of Wundt's students, opens first major psychology laboratory in the United States, at Johns Hopkins University

1888: James McKeen Cattell becomes first professor of psychology in the United States

1889: Sir Francis Galton introduces concept of correlation, allowing psychologists to quantify associations among variables

1890: William James writes *Principles of Psychology*

1892: American Psychological Association (APA) founded

1896: Lightmer Witmer creates first psychological clinic at the University of Pennsylvania, launching field of clinical psychology

1900: Sigmund Freud writes *The Interpretation of Dreams*, landmark book in the history of psychoanalysis

1904: Mary Calkins is first woman elected president of the American Psychological Association

1967: Ulric Neisser writes *Cognitive Psychology*; helps to launch field of cognitive psychology

1963: Stanley Milgram publishes classic laboratory studies of obedience

1958: Joseph Wolpe writes *Psychotherapy by Reciprocal Inhibition*, helping to launch field of behavioral therapy

1954: Paul Meehl writes *Clinical versus Statistical Prediction*, first major book to describe both the strengths and weaknesses of clinical judgment

1953: Rapid eye movement (REM) sleep discovered

1953: Francis Crick and James Watson discover structure of DNA, launching genetic revolution

1952: Antipsychotic drug Thorazine tested in France, launching modern era of psychopharmacology

1949: Conference held at University of Colorado at Boulder to outline principles of scientific clinical psychology; founding of the "Boulder" (scientist-practitioner) model of clinical training

1938: B. F. Skinner writes *The Behavior of Organisms*

1935: Kurt Koffka writes *Principles of Gestalt Psychology*

1920s: Gordon Allport helps to initiate field of personality trait psychology

1920: Jean Piaget writes *The Child's Conception of the World*

1913: John B. Watson writes *Psychology as Behavior*, launching field of behaviorism

1911: E. L. Thorndike discovers instrumental (later called operant) conditioning

1910: Ivan Pavlov discovers classical conditioning

1907: Oscar Pfungst demonstrates that the amazing counting horse, Clever Hans, responds to cues from observers; demonstrates power of expectancies

1905: Alfred Binet and Henri Simon develop first intelligence test

1974: Positron emission tomography (PET) scanning introduced, launching field of functional brain imaging

1974: Elizabeth Loftus and Robert Palmer publish classic paper on the malleability of human memory, showing that memory is more reconstructive than previously believed

1976: Founding of Committee for the Scientific Investigation of Claims of the Paranormal, first major organization to apply scientific skepticism to paranormal claims

1977: First use of statistical technique of meta-analysis, which allows researchers to systematically combine results of multiple studies; demonstrated that psychotherapy is effective

1980: *Diagnostic and Statistical Manual of Mental Disorders*, Third Edition (*DSM-III*) published; helps standardize the diagnosis of major mental disorders

1980s: Recovered memory craze sweeps across America; pits academic researchers against many clinicians

1988: Many scientifically oriented psychologists break off from American Psychological Association to found American Psychological Society (APS)

1990: Thomas Bouchard and colleagues publish major results of Minnesota Study of Twins Reared Apart, demonstrating substantial genetic bases for intelligence, personality, interests, and other important individual differences

1995: Task force of Division 12 (Society of Clinical Psychology) of American Psychological Association publishes list of, and criteria for, empirically supported psychotherapies

2000: Human genome sequenced

2002: Daniel Kahneman becomes first Ph.D. psychologist to win Nobel Prize; honored for his pioneering work (with the late Amos Tversky) on biases and heuristics

2004: APS members vote to change name to Association for Psychological Science

Figure 1.5 Timeline of Major Events in Scientific Psychology.

Table 1.4 The Theoretical Perspectives That Shaped Psychology.

	Perspective	Leading Figures	Goal	Lasting Influence
◀ E.B. Titchener	Structuralism	Founded by E. B. Titchener	Uses introspection to identify basic elements or "structures" of experience	Emphasis on the importance of systematic observation to the study of conscious experience
◀ William James	Functionalism	Founded by William James; influenced by Charles Darwin	To understand the functions or adaptive purposes of our thoughts, feelings, and behaviors	Has been absorbed into psychology and continues to influence it indirectly in many ways
◀ B. F. Skinner	Behaviorism	John B. Watson; B. F. Skinner	To uncover the general principles of learning that explain all behaviors; focus is largely on observable behavior	Influential in models of human and animal learning and among the first to focus on need for objective research
◀ Jean Piaget	Cognitivism	Jean Piaget; Ulric Neisser	To examine the role of mental processes on behavior	Influential in many areas, such as language, problem solving, concept formation, intelligence, memory, and psychotherapy
◀ Sigmund Freud	Psychoanalysis	Sigmund Freud	To uncover the role of unconscious psychological processes and early life experiences in behavior	Understanding that much of our mental processing goes on outside of conscious awareness

Structuralism: The Elements of the Mind.

Edward Bradford Titchener (1867–1927), a British student of Wundt who emigrated to the United States, founded the field of structuralism. **Structuralism** aimed to identify the basic elements, or "structures," of psychological experience. Adopting Wundt's method of introspection, structuralists dreamed of creating a comprehensive "map" of the elements of consciousness—which they believed consisted of sensations, images, and feelings—much like the periodic table of the elements we can find in every chemistry classroom (Evans, 1972).

Structuralism eventually ran out of steam. At least two major problems eventually did it in. First, even highly trained introspectionists often disagreed on their subjective reports. Second, German psychologist Oswald Kulpe (1862–1915) showed that subjects asked to solve certain mental problems engage in *imageless thought:* thinking unaccompanied by conscious experience. If we ask an introspecting subject to add 10 and 5, she'll quickly respond "15," but she'll usually be unable to report what came to her mind when performing this calculation (Hergenhahn, 2000). The phenomenon of imageless thought dealt a serious body blow to structuralism because it demonstrated that some important aspects of human psychology lie outside of conscious awareness.

Structuralism correctly emphasized the importance of *systematic observation* to the study of conscious experience. Nevertheless, structuralists went astray by assuming that a

GLOSSARY

structuralism
school of psychology that aimed to identify the basic elements of psychological experience

single, imperfect method—introspection—could provide all of the information needed for a complete science of psychology.

Functionalism: Psychology Meets Darwin.
Proponents of **functionalism** hoped to understand the adaptive purposes, or functions, of psychological characteristics, such as thoughts, feelings, and behaviors (Hunt, 1993). Whereas structuralists asked "what" questions, like "What is conscious thought like?" functionalists asked "why" questions, like, "Why do we sometimes forget things?" The founder of functionalism, William James, rejected structuralists' approach and methods, arguing that careful introspection doesn't yield a fixed number of static elements of consciousness but rather an ever-changing "stream of consciousness," a famous phrase he coined.

The functionalists of the late 1800s were influenced substantially by biologist Charles Darwin's (1809–1882) still-young theory of natural selection, which emphasized that many physical characteristics evolved because they were useful for organisms. The functionalists believed that Darwin's theory applied to psychological characteristics too. Just as the trunk of an elephant serves useful functions for survival, such as snaring distant water and food, the human memory system, for example, must similarly serve a purpose. It's the job of psychologists, functionalists maintained, to act as "detectives," figuring out the evolved functions that psychological characteristics serve for organisms.

Like structuralism, functionalism doesn't exist in its original form today. Instead, functionalism was gradually absorbed into mainstream scientific psychology and continues to influence it indirectly in many ways.

Charles Darwin's theory of evolution by natural selection was a significant influence on functionalism, which strove to understand the adaptive purposes of psychological characteristics.

Behaviorism: The Laws of Learning.
In the early twentieth century, many American psychologists were growing impatient with the touchy-feely nature of their discipline. In particular, they believed that Titchener and other introspectionists were leading psychology down a misguided path. For these critics, the study of consciousness was a waste of time because researchers could never verify conclusively the existence of the basic elements of psychological experience. Psychological science, they contended, must be objective, not subjective.

Foremost among these critics was a flamboyant American psychologist, John B. Watson (1878–1958). Watson was a founder of the still-influential school of **behaviorism,** which focuses on uncovering the general principles of learning underlying human and animal behavior. For Watson (1913), the proper subject matter of psychology was observable behavior, plain and simple. Subjective reports of conscious experience should play no part in psychology. If it followed his brave lead, Watson proclaimed, psychology could become just as scientific as physics, chemistry, and other "hard" sciences.

Watson further insisted that psychology should aspire to uncover the general laws of learning that explain all behaviors, whether they be riding a bicycle, eating a sandwich, or becoming depressed. All of these behaviors, Watson proposed, were products of a handful of basic learning principles (see Chapter 5). Moreover, according to Watson, we don't need to peer "inside" the organism to grasp these principles. We can comprehend human behavior exclusively by looking *outside* the organism, to rewards and punishments delivered by the environment. For traditional behaviorists, the human mind is a black box: We know what goes into it and what comes out of it, but we needn't worry about what happens between the inputs and the outputs. For this reason, psychologists sometimes call behaviorism *black box psychology.*

John B. Watson, one of the founders of behaviorism. Watson's stubborn insistence on scientific rigor made him a hero to some and an enemy to others.

GLOSSARY

functionalism
school of psychology that aimed to understand the adaptive purposes of psychological characteristics

behaviorism
school of psychology that focuses on uncovering the general laws of learning by looking at observable behavior

Behaviorism has left a stamp on scientific psychology that continues to be felt today. By identifying the fundamental laws of learning that help to explain human and animal behavior, behaviorists placed psychology on firmer scientific footing. Although early behaviorists' deep mistrust of subjective observations of conscious experience probably went too far, these psychologists properly warned us of the hazards of relying too heavily on reports that we can't verify objectively.

Cognitivism: Opening the Black Box.

Beginning in the 1950s and 1960s, growing numbers of psychologists grew disillusioned with behaviorists' neglect of **cognition,** the term psychologists use to describe the mental processes involved in different aspects of thinking. Although some behaviorists acknowledged that humans and even many intelligent animals do think, they viewed thinking as merely another form of behavior. The cognitivists, in contrast, argued that our thinking affects our behavior in powerful ways. For example, Swiss psychologist Jean Piaget (1896–1980) argued compellingly that children conceptualize the world in markedly different ways than do adults (see Chapter 8). Later, led by Ulric Neisser (1928–), cognitivists argued that thinking is so central to psychology that it merits a separate discipline in its own right (Neisser, 1967; see Chapter 7).

According to cognitivists, a psychology based solely on rewards and punishments from the environment will never be adequate because our *interpretation* of rewards and punishments is a crucial determinant of our behavior. Take a student who receives a B+ on his first psychology exam. A student accustomed to getting Fs on his tests might regard this grade as a reward, whereas a student accustomed to As might view it as a punishment. Without understanding how people evaluate information, cognitivists maintain, we'll never fully grasp the causes of their behavior. Moreover, according to cognitivists, we often learn not merely by rewards and punishments but by *insight,* that is, by grasping the underlying nature of problems (see Chapter 5).

Cognitive psychology is a thriving approach today, and its tentacles have spread to such diverse domains as language, problem solving, concept formation, intelligence, memory, and psychotherapy. By focusing not merely on rewards and punishments but on organisms' interpretation of them, cognitivism has encouraged psychologists to peek inside the black box to examine the connections between inputs and outputs.

Psychoanalysis: The Depths of the Unconscious.

Around the time that behaviorism was becoming dominant in the United States, a parallel movement was gathering momentum in Europe. This field, psychoanalysis, was founded by the Viennese neurologist Sigmund Freud (1856–1939). In sharp contrast to behaviorism, **psychoanalysis** focused on internal psychological processes, especially impulses, thoughts, and memories of which we're unaware. According to Freud (1900) and other psychoanalysts, the primary influences on behavior aren't forces outside the organism, like rewards and punishments, but rather unconscious drives, especially sexuality and aggression.

Psychoanalysts maintain that much of our everyday psychological lives is filled with symbols—things that represent other things (Loevinger, 1987; Moore & Fine, 1995). For example, if you refer accidentally to one of your female professors as "Mom," Freudians would be unlikely to treat this embarrassing blooper as an isolated mistake. Instead, they'd quickly suggest that your professor probably reminds you of your mother, which may be a good reason to transfer to a different course. The goal of the psychoanalyst is to decode the symbolic meaning of our slips of the tongue (or *Freudian slips,* as they're often called), dreams, and psychological symptoms. By doing so, psychoanalysts contend, they can get to the roots of our deep-seated psychological conflicts. Psychoanalysts also

GLOSSARY

cognition
mental processes involved in different aspects of thinking

psychoanalysis
school of psychology, founded by Sigmund Freud, that focuses on internal psychological processes of which we're unaware

place considerably more emphasis than do other schools of thought on the role of early experience. For Freud and others, the core of our personalities are molded in the first few years of life.

The influence of Freud and psychoanalysis on scientific psychology is controversial. On the one hand, some critics insist that psychoanalysis retarded the progress of scientific psychology because it focused heavily on unconscious processes that are difficult or impossible to verify. As we'll learn in Chapter 12, these critics probably have a point (Crews, 2005; Esterson, 1993). On the other hand, at least some psychoanalytic claims, such as the assertion that a great deal of important mental processing goes on outside of conscious awareness, have held up well in scientific research (Westen, 1998; Wilson, 2002). It's not clear, however, whether the Freudian view of the unconscious bears anything more than a superficial resemblance to more contemporary views of unconscious processing (Kihlstrom, 1987; see Chapter 12).

The couch that Sigmund Freud used to psychoanalyze his patients, now located in the Freud museum in London, England. Contrary to popular conception, most psychologists aren't psychotherapists, and most psychotherapists aren't even psychoanalysts. Nor do most modern therapists ask patients to recline on couches.

THE MULTIFACETED WORLD OF MODERN PSYCHOLOGY

Psychology isn't just one discipline, but rather an assortment of many subdisciplines. In most major psychology departments, we can find researchers examining areas as varied as the brain bases of visual perception, the mechanisms of memory, the causes of prejudice, and the treatment of depression.

The Growth of a Field.
Today, there are about 500,000 psychologists worldwide (Kassin, 2004), with more than 100,000 in the United States alone (McFall, 2006). The American Psychological Association (APA), founded in 1892 and now the world's largest association of psychologists, consists of more than 150,000 members. (To give us a sense of how much the field has grown, there were only 150 APA members in 1900.) The percentage of women and minorities within the APA has grown steadily, too (see **Figure 1.6**). These members' interests span such topics as addiction, art psychology, clinical psychology, hypnosis, law and psychology, media psychology, mental retardation, neuroscience, psychology and religion, sports psychology, the psychology of women, and gay, lesbian, bisexual, and transgendered issues.
[LEARNING OBJECTIVE 1.8]

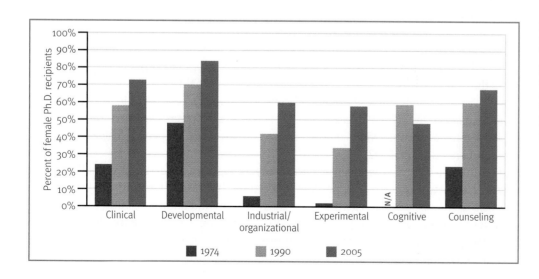

Figure 1.6 The Face of Psychology Has Changed Dramatically over the Past Three Decades. Across most areas, the percentage of women earning doctoral degrees has increased. In clinical and developmental psychology, women comprise three-fourths to four-fifths of those attaining Ph.D.s. (*Source:* wwwapa.org/monitor/jun07/changing.html)

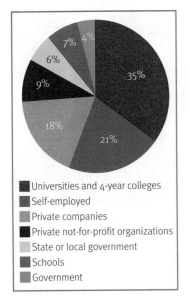

Figure 1.7 Approximate Distribution of Psychologists in Different Settings. Psychologists are employed in a diverse array of settings. (*Source:* Data from National Science Foundation, 2003)

Fict-OID

MYTH: If you want to become a psychotherapist, you don't need to learn about research.

REALITY: The "scientist–practitioner model" of training—often called the "Boulder model" because it was formulated over a half century ago at a conference in Boulder, Colorado—is the predominant model for educating clinical psychology Ph.D. students. This model requires all graduate students, even those who intend to become therapists, to receive extensive training in how to interpret psychological research.

Types of Psychologists: Fact and Fiction. **Figure 1.7** shows a breakdown of the settings in which psychologists work. As we can see, some work primarily in research settings, others primarily in practice settings. **Table 1.5** describes a few of the most important types of psychologists whose work we'll encounter in this book. It also dispels common misconceptions about what each type of psychologist does.

As we can see, the field of psychology is remarkably diverse, as are the types of careers psychology majors pursue. Moreover, the face of psychology is changing, with more women and minorities entering many of its subfields. Despite their differences in content, all of these areas of psychology have one thing in common: Most of the psychologists who specialize in them rely on scientific methods (see Chapter 2). Specifically, they use scientific methods to generate new findings about human or animal behavior or use existing findings to enhance human welfare. But as we've discussed, many pseudoscientists try to lead us to believe that they're using a true scientific approach. Throughout this text, we'll highlight ways that pseudoscience has infiltrated popular beliefs about psychology and ways to guard against pseudoscience.

WHAT DO *you* THINK?

You're working as a career advisor at a campus career center. A student visits you and says that she plans to apply to only the top five graduate programs in clinical psychology because she loves helping people, even though she thinks research is boring. What types of graduate programs might you advise her to explore instead and why?

THE GREAT DEBATES OF PSYCHOLOGY

Now that we've learned a bit about the past and present of psychology, we need to set the stage for things to come. Two great debates have shaped the field of psychology since its inception and seem likely to continue to shape it in the future. **[LEARNING OBJECTIVE 1.9]** Because these debates are alive and well, we'll find traces of them in virtually all of the chapters of this text.

The Nature–Nurture Debate. The nature–nurture debate poses the following question: *Are our behaviors attributable mostly to our genes (nature) or to our rearing environments (nurture)?*

As we'll discover later in this text, the nature-nurture debate has proven especially controversial in the domains of intelligence, personality, and psychopathology (mental illness). Like most major debates in psychology, this one has a lengthy history. Many early thinkers, such as British philosopher John Locke (1632–1704), likened the human mind at birth to white paper that hadn't been written on. Others after him referred to the mind as a *tabula rasa* ("blank slate"). For Locke and his followers, we enter the world with no genetic preconceptions or preconceived ideas: We're shaped exclusively by our environments (Pinker, 2002).

For much of the twentieth century, most psychologists assumed that virtually all human behavior was exclusively a product of learning. But research conducted by *behavior geneticists,* who use sophisticated designs such as twin and adoption studies (see Chapter 3), shows that most important psychological traits, including intelligence, interests, personality, and many mental illnesses, are influenced substantially by genes. Increasingly, modern psychologists have come to recognize that human behavior is

Table 1.5 Types of Psychologists, What They Do, and What They Don't Do.

Type of Psychologist	What Do They Do?	Frequent Misconception and Truth
Clinical Psychologist	• Perform assessment, diagnosis, and treatment of mental disorders • Conduct research on people with mental disorders • Work in colleges and universities, mental health centers, or private practice	*Misconception: You need a Ph.D. to become a therapist.* • *Truth*: Most clinical psychology Ph.D. programs are highly research oriented. Other options for therapists are a Psy.D. (doctor of psychology), which focuses on training therapists rather than researchers, or an M.S.W., a master's degree in social work, which also focuses on training therapists.
Counseling Psychologist	• Work with people experiencing temporary or relatively self-contained life problems, like marital conflict, sexual difficulties, occupational stressors, or career uncertainty • Work in counseling centers, hospitals, or private practice (although some work in academic and research settings)	*Misconception: Counseling psychology is pretty much the same as clinical psychology.* • *Truth*: Whereas clinical psychologists work with people with serious mental disorders like severe depression, most counseling psychologists don't.
School Psychologist	• Work with teachers, parents, and children to remedy students' behavioral, emotional, and learning difficulties	*Misconception: School psychology is another term for educational psychology.* • *Truth*: Educational psychology is a substantially different discipline that focuses on helping instructors identify better methods for teaching and evaluating learning.
Developmental Psychologist	• Study how and why people change over time • Conduct research on infants', childrens', and sometimes adults' and elderly people's emotional, physiological, and cognitive processes and how these change with age	*Misconception: Developmental psychologists spend most of their time on their hands and knees playing with children.* • *Truth*: Most spend their time in the laboratory, collecting and analyzing data.
Experimental Psychologist	• Use research methods to study memory, language, thinking and social behaviors of humans • Work primarily in research settings	*Misconception: Experimental psychologists do all of their work in psychological laboratories.* • *Truth*: Many conduct research in real-world settings, examining how people acquire language, remember events, apply mental concepts, and the like, in everyday life.
Biopsychologist	• Examine the physiological bases of behavior in animals and humans • Most work in research settings	*Misconception: All biopsychologists use invasive methods in their research.* • *Truth*: Although many biopsychologists create brain lesions in animals to examine their effects on behavior, others use brain imaging methods that don't require investigators to damage organisms' nervous systems.
Forensic Psychologist	• Work in prisons, jails, and other settings to assess and diagnose inmates and assist with their rehabilitation and treatment • Others conduct research on eyewitness testimony or jury decision making • Typically hold degrees in clinical or counseling psychology	*Misconception: Most forensic psychologists are criminal profilers, like those employed by the FBI.* • *Truth*: Criminal profiling is a small and controversial (as we'll learn in Chapter 11) subspecialty within forensic psychology.
Industrial/Organizational Psychologist	• Work in companies and businesses to help select productive employees, evaluate performance, examine the effects of different working or living conditions on people's behavior (called *environmental psychologists*) • Design equipment to maximize employee performance and minimize accidents (called *human factors* or *engineering psychologists*)	*Misconception: Most industrial/organizational psychologists work on a one-to-one basis with employees to increase their motivation and productivity.* • *Truth*: Most spend their time constructing tests and selection procedures or implementing organizational changes to improve worker productivity or satisfaction.

attributable not only to our environments but to our genes (Bouchard, 2004; Harris, 2002; Pinker, 2002).

Current Status of the Nature–Nurture Debate.   Some people have declared the nature–nurture debate dead (Ferris, 1996) because just about everyone now agrees that both genes and environment play crucial roles in most human behaviors. Yet this debate is far from dead because we still have a great deal to learn about how much nature or nurture contributes to different behaviors and how nature and nurture work together. Indeed, we'll discover in later chapters that the old dichotomy between nature and nurture is far less clear-cut—and far more interesting—than once believed. Nature and nurture sometimes intersect in complex and surprising ways (see Chapters 5, 8, and 13).

Evolutionary Psychology.   One domain of psychology that's shed light on the nature–nurture debate is **evolutionary psychology,** sometimes also called *sociobiology:* a discipline that applies Darwin's theory of natural selection to human and animal behavior (Barkow, Cosmides, & Tooby, 1992; Dennett, 1995; Tooby & Cosmides, 1989). It begins with the assumption, shared by William James and other functionalists, that many human psychological systems, like memory, emotion, and personality, serve key adaptive functions: They help organisms survive and reproduce. Darwin and his followers suggested that natural selection favored certain kinds of mental traits, just as it did physical ones, like our hands, livers, and hearts.

Biologists refer to *fitness* as the extent to which a trait increases the chances that organisms that possess this trait will survive and reproduce at a higher rate than competitors who lack it (see Chapter 3). Fitness has nothing to do, by the way, with how strong or powerful an organism is. By surviving and reproducing at higher rates than other organisms, more fit organisms pass on their genes more successfully to later generations. For example, humans who have at least some degree of anxiety probably survived at higher rates than humans who lacked it, because anxiety serves an essential function: It warns us of impending danger (Barlow, 2000).

Still, evolutionary psychology has received more than its share of criticism (Kitcher, 1985; Panksepp & Panksepp, 2000). Many of its predictions are extremely difficult to falsify. In part, that's because behavior, unlike the bones of dinosaurs, early humans, and other animals, doesn't leave fossils. As a consequence, it's far more challenging to determine the evolutionary functions of anxiety or depression than the functions of birds' wings. For example, two researchers speculated that male baldness serves an evolutionary function, because women supposedly perceive a receding hairline as a sign of maturity (Muscarella & Cunningham, 1996). But if it turned out that women preferred men with lots of hair to bald men, it would be easy to cook up an explanation for that finding ("Women perceive men with a full head of hair as stronger and more athletic"). Evolution can account for either outcome. Evolutionary psychology has the potential to be an important unifying framework for psychology (Buss, 1995), but we should beware of evolutionary explanations that can fit almost any piece of evidence after the fact (de Waal, 2002).

The Free Will–Determinism Debate.   The free will–determinism debate poses the following question: *To what extent are our behaviors freely selected rather than caused by factors outside of our control?*

Most of us like to believe that we're free to select any course of events we wish. Fewer truths seem more self-evident than the fact that we're free to do what we want whenever we want. For example, you may believe that at this very moment you can decide to either continue reading to the end of the chapter or take a well-deserved break to watch TV. Indeed, our legal system is premised on the concept of free will. We punish criminals

---

FALSIFIABILITY
Can the claim be disproved?

The fact that American men spend billions of dollars per year on hair replacement treatments is difficult to square with evolutionary hypotheses suggesting that women prefer bald men. The bottom line: Beware of unfalsifiable evolutionary stories.

GLOSSARY

evolutionary psychology
discipline that applies Darwin's theory of natural selection to human and animal behavior

because they're supposedly free to abide by the law but choose otherwise. One major exception, of course, is the insanity defense, in which the legal system assumes that severe mental illness can interfere with people's free will (Hoffman & Morse, 2006; Stone, 1982).

Yet many psychologists maintain that free will is actually an illusion (Wegner, 2002). It's such a powerful illusion, they insist, that we have a hard time imagining it could be an illusion. Some psychologists, like behaviorist B. F. Skinner, argue that our sense of free will stems from the fact that we aren't consciously aware of the thousands of subtle environmental influences impinging on our behavior at any given moment. Much like puppets in a play who don't realize that actors are pulling their strings, we conclude mistakenly that we're free simply because we don't realize all of the influences acting on our behavior. For Skinner and others, our behaviors are completely determined: caused by preceding influences.

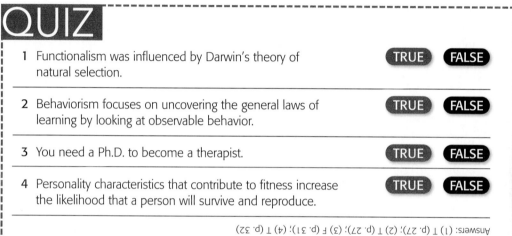

QUIZ

1. Functionalism was influenced by Darwin's theory of natural selection.　　TRUE　FALSE

2. Behaviorism focuses on uncovering the general laws of learning by looking at observable behavior.　　TRUE　FALSE

3. You need a Ph.D. to become a therapist.　　TRUE　FALSE

4. Personality characteristics that contribute to fitness increase the likelihood that a person will survive and reproduce.　　TRUE　FALSE

Answers: (1) T (p. 27); (2) T (p. 27); (3) F (p. 31); (4) T (p. 32).

PEARSON mypsych·lab

▼ Why has the percentage of women in the field of psychology increased in recent years? Watch the video titled "Women and the Field of Psychology: Florence Denmark" at www.mypsychlab.com to find out.

Applying Psychological Science and Thinking to Everyday Life

Psychological scientists often distinguish basic from applied research. **Basic research** examines how the mind works, whereas **applied research** examines how we can use basic research to solve real-world problems. Within most large psychology departments, we'll find a healthy mix of people conducting basic research, such as investigators who study the laws of learning, and applied research, such as investigators who study how to help people cope with the psychological burden of cancer.

As we'll discover throughout this text, psychological science offers important applications for a variety of aspects of everyday life. **[LEARNING OBJECTIVE 1.10]** Psychological science has found its way into far more aspects of contemporary society than most of us realize (Salzinger, 2002; Zimbardo, 2004a).

HOW PSYCHOLOGY AFFECTS US

Let's look at a sampling of these applications; we can discover more about these and other examples on a website maintained by the American Psychological Association: www.psychologymatters.apa.org.

GLOSSARY

basic research
research examining how the mind works

applied research
research examining how we can use basic research to solve real-world problems

- If you live in or near a big city, you've probably noticed a gradual change in the color of fire engines. Although old fire engines were bright red, most new ones are an odd color called lime-yellow. That's because psychological researchers who study perception found that lime-yellow objects are easier to detect in the dark. Indeed, lime-yellow fire trucks are only about half as likely to be involved in traffic accidents as red fire trucks (American Psychological Association, 2003; Solomon & King, 1995: www.psychologymatters.apa.org/solomon.html).

- As a car driver, have you ever had to slam on your brakes to avoid hitting a driver directly in front of you who stopped short suddenly? If so, and if you managed to avoid a bad accident, you may have John Voevodsky to thank. For decades, cars had only two brake lights. In the early 1970s, Voevodsky hit on the bright (pun intended) idea of placing a third brake light at the base of cars' back windshields. He reasoned that this additional visual information would decrease the risk of rear-end collisions. He conducted a 10-month study of taxis with and without the new brake lights and found a 61 percent lower rate of rear-end accidents in the first group (Voevodsky, 1974). As a result of his research, all new American cars have three brake lights (http://www.psychologymatters.apa.org/voevodsky.html).

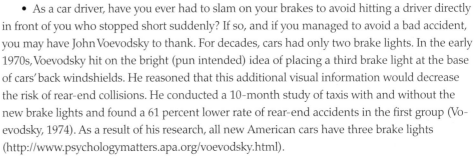

- If you're anything like the average American, you see more than 100 commercial messages every day. The chances are high that psychologists had a hand in crafting many of them. The founder of behaviorism, John B. Watson, pioneered the application of psychology to advertising in the 1920s and 1930s. Today, psychological researchers still contribute to the marketing success of companies. For instance, psychologists who study magazine advertisements have discovered that human faces better capture readers' attention on the left rather than on the right side of pages. Written text, in contrast, better captures readers' attention on the right rather than on the left side of pages (Clay, 2002).

- To get into college, you probably had to take one or more tests, like the Scholastic Assessment Test (SAT) or American College Test (ACT). If so, you can thank—or blame—psychologists with expertise in measuring academic achievement and knowledge, who were primarily responsible for developing these measures (Zimbardo, 2004a). Although these tests are far from perfect predictors of academic performance, they do significantly better than chance in forecasting how students perform in college (Geiser & Studley, 2002).

- Police officers often ask victims of violent crimes to select a suspect from a lineup. When doing so, they've traditionally used *simultaneous lineups,* in which one or more suspects and several decoys (people who aren't really suspects) are lined up in a row, often of five to eight individuals (see Chapter 6). These are the kinds of lineups we've most often seen on television crime shows. Yet psychological research generally shows that *sequential lineups*—those in which victims view each person individually and then decide whether he or she was the perpetrator of the crime—are more accurate than simultaneous lineups (Steblay et al., 2003; Wells, Memon, & Penrod, 2006; Wells & Olson, 2003). As a result of this research, police departments around the United States are increasingly using sequential rather than simultaneous lineups.

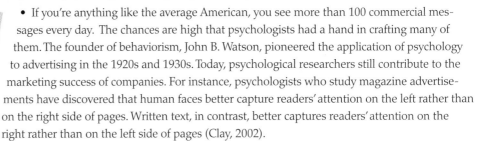

- For many years, many American public schools were legally required to be racially segregated. Before 1954, the law of the land in the United States was that "separate but equal" facilities were sufficient to guarantee racial equality. But based in part on the pioneering research of psychologists Kenneth and Mamie Clark (1950), shown here, who demonstrated that African American children preferred white to African American dolls, the U.S. Supreme Court decided—in the landmark 1954 case of *Brown v. Board of Education of Topeka, Kansas*—that school segregation exerted a negative impact on the self-esteem of African American children.

So, far more than most of us realize, the fruits of psychological research are all around us. Psychology has dramatically altered the landscape of everyday life.

THINKING SCIENTIFICALLY: IT'S A WAY OF LIFE

As you embark on your journey to the rest of the field of psychology, we leave you with one crucial point: Learning to think scientifically will help you make better decisions not only in this course and other psychology courses, but in everyday life. **[LEARNING OBJECTIVE 1.10]** Each day, the news and entertainment media bombard us with confusing and contradictory claims about a host of topics: herbal remedies, weight loss plans, parenting methods, insomnia treatments, speed reading courses, urban legends, political conspiracy theories, unidentified flying objects, and "overnight cures" for mental disorders, to name only a few. Some of these claims are at least partly true, whereas others are entirely bogus. Yet the media typically offer little guidance for sorting out which claims are scientific, pseudoscientific, or a bit of both. It's scarcely any wonder that we're often tempted to throw up our hands in despair and ask "What I am supposed to believe?"

Fortunately, the scientific thinking skills you've encountered in this chapter—and that you'll come to know and (we hope!) love in later chapters—can assist you in successfully navigating the bewildering world of popular psychology and popular culture. The trick is to bear three words in mind throughout this text and in daily life: "Insist on evidence." By recognizing that common sense can take us only so far in evaluating claims, we can come to appreciate that we need scientific evidence to avoid being fooled and to avoid fooling ourselves. But how exactly do we collect this scientific evidence, and how do we evaluate it? We'll find out in the next chapter.

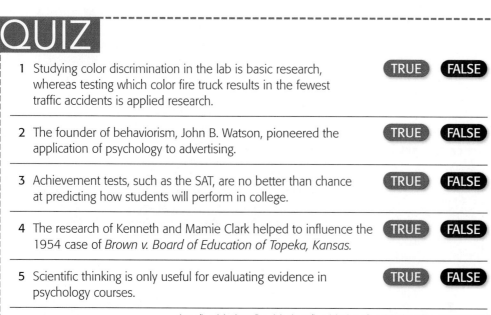

QUIZ

1 Studying color discrimination in the lab is basic research, whereas testing which color fire truck results in the fewest traffic accidents is applied research. **TRUE FALSE**

2 The founder of behaviorism, John B. Watson, pioneered the application of psychology to advertising. **TRUE FALSE**

3 Achievement tests, such as the SAT, are no better than chance at predicting how students will perform in college. **TRUE FALSE**

4 The research of Kenneth and Mamie Clark helped to influence the 1954 case of *Brown v. Board of Education of Topeka, Kansas.* **TRUE FALSE**

5 Scientific thinking is only useful for evaluating evidence in psychology courses. **TRUE FALSE**

Answers: (1) T (p. 33); (2) T (p. 34); (3) F (p. 34); (4) T (p. 34); (5) F (p. 35)

PEARSON **mypsychlab**

▼ Are these exciting times for psychologists and psychology students? Watch the video titled "So much to choose from: Phil Zimbardo" at www.mypsychlab.com to decide.

Your Complete Review System

1.1 Explain why psychology is more than just common sense

Psychology is the scientific study of the mind, brain, and behavior. Although we often rely on our common sense to understand the world, our commonsensical understanding of it is sometimes wrong. Naive realism is the error of believing that we see the world precisely as it is. It can lead us to false beliefs about ourselves and our world, such as believing that our perceptions and memories are always accurate.

1. Which would be a better description of naive realism, "seeing is believing" or "believing is seeing"? (p. 7)

2. What does Shepard's table illusion tell us about our ability to trust our own intuitions and experiences? (p. 7)

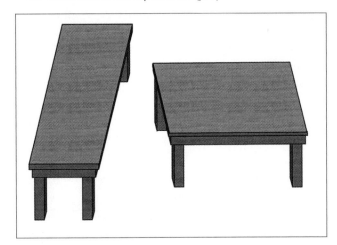

3. Our common sense (is/isn't) always wrong. (p. 8)

1.2 Explain the importance of science as a set of safeguards against biases

Confirmation bias is the tendency to seek out evidence that supports our hypotheses and disregard or distort evidence that doesn't. Belief perseverance is the tendency to cling to our beliefs despite contrary evidence. The scientific method is a set of safeguards against these two errors.

4. Science is an _____ to evidence. (p. 8)

5. When presented with both contradictory and supportive evidence regarding a hypothesis we are researching, our tendency to disregard the contradictory evidence is our _____ _____ . (p. 8)

6. Our _____ _____ kicks in when we refuse to admit our beliefs are incorrect in the face of evidence that contradicts them. (p. 9)

7. Initial scientific conclusions are (often/rarely) wrong. (pp. 9–10)

8. A scientific model like the Big Bang theory, which provides an explanation for a large number of findings in the natural world, is known as a _____ _____ . (p. 10)

9. In scientific research, _____ are general explanations, whereas _____ are specific predictions derived from these explanations. (p. 10)

10. Review each of the statements in the table below and identify whether each is a theory (T) or hypothesis (H). (p. 10)

T or H	Explanation
(1) _____	Sarah's motivation for cheating on the test was fear of failure.
(2) _____	Darwin's evolutionary model explains the changes in species over time.
(3) _____	The universe began in a gigantic explosion about 14 billion years ago.
(4) _____	Our motivation to help a stranger in need is influenced by the number of people present.
(5) _____	Crime rates in Nashville increase as the temperature rises.

succeed with mypsych lab

1. Participate in a replication of a psychological study and see if you can be bias free in your judgment.
   Confirmation Bias

2. What does a typical student think about psychology? Watch this video to learn whether certain psychological myths are misconceptions or have some validity to them.
   How much do you know about psychology?

1.3 Describe psychological pseudoscience and distinguish it from psychological science

Pseudoscientific claims appear scientific but don't play by the rules of science. In particular, pseudoscience lacks the safeguards against confirmation bias and belief perseverance that characterize science. Metaphysical claims, in contrast, aren't testable and therefore lie outside the boundaries of science. We are drawn to pseudoscientific beliefs because the human mind tends to perceive sense in nonsense and order in disorder.

Although generally adaptive, this tendency can lead us to see patterns when they don't exist.

11. The growth of popular psychology has led to a _____ explosion (p. 12)

12. About _____ percent of self-help books remain untested. (p. 12)

13. There are over 500 "brands" of _____ , with new ones being added every year. (p. 12)

14. A recent survey of the American public shows that pseudoscientific and other questionable beliefs are (rare/widespread). (p. 13)

Answers are located at the end of the text.

15. Match the warning signs of pseudoscience with the examples shown. (p. 14)

Example	Sign of Pseudoscience
(1) ___ Three simple steps will change your love life forever!	a. Meaningless "psychobabble" that uses fancy scientific-sounding terms that don't make sense
(2) ___ This woman practiced yoga daily for three weeks and hasn't had a day of depression since.	b. Exaggerated claims
(3) ___ Amazing new innovations in research have shown that eye massage results in reading speeds 10 times faster than average!	c. Overreliance on anecdotes
(4) ___ Fifty studies conducted by the company all show overwhelming success!	d. Lack of self-correction when contrary evidence is published
(5) ___ Although some scientists say that we use almost all our brains, we've found a way to harness additional brain power previously undiscovered.	e. Absence of connectivity to other research
(6) ___ Sine-wave filtered auditory stimulation is carefully designed to encourage maximal orbitofrontal dendritic development.	f. Talk of "proof" instead of "evidence"
(7) ___ Our new program is proven to reduce social anxiety by at least 50 percent!	g. Lack of review by other scholars (called *peer review*) or replication by independent labs

16. Apophenia is the tendency for us to make meaningful connections among (related/unrelated) phenomena. (p. 15)

17. We may attribute paranormal significance to coincidences that are probably due to _____. (p. 15)

18. Metaphysical claims, such as the existence of God, the soul, or the afterlife, differ from pseudoscientific claims in that they are not _____. (p. 15)

1.4 **Describe the dangers of pseudoscience**

Pseudoscientific claims can result in opportunity costs and direct harm due to dangerous treatments. They may also lead us to think less scientifically about other important domains of modern life.

19. What does the case of Candace Newmaker tell us about the dangers of pseudoscientific treatments? (p. 17)

20. Pseudoscientific treatments for mental disorders can lead people to forgo _____ _____. (p. 17)

succeed with **mypsychlab**

1. What is your sign? See what science has to say about whether your horoscope is a good predictor of your personality. **The Pseudoscience of Astrology**

2. Betting that the next coin flip will be heads or tails? Save your money and toss a virtual coin to learn about random events. **Coin Toss**

3. Want to be a better consumer of information in the media? Listen to this podcast and learn how to evaluate reports of psychological findings in the news. **Psychology in the News**

SCIENTIFIC THINKING: DISTINGUISHING FACT FROM FICTION (pp. 17–23)

1.5 **Identify the key features of scientific skepticism**

Scientific skepticism requires us to evaluate all claims with an open mind but to insist on compelling evidence before accepting them. Scientific skeptics evaluate claims on their own merits and are unwilling to accept them on the basis of authority alone.

21. Being open-minded but conservative about accepting claims without evidence is _____ _____. (p. 18)

1.6 **Identify and explain six key principles of scientific thinking that will be used throughout the text**

Six key scientific thinking principles are ruling out rival hypotheses, correlation vs. causation, falsifiability, replicability, extraordinary claims, and Occam's Razor.

22. The skill set for evaluating all claims in an open-minded and careful manner, both inside and outside the classroom or laboratory, is called _____ _____. (p. 18)

23. Scientific thinking (can/can't) be applied to claims in the media, Internet, self-help books, and any other information outlet outside the psychology laboratory. (p. 18)

24. When evaluating a claim, we should ask ourselves whether we're excluded other plausible _____ for it. (p. 20)

25. The assumption that because one thing is associated with another, it must cause the other is the definition of the _____ _____. (p. 20)

succeed with
mypsychlab

Do You Know All of the Terms in This Chapter?

Find out by using our Flashcards. Want more practice? Take additional quizzes, try simulations, and watch video to be sure you are prepared for the test!

26. A claim is considered _____ if it could in principle be disproved. (p. 21)

27. The ability of others to consistently duplicate a study's findings is called _____ . (p. 22)

28. Occam's Razor is also called the principle of _____ . (p. 23)

29. How would you use Occam's Razor to select among different explanations for crop circles such as this? (p. 23)

succeed with mypsychlab

1. Listen to two psychologists discuss the six critical thinking principles and how they can be applied to scientific and pseudoscientific topics.
Science and Pseudoscience

2. Six easy steps to becoming a more educated, critical thinker.
How To Be a Critical Thinker

3. Can you think yourself wealthy or think yourself to good grades? What do scientists say about the power of thought?
The Secret

30. Match the scientific thinking principle (left) with the accurate description (right). (pp. 18–23).

Name of Scientific Thinking Principle	Explanation of Scientific Thinking Principle
(1) ___ Extraordinary Claims	a. Claims must be capable of being disproved.
(2) ___ Falsifiability	b. If two hypotheses explain a phenomenon equally well, we should generally select the simpler one.
(3) ___ Occam's Razor	c. The fact that two things are associated with each other doesn't mean that one causes the other.
(4) ___ Replicability	d. The more a claim contradicts what we already know, the more persuasive the evidence for this claim must be before we should accept it.
(5) ___ Ruling Out Rival Hypotheses	e. A finding must be capable of being duplicated by independent researchers following the same "recipe."
(6) ___ Correlation versus Causation	f. Findings consistent with several hypotheses require additional research to eliminate these hypotheses.

PSYCHOLOGY'S PAST AND PRESENT: WHAT A LONG, STRANGE TRIP IT'S BEEN (pp. 24–33)

1.7 Identify the major theoretical frameworks of psychology

Five major theoretical orientations have played a role in shaping the field. Structuralism aimed to identify the basic elements of experience through the method of introspection. Functionalism hoped to understand the adaptive purposes of behavior. Behaviorism grew out of the belief that psychological science must be completely objective. The cognitive view emphasized the importance of mental processes in understanding behavior. Psychoanalysis, focusing on unconscious processes and urges, has been criticized as retarding the progress of scientific psychology because of its lack of scientific rigor.

31. Structuralism aimed to identify the basic elements of thought through _____. (p. 26)

32. The founder of functionalism, _____ _____, rejected structuralists' approach and methods, arguing that thought is an ever-changing "stream of consciousness." (p. 27)

33. For traditional behaviorists, the human mind is a _____ _____: We know what goes into it and what comes out of it, but we needn't worry about what happens between inputs and outputs. (p. 27)

34. Cognitivists believe our _____ of rewards and punishments is a crucial determinant of our behavior. (p. 28)

35. Psychoanalysts believe that dreams and verbal mistakes called _____ _____ reveal our inner conflicts. (pp. 28–29)

1.8 Describe the different roles psychologists fill

There are many types of psychologists. Clinical and counseling psychologists often conduct therapy. School psychologists develop intervention programs for children in school settings. Industrial/organizational psychologists often work in companies and business and are involved in maximizing performance. Many forensic psychologists work in prisons or court settings. Many other psychologists conduct research. Developmental psychologists study systematic change over time. Experimental psychologists study learning and thinking and biopsychologists study biological basis of behavior.

36. You (need/don't need) a Ph.D. to become a therapist. (p. 31)

37. Educational psychology is the (same as/different than) school psychology. (p. 31)

38. How do developmental psychologists spend the bulk of their time? (p. 31)

Developmental Psychologist

1.9 Describe the two great debates that have shaped the field of psychology

The two great debates are the nature–nurture debate, which questions whether our behaviors are attributable mostly to our genes (nature) or our rearing environments (nurture), and the free will–determinism debate, which asks to what extent our behaviors are freely selected rather than caused by factors outside our control. Both debates continue to shape the field of psychology.

39. _____ _____, a discipline that applies Darwin's theory of natural selection to human and animal behavior, has shed light on the nature–nurture debate. (p. 32)

40. Many psychologists, such as B. F. Skinner, believe that free will is a(n) _____. (p. 33)

succeed with mypsychlab

1. Use this interactive timeline to see how world events correspond with psychological discoveries. **Psychology Timeline**

2. Do psychologists work directly with athletes or juries? Learn more about the different specialties within the field of psychology. **Psychologists at Work**

APPLYING PSYCHOLOGICAL SCIENCE AND THINKING TO EVERYDAY LIFE (pp. 33–35)

1.10 Describe how psychological research affects our daily lives

Psychological research has shown how psychology can be applied to such diverse fields as adverting, public safety, the criminal justice system, and education.

41. _____ research examines how the mind works, whereas _____ research examines how we use research to solve real-world problems. (p. 33)

42. Psychological research on perception led to the change in color of fire trucks from red to _____. (p. 34)

43. As a result of research by John Voevodsky, all new American cars have _____ brake lights. (p. 34)

44. According to a 10-month study, taxis with the new brake lights had a _____ percent lower rate of rear-end accidents than taxis without the new lights. (p. 34)

45. _____ _____ pioneered the application of psychology to advertising in the 1920s and 1930s. (p. 34)

46. What have psychologists who study magazine advertisements learned about how best to capture readers' attention? (p. 34)

47. Psychologists with expertise in measuring academic achievement and knowledge were primarily responsible for developing the _____ and _____ tests. (p. 34)

48. Police departments have traditionally used _____ lineups, in which one or more suspects and several decoys are lined up in a row. (p. 34)

49. Based on psychological research, police departments increasingly now use _____ lineups. (p. 34)

50. How did the research of Kenneth and Mamie Clark affect public education in the United States? (p. 34)

succeed with mypsychlab

1. Can psychology change your life? **The Complexity of Humans: Phil Zimbardo**

SCIENTIFIC THINKING SKILLS
Questions and Summary

1 Your friend is trying a new diet that is made up entirely of fruits and vegetables. She assures you that it works because co-workers have lost 10 pounds in a single week. How would you convince her to evaluate it more carefully?

2 If a researcher finds that children whose parents use complicated vocabulary end up with higher vocabulary themselves, can the researcher conclude that the parents' use of vocabulary caused higher vocabulary in their children? Why or why not?

RULING OUT RIVAL HYPOTHESES p. 20

CORRELATION vs. CAUSATION p. 21

FALSIFIABILITY pp. 21, 32

REPLICABILITY p. 22

EXTRAORDINARY CLAIMS p. 23

OCCAM'S RAZOR p. 23

Research Methods

Do we really need research designs to figure out the answers to psychological questions? (p. 43)

How do our intuitions sometimes deceive us? (p. 52)

What are the major pitfalls to watch out for when evaluating experiments? (pp. 55–58)

How can we be fooled by statistics? (pp. 67–69)

What are the pluses and minuses of asking people to describe themselves? (pp. 58–59)

Confounds: A Source of False Conclusions. For an experiment to be valid, the level of the independent variable must be the *only* difference between the experimental group and the control group. If there's some other difference between groups, there's no way of knowing whether the independent variable really exerted an effect on the dependent variable. Psychologists use the term **confounding variable,** or **confound,** to refer to any difference between the experimental and control groups other than the independent variable. In our earlier depression treatment example, let's imagine that the patients who received Miraculin also received a few sessions of psychotherapy. This additional psychotherapy would be a confound, because it's a variable in addition to the independent variable that differed between the experimental and control groups. This confound makes it impossible for us to determine whether the differences between groups concerning the dependent variable (level of depression) were due to Miraculin, to psychotherapy, or to both.

Cause and Effect: Permission to Infer. The two major features of an experiment—random assignment to conditions and manipulation of an independent variable—permit us to infer cause-and-effect relations if we've conducted the study correctly.

Before going further, let's make sure the major points concerning experimental designs are clear. Read this description of a study, and then answer the four questions below it. (You can find the answers upside down on the bottom of this page.)

Acupuncture Study: Assess Your Knowledge.

A researcher hypothesizes that acupuncture, an ancient Chinese medical practice that involves inserting thin needles in specific places on the body (see Chapter 10), can allow stressed-out psychology students to decrease their levels of anxiety. She randomly assigns half of her participants to undergo acupuncture and half to receive no treatment. Two months later, she measures their levels of anxiety and finds that people who received acupuncture are less stressed out than other participants, who received no treatment.

(1) Is this a correlational or an experimental design?

(2) What are the independent and dependent variables?

(3) Is there a confound in this design? If so, what is it?

(4) Can we infer cause and effect from this study? Why or why not?

Pitfalls in Experimental Design. Like correlational designs, experimental designs can be tricky to interpret because there are numerous pitfalls to beware of when evaluating them. We'll focus on the most important of these traps here.

The Placebo Effect. To understand the first major pitfall in experiments, imagine we've developed what we believe to be a new wonder drug that treats hyperactivity (now called attention-deficit/hyperactivity disorder; see Chapter 13) in children. We randomly assign half of our participants with this condition to receive the drug and the other half to receive no treatment. At the conclusion of our study, we find that children who received the drug are much less hyperactive than children who received nothing. That's good news, to be sure, but does it mean we can now break out the champagne and celebrate the news that the drug is effective? Unfortunately, no.

The reason we can't pop the corks on our champagne bottles is that we haven't controlled for the placebo effect. The term *placebo* is derived from the Latin for "I will please." The **placebo effect** is improvement resulting from the mere expectation of improvement (Kirsch, 1999). Participants who received the drug may have gotten better merely because they knew they were receiving treatment. This knowledge could have instilled confidence or exerted a calming influence. The placebo effect is a powerful reminder that expectations can become reality.

"Find out who set up this experiment. It seems that half of the patients were given a placebo, and the other half were given a different placebo."

(© ScienceCartoonsPlus.com)

Answers to Assess Your Knowledge Questions

(1) This study is experimental because there's random assignment to groups and the experimenter manipulated whether or not participants received treatment.

(2) The independent variable is the presence versus absence of acupuncture treatment. The dependent variable is the anxiety level of participants.

(3) There is a potential confound in that those who received acupuncture knew they were receiving treatment. Their lower anxiety may have been the result of expectations that they'd be feeling better following treatment.

(4) Yes. Because of the confound, we don't know why the experimental group was less anxious. But we can conclude that something about the treatment reduced anxiety.

In medication research, researchers typically control for the placebo effect by administering a sugar pill, which is itself often called a *placebo,* to the members of the control group. In this way, patients in both the experimental and control groups don't know whether they're taking the actual medication or a placebo, so they're roughly equated in their expectations of improvement.

To avoid placebo effects, it's critical that patients not know whether they're receiving the real medication or a placebo. That is, patients must remain **blind** to the condition to which they've been assigned, namely, experimental or control. If patients aren't blind to this condition, then the experiment is essentially ruined, because the patients differ in their expectations of improvement. Those in the placebo group expect to show no improvement and so will be less likely to display improvement or recognize improvement, even if they experience it.

Some researchers refer to the placebo effect as though it were purely an uninteresting artifact. Yet placebo effects are just as real as those of actual drugs and are worthy of psychological investigation in their own right (see Chapters 10 and 14). Placebos show many of the same characteristics as do real drugs, such as having a more powerful effect at higher doses (Buckalew & Ross, 1981; Rickels, Hesbacher, Weise, et al., 1970). Moreover, some researchers maintain that up to 80 percent of the effectiveness of antidepressants is attributable to placebo effects (Kirsch & Sapirstein, 1998), although some others suspect the true percentage is somewhat lower (Dawes, 1998; Klein, 1998).

The Experimenter Bias Effect. It's clear that including a control condition that provides a placebo treatment is extremely important, as is keeping participants blind to their condition assignment. Still, there's one more potential concern with experimental designs. In some cases, the subject doesn't know the condition assignment, but the experimenter does.

When this happens, a problem can arise: the **experimenter bias effect** or *Rosenthal effect.* It occurs when researchers' hypotheses lead them to unintentionally bias the outcome of a study. This effect doesn't refer to deliberate "fudging" or making up of data, which fortunately happens only rarely in science. Instead, in the experimenter bias effect, researchers' biases subtly affect the results. In some cases, researchers may end up confirming their hypotheses even when these hypotheses are wrong.

Because of this effect, it's essential that experiments be conducted whenever possible in a **double-blind** fashion. By double-blind, we mean that neither researchers nor participants know who's in the experimental or control group. By voluntarily shielding themselves from the knowledge of which subjects are in which group, researchers are once again guarding themselves against confirmation bias.

One of the oldest and best-known examples of the experimenter bias effect is the infamous tale of a man and his horse. In 1900, a man named Wilhem van Osten purchased a handsome Arabian stallion, now known in the psychological literature as Clever Hans, who seemingly displayed astonishing mathematical abilities. By tapping with his hooves, Clever Hans responded correctly to mathematical questions from van Osten (such as, "How much is 8 plus 3?"). He even calculated square roots and could tell the time of day. Understandably, van Osten was so proud of Clever Hans that he began showing him off in public. Eventually, Clever Hans's performances drew large throngs of amazed spectators.

You might be wondering whether Clever Hans's feats were the result of trickery. A panel of 13 psychologists investigated Clever Hans, found no evidence of fraud on van Osten's part, and concluded that Clever Hans possessed the arithmetic abilities of a 14-year-old human.

Nevertheless, psychologist Oscar Pfungst was skeptical of just how clever Clever Hans really was, and in 1904 he launched a series of careful observations. In this case, Pfungst did something that previous psychologists didn't think to do: He focused not

Clever Hans performing in public. If one can observe powerful experimenter (in this case, owner) bias effects even in animals, how powerful might such effects be in humans?

GLOSSARY

blind
unaware of whether one is in the experimental or control group

experimenter bias effect
phenomenon in which researchers' hypotheses lead them to unintentionally bias the outcome of a study

double-blind
when neither researchers nor participants are aware of who's in the experimental or control group

on the horse, but on the people asking him questions. When he did, he found that van Osten and others were *unintentionally cuing* the horse to produce correct answers. Specifically, Pfungst found that Clever Hans's questioners almost invariably tightened their muscles immediately before the correct answer. When Pfungst prevented Clever Hans from seeing the questioner or anyone else who knew the correct answer, the horse did no better than chance. The puzzle was solved: Clever Hans was cleverly detecting subtle physical cues unintentionally produced by questioners.

The Clever Hans story was one of the first demonstrations of the experimenter bias effect. It showed that people can—even without their knowledge—give off cues that affect a subject's behavior, even when that subject is a horse. This story also reminds us that an extraordinary claim, in this case that a horse can perform arithmetic, requires extraordinary evidence. Van Osten's claims were extraordinary, but his evidence wasn't.

EXTRAORDINARY CLAIMS
Is the evidence as convincing as the claim?

We mentioned that the experimenter bias effect is also called the Rosenthal effect. That's because in the 1960s psychologist Robert Rosenthal conducted an elegant series of experiments that persuaded the psychological community that experimenter bias effects were genuine. Rosenthal and his colleagues were so adept at identifying experimental artifacts that they became known as "artifactologists."

In one of these experiments, Rosenthal and Fode (1963) randomly assigned some psychology students a group of five so-called maze-bright rats—rats bred over many generations to run mazes quickly—and other students a group of five so-called maze-dull rats—rats bred over many generations to run mazes slowly. Note that this is an experiment because Rosenthal and Fode randomly assigned students to groups and manipulated which type of rat the students supposedly received. They then asked the students to run the rats in mazes and to record each rat's completion time. But there was a catch: Rosenthal and Fode had told a fib. They had randomly assigned rats to the students rather than the other way around. The story about the "maze-bright" and "maze-dull" rats was all cooked up. Yet when Rosenthal and Fode tabulated their results, they found that students assigned the "maze-bright" rats reported 29 percent faster maze running times than did students assigned the "maze-dull" rats. In some unknown fashion, the students had influenced their rats' running times.

Even experiments with rats can create experimenter bias effects. Rats that experimenters think are smarter learn to run a maze more quickly than those that experimenters believe are slower.

Demand Characteristics. A final potential pitfall of psychological research can be difficult to eliminate. Research participants can pick up cues, known as **demand characteristics,** from an experiment that allow them to generate guesses regarding the experimenter's hypotheses (Orne, 1962; Rosnow, 2002). In some cases, participants' guesses about what the experimenter is up to may be correct; in other cases, they may not. The problem is that when participants think they know how the experimenter wants them to act, they may alter their behavior accordingly. So whether they've guessed right or wrong, their beliefs are preventing the researchers from getting an unbiased view of the participants' thoughts and behaviors. To combat demand characteristics, researchers will often include "distractor" tasks or "filler" items — measures that are unrelated to the question of interest. These help to prevent participants from altering their responses in ways they think the experimenters are looking for.

ASKING PEOPLE ABOUT THEMSELVES AND OTHERS

Imagine being hired by a research firm to estimate people's attitudes toward a newly released brand of toothpaste, Brightooth, which supposedly prevents 99.99 percent of cavities. How will we do it? We could flag people down on the street, pay them money to brush their teeth with Brightooth, and measure their reactions to Brightooth on a survey. Is this a good approach?

GLOSSARY

demand characteristics
cues that participants pick up from a study that allow them to generate guesses regarding the researcher's hypotheses

No, because the people on your neighborhood street probably aren't typical of people in general. Moreover, some people will almost surely refuse to participate, and they may differ from those who agreed to participate. For example, people with especially bad teeth might refuse to try Brightooth, and they may be the very people to whom Brightooth executives would most want to market their product.

Random Selection: The Key to Generalizability.

A better approach would be to identify a representative sample of the population and then administer our survey to people drawn from that sample. For example, we could look at U.S. population census data and try to contact every 10,000th person listed. This approach, often used in survey research, is called **random selection.** In random selection, every person in the population has an equal chance of being chosen to participate. Random selection is crucial if we want our results to generalize to the broader population because we're more likely to select a sample that accurately reflects characteristics that are true of the population as a whole. Political pollsters keep themselves awake at night worrying about random selection. If their selection of survey respondents from the population is nonrandom (that is, biased), their election forecasts will be hopelessly skewed.

Incidentally, we shouldn't confuse random selection with *random assignment,* which, as we discussed earlier, is one of the two ingredients of an experiment. Here's how to remember the difference: Random selection deals with how we initially choose our participants, whereas random assignment deals with how we assign our participants *after we've already chosen them.*

An example of how nonrandom selection can lead to disastrously misleading conclusions comes from the infamous *Hite Report* (1987). In the mid-1980s, sex researcher Shere Hite sent out 100,000 surveys to American women inquiring about their romantic and sexual relationships. She'd identified potential survey respondents from lists of subscribers to women's magazines. Hite's findings were so startling that *Time* magazine and other prominent publications featured them as their cover story. Here's a sampling of Hite's findings:

- 70 percent of women married 5 or more years say they've had extramarital affairs.
- 87 percent of married women say their closest emotional relationship is with someone other than their husband.
- 95 percent of women say they're "emotionally and psychologically harassed" by their love partner.
- 98 percent of women say they're generally unsatisfied with their present love relationship.

That's pretty depressing news, to put it mildly. Yet lost in the furor over Hite's findings was one crucial point: Only 4.5 percent of her sample had responded to her survey. What's more, Hite had no way of knowing whether this 4.5 percent was representative of her full sample. Interestingly, a poll conducted by the Harris organization at around the same time used random selection and reported results virtually opposite to Hite's. In their better-conducted survey, 89 percent of women said they were generally satisfied with their current relationship, and only a small minority reported extramarital affairs. More likely than not, Hite's high percentages were a result of nonrandom selection: The 4.5 percent of participants who responded to her survey were probably the very women experiencing the most relationship problems to begin with and therefore the most motivated to participate.

Self-Report Measures and Surveys.

Psychologists frequently use *self-report measures,* often called questionnaires, to assess a variety of characteristics, such as personality traits, mental illnesses, and interests. Closely related to self-report measures are *surveys,* which psychologists typically use to measure people's opinions and attitudes (say, their reactions to Brightooth and other toothpastes). Yet not all self-report measures and surveys

---

Fict -OID

MYTH: When conducting surveys, larger samples are always better.

REALITY: A poll of over 100,000 people is virtually useless if it's nonrandom. In fact, it's far better to conduct a poll of 100 people we've selected randomly than a poll of 100 million people we've selected nonrandomly. In large samples, biases become magnified.

GLOSSARY

random selection
procedure that ensures every person in a population has an equal chance of being chosen to participate

are created equal; some have high levels of reliability and validity, but others don't.

When interpreting the results of self-report measures and surveys, we should bear in mind that we can obtain quite different answers depending on how we phrase the questions (Schwarz, 1999). One researcher administered surveys to 300 women homemakers. In some surveys, women answered a question that asked, "Would you like to have a job, if this were possible?" whereas others answered a question that asked, "Would you prefer to have a job, or do you prefer to do just your housework?" These two questions seem remarkably similar. Yet although 81 percent answered yes to the first question, only 32 percent answered yes to the second (Noelle-Neumann, 1970; Walonick, 1994). The reason for this whopping difference isn't clear, although the use of the words "if this were possible" in the first question might have encouraged respondents to think about employment options that wouldn't ordinarily have occurred to them. Moreover, we shouldn't assume that people who respond to survey questions even understand the answers they're giving. In one survey study, researchers asked subjects their opinions about the "Agricultural Trade Act of 1978." About 30 percent of subjects expressed an opinion about this act, even though no such act exists (Bishop, Oldendick, & Tuchfarber, 1986; Schwarz, 1999).

Self-report measures have an important advantage: They're easy to administer. All we need are a pencil and paper or a web survey, and a willing participant, and we're ready to go. Self-report measures of personality traits and behaviors often work reasonably well (see Chapter 12). For example, people's reports of how outgoing or shy they are tend to be moderately correlated (often about $r = .5$) with the reports of people who know them well. The correlations tend to be somewhat higher for more observable traits, like extraversion, than for less observable traits, like anxiety (Kenrick & Funder, 1988).

Yet self-report measures have their disadvantages too. First, they typically assume that respondents possess enough insight into their own personality characteristics to report on them accurately. This assumption is questionable for certain groups of people. For example, people with high levels of narcissistic personality traits, like self-centeredness and excessive self-confidence (the word *narcissistic* derives from the Greek mythological character Narcissus, who fell in love with his reflection in the water), tend to view themselves more positively than others do (John & Robins, 1994).

Second, self-report questionnaires typically assume that participants are honest in their responses. But not surprisingly, some questionnaire respondents engage in **response sets**—tendencies to distort their answers to items to appear more positive, for example, than they actually are.

Democrat Harry Truman famously holding up an early edition of the *Chicago Daily Tribune* incorrectly proclaiming Republican Thomas Dewey the winner of the 1948 presidential election. In fact, Truman won by nearly 5 percentage points. The pollsters got it wrong largely because they based their survey results on people with telephones. Back in 1948, considerably more Republicans (who tended to be richer) owned telephones than Democrats, resulting in a skewed preelection prediction.

Fact-OID A widely publicized 1992 poll by the Roper organization asked Americans the following confusing question, which contained two negatives: "Does it seem possible or does it seem impossible to you that the Nazi extermination of the Jews never happened?" A shocking 22 percent of respondents replied that the Holocaust may not have happened. Yet when a later poll asked the question more clearly, this number dropped to only 1 percent. Survey wording counts.

LABORATORY RESEARCH DOESN'T APPLY TO THE REAL WORLD, RIGHT?

It's easy to assume that laboratory research doesn't generalize to the real world. This assumption seems reasonable at first blush, because behavior that emerges in the artificial confines of the laboratory doesn't always mirror behavior in natural settings. Moreover, psychologists conduct a great deal of their research on college students, who tend to be more intelligent, more self-absorbed, less certain of their identities, and more reliant on social approval than noncollege participants. For example, about 75 percent of published studies of interpersonal interactions are conducted on undergraduates (Sears, 1986). It's not always clear how generalizable these findings are to the rest of humanity (Peterson, 2000).

GLOSSARY

response sets
tendencies of research participants to distort their responses to questionnaire items

REPLICABILITY
Can the results be duplicated in other studies?

Is the belief that laboratory research is low in external validity really true? As Douglas Mook (1983) pointed out, high internal validity can often lead to high external validity. That's because carefully controlled experiments generate conclusions that are more trustworthy and more likely to apply to the real world than are loosely controlled studies. In addition, the results of carefully controlled experiments are typically more likely to replicate than the results of loosely controlled studies.

Craig Anderson, James Lindsay, and Brad Bushman (1999) decided to take a systematic look at this issue. They examined the correspondence between laboratory studies of various psychological phenomena—including aggression, helping, leadership, interpersonal perception, performance on exams, and the causes of depressed mood—as measured in both the laboratory and real world. Anderson and his colleagues computed how large the effects were in both laboratory and real-world studies and then correlated these effects. For example, in studies of the relation between watching violent television and aggressive behavior, they examined the correspondence between findings from controlled laboratory studies—in which investigators randomly assign participants to watch either violent television or nonviolent television, and then measure their aggression—and real-world studies—in which investigators observe people's television viewing habits and aggression in daily life.

Anderson and his collaborators found the correlation between the sizes of the effects in laboratory and real-world studies to be $r = .73$, which is a high association (see **Figure 2.6**). That is to say, laboratory research often generalizes surprisingly well to the real world.

Even so, we shouldn't simply assume that a laboratory study has high external validity. The best approach is to examine both well-controlled laboratory experiments and studies using naturalistic observation to make sure that the results from both research designs converge. If they do, that should make us even more confident in our conclusions (Shadish, Cook, & Campbell, 2002). If they don't, that should make us scratch our heads and try to figure out what's accounting for the difference.

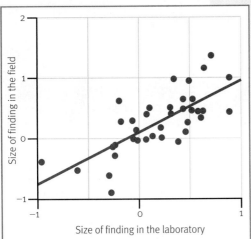

Figure 2.6 Does Laboratory Research Relate to the Real World? This scatterplot displays the data from the findings of studies in the laboratory versus the real world. (*Source:* Anderson, Lindsay, and Bushman, 1999)

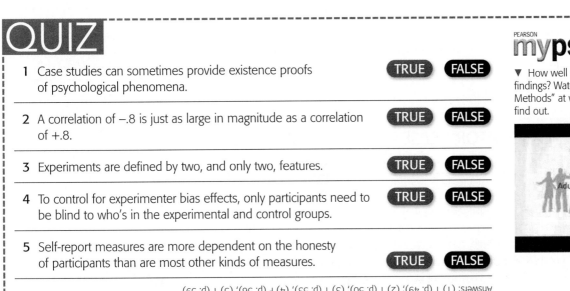

QUIZ

1 Case studies can sometimes provide existence proofs of psychological phenomena. TRUE FALSE

2 A correlation of −.8 is just as large in magnitude as a correlation of +.8. TRUE FALSE

3 Experiments are defined by two, and only two, features. TRUE FALSE

4 To control for experimenter bias effects, only participants need to be blind to who's in the experimental and control groups. TRUE FALSE

5 Self-report measures are more dependent on the honesty of participants than are most other kinds of measures. TRUE FALSE

▼ How well can you evaluate research findings? Watch the video "Research Methods" at www.mypsychlab.com to find out.

Answers: (1) T (p. 49); (2) T (p. 50); (3) T (p. 53); (4) F (p. 56); (5) T (p. 59)

Ethical Issues in Research Design

When designing and conducting research studies, psychologists need to worry about more than their scientific value. The ethics of these studies also matter. Although psychology adheres to the same basic scientific principles as other sciences, let's just face it: A chemist needn't worry about hurting the mineral's feelings, and a physicist needn't be concerned about the long-term emotional well-being of a neutron. The scientific study of people and their behavior raises unique concerns.

Many philosophers believe—and the authors of this text agree—that science itself is value neutral. In less technical terms, this means that because science is a search for the truth, it's neither inherently good nor bad. Truth is what it is. This fact doesn't imply, though, that scientific *research,* including psychological research, is value neutral. There are both ethical and unethical ways of searching for the truth. Moreover, we may not all agree on which ways of searching for the truth are ethical. We'd probably all agree that it's perfectly acceptable to learn about brain damage by studying the behavior of people with brain damage on laboratory tasks of learning, just so long as these tasks don't cause participants much stress. We'd also all agree (we hope!) that it's unacceptable for us to learn about brain damage by hitting people over the head with baseball bats and then testing their motor coordination by measuring how often they fall down a flight of stairs. Nevertheless, we might not all agree on whether it's acceptable to learn about brain damage by creating severe lesions (wounds) in the brains of cats and examining their effects on cats' responses to fear-provoking stimuli (like scary dogs). In many cases, the question of whether research is ethical isn't clear cut.

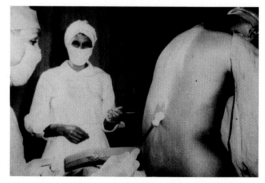

From 1932 to 1972, the United States Health Service conducted the Tuskegee Study in which 399 African American men infected with syphillis were studied. Incredibly, the researchers withheld information from the subjects about their diagnosis and about the availability of treatment for 30 years.

ETHICAL GUIDELINES FOR HUMAN RESEARCH

Throughout the history of psychology, a host of ethically questionable studies have been conducted—ones that had the potential to inflict serious psychological harm on participants. To address concerns about ethically problematic research, and to prevent researchers from inadvertently harming participants, stringent ethical guidelines are now in place. **[LEARNING OBJECTIVE 2.5]** For example, the American Psychological Association has developed a set of ethical guidelines that all psychologists are expected to follow (see **Table 2.1**).

Table 2.1: **APA Ethical Principles for Human Research** Psychological researchers must carefully weigh the potential scientific benefits of their research against the potential danger to participants. In 2002, the American Psychological Association (APA) published a code of ethics to govern all research with human participants. The following is a summary of the key ethical principles.

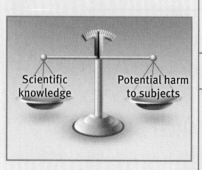

Scientific knowledge — Potential harm to subjects

Informed Consent
- Research participants should be fully informed of the purpose of the research, its expected duration, and any potential risks, discomfort, or adverse effects associated with it.
- Participants should enter the study voluntarily and be informed of their right to withdraw from it at any time.
- A contact who can answer questions about the research and the participant's rights should be provided.

Protection from Harm and Discomfort
- Psychologists must take reasonable steps to avoid harm to research participants.

Deception and Debriefing
- When deceptive techniques are used in research, the participants should be informed of the deception as soon as possible after the deception takes place.
- Participants should not be deceived about research procedures that may cause the participants physical pain or emotional distress.
- Once the research study has concluded, participants should be not only informed of the deception but fully debriefed about the true nature of the research and its results.

What's more, every major American research college and university has at least one *institutional review board* (IRB), which reviews all research carefully with an eye toward protecting participants against abuses. IRBs typically consist of faculty members drawn from various departments within a college or university, as well as one or more outside members, such as a person drawn from the community surrounding the college or university.

Informed Consent. IRBs insist on a procedure called **informed consent:** Researchers must tell subjects what they're getting into before asking them to participate, and the participants must agree to undergo the procedure. During the informed consent process, participants can ask questions about the study and learn more about what will be involved.

However, IRBs may sometimes allow researchers to forgo at least some elements of informed consent. In particular, some psychological research entails *deception.* When researchers use deception, they deliberately mislead participants about the study's purpose. In one of the most controversial and best-known studies in the history of psychology (conducted before IRBs existed), Stanley Milgram (1963) invited volunteers to participate in a study (see Chapter 11) in which the participants believed they were administering painful electric shocks of increasing intensity to another participant. In reality, no shocks were delivered, and the other "participant" was actually a *confederate* (a research assistant who plays the part of a participant) of the experimenter. Milgram was interested in the influence of authority figures (such as the experimenter) on obedience. Many of the actual participants were understandably distressed by the fact that they delivered what they believed to be extremely painful electric shocks to an innocent person.

Was Milgram's elaborate deception justified? Milgram (1964) argued that the hoax was required to pull off the study because informing subjects of the true purpose of the study would have generated obvious demand characteristics. He further noted that he went out of his way to later explain the study's true purpose to participants.

The debate concerning the ethics of Milgram's study continued long after the study was completed (Blass, 2004). Over the years, IRBs—which didn't exist in Milgram's day—have become more stringent about the need for informed consent. Milgram's study almost certainly wouldn't be approved by any college or university IRBs in the United States today.

WHAT DO *you* THINK ?

You are a participant in a research study. After hearing from the experimenter about what to expect in the study, you are still confused about what is involved. How would you assert your rights as a subject to find out more information before consenting?

Debriefing: Educating Participants. IRBs may also request that a full debriefing be performed at the conclusion of the research session. *Debriefing* is a process whereby researchers inform participants what the study was about. In some cases, researchers even use debriefings to explain their hypotheses in nontechnical language. In these cases the research study becomes a learning experience for not only the investigator but also the subject.

ETHICAL ISSUES IN ANIMAL RESEARCH

Few topics generate as much anger and discomfort as animal research. This is especially true of *invasive* research, in which investigators cause physical harm to animals. In psychology departments, invasive research most often takes the form of producing lesions in animals' brains, usually by means of surgery, and observing their effects on animals' behavior (see

GLOSSARY

informed consent
informing research participants of what is involved in a study before asking them to participate

Chapter 3). About 7 to 8 percent of published research in psychology relies on animals (American Psychological Association, 2008) with the overwhelming majority of studies conducted on rodents (especially rats and mice) and birds. The goal of such research is to generate ideas about how the brain relates to behavior in humans without having to inflict harm on people.

Many animal rights protestors have raised important concerns regarding the ethical treatment of animals and have underscored the need for adequate housing and feeding conditions (Ott, 1995). In contrast, others have gone to extremes that many critics would describe as unethical in themselves. **[LEARNING OBJECTIVE 2.6]** Some have ransacked laboratories and "liberated" animals. In 1999, the Animal Liberation Front attacked several psychology laboratories at the University of Minnesota, releasing rats and pigeons and inflicting about $20 million worth of damage (Azar, 1999; Hunt, 1999). Most individuals on both sides of the animal rights debate agree that liberating animals is a dreadful idea because most animals die shortly after being released due to lack of adequate care and feeding.

A great deal of animal research remains intensely controversial. It will probably always remain this way, given the complex ethical questions involved.

These excessive tactics aside, the ethical issues aren't easily resolved. Some commentators maintain that the deaths of approximately 20 million laboratory animals every year (Cunningham, 1993; Regan, 2004) aren't worth the benefits. They argue that the knowledge gleaned from animal research on aggression, fear, learning, memory, and related topics is of such doubtful external validity to humans as to be virtually useless (Ulrich, 1991).

However, some animal research has led to direct benefits to humans, as well as immensely useful knowledge in its own right. For example, many psychological treatments, especially those based on principles of learning (see Chapter 5), were derived from animal research. Without animal research, we'd know relatively little about the physiology of the brain (Domjan & Purdy, 1995). Moreover, to answer many critical psychological questions, there are simply no good alternatives to using animals (Baldwin, 1993; Gallup & Suarez, 1985). For example, without animals we'd be unable to test the safety and effectiveness of many medications.

None of this tells us when we should and shouldn't use animals in research. Nevertheless, it's clear that animal research has yielded enormously important insights about the brain and behavior and that psychologists are likely to rely on such research for some time to come. It's also clear that animal researchers must weigh carefully the potential scientific gains of their inquiries against the costs in death and suffering they produce. Because reasonable people will inevitably disagree about how to weigh these pros and cons, the intense controversy surrounding animal research is unlikely to subside anytime soon.

QUIZ

PEARSON mypsychlab

▼ Can participants die in experiments? Watch the video titled "Before Informed Consent: Robert Guthrie" at www.mypsychlab.com to find out.

1 IRBs review research procedures to ensure that studies are ethical before researchers are permitted to conduct them. **TRUE FALSE**

2 Milgram's study would be considered unethical today because the shock could have caused injury or death. **TRUE FALSE**

3 In debriefing, the researcher informs participants of what will happen in the procedure before asking them to participate. **TRUE FALSE**

4 Before conducting invasive research on animals, investigators should weigh carefully the potential scientific benefits of this research against the costs of animal death and suffering. **TRUE FALSE**

Answers: (1) T (p. 62); (2) F (p. 62); (3) F (p. 62); (4) T (p. 63)

Statistics: The Currency of Psychological Research

Up to this point in the chapter, we've mostly spared you the gory mathematical details of psychological research. Aside from correlation coefficients, we haven't said much about how psychologists analyze their findings. Still, to understand psychological research and how to interpret it, we need to know a bit about **statistics:** the application of mathematics to describing and analyzing data. Statistics are considered the "currency" of research because they help us determine the value of a particular hypothesis. For you math phobics out there, there's no cause for alarm. We promise to keep things simple.

Psychologists use two kinds of statistics. The first are **descriptive statistics.** They do exactly what the name implies: describe data. In addition to descriptive statistics, psychologists use **inferential statistics,** which allow us to determine whether we can generalize findings from our sample to the full population.

DESCRIPTIVE STATISTICS: WHAT'S WHAT?

Descriptive statistics allow us to summarize the nature of our data. For example, using descriptive statistics on a sample of 100 men and 100 women whose levels of friendliness we assess using a self-report measure, we could ask the following questions:

- What's the average level of friendliness in this sample?
- What's the average level of friendliness among men, and what's the average level of friendliness among women?
- How much do all of our participants, as well as men and women separately, vary in how friendly they are?

To maintain our promise we'd keep things simple, we'll discuss only two major types of descriptive statistics, central tendency and dispersion.

Central Tendency: The 3 Ms. The first is the **central tendency,** which gives us a sense of the "central" score in our data set or where the group tends to cluster. There are three measures of central tendency: mean, median, and mode (known as the "three Ms"). Follow along in **Table 2.2a** (the left half of the table below) as we calculate each. **[LEARNING OBJECTIVE 2.7]**

The **mean,** also known as the average, is just the total score divided by the number of people. If our sample consists of five people, as shown in **Table 2.2,** the mean IQ is simply the total of the five scores divided by five, which happens to be 102.

GLOSSARY

statistics
application of mathematics to describing and analyzing data

descriptive statistics
numerical characterizations that describe data

inferential statistics
mathematical methods that allow us to determine whether we can generalize findings from our sample to the full population

central tendency
measure of the "central" scores in a data set, or where the group tends to cluster

mean
average; a measure of central tendency

median
middle score in a data set; a measure of central tendency

mode
most frequent score in a data set; a measure of central tendency

Table 2.2 The Three Ms: Mean, Median, and Mode.

(a)	(b)
Sample IQ scores: 100, 90, 80, 120, 120	**Sample IQ scores:** 80, 85, 95, 95, 220
Mean: (100 + 90 + 80 +120 +120)/5 = 102	**Mean:** (80 + 85 + 95 + 95 + 220)/5 = 116
Median: order scores from lowest to highest: 80, 90, 100, 120, 120; middle score is 100	**Median:** 95
	Mode: 95
Mode: only 120 appears twice in the data set, so it's the most common score	**Note:** Mean is affected by one extreme score, but median and mode aren't

The **median,** which we shouldn't confuse with that patch of grass in the middle of a highway, is the middle score in our data set. We obtain the median by lining up our scores in order and then finding the middle one. So in this case, we'd line up the five IQ scores in order from lowest to highest and then find that 100 is the median because that's the score smack in the middle of the distribution.

The **mode** is the most frequent score in our data set. In this case, the mode is 120, because two people in our sample received scores of 120 on the IQ test and one person received each of the other scores.

As we can see, the three Ms sometimes give us rather different measures of central tendency. In this case, the mean and median were close to each other, but the mode was much higher than both. The mean is generally the best statistic to report when our data form a bell-shaped or "normal" distribution, as we can see in the top panel of **Figure 2.7**. But what happens when our distribution is "skewed," that is, tilted sharply to one side or the other, as in the lower panels of Figure 2.7? Here the mean provides a misleading picture of the central tendency, so it's better to use the median or mode instead. **[LEARNING OBJECTIVE 2.8]**

To hammer this point home, let's now look at **Table 2.2b** to see what happens to our measures of central tendency. The mean of this distribution is 116, but four of the scores are much below 116, and the only reason the mean is this high is the presence of one person who scored 220 (who in technical terms we call an *outlier,* because his or her score lies way outside the other scores). In contrast, both the median and mode are 95, which capture the central tendency of the distribution much better.

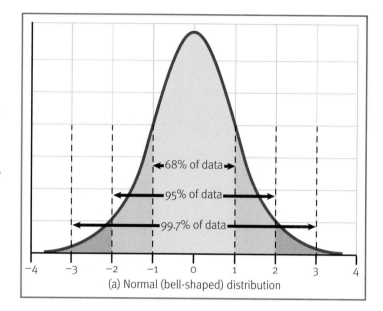

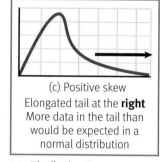

(a) Normal (bell-shaped) distribution

(b) Negative skew
Elongated tail at the **left**
More data in the tail than would be expected in a normal distribution

(c) Positive skew
Elongated tail at the **right**
More data in the tail than would be expected in a normal distribution

Figure 2.7 Distribution Curves. (a) a normal (bell-shaped) distribution, (b) a markedly negative skewed distribution, and (c) a markedly positive skewed distribution.

Dispersion: How the Data Scatter.
The second type of descriptive statistic is **dispersion,** which gives us a sense of how loosely or tightly bunched the scores are. Consider the following two sets of IQ scores from five people:

- 80, 85, 85, 90, 95
- 25, 65, 70, 125, 150

In both groups of scores, the mean is 87. But the second set of scores is much more spread out (dispersed) than the first. So we need some way of describing the differences in dispersion in these two data sets.

Although there are several measures of dispersion, the simplest is the **range.** The range is the difference between the highest and lowest scores. In the first set of IQ scores, the range is only 15, whereas in the second set the range is 125. So the range tells us that, although the two sets of scores have a similar central tendency, their dispersion is wildly different. Although the range is the easiest measure of dispersion to calculate, it can be deceptive because, as shown in **Figure 2.8** two data sets with the same range can display a very different distribution of scores across that range. To compensate for this fact, psychologists often use another measure called the

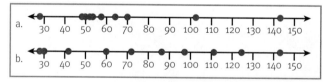

Figure 2.8 The Range versus the Standard Deviation. These two number lines display data sets with the same *range* but different *standard deviations*. The dispersion is more tightly clustered in (a) than in (b), so the standard deviation in (a) will be smaller.

GLOSSARY

dispersion
measure of how loosely or tightly bunched scores are

range
difference between the highest and lowest scores; a measure of dispersion

standard deviation to depict dispersion. Without getting into the mathematical details, this measure is less likely to be deceptive than the range because it takes into account how far *each* data point is from the mean, rather than simply looking at how widely scattered the most extreme scores are.

INFERENTIAL STATISTICS: TESTING HYPOTHESES

The second type of statistic psychologists use is inferential statistics. When we use inferential statistics, we're asking whether we can draw "inferences" (conclusions) regarding whether the differences we've observed in our sample apply to similar samples. Previously, we mentioned a study of 100 men and 100 women who took a self-report measure of friendliness. In this study, inferential statistics allow us to answer the following question: Are the differences we've found in friendliness between men and women believable, or are they just a fluke occurrence in our sample? Let's imagine we calculated the means for men and women (we first verified that the distribution of scores in both men and women approximated a bell curve). After doing so, we found that men scored 10.4 on our friendliness scale (the scores range from 0 to 15) and that women scored 9.9. So, *in our sample,* men report being more friendly than women. Can we conclude from this finding that men are more friendly than women in general? How can we rule out the possibility that this small sex difference in our sample is due to chance? That's where inferential statistics enter the picture.

Statistical Significance.
To figure out whether the difference we've observed in our sample is a believable (real) one, we need to conduct statistical tests to determine whether we can generalize our findings to the broader population. To do so, we can use a variety of statistics, depending on the research design. But regardless of which test we use, we generally use a .05 level of confidence when deciding whether a finding is believable. This means that we don't typically accept a finding as believable unless it has a probability of happening less than 5 percent of the time by chance or less than 1 out of every 20 times we conducted the study. When the finding meet the .05 confidence level, we say that the finding is *statistically significant*. Statistical significance means that it is very likely a real difference. In psychology journals, we'll often see the expression "$p < .05$," meaning that the probability (the lowercase p stands for probability) that our finding would have occurred by chance alone is less than 1 in 20.

A large sample size can yield a statistically significant result, but this result may have little or no practical significance.

Practical Significance.
Writer Gertrude Stein said that "a difference is a difference that makes a difference." Stein's quotation reminds us not to confuse statistical significance with *practical significance,* that is, real-world importance. A finding can be statistically significant yet be of virtually no importance in real-world predictions. To understand this point, we need to understand that a major determinant of statistical significance is sample size. The larger the sample size, the greater the odds (all else being equal) that a result will be statistically significant. With huge sample sizes, almost any finding—even tiny ones—can be statistically significant.

If we were to find a correlation of $r = .06$ between IQ and nose length in a sample of 500,000 people, this correlation would be statistically significant at the $p < .05$ level. Yet

GLOSSARY

standard deviation
measure of dispersion that takes into account how far each data point is from the mean

this value is so close to zero (no correlation) that it would be essentially useless for predicting anything.

HOW PEOPLE LIE WITH STATISTICS

American humorist Mark Twain once said there are three kinds of untruths: "lies, damned lies, and statistics." He was right: Because many people's eyes glaze over when they see lots of numbers, it's easy to fool them with statistical sleight of hand. Here, we'll provide two examples of how people can misuse statistics. **[LEARNING OBJECTIVE 2.9]** Our goal, of course, isn't to encourage you to lie with statistics but to equip you with critical thinking skills for spotting widespread statistical abuses (Huff, 1954).

Example 1. Your Congressional Representative, Ms. Dee Section, is running for reelection. As part of her platform, she's just proposed a new tax plan for everyone in your state. According to the "fine print" in Ms. Section's plan, 99 percent of the people in your state will receive a $100 tax cut this year. The remaining 1 percent, who make over $3 million per year, will receive a tax cut of $500,000 (according to Ms. Section, this large tax cut for the people in the uppermost 1 percent of the population is necessary because she gets her biggest campaign contributions from them).

Based on this plan, Ms. Dee Section announces at a press conference, "If I'm elected and my tax plan goes through, the average person in our state will receive a tax cut of $5,099." Watching this press conference on television, you think, "Wow . . . what a deal! I'm definitely going to vote for Dee Section. If she wins, I'll have over 5,000 extra bucks in my bank account."

Question: *Why should you be skeptical of Dee Section's claim?*

Answer: Ms. Dee Section has engaged in a not especially subtle deception. She assures us that under her plan the "average person" in her state will receive a tax cut of $5,099. In one respect she's right, because the *mean* tax cut is indeed $5,099. But in this case, the mean is highly misleading, because under Section's plan virtually everyone in her state will receive only a $100 tax cut. Only the richest of the rich will receive a tax cut of $500,000, making the mean highly unrepresentative of the central tendency. Dee Section should have instead reported the median or mode, which are both only $100, as measures of central tendency.

Example 2. A researcher, Dr. Faulty Conclusion, conducts a study to demonstrate that transcendental meditation (TM), a form of relaxation that originated in East Asian cultures, reduces crime rates. According to Dr. Conclusion, towns whose citizens are taught to practice TM will experience a dramatic drop in numbers of arrests. He finds a small town, Pancake, Iowa (population 300), and teaches all of the citizens of Pancake to practice TM. For his control group, he identifies a small neighboring town in Iowa, called Waffle (population also 300), and doesn't introduce them to TM. According to Dr. Conclusion, Waffle is a good control group for Pancake, because it has the same population, ethnic makeup, income, and initial arrest rates.

Two months after the introduction of TM to Pancake, Dr. Conclusion measures the arrest rates in Pancake and Waffle. At a major conference, he proudly announces that although the arrest rates in Waffle stayed exactly the same, the arrest rates in Pancake experienced a spectacular plunge. To demonstrate this astonishing effect in Pancake, he

"There are lies, damn lies, and statistics. We're looking for someone who can make all three of these work for us."

(© www.CartoonStock.com)

The Psychologist

09-04-2010

NEWSWIRE

50% of Americans Below Average in IQ

Rutters News Agency: A shocking 50% of Americans are below average in IQ, reported a team of psychologists today at the Annual Meeting of the American Society of Psychology and Pseudoscience. The researchers, from Nonexistent State University, administered IQ tests to a sample of 6,000 Americans and found that fully half scored below the mean of their sample.

To evaluate claims about statistics in the news and on the Internet, we must equip ourselves with tools to guard against errors in reasoning.

directs the audience to a graph (see **Figure 2.9** to see this effect). "As you can see from this graph," Conclusion proclaims, "the arrest rates in Pancake were initially very high. But after I taught Pancake's citizens TM, their arrest rates were much, much lower." Dr. Conclusion concludes triumphantly, "Our findings show beyond a shadow of a doubt that TM reduces crime rates."

Question: *What's wrong with Dr. Conclusion's conclusion?*

Answer: Dr. Conclusion's graph in Figure 2.9 sure looks impressive, doesn't it? The arrest rates have indeed gone down from the beginning to the end of the study. But let's take a good close look at the scale of the graph. Can we see anything suspicious about it?

Dr. Conclusion has tricked us, or perhaps he's tricked himself. The *y* axis (that's the vertical axis) starts at 15.5 arrests per month and goes up to 16 arrests per month. In fact, Dr. Conclusion has demonstrated only that the arrest rate in Pancake declined from 15.9 arrests per month to 15.6 arrests per month—a grand total of less than one-third of an arrest per month! That's hardly worth writing home about, let alone mastering transcendental meditation for.

Dr. Conclusion used what's termed a "truncated line graph." That kind of graph is a real "no-no" in statistics, although researchers use it all the time (Huff, 1954; Smith, 2001). In a truncated line graph, the *y* axis starts not at the lowest possible score, where it should start (in this case, it should start at 0, because the lowest possible number of arrests per month is 0), but somewhere close to the highest possible score. By using a truncated line graph, Dr. Conclusion made the apparent effects of TM appear huge. In fact, they were pitifully small.

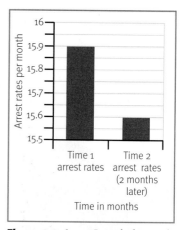

Figure 2.9 Arrest Rates before and after Transcendental Meditation.
Arrest rates per month in Pancake before (*left*) and after (*right*) introduction of transcendental meditation.

WHAT DO *you* THINK?

You are hired by a research and development company to conduct a study on behalf of a local corporation to explore the benefits of their product on learning. The research results fail to support the company's claim that the product improves learning. How would you report your findings to the company and how would you characterize the results in your conclusions?

QUIZ

1 The mean is not always the best measure of central tendency. **TRUE** **FALSE**

2 The mode and standard deviation are both measures of dispersion. **TRUE** **FALSE**

3 All statistically significant findings are important and large in size. **TRUE** **FALSE**

4 Researchers can easily manipulate statistics to make it appear that their hypotheses are confirmed. **TRUE** **FALSE**

Answers: (1) T (p. 65); (2) F (pp. 65–66); (3) F (p. 66); (4) T (p. 67)

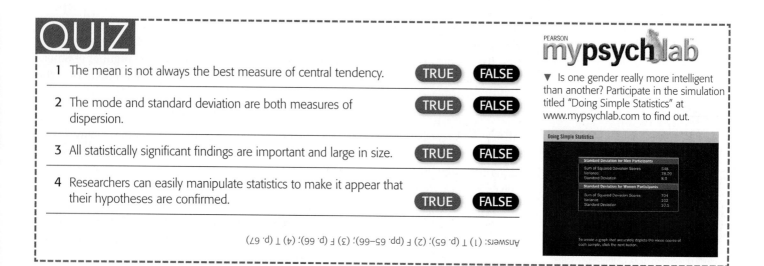

PEARSON
mypsych lab

▼ Is one gender really more intelligent than another? Participate in the simulation titled "Doing Simple Statistics" at www.mypsychlab.com to find out.

Becoming a Peer Reviewer of Psychological Research

"That's it? That's peer review?"

(© ScienceCartoonsPlus.com)

Almost all psychological journals send submitted articles to outside reviewers, who screen the articles carefully for quality control. This often ego-bruising process is called **peer review.** One crucial task of peer reviewers is to identify flaws that could undermine a study's findings and conclusions. Now that we've learned the key ingredients of a psychological experiment and the pitfalls that can cause experiments to go wrong, let's try our hands at becoming peer reviewers.

TRYING YOUR HAND AT PEER REVIEW

We're going to present descriptions of three studies, each of which contains at least one hidden flaw. Read each study and try to figure out what's wrong with it. **[LEARNING OBJECTIVE 2.10]** Once you've done so, read the paragraph below it to see how close you came. Ready? Here goes.

Study 1. An investigator, Dr. Sudo Sigh-Ents, sets out to test the hypothesis that subliminal self-help tapes (see Chapter 4) are effective in increasing self-esteem. She randomly selects 50 college freshmen from the subject pool to receive a commercially available subliminal self-help tape. She asks them to play the tape for 2 months each night for 1 hour before going to sleep (which is consistent with the standard instructions on the tape). Dr. Sigh-Ents measures participants' self-esteem at the start of the study and again after the 2-month period. She finds that their self-esteem has increased significantly over these 2 months. On the basis of this finding, Dr. Sigh-Ents concludes that "subliminal self-help tapes increase self-esteem."

Question: *What's wrong with this experiment?*

Answer: What's wrong with this "experiment" is that it's not even an experiment. There's no random assignment of participants to experimental and control groups; in fact, there's no control group at all. There's also no manipulation of an independent variable. Remember that a variable is something that varies. In this case, there's no independent variable because all participants received the same manipulation, namely, playing the subliminal self-help tape every night. As a result, we can't know whether the increase in self-esteem was really due to the tape. It could have been due to any number of other factors, such as placebo effects or increases in self-esteem that might often occur over the course of one's freshman year.

Study 2. A researcher, Dr. Art E. Fact, is interested in determining whether a new form of therapy, Anger Expression Therapy, is effective in treating anxiety. He randomly assigns 100 individuals with anxiety disorders to two groups. The experimental group receives Anger Expression Therapy (which is administered by Dr. Fact himself), whereas the control group is placed on a waiting list and receives no treatment. At the conclusion of 6 months, Dr. Fact finds that the rate of anxiety disorders is significantly lower in the experimental group than in the control group. He concludes, "Anger Expression Therapy is helpful in the treatment of anxiety disorders."

GLOSSARY

peer review
mechanism by which experts in a field carefully screen the work of their colleagues

Question: *What's wrong with this experiment?*

Answer: On its surface, this experiment looks OK. There's random assignment of participants to experimental and control groups and manipulation of an independent variable, namely, the presence versus absence of Anger Expression Therapy. But Dr. Fact hasn't controlled for two crucial pitfalls. First, he hasn't controlled for the placebo effect because the people receiving Anger Expression Therapy know they're receiving a treatment and the people in the control group know they're not. To control for this problem, Dr. Fact should probably have built in an *attention-placebo control condition:* A condition in which a counselor provides attention, but no formal psychotherapy, to patients (for example, the counselor could simply chat with his or her patients once a week). Second, Dr. Fact hasn't controlled for the experimenter bias effect. He knows which patients are in which group and could therefore subtly influence patients who are receiving Anger Expression Therapy to improve or report better results.

In an attention-placebo control condition, a counselor typically chats with patients but provides no formal treatment.

Study 3. Dr. E. Roney Us wants to find out whether listening to loud rock music impairs college students' performance on psychology tests. She randomly assigns 50 college students in Psychology 101 to listen to loud rock music for 2 hours (from 7 P.M. to 9 P.M.) every day for 1 week. Dr. Us asks her research assistant to randomly assign 50 other college students in Psychology 101 to use these same 2 hours to do whatever they like, except that they can't listen to loud rock music during this time period. She has no contact with the subjects in either group throughout the week and doesn't know who's in which group. At the end of the week, she examines their scores on their first Psychology 101 test (she doesn't know the Psychology 101 instructor and has no contact with him) and finds that students who listen to rock music do significantly worse than other students. Dr. Us concludes that "listening to loud rock music impairs students' performance on psychology tests."

Question: *What's wrong with this experiment?*

Answer: This study looks pretty decent at first glance. There's random assignment of participants to conditions, and there's also manipulation of an independent variable—either listening to or not listening to loud rock music. In addition, Dr. Us has ensured that she's blind to who's in the experimental and control groups and that she has no contact with either participants or the Psychology 101 instructor during this time. But Dr. Us has forgotten to control for one crucial confound: Subjects in the control group could have used the extra time to study for their exams. Because of this confound, it's impossible to know whether rock music leads to poorer test performance or whether extra study time leads to better test performance. Of course, both could be true, but we don't know for sure.

MOST REPORTERS AREN'T SCIENTISTS: EVALUATING PSYCHOLOGY IN THE MEDIA

Few major American newspapers hire reporters with any formal psychological training—the *New York Times* is a notable exception—so we shouldn't assume that people who write news stories about psychology are trained to distinguish psychological fact from fiction. Most aren't. This means that news stories are prone to faulty conclusions because reporters rely on the same heuristics and biases that we all do.

News coverage of scientific claims isn't always trustworthy.

When it comes to evaluating psychological claims in the news or entertainment media, there's a simple bottom-line message: We should always insist on rigorous research evidence.

When evaluating the legitimacy of psychological reports in the media, here are some tips to keep in mind. **[LEARNING OBJECTIVE 2.11]** First, we should *consider the source* (Gilovich, 1991). We should generally place more confidence in a finding reported in a reputable science magazine (like *Scientific American Mind* or *Discover*) than one reported in a supermarket tabloid (like the *National Enquirer*) or a popular magazine (like *People* or *Vogue*). The "consider the source" principle also applies to websites. We should generally place more trust in findings reported on websites of well-established psychological organizations, such as the American Psychological Association (www.apa.org) or Association for Psychological Science (www.psychologicalscience.org), than on websites that aren't hosted by a formal organization. Moreover, we should place more trust in findings from primary sources, such as the original journal articles themselves (if we can look them up in the library or on the Internet) than from secondary sources, such as newspapers, magazines, or websites that merely report findings from primary sources.

Second, we need to be on the lookout for excessive *sharpening* and *leveling* (Gilovich, 1991). *Sharpening* refers to the tendency to exaggerate the gist, or central message, of a study, whereas *leveling* refers to the tendency to minimize the less central details of a study. Sharpening and leveling often result in a "good story" because they end up bringing the most important facts of a study into sharper focus. But too much sharpening and leveling can result in a misleading picture. If an investigator discovers that a new medication is effective for 35 percent of people with anxiety disorders but that a placebo is effective for 33 percent of people with anxiety disorders, the newspaper editor may lead off the story with this eye-popping headline: "Breakthrough: New Medication Outperforms Other Pills in Treating Anxiety." This headline isn't literally wrong, but it oversimplifies greatly what the researcher found.

WHAT DO *you* THINK?

You are a member of your college debate team. When researching online articles on your upcoming debate topics, how would you detect sharpening and leveling by the writers to ensure that the information is not misleading?

Third, we can easily be misled by seemingly "balanced" coverage of a story. There's a crucial difference between genuine scientific controversy and the kind of balanced coverage that news reporters create by ensuring that representatives from both sides of the story receive equal air time. When covering a psychological story, the news media usually try to include comments from "experts" (we place this term in quotation marks, because they're not always genuine experts) on opposing sides of an issue. In this way, the media make their coverage appear more balanced. They also help to generate greater reader interest because almost everybody enjoys a juicy controversy.

The problem is that "balanced coverage" sometimes creates *pseudosymmetry* (Park, 2000): the appearance of a scientific controversy where none exists. For example, a newspaper might feature a story about a study that provides scientific evidence against extrasensory perception (ESP). They might devote the first four paragraphs to

a description of the study but the last four paragraphs to impassioned critiques of the study from advocates of ESP. This coverage may create the impression that the scientific evidence for ESP is split right down the middle, with about half of the research supporting it and about half disputing it. It's easy to overlook the fact that there was no scientific evidence in the last four paragraphs, only criticisms of the evidence against ESP.

One reason that most of us find it difficult to think critically about scientific evidence is that we're constantly bombarded by media reports that (unintentionally) provide us with poor role models for interpreting research (Lilienfeld, Ruscio, & Lynn, 2008; Stanovich, 2006). Fortunately, keeping these tips in mind should help us to become better consumers of psychological science in everyday life.

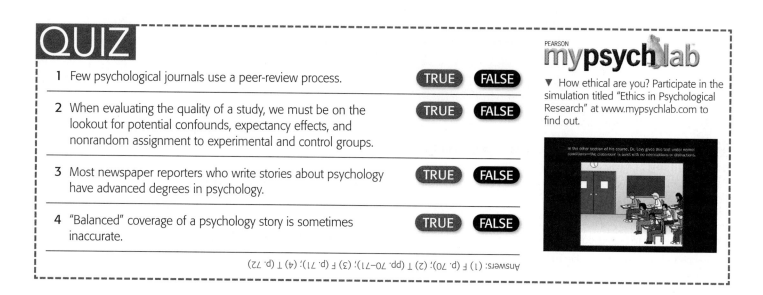

QUIZ

1 Few psychological journals use a peer-review process. **TRUE** **FALSE**

2 When evaluating the quality of a study, we must be on the lookout for potential confounds, expectancy effects, and nonrandom assignment to experimental and control groups. **TRUE** **FALSE**

3 Most newspaper reporters who write stories about psychology have advanced degrees in psychology. **TRUE** **FALSE**

4 "Balanced" coverage of a psychology story is sometimes inaccurate. **TRUE** **FALSE**

PEARSON mypsychlab

▼ How ethical are you? Participate in the simulation titled "Ethics in Psychological Research" at www.mypsychlab.com to find out.

Answers: (1) F (p. 70); (2) T (pp. 70–71); (3) F (p. 71); (4) T (p. 72).

Your Complete Review System

2.1 Explain what research designs accomplish that we can't discover by intuition alone

Numerous examples from history and recent times demonstrate that our intuitions that a particular phenomenon has occurred can be wrong. Only when there is an objective, consistent, replicable measure can we confirm our subjective hunches.

1. Bias can get in the way of our evaluation of claims unless we use dependable _____ _____. (p. 43)

2. Using your knowledge of research design, explain the flaws in Biklen's claims regarding facilitated communication. (p. 43)

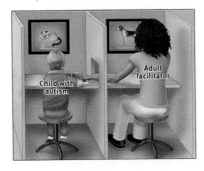

2.2 Identify heuristics and biases that prevent us from thinking clearly about psychology

Our heuristics are highly useful but can sometimes steer us wrong. Representativeness and availability heuristics can lead us to rely too heavily on inaccurate measures of the probability of events. Biases such as hindsight bias and overconfidence can lead us to over-estimate our ability to predict outcomes accurately.

3. Kahneman and Tversky pioneered the study of _____, mental shortcuts that help us make sense of the world. (p. 45)

4. When we use a _____ heuristic, we are essentially judging a book by its cover. (p. 45)

5. A _____ _____ is another term for how common a characteristic or behavior is. (p. 45)

6. The _____ heuristic involves estimating the likelihood of an occurrence based on the ease with which it comes to our minds. (p. 46)

7. How can we explain that most people say they'd have to travel southwest to get from Reno to San Diego? (p. 46)

8. In addition to heuristics, we can also fall prey to a variety of _____ _____—systematic errors in thinking. (p. 46)

9. Once an event occurs, if you say, "I knew that was going to happen," you might be engaging in _____ _____. (p. 46)

10. Most of us tend to engage in _____ when we overestimate our ability to make correct predictions. (p. 47)

succeed with mypsychlab

1. Is bias in the mind of the beholder? Learn how to avoid bias in everyday thinking.
   Anchoring and Adjustment

2.3 Distinguish the types of designs and the conclusions that we can draw from each

Four key types of research designs are naturalistic observation, case studies, correlational designs, and experimental designs. Naturalistic observation involves recording behaviors in real-world settings but is often not carefully controlled. Case studies involve examining one or a few individuals over long periods of time; these designs are often useful in generating hypotheses but limited in testing them rigorously. Correlational studies allow us to establish the relations among two or more measures but do not allow causal conclusions. Experimental designs involve random assignment of participants to conditions and manipulation of an independent variable, and they allow us to draw conclusions about the causes of a particular behavior.

11. A _____ _____ examines one person or a small group of people, and a _____ _____ examines the extent to which two variables are associated. (pp. 48–49)

12. A positive correlation is one in which the value of one variable goes up while the other one goes (up/down). (p. 49)

13. Why can't we use exceptions to argue against the existence of a correlation? (p. 51)

14. An _____ is a research design that consists of two components: (1) a random assignment of participants to conditions and (2) manipulation of an independent variable. (p. 53)

15. If a study is an experiment we (can/can't) infer cause and effect, but if the study is correlational we (can/can't). (p. 53)

16. The group of participants in a study that doesn't receive the manipulation is the _____ group. (p. 53)

Answers are located at the end of the text.

2.4 Identify the potential pitfalls of each design that can lead to faulty conclusions

Placebo effects, experimenter bias effects, and response sets are examples of problems in research designs that can lead to faulty conclusions.

17. When evaluating results, we need to be able to evaluate the consistency of the measurement, or _____, and the extent to which a measure assesses what it claims to measure, or _____. (p. 54)

18. To avoid the _____ effect it is crucial that the subject remain _____ to whether he or she has been assigned to the experimental group. (p. 56)

succeed with mypsychlab

1. Challenge your assumptions about explanations of behavior. **Correlations Do Not Show Causation**

2. Be a participant in a psychological experiment and practice your knowledge of research methods. **Distinguishing Independent and Dependent Variables**

3. Test your knowledge of the scientific method. **The Scientific Method: A Toolbox of Skills**

19. The Clever Hans example demonstrates how _____ _____ can influence the results of a study. (p. 57)

20. Using your knowledge of random selection, what did the pollsters do wrong in reporting the 1948 presidential election results? (p. 59)

ETHICAL ISSUES IN RESEARCH DESIGN (pp. 61–63)

2.5 Explain the ethical obligations of researchers toward their research participants

Concerns about ethical treatment of research participants have led research institutions to establish institutional review boards that review all research and require informed consent by participants. In some cases, they may also require a full debriefing at the conclusion of the research session.

21. Psychologists need to be concerned about the scientific value of their research studies but also the _____ of these studies. (p. 61)

22. Every major American research college and university now has an _____ _____ _____, which reviews all research and seeks to protect study participants against abuses. (p. 62)

23. The process during which researchers tell participants what's involved in a study is called _____ _____. (p. 62)

24. Milgram's controversial study relied on _____ because he deliberately misled the participants about the study's purpose. (p. 62)

25. Milgram's study likely (would/would not) be approved by a college or university IRB today in the United States. (p. 62)

26. What important changes have been made to research procedures in the United States to ensure that an ethical catastrophe like the Tuskegee study doesn't happen again? (pp. 61–63)

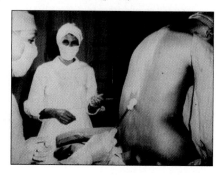

2.6 Describe both sides of the debate on the use of animals as research subjects

Animal research has led to clear benefits in our understanding of human-learning, brain physiology, and psychological treatment. To answer many critical psychological questions, there are simply no good alternatives to using animals. Those who question the ethics of animal research have raised useful questions about the treatment of these animals and emphasized the need for adequate housing and feeding conditions. Many protest the large number of laboratory animals that are used each year and question whether animal research offers sufficient external validity to justify such uses.

27. The goal of an _____ research study on animals is to learn how the brain relates to behavior in humans without having to inflict harm on people. (pp. 62–63)

succeed with mypsychlab

Do You Know All of the Terms in This Chapter?

Find out by using the Flashcards. Want more practice? Take additional quizzes, try simulations, and watch video to be sure you are prepared for the test!

28. About _____ percent of published psychology research relies on animals. (p. 63)

29. What are some of the ethical arguments for and against animal testing? (p. 63)

30. Animal researchers must carefully weigh the potential _____ _____ against the costs in death and suffering they produce. (p. 63)

succeed with mypsychlab

1. 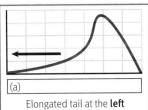 Learn about the extreme methods of animal rights terrorists. **Animal Rights Terrorists**

STATISTICS: THE CURRENCY OF PSYCHOLOGICAL RESEARCH (pp. 64–69)

2.7 Explain how to calculate measures of central tendency

Three measures of central tendency are the mean, median, and mode. The mean is the average of all scores. The median is the middle score. The mode is the most frequent score.

31. The application of mathematics to describing and analyzing data is called _____. (p. 64)

32. In _____ statistics, the _____ _____ provides a sense of the "central" score in a data set, or where the group tends to cluster. (p. 64)

33. Match up the measure to the definition. (pp. 64–65)

___ Mode	1. Middle score in a data set
___ Mean	2. Most frequent score in a data set
___ Median	3. Average score in a data set

2.8 Identify uses of various measures of central tendency and dispersion

Among the three measures of central tendency, the mean is the most widely used measure and is also the most sensitive to extreme scores. Two measures of dispersion are the range and standard deviation. The range is a more intuitive measure of variability but can yield a deceptive picture of how spread out or clustered individual scores are. The standard deviation is a better measure of dispersion, although it is more difficult to calculate.

34. The best measure of central tendency to report when the data form a "bell-shaped" or normal distribution is the _____. (p. 65)

35. The difference between the highest and lowest scores is the _____. (p. 65)

36. Another type of descriptive statistic is _____, which gives a sense of how loosely or tightly bunched the data are. (p. 65)

37. Using your knowledge of distribution curves, label these two different types of skews. (p. 65)

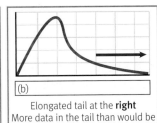

(a) Elongated tail at the **left**
More data in the tail than would be expected in a normal distribution

(b) Elongated tail at the **right**
More data in the tail than would be expected in a normal distribution

38. The _____ _____ takes into account how far each data point is from the mean. (p. 66)

39. By using _____ statistics, psychologists can determine whether they can generalize findings from a sample to the full population. (p. 66)

2.9 Show how statistics can be misused for purposes of persuasion

Reporting measures of central tendency that are nonrepresentative of most participants, creating visual representations that exaggerate effects, and failing to take base rates into account are all frequent methods of manipulating statistics for the purposes of persuasion.

40. In a _____ _____ _____, the y axis starts somewhere close to the highest possible score, instead of at the lowest score, where it should start. (p. 69)

succeed with mypsychlab

1. 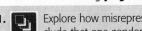 Explore how misrepresenting statistics could lead us to conclude that one gender is more intelligent than the other. **Doing Simple Statistics**

2. What does it mean to be "normal"? Familiarize yourself with the bell curve and see where you fall under it. **The Normal Curve**

BECOMING A PEER REVIEWER OF PSYCHOLOGICAL RESEARCH (pp. 70–73)

2.10 Identify flaws in research designs

Good research design requires not only random assignment and manipulation of an independent variable, but also inclusion of an appropriate control condition to rule out placebo effects. Most important, it requires careful attention to the possibility of alternative explanations of observed effects.

41. The crucial task of a _____ _____ is to identify flaws that could undermine a study's findings. (p. 70)

42. By definition, an experiment is flawed if it doesn't include a manipulation of an _____ _____. (p. 70)

43. In Study 1, the researcher puts all the subjects in a single group and is therefore lacking a necessary _____ group. (p. 70)

44. In Study 2, the researcher has not controlled for the _____ effect because the participants are aware of whether they are receiving treatment or not. (p. 71)

45. In Study 2, the researcher knows which participants are in which groups so he has created an opportunity for the _____ _____ effect. (p. 71)

46. In Study 3, the researcher's design had a potential _____ that prevents us from concluding that listening to rock music was the reason for the group differences. (p. 71)

2.11 Identify skills for evaluating psychological claims in the popular media

To evaluate psychological claims in the news and elsewhere in the popular media, we should bear in mind that few psychology reporters have formal psychological training. When considering media claims, we should consider the source, beware of excessive sharpening and leveling, and be on the lookout for pseudosymmetry.

47. News stories about psychology (are/are not) typically written by people who have formal training in psychology. (p. 71)

48. When evaluating the legitimacy of psychological reports in the media, one should consider the _____. (p. 72)

49. Newspapers, magazines, and websites tend to engage in a certain amount of _____ and _____ to make a good story. (p. 72)

50. When a news story mistakenly suggests that experts are equally divided over a topic, it creates _____. (p. 72)

succeed with mypsych lab

1. Should we be allowed to conduct this study? You decide.
Ethics in Psychological Research

SCIENTIFIC THINKING SKILLS
Questions and Summary

1 There is a widely held myth that sugar causes hyperactivity in children. Yet although many believe they have observed a causal relation between children's consumption of sugary food and high activity level, objective research suggests any carbohydrate would give the same level of energy. But no one has heard of a "rice high" or "potato buzz." What cognitive biases contribute to this misconception?

2 The *Journal of American Pediatrics* reports a link between TV watching and obesity. Does this link imply a causal relation? What alternative explanations can you think of?

RULING OUT RIVAL HYPOTHESES
pp. 43, 49

CORRELATION vs. CAUSATION
p. 52

FALSIFIABILITY
p. 49

REPLICABILITY
p. 60

EXTRAORDINARY CLAIMS
pp. 42, 57

Biological Psychology

Do specific regions on the brain's surface correspond to different personality traits? (pp. 97–98)

Do we use only about 10 percent of our brain's capacity? (p. 100)

EXTRAORDINARY CLAIMS
Is the evidence as convincing as the claim?

Jenny Storch was 14 years old, but she was no ordinary 14-year-old. She was mute. Like all people with infantile autism, a severe psychological disorder that begins in early childhood (see Chapter 13), Jenny's language and ability to bond with others were severely impaired. Like three-fourths of individuals with infantile autism (American Psychiatric Association, 2000), Jenny had mental retardation. And, like all parents of children with infantile autism, Mark and Laura Storch were desperate to find some means of connecting emotionally with their child.

In the fall of 1991, Mark and Laura Storch had enrolled Jenny in the Devereux School, in upstate New York, which was interested in trying out a new therapy with Jenny. Only the year before, Douglas Biklen, a professor of education, had published an article announcing the development of a technique called *facilitated communication*. Developed in Australia, facilitated communication was a stunning breakthrough in the treatment of infantile autism—or so it seemed.

Indeed, facilitated communication possessed a charming simplicity that somehow rang true. Here's how it works. A "facilitator" sits next to the child with autism, who in turn sits in front of a computer keyboard or letter pad. According to Biklen, the facilitator is required to be present because infantile autism is actually a motor (movement) disorder, not a mental disorder as scientists had long assumed. Boldly challenging conventional wisdom, Biklen (1990) proclaimed that children with autism are just as intelligent as other children. But they suffer from a severe motor disorder that prevents them from talking or typing on their own. By guiding the child's hands ever so gently across the letters, the facilitator permits the child to communicate by typing out words. Not just isolated words, like *Mommy,* but complete sentences like, *Mommy, I want you to know that I love you even though I can't speak.* Facilitated communication was the long-sought-after bridge between the hopelessly isolated world of the child with autism and the adult world of social interaction.

The psychiatric aides at Devereux had heard about facilitated communication, which was being used by thousands of mental health and education professionals across America with apparently astonishing effects. Almost immediately after trying facilitated communication with Jenny, the Devereux aides similarly reported amazing results. For the first time, Jenny produced eloquent statements describing her innermost thoughts and feelings, including her deep love for her parents. The emotional bond with Jenny that Mark and Laura Storch had dreamt of for 14 years was at last a reality.

Yet the Storchs' joy proved to be short lived. In November 1991, Mark Storch received a startling piece of news that was to forever change his life. With the aid of a facilitator, Jenny had begun to type out allegations of brutal sexual abuse against him. When all was said and done, Jenny had typed out 200 gruesome accusations of rape, all supposedly perpetrated by her father. A second facilitator, who'd heard about these accusations, reported similar findings while assisting Jenny at the keyboard.

Although there was no physical evidence against Mark Storch, the Department of Social Services removed Jenny from the Storch home. Jenny was eventually returned to her parents following a legal challenge, but not before Mark Storch's reputation had been forever stained.

The claims of facilitated communication proponents seemed extraordinary. Was the evidence for these claims equally extraordinary?

Since Douglas Biklen introduced facilitated communication to thousands of eager mental health professionals in the United States, dozens of investigators have examined this procedure under tightly controlled experimental conditions. In a typical study, the facilitator and child with autism are seated in adjoining cubicles. A wall separates them, but an opening between them permits hand-to-hand contact on a keyboard (see **Figure 2.1**). Then, researchers flash two different pictures on adjacent screens, one of which is seen only by the facilitator and the other of which is seen only by the child. For example, the facilitator might view a photograph of a dog, but the child, a photo of a cat. The crucial question is this: Will the word typed out by the child be the picture shown to the facilitator—*dog*—or the picture shown to the child—*cat*?

The results of these studies were as stunning as they were unanimous. In virtually 100 percent of trials, the typed word corresponded to the picture flashed to the facilitator, not the child (Jacobson, Mulick, & Schwartz, 1995; Romanczyk, Arnstein, Soorya, et al., 2003; Smith, 2008). Unbelievable as it seems, facilitated communication originates entirely from the minds of facilitators. *Unbeknownst to facilitators, their hands are effortlessly guiding the fingers of the child with autism toward the keyboard, and the resulting words are coming from their minds, not the child's.* Scientists, who'd known about a similar phenomenon for decades before facilitated communication appeared on the scene, term it the *ideomotor effect,* because facilitators' ideas are unknowingly influencing their movements (Wegner, 2002). The facilitated communication keyboard turns out to be nothing more than a modern version of the Ouija board, a popular device used by spiritualists to communicate with the dead. Regrettably, proponents of facilitated communication neglected to consider rival hypotheses for its apparent effects.

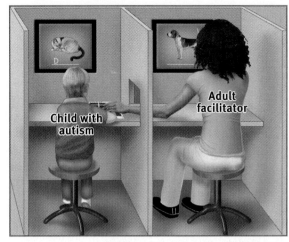

Figure 2.1 How Facilitated Communication Works. By placing the child with autism and the facilitator in neighboring cubicles and flashing different pictures to each of them on some trials, researchers demonstrated that the "facilitated communications" originated in the mind of the facilitator, not the child.

RULING OUT RIVAL HYPOTHESES
Have important alternative explanations for the findings been excluded?

The Beauty and Necessity of Good Research Design

The facilitated communication story imparts an invaluable lesson that we'll highlight throughout this book: *Research design matters.* This story is also a powerful illustration of the triumph of good science over pseudoscience.

WHY WE NEED RESEARCH DESIGNS

Many beginning psychology students understandably wonder why they need to learn about research design. Indeed, some of you may be puzzling over the same thing: I took this course to learn about people. Why do I need to learn how to design research studies?

The facilitated communication story tells us the answer. Without research designs, even intelligent and well-educated people can be fooled. Had the proponents of facilitated communication made use of some of the research designs we'll discuss in this chapter, they wouldn't have been fooled either. As we learned in Chapter 1, the scientific method is a set of tools that helps us to avoid being tricked by our own biases. In this chapter, we'll learn what these tools are and how we can use them to evaluate psychological claims, not only in psychology courses but in everyday life.

The facilitated communication keyboard appears to be little more than a modern version of the Ouija board, which is used widely in spiritual circles to supposedly "contact" the dead. Both rely on the ideomotor effect.

If we're really persistent, we might ask, Do I really need to use research methods to avoid being fooled? Can't I just rely on my experience and common sense? Yet experience and common sense, although enormously helpful in generating hypotheses, are extremely limited for the purposes of testing hypotheses (see Chapter 1). After all, the Devereux aides who worked with Jenny Storch "knew" that facilitated communication worked: They saw Jenny's abuse allegations with their own eyes. But like so many advocates of pseudoscientific techniques, they were the victims of an illusion. Their confirmation bias led them to see what they hoped to see. By relying on the faulty assumption that "seeing is always believing," these aides were fooled.

If the history of psychology teaches us anything, it's that we should be deeply skeptical of the "Trust me; I know it works" claim. We need rigorous research methods to find out whether a technique really works. Firsthand experience can be helpful in this regard as a starting point, but it's never sufficient, because it's not an adequate safeguard against confirmation bias (see Chapter 1) and other sources of human error. **[LEARNING OBJECTIVE 2.1]**

HEURISTICS: HOW WE CAN BE FOOLED

At this point, you may be feeling a bit defensive. At first glance, the authors of your text may seem to be implying that many people, perhaps you included, are foolish. But we shouldn't take any of this personally, because one of this text's central themes is that we're *all* capable of being fooled, and that includes your text's authors. That doesn't make you—or us—foolish. It merely makes us human.

How can we all be fooled so easily? A key finding emerging from the past few decades of research is that *the same psychological processes that serve us well in most situations also predispose us to errors in thinking*. Putting it differently, most mistaken thinking is cut from the same cloth as our most useful thinking (Pinker, 1997).

Heuristics: Double-Edged Swords.

Humans are cognitive misers; we try to economize on our use of brain power to understand situations and solve problems efficiently.

Psychologists have identified several **heuristics**—mental shortcuts or rules of thumb—that help us to streamline our thinking and make sense of our world. These heuristics probably have evolutionary survival value, because without them we'd quickly become overwhelmed by the tens of thousands of pieces of information with which we're bombarded every day. According to cognitive psychologists (psychologists who study thought; see Chapter 7), we're all *cognitive misers* (Fiske & Taylor, 1991). That is, we're mentally lazy and try to conserve our mental energies by simplifying the world. Just as a miser doesn't spend much money, a cognitive miser doesn't expend any more effort in thinking than is necessary.

Although our heuristics work well most of the time (Gigerenzer, 2007; Krueger & Funder, 2004; Shepperd & Koch, 2005), they occasionally get us into trouble. Typically, heuristics cause problems when we use them either too often or in inappropriate situations. In these cases, they can lead us to not merely simplify reality, but to *oversimplify* it. Although most heuristics are probably useful overall, the modern world sometimes presents us with complicated information for which these shortcuts were never intended. The good news is that research designs can help us avoid the pitfalls that can result from misapplying heuristics.

To understand the concept of a heuristic, try to answer the following question. *Imagine that you are in Reno, Nevada. If you wanted to get to San Diego, California, what compass direction would you take? Close your eyes for a moment and picture how you'd get there* (Piatelli-Palmarini, 1994).

Well, of course we'd need to go southwest to get to San Diego from Reno, because California is west of Nevada, right? Wrong! Actually, to get from Reno to San

GLOSSARY

heuristic
mental shortcut that helps us to streamline our thinking and make sense of our world

Diego, we would go *southeast,* not southwest. If you don't believe us, look at **Figure 2.2** on page 46.

If you got this one wrong (and, if you did, don't feel bad, because your authors got it wrong too!), you almost certainly relied on a heuristic. The mental shortcut you probably used was this: *California is west of Nevada, and San Diego is at the bottom of California, whereas Reno has a lot more land south of it before you hit Mexico.* What you either forgot or didn't know is that a large chunk of California (the bottom third or so) is actually *east* of the Nevada-California border. Of course, for most geographical questions (such as, "Is St. Louis east or west of Los Angeles?") these kinds of mental shortcuts work just fine. But in this case the heuristic tripped us up.

The Representativeness Heuristic: Like Goes with Like.
Two Israeli psychologists who later emigrated to the United States, Daniel Kahneman and Amos Tversky, pioneered the study of heuristics. Their research fundamentally changed how psychologists think about thinking. Kahneman and Tversky focused on several heuristics, two of which we'll discuss. They termed the first heuristic *representativeness* (Kahneman, Slovic, & Tversky, 1982; Tversky & Kahneman, 1974). When we use the **representativeness** heuristic, we judge the probability of an event by its superficial similarity to a prototype. According to this heuristic, "Like goes with like." Imagine that on the first day of your introductory psychology class you sit next to Roger Davis, whom you've never met. You have a few minutes before the first class begins, so you try to strike up a conversation with him. Despite your best efforts, Roger says almost nothing. He appears painfully shy, looks away from you when you ask him a question, stammers, and finally manages to blurt out a few awkward words about being a member of the college chess team and treasurer of the local Star Trek fan club.

Based on your brief interaction with him, would you say that Roger is more likely to be a major in communications or a major in computer science? You're more likely to pick the latter than the former, and you'd probably be right. You relied on a representativeness heuristic to answer this question, because Roger matched your stereotype (see Chapter 11) of a computer science major far better than your stereotype of a communications major. According to the representativeness heuristic, we judge the similarity between two things by gauging the extent to which they resemble each other superficially.

Now consider a slightly different example. Imagine that on the second day of class you sit next to Amy Chang. Amy is polite and soft-spoken, but friendly, and describes herself as having grown up in the Chinatown section of San Francisco. In response to a question about her interests, she mentions that she's vice president of the college Chinese Students' Association.

Based on your brief interaction with Amy, would you say that she's more likely to be a psychology major or an Asian American studies major? You'd probably be more likely to pick the latter than the former. Yet in this case, you'd probably be wrong. Why?

Although Amy fits your stereotype of an Asian American studies major better than your stereotype of a psychology major, you probably forgot one crucial fact: There are many more psychology majors in your college than Asian American studies majors. By focusing too heavily on the superficial similarity of Amy to your stereotype of an Asian American studies major—that is, by relying too heavily on the representativeness heuristic—you neglected to consider what psychologists call the extremely low *base rate* of this major. **[LEARNING OBJECTIVE 2.2]**

Base rate is just a fancy term for how common a behavior or characteristic is (Finn & Kamphuis, 1995; Meehl & Rosen, 1955). When evaluating the probability that a person (for example, Amy) belongs to a category (for example, Asian American studies major), we need to consider not only how similar that person is to other members of the category, but also the base rate of this category.

Daniel Kahneman of Princeton University (*left*) was the first Ph.D. psychologist to be awarded a Nobel Prize. The Nobel Committee recognized him for his groundbreaking work on the cognitive sources of human irrationality.

GLOSSARY

representativeness
heuristic that involves judging the probability of an event by its superficial similarity to a prototype

base rate
how common a characteristic or behavior is

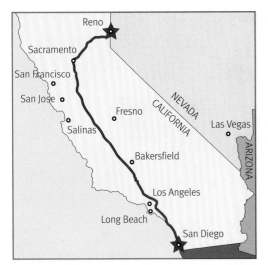

Figure 2.2 In Which Compass Direction Would You Travel to Get from Reno, Nevada, to San Diego, California? If you didn't guess southeast (which is the correct answer), you're not alone. By relying on a heuristic—that is, a mental shortcut—we can sometimes be fooled.

If a couple of your friends were dating and later became happily married, would you say, "I knew from the start they were made for each other!"? If so, you might be engaging in hindsight bias.

The Availability Heuristic: "Off the Top of My Head . . .". Kahneman and Tversky termed the second heuristic *availability.* Using the **availability** heuristic, we estimate the likelihood of an occurrence based on the ease with which it comes to our minds—that is, on how "available" it is in our memories (Kahneman et al., 1982). Like representativeness, availability often works well.

Try answering the following question: Are there more words in the English language with the letter *k* as the first letter in the word or the third letter in the word? If you're like most people, you responded that there are more English words beginning with the letter *k* than with *k* in the third position. In fact, there are more than twice as many words with *k* in the third position as there are words beginning with the letter *k*. Why do most of us get this question wrong? We rely on the availability heuristic: Because of how our brains categorize words, we find it easier to think of words with *k* in the first position (like *kite* and *kill*) than words with *k* in the third position (like *bike* and *cake*).

We should keep the representativeness and availability heuristics in mind, because we'll soon learn that many research methods help us to avoid the mistakes that arise from applying these heuristics uncritically. As Kahneman and Tversky noted, however, it's not only heuristics that can lead us astray. We can also fall prey to a variety of **cognitive biases**—systematic errors in thinking.

COGNITIVE BIASES

As we'll recall from Chapter 1, *confirmation bias* is our natural tendency to seek out evidence that supports our hypotheses and to ignore, downplay, or distort evidence that doesn't. One crucial function of the scientific method, as we've seen, is to help us compensate for confirmation bias. By forcing us to adopt safeguards against confirming our pet hypotheses, the scientific method makes us less likely to fool ourselves.

Yet confirmation bias is only one bias that can lead us to draw misleading conclusions. Two others are hindsight bias and overconfidence.

WHAT DO *you* THINK?

You are a consultant for the International Skating Union (which governs all professional figure skating competitions). You have been hired to design a judging system with less potential for the panel of judges (who are all from different countries) to show bias for skaters from their own countries. What changes would you suggest?

Hindsight Bias. **Hindsight bias,** sometimes known also as the "I knew it all along effect," refers to our tendency to overestimate how well we could have successfully forecasted known outcomes (Fischoff, 1975; Kunda, 1999). As the old saying goes, "Hindsight is always 20/20." This is one case in which common wisdom appears to be correct. Sports commentators routinely engage in hindsight bias, analyzing sporting events after the fact and suggesting that different strategies than the ones the losing teams used would have been more effective. The term "Monday Morning Quarterbacking" was coined to describe precisely this bias—thinking we could have quarterbacked the Sunday evening football game better after the fact. There may well have been some truth to each of these after-the-fact recommendations, but they all miss a crucial point: Once an event has occurred, it's

GLOSSARY

availability
heuristic that involves estimating the likelihood of an occurrence based on the ease with which it comes to our minds

cognitive bias
systematic error in thinking

hindsight bias
tendency to overestimate how well we could have successfully forecasted known outcomes

awfully easy in retrospect to "predict" it and then suggest ways in which we could have prevented it.

Overconfidence. Related to hindsight bias is **overconfidence:** our tendency to overestimate our ability to make correct predictions. Across a wide variety of tasks, most of us are more confident in our predictive abilities than we should be (Hoffrage, 2004; Smith & Dumont, 2002).

We're overconfident in many domains of our lives. A national survey of nearly a million high school seniors revealed that 100 percent (yes, all of them!) believed they were *above* average in their ability to get along with others. Twenty-five percent believed that that they were in the top 1 percent (College Board, 1976–1977). A survey of college professors revealed that 94 percent believed they were better scholars than their colleagues (Cross, 1977).

The heuristics and biases we've discussed can make us certain we're right even when we're not. As a consequence, we can not only draw false conclusions, but become convinced of them. Not to worry: The scientific method is here to the rescue.

Overconfidence is sometimes referred to as the "Lake Wobegone effect." In the fictional town of Lake Wobegone from the radio series *A Prairie Home Companion*, the show's narrator, Garrison Keillor, says that "all the women are strong, all the men are good looking, and all the children are above average."

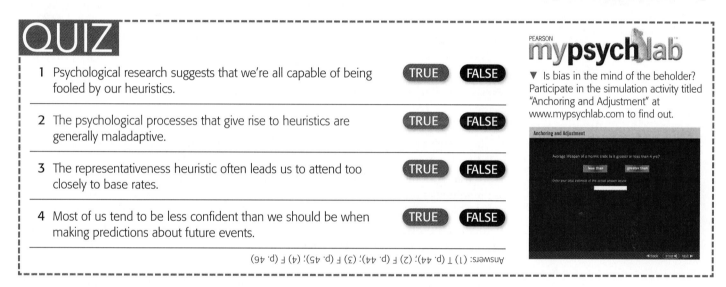

QUIZ

1 Psychological research suggests that we're all capable of being fooled by our heuristics. TRUE   FALSE

2 The psychological processes that give rise to heuristics are generally maladaptive. TRUE   FALSE

3 The representativeness heuristic often leads us to attend too closely to base rates. TRUE   FALSE

4 Most of us tend to be less confident than we should be when making predictions about future events. TRUE   FALSE

PEARSON
mypsychlab

▼ Is bias in the mind of the beholder? Participate in the simulation activity titled "Anchoring and Adjustment" at www.mypsychlab.com to find out.

Anchoring and Adjustment

Answers: (1) T (p. 44); (2) F (p. 44); (3) F (p. 45); (4) F (p. 46)

The Scientific Method:
A Toolbox of Skills

As we discovered in Chapter 1, the scientific method is a toolbox of skills designed to counteract our tendency to fool ourselves. All of the tools we'll describe have one major thing in common: They permit us to test *hypotheses,* which as we learned in Chapter 1 are specific predictions. Psychologists often derive these hypotheses from broader theories. If these hypotheses are confirmed, our confidence in the theory is strengthened, although we should remember that this theory is never truly "proven." If these hypotheses are disconfirmed, scientists often revise this theory or eventually abandon it entirely. Using the toolbox of the scientific method allows us to test hypotheses in a way that minimizes our biases. This toolbox isn't foolproof by any means, but it's the best set of safeguards against bias we have at our disposal. Let's now open up this toolbox and take a peek at what's inside.

GLOSSARY

overconfidence
tendency to overestimate our ability to make correct predictions

NATURALISTIC OBSERVATION: STUDYING HUMANS "IN THE WILD"

Let's say we wanted to conduct a study to find out about laughter. How often do people laugh in the real world, and what kinds of things make them laugh? Do men laugh more often than women? In what settings are people most likely to laugh? We could try to answer these questions by bringing people into our laboratory and observing their laughter across various situations. But it's unlikely we'd be able to re-create the full range of situations that trigger laughter. Moreover, their laughter could still have been influenced by the fact that they knew they were being observed.

Researcher Jane Goodall has spent much of her career using techniques of naturalistic observation with chimpanzees in Gombe, Kenya. As we'll learn in Chapter 11, her work strongly suggests that warfare is not unique to humans.

One way of getting around these problems is **naturalistic observation:** watching behavior in real-world settings. We can perform naturalistic observation using a video camera or tape recorder or, if we're willing to go low-tech, only a paper and pencil. Many psychologists who study animals, such as chimpanzees or gorillas, in their natural habitats use naturalistic observation, although psychologists who study humans sometimes use it, too. By doing so, we can better understand the range of behaviors displayed by individuals in the "real world," as well as the situations in which they exhibit them. **[LEARNING OBJECTIVE 2.3]**

The major advantage of naturalistic designs is that they are often high in **external validity:** the extent to which we can generalize our findings to real-world settings (Neisser & Hyman, 1999). Because psychologists apply these designs to organisms as they go about their everyday business, their findings are often directly applicable to the real world.

Still, naturalistic designs have a major disadvantage. They tend to be low in **internal validity:** the extent to which we can draw cause-and-effect inferences. As we'll soon learn, well-conducted laboratory experiments are high in internal validity, because we can manipulate the key variables ourselves. In contrast, in naturalistic designs we have no control over these variables and need to wait for behavior to unfold before our eyes. Naturalistic observation provides an opportunity to *describe* behavior but little opportunity to *explain* it. **[LEARNING OBJECTIVE 2.4]**

Robert Provine (1996, 2000) relied on naturalistic observation in an investigation of human laughter. Provine and his research assistants eavesdropped on 1,200 instances of laughter in social situations—shopping malls, restaurants, and street corners—and recorded the gender of participants, the remarks that preceded laughter, and others' reactions to laughter. Provine found that women laugh much more than men in social situations. Surprisingly, he discovered that less than 20 percent of laughing incidents are preceded by statements that could remotely be described as funny. Instead, most cases of laughter are preceded by nonhumorous, often quite ordinary, comments (such as, "It was nice meeting you, too"). Provine also found that speakers laugh considerably more than listeners. Provine's work, which would have been difficult to pull off in a laboratory, raised new ideas about the interpersonal triggers and consequences of laughter.

GLOSSARY

naturalistic observation
watching behavior in real-world settings

external validity
extent to which we can generalize findings to real-world settings

internal validity
extent to which we can draw cause-and-effect inferences from a study

case study
research design that examines one person or a small number of people in depth, often over an extended time period

CASE STUDY DESIGNS: GETTING TO KNOW YOU

One of the simplest designs in the psychologist's investigative toolbox is the case study. In a **case study,** researchers examine either one person or a small number of people, often over an extended period of time (Davison & Lazarus, 2007). An investigator could spend 10 or even 20 years studying one man with schizophrenia, carefully documenting his childhood experiences, academic and job performance, family life, friendships, psychological treatment, and the ups and downs of his mental problems. There's no single "recipe" for how to perform a case study. Some researchers might observe a person over time, others might administer questionnaires, and still others might conduct repeated interviews. The richness of detail yielded by case studies often gives researchers a valuable source of fruitful hypotheses. Case studies can be helpful in providing **existence proofs:** demonstrations that a given psychological phenomenon can occur. For example, although scientists have claimed that it is impossible for humans to remember their own births, all it would take is one clear-cut case of birth memory to falsify the claim. Case studies can also offer useful insights that researchers can later test in systematic investigations (Davison & Lazarus, 2007). For example, the observation that someone with a phobia (severe and irrational fear) didn't display anxiety when extremely relaxed led to systematic investigation of a phobia treatment (discussed in more detail in Chapter 14) called *systematic desensitization.* Yet, if we're not careful, case studies can lead to misleading, even disastrously wrong, conclusions, as we saw in the case of facilitated communication.

Because of the limitations of case studies, psychologists are cautious about relying on them too heavily to draw conclusions. As a consequence, they've turned to research designs that are more systematic, that is, that allow more rigorous conclusions. We'll review several research designs that allow us to draw more definite conclusions.

CORRELATIONAL DESIGNS

The first important systematic research method we'll discuss is the correlational design. When using a **correlational design,** psychologists examine the extent to which two variables are associated. Recall from Chapter 1 that a *variable* is anything that can take on different values across individuals, like impulsivity, creativity, brain size, and religiosity. When we think of the word *correlate,* we should decompose it into its two parts: *co-* and *relate.* If two things are correlated, they relate to each other—not interpersonally, but statistically.

Identifying Correlational Designs. Identifying a correlational design can be tricky at first, because investigators who use this design—and news reporters who describe it—don't always use the word *correlated* in their description of findings. Instead, they'll often use terms like *associated, related, linked,* or *went together.* Any time researchers conduct a study of the extent to which two variables tend to "go together," their design is correlational even if they don't describe it that way explicitly.

Correlations: A Beginner's Guide. Before we go any further, let's lay some groundwork by examining two basic facts about correlations:

(1) Correlations can be *positive, zero,* or *negative.* A positive correlation means that as the value of one variable goes up, the other also goes up. If the number of friends children have is positively correlated with how outgoing they are, then more outgoing children have more friends and less outgoing children have fewer friends. A zero correlation means that the variables don't go together. If math ability has a zero correlation with singing ability, then knowing that someone is good at math tells us nothing about whether his singing ability is good, bad, or mediocre. Finally, a negative correlation means that when the value of one variable goes up, the other goes down, and vice versa. If social anxiety is negatively correlated with perceived physical attractiveness, then more socially anxious people would be rated as less attractive, and less socially anxious people as more attractive.

(2) Correlations, at least the ones we'll be discussing in this textbook, range in value from $r = -1.0$ to 1.0. (The lowercase r, by the way, is the letter used to indicate a correlation.) A correlation of -1.0 is a perfect negative correlation, whereas a correlation of $+1.0$ is a perfect positive correlation. We won't talk about how to calculate correlations, because the mathematics of doing so

FALSIFIABILITY
Can the claim be disproved?

RULING OUT RIVAL HYPOTHESES
Have important alternative explanations for the findings been excluded?

Case studies helped to inspire a scientifically supported phobia treatment called *systematic desensitization* that combines deep muscle relaxation with gradual exposure to anxiety-provoking experiences.

GLOSSARY

existence proof
demonstration that a given psychological phenomenon can occur

correlational design
research design that examines the extent to which two variables are associated

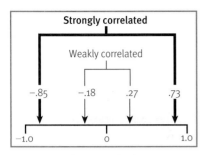

Figure 2.3 The Strength of a Correlation Is Unrelated to the Direction of the Correlation. Values close to positive or negative 1.0 are strong and those close to zero are weak.

GLOSSARY

scatterplot
grouping of points on a two-dimensional graph in which each dot represents a single person's data

gets pretty technical. Values lower than 1.0 (either positive or negative values), such as .23 or −.69, indicate a less-than-perfect correlation. To find out how strong a correlation is, we should look at its *absolute value,* that is, the size of the correlation without the plus or minus sign in front of it (see **Figure 2.3**). Thus, the absolute value of a correlation of +.27 is .27, and the absolute value of a correlation of −.27 is also .27. Interestingly, both correlations are equally large in size—and equally informative—but they're going in opposite directions.

The Scatterplot. **Figure 2.4** shows three panels depicting three types of correlations. Each panel shows a **scatterplot:** a grouping of points on a two-dimensional graph. Each dot on the scatterplot represents a person. As we can see, each person differs from other persons in his or her scores on one or both variables displayed on the scatterplot.

In the panel on the left is a fictional scatterplot of a moderate ($r = -.5$) negative correlation; this correlation shows the association between the average number of beers that students drank the night before their first psychology exam and their scores on their exam. We can tell that this correlation is negative because the clump of dots goes from higher on the left of the graph to lower on the right of the graph. Because this correlation is negative, it means that the more beers students drink, the worse they tend to do on their first psychology exam. Note that this negative correlation isn't perfect (that is, it's not $r = -1.0$). That means that some students drink a lot of beers and still do well on their exam and that some students drink almost no beer and still do poorly on their exam.

In the middle panel is a fictional scatterplot of a zero ($r = 0$) correlation; this correlation displays the association between the students' shoe sizes and scores on their first psychology exam. The easiest way to identify a zero correlation is that the scatterplot looks like a blob of dots that's pointing neither upward nor downward. This zero correlation means

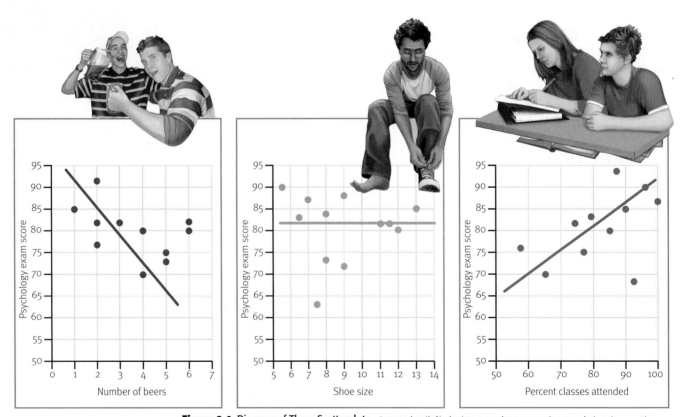

Figure 2.4 Diagram of Three Scatterplots. Scatterplot (*left*) depicts a moderate negative correlation ($r = -.5$); scatterplot (*middle*) depicts a zero correlation; and scatterplot (*right*) depicts a moderate positive correlation ($r = .5$).

there's no association whatsoever between students' shoe sizes and how well they do on their first psychology exam. Knowing one variable tells us absolutely nothing about the other (that's good news for those of us with tiny feet).

The panel on the right shows a fictional scatterplot of a moderate ($r = .5$) positive correlation; this correlation shows the association between students' attendance in their psychology course and their scores on their first psychology exam. Here, the clump of dots goes from lower on the left of the graph to higher on the right of the graph. This positive correlation means that the more psychology classes students attend, the better they tend to do on their first psychology exam. Again, because the correlation isn't perfect (it's not $r = 1.0$), there will always be the inevitable annoying students who don't attend any classes yet do well on their exams, and the incredibly frustrated souls who attend all of their classes and still do poorly.

Remember that unless a correlation is perfect, that is, 1.0 or –1.0, there will always be exceptions to the general trend. Because virtually all correlations in psychology have an absolute value of less than 1, *psychology is a science of exceptions.* To argue against the existence of a correlation, it's tempting to resort to "I know a person who . . ." reasoning (see Chapter 1). We have to keep in mind that exceptions, intriguing as they are, don't refute the existence of the correlation. If a correlation is less than 1.0, such exceptions are to be completely expected—in fact, they're mathematically required.

Illusory Correlation.

Why do we need to calculate correlations? Can't we just "eyeball" the data to estimate how well two variables go together?

No, we can't, because psychological research demonstrates that we're remarkably poor at accurately estimating the sizes of correlations. In fact, we're often prone to an extraordinary phenomenon termed **illusory correlation:** the perception of a statistical association between two variables where none exists (Chapman & Chapman, 1967, 1969). An illusory correlation is a statistical mirage. Here are two striking examples:

(1) Many people are convinced of a strong statistical association between the full moon and a variety of strange occurrences, like violent crimes, suicides, psychiatric hospital admissions, and births—the so-called lunar lunacy effect (the word *lunatic* derives from *Luna,* the Roman goddess of the moon). Some police departments even put more cops on the beat on nights when there's a full moon, and many emergency room nurses insist that more babies are born during full moons (Hines, 2003). Yet a mountain of data shows that the full moon isn't correlated with any of these events: That is, the true correlation is almost exactly $r = 0$ (Rotton & Kelly, 1985).

(2) Many individuals with arthritis are convinced that their joint pain increases during rainy weather, yet several carefully conducted studies show no association between joint pain and rainy weather (Quick, 1999).

Why are people so susceptible to illusory correlation? The primary reason is the confirmation bias (see Chapter 1). We all tend to pay too much attention to examples that confirm our expectations and ignore examples that challenge them. In the case of the lunar lunacy effect, instances in which there was both a full moon and a crime are especially interesting and memorable ("See, just like I've always said, weird things happen during full moons").

Unfortunately, our minds aren't good at detecting and remembering *nonevents,* that is, things that don't happen. It's unlikely we're going to rush home excitedly to tell our friend, "Wow, you're not going to believe this. There was a full moon tonight, and guess what happened? Nothing!" Our uneven attention to events over nonevents leads us to perceive illusory correlations.

Just because we know one person who was a lifelong smoker and lived to a ripe old age doesn't mean there's no correlation between smoking and serious illnesses, like lung cancer and heart disease. Exceptions don't invalidate the existence of correlations.

Fict-OID

MYTH: People who adopt a child after years of unsuccessfully trying to have one of their own are more likely to conceive successfully shortly following the adoption.

REALITY: Studies show that this correlation is entirely illusory (Gilovich, 1991). We remember such cases more readily because they are ironic.

GLOSSARY

illusory correlation
perception of a statistical association between two variables where none exists

How can we avoid or at least minimize our tendencies toward illusory correlation? Probably the best way is to force ourselves to keep track of disconfirming instances. For example, when James Alcock and his students asked a group of participants who claimed they could predict the future from their dreams—so-called prophetic dreamers—to keep careful track of their dreams by using a diary, their beliefs that they were prophetic dreamers vanished (Hines, 2003). By forcing participants to record all of their dreams, Alcock forced them to notice cases that disconfirmed prophetic dreams.

The phenomenon of illusory correlation explains why we can't rely on our subjective impressions to tell us whether two variables are associated. Our intuitions often mislead us, especially when we've learned to expect two things to go together (Myers, 2002). Indeed, adults may be more prone to illusory correlation than children because they've built up expectations about whether certain events—like full moons and odd behavior—go together (Kuhn, 2007).

Correlation versus Causation: Jumping the Gun.

Correlational designs can be extremely useful for determining whether two (or more) variables are related. Nevertheless, there are important limitations to the conclusions we can draw from them. As we learned in Chapter 1, the most common mistake we make when interpreting correlational designs is to jump the gun and draw *causal* conclusions from them. Correlation doesn't necessarily mean causation. Although a correlation *sometimes* results from a causal relationship, we can't determine from a correlational study alone whether the relationship is causal.

Incidentally, we shouldn't confuse the error of equating correlation with causation (see Chapter 1) with illusory correlation. Illusory correlation refers to perceiving a correlation where none exists. In the case of the correlation versus causation fallacy, a correlation exists, but we mistakenly interpret it as implying a causal association.

CORRELATION vs. CAUSATION
Can we be sure that A causes B?

Let's look at an example of how a correlation between variables *A* and *B* can actually be due to a third variable, *C*, rather than to a direct causal association between variables *A* and *B*.

There's a substantial positive correlation between the amount of ice cream people eat on a given day and the number of violent crimes committed on that day. It's unlikely that eating ice cream (*A*) causes violent crime (*B*) or that violent crime (*B*) causes people to eat ice cream (*A*). Instead, it's far more likely that a third variable, *C*, accounts for this correlation. What could it be? The most likely candidate for *C* is temperature. When the temperature is warm, more people consume ice cream; also, when the temperature is warm, more people commit violent crimes (Anderson, Bushman, & Groom, 1997).

There's a positive correlation between the amount of ice cream consumed and the number of violent crimes committed on the same day. But does eating ice cream cause crime?

Observational and case studies allow us to describe the state of the psychological world but rarely allow us to make general predictions about the future. In contrast, correlational designs often allow us to make predictions. For example, if SAT scores are correlated with college grades, then knowing people's SAT scores allows us to predict—although by no means perfectly—what their grades will be. Nevertheless, our conclusions from correlational research are always limited because we can't be sure *why* these predicted relationships exist. We should always be on the alert for cases where cause is being concluded from a correlational study. As the examples in **Figure 2.5** demonstrate, the news media are especially prone to making this type of mistake.

The bottom line: Be on the lookout for headlines or news stories that proclaim a causal association between two variables. If the study is based on correlational data alone, we know they're taking their conclusions too far.

WHAT DO *you* THINK?

You are leading a support group for parents of teens. One parent reports that she read somewhere that parents who supervise their children more closely have children who are less likely to be sexually active or abuse drugs. How would you help the parents evaluate whether this finding means they should alter their parenting styles?

EXPERIMENTAL DESIGNS

If correlational designs don't allow us to draw cause-and-effect conclusions, what kinds of designs do? The answer: experimental designs, often known simply as "experiments." These designs differ from correlational designs in one crucial way: *They permit cause-and-effect inferences.* To see why, it's important to understand that in correlational designs researchers are measuring preexisting differences in participants, like age, gender, IQ, and extraversion. In contrast, in experimental designs researchers are *manipulating* variables to see whether these manipulations produce differences in participants' behavior. Putting it another way, in correlational designs the differences among participants are *measured*, whereas in experimental designs they're *created*.

What Makes a Study an Experiment: Two Components. Although news reporters frequently use the term *experiment* rather loosely to refer to any kind of research study, this term actually carries a specific meaning in psychology. To be precise, to be an **experiment,** a study requires *two* particular ingredients:

(1) Random assignment of participants to conditions.

(2) Manipulation of an independent variable.

Both of these ingredients are necessary for the recipe; if a study doesn't contain both of them, it's *not* an experiment. Let's look at each in turn.

Random Assignment. By **random assignment,** we mean that the experimenter randomly sorts participants into two groups. One of these groups is called the **experimental group:** This group receives the manipulation. The other is called the **control group:** This group doesn't receive the manipulation. As we learned in Chapter 1, scientific thinking doesn't come naturally to the human species. When viewed through this lens, it's perhaps not surprising that the concept of the control group didn't clearly emerge in psychology until the turn of the twentieth century (Coover & Angell, 1907; Dehue, 2000).

To take an example of random assignment, let's imagine that we wanted to determine whether a new drug, Miraculin, is effective for treating depression. We'd first start with a large sample of individuals with depression. We'd then randomly assign (say, by flipping a coin) half of the participants to an experimental group, which receives Miraculin, and the other half to a control group, which receives baby aspirin instead. By randomly assigning participants to experimental and control groups, we're helping to cancel out any preexisting differences between these groups.

Manipulation of an Independent Variable. The second ingredient of an experiment is manipulation of an independent variable. An **independent variable** is the treatment or intervention that the experimenter "manipulates" or varies. The **dependent variable** is the variable that the experimenter measures to see whether this manipulation has had an effect. In the experiment using Miraculin as a treatment for depression, the independent variable is the presence versus absence of Miraculin. The dependent variable is the level

Low Self-Esteem "Shrinks Brain"

A Surprising Secret to a Long Life: Stay in School

Housework Cuts Breast Cancer Risk

Fear of hell makes us richer, Fed says

Wearing a helmet puts cyclists at risk, suggests research

Winning World Cup lowers heart attack deaths

Eating fish prevents crime

Figure 2.5 Examples of Newspaper Headlines That Confuse Correlation with Causation. Here are some actual newspaper headlines that suggest a causal association between two variables. Can you think of alternative explanations for the findings reported in each headline?

GLOSSARY

experiment
research design characterized by random assignment of participants to conditions and manipulation of an independent variable

random assignment
randomly sorting participants into two groups

experimental group
in an experiment, the group of participants that receives the manipulation

control group
in an experiment, the group of participants that doesn't receive the manipulation

independent variable
treatment or intervention that the experimenter "manipulates" or varies

dependent variable
variable that an experimenter measures to see whether the manipulation has an effect

of participants' depression following the experimental manipulation. When we define our independent and dependent variables for the purposes of a study, we are performing **operationalization.** Operationalizing a variable is specifying how we are measuring our variables of interest. This is important because different researchers may operationalize the same variables in different ways and end up with different conclusions as a result. For example, imagine that two researchers used two different doses of Miraculin and also measured depression using two different scales. They might end up drawing different conclusions about Miraculin's effectiveness because their measures told different stories.

Evaluating Measures.
When evaluating the results from any dependent variable or measure, we need to ask two critical questions: Is the measure reliable? Is it valid?

Reliability. **Reliability** refers to consistency of measurement. For example, a reliable questionnaire yields similar scores within a group of people over time; this type of reliability is called *test-retest reliability*. To assess test-retest reliability, we could administer a personality questionnaire to a large group of people today and readminister it in 2 months. If the measure is reasonably reliable, the correlation between these scores should be at least $r = .80$, which is a high level of association. Reliability also applies to interviews and observational data. *Interrater reliability* is the extent to which different people who conduct an interview, or make behavioral observations, agree on the characteristics, like depression, that they're measuring.

Validity. **Validity** is the extent to which a measure assesses what it claims to measure. We can think of validity as "truth in advertising." We discussed two different types of validity on page 48. If we went to the grocery store, purchased a can labeled "Aunt Barbara's Baked Beans," and opened it to discover artichoke hearts, we'd demand our money back (unless we really like artichokes)—the label would not be valid. Similarly, if a questionnaire we're administering claims to be a valid measure of introversion, but studies show it's really measuring anxiety, then this measure isn't valid.

Reliability and Validity: The Differences. Reliability and validity are different concepts, although people routinely confuse them. In courts of law, we'll frequently hear debates about whether the polygraph (or so-called lie-detector) test is scientifically "reliable." But as we'll learn in Chapter 9, the central question concerning the polygraph isn't its reliability, because it typically yields fairly consistent scores over time. Instead, the central question is its validity, because many critics maintain that the polygraph isn't a detector of lies at all. Instead, they maintain that the polygraph detects emotional arousal, which can be produced not only by lies but by anxiety, anger, surprise, and other emotions (Lykken, 1998).

Reliability is necessary for validity. In other words, we need to measure something consistently before we can measure it well. Imagine trying to measure the floors and walls of our apartment or house using a ruler made of Silly Putty, that is, a ruler whose length changes every time we pick it up. Our efforts at accurate measurement would be doomed. The same goes for personality questionnaires, because we can't expect a measure that yields very different scores each time we administer it to measure anything well.

Nevertheless, reliability isn't sufficient for validity. Although a test must be reliable to be valid, a reliable test can still be completely invalid. Imagine we've developed a new measure of intelligence, the "Distance Index-Middle Width Intelligence Test" (DIMWIT), which computes the average width of our middle finger and the average width of our index finger and then subtracts the lesser of these from the greater one. The DIMWIT would be a highly reliable measure of intelligence because the widths of our middle and index fingers are unlikely to change much over time. But the DIMWIT would be a completely invalid measure of intelligence because finger width has nothing to do with intelligence.

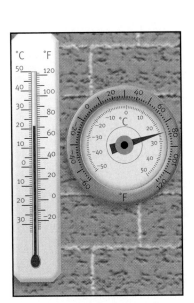

These two thermometers are providing different readings for temperature in almost the identical location. Psychologists might say that these thermometers display less-than-perfect interrater reliability.

GLOSSARY

operationalization
specification of how a variable is being measured for the purposes of a particular study

reliability
consistency of measurement

validity
extent to which a measure assesses what it claims to measure

confounding variable or **confound**
any difference between the experimental and control groups other than the independent variable

placebo effect
improvement resulting from the mere expectation of improvement

Can we trace complex psychological functions, like religious belief, to specific brain regions? (p. 101)

Are there left- and right-brained people? (pp. 102–103)

Is heritability a fixed value, or can it change over time? (p. 106)

CORRELATION vs. CAUSATION

Can we be sure that A causes B?

GLOSSARY

neuron
nerve cell specialized for communication

In the early twenty-first century, we take for granted the fact that the brain is the seat of psychological activity. When we struggle mightily with a difficult homework problem, we say that "our brains hurt," when we consult friends for advice about a complicated question, we "pick their brains," and when we insult others' intelligence, we call them "bird brains." Yet throughout much of human history, it seemed obvious that the brain *wasn't* the prime location for our thoughts, memories, and emotions.

For example, the ancient Egyptians believed that the heart was the seat of the human soul and the brain was irrelevant to mental life (Finger, 2000; Raulin, 2003). Egyptians often prepared corpses for mummification by scooping their brains out through the nostrils using an iron hook (you'll be pleased to know that no drawings of this practice survive today) (Leek, 1969). Although some ancient Greeks correctly pinpointed the brain as the source of the psyche, others, like the great philosopher Aristotle, were convinced that the brain functions merely as a radiator, cooling the heart when it becomes overheated. Even today, we can find holdovers of this way of thinking in our everyday language. When we memorize something, we come to know it "by heart" (Finger, 2000). When we're devastated by the loss of a romantic relationship, we feel "heartbroken."

Why were so many of the ancients certain that the heart, not the brain, was the source of mental activity? It's almost surely because they trusted their "common sense," which as we've learned is often a poor signpost of scientific truth. They noticed that when people become excited, angry, or scared, their hearts pound quickly, whereas their brains seem to do little or nothing. Therefore, they reasoned, the heart must be causing these emotional reactions. By confusing correlation with causation, the ancients' intuitions misled them.

Today, we recognize that the mushy organ lying between our two ears is the most complicated structure in the known universe. Our brain has the consistency of gelatin, and it weighs a mere 3 pounds. Despite its rather unimpressive appearance, it is almost incomprehensibly complex and capable of astonishing feats. Scientists have made numerous technological breakthroughs in recent years that have told us a lot about how the brain works. We call researchers who study the brain and behavior *biological psychologists* or *neuroscientists*. As we discuss what these scientists have discovered about the brain, we'll compare our current state-of-the-art knowledge with the many misconceptions that have arisen along the way. Even experts sometimes subscribe to certain myths about brain, behavior, and mind.

Nerve Cells: Communication Portals

To understand how the brain works, we first need to understand the pieces of which it is made. To determine the strength of a chain, we need to know the strength of the individual links in that chain. Similarly, to understand how the brain functions, we need to understand the function of individual brain cells.

NEURONS: THE BRAIN'S COMMUNICATORS

The workings of the brain depend on cross-talk among **neurons**—that is, nerve cells specialized for communication with each other (see **Figure 3.1**). Our brains contain about 100 billion neurons. To give you a sense of how

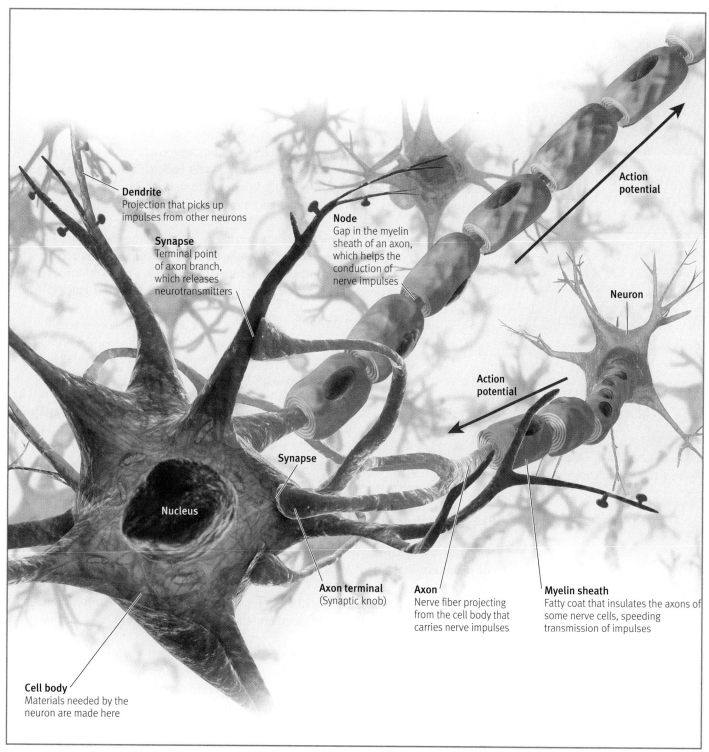

Dendrite
Projection that picks up
impulses from other neurons

Synapse
Terminal point
of axon branch,
which releases
neurotransmitters

Node
Gap in the myelin
sheath of an axon,
which helps the
conduction of
nerve impulses

Action
potential

Neuron

Action
potential

Synapse

Nucleus

Axon terminal
(Synaptic knob)

Axon
Nerve fiber projecting
from the cell body that
carries nerve impulses

Myelin sheath
Fatty coat that insulates the axons of
some nerve cells, speeding
transmission of impulses

Cell body
Materials needed by the
neuron are made here

Figure 3.1 A Neuron with a Myelin Sheath. Neurons receive chemical messages from other neurons by way of
synaptic contacts with dendrites. Next, neurons send action potentials down along their axons, some of which are coated
with myelin to make the electrical signal travel faster. (*Source:* Modified from Dorling Kindersley)

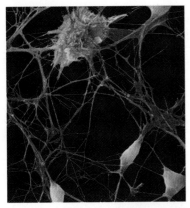

Neurons and their dendrites (shown stained pink) with their nuclei (shown stained blue).

large this number is, there are more than 15 times as many neurons in our brains as there are people on Earth. More graphically, 100 billion neurons lined up side to side would reach back and forth from New York to California five times. In addition, many neurons make tens of thousands of connections with other neurons. In total, there are about 160 trillion—that's a whopping 160,000,000,000,000—connections in the human brain (Tang, Nyengaard, De Groot, et al., 2001).

Although many cells have simple and regular shapes, neurons are different. They have long extensions, which help them respond to stimulation and communicate with each other. Cells have several key parts that work together to make the brain function. **[LEARNING OBJECTIVE 3.1]**

The Cell Body.

The *cell body* is the central region of the neuron that manufactures new cell components, consisting of small and large molecules (refer back to Figure 3.1). A neuron won't survive severe damage to the cell body because it contains the nucleus where proteins are manufactured and it provides continuous renewal of cell components.

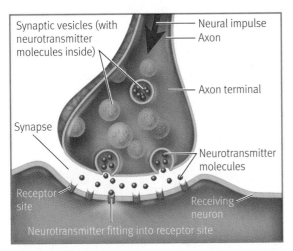

Figure 3.2 The Axon Terminal. The axon terminal contains synaptic vesicles filled with neurotransmitter molecules.

Dendrites.

Neurons differ from other cells in that they have branchlike extensions for receiving information from other neurons. These receiving parts are called **dendrites.** Dendrites spread out to pick up information from neighboring neurons and pass it on to the nucleus (refer to Figure 3.1).

Axons and Axon Terminals.

Axons are long tail-like extensions protruding from the cell body of a neuron specialized for sending messages to other neurons. Unlike dendrites, axons are usually very thin near the cell body. This narrowness creates a *trigger zone,* an area that's easy to activate. The *axon terminal* is a knoblike structure at the far end of the axon (see **Figure 3.2**). Axon terminals contain **synaptic vesicles,** spheres that contain **neurotransmitters,** the chemical messengers that neurons use to communicate with each other. Synaptic vesicles are constructed in the cell body and travel down along the length of the axon. We might think of the synaptic vesicles as similar to gel capsules filled with cold medicine. When we swallow each capsule, it's carried down our digestive tracts. This is similar to how synaptic vesicles travel down the axon to the axon terminal. In our stomachs, the gel capsules dissolve and release the medicine. Similarly, the synaptic vesicle releases neurotransmitters when it reaches the end of the axon terminal.

Synapses.

A **synapse** is the space between neurons through which neurotransmitters travel. As neurotransmitters are released into the synapse, they are picked up by the dendrites of nearby neurons.

Sir Charles Sherrington was one of the first to hypothesize the existence of synapses. He measured the time it took for muscles to become active following nerve stimulation. From this data, he deduced the existence of microscopic physical spaces between neurons and between neurons and muscle cells (Pearce, 2004). At the time, no microscopes were powerful enough to observe these spaces. Consequently, some scientists believed that all neurons melded together into one giant net. But Sherrington (1906), among others, argued strongly for neurons being separate, individual cells that nonetheless communicated with each other and with muscle cells. What Sherrington hypothesized could have been falsified had he been wrong. A Spanish scientist named Santiago Ramón y Cajal showed that Sherrington was right using a staining technique to demonstrate the existence of individual neurons. Later studies using a powerful *electron microscope* confirmed that tiny gaps responsible for transmitting messages between neurons, which we now call synapses, indeed exist.

GLOSSARY

dendrite
portion of neuron that receives signals

axon
portion of neuron that sends signals

synaptic vesicle
spherical sac containing neurotransmitters

neurotransmitter
chemical messenger specialized for communication from neuron to neuron

FALSIFIABILITY
Can the claim be disproved?

GLIAL CELLS: SUPPORTING ROLES

Glial cells are the supporting actors in the nervous system; among other things, they protect neurons. Glial cells are about ten times more numerous than neurons but are also considerably smaller; different types play various supporting roles. Certain glial cells respond to injury by releasing chemicals that promote healing. Glial cells are also found in a fatty coating called the **blood–brain barrier** that wraps around tiny blood vessels. As a result, large molecules, highly charged particles, and molecules that dissolve in water but not in fat are blocked from entering the brain. The blood–brain barrier is the brain's way of protecting itself from bacterial infection.

Still other glial cells wrap around axons, which speeds up the passage of electrical messages inside the neuron by insulating the axons. This wrapper is called the **myelin sheath.** This sheath has numerous gaps all the way along the neuron called *nodes,* which help the neuron conduct electricity more efficiently (refer again to Figure 3.1). In the autoimmune disease *multiple sclerosis,* the myelin sheaths surrounding neurons are "eaten away," resulting in a progressive loss of insulation of neural messages. As a consequence, these messages become hopelessly scrambled, eventually resulting in a wide variety of physical and emotional symptoms. Glial cells also clear away debris, acting as the brain's cellular garbage disposals.

CHEMICAL COMMUNICATION: NEUROTRANSMISSION

Neurotransmitters enable communication among neurons. After these molecules are released into the synapse, they connect to specific **receptor sites** along the dendrites of neighboring neurons. Different receptor sites recognize different types of neurotransmitters. **[LEARNING OBJECTIVE 3.2]** Psychologists often use a lock-and-key analogy to describe this specificity (see **Figure 3.3**). We can think of each neurotransmitter as a key that fits only its own type of receptor, or lock.

Neurotransmission can also be halted by **reuptake** of the neurotransmitter back into the axon terminal—a process by which the synaptic vesicle re-absorbs the neurotransmitter. We might think of release and reuptake as similar to letting some liquid drip out of the bottom of a straw and then sucking it back up again. It's one of nature's recycling mechanisms.

Neurotransmitters. Different neurotransmitters are like messengers with slightly different things to say. Some act to arouse or stimulate the nervous system, others act to inhibit or reduce activity. Some play a role in movement, and others in pain perception. We introduce some of the most prominent neurotransmitters here (see **Table 3.1** on page 84).

Glutamate and GABA. *Glutamate* and gamma-aminobutyric acid (*GABA*) are the most common neurotransmitters in the brain. Neurons in virtually every brain area use these neurotransmitters to communicate with other neurons (Fagg & Foster, 1983). Glutamate excites the neurons it acts on, increasing the likelihood that it will communicate with other neurons. GABA, in contrast, inhibits neurons, dampening neural activity. That's why most antianxiety drugs activate GABA receptor sites.

Acetylcholine. Acetylcholine plays a role in arousal, selective attention, and memory (McKinney & Jacksonville, 2005; Woolf, 1991). Neurons that connect directly to muscle cells also release acetylcholine, which plays a key role in movement.

Monoamine Neurotransmitters. *Norepinephrine, dopamine,* and *serotonin* are the monoamine neurotransmitters. Dopamine plays a role in movement and the reward experience that occurs when we accomplish our movement goals or experience pleasure. Norepinephrine and serotonin activate or deactivate different parts of the brain to control arousal or readiness to respond (Jones, 2003).

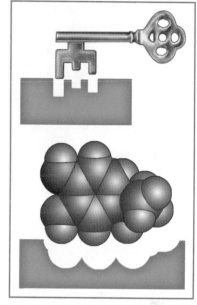

Figure 3.3 The Lock-and-Key Model of Neurotransmitter Binding to Receptor Sites. Receptor sites are specialized to receive only certain types of neurotransmitters.

GLOSSARY

synapse
space between two connecting neurons through which messages are transmitted chemically

glial cell
support cell in nervous system that plays a role in the formation of myelin and blood–brain barrier, responds to injury, and removes debris

blood–brain barrier
glial cells forming a fatty coating that prevents certain substances from entering the brain

myelin sheath
glial cells wrapped around axons that act as insulators of the neuron's signal

receptor site
location that uniquely recognizes a neurotransmitter

reuptake
means of recycling neurotransmitters

Neuropeptides. Neuropeptides are short strings of amino acids in the nervous system. They act somewhat like neurotransmitters, the difference being that their roles are typically specialized. **Endorphins** are a type of neuropeptide that play a specialized role in pain reduction (Holden, Jeong, & Forrest, 2005). Our brains contain a host of other neuropeptides; some of them regulate hunger and satiety (fullness).

Athletes, like this bicyclist, often rely on their endorphins to push them through intense pain.

Neurotransmitters and Psychoactive Drugs.

Particular drugs have been developed that target production or inhibition of particular neurotransmitters (refer again to Table 3.1). Drugs that interact with neurotransmitter systems are called *psychoactive*, meaning they affect mood, arousal, or behavior in some way (see Chapter 10). At high doses virtually any psychoactive drug can be toxic. A few are toxic at very low doses. For example, botulinum toxin, also known as the cosmetic agent *Botox*, causes paralysis by blocking acetylcholine's actions on muscles. This paralysis temporarily decreases small wrinkles, such as those on the forehead and around the eyes, by relaxing those muscles. Whereas it takes 1–2 teaspoons of the poison arsenic to kill a person, a microscopic amount of Botox is lethal (Kamrin, 1988).

Knowing how psychoactive drugs interact with neurotransmitter systems enables us to predict how they affect our mental state, mood, or behavior. Opiate drugs, such as codeine and morphine, function as *agonists,* meaning they enhance receptor site activity. Specifically, they reduce pain and the emotional response to painful stimuli by binding with opioid receptors and mimicking endorphins (Evans, 2004). Tranquilizers, like Xanax, which relax people with high levels of anxiety, stimulate GABA receptor sites, thereby reducing neuronal activity (Roy-Byrne, 2005). Still other drugs block reuptake of neurotransmitters into the axon terminal. Many antidepressants, like Prozac, prevent the reuptake of serotonin, norepineph-

Table 3.1 Neurotransmitters and Their Major Functional Roles.

Neurotransmitter	Selected Roles	Drugs That Interact with the Neurotransmitter System
Glutamate	Main excitatory neurotransmitter in the nervous system; participates in relay of sensory information and learning	*Alcohol* and *memory enhancers* interact with *N*-methyl-ᴅ-aspartate (NMDA) receptors, a specific type of glutamate receptor.
Gamma-aminobutyric acid (GABA)	Main inhibitory neurotransmitter in the nervous system	*Alcohol* and *antianxiety drugs* increase GABA activity.
Acetylcholine (ACh)	Muscle contraction (PNS) Cortical arousal (CNS)	*Nicotine* stimulates ACh receptors. *Memory enhancers* increase ACh. *Insecticides* block the breakdown of ACh. *Botox* causes paralysis by blocking ACh.
Norepinephrine (NE)	Brain arousal and other functions like mood, hunger, and sleep	*Amphetamine* and *methamphetamine* increase NE.
Dopamine	Motor function and reward	*ʟ-Dopa,* which increases dopamine, is used to treat *Parkinson* disease. *Antipsychotic drugs,* which block dopamine action, are used to treat schizophrenia.
Serotonin	Mood and temperature regulation, aggression, and sleep cycles	*Serotonin-selective reuptake inhibitor (SSRI) antidepressants* are used to treat depression.
Endorphins	Pain reduction	*Narcotic drugs*—codeine, morphine, and heroin—reduce pain and produce euphoria.
Anandamide	Pain reduction, increase in appetite	*Tetrahydrocannabinol (THC)*—found in marijuana—produces euphoria.

(*Source:* Adapted from Carlson et al., 2007)

GLOSSARY

endorphin
chemical in the brain that plays a specialized role in pain reduction

resting potential
electrical charge difference (–60 millivolts) across the neuronal membrane, when the neuron is not being stimulated or inhibited

threshold
membrane potential necessary to trigger an action potential

action potential
electrical impulse that travels down the axon triggering the release of neurotransmitters

absolute refractory period
time during which another action potential is impossible; limits maximal firing rate

rine, or dopamine from the synapse (Schatzberg, 1998). Allowing these neurotransmitters to remain in the synapse longer than usual enhances their effects on the receptor sites.

Some drugs work in the opposite way, functioning as receptor *antagonists*, meaning they decrease receptor site activity. Drugs used to treat schizophrenia—a complex mental disorder we'll describe more fully in Chapter 13—typically block dopamine receptors by binding to them and then blocking dopamine from binding to the receptors themselves (Bennett, 1998).

ELECTRIFYING THOUGHT

Neurons respond to neurotransmitters by generating electrical activity (see **Figure 3.4**). We know this because scientists have recorded electrical activity from neurons using tiny *electrodes,* small devices made from wire or fine glass tubes. These electrodes allowed them to measure what's called the *potential difference* in electrical charge inside versus outside the neuron. The basis of all electrical responses in neurons depends on an uneven distribution of charged particles across the membrane that surrounds the neuron (see Figure 3.4). Some particles are positively charged, others negatively charged. When there are no neurotransmitters acting on the neuron, the membrane is at the **resting potential.** In this resting state, there are more negative particles inside than outside the neuron. In some large neurons, the voltage of the resting potential can be about one-twentieth that of a flashlight battery, or about –60 millivolts (inside charge is more negative than outside). While at rest, particles of both types are flowing in and out of the membrane. If the charge inside the neuron reaches a high enough level relative to the outside, called the **threshold,** an action potential occurs. **[LEARNING OBJECTIVE 3.3]**

Action Potentials. **Action potentials** are abrupt waves of electric discharge caused by a change in charge inside the axon. When this occurs, we can describe the neuron as "firing," similar to the firing of a gun. Action potentials begin in the trigger zone near the cell body and then continue all the way down the axon to the axon terminal. During an action potential, positively charged particles flow rapidly into the axon and then rapidly flow out again, causing a spike in positive charge followed by a sudden decrease in charge, with the inside charge ending up at a slightly more negative level than at its original resting value (see **Figures** 3.4 and **3.5**). These sudden shifts in charge cause a release of electrical charge. When the electrical charge reaches the axon terminal, it triggers the release of neurotransmitters into the synapse.

Neurons can fire extremely rapidly, at rates of 100 to 1,000 times per second. Energy travels down the axon at speeds of about 220 miles per hour. After each action potential there's an **absolute refractory period,** a brief time during which another action potential can't occur. The absolute refractory period limits the *maximal firing rate,* the fastest rate at which a neuron can fire. The rate at which action potentials travel becomes an issue in very long axons, such as the sciatic nerve, which runs from the spinal cord down the leg. Believe it or not, in humans this axon extends an average of 3 feet.

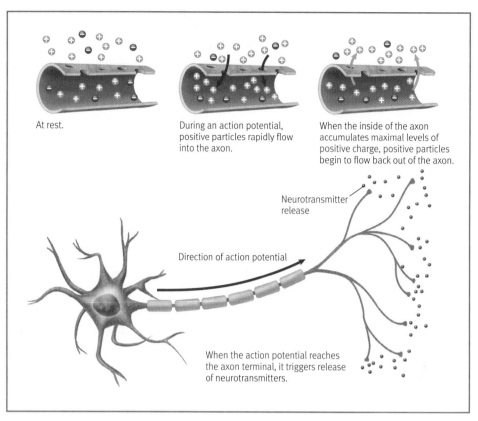

At rest.

During an action potential, positive particles rapidly flow into the axon.

When the inside of the axon accumulates maximal levels of positive charge, positive particles begin to flow back out of the axon.

Neurotransmitter release

Direction of action potential

When the action potential reaches the axon terminal, it triggers release of neurotransmitters.

Figure 3.4 The Action Potential. When a neuron is at rest there are positive and negative ions on both sides of the membrane. During an action potential, positive ions rush in and then out of the axon. This process re-occurs along the axon until the axon terminal releases neurotransmitters. (*Source:* Adapted from Sternberg, 2004a)

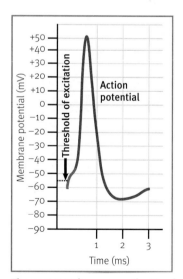

Figure 3.5 Voltage across the Membrane during the Action Potential. The membrane potential needed to trigger an action potential is called the *threshold*. Many neurons have a threshold of –55 mV. That means only 5 mV of current above resting (at –60 mV) is needed to trigger an action potential. (*Source:* Adapted from Sternberg, 2004a)

NEURAL PLASTICITY: HOW AND WHEN THE BRAIN CHANGES

We'll conclude our examination of neurons by looking at the ability of the nervous system to change. Scientists use the term **plasticity** to describe the nervous system's ability to change. We talk about brain circuits being "hardwired" when they don't change very much, if at all. The nervous system is constantly changing, by leaps and bounds, as a result of both maturation and experience.

Neural Plasticity over Development.
The nervous system is most capable of changing during early development. But our brains don't mature fully until late adolescence or early adulthood. This means the period of heightened plasticity in the human brain is lengthy, with some parts maturing faster than others. **[LEARNING OBJECTIVE 3.4]**

The network of neurons in the brain changes over the course of development in four primary ways:

(1) *growth* of dendrites and axons;

(2) *synaptogenesis,* or the formation of new synapses;

(3) *pruning,* consisting of the death of certain neurons and the retraction of axons to remove connections that aren't useful; and

(4) *myelination,* or the insulation of axons with a myelin sheath.

Of these four steps, pruning is probably the most surprising one. During pruning, as many as 70 percent of neurons die off. This process is helpful, though, because it streamlines neural organization, enhancing communication among brain structures (Oppenheim, 1991).

WHAT DO *you* THINK *?*

You are guest-lecturing on brain development in a high school biology class, and you are concerned that the concept of pruning might be confusing. How might you use an analogy to gardening and landscaping to get the point across?

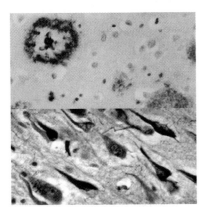

Senile plaques (*top*) and neurofibrillary tangles (*bottom*) in a brain of a patient with Alzheimer's disease. This degeneration in hippocampus and association cortex may contribute to the memory loss and intellectual decline associated with the disorder (see Chapter 6).

Neural Plasticity Following Injury and Degeneration.
In adults, plasticity in the brain decreases markedly, occurring only on a small scale, such as with learning. The human brain and spinal cord exhibit only a limited degree of regeneration following injury. Not surprisingly, scientists are focused on finding ways to get around the barriers that prevent brain and spinal cord axons from growing back following injury (Maier & Schwab, 2006). Some patients and experimental animals recover sensory and motor function following certain treatments, but the degree of recovery varies greatly (Bradbury & McMahon, 2006; Jones, Oudega, Bunge, et al., 2001). Because degenerative disorders, such as Alzheimer's disease and Parkinson disease, pose enormous challenges to society, scientists are actively investigating ways of preventing damage or enabling the brain to heal itself. Deposits, known as *senile plaques* and *neurofibrillary tangles,* accumulate in the brains of Alzheimer's disease patients. Many scientists agree that by better understanding neural plasticity we may someday be able to partly reverse neural degeneration or at least prevent it from occurring.

There's another way that researchers may be able to get around the problems associated with lack of regeneration following injury and with neural degeneration. **Neurogenesis** is the creation of new neurons in the adult brain. Less than 20 years ago, scientists believed that we're born with all the neurons we'll ever have. Then Fred Gage, Elizabeth Gould, and their colleagues discovered that neurogenesis occurs in some brain areas (Gage, 2002; Gould & Gross, 2002).

GLOSSARY

plasticity
ability of the nervous system to change

neurogenesis
creation of new neurons in the adult brain

Neurogenesis is exciting because it opens up new possibilities. Why does neurogenesis occur in adults? One possibility is that it plays a role in learning (Aimone, Wiles, & Gage, 2006). Another role may be aiding recovery following brain injury. By activating neurogenesis, scientists may be able to induce the adult nervous system to heal itself (Kozorovitskiy & Gould, 2003; Lie, Song, Colamarino, et al., 2004).

Today we know more about neurons than ever before. We're on firm ground when it comes to understanding the electrical and chemical processes by which neurons communicate. We've yet to fully understand how to heal the nervous system, but the rapid pace of research in this critical area gives us considerable hope.

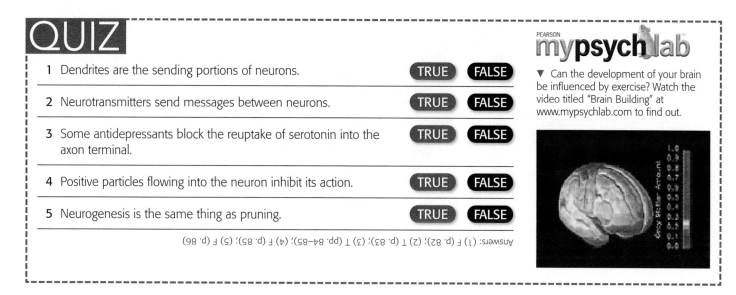

QUIZ

1 Dendrites are the sending portions of neurons. **TRUE** **FALSE**

2 Neurotransmitters send messages between neurons. **TRUE** **FALSE**

3 Some antidepressants block the reuptake of serotonin into the axon terminal. **TRUE** **FALSE**

4 Positive particles flowing into the neuron inhibit its action. **TRUE** **FALSE**

5 Neurogenesis is the same thing as pruning. **TRUE** **FALSE**

Answers: (1) F (p. 82); (2) T (p. 83); (3) T (pp. 84–85); (4) F (p. 85); (5) F (p. 86)

PEARSON mypsychlab

▼ Can the development of your brain be influenced by exercise? Watch the video titled "Brain Building" at www.mypsychlab.com to find out.

The Brain–Behavior Network

The connections among neurons determine all our thoughts and behaviors. So when we behave in a specific manner or ponder a certain thought, we can thank our neurons. But how do we get from electric charges and release of neurotransmitters to such complex behaviors as writing a term paper or singing a song? Let's say we decide to walk to a vending machine to buy a can of soda. How does our brain, this collection of neurons, accomplish this? First, our brain makes a conscious decision to do so—or so it would seem. Second, our nervous system, composed of the brain, spinal cord, and nerves, propels our body into action. Then we need to locate and operate the vending machine. We must be able to accurately identify the vending machine on the basis of how it looks and feels, put in the right amount of money, and finally retrieve our soda and take a well-deserved sip. Communication among neurons in the vast network of connections we call our brains is what allows us to take for granted such complex actions.

We can think of this set of connecting neurons within the nervous system as a superhighway with a two-way flow of traffic. Sensory information comes into—and decisions to act go away from—the **central nervous system (CNS),** composed of the brain and spinal cord. Scientists call all the nerves that extend outside of the CNS the **peripheral nervous system (PNS)** (see **Figure 3.6** on page 88). The peripheral nervous system is further divided into the somatic nervous system, which controls voluntary

GLOSSARY

central nervous system (CNS)
part of nervous system containing brain and spinal cord that controls the mind and behavior

peripheral nervous system (PNS)
nerves in the body that extend outside the central nervous system (CNS)

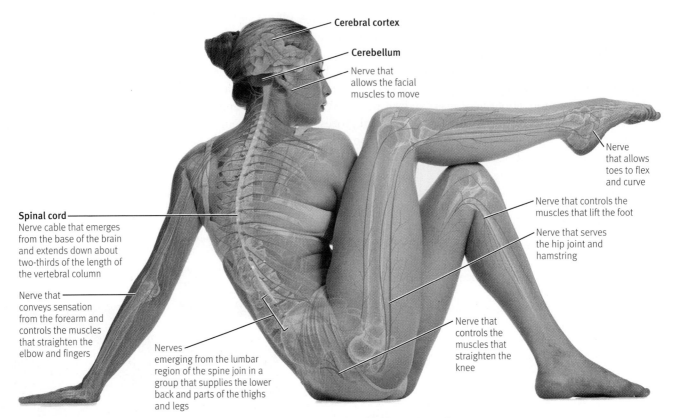

Cerebral cortex

Cerebellum

Nerve that allows the facial muscles to move

Nerve that allows toes to flex and curve

Nerve that controls the muscles that lift the foot

Nerve that serves the hip joint and hamstring

Nerve that controls the muscles that straighten the knee

Spinal cord
Nerve cable that emerges from the base of the brain and extends down about two-thirds of the length of the vertebral column

Nerve that conveys sensation from the forearm and controls the muscles that straighten the elbow and fingers

Nerves emerging from the lumbar region of the spine join in a group that supplies the lower back and parts of the thighs and legs

Figure 3.6 The Nervous System Exerts Control over the Body. (*Source:* Modified from Dorling Kindersley)

behavior, and the autonomic nervous system, which controls nonvoluntary or automatic functions of the body (see Chapter 9). **[LEARNING OBJECTIVE 3.5]**

CNS: THE COMMAND CENTER

So what do contemporary psychologists know about the brain, and what insights does that knowledge provide? To start with, scientists divide the CNS into distinct sections or systems (see **Table 3.2**). We'll begin our guided tour of the brain with the part of the brain studied most extensively by psychologists.

The Cerebral Cortex. The *cerebrum* or **forebrain,** is the most highly developed area in the human brain. Our forebrains give us our advanced intellectual abilities—which explains why it is of such interest to psychologists.

The largest component of the cerebrum is the **cerebral cortex,** which contains some 12 to 20 billion neurons. The cortex is the outermost part of the forebrain and is aptly named, because *cortex* means "bark." The cerebral cortex is responsible for analyzing sensory information and performing complex brain functions, including our ability to think, talk, and reason.

The cerebral cortex is divided into two **cerebral hemispheres** (see **Figure 3.7**). The two cerebral hemispheres look alike but serve different functions. However, the two hemispheres work closely together to coordinate functions. A band of fibers connecting the two cerebral hemispheres is called the **corpus callosum** (see Figure 3.7). The cortex contains four regions called *lobes,* each associated with somewhat different functions (see **Figure 3.8** on page 90). Each of the brain's hemispheres has the same four lobes.

GLOSSARY

forebrain (cerebrum)
forward part of the brain that allows advanced intellectual abilities

cerebral cortex
outermost part of forebrain, responsible for analyzing sensory processing and higher brain functions

cerebral hemispheres
two halves of the cerebral cortex, each of which serve distinct yet highly integrated functions

corpus callosum
large band of fibers connecting the two cerebral hemispheres

Table 3.2 The Organization of the Central Nervous System.

Central Nervous System		
Cortex	**Frontal Lobe:** executive function coordinating other brain areas, motor planning, language, and memory	
	Parietal Lobe: processes touch information, integrates vision and touch	
	Temporal Lobe: processes auditory information, language, and autobiographical memory	
	Occipital Lobe: processes visual information	
Basal Ganglia	control movement and motor planning	
Limbic system	**Thalamus:** conveys sensory information to cortex	
	Hypothalamus: oversees endocrine and autonomic nervous system	
	Amygdala: regulates arousal and fear	
	Hippocampus: processes memory for spatial locations	
Cerebellum	controls balance and coordinated movement	
Brain Stem	**Midbrain:** tracks visual stimuli and reflexes triggered by sound	
	Pons: conveys information between the cortex and cerebellum	
	Medulla: regulates breathing and heartbeats	
Spinal Cord	conveys information between the brain and the body	

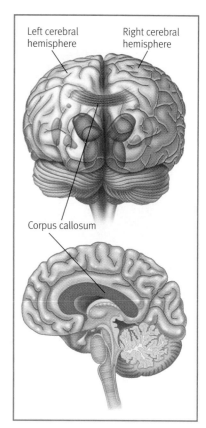

Figure 3.7 The Cerebral Hemispheres and the Corpus Callosum. The corpus callosum connects the two cerebral hemispheres.

Frontal Lobes. The **frontal lobes** lie in the forward part of the cerebral cortex. If you touch your forehead right now, your fingers are less than an inch away from your frontal lobes. The frontal lobes are responsible for motor function (movement), language, and memory, as well as overseeing and organizing most other mental functions, a process called *executive function.* Just as the U.S. president exerts control over the members of his Cabinet, the brain's executive function provides a kind of top-level governance over simpler cognitive functions.

In most people's brains a deep groove, called the *central sulcus,* separates the frontal lobe from the rest of the cortex. The **motor cortex** is the part of the frontal lobe that lies next to the central sulcus. We know a great deal about motor cortex function because of the research of neurosurgeon Wilder Penfield. Penfield (1958) applied mild electrical shocks to the motor cortex of patients who were awake during surgery for epilepsy. He elicited movements ranging from small muscle twitches to large and complex bodily movements. Penfield found that each part of the motor cortex controlled a specific part of the body (see **Figure 3.9** on page 90).

In front of the motor cortex in each brain hemisphere lies a large expanse of the frontal lobe called the **prefrontal cortex,** the part of the frontal lobe responsible for thinking, planning, and language (see **Figure 3.10** on page 91). One region of the prefrontal cortex, **Broca's area,** was named after French surgeon Paul Broca after he discovered that this brain site plays a key role in language production (Broca, 1861). Broca discovered that this site was damaged in many patients who were having trouble producing speech. It didn't take long for Broca and others to notice that brain damage in these patients was almost always located in the left cerebral hemisphere. Many researchers have since replicated this finding.

The prefrontal cortex serves additional functions, including memory, abstract thinking, and decision making. Part of the reason the prefrontal area assumes an executive role is that

GLOSSARY

frontal lobe
forward part of cerebral cortex responsible for motor function, language, memory, and planning

motor cortex
part of frontal lobe responsible for body movement

prefrontal cortex
part of frontal lobe responsible for thinking, planning, and language

Broca's area
language area in the prefrontal cortex that helps to control speech production

REPLICABILITY
Can the results be duplicated in other studies?

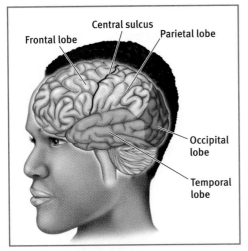

Figure 3.8 The Four Lobes of the Cerebral Cortex. The cerebral cortex consists of four interacting lobes: frontal, parietal, temporal, and occipital.

it receives information from many other regions of the cerebral cortex (Fuster, 2000). The prefrontal cortex also contributes to mood, personality, and self-awareness (Chayer & Freedman, 2001). The tragic story of Phineas Gage demonstrates how the prefrontal cortex can be crucial to personality.

Phineas Gage was a railroad foreman who experienced a horrific accident in 1848. His job at the time was to build railroad tracks running through rural Vermont. Gage was doing his usual job of filling holes with gunpowder to break up stubborn rock formations. He was pressing gunpowder into one hole with a tamping iron when suddenly an explosion propelled the iron with great thrust through his head. The iron pierced Gage's face under his cheekbone and destroyed much of his prefrontal cortex. Remarkably, Gage survived the accident, but he was never the same. His physician, J.M. Harlow (1848), describes Gage's personality after the accident as

fitful, irreverent, indulging at times in the grossest profanity (which was not previously his custom) . . . his mind was radically changed, so decidedly that his friends and acquaintances said he was "no longer Gage."

Admittedly, we don't know exactly what Gage was like before the accident, and some scholars have contended that his personality didn't change as much as is often claimed (Macmillan, 2000). We do know more about the exact location of Gage's brain damage, however. Hanna Damasio and colleagues (1994) examined the skull of Phineas Gage with modern brain imaging techniques and confirmed that both the right and left sides of his prefrontal cortex were seriously damaged.

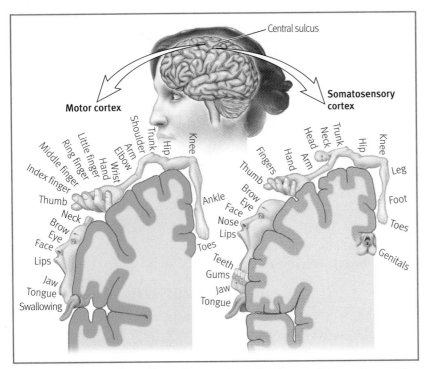

Figure 3.9 Representation of the Body Mapped onto the Motor and Sensory Areas of the Cerebral Cortex. The brain networks with the body in a systematic way, with specific regions of both the motor and somatosensory cortex mapping onto specific regions of the body. (*Source:* Adapted from Marieb & Hoehn, 2007)

Parietal Lobe. The **parietal lobe** is the upper middle part of the cerebral cortex lying behind the frontal lobe (refer to Figure 3.8). The part of the parietal lobe that lies just behind the central sulcus next to the motor cortex is the somatosensory cortex, devoted to touch (Figure 3.9). It's sensitive to pressure, temperature, and pain. The parietal lobe plays a role in tracking objects' locations (Nachev & Husain, 2006; Shomstein & Yantis, 2006), shapes, and orientations. It also helps us process others' actions and represent numbers (Gobel & Rushworth, 2004). The parietal lobe communicates visual and touch information to the motor cortex every time we reach, grasp, and move our eyes (Culham & Valyear, 2006). For example, imagine that you ask your roommate to put a blank CD in your jacket pocket because you're going to copy an assignment for him. You grab your jacket, go to school, and forget about it until you're in the library sitting at the computer terminal and then you reach into your pocket. What do you expect to feel? A CD or disk case, or maybe a soft sleeve? You're probably not sure how, or even if, your roommate packaged the blank CD, but you can envision how the possibilities look. So you can translate what your fingers feel into how it will look when you pull it out of your pocket. That's a parietal lobe function.

GLOSSARY

parietal lobe
upper middle part of the cerebral cortex lying behind the frontal lobe that is specialized for touch and perception

temporal lobe
lower part of cerebral cortex that plays roles in hearing, understanding language, and memory

Wernicke's area
part of the temporal lobe involved in understanding speech

Temporal Lobe. The **temporal lobe** is the site of hearing, understanding language, and storing autobiographical memories (look again at Figure 3.8). This lobe is separated from the rest of the cortex by a horizontal groove called the *lateral fissure*.

The top of the temporal lobe contains the *auditory cortex,* the part of the cortex devoted to hearing (see Chapter 4). The language area in the temporal lobe is called **Wernicke's area,** although this area also includes the lower parietal lobe (look again at Figure 3.10). Damage to Wernicke's area results in difficulties with understanding speech.

The lower part of the temporal lobe is critical to storing memories of autobiographical events (see Chapter 6). Penfield (1958) discovered that stimulating this region with electrical probes elicited memories, like vivid recollections of "a certain song" or "the view from a childhood window." Amazing as these descriptions seem, psychologists today aren't certain if stimulating the brain elicits genuine memories of past events or rather altered perceptions, making them closer to hallucinations (Schacter, 1996).

Occipital Lobe. At the very back of the brain lies the **occipital lobe,** containing the *visual cortex,* dedicated to vision. We human beings are highly dependent on our visual systems, so it stands to reason that we have a lot of visual cortex. Not all animals rely as much on vision as we do, but we're not the only highly visual creatures. For each species, the amount of sensory cortex of each type is proportional to the degree to which it relies on that sense. Ghost bats depend highly on auditory cues and have proportionally more auditory cortex; the platypus relies heavily on touch cues and has proportionally more touch cortex; and squirrels, like humans, rely strongly on visual inputs and have proportionally more visual cortex (Krubitzer & Kaas, 2005).

Cortical Hierarchies. When information from the outside world is transmitted by a particular sense (sight, hearing, touch), it reaches the **primary sensory cortex** specific to that particular sense (look at Figure 3.10 again). After sense information has been transmitted from the eye, ear, or skin to the primary sensory cortex, it is passed on to another area for that sense called the **association cortex.** The association cortex integrates information to perform more complex functions, such as pulling together size, shape, color, and location information to identify an object. These areas play key roles in perception, memory, attention, and conscious awareness. The overall organization of the cortex is "hierarchical" because processing becomes increasingly complex as information is passed along within the network.

The Basal Ganglia. The **basal ganglia** are two sets of structures buried deep inside the cortex that help to control movement. Damage to the basal ganglia plays a key role in Parkinson disease, resulting in a lack of control over movement. After sensory information reaches primary and association areas, it is transmitted to the basal ganglia, which in turn calculate a course of action and transmit that plan to the motor cortex.

The basal ganglia are also responsible for making sure our movements help us obtain rewards, that is, pleasurable activities (Graybiel et al., 1994). When we anticipate rewards, such as a tasty sandwich or hot date, we depend on activity in our basal ganglia.

RULING OUT RIVAL HYPOTHESES
Have important alternative explanations for the findings been excluded?

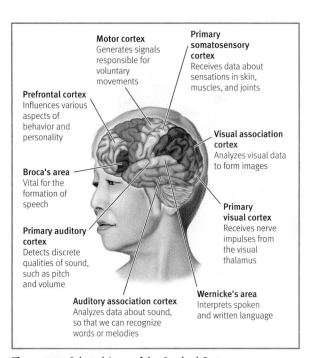

Motor cortex
Generates signals responsible for voluntary movements

Primary somatosensory cortex
Receives data about sensations in skin, muscles, and joints

Prefrontal cortex
Influences various aspects of behavior and personality

Visual association cortex
Analyzes visual data to form images

Broca's area
Vital for the formation of speech

Primary visual cortex
Receives nerve impulses from the visual thalamus

Primary auditory cortex
Detects discrete qualities of sound, such as pitch and volume

Auditory association cortex
Analyzes data about sound, so that we can recognize words or melodies

Wernicke's area
Interprets spoken and written language

Figure 3.10 Selected Areas of the Cerebral Cortex. The prefrontal cortex controls various aspects of behavior and personality. Broca's area is vital for the formation of speech, and Wernicke's area interprets spoken and written language. Other cortical areas include the motor cortex, primary sensory areas, and association areas.

GLOSSARY

occipital lobe
back part of cerebral cortex specialized for vision

primary sensory cortex
regions of the cerebral cortex that initially process information from the senses

association cortex
regions of the cerebral cortex that integrate simpler functions to perform more complex functions

basal ganglia
structures in the forebrain that help to control movement

THE LIMBIC SYSTEM

The parts of the brain dedicated to emotion are housed within the **limbic system.** This specialized set of brain regions is highly interconnected. In contrast to the cortex, which processes information about external stimuli, the limbic system processes information about our internal states, such as blood pressure, heart rate, respiration rate, and perspiration, as well as emotional state.

We can think of the limbic system as the *emotional center* of the brain (see **Figure 3.11**). Limbic system structures also play roles in smell, motivation, and memory. The limbic system evolved out of the primitive olfactory system (dedicated to smell), that controlled various survival behaviors in early mammals. As anyone who's walked a dog knows, smell remains vitally important to many animals.

We'll next explore four areas of the limbic system called the thalamus, the hypothalamus, the amygdala, and the hippocampus. Each area has specific roles, although different areas cooperate in many shared functions.

The term **thalamus** derives from the Greek word for bedroom or chamber. But the thalamus is actually more than one room. It contains many areas, each of which connects to a specific region of the cerebral cortex. We might think of the thalamus as the gateway to the sensory areas. The vast majority of sensory information passes through its doors (refer again to Figure 3.11).

The **hypothalamus** regulates and maintains constant internal bodily states. It's located on the floor of the brain. Separate areas of the hypothalamus play different roles in emotion and motivation. Some parts of the hypothalamus play a role in regulating hunger, thirst, temperature, sexual motivation, and other emotional behaviors (see Chapter 9).

The **amygdala** is named for its almond shape (*amygdala* is Greek for "almond"). Excitement, arousal, and fear are all part of the amygdala's job description. For example, the amygdala kicks into high gear when teenagers play violent video games (Mathews, Gump, Harris, et al., 2006). The amygdala also plays a role in fear conditioning, a process by which animals (including human animals) learn to predict when something scary is about to happen (LeDoux, 2000).

Ralph Adolphs and his colleagues showed this by studying a 30-year-old woman whose left and right amygdala were both almost entirely destroyed by disease. Although

Snakes evoke fear in many animals, including squirrels, by activating the amygdala.

GLOSSARY

limbic system
emotional center of brain that also plays roles in smell, motivation, and memory

thalamus
gateway from the sense organs to the primary sensory cortex

hypothalamus
part of the brain responsible for maintaining a constant internal state

amygdala
part of limbic system that plays key roles in fear, excitement, and arousal

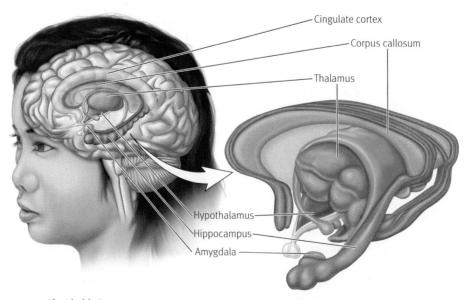

Figure 3.11 The Limbic System. The limbic system consists mainly of the thalamus, hypothalamus, amygdala, and hippocampus. (Left brain modified from Dorling Kindersley and right art from Kalat, 2007)

she had no difficulty identifying faces, she was markedly impaired in detecting fear in these faces (Adolphs et al., 1994).

The **hippocampus** performs several memory functions, particularly maintaining spatial memory. When we make a mental map of how to get from one place to another, we're using our hippocampus. This may explain why a portion of the hippocampus is larger in London taxi drivers than in non–taxi drivers and is especially large in more experienced taxi drivers (Maguire et al., 2000). This correlation could mean either that people with greater amounts of experience navigating complex environments develop larger hippocampi or that people with larger hippocampi seek out occupations, like taxi driving, that depend on spatial navigation.

CORRELATION vs. CAUSATION
Can we be sure that A causes B?

Damage to the hippocampus causes problems with forming new memories but leaves old memories intact. One hypothesis is that the hippocampus temporarily stores memories and then transfers them to other sites, such as the cortex, for permanent storage (Sanchez-Andres, Olds, & Alkon, 1993). The *multiple trace theory* is a rival hypothesis of memory storage in the hippocampus (Moscovitch et al., 2005). According to this theory, memories are initially stored at multiple sites. Over time, storage strengthens at some sites but weakens at others. The multiple trace theory avoids the need to "transfer" memory from the hippocampus to the cortex. The memory is already stored in the cortex and merely strengthens over time.

RULING OUT RIVAL HYPOTHESES
Have important alternative explanations for the findings been excluded?

THE BRAIN STEM

The **brain stem,** located inside the cortex, contains the *midbrain,* the *cerebellum,* the *pons,* and the *medulla* (see **Figure 3.12**). The brain stem performs some of the basic bodily functions that keep us alive and also serves as a relay station between the cortex and the rest of the nervous system.

The **midbrain** plays an important role in movement. It also controls the tracking of visual stimuli and reflexes triggered by sound. Below the midbrain lie the **cerebellum, pons,** and **medulla.** *Cerebellum* is the Latin word for "little brain," and in many respects the cerebellum is a miniature version of the cortex. The cerebellum plays a prodominant role in our sense of balance and enables us to coordinate movement and learn motor skills. Among other things, it helps us prevent ourselves from falling down. Additionally, the cerebellum contributes to executive, spatial, and linguistic abilities (Schmahmann, 2004). The pons connects the cortex with the cerebellum.

The medulla regulates breathing, heartbeat, and other vital functions. Damage to the medulla can cause *brain death,* which is defined as irreversible coma. People who are brain dead are totally unaware of their surroundings and unresponsive, even to ordinarily very painful stimuli. They show no signs of spontaneous movement, respiration, or reflex activity.

People often confuse a *persistent vegetative state,* or cortical death, with brain death, but the two aren't the same. Terri Schiavo made history as the woman who had lain unconscious in a hospital bed for 15 years. Schiavo collapsed in her Florida home in 1990 following temporary cardiac arrest. Her heart stopped long enough to deprive her brain of vital oxygen, such that when her heart was restarted, the brain damage she suffered left her in a persistent vegetative state. The deep structures in her brain stem that control breathing, heart rate, digestion, and certain reflexive responses were still operating, so Schiavo wasn't brain dead, as much of the news media incorrectly reported. Nevertheless, her higher cerebral structures, necessary for awareness of herself and her environment, were damaged permanently. Her doctors knew that much of her cortex had withered away, and an autopsy later showed that she'd lost about half of her brain.

Those who believe that death of the higher brain centers essential for consciousness and behavior is equivalent to actual death felt that Terri had, in fact, died 15 years earlier.

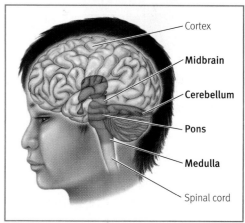

Figure 3.12 The Brain Stem. The brain stem is located at the top of the spinal cord, below the cortex.

GLOSSARY

hippocampus
part of the brain that plays a role in spatial memory

brain stem
part of the brain between the spinal cord and cerebral cortex that contains the medulla, midbrain, pons, and cerebellum

midbrain
part of the brain stem that contributes to movement, tracking of visual stimuli, and reflexes triggered by sound

cerebellum
brain structure responsible for our sense of balance

pons
part of the brain stem that connects the cortex with the cerebellum

medulla
part of brain stem involved in basic functions, such as heartbeat and breathing

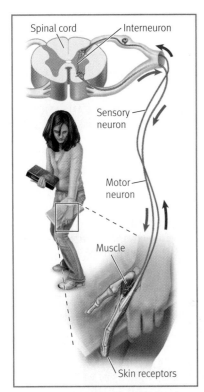

Figure 3.13 The Spinal Reflex. We detect even small amounts of muscle stretch and compensate by contraction. In this way we can maintain balance or keep from losing our grip.

GLOSSARY

spinal cord
thick bundle of nerves that conveys signals between the brain and the body

interneuron
neuron that sends messages to other neurons nearby

reflex
an automatic motor response to a sensory stimulus

cerebral ventricles
pockets in the brain that contain cerebrospinal fluid (CSF), which provide the brain with nutrients and cushion against injury

somatic nervous system
part of the nervous system that conveys information between the CNS and the body, controlling and coordinating voluntary movement

autonomic nervous system
part of the nervous system controlling the involuntary actions of our internal organs and glands, which (along with the limbic system) participates in emotion regulation

Nevertheless, Schiavo's death raises difficult and troubling questions that science can't fully resolve: Should brain death be the true criterion for death, or should this criterion instead be the permanent loss of consciousness?

The Spinal Cord. The **spinal cord** runs down the middle of the back, conveying information back and forth between the brain and the body. *Nerves* extend from neurons to the body, traveling in two directions. Sensory information is carried from the body to the brain by way of *sensory nerves* and motor commands move from the brain to the body by way of *motor nerves*. The spinal cord also contains sensory neurons that contact **interneurons,** neurons that send messages to other neurons located nearby. Interneurons connect sensory nerves with motor nerves within the spinal cord without having to report back to the brain. Interneurons explain how **reflexes,** automatic motor responses to sensory stimuli, can occur.

Consider an automatic behavior called the stretch reflex, which relies only on the spinal cord. We're carrying our books in our arms, but over time our grasp releases ever so slightly without our even noticing. Our sensory nerves detect the muscle stretch and relay this information to the spinal cord. Interneurons intervene and the motor neurons automatically send messages causing our arm muscles to contract. Without our ever knowing it, a simple reflex causes our arm muscles to tighten, preventing us from dropping our books (see **Figure 3.13**).

The Cerebral Ventricles. The **cerebral ventricles** are pockets within the CNS that extend throughout the entire brain and spinal cord. A clear liquid, called *cerebrospinal fluid* (CSF), runs through the cerebral ventricles and bathes the brain and spinal cord, providing nutrients and cushioning against injury.

THE SOMATIC NERVOUS SYSTEM

Now that we've completed our tour of the CNS, let's see how the CNS is hooked up to the body through the somatic nervous system. The **somatic nervous system** carries messages from the CNS to muscles throughout the body, controlling movement (look back to Figure 3.6). Whenever we stabilize or move our many joints, the CNS works with the somatic nervous system to regulate posture and bodily movement.

Let's review what happens when we decide to walk over to the vending machine to purchase a can of soda. Sensory inputs of all types reach the cortex. Then all parts of the cortex send information to the basal ganglia. The basal ganglia contribute to our decision about what to do and send that information to the motor cortex. Next the motor cortex sends commands to the spinal cord, activating certain motor neurons. These motor neurons send messages through nerves that reach muscles throughout the body and trigger muscle contractions. We walk, reach, touch, and grasp. Our brain triggers all these movements, but our somatic nervous system executes them. And after we finish our drink, our somatic nervous system keeps on working, enabling us to walk away—hopefully to the nearest recycling container.

THE AUTONOMIC NERVOUS SYSTEM

The brain and spinal cord interact with the somatic nervous system to bring about sensation and behavior. In much the same manner, the brain and particularly the limbic system interact with the **autonomic nervous system** to regulate emotion and internal physical states.

There are two divisions of the autonomic nervous system: the **sympathetic division** and the **parasympathetic division.** These two divisions work in opposing directions: When one division is active, the other is passive. The sympathetic nervous system is active during emotional arousal, especially during a crisis, whereas the parasympathetic nervous system is active during rest and digestion. The sympathetic nervous system mobilizes the *fight-or-flight response,* first described by Walton Cannon in 1929 (see also Chapter 10). Cannon noticed that when animals encounter threats, the sympathetic nervous system becomes aroused and prepares animals for fighting or fleeing. Sympathetic activation triggers a variety of physical responses, including increased heart rate, respiration, and perspiration. Autonomic nerves that reach the heart, diaphragm, and sweat glands control these reactions. **[LEARNING OBJECTIVE 3.6]**

THE ENDOCRINE SYSTEM

The limbic system in the brain also cooperates with the **endocrine system** in the body to regulate emotion. The endocrine system consists of glands that release **hormones,** molecules that influence particular organs, into the bloodstream (see **Figure 3.14**).

The Pituitary Gland and Pituitary Hormones.
The **pituitary gland** controls the other glands in the body; for this reason, it's known as the "master gland." The pituitary gland is under the control of the hypothalamus. The pituitary releases a variety of hormones into the bloodstream, serving a variety of different functions, ranging from regulating physical growth to controlling blood pressure to determining how much water is retained in the kidneys. One pituitary hormone called oxytocin is responsible for a variety of important reproductive functions including stretching the cervix and vagina during birth and aiding milk flow in nursing mothers. Oxytocin also plays roles in maternal and romantic love (Esch & Stefano, 2005). **[LEARNING OBJECTIVE 3.7]** Oxytocin may also be a key player in interpersonal trust. In one study, men exposed to a nasal spray containing oxytocin were more likely than other men to hand over money to their team partners in a risky investment game (Kosfeld, Heinrichs, Zaks, et al., 2005).

The Adrenal Glands and Adrenaline.
Psychologists sometimes call the **adrenal glands** the emergency centers of the body. Located on top of the kidneys, they manufacture *adrenaline* and *cortisol.* Adrenaline boosts energy production in muscle cells, thrusting them into action, while conserving as much energy as possible outside of muscle cells. Nerves of the sympathetic nervous system signal the adrenal glands to release adrenaline. Adrenaline triggers many actions, including (1) contraction of the heart muscle and constriction of the blood vessels to provide more blood to the body, (2) opening of the bronchioles (small airways) of the lungs to allow inhalation of more air, (3) breakdown of fat into fatty acids, providing more fuel, (4) breakdown of glycogen (a carbohydrate) into glucose (a sugar) to energize muscles, and (5) opening the pupils of the eye to enable better sight in low levels of light during emergencies. Adrenaline also inhibits gastrointestinal secretions. This last fact helps explain why we often lose our appetites when we feel nervous, as when we're preparing for a big test or anticipating a long-awaited date.

Adrenaline allows people to perform amazing feats in crisis situations, although these acts are constrained by people's physical limits. One desperate mother was energized to

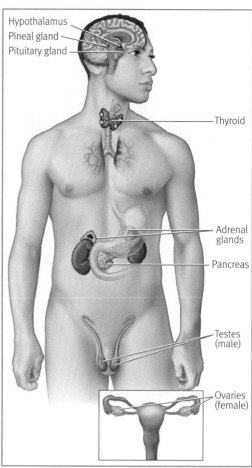

Figure 3.14 The Major Endocrine Glands of the Body. Endocrine glands throughout the body play specialized roles.

GLOSSARY

sympathetic division
part of the autonomic nervous system engaged during a crisis or after actions requiring fight or flight

parasympathetic division
part of autonomic nervous system that controls rest and digestion

endocrine system
system of glands and hormones that controls secretion of blood-borne chemical messengers

hormone
chemical released into the bloodstream that influences particular organs and glands

pituitary gland
master gland that, under the control of the hypothalamus, directs the other glands of the body

adrenal gland
tissue located on top of the kidneys that releases adrenaline and cortisol during states of emotional arousal

When under threat or attack, the sympathetic nervous system takes charge, preparing the body for fight or flight.

lift a heavy automobile to save her trapped infant (Solomon, 2002). Why do threatening or stressful situations activate the sympathetic nervous system? Evolution has probably predisposed this system to detect dangerous stimuli so we can better prepare for counterattack or escape. We're especially likely to interpret sudden and intense stimuli as threatening (Graham et al., 2005). But adrenaline isn't activated only during threatening situations. Pleasurable and exciting activities, like race car driving and skydiving, can also produce adrenaline surges.

Like adrenaline, cortisol also increases in response to physical and psychological stress. Cortisol regulates blood pressure and cardiovascular function, as well as the body's use of proteins, carbohydrates, and fats. The way in which cortisol regulates nutrients has suggested to some researchers that it might regulate body weight, leading to the development of the popular *cortisol diet*. Proponents of this diet claim that elevated levels of cortisol produced by stress cause weight gain (Talbott, 2002). The solution: reduce stress, increase exercise, and monitor nutrition—reasonable advice for those of us who want to lose weight—and it doesn't require us to take supplements. Some people get frustrated or want faster results, however, so health food supplement outlets are happy to oblige by selling cortisol blockers and other dieting supplements. Unfortunately, there's little scientific evidence that these supplements work better than dieting measures that naturally inactivate the body's cortisol.

Sexual Reproductive Glands and Sex Hormones. The sexual reproductive glands are the testes in males and ovaries in females (refer back to Figure 3.14 on page 95). We think of *sex hormones* as traditionally male or female. After all, the testes make the male sex hormone, called *testosterone,* and the ovaries make the female sex hormone, called *estrogen.* Although males and females do have more of their own type of sex hormone, both sexes manufacture some amount of the sex hormone associated with the opposite sex. For example, women's bodies produce about one-twentieth the amount of testosterone as those of males. This is because the ovaries also make testosterone, and the adrenal gland makes low amounts of testosterone in both sexes. Conversely, the testes manufacture low levels of estrogen (Hess, 2003).

Scientists have long debated the relationship between sex hormones and sex drive (Bancroft, 2005). Most scientists believe that testosterone, which increases sex drive in men, also increases sex drive in women, but to a lesser degree. Australian researchers conducted a survey of 18- to 75-year-old women regarding their sexual arousal and frequency of orgasm (Davis et al., 2005). Before they administered the survey, they took blood samples from women and measured their testosterone. The researchers found no correlation between the levels of male sex hormone in a woman's blood and her sex drive. However, the study relied on self-reports, and there weren't controls for demand characteristics (see Chapter 2). Most researchers still accept the idea that testosterone influences female sex drive. Nevertheless, given mixed reports, more research from multiple laboratories must be conducted before we can draw firm conclusions.

REPLICABILITY
Can the results be duplicated in other studies?

WHAT DO *you* THINK?

If you wanted to design a study on the relationship between hormones and friendship, which hormone would you hypothesize would be most relevant and why?

QUIZ

1 The cortex is divided into the frontal, parietal, temporal, and hippocampal lobes. **TRUE** **FALSE**

2 The basal ganglia control sensation. **TRUE** **FALSE**

3 The amygdala plays a key role in fear. **TRUE** **FALSE**

4 The cerebellum regulates only our sense of balance. **TRUE** **FALSE**

5 There are two divisions of the autonomic nervous system. **TRUE** **FALSE**

Answers: (1) F (p. 88); (2) F (p. 91); (3) T (p. 92); (4) F (p. 93); (5) T (p. 95)

PEARSON
mypsychlab

▼ How do individuals cope with brain injury? Watch the video titled "Connie: Head Injury" at www.mypsychlab.com to find out.

Mapping the Mind: The Brain in Action

Although many questions remain unanswered, we know far more about the brain and mind today than we did 200, or even 20, years ago. For this, we can thank psychologists and related scientists who've developed a host of methods to explore the brain and test hypotheses about its functioning. How do we know what we know about brain function and organization?

A TOUR OF BRAIN-MAPPING METHODS

Many advances and major breakthroughs of the past two centuries have enabled scientists to measure brain activity. We know a great many facts about the brain and behavior today because our current methods have been scrutinized and substantiated again and again. Nonetheless, brain research tools weren't always reliable or valid. Some of the earliest methods turned out to be fundamentally flawed, but they paved the way for the sounder methods used today.

Phrenology: A Questionable Map of the Mind. Phrenology was one of the earliest attempts to map mind onto brain. Phrenology was wildly popular in the 1800s, when phrenologists assessed enlargements of the skull—literally bumps on the head—and attributed various personality traits and abilities to those who sought their "expertise." Phrenologists assumed that bumps on the head were related to brain enlargements. From the 1820s through the 1840s, thousands of phrenology shops popped up in Europe and North America. Anyone could go to a phrenology parlor to discover his or her psychological makeup. This popular practice was the origin of the familiar expression "having one's head examined."

The founder of phrenology, Viennese physician Franz Joseph Gall (1758–1828), began with some valid assumptions about the brain. He correctly predicted a positive relationship between enlargements in specific brain areas and certain traits and abili-

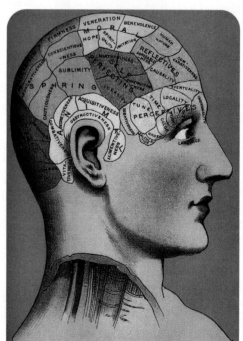

A phrenologist's chart showing where certain psychological traits are supposedly associated with bumps on the skull.

ties, like language. Gall was incorrect, however, in assuming that brain area enlargements created bumps that made impressions on the overlying parts of the skull. Moreover, the 37 different traits that phrenologists described—aggressiveness, vanity, friendliness, and happiness among them—are vastly different from the functions scientists studying the brain today assign to different brain areas.

Phrenology isn't a valid method of assessment. Still, it had one virtue: It was falsifiable. Ironically, this lone asset proved to be its undoing. Eventually, researchers discovered that patients with damage to specific brain areas didn't suffer the kinds of psychological deficits the phrenologists predicted. Even more critically, because the shape of the outer surface of the skull doesn't closely match that of the underlying brain, phrenologists weren't even measuring bumps on the brain, as they'd believed. These discoveries led to the demise of phrenology as an approach.

Brain Damage: Studying How the Brain Works by Seeing How It Doesn't. New methods quickly arose to fill the void left by phrenology. These included methods of studying brain function following damage. We've already mentioned studies conducted by Broca and others that linked specific areas of the cerebral cortex to precise functions. More recently, scientists have created **lesions,** that is, areas of damage, in experimental animals using *stereotaxic methods,* techniques that permit them to pinpoint the location of specific brain areas using coordinates, much like those that navigators use on a map. Today, *neuropsychologists* rely on sophisticated psychological tests, like measures of reasoning, attention, and verbal and spatial ability, to infer the location of brain damage in human patients.

Electrical Stimulation and Recording of Nervous System Activity. Although early studies of function following brain damage provided valuable insights into which brain areas are responsible for which behaviors, many questions concerning the workings of neurons remained. Gustav Fritsch and Eduard Hitzig (1870) were the first to show that stimulating the cortex in an experimental animal caused specific movements. Nearly 90 years later, Penfield (1958) stimulated selected parts of the human motor cortex in patients who were having brain surgery and produced specific movements in those patients. These experiments and others like them showed that neurons respond to electrical stimulation, leading to the hypothesis that neurons themselves might use electrical activity to send information. To test that hypothesis, scientists would need to record electrical activity from the nervous system.

To that end, another method arose that enabled scientists to probe the brain's electrical activity. In the late 1920s, Hans Berger (1929) developed the **electroencephalograph (EEG),** a device that measures electrical activity generated by the brain (see **Figure 3.15**). Patterns and sequences in the EEG allow scientists to infer whether a person is awake or asleep, dreaming or not, and to tell what regions of the brain are active during specific tasks. To obtain an EEG record, researchers record electrical activity from electrodes placed on the scalp's surface. **[LEARNING OBJECTIVE 3.8]**

Because it's noninvasive, researchers frequently use the EEG in both animal and human experiments. The method has a high *temporal resolution* ("temporal" refers to time and "resolution" to sharpness of image), meaning it can detect very rapid changes in the overall electrical activity of the brain occurring in the range of milliseconds (one-thousandths of seconds). Even though the EEG is an old method, researchers still use it to study brain activity in normal brains and in brains of individuals afflicted with schizophrenia, epilepsy, and other psychiatric and neurological disorders. But EEGs have a few disadvantages. Because they show averaged activity that reaches the surface of the scalp, they tell us little, if anything, about what's happening inside neurons. Furthermore, EEGs have low *spatial resolution,* meaning that they aren't especially good for determining where in the brain the activity is occurring.

FALSIFIABILITY
Can the claim be disproved?

Fict -OID **MYTH:** Research using brain imaging is more "scientific" than other psychological research.

REALITY: Brain imaging research can be extremely useful but, like all research, can be misused and abused. Yet because it seems scientific, we can be more persuaded by brain imaging research than we should be (McCabe & Castel, 2008; Weisberg et al., 2008).

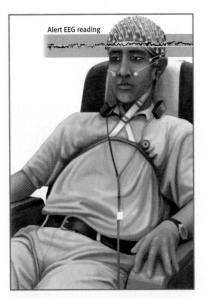

Alert EEG reading

Figure 3.15 Electroencephalograph (EEG). An EEG reading during wakefulness.

GLOSSARY

lesion
area of damage due to surgery, injury, or disease

electroencephalograph (EEG)
recording of brain's electrical activity at the surface of the skull

Brain Scans. Although electrical recording and stimulation provided the initial routes for mapping mind functions onto brain areas, a virtual explosion of brain research occurred with the advent of brain scans, or *neuroimaging*. Researchers developed imaging methods to satisfy clinical and research needs unmet by other techniques. As a group, these imaging methods enable us to peer inside the brain or body. Let's first look at imaging methods that provide a picture of the brain's structure.

CT Scans and MRI Images. In the mid-1970s, independent teams of researchers developed **computed tomography (CT)** and **magnetic resonance imaging (MRI)** (Hounsfield, 1973; Lauterbur, 1973). The discovery of the CT scan earned its developers the Nobel Prize. It's a three-dimensional reconstruction of many x-rays taken through a part of the body, such as the brain. It shows much more detail than an individual X-ray. The MRI shows structural detail using a totally different principle. The MRI scanner measures the release of energy from water in biological tissues following exposure to a magnetic field. MRI images are superior to CT scans for detecting soft tissues, such as brain tumors. However, neuroscientists interested in thought and emotion typically don't use CT or MRI scans, except to localize brain damage, because these scans show only the structure of the brain, not its activity. Instead, they typically use what are called *functional* imaging techniques.

PET. Martin Reivich and colleagues (1979) developed **positron emission tomography (PET),** which is a *functional imaging* technique, meaning it measures changes in the brain's activity levels as a result of physical and mental activity. PET relies on the fact that neurons, like other cells in the body, increase their consumption of glucose (sugar) when they're active. We can think of glucose as the brain's gasoline. PET requires the injection of radioactive glucoselike molecules into patients. Although they're radioactive, they're shortlived, so they do little or no harm. The scanner measures where in the brain the most glucoselike molecules are consumed, allowing neuroscientists to figure out which parts of the brain are most active during a particular task. Clinicians can also use PET scans to see how brain activity changes when patients take a medication. Because PET is invasive, researchers continued to work to develop functional imaging methods that wouldn't require injections of radioactive molecules.

BOLD Response and fMRI. Seiji Ogawa and his colleagues first reported the *blood oxygenation level dependent* (BOLD) response in 1990. The discovery of the BOLD response enabled the development of the **functional MRI,** known as **fMRI.** As neural activity picks up its pace, there's an increase in oxygenated blood in response to heightened demand. Because fMRI measures the change in blood oxygen level, it's an indirect correlate of neural activity. Neuroscientists frequently use fMRI to image brain activity. The fMRI relies on magnetic fields, as does MRI. Whereas MRI has a high resolution, fMRI operates at a low resolution so that researchers can perform many scans in rapid succession. Individual fMRI images aren't very sharp, but the method shows changes in brain activity level over time because it creates a sequence of images.

Magnetic Stimulation and Recording. To provide access to surface brain structures and improve on the resolution, researchers developed methods such as MRI and fMRI that relied on magnetic fields. Anthony Barker and colleagues (1985) were the first to report on a method called **transcranial magnetic stimulation (TMS),** which applies strong and quickly changing magnetic fields to the skull to create electric fields in the brain. Depending on the level of stimulation, TMS can either enhance or interrupt brain

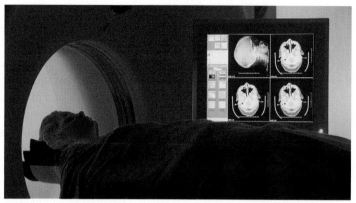

Magnetic resonance imaging (MRI) is a noninvasive procedure that reveals high-resolution images of soft tissue, such as the brain.

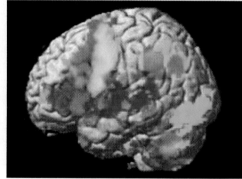

An fMRI of the brain showing areas that were active when subjects remembered something they saw (*green*), something they heard (*red*), or both (*yellow*). (*Source:* M. Kirschen/ Stanford University)

GLOSSARY

computed tomography (CT)
a scanning technique using multiple x-rays to construct three-dimensional images

magnetic resonance imaging (MRI)
technique that uses magnetic fields to indirectly visualize brain structure

positron emission tomography (PET)
imaging technique that measures consumption of glucoselike molecules, yielding a picture of neural activity in different regions of the brain

functional MRI (fMRI)
technique that uses magnetic fields to visualize brain activity using the BOLD response

transcranial magnetic stimulation (TMS)
technique that applies strong and quickly changing magnetic fields to the surface of the skull that can either enhance or interrupt brain function

function in a particular region. Some reports suggest that TMS provides relief for depression and may decrease auditory hallucinations, that is, the hearing of sounds, typically voices (Saba, Schurhoff, & Leboyer, 2006). *Repetitive TMS* (rTMS) additionally shows promise as a treatment for depression (Rachid & Bertschy, 2006). However, TMS also offers important insights for researchers attempting to understand which areas of the brain are involved in different types of psychological processes. For example, if TMS interrupts functioning in the temporal lobe and the subject displays (temporary!) language impairment as a result, we can conclude that the temporal lobe is important for language processing. This is the only noninvasive technique for studying the brain that allows us to infer cause—all other techniques can only correlate brain activation with psychological processing.

Another technique that uses magnetic fields is **magnetoencephalography (MEG),** which measures tiny magnetic fields and in this way detects electrical activity in the brain and the rest of the nervous system. The resulting images produced by MEG reveal patterns of magnetic fields on the surface of the skull. MEG has good spatial resolution and excellent temporal resolution—measuring activity changes millisecond by millisecond—whereas PET and fMRI scans measure activity changes second by second.

CORRELATION vs. CAUSATION
Can we be sure that A causes B?

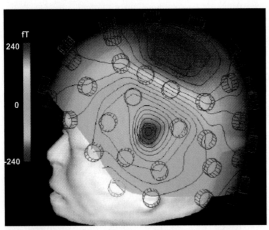

An example of magnetoencephalography (MEG) illustrating the presence of magnetic fields on the surface of the cerebral cortex. (*Source:* Arye Nehorai/Washington University, St. Louis)

HOW MUCH OF OUR BRAIN DO WE USE?

Despite having so much information available today regarding the relationship between brain and behavior, misconceptions about the brain still survive. One widely held myth is that most people use only 10 percent of their brain (Beyerstein, 1999). What could we do if we could access the 90 percent of the brain that's supposedly inactive? Would we find the cure for cancer, acquire wealth beyond belief, or write our own psychology textbook?

The 10 percent myth gained its toehold at around the same time as phrenology, in the late 1800s. William James (1842–1910), one of the fathers of modern psychology (see Chapter 1), wrote that most people fulfill only a small percent of their intellectual potential. Some people misconstrued this quote as meaning that we only use about 10 percent of our brains. As the 10 percent myth was repeated, it acquired the status of an urban legend.

Early difficulties in identifying which brain regions controlled which functions probably reinforced this misconception. In 1929, Karl Lashley showed that there was no single memory area in the brain (see Chapter 6). He made multiple knife cuts in the brains of rats and tested them on a series of mazes. The result was that no specific cortical area was more critical to maze learning than any other. Unfortunately, Lashley's results were ripe for misinterpretation as evidence for "silent" areas in the cerebral cortex.

Given how appealing the idea of tapping into our full potential is, it's no wonder that scores of pop psychology writers, media figures, and so-called self-improvement experts have assured us they know how to harness our brain's full potential. Some authors of self-help books who were particularly fond of the 10 percent myth liberally misquoted scientists as saying that 90 percent of the brain isn't doing anything. Believers in psychic phenomena have even spun the yarn that because scientists don't know what 90 percent of the brain is doing, it must be serving a psychic purpose, like extrasensory perception (ESP) (Clark, 1997).

We now know enough about all parts of the brain that we can safely conclude that every part of the brain has a function. Specialists in the fields of clinical neurology and neuropsychology, who deal with the effects of brain damage, have shown that losses of small areas of certain parts of the brain can cause devastating, often permanent, losses

GLOSSARY

magnetoencephalography (MEG)
measure of brain activity that measures tiny magnetic fields generated by the brain

of function (Sacks, 1985). Even when brain damage doesn't cause severe deficits, it produces some change in behavior, however subtle.

The fatal blow against the 10 percent myth, however, comes from neuroimaging and brain stimulation studies. No one's ever discovered any perpetually silent areas, nor is it the case that 90 percent of the brain produces nothing of psychological interest when stimulated. All brain areas become active on brain scans at one time or another as we think, feel, and perceive (Beyerstein, 1999).

WHICH PARTS OF OUR BRAIN DO WE USE FOR WHAT?

Scientists refer to *localization of function* when they identify brain areas that are active during a particular psychological task over and above a baseline rate of activity. We should be careful not to overemphasize localization of function, however, and particularly cautious in our interpretations of neuroimaging results. William Uttal (2001) warned that researchers are too quick to assign narrowly defined functions to specific brain regions. He argued that we can't always dissect higher brain functions into narrower components. Take visual perception, for example: Can we divide it into subcomponents dealing with color, form, and motion, as cortical localization of functions might imply, or is visual perception a unified experience supported by multiple regions?

The notion that the brain contains a "God spot" that is activated when people pray or think about God caught the attention of the public, but brain organization is nowhere near this simple.

Regrettably, much of the popular media hasn't taken Uttal's useful cautions to heart. To take one example, some newspapers announced the discovery of a specific "God spot" in the brain when scientists found that areas of the frontal lobe become active when individuals think of God. Yet later brain imaging research showed that religious experiences activate a wide variety of brain areas, not just one (Beauregard & Paquette, 2006). As Uttal reminds us, few if any complex psychological functions are likely to be confined to a single brain area.

Just as multiple brain regions contribute to each psychological function, individual brain areas contribute to multiple psychological functions. Broca's area, well known to play a role in speech, is also active when we notice that a musical note is off key (Limb, 2006). There's enhanced activity in such emotional centers as the amygdala when we listen to inspiring music, even though these regions aren't traditionally known as "musical areas" (Blood & Zatorre, 2001). The rule of thumb is that each brain region participates in many functions—some expected, some unexpected—so coordination across multiple brain regions contributes to each function.

WHICH SIDE OF OUR BRAIN DO WE USE FOR WHAT?

Just as we can localize certain functions to specific parts of the brain, we can localize certain functions to our right or left hemispheres. Roger Sperry (1974) won the Nobel Prize for his studies revealing that the two cerebral hemispheres possess different functions, in particular different levels of language ability. These studies examined patients who underwent **split-brain surgery** because their doctors couldn't control their epilepsy with medication. In this rare operation, neurosurgeons separate a patient's cerebral hemispheres by severing the corpus callosum. Split-brain surgery typically offers marked relief from seizures, and patients behave normally under most conditions. **[LEARNING OBJECTIVE 3.9]**

Nevertheless, carefully designed experiments have revealed unusual fragmenting of cognitive functions that we normally experience as fused into indivisible wholes. The two hemispheres of split-brain subjects have different abilities and even different "personalities" (Gazzaniga, 2000; Zaidel, 1994). Nonetheless, a split-brain subject usually experiences him- or herself as a single, unified person.

GLOSSARY

split-brain surgery
procedure that involves severing the corpus callosum to reduce the spread of epileptic seizures

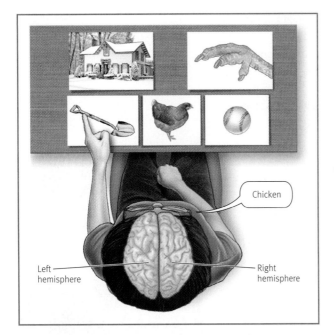

Figure 3.16 Split-Brain Subject. This woman's right hemisphere recognizes the snow scene and leads her to point to the shovel, but her left hemisphere recognizes the claw and indicates verbally that the chicken is the matching object.

Table 3.3 Lateralized Functions

Left Hemisphere
Fine-tuned language skills
• Speech comprehension
• Speech production
• Phonology
• Syntax
• Reading
• Writing
Actions
• Making facial expressions
• Motion detection

Right Hemisphere
Coarse language skills
• Simple speech
• Simple writing
• Tone of voice
Visuospatial skills
• Perceptual grouping
• Face perception

(*Source:* Adapted from Gazzaniga, 2000)

Right and Left Hemispheres: Worlds Apart. Split-brain surgery showed that many cognitive functions rely on one cerebral hemisphere more than the other; scientists call this phenomenon **lateralization.** The left or the right hemisphere demonstrates specialization for various cognitive functions (see **Table 3.3**). Many of the lateralized functions concern specific language and verbal skills.

A classic way to study split-brain subjects is for researchers to present stimuli, such as written words, to either their right or left *visual field*. The right visual field is the right half of information entering each eye, and the left visual field is information from the left half of each eye's viewing area. To understand why researchers present stimuli to only one visual field, we need to know where visual information goes in the brain. In a normal brain, most visual information from either the left or right visual field ends up on the opposite side of the visual cortex. There's also crossing over for motor control. The left hemisphere controls the right hand and the right hemisphere controls the left hand.

The corpus callosum transfers information between the two halves of the cerebral cortex. As a result, cutting the corpus callosum prevents most visual information in each visual field from reaching the visual cortex on the same side. When the corpus callosum is cut, there's a striking separation of functions. In one extreme case, a split-brain subject complained that his left hand wouldn't cooperate with his right hand. His left hand misbehaved frequently; it turned off TV shows while he was in the middle of watching them and frequently struck at family members against his will (Joseph, 1988).

Split-brain subjects often experience difficulties integrating information presented to separate hemispheres but frequently find a way to rationalize or make sense of their puzzling behaviors. In one experiment, researchers flashed a chicken claw to a split-brain patient's left hemisphere and a snow scene to his right hemisphere (see **Figure 3.16**). When asked to match what he saw with a set of choices, he pointed to a shovel with his left hand (controlled by his right hemisphere) but said, "chicken" (since speech is controlled by his left hemisphere). When asked to explain these actions, he said, "I saw a claw and I picked the chicken, and you have to clean out the chicken shed with a shovel."

We should guard against placing too much emphasis on lateralization of function and taking it to an extreme. Remarkably, it's possible to live with only half of a brain, that is, only one hemisphere. Indeed, a number of people have survived operations to remove one hemisphere to spare the brain from serious disease. The outlook for such individuals is best when surgeons perform the operation in childhood, which gives the remaining hemisphere a better chance to assume the functions of the missing hemisphere (Kenneally, 2006). The fact that children who undergo this procedure develop almost normally suggests that functional localization is not a foregone conclusion.

myth
CONCEPTIONS
ARE THERE LEFT-BRAINED VERSUS RIGHT-BRAINED PERSONS?

Despite the great scientific contribution of split-brain studies, the popular notion that normal people are either "left brained" or "right brained" is a myth. According to this myth, left-brained people are scholarly, logical, and analytical, and right-brained people are artistic, creative, and emotional. One Internet blogger tried to explain the differences between people's political beliefs in terms of the left–right brain distinction; conservatives, he claimed, tend to be left brained and liberals right brained (Block, 2006). Yet these claims are vast oversimplifications (Hines, 1987). After reviewing numerous studies, Michael Corballis (1999) concluded that we use both sides of our brains in a complementary way. Furthermore, the corpus callosum and other interconnections ensure that both hemispheres are in constant communication. If the left-brained versus right-brained dichotomy were accurate, then people who were artistic would be unlikely to be verbally gifted. In reality, there are scores of multitalented people: Consider actors who are also screenwriters (like Sean Penn or Tina Fey).

We can trace the myth of exaggerated left-brain versus right-brain differences to misinterpretations of what scientists reported. Self-help books incorporating the topic have flourished. Robert E. Ornstein was among those to promote the idea of using different ways to tap into our creative right brains versus our intellectual left brains in his 1997 book *The Right Mind: Making Sense of the Hemispheres*. Right brain–oriented educational programs for children sprang up that deemphasized getting the correct answers on tests in favor of developing creative ability. Such programs as the "Applied Creative Thinking Workshop" trained business managers to use their right brains (Herrmann, 1996). For a mere $195, "whole brain learning" supposedly expanded the mind in new ways using "megasubliminal messages," heard only by the left or the right brain (Corballis, 1999). Although there's nothing wrong with trying to be more creative by using our minds in different ways, using both hemispheres in tandem works far better.

Left-brain, right-brain differences supposedly can also be used to treat mood disorders or anger. There are even sunglasses with flip-up side panels designed to selectively increase light to either the left or right hemisphere. Nevertheless, there's little or no scientific support for "goggle therapy" (Lilienfeld, 1999a). The magazine *Consumer Reports* (2006) couldn't confirm the claim that the sunglasses reduced anger or other negative feelings, with 7 out of 12 subjects reporting no change. Surely, more evidence is required before we can interpret an extraordinary claim of this type as scientifically supported.

Left-side, right-side flip-up sunglasses designed to improve mental state.

EXTRAORDINARY CLAIMS
Is the evidence as convincing as the claim?

WHAT DO *you* THINK?

Your employer asks you to participate in a creativity workshop in which the company will engage in exercises to help strengthen the right side of the brain. Your manager believes this will help staff think up more creative innovations and solutions. What is your assessment of whether this will be a worthwhile endeavor?

GLOSSARY

lateralization
cognitive function that relies more on one side of the brain than the other

QUIZ

1 PET scans detect changes in cerebral blood flow that tend to accompany neural activity.   `TRUE` `FALSE`

2 Most people use only about 10 percent of their brain.   `TRUE` `FALSE`

3 Psychological functions are strictly localized to specific areas of the cerebral cortex.   `TRUE` `FALSE`

4 Split-brain subjects are impaired at integrating information from both visual fields.   `TRUE` `FALSE`

Answers: (1) F (p. 99); (2) F (p. 100); (3) F (p. 101); (4) T (p. 102).

PEARSON
mypsychlab

▼ How do neurosurgeons use computers to talk to the brain? Watch the video titled "MKM and Brain Scans" at www.mypsychlab.com to find out.

Nature and Nurture: Did Your Genes—or Parents—Make You Do It?

By this point in the chapter, we've learned a fair amount about the brain and nervous system and how they contribute to behavior. Now we're ready to tackle an equally complex set of questions. How much does what we inherit from our parents—as opposed to the events in our lives—influence our behavior and mental activities?

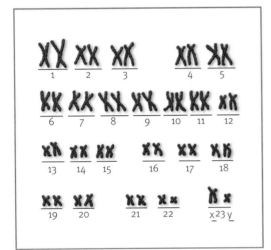

Figure 3.17 Human Chromosomes.
Humans have 46 chromosomes. Males have an XY pair and females have an XX pair. The other 22 pairs of chromosomes aren't sex linked.

GLOSSARY

chromosome
slender thread inside a cell's nucleus that carries genes

gene
genetic material, composed of deoxyribonucleic acid (DNA)

genotype
our genetic makeup

phenotype
our observable traits

dominant gene
gene that masks other genes' effects

recessive gene
gene that is expressed only in the absence of a dominant gene

natural selection
principle that organisms that possess adaptations survive and reproduce at a higher rate than other organisms

HOW WE CAME TO BE WHO WE ARE

As little as 150 years ago, even the smartest of scientists knew almost nothing about how we humans came to be. Today, the average educated person knows more about the origins of human life and the human brain than did Charles Darwin. We're remarkably fortunate to be armed with scientific principles concerning heredity, adaptation, and evolution that enable us to understand the origins of our psychological characteristics.

The Biological Material of Heredity. In 1866 Gregor Mendel published his classic treatise on inheritance based on his research on pea plants. We now know that humans have 46 **chromosomes** (see **Figure 3.17**). Chromosomes are the slender threads inside the cell's nucleus that carry **genes:** genetic material. Genes are made of deoxyribonucleic acid (DNA), the material that stores everything cells need to replicate (reproduce) themselves. **[LEARNING OBJECTIVE 3.10]** The genome is what we call a full set of chromosomes and the heritable traits associated with them. The *Human Genome Project,* which characterized all the human genes, was completed in 2001.

Genotype versus Phenotype. People's genetic makeup, or the set of genes transmitted from the parents to offspring, is their **genotype.** Their **phenotype** is their set of observable traits. We can't tell people's genotypes by observing their phenotypes in part because some genes are **dominant,** meaning they mask other genes' effects, or **recessive,** meaning they're expressed only in the absence of a dominant gene.

Eye color, hair color, and even skin color are determined by combinations of recessive and dominant genes. For example, two brown-eyed parents could have a blue-eyed child, because the child inherited recessive genes for blue eyes from both parents.

Behavioral Adaptation. Charles Darwin's classic book *On the Origin of Species* (1859) introduced the concept of **natural selection** and the broad strokes of his theory of evolution. Darwin hypothesized that populations of organisms change over time by selective breeding among individuals within the population who possess some apparent advantage. According to these principles, some organisms possess *adaptations* that make them better suited to their environments. Those individuals survive and reproduce at a higher rate than other organisms. Some adaptations that offer advantages are physical changes that enable animals to better manipulate their environments. An opposable thumb (one that can be moved away from the other fingers), for example, greatly improved our hand function.

Other adaptations are behavioral. According to most evolutionary psychologists, aggressive behavior is an adaptation because it enables organisms to obtain more resources. Too much aggression, however, is usually maladaptive, meaning it often fails to increase organisms' chances of survival or reproduction, perhaps because they are likely to be killed in a fight or because their aggression scares off potential mates. Organisms with many successful adaptations have high levels of **fitness,** meaning that they have a better chance of passing their genes on to later generations.

Brain Evolution.
The relationship between the human nervous system and behavior has been finely tuned over millions of years of evolution (Cartwright, 2000). Brain regions with complicated functions, such as the cortex, have evolved the most (Karlen & Krubitzer, 2006). As a result, our behaviors are more complex and flexible than those of other animals, allowing us to respond in many more ways to a given situation.

What makes us so distinctive in the animal kingdom? Fossil and genetic evidence suggests that somewhere between 6 and 7 million years ago, humans and apes split off from a shared ancestor. After that critical fork in the evolutionary road, we went our separate ways. The human line eventually resulted in our species, *Homo sapiens,* whereas the ape line resulted in chimpanzees, gorillas, and orangutans (the "great apes"). We often fail to appreciate that *Homo sapiens*—modern humans—have been around for only about 1 percent of the total time period of the human race (Calvin, 2004).

Around the time of our divergence from apes, our brains weren't that much larger than theirs. Then, around 3 to 4 million years ago, something dramatic happened, although we don't know why. We do know that within a span of only a few million years—a mere blink of an eye in the earth's 4.5-billion-year history—one tiny area of the human genome changed about 70 times more rapidly than other areas, resulting in significant changes in the cortex (Pollard et al., 2006). The human brain mushroomed in size, more than tripling from less than 400 grams—a bit less than a pound—to its present hefty weight of 1,300 grams—about 3 pounds (Holloway, 1983). The brains of modern great apes weigh between 300 and 500 grams, even though their overall body size doesn't differ that much from humans' (Bradbury, 2005).

Relative to our body size, we're proportionally the biggest brained animals in existence (we need to correct for body size, because large animals, like whales and elephants, have huge brains in part because their bodies are also huge). Second in line are dolphins (Marino, McShea, & Uhen, 2004), followed by chimpanzees and other great apes. Research suggests that across species, relative brain size—brain size corrected for body size—is associated with behaviors we typically regard as intelligent (Jerison, 1983). For example, big-brained animals tend to have especially large and complex social networks (Dunbar, 2003).

BEHAVIORAL GENETICS: HOW WE STUDY HERITABILITY

Scientists use *behavioral genetics* to examine the roles of nature and nurture in the origins of traits, such as intelligence (see Chapter 7). In reality, behavioral genetic designs are misnamed, because they permit us to look at the roles of both genetic *and* environmental influences on behavior (Waldman, 2005).

Behavioral genetic designs also allow us to estimate the **heritability** of traits and diseases. By heritability, we mean the extent to which genes contribute to differences in a trait *among individuals.* Typically, we express heritability as a percentage. So, if we say that the heritability of a trait is 60 percent, we mean that more than half of the differences *among individuals* in their levels of that trait are due to differences in their genes. By definition, the other 40 percent is due to differences in their environments. Some traits, like height, are highly heritable; the heritability of height in adults is between 70 and 80 percent (Silventoinen et al., 2003). In contrast, other traits, like the accent in speech, are due almost entirely to environment; the heritability of accent is essentially 0. That's because our accents are almost entirely a product of the dialect spoken by our parents or in the community in which we're raised. **[LEARNING OBJECTIVE 3.11]**

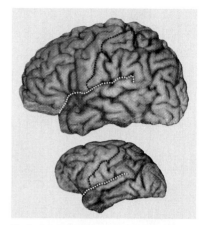

The brain of a human (*top*) and that of a chimpanzee (*bottom*). The human brain is about three times larger, even though humans are only about two times as large overall.

The distinction of the largest brain in the animal kingdom—between 15 and 20 pounds—goes to the sperm whale. Still, this fact doesn't make the sperm whale the "brainiest" creature on the planet because we must correct for its huge body size when determining its relative brain size.

GLOSSARY

fitness
organisms' capacity to pass on their genes

heritability
percentage of the variability in a trait across individuals that is due to genes

Even though differences in height among plants may be largely heritable, watering these plants—an environmental manipulation—can result in substantial increases in their height. Bottom line: High heritability doesn't imply unchangeablility.

Three Major Misconceptions about Heritability.

Heritability isn't as simple a concept as it seems, and it confuses even some psychologists. So before discussing how psychologists use heritability in different kinds of experiments, we'll first address three widespread misunderstandings about it:

- *Misconception #1:* *Heritability applies to a single individual rather than to differences among individuals.* Heritability applies only to groups of people. If someone asks you, "What's the heritability of your IQ?" you should promptly hand that person a copy of this chapter. Heritability tells us about the causes of differences among people, not within a person.

- *Misconception #2:* *Heritability tells us whether a trait can be changed.* Many people believe that if a trait is highly heritable, then by definition we can't change it. Yet, logically speaking, heritability says little or nothing about how malleable (alterable) a trait is. In fact, a trait can, in principle, have a heritability of 100 percent and still be extremely malleable. Here's how. Imagine 10 plants that differ markedly in height, with some of them only 2 or 3 inches tall and others 5 or 6 inches tall. Imagine they're only a few days old and that since their germination we've exposed them to *exactly equal* environmental conditions: the same amount of water and identical soil and lighting conditions. What's the heritability of height in this group of plants? It's 100 percent: The causes of differences in their heights *must be* completely genetic, because we've kept all environmental influences constant. Now imagine that we suddenly decide to stop watering these plants and providing them with light. All of the plants will soon die, and their heights will all become 0 inches. So, even though the heritability of height in these plants was 100 percent, we can easily change their heights by changing their environments.

- *Misconception #3:* *Heritability is a fixed number.* Heritability can differ dramatically across different time periods and populations. Remember that heritability is the extent to which differences among people in a trait are due to genetic influences. So if we reduce the range of environmental influences on a trait within a population, heritability will increase because more of the differences in that trait will be due to genetic factors. Conversely, if we increase the range of environmental influences on a trait within a population, heritability will go down because fewer of the differences in that trait will be due to genetic factors.

⌐ WHAT DO *you* THINK ?

Your nephew has been diagnosed with phenylketonuria (PKU), a highly heritable disease that prevents normal brain development but that can be treated by a special diet. How would you explain to your family that heritability doesn't mean "untreatable"?

GLOSSARY

family study
analysis of how traits run in families

twin study
analysis of how traits differ in identical versus fraternal twins

RULING OUT RIVAL HYPOTHESES
Have important alternative explanations for the findings been excluded?

Behavioral Genetic Designs.

Scientists estimate heritability by means of one of three behavioral genetic designs: *family studies, twin studies,* and *adoption studies.* In such studies, scientists track the presence or absence of a trait among different relatives. These studies help them determine how much both genes and environment contribute to the causes of that trait.

Family Studies. In **family studies,** researchers examine the extent to which a trait "runs" or goes together in intact families, namely, those in which all family members are raised in the same home. In these studies, there is a crucial limitation: Relatives share a similar environment as well as similar genetic material. As a consequence, family studies don't allow us to disentangle the effects of nature from nurture. Investigators have therefore turned to more informative research designs to separate these influences.

Twin Studies. To understand **twin studies,** we first need to say a bit about the birds and the bees. Two different things can happen when a sperm fertilizes an egg. First, a single sperm may fertilize a single egg, producing a *zygote,* or fertilized egg (see Chapter 8). For reasons that scientists still don't fully understand, that zygote occasionally (in about 1 in 250 births) splits into two, yielding two identical genetic copies. Researchers refer to these identical twins as *monozygotic* (MZ), because they originate from one zygote. Identical twins are essentially genetic clones of each other because they share 100 percent of their genes. In other cases, two different sperm may fertilize two different eggs, resulting in two zygotes. These twins are *dizygotic* (DZ), or, more loosely, fraternal. In contrast to identical twins, fraternal twins share only 50 percent of their genes on average and are no more alike genetically than ordinary brothers or sisters. Fraternal twins (and triplets, quadruplets, and so on) are more likely to occur in women undergoing fertility treatments to encourage eggs to be produced and released, but fertility treatment has no effect on frequency of identical twins, because it doesn't affect whether a single egg will split.

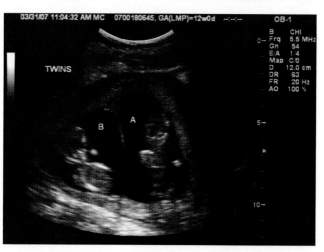

Identical twin fetuses developing in utero. Behavior geneticists compare identical with fraternal twins to estimate genetic and environmental influences on psychological traits.

The logic of *twin studies* rests on the fact that identical twins are more similar genetically than are fraternal twins. Consequently, if identical twins are more alike on a psychological characteristic, such as intelligence or extraversion, than are fraternal twins, we can infer that this characteristic is genetically influenced, assuming that the environmental influences on the characteristic we're studying are the same in identical and fraternal twins.

Adoption Studies. As we've noted, studies of intact family members are limited because they can't disentangle genetic from environmental influences. To address this shortcoming, psychologists have turned to **adoption studies,** which examine the extent to which children adopted into new homes resemble their adoptive as opposed to biological parents. Children adopted into other homes share genes with their biological relatives but not environment. As a consequence, if adopted children resemble their biological parents on a psychological characteristic, we can typically assume that it's genetically influenced.

One potential confound in adoption studies is *selective placement:* Adoption agencies frequently place children in homes similar to those of their biologic parents (DeFries & Plomin, 1978). This confound can lead investigators to mistakenly interpret the similarity between adoptive children and their biological parents as a genetic effect. In adoption studies, researchers try to control for selective placement by correcting statistically for the correlation between biological and adoptive parents.

GLOSSARY

adoption study
analysis of how traits vary in individuals raised apart from their biological relatives

QUIZ

1	Brain evolution is responsible for humans' advanced abilities.	TRUE	FALSE
2	The fact that the human brain is smaller than an elephant's shows that brain size is unrelated to intelligence.	TRUE	FALSE
3	Heritability values can't change over time.	TRUE	FALSE
4	Identical twins have similar phenotypes (observable traits) but may have different genotypes (sets of genes).	TRUE	FALSE
5	Adoption studies are useful for distinguishing nature influences from nurture influences.	TRUE	FALSE

PEARSON
mypsychlab

▼ How do your genes impact your medical treatment? Watch the video titled "How the Human Genome Map Affects You" at www.mypsychlab.com to find out.

Answers: (1) T (p. 105); (2) F (p. 105); (3) F (p. 106); (4) F (p. 107); (5) T (p. 107)

NERVE CELLS: COMMUNICATION PORTALS (pp. 80–87)

3.1 Distinguish the parts of neurons and what they do

The neuron has a cell body, which contains the nucleus filled with deoxyribonucleic acid (DNA), responsible for manufacturing the proteins that make up our cells. Neurons have dendrites, long extensions that receive messages from other neurons and an axon extending from the cell body of each neuron, which is responsible for sending messages.

1. The central region of the neuron which manufactures new cell components is called the _____ _____ . (p. 82)

2. The receiving ends of a neuron, extending from the cell body like tree branches, are known as _____ . (p. 82)

3. The space between two connecting neurons where neurotransmitters are released is called the _____ . (p. 82)

4. _____ are long extensions from the neuron at the cell body that _____ messages from one neuron to another. (p. 82)

5. The autoimmune disease multiple sclerosis is linked to the destruction of the glial cells wrapped around the axon—called the _____ _____ . (p. 83)

3.2 Explain how neurons use neurotransmitters to communicate with each other

Neurotransmitters are the chemical messengers neurons use to communicate with each other or to cause muscle contraction. The axon terminal releases neurotransmitters at the synapse. This process then produces excitatory or inhibitory responses in the recipient neuron.

6. What "natural narcotic" produced by the brain helps athletes endure intense workouts or pain? (p. 84)

3.3 Describe electrical responses of neurons and what makes them possible

Neurons exhibit excitatory and inhibitory responses to inputs from other neurons. When excitation is strong enough, the neuron generates an action potential, which travels all the way down the axon to the axon terminal. Charged particles crossing the neuronal membrane are responsible for these events.

7. The electrical charge difference across the membrane of the neuron when it is not being stimulated is called the _____ _____ . (p. 85)

8. Action potentials are abrupt waves of _____ _____ that allow neurons to communicate. (p. 85)

9. Label the image showing the process of action potential in a neuron. Include (a) axon, (b) arrow depicting the direction of the action potential, and (c) neurotransmitters. (p. 85)

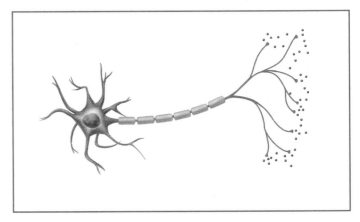

3.4 Recognize when the brain changes most and least

The brain changes the most before birth and during early development. Throughout the life span the brain demonstrates some degree of plasticity, which plays a role in learning and memory. Later in life, healthy brain plasticity decreases and neurons can show signs of degeneration.

10. Scientists are working to improve ways to encourage neurogenesis, the adult brain's ability to create new _____ . (p. 86)

succeed with mypsychlab

1. Use this interactive visual quiz to test your knowledge of the synapse.
   The Synapse

2. How do chemicals in the brain send messages to control our behaviors?
   Neuronal Transmission

3. See if you can identify the structures of a brain cell, using this image of a neural cell.
   Structure of a Neuron

succeed with mypsychlab

Do You Know All of the Terms in This Chapter?

Find out by using the Flashcards. Want more practice? Take additional quizzes, try simulations, and watch video to be sure you are prepared for the test!

Answers are located at the end of the text.

THE BRAIN–BEHAVIOR NETWORK (pp. 87–97)

3.5 **Identify what roles different parts of the central nervous system play in behavior**

The cerebral cortex consists of the frontal, parietal, temporal, and occipital lobes. Cortex involved with vision lies in the occipital lobe, cortex involved with hearing in the temporal lobe, and cortex involved with touch in the parietal lobe. Association areas throughout the cortex analyze and reanalyze sensory inputs to build up our perceptions. The motor cortex in the frontal lobe, the basal ganglia, and the spinal cord work together with the somatic nervous system to bring about movement and action. The somatic nervous system has a sensory as well as a motor component, which enables touch and feedback from the muscles to guide our actions.

11. The brain and spinal cord combine to form the superhighway known as the _____ _____ _____. (p. 87)

12. Outside of the CNS, the _____ _____ system works to help us control behavior and express emotion. (pp. 87–88)

13. The brain component responsible for analyzing sensory information and our ability to think, talk, and reason is called the _____. (p. 88)

14. Label the various parts of the central nervous system. (p. 89)

Central Nervous System	
(a)	**Frontal Lobe:** executive function coordinating other brain areas, motor planning, language, and memory **Parietal Lobe:** processes touch info, integrates vision and touch **Temporal Lobe:** processes auditory info, language, and autobiographical memory **Occipital Lobe:** processes visual info
(b)	control movement and motor planning
(c)	**Thalamus:** conveys sensory info to cortex **Hypothalamus:** oversees endocrine and autonomic nervous system **Amygdala:** regulates arousal and fear **Hippocampus:** processes memory for spatial locations
(d)	controls balance and coordinated movement
(e)	**Midbrain:** tracks visual stimuli and reflexes triggered by sound **Pons:** conveys information between the cortex and cerebellum **Medulla:** regulates breathing and heartbeats
(f)	conveys information between the brain and the body

succeed with mypsychlab

1. What brain parts go where? See if you can identify parts of the brain on this image.
The Limbic System

2. How do your eyes communicate with your brain? Learn how you know what you are seeing with this simulation.
The Visual Cortex

3. The fight-or-flight response originates in the ANS. Test your knowledge of what bodily functions are stimulated or slowed down.
The Autonomic Nervous System

15. Fill in the function of each brain component identified in this figure. (p. 91)

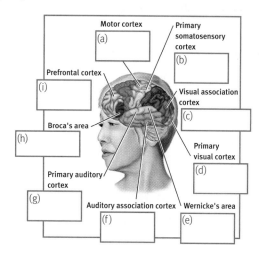

16. Parkinson disease is the result of damage to the _____ _____, which play a critical role in voluntary movement. (p. 91)

3.6 **Clarify how the autonomic nervous system works in emergency and everyday situations**

The autonomic nervous system consists of the parasympathetic and sympathetic divisions. Whereas the parasympathetic nervous system is active during rest and digestion, the sympathetic division propels the body into action during an emergency or crisis. Sympathetic arousal also occurs in response to everyday stress.

17. Our ability to react physically to a perceived threat is dependent on the _____ division of the autonomic system. (p. 95)

18. Sympathetic activation triggers a variety of physical responses, including increased heart rate, _____, and _____. (p. 95)

3.7 **Describe what hormones are and how they affect behavior**

Hormones are chemicals released into the bloodstream that trigger specific effects in the body. Activation of the sympathetic nervous system triggers the release of adrenaline and cortisol by the adrenal glands, which energize our bodies. Sex hormones control sexual responses.

19. The body's "master gland" that, under the control of the hypothalamus, directs all other body glands is known as the _____ _____. (p. 95)

20. Males and females (do/don't) both manufacture estrogen and testosterone. (p. 96)

MAPPING THE MIND: THE BRAIN IN ACTION (pp. 97–103)

3.8 Identify the different brain-stimulating, recording, and imaging techniques

Electrical stimulation of the brain can elicit vivid imagery or movement. Methods such as electroencephalography (EEG) and magnetoencephalography (MEG) enable researchers to record brain activity. Imaging techniques provide a way to see the brain. The first imaging techniques included computed tomography (CT) and magnetic resonance imaging (MRI). Brain-imaging techniques that allow us to see where activity changes during psychological function include positron emission tomography (PET) and functional MRI (fMRI).

21. Franz Joseph Gall made one of the earliest attempts to connect mind and brain by measuring head bumps, otherwise known as _____. (p. 97)

22. Early efforts by Hans Berger to measure electrical activity in the brain resulted in the development of the _____. (p. 98)

23. Neuroscientists interested in measuring thought and emotion (would/wouldn't) employ an MRI scan. (p. 99)

24. What do functional MRIs (fMRI), such as the one pictured here, measure? (p. 99)

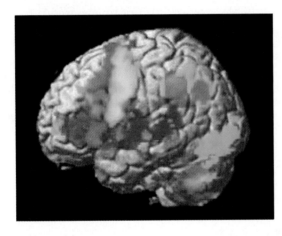

3.9 Evaluate results demonstrating the brain's localization of function

Stimulating, recording, and imaging techniques have shown that specific brain areas correspond to specific functions. Although these results provide valuable insight into how our brains divide up the many tasks we perform, many parts of the brain contribute to each specific task. Because individual brain areas participate in multiple functions, many cognitive functions cannot be neatly localized.

25. Neuroscientists have confirmed that there (are/aren't) parts of the brain that remain completely inactive and unutilized. (p. 101)

26. Severing the corpus callosum to reduce the incidence of epileptic seizures is known as _____ surgery. (p. 101)

27. The phenomenon known as _____ explains how many cognitive functions rely on one cerebral hemisphere more than another. (p. 102)

28. In this experiment, researchers flashed a chicken claw to a split-brain patient's left hemisphere and a snow scene to his right hemisphere. How can we explain his response? (p. 102)

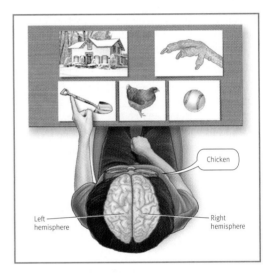

29. The _____ hemisphere of the brain is related to coarse language skills and visuospatial skills whereas the _____ hemisphere is related to fine-tuned language skills and actions. (p. 102)

30. Artists and other creative thinkers (are/aren't) able to make use only of their right hemisphere. (p. 103)

succeed with mypsych lab

1. Is one side of your brain working harder? Participate in this study on language and see how your results compare to others.
Hemispheric Experiment

2. Play the role of researcher and see if you can determine how the brain of a split-brain patient would see, hear, and touch certain stimuli.
Split-Brain Experiments

3. What does your brain look like? Listen as two psychologists discuss the different brain-mapping techniques used to see how your brain functions.
Brain Mapping

NATURE AND NURTURE: DID YOUR GENES—OR PARENTS—MAKE YOU DO IT? (pp. 104–107)

3.10 **Describe genes and how they influence observable traits**

Genes are made of deoxyribonucleic acid (DNA). They are arranged on chromosomes. We inherit this genetic material from our parents. Each gene carries a code to manufacture a particular protein. These proteins determine our observable traits.

31. _____ are the thin threads within a nucleus that carry genes. (p. 104)

32. _____ are made up of deoxyribonucleic acid (DNA), the material that stores everything cells need to reproduce themselves. (p. 104)

33. Our _____ is the set of our observable traits, and our genetic makeup is our _____ . (p. 104)

34. (Recessive/Dominant) genes work to mask other genes' effects. (p. 104)

35. How many chromosomes do humans have? How many are sex-linked? (p. 104)

36. The principle that organisms that possess adaptations survive and reproduce at a higher rate than other organisms is known as _____ _____ . (p. 104)

3.11 **Explain the concept of heritability and the misconceptions surrounding it**

Heritability refers to how differences in a trait across people are influenced by our genes as opposed to environmental factors. Highly heritable traits can sometimes change and the heritability of a trait can also change over time.

37. Scientists use _____ _____ to examine the roles of nature and nurture in the origins of traits, such as intelligence. (p. 105)

38. Heritability applies only to (a single individual/ groups of people). (p. 106)

39. Does high heritability imply a lack of malleability? Why or why not? (p. 106)

40. Analyses of how traits vary in individuals raised apart from their biological relatives are called _____ _____ . (p. 107)

SCIENTIFIC THINKING SKILLS
Questions and Summary

1 An analogy is often made between action potentials and the flushing of a toilet. Develop that analogy here and think of ways that they function in common. Be sure to consider all aspects of neural transmission of the messages.

2 While you are watching TV, you decide you need a snack but you want to wait for a commercial to come on before heading out to the kitchen. Describe the activity of your somatic nervous system in helping you get up and get a snack from the kitchen and then get back to watching TV. Be sure to consider that you want to inhibit going to the kitchen until the commercial comes on, that you then want to navigate over to the kitchen and remember that you went there to get a snack and return to the TV room before the commercials are over, and that you finally want to be able to pick up the story on the TV program when you return.

RULING OUT RIVAL HYPOTHESES
pp. 91, 93, 106

CORRELATION vs. CAUSATION
pp. 80, 93, 100

FALSIFIABILITY
pp. 82, 98

REPLICABILITY
pp. 89, 96

EXTRAORDINARY CLAIMS
p. 103

succeed with mypsychlab

1. Gain a better understanding of DNA and how it stores genetic information.
Building Blocks of Genetics

2. Will my child look like me? Explore how our genes dictate the color of our hair.
Dominant and Recessive Traits

3. How might your genes affect your offspring? Learn about the role a genetic counselor can play in helping patients understand their risk of passing along a disorder to a child.
Should You Consult a Genetic Counselor?

Sensation and Perception

What causes déjà vu? (p. 142)

Can our eyes detect only
a single particle of light? (p. 120)

Can certain blind people still "see" some of their surroundings?  (p. 123)

Do some people "taste" shapes or "hear" colors? (p. 117)

Why can't we taste food when we have a bad cold? (p. 133)

Figure 4.1 Separating Sensation from Perception. Hold this page about 10 inches from your face. Close your right eye and keep focusing on the white circle. Can you see the white *X*? Now slowly move the page toward your face and then away from it; at some point the white *X* will disappear and then reappear. Surprisingly, your brain supplies an illusory background pattern that fills in the white space occupied by the *X*. (*Source:* Glynn, 1999)

Before you read any further, try the exercise in **Figure 4.1** above. Were you surprised that the white *X* disappeared from view? Were you even more surprised that you filled the missing space occupied by the *X* with a mental image exactly matching the fancy background pattern?

Sensation and perception are the underlying processes operating in this visual illusion; it's an illusion because your brain perceived a complete pattern even though some of it was missing. **Sensation** refers to the detection of physical energy by the sense organs including the eyes, ears, skin, nose, and tongue, which then send information to the brain (see Chapter 3). **Perception** is the brain's interpretation of these raw sensory inputs. Sensation allows us to pick up the signals in our environments, and perception allows us to assemble these signals into something meaningful.

We often assume that our sensory systems are infallible and that our perceptions are perfect representations of the world around us. As we learned in Chapter 1, we term these beliefs *naive realism*. We'll discover in this chapter that naive realism is wrong; the world isn't precisely as we see it. Somewhere in our brains we reconstructed that fancy pattern in the figure and put it smack in the middle of the empty space; this perceptual process is called *filling-in*. Most of the time, filling-in is adaptive, as it helps us to make sense of our often confusing and chaotic perceptual worlds. But sometimes it can fool us, as in the case of illusions. We often blend the real with the imagined, going beyond the information given to us. By doing so, we simplify the world but make better sense of it in the process.

Two Sides of the Coin: Sensation and Perception

How do signals that make contact with our sense organs—like our eyes, ears, and tongue—become translated into information that our brains can interpret and act on? And how does the raw sensory information delivered to our brains become integrated with what we already know about the world, allowing us to recognize objects, avoid accidents, and (we hope) find our way out the door each morning?

Here's how. Our brain picks and chooses among the types of sensory information it uses, often relying on expectations and prior experiences to fill in the gaps and simplify processing. The end result is often more than the sum of its parts—and in some cases it's completely wrong! Errors in perception, like the illusion in Figure 4.1 and others we'll present in this chapter, are often extremely informative. They show us which parts of our sensory experiences are accurate and which parts our brains fill in for us. We'll first review what our sensory systems can accomplish and how they manage to transform physical signals in the outside world into neural activity in the "inside world"—our brains. Then we'll explore how and when our brains flesh out the details, moving beyond the raw sensory information available to us.

SENSATION: OUR SENSES AS DETECTIVES

Our senses enable us to see and hear, to feel a touch, determine body position, maintain balance, and smell and taste. Despite their differences, all of these senses rely on a mere handful of basic principles. **[LEARNING OBJECTIVE 4.1]**

Transduction: Going from the Outside World to Within. The first step in sensation is to convert external energies or substances into a "language" the nervous system understands. The process by which the nervous system converts an external energy or a substance into excitation or inhibition of neurons in the brain is **transduction.** A particular type of **sense receptor,** or specialized cell, transduces a specific stimulus. For example, specialized cells at the back of the eye transduce light and cells in a spiral-shaped organ in the ear transduce sound.

For all of our senses, activation is greatest when we first detect a stimulus. After that, the response declines in strength, a process called **sensory adaptation.** A good example is feeling the seat of a chair when we first sit on it. What happens in a matter of seconds? We no longer feel the chair, unless it's an extremely hard seat, or worse, has a thumbtack on it. The adaptation takes place at the level of the sense receptor. This receptor reacts strongly at first and then turns down its level of responding. Our nervous systems are probably arranged this way to conserve energy and attentional resources. If we didn't engage in sensory adaptation, we'd be attending to just about everything around us all of the time and wouldn't be able to devote our attention to the important things.

Psychophysics: Measuring the Barely Detectable. One of the earliest areas of psychological research was *psychophysics,* the study of how we perceive sensory stimuli based on their physical characteristics.

Absolute Threshold. Imagine that a researcher fits us with a pair of headphones and places us in a quiet room. She asks repeatedly if we've heard one of many very faint tones. Detection isn't an all-or-none state of affairs because human error increases as stimuli become weaker. Psychophysicists study phenomena like the **absolute threshold** of a stimulus—the lowest level of a stimulus we can detect on 50 percent of trials when that stimulus appears by itself, that is, with no other stimuli of that type present. Our absolute thresholds demonstrate how remarkably sensitive our sensory systems are. On a clear night, our visual systems can detect a single candle from 30 miles away. We can detect a smell from as few as fifty airborne odorant molecules; salamanders can pull off this feat with only one (Menini, Picco, & Firestein, 1995).

Just Noticeable Difference. Related to the absolute threshold is the **just noticeable difference (JND).** The JND is the smallest change in the intensity of a stimulus that we can

(© ScienceCartoonsPlus.com)

GLOSSARY

sensation
detection of physical energy by sense organs, which then send information to the brain

perception
the brain's interpretation of raw sensory inputs

transduction
the process of converting an external energy or substance into neural activity

sense receptor
specialized cell responsible for converting external stimuli into neural activity for a specific sensory system

sensory adaptation
a decline in activation within a sense receptor after initial activation

absolute threshold
lowest level of a stimulus needed for the nervous system to detect a stimulus 50 percent of the time

just noticeable difference (JND)
the smallest change in the intensity of a stimulus that we can detect

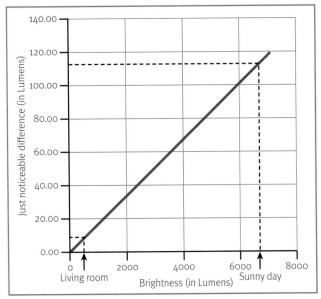

Figure 4.2 Just Noticeable Differences (JNDs) Adhere to Weber's Law. In this example, changes in light are shown measured in lumens, which are units equaling the amount of light generated by one candle standing one foot away. Weber's law states that the brighter the light, the more change in brightness is required for us to be able to notice a difference.

detect. The JND is relevant to our ability to distinguish a stronger from a weaker stimulus, like a soft noise from a slightly louder noise.

Weber's law says that there's a constant proportional relationship between the JND and the original stimulus intensity (see **Figure 4.2**). In plain language, the stronger the stimulus, the bigger the change needed for a change in stimulus intensity to be noticeable. Think of how much light we'd need to add to a brightly lit kitchen to notice an increase in illumination compared with the amount of light we'd need to add to a dark bedroom to notice a change in illumination. We'd need a lot of light in the first case and only a smidgeon in the second.

Signal Detection Theory. David Green and John Swets (1966) developed *signal detection theory* to help psychologists determine how we detect stimuli under uncertain conditions, as when we're driving on a foggy night and trying to decide whether there's an animal on the road in front of us. Think of how difficult it is to talk on a cell phone when there's static in the connection; that's high background noise. We need to increase the signal by shouting over the static or the other party won't understand us. If we have a good connection, however, others can easily understand us without our shouting. This point illustrates the concept of the *signal-to-noise ratio:* It becomes harder to detect a signal as background noise increases. Low signal-to-noise ratios may lead us to miss detecting a stimulus. They may also lead us to say we detect a stimulus when there wasn't one, a behavior Green and Swets called a "false alarm." Different individuals and different contexts can result in different "thresholds" or levels of signal that result in someone saying she or he detects a stimulus. For example, if you're lounging in a park on a Saturday morning, you may be less likely to notice a rustling sound in a nearby tree than if you're a bird watcher hoping for a sighting of a rare species of hawk known to live in the area.

WHAT DO *you* THINK?

If you were anticipating a crucial telephone call and kept jumping up at the slightest noise to grab the phone, how would signal detection theory classify your behavior?

Sensory Systems Stick to One Sense—Or Do They?
It would make sense for the different sensory systems to operate completely independently in the brain. Specific nerve energies follow specific pathways up to the cerebral cortex, right? As a result, we might not expect much in the way of *cross-modal processing,* that is, the mixing of senses across brain areas.

Yet this expectation turns out to be false. Scientists have found many examples of cross-modal processing that produce different perceptual experiences than either modality provides by itself. One striking example is the *McGurk effect* (McGurk & MacDonald, 1976). This effect demonstrates that we integrate visual and auditory information when processing spoken language, and our brains automatically calculate the most probable sound, given the information from the two sources. In the McGurk effect, hearing the audio track of one syllable (such as "ba") spoken repeatedly while seeing a video track of a different syllable being spoken (such as "ga") results in the perceptual experience of a different third sound (such as "da"). This third sound is the brain's best "guess" at integrating the two conflicting sources of information.

Sir Francis Galton (1880) was the first to describe another example of cross-modal processing called *synesthesia,* a condition in which people experience cross-modal sensations, like hearing sounds when they see colors—sometimes called "colored hearing"—or even tasting colors (Cytowic, 1993). Synesthesia may be an extreme version of the cross-modal responses that most of us experience from time to time, as we described earlier (Rader & Tellegen, 1987). The great Finnish composer Jean Sibelius saw notes as colors and even claimed to smell them. In one case, he asked a worker to repaint his kitchen stove in the key of F major. No one knows for sure how widespread synesthesia is, but some estimates put it at no higher than about 1 in 2,500 people (Baron-Cohen et al., 1993). **Figure 4.3** illustrates a clever test that detects one type of synesthesia.

These cross-modal effects may reflect "cross-talk" among different brain regions. Visual areas may connect directly to auditory areas, for example. But there's an alternative explanation: In some cases, a single brain region may serve double duty, helping to process multiple senses. For example, neurons in the auditory cortex tuned to sound also respond weakly to touch (Fu et al., 2003).

Figure 4.3 Are You Synesthetic? Although most of us see the image on the left as a bunch of jumbled numbers, some synesthetes perceive it as looking like the image on the right. Synesthesia makes it much easier to find the 2s embedded in a field of 5s. (*Source:* Adapted from Ramachandran & Hubbard, 2001)

RULING OUT RIVAL HYPOTHESES
Have important alternative explanations for the findings been excluded?

PERCEPTION: WHEN OUR SENSES MEET OUR MINDS

Now that we've encountered the basic principles governing how we process sensory information, we'll embark on an exciting voyage into how our minds organize the little pieces of sensory data into more meaningful concepts. What's so remarkable about our mind's ability to bring together so much data? The answer is that our mind doesn't rely only on what's out there in the sensory field: It pieces together (a) what's in the sensory field, along with (b) what was just there a moment ago and (c) what we remember from our past. **[LEARNING OBJECTIVE 4.2]** Because our brains rely so much on what we know and have experienced, we can usually get away with economizing in our sensory processing and making educated guesses about what sensory information is telling us. Moreover, a pretty decent guess with fewer neurons is more efficient than a more sure answer with a huge number of neurons. As cognitive misers (see Chapter 2), we generally try to get by with as little neural firepower as we can.

Figure 4.4 What Do You See? Due to the influence of top-down processing, reading the caption "saxophone player" beneath this ambiguous figure tends to produce a different perception than reading the caption "woman."

Parallel Processing. We can attend to many sense modalities simultaneously, a phenomenon called *parallel processing* (Rumelhart & McClelland, 1986). Two important concepts that go along with parallel processing are **bottom-up** and **top-down processing.** In bottom-up processing, we construct a whole stimulus from its parts. An example is perceiving an object on the basis of its edges. This kind of processing is stimulus-driven and results from activity in the primary visual cortex (see Chapter 3), followed by processing in the association cortex. In contrast, top-down processing is conceptually driven and influenced by our beliefs and expectations.

Some perceptions rely more heavily on bottom-up processing (Koch, 1993), others on top-down processing (McClelland & Plaut, 1993). In most cases, though, bottom-up and top-down processing work hand in hand (Patel & Sathian, 2000). We can illustrate this point by how we process ambiguous figures. Depending on our expectations, we typically perceive these figures differently. The top-down influence of thinking of a jazz musician biases our bottom-up processing of the shapes in **Figure 4.4** and increases the chances we'll perceive a saxophone player. In contrast, if our top-down expectation were

GLOSSARY

bottom-up processing
constructing a mental understanding of a stimulus by putting together the raw sensory information into a complete whole

top-down processing
constructing a mental understanding of a stimulus using our existing knowledge and expectations

of a woman's face, our sensory-based bottom-up processing would change accordingly. (Can you see both figures?) The influence that our expectations have on our perceptions is called a **perceptual set.**

Selective Attention: How We Focus on Particular Inputs.

Like a TV set with all channels switched on at once, our brains are constantly receiving inputs from all our sensory channels. How do we keep from becoming hopelessly confused? **Selective attention** allows us to select one channel and turn off the others or at least turn down their volume. Donald Broadbent's (1957) *filter theory of attention* views attention as a bottleneck through which information passes. This narrow entryway allows only the most important information through—and only as much of it as we can process at one time, filtering out the less important stimuli from our focus of attention. This theory accounts for a lot of the evidence regarding how we selectively attend to some stimuli over others. However, Anne Treisman (1960) presented an alternative account suggesting that "filtered out" information isn't being discarded completely. Information we've supposedly filtered out of our attention is still being processed at some level—even when we're not aware of it (Beaman, Bridges, & Scott, 2007). One phenomenon that illustrates this is the *cocktail party effect.* This refers to our ability to detect important information such as our own names even in a conversation that doesn't involve us in a noisy restaurant or at a crowded party. This finding tells us that the filter inside our brain, which selects what will and won't receive our attention, is more complex than just an "on" or "off" switch (see **Figure 4.5**)—there is some monitoring of "unattended" stimuli going on after all.

RULING OUT RIVAL HYPOTHESES
Have important alternative explanations for the findings been excluded?

Figure 4.5 The Cocktail Party Effect. The cocktail party effect helps explain how we can become aware of stimuli outside of our immediate attention when it's relevant to us—like our names.

I saw Jenny yesterday...

The Binding Problem: Putting the Pieces Together.

The *binding problem* is one of the great mysteries of psychology. It refers to how our brains take multiple pieces of information and combine them to represent something concrete, like an apple. An apple looks red and round, feels smooth, tastes sweet and tart, and smells, well, apple-ish. Any one of its characteristics in isolation isn't an apple or even a part of an apple. How do our brains put together all of the information to recognize an object from its various parts? We don't know for sure, but one suggestion is that fast, coordinated activity across multiple cortical areas does the trick (Engel & Singer, 2001). Binding may explain many aspects of perception and attention. When we see the world, we rely on shape, motion, color, and depth cues, each of which requires different amounts of time to detect individually (Bartels & Zeki, 2006). Yet our minds seamlessly combine these visual cues into a single unified perception of a scene. That's binding.

SUBLIMINAL INFORMATION PROCESSING

You're home on a Sunday afternoon, curled up on your couch watching a movie on TV. Within a span of a few minutes you see three or four quick flashes of light on the screen. Only a few minutes later, you're seized with an uncontrollable desire to eat a hamburger. Did an advertiser sneak several photographs of a hamburger in the midst of the movie, so quickly you didn't realize it? If we can detect stimuli without knowing it, does that affect our behavior?

Subliminal Perception.

The American public has long been fascinated with the possibility of *subliminal perception*—the processing of sensory information that occurs below the level of conscious awareness (Cheesman & Merikle, 1986; Rogers & Smith, 1993). To study subliminal perception, researchers typically present a word or photo-

GLOSSARY

perceptual set
the influence that expectations have on perception

selective attention
process of selecting one sensory channel and ignoring or minimizing others

graph extremely quickly, say at 50 milliseconds ($\frac{1}{20}$ of a second). They frequently follow this stimulus immediately with a *mask,* another stimulus (like a pattern of dots or lines) that blocks out mental processing of the subliminal stimulus. When subjects can't correctly identify the content of the stimulus at better than chance levels, researchers deem it subliminal.

The claim for subliminal perception is extraordinary, but the evidence supporting it is compelling (Seitz & Watanabe, 2003). When investigators subliminally trigger emotions by exposing subjects to words related to anger, these subjects are more likely to rate other people as hostile (Bargh & Pietromonaco, 1982). Similarly, graduate students in psychology who are subliminally exposed to photographs of the smiling face of a postdoctoral research assistant in their laboratory rate their research projects more positively than those exposed to the disapproving face of their primary professor (Baldwin, Carrell, & Lopez, 1990).

Subliminal Persuasion. Even though we're subject to subliminal perception, that doesn't mean we numbly succumb to *subliminal persuasion.* In other words, subliminal information doesn't necessarily influence our product choices, votes in elections, and life decisions. For decades, Americans have envisioned nightmare scenarios in which advertisers flash subliminal messages in movies and television programs, leading them to buy merchandise against their will (Key, 1973). Yet research demonstrates that subliminal persuasion, although not impossible (Epley, Savitsky, & Kachelski, 1999; Weinberger & Hardaway, 1990), is unlikely in most cases. That's because we can't engage in much, if any, in-depth processing of the *meaning* of subliminal stimuli (Rosen, Glasgow, & Moore, 2003). As a result, these stimuli probably can't produce large-scale or enduring changes in our attitudes, let alone our everyday decisions.

Still, subliminal self-help audiotapes and videotapes are a multimillion-dollar-a-year industry in the United States alone. They purportedly contain repeated subliminal messages (such as "Feel better about yourself") designed to influence our behavior or emotions. In stores and on the Internet, we can find subliminal tapes for self-esteem, memory, sexual performance, and weight loss (Rosen et al., 2003). Yet scores of studies show that subliminal self-help tapes are ineffective (Eich & Hyman, 1991; Moore, 1992).

EXTRAORDINARY CLAIMS
Is the evidence as convincing as the claim?

Fict-OID

MYTH: In the late 1950s, advertisers subliminally flashed the words "Eat popcorn" and "Drink Coke" during films in a New Jersey movie theater over the span of several weeks. The rates of popcorn and Coca-Cola consumption in the theater skyrocketed.

REALITY: The originator of this claim, advertising expert James Vicary, later admitted that it was a hoax cooked up to generate publicity for his failing business (Pratkanis, 1992).

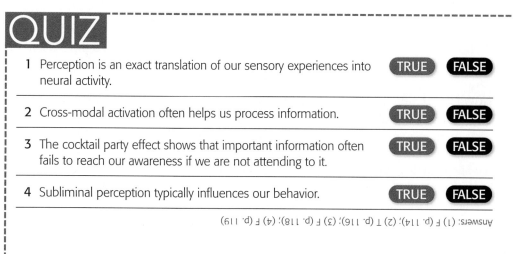

QUIZ

1 Perception is an exact translation of our sensory experiences into neural activity. `TRUE` `FALSE`

2 Cross-modal activation often helps us process information. `TRUE` `FALSE`

3 The cocktail party effect shows that important information often fails to reach our awareness if we are not attending to it. `TRUE` `FALSE`

4 Subliminal perception typically influences our behavior. `TRUE` `FALSE`

Answers: (1) F (p. 114); (2) T (p. 116); (3) F (p. 118); (4) F (p. 119)

PEARSON
mypsych lab

▼ Are our minds being bombarded with subliminal messages by the media? Listen to the podcast titled "Subliminal Messages" at www.mypsychlab.com to find out.

Podcast: Subliminal Messages
January 10, 2008 — editor

This podcast episode features a conversation between two psychologists who discuss the controversial topic of subliminal messages.

◀) Click here to listen to this podcast.

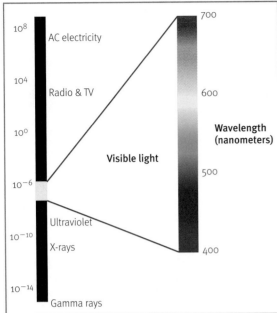

Figure 4.6 The Visible Spectrum Is a Subset of the Electromagnetic Spectrum. Visible light is electromagnetic energy between ultraviolet and infrared. Humans are sensitive to wavelengths ranging from slightly less than 400 nanometers (violet) to slightly more than 700 nanometers (red).

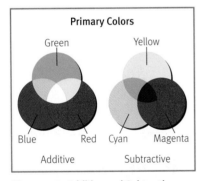

Figure 4.7 Additive and Subtractive Color Mixing. Additive color mixing of light differs from subtractive color mixing of paint.

GLOSSARY

brightness
intensity of reflected light that reaches our eyes

hue
color of light

cornea
part of the eye containing transparent cells that focus light on the retina

Seeing: The Visual System

Sight is the most heavily studied sense—perhaps because it plays such a fundamental role in most people's everyday lives. Have you ever tried walking through a familiar space like your room or a neighborhood street with your eyes closed or the lights out? No matter how many times you've walked through the space, you're likely to trip or become disoriented. We are highly dependent on our visual sense.

LIGHT: THE ENERGY OF LIFE

One of the central players in our visual perception of the world is light, a form of electromagnetic energy composed of fluctuating electric and magnetic waves. Visible light has a *wavelength* in the hundreds of nanometers (a nanometer is one billionth of a meter).

As we can see in **Figure 4.6,** humans can detect only a narrow range of wavelengths of light; this range is the human visible spectrum. Each animal species detects a specific visible range, which can extend slightly above or below the human visible spectrum. For example, butterflies are sensitive to all of the wavelengths we detect in addition to ultraviolet light, which has a shorter wavelength than violet light.

When light reaches an object, part of that light gets reflected by the object and part gets absorbed. **Brightness** is the intensity of the reflected light that reaches our eyes. Completely white objects reflect all the light shone on them and absorb none of it, whereas black objects do the opposite. Psychologists call the color of light **hue.** We're sensitive to three primary colors of light: red, green, and blue. The mixing of varying amounts of these three primary colors—called *additive color mixing*—can produce any color **(Figure 4.7)**. Mixing equal amounts of red, green, and blue light produces white light. This process is quite different from the mixing of colored pigments in paint or ink, called *subtractive color mixing*. As we can see in most printer color ink cartridges, the primary colors of pigment are yellow, cyan, and magenta, and mixing them all together produces a dark color (Figure 4.7).

THE EYE: HOW WE REPRESENT THE VISUAL REALM

Without our eyes we couldn't sense or perceive much of anything about light, aside from the heat it generates. Keep an "eye" on **Figure 4.8** as we tour the structures of the eye.

How Light Enters the Eye. Different parts of the eye allow in varying amounts of light. This feature is critical to our ability to see in bright sunshine or in a dark room. Other parts of the eye ensure that what we see stays in focus. **[LEARNING OBJECTIVE 4.3]**

Although poets have told us that the eyes are windows into the soul, when we look people squarely in the eye all we can see is their sclera, iris, and pupil (see Figure 4.8). The sclera is simply the white of the eye.

The iris is the colored part of the eye, usually blue, brown, green, or hazel. The chemicals responsible for eye color are called *pigments*. Only two pigments—melanin, which is brown, and lipochrome, which is yellowish-brown—account for all of the remarkable variations in eye colors across people. Blue eyes contain a small amount of yellow pigment and little or no brown pigment; green and hazel eyes, an intermediate amount of brown pigment; and brown eyes, a lot of brown pigment. The reason blue eyes appear blue and not yellow, is that blue light is scattered more by irises containing less pigment. Popular

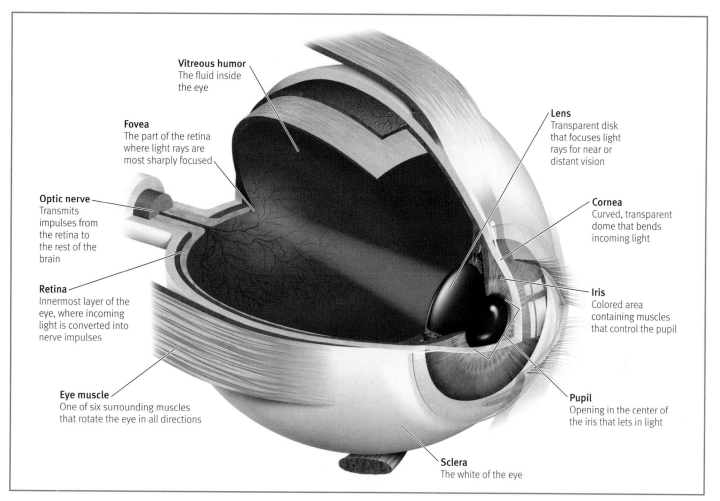

Vitreous humor
The fluid inside
the eye

Fovea
The part of the retina
where light rays are
most sharply focused

Optic nerve
Transmits
impulses from
the retina
to the rest of the
brain

Retina
Innermost layer of the
eye, where incoming
light is converted into
nerve impulses

Eye muscle
One of six surrounding muscles
that rotate the eye in all directions

Lens
Transparent disk
that focuses light
rays for near or
distant vision

Cornea
Curved, transparent
dome that bends
incoming light

Iris
Colored area
containing muscles
that control the pupil

Pupil
Opening in the center of
the iris that lets in light

Sclera
The white of the eye

Figure 4.8 The Key Parts of the Eye. (*Source:* Adapted from Dorling Kindersley)

belief notwithstanding, our irises don't change color over brief periods of time, although they may seem to do so depending on lighting conditions.

The pupil is a circular hole through which light enters the eye. The shrinking of the pupil is a reflex response to light or objects coming toward us. If we walk out of a building into bright sunshine, our eyes respond with the *pupillary reflex* to decrease the amount of light allowed into them. This reflex occurs simultaneously in both eyes, so shining a flashlight into one eye triggers it in both.

The dilation (expansion) of the pupil also has psychological significance. Our pupils dilate when we're trying to process complex information, like difficult math problems (Beatty, 1982; Karatekin, 2004). They also dilate when we view someone we find physically attractive (Tombs & Silverman, 2004). This finding may help to explain why people find faces with large pupils more attractive than faces with small pupils, even when they're oblivious to this physical difference (Hess, 1965; Tomlinson, Hicks, & Pellegrini, 1978).

The Cornea, Lens, and Retina.

The **cornea** is a curved, transparent layer covering the iris and pupil. Its curvature is responsible for bending incoming light to focus it on the **retina,** a thin membrane at the back of the eye. We can think of the retina as a "movie screen" onto which light from the world is projected. It contains a hundred million sense receptor cells. The **fovea** is the central part of the retina and is responsible for **acuity,** or sharpness of vision. We need a sharp image to read, drive, sew, or do just about anything requiring fine detail.

We tend to find faces with larger pupils (in this case, the face on the left) more attractive than those with smaller pupils. (*Source:* Hess, 1965; Tombs & Silverman, 2004)

GLOSSARY

retina
membrane at the back of the eye responsible for converting light into neural activity

fovea
central portion of the retina

acuity
sharpness of vision

The **lens** also bends light, but unlike the cornea, the lens changes its curvature. In a process called **accommodation,** the lenses change shape to focus light on the back of the eyes; in this way, they adapt to different lighting conditions. Accommodation can either make the lens "flat," enabling us to see distant objects, or "fat," enabling us to focus on nearby objects. For nearby objects, a fat lens works better because it more effectively bends the scattered light and focuses it on a single point at the back of the eye.

How much our eyes need to bend the path of light to focus properly depends on the curve of our corneas and overall shape of our eyes. Nearsightedness, or *myopia,* results when images are focused in front of the retina, due to our cornea being too steep or our eyes too long (see **Figure 4.9a**). Nearsightedness, as the name implies, is an ability to see close objects well coupled with an inability to see far objects well. Farsightedness, or *hyperopia,* results when our cornea is too flat or our eyes too short **(Figure 4.9b).** Farsightedness, as the name implies, is an ability to see far objects well coupled with an inability to see near objects well.

Rods and Cones. The retina contains two types of cells. The far more plentiful **rods,** which are long and narrow, enable us to see basic shapes and forms. We rely on rods to see in low levels of light. There are no rods in the fovea, so we rely more on our peripheral vision at night or in a darkened room. Rods detect light but not color.

The less numerous **cones,** which are shaped like small cones, give us our color vision. Cones require more light than do rods. However, rods are slower to adapt to light changes than cones which explains why we go through a period of *dark adaptation,* during which our ability to make things out in the dark gradually improves.

The Optic Nerve. The *optic nerve* travels from the retina to the rest of the brain. At the spot where the optic nerve connects to the retina, we have a **blind spot,** a part of the visual field that we can't see. Why don't we notice our blind spots? Fortunately, our two eyes provide slightly different perspectives so that the blind spot in one eye is filled in by information from the other. And, as we saw at the beginning of the chapter (refer back to Figure 4.1), the visual areas of our brains also help us to fill in the gaps.

After the optic nerves leave both eyes, they come to a fork in the road called the *optic chiasm.* Half the axons cross in the optic chiasm, and the other half stay on the same side. Within a short distance, the optic nerves enter the brain, sending most of their axons to the visual thalamus and then to the primary visual cortex—called V1—the primary route for visual perception (see **Figure 4.10**).

VISUAL PERCEPTION

Now that we know how our nervous system gathers and transmits visual information from the eye, we can examine how we perceive shape, motion, color, and depth, all of

GLOSSARY

lens
part of the eye that changes curvature to keep images in focus

accommodation
changing the shape of the lens to focus on objects near or far

rods
receptor cells in the retina allowing us to see in low levels of light

cones
receptor cells in the retina that allow us to see in color

blind spot
part of the visual field we can't see, where the optic nerve connects to the retina

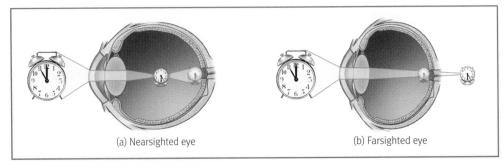

(a) Nearsighted eye　　　　(b) Farsighted eye

Figure 4.9 Nearsighted and Farsighted Eyes. Nearsightedness or farsightedness results when light is focused in front of or behind the retina, respectively. (*Source:* Adapted from St. Luke's Cataract & Laser Institute)

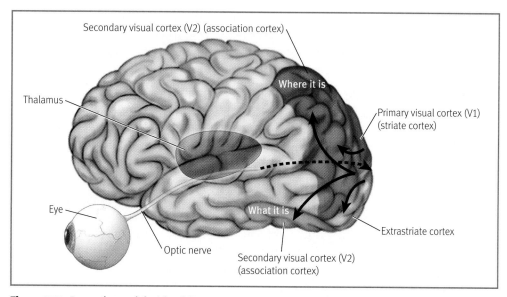

Figure 4.10 Perception and the Visual Cortex. Visual information from the retina travels to the visual thalamus. Next, the visual thalamus sends inputs to the primary visual cortex (V1), then along two visual pathways to the secondary visual cortex (V2). One pathway leads to the parietal lobe, which processes visual form, position, and motion; and one to the temporal lobe, which processes visual form and color.

which are handled by different parts of the visual cortex (see Figure 4.10). Even though different parts of the brain process different aspects of visual perception, we perceive whole objects and unified scenes, not isolated components. By compensating for missing information, our perceptual systems help us make sense of the world. **[LEARNING OBJECTIVE 4.4]**

How We Perceive Shape and Contour. In the 1960s, David Hubel and Torsten Wiesel sought to unlock the secrets of how we perceive shape and form; their work eventually led to a Nobel Prize. They used cats as their subjects because their visual responses are much like ours. Hubel and Wiesel (1962, 1963) recorded electrical activity in the visual cortexes of cats while presenting them with visual stimuli on a screen **(Figure 4.11).** They found that many cells in V1 respond to slits of light of a specific orientation, for example, vertical, horizontal, or oblique lines or edges.

Feature Detection. Neurons that fire in response to specific patterns are called *feature detectors* because they detect lines and edges. But there are other neurons that act as feature detectors for other kinds of perceptual information, including lines of specific lengths, complex shapes, and even moving objects.

As we saw in Figure 4.10, visual information travels from V1 to higher visual areas along two major routes. One path goes to the upper parts of the parietal lobe where location and motion information are processed. The other path goes to the lower part of the temporal lobe where form and color of objects are processed.

Blindsight. *Blindsight* is a remarkable phenomenon that demonstrates the involvement of secondary association areas in visual processing. People whose blindness results from damage to V1 can sometimes make correct guesses about things in their environment, even though they can't see them and report that they are just guessing. Because blindsight operates outside the bounds of conscious activity, some nonscientists have suggested that it may be a supernatural phenomenon. Yet there's a parsimonious natural explanation: People with

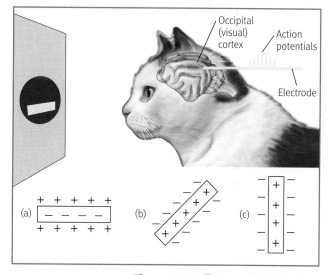

Figure 4.11 Cells Respond to Slits of Light of a Particular Orientation.
Top: Hubel and Wiesel studied activity in the visual cortex of cats viewing slits of light on a screen. *Bottom:* Visual responses were specific to slits of dark on light (minuses on pluses—a) or light on dark (pluses on minuses—b), which were of particular orientations, such as horizontal, oblique, or vertical—(c). Cells in the visual cortex also detected edges.

OCCAM'S RAZOR
Does a simpler explanation fit the data just as well?

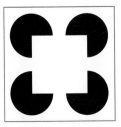

Figure 4.12 Kanizsa Square. This Kanizsa square illustrates subjective contours. The square you perceive in the middle of this figure is imaginary. (*Source:* Herrmann & Friederici, 2001)

blindsight have suffered damage to V1, so that route of information flow to visual association areas is blocked. Coarser visual information still reaches the visual association cortex without going through V1, so this visual information probably accounts for blindsight (Moore, Rodman, Repp, et al., 1995; Stoerig & Cowey, 1997; Weiskrantz, 1986).

Gestalt: Filling in the Blanks. Our brains often provide missing information to help us make sense of a stimulus, a phenomenon called *subjective contours.* Gaetano Kanizsa sparked interest in this phenomenon in 1955. As **Figure 4.12** illustrates, a mere hint of four corners can give rise to the perception of an imaginary square.

Gestalt principles are rules governing how we perceive objects as wholes within their overall context (*Gestalt* is a German word meaning "whole"). Gestalt principles of perception help to explain why we see much of our world as unified figures or forms rather than as a confusing jumble of lines and curves. These principles provide a road map for how we organize and make sense of our perceptual world. Gestalt psychologists identified a set of principles that they believed accounted for the ways we impose organization on our perceptual experiences. For example, objects physically close to each other tend to be perceived as unified wholes such as the columns of lines we perceive in **Figure 4.13a.** This illustrates the Gestalt principle of proximity. Also when partial visual information is present, the mind fills in what's missing to create a coherent whole, demonstrating the principle of closure **(Figure 4.13b).**

Figure-ground is another Gestalt principle. Perceptually, we make an instant decision to focus attention on what we believe to be the central figure and largely ignore what we believe to be the background. We can view some figures, such as Rubin's vase illusion, shown in **Figure 4.13c,** in two ways. The vase can be the figure, in which case we ignore the background. If we look again, we can see an image in the background: two faces looking at each other. Rubin's vase illusion is also an example of a *bistable* image, an image we can perceive in one of two ways. When we look at bistable images, we can typically perceive them only one way at a time.

The Gestalt principle of similarity says that we group items based on their similar appearance. In **Figure 4.13d,** we perceive the dots as forming 6 horizontal lines rather than 6 vertical lines. The Gestalt principle of continuity leads us to perceive the cross shown in **Figure 4.13e** as one long vertical line crossing over one long horizontal line rather than 4 smaller line segments joining together. Finally, the principle of symmetry depicted in **Figure 4.13f** demonstrates that two symmetrical figures tend to be grouped together as a single unit. Each of these principles (and many more) accurately describes the subjective organization that our brains impose on sensory information.

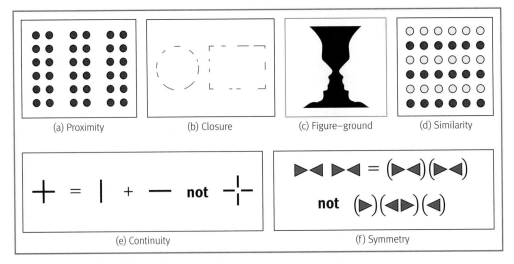

(a) Proximity (b) Closure (c) Figure–ground (d) Similarity

(e) Continuity (f) Symmetry

Figure 4.13 Gestalt Principles of Perception. As Gestalt psychologists discovered, we use a variety of principles to help us organize the world.

Face Recognition. Our ability to recognize familiar faces is one of our most important perceptual tasks. What features of a face do we use to recognize it? We don't need an exact replica every time to do so. Caricature artists have known this fact for a long time and amused us with their versions of famous faces, usually with some feature exaggerated way out of proportion. Why can we recognize these wacky faces? As we've already learned, our brains get by with only partial information, because we acquire information from the surrounding context and our preconceptions.

Do individual neurons respond specifically to certain faces? Scientists have known for some time that the lower part of the temporal lobe responds to faces (refer back to Figure 4.10). As we'll learn in Chapter 6, researchers have recently identified neurons in the human hippocampus that fire selectively in response to celebrity faces, such as Halle Berry (Quiroga, Reddy, Kreiman, et al., 2005). In the 1960s, Jerry Lettvin half-jokingly proposed that each neuron in the brain might store a single memory, like the recollection of our grandmother sitting in our living room when we were children. Lettvin coined the term *grandmother cell* to represent this argument, assuming it could be easily falsified (Horgan, 1999). Certain neurons, such as those responding to Halle Berry, are suggestive of the grandmother cell idea, but we shouldn't be too quick to accept this possibility. Even though individual cells may respond to Berry, many other neurons in other lobes of the brain probably chime in too. Researchers can make recordings from only a small number of neurons at a time, so we don't know what the rest of the brain is doing. At present, the most parsimonious hypothesis is that sprawling networks of neurons, rather than single cells, are responsible for face recognition.

How We Perceive Motion.

The brain judges how things in our world are constantly changing by comparing visual frames, like those in a movie. Perceiving the motion of a car coming toward us relies on this kind of motion detection, and we couldn't cross the street, let alone drive a car, without it. We can also be fooled into seeing motion when it's not there. Moving closer to and farther from certain images produces the illusion of motion, as we can see in **Figure 4.14.** The *phi phenomenon,* discovered by Gestalt psychologist Max Wertheimer, is the illusory perception of movement produced by the successive flashing of images, like the flashing lights that seem to circle around a movie marquee. These lights are actually jumping from one spot on the marquee to another, but they appear continuous. The phi phenomenon and other illusions show that our perceptions of what's moving and what's not are based on only partial information, with our brains making their best guesses about what's missing. Luckily, many of these guesses are accurate or at least accurate enough for us to get along in everyday life.

How We Perceive Color.

Color delights our senses and stirs our imagination. We use the lower visual pathway leading to the temporal lobe to process color information (refer back to Figure 4.10), but it hardly starts there. Different theories of color perception explain different aspects of our ability to detect color, enabling us to see the world, watch TV, and enjoy movies, all in vibrant color.

Trichromatic theory is the idea that we base our color vision on three primary colors—blue, green, and red. Trichromatic theory is consistent with the fact that we have three kinds of cones, each most sensitive to a particular wavelength (color) of light. Given that the three types of cones were discovered in the 1960s (Brown & Wald, 1964), it's perhaps surprising that Thomas Young and Hermann von Helmholtz described trichromatic theory over 100 years earlier. Young's theory (1802) proposed that our vision is sensitive to three primary colors of light. Hermann von Helmholtz (1850) replicated and extended Young's proposal by testing the colors that color-blind subjects could distinguish, and the Young-Helmholtz trichromatic theory of color vision was born.

FALSIFIABILITY
Can the claim be disproved?

OCCAM'S RAZOR
Does a simpler explanation fit the data just as well?

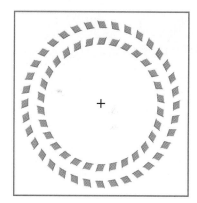

Figure 4.14 Moving Spiral Illusion. Focus on the plus sign in the middle of the figure and move the page closer to your face and then farther away. The two rings should appear to move in opposite directions, and those directions should reverse when you reverse the direction in which you move the page. (*Source:* cooloptical illusions.com)

GLOSSARY

trichromatic theory
idea that color vision is based on our sensitivity to three different colors

REPLICABILITY
Can the results be duplicated in other studies?

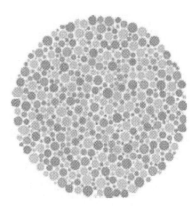

Figure 4.15 The Ishihara Test for Red-Green Color Blindness. If you can't see the two-digit number, you probably have red-green color blindness. This condition is common, especially among males.

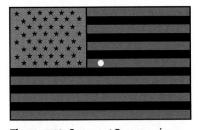

Figure 4.16 Opponent Processes in Action. Find a patch of blank white wall or place a blank sheet of white paper nearby before you begin. Then relax your eyes and fix your gaze on the white dot in the image above for at least 30 seconds without looking around or away. Afterwards, stare at the white wall or paper for a few seconds. What do you see?

Persons with **color blindness** can't see all colors. Color blindness is most often due to the absence or reduced number of one or more types of cones stemming from genetic abnormalities. Most color-blind individuals are missing only one type of cone. Most common is red-green color blindness. Those with red-green color blindness see considerable color but are missing the cone that allows them to distinguish red from green. A common test for red-green color blindness is shown in **Figure 4.15;** many males have this condition but don't even know it because it doesn't interfere much with their everyday functioning.

WHAT DO *you* THINK?

What evolutionary advantage might there be in seeing in color rather than black and white? Can you think of situations in which people with red-green color blindness might be at a disadvantage?

Trichromatic theory does a good job of accounting for the different types of cones in the eye and how they work together to detect the full range of colors. But further research revealed a phenomenon that trichromatic theory can't explain—afterimages. Afterimages occur when we've stared at one color for a long time and then look away and see a different colored replica of the same image mysteriously appear as in **Figure 4.16.** What was difficult to explain was why each color always resulted in the same afterimage color (such as afterimages for red always appearing green). It turns out that afterimages are a result of how the visual cortex processes information delivered from the rods and cones. A new theory called *opponent process* theory was developed to explain how the visual cortex allows red and green, blue and yellow, and black and white to compete for activation. When the color red has been activated in the brain for a particular area of a visual display, the neurons respond by rebounding to the opposite extreme, leading to the experience of seeing green. Although trichromatic theory accurately explains how color information is processed by the sense receptors in the eye, opponent process theory better explains how the visual cortex interprets the color information it receives.

How We Perceive Depth. **Depth perception** is the ability to see spatial relations in three dimensions; it enables us to reach for a glass and grasp it rather than knock it over and spill its contents. We need to have some idea of how close or far we are from objects to navigate around our environments. We use two kinds of cues to gauge depth: **monocular depth cues,** which rely on one eye alone, and **binocular depth cues,** which require both eyes.

Monocular Cues. We can perceive three dimensions using only one eye. Each eye provides independent cues to depth including:

- *Relative size:* More distant objects look smaller than closer objects.
- *Texture gradient:* The texture of objects becomes less apparent as objects move farther away.
- *Interposition:* One object that's closer blocks our view of an object behind it. From this fact, we know which object is closer and which is farther away.
- *Linear perspective:* The outlines of rooms or buildings converge as distance increases. In reality, lines in parallel never meet, but they appear to do so at great distances.

GLOSSARY

color blindness
inability to see some or all colors

depth perception
ability to judge distance and three-dimensional relations

monocular depth cues
stimuli that enable us to judge depth using only one eye

binocular depth cues
stimuli that enable us to judge depth using both eyes

- *Light and shadow:* Objects cast shadows that give us a sense of their three-dimensional form.
- *Motion parallax:* Nearby objects seem to move faster than those far away traveling at the same speed because near objects move across the retina more quickly.

Binocular Cues. Our visual system is set up so that half of the axons in the optic nerve for each eye cross to the other side and half stay on the same side before entering the brain. Our brains compare visual information from both eyes. These comparisons form the basis of binocular depth perception.

- *Binocular disparity:* Like the two lenses from a pair of binoculars, our left and right eyes transmit quite different information for near objects but see distant objects similarly. This depth cue is easy to demonstrate. Close one of your eyes and hold a pen up about a foot away from your face, lining the top of it up with a distant point on the wall (like a doorknob or corner of a picture frame). Then, hold the pen steady while alternating which of your eyes is open. You'll find that although the pen is lined up with one eye, it's no longer lined up when you switch to the other eye, whereas the distant object remains lined up. Each eye sees the world a bit differently, and our brains ingeniously make use of this information to judge depth.

- *Binocular convergence:* When we look at nearby objects, we reflexively focus on them by using our eye muscles to turn our eyes inward, a phenomenon called *convergence.* Our brains are aware of how much our eyes are converging, and they use this information to estimate distance.

This painting depicts a scene that provides monocular cues to depth.

(a) *Relative size:* The house is drawn approximately as high as the fence post, but we know the house is much bigger, so it must be considerably farther away.
(b) *Texture gradient:* The grasses in front of the fence are drawn as individual blades but those in the field behind are shown with almost no detail.
(c) *Interposition:* The tree at the corner of the house is blocking part of the house, so we know that the tree is closer to us than the house is.

Depth Perception Appears in Infancy. We can judge depth as soon as we learn to crawl. Eleanor Gibson established this phenomenon in a classic experimental setup called the *visual cliff* (Gibson, 1991; Gibson & Walk, 1960). The typical visual cliff consists of a table covered with a checkered cloth that drops to the floor, which is covered by the same checkered cloth. A clear glass surface extends from the table out over the floor. Infants between 6 and 14 months of age hesitate to crawl over the glass elevated several feet above the floor, even when their mothers beckon. The visual cliff findings tell us that depth cues are present soon after birth.

The visual cliff tests infants' ability to judge depth.

Perceptual Constancy. The process by which we perceive stimuli consistently across varied conditions is **perceptual constancy.** There are several kinds of perceptual constancy—shape, size, and color constancy. Consider a door we view from differing perspectives. Because of *shape constancy,* we still see a door as a door whether it's completely shut, barely open, or more fully open, even though these shapes differ markedly from each other.

Color constancy is our ability to perceive color consistently across different levels of illumination. Consider a group of firemen dressed in bright yellow jackets. Their jackets look bright yellow even in very low levels of ambient light. That's because our perceptual apparatus evaluates the color of an object in the context of background light and surrounding colors.

GLOSSARY

perceptual constancy
the process by which we perceive stimuli consistently across varied conditions

The man standing toward the back of the bridge looks to be of normal size, but when the exact duplicate image appears in the foreground, it looks like a toy because of size constancy.

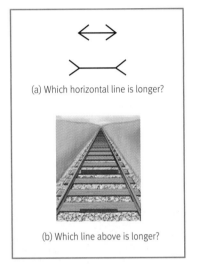

(a) Which horizontal line is longer?

(b) Which line above is longer?

Figure 4.17 **How Well Can You Judge Relative Size?** The Müller-Lyer (a) and Ponzo (b) illusions.

Or take *size constancy,* our ability to perceive objects as the same size no matter how near or far away they are from us. When a friend walks away from us, her image becomes smaller. But we almost never realize this is happening, nor do we conclude that our friend is mysteriously shrinking. Outside of our conscious awareness, our brains mentally enlarge figures far away from us so that they appear more like similar objects in the same scene.

When Perception Deceives Us. Sometimes the best way to understand how something works is to understand situations where it doesn't work—or works in unusual circumstances. We've already examined a number of illusions that illustrate principles of sensation and perception. Now we'll examine further how optical size illusions help us to understand everyday perception.

The *moon illusion* has fascinated laypersons, philosophers, and scientists for centuries (Ross & Plug, 2002). The illusion is that the moon appears larger when it's near the horizon than high in the sky. One likely explanation for this is that there's nothing else around for comparison when the moon is high in the sky. In contrast, when the moon is near the horizon, we may unconsciously perceive it as farther away because we can see it next to things we know to be far away, like buildings, mountains, and trees. Because we know these things are large, we perceive the moon as larger still.

In the *Müller-Lyer illusion,* a line of identical length appears longer when it ends in a set of arrowheads pointing inward than in a set of arrowheads pointing outward (see **Figure 4.17a**). That's because we perceive lines as part of a larger context. Three researchers (Segall, Campbell, & Herskovits, 1966) found that people from different cultures displayed differing reactions to the Müller-Lyer illusion. The Zulu, who live in round huts and plow their fields in circles rather than rows, are less susceptible to the Müller-Lyer illusion, probably because they have less experience with linear environments.

In the *Ponzo illusion,* known also as the railroad tracks illusion, converging lines enclose two objects of identical size, leading us to perceive the object closer to the converging lines as larger (see **Figure 4.17b**). Our brain "assumes" that the object closer to the converging lines is farther away, and compensates for this knowledge by making the object look bigger.

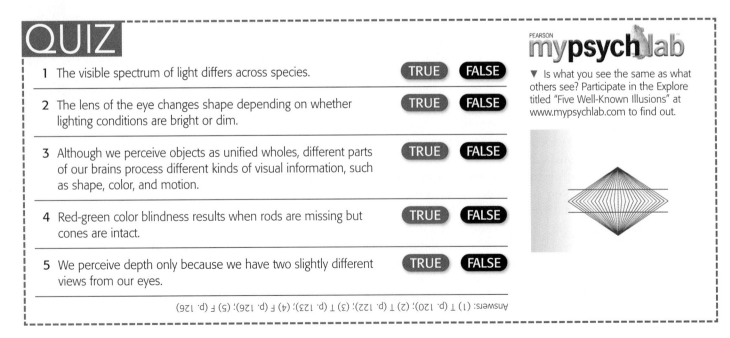

QUIZ

1 The visible spectrum of light differs across species. **TRUE** **FALSE**

2 The lens of the eye changes shape depending on whether lighting conditions are bright or dim. **TRUE** **FALSE**

3 Although we perceive objects as unified wholes, different parts of our brains process different kinds of visual information, such as shape, color, and motion. **TRUE** **FALSE**

4 Red-green color blindness results when rods are missing but cones are intact. **TRUE** **FALSE**

5 We perceive depth only because we have two slightly different views from our eyes. **TRUE** **FALSE**

PEARSON
mypsychlab

▼ Is what you see the same as what others see? Participate in the Explore titled "Five Well-Known Illusions" at www.mypsychlab.com to find out.

Answers: (1) T (p. 120); (2) T (p. 122); (3) T (p. 123); (4) F (p. 126); (5) F (p. 126)

Hearing: The Auditory System

Next to vision, **audition,** our sense of hearing, is probably the sensory modality we rely on most to acquire information about our world.

SOUND: MECHANICAL VIBRATION

Sound is vibration, a kind of mechanical energy traveling through a medium, usually air. The disturbance created by vibration of molecules of air produces sound waves. The precise nature of the vibrations (and the precise sound that we experience) is determined by a combination of pitch, timbre, and loudness.

The *pitch* of a sound corresponds to the frequency of the wave. Higher frequency corresponds to higher pitch, lower frequency to lower pitch. Scientists measure pitch in cycles per second, or hertz (Hz) (see **Figure 4.18**). The human ear is sensitive to frequencies ranging from 20 to 20,000 Hz. When it comes to sensitivity to pitch, age matters. Younger people are more sensitive to higher pitch tones than older adults. A recently developed ring tone for cell phones has ingeniously exploited this simple fact of nature, allowing teenagers to hear their cell phones ring while many of their parents or teachers can't (Vitello, 2006). However, the tables have been turned. Some stores have taken to blasting the same high-pitched tones outside their stores to discourage teenage loiterers without disturbing adult customers.

The amplitude—or height—of the sound wave corresponds to *loudness,* measured in decibels (dB). Loud noise results in increased wave amplitude because there's more mechanical disturbance, that is, more vibrating airborne molecules. **Table 4.1** on page 130 lists various common sounds and their typical loudness. *Timbre* refers to the quality or complexity of the sound. Different musical instruments sound different because they differ in timbre, and human voices are recognizably different from each other for the same reason.

A high school student responds to the "teenagers only" ringtone.

WHAT DO *you* THINK ?

You've just been appointed the director of noise pollution control for a major city. What changes might you recommend to minimize city noise and reduce the risk of hearing loss among residents?

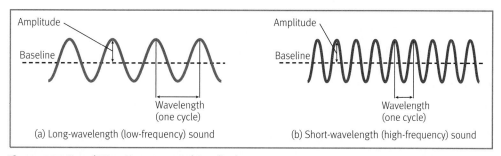

(a) Long-wavelength (low-frequency) sound (b) Short-wavelength (high-frequency) sound

Figure 4.18 Sound Wave Frequency and Amplitude. Sound wave frequency (cycles per second) is the inverse of wavelength (cycle width). Sound wave amplitude is the height of the cycle. The frequency for middle C (a) is lower than that for middle A (b).

GLOSSARY

audition
our sense of hearing

Table 4.1 Common Sounds. This decibel (dB) table compares some common sounds and shows how they rank in potential harm to hearing.

Sound	Level Noise (dB)	Effect
Jet Engines (near)	140	
Rock Concerts (varies)	110–140	We begin to feel pain at about 125 dB
Thunderclap (near)	120	
Power Saw (chainsaw)	110	Regular exposure to sound over 100 dB of more than 1 minute risks permanent hearing loss
Garbage Truck/Cement Mixer	100	No more than 15 minutes of unprotected exposure is recommended for sounds between 90 and 100 dB
Motorcycle (25 ft)	88	Very annoying
Lawnmower	85–90	85 dB is the level at which hearing damage (after 8 hr.) begins
Average City Traffic	80	Annoying; interferes with conversation; constant exposure may cause damage
Vacuum Cleaner	70	Intrusive; interferes with telephone conversation
Normal Conversation	50–65	Comfortable hearing levels are under 60 dB
Whisper	30	Very quiet
Rustling Leaves	20	Just audible

(*Source:* NIDCD)

HOW THE EAR WORKS

Just as sense receptors for vision transduce light into neural activity, sense receptors for hearing transduce sound into neural activity.

The Structure of the Ear. The ear has three parts: outer, middle, and inner, each of which performs a different job (see **Figure 4.19**). The outer ear, consisting of the *pinna* (the part of the ear we see, namely, its skin and cartilage flap) and ear canal, has the simplest function; it funnels sound waves onto the *tympanic membrane,* commonly called the eardrum. On the other side of the tympanic membrane lies the middle ear, containing the *ossicles*—the three tiniest bones in the body—named the hammer, anvil, and stirrup, after their shapes. These ossicles vibrate at the frequency of the sound wave, transmitting it from the tympanic membrane to the inner ear. **[LEARNING OBJECTIVE 4.5]**

GLOSSARY

cochlea
bony, spiral-shaped sense organ used for hearing

organ of Corti
tissue containing the hair cells necessary for hearing

basilar membrane
membrane supporting the organ of Corti and hair cells in the cochlea

The Cochlea and Organ of Corti. The **cochlea** lies in the inner ear and converts vibration into neural activity. The term *cochlea* derives from the Greek word *kokhlias,* meaning "snail" or "screw," and as its name implies, it has a spiral shape (refer again to Figure 4.19). The outer part of the cochlea is bony, but its inner cavity is filled with a thick fluid. Vibrations from sound waves disturb this fluid, and travel to the base of the cochlea, where pressure is released and transduction occurs.

The **organ of Corti** and **basilar membrane** are critical to hearing because *hair cells* are embedded within them. Hair cells are where transduction of auditory information

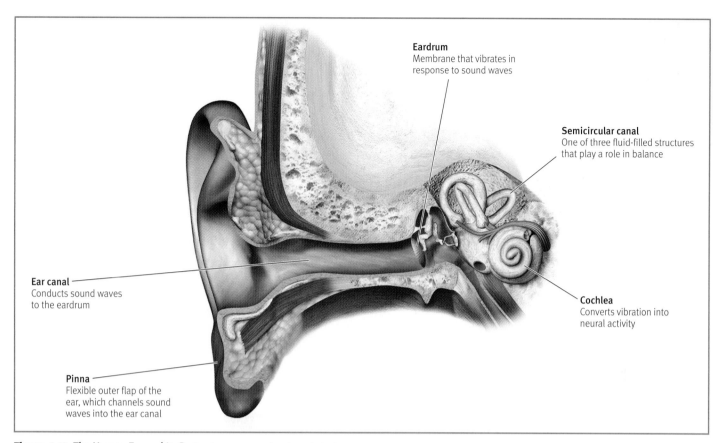

Eardrum
Membrane that vibrates in
response to sound waves

Semicircular canal
One of three fluid-filled structures
that play a role in balance

Ear canal
Conducts sound waves
to the eardrum

Cochlea
Converts vibration into
neural activity

Pinna
Flexible outer flap of the
ear, which channels sound
waves into the ear canal

Figure 4.19 **The Human Ear and Its Parts.** A cutaway section through the human ear.
(*Source:* Adapted from Dorling Kindersley)

takes place: They convert acoustic information into action potentials. Here's how. Hair cells contain cilia (hairlike structures) that protrude into the fluid of the cochlea. When sound waves travel through the cochlea, the resulting pressure deflects these cilia, exciting the hair cells (Roberts, Howard, & Hudspeth, 1988). That information feeds into the *auditory nerve,* which travels to the brain.

AUDITORY PERCEPTION

Once the auditory nerve enters the brain, it makes contacts in the brain stem, which sends auditory information higher—all the way up the auditory cortex. At each stage, perception becomes increasingly complex. In this respect, auditory perception is like visual perception.

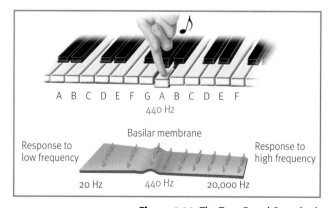

Figure 4.20 **The Tone-Based Organization of the Basilar Membrane.** Hair cells at the base of the basilar membrane respond to high-pitched tones, whereas hair cells at the top of the basilar membrane respond to low-pitched tones.

Pitch Perception. Different tones are represented in different places in the primary auditory cortex (see **Figure 4.20**). This is because each place receives information from a specific place in the basilar membrane. Hair cells located at the base of the basilar

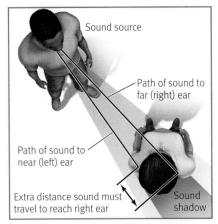

Figure 4.21 How We Locate Sounds. When someone standing to our left speaks to us, the sound reaches our left ear slightly earlier than it reaches our right. Also, the intensity detected by the left ear is greater than the intensity detected by the right ear, because the right ear lies in a sound shadow produced by the head and shoulders.

membrane are most excited by high-pitched tones, whereas hair cells at the top of the basilar membrane are most excited by low-pitched tones. **[LEARNING OBJECTIVE 4.6]** Scientists call this mode of pitch perception *place theory,* because a specific place along the basilar membrane (and also in the auditory cortex) matches a tone with a specific pitch.

Localization of Sound.

We use various brain centers to determine the location of a sound source with respect to our bodies. When the auditory nerve enters the brain stem, some of the axons connect with cells on the same side of the brain, whereas others cross over to the other side of the brain. This clever arrangement enables information from both ears to reach the same structures in the brain stem. Because the two sources of information take different routes, they arrive at the brain stem slightly out of sync with each other. Our brains compare this difference to localize sound sources (**Figure 4.21**). The presentation of dissimilar sounds to the two ears is called *binaural cues.* There's also a loudness difference between our ears, because the ear closest to the sound source is in the direct path of the sound wave, whereas the ear farthest away is in a *sound shadow,* created by the head.

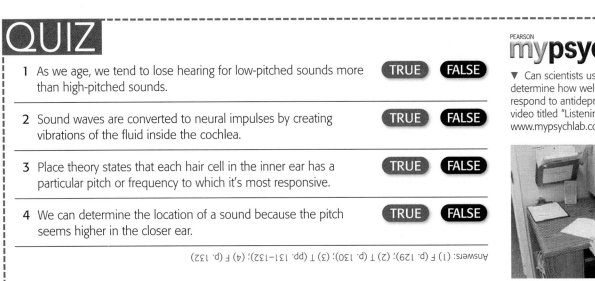

QUIZ

1. As we age, we tend to lose hearing for low-pitched sounds more than high-pitched sounds. **TRUE** **FALSE**

2. Sound waves are converted to neural impulses by creating vibrations of the fluid inside the cochlea. **TRUE** **FALSE**

3. Place theory states that each hair cell in the inner ear has a particular pitch or frequency to which it's most responsive. **TRUE** **FALSE**

4. We can determine the location of a sound because the pitch seems higher in the closer ear. **TRUE** **FALSE**

Answers: (1) F (p. 129); (2) T (p. 130); (3) T (pp. 131–132); (4) F (p. 132)

PEARSON
mypsychlab

▼ Can scientists use a hearing test to determine how well your body will respond to antidepressants? Watch the video titled "Listening to the Blues Test" at www.mypsychlab.com to find out.

Smell, Taste, and Touch: The Sensual Senses

Without smell and taste, many of our everyday experiences would be bland. Cuisines of the world feature characteristic spices that enliven their dishes. Similarly, smell and taste stimulate our senses and elevate our spirits. The term *comfort food* refers to familiar dishes that we seek because of the warm memories they evoke.

Smell is also called **olfaction** and taste **gustation.** These senses work hand in hand, enhancing our liking of some foods and our disliking of others. Smell and taste are called the *chemical senses* because we derive these sensory experiences from chemicals in sub-

GLOSSARY

olfaction
our sense of smell

gustation
our sense of taste

stances. The most critical function of our chemical senses is to sample our food before swallowing it. The smell and taste of sour milk are powerful stimuli that few of us can ignore even if we want to. An unfamiliar bitter taste may signal dangerous bacteria or poison in our food. We develop food preferences for "safe" foods and base them on a combination of smell and taste.

Somatosensation, our sense of touch, is responsible for our ability to detect pressure ranging from a gentle tickle of a stray hair to the crushing sensation of having someone trip and land on top of us. This sense is also used to sense pain and temperature. The ability to feel pain may not sound like such a desirable asset; but, in fact, the ability to detect pain and temperature plays a critical role in our survival by alerting us to injury and illness. Imagine having a thorn prick your hand as you are picking a rose, but not perceiving the prick as painful. You might go on to grasp the stem firmly, embedding the thorn into your finger and causing injury and infection.

We will discuss each of the remaining senses in turn.

TASTE AND SMELL GO HAND IN HAND

Odors are airborne chemicals that interact with receptors in the lining of our nasal passages. Estimates suggest that our noses are capable of detecting between 2,000 and 4,000 different odors. Not everything, though, has an odor. (We bet you're pleased to hear that!) Clean water, for example, has no odor. In contrast to our sense of smell, we can detect only a few tastes. We're sensitive to five basic tastes—sweet, salty, sour, bitter, and umami, which is a recently discovered "meaty" or "savory" taste. There's preliminary evidence for a sixth taste, one for fatty foods (Gilbertson et al., 1997).

With only five or six taste categories, how can we taste so many flavors? The secret lies in the fact that our taste perception is biased strongly by our sense of smell, which explains why we find food much less tasty when our noses are stuffed. Far more than we realize, we find certain foods "delicious" because of their smell. Indeed, we perceive a combination of taste and smell. If you're not persuaded, try this exercise. Buy some multiflavored jelly beans, open the bag, and close your eyes so you can't see which flavor you're picking. Then pinch your nose with one hand and pop a jelly bean in your mouth. At first you won't be able to identify the flavor. You'll only be able to tell that it's sweet. Then release your fingers from your nose and you'll soon be able to perceive the jelly bean's flavor.

We detect taste with **taste buds** on our tongues. Bumps on the tongue called *papillae* contain numerous taste buds **(Figure 4.22).** There are separate taste buds for sweet, salty, sour, bitter, and the "meaty flavor" umami (Chandrashekar et al., 2006).

Umami taste receptors were controversial until physiological studies replicated earlier results and showed that these receptors were present on taste buds (Chandrashekar et al., 2006). That was nearly a century after 1908, when Kikunae Ikeda isolated the molecules responsible for the savory flavor found in many Japanese foods, such as broth or dried seaweed (Yamaguchi & Ninomiya, 2000). Today, most scientists consider umami the fifth taste.

PERCEPTION OF SMELL AND TASTE

Our perceptions of smell and taste are often remarkably sensitive—and more informative than we consciously realize. Studies show that babies can identify their mothers' odor and siblings can recognize each other on the basis of odor. Research suggests that women can even tell whether people just watched a happy or a sad movie from samples of their armpit odor (Wysocki & Preti, 2004).

Ashlyn Blocker was born with an insensitivity to pain. This rare disorder renders people unable to detect pain or temperature. Her parents and teachers need to monitor her constantly to ensure that she doesn't hurt herself inadvertently. Many people with this disorder die prematurely due to injury or infection.

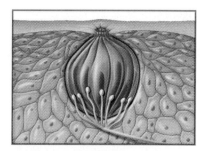

Figure 4.22 How We Detect Taste.
The tongue contains many taste buds, which transmit information to the brain as shown in this close-up.

REPLICABILITY
Can the results be duplicated in other studies?

GLOSSARY

somatosensation
our sense of touch

taste buds
sense receptors in the tongue that respond to sweet, salty, sour, bitter, umami, and perhaps fat

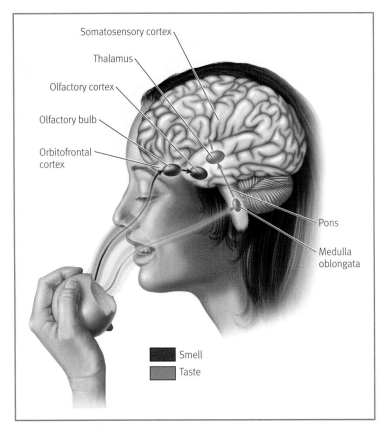

Somatosensory cortex
Thalamus
Olfactory cortex
Olfactory bulb
Orbitofrontal cortex
Pons
Medulla oblongata

Smell
Taste

Figure 4.23 Smell and Taste. Our senses of smell and taste enter the brain by different routes but converge on the orbitofrontal cortex.

RULING OUT RIVAL HYPOTHESES
Have important alternative explanations for the findings been excluded?

GLOSSARY

pheromone
odorless chemical that serves as a social signal to members of one's species

How are odors and tastes interpreted in the brain? After odors interact with sense receptors in the nasal passages, the information is transmitted to the olfactory cortex and parts of the limbic system (see **Figure 4.23**). Similarly, after taste information interacts with taste buds, it enters the brain, reaching the gustatory cortex, somatosensory cortex (because food also has texture), and parts of the limbic system. **[LEARNING OBJECTIVE 4.7]** The orbitofrontal cortex is a site of convergence for smell and taste (Rolls, 2004) that allows us to experience more complex tastes based on the combination of taste and smell.

Parts of the limbic system, such as the amygdala and the orbitofrontal cortex, help us to distinguish pleasant from disgusting smells (A.K. Anderson et al., 2003). Taste can also be pleasant or disgusting; *disgust,* not surprisingly, means "bad taste." Both tasting disgusting food and viewing facial expressions of disgust (see Chapter 9) activate the gustatory cortex (Wicker et al., 2003). Moreover, persons who suffer damage to the gustatory cortex don't experience disgust (Calder et al., 2000). These results underscore the powerful links among smell, taste, and emotion.

Smell also plays a particularly strong role in many animals' sexual behavior. In fact, mice with a genetic defect in smell don't even bother to mate (Mandiyan, Coats, & Shah, 2005). Is smell central to human sexuality too? Many perfume and cologne manufacturers sure seem to think so. Curiously, though, it may not be fragrant odors, but **pheromones**—odorless chemicals that serve as social signals to members of one's species—that alter our sexual behavior. There's evidence that rodents respond to pheromones during mating and social behavior (Biasi, Silvotti, & Tirindelli, 2001). So do most other mammals, including whales and horses (Fields, 2007). Most mammals use the *vomeronasal organ,* located in the bone between the nose and the mouth, to detect pheromones. However, humans don't have a vomeronasal organ (Witt & Wozniak, 2006), causing some to suggest that humans are insensitive to pheromones. An alternative hypothesis is that humans detect pheromones via a different route. This idea is supported by the fact that humans do produce pheromones (Pearson, 2006).

Still, we should be cautious about shelling out sizeable chunks of money on pheromone-based products that promise to stir up romance. Scientific evidence suggests they probably won't work. Pheromones are large molecules, so although it's easy to transfer a pheromone from one person to another during a passionate kiss, sending them across a restaurant table is definitely a stretch.

TOUCH AND PAIN

The stimuli that activate the somatosensory system come in a variety of types. In this respect, this sense differs from vision and audition, each of which is devoted mainly to a single stimulus type.

Pressure, Temperature, and Injury. Our somatosensory system responds to stimuli applied to the skin, such as light touch or deep pressure, hot or cold temperature, or chemical or mechanical (touch-related) injury that produces pain. Somatosensory stimuli

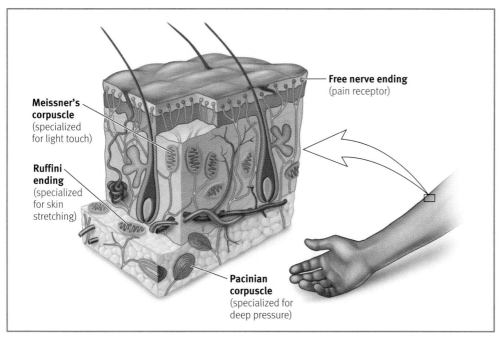

Meissner's corpuscle (specialized for light touch)

Ruffini ending (specialized for skin stretching)

Free nerve ending (pain receptor)

Pacinian corpuscle (specialized for deep pressure)

Figure 4.24 The Sense of Touch. The skin contains many specialized and free nerve endings that detect mechanical pressure, stretching, and pain.

can be very specific, such as the embossed patterns of a letter written in Braille, or generalized to a large area of the body.

We sense light touch and deep pressure with *mechanoreceptors* located on the ends of sensory nerves in the skin (see **Figure 4.24**). One example of a mechanoreceptor is the Pacinian corpuscle, named after anatomist Filippo Pacini, who discovered it in 1831. This receptor is specialized to detect deep pressure.

We sense touch, temperature, and especially pain with *free nerve endings* (refer once more to Figure 4.24). There are many more free nerve endings than specialized endings. Nerve endings of all types are distributed unevenly across our body surface. We have the greatest number of nerve endings in our fingertips (which explains why it really hurts when we cut our finger, say, in a paper cut), followed by our lips, face, hands, and feet. We have the fewest in the middle of our backs, perhaps explaining why even a strenuous deep back massage rarely makes us scream out in agony.

How We Perceive Touch and Pain.
Information about body touch, temperature, and painful stimuli travels from the skin to the spinal cord. Touch information travels more quickly than information about pain stimuli. Many of us have discovered this fact when stubbing our toes on a piece of furniture: We first feel our toes hitting the furniture, but don't experience the stinging pain (ouch!) until a second or two later. That's because touch and pain have different functions. Touch informs us of our immediate surroundings, which is often an urgent matter, whereas pain alerts us to take care of that part of our bodies. **[LEARNING OBJECTIVE 4.8]**

As we've all discovered, there are different kinds of pain: sharp, stabbing, throbbing, burning, and aching. Many of the types of pain perceptions relate to the pain-causing stimulus—thermal (heat-related), chemical, or mechanical. Pain can also be acute, that is, short lived, or chronic, that is, enduring, perhaps even lasting years. Each kind of pain-producing stimulus has a *threshold,* or point at which we perceive it as painful. People differ in their pain thresholds. Surprisingly, one study showed that

Fict-OID

MYTH: Consuming ice cream or other cold substances too quickly causes pain in our brains.

REALITY: "Brain freeze," as it's sometimes called, doesn't affect the brain at all. It's produced by a constriction of blood vessels in the roof of our mouths in response to intense cold temperatures, followed by an expansion of these blood vessels, producing pain that is felt as a headache.

CORRELATION vs. CAUSATION
Can we be sure that A causes B?

RULING OUT RIVAL HYPOTHESES
Have important alternative explanations
for the findings been excluded?

people with naturally red hair require more anesthetic than do people with other hair colors (Liem et al., 2004). Of course, this correlational finding doesn't mean that red hair causes lower pain thresholds. Instead, it suggests that some of the differences in people's thresholds are due to genetic factors that happen to be associated with hair color.

For many years the scientific consensus has been that we can ignore pain, or at least withstand it, with a stoic mind-set. There's evidence that people of certain cultural backgrounds, such as American Indians, Cambodians, Chinese, and Germans, are more reserved and less likely to communicate openly about pain, whereas South and Central Americans consider it more acceptable to moan and cry out when in pain (Ondeck, 2003). Although these descriptions of average behavior may help physicians deal with diverse populations, the premise that pain perception varies with ethnicity isn't universally accepted. An alternative hypothesis is that health care professionals treat certain ethnic groups differently. Blacks and Hispanics are less likely than Caucasians to receive analgesic (antipain) medication during emergency room visits (Bonham, 2001), which could account for some of the differences in reports of pain.

Firewalkers, popular in India, Japan, North Africa, and the Polynesian islands, have walked 20- to 40-foot-long beds of burning embers. The practice has been around since as early as 1200 B.C. Do firewalkers experience less pain than the rest of us? Success in firewalking has nothing to do with our pain sensitivity and everything to do with physics. The type of coal or wood used in firewalking has a low rate of heat exchange, such that it burns red hot in the center while remaining less hot on the outside (Kurtus, 2000). So any of us can firewalk successfully just so long as we walk over the burning embers quickly enough. Still, serious accidents can occur if the fire isn't prepared properly or if the firewalker walks too slowly.

Firewalking, though potentially dangerous, can be done pain free by anyone walking quickly enough.

WHAT DO *you* THINK *?*

You are an intake nurse at an emergency room serving a diverse population, and you routinely ask patients to estimate their pain on a ten-point scale as a way of evaluating the urgency of their medical problems. What factors should you consider when judging the severity of a patient's case?

BODY POSITION AND BALANCE

We usually think of ourselves as having five senses: sight, hearing, taste, smell, and touch. But we actually have two more sensory systems that are fundamental to our basic everyday functioning. Every time we move, we need to maintain posture and balance, as well as navigate bodily motion. **Proprioception,** also called our kinesthetic sense, helps us keep track of where we are and move efficiently. The **vestibular sense,** also called our sense of equilibrium, enables us to sense and maintain our balance as we move about. **[LEARNING OBJECTIVE 4.9]** Our senses of body position and balance work together.

Proprioceptors: Telling the Inside Story. We use *proprioceptors* to sense how much muscles stretch and with how much force. From these two sources of information we can tell what our bodies are doing, even with our eyes closed. Proprioceptive information enters the spinal cord and travels upward through the brain stem and thalamus to reach the somatosensory and motor cortexes (Naito, 2004). Here our

GLOSSARY

proprioception
our sense of body position

vestibular sense
our sense of equilibrium or balance

brains combine information from our muscles and tendons, along with a sense of our intentions to obtain a perception of our body's location (Proske, 2006).

The Vestibular Sense: A Balancing Act.

In addition to the cochlea, the inner ear contains three tiny tunnels called *semicircular canals* named for their curved half-circle shape **(Figure 4.25).** The semicircular canals are filled with fluid. They help us maintain our balance by detecting movement. When movement or the pull of gravity displaces fluid in the canals, this stimulates hair cells that line the inside of the semicircular canals and feed into the vestibular nerve. The vestibular nerve transmits information to the brain.

Vestibular information reaches parts of the brain stem that control eye muscles and triggers reflexes that coordinate eye and head movements (Highstein, Fay, & Popper, 2004). Vestibular information also travels to the cerebellum, which controls bodily responses that enable us to catch our balance when we're falling. We are typically completely unaware of this sense, noticing it only when we lose our sense of balance.

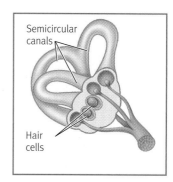

Figure 4.25 How We Sense Motion. The semicircular canals of the inner ear detect movement and gravity.

Ergonomics: Human Engineering.

How do our bodies interact with new technologies? A field of psychology called *human factors* optimizes technology to better suit our sensory and perceptual capabilities. We can use what we know about human sensory systems—ranging from our body position sense to vision—to build more *ergonomic,* or worker-friendly, gadgets and tools of the trade.

Have you ever tried to repeatedly push open a door that needed to be pulled open or spent several minutes trying to figure out how to turn on a shower in an apartment or hotel room? Fortunately, human factors psychologists have been able to apply their extensive knowledge of sensation and perception to improve the design of many everyday devices such as a new design for a computer screen, keyboard, or mouse that enables users to better reach for their computers or see their screens, increasing their efficiency. Human factors psychologists design not only computer components but also devices like control panels on aircraft carriers to make them safer and easier to use. Human factors remind us that much of what we know about sensation and perception has useful applications to many domains of everyday life.

The cockpit of an airplane contains many controls that human factors psychologists can make safer and more user friendly.

QUIZ

1 Humans can detect only a small number of odors but thousands of tastes. **TRUE** **FALSE**

2 The vomeronasal organ helps to detect pheromones in many mammals but doesn't develop in humans. **TRUE** **FALSE**

3 Pain information travels more quickly to the spinal cord than does touch information. **TRUE** **FALSE**

4 Proprioception enables us to coordinate our movements without having to look at our bodies. **TRUE** **FALSE**

▼ Does your sense of smell relate to memory problems? Watch the video titled "Alzheimer's Smell Test" at www.mypsychlab.com to find out.

Answers: (1) F (p. 133); (2) T (p. 134); (3) F (p. 135); (4) T (p. 136)

Alterations in Sensation and Perception

We started this chapter discussing the fact that sensation and perception are two different things—that our perceptual experiences often go well beyond the information provided by our sensory organs. In some cases, our top-down processing can lead to perceptual experiences that deviate significantly from the actual sensory input. In this section, we'll explore several ways in which our perception of the world may be altered in the absence of sensory information.

EXTRASENSORY PERCEPTION (ESP): FACT OR FICTION?

As we've seen, scientists have learned a great deal about perception. Yet might some forms of perception remain to be discovered? This question takes us into the mysterious realm of **extrasensory perception (ESP).** Proponents of ESP argue that we can perceive events outside of the known channels of sensation, such as seeing, hearing, and touch.

What's ESP, Anyway?

ESP isn't one thing. Instead, *parapsychologists*—investigators who study ESP and related psychic phenomena—have subdivided ESP into three major types (Hines, 2003; Hyman, 1989):

(1) *Precognition:* predicting specific events before they occur through paranormal means, that is, mechanisms that lie outside of traditional science

(2) *Telepathy:* reading other people's minds

(3) *Clairvoyance:* detecting the presence of objects or people that are hidden from view

Closely related to ESP, although usually distinguished from it, is *psychokinesis:* moving objects by mental power alone.

Surveys indicate that 41 percent of American adults believe in ESP (Haraldsson & Houtkooper, 1995; Moore, 2005). Moreover, two-thirds of Americans say they've had a psychic experience, like a dream foretelling the death of a loved one or a premonition about a car accident that came true (Greeley, 1987).

Scientific Evidence for ESP.

The real-world implications of ESP are mind-boggling. Imagine that we could forecast catastrophic events, like the terrorist attacks of September 11, 2001, or figure out whether a romantic partner is cheating by viewing his actions at a distance or reading his mind.

In the 1930s, Joseph B. Rhine, who coined the term *extrasensory perception,* launched the full-scale study of ESP in the United States. Rhine used a set of stimuli called *Zener cards,* which consist of five standard symbols: squiggly lines, star, circle, plus sign, and square. He presented these cards to subjects in random order and asked them to guess which card would appear (precognition), which card another subject had in mind (telepathy), and which card was hidden from view (clairvoyance). Rhine (1934) initially reported positive results, as his subjects averaged about 7 correct Zener card identifications per deck of 25, where 5 would be chance performance.

But there was a problem, one that has dogged ESP research for well over a century: Try as they might, other investigators couldn't replicate Rhine's findings. **[LEARNING OBJECTIVE 4.10]** Moreover, scientists later pointed out serious flaws in Rhine's methods. For example, some of the Zener cards were so worn down or poorly manufactured that subjects could see the imprint of the symbols through the backs of the cards (Alcock, 1990; Gilovich, 1991).

The Zener cards, named after a collaborator of Joseph B. Rhine, have been used widely in ESP research.

REPLICABILITY

Can the results be duplicated in other studies?

GLOSSARY

extrasensory perception (ESP)
perception of events outside the known channels of sensation

Other attempts to document ESP have proven equally disappointing (Bem & Honorton, 1994; Lilienfeld, 1999c; Milton & Wiseman, 1999; Moulton & Kosslyn, 2008). For example, research conducted over three decades ago suggested that people could mentally transmit images to dreaming subjects (Ullman, Krippner, & Vaughn, 1973). Yet later investigators couldn't replicate these results.

The negative findings we've reviewed suggest that the extraordinary claim of ESP isn't matched by equally extraordinary evidence. But these findings don't demonstrate that ESP doesn't exist. In science, it's exceedingly difficult to prove a negative. But more than 150 years of failed replications suggest that the research evidence for it is awfully weak.

Tricks of the Psychics. When a psychic forecaster predicts correctly that a major event will happen, people take special notice of it. But people forget about all of the events the psychic predicted that didn't occur, not to mention all of the events that occurred that the forecaster didn't predict. As a consequence, people tend to overestimate the psychic's accuracy. Why do psychics sometimes seem so convincing?

Most of these psychics probably rely on a set of skills known as *cold reading,* the art of persuading people we've just met that we know all about them (Hines, 2003; Hyman, 1977). If you want to impress your friends with a cold reading, **Table 4.2** contains some tips to keep in mind. Cold reading works for one major reason: As we've learned in earlier chapters, we humans seek meaning in our worlds and often find it even when it's not there. So in many respects we're reading into the cold reading at least as much as the cold reader is reading into us.

HALLUCINATIONS: EXPERIENCING WHAT ISN'T THERE

The most extreme example of separation between sensation and perception is *hallucinations*, realistic perceptual experiences in the absence of any external stimuli. Hallucinations can occur in any sensory modality, including auditory (such as voices), olfactory (such as the smell of gasoline), gustatory (such as the taste of lemonade), or tactile (such as sensations of bugs crawling on the skin). Brain scans reveal that when people report visual hallucinations, their visual cortex becomes active, just as it does when they see a real object (Allen, Laroi, McGuire, & Aleman, 2008; Bentall, 2000). **[LEARNING OBJECTIVE 4.11]** A frequent misconception is that hallucinations occur only in psychologically disturbed individuals (Aleman & LaRoi, 2008). But hallucinations are far more common than many people realize. Surveys reveal that between 10 and 14 percent (Sidgwick, 1894; Tien, 1991; West, 1948) to as many as 39 percent (Ohayon, 2000; Posey & Losch, 1983) of college students

REPLICABILITY
Can the results be duplicated in other studies?

EXTRAORDINARY CLAIMS
Is the evidence as convincing as the claim?

Table 4.2 Cold Reading Techniques.

Technique	Example	
Start off with a stock spiel, a list of general statements that apply to just about everyone.	"You've recently been struggling with some tough decisions in life."	
Fish for details by peppering your reading with vague probes.	"I'm sensing that someone with the letter M or maybe N has been important in your life lately."	
Use the technique of *sleight of tongue*, meaning that you toss out so many guesses in rapid-fire fashion that at least a few of them are bound to be right.	"Has your father been ill?"; "How about your mother?"; "Hmmm . . . I sense that someone in your family is ill or worried about getting ill."	
Look for physical cues to the individual's personality or life history.	A traditional manner of dress often suggests a conventional and proper person, a great deal of shiny jewelry often suggests a flamboyant person, and so on.	
Remember that "flattery will get you everywhere."	Tell people what they want to hear, like "I see a great romance on the horizon."	

(*Source:* Hines, 2003; Hyman, 1977; Rowland, 2001)

and people in the general population report having hallucinated at least once, even when not taking drugs or experiencing psychological problems (Ohayon, 2000).

Hallucinations vary a great deal across people and occasions. Some experience frightening and disturbing hallucinations, but others report pleasant and even comforting hallucinations. The meaning and types of hallucinations also vary across cultures. Some non-Western cultures, including some in Africa, believe that hallucinations impart wisdom. Some of these cultures value hallucinations as gifts from the gods and incorporate them into their religious rituals. People in these societies may even go out of their way to induce hallucinations by means of prayer, sensory deprivation, fasting, and hallucinogenic drugs (Al-Issa, 1995; Bourguignon, 1970).

OUT-OF-BODY AND NEAR-DEATH EXPERIENCES

Carlos Alvarado (2000) described a 36-year-old police officer's account of an out-of-body experience (OBE), an extraordinary sense of her consciousness leaving her body, when she pursued an armed suspect on her first night on patrol. "When I and three other officers stopped the vehicle and started getting (to) the suspect . . . I was afraid. I promptly went out of my body and up into the air maybe 20 feet above the scene. I remained there, extremely calm, while I watched the entire procedure."

OBEs are surprisingly common: About 25 percent of college students and 10 percent of the general population report having experienced one or more OBEs (Alvarado, 2000). In many cases, individuals describe themselves as floating above their bodies, calmly observing themselves from high above.

Are people really outside of their bodies during an OBE? Laboratory studies have compared what's reported during an OBE against sights and sounds known to be present in a given location. Interestingly, even though participants report they can see or hear what's occurring at a faraway place, their reports are generally inaccurate or, at best, a "good guess" when they are accurate. When researchers have reported positive results, these results have rarely been replicated (Alvarado, 2000). So there's no good evidence that people are truly floating above their bodies during an OBE, although it certainly seems that way to them (Cheyne & Girard, 2009; Ehrsson, 2007; Lenggenhager et al., 2007).

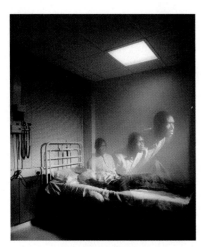

As real as an out-of-body experience seems to the person having it, research has found no evidence that consciousness exists outside the body.

REPLICABILITY
Can the results be duplicated in other studies?

WHAT DO *you* THINK?

You are interested in designing a study that provides a strong and objective evaluation of OBEs. Can you think of a research design that would enable you to ask participants questions that only those who have had a true OBE could answer?

Near-death experiences (NDEs) are OBEs reported by people who have nearly died or thought they were going to die. Roughly 12 to 33 percent of people who've been close to death report NDEs (Greyson, 2000; Ring, 1984; Sabom, 1982; van Lommel et al., 2001). Ever since Raymond Moody (1975) cataloged them some 30 years ago, Americans have become familiar with some of the "classical" elements of the NDE (see **Table 4.3**)."

NDEs differ across persons and cultures, suggesting they don't provide a genuine glimpse of the afterlife, but are constructed from prevalent beliefs about the hereafter in response to the threat of death (Ehrenwald, 1974; Noyes & Kletti, 1976). People from Christian and Buddhist cultures frequently report the sensation of moving through a tunnel, but native people in North America, the Pacific Islands, and Australia rarely do (Kellehear, 1993).

Table 4.3 Common Elements in Adult Near-Death Experiences.

- Difficulty describing the experience in words
- Hearing oneself pronounced dead
- Feelings of peace and quiet
- Hearing unusual noises
- Meeting "spiritual beings"
- Experiencing a bright light as a "being of light"
- Panoramic "life review," that is, seeing our entire life pass before our eyes
- Experiencing a realm in which all knowledge exists
- Experiencing cities of light
- Experiencing a realm of ghosts and spirits
- Sensing a border or limit
- Coming back "into the body"

(*Source:* Moody, 1975, 1977; adapted from Greyson, 2000)

EXTRAORDINARY CLAIMS
Is the evidence as convincing as the claim?

RULING OUT RIVAL HYPOTHESES
Have important alternative explanations for the findings been excluded?

Fact
-OID

Some people experience a phenomenon called "jamais vu," French for "never seen," which is essentially the opposite of déjà vu. In jamais vu, the person reports feeling as though a previously familiar experience suddenly seems unfamiliar. Jamais vu is sometimes seen in neurological disorders, such as amnesia (see Chapter 6) and epilepsy (Brown, 2004a, b).

FALSIFIABILITY
Can the claim be disproved?

GLOSSARY

déjà vu
feeling of reliving an experience that's new

hypnosis
set of techniques that provides people with suggestions for alterations in their perceptions, thoughts, feelings, and behaviors

It's tempting to believe that NDEs prove that when we die we'll all be ushered into the afterlife by friends or loved ones. Nevertheless, the evidence at this point is insufficient to support this extraordinary claim. Scientists have offered alternative explanations based on changes in the chemistry of the brain associated with cardiac arrest, anesthesia, and other physical traumas (Blackmore, 1993). For example, a feeling of complete peace may result from a massive release of *endorphins* and buzzing, ringing, or other unusual sounds may be the rumblings of an oxygen-starved brain (Blackmore, 1993). NDE-like experiences can be triggered by electrical stimulation of the brain's temporal lobes (Persinger, 1994). Temporary lack of oxygen to the brain in rapid acceleration during fighter pilot training (Whinnery, 1997) and some drugs (Jansen, 1991) can also result in NDEs.

DÉJÀ VU EXPERIENCES

Have you ever had the mind-boggling sense that you've "been there" or "done that" before? Or have you ever felt you were reliving something, scene by scene, even though you knew that the situation was new or unfamiliar? Maybe you even had the spooky feeling you could predict what would happen next. If you've had one or more of these eerie flashes of familiarity, then you've experienced **déjà vu,** which is French for "already seen." More than two-thirds of us have experienced at least one episode of déjà vu (Adachi et al., 2008). For reasons that aren't well understood, these 10- to 30-second illusions are more likely to be reported by people who remember their dreams, travel frequently, are young, and have liberal political and religious beliefs, a college education, and a high income (Brown, 2003, 2004a, b).

Scientists don't fully understand these fascinating changes in consciousness. Some people believe that the déjà vu experience is a memory from a past life. Although not impossible, this explanation is unfalsifiable and therefore outside the boundaries of scientific study (Stevenson, 1960).

Other explanations are testable. One hypothesis is that déjà vu is triggered by small seizures in the right temporal lobe, which is largely responsible for feelings of familiarity (Bancaud et al., 1994). This explanation is consistent with the finding that people with temporal lobe epilepsy often report déjà vu just before a seizure. An excess of the neurotransmitter dopamine in the temporal lobes may also play a role in déjà vu (Taiminen & Jääskeläinen, 2001).

Another possibility is that déjà vu is related to situations in which we're mentally or physically distracted and don't consciously register something we're seeing. For example, imagine we visit a park we know we've never seen, but we experience déjà vu. Perhaps we've driven by this park many times without ever noticing it, but our minds processed the information unconsciously (Strayer, Drews, & Johnston, 2003).

A final possibility is that déjà vu is triggered by a present experience that resembles, in whole or in part, an earlier experience. The familiar feeling arises because we don't consciously recall the previous experience, which may have originated in childhood or earlier in life. This account implies that the situation feels familiar because it is, in some unrecognized sense, familiar.

HYPNOSIS

Hypnosis is a set of techniques that provides people with suggestions for alterations in their perceptions, thoughts, feelings, and behaviors (Kirsch & Lynn, 1998). Today, we have a much better understanding of hypnotic phenomena than when such renowned late nineteenth- and early twentieth-century scholars as Sigmund Freud, Alfred Binet, and William James began to explore hypnosis. It's safe to say that hypnosis has since moved into the mainstream of science.

Myths and Misconceptions about Hypnosis: What Hypnosis Is and Isn't.
Hypnosis can produce profound changes in perception (Cardeña, 2005; Nash & Barnier, 2008). Still, public knowledge about hypnosis hasn't kept pace with scientific developments. We'll first examine five misconceptions about hypnosis before evaluating two prominent theories of how it works.
[LEARNING OBJECTIVE 4.12]

People who perform in stage hypnosis shows are carefully selected before the performance for high suggestibility.

• **Myth 1: Hypnosis Produces a Trance State in Which "Amazing" Things Happen.** Popular stereotypes of hypnosis derive from *stage hypnosis* shows, in which hypnotists seemingly program people to enact commands ranging from quacking like a duck to playing a wicked air guitar (MacKillop, Lynn, & Meyer, 2004). But the wacky actions of people in movies and on-stage have nothing to do with a trance state. Actually, hypnosis doesn't have a great impact on suggestibility. People who are highly receptive to hypnotic suggestions (for example, "your hands are moving together because of a magnetic force") also turn out to be highly susceptible to following such suggestions without being hypnotized (Kirsch & Lynn, 1995). Hollywood thrillers aside, hypnosis can't turn a mild-mannered person into a cold-blooded murderer.

• **Myth 2: Hypnosis Is a Sleeplike State.** James Braid (1843), a Scottish physician, claimed that the hypnotized brain produces a condition akin to sleep. Braid labeled the phenomenon *neurohypnosis* (from the Greek word *hypno*, meaning "sleep"), and the shortened term "hypnosis" eventually stuck. Yet people who are hypnotized don't show brain waves similar to those of sleep.

• **Myth 3: Hypnotized People Are Unaware of Their Surroundings.** Another popular idea is that hypnotized people are so "entranced" that they lose touch with their surroundings. In actuality, most hypnotized people are fully aware of their immediate surroundings, and can even recall the details of an overheard telephone conversation that took place during hypnosis (Lynn, Weekes, & Milano,1989).

• **Myth 4: Hypnotized People Forget What Happened during Hypnosis.** In the popular 1962 film *The Manchurian Candidate,* remade in 2004, a person is programmed by hypnosis to commit an assassination and has no memory of what transpired during hypnosis. In real life, *spontaneous amnesia* for what happens during hypnosis is rare and mostly limited to people who expect to be amnesic following hypnosis (Simon & Salzberg, 1985; Young & Cooper, 1972).

• **Myth 5: Hypnosis Enhances Memory.** Scientific studies generally reveal that hypnosis doesn't improve memory (Erdelyi, 1994; Scoboria et al., 2002). Hypnosis does lead to an increase in recalling information, but not all of it is accurate (Erdelyi, 1994; Steblay & Bothwell, 1994; Wagstaff, 2008). Courts in most U.S. states have banned the testimony of hypnotized witnesses out of concerns that their inaccurate statements will sway a jury and lead to wrongful convictions.

Fict OID

MYTH: Most hypnotists use a swinging watch to lull subjects into a state of relaxation.

REALITY: Few hypnotists today use a watch; any procedure that effectively induces expectancies of hypnosis can boost suggestibility in most people (Kirsch, 1991).

CAN HYPNOSIS LEAD US TO EXPERIENCE AGE REGRESSION AND PAST LIVES?

One of the most popular myths of hypnosis is that it can help people to retrieve memories of events as far back in time as birth. A televised documentary (Bikel, 1995) showed a group therapy session in which a woman was age-regressed through childhood, to the womb, and eventually to being trapped in her mother's Fallopian tube. The woman provided a highly emotional demonstration of the discomfort that one would experience if one were indeed stuck in such an uncomfortable position. Although the woman may have believed in the reality of her experience, we can be quite certain that it wasn't memory based (after all, she didn't have a brain yet—she wasn't even a fertilized egg at that point). Instead, age-regressed subjects behave the way they believe children of that age should behave. Age-regressed adults don't show the expected patterns on many indices of development. For example, when regressed to childhood, they exhibit the brain waves (EEGs) typical of adults rather than of children. **Figure 4.26** describes another example.

Some therapists believe that current problems can be traced to previous lives and use **past life regression therapy** with their patients (Weiss, 1988). Typically, they hypnotize and age-regress patients to "go back to" the source of their present-day psychological and physical problems. For example, some practitioners of past life regression therapy claim that neck and shoulder pains may be a sign of having been executed by hanging or by a guillotine in a previous life.

With some rare exceptions (Stevenson, 1974), scientists agree that reports of a past life are the products of imagination and what's known about a given time period. When checked against known facts (such as whether the country was at war or peace, the face on the coin of the time), subjects' descriptions of the historical circumstances of their past lives are rarely accurate. When they are, we can often explain this accuracy by "educated guesses" and knowledge about history (Spanos et al., 1991). One participant regressed to ancient times claimed to be Julius Caesar, emperor of Rome, in 50 B.C., even though the designations of B.C. and A.D. weren't adopted until centuries later and even though Julius Caesar died decades before the first Roman emperor came to power.

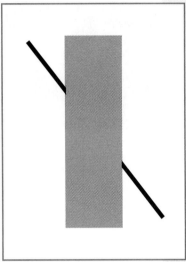

Figure 4.26 The Poggendorf Illusion Falsifies Age Regression. Researchers have used the Poggendorf illusion, shown above, to study the effects of hypnotic age regression. Adults tend to see the two segments of the black line as misaligned (in reality, they're perfectly aligned), whereas children don't. When adult subjects are age-regressed to childhood, they still see the two segments of the black line as misaligned, suggesting that hypnotic age regression doesn't make adults' perceptions more childlike (*Source:* Ascher, Barber, & Spanos, 1972; Nash, 1987)

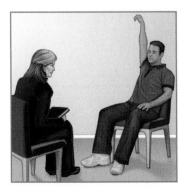

Hypnotists frequently present subjects with the suggestion that one of their arms is lifting involuntarily.

Theories of Hypnosis. The sociocognitive theory and the dissociation theory are the two most influential explanations of hypnosis. Sociocognitive theorists (Barber, 1969; Coe & Sarbin, 1991; Lynn, Kirsch, & Hallquist, 2008; Spanos, 1986) reject the idea that hypnosis is a trance state or unique state of consciousness. Instead, they explain hypnosis in the same way they explain everyday social behaviors. According to sociocognitive theory, people's attitudes, beliefs, and expectations about hypnosis shape their responses to hypnosis. Participants who are told that hypnotized people can resist suggestions find themselves able to resist, whereas those told that hypnotized people can't resist suggestions often fail to resist (Lynn, Nash, Rhue, et al., 1984; Spanos, Cobb, & Gorassini, 1985).

Ernest Hilgard's (1977, 1986, 1994) dissociation theory is an influential alternative to sociocognitive theories of hypnosis (Kihlstrom, 1992, 1998; Woody & Sadler, 2008). Hilgard (1977) defined *dissociation* as a division of consciousness, in which attention, effort, and planning are carried out without awareness. He hypothesized that hypnotic suggestions result in a separation between aspects of thought that are normally well integrated. Thus, suggestions directly bring about responses with little or no sense of effort or conscious control (Jamieson & Sheehan, 2004; Sadler & Woody, 2006). This theory does a good job of describing what people experience during hypnosis. Nevertheless, contrary to popular belief, people never completely "give up control" during hypnosis to the point that they'd do something objectionable.

Many advertisements for the effectiveness of hypnosis in treating smoking are misleading and exaggerated. Still, hypnosis can sometimes be combined with well-established treatment approaches as a cost-effective means of helping some people quit smoking.

Hypnosis in Clinical Practice.
Hypnosis has a wide range of clinical applications. Hypnosis is useful for treating pain, medical conditions, and habit disorders (such as smoking addiction), and it boosts the effectiveness of therapies for anxiety, obesity, and other conditions (Lynn & Kirsch, 2006). Nevertheless, there's no scientific evidence that hypnosis is an effective treatment by itself, so we should be skeptical of professional "hypnotherapists" who use nothing but hypnosis to treat serious psychological problems.

GLOSSARY

past life regression therapy
therapeutic approach that hypnotizes and supposedly age-regresses patients back to a previous life to identify the source of a present-day problem

QUIZ

1 Belief in psychics' cold reading techniques can be partly explained by our desire to find meaning even when it isn't there.   **TRUE** **FALSE**

2 Many of the experiences associated with an NDE can be created in circumstances that have nothing to do with being "near death."   **TRUE** **FALSE**

3 Déjà vu experiences often last for as long as an hour.   **TRUE** **FALSE**

4 A hypnosis induction greatly increases suggestibility beyond waking suggestibility.   **TRUE** **FALSE**

Answers: (1) T (p. 139); (2) T (p. 142); (3) F (p. 142); (4) F (p. 143)

▼ Can psychics really read your mind? Watch the video titled "Cold Reading: Talking to Heaven Popular Medium James Van Praagh" at www.mypsychlab.com to find out.

Your Complete Review System

4.1 Identify the basic principles that apply to all senses

Transduction is the process of converting an external energy, such as light or sound vibration, into activity in the nervous system. Evidence suggests that even though most connections in the brain are faithful to one sense modality, brain regions often respond to information from a different sense. For example, what we see affects what we hear when watching video with sound.

1. The detection of physical energy by means of the activation of sense organs, followed by transmission of this activation to higher brain areas, is called _____. (p. 114)

2. _____ is the interpretation of raw sensory inputs. (p. 114)

3. The process of converting external stimulus energy into neural activity is called _____. (p. 115)

4. A _____ _____ is a specialized cell that transduces a specific stimulus. (p. 115)

5. The _____ _____ is the lowest level of a stimulus needed for the nervous system to detect a change 50 percent of the time. (p. 115)

6. The _____ _____ _____ tells us how easily we can detect changes in stimulus intensity. (pp. 115–116)

4.2 Track how our minds build up perceptions

Information travels from primary sensory to secondary sensory cortex and then on to association cortex. Along the way, perception becomes increasingly complex and is influenced by our prior knowledge and expectations. We also process many different inputs simultaneously, a phenomenon called parallel processing. All the processing comes together to generate an integrated perceptual experience referred to as *binding*.

7. In (top-down/bottom-up) processing, we construct a whole stimulus from its parts. (p. 117)

8. Name the processing model taking place when you look at this image with a caption of "woman" versus a caption of "saxophone player." (p. 117)

9. We are able to focus on one object or idea while ignoring others thanks to _____ _____. (p. 118)

10. What does the cocktail party effect tell us about our ability to monitor stimuli outside of our immediate attention? (p. 118)

succeed with mypsychlab

1. Can past information change how you interpret what you see? Participate in this experiment to find out.
   Ambiguous Figures

2. Can you always tell the volume difference when someone turns up the volume of your favorite song?
   Weber's Law

3. Are there hidden messages in advertisements that may change our behavior? Listen as two psychologists discuss research on subliminal messages.
   Subliminal Messages

succeed with mypsychlab

Do You Know All of the Terms in This Chapter?

Find out by using the Flashcards. Want more practice? Take additional quizzes, try simulations, and watch video to be sure you are prepared for the test!

4.3 Explain how the eye starts the visual process

The lens in the eye accommodates to focus on images both near and far by changing from "fat" to "flat." The lens optimally focuses light on the retina, which lies at the rear of the eye. The retina contains rods which allow us to see shapes and cones which allow us to see colors. Additional cells in the retina transmit information about light to the brain by way of the optic nerve.

11. The _____ _____ spectrum refers to the range of wavelengths of light that humans can see. (p. 120)

12. The intensity of reflected light that reaches our eyes is called _____. (p. 122)

13. We can think of the _____ as a "movie screen" onto which light from the world is projected. (p. 121)

14. Consisting of cells that are completely transparent, the _____ changes its curvature to keep images in focus. (p. 122)

15. _____ are receptor cells that allow us to see in low light, and _____ are receptor cells that allow us to see in color. (p. 122)

Answers are located at the end of the text.

16. Identify each eye component and its function (p. 121)

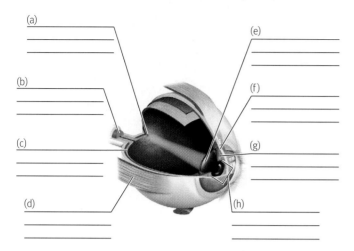

(a) _____

(b) _____

(c) _____

(d) _____

(e) _____

(f) _____

(g) _____

(h) _____

4.4 **Identify the different kinds of visual perceptions**

Our visual system is sensitive to shape, color, and motion. We use different parts of the visual cortex to process these different aspects of visual perception. Cells in the primary visual cortex, called V1, are sensitive to lines of a particular orientation, like a horizontal line or a vertical line. Color perception involves comparing the reflectance from an object with the reflectance of surrounding elements in the scene. Our visual system detects motion by comparing individual "still frames" of visual content.

17. Different parts of our _____ _____ help us to perceive shape, motion, color, and depth. (pp. 122–123)

18. Apply what you have learned about the Gestalt principles of visual perception by identifying the two rules that are shown here. (p. 124)

19. Our ability to see spatial relations in three dimensions is called _____ _____. (p. 126)

20. The process by which we perceive stimuli consistently across varied conditions is _____ _____. (p. 127)

(a)

(b)

succeed with mypsychlab

1. If you are a 9-month-old infant, will you crawl to your mother when she calls you? Find out with this simulation. **The Visual Cliff**

2. Experience how the world looks when an individual wears corrective lenses. **Normal Vision, Nearsightedness**

3. Explore how light waves are processed through the visual system. **Light and the Optic Nerve**

HEARING: THE AUDITORY SYSTEM (pp. 129–132)

4.5 **Explain how the ear starts the auditory process**

Sound waves created by vibration of air molecules are funneled into the outer ear. These vibrations perturb the eardrum, causing the three small bones in the middle ear to vibrate. This process creates pressure in the cochlea containing the basilar membrane and organ of Corti, in which hair cells are embedded. The hair cells then bend, thereby exciting them. The message is relayed to the brain through the auditory nerve.

21. _____ refers to the frequency of the sound wave and is measured in hertz (Hz). (p. 129)

22. The height of the sound wave corresponds to _____ and is measured in decibels (dB). (p. 129)

23. We refer to _____ to describe the complexity or quality of a sound. (p. 129)

24. The _____ lies in the inner ear and converts vibration into neural activity. (p. 130)

25. The organ of Corti and basilar membrane are especially critical to hearing because _____ _____ are embedded within them. (p. 130)

26. Identify both the component and its function in the hearing process. (p. 131)

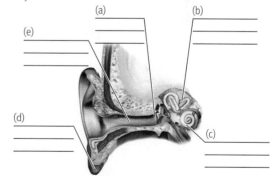

(a) _____

(b) _____

(c) _____

(d) _____

(e) _____

4.6 **Identify the different kinds of auditory perceptions**

We perceive pitch based on where along the basilar membrane hair cells were maximally excited. We also perceive where a sound is coming from, a phenomenon called "sound localization." Loudness and timbre are also important aspects of sound perceptions.

27. The perception of high-pitched tones by the basilar membrane can be explained by _____ theory. (pp. 131–132)

28. We use various brain centers to _____ sounds with respect to our bodies. (p. 132)

29. Demonstrate how we locate sound starting from the "sound source." (p. 131)

30. The presentation of dissimilar sounds to the two ears is called _____ _____. (p. 132)

Sound source

succeed with mypsychlab

1. Test your knowledge of the auditory system.
   Major Structures of the Ear

2. How do you hear your favorite music? Take an interactive tour of the ear.
   Virtual Tour of the Human Ear

3. Listen to and watch different sound waves.
   Frequency and Amplitude of Sound Waves

SMELL, TASTE, AND TOUCH: THE SENSUAL SENSES (pp. 132–137)

4.7 Identify how we sense and perceive tastes and odors

Gustation (taste) and olfaction (smell) are chemical senses because our sense receptors interact with molecules containing flavor and odor. The tongue contains taste receptors for sweet, sour, salty, and umami (a "meaty" or "savory" flavor). Our ability to taste different food also relies largely on smell. Olfactory receptors in our noses are sensitive to hundreds of different airborne molecules. We use our senses of taste and smell to sample our food. We also appear sensitive to pheromones, odorless molecules that can affect sexual response.

31. We detect taste with _____ _____ that are on our tongue. (p. 133)

32. We're sensitive to _____ basic tastes, the last of which, _____, was recently discovered. (p. 133)

33. A part of the limbic system, the _____ _____ is a site of convergence for smell and taste. (p. 134)

34. Label the brain components involved in the processes of smell and taste. (p. 134)

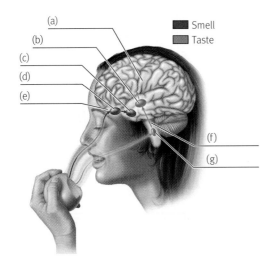

(a)
(b)
(c)
(d)
(e)

■ Smell
■ Taste

(f)
(g)

35. _____ are odorless chemicals that serve as social signals to one's species and alter animals' sexual behavior. (p. 134)

4.8 Explain how pain perception differs from touch perception

Different receptors process touch and pain and there's a large emotional component to pain not present with touch. This is because pain information activates parts of the limbic system in addition to the somatosensory cortex. As unpleasant as pain may be, it's essential to our survival.

36. Explain the process by which humans detect physical pressure, temperature, and pain. (p. 135)

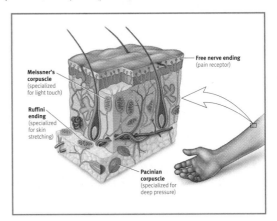

Free nerve ending (pain receptor)

Meissner's corpuscle (specialized for light touch)

Ruffini ending (specialized for skin stretching)

Pacinian corpuscle (specialized for deep pressure)

37. We sense touch, temperature, and especially pain, with _____ _____ _____. (p. 135)

38. Touch information travels more (slowly/quickly) than pain stimuli information. (p. 135)

4.9 Describe the different body senses

We process information about touch to the skin, muscle activity, and acceleration. These are called "somatosensory" for body sensation, "proprioception" for muscle position sense, and "vestibular sense" for the sense of balance and equilibrium. The somatosensory system responds to light touch, deep pressure, hot and cold temperature, and tissue damage. Our muscles contain sense receptors that detect stretch and others that detect force. We calculate where our bodies are located from this information. We're typically unaware of our sense of equilibrium.

39. Our sense of body position is called _____. (p. 136)

40. The _____ _____, also called the sense of equilibrium, enables us to sense and maintain our balance. (p. 136)

succeed with mypsychlab

1. Watch how sense of smell may predict early memory loss.
   Alzheimer's Smell Test

2. Watch as scientists explain how your perfume may change your self-perception.
   Aromatherapy

ALTERATIONS IN SENSATION AND PERCEPTION (pp. 138–145)

4.10 Analyze the scientific support for and against ESP

Most people accept the existence of ESP without the need for scientific evidence in part because we greatly underestimate how likely it is that coincidences, like two people at a gathering having the same birthday, occur by chance.

41. Proponents of _____ _____ argue that we can perceive events outside of the known channels of sensation. (p. 138)

4.11 Determine how scientists explain seemingly "mystical" alterations in perception

Hallucinations are associated with sensory deprivation, hallucinogenic drug use, and altered states of consciousness. Out-of-body experiences and near-death experiences seem to vary by culture and are likely explained by a combination of physiological factors and cultural expectations. Déjà vu experiences may be triggered by small seizures in the temporal lobe creating a sense of familiarity or by unconscious information processing.

42. The most extreme example of separation between sensation and perception is _____. (p. 139)

43. During a state of high stress or extreme relaxation, if you feel like your consciousness has left your body, you may be having an _____ experience. (p. 140)

44. Although there are many variations depending on one's religion and culture, many people in our culture associate a _____ _____ experience with approaching a bright light. (p. 141)

45. The sensation that you're reliving something even though you know the situation is new, or that you've been somewhere even though you've never been there before is called _____. (p. 142)

4.12 Distinguish myths from realities concerning hypnosis

Contrary to popular belief, hypnosis is not a sleep-like state, subjects are not in a trances, and they don't forget what happened during hypnosis. Hypnosis does not improve memory and may lead to a higher incidence of false memory. Sociocognitive models of hypnosis attribute hypnosis to preexisting expectations about what impact hypnosis will have. The dissociation model suggests that a division of conscious experience from perception and attention may explain the experience of hypnosis.

46. Most hypnotized people (are/aren't) fully aware of their surroundings. (p. 143)

47. One of the most popular myths about hypnosis is that it can make people remember a past life using a therapy called _____ _____ _____ _____. (p. 144)

48. What is the name of the illusion (pictured here) that researchers have used to study the effects of hypnotic age regression? (p. 144)

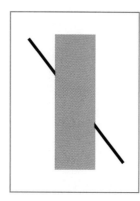

49. Hilgard's _____ theory explains hypnosis based on a separation of the part of the personality responsible for planning from the part of the personality that controls memories. (p. 144)

50. Hypnosis in clinical practice (has/has not) demonstrated positive effects in treating pain or habit disorders, such as smoking. (p. 145)

succeed with mypsychlab

1. Experience hypnosis for yourself
Hypnosis

SCIENTIFIC THINKING SKILLS
Questions and Summary

1 Your friends plan to spend an afternoon trying to expose the subliminal messages they believe are hidden on a CD of your favorite band. What would you do to help them understand how subliminal messaging works (or doesn't work)?

2 Your new part-time job as a theatre stage director involves selecting audience members to participate in a hypnotist's show. What characteristics would you look for as you screen potential audience participants?

RULING OUT RIVAL HYPOTHESES
pp. 117, 118, 134, 136, 142

CORRELATION vs. CAUSATION
p. 136

FALSIFIABILITY
pp. 125, 142

REPLICABILITY
pp. 125, 133, 138, 139, 140

EXTRAORDINARY CLAIMS
pp. 119, 139, 142

OCCAM'S RAZOR
pp. 123, 125

Learning

Can we learn in our sleep? (p. 180)

How do trainers get animals to do cute tricks like dancing or water skiing? (p. 168)

Does watching violence on TV really teach children to become violent? (p. 174)

How do phobias develop? (pp. 158–159)

Do different people have different learning styles that work best for them? (p. 181)

Before reading further, try your hand at the following four items.

(1) Ivan Pavlov, the discoverer of classical conditioning, was well known as a
   (a) slow eater.
   (b) fast walker.
   (c) terrible cook.
   (d) I have no idea.

(2) John B. Watson, the founder of behaviorism, was tossed out of Johns Hopkins University for
   (a) plagiarizing a journal article.
   (b) stabbing one of his faculty colleagues.
   (c) having an affair with his graduate student.
   (d) I have no idea.

(3) Watson believed that parents should do which of the following to their children before bedtime?
   (a) spank them
   (b) kiss them on the cheek
   (c) shake their hands
   (d) I have no idea.

(4) As a college student, B.F. Skinner, the founder of radical behaviorism, once spread a false rumor that which of the following individuals was coming to campus?
   (a) silent movie comedian Charlie Chaplin
   (b) psychoanalyst Sigmund Freud
   (c) President Theodore Roosevelt
   (d) I have no idea.

Now, read the following paragraph.

The three most famous figures in the psychology of learning were each colorful characters in their own way. The discoverer of classical conditioning, Ivan Pavlov, was a notoriously compulsive fellow. He ate lunch every day at precisely 12 noon, went to bed at exactly the same time every night, and departed St. Petersburg, Russia, for vacation the same day every year. Pavlov was also such a rapid walker that his wife frequently had to run frantically to keep up with him. The life of the founder of behaviorism, John B. Watson, was rocked with scandal. Despite becoming one of the world's most famous psychologists, he was unceremoniously booted out of Johns Hopkins University for having an affair with his graduate student, Rosalie Rayner. Watson also had rather unusual ideas about parenting; for example, he believed that all parents should shake hands with their children before bedtime. B.F. Skinner, the founder of radical behaviorism, was something of a prankster in his undergraduate years at Hamilton College in New York. He and a friend once spread a false rumor that comedian Charlie Chaplin was coming to campus. This rumor nearly provoked a riot when Chaplin didn't materialize as expected.

Now go back and try again to answer the four questions at the beginning of this chapter.

If you got more questions right the second time than the first—and odds are you did—then you've experienced something we all take for granted: learning. (The answers, by the way, are b, c, c, and a.) By **learning,** we mean a change in an organism's behavior or thought as a result of experience. As we discovered in Chapter 3, when we learn our brains change along with our behaviors. Remarkably, your brain is physically different now than it was just a few minutes ago, because it underwent chemical changes that allowed you to learn novel facts.

Learning lies at the heart of just about every domain of psychology. Virtually all behaviors are a complex stew of genetic predispositions and learning. Without learning, we'd be unable to do much; we couldn't walk, talk, or read an introductory psychology textbook chapter about learning.

Psychologists have long debated how many distinct types of learning there are. We're not going to try to settle this controversy here. Instead, we'll review several types of learning that psychologists have studied in depth, starting with the most basic.

Before we do, place your brain on pause, put down your pen or highlighter, close your eyes, and attend to several things that you almost never notice: the soft buzzing of the lights in the room, the feel of your clothing against your skin, the sensation of your tongue on your teeth or lips. Unless someone draws our attention to these stimuli, we don't even realize they're there because we've learned to ignore them. **Habituation** is the process by which we respond less strongly over time to repeated stimuli. It helps explain why loud snorers can sleep peacefully through the night while keeping their irritated roommates wide awake. Chronic snorers have become so accustomed to the sound of their own snoring that they no longer notice it.

Habituating to background noise while studying can be difficult, especially if the noise is loud.

Habituation is the simplest form of learning. We can find it even in the lowly single-celled amoeba that we see under our microscope. Shine a light on an amoeba, and it will contract into a ball. But keep shining the light, and soon it will resume its normal activities, like busily swimming around on our microscope slide. Habituation is probably the earliest form of learning to emerge in humans. Unborn fetuses as young as 32 weeks display habituation when we apply a gentle vibrator to the mother's stomach. At first, the fetus jerks around in response to the stimulus, but after repeated vibrations it stops moving (Morokuma et al., 2004). What was first a shock to the fetus's system later became a mere annoyance that it could safely ignore.

Habituation makes good adaptive sense. We wouldn't want to attend to every tiny sensation that comes across our mental radar screens because most pose no threat. Yet we wouldn't want to habituate to stimuli that might be dangerous. Fortunately, not all repeated stimuli lead to habituation; only those that we deem safe or worth ignoring do. We typically don't habituate to powerful stimuli, like extremely loud tones or painful electric shocks.

Classical Conditioning

The story of habituation could hardly be more straightforward. We experience a stimulus, respond to it, and then stop responding after repeated exposure. We've learned something significant, but we haven't learned to forge connections between two stimuli. Yet a great deal of learning depends on associating one thing with another. If we never learned to connect one stimulus, like the appearance of an apple, with another stimulus, like its taste, our world would be what William James (1890) called a "blooming, buzzing confusion"—a world of disconnected sensory experiences.

PAVLOV'S DISCOVERIES

The history of science teaches us that many discoveries arise from *serendipity*, or accident. Yet it takes a great scientist to capitalize on serendipitous observations that others regard as meaningless flukes. As French microbiologist Louis Pasteur, who discovered the process of pasteurizing milk, observed, "Chance favors the prepared mind." So it was with the discoveries of Russian scientist Ivan Pavlov. His landmark understanding of classical

GLOSSARY

learning
change in an organism's behavior or thought as a result of experience

habituation
process of responding less strongly over time to repeated stimuli

The Rolling Stones may be the only major rock band to accurately describe the process of classical conditioning. One of their well-known songs refers to a man salivating like one of Pavlov's dogs whenever the object of his affection calls his name. Not bad for a group of nonpsychologists!

GLOSSARY

classical (Pavlovian) conditioning
form of learning in which animals come to respond to a previously neutral stimulus that had been paired with another stimulus that elicits an automatic response

conditioned stimulus (CS)
initially neutral stimulus that comes to elicit a response due to association with an unconditioned stimulus

unconditioned stimulus (UCS)
stimulus that elicits an automatic response

unconditioned response (UCR)
automatic response to a nonneutral stimulus that does not need to be learned

conditioned response (CR)
response previously associated with a nonneutral stimulus that is elicited by a neutral stimulus through conditioning

REPLICABILITY
Can the results be duplicated in other studies?

acquisition
learning phase during which a conditioned response is established

extinction
gradual reduction and eventual elimination of the conditioned response after the conditioned stimulus is presented repeatedly without the unconditioned stimulus

conditioning emerged from a set of unforeseen observations that were unrelated to his main research interests.

Pavlov's primary research was digestion in dogs—in fact, his discoveries concerning digestion, not classical conditioning, earned him the Nobel Prize in 1904. Pavlov placed dogs in a harness and inserted a *cannula,* or collection tube, into their salivary glands to study their salivary responses to meat powder. In doing so, he observed something unexpected: He found that dogs began salivating not only to the meat powder itself but to previously neutral stimuli that had become associated with it, such as research assistants who brought in the powder. Indeed, the dogs even salivated to the sound of these assistants' footsteps as they approached the laboratory. The dogs seemed to be anticipating the meat powder and responding to stimuli that signaled its arrival.

We call this process of association **classical conditioning** (or **Pavlovian conditioning**): a form of learning in which animals come to respond to a previously neutral stimulus that had been paired with another stimulus that elicits an automatic response. Yet Pavlov's initial observations were merely anecdotal, so like any good scientist he put his informal observations to a more rigorous test.

THE CLASSICAL CONDITIONING PHENOMENON

Here's how Pavlov first demonstrated classical conditioning systematically (see **Figure 5.1**):

(1) He started with an initially neutral stimulus, one that didn't elicit any particular response. In this case, Pavlov used a metronome, a clicking pendulum that keeps time (in other studies, Pavlov used a tuning fork or whistle; contrary to popular belief, Pavlov didn't use a bell).

(2) He then paired the neutral stimulus again and again with an **unconditioned stimulus (UCS).** In the case of Pavlov's dogs, the UCS was the meat powder. The UCS elicits an automatic, reflexive response called the **unconditioned response (UCR),** in this case salivation. The key point is that the animal doesn't need to learn to respond to the UCS with the UCR. It produces the UCR without any training at all, because the response is a product of biology, not experience.

(3) As Pavlov repeatedly paired the neutral stimulus with the UCS he observed something remarkable. If he now presented the metronome alone, it elicited a response, namely, salivation. This new response is the **conditioned response (CR):** a response previously associated with a nonneutral stimulus that comes to be elicited by a neutral stimulus. The previously neutral stimulus (the metronome) had now become a **conditioned stimulus (CS)** —a previously neutral stimulus that comes to elicit a conditioned response as a result of its association with an unconditioned stimulus.

Once the dog began to salivate (CR) to the metronome (CS), we could conclude that learning had occurred. **[LEARNING OBJECTIVE 5.1]** The dog, which previously did nothing when it heard the metronome except perhaps turn its head toward it, now salivates when it hears the metronome. The CR, in contrast to the UCR, is a product of experience, not biology.

In most cases, the CR is similar to the UCR, but it's rarely identical to it. For example, Pavlov found that dogs salivated less in response to the metronome (the CS) than to the meat powder (the UCS).

Few findings in psychology are as replicable as classical conditioning. We can apply the classical conditioning paradigm to just about any animal with an intact nervous system and demonstrate it repeatedly without fail. If only all psychological findings were so dependable!

ACQUISITION, EXTINCTION, AND SPONTANEOUS RECOVERY

Pavlov noted, and many others have confirmed, that classical conditioning occurs in three phases—acquisition, extinction, and spontaneous recovery.

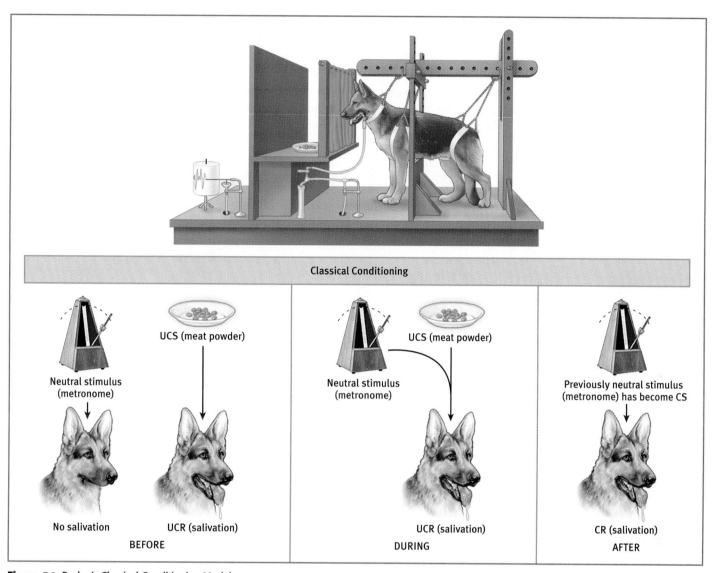

Figure 5.1 Pavlov's Classical Conditioning Model. UCS (meat powder) is paired with a neutral stimulus (metronome clicking) and produces UCR (salivation). Then the metronome is presented alone, and CR (salivation) occurs.

Acquisition. In **acquisition,** we gradually learn—or acquire—the CR. If we look at **Figure 5.2a,** we'll see that, as the CS and UCS are paired over and over again, the CR increases progressively in strength. The steepness of this curve varies somewhat depending on how close together in time the CS and UCS are presented. In general, the closer in time the pairing of CS and UCS, the faster learning occurs, with about a half-second delay typically being the optimal pairing for learning. **[LEARNING OBJECTIVE 5.2]** Longer delays usually decrease the speed and strength of the organism's response.

Extinction. In a process called **extinction,** the CR decreases in magnitude and eventually disappears when the CS is repeatedly presented alone, that is, without the UCS (see **Figure 5.2b**). After numerous presentations of the metronome without meat powder, Pavlov's dogs eventually stopped salivating. Most psychologists once believed that extinction was similar to forgetting: The CR fades away over repeated trials, just as many memories gradually decay (see Chapter 6). Yet the truth

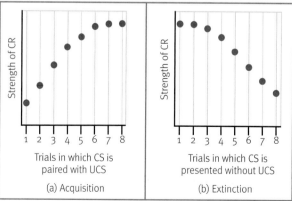

Figure 5.2 Acquisition and Extinction. Acquisition is the repeated pairing of UCS and CS, increasing the CR's strength (a). In extinction, the CS is presented again and again without the UCS, resulting in the gradual disappearance of the CR (b).

Fact-OID Backward conditioning—in which the UCS is presented *before* the CS—is extremely difficult to achieve. Because the CS fails to predict the UCS and the UCR often begins before the CS has even occurred, organisms have difficulty using the CS to anticipate the UCS.

is more complicated and interesting than that. Extinction is an active, rather than passive, process. During extinction a new response, which in the case of Pavlov's dogs was the *absence* of salivation, gradually "writes over" or inhibits the CR, namely, salivation. The extinguished CR doesn't vanish completely; it's merely overshadowed by the new behavior. This contrasts with most forms of traditional forgetting, in which the memory itself disappears. Interestingly, Pavlov had proposed this hypothesis in his writings, although few people believed him at the time. How do we know he was right? Read on.

Spontaneous Recovery. In a phenomenon called **spontaneous recovery,** a seemingly extinct CR reappears (often in somewhat weaker form) if the CS is presented again. It's as though the CR were lurking in the background, waiting to appear following another presentation of the CS. In a classic study, Pavlov (1927) presented the CS (tone from a metronome) alone again and again and extinguished the CR (salivation) because there was no UCS (mouthwatering meat powder) following it. Two hours later, he presented the CS again, and the CR returned. The animal hadn't really forgotten the CR, just suppressed it.

WHAT DO *you* THINK?

You are a veteran of the Vietnam War who suffered emotional trauma for several years following your combat experience. You are currently re-experiencing symptoms of trauma after viewing coverage of the current conflicts in Iraq and Afghanistan. How could spontaneous recovery help explain the return of your symptoms?

GLOSSARY

spontaneous recovery
sudden reemergence of an extinct conditioned response after a delay in exposure to the conditioned stimulus

stimulus generalization
process by which conditioned stimuli similar, but not identical to, the original conditioned stimulus elicit a conditioned response

stimulus discrimination
displaying a less pronounced conditioned response to conditioned stimuli that differ from the original conditioned stimulus

STIMULUS GENERALIZATION AND DISCRIMINATION

As much as classical conditioning helps us adapt to and learn new things, it would be virtually useless if we couldn't apply it to new situations. No two stimuli are identical; even our friends and family look a tiny bit different every time we see them. We need to learn to respond to stimuli that differ somewhat from those we originally encountered during conditioning. By the same token, we don't want to go around shouting "Mom!" at every woman who has the same height and hair style as our mothers.

Stimulus Generalization. Pavlov found that, following classical conditioning, his dogs salivated not merely to the original metronome sound but to sounds similar to it. This phenomenon is **stimulus generalization:** the process by which CSs that are similar, but not identical, to the original CS elicit a CR. Stimulus generalization occurs along a *generalization gradient:* The more similar to the original CS the new CS is, the stronger the CR will be (see **Figure 5.3**). Pavlov found that his dogs showed their largest amount of salivation to the original sound, with progressively less salivation to sounds that were less and less similar to it in pitch. Stimulus generalization allows us to transfer what we've learned to new things. For example, this is why we can borrow a friend's car without needing a full tutorial on how to drive it, once we've learned to drive our own car.

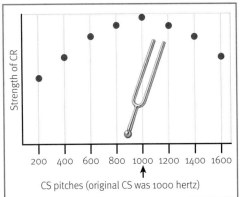

Figure 5.3 Generalization Gradient. The more similar to the original CS the new CS is (for example, Pavlov using a tone pitched close to the original tone's pitch), the stronger the CR will be.

Stimulus Discrimination. **Stimulus discrimination** is the flip side of the coin to stimulus generalization; it occurs when we exhibit a less pronounced CR to CSs that differ from the original CS. Stimulus discrimination helps us understand why we can enjoy scary movies. Although we may hyperventilate a bit while watching sharks circle the divers in the movie *Open Water,* we'd respond much more strongly if a shark chased us around in a tank at the aquarium. We've learned to discriminate between a motion picture stimulus and the real-world version of it and to modify our response as a result.

HIGHER-ORDER CONDITIONING

Taking conditioning a step further, organisms learn to develop conditioned associations to CSs that are associated with the original CS. If after we condition a dog to salivate to a tone we pair a picture of a circle with the tone, the dog eventually salivates to the circle as well as to the tone. This finding demonstrates **higher-order conditioning:** the process by which organisms develop classically conditioned responses to CSs associated with the original CS (Gewirtz & Davis, 2000). As we might expect, second-order conditioning—in which a new CS is paired with the original CS—tends to be weaker than garden-variety classical conditioning, and third-order conditioning—in which a third CS is paired with the second-order CS—is even weaker. Fourth-order conditioning and beyond are typically difficult or impossible.

Higher-order conditioning also helps to explain how some people develop addictions to cigarettes, heroin, and other drugs. Many addictions are shaped in part by higher-order conditioning, with the context in which people take the drugs serving as a higher-order CS. People who don't generally smoke cigarettes may find themselves craving one at a party because they've smoked occasionally at previous parties with their friends who smoke. Behaviorists refer to these higher-order CSs as *occasion setters,* because they refer to the setting in which the CS occurs.

APPLICATIONS OF CLASSICAL CONDITIONING TO DAILY LIFE

Without classical conditioning, we couldn't develop physiological associations to stimuli that signal biologically important events, like things we want to eat—or that want to eat us. Many of the physiological responses we display in classical conditioning contribute to our survival. Salivation, for instance, helps us to digest food. Moreover, without classical conditioning, we couldn't learn many important associations that help us survive, such as the connection between a car horn and the risk of being hit by a large metal object.

Classical conditioning applies to various areas of everyday life. We'll consider four here: advertising and the acquisition of fears, phobias, and fetishes. **[LEARNING OBJECTIVE 5.3]**

Higher-order conditioning helps explain the seemingly mysterious "power of suggestion." Merely hearing "Want a Coke?" can make us feel thirsty on a hot summer day.

Classical Conditioning and Advertising.
Few people grasp the principles of classical conditioning, especially higher-order conditioning, better than advertisers. By repeatedly pairing the sights and sounds of products with photographs of handsome hunks and scantily clad beauties, marketing whizzes try to establish classically conditioned connections between their brands and positive emotions (Gibson, 2008). They do so for a good reason: It works.

One researcher (Gorn, 1982) paired slides of either blue or beige pens (the CSs) with music that participants had rated as either enjoyable or not enjoyable (the UCSs). Then he gave participants the opportunity to select a pen as they left the lab. Whereas 79 percent of participants who heard music they liked picked the pen that had been paired with music, only 30 percent of those who heard music they disliked picked the pen that had been paired with music.

Nevertheless, not all researchers who've paired products with pleasurable stimuli have succeeded in demonstrating classical conditioning effects (Smith, 2001). Two researchers (Gresham & Shimp, 1985) paired various products, like Coke, Colgate toothpaste, and Grape-Nuts cereal, with television commercials that previous subjects had rated as generating pleasant, unpleasant, or neutral emotions. They found little evidence that these pairings affected participants' preferences for the ads. Nevertheless, their negative findings are open to a rival explanation: latent inhibition. *Latent inhibition* refers to the fact that when we've experienced a CS alone many times, it's difficult to classically condition it to another stimulus (Vaitl & Lipp, 1997). Because the investigators relied on brands

Advertisers use higher-order classical conditioning to get customers to associate their products with an inherently enjoyable stimulus.

GLOSSARY

higher-order conditioning
developing a conditioned response to a conditioned stimulus by virtue of its association with another conditioned stimulus

RULING OUT RIVAL HYPOTHESES
Have important alternative explanations for the findings been excluded?

with which participants were already familiar, their negative findings may be attributable to latent inhibition. Indeed, when researchers have used novel brands, they've generally been able to show classical conditioning effects (Stuart, Shimp, & Engle, 1987).

The Acquisition of Fears: The Strange Tale of Little Albert.
Can classical conditioning help explain how we come to fear, despise, or avoid stimuli? John B. Watson, the founder of behaviorism, answered this question in 1920 when he and his graduate student, Rosalie Rayner, performed what must be regarded as one of the most ethically questionable studies in the history of psychology. Here's what they did.

Watson and Rayner (1920) set out in part to falsify the Freudian view (see Chapter 12) that phobias stem from deep-seated conflicts buried in the unconscious. They recruited a 9-month-old infant who'll be forever known in the psychological literature as Little Albert. Little Albert was fond of furry little creatures, like white rats. But Watson and Rayner were about to change that.

Watson and Raynor first allowed Little Albert to play with a rat. But only seconds afterward, Watson snuck up behind Little Albert and struck a gong with a steel hammer, creating an earsplitting noise, startling him out of his wits and making him cry. After seven such pairings of the rat and UCS (loud sound from gong), Little Albert displayed a CR (crying) to the rat alone, indicating that the rat had now become a CS. The conditioned response was still present when Watson and Rayner exposed Little Albert to the rat five days later. Little Albert also displayed stimulus generalization, crying not only in response to rats, but also to a rabbit, a dog, a furry coat, and, to a lesser extent, a Santa Claus mask and John B. Watson's hair. Fortunately, Little Albert also demonstrated at least some stimulus discrimination, as he didn't display much negative reaction toward cotton balls or the hair of Dr. Watson's research assistants.

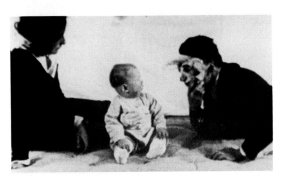

Nine-month-old Little Albert, crying in response to a Santa Claus mask after he was conditioned to fear white furry objects.

FALSIFIABILITY
Can the claim be disproved?

REPLICABILITY
Can the results be duplicated in other studies?

Watson and Rayner's demonstration is only a case study. As we saw in Chapter 2, case studies are limited in the conclusions they allow; for example, we can't generalize from Little Albert's case to the development of fears in other children. But the Little Albert case provides an *existence proof* (see Chapter 2) that classical conditioning can produce fears in humans. Although not everyone has successfully replicated Watson and Rayner's findings (Harris, 1979; Jones, 1930), Watson and Rayner were probably right that Little Albert's fears arose in part from classical conditioning. Nevertheless, these replication failures may imply that there's more to fear reactions than classical conditioning alone; we'll come back to this point later in the chapter.

Incidentally, no one knows what became of poor Little Albert. His mother withdrew him from the study about a month after it began, never to be heard from again. Needless to say, because inducing prolonged fear responses in an infant raises a host of serious ethical questions, Watson and Rayner's Little Albert study would never get past a modern-day college or university IRB (see Chapter 2).

Phobias.
Do you suffer from *paraskavedekatriaphobia*? If so, don't be concerned, because you aren't the only person who's afraid of Friday the 13th.

Higher-order conditioning allows our learning to be remarkably flexible. We can develop fears of many stimuli, although certain phobias, such as those of snakes, spiders, heights, water, and blood, are considerably more widespread than others (American Psychiatric Association, 2000). Other, more exotic phobias, like fear of being tickled by feathers (*pteronophobia*), fear of clowns (*coulrophobia*), fear of flutes (*aulophobia*), and fear of bald people (*peladophobia*), are exceedingly rare.

The good news is that classical conditioning can contribute not only to the acquisition of phobias but also to their elimination. Mary Cover Jones, a student of Watson, treated a 3-year-old named Little Peter, who had a phobia of rabbits. Jones (1924) treated Peter's fear successfully by gradually introducing him to a white rabbit while giving him a piece of his favorite candy. As she moved the rabbit increasingly closer to him, the sight of the rabbit eventually came to elicit a new CR: pleasure rather than fear. Modern-day psychotherapists, although rarely feeding their clients candy, use similar practices to eliminate phobias. They may pair feared stimuli with relaxation or other pleasurable stimuli (Wolpe, 1990; see Chapter 14).

Fetishes. There's also good reason to believe that *fetishism*—sexual attraction to nonliving things—often arises in part from classical conditioning (Akins, 2004). Like phobias, fetishes come in a bewildering variety of forms: People can become attached to shoes, stockings, and just about anything else.

Although the origins of human fetishes are controversial, Michael Domjan and his colleagues were successful in classically conditioning fetishes in male Japanese quails. In one study, they presented male quails with a cylindrical object made of terrycloth, followed by a female quail with which they happily mated. After 30 such pairings, about half of the male quails attempted to mate with the cylindrical object when it appeared alone (Köksal et al., 2004). Although the generalizability of these findings to humans is unclear, there's good evidence that at least some people develop fetishes by the repeated pairing of neutral objects with sexual activity (Rachman & Hodgson, 1968; Weinberg, Williams, & Calhan, 1995).

Some researchers have suggested that classical conditioning may help to explain some human fetishes, such as a shoe fetish.

myth CONCEPTIONS — ARE WE WHAT WE EAT?

Many of us have heard that "we are what we eat," but in the 1950s, psychologist James McConnell took this proverb quite literally. McConnell became convinced he'd discovered a means of chemically transferring learning from one animal to another. Indeed, for many years psychology textbooks informed undergraduates that scientists could chemically transfer learning across animals.

James McConnell and his colleagues paired a light with an electric shock, which caused the *planaria* worm to contract reflexively.

McConnell's animal of choice was the *planaria,* a flatworm a few inches long. Using classical conditioning, McConnell and his colleagues exposed planaria to a light, which served as the CS, while pairing it with a 1-second electric shock, which served as the UCS. When planaria receive an electric shock, they contract reflexively. After numerous pairings between light and shock, the light itself causes planaria to contract (Thompson & McConnell, 1955).

McConnell wanted to find out whether he could chemically transfer the memory of this classical conditioning experience to another planaria. His approach was brutally simple. Relying on the fact that many planaria are miniature cannibals, he chopped up the trained planaria and fed them to their fellow worms. Remarkably, McConnell (1962) reported that planaria who'd gobbled up classically conditioned planaria acquired classically conditioned reactions to the light more quickly than planaria who hadn't.

Understandably, McConnell's memory transfer studies generated enormous excitement. Imagine if McConnell were right! You could sign up for your introductory psychology class, swallow a pill containing all of the psychological knowledge you'd need to get an A, and . . . voilà, you're now an expert psychologist. Indeed, McConnell went directly to the general public with his findings, proclaiming in *Time, Newsweek,* and other popular magazines that scientists were on the verge of developing a "memory pill" (Rilling, 1996).

Yet it wasn't long before the wind went out of McConnell's scientific sails: Scientists couldn't replicate his findings. Eventually, after years of intense debate and failed replications, the scientific community concluded that McConnell had fooled himself into seeing something that was never there. His planaria lab closed its doors in 1971.

REPLICABILITY
Can the results be duplicated in other studies?

QUIZ

1 Habituation to meaningless stimuli is generally adaptive. **TRUE** **FALSE**

2 In classical conditioning, the conditioned stimulus (CS) initially yields a reflexive, automatic response. **TRUE** **FALSE**

3 Conditioning is most effective when the CS precedes the UCS by a short period of time. **TRUE** **FALSE**

4 Extinction is produced by the gradual "decay" of the CR over time. **TRUE** **FALSE**

Answers: (1) T (p. 153); (2) F (p. 154); (3) T (p. 155); (4) F (p. 156)

PEARSON
mypsychlab

▼ How was Little Albert conditioned to fear furry objects? Watch the video titled "Archived Footage of Little Albert" at www.mypsychlab.com to find out.

Operant Conditioning

What do the following three examples have in common?

- Using bird feed as a reward, a behavioral psychologist teaches a pigeon to distinguish paintings by Monet from paintings by Picasso. By the end of the training, the pigeon is a veritable art expert.

- Using fish as a treat, a trainer teaches a dolphin to jump out of the water, spin three times, splash in the water, and propel itself through a hoop.

- In his initial attempt at playing tennis, a frustrated 12-year-old hits his opponent's serve into the net the first 15 times. After two hours of practice, he returns his opponent's serve successfully more than half the time.

The answer: All are examples of operant conditioning. The first, incidentally, comes from an actual study (Watanabe, Sakamoto, & Wakita, 1995). **Operant conditioning** is learning controlled by the consequences of the organism's behavior. In each of these examples, superficially different as they are, the organism's behavior is shaped by what comes after it, namely, reward. Psychologists also refer to operant conditioning as *instrumental conditioning,* because the organism's response serves an instrumental function. That is, the organism "gets something" out of the response, like food, sex, attention, or avoiding something unpleasant. **[LEARNING OBJECTIVE 5.4]**

Behaviorists refer to the behaviors emitted by the animal to receive a reward as *operants,* because the animal "operates" on its environment to get what it wants. Dropping 75 cents into a soda machine is an operant, as is asking out an attractive classmate. In the first case, our reward is a refreshing drink and, in the second, a hot date—if we're lucky.

Through operant conditioning, researchers taught pigeons to distinguish paintings by Monet (*top*) from those of Picasso (*bottom*).

OPERANT CONDITIONING: WHAT IT IS AND HOW IT DIFFERS FROM CLASSICAL CONDITIONING

Operant conditioning differs from classical conditioning in three important ways, which we've highlighted in **Table 5.1. [LEARNING OBJECTIVE 5.5]**

(1) In classical conditioning, the organism's response is *elicited,* that is, "pulled out" of the organism by the UCS and later the CS. Remember that in classical conditioning the UCR is an automatic response that doesn't require training. In operant conditioning, the organism's response is *emitted,* that is, generated by the organism in a seemingly voluntary fashion.

GLOSSARY

operant conditioning
learning controlled by the consequences of the organism's behavior

(2) In classical conditioning, the animal's reward is independent of what it does. Pavlov gave his dogs meat powder regardless of whether, or how much, they salivated. In operant conditioning, the animal's reward is contingent—that is, dependent—on what it does. If the animal doesn't emit a response in an operant conditioning paradigm, it comes out empty handed (or in the case of a dog, empty pawed).

(3) In classical conditioning, the organism's responses depend primarily on the autonomic nervous system (see Chapter 3). In operant conditioning, the organism's responses depend primarily on the skeletal muscles. That is, in contrast to classical conditioning, in which learning involves changes in heart rate, breathing, perspiration, and other bodily systems, in operant conditioning learning involves changes in voluntary motor behavior.

Table 5.1 Key Differences between Operant and Classical Conditioning.

	Classical Conditioning	**Operant Conditioning**
Target behavior is . . .	Elicited automatically	Emitted voluntarily
Reward is . . .	Provided unconditionally	Contingent on behavior
Behavior depends primarily on . . .	Autonomic nervous system	Skeletal muscles

THE LAW OF EFFECT

The famous **law of effect,** put forth by psychologist E.L. Thorndike is the first and most important commandment of operant conditioning: *If a response, in the presence of a stimulus, is followed by a satisfying state of affairs, the bond between stimulus and response will be strengthened.* This statement means simply that if we're rewarded for a response to a stimulus, we're more likely to repeat the behavior in response to that stimulus in the future. Psychologists sometimes refer to early forms of behaviorism as S-R psychology (*S* stands for *stimulus, R* for *response*). According to S-R theorists, most of our complex behaviors reflect the accumulation of associations between stimuli and responses: the sight of a close friend and the behavior of saying hello or the smell of a delicious hamburger and reaching for it on our plate. S-R theorists maintain that almost everything we do voluntarily—driving a car, eating a sandwich, or planting a kiss on someone's lips—results from the gradual buildup of S-R bonds due to the law of effect.

Thorndike's law of effect holds true for many but not all learning situations. Some learning tasks involve gradual increases in the likelihood of success built up over time through reward, such as training a dog to roll over or teaching a group of elementary school students to quiet down when the teacher flickers the lights. But other learning experiences are accomplished through sudden flashes of **insight,** suddenly grasping the solution to a problem or appropriate response to a stimulus. Insights don't need to be gradually solidified through rewards. Many of us can relate to the feeling of having a light bulb click on in our brains when we suddenly realize how something works. This type of learning is illustrated in **Figure 5.4.** There is good evidence that humans solve many problems through insight learning (Dawes, 1994). But whether we realize it or not, the law of effect still applies to many behaviors in both humans and other animals. How do we know? Thorndike's work laid the groundwork for demonstrating the law of effect. B.F. Skinner kicked it up a notch by using electronic technology to push the law of effect to the extreme.

B.F. SKINNER AND OPERANT CONDITIONING

Skinner wanted to put the law of effect to the test in as controlled an environment as possible. He wanted to be able to study the continual buildup of associations in ongoing operant behavior over hours, days, or weeks. So he developed what came to be known as a **Skinner box**

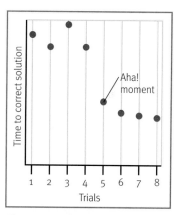

Figure 5.4 "Aha!" Reaction. Insight learning: Once an individual solves the problem, he or she gets the answer right almost every time after that.

GLOSSARY

law of effect
principle asserting that if a stimulus followed by a behavior results in a reward, the stimulus is more likely to elicit the behavior in the future

insight
grasping the nature of a problem

Skinner box
small animal chamber constructed by Skinner to allow sustained periods of conditioning to be administered and behaviors to be recorded unsupervised

"Oh, not bad. The light comes on, I press the bar, they write me a check. How about you?"

(© The New Yorker Collection 1993 Tom Cheney from cartoonbank.com. All Rights Reserved)

GLOSSARY

reinforcement
outcome or consequence of a behavior that strengthens the probability of the behavior

positive reinforcement
presentation of a stimulus that strengthens the probability of the behavior

negative reinforcement
removal of a stimulus that strengthens the probability of the behavior

(more formally, an *operant chamber*), which electronically records an animal's responses and prints out a *cumulative record,* or graph, of the animal's activity. A Skinner box typically contains a bar that delivers food when pressed, a food dispenser, and often a light that signals when reward is forthcoming (see **Figure 5.5**). With this setup, Skinner studied the operant behavior of rats, pigeons, and other animals and mapped out their responses to reward. By allowing a device to record behavior without any direct human observation, Skinner ran the risk of missing some important behaviors that the box wasn't designed to record. Nonetheless, the detailed, comprehensive data he collected forever altered the landscape of psychology.

To understand Skinner's research, you need to learn a bit of psychological jargon. There are three key concepts in Skinnerian psychology: reinforcement, punishment, and discriminative stimulus.

Reinforcement. Up to this point, we've used the term *reward* to refer to any consequence that makes a behavior more likely to occur. But Skinner found this term imprecise. He preferred the term **reinforcement,** meaning any outcome that strengthens the probability of a response (Skinner, 1953, 1971).

Skinner distinguished **positive reinforcement,** when we administer a stimulus, from **negative reinforcement,** when we take away a stimulus. Positive reinforcement could be giving a child a Hershey's Kiss when he picks up his toys; negative reinforcement could be ending a child's time-out for bad behavior once she's stopped whining. **[LEARNING OBJECTIVE 5.6]** In both cases, assuming the child finds the result satisfying, the outcome is an increase or strengthening of the response.

Hundreds of psychology students over the years have demonstrated the power of reinforcement using an unconventional participant: their professor. In the game Condition Your

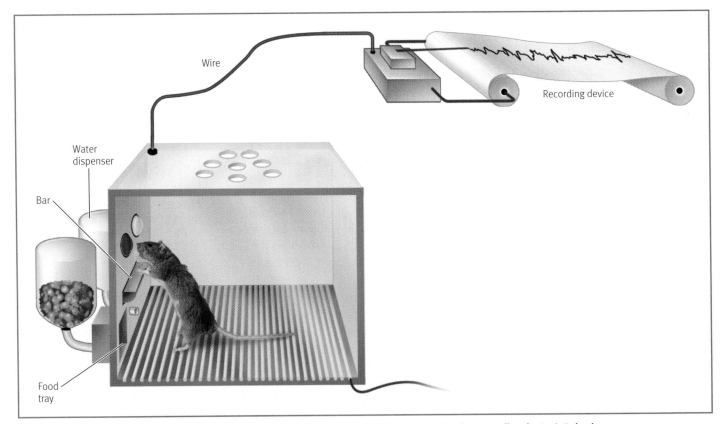

Figure 5.5 **Rat in Skinner Box and Electronic Device for Recording the Rat's Behavior.** B.F. Skinner devised a small chamber (the Skinner box) containing a bar that the rat presses to obtain food, a food dispenser, and often a light that signals when reward is forthcoming. An electronic device graphs the rat's responses in the researcher's absence.

Professor (Vyse, 1997), a class of introductory psychology students agrees to provide positive reinforcement—such as smiling or nodding their heads—to their professor whenever he or she moves in a particular direction, such as to the far left side of the room. Your authors know of one famous introductory psychology teacher who spent almost all of his time lecturing from behind his podium. During one class, his students smiled profusely and nodded their heads whenever he ventured out from behind the podium. Sure enough, by the end of class the professor was spending most of his time away from the podium.

Punishment. We shouldn't confuse negative reinforcement with **punishment,** which is any outcome that weakens the probability of a response. Punishment typically involves administering a stimulus that the organism wishes to avoid, such as a physical shock or a spanking, or an unpleasant social outcome, like laughing at someone. It can also involve the removal of a stimulus that the organism wishes to experience, such as a favorite toy or article of clothing. This means that we actually characterize punishments as both positive and negative as well, depending on whether they involve administering a stimulus or taking one away (see **Table 5.2**).

We also shouldn't confuse punishment with the disciplinary practices often associated with it. Skinner, who insisted on precision in language, argued that certain actions that might superficially appear to be punishments are actually reinforcers. He defined reinforcers and punishments solely in terms of their consequences. Consider this scenario: A mother rushes into her 3-year-old son's bedroom and yells "Stop that!" each time she hears him kicking the wall. Is she punishing the child's demanding behavior? There's no way to tell without knowing the consequences. If the bad behavior increases following the scolding, then perhaps the child is kicking the wall to get attention. If so, the mother is reinforcing, rather than punishing, his angry demands. Reinforcement strengthens the probability of a response. In contrast, punishment weakens it. **[LEARNING OBJECTIVE 5.7]**

Table 5.2 Distinguishing Reinforcement from Punishment.

	Procedure	**Effect on Behavior**	**Typical Example**
Positive Reinforcement	Presenting a stimulus	Increases target behavior	Gold star on homework that makes a student feel special
Negative Reinforcement	Removing a stimulus	Increases target behavior	Static on phone that subsides when you move to a different spot in your room
Positive Punishment	Presenting a stimulus	Decreases target behavior	Scolding by owners to stop a dog from chewing on shoes
Negative Punishment	Removing a stimulus	Decreases target behavior	Confiscating a favorite toy to stop a child from throwing a tantrum

Try labeling each of the following examples as an instance of either negative reinforcement or punishment and explain why (you can find the answers written upside-down in the margin at the bottom of the next page):

(1) A boy keeps making noise in the back of a classroom despite a teacher's repeated warnings. The teacher finally sends him to the principal's office. When he returns two hours later, he's much quieter.

(2) A woman with adult onset diabetes works hard to control her blood sugar through diet and exercise. As a result, her doctor allows her to discontinue administering her unpleasant daily insulin shots, which increases her attempts to eat healthily and exercise.

Does punishment work in the long run? Popular wisdom tells us that it usually does. Yet Skinner (1953) and most of his followers argued against the routine use of punishment to change behavior. They believed that reinforcement alone could shape most human behaviors for the better.

GLOSSARY

punishment
outcome or consequence of a behavior that weakens the probability of the behavior

Skinner and his followers believed that reinforcement was generally much more effective in shaping children's behavior than punishment.

CORRELATION vs. CAUSATION
Can we be sure that A causes B?

In some countries, such as China and Thailand, spanking is uncommon.

GLOSSARY

discriminative stimulus
stimulus associated with the presence of reinforcement

rates of eating well and exercising
her doctor increased the woman's
(2) negative reinforcement; because
noise making
the boy's teacher reduced his rate of
Answers: (1) punishment; because

According to Skinner and others (Azrin & Holz, 1966), punishment has several disadvantages:

(1) Punishment tells the organism only what *not* to do, not what *to* do. A child who's punished for throwing a tantrum won't learn how to deal with frustration more constructively.

(2) Punishment often creates anxiety, which in turn interferes with future learning.

(3) Punishment may encourage subversive behavior, prompting people to become sneakier about finding ways to display forbidden behavior.

(4) Punishment from parents may provide a model for children's aggressive behavior (Straus, Sugarman, & Giles-Sims, 1997). A child whose parents slap him when he misbehaves may "get the message" that slapping is acceptable.

Numerous researchers have reported that the use of physical punishment by parents is positively correlated with aggressive behavior in children (Fang & Corso, 2007; Gershoff, 2002). Across many studies, Murray Strauss and his colleague (Strauss & McCord, 1998) found that physical punishment is associated with more behavioral problems in children.

Yet we must remember that these studies are correlational and don't demonstrate causality. Other interpretations are possible. For example, because children share half of their genes with each parent, and because aggression is partly heritable (Krueger, Hicks, & McGue, 2001), the correlation between parents' physical punishment and their children's aggression may be due to the fact that parents who respond to adverse situations physically pass on this genetic predisposition to their children (DiLalla & Gottesman, 1991). It's also conceivable that the causal arrow is reversed: Children who are aggressive may be difficult to control and therefore elicit physical responses from their parents.

The association between physical punishment and childhood behavior problems may depend on race and culture. Spanking and other forms of physical discipline result in more childhood behavior problems in Caucasian families but fewer in African American families (Lansford, Deater-Deckard, Dodge, et al., 2004). Moreover, spanking tends to be more predictive of higher levels of childhood aggression and anxiety in countries in which spanking is rare, like China or Thailand, than in countries in which it's common, like Kenya or India (Lansford et al., 2005). The reasons for this difference aren't clear, although children who are spanked in countries in which spanking is more culturally accepted may feel less stigmatized than children in countries in which it's culturally condemned.

Still, that's not to say that we should never use punishment, only that we should use it sparingly. Most research suggests that punishment works best when it's delivered consistently and follows the undesired behavior promptly (Brennan & Mednick, 1994). In particular, immediate punishment sometimes tends to be effective, whereas delayed punishment is often useless (Church, 1969; McCord, 2006; Moffitt, 1983). Punishment of an undesired behavior also works best when we simultaneously reinforce a desired behavior (Azrin & Holz, 1966).

Discriminative Stimulus. The final critical term in operant conditioning lingo is **discriminative stimulus,** which is any stimulus that signals the presence of reinforcement. When we snap our fingers at a dog in the hopes of having it come over to us, the dog may approach us to get a much-appreciated petting. For the dog, our finger snapping is a discriminative stimulus. It's a signal that if it comes near us, it will receive reinforcement. According to behaviorists, we're responding to a discriminative stimulus virtually all the time, even if we're not consciously aware of it. An example is when a friend waves at us and we walk over to her to say hi in return.

Same Song, Second Verse. *Acquisition, extinction, spontaneous recovery, stimulus generalization,* and *stimulus discrimination* are all terms that we introduced in our discussion of

Table 5.3 Definition Reminders of Important Concepts in Both Classical and Operant Conditioning.

Term	Definition
Acquisition	Learning phase during which a response is established
Extinction	Gradual reduction and eventual elimination of the response after a stimulus is presented repeatedly
Spontaneous Recovery	Sudden reemergence of an extinguished response after a delay
Stimulus Generalization	Eliciting a response to stimuli similar to but not identical to the original stimulus
Stimulus Discrimination	Displaying a less pronounced response to stimuli that differs from the original stimulus

classical conditioning. These terms apply just as much to operant conditioning as well. We can find the definitions in **Table 5.3.** Below, we'll examine how three of these concepts apply to operant conditioning.

Extinction. In operant conditioning, extinction occurs when we stop delivering reinforcers to a previously reinforced behavior. Gradually, this behavior declines in frequency and disappears. If parents give a screaming child a toy to quiet her, they may be inadvertently reinforcing her behavior, because she's learning to scream to get something. If parents buy earplugs and stop placating the child by giving toys, the screaming behavior gradually extinguishes. In such cases we often see an *extinction burst.* That is, shortly after withdrawing the reinforcer the undesired behavior initially increases in intensity, probably because the child is trying harder to get reinforced. So there's some truth to the old saying that things sometimes need to get worse before they get better.

Stimulus Discrimination. As we mentioned earlier, one group of investigators used food reinforcement to train pigeons to distinguish paintings by Monet from those of Picasso (Watanabe et al., 1995). That's stimulus discrimination because the pigeons are learning to tell the difference between two different types of stimuli.

Stimulus Generalization. Interestingly, these investigators also found that their pigeons displayed stimulus generalization. Following operant conditioning, they distinguished paintings by impressionist artists whose styles were similar to Monet's, such as Renoir, from paintings by cubist artists similar to Picasso, such as Braque.

PRINCIPLES OF REINFORCEMENT

Before we tackle a new principle of behavior, try answering this question: If we want to train a dog to perform a trick, like catching a Frisbee, should we reinforce it for (a) each successful catch or (b) only some of its successful catches? If you're like most people, you'd answer (a), which seems to match our commonsense notions regarding the effects of reinforcement. It seems logical to assume that the more consistent the reinforcement, the more consistent will be the resulting behavior. But, in fact, our intuitions about reinforcement are backward.

Partial Reinforcement. According to Skinner's principle of **partial reinforcement,** sometimes called *Humphrey's paradox* after psychologist Lloyd Humphreys (1939) who first described it, behaviors we reinforce only occasionally are slower to extinguish than those we reinforce every time. Although this point may seem counterintuitive, consider that an animal that expects to be rewarded every time it performs the target behavior may become reluctant to continue performing the behavior if the reinforcement becomes undependable. However, if an animal has learned that the behavior will be rewarded

If parents stop giving this boy his favorite toy when he screams, he'll initially scream harder to get what he wants. Eventually he'll realize it won't work and give up the screaming behavior.

Behaviors that we reinforce only occasionally (partial reinforcement) are slowest to extinguish. So to train a dog to catch a Frisbee, we should reinforce it only intermittently.

GLOSSARY

partial reinforcement
only occasional reinforcement of a behavior, resulting in slower extinction than if the behavior had been reinforced continually

only occasionally, it's more likely to continue the behavior in the hopes of being reinforced.

So if we want an animal to maintain a trick for a long time, we should actually reinforce it for correct responses only occasionally. Skinner (1969) noted that **continuous reinforcement,** reinforcing an animal everytime it performs the behavior, allows animals to learn new behaviors more quickly, but that partial reinforcement leads to a greater resistance to extinction. This principle may help to explain why some people remain trapped for years in terribly dysfunctional, even abusive, relationships. Some relationship partners provide intermittent reinforcement to their significant others, treating them miserably most of the time but treating them well on rare occasions. This pattern of partial reinforcement may keep individuals "hooked" in relationships that aren't working.

Schedules of Reinforcement.

Skinner (1938) found that animals' behaviors differ depending on the **schedule of reinforcement,** that is, the pattern of delivering reinforcement. Remarkably, the effects of these reinforcement schedules are consistent across species as diverse as cockroaches, pigeons, rats, and humans. Although there are numerous schedules of reinforcement, we'll discuss the four major ones here. **[LEARNING OBJECTIVE 5.8]** The principal reinforcement schedules vary along two dimensions:

(1) *The consistency of administering reinforcement.* Some reinforcement contingencies are *fixed,* whereas others are *variable.* That is, in some cases experimenters provide reinforcement on a regular (fixed) basis, whereas in others they provide reinforcement on an irregular (variable) basis.

(2) *The basis of administering reinforcement.* Some reinforcement schedules operate on *ratio* schedules, whereas others operate on *interval* schedules. In ratio schedules, the experimenter reinforces the animal based on the *number of responses* it's emitted. In interval schedules, the experimenter reinforces the animal based on the *amount of time* elapsed since the last reinforcement.

We can combine these two dimensions to arrive at four schedules of reinforcement (see **Figure 5.6**):

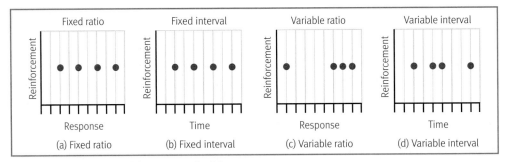

Figure 5.6 Four Major Reinforcement Schedules. The four major reinforcement schedules are (a) fixed ratio, (b) fixed interval, (c) variable ratio, and (d) variable interval.

(1) In a **fixed ratio (FR) schedule,** we provide reinforcement after a regular number of responses. For example, we could give a rat a pellet after every 15 times it presses the lever in a Skinner box.

(2) In a **fixed interval (FI) schedule,** we provide reinforcement for producing the response at least once during a specified period of time. For example, a worker in a toy factory might get paid at the same time every Friday afternoon for the work she's done, as long as she's generated at least one toy during that one-week interval.

(3) In a **variable ratio (VR) schedule,** we provide reinforcement after a specific number of responses on average, but the precise number of responses required during any given period

Fact -OID

The *gambler's fallacy* describes the error of believing that random events have "memories." After losing ten roulette spins in a row, the gambler often concludes that he's now "due" to win. Yet his odds of winning on the eleventh spin are no higher than they were on his first ten spins.

GLOSSARY

continuous reinforcement
reinforcing a behavior every time it occurs, resulting in faster learning but faster extinction than only occasional reinforcement

schedule of reinforcement
pattern of reinforcing a behavior

fixed ratio (FR) schedule
pattern in which we provide reinforcement following a regular number of responses

fixed interval (FI) schedule
pattern in which we provide reinforcement for producing the response at least once following a specified time interval

variable ratio (VR) schedule
pattern in which we provide reinforcement after a specific number of responses on average, with the number varying randomly

varies randomly. Playing the slot machines and other forms of gambling are examples of variable ratio schedules.

(4) In a **variable interval (VI) schedule,** we provide reinforcement for producing the response at least once during an average time interval, with the actual interval varying randomly. For example, we could give a dog a treat for performing a trick on a variable interval schedule with an average interval of 8 minutes. This dog may have to perform the trick at least once during a 7-minute interval the first time, but then during only a 1-minute interval the second time, then a longer 20-minute interval, and then a 4-minute interval, with the average of these intervals being 8 minutes.

Skinner discovered that different reinforcement schedules yield distinctive patterns of responding (see **Figure 5.7**). Ratio schedules tend to yield higher rates of responding than do interval schedules. This finding makes intuitive sense. If a dog gets a treat every five times he rolls over, he's going to roll over more often than if he gets a treat every 5 minutes, regardless of whether he rolls over once or twenty times during that interval. In addition, variable schedules tend to yield more consistent rates of responding than do fixed schedules. This finding also makes intuitive sense. If we never know when our next treat is coming, it's in our best interests to keep emitting the response to ensure we've emitted it enough times to earn the reward.

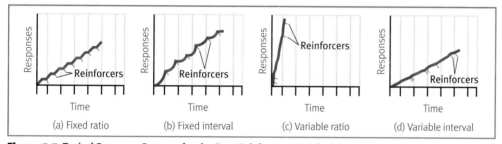

Figure 5.7 Typical Response Patterns for the Four Reinforcement Schedules. Note the "scalloped" pattern in (b), the fixed interval response pattern. The subject decreases the reinforced behavior immediately after receiving a reinforcer, then increases the behavior in anticipation of reinforcement as the time for reinforcement approaches.

Two other features of reinforcement schedules are worth noting. First, fixed interval schedules are associated with a "scalloped" pattern of responding. This *FI scallop* reflects the fact that the animal "waits" for a time after it receives reinforcement and then increases its rate of responding just before the interval is up as it begins to anticipate reinforcement.

Second, variable ratio (VR) schedules usually yield the highest rates of responding of all. It's for this reason that there's one place where we can be guaranteed to find a VR schedule: a casino (Madden, Ewan, & Lagorio, 2007). Roulette wheels, slot machines, and the like deliver cash rewards on an irregular basis, and they do so based on the gambler's responses. Sometimes the gambler has to pull the arm of the slot machine (the "one-armed bandit") hundreds of times before receiving any money at all. At other times, the gambler pulls the arm only once and makes out like a bandit himself, perhaps walking away with thousands of dollars for a few seconds of work. The extreme unpredictability of the VR schedule is precisely what keeps gamblers addicted, because reinforcement can come at any time.

APPLICATIONS OF OPERANT CONDITIONING

Operant conditioning plays a role in a surprising number of everyday experiences and in some special circumstances as well. As we've already noted, operant conditioning

Gambling is a prime example of a behavior reinforced by a variable ratio reinforcement schedule. The big pay-off may come at any time, so people keep rolling the dice.

GLOSSARY

variable interval (VI) schedule
pattern in which we provide reinforcement for producing the response at least once during an average time interval, with the interval varying randomly

is central to some parenting practices. It's also relevant to a wide array of other situations ranging from animal training to weight loss plans—even to learning to master a video game! Here we review a few well-studied examples of operant conditioning in action.

Using Shaping to Train Animals. If you've ever seen animals perform at a circus, zoo, or aquarium, you might wonder how on Earth the animals learned such elaborate routines. They typically do so by means of a procedure called **shaping by successive approximations,** or *shaping* for short. Using shaping, we reinforce behaviors that aren't exactly the target behavior but that are progressively closer versions of it. Typically, we shape an organism's response by initially reinforcing most or all responses that are close to the desired behavior, and then gradually *fading* (that is, decreasing the frequency of) our reinforcement for the not-exactly-right behaviors over time.

Animal trainers often combine shaping with a technique called *chaining,* in which they link a number of interrelated behaviors to form a longer series. Each behavior in the chain becomes a cue for the next behavior in the chain. By means of shaping and chaining, Skinner taught pigeons to play Ping-Pong, although they weren't exactly Olympic-caliber table tennis players. During World War II, he also taught pigeons to guide missiles from airplanes to enemy targets by pecking at an image on a screen whenever the missile got closer to the target, although the U.S. military never adopted his creative approach to aerial warfare. In both cases, Skinner began by reinforcing initial approximations to the desired response. When teaching pigeons to play Ping-Pong, he first reinforced them for turning toward the paddles, then approaching the paddles, then placing the paddles in their beaks, then picking up the paddles with their beaks, and so on. Then, he chained later behaviors, like swinging the paddle and then hitting the ball, to the earlier behaviors. As we might imagine, shaping and chaining complex animal behaviors requires patience, as the process can take days or weeks. Still, the payoff can be substantial, because we can train animals to engage in numerous behaviors that lie well outside their normal repertoires. Indeed, all contemporary animal trainers rely on Skinnerian principles.

Skinner's shaping principles are used today to train service animals.

WHAT DO *you* THINK?

You are a new Sea World intern, assisting trainers to teach their youngest dolphin to jump from the water and hit a ball with her fin. What principles of operating conditioning would be useful in accomplishing this learning goal?

Premack Principle. Be honest: Did you put off reading this chapter until the last moment? If so, don't feel ashamed, because procrastination is one of the most frequent study problems that college students report. Unfortunately, procrastinators tend to perform more poorly in their classes than do early birds (Tice & Baumeister, 1997). Although these findings are correlational and don't establish that procrastination causes bad grades, they certainly suggest that putting things off isn't ideal.

How can we overcome procrastination? Although there are several potential solutions for procrastination, among the best is probably the one discovered by David Premack (1965) in his research on monkeys. The **Premack principle** states that we can positively reinforce a less frequently performed behavior with a more frequently performed behavior (Danaher, 1974). Although not a foolproof rule (Knapp, 1976), this guideline typically works surprisingly well. The Premack principle is also called

GLOSSARY

shaping by successive approximations
conditioning a target behavior by progressively reinforcing behaviors that come closer and closer to the target

CORRELATION vs. CAUSATION
Can we be sure that A causes B?

Premack principle
principle that a less frequently performed behavior can be increased in frequency by reinforcing it with a more frequent behavior

"grandma's rule," because our grandmother reminded us to finish our vegetables before moving on to dessert. So, if you find yourself putting off a reading or writing task, think of behaviors you'd typically perform if given the chance—perhaps hanging out with a few close friends, watching a favorite TV program, or treating yourself to an ice cream cone. Then, reinforce yourself with these higher frequency behaviors only *after* you've completed your homework.

Superstitious Behavior.
How many of the following behaviors do you perform?

- Never opening an umbrella indoors
- Not walking under a ladder
- Carrying a lucky charm or necklace
- Knocking on wood
- Crossing your fingers
- Avoiding the number 13 (as in not stopping on the thirteenth floor of a building)

If you've engaged in several of these actions, you're at least somewhat superstitious. So are many Americans. For example, 12 percent of Americans are afraid of walking under a ladder (Vyse, 1997). So many people are afraid of the number 13 (*triskaidekaphobia*) that the floor designations in many tall buildings skip directly from 12 to 14 (Hock, 2002). This phobia isn't limited to North America; in Paris, triskaidekaphobics who are going out to dinner with 12 other people can hire a *quatorzieme*, a person paid to serve as a fourteenth guest.

How do superstitions relate to operant conditioning? In a classic study, Skinner (1948) placed eight food-deprived pigeons in a Skinner box while delivering reinforcement (bird feed) every 15 seconds *independent of their behavior.* That is, the birds received reinforcement regardless of what they did. After a few days, Skinner found that six of the eight pigeons had acquired remarkably strange behaviors. In the words of Skinner:

> One bird was conditioned to turn counterclockwise about the cage, making two or three turns between reinforcements. Another repeatedly thrust its head into one of the upper corners of the cage. A third developed a tossing response as if placing its head beneath an invisible bar and lifting it repeatedly. (p. 168)

You may have observed similarly odd behaviors in large groups of birds that people are feeding in city parks; for example, some pigeons may prance around or walk rapidly in circles in anticipation of reinforcement.

According to Skinner, his pigeons had developed *superstitious behavior:* Actions linked to reinforcement by sheer coincidence (Morse & Skinner, 1957). There's no actual association between superstitious behavior and reinforcement, although the animal acts as though there is. The behavior that the pigeon just happened to be performing immediately prior to being reinforced was strengthened—remember that reinforcement increases the probability of a response—so the pigeon kept on doing it (this kind of accidental operant conditioning is sometimes called *superstitious conditioning*). Not all studies have been able to replicate these findings in pigeons (Staddon & Simmelhag, 1971), although it's likely that at least some animal superstitions develop in the fashion Skinner described.

MYTH: Few educated people are superstitious.

REALITY: People are prone to certain superstitious behaviors regardless of educational level. As many as 90 percent of college students engage in one or more superstitious rituals before taking an exam (Vyse, 1997). More than half use a "lucky" pen or wear a "lucky" piece of jewelry or clothing. Others recite particular words, eat a special food, or skip showering or shaving.

Bowlers often contort themselves into odd positions as if trying to coax the ball in the desired direction. These behaviors are probably a result of superstitious conditioning.

REPLICABILITY
Can the results be duplicated in other studies?

Athletes may engage in superstitious behaviors, such as Tiger Woods's "red shirt on Sundays" superstition, because the outcome of many athletic events depends heavily on chance.

One study has shown similar effects in children (Wagner & Morris, 1987). This study found that about three-fourths of the children involved in the study developed superstitious behaviors following periodic reinforcement.

Few people are more prone to superstitions than athletes. That's probably because the outcome of so many sporting events, even those requiring a great deal of skill, depends heavily on chance. Baseball Hall of Famer Wade Boggs became famous for eating chicken before each game. Hall of Fame football player Jim Kelly forced himself to vomit before every game, and basketball player Chuck Person ate exactly two candy bars (always Snickers or Kit Kats) before every game (Vyse, 1997). Superstar golfer Tiger Woods always wears a red shirt when playing on Sundays.

Token Economies. One of the most successful applications of operant conditioning has been the *token economy*. Token economies are systems, often set up in psychiatric hospitals, for reinforcing appropriate behaviors and extinguishing inappropriate ones (Carr, Fraizer, & Roland, 2005; Kazdin, 1982). In token economies, staff members reinforce patients who behave in a desired fashion using tokens, chips, points, or other **secondary reinforcers.** Secondary reinforcers are neutral objects that become associated with **primary reinforcers**—things that naturally increase the target behavior, like a favorite food or drink. Typically, psychologists who construct token economies begin by identifying *target behaviors,* that is, actions they hope to make more frequent, such as talking quietly or being polite. Research suggests that token economies are often effective in improving behavior in hospitals, group homes, and juvenile detention units (Ayllon & Milan, 2002; Paul & Lentz, 1977) although they may not be as effective outside these highly institutional settings.

TWO-PROCESS THEORY: PUTTING CLASSICAL AND OPERANT CONDITIONING TOGETHER

Up to this point, we've discussed classical and operant conditioning as though they were two entirely independent processes. Brain imaging studies provide some support for this distinction, showing that these two forms of learning are associated with activations in different brain regions. Classically conditioned fear reactions are based largely in the amygdala (LeDoux, 1996; Veit et al., 2002), whereas operantly conditioned responses are based largely in parts of the limbic system linked to reward (Robbins, Granon, Muir, et al., 1998; see Chapter 3).

However these two types of conditioning often interact. To see how, let's revisit the question of how people develop phobias. We've seen that certain phobias arise in part by classical conditioning: A previously neutral stimulus (the CS)—say, a dog—is paired with an unpleasant stimulus (the UCS)—a dog bite—resulting in the CR of fear. So far, so good.

But why doesn't the CR of fear eventually extinguish? Given what we've learned about classical conditioning, we might expect the CR of fear to fade away over time with repeated exposure to the CS of dogs. Yet this often doesn't happen (Rachman, 1977).

We probably need both classical and operant conditioning to explain the persistence of such phobias (Mowrer, 1947). Here's how: People acquire phobias by means of classical conditioning. Then, once they're phobic, they start to avoid their feared stimulus whenever they see it. If they have a dog phobia, they may cross the street whenever they see someone walking toward them with a large German shepherd. When they do, they experience a reduction in anxiety—a surge of relief. They are *negatively reinforcing* their own fear by removing the fear-inducing stimulus.

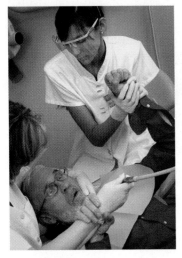

Fears of dental procedures are often reinforced by avoidance behavior over many years, such as a refusal to go to the dentist until it's absolutely necessary.

GLOSSARY

secondary reinforcer
neutral object that becomes associated with a primary reinforcer

primary reinforcer
item or outcome that naturally increases target behavior

QUIZ

1 In classical conditioning, responses are emitted; in operant conditioning, they're elicited. **TRUE** **FALSE**

2 Negative reinforcement and punishment are superficially different, but they produce the same short-term effects on behavior. **TRUE** **FALSE**

3 The correlation between spanking and children's behavioral problems appears to be positive in Caucasians but negative in African Americans. **TRUE** **FALSE**

4 The principle of partial reinforcement states that behaviors reinforced only some of the time extinguish more rapidly than behaviors reinforced continuously. **TRUE** **FALSE**

5 According to the Premack principle, we can reinforce less frequent behaviors with more frequent behaviors. **TRUE** **FALSE**

Answers: (1) F (p. 160); (2) F (p. 163); (3) T (p. 164); (4) F (p. 165); (5) T (p. 168)

PEARSON
mypsychlab

▼ How can reinforcement be used to teach pigeons to play Ping Pong? Watch the video titled "Pigeon Ping Pong" at www.mypsychlab.com to find out.

Cognitive Models of Learning

Thus far, we've omitted one word when discussing how we learn: *thinking.* That's not accidental, because early behaviorists didn't believe that thought played much of a causal role in learning.

WATSON, SKINNER, AND THINKING

Watson and Skinner held different views on thinking. Watson (1913) argued that psychology should focus exclusively on overt (that is, observable) behaviors. From Watson's perspective, thinking and emotion lay outside the domain of scientific psychology.

In contrast, Skinner (1953) firmly believed that observable behavior, thinking, and emotion are all governed by the same laws of learning, namely, classical and operant conditioning. In other words, thinking and emotion *are* behaviors, they're just covert—that is, unobservable—behaviors.

One frequent misconception about Skinner is that he didn't believe in thinking. On the contrary, Skinner clearly thought—he wouldn't have objected to our use of that word here—that humans and other intelligent animals think, but he insisted that thinking is no different in principle from any other behavior. For Skinner, this view is far more parsimonious than invoking different laws of learning for thinking than for other behaviors.

S-O-R PSYCHOLOGY: THROWING THINKING BACK INTO THE MIX

Over the past 30 or 40 years, psychology has moved increasingly away from a simple S-R (stimulus-response) psychology to a more complex S-O-R psychology, with *O* being the

Where did I come from? Why am I here?

Most early behaviorists believed that thinking lies outside the boundaries of scientific psychology. In contrast, Skinner regarded thinking as a behavior, just one that happens to be unobservable.

OCCAM'S RAZOR
Does a simpler explanation fit the data just as well?

Although few of us enjoy criticism, some of us react to it well, whereas others of us don't. According to S-O-R psychologists, this difference hinges on our interpretation of what the criticism means.

organism that interprets the stimulus before producing a response (Mischel, 1973; Woodworth, 1929). For S-O-R psychologists, the link between S and R isn't mindless or automatic. Instead, the organism's response to a stimulus depends on what this stimulus *means* to it. The S-O-R principle helps to explain a phenomenon we've probably all encountered. You've probably had the experience of giving two friends the same mild criticism (like, "It bothers me a little when you show up late") and found that they reacted quite differently: One was apologetic, the other defensive.

To explain these differing reactions, Skinner would probably invoke your friends' differing *learning histories,* in essence how each friend had been trained to react to criticism. In contrast, S-O-R theorists, who believe that cognition is central to explaining learning, would contend that the differences in your friends' reactions stem from how they *interpreted* your criticism. Your first friend may have viewed your criticism as constructive feedback, your second friend as a personal attack.

Although S-O-R theorists attempted to integrate classical and operant conditioning with a more thought-based account, the Gestalt psychologists, about whom we learned in Chapter 4, had long argued for a critical role for the organism. As we'll recall, Gestalt psychologists noted that what we perceive is different from and greater than the sum of the stimuli our sense organs receive. This fact implies that as organisms we're performing mental operations, or transformations, on our experience of stimuli.

S-O-R theorists don't deny that classical and operant conditioning occur, but they believe that these forms of learning usually depend on thinking. Take a person who's been classically conditioned by tones and shock to sweat in response to the tones. Her skin conductance response will extinguish suddenly if she's told that no more shocks are on the way (Grings, 1973). This phenomenon of *cognitive conditioning,* whereby our interpretation of the situation affects conditioning, suggests that conditioning is more than an automatic, mindless process (Brewer, 1974; Kirsch, Lynn, Vigorito, et al., 2004).

To explain psychology's gradual transition away from behaviorism, we need to tell the story of a pioneering psychologist and his rats.

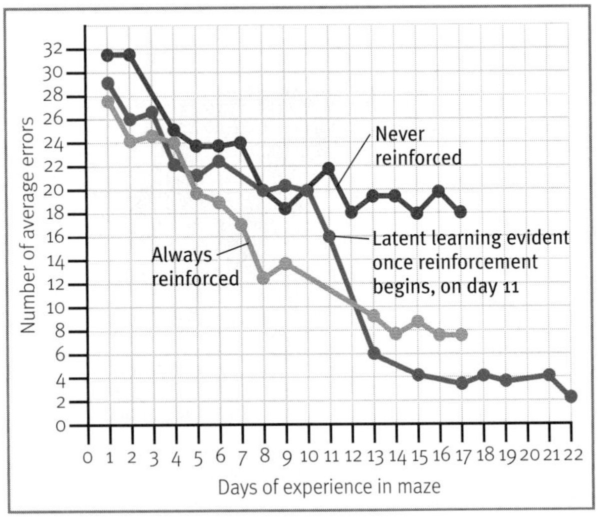

LATENT LEARNING

One of the first serious challenges to purely behaviorist accounts of learning was mounted by Edward Chace Tolman (1886–1959), whose contributions to the psychology of learning cannot be overestimated.

Tolman suspected that reinforcement wasn't the be-all and end-all of learning. To understand why, answer this question: "Who was one of the first psychologists to challenge pure behaviorism?" If you've been paying attention, you answered "Tolman." Yet immediately before we asked that question, you knew the answer, even though you had no opportunity to demonstrate it. According to Tolman (1932), you engaged in **latent learning:** learning that isn't directly observable (Blodgett, 1929). We learn many things without showing them. Putting it a bit differently, there's a crucial difference between *competence*—what we know—and *performance*—showing what we know (Bradbard, Martin, Endsley, et al., 1986).

Why is this distinction important? Because it implies that *reinforcement isn't necessary for learning.* **[LEARNING OBJECTIVE 5.9]** Here's how Tolman and C.H. Honzik (1930) demonstrated this point systematically.

They randomly assigned three groups of rats to go through a maze over a three-week period (see **Figure 5.8**). One group always received reinforcement in the form of cheese when it got to the end of the maze. A second group never received reinforcement when it got to the end of the maze. The first group made far fewer errors; that's no great surprise. The third group of rats received no reinforcement for the first 10 days and then started receiving reinforcement on the eleventh day.

Figure 5.8 Tolman and Honzik's Maze Trials. Graphs from Tolman and Honzik's classic study of latent learning in rats. Pay particular attention to the blue line. The rats in this group weren't reinforced until day 11; note the sudden drop in the number of their errors on receiving reinforcement. The rats were learning all along, even though they weren't showing it. (*Source:* Tolman & Honzik, 1930)

[Graph: x-axis "Days of experience in maze" (0–22); y-axis "Number of average errors" (0–32). Labels: "Never reinforced", "Always reinforced", "Latent learning evident once reinforcement begins, on day 11"]

GLOSSARY

latent learning
learning that's not directly observable

As we can see in Figure 5.8, the rats in the third group showed a large and abrupt drop in their number of errors on receiving their very first reinforcer. In fact, within only a few days their number of errors didn't differ significantly from the number of errors among the rats who were always reinforced.

According to Tolman, this finding means that the rats in the third group had been learning all along. They just hadn't bothered to show it because they had nothing to gain. Once there was a payoff for learning, namely, a tasty morsel of cheese, they promptly became miniature maze masters.

According to Tolman (1948), the rats had developed **cognitive maps**—that is, spatial representations—of the maze. If you're like most college students, you were hopelessly confused the first day you arrived on campus. Over time, however, you probably developed a mental sense of the layout of the campus, so that you now hardly ever become lost. That internal spatial blueprint, according to Tolman, is a cognitive map.

In a clever demonstration of cognitive maps, three investigators (McNamara, Long, & Wike, 1956) had one set of rats run repeatedly through a maze to receive reinforcement. They put another set of rats in little moving "trolley cars," in which the rats could observe the layout of the maze but not obtain the experience of running through it. When the researchers gave the second group of rats the chance to run through the maze, they did just as well as the rats in the first group. As rodent tourists in trolley cars, they'd acquired cognitive maps of the maze.

The latent learning research of Tolman and others challenged strict behaviorist accounts of learning because their work showed that learning could occur without reinforcement. To many psychologists, this research falsified the claim that reinforcement is necessary for all forms of learning. It also suggested that thinking, in the form of cognitive maps, plays a central role in at least some forms of learning.

Cats have cognitive maps, too. (Rhymes With Orange (105945) © Hilary B. Price. King Features Syndicate)

FALSIFIABILITY
Can the claim be disproved?

OBSERVATIONAL LEARNING

According to some psychologists, one important variant of latent learning is **observational learning:** learning by watching others (Bandura, 1965). In many cases, we learn by watching *models:* parents, teachers, and others who are influential to us. Many psychologists regard observational learning as a form of latent learning because it allows us to learn without reinforcement. **[LEARNING OBJECTIVE 5.10]** We can merely watch someone else being reinforced for doing something and take our cues from that person.

Observational learning spares us the expense of having to learn everything firsthand (Bandura, 1977). Most people have never been skydiving, but from our observations of people who've gone skydiving we have the distinct impression that it's generally a good idea to have a parachute on before you jump out of a plane. Note that we didn't need to learn this useful tidbit of advice by trial and error, or else we wouldn't be here to talk about it. Observational learning can spare us from serious, even life-threatening, mistakes. But it can also contribute to our learning of maladaptive habits.

Observational Learning of Aggression. In classic research in the 1960s, Albert Bandura and his colleagues demonstrated that children can learn to act aggressively by watching aggressive role models (Bandura, Ross, & Ross, 1963).

Bandura and his colleagues asked preschool boys and girls to watch an adult (the model) interact with a large Bobo doll, a doll that bounces back to its original upright position after being hit (Bandura, Ross, & Ross, 1961). The experimenters randomly assigned some children to watch the adult model playing quietly and ignoring the Bobo doll, and others to watch the adult model punching the Bobo doll in the nose, hitting it with a mallet, sitting on it, and kicking it around the room. As though that weren't enough, the model in the latter condition shouted out insults and vivid descriptions of his actions while inflicting violence: "Sock him in the nose," "Kick him," "Pow."

Children acquire a great deal of their behavior by observational learning of adults, especially their parents.

GLOSSARY

cognitive map
mental representation of how a physical space is organized

observational learning
learning by watching others

Bandura and his coworkers then brought the children into a room with an array of appealing toys, including a miniature fire engine, a jet fighter, and a large doll set. Just as children began playing with these toys, the experimenter interrupted them, informing them that they needed to move to a different room. This interruption was intentional, as the investigators wanted to frustrate the children to make them more likely to behave aggressively. Then the experimenter brought them into a second room, which contained a Bobo doll identical to the one they'd seen.

On a variety of dependent measures, Bandura and his colleagues found that previous exposure to the aggressive model triggered significantly more aggression against the Bobo doll than did exposure to the nonaggressive model. The children who'd watched the aggressive model yelled at the doll much as the model had done, and they even imitated many of his verbal insults.

Media Violence and Real-World Aggression.

The Bandura studies and scores of later studies of observational learning led psychologists to examine a theoretically and socially important question: Does exposure to media violence, such as in films or movies, contribute to real-world violence? Hundreds of investigators using correlational designs have reported that children who watch many violent television programs are more aggressive than other children (Twemlow & Bennett, 2008; Wilson & Herrnstein, 1985). These findings, though, don't demonstrate that media violence causes real-world violence (Freedman, 1984). They could simply indicate that highly aggressive children are more likely than other children to tune in to aggressive television programs. Alternatively, these findings could be due to a third variable, such as children's initial levels of aggressiveness. That is, highly aggressive children may be more likely than other children to both watch violent television programs and to act aggressively.

Investigators have tried to get around this problem by using longitudinal designs (see Chapter 8), which track individuals' behavior over time. Longitudinal studies show that children who watch many violent television shows commit more aggressive acts years later than do children who watch fewer violent television shows, even when researchers have equated children in their initial levels of aggression (Huesmann, Moise-Titus, Podolski, et al., 2003; see **Figure 5.9**). These studies offer somewhat more compelling evidence for a causal link between media violence and aggression than do correlational studies, but even they don't demonstrate the existence of this link. For example, an unmeasured personality variable, like impulsivity, or a social variable, like weak parental supervision, might account for these findings. Moreover, just because variable *A* precedes variable *B* doesn't mean that variable *A causes* variable *B* (see Chapter 8). For example, if we found that most common colds start with a scratchy throat and a runny nose, we shouldn't conclude that scratchy throats and runny noses cause colds, only that they're early signs of a cold.

CORRELATION vs. **CAUSATION**
Can we be sure that A causes B?

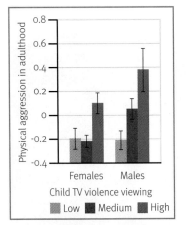

Figure 5.9 Longitudinal Study of Individuals Who Watched Violent TV as Children. In both females and males, there's a positive correlation between viewing violent television in childhood and violent behavior in adulthood. But this correlation doesn't demonstrate causality. Why? (*Source:* Huesmann et al., 2003)

WHAT DO *you* THINK?

As the media director for student affairs, you are responsible for selecting the movies for the weekly movie night on campus. Following a violent incident last semester, the administration is concerned that showing violent movies will provoke violent behavior from students. How would you evaluate whether violent movie viewing relates to campus violence?

Finally, some investigators have conducted *field studies* of the link between media violence and aggression (Anderson & Bushman, 2002c). In field studies, researchers examine the relation between naturally occurring events and aggression in the real world. For example, one investigator (Williams, 1986) conducted a field study of a small, isolated mountain town in Canada that had no television before 1973. She called it "Notel," short for "*no tele*vision." Compared with school-age children in two other Canadian towns that already had television, children in Notel showed a marked increase in physical and verbal aggression two years later. Nevertheless, these findings are difficult to interpret in light of a potential confound: At around the same time that Notel received television, the Canadian government constructed a large highway that connected Notel to nearby towns. This highway might have introduced the children in Notel to negative outside influences, including crime spilling over from other cities.

> **RULING OUT RIVAL HYPOTHESES**
> **Have important alternative explanations for the findings been excluded?**

So what can we make of the literature on media violence and aggressive behaviors? Most psychological scientists today agree that media violence contributes to aggression in at least some circumstances (Anderson & Bushman, 2002a; Bushman & Anderson, 2001). Nevertheless, it's equally clear that media violence is only one small piece of a multifaceted puzzle. We can't explain aggression by means of media violence alone because the substantial majority of individuals exposed to high levels of such violence don't become aggressive (Freedman, 2002; Wilson & Herrnstein, 1985). We'll examine other causal factors in aggression in Chapter 11.

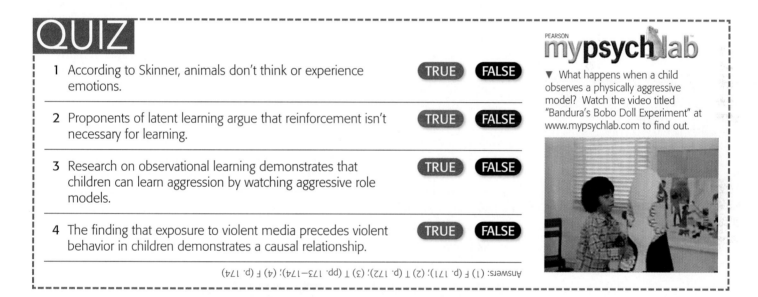

QUIZ

1 According to Skinner, animals don't think or experience emotions. **TRUE FALSE**

2 Proponents of latent learning argue that reinforcement isn't necessary for learning. **TRUE FALSE**

3 Research on observational learning demonstrates that children can learn aggression by watching aggressive role models. **TRUE FALSE**

4 The finding that exposure to violent media precedes violent behavior in children demonstrates a causal relationship. **TRUE FALSE**

Answers: (1) F (p. 171); (2) T (p. 172); (3) T (pp. 173–174); (4) F (p. 174)

PEARSON
mypsychlab

▼ What happens when a child observes a physically aggressive model? Watch the video titled "Bandura's Bobo Doll Experiment" at www.mypsychlab.com to find out.

Biological Influences on Learning

For many decades, most behaviorists regarded learning as entirely distinct from biology. The animal's learning history and genetic makeup were like two ships passing in the night. Yet we now understand that our biology influences the speed and nature of our learning in complex and fascinating ways. Here are three powerful examples.

CONDITIONED TASTE AVERSIONS

One day in the 1970s, psychologist Martin Seligman went out to dinner with his wife. He ordered a filet mignon steak flavored with sauce béarnaise. Approximately six hours later, while at the opera, Seligman felt nauseated and became violently ill. He and his stomach recovered, but his love of sauce béarnaise didn't. From then on, Seligman couldn't even think of, let alone taste, sauce béarnaise without feeling like vomiting (Seligman & Hager, 1972).

The *sauce béarnaise syndrome,* also known as *conditioned taste aversion,* refers to the fact that classical conditioning can lead us to develop avoidance reactions to the taste of food. Before reading on, ask yourself a question: Does Seligman's story contradict the other examples of classical conditioning we've discussed, like that of Pavlov and his dogs?

In fact, it does in at least three ways (Garcia & Hankins, 1977; Reilly & Schachtman, 2009):

(1) In contrast to most classically conditioned reactions, which require repeated pairings between CS and UCS, conditioned taste aversions typically require *only one trial* to develop.

(2) The delay between CS and UCS in conditioned taste aversions can be as long as six or even eight hours (Rachlin & Logue, 1991).

(3) Conditioned taste aversions tend to be remarkably specific and display little evidence of stimulus generalization. For example, an aversion to fried chicken may not generalize to baked chicken or fried fish.

These differences make good sense. We wouldn't want to have to experience horrific food poisoning again and again to learn a conditioned association between taste and illness. Not only would doing so be incredibly unpleasant, but, in some cases, we'd be dead after the first trial. The lag time between eating and illness violates typical classical conditioning because close timing between the CS and UCS is usually necessary for learning. But, in this case, because food poisoning often sets in many hours rather than a few seconds after eating toxic food, making this association is appropriate and adaptive. **[LEARNING OBJECTIVE 5.11]**

Conditioned taste aversions are a particular problem among cancer patients undergoing chemotherapy, which frequently induces nausea and vomiting. As a result, they often develop an aversion to food that preceded chemotherapy, even though they realize it bears no logical connection to the treatment. Fortunately, health psychologists have developed a clever way around this problem. Capitalizing on the specificity of conditioned taste aversions, they ask cancer patients to eat an unfamiliar *scapegoat food*—a novel food of which they aren't fond—prior to chemotherapy. In general, the taste aversion becomes conditioned to the scapegoat food rather than to patients' preferred foods (Andresen, Birch, & Johnson, 1990).

Psychological science has helped many cancer patients undergoing chemotherapy to minimize conditioned taste aversions to their favorite foods.

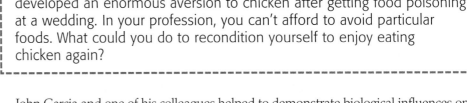

WHAT DO *you* THINK?

You are a professional food critic for the local newspaper who has developed an enormous aversion to chicken after getting food poisoning at a wedding. In your profession, you can't afford to avoid particular foods. What could you do to recondition yourself to enjoy eating chicken again?

John Garcia and one of his colleagues helped to demonstrate biological influences on conditioned taste aversions (Garcia & Koelling, 1966). They found that rats exposed to X-rays, which make them nauseated, developed conditioned aversions to a specific taste but not to a specific visual or auditory stimulus presented after the X-rays (Garcia & Koelling, 1966). In other words, the rats more readily associated nausea with taste than with other sensory stimuli after a single exposure. Conditioned taste aversions aren't much fun, but they're often adaptive. In the real world, poisoned drinks and foods, not sights and sounds, make animals feel sick. As a consequence, animals more easily develop conditioned aversions to stimuli that tend to trigger nausea in the real world (see **Figure 5.10**).

Because certain stimuli are more easily associated with particular outcomes, this finding contradicts the assumption of **equipotentiality**—the claim that we can pair all CSs

This coyote, eating from a sheep carcass that's been tainted with a mild poison, will become sick several hours later. The coyote will avoid sheep from then on. Ranchers have made use of this technique to keep coyotes from attacking their livestock.

GLOSSARY

equipotentiality
assumption that any conditioned stimulus can be associated equally well with any unconditioned stimulus

Figure 5.10 Conditioned Taste Aversion. The work of John Garcia and his colleagues demonstrated that animals tend to develop conditioned taste aversions only to certain stimuli, namely, those that trigger nausea in the real world.

US (radiation box) → UR (nausea)

Neutral stimulus (flavored water) → No response

The CS is paired with the US

CS (flavored water) US (radiation box)

CS (flavored water) → CR (nausea)

equally well with all UCSs—a belief held by many traditional behaviorists (Plotkin, 2004). Notice that Martin Seligman felt nauseated at the thought of sauce béarnaise, but not at the thought of the opera or—fortunately—his wife.

PREPAREDNESS AND PHOBIAS

A second challenge to the equipotentiality assumption comes from research on phobias. If we look at the distribution of phobias in the general population, we'll find something curious: People aren't always afraid of things with which they've had the most frequent unpleasant experiences. Phobias of the dark, heights, snakes, spiders, deep water, and blood are commonplace, even though many people who fear these stimuli have never had a frightening encounter with them. In contrast, phobias of razors, knives, the edges of furniture, ovens, and electrical outlets are extremely rare, although many of us have been cut, bruised, burned, or otherwise hurt by them.

Mineka and Cook (1993) showed that monkeys can acquire fears of snakes by means of observational learning. Nevertheless, these monkeys didn't acquire fears of nondangerous stimuli, like flowers, suggesting a role for evolutionary predispositions in the development of fears.

Seligman (1971) proposed that we can explain the distribution of phobias in the population by means of **prepared learning:** We're evolutionarily predisposed to fear certain stimuli more than others. According to Seligman, that's because certain stimuli, like steep cliffs and poisonous animals, posed a threat to our early human ancestors (Ohman & Mineka, 2001; Weiek, Schupp, & Hamm, 2007). In contrast, household items and appliances didn't, because they weren't around back then. In the words of Susan Mineka and Michael Cook (1993), prepared fears are "evolutionary memories."

Mineka and Cook (1993) tested prepared learning by first exposing lab-reared rhesus monkeys, who had no previous exposure to snakes, to a snake. These monkeys displayed no fear of snakes. Next, the researchers showed the monkeys a videotape of fellow monkeys reacting in horror to snakes. Within less than half an hour, the monkeys acquired a fear of snakes by observational learning. The researchers then edited the videotape so that it looked as though the same monkeys were reacting in horror, but this time in response to flowers, a toy rabbit, a toy snake, or a toy crocodile. They then showed these doctored videotapes to different groups of monkeys who had no experience with flowers, rabbits, snakes, or crocodiles. The monkeys who observed these altered videotapes acquired fears of the toy snake and toy crocodile but not the flowers or toy rabbit. From the standpoint of preparedness, this finding is understandable. Snakes and crocodiles were dangerous to our primate ancestors, but flowers and rabbits weren't (Ohman & Mineka, 2003). What's most fascinating is that these fears were clearly learned, because the monkeys showed no fear until they observed the videos. But the video was much more effective in creating fear reactions to some stimuli than to others. The monkeys were apparently predisposed to learn some fears more readily than others but needed to observe others' fear before that learning predisposition was activated.

Still, the laboratory evidence for preparedness isn't completely consistent. When researchers have paired either prepared stimuli—like snakes or spiders—or unprepared stimuli—like flowers or mushrooms—with electric shocks, they haven't invariably replicated the finding that subjects more rapidly acquire fears to prepared than unprepared stimuli (Davey, 1995; McNally, 1987).

INSTINCTIVE DRIFT

Animal trainers Marian and Keller Breland taught pigeons, chickens, raccoons, pigs, and a host of other creatures to perform a variety of tricks—much like those we might see on David Letterman's Stupid Pet Tricks segment—for circuses and television advertisers. As students of B.F. Skinner at Harvard, they relied on traditional methods of operant conditioning to shape their animals' behavior.

In the process of their animal training adventures, the Brelands discovered that their little charges didn't always behave as anticipated. In one case they tried to train raccoons to drop

REPLICABILITY
Can the results be duplicated in other studies?

GLOSSARY

prepared learning
evolutionary predisposition to learn some pairings of feared stimuli over others owing to their survival value

instinctive drift
tendency for animals to return to innate behaviors following repeated reinforcement

tokens into a piggy bank. Although they successfully trained the raccoons to pick up the coins using food reinforcement, they soon ran headfirst into a surprising problem. Despite repeated reinforcement for dropping the coins into the piggy bank, the raccoons began rubbing the coins together, dropping them, and rubbing them together again instead.

The raccoons had reverted to an innate behavior, namely, rinsing. They were treating the tokens like pieces of food, like the small hard shells they extract from the beds of ponds and streams (Timberlake, 2006). Breland and Breland (1961) referred to this phenomenon as **instinctive drift:** the tendency for animals to return to innate behaviors following repeated reinforcement. Researchers have observed instinctive drift in other animals, including rats (Powell & Curley, 1984; Staddon, 2007). Psychologists don't fully understand the reasons for such drift. Nevertheless, instinctive drift suggests that we can't fully understand learning without taking into account innate biological influences because these influences place limits on what kinds of behaviors we can train through reinforcement.

Instinctive drift is the tendency to return to an evolutionarily selected behavior.

QUIZ

1 Many conditioned taste aversions are acquired in only a single trial.   **TRUE**   **FALSE**

2 Most research suggests that the assumption of equipotentiality is false.   **TRUE**   **FALSE**

3 The phenomenon of preparedness helps explain why virtually all major phobias are equally common in the general population.   **TRUE**   **FALSE**

4 With progressively more reinforcement, animals typically drift further and further away from their instinctual patterns of behavior.   **TRUE**   **FALSE**

Answers: (1) T (p. 176); (2) T (p. 176–178); (3) F (p. 178); (4) F (p. 179)

PEARSON
mypsychlab

▼ Why do you avoid certain food? Watch the explore activities titled "Taste Aversion" at www.mypsychlab.com to find out.

Learning Fads: Do They Work?

Learning is hard work. It requires mental energy and concentration.

Perhaps because learning new things requires so much time and effort on our part, many mental health professionals have marketed a motley assortment of techniques that supposedly help us to learn more quickly, or more easily, than we currently do. Do these newfangled methods work? We'll find out by examining three popular techniques. **[LEARNING OBJECTIVE 5.12]**

SLEEP-ASSISTED LEARNING

Imagine that you could master all of the information in this book while getting a few nights of sound sleep. You could pay someone to audiorecord the entire book, play the recording over the span of several weeknights, and you'd be all done. You could say good-bye to those late nights in the library reading about psychology.

Although the prospect of learning new languages while sleeping is immensely appealing, psychological research offers no support for it.

EXTRAORDINARY CLAIMS
Is the evidence as convincing as the claim?

As in many areas of psychology, hope springs eternal. Many proponents of *sleep-assisted learning*—learning new material while asleep—have made some extraordinary claims regarding this technique's potential. Companies offer a variety of CDs that they claim can help us to learn languages, stop smoking, lose weight, or reduce stress, all while we're comfortably catching up on our *zzzzs*. These assertions are certainly quite remarkable. Does the scientific evidence for sleep-assisted learning stack up to its proponents' impressive claims?

As is so often the case in life, things that sound too good to be true often are. Admittedly, the early findings on sleep-assisted learning were encouraging. One group of investigators exposed sailors to Morse code (a shorthand form of communication that radio operators sometimes use) while asleep. These sailors mastered Morse code three weeks faster than did other sailors (Simon & Emmons, 1955). Other studies from the former Soviet Union seemingly provided support for the claim that people could learn new material, such as tape-recorded words or sentences, while asleep (Aarons, 1976).

RULING OUT RIVAL HYPOTHESES
Have important alternative explanations
for the findings been excluded?

Nevertheless, these early positive reports neglected to rule out a crucial alternative explanation: The recordings may have awakened the subjects. The problem is that almost all of the studies showing positive effects didn't monitor subjects' electroencephalograms (EEGs; see Chapter 3) to ensure they were asleep while listening to the tapes (Druckman & Swets, 1988; Druckman & Bjork, 1994). Better-controlled studies that monitored subjects' EEGs to make sure they were asleep offered little evidence for sleep-assisted learning. So to the extent that sleep-learning tapes "work," it's because subjects hear snatches of them while drifting in and out of sleep. As for that quick fix for reducing stress, we'd recommend skipping the tapes and just getting a good night's rest.

DISCOVERY LEARNING

RULING OUT RIVAL HYPOTHESES
Have important alternative explanations
for the findings been excluded?

As we've discovered throughout this text, learning how to *rule out rival explanations* for findings is a key ingredient of critical thinking. But science educators haven't always agreed on how to teach this crucial skill.

One increasingly popular way of imparting this knowledge is *discovery learning:* giving students experimental materials and asking them to figure out the scientific principles on their own (Klahr & Nigam, 2004). For example, a psychology professor who's teaching operant conditioning might set her students up with a friendly rat, a maze, and a bountiful supply of cheese and ask them to determine which variables affect the rat's learning. For instance, does the rat learn the maze most quickly when we reinforce it continuously or only occasionally?

Nevertheless, as David Klahr and his colleagues have shown, the old-fashioned method of *direct instruction,* in which we simply tell students how to solve problems, is often more effective and efficient than discovery learning. In one study, they examined third- and fourth-graders' ability to isolate the variables that influence how quickly a ball rolls down a ramp, such as the ramp's steepness or length. Only 23 percent of students assigned to a discovery learning condition later solved a slightly different problem on their own, whereas 77 percent of students assigned to a direct instruction condition did (Klahr & Nigam, 2004).

That's not to say that discovery learning has no role in education, as in the long term it may encourage students to learn how to pose scientific questions on their own (Alferink, 2007; Kuhn & Dean, 2005). It may be a more effective technique for advanced students than beginning learners. Because many students may never figure out how to solve certain scientific problems independently, it's ill advised as a standalone approach (Kirschner, Sweller, & Clark, 2006).

LEARNING STYLES

Few beliefs about learning are as widespread as the idea that all individuals have their own distinctive **learning styles**—their preferred means of acquiring information. According to proponents of this view, some students are "analytical" learners who excel at breaking down problems into different components, whereas others are "holistic" learners who excel at viewing problems as a whole. Still others are "verbal" learners who prefer to talk through problems, whereas others are "spatial" learners who prefer to visualize problems in their heads (Cassidy, 2004; Desmedt & Valcke, 2004). Some educational psychologists have claimed to boost learning dramatically by matching methods of instructions to people's learning styles. According to them, children who are verbal learners should learn much faster and better with written material, children who are spatial learners should learn much faster and better with visual material, and so on.

The view that students with certain learning styles benefit from specific types of instructional materials is popular in educational psychology. Yet scientific research provides little evidence for this belief.

Appealing as these assertions are, they haven't stood the test of careful research. For one thing, it's difficult to assess learning style reliably (Snider, 1992; Stahl, 1999). As we'll recall from Chapter 2, *reliability* refers to consistency in measurement. In this case, researchers have found that different measures designed to assess people's learning styles often yield very different answers about their preferred mode of learning. In part, that's probably because few of us are purely analytical or holistic learners, verbal or spatial learners, and so on; most of us are a blend of both styles. Moreover, studies have generally revealed that tailoring different methods to people's learning styles doesn't result in enhanced learning (Kavale & Forness, 1987; Kratzig & Arbuthnott, 2006; Tarver & Dawson, 1978). Like a number of other fads in popular psychology, the idea of learning styles seems to be more fiction than fact (Alferink, 2007; Stahl, 1999).

WHAT DO *you* THINK?

You are a sixth grade teacher meeting with the parents of one of your students. The parents insist their child is strictly a visual learner and that your teaching style is preventing her from learning. How would you persuade them that their child's learning isn't being hindered?

GLOSSARY

learning style
an individual's preferred or optimal method of acquiring new information

QUIZ

1 Sleep-assisted learning techniques work only if subjects stay completely asleep during learning.   **TRUE** **FALSE**

2 Discovery learning tends to be more efficient than direct instruction for solving most scientific problems.   **TRUE** **FALSE**

3 There's little evidence that matching teaching methods to people's learning styles enhances learning.   **TRUE** **FALSE**

Answers: (1) F (p. 180); (2) F (p. 180); (3) T (p. 181)

PEARSON
mypsychlab

▼ Can we really learn while we sleep? Watch the explore activities titled "Accelerated Learning" at www.mypsychlab.com to find out.

"Imagine that you could learn 100 times faster than you do now!"

"You can improve your IQ while you sleep."

CLASSICAL CONDITIONING (pp. 153–160)

5.1 Describe the process of classical conditioning and discriminate conditioned stimuli and responses from unconditioned stimuli and responses

In classical conditioning, animals come to respond to a previously neutral stimulus (the CS) that has been paired with another stimulus (the UCS) that elicits an automatic response (the UCR). After repeated pairings with the UCS, the CS comes to elicit a conditioned response (CR) similar to the UCR.

1. A change in an organism's behavior or thought as a result of experience is called _____ . (p. 152)

2. If the dog continues to salivate at the sound of the metronome when the meat powder is absent, this is called _____ _____ . (p. 154)

3. Identify the components of the classical conditioning model used in Pavlov's dog research. (p. 155)

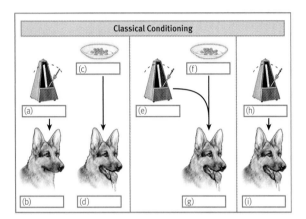

Classical Conditioning

(a) (b) (c) (d) (e) (f) (g) (h) (i)

4. If Lynne has a crush on her neighborhood mail carrier and her heart starts to race every time she sees a mail truck as a result, the mail truck is the (conditioned/unconditioned) stimulus and the mail carrier is the (conditioned/unconditioned) stimulus. (p. 155)

5.2 Explain how conditioned responses are acquired, maintained, and extinguished

Acquisition is the process by which we gradually learn the CR. Extinction occurs when, following repeated presentation of the CS alone, the CR decreases in magnitude and eventually disappears. Extinction appears to involve an "overwriting" of the CR by new information.

5. The learning phase during which a conditioned response is established is called _____. (p. 155)

6. After numerous presentations of the metronome without meat powder, Pavlov's dogs eventually stopped salivating; this is the process of _____. (p. 155)

7. A sudden reemergence of an extinguished conditioned response after a delay in exposure to the conditioned stimulus is called _____ _____. (p. 156)

8. Being able to enjoy a scary movie is an example of stimulus (generalization/discrimination). (p. 156)

5.3 Explain how complex behaviors can result from classical conditioning and how they emerge in our daily lives

Higher-order conditioning occurs when organisms develop classically conditioned responses to other CSs associated with the original CS.

9. Advertisers use _____ _____ to get customers to associate their products with an enjoyable stimulus. (p. 157)

10. Describe the methods used by Watson and Rayner to condition fear in Little Albert and explain why their work could not be conducted today for ethical reasons. (p. 158)

succeed with mypsychlab

1. Can a controversial study of a young child help psychologists understand phobias?
   Classical Conditioning of Little Albert

2. Can we condition a dog to salivate to a light without ever pairing the light with a UCS such as food?
   Higher-Order Conditioning

OPERANT CONDITIONING (pp. 160–171)

5.4 Describe how behaviors are acquired through operant conditioning

Operant conditioning is learning that is controlled by the consequences of the organism's behavior. It is also referred to as instrumental conditioning since the organism "gets something" out of the response.

11. The behaviors emitted by the animal to receive a reward are known as _____. (p. 160)

5.5 Identify the similarities and differences between operant and classical conditioning

Both forms of conditioning involve many of the same processes, including acquisition and extinction. Nevertheless, in operant conditioning, responses are emitted rather than elicited, the reward is contingent on behavior, and responses mostly involve skeletal muscles rather than the autonomic nervous system.

12. Complete the table to show the differences between classical and operant conditioning. (p. 161)

	Classical Conditioning	Operant Conditioning
Target behavior is . . .		
Reward is . . .		
Behavior depends primarily on . . .		

Answers are located at the end of the text.

5.6 Describe reinforcement and its effects on behavior

Thorndike's law of effect tells us that if a response, in the presence of a stimulus, is followed by a reward, it is likely to be repeated, resulting in the gradual "stamping in" of S-R connections. Reinforcement can be positive (administering a stimulus) or negative (withdrawing a stimulus).

13. Positive reinforcement and negative reinforcement can both be considered "rewards" because they both _____ the likelihood of performing a behavior. (p. 162)

14. A physics professor announces to his class that students who are earning 90 percent or higher in the class do not have to take the midterm exam. This is an example of (positive/negative reinforcement). (p. 162)

5.7 Distinguish negative reinforcement from punishment as influences on behavior

Negative reinforcement increases a behavior, whereas punishment weakens a response. One disadvantage of punishment is that it tells the organism only what *not* to do, not what *to* do.

15. Whereas _____ _____ is the removal of a negative outcome or consequence of a behavior that strengthens the probability of the behavior, _____ is the outcome or consequence of a behavior that weakens the probability of the behavior. (p. 163)

16. According to Skinner, one of the disadvantages of punishment is that it often creates _____, which interferes with future learning. (p. 164)

5.8 Describe the four major schedules of reinforcement and their effects on behavior

Partial reinforcement tends to result in slower acquisition but also slower extinction than reinforcement on every instance. The pattern of behavior exhibited by the animal experiencing partial reinforcement varies, depending on the schedule of reinforcement. The four most common

schedules are determined by whether the schedule of reinforcement is fixed or variable and whether it is based on the ratio of behaviors produced or the amount of time that has elapsed, and each has a distinct pattern of behavior associated with it.

17. According to the principle of partial reinforcement, behaviors we reinforce only occasionally are (slower/quicker) to extinguish than those we reinforce every time. (p. 165)

18. Skinner discovered that different _____ _____ yield distinctive patterns of responding. (p. 166)

19. Casino gambling is a prime example of a _____ _____ _____. (p. 167)

20. Identify the typical response patterns for the four reinforcement schedule types. (p. 167)

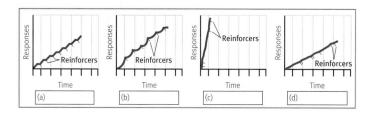

succeed with mypsychlab

1. Do you need a reinforcer every time you engage in a desirable behavior?
Schedules of Reinforcement

2. How do animals at Sea World learn to perform tricks for the first time?
The Shaping Process

COGNITIVE MODELS OF LEARNING (pp. 171–175)

5.9 Outline the evidence that supports learning in the absence of conditioning

S-O-R psychologists believe that the organism's interpretation of stimuli plays a central role in learning. Tolman's work on latent learning, which showed that animals can learn without reinforcement, challenged the radical behaviorist view of learning.

21. Early behaviorists (believed/didn't believe) that thought played an important causal role in learning. (p. 171)

22. Watson believed psychologists should focus only on _____ behaviors. (p. 171)

23. Skinner believed that observable behavior, _____, and _____ are all governed by the laws of learning. (p. 171)

24. In the past few decades, psychology has increasingly moved away from a simple S-R psychology to a more complex _____ psychology. (p. 171)

25. When talking to employees about their performance, why might managers want to adapt their style depending on the person they're talking to? (p. 172)

26. According to Tolman, the rats in his study had developed spatial representations of the maze that he called _____ _____. (p. 173)

5.10 Explain how learning can occur through observation

Research suggests that individuals can acquire aggressive behavior by observational learning. Correlational studies, longitudinal studies, laboratory studies, and field studies suggest that media violence contributes to aggression.

27. According to some psychologists, an important variant of latent learning is _____ learning, in which one learns by watching others without instruction or reinforcement. (p. 173)

28. In classic research in the 1960s, _____ _____ and his colleagues demonstrated that children can learn to act aggressively by watching aggressive role models. (p. 173)

29. Longitudinal studies that correlate the amount of violent TV watched in childhood with the number of aggressive acts they committed in adulthood (have/have not) demonstrated causality. (p. 174)

30. What type of learning is taking place in this photo, and what is the basis of the learning process shown? (p. 173)

succeed with mypsych lab

1. Play the role of researcher and evaluate findings of psychological studies on violence and the media.
Media Violence

2. Get a chance to be a participant in a psychological experiment.
Latent Learning

BIOLOGICAL INFLUENCES ON LEARNING (pp. 175–179)

5.11 Explain how biological predispositions can facilitate learning of some associations

Most psychologists have increasingly recognized that our genetic endowment influences learning. Conditioned taste aversions refer to the phenomenon whereby classical conditioning can lead us to develop avoidance reactions to the taste of food. John Garcia and his colleagues showed that conditioned taste aversions violate the principle of equipotentiality, because they demonstrated that certain CSs are more easily conditioned to certain UCSs. Research on preparedness suggests that we are evolutionarily predisposed to learn to fear some stimuli more easily than others.

31. Classical conditioning can lead us to develop an avoidance reaction to the taste of food known as _____ _____ _____. (p. 176)

32. Explain how conditioned taste aversions can actually help cancer patients undergoing chemotherapy. (p. 176)

33. Through his research with rats, Garcia helped to demonstrate the _____ influences on conditioned taste aversions. (p. 176)

34. The rats in Garcia's study more readily associated nausea with _____ than with any other sensory stimuli. (p. 176)

35. Garcia's finding challenged the assumption of _____, the belief of many behaviorists that we can pair all CSs equally well with all UCSs. (pp. 176–178)

36. Conditioned taste aversions aren't much fun, but they're often _____ in the real world. An example would be an animal that develops a conditioned taste aversion to a poisoned food or drink. (p. 176)

37. According to Seligman, we're evolutionarily predisposed to fear certain stimuli more than others by means of _____ _____. (p. 178)

38. In Mineka's and Cook's study, the monkeys (acquired/didn't acquire) fears of nondangerous stimuli, such as flowers. (p. 178)

39. Mineka's and Cook's study was clearly a case of learning because the monkeys were (afraid/unafraid) of snakes prior to the experiment. (p. 178)

40. Describe the phenomenon whereby animals return to evolutionarily selected behavior and how that behavior has affected researchers' understanding of learning. (p. 179)

succeed with mypsych lab

1. Cells in the motor cortex fire when monkeys perform a particular task, but will they also fire just watching another monkey perform the same task?
Mirror Neurons

2. Test if you understand what would account for never wanting to eat chocolate again!
Biological Influences on Learning

LEARNING FADS: DO THEY WORK? (pp. 179–181)

5.12 Evaluate popular techniques marketed to enhance learning

Proponents of sleep-assisted learning claim that individuals can learn new material while asleep, but studies have yielded negative results. Although popular in science education, discovery learning approaches often appear to be less effective and efficient than direct instruction. Some educational psychologists claim to be able to boost learning by matching individuals' learning styles with different teaching methods. Nevertheless, learning styles are difficult to assess reliably; moreover, studies that have matched learning styles with teaching methods have typically yielded negative results.

41. Proponents of _____ _____ claim that, just by listening to instructional tapes while you sleep, you can learn any number of new things, such as a foreign language. (p. 180)

42. Controlled studies that monitored subjects' EEGs to make sure the subjects were asleep while listening to the instructional tapes revealed evidence (supporting/refuting) the effectiveness of sleep-assisted learning. (p. 180)

43. Explain the extraordinary claims about how sleep-assisted learning works and identify shortcomings in researchers' attempts to validate those claims. (pp. 179–180)

44. When you give students experimental materials and ask them to figure out a scientific principle on their own, this is known as _____ _____. (p. 180)

succeed with mypsych lab

1. ☼ Look past the hype and pick out the learning techniques that really work.
   Learning Fads: Do They Work?

45. Klahr and his colleagues have shown that the old-fashioned method of _____ _____, in which we simply tell students how to solve problems, is often most efficient and effective. (p. 180)

46. Discovery learning may be a more effective technique for _____ students than for _____ students. (p. 180)

47. Individuals' preferred or optimal method of acquiring new information is referred to as _____ _____. (p. 181)

48. Proponents of this view believe that some students are _____ learners who excel at breaking down problems into different components, while others are _____ learners who excel at viewing problems as a whole. (p. 181)

49. Studies have generally shown that tailoring different methods to people's learning styles (does/doesn't) result in enhanced learning. (p. 181)

50. Provide a valid argument against teaching to students' learning styles. (p. 181)

succeed with mypsych lab

Do You Know All of the Terms in This Chapter?
 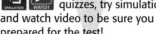 Find out by using the Flashcards. Want more practice? Take additional quizzes, try simulations, and watch video to be sure you are prepared for the test!

SCIENTIFIC THINKING SKILLS
Questions and Summary

1 Many people believe that punishment is necessary for raising children properly, while others believe that any form of physical punishment, no matter how mild, constitutes abuse and creates a potential for future aggression in the child. Synthesize the arguments both in favor of and against physical punishment. Which side are you more inclined to side with? Why?

2 Drugs such as Antabuse are often used to help people with a substance abuse disorder, in this case alcohol abuse, stop drinking. These drugs act by inducing severe vomiting whenever alcohol is consumed. Consider how the effects of such drugs might continue long after the drugs have stopped, in helping people to avoid drinking alcohol.

RULING OUT RIVAL HYPOTHESES
pp. 157, 175, 180

CORRELATION vs. CAUSATION
pp. 164, 168, 174

FALSIFIABILITY
pp. 158, 173

REPLICABILITY
pp. 154, 158, 159, 169, 178

EXTRAORDINARY CLAIMS
p. 180

OCCAM'S RAZOR
p. 171

Memory

How long do memories last? (p. 196)

Can people recover repressed memories of traumatic experiences? (p. 218)

Do memory aids like "ROYGBIV" (for the colors of the rainbow) really help us to remember? (p. 200)

What are infants' earliest memories? (p. 211)

Do witnesses to a crime always remember what they observed accurately? (pp. 216–217)

Consider the following two memorable tales of memory, both true.

True Story 1. A woman in her forties, known only by the initials A.J., has such an astounding memory that she's left even seasoned psychological researchers shaking their heads in amazement. Although emotionally quite normal, A.J. is markedly abnormal in one way: She remembers the details of just about every day she's lived. When researchers give her a date, like March 17, 1989, she can tell them precisely what she was doing on that day—taking a test, eating dinner with a good friend, or traveling to a new city. Researchers have confirmed that she's almost always right. Moreover, she remembers on what day of the week that date fell. In 2003, a team of investigators asked A.J. to remember all of the dates of Easter over the past 24 years. She got all but two correct and reported accurately what she'd done each day (Parker, Cahill, & McGaugh, 2006).

A.J. "suffers" from an exceedingly rare condition called hyperthymestic syndrome: memory that's too good. Or does she really suffer? It's not entirely clear because she regards her remarkable memory as both a curse and a blessing. A.J. says that she sometimes remembers painful events that she'd prefer to forget, but also that she'd never want to give up her special memory "gift." As to the causes of hyperthymestic syndrome, scientists are baffled (Foer, 2007).

True Story 2. In 1997, Nadean Cool, a 44-year-old nurse's aide in Wisconsin, won a $2.4 million malpractice settlement against her psychotherapist. Nadean entered treatment with relatively mild emotional problems, such as a depressed mood and binge eating. Yet after five years of treatment, Nadean supposedly "recovered" childhood memories of having been a member of a murderous satanic cult, of being raped, and of witnessing the murder of her 8-year-old childhood friend. Her therapist also persuaded her that she harbored more than 130 personalities, including demons, angels, children, and a duck. (Her therapist even listed her treatment as group therapy on the grounds that he needed to treat numerous different personalities.)

All of these memories surfaced after Nadean participated in repeated sessions involving *guided imagery*—in which therapists ask clients to imagine past events—and *hypnotic age regression*—in which therapists use hypnosis to "return" clients to the psychological state of childhood. The therapist also subjected Nadean to an exorcism and 15-hour marathon therapy sessions. As therapy progressed, she became overwhelmed by images of terrifying memories she was convinced were genuine. Eventually, however, Nadean came to doubt the reality of these memories, and she terminated treatment.

In a very real sense, we *are* our memories. Our memories define not only our past, but who we are. For A.J., life is like "a movie in her mind that never stops," as she puts it. Her recollections of her life and interactions with friends are remarkably vivid and emotionally intense. A.J.'s memory has shaped her personality in profound ways.

Moreover, when our memories change, as did Nadean Cool's, so do our identities. Following psychotherapy, Nadean came to believe she was a victim of brutal and repeated child abuse. She even came to believe she suffered from a severe condition, namely, *dissociative identity disorder,* or DID (known formerly as multiple personality disorder; see Chapter 13), characterized by the existence of "alter" personalities, or *alters*.

How Memory Operates:
The Memory Assembly Line

We can define **memory** as the retention of information over time. We have memories for many different kinds of information, ranging from our sixteenth birthday party, to how to ride a bike, to the shape of a pyramid. Our memories work pretty well most of the time. Odds are high that tomorrow you'll find your way into school or work just fine and that, with a little luck, you'll even remember some of what you read in this chapter. Yet in other cases, our memories fail us, often when we least expect it. How many times have you misplaced your keys or cell phone? Or how often have you forgotten the names of people you've met over and over again? We call this seeming contradiction the *paradox of memory:* Our memories are surprisingly good in some situations and surprisingly poor in others.

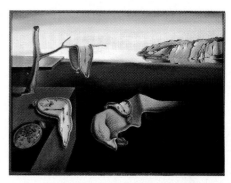

Salvador Dali's classic painting, *The Persistence of Memory,* is a powerful reminder that our memories are much more like melting wax than hardened metal. They often change over time, far more than we realize.

THE PARADOX OF MEMORY

To a large extent, this chapter is the story of this mysterious paradox. As we'll see, the answer to the paradox of memory hinges on a crucial fact: *The same memory mechanisms that serve us well in most circumstances can sometimes cause us problems in others.* Research shows that our memories are often astonishingly accurate. Most of us can recognize our schoolmates decades later and recite the lyrics to dozens, even hundreds, of songs. **[LEARNING OBJECTIVE 6.1]** Consider a study by a group of investigators (Standing, Conezio, & Haber, 1970) who showed college students 2,560 photographs of various objects or scenes for only a few seconds each. Three days later, the researchers showed these students each of the original photographs paired with one new photograph, and asked them to say which was which. Remarkably, the students picked out the original photographs correctly 93 percent of the time. In another case, a researcher contacted subjects 17 years after they'd viewed over 100 line drawings for one to three seconds in a laboratory study. Remarkably, they identified these drawings at better than chance rates when compared with a control group of participants who'd never seen the drawings (Mitchell, 2006).

Some individuals possess remarkable memory capacities. Consider the case of Rajan Mahadevan (better known simply as Rajan). Rajan displayed memory feats so spectacular that they were spoofed on an episode of the cartoon show *The Simpsons.* Rajan had somehow managed to memorize the number *pi*—the ratio of a circle's diameter to its radius—to 38,811 digits (see **Figure 6.1**). When he recited them, it took him three hours at a rate of more than three digits per second. How did Rajan pull off his amazing pi feat? We'll find out later in the chapter.

```
Pi=3.
1415926535 8979323846 2643383279 5028841971 6939937510 (50)
5820974944 5923078164 0628620899 8628034825 3421170679 (100)
8214808651 3282306647 0938446095 5058223172 5359408128 (150)
4811174502 8410270193 8521105559 6446229489 5493038196 (200)
4428810975 6659334461 2847564823 3786783165 2712019091 (250)
4564856692 3460348610 4543266482 1339360726 0249141273 (300)
7245870066 0631558817 4881520920 9628292540 9171536436 (350)
7892590360 0113305305 4882046652 1384146951 9415116094 (400)
3305727036 5759591953 0921861173 8193261179 3105118548 (450)
0744623799 6274956735 1885752724 8912279381 8301194912 (500)
9833673362 4406566430 8602139494 6395224737 1907021798 (550)
6094370277 0539217176 2931767523 8467481846 7669405132 (600)
0005681271 4526356082 7785771342 7577896091 7363717872 (650)
1468440901 2249534301 5654958537 1050792279 6892589235 (700)
4201995611 2129021960 8640344181 5981362977 4771309960 (750)
5187072113 4999999837 2978049951 0597317328 1609631859 (800)
5024459455 3469083026 4252230825 3344685035 2619311881 (850)
7101000313 7838752886 5875332083 8142061717 7669147303 (900)
5982534904 2875546873 1159562863 8823537875 9375195778 (950)
1857780532 ...68065 ...787 661119... ...409 (1000)
```

Figure 6.1 Rajan's Demonstration Sheet of Digits of Pi. Rajan's feats demonstrate the uppermost end of the capacity of human memory.

THE FALLIBILITY OF MEMORY

In some exceedingly rare cases, as with A.J., memory is virtually perfect. Many others of us have extremely good memories in one or two narrow domains, like art history, baseball batting averages, or Civil War trivia. Yet as the case of Nadean Cool illustrates, memory can be surprisingly malleable and prone to error.

Most and perhaps all of us are prone to false memories under the right conditions. Here's a simple demonstration that requires only a pen or pencil and a piece of paper.

GLOSSARY

memory
retention of information over time

Read the list of words below, taking about a second per word. Read the left column first, then the middle column, then the right.

Bed	Cot	Sheets
Pillow	Dream	Rest
Tired	Snore	Yawn
Darkness	Blanket	Couch

Now, put down your textbook, and take a minute or so to jot down as many of these words as you can recall without peeking.

Did you remember *couch?* If so, give yourself a point. How about *snore?* If so, good—give yourself another point.

OK, how about *sleep?* If you're like about a third of typical subjects, you "remembered" seeing the word *sleep.* But now take a close look at the list. The word *sleep* isn't there.

If you remembered seeing this word on the list, you experienced a **memory illusion:** a false but subjectively compelling memory (Deese, 1959; Roediger & McDermott, 1995, 1999). Like optical illusions (see Chapter 4), most memory illusions are by-products of our brain's generally adaptive tendency to go beyond the information it has at its disposal. By doing so, our brains help us to make sense of the world, but they sometimes lead us astray (Gilovich, 1991). In this case, you may have remembered seeing the word *sleep* because it was linked closely in meaning to the other words on the list. Your brain correctly extracted the *gist* or central theme of the list, namely, sleeping, dreaming, and resting. As a consequence, it may have been fooled into remembering that the word *sleep* was there. By relying on the *representativeness heuristic* (Chapter 2), we simplify things to make them easier to remember. In this case, though, our use of this handy heuristic comes with a modest price: a memory illusion.

WHAT DO *you* THINK?

You are an evolutionary psychologist trying to explain why we remember the gist of complex information rather than remembering it literally. What advantages might there be to not remembering things exactly as they happened?

Moreover, most of us have surprisingly poor memories for everyday objects we've seen hundreds, even thousands, of times. Take a look at **Figure 6.2,** where you'll see an array of six pennies. Which of these pennies is the real one? Fewer than half of 203 Americans tested identified the correct penny (Nickerson & Adams, 1979).

THE RECONSTRUCTIVE NATURE OF MEMORY

These demonstrations drive home a crucial point: Our memories frequently fool us and fail us. Indeed, a central theme of this chapter is that our memories are far more reconstructive than reproductive. When we try to recall an event, we *actively reconstruct* our memories using the cues and information available to us. We don't *passively reproduce* our memories, as we would if we were downloading information from a web page on the Internet. Remembering is largely a matter of patching together our often fuzzy recollection with our best hunches about what really happened. When we recall our past experiences, we rarely, if ever, reproduce precise replicas of them (Neisser & Hyman, 1999). We should

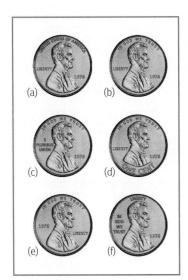

Figure 6.2 Penny Array from Nickerson and Adams (1979). Which of these pennies is the real one? Try to guess before pulling one out of your pocket. See the answer upside down at the bottom of the next page. (*Source:* Nickerson & Adams, 1979)

GLOSSARY

memory illusion
false but subjectively compelling memory

therefore be skeptical of widespread claims that certain vivid memories or even dreams are exact "photocopies" of past events (van der Kolk, Britz, Burr, et al., 1984).

In fact, it's easy to show that our memories are often reconstructive. After reading this sentence, close your eyes for a few moments and picture your most recent walk along a beach, lake, or pond. Then, after opening your eyes, ask yourself what you "saw."

Did you see yourself as if from a distance? If so, you experienced what cognitive psychologists Georgia Nigro and Ulric Neisser termed an *observer memory,* meaning a memory in which we see ourselves as an outside observer would (Nigro & Neisser, 1983). As Sigmund Freud noted well over a century ago, observer memories provide an existence proof (see Chapter 2) that at least some of our memories are reconstructive (Schacter, 1996). You couldn't possibly have seen yourself from a distance because you don't see yourself when you look at your surroundings. Incidentally, if you instead pictured the scene as you would have seen it through your own eyes, you experienced what Nigro and Neisser called a *field memory:* seeing the world through your visual field.

How can our memories be both so good in some cases and so bad in others? How can we explain both the astonishing memories of people like A.J. and Rajan and the faulty memories of people like Nadean Cool? To grasp the paradox of memory, we need to figure out how some of our experiences make it into our memories, whereas so many others never do. To do so, let's embark on a guided tour of the factory assembly line inside our heads.

When you picture yourself taking a recent walk on the beach, do you see yourself as an outside observer would (an "observer memory")? If so, such a recollection provides compelling evidence that memory can be reconstructive.

THE THREE SYSTEMS OF MEMORY

Up to this point, we've been talking about memory as though it were a single thing. It isn't. Most psychologists distinguish among three major systems of memory: sensory memory, short-term memory, and long-term memory, as depicted in **Figure 6.3** (Atkinson & Shiffrin, 1968; Waugh & Norman, 1965). These systems serve different purposes and differ along at least two important dimensions: **span**—how much information each system can hold—and **duration**—over how long a period of time that system can hold information.

We can think of these three systems much like different factory workers along a factory assembly line. The first system, *sensory memory,* is tied closely to the raw materials of our experiences, our perceptions of the world; it holds these perceptions for just a few seconds or less before passing *some* of them on to the second system. This second system, *short-term memory,* works actively with the information handed to it, transforming it into more meaningful material before passing *some* of it on to the third system. Short-term memory holds on to information longer than sensory memory does, but not much longer. The third and final system, *long-term memory,* permits us to retain important information for minutes, days, weeks, months, or even years. **[LEARNING OBJECTIVE 6.2]** In some cases, the information in long-term memory lasts for a lifetime. The odds are high, for example, that you'll remember your first kiss and your high school graduation for many decades, perhaps until the last day of your life. As you can tell from our use of the word *some* in the previous sentences, we lose a great deal of information at each stage of the memory assembly line.

Sensory Memory. If you're anywhere near a television set, turn it on for 10 seconds or so. What did you see?

Regardless of what program you were watching, you almost certainly experienced a steady and uninterrupted stream of visual information. In reality, that continuous stream of images was an illusion, because television programs and movies consist of a series of disconnected frames, each separated by an extremely brief interlude of darkness that you

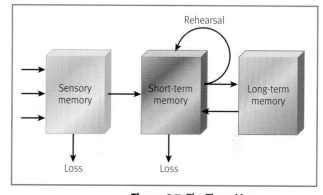

Figure 6.3 The Three-Memory Model. This model subdivides memory into sensory, short-term, and long-term memory. Information flows from left to right, but also from right to left in the case of information retrieved from long-term memory and moved into short-term memory. (*Source:* Atkinson & Shiffrin, 1968)

GLOSSARY

span
how much information a memory system can retain

duration
length of time for which a memory system can retain information

Iconic memory: After a lightning strike, we retain a visual image of it for about one second. (© Ralph Wetmore)

can't perceive. Yet your brain sees these frames as blending together into a seamless whole, in part because it continues to detect each frame for an extremely brief period of time after it disappears.

That is, our brains retain each frame in our **sensory memory,** which is the first factory worker in the assembly line of memory. Sensory memory briefly maintains our perceptions before passing them on to the next memory system, which is short-term memory. Sensory memory is a helpful system because it buys our brains a bit of extra time to process incoming sensations. It also allows us to "fill in the blanks" in our perceptions and see the world as an unbroken stream of events.

Psychologists believe each sense, including vision, hearing, touch, taste, and smell, has its own form of sensory memory. In the case of television or movie clips, we experience an *iconic memory,* the type of sensory memory that applies to vision. Iconic memories last for only about a second, and then they're gone forever.

Psychologist George Sperling (1960) conducted a pioneering study that demonstrated the existence of iconic memory. He quickly flashed participants a display of 12 letters, 4 letters in each of three rows, as shown in **Figure 6.4.** The display lasted only about one-twentieth of a second. Sperling found that most participants could remember 4 or 5 letters. Surprisingly, different participants remembered different letters. This finding suggested to Sperling that all 12 letters had an equal chance of being recalled but that no one person could recall them all.

This finding was puzzling. After all, if participants had remembered the whole visual display, why could they recall only a handful of letters and no more?

To test whether all 12 letters were making it into iconic memory, Sperling played a tone (high, medium, or low) to signal participants which of the three rows (top, middle, or bottom) he wanted them to report. The key to his experiment was that he didn't play the tone until after the letters flashed up, so participants couldn't plan ahead and only focus on one row of letters. He found that virtually all participants now got almost all letters in that row correct. This finding confirmed Sperling's hunch: Participants had access to all 12 letters in their memories and could recall any row. Sperling concluded that our iconic memories fade so quickly that we can't access all the information before it disappears. So Sperling's participants were able to take in all of the information but retained it in memory only long enough to read off a few letters.

Sensory memory also applies to hearing. Now read that last sentence out loud: "Sensory memory also applies to hearing." If you pause for a few moments after saying it, you'll be able to replay the words precisely as you heard them for a few seconds, much like a soft echo. That's why psychologists call this form of sensory memory *echoic memory* (Neisser, 1967). In contrast to iconic memories, echoic memories can last as long as 5 to 10 seconds (Cowan, Lichty, & Grove, 1990), conveniently permitting you to take notes on your psychology professor's most recent sentence even after he or she has finished saying it.

S D F G
P W H J
X C V N

Figure 6.4 Display of Twelve Letters as Used in Sperling's 1960 Study. Sperling's partial report method demonstrated that all displayed letters were held in sensory memory but decayed rapidly before all of them could be transferred to short-term memory. (*Source:* Sperling, 1960)

Short-Term Memory. Once information makes it past our sensory storage, it passes into our **short-term memory,** a second system for retaining information in our memories for brief periods of time. Short-term memory is the second factory worker in our memory assembly line. Some psychologists also refer to short-term memory as *working memory*— although working memory tends to refer specifically to our ability to hold on to information we're currently thinking about, attending to, or processing actively (Baddeley, 1993; Baddeley & Hitch, 1974). If sensory memory is what feeds raw materials into the assembly line, then short-term memory is the work space where construction happens. After construction takes place, we either move the product into the warehouse for long-term storage or, in some cases, scrap it altogether.

GLOSSARY

sensory memory
brief storage of perceptual information before it is passed to short-term memory

short-term memory
memory system that retains the information we are currently thinking about for limited durations

If short-term memory is a short stop on the assembly line, just how brief is it? In the late 1950s, a husband-and-wife psychologist team decided to find out.

The Duration of Short-Term Memory.

The Duration of Short-Term Memory. Lloyd and Margaret Peterson (1959) presented participants with lists of three letters each, such as MKP or ASN, and then asked them to recall these three-letter strings. In some cases, they made participants wait only 3 seconds before recalling the letters; in other cases, they made them wait up to 18 seconds. Each time, they told participants to count backward by threes while they were waiting.

Many psychologists were surprised by the Petersons' results, and you may be too. They found that after about 10 or 15 seconds, most participants *did no better than chance.* So the duration of short-term memory is quite brief; it's probably no longer than about 20 seconds. Incidentally, many people misuse the term *short-term memory* in everyday language. For example, they may say that their "short-term memory isn't working" because they forgot what they had for dinner yesterday. As we've seen, the duration of short-term memory is far briefer than that.

Memory Loss from Short-Term Memory: Decay versus Interference. Why did the Petersons' participants lose their short-term memories so quickly? The most obvious explanation is that short-term memories **decay,** that is, fade away. The longer we wait, the less is left. Yet there's a competing explanation for the loss of information from short-term memory: **interference.** According to this view, our memories get in the way of each other. That is, our memories are very much like radio signals. They don't change over time, but they're harder to detect if they're jammed by other signals.

Research indicates that interference is the prime culprit in forgetting (Waugh & Norman, 1965). Most researchers believe that decay also plays some role in short-term memory loss (Altmann & Schunn, 2002). It turns out that there are two different kinds of interference (Underwood, 1957). One kind, **retroactive interference,** occurs when learning something new hampers earlier learning (think of the prefix *retro-*, because retroactive interference works in a reverse direction). For example, if you've learned one language, say Spanish, and then later learned a somewhat similar language, perhaps Italian, you've probably found that you started making mistakes in Spanish you'd never made before. Specifically, you may have found yourself using Italian words, like *buono,* for Spanish words, like *bueno* (both *buono* and *bueno* mean "good").

In contrast, **proactive interference** occurs when earlier learning gets in the way of new learning. For example, knowing how to play tennis might interfere with our attempt to learn to play racquetball, which requires a much smaller racquet. Not surprisingly, both retroactive and proactive interference are more likely to occur when the old and new stimuli that we've learned are similar. Learning a new language doesn't much affect our ability to master a new lasagna recipe.

The Capacity of Short-Term Memory: The Magic Number.

The Capacity of Short-Term Memory: The Magic Number. We've already seen that short-term memory doesn't last very long. Twenty seconds, or even less—and—poof!—the memory is gone, unless we've made an extra-special effort to retain it. But how large is the span of short-term memory? Find out for yourself by taking the test in **Figure 6.5.**

This exercise is a test of "digit span." How did you make out? Odds are that you breezed through 3 digits, started to find 4 digits a bit tricky, and maxed out at somewhere between 5 and 9 digits. It's unlikely you got the ten-digit list completely right; if you did, you've earned the right to call yourself a memory superstar.

That's because the digit span of most adults is between five and nine digits, with an average of seven digits. Indeed, this finding is so consistent across people that Princeton University psychologist George Miller (1956) referred to seven plus or minus two pieces of information as the **Magic Number.**

RULING OUT RIVAL HYPOTHESES
Have important alternative explanations for the findings been excluded?

$$9-5-2$$
$$2-9-7-3$$
$$5-7-4-9-2$$
$$6-2-7-3-8-4$$
$$2-4-1-8-6-4-7$$
$$3-9-5-7-4-1-8-9$$
$$8-4-6-3-1-7-4-2-5$$
$$5-2-9-3-4-6-1-8-5-7$$

Figure 6.5 A Test of Short-Term Memory Span. Try reading each row of numbers, one row at a time, at a rate of one number per second. Once you're done with each row, cover the line and write down what you remember. How far did you get before making a mistake?

GLOSSARY

decay
fading of information from memory

interference
loss of information from memory because of competition from additional incoming information

retroactive interference
interference with retention of old information due to acquisition of new information

proactive interference
interference with acquisition of new information due to previous learning of information

Magic Number
the span of short-term memory, according to George Miller: seven plus or minus two pieces of information

According to Miller, the Magic number applies to much more than digits. It's the universal limit of short-term memory, and it applies to just about all information we encounter: numbers, letters, people, vegetables, and cities. Because it's hard to retain much more than seven plus or minus two pieces of information in our short-term memory, it's almost surely not a coincidence that telephone numbers are exactly seven digits long, not counting the area code. When telephone numbers exceed seven digits, we start making mistakes. Some psychologists have since argued that Miller's Magic Number may even overestimate the capacity of short-term memory, and that the true Magic Number may be as low as four (Cowan, 2001). Regardless of who's right, it's clear that the capacity of short-term memory is extremely limited.

Chunking: Multiplying the Magic Number. If our short-term memory capacity is no more than nine digits, how do we manage to remember larger amounts of information than this for brief periods of time? For example, read the following sentence, then wait a few seconds and recite it back to yourself: **Harry Potter's white owl Hedwig flew off into the dark and stormy night.** Were you able to remember most or even all of it? The odds are high that you were. Yet this sentence contained 13 words, which exceeds the Magic Number. How did you accomplish this feat?

We can expand our ability to remember things in the short term by using a technique called **chunking:** organizing material into meaningful groupings. For example, look at the following string of 15 letters for a few seconds and then try to recall them:

G T I Q A K B N R D W E L F O

How'd you do? Probably right around the Magic Number, which is only a subset of the letters listed. Okay, now try this 15-letter string instead.

C I A U S A F B I N B C J F K

Did you do any better this time? If so, it's probably because you noticed something different about this group of 15 letters than the first group: They consisted of meaningful abbreviations. So you probably "chunked" these 15 letters into five meaningful groups of 3 letters each: CIA, USA, FBI, NBC, JFK. In this way, you reduced the number of items you needed to remember from 15 to only 5. In fact, you might have even gotten this number down to less than 5 by combining CIA and FBI (both the initials of U.S. government intelligence agencies) into one chunk.

Chunking explains Rajan's remarkable pi memorization feats. Rajan memorized enormous numbers of area codes, dates of famous historical events, and other meaningful numbers embedded within the list of pi digits to effectively reduce more than 30,000 digits to a much smaller number.

Experts rely on chunking to help them process complex information. William Chase and Nobel Prize–winning researcher Herbert Simon showed chess masters and chess novices various sets of chess positions from a point midway through a game for 5 seconds each. Experts correctly recalled the positions of 16 chess pieces on average, whereas beginners correctly recalled only four on average. Yet when the researchers showed both groups *random* chess positions—those that would be extremely unlikely to occur in actual games—both did equally poorly (Chase & Simon, 1973). By chunking the chess pieces into patterns they found meaningful, the chess experts easily remembered the complete positions (see **Figure 6.6**). Yet their overall memories were no better than anyone else's when the chess positions were nonsensical. Researchers have reported the same finding when comparing professional basketball players with nonplayers. Players recall actual basketball positions much better than do nonplayers (Didierjean & Marmèche, 2005).

Fact -OID One man named S.F. was able to get his digit span memory up to 79 digits using chunking. Among other tricks, S.F., who was a runner, memorized enormous numbers of world record times for track events and used them to chunk numbers into bigger units. Yet S.F. hadn't really increased his short-term memory capacity at all, only his chunking ability. His memory span for letters was only a measly six, well within the range of the Magic Number achieved by the rest of us memory slackers.

Figure 6.6 Chunking Chess Position. Experienced chess players recall the positions above much better than chess novices by using chunking.

GLOSSARY

chunking
organizing information into meaningful groupings, allowing us to extend the span of short-term memory

Rehearsal: Keeping Information Onstage. Whereas chunking increases the span of short-term memory, a strategy called rehearsal extends the duration of information in short-term memory. **Rehearsal** is repeating the information mentally (or even out loud). In that way, we keep the information active in our short-term memories, just as a juggler keeps a bunch of bowling pins in action by continuing to catch them and toss them back into the air. Of course, if he pauses for a second to scratch his nose, the bowling pins come crashing to the ground. Similarly, if we stop rehearsing and shift our attention elsewhere, we'll quickly lose material from our short-term memory.

There are two major types of rehearsals. The first, **maintenance rehearsal,** simply involves repeating the stimuli in their original form; we don't attempt to change the original stimuli in any way. We engage in maintenance rehearsal whenever we hear a phone number and keep on repeating it—either out loud or in our minds—until we're ready to dial the number. Of course, if someone interrupts us while we're rehearsing, we'll forget the number.

The second type of rehearsal, **elaborative rehearsal,** usually takes more effort. In this type of rehearsal, we "elaborate" on the stimuli we need to remember by linking them in some meaningful way, perhaps by visualizing them or trying to understand how they relate to each other (Craik & Lockhart, 1972).

To grasp the difference between maintenance and elaborative rehearsal, let's imagine that a researcher gave us a *paired-associate task*. In this task, the investigator first presents us with various pairs of words, such as dog–shoe, tree–pipe, key–monkey, and kite–president. Then, she presents us with the first word in each pair—dog, tree, and so on—and asks us to remember the second word in the pair. If we used maintenance rehearsal, we'd simply repeat the words in each pair over and over again as soon as we heard it—dog–shoe, dog–shoe, dog–shoe, and so on. In contrast, if we used elaborative rehearsal, we'd try to link the words in each pair in a meaningful way. One effective way of accomplishing this goal is to come up with a meaningful, visual image that combines both stimuli (see **Figure 6.7**) (Paivio, 1969). So to remember the word pair dog–shoe, for example, we could picture a dog wearing a shoe or a shoe shaped like a dog.

Elaborative rehearsal usually works better than maintenance rehearsal (Harris & Qualls, 2000). This finding demolishes a widely held misconception about memory: that rote memorization is typically the best means of retaining information. There's a take-home lesson here when it comes to our study habits. To remember complex information, it's almost always better to connect that information with things we already know than to merely keep repeating it.

Figure 6.7 Word Pairs. Using elaborative rehearsal helps us recall the word pair dog–shoe. (*Source:* Paivio, 1969)

Depth of Processing: Everyone into the Deep End! This finding is consistent with a **levels-of-processing model** of memory. According to this model, the more deeply we process information, the better we tend to remember it. This model identifies three levels of processing of verbal information (Craik & Lockhart, 1972): For example, look at the following sentence:

ALL PEOPLE CREATE THEIR OWN MEANING OF LIFE

If you made judgments about aspects of the sentence such as whether it consists of capital or lowercase letters, you would be unlikely to remember much about what the sentence said. If you repeated the sentence out loud over and over, you'll be more likely to remember something about the sentence. However, the most effective way to remember is to consider its meaning. You might think about whether you've tried to create your own meaning of life and how doing so has been beneficial to you. Research shows that deeper levels of processing, especially processing of meaning, tend to produce more enduring long-term memories (Craik & Tulving, 1975).

GLOSSARY

rehearsal
repeating information to extend the duration of retention in short-term memory

maintenance rehearsal
repeating stimuli in their original form to retain them in short-term memory

elaborative rehearsal
linking stimuli to each other in a meaningful way to improve retention of information in short-term memory

levels-of-processing model
model stating that the more deeply we process information, the better we remember it

FALSIFIABILITY
Can the claim be disproved?

Still, some psychologists have criticized the levels-of-processing model as largely unfalsi-fiable (Baddeley, 1993). According to them, it's virtually impossible to determine how deeply we've processed a memory in the first place. Moreover, they claim, proponents of the levels-of-processing model are merely equating "depth" with how well subjects later remember. There may well be some truth to this criticism. Still, it's safe to say that the more meaning we can supply to a stimulus, the more likely we are to recall it in the long term.

Long-Term Memory.
Now that the second factory assembly line worker—short-term memory—has finished her construction job, what does she pass on to the third and final worker? And how does what the third worker receives differ from what the second worker started out with? **Long-term memory,** the third worker, is our lasting store of information. It includes the facts, experiences, and skills we've acquired over our life span.

Differences between Long-Term and Short-Term Memory. Long-term memory differs from short-term memory in several important ways. First, in contrast to short-term memory, which can hold only about seven stimuli at a single time, the capacity of long-term memory is huge. Just how huge? No one knows for sure. Some scientists estimate that a typical person's memory holds about as much information as 500 complete sets of *Encyclopaedia Britannica* (Cardón, 2005).

Second, although information in short-term memory vanishes after only about 20 seconds at most, information in long-term memory often endures for years, even decades. Consider the work of psychologist Harry Bahrick, who has studied individuals' memory for languages they learned in school over many decades. In **Figure 6.8,** we can see that people's memory declines markedly about 2 to 3 years after taking a Spanish course. Yet after about 2 years, the decline becomes quite gradual. Indeed, it begins to level out after a while, with almost no additional loss for up to 50 years after they took the course (Bahrick & Phelps, 1987).

GLOSSARY

long-term memory
sustained (from minutes to years) retention of information stored regarding facts, our experiences, and skills

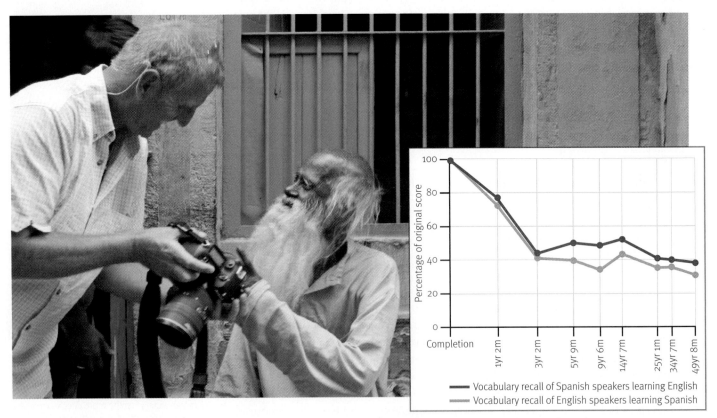

Figure 6.8 Long-Term Memory Retention. The classic work of Harry Bahrick (1984) shows that retention of a foreign language remains remarkably constant for spans of almost 50 years after an initial drop. (*Source:* Bahrick, 1984)

Third, the types of mistakes we commit in long-term memory differ from those we make in short-term memory. Long-term memory errors tend to be *semantic,* that is, based on the meaning of the information we've received. So we might misremember a "poodle" as a "terrier." In contrast, short-term memory errors tend to be *acoustic,* that is, based on the sound of the information we've received (Conrad, 1964; Wickelgren, 1965). So, we might misremember hearing "noodle" rather than "poodle."

Primacy and Recency Effects: Forgetting Isn't Random. When we try to remember a large number of items, such as a grocery list or a schedule of events, we often forget some of them. To some extent, psychologists can predict which items we're more likely to forget and which we're more likely to remember.

To demonstrate this point, read the list of 21 words below, either to yourself or out loud. Read the left column first, then the middle column, then the right one. Then, turn away from your book and take a few minutes to try to recall as many of these words as you can in any order you'd like. Psychologists call this a *free recall* task because you're free to recall the words in whatever order they come to mind. Ready? Begin.

Ball	Sky	Store
Shoe	Desk	Pencil
Tree	Car	Grass
Dog	Rope	Man
Paper	Dress	Cloud
Bird	Xylophone	Hat
House	Knife	Vase

When you're done, check off which words you got right. This demonstration may not work as well as the others in this chapter because it works best when the results are averaged across a large group of people. Still, let's take a peek at how you did.

If you're like most people, you probably did a bit better with the early words, like *ball, shoe,* and *tree,* than with the words in the middle of the list. That's the **primacy effect:** the tendency to remember stimuli, like words, early in a list. Also, you may have done a bit better with the later words, like *cloud, hat,* and *vase.* That's the **recency effect:** the tendency to remember stimuli later in a list. You may also have remembered the word *xylophone,* which seems to be something of an oddball in the list. We also tend to remember stimuli that are distinctive (Neath & Surprenant, 2003).

If we averaged your results along with those of a few hundred other subjects, we'd end up with the graph depicted in **Figure 6.9,** called the **serial position curve.** As we can see from the figure, this curve clearly displays the primacy and recency effects. What do the terms primacy and recency effect mean? There's still some controversy concerning this question, but most researchers agree that primacy and recency effects reflect the operation of different memory systems. The last few words in the list were probably recalled because they still lingered in your short-term memory. The primacy effect is trickier to explain, but there's good evidence that you were more likely to recall the earlier words in the list because you had more opportunity to rehearse them silently. As a consequence, these words were more likely to be transferred from short-term memory into long-term memory.

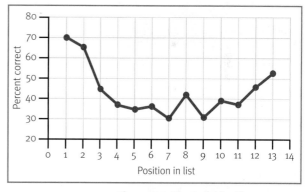

Figure 6.9 The Serial Position Curve. Most psychologists believe that the primacy and recency effects in this curve are the telltale signs of two different memory systems: long-term and short-term memory, respectively.

GLOSSARY

primacy effect
tendency to remember words at the beginning of a list especially well

recency effect
tendency to remember words at the end of a list especially well

serial position curve
graph depicting the effect of both primacy and recency on people's ability to recall items on a list

Types of Long-Term Memory: Different Flavors or Different Meals? Long-term memory isn't just one system, but many.

To find out why, try your hand at the following four questions:

(1) In what year did the United States become independent from Great Britain?

(2) What Middle Eastern country did the United States invade in 2003?

(3) How old were you when you first tried to ride a bicycle?

(4) Where did you celebrate your last birthday?

According to Endel Tulving (1972) and many other memory researchers, our answers to the first two questions rely on different memory systems than our answers to the last two. Our answers to the first two questions (1776 and Iraq) depend on **semantic memory,** our knowledge of facts about the world. **[LEARNING OBJECTIVE 6.3]** In contrast, our answers to the last two questions, which are unique to each of us, depend on **episodic memory,** our recollection of events in our lives. There's good evidence that these two types of memory are housed in different brain regions. Semantic memory tends to activate the left frontal cortex more than the right frontal cortex, and vice versa for episodic memory (Cabeza & Nyberg, 1997). Still, both semantic and episodic memory share one important feature: They require conscious effort and awareness. Whether we're trying to recall the definition of "chunking" from earlier in this chapter or our first kiss, we *know* we're trying to remember. Moreover, when we recall this information, we have a conscious experience of accessing it. That is, both semantic and episodic memory are examples of **explicit memory,** the process of recalling information intentionally. (Some researchers refer to the information recalled by explicit memory as *declarative memory*.)

Explicit memory differs from **implicit memory,** which is the process of recalling information we don't remember deliberately. Implicit memories don't require conscious effort on our part. For example, each of us can go through the steps of unlocking our front doors without consciously recalling the sequence of actions required to do so. In fact, we probably can't tell without reenacting it in our heads or actually standing in front of our doors which way the key turns in the lock and how we'd hold the key in our hands while unlocking the door.

There are several subtypes of implicit memory. We'll discuss two of them here: procedural memory and priming. According to most psychologists, implicit memory also includes habituation, classical conditioning, and other forms of learning we've encountered in Chapter 5.

One subtype of implicit memory, **procedural memory,** refers to memory for motor skills and habits. Whenever we ride a bicycle or open a soda can, we're relying on procedural memory. Our procedural and semantic memories for the same skills are sometimes surprisingly different. For example, most college students are experienced enough typists to type the word *the* without difficulty. But now try to remember where the *t, h,* and *e* are located on the keyboard without looking at it or moving your fingers. If you're like most people, you draw a blank. You may even find that the only way to remember their location is to use your fingers to type the imaginary letters in midair. Although your procedural memory for locating letters on a keyboard is effortless, your semantic memory for locating them is a different story.

A second subtype of implicit memory, **priming,** refers to our ability to identify a stimulus more easily or more quickly when we've previously encountered similar stimuli. Imagine that a researcher flashes the word QUEEN, interspersed with a few hundred other words, very quickly on a computer screen. An hour later, she asks you

Procedural memory is memory for how to do things, even things we do automatically without thinking about how to do them.

GLOSSARY

semantic memory
our knowledge of facts about the world

episodic memory
recollection of events in our lives

explicit memory
memories we recall intentionally and of which we have conscious awareness

implicit memory
memories we don't deliberately remember or reflect on consciously

procedural memory
memory for how to do things, including motor skills and habits

priming
our ability to identify a stimulus more easily or more quickly after we've encountered similar stimuli

to perform a *stem completion task,* which requires you to fill in the missing letters of a word. In this case, the stem completion task is K __ __ __. Research shows that having seen the word QUEEN, you're more likely to complete the stem with KING (as opposed to KILL or KNOW, for example) than are subjects who haven't seen QUEEN (Neely, 1976). This is true, incidentally, even for subjects who insist they can't even remember having seen the word QUEEN (Bargh, 1994). This memory is implicit because it doesn't involve any deliberate effort or conscious access on our part.

Priming occurs in everyday life too. During the infamous O.J. Simpson murder trial in 1995, many Americans "suddenly" reported seeing dozens of license plates with the letters "OJ" in them. Almost surely, these license plates had been there all along, but the virtual round-the-clock press coverage of the O.J. trial primed people to see these two letters on the backs of cars.

If you're having a hard time keeping all of these subtypes of long-term memory straight, **Figure 6.10** summarizes the major subtypes of explicit and implicit memory.

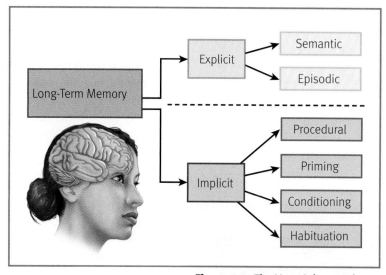

Figure 6.10 The Many Subtypes of Memory. A summary of the subtypes of explicit and implicit memory.

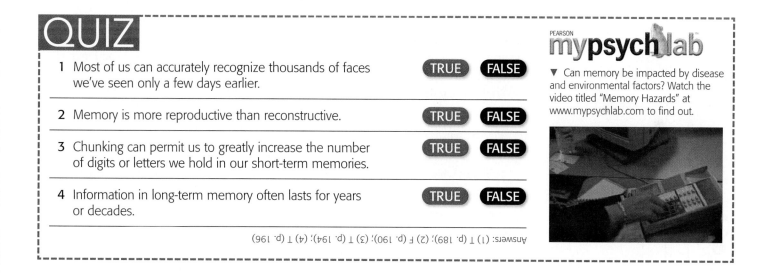

QUIZ

1 Most of us can accurately recognize thousands of faces we've seen only a few days earlier. **TRUE** **FALSE**

2 Memory is more reproductive than reconstructive. **TRUE** **FALSE**

3 Chunking can permit us to greatly increase the number of digits or letters we hold in our short-term memories. **TRUE** **FALSE**

4 Information in long-term memory often lasts for years or decades. **TRUE** **FALSE**

PEARSON mypsychlab

▼ Can memory be impacted by disease and environmental factors? Watch the video titled "Memory Hazards" at www.mypsychlab.com to find out.

Answers: (1) T (p. 189); (2) F (p. 190); (3) T (p. 194); (4) T (p. 196).

The Three Stages of Remembering

How do we get information into our long-term memories? Memory psychologists agree that there are three major *stages* of memory: *encoding, storage,* and *retrieval.* By the way, we shouldn't confuse these stages with the three major *systems* of memory we've just discussed (sensory, short-term, and long-term). Instead, these three stages refer to *processes* that explain how information gets into long-term memory and gets back out again when we need it.

To understand these three memory stages, picture yourself working as a librarian at your college or university library. When a new book arrives, you first give it a number to identify it; that's encoding. Then you file it away on the bookshelf; that's storage. Then, when you want to find the book a few weeks, months, or even years later, you go to the shelves and fetch it; that's retrieval. Of course, like all metaphors, this one is an oversimplification because the memories we retrieve are rarely identical to those we initially encoded. Some of the "books" in our mental library may become yellow with age; others are marked up or even damaged beyond recognition.

ENCODING: THE "CALL NUMBERS" OF THE MIND

Encoding refers to the process of getting information into our memory banks. To remember something, we first need to make sure the information is in a format our memories can use. To a far greater extent than we realize, many of our memory failures are actually failures of encoding. Have you ever had the embarrassing experience of going to a party and being introduced to several people at the same time and then immediately realizing that you'd forgotten all of their names? Odds are high you were so nervous or distracted that you never encoded their names in the first place. Once we lose the chance to encode an event, we'll never remember it. To go back to our library analogy, imagine that the librarian assigns some of the books that come in for processing an identification number but tosses some of them in the trash instead. These books never make it to the shelves.

"In one ear and out the other," the saying goes. If you've met someone and have forgotten his or her name a minute later, you probably never encoded it in the first place.

That principle helps to explain why the popular belief that our brains preserve a record of every event we've ever encountered (Alvarez & Brown, 2001) is almost surely a myth. Most events we've experienced are never encoded, and almost all events we do encode include only some of the details of the experience. Much of our everyday experience never gets into our brains in the first place.

What can we do to help ourselves encode important information? Read the following passages for a clue:

(1) Please Excuse My Dear Aunt Sally.

(2) Thirty days hath September, April, June, and November. All the rest have 31, except for February, which has twenty-eight, and you probably think it's great. Or maybe it's fine, when on leap year, it has twenty-nine.

(3) Every Good Boy Does Fine.

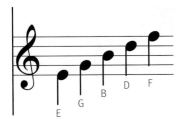

Music students use the mnemonic "Every good boy does fine" to remember the names of the lines (E, G, B, D, F) in the treble clef.

What do these strange passages have in common? Each is a **mnemonic** (pronounced "nuh-mon-ick"): a learning aid, strategy, or device that enhances recall. Mnemonics help us encode memories in a way that makes them easier to recall. **[LEARNING OBJECTIVE 6.4]** From time to time, virtually all of us use recall boosters, like making lists or writing appointments on a calendar or PDA (Intons-Peterson & Fournier, 1986). Mnemonics are *mental* strategies that help us organize information meaningfully during encoding so that we can get it back out again during retrieval. Item 1 specifies the proper order of mathematical operations (parentheses, exponents, multiplication, division, addition, subtraction) by having each word start with the same letter as the mathematical operation. Item 2 is a rhyme that's a handy way of remembering the number of days in each month. Item 3, as everyone who's ever taken music lessons will recall, stands for the note names on the lines of the treble clef in musical notation (E, G, B, D, F).

Generally speaking, mnemonics can be helpful if we're motivated to practice them on a regular basis. Many people seem to prefer external aids, such as making lists (Park, Smith, & Cavanaugh, 1990), to mnemonics, probably because they take less work and effort. Mnemonics require training, patience, and even a dash of creativity.

GLOSSARY

encoding
process of getting information into our memory banks

mnemonic
a learning aid, strategy, or device that enhances recall

myth CONCEPTIONS DO MEMORY BOOSTERS WORK?

The next time you're in your local drug store, stop by the aisle containing herbal remedies. There you'll find a variety of so-called "smart pills" designed to enhance memory: ginkgo, vitamin E, and even drugs with unpronounceable, but scientific-sounding names like phosphatidylserine, citicoline, and piracetam. Can any of them help us remember where we mislaid our keys this morning, memorize the names of the ten people we met at last night's party, or recall how to spell "phosphatidylserine"?

You might reasonably assume that you wouldn't find these products lining your drugstore shelves unless researchers had first demonstrated that they work. You'd be wrong. In 1994, the U.S. Congress passed the Dietary Supplement Health and Education Act (DSHEA), which prevented the Food and Drug Administration (FDA) from regulating diet supplements and herbal remedies, including those intended to enhance memory. Before allowing drugs to enter the market, the FDA normally demands controlled experiments to demonstrate their safety and effectiveness. Following the passage of DSHEA, however, there's been no quality control over most diet supplements or herbal remedies. It's anybody's guess whether they work or even whether any might be harmful.

Probably the best-known herbal remedy for memory is ginkgo (whose scientific name is *Ginkgo biloba*), an ancient Chinese medicine extracted from the leaves of the ginkgo tree. The manufacturers of ginkgo claim that it can markedly improve normal people's memory in as little as four weeks. Like many other memory boosters, ginkgo presumably works in part by increasing the amount of acetylcholine in the brain. Acetylcholine is a neurotransmitter that plays a key role in memory.

Ginkgo is remarkably popular; Americans spend several hundred million dollars on it per year. Yet controlled studies comparing ginkgo with a placebo show that its effects on memory in normal individuals are minimal, even nonexistent (Gold, Cahill, & Wenk, 2002; Solomon, Adams, Silver, et al., 2002). If ginkgo produces any effects on normal memory at all, they appear to be about equal to those of drinking a glass of lemonade or any sugary liquid (as you'll recall from Chapter 3, sugar is the brain's fuel). Ginkgo's effects on memory in people with Alzheimer's disease or other forms of dementia are only slightly more promising (Gold et al., 2002). There's no good evidence that it can reverse severe memory loss. Moreover, like many herbal remedies, ginkgo can be harmful in certain cases. For example, it can interact with blood-thinning medicines and thereby cause excessive bleeding.

As for all of the other smart pills with fancy names, the evidence for their effects on memory is too preliminary to draw any strong conclusions (McDaniel, Maier, & Einstein, 2002). As is so often the case in pop psychology, the best advice for those of us hoping to become memory whizzes overnight is *caveat emptor:* Let the buyer beware.

Ginkgo and other supposed memory-enhancing drugs are a multimillion dollar industry in the United States. These pills are popular, but do they work?

STORAGE: FILING OUR MEMORIES AWAY

Once we've filed away a library book on the shelf, it sits there, often for years at a time, collecting dust and cobwebs. We've stored it, perhaps to be retrieved one day by a student or professor who needs it for a writing project. **Storage** refers to the process of keeping information in memory.

Yet, where in the library we choose to file this book depends on our *interpretation* and *expectations* regarding the book's content. For example, let's imagine a new book entitled *The Psychology of Dating* has just arrived in the library. Should we file this book in the

GLOSSARY

storage
process of keeping information in memory

Our interpretation of ambiguous events in everyday life, like an animated conversation on the street, depends in part on our schemas.

Figure 6.11 **The Danger of Schemas.** Look carefully at this drawing. Allport and Postman (1956) used a similar drawing to show how schemas involving racial stereotyping can shape our memories.

GLOSSARY

schema
organized knowledge structure or mental model that we've stored in memory

retrieval
reactivation or reconstruction of experiences from our memory stores

psychology section, along with books on personality, emotion, and social psychology, or in the relationships section, along with books on dating, attraction, and marriage? The answer depends on what we think is most important or relevant about the book's content. Similarly, how we store our experiences in memory depends on our interpretations and expectations of these events.

Consider this scenario. You and your friends go to a brand-new sit-down restaurant. Although this is your first visit, you've got a pretty good idea of what's in store. That's because you possess a schema for eating at a nice restaurant. A **schema** is an organized knowledge structure or mental model that we've stored in memory. Our schema for restaurants is characterized by a set order of events, sometimes called a *script* (Schank & Abelson, 1977). You're seated at a table, given menus from which you order food, wait while your food is prepared, eat the food, get the check, and pay for the food before leaving. And don't forget the tip! There's even a standard sequence in ordering, at least in U.S. culture. We order drinks first, followed by appetizers, soup or salad, entrees, and finally dessert and coffee.

Schemas serve a valuable function: They equip us with frames of reference for interpreting new situations. Valuable as they are, schemas can sometimes create memory problems, because they can lead us to remember things that never happened simply because our schemas led us to expect them. Schemas simplify, which is good because they help to make sense of the world. But schemas sometimes *oversimplify,* which is bad because they can produce memory illusions. Schemas provide one key explanation for the paradox of memory: They enhance memory in some cases but lead to memory errors in others.

In a classic study, Gordon Allport and Leo Postman (1956) showed subjects a picture of a scene on a subway. As we can see from a similar drawing in **Figure 6.11,** this picture clearly shows a Caucasian man wielding a razor at a well-dressed African American man as bystanders looked on. Allport and Postman asked Caucasian subjects to recount the scene to others. After repeated tellings, subjects tended to recall the African American man, rather than the Caucasian man, as the person brandishing the razor, presumably because their stereotype of African Americans as violent had biased their memory.

It can sometimes be helpful to lump people into categories. But if we're not careful, our schemas can lead us to overgeneralize. As we'll discover in Chapter 11, we can think of racial stereotypes as schemas gone haywire.

RETRIEVAL: HEADING FOR THE "STACKS"

To remember something, we need to fetch it from our long-term memory banks. This is **retrieval,** the third and final stage of memory. Yet, as we mentioned earlier, this is where our metaphor of a library begins to break down, because what we retrieve from our memory often doesn't match what we put into it. Our memories are reconstructive, often transforming our recollections to fit our beliefs and expectations.

Many types of forgetting result from failures of retrieval: Our memories are still present, but we can't access them. It's pretty easy to demonstrate this point. If a friend is nearby, try the following demonstration, courtesy of psychologist Endel Tulving (even if you don't have a friend handy, you can still follow along). Read each category in **Table 6.1** to your friend, followed by the word that goes along with it. Tell your friend that after you're done reading all of the categories and their corresponding words, you'll ask him or her to recall just the words—in any order—not the categories.

After you read the list to your friend, ask him or her to take a few minutes to write down as many words as he or she can remember. Almost certainly, your friend missed some of them. For those missing words, prompt your friend with the category. So if your friend missed *Finger,* ask, "Do you remember the word that went with 'A part of the body'?" You'll probably find that these prompts help your friend to remember some of the forgotten words. In psychological lingo, the category names serve as **retrieval cues:** hints that make it easier for us to recall information. So your friend's long-term memory contained these missing words, but he or she needed the retrieval cues to remember them.

Measuring Memory. Psychologists assess people's memory in three major ways: recall, recognition, and relearning. **[LEARNING OBJECTIVE 6.5]** Think of them as the three Rs (another mnemonic device, by the way).

Recall and Recognition. What kind of exam do you find the toughest, essay or multiple choice? For sure, we've all taken multiple-choice tests that are "killers." Still, all else being equal, essay tests are usually harder than multiple-choice tests. That's because **recall,** that is, generating previously remembered information on our own, tends to be less accurate and complete than **recognition,** selecting previously remembered information from an array of options (Bahrick, Bahrick, & Wittlinger, 1975). To demonstrate what we mean, try recalling the sixth president of the United States. Unless you're an American history buff, you may be stumped. If so, try this question instead:

The sixth president of the United States was:

    (a) George Washington   (c) George W. Bush
    (b) John Quincy Adams   (d) Arnold Schwarzenegger

With a bit of thought, you probably figured out that (b) was the correct answer. You could safely eliminate (a) because you know George Washington was the first president, (c) because you know George W. Bush is a much more recent president, and (d) because you know Arnold Schwarzenegger hasn't been president. Moreover, you may well have recognized John Quincy Adams as an early U.S. president, even if you didn't know that he was number six.

Why is recall usually harder than recognition? In part, it's because recalling an item requires two steps—generating an answer and then determining whether it seems correct—whereas recognizing an item takes only one step: determining which item from a list seems most correct (Haist, Shimamura, & Squire, 1992).

Relearning. A third way of measuring memory is **relearning:** how much more quickly we learn information when we study something we've already studied relative to when we studied it the first time. The concept of relearning originated with the pioneering work of German researcher Hermann Ebbinghaus (1885) well over a century ago. Ebbinghaus used hundreds of "nonsense syllables," like ZAK and BOL, to test his own recollection. He found that most of our forgetting occurs almost immediately after learning new material, with less and less forgetting after that. However, he also found that when he attempted to relearn nonsense syllables that he'd forgotten, he learned them much more quickly the second time around. That's relearning. The fact that relearning was faster shows that a memory for this information was still in your brain—somewhere.

When memorizing his nonsense syllables, Ebbinghaus happened on a crucial principle that applies to most forms of learning: the law of **distributed versus massed practice** (Donovan & Radosevich, 1999; Willingham, 2002). Simply put, this law tells us that we tend to remember things better in the long run when we spread our learning over long intervals than when we pack it into short intervals. This principle is probably one of the best-replicated effects in all of psychology (Cepeda, Pashler, Vul, et al., 2006). Even infants show it (Cornell, 1980).

Herein lies another word to the wise. Cramming for an exam helps us remember the information for *that exam,* but it typically produces poor long-term retention. If you want to master the information in your psychology course—or any course, for that matter—you should spread out your review of the material over long intervals. So, when one of your

Table 6.1 Demonstration of Retrieval Cues. Find a friend and read each category, followed by the word that goes along with it. Then, ask your friend to recall only the words, in any order. For each word your friend forgot, ask whether he or she remembers something from that word's category. As you'll see, this demonstration helps to make a simple point: Many memory failures are actually failures of retrieval.

Category	Word
A metal	Silver
A bird	Canary
A color	Violet
A four-legged animal	Mouse
A piece of furniture	Dresser
A part of the body	Finger
A fruit	Cherry
An alcoholic beverage	Brandy
A crime	Kidnapping
An occupation	Plumber
A sport	Lacrosse
An article of clothing	Sweater
A musical instrument	Saxophone
An insect	Wasp

GLOSSARY

retrieval cues
hints that make it easier for us to recall information

recall
generating previously remembered information

recognition
selecting previously remembered information from an array of options

relearning
reacquiring knowledge that we'd previously learned but largely forgotten over time

REPLICABILITY
Can the results be duplicated in other studies?

distributed versus massed practice
studying information in small increments over time (distributed) versus in large increments over a brief amount of time (massed)

Fact-OID TOT occurs in those who use sign language as well as spoken language; psychologists call this the *tip-of-the-fingers* phenomenon. Deaf signers who are unable to retrieve the names of fairly famous people but feel that they're on the verge of remembering can depict at least some part of the famous person's name with their fingers about 80 percent of the time (Thompson, Emmorey, & Gollan, 2005).

GLOSSARY

encoding specificity
phenomenon of remembering something better when the conditions under which we retrieve information are similar to the conditions under which we encoded it

context-dependent learning
superior retrieval of memories when the external context of the original memories matches the retrieval context

teachers nags you to "start studying at least a week before the exam rather than waiting until the last minute," you have Ebbinghaus to thank—or blame.

Tip-of-the-Tongue Phenomenon.
We've all experienced retrieval failure in the form of the frustrating *tip-of-the-tongue (TOT) phenomenon,* in which we're sure we know the answer to a question, but can't come up with it (Brown, 1991; Schwartz, 1999). It's surprisingly easy to generate this phenomenon (Baddeley, 1993). Read the names of the 10 U.S. states in **Table 6.2,** and try to name their capital cities. Now focus on the states for which you're *unsure* of whether you know the right answer and keep trying. If you're still stuck, look at the list that follows, which gives you the first letter of the capital of each state: Georgia (A), Wisconsin (M), California (S), Louisiana (B), Florida (T), Colorado (D), New Jersey (T), Arizona (P), Nebraska (L), and Kentucky (F).

Did the first letters help? Research shows when we experience the TOT phenomenon, they often will. The fact that we sometimes experience TOT tells us that there's a difference between something we've forgotten because it didn't get *stored* in memory and something that's in there somewhere that we can't quite retrieve.

Encoding Specificity: Finding Things Where We Left Them.
Why is it easier to retrieve some things from memory than others? One answer to this mystery lies in the principle of **encoding specificity** introduced by Endel Tulving (1982; Tulving & Thomson, 1973). We're more likely to remember something when the conditions present at the time we encoded it are also present at retrieval. **[LEARNING OBJECTIVE 6.6]** We can see this principle at work in several psychological phenomena, two of which we'll examine here: context-dependent learning and state-dependent learning.

Context-dependent learning refers to superior retrieval when the external context of the original memories matches the retrieval context. Duncan Godden and Alan Baddeley (1975) provided an ingenious example of this effect in a study of scuba divers. They presented divers with 40 unrelated words while the divers were either standing on the beach or submerged in about 15 feet of water. Godden and Baddeley then tested the divers in either the same or a different context from which they originally presented the words. The divers' memory was best when the original context matched the retrieval con-

Table 6.2 TOT Phenomenon. First try to come up with the capital of each state. Then, return to the text for some hints.

State	Capital
Georgia	
Wisconsin	
California	
Louisiana	
Florida	
Colorado	
New Jersey	
Arizona	
Nebraska	
Kentucky	

Answers: Atlanta, Madison, Sacramento, Baton Rouge, Tallahassee, Denver, Trenton, Phoenix, Lincoln, Frankfort

text, regardless of whether they were on land or underwater, as shown in **Figure 6.12.** Undergraduates also display context-dependent learning. Students tend to do slightly better on their exams when tested in the same classroom in which they learned the material (Smith, 1979). Still, this effect isn't all that powerful, and not all researchers have replicated it (Saufley, Otaka, & Bavaresco, 1985). That's probably because you've acquired the information not only in the classroom but in other settings, such as the room in which you're now reading this textbook.

WHAT DO *you* THINK?

Imagine that your organic chemistry exam is scheduled for a different room than the one where the class is held. What could you do to ensure you perform your best?

REPLICABILITY
Can the results be duplicated in other studies?

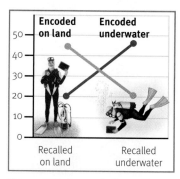

Figure 6.12 Research Shows That the Word Learning of Scuba Divers Depends on Context. If the divers learned words underwater, they recalled them best when underwater again.

State-dependent learning is similar to context-dependent learning, except that it refers to the internal "state" of the organism rather than the external context. That is, state-dependent learning refers to superior retrieval of memories when the organism is in the same physiological or psychological state as it was during encoding.

There's anecdotal evidence for this phenomenon among alcoholics, who often report that they need to get drunk to locate items—including their favorite bottles of liquor— that they'd hidden while drinking (Goodwin, 1995). Of course, we've learned that anecdotes are limited as sources of scientific evidence (see Chapter 2). However, in this case, controlled studies bear out the anecdotes: People who've learned a task while under the influence of alcohol tend to remember it better when under the influence than when sober (Goodwin, Powell, Brenner, et al., 1969). Still, researchers haven't always replicated these findings (Lisman, 1974), suggesting that state-dependent effects probably depend in complex ways on the participants tested and stimuli administered.

REPLICABILITY
Can the results be duplicated in other studies?

Using Memory Research to Study More Effectively.
A number of the memory concepts that we've covered in this chapter can be applied to help you study more effectively and efficiently. **Table 6.3** provides a handy list of studying pointers based on several memory concepts introduced in this chapter.

Table 6.3 Helpful Study Hints Derived from Memory Research.

Memory Concept	Pointer
(1) Distributed versus massed study	Spread your study time out—review your notes and textbook in increments rather than cramming.
(2) Elaborative rehearsal	Connect new knowledge with existing knowledge rather than simply memorizing facts or names.
(3) Levels of processing	Work to process ideas deeply and meaningfully—avoid writing notes down word-for-word from instructors' lectures or slides. Try to capture the information in your own words.
(4) Mnemonic devices	The more reminders or cues you can connect from your knowledge base to new material, the more likely you are to recall new material when tested.

For instance, let's see how a mnemonic device known as the pegword method can be used to help us remember the key terms associated with memory.

When we were children, nursery rhymes captivated our attention. By elementary school age, most of us were well acquainted with the exploits of Jack and Jill, Little Bo

GLOSSARY

state-dependent learning
superior retrieval of memories when the organism is in the same physiological or psychological state as it was during encoding

Figure 6.13 Pegword Method. The pegword method can be a useful mnemonic for helping us recall lists of objects in order. See the text for an explanation of this fanciful illustration.

Peep, and Little Jack Horner. Songs ranging from "Twinkle, Twinkle Little Star" to the rap music of Eminem are easy to remember because they contain rhymes.

Rhyming is a key component of the *pegword method,* often used to recall lists of words. To master this mnemonic, first associate each number in a list with a word that rhymes with each number, such as "One is a bun." The word associated with the number is a "pegword." It's essential to memorize a list like the one that follows, but the fact that the numbers and words rhyme makes it easy to do so: (1) One is a bun, (2) Two is a shoe, (3) Three is a tree, and (4) Four is a door.

Suppose you need to learn four words associated with memory concepts for your psychology class (don't you wish there were only four new terms in this chapter?) and that you need to recall them in the following order: chunking, elaboration, hippocampus, decay. After you've memorized the pegword associated with each number (such as "one is a bun"), create an image that associates the word you want to remember with the pegword (such as *bun*). For the first word, *chunking,* you could imagine a bun (the pegword) with a chunk missing or broken up into chunks. For two—*elaboration*—you might imagine a shoe with elaborate beading, sequins, and bows. For three—*hippocampus*—imagine a tree with a hippo camping under it. For number four, *decay,* you might picture a rotting, decaying door on an old house. When you need to remember the third thing on your list, for example, you'd say to yourself that three is a tree, which would prompt recall of the hippo camping under it, and you'd know that the third word on the list is hippocampus (see **Figure 6.13**).

QUIZ

PEARSON
mypsych lab

1 We encode virtually all of our life experiences, even though we can't retrieve more than a tiny proportion of them.   **TRUE** **FALSE**

2 We need to practice mnemonics to use them successfully.   **TRUE** **FALSE**

3 Schemas distort memories but don't enhance them.   **TRUE** **FALSE**

4 In general, recall is less accurate than recognition.   **TRUE** **FALSE**

5 Cramming for exams, although stressful, is actually a good strategy for enhancing long-term recall of material.   **TRUE** **FALSE**

▼ How does memory loss affect our interactions? Watch the video titled "Dementia: Judy" at www.mypsychlab.com to find out.

Answers: (1) F (p. 200); (2) T (p. 200); (3) F (p. 202); (4) T (p. 203); (5) F (p. 203)

Karl Lashley attempted to find the engram for maze learning in rats by testing their memory for the maze when various parts of the cortex were removed.

The Biology of Memory

Although few of us think about it, the biology of memory plays a pivotal role in our daily lives, whether it's remembering where we left our keys or the name of that friendly person we met at last night's party. What's more, understanding how our brains store memory may help us find ways of treating devastating diseases that impair our ability to recall everyday events.

THE NEURAL BASIS OF MEMORY STORAGE

Locating where a library book is stored is generally pretty easy. We look it up in our library's computer system or card catalog, write down its number, go to the shelf, and—unless someone's recently plucked it away—find it. If we're lucky, it's right there on the shelf where it's supposed to be. Yet as we'll soon see, memory storage in the brain isn't quite this cut and dried.

The Elusive Engram.
Beginning in the 1920s, psychologist Karl Lashley went in search of the *engram:* the physical trace of each memory in the brain. He taught rats how to run mazes and then lesioned different parts of their brains to see if they forgot how to find their way. By doing so, Lashley hoped to discover where memory is stored in the brain. Yet after years of painstaking work, he came up empty handed in his quest.

Still, Lashley learned two important things. First, the more brain he removed, the worse the rat performed on the maze: There's no great surprise there. Second, no matter where he removed brain tissue, the rats retained at least some memory of the maze (Lashley, 1929). Even removing up to half of the rat's cortex didn't erase the memory. These findings led Lashley to conclude that we can't simply point to a spot in the brain and say, "There's the memory of my first kiss," because that memory isn't located in a single place. In the words of writer Gertrude Stein, there's "no there there." Lashley's engram doesn't seem to exist, at least in the sense of being in one location, like a library book sitting on a shelf.

Long-Term Potentiation—A Physiological Basis for Memory.
As we learned in Chapter 3, connections among neurons are strengthened by repetitive stimulation, a process called **long-term potentiation (LTP)** (Bliss, Collingridge, & Morris, 2004). LTP is a result of an increase in the release of a neurotransmitter called glutamate into the synapse, which enhances learning as shown in **Figure 6.14** (Lisman & Raghavachari, 2006). **[LEARNING OBJECTIVE 6.7]**

Today, many researchers believe that our ability to store memories depends on strengthening the connections among neurons arranged in sprawling networks that extend to the far and deep recesses of our brains (Shors & Matzel, 1999). The question of whether LTP is directly responsible for the storage of memories, or whether it affects learning indirectly by increasing arousal and attention, remains unresolved (Shors & Matzel, 1999). Still, most scientists agree that LTP plays a key role in learning.

The hippocampus plays a particularly important role in forming lasting memories and exhibits clear evidence of LTP. Like the hippocampus, the amygdala exhibits LTP-like activity following the creation of a fear memory (Maren, 2005; Sigurdsson et al., 2007). These results establish that LTP-like activity is correlated with memory, but don't necessarily demonstrate that LTP serves as the basis of memory.

WHERE IS MEMORY STORED?

Clearly, the hippocampus is critical to memory. Some researchers have even identified neurons in the hippocampus that fire in response only to certain celebrities, such as actress Halle Berry (Quiroga et al., 2005) (see **Figure 6.15**).

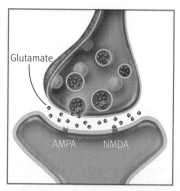

Figure 6.14 Neural Basis of Long-Term Potentiation. LTP enhances the release of glutamate which appears to enhance learning.

Figure 6.15 Halle Berry Neuron. Scientists have discovered cells in the human hippocampus that respond preferentially to actress Halle Berry, including when she's dressed as Catwoman and even to her name (see *top row*). These cells don't respond to other celebrities or other beautiful women (see *bottom row*). The graphs below each figure show the firing rates of the neuron to the picture above it. (*Source:* Quiroga et al., 2005)

CORRELATION vs. CAUSATION
Can we be sure that A causes B?

GLOSSARY

long-term potentiation (LTP)
gradual strengthening of the connections among neurons from repetitive stimulation

But is the hippocampus, or any single brain structure, the site of the elusive engram? We can say with some certainty that the answer is no. fMRI studies reveal that learned information isn't stored permanently in the hippocampus itself. Rather, the prefrontal cortex seems to be one of the major "banks" from which we withdraw our memories (Zeinah, Engel, Thompson, et al., 2003). But, as Lashley discovered, damage to isolated areas of the prefrontal cortex—or other cortical regions, for that matter—doesn't wipe out long-established memories. Much as the smell of a rose diffuses throughout a room, our memories distribute themselves throughout many areas of the cortex.

Amnesia—Biological Bases of Explicit and Implicit Memory.

Earlier we learned about explicit and implicit memory. Are these two forms of memory governed by different brain systems? The answer seems to be yes (Squire, 1987). The best evidence comes from individuals with severe amnesia. **[LEARNING OBJECTIVE 6.8]** The two most common types of amnesia are **retrograde amnesia,** in which we lose some memories of our past, and **anterograde amnesia,** in which we lose the capacity to form new memories.

The general public holds a host of misconceptions about amnesia. Perhaps the most prevalent myth is that many amnesics have lost all memories of their previous life, even of who they are. In fact, such *generalized amnesia* is exceedingly rare (American Psychiatric Association, 2000), although it's a favorite plot device of Hollywood moviemakers (Baxendale, 2004). Another myth, also perpetuated by Hollywood, is that memory recovery from amnesia is usually abrupt. Although sudden recoveries from amnesia make for good drama, they don't make for good science. In fact, memory recovery from amnesia tends to occur gradually, if at all (American Psychiatric Association, 2000).

A Case Study of Amnesia: H.M.

A man known for decades only by the initials of H.M. was by far the best-known amnesic in the psychological literature. H.M. suffered from severe epileptic seizures that his doctors couldn't control with medication. In March 1953, in a last-ditch attempt to eliminate these seizures, surgeons removed large chunks of H.M.'s temporal lobes, including both his left and right hippocampi, where they had reason to believe the seizures originated; the surgeons of the time didn't anticipate the disastrous impact of this radical operation. At the time, H.M. was 26 years old. Recall that the hippocampus plays a key role in long-term memory. Following the operation, H.M. developed virtually complete anterograde amnesia: He could recall almost no new information. Although he also experienced some retrograde amnesia for the 11 years prior to the surgery (Corkin, 1984), his memories from the first 15 years of his life remained pretty much intact.

Although H.M.'s surgery took place in 1953, his life from that moment on was, for all intents and purposes, frozen in time. He was oblivious to the fact that he underwent surgery. Two years after the operation, in 1955, he reported the current date as March 1953. H.M. read the same magazines and completed the same jigsaw puzzles over and over again without any awareness of having seen them before. He didn't recall having met physicians whom he met just a few minutes earlier or remember what he ate for lunch 30 minutes ago (Milner, 1972; Scoville & Milner, 1957). When informed repeatedly of the death of his uncle, he showed the same dramatic grief reaction to this news each time (Shimamura, 1992). H.M.'s true identity was revealed as Henry Molaison only after his recent death in December, 2008 at the age of 82. He lived for 55 years without acquiring any new explicit memories.

H.M.'s tragic case illustrates a striking dissociation between explicit and implicit memory. Researchers repeatedly asked H.M. to trace simple geometrical shapes from a mirror (**Figure 6.16**), a task that just about all people find infuriatingly difficult when

The 2000 film *Memento* offers a largely accurate portrayal of an individual with virtually complete anterograde amnesia stemming from an accident. The main character in the movie (portrayed by Guy Pearce) tattooed numerous messages on his body in a desperate effort to remind himself of his preamnesia life. In reality, such messages rarely help people with anterograde amnesia because they usually don't remember to look at them.

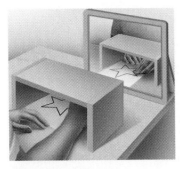

Figure 6.16 A Mirror Tracing Task Similar to That Administered to H.M. On this task, used to assess implicit memory, subjects must trace a star while looking only at a mirror.

GLOSSARY

retrograde amnesia
loss of memories from our past

anterograde amnesia
inability to encode new memories from our experiences

they first try it. Although H.M. had no recollection of ever having performed this task before, his performance improved steadily over time (Milner, 1964, 1965). So although H.M. has no explicit memory for this task, he displayed clear-cut implicit—specifically, procedural—memory for it.

When researchers examined H.M.'s brain using imaging techniques, they found that not only his hippocampus but his surrounding cortex and neighboring amygdala (see Chapter 3) were damaged by the surgery (Corkin, Amaral, Gonzalez, et al., 1997). This finding led researchers to hypothesize that large circuits connecting different parts of the limbic system—consisting of the hippocampus, hypothalamus, and amygdala—are critical to memory.

THE BIOLOGY OF MEMORY DETERIORATION

As humans pass the ripe old age of 65 years, we usually begin to experience memory problems and some degeneration in the brain. At least some loss of memory and brain tissue is virtually inevitable if we make it to 100 years of age. Yet despite what many people believe, senility isn't an unavoidable part of aging, and some manage to make it past 100 with only modest amounts of everyday forgetfulness. But scientists disagree as to how much memory loss is "normal" during the advanced years.

Many people equate senility with one cause: Alzheimer's disease. Although Alzheimer's disease is the most frequent cause of senility, it accounts for only about 50 to 60 percent of cases of *dementia,* that is, severe memory loss; another common cause of senility is the accumulation of multiple strokes in the brain. Alzheimer's disease occurs at alarming rates as people age. The risk for Alzheimer's disease is 13 percent for those over 65 years of age but a whopping 42 percent for those over 85 years of age. The cognitive impairments of Alzheimer's disease are both memory and language related, which corresponds to the patterns of cortical loss in this illness. The memory loss begins with recent events, with memories of the distant past being the last to go. Alzheimer's patients forget their grandchildren's names well before forgetting their children's names. Alzheimer's disease patients also experience disorientation and are frequently at a loss as to where they are, what year it is, or who the current president is. **[LEARNING OBJECTIVE 6.9]**

Physical activity after the age of 65 reduces the risk of cognitive decline associated with aging.

As we learned in Chapter 3, the Alzheimer's brain contains many senile plaques and neurofibrillary tangles. These abnormalities contribute to the loss of synapses and death of cells in the hippocampus and cerebral cortex. They may also contribute to memory loss and intellectual decline. Loss of synapses is correlated with intellectual status, with greater loss as the disease progresses (Scheff, Price, Schmitt, et al., 2007). But this result doesn't necessarily mean that the reduction in synapses causes the memory decline. Along with loss of synapses comes degeneration and death of acetylcholine neurons in the basal forebrain. No treatment to date halts or reverses the course of Alzheimer's disease. At best, drug treatments only slow its progression.

For this reason, researchers have evaluated people's lifestyles to see if anything can be done to reduce the risk of Alzheimer's disease. A massive study assessing more than 4,000 people over 65 years of age showed that being physically active reduces the risk of cognitive impairment and Alzheimer's disease (Laurin, Verreault, Lindsay, et al., 2001). Numerous other studies suggest that people who are highly educated and intellectually active are at decreased risk of Alzheimer's disease (Ngandu et al., 2007). Admittedly, these correlational findings are ambiguous in their causal direction: Perhaps people who are more mentally and physically fit have more brain capacity to begin with. Yet these findings certainly raise the possibility that the old maxim "use it or lose it" may contain more than a grain of truth (Wilson, Scherr, Schneider, et al., 2007).

CORRELATION vs. CAUSATION
Can we be sure that A causes B?

CORRELATION vs. CAUSATION
Can we be sure that A causes B?

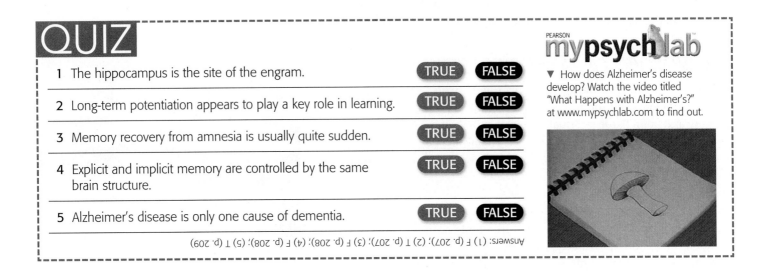

┌─ **WHAT DO** *you* **THINK** ─────────────────────

Your parents are about to retire and relax at their condo on the beach. What recommendations would you give them about their new lifestyle that will help prevent memory loss as they age?

QUIZ

1 The hippocampus is the site of the engram. **TRUE** **FALSE**

2 Long-term potentiation appears to play a key role in learning. **TRUE** **FALSE**

3 Memory recovery from amnesia is usually quite sudden. **TRUE** **FALSE**

4 Explicit and implicit memory are controlled by the same brain structure. **TRUE** **FALSE**

5 Alzheimer's disease is only one cause of dementia. **TRUE** **FALSE**

Answers: (1) F (p. 207); (2) T (p. 207); (3) F (p. 208); (4) F (p. 208); (5) T (p. 209)

PEARSON
mypsychlab

▼ How does Alzheimer's disease develop? Watch the video titled "What Happens with Alzheimer's?" at www.mypsychlab.com to find out.

The Development of Memory: Acquiring a Personal History

How early can children remember, and what do they remember? The answer depends on what kind of memory we're discussing. In at least one sense, we can remember information even before we're born. That's because fetuses display *habituation*—a decrease in attention to familiar stimuli. As we learned in Chapter 5, fetuses as young as 32 weeks exhibit a decline in their reactions to vibratory stimulators over time. Habituation is a form of implicit memory—to interpret a stimulus as familiar, we need to recall we've experienced it before. It's a far cry from explicitly recalling the words to a song or remembering what we wore to our last birthday party, but it's still a form of remembering.

MEMORY OVER TIME

Memory changes as we age, but there's considerable continuity over the course of development. Infants have worse memories than children, who have worse memories than adults, and young adults have better memories than older adults. But the same basic processes operate across the life span. For example, infants display a serial position curve just as adults do (Cornell & Bergstrom, 1983; Gulya, Galluccio, Wilk, et al., 2001). Nevertheless, the span of memory and the ability to use strategies increase dramatically across the infant, toddler, preschool, and elementary school years.

Over time, children's memories become increasingly sophisticated. **[LEARNING OBJECTIVE 6.10]** Several factors explain why. First, children's memory spans increase with age (Pascual-Leone, 1989). In fact, their Magic Number doesn't become seven plus or minus two until age 12 or so. If we ask a 3-year-old to remember a string of letters or numbers, she'll remember only about three on average. A 5-year-old will remember about four. By age 9, children are getting close to the adult's Magic Number, remembering six items on average.

Is this increase in span a result of better use of strategies, like rehearsal? That's certainly part of the story (Flavell, Beach, & Chinsky, 1966; McGilly & Siegler, 1989), but there's a large physical maturational component too. So, in an odd turn of events, shoe size is actually more highly correlated with memory span in children than is either age or intelligence. Nevertheless, we can assure you that this correlation isn't a causal one! Because different children grow at different rates, this correlation reflects a biological maturity component to memory span, for which variables like shoe size or height are the best predictors.

CORRELATION vs. **CAUSATION**
Can we be sure that A causes B?

Second, our conceptual understanding increases with age. This fact is important because our ability to chunk related items and store memories in meaningful ways depends on our knowledge of the world. For example, without knowing that "CIA" stands for Central Intelligence Agency, children can't chunk the letters *C, I,* and *A* into one unit.

Third, over time children develop enhanced *metamemory* skills: knowledge about their memory abilities and limitations. These skills help children to identify when they need to use strategies to improve their memories, as well as which strategies work best (Schneider & Bjorklund, 1998; Weinert, 1989; Zabrucky & Ratner, 1986).

INFANTS' IMPLICIT MEMORY: TALKING WITH THEIR FEET

Carolyn Rovee-Collier has developed an innovative technique to study infants' implicit memory. Her research capitalizes on the fact that we can operantly condition (see Chapter 5) infants to perform specific behaviors. Rovee-Collier placed infants in a crib with a mobile positioned over their heads. She first watched their behaviors for a few minutes to assess their activity levels in a "baseline" condition. Then, she took a ribbon tied to the mobile and attached it to the infant's ankle. The next time the infant kicked her foot, she was in for a pleasant surprise: The mobile shook and jiggled in response. Infants find the motion of the mobile inherently reinforcing. Because the movement is dependent on infants' behavior, they quickly become conditioned to kick their legs to get the mobile moving.

Once she conditioned infants to kick their legs in response to the mobile, Rovee-Collier sent them home. Then, after a delay—of a day, a week, or even a month—she brought them back to the lab and placed them in the crib again. This time, the mobile wasn't attached to the infant's leg, so there was no reinforcement. The question was: Would infants show an increased kicking rate in response to seeing the mobile? If so, it would imply that they remembered the conditioning experience.

Rovee-Collier (1993) found that children as young as 2 months retained a memory of this experience, although they forgot it after just a few days. Nevertheless, their span of recall increased quickly. Three-month-olds could remember the conditioning for over a week, and 6-month-olds for over 2 weeks. Infants' memories of the experience were surprisingly specific. If researchers modified even a few elements of the mobile or changed the pattern of the crib liner ever so slightly, infants didn't seem to recognize the mobile: Their kicking rate returned to baseline.

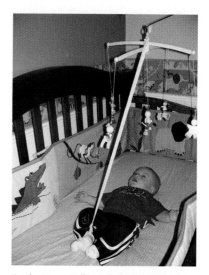

Carolyn Rovee-Collier and other researchers have used mobiles to study infants' implicit memory. Although infants can't tell you they remember the mobiles, their kicking behavior gives us insight into what they recall and for how long.

INFANTILE AMNESIA

Try to recall your earliest memory. What was it, and how old were you? Most students say their earliest memory falls somewhere between 3 and 5 years of age. **Infantile amnesia** is the inability of adults to retrieve accurate memories before an early age (Malinoski, Lynn, & Sivec, 1998; Wetzler & Sweeney, 1986).

Few, if any, of us correctly recall events before 2 or 3 years of age, the lowest cutoff for infantile amnesia (West & Bauer, 1999; Winograd & Killinger, 1983). Memories before that age just aren't trustworthy. **[LEARNING OBJECTIVE 6.11]** So if you have a distinct memory of something that happened at age 1 or before, it's almost certainly either a false memory or a true memory of something that happened later.

Recent research suggests that culture may shape the age and content of our first memories. European Americans report earlier first memories than do people from Taiwan. Moreover, European Americans' earliest memories more often focus on themselves, whereas Taiwanese's earliest memories more often focus on others (Wang, 2006) which may relate to living in individualistic versus collectivist cultures (Lehman, Chiu, & Schaller, 2004).

Infantile Amnesia and Pop Psychology.

Proponents of some fringe psychological treatments have largely ignored the scientific evidence concerning infantile amnesia. Many advocates of hypnotic age regression, which Nadean Cool's therapist used, claim to be able to retrieve memories from well before age 2, sometimes even before birth (Nash, 1987). For example, proponents of Scientology believe that long-buried memories of negative statements overheard by fetuses, embryos, and even zygotes can be reactivated in adulthood, especially under stress. These memories, Scientologists claim, can trigger low self-esteem and other psychological problems (Carroll, 2003; Gardner, 1958). Fortunately, for both fetuses and adults, there's no evidence for this extraordinary claim. Fetuses can't accurately make out most sentences they hear from outside the womb (Smith, Genhardt, Griffiths, et al., 2003), let alone remember them decades later.

What's your earliest memory? How old were you when the event took place? Research suggests that at least some distinctly recalled early memories, especially those prior to age 3, are either false memories or memories we've dated incorrectly.

EXTRAORDINARY CLAIMS
Is the evidence as convincing as the claim?

WHAT DO *you* THINK?

Your best friend claims that she can remember things that happened during her first year of life. How would you explain whether these memories are real and where they might have come from?

Explanations for Infantile Amnesia.

No one knows for sure why the first few years of our lives are lost to us forever, but psychologists have a few promising leads (Bauer, 2006). The hippocampus, which as we've learned plays a key role in long-term memory, especially episodic memory, is only partially developed in infancy (Mishkin, Malamut, & Bachevalier, 1984; Schacter & Moscovitch, 1984). So before age 2 or so, we may not possess the brainpower needed to retain memories of events.

Also, as infants, we possess little or no concept of self (Fivush, 1988; Howe & Courage, 1993). Before about 18 months of age, infants can't recognize themselves in mirrors (Lewis, Brooks-Gunn, & Jaskir, 1985). Without a well-developed sense of self, some psychologists maintain, infants can't encode or store memories of their experiences in a meaningful fashion.

Finally, the fact that infants have limited language skills prior to the age of 2 may be a factor. Perhaps we begin storing memories using a more verbal form of encoding as we age. The lack of verbal encoding for earlier memories may make them inaccessible.

Research suggests that, other than humans, chimpanzees, gorillas, and dolphins are among the handful of species that exhibit mirror self-recognition—often regarded as one important indicator of the presence of a self-concept (Gallup, 1979; Reiss & Marino, 2001). Here a baby reacts to his mirror image.

GLOSSARY

infantile amnesia
inability of adults to remember personal experiences that took place before an early age

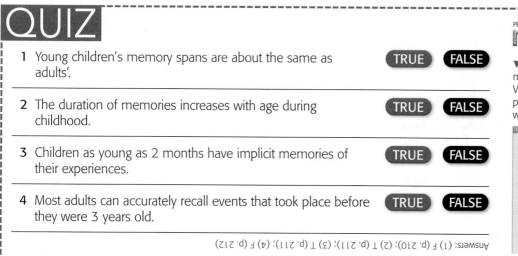

QUIZ

1 Young children's memory spans are about the same as adults'.　TRUE　FALSE

2 The duration of memories increases with age during childhood.　TRUE　FALSE

3 Children as young as 2 months have implicit memories of their experiences.　TRUE　FALSE

4 Most adults can accurately recall events that took place before they were 3 years old.　TRUE　FALSE

Answers: (1) F (p. 210); (2) T (p. 211); (3) T (p. 211); (4) F (p. 212).

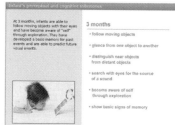

PEARSON
mypsychlab

▼ When do infants show signs of memory along with other milestones? View the simulation titled "Infant's perceptual and Cognitive Milestones" at www.mypsychlab.com to find out.

When Good Memory Goes Bad: False Memories

We generally trust our memories to provide us with an accurate recounting of our past. In many cases, our memories do the job well enough. Over the past few decades, however, researchers have shown that our memories can be more fallible than any of us could have imagined. Moreover, we're often far more confident of our recollections of events than we should be.

FALSE MEMORIES

At first blush, our everyday experience strongly suggests that we can safely rely on our memories, because many of our recollections seem to be as crisp as scenes from a movie. Do you remember where you were and what you were doing when you heard about the terrorist attacks on September 11, 2001? Most Americans say yes, and many say that, even today, they can "relive" those frightening moments with astonishing clarity. Many older Americans report equally vivid memories of the assassination of President John F. Kennedy on November 22, 1963. Powerful memories of the attempted assassination of President Ronald Reagan (Pillemer, 1984), the explosion of the space shuttle *Challenger* (McCloskey, Wible, & Cohen, 1988), and the death of Princess Diana (Krackow, Lynn, & Payne, 2005–2006) are other examples.

Flashbulb Memories.

It's no wonder that Roger Brown and James Kulik (1977) referred to these recollections as **flashbulb memories,** emotional memories that seem so vivid that people seem able to recount them in remarkable, even photographic, detail. They further argued that flashbulb memories don't decay over time like ordinary memories. So flashbulb memories suggest that our memories sometimes operate like video cameras after all, right?

Ulrich Neisser and Nicole Harsch (1992) decided to find out whether extremely vivid memories were accurate by studying college students' recollection of the explosion of the space shuttle *Challenger* in 1986. For many people, this was a particularly tragic and

Do you recall precisely where you were and what you were doing on the morning of September 11, 2001? If so, some researchers would claim that you have a flashbulb memory of this event. In reality, however, there's scant evidence that flashbulb memories are either distinctive from other memories or infallible.

GLOSSARY

flashbulb memories
emotional memories that are thought to be extraordinarily vivid and detailed

memorable event because, for the first time, a nonastronaut—a schoolteacher named Christa McAuliffe—was onboard. Neisser and Harsch discovered that $2\frac{1}{2}$ to 3 years after the *Challenger* explosion, 75 percent of college students' reports of the event didn't match their recollections from only a few days following this event. Moreover, about a third of the students' stories changed dramatically over time. Consider this recollection from one of their subjects almost immediately after the *Challenger* explosion.

Initial Recollection. (January 1986): "I was in my religion class and some people walked in and started talking about the explosion. I didn't know any details except that it had exploded and the schoolteacher's students had all been watching, which I thought was so sad. Then after class I went to my room and watched the TV program talking about it and I got all the details from that."

Here's the recollection from the *same* student more than $2\frac{1}{2}$ years later:

Later Recollection. (September 1988): "When I first heard about the explosion I was sitting in my freshman dorm room with my roommate and we were watching TV. It came on a news flash and we were both totally shocked. I was really upset and went upstairs to talk to a friend of mine and then I called my parents."

When Neisser and Harsch presented students with their written recollections from several years earlier, some insisted that they must have been written by someone else! The authors coined the term *phantom flashbulb memory* to capture the idea that many seeming flashbulb memories are false. **[LEARNING OBJECTIVE 6.12]** This phenomenon has been replicated with a group of students asked to recall their memory of the verdict of the O.J. Simpson trial (Schmolk, Buffalo, & Squire, 2000). After 32 months, 40 percent of the memory reports contained "major distortions" relative to their initial recollection only three days after the verdict.

This research indicates that flashbulb memories change over time, just like all other memories. They remind us that much as our memories may seem to work like video cameras, they don't. We don't need to invoke an entirely new set of explanations to explain vivid recollections. The most parsimonious hypothesis is that flashbulb memories aren't a separate class of memories; they're much like other memories, just more intense.

REPLICABILITY
Can the results be duplicated in other studies?

OCCAM'S RAZOR
Does a simpler explanation fit the data just as well?

Source Monitoring: Who Said That?

Think back to a conversation you had yesterday with a friend. How do you know it really happened? About 25 percent of undergraduates report experiencing a distinct memory of an event but feeling unsure of whether it actually occurred or was part of a dream (Rassin, Merckelbach, & Spaan, 2001). This is an example of a *source monitoring confusion,* a lack of clarity about the origin of a memory.

According to a **source monitoring** view of memory (Johnson, Hashtroudi, & Lindsay, 1993; Johnson & Raye, 1981), we try to identify the origins of our memories by seeking cues about how we encoded them. Source monitoring refers to our efforts to identify the origins (sources) of a memory. Whenever we try to figure out whether a memory really reflects something that happened or whether we merely imagined it, we're engaging in source monitoring. We also rely on source monitoring to recall which possible information source provided the information—did you hear it on the news or from a friend? Have you ever started to tell someone a joke or story only to realize that he was the one who told it to you in the first place? That's an example of a source monitoring failure.

Many memory errors reflect confusions in source monitoring. Take the phenomenon of *cryptomnesia* (literally meaning "hidden memory"), whereby we mistakenly forget that one of "our" ideas originated with someone else. Some cases of plagiarism probably reflect cryptomnesia. When George Harrison, a former member of the Beatles, wrote his hit song, "My Sweet Lord," he apparently forgot that the melody of this song

In 2006, reporters revealed that Kaavya Viswanathan, author of the book *How Opal Mehta Got Kissed, Got Wild, and Got a Life,* had numerous passages in her book that were suspiciously similar to those in several other books. Viswanathan's defense was cryptomnesia: She claimed to have read these books and forgotten their source.

GLOSSARY

source monitoring
ability to identify the origins of a memory

was virtually identical to that of the Chiffons' song, "He's So Fine," which had appeared about 10 years earlier. After the copyright owners of the Chiffons' song sued Harrison, he used cryptomnesia as a legal defense, arguing that he mistakenly believed he'd invented the melody himself. The judge awarded money to the copyright owners of the original song, although he ruled that Harrison probably didn't commit the plagiarism intentionally.

Implanting False Memories in the Lab.

Three decades ago, psychologist Elizabeth Loftus (Loftus, 1979; Loftus, Miller, & Burns, 1978; Wells & Loftus, 1984) opened researchers' eyes to the dramatic effects of misleading suggestions on both everyday memories and eyewitness reports. Her pioneering work demonstrated that our memories are far more easily manipulated than most psychologists had assumed. She found that **suggestive memory techniques**—procedures that strongly encourage people to recall memories—often create recollections that were never present to begin with (Lynn, Lock, Loftus, et al., 2003a).

Misinformation Effect. In a classic study, Loftus and John Palmer (1974) took advantage of a finding (Marshall, 1969) that people's estimates of the speed of a car traveling at 12 miles per hour varied between 10 and 50 miles per hour. That is, people aren't especially good at estimating the speed of moving vehicles, and can be influenced by subtle suggestions. Loftus, Miller, and Burns showed participants brief clips of traffic accidents and asked them to estimate the speed of the vehicles involved. They varied the wording of their question, "About how fast were the cars going when they _____ each other?" When participants heard the word *smashed,* they rated the speed as 9 miles per hour faster than when they heard the word *contacted* (40.8 when *smashed* was used versus 31.8 when *contacted* was used).

In a later study, Loftus and her colleagues asked participants to watch a slide sequence of an accident in which a car passed through an intersection and struck a pedestrian. They asked participants questions about the event. Some of the questions contained misleading suggestions. For example, in the actual slide sequence, the sign at the intersection was a yield sign. Yet Loftus and her colleagues phrased one of the questions, "While the car was stopped at the stop sign, did a red Datsun pass by?" A moment's reflection suggests that the question is misleading because it implies that a different sign—a stop sign—was located at the intersection. Afterward, participants who received the misleading questions were more likely to say that the sign was a stop sign than a yield sign. In contrast, most subjects who didn't receive the phony information recalled the yield sign accurately. This phenomenon is the **misinformation effect:** Providing people with misleading information after an event can lead to fictitious memories (Loftus et al., 1978).

In the 1978 study by Loftus, Miller, and Burns, subjects saw a car stopped at a yield sign (*left*). Yet when prompted with the information that the car had been stopped at a stop sign (*right*), they later "remembered" seeing the stop sign.

Lost in the Mall and Other Implanted Memories. Loftus's famous "lost in the mall study" demonstrates that we can implant elaborate memories of a made-up event that never happened. Loftus and her colleagues (Loftus, Coan, & Pickrell, 1996; Loftus & Pickrell, 1995) asked the relatives of 24 participants to describe events that participants had experienced in childhood. They then presented participants with a booklet that contained the details of three events the relatives reported, along with a fourth event that the relatives verified never occurred: being lost in a shopping mall as a child. Participants wrote about each event they could recall. In follow-up interviews, a quarter of the subjects claimed to distinctly remember being lost in the mall as a child. Some even provided surprisingly detailed accounts of the event.

GLOSSARY

suggestive memory techniques
procedures that encourage patients to recall memories that may or may not have taken place

misinformation effect
creation of fictitious memories by providing misleading information about an event after it takes place

REPLICABILITY
Can the results be duplicated in other studies?

RULING OUT RIVAL HYPOTHESES
Have important alternative explanations
for the findings been excluded?

Researchers have used fake photographs to
convince subjects that they'd experienced a
hot-air balloon ride as a child even when they
hadn't.

REPLICABILITY
Can the results be duplicated in other studies?

Many investigators followed in the path of Loftus's groundbreaking work. Using suggestive questions and statements, researchers have replicated these findings, implanting memories of a wide variety of events, ranging from accidentally spilling a bowl of punch on the parents of the bride at a wedding reception to a serious animal attack to demonic possession, in about 20 to 25 percent of college students (Bernstein et al., 2005; DeBreuil, Garry, & Loftus, 1998; Hyman, Husband, & Billings, 1995; Mazzoni, Loftus, & Kirsch, 2001; Porter, Yuille, & Lehman, 1999). Of course, these percentages imply that many students aren't especially prone to false memories, although some clearly are.

Most of the studies we've reviewed so far are open to at least one major criticism. Perhaps participants actually experienced the suggested event, such as being lost in a mall, but forgot about it until the suggestion reminded them of it. Studies of impossible or highly implausible memories rule out this alternative hypothesis. Indeed, researchers have devised clever *existence proofs* (see Chapter 2) demonstrating that it's possible to create elaborate memories of events that never happened. Here's a "memorable" example. One team of researchers (Wade, Garry, Read, et al., 2002) showed participants a fake photograph of a hot-air balloon, into which they'd pasted photographs of the participant and a relative (ah, the wonders of computers!). Family members had confirmed that the participant had never experienced a hot-air balloon ride. When investigators showed participants the fake photograph, several recalled at least something about this fictitious experience. After two further interviews, 50 percent of subjects recalled at least some of the fictitious hot-air balloon ride, and some embellished their reports with sensory details (such as seeing a road from high up in the air).

Generalizing from Lab to Real World.

Studies like those we've reviewed, and dramatic cases like that of Nadean Cool, provide vivid examples of how suggestive memory recovery techniques can shape our memories and identities. But we should be cautious about generalizing experimental findings to the real world, because these laboratory studies may be low in *external validity* (see Chapter 2). Many investigators, using different methods, have replicated the finding that memories are malleable provides strong support for the claim that memory is reconstructive.

Eyewitness Testimony. As of today, 218 prisoners have been acquitted of a crime and released because their DNA didn't match genetic material left by perpetrators. Since the mid-1980s, when scientists developed techniques to analyze genetic material, the number of prisoners who've been released due to DNA testing has increased each year. Consider Gene Bibbons, "Number 125," sentenced to life imprisonment for the sexual assault of a 16-year-old girl. The victim described the perpetrator as a man with long curly hair, wearing jeans, while Bibbons had short, cropped hair at the time and was wearing shorts. Still, she identified Bibbons as the assailant. Years later, investigators located a biological specimen, and genetic testing confirmed that Bibbons's DNA didn't match the DNA at the crime scene. After maintaining his innocence for 16 years, Bibbons walked out of prison a free man.

If there's a thread that ties Bibbons to the 217 other unjustly imprisoned individuals, it's that an eyewitness misidentified him as guilty. Three-quarters or more of prisoners acquitted by DNA testing are mistakenly identified by eyewitnesses (Scheck, Neufeld, & Dwyer, 2000). This fact isn't surprising when we consider that when witnesses seem sure they've identified a culprit, juries tend to believe them (Smith, Lindsay, Pryke, et al., 2001; Wells & Bradford, 1998). Yet contrary to popular (mis)conception, the correlation between witnesses' confidence in their testimony and the accuracy of this testimony is weak (Bothwell, Deffenbacher, & Brigham, 1987; Kassin, Ellsworth, & Smith, 1989).

Eyewitnesses sometimes provide invaluable evidence, especially when they have ample time to observe the perpetrator under good lighting conditions, when the criminal isn't disguised, and when little time elapses between witnessing the crime and identifying the guilty party (Memon, Hope, & Bull, 2003). But eyewitness testimony is far from accurate when these optimal conditions aren't met. Moreover, eyewitness testimony is less likely to be accurate when people observe individuals of races different from their own (Kassin, Tubb, Hosch, et al., 2001; Meissner & Brigham, 2001; Pezdek, Blandon-Gitlin, & Moore, 2003), when they talk to other witnesses (Wells, et al., 2006), or when they view a crime under stressful circumstances, such as when they feel threatened (Deffenbacher, Bornstein, Penrod, et al., 2004). Psychologists can play a critical role in educating jurors about the science of eyewitness recall, so that they can better weigh the evidence. For example, psychologists can inform juries about the best way to conduct eyewitness lineups. In a lineup, police instruct the witness to select the culprit from among potential suspects. In a *simultaneous lineup* the witness can make the selection "live" from among six people standing behind glass or from photographs. But when the real criminal isn't in the lineup, witnesses are likely to mistakenly identify the person who most closely resembles the real perpetrator relative to other people in the lineup. As we discussed in Chapter 1, a better solution is the use of *sequential lineups,* in which witnesses view one person at a time (Lindsay & Wells, 1985). Laboratory evidence suggests that identification of suspects is more accurate with sequential than with simultaneous lineups (Steblay, Dysart, Fulero, et al., 2001), although important questions about the real-world difference between these two types of lineups remain (McQuiston-Surrett, Malpass, & Tredoux, 2006).

In 1984, Jennifer Thompson, a 22-year-old college student, was raped. Shortly after, she confidently identified Ronald Cotton (*right*) as the man who raped her, and he was imprisoned following a trial. In 1995, a DNA test showed conclusively that Bobby Poole (*left*) was the actual rapist, and Cotton was released after spending 11 years in prison for a crime he didn't commit. Consumed by guilt, Thompson sought out Cotton following his release from prison; they've since become friends.

WHAT DO *you* THINK?

You are a police detective investigating an assault. What would you do to optimize the chance that the victim will correctly identify the guilty party?

Suggestibility And Child Testimony.   Children are especially vulnerable to suggestions to recall events that didn't occur (Ceci & Bruck, 1993). Stephen Ceci and his colleagues (Ceci, Crotteau-Huffman, Smith, et al., 1994) asked preschool children to imagine real and fictitious events. Once a week, for a total of seven to ten interviews, they instructed children to "think real hard" about whether the events had occurred. For example, they asked the children to try to remember made-up events, like going to the hospital with a mousetrap on their fingers. Fifty-eight percent of children generated stories regarding at least one of these fictitious events. Interestingly, about a quarter of the children continued to insist their memories were real even when their parents and the experimenter assured them the events never happened. The fact that children cling to their false memories even when an authority figure tells them the memories are wrong suggests that such memories can be convincing. **[LEARNING OBJECTIVE 6.13]** These findings are important for another reason: Many social workers and police officers who suspect that a child was abused question the child about this abuse repeatedly. Repeated questioning comes with a risk: Children may give investigators the answers they're seeking, even if these answers are wrong.

MYTH: People who think they might have been sexually abused, but aren't sure, can use symptom checklists in self-help books to help them find out.

REALITY: Many therapists who treat patients with suspected sexual abuse histories prescribe "survivor books"—self-help books that often contain checklists of supposed telltale symptoms of past sexual abuse, such as fears of sex, low self-esteem, insecurity about one's appearance, or excessive dependency (Lynn, Pintar, Sandberg, et al., 2003b). Yet research shows that most of these symptoms are so vague and general that they can apply to virtually everyone (Emery & Lilienfeld, 2004).

Gary Ramona, a successful California wine executive, was accused by his daughter, Holly, of sexually abusing her in childhood. Ramona eventually won a half-million-dollar lawsuit against Holly's psychiatrist. The jury ruled that the psychiatrist's suggestive techniques had triggered false memories of sexual abuse in Holly.

The False Memory Controversy. One of the most divisive controversies in all of psychology centers on the possibility that memories of child abuse and other traumatic experiences can be shaped by suggestive techniques in psychotherapy. On one side of the battle are memory recovery therapists, who claim that patients *repress* memories of traumatic events, such as childhood sexual abuse, and then *recover* them years, even decades, later (Brown, Scheflin, & Hammond, 1997). As we'll learn in Chapter 12, most followers of Sigmund Freud believe that repression is a form of forgetting in which people push painful memories into their unconscious. According to recovered memory therapists, these repressed memories are the root cause of current life problems and must be addressed to make progress in psychotherapy (McNally, 2003). By the mid-1990s, approximately 25 percent of psychotherapists reported in surveys (Polusny & Follette, 1996; Poole, Lindsay, Memon, et al., 1995) that they used two or more potentially suggestive procedures, including dream interpretation, guided imagery, and hypnosis, to help patients who initially had no recollection of sexual abuse to recover memories of it.

Lined up on the opposing side of the false memory debate is a growing chorus of researchers who claim that there's slim evidence that people repress traumatic memories, including childhood sexual abuse. These researchers point to a mounting body of evidence that painful memories are well remembered and, if anything, remembered too well (Loftus, 1993; McNally, 2003; Pope, Poliakoff, Parker, et al., 2007). According to them, there's serious reason to doubt that many memories can be repressed and then recovered years or decades later. These researchers have also voiced serious concerns about whether suggestive procedures can lead patients to conclude erroneously that family members abused them in childhood. Indeed, hundreds of individuals have been separated from their families, and in some cases even imprisoned, solely on the basis of recovered memory claims of child sexual abuse.

From a scientific and ethical standpoint, this state of affairs is deeply troubling, often tragic. Given what we now know about how fallible human memory is, recovered memories of child abuse shouldn't be trusted completely unless they're accompanied by corroborating evidence although any allegation of abuse should certainly be investigated thoroughly.

THE SEVEN SINS OF MEMORY

By this point in the chapter, we hope we've persuaded you that although our memories generally work well and are often accurate, they're anything but perfect. Daniel Schacter (2001) elegantly summarized the tricks that memory can play on us by describing the "seven sins of memory." Schacter's analogy to the ancient seven deadly sins (pride, anger, envy, greed, gluttony, lust, and sloth) is hardly accidental. Just as these sins can get us into big trouble, the seven sins of memory listed in **Table 6.4** can lead to a host of memory errors.

The seven sins of memory needn't lead us to despair. As Schacter (2001) pointed out, if we look at the flip side of each of the seven sins, we'll find an adaptive function. For instance, the fact that older memories aren't as accessible as new ones is adaptive because many new memories are relevant to current life tasks and challenges. In this way, we're likely to keep in mind memories that are distinctive, interesting, and emotionally meaningful. Even absentmindedness has its upside, because paying attention to unnecessary details can derail us from pursuing important life goals. So these seven sins help us resolve the paradox of memory, because most memory errors stem from basic mechanisms of memory that usually serve us well.

Absentmindedness (such as forgetting to take items we've paid for, or that we had scheduled a coffee date with a friend) happens to everyone occasionally. Cellist Yo-Yo Ma left his $2.5 million Venetian cello made in 1733 in a cab. The taxi driver discovered the rare instrument in his trunk after completing his shift and gave it to the police.

Table 6.4 The Seven Sins of Memory.

Memory Sin	How It Leads to Errors
(1) Suggestibility	Leading questions and suggestions can increase the chances of our believing that fictitious events occurred.
(2) Misattribution	Suggestions lead us to misattribute memories to incorrect sources or mistake what's imagined for a real memory.
(3) Bias	Our schemas and expectations can bias us to remember things as more consistent with our beliefs than they actually were.
(4) Transience	Memories fade with time. As we age, it becomes particularly difficult to access memories.
(5) Persistence	Memories for upsetting or extremely exciting events can linger in our minds for days or weeks and intrude into our thoughts, even disrupting our ability to sleep.
(6) Blocking	We may suddenly and inexplicably lose all memory of what we were trying to think of. Fortunately, this inability to access information is temporary.
(7) Absentmindedness	Virtually all of us suffer from occasional absentmindedness (forgetting due to lack of attention) when we're tired or distracted.

QUIZ

1 Flashbulb memories almost never change over time. TRUE FALSE

2 People often find it difficult to tell the difference between a true and a false memory. TRUE FALSE

3 One powerful way of creating false memories is to show people fake photographs of events that didn't happen. TRUE FALSE

4 The correlation between witnesses' confidence in their testimony and the accuracy of this testimony is strong. TRUE FALSE

Answers: (1) F (p. 214); (2) T (p. 214); (3) T (p. 216); (4) F (p. 216)

PEARSON
mypsychlab

▼ Can another individual change our memory? Watch the video titled "Memory: Elizabeth Loftus" at www.mypsychlab.com to find out.

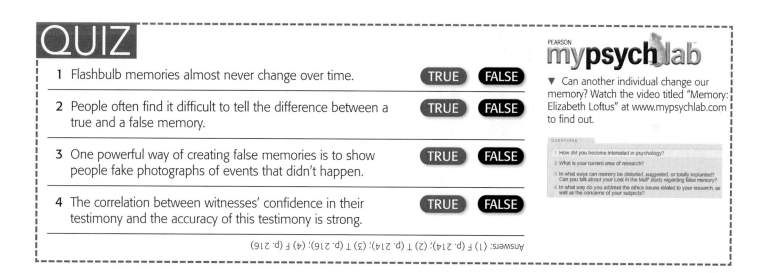

HOW MEMORY OPERATES: THE MEMORY ASSEMBLY LINE (pp. 189–199)

6.1 Identify the ways that memories do and do not accurately reflect experiences

Memories can be surprisingly accurate over very long periods of time but tend to be reconstructive rather than reproductive.

1. A _____ _____ is a false but subjectively compelling memory. (p. 190)

2. Our memories are far more (reproductive/reconstructive) rather than (reproductive/reconstructive). (p. 190)

3. An _____ memory is a memory in which we see ourselves as an outside observer would. (p. 191)

6.2 Explain the function, span, and duration of each of the three memory systems

Sensory memory, short-term memory, and long-term memory are stages of information processing that vary in how much information they hold and for how long they retain it. Short-term memory has a limited span of seven plus or minus two that can be extended by grouping things together into larger, meaningful units called chunks.

4. The three major systems of memory are measured by _____, or how much information each system can hold, and _____ or how long a period of time the system can hold information. (p. 191)

5. Map out the three-memory model process proposed by Atkinson and Shiffrin depicting memory flow. (p. 191)

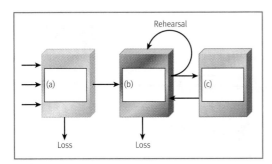

6. _____ memory is the brief storage of perceptual information before it is passed to _____ memory. (p. 192)

7. To extend the span of short-term memory, we organize information into meaningful groupings using a process called _____. (p. 194)

8. The tendency to remember words at the beginning of a list better than those in the middle is known as the _____ _____. (p. 197)

6.3 Differentiate the subtypes of long-term memory

Explicit memory subtypes include semantic and episodic memory. Implicit memory types include procedural and priming memory.

9. _____ memory is the process of recalling information intentionally, and _____ memory is the process of recalling information we don't remember deliberately. (p. 198)

10. Complete the diagram to show the subtypes of explicit and implicit memory. (p. 199)

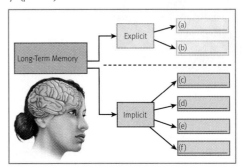

succeed with mypsychlab

1. Can you memorize a phone number? Let's test the "magic" number 7.
   Simulation: Digit Span

2. Can the order that we hear a grocery list in affect our memory for certain food items?
   The Serial Position Curve

3. Can memories be created that are not true?
   Creating False Memories

succeed with mypsychlab

Do You Know All of the Terms in This Chapter?

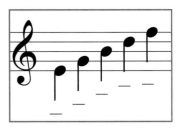

Find out by using the Flashcards. Want more practice? Take additional quizzes, try simulations, and watch video to be sure you are prepared for the test!

THE THREE STAGES OF REMEMBERING (pp. 199–206)

6.4 Determine methods for connecting new information to existing knowledge

Mnemonics are memory aids that link new information to more familiar knowledge. There are many kinds of mnemonics; they take effort to use but can assist recall.

11. The three major stages of memory are _____, _____, and _____. (p. 199)

12. _____ is the process of organizing information in a format that our memories can use. (p. 200)

13. A learning aid, strategy, or device that enhances recall is a _____. (p. 202)

14. Label the lines in the treble clef using the mnemonic "Every good boy does fine" as a memory aid. (p. 200)

Answers are located at the end of the text.

6.5 Distinguish ways of measuring memory

Recall requires generating previously encountered information on our own, whereas recognition simply requires selecting the correct information from an array of choices. How quickly we relearn material previously learned and forgotten is another measure of memory.

15. _____ is reacquiring knowledge that we'd previously learned but largely forgotten over time. (p. 203)

16. The law of _____ _____ _____ _____ explains why cramming for a test is not the best way to remember things well in the long run. (p. 203)

6.6 Describe how the relation between encoding and retrieval conditions influences remembering

Individuals remember better if they're tested under the same physical and emotional conditions as when they encoded the information.

17. The _____ phenomenon is a form of retrieval failure in which we're sure we know the answer to a question but can't come up with it. (p. 204)

18. _____ _____ is the phenomenon of remembering something better when the conditions under which we retrieve information are similar to the conditions under which we encoded it. (p. 204)

19. In _____ _____, our retrieval of memories is superior when the external context of the original memories matches the retrieval context. (p. 204)

20. Identify the concepts from memory researchers that can help you in studying for this and other courses. (p. 205)

Memory Concept	Pointer
1. _____	Spread your study time out—review your notes and textbook in increments rather than cramming.
2. _____	Connect new knowledge with existing knowledge rather than simply memorizing facts or names.
3. _____	Work to process ideas deeply and meaningfully—avoid writing notes down word-for-word from instructors' lectures or slides. Try to capture the information in your own words.
4. _____	The more reminders or cues you can connect from your knowledge base to new material, the more likely you are to recall new material when tested.

succeed with mypsychlab

1. What goes in doesn't always come out.
Encoding, Storage, and Retrieval in Memory

2. How good is your memory? Practice your understanding of the stages of memory.
Key Processes in Stages of Memory

THE BIOLOGY OF MEMORY (pp. 206–210)

6.7 Describe the role of long-term potentiation in memory

Most scientists believe that long-term potentiation—a gradual strengthening of the connections among neurons from repetitive stimulation—plays a key role in the formation of memories and memory storage.

21. Scientists agree that LTP plays a key role in _____. (p. 207)

22. The _____ plays a key role in forming lasting memories. (p. 207)

6.8 Explain how amnesia helps to clarify the distinction between explicit and implicit memory

Patients with severe anterograde amnesia, like H.M., often display grossly impaired explicit memory yet intact implicit memory for certain tasks.

23. A person with _____ amnesia has lost some memories of his or her past. (p. 208)

24. The inability to encode new memories from our experiences is called _____ amnesia. (p. 208)

25. If there is memory recovery from amnesia, it tends to occur (gradually/suddenly). (p. 208)

26. Large circuits connecting different parts of the limbic system—consisting of the _____, _____, and _____ are critical to memory. (p. 209)

27. How effective, according to researchers' understanding of anterograde amnesia, would it be for someone with this condition to write notes to (or on) himself in an effort to recall previous experiences? (p. 208)

28. On this task, subjects must trace a star while looking only at a mirror. What type of memory is this task designed to assess? (p. 208)

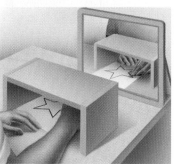

6.9 Identify the key impairments of Alzheimer's disease

The memory loss of patients with Alzheimer's disease begins with that of recent events, with memories of events of the distant past typically being the last to go. Alzheimer's disease is marked by loss of synapses and acetylcholine neurons.

29. Senility (is/isn't) an unavoidable part of aging. (p. 209)

30. Alzheimer's disease accounts for only 50 to 60 percent of cases of _____, or severe memory loss. (p. 209)

succeed with mypsychlab

1. Explore competing theories of what leads to Alzheimer's disease.
What Happens with Alzheimer's?

THE DEVELOPMENT OF MEMORY: ACQUIRING A PERSONAL HISTORY (pp. 210–213)

6.10 Identify how children's memory abilities change with age

Infants display implicit memory for events; both infants' and children's memories are influenced by some of the same factors as adults' memory. Children's memory improves in part because of maturational changes in the brain that extend the span of memory. Over time, children become better able to use mnemonic and rehearsal strategies and become more aware of their memory limitations.

31. Over time, children develop enhanced _____ skills that provide knowledge about one's own memory ability and limitations. (p. 211)

32. Rovee-Collier's experiments utilized operant conditioning to study infants' _____ _____. (p. 211)

33. How did Carolyn Rovee-Collier and others use infants' kicking behavior to study memory in infants? (p. 211)

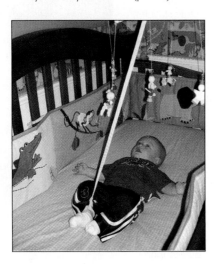

34. Rovee-Collier found that infants' memories of the experience were surprisingly (general/specific). (p. 211)

6.11 Examine why we fail to remember experiences from early childhood

The hippocampus, which is critical for the establishment of long-term memory, isn't fully developed in infancy or early childhood. Infants have little sense of self, which makes it difficult for them to encode and store experiences in ways that are meaningful. They also haven't learned language yet.

35. _____ _____ is the inability to remember personal experiences that took place before the age of 3 or so. (p. 212)

36. European Americans report (earlier/later) first memories than do people from Taiwan. (p. 212)

37. There (is/isn't) evidence that we can remember things that took place at or prior to birth. (p. 212)

38. Infants have little sense of _____, which makes it difficult for them to encode or store experiences in ways that are meaningful. (p. 212)

39. The fact that infants have limited _____ _____ prior to age 2 may be another factor in infantile amnesia. (p. 212)

40. Which important indicator of the presence of a self-concept do humans and chimpanzees exhibit? (p. 212)

succeed with mypsychlab

1. At what age do infants develop a memory for past events?
Infant's Perceptual and Cognitive Milestones

WHEN GOOD MEMORY GOES BAD: FALSE MEMORIES (pp. 213–219)

6.12 **Identify factors that influence people's susceptibility to false memories and memory errors**

Flashbulb memories for highly significant events seem more crisp and vivid than other memories but are just as vulnerable to errors as other kinds of memory. One source of memory errors is source monitoring difficulty, sometimes resulting in cryptomnesia. Our memories for events are easily influenced by suggestions from others that the event happened differently than our observations suggested. The fact that we're receptive to suggestions about whether and how events took place has important implications for eyewitness testimony.

41. _____ _____ are memories that are extremely vivid and detailed, and often highly emotional. (p. 213)

42. Whenever we try to figure out whether a memory reflects something that really happened, we are engaging in _____ _____. (p. 214)

43. The failure to recognize that our ideas come from another source is called _____. (p. 214)

44. Explain Elizabeth Loftus's misinformation effect and its influence on our memory. (p. 215)

45. Explain how we could have vivid memories of events we never experienced. (p. 216)

46. Research suggests that some _____ may be unintentionally planting memories of traumatic events by means of suggestive procedures. (p. 218)

47. In a well-known example of _____, cellist Yo-Yo Ma once left his $2.5 million cello in a cab. (p. 219)

48. Most of us recover quickly from _____, a temporary inability to access information. (p. 219)

49. As we age, it is (typical/atypical) to find it increasingly difficult to access memories. (p. 219)

6.13 **Explain how suggestions can shape children's memories**

Children prompted over repeated trials to remember something that never occurred sometimes report that the event actually took place. Children's memories are affected by their expectations about how someone will behave; they're likely to report that an experience consistent with their expectations took place even if they didn't see it happen.

50. _____ may cause children to provide authority figures with the answers they are seeking, even if those answers are wrong. (p. 217)

succeed with mypsychlab

1. Be a participant in a psychological test of story telling. **How Good Is Your Memory for Stories?**

SCIENTIFIC THINKING SKILLS
Questions and Summary

1 Imagine that you are a psychologist testifying in court as an expert witness for the benefit of a jury regarding the relationship between confidence and accuracy among criminal eyewitnesses. Present a case for why line-ups are particularly prone to errors of identification and why confidence should *not* be taken into account.

2 This chapter presents a wealth of evidence that memory is reconstructive. How then might you explain the extraordinary accuracy with which actors learn long parts, especially in stage plays? Are there other examples where memory is primarily reproductive rather than reconstructive?

RULING OUT RIVAL HYPOTHESES
pp. 193, 216

CORRELATION vs. CAUSATION
pp. 207, 209, 211

FALSIFIABILITY
p. 196

REPLICABILITY
pp. 203, 205, 214, 216

EXTRAORDINARY CLAIMS
p. 212

OCCAM'S RAZOR
p. 214

Language, Thinking, and Intelligence

Is the babbling of babies
meaningful**?** (p. 227)

Do nonhuman animals
have language**?** (p. 232)

Is human intelligence
related to brain size**?** (p. 243)

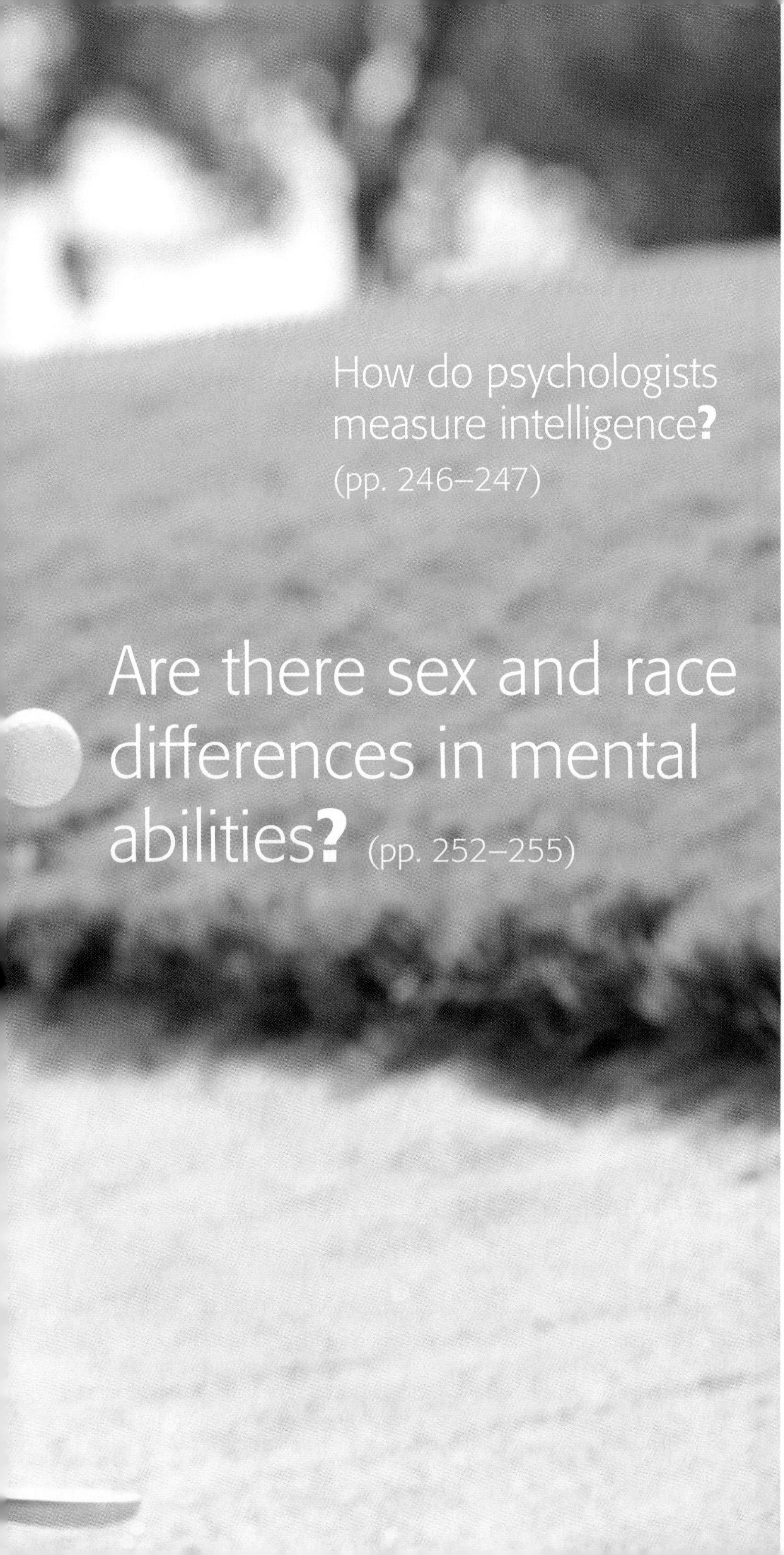

CHAPTER 7

How do psychologists
measure intelligence?
(pp. 246–247)

Are there sex and race
differences in mental
abilities? (pp. 252–255)

One of the most valuable lessons psychology can teach us is to appreciate mental capacities we normally take for granted. Take language and thinking. We rely on them almost every second of our waking hours but rarely notice the complexity that goes into them.

Picture this brief conversation between two students:

Male student:	"Just scored us some free tickets to the game!"
Female student:	"Shut up! How?"
Male student:	"I heard this guy at the bank say he had some he couldn't use, did a little back slapping and high-fiving and . . . tah-da!"

Most native speakers of English can follow that conversation with ease. Yet all sorts of complex cognitive processes we take for granted go into comprehending that conversation. Let's look at some of the behind-the-scenes thinking that was probably going on as you read that passage.

(1) You filled in the gaps in grammar. For example, "Just scored us some free tickets" is an incomplete phrase that needs the word "I" at the beginning to make it grammatical, but you realized that the male student was referring to himself.

(2) You figured out that "the game" is either important to the students, about to take place in the near future, or both. You also figured out that the female student knew which game the male was talking about, even though you didn't know which one it was.

(3) You inferred that "shut up" wasn't a literal command to be quiet, but instead an expression of surprise, even skepticism.

(4) You realized that the male student engaged in a bit of friendly social interaction to persuade the man at the bank to hand over his tickets. This realization goes well beyond the literal action reported in the conversation—he reported only backslapping and high-fiving.

We can probably think of other aspects of the conversation that required us to go beyond the literal information given to us. What enables us to draw these behind-the-scenes inferences? Our implicit ability to access knowledge, draw conclusions, make decisions, and interpret new phrases all contribute to our understanding of this and every other conversation.

In this chapter, we'll examine how we communicate, and the challenges we face when doing so. Then we'll explore our thinking and reasoning processes in everyday life and learn to avoid commonplace pitfalls in logic that can lead us to draw mistaken conclusions about the world around us. We'll conclude by asking what it means for some of us to be better thinkers than others. In other words, what is intelligence and what accounts for differences in intellect among individuals?

How Does Language Work?

Language is a system of communication that combines symbols, such as words or gestural signs, in rule-based ways to create meaning. One hallmark of language is that it tends to be arbitrary—the sounds, words, and sentences bear no clear relation to their meaning. Language serves several functions. The most obvious is the transmission of information. When we tell our roommate "The party starts at 9" or place an order at a coffee shop for a "skim latte," we're communicating information that enables us or someone else to accomplish a goal, like getting to the party on time or making sure our latte is fat free.

Language serves key social and emotional functions too. It enables us to express our thoughts and views about social interactions, such as conveying, "I thought you were mad at me" or "That guy was hilarious." We spend much of our conversational time using language in ways that help us to establish or maintain relationships with others (Dunbar, 1996).

THE FEATURES OF LANGUAGE

We take language for granted because it's a highly practiced and automatic cognitive process, like driving a car once we've done it for a few months. By *automatic,* we mean that using and interpreting language usually require little attention, enabling us to perform other tasks like walking, cooking, or exercising without speech getting in the way (Posner & Snyder, 1975). We don't realize how complex language is until we try to learn or use a new one. In fact, our ability to use language requires the coordination of an enormous number of cognitive, social, and physical skills. Even the mere ability to produce the sounds of our language requires the delicate coordination of breath control, vocal cords, throat and mouth position, and tongue movement.

We can think about language at four different levels of analysis, all of which we need to coordinate to communicate effectively. These levels are (1) *phonemes,* the sounds of our language; (2) *morphemes,* the smallest units of speech that are meaningful; (3) *syntax,* the grammatical rules that govern how we compose words into meaningful strings; and (4) *extralinguistic information,* elements of communication that aren't part of the content of language but are critical to interpreting its meaning, such as facial expressions and tone of voice. We can think of each level as similar to the different levels of specificity involved in preparing a meal, ranging from the individual ingredients to the menu items to the meal itself and, last but not least, to the overall dining experience. Just as different cuisines involve differences at all of these levels, different languages vary at all four levels of analysis.

Clearly, language is more complex than we typically realize. Successful communication depends on (1) the content of the language, (2) the social environment and nonverbal behavior of the speaker, and (3) the knowledge and reasoning ability of the listener to "fill in the gaps" to make sense of the context of the linguistic material. Successful communication between people relies on the language used but also on a lot of other aspects of social interaction and context that are not part of the language system itself.

HOW DO CHILDREN LEARN LANGUAGE?

Language is among the few documented cases in which children are more efficient learners than adults. The language-learning process starts long before children begin talking. Although children don't begin using words until around their first birthday or later, infants begin learning about their language even before birth. **[LEARNING OBJECTIVE 7.1]** How? Babies begin to hear inside the womb by the fifth month of pregnancy. Although what they hear is a rather muffled version of what we hear, they can make out their mothers' voices, learn to recognize some characteristics of their mothers' native language, and even recognize specific songs or stories they've heard over and over again (DeCasper & Spence, 1988).

Babbling. During the first year or so after birth, infants learn much more about the sounds of their native languages. They begin to figure out the phonemes of their languages and how to use their vocal apparatus to make specific sounds. Although children's babbling seems like nonsense (and usually is), babbling plays an important role in language development by enabling babies to figure out how to move their vocal tracts to generate

More than we typically realize, our ability to follow a conversation depends on a host of sophisticated inferences.

Fetuses can recognize their native language, their mother's voice, and a specific story read to them before birth. (*Source:* DeCasper & Spence, 1988)

GLOSSARY

language
a largely arbitrary system of communication that combines symbols (such as words or gestural signs) in rule-based ways to create meaning

specific sounds. **Babbling** refers to any intentional vocalization (other than crying, burping, sighing, and laughing, which are less intentional) that lacks specific meaning. Babbling becomes increasingly complex as infants' control of their vocal tracts increases (Kent & Miolo, 1995). By the end of their first year, their babbling takes on a conversational tone that sounds meaningful even though it isn't (Goldstein & Schwade, 2008).

As infants are fine-tuning their vocal tracts, they're also fine-tuning their ears. Different languages have different phoneme categories, so to be successful users of their native languages infants must learn how to classify sounds (Eimas, Siqueland, Jusczyk, et al., 1971; Werker, Gilbert, Humphrey, et al., 1981). By 10 months, infants' phonemes are very much like those of the adult speakers of their native language (Werker & Tees, 1984).

Learning Words. How and when do children start to learn to talk? One key principle characterizes early word learning: *Comprehension precedes production.* Children are learning to recognize and interpret words well before they can produce them (see **Figure 7.1**). This is because they have only a tentative grasp of how to produce sounds. They may be perfectly aware that "elephant" refers to a large gray animal with a long trunk and large ears but be unable to produce this big word.

GLOSSARY

babbling
intentional vocalization that lacks specific meaning

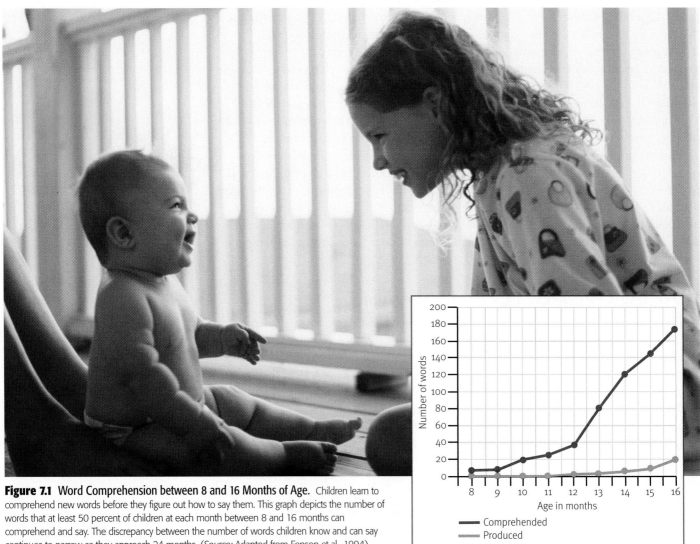

Figure 7.1 Word Comprehension between 8 and 16 Months of Age. Children learn to comprehend new words before they figure out how to say them. This graph depicts the number of words that at least 50 percent of children at each month between 8 and 16 months can comprehend and say. The discrepancy between the number of words children know and can say continues to narrow as they approach 24 months. (*Source:* Adapted from Fenson et al., 1994)

Most infants start understanding words around 9 or 10 months. Children start to *produce* their first words around their first birthday, although there's considerable variability in this milestone. They acquire their first words slowly. Between 1 and 1½ years of age, they gradually accumulate a vocabulary of between 20 and 100 words. As children become more experienced in learning new words, the rate at which they acquire words increases (Goldfield & Reznick, 1990). By the time they turn 2, most children can produce several hundred words. By kindergarten, their vocabulary has ballooned to several thousand words.

WHAT DO *you* THINK?

Your sister is concerned that your 1-year-old niece isn't talking yet. You know that comprehension precedes production so she understands a lot more than she's saying. What method could you use to evaluate what words she understands?

Syntactic Development: Putting It All Together.

By the time children turn 2, most start to combine words into simple two-word phrases such as "more juice" and "kitty run." Although these phrases are still simplistic, children at this phase have already grasped something about syntactic rules. They tend to use words in the correct order, even if they're leaving some of them out.

As is the case with word learning, children understand some basic syntactic rules before they can display them. For example, they understand how word order relates to meaning before they can generate complete sentences. Seventeen-month-olds can understand that "Cookie Monster is tickling Big Bird" means something different than "Big Bird is tickling Cookie Monster" (Hirsh-Pasek & Golinkoff, 1996) (see **Figure 7.2** for a different example using a pig and a dog).

Several months after they've begun using two-word phrases, children use more complex sentences involving three- or four-word combinations. Around the same time, they begin to produce morphological markers such as *-s* for plural and *-ed* for past tense in English. They acquire most syntactic rules by preschool age but continue to acquire more complex rules in their early school years (Dennis, Sugar, & Whitaker, 1982).

Figure 7.2 Children Display Comprehension of Word Order Prior to Sentence Production. Children can display their grasp of syntax by pointing to a video that matches a sentence they have heard. Here, a 17-month-old child is displaying his comprehension of the sentence "The pig is tickling the dog" by pointing to the video that corresponds to the sentence.

Theoretical Accounts of Language Acquisition.

Given that we acquire so much of our capacity to learn language at such an early age, how do children solve this challenge? There are several explanations: Some fall more heavily on the nature side of the nature–nurture debate, others on the nurture side. Ultimately, language learning requires both nature and nurture.

The simplest explanation of children's language learning is that they learn through imitation. Babies hear language used in systematic ways and learn to use language as adults use it. This is certainly true in one sense, because babies learn the language they hear. But a purely imitation-based explanation can't be completely right for one reason: Language is **generative.** *Generativity* means that language is a system that allows us to create an infinite number of sentences, producing new statements, thoughts, and ideas never previously

GLOSSARY

generative
allowing an infinite number of unique sentences to be created by combining words in novel ways

uttered. The fact that even very young children use language in generative ways—producing sentences or combinations of words they've never heard—means they're producing things for which they were never directly reinforced, refuting a purely behavioral view.

The strongest nature view is the *nativist* account, which says that children come into the world knowing how language works. Nativists propose that children are born with syntactic rules that determine how sentences are constructed (Chomsky, 1972). Noam Chomsky, who essentially invented the field of contemporary linguistics, even hypothesized that humans are born with a specific language "organ" in the brain called the *language acquisition device* that houses these rules. Critics of this view have pointed out that children learn syntax gradually and that even adults use grammatically incorrect sentences.

The *social pragmatics* account suggests that particular aspects of the social environment help structure language learning. According to this account, children use the context of a conversation to infer its topic from the actions, expressions, gestures, and other behaviors of speakers. Another explanation for how children learn language is the *general cognitive processing* account. It proposes that children's ability to learn language is a result of general skills that children apply across a variety of activities. For example, children's ability to perceive, learn, and recognize patterns may be all they need to learn language.

As we've seen, the imitation account can't explain the complexity of language. Nevertheless, each of the other three theoretical views has its strengths, and there's some evidence consistent with each. Yet only the social pragmatics theory and the general cognitive processing theory are clearly falsifiable. Researchers are making important strides in generating experiments that pit these two accounts against each other (Namy & Waxman, 2000; Samuelson & Smith, 1998). Nativism may ultimately be correct about some aspects of language processing. But because scientists can't easily test all of its claims, they'll need to rule out competing accounts before accepting it as a viable explanation for language learning.

FALSIFIABILITY
Can the claim be disproved?

Language clearly has an important learned component, because children adopted from a different country learn to speak the language of their adopted rather than biological parents.

FALSIFIABILITY
Can the claim be disproved?

RULING OUT RIVAL HYPOTHESES
Have important alternative explanations for the findings been excluded?

myth CONCEPTIONS
DO TWINS HAVE THEIR OWN LANGUAGE?

Popular psychology tells us that twins sometimes develop their own language. Is this fact or fiction?

The idea of being a twin has a certain appeal and allure. Twins share their mother's womb, potty train together, and go through school at the same time. It's only natural to expect there to be a special bond between twins. One commonly held belief is that twins invent their own secret language, one only they can understand. This phenomenon is known as **cryptophasia.**

As fascinating as this notion is, the truth is less exotic. Cases of apparent cryptophasia among twins turn out to be a result of phonological impairment and other types of language delays (Bishop & Bishop, 1998; Dodd & McEvoy, 1994) that are more prevalent among twins than among singletons (children born one at a time). Twin pairs who've supposedly developed a secret language are simply attempting to use their native language but with poor articulation and significant pronunciation errors. These difficulties are serious enough to render their speech largely incomprehensible. Because twin pairs tend to make similar kinds of phonological errors, their speech is more understandable to each other than it is to their parents or nonrelated children (Dodd & McEvoy, 1994; Thorpe, Greenwood, Eivers, et al., 2001).

There *are* interesting, but rare, cases of children inventing their own communication systems. One example is deaf children of hearing parents who sometimes invent their own signs when not being instructed in sign language. This phenomenon is called

GLOSSARY

cryptophasia
secret language developed and understood only by a small number of people, typically twins

homesign and shows impressive ingenuity (and motivation to communicate) on the part of children, because they're inventing these signs without guidance from adults (Goldin-Meadow & Mylander, 1998).

Still, in the cases of homesign, children didn't invent a full-blown secret language. Homesigners generate some basic sign combinations, but not a full syntax. Languages evolve gradually across large groups of people, not privately within a pair.

SPECIAL CASES OF LANGUAGE LEARNING

Children learning language sometimes confront special challenges. These challenges may prevent, slow down, or complicate acquiring a language. In this section, we review two of them: sign language learning in deaf children and bilingual language acquisition.

Sign Language. A type of language developed by members of deaf communities that allows them to use visual rather than auditory communication is **sign language.** It involves using the hands, face, body, and "sign space"—the space in front of the signer—to communicate. Just as there are many spoken languages, there are many sign languages used in different countries and deaf communities.

Many people think of sign language as an elaborate form of gesturing, a charades-type attempt to act out silently what people would otherwise speak. This couldn't be further from the truth. Sign language is called "language" for a reason. It's a linguistic system of communication with its own phonemes, words, syntax, and extralinguistic information (Poizner, Klima, & Bellugi, 1987; Stokoe, Casterline, & Croneberg, 1976). Deaf babies pass through the same stages as hearing babies at about the same time (Newport & Meier, 1985; Orlanksy & Bonvillian, 1984; Petitto & Marentette, 1991). Each of these similarities confirms that sign languages work the same way that spoken languages do. **[LEARNING OBJECTIVE 7.2]** So what makes sign language learning a challenge? For babies learning sign from parents who are fluent signers, there is no challenge. But more than 90 percent of deaf children are born to hearing parents who then have to learn sign right along with their children, making for a very challenging learning environment for everyone. There are many common misconceptions about deafness and sign language. **Table 7.1** lists a few popular misconceptions.

Bilingualism. Most of us have tried to learn a second language, and some of us are **bilingual,** adept at speaking and comprehending two distinct languages. How do individuals who are bilingual manage to learn two languages and become fluent in both? In most bilingual persons, one language is dominant. It's typically the first language learned, the one they heard most often as a child, and the one they use most often. How do bilingual

GLOSSARY

homesign
system of signs invented by deaf children of hearing parents who receive no language input

sign language
language developed by members of deaf communities that uses visual rather than auditory communication

bilingual
proficient and fluent at speaking and comprehending two distinct languages

Table 7.1 Common Misconceptions about Deafness and Sign Language.

Myth	Reality
1. Deaf people don't need sign language because they can lip read.	Even the most skilled lip-readers can pick up only about 30 to 35 percent of what's being said because most of the work is done behind the scenes by the throat, tongue, and teeth. Our lips look virtually identical when saying "nice" and "dice"—even words like "queen" and "white" look the same to lip readers.
2. Learning to sign slows down deaf children's ability to learn to speak.	Historically, deaf education programs tried to prevent deaf children from learning to sign because they feared children would never learn to talk. It's now clear that learning a sign language actually speeds up the process of learning to talk.
3. American Sign Language is English translated word-for-word into signs.	American Sign Language (ASL) bears no resemblance to English; the syntax in particular differs completely from English syntax. Some deaf communities use what's called Signed English instead of ASL which translates English sentences word-for-word into signs from ASL.

A growing number of children hear one language spoken at home and another at school. Although bilingualism may slow the learning of some aspects of both languages, it may promote linguistic ability in the long run.

Figure 7.3 A Chimpanzee Uses Lexigrams to Communicate with Caretakers. This ape has been trained to associate colored shapes with meanings such as "juice," "fruit," and "tickle" (a favorite pastime for chimpanzees raised in captivity).

Figure 7.4 Nonhuman Animals Can Learn to Use Language. Alex (an African gray parrot) was famous for his impressive language skills.

persons fluent in two languages keep them straight, and how are these languages organized in their brains?

Children learning two languages seem to go about it the same way that *monolingual* children—those learning a single language—do. They follow the same stages in the same order for each language as do monolingual children. There's some evidence that bilingual children experience some delay in each of their languages relative to their monolingual counterparts (Gathercole, 2002a, b). However, this delay depends on what aspects of language researchers measure. **[LEARNING OBJECTIVE 7.4]** Vocabulary development is relatively unimpaired (Pearson & Fernàndez, 1994; Pearson, Fernàndez, & Oller, 1993), whereas syntax is more affected (Gathercole, 2002a, b) and the delays that occur early in the acquisition process are often offset by a variety of long-term benefits (Sorace, 2007). In fact, in some cases the process of figuring out how two languages work enables bilinguals to perform better on some language tasks (Bialystok, 1988; Galambos & Hakuta, 1988; Ricciardelli, 1992).

NONHUMAN ANIMAL COMMUNICATION

The communication systems of different animal species differ in type and complexity. Some species use scent marking as their primary form of communication. Others rely on visual displays, such as baring their teeth or flapping their wings. Still others, like humans, use vocal communication. Human language differs from the communication systems of other species on several fronts. First, language appears to be significantly more complex in its structure and rules than other communication systems. Second, language's generativity is unique relative to the natural communication systems of other species. Most species have a fixed number of ways of expressing a fixed number of messages but have no way of communicating completely new thoughts or messages. Third, the range of contexts in which nonhuman animals communicate is much more limited than the range of contexts for human language. In most nonhuman animals, aggression and mating are the two circumstances in which communication most often takes place. For example, male songbirds, such as canaries and finches, produce a specific song to convey the message, "This is my territory, back off," and another song to attract mates (Kendeigh, 1941). Chimpanzees use a combination of vocalizations and visual displays, such as facial expressions and slapping the ground, to convey aggression (de Waal, 1989a). These communicative goals are important, of course, but differ greatly from the wide array of messages we communicate every day. **[LEARNING OBJECTIVE 7.2]**

Concerted efforts to teach animals to use human language have been largely unsuccessful. The earliest attempts to teach chimpanzees, one of our nearest living genetic relatives, fell flat. Later attempts were more successful, but there were still crucial limits. Although chimpanzees can learn words, they differ from human infants in that they require thousands of trials to learn to associate signs or lexigrams with their meanings and typically only learn through conditioning (see **Figure 7.3**). Chimpanzees can also combine words into more complex utterances, but they never master syntactic rules.

Two animal species may do better than chimpanzees at learning language. One is the bonobo, a primate species that's genetically even more closely related to humans than chimpanzees. The few studies conducted on bonobos suggest a different learning pathway, which more closely resembles human learning (Savage-Rumbaugh, 1986). Bonobos (1) learn better as young animals than as adults, (2) tend to learn through observation rather than reinforcement, and (3) use symbols to comment on or engage in social interactions, rather than simply for food treats. Yet bonobos seem to get stuck when learning syntax.

One other species that seems able to use spoken language much as we do is the African gray parrot. An Einstein of a parrot named Alex, who died in 2007 at the age of 31, was particularly well known for his ability to speak and to solve cognitive tasks (see **Figure 7.4**).

Moreover, he was able to generate new and meaningful combinations of words (Pepperberg, 1999). Yet the learning process for Alex and other African gray parrots is more similar to that of chimpanzees than bonobos and humans. It's a result of many repetitions rather than of observing and interacting with the world.

DO WE THINK IN WORDS? THE RELATION BETWEEN LANGUAGE AND THOUGHT

We've all had times when we realized we were conversing with ourselves; we may have even started talking out loud to ourselves. Clearly, we sometimes think in words. What about the rest of the time? Do we usually think in a nonlinguistic fashion, or do we just not notice our internal conversation? One early hypothesis was that thinking is a form of internal speech. The view that all thinking is represented linguistically is called **linguistic determinism.** One of the best-known examples of how language can influence thought is the belief that Inuits (formerly called Eskimos) have about a thousand words for snow. Linguistic determinists argue that having so many words for snow enables Inuits to perceive incredibly subtle distinctions among types of snow. It's a good story. But there are several reasons to believe it's all a myth:

(1) Analysis of Inuit languages reveals that although Inuits make several fine distinctions among types of snow, a thousand is a substantial exaggeration of these types.

(2) English speakers also use many different terms to describe snow, such as "slush," "powder," or even "crud."

(3) We can't infer that having a greater number of terms *caused* the Inuit to make finer distinctions. Instead, perhaps Inuits and other people who work in snowy conditions, like skiers and hikers, find it helpful to draw fine distinctions among types of snow. If so, language may reflect people's thinking about snow rather than the other way around.

There are other reasons to doubt linguistic determinism. First, children can perform many complex cognitive tasks long before they can talk about them. Second, recent neuroimaging studies show that although language areas often become activated when people engage in certain cognitive tasks, such as reading, they aren't activated during others, such as spatial tasks or visual imagery (Gazzaniga, Ivry, & Mangun, 2002). These studies suggest that thought can occur without language.

Although linguistic determinism doesn't have a lot going for it, there's some promise for **linguistic relativity,** a less radical perspective. Proponents of linguistic relativity maintain that characteristics of language shape our thought processes. **[LEARNING OBJECTIVE 7.3]** This idea is also known as the Sapir-Whorf hypothesis, named after the two scholars who proposed it (Sapir, 1929; Whorf, 1956). Several studies suggest that language can affect thinking. One study examined the memories of Russians who moved to the United States and achieved fluency in Russian and English. These participants recalled events that happened in Russia more accurately when speaking Russian and recalled events that happened in the United States more accurately when speaking English (Marian & Neisser, 2000).

Yet in other cases, researchers have been surprised to discover that language doesn't influence thought. One example is color categorization (Lenneberg, 1967). Different languages contain different numbers of basic color terms. Although English uses a set of 11 basic color terms (red, blue, green, yellow, white, black, purple, orange, pink, brown, and gray), some languages contain fewer basic color terms. A language community may use a single word to refer to all things that are either blue or green. In a small number of non-Westernized cultures such as the Dani of New Guinea, there are no true color

The Inuit commonly live in Arctic climates. It's common lore that the Inuit have a thousand words for different types of snow, and as a result, they make finer distinctions among types of snow than do people who speak English. In fact, Inuit languages have about the same number of words for snow as does English.

GLOSSARY

linguistic determinism
view that all thought is represented verbally and that, as a result, our language defines our thinking

linguistic relativity
view that characteristics of language shape our thought processes

CORRELATION vs. CAUSATION
Can we be sure that A causes B?

The Dani language has only words for "dark" and "bright," not individual colors, but Dani people can distinguish colors, just as we do.

terms at all, only "dark" and "bright." Eleanor Rosch (1973) demonstrated that the Dani perceive colors as dividing up into roughly the same color categories as do English speakers even though they don't have terms to distinguish them.

Overall the evidence suggests that language shapes some, but not all, aspects of perception, memory, and thought. Nevertheless, when researchers identify language-related differences in thought, it's not easy to disentangle the influences of language from culture. In fact, nearly all cross-linguistic comparisons are correlational rather than experimental because we can't randomly assign people to learn different languages. As a result, language and culture are nearly always confounded. We must be careful when drawing causal conclusions about the impact of language on thinking.

CORRELATION vs. CAUSATION
Can we be sure that A causes B?

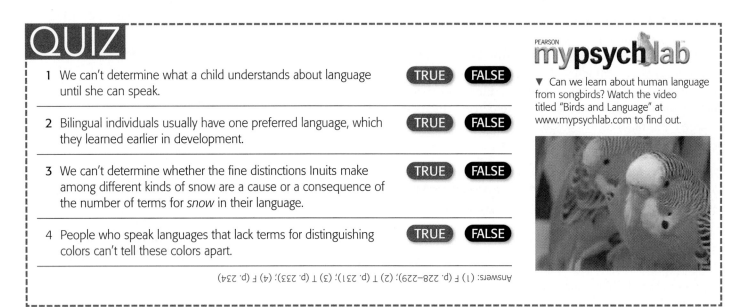

QUIZ

1 We can't determine what a child understands about language until she can speak.   **TRUE** **FALSE**

2 Bilingual individuals usually have one preferred language, which they learned earlier in development.   **TRUE** **FALSE**

3 We can't determine whether the fine distinctions Inuits make among different kinds of snow are a cause or a consequence of the number of terms for *snow* in their language.   **TRUE** **FALSE**

4 People who speak languages that lack terms for distinguishing colors can't tell these colors apart.   **TRUE** **FALSE**

Answers: (1) F (p. 228–229); (2) T (p. 231); (3) T (p. 233); (4) F (p. 234)

PEARSON
mypsychlab

▼ Can we learn about human language from songbirds? Watch the video titled "Birds and Language" at www.mypsychlab.com to find out.

Thinking and Reasoning

Language may shape our thinking in some respects and certainly allows us to express our thoughts but a great deal of our thinking goes on "behind the scenes" unexpressed and sometimes even beyond our awareness. Generally speaking, we can define **thinking** as any mental activity or processing of information. It includes learning, remembering, perceiving, believing, and deciding.

As we discovered in Chapter 5, behaviorists attempted to explain thinking in terms of stimulus and response, reinforcement and punishment. Yet psychologists have long known that our minds often go beyond the available information and fill in the gaps to create information that isn't present (see Chapters 2 and 4). Behaviorism's "black box psychology" (see Chapter 5) can't easily account for this phenomenon.

COGNITIVE ECONOMY—IMPOSING ORDER ON OUR WORLD

GLOSSARY

thinking
any mental activity or processing of information, including learning, remembering, perceiving, believing, and deciding

We process an enormous amount of information every minute of every day. From the moment we wake up, we must take into account what time it is, notice if there are any obstacles on the floor (like a roommate's shoes) between us and the shower, plan what time we need to get to class or work, and collect everything we need to bring with us. Of course, that's all before we've even gone out the door. If we were to attend to and draw conclusions about every aspect of our experience all of the time, we'd be so over-whelmed that we'd be paralyzed psychologically. As we learned in Chapter 2, we're cog-nitive misers who economize our thinking efforts whenever possible. Cognitive economy allows us to simplify what we attend to and keep the information we need for decision making to a manageable minimum.

Categories and Concepts.

Categories and **concepts** help us to achieve cognitive economy. Categories are collections of real or imagined objects, actions, and characteris-tics that share core properties, such as *motorcycles, fruit, dancing,* and *purple.* We can think of concepts as the general ideas or thoughts associated with members of a category. For example, if the category of flowers is the group of all individual items that can be classified as flowers, the concept of flowers is the idea of colorful, scented blooms growing on plants. As we acquire knowledge, we create stored categories that enable us to draw on knowledge when we experience something new. For example, when encountering an ani-mal we've never seen, we use our knowledge of an animal's characteristics to recognize whether it's a mammal or a reptile, harmless or dangerous. **[LEARNING OBJECTIVE 7.4]**

Categorizing allows us to have all of our general knowledge about dogs at our dis-posal when dealing with Rover. We don't need to discover from scratch that Rover barks, pants when he's hot, and has a stomach. These things all come "for free" once we recog-nize Rover as a dog. Of course, our categories and concepts don't apply to all real-world situations. Rover may be unable to bark because of a throat disorder. Yet most of the time, our concepts safely allow us to exert less cognitive effort over basic knowledge, freeing us up to engage in more complex reasoning and emotional processing.

We organize mental categories so that they're optimally useful to us. For example, we notice which members of a category are typical or atypical, and we use this infor-mation as a basis for building categories. When thinking about birds, for example, we rely more heavily on our knowledge of typical birds, such as robins and sparrows, than on atypical birds, such as ostriches or penguins (Smith, Shoben, & Rips, 1974). This suggests that when we acquire a category we form what is called a *prototype,* an idealized or average example that most closely resembles a typical example of the category. However, our prototypes depend on our cultural and social experience (Bailenson, Shum, Atrin, et al., 2002). Someone from Brazil or Mexico may have a dif-ferent notion than a North American of a typical fruit because the kinds of fruit people encounter in tropical climates differ from those people encounter in the Northern Hemisphere (Pinto, 1992).

Decision Making–Playing the Odds.

We often must make snap decisions with incomplete or even misleading information. When that happens, we try to calculate which of a variety of possible solutions is our best bet and then hazard an educated guess. As we learned in Chapter 2, we engage in these calculations all the time utilizing a variety of heuristics and biases to help us streamline our decision making. We may decide that the week-old milk in our refrigerator has gone bad based on its smell without tast-ing it, let alone conducting a microscopic bacterial analysis of it. We may decide that the stressed-out-looking woman with an unfriendly expression on her face isn't a good choice to approach for a donation to our local charity. These guesses may not always be right, but they're probably good bets.

Gerd Gigerenzer (2001, 2007; Gigerenzer & Goldstein, 1996) referred to this type of cognitive economy as "fast and frugal" thinking. He argued that it serves us well most of the time. In fact, in many cases, the heuristics we use are more valid than an exhaustive (and exhausting!) analysis of all potential factors.

What's considered a prototype for the fruit category differs for people from the tropics compared with North Americans.

GLOSSARY

category
collection of real or imagined objects, actions, and characteristics that share core properties

concept
the general ideas or thoughts associated with members of a category

Research by Samuel Gosling and his collaborators suggests that observers can often infer people's personality traits at better than chance levels merely by inspecting their rooms. What might you guess about the level of conscientiousness of this room's occupant?

For example, Samuel Gosling and his colleagues asked a group of untrained observers to make personality judgments about students by viewing their dorm rooms or bedrooms for a few minutes. They gave observers no instructions about what features of the room to focus on and covered all photos in the rooms so that observers couldn't determine the sex, race, or age of the rooms' occupants. Yet observers were surprisingly accurate at judging aspects of the occupants' personalities, such as their emotional stability, openness to new experiences, and conscientiousness (Gosling, Ko, Mannarelli, et al., 2002). Observers' fast and frugal processing steered them right.

These studies highlight the upsides of cognitive economy. Snap judgments and heuristics make us quick, efficient, and often accurate processors of information (Ambady & Rosenthal, 1993; Gladwell, 2005). This processing affords us some mental legroom, allowing us to engage in more complex mental tasks.

The Risks of Economizing: You Get What You Pay For. There are also significant downsides to cognitive economy (Myers, 2002; Stewart, 2009). As we've noted in earlier chapters, we need to guard against cognitive errors when drawing conclusions about behavior. In Chapters 1 and 2, we encountered several biases and heuristics that can lead us to draw faulty conclusions about scientific evidence.

For many decisions, heuristic-based errors aren't the end of the world. An error in judgment about who might donate to our charity isn't catastrophic because we can easily find other potential donors. Nevertheless, some cognitive mistakes are expensive financially, socially, and even physically. For example, tens of thousands of people stopped flying during the several months following the terrorist attacks of September 11, 2001. This response was probably a consequence of a heightened sense of fear and vulnerability stemming from the *availability heuristic* (see Chapter 2), that is, the prominence of these attacks in people's memories. Ironically, during the 3 months following September 11, more Americans who opted to travel by car instead of plane died in traffic fatalities than in the four hijacked planes combined (Gigerenzer, 2004).

Our cognitive economy can sometimes lead us to make incorrect snap judgments, such as hiring the well-dressed socially skilled applicant over the one with the most talent and experience.

Faulty conclusions based on cognitive economy can lead us to misinterpret the causes of people's behaviors and make mistaken judgments about their personalities. This fact probably helps to explain why brief open-ended interviews of people, such as college students, job applicants, and psychiatric patients, often yield inaccurate judgments of their personalities (Garb, 1998; see Chapter 12). We should listen to our first impressions but not be imprisoned by them.

PROBLEM SOLVING: MORE THINKING HURDLES

Keeping track of when heuristics are and aren't useful is challenging enough. But still other aspects of our cognitive functioning put us at a disadvantage when making decisions and solving complicated problems. **Problem solving** is generating a cognitive strategy to accomplish a goal. We often encounter four hurdles when solving problems: salience of surface similarities, mental sets, functional fixedness, and context and consequence effects. **[LEARNING OBJECTIVE 7.5]**

Salience of Surface Similarities. Salience refers to how attention-grabbing something is. We tend to focus our attention on the surface-level (superficial) properties of a problem, such as the topic of an algebra word problem, and to try to solve problems in the same way we solved problems that exhibited similar surface characteristics. When one algebra word problem calls for subtraction and another calls for division,

GLOSSARY

problem solving
generating a cognitive strategy to accomplish a goal

the fact that they both deal with trains isn't going to help us. Ignoring the surface features of a problem and focusing on the underlying reasoning needed to solve it can be challenging.

One way to combat the tendency to focus on surface properties is to practice solving multiple problems that require the same reasoning (so they should be solved the same way) but possess different surface features. Comparing the commonalities across these different problems can help us focus on the problem's structure (Loewenstein, Thompson, & Gentner, 1999; Markman & Gentner, 1993).

Mental Sets. Once we find a workable solution that's dependable, we often get stuck in that solution mode; we have trouble generating alternatives. Psychologists term this phenomenon a **mental set.** For example, when attempting to identify the topic for a term paper, we may have trouble thinking of topics that the professor hasn't already covered in class. In fact, a friend or roommate who hasn't taken the class may be able to come up with more creative ideas because our thinking has become boxed in by our experiences.

In a classic study of mental sets, participants had to solve a series of problems that required measuring out a precise amount of water by adding and subtracting water, given only three odd measuring jars (such as filling a jug with precisely 100 quarts using only a 21-quart jar, a 127-quart jar, and a 3-quart jar). Participants either solved eight problems that used the same formula ($A - B - C - C =$ Target amount) before working on a problem that used a different formula, or they solved the ninth problem without working on the first eight. Only 36 percent of participants who solved the first eight problems the same way generated the correct solution on the ninth one. In contrast, participants who solved the ninth problem first generated a correct solution 95 percent of the time (Luchins, 1946). Solving the first eight problems actually made solving the ninth more difficult, because the eight problems created a mental set from which subjects had a hard time breaking free.

WHAT DO *you* THINK?

As the vice president of an exotic foods importing business, you notice that your staff tend to negotiate one type of contract for perishable foods and a different type of contract for nonperishable foods. What can you do to encourage your staff to ignore the surface-level property of food type to arrange the most appropriate contracts?

Functional Fixedness. When we experience difficulty conceptualizing that an object typically used for one purpose can be used for another, we experience **functional fixedness** (German & Defeyter, 2000). That is, we become "fixated" on one conventional use for an object. Have you ever needed a hammer, tape, or scissors but didn't have any of these items around? What alternative solutions did you come up with? Functional fixedness can make it difficult for us to realize that we could use a shoe as a hammer, a mailing label as tape, or a key to cut a piece of string.

One famous demonstration asked participants to figure out a way to mount a candle on a wall given only a candle, book of matches, and box of tacks, as shown in **Figure 7.5** (Duncker, 1945). Can you think of how to do it? Most of us find this problem difficult because it forces us to use conventional objects in unconventional ways. In one

Figure 7.5 Functional Fixedness.
A classic demonstration of functional fixedness requires participants to figure out how to mount a candle on a wall given only a candle, book of matches, and a box of tacks (Duncker, 1945). To see the solution, see the upside-down figure at the top of page 238.

GLOSSARY

mental set
phenomenon of becoming stuck in a specific problem-solving strategy, inhibiting our ability to generate alternatives

functional fixedness
difficulty conceptualizing that an object typically used for one purpose can be used for another

Solution to Figure 7.5

study, two investigators tested individuals from a rural area of Ecuador who live in a traditional nontechnological society and consequently have few expectations about the functional roles of these objects. Even they displayed functional fixedness (German & Barrett, 2005).

Context and Consequence Effects. A problem's context often influences our problem-solving approach. Our goals, the setting, and the consequences of getting the problem right or wrong can all influence what approach we take, for better or for worse. For example, whether children and adults adopt a confirming or a disconfirming strategy when testing a hypothesis—recall from Chapter 2 that a disconfirming strategy is better—depends on the consequences. If people hold a hypothesis about what made a cake taste terrible, they'll test that hypothesis by removing the offending ingredient, a disconfirming strategy. In contrast, if they hold a hypothesis about what made a cake taste delicious, they'll test the hypothesis by keeping the ingredient in, a confirming strategy (Tschirgi, 1980).

THE SCIENTIFIC METHOD DOESN'T COME NATURALLY

Clearly scientific reasoning isn't a terribly natural or intuitive process—cognitive economizing is much more natural for us. (Cromer, 1993; Wolpert, 1993). The moral of the story isn't that we should change our ways entirely because our cognitive economy often serves us well.

Nevertheless, we need to be able to recognize situations in which we're vulnerable to faulty reasoning and think twice about our intuitions. When we hear on the news that vaccines cause autism or that watching violent TV turns entirely normal kids into violent monsters, we should stop to think about the information on which the media based these conclusions. When evaluating political candidates' extravagant promises or deciding whether that incredible deal on laptops is too good to be true, we should consider whether the information was sufficient to warrant the extreme claims. Cognitive economy has a lot going for it, but being aware of its pitfalls will make us more informed consumers of information in our everyday lives.

EXTRAORDINARY CLAIMS
Is the evidence as convincing as the claim?

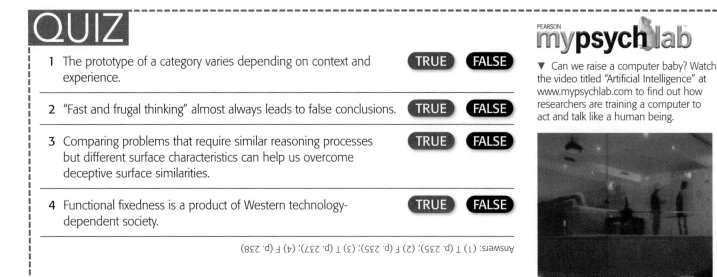

QUIZ

1 The prototype of a category varies depending on context and experience. **TRUE** **FALSE**

2 "Fast and frugal thinking" almost always leads to false conclusions. **TRUE** **FALSE**

3 Comparing problems that require similar reasoning processes but different surface characteristics can help us overcome deceptive surface similarities. **TRUE** **FALSE**

4 Functional fixedness is a product of Western technology-dependent society. **TRUE** **FALSE**

Answers: (1) T (p. 235); (2) F (p. 235); (3) T (p. 237); (4) F (p. 238)

PEARSON
mypsychlab

▼ Can we raise a computer baby? Watch the video titled "Artificial Intelligence" at www.mypsychlab.com to find out how researchers are training a computer to act and talk like a human being.

What Is Intelligence?
Definitional Confusion

We've learned about ways to improve our thinking and pitfalls that hinder thought. We all encounter challenges in thinking and reasoning. But, of course, some of us seem to think more clearly or quickly than others. In other words, some of us seem to be more intelligent than others. But what does it actually mean to be more or less intelligent? Psychologists have heavily debated the precise definition of intelligence (Sternberg, 2003b; Sternberg & Detterman, 1986).

Edwin Boring (1923) discovered an easy way around the nagging question of what intelligence is. According to *Boring's dictum,* intelligence is whatever intelligence tests measure. Yes, it's that simple. Some modern psychologists have embraced this definition, which lets us off the hook from having to figure out what intelligence is. Yet because this definition sidesteps the central question of what makes some people smarter than others—or whether some people really are smarter than others across the board—it doesn't really get us all that far. The definition of intelligence must go beyond Boring's dictum. With that point in mind, let's examine the five most influential attempts to define and understand intelligence. **[LEARNING OBJECTIVE 7.6]**

DEFINITIONS OF INTELLIGENCE

(1) **Intelligence as Sensory Capacity.** Sir Francis Galton (1822–1911) proposed that intelligence is the by-product of sensory capacity. He reasoned that most knowledge first comes through the senses, especially vision, hearing, and a good sensitivity to the difference in weight between two objects. Therefore, he assumed, people with superior sensory capacities, like better eyesight, should acquire more knowledge than other people. Yet later research showed that different measures of sensory capacities, like the ability to distinguish similar sounds from one another or similar colors from one another, are only weakly correlated with each other (Acton & Schroeder, 2001). Nor are measures of sensory ability highly correlated with assessments of overall intelligence (Li, Jordanova, & Lindenberger, 1998). These findings falsify Galton's claim that intelligence equals sensory ability. Sensory ability and intelligence clearly aren't identical.

(2) **Intelligence as Abstract Thinking.** Early in the last century, the French government wanted to find a way to identify children in need of special educational assistance. In 1904, Alfred Binet (pronounced "Bee-NAY") and Henri Simon (pronounced "See-MOAN") developed a psychological test designed to separate "slower" learners from other children without having to rely on the subjective judgments of teachers. Binet and Simon developed what most psychologists today regard as the first **intelligence test,** a diagnostic tool designed to measure overall thinking ability. Binet and Simon's items were remarkably diverse in content, ranging from drawing pictures to drawing analogies, but they had one thing in common: *higher mental processes.* These processes included reasoning, understanding, and judgment (Siegler, 1992). Most experts today agree that whatever intelligence is, it has something to do with **abstract thinking:** the capacity to understand hypothetical concepts, rather than concepts in the here-and-now (Gottfredson, 1997; Sternberg, 2003b).

(3) **That Controversial Little Letter: *g.*** Even though Binet and Simon's items differed enormously in content, the correlations among them were all positive: People who got one item correct were more likely than chance to get the others correct. The phenomenon of positive correlations among intelligence test items caught the attention of psychologist Charles Spearman (1927). To account for these correlations, Spearman hypothesized the

FALSIFIABILITY
Can the claim be disproved?

GLOSSARY

intelligence test
diagnostic tool designed to measure overall thinking ability

abstract thinking
capacity to understand hypothetical concepts

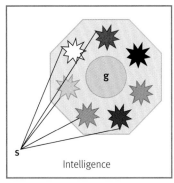

Figure 7.6 Schematic of Spearman's Model of *g*. Spearman's model of intelligence posits the existence of *g* (general intelligence) along with specific factors (*s*).

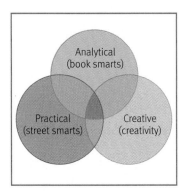

Figure 7.8 Sternberg's Triarchic Model of Intelligence. Sternberg's model proposes three kinds of intelligence: analytical, practical, and creative.

GLOSSARY

***g* (general intelligence)**
hypothetical factor that accounts for overall differences in intellect among people

FALSIFIABILITY
Can the claim be disproved?

***s* (specific abilities)**
particular ability levels in a narrow domain

fluid intelligence
capacity to learn new ways of solving problems

crystallized intelligence
accumulated knowledge of the world acquired over time

multiple intelligences
idea that people vary in their ability levels across different domains of intellectual skill

triarchic model
model of intelligence proposed by Robert Sternberg positing three distinct types of intelligences: analytical, practical, and creative

existence of a single factor across all these aspects—***g***, or **general intelligence**—that accounted for the overall differences in intellect among people. All intelligence test items are positively correlated, he thought, because they reflect the influence of overall intelligence. Spearman wasn't sure what produces individual differences in *g*, although he speculated that it corresponds to the strength of our mental engines. Some people have more "powerful"—more effective and efficient—brains than others. They have more *g*. Spearman didn't believe that *g* tells the whole story about intelligence. For every intelligence test item, Spearman (1927) also proposed the existence of a factor called ***s***, or **specific abilities,** that is unique to each item (see **Figure 7.6**) such as quantitative abilities, spatial reasoning, or language.

(4) **Fluid versus Crystallized Intelligence.** Raymond Cattell and John Horn distinguished fluid from crystallized intelligence. **Fluid intelligence** refers to the capacity to learn new ways of solving problems, such as solving a puzzle we've never seen or trying to operate a motorcycle for the first time. In contrast, **crystallized intelligence** refers to the accumulated knowledge of the world we acquire over time (Cattell, 1971; Horn, 1994). We rely on our crystallized intelligence to answer questions such as "What's the capital of Italy?" or "How many justices sit on the U.S. Supreme Court?" Most modern researchers view fluid and crystallized intelligence as "facets" or more specific aspects of *g* (Messick, 1992).

(5) **Multiple Intelligences.** Up to this point, we've been talking about "intelligence" as though it were one and only one overarching intellectual ability. But since at least the 1930s, some psychologists have argued for the existence of **multiple intelligences:** different domains of intellectual skill (Thurstone, 1938). According to them, there are many ways of being smart (Guilford, 1967). Howard Gardner's (1983, 1999) theory of multiple intelligences proposes that there are numerous "frames of mind," or different ways of thinking about the world. Each frame of mind is a different and fully independent intelligence in its own right. Gardner (1999) proposed eight different intelligences ranging from linguistic and spatial to musical and interpersonal, as described in **Figure 7.7** on the facing page. He's also tentatively proposed the existence of a ninth intelligence, called *existential* intelligence: the ability to grasp deep philosophical ideas, like the meaning of life.

The scientific reaction to Gardner's model has been mixed. It's not clear why certain mental abilities (such as naturalistic and intrapersonal abilities) but not others (such as humor or romantic abilities) qualify as intelligences. It's also not clear that all of Gardner's "intelligences" are genuinely related to intelligence. For example, bodily-kinesthetic intelligence may depend more heavily on nonmental abilities (Scarr, 1985; Sternberg, 1988b). Moreover, Gardner hasn't developed formal tests to measure the independence of these intelligences, so his model is virtually impossible to falsify (Klein, 1998).

Like Gardner, Robert Sternberg has argued that there's more to intelligence than *g*. Sternberg's (1983, 1988b) **triarchic model** posits the existence of three largely distinct intelligences: analytical, practical, and creative intelligence (see **Figure 7.8**). *Analytical intelligence* is the ability to reason logically: "book smarts." It's the kind of intelligence we need to do well on traditional intelligence tests and standardized exams. *Practical intelligence* is also called "tacit intelligence": the ability to solve real-world problems, especially those involving other people. This form of intelligence is akin to "street smarts." *Creative intelligence* is our ability to come up with novel and effective answers to questions. It's the kind of intelligence we need to find new and effective solutions to problems (Sternberg & Wagner, 1993; Sternberg, Wagner, Williams, et al., 1995). Our intuitions tell us that these three types of intellects don't always go hand-in-hand. Yet the concept of multiple intelligences remains controversial. Unquestionably, we all possess different intellectual strengths and weaknesses, but it's not clear that they're as independent of each other as Gardner and Sternberg assert.

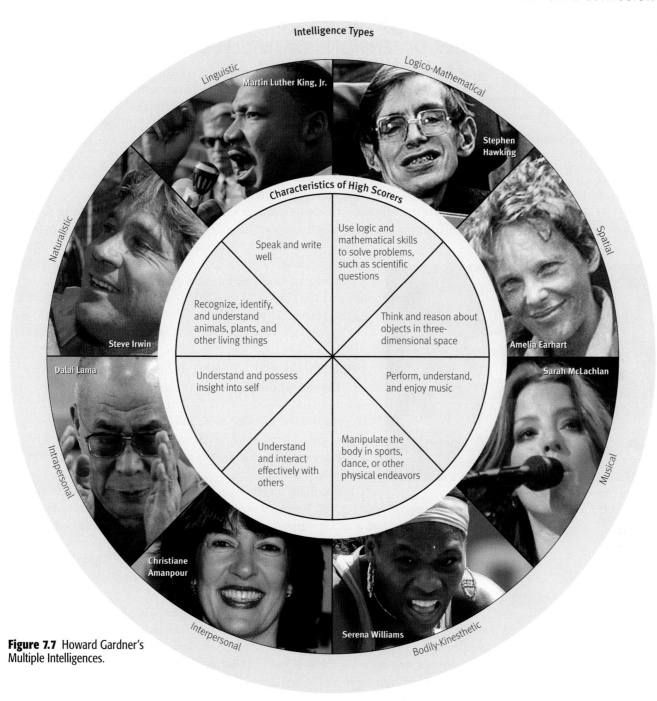

Figure 7.7 Howard Gardner's Multiple Intelligences.

WHAT DO *you* THINK?

You are a peer tutor to a varsity athlete who is struggling with his grades but is also a gifted piano player. He tells you he realizes he's just not smart. How might you use the concept of multiple intelligences to make him feel better about himself?

MYTH: Most creative ideas arrive in sudden flashes of insight.

REALITY: Studies of brain activity indicate that well before people report a sudden creative answer to a problem, brain areas involved in problem solving (particularly those in the frontal and temporal lobes) have already been active (Kounios et al., 2006).

THE REST OF THE STORY: OTHER DIMENSIONS OF INTELLECT

Do intelligent people always behave intelligently? If you have any doubt, just look at the string of high-profile corporate scandals over the past 10 years, in which well-educated and highly intelligent CEOs got caught red-handed doing remarkably dumb things. Let's consider two other psychological variables that can make us act intelligently—and not so intelligently.

Creativity. Psychologists have found creativity difficult to define. Nevertheless, most psychologists agree that creative accomplishments consist of two features: They are *novel* and *successful*. Psychologists often measure creativity using tests of **divergent thinking** (Guilford, 1967; Razoumnikova, 2000): the capacity to generate many different solutions to problems. It's likely, though, that tests of divergent thinking don't capture everything about creativity. To be creative, we also need to be good at **convergent thinking:** the capacity to find the single best answer to a problem (Bink & Marsh, 2000). As two-time Nobel Prize winner Linus Pauling said, to be creative we need to first come up with lots of ideas, and then toss out all the bad ones. **[LEARNING OBJECTIVE 7.7]**

Frank Lloyd Wright's architectural masterpiece, "Fallingwater," a house built on top of a water fall is a prime example of a remarkable creative achievement.

Emotional Intelligence: Is EQ as Important as IQ?

Emotional intelligence is the ability to understand our emotions and those of others, and to apply this information to our everyday lives (Goleman, 1995; Salovey & Mayer, 1990). Most proponents of emotional intelligence maintain that this ability is just as important as traditional intelligence for effective functioning in the world.

Some items on emotional intelligence tests ask subjects to report how good they are at handling their emotions under stress. Others ask subjects to identify which emotion a face is expressing. Still others ask subjects to predict what emotion a person will experience in a given situation, like meeting future in-laws for the first time or being asked an embarrassing question during a job interview (**Figure 7.9**). Many American companies now provide their employees and bosses with formal training for boosting their emotional intelligence (Locke, 2005).

The concept of emotional intelligence has its critics. In particular, it's not clear that this concept measures much beyond personality (Matthews, Zeidner, & Roberts, 2002). Most measures of emotional intelligence assess personality traits, such as extraversion, agreeableness, and openness to experience, at least as much they do intelligence (Conte, 2005). Moreover, emotional intelligence doesn't predict job performance any better than measures of general intelligence (Van Rooy & Viswesvaran, 2004). Nor is there much evidence that different measures of emotional intelligence are highly correlated (Conte, 2005).

GLOSSARY

divergent thinking
capacity to generate many different solutions to a problem

convergent thinking
capacity to generate the single best solution to a problem

emotional intelligence
ability to understand our own emotions and those of others, and to apply this information to our daily lives

---

When Anne's friend Maggie was feeling depressed over a recent break-up with her boyfriend, Anne took several hours off from studying for a big test to drive to Maggie's apartment and comfort her. Two weeks later, Anne was upset over an argument with her sister, and phoned Maggie to talk about it. Maggie told Anne she was busy packing for an upcoming trip and asked if they could put off talking until the following week. Anne felt _____. (Select the best choice.)

(a) sad   (b) nervous   (c) embarrassed   (d) resentful   (e) envious

Figure 7.9 **Item Similar to That on a Test of Emotional Intelligence.** How would you do on a test of emotional intelligence? Try your hand at this item, modeled after those on actual emotional intelligence measures. The correct answer is upside-down at the bottom of the next page.

The most parsimonious hypothesis is that emotional intelligence isn't anything new and that it's instead a mixture of personality traits that psychologists have studied for decades.

OCCAM'S RAZOR
Does a simpler explanation fit the data just as well?

BIOLOGICAL BASES OF INTELLIGENCE

One popular notion about intelligence is that it's related positively to brain size. We speak of smart people as "brainy." When researchers have asked people to draw pictures of aliens—who supposedly have high levels of extraterrestrial "intelligence"—they've found that depictions of these otherworldly creatures share surprisingly similar features, like big heads, big eyes, and tiny bodies (Blackmore, 1998). But to what extent is intelligence actually related to the brain's size and efficiency? Several studies demonstrate that brain volume, as measured by structural MRI scans (see Chapter 3), correlates positively— between .3 and .4—with measured intelligence (McDaniel, 2005; Willerman et al., 1991). **[LEARNING OBJECTIVE 7.8]** But we don't know whether these findings reflect a direct causal association. Perhaps higher intelligence leads to bigger brains. Or perhaps some third variable, like better nutrition before or shortly after birth, leads to both. Recent studies on brain development suggest that highly intelligent (children in the top 10 percent) 7-year-olds have a *thinner* cerebral cortex than other children of the same age. The cortexes of these children then thicken rapidly, peaking at about age 12 (Shaw et al., 2006). This may indicate that, like fine wines, intelligent brains take longer to mature than others.

CORRELATION vs. CAUSATION
Can we be sure that A causes B?

Functional brain imaging studies and laboratory studies of information processing indicate that subjects with higher levels of intelligence exhibit less brain activity while performing cognitive tasks than subjects with lower levels of intelligence (Haier et al., 1992). It seems that the brains of the more intelligent students were especially efficient. Admittedly, not all researchers have replicated this finding (Fidelman, 1993), but it raises the possibility that intelligence in part reflects efficiency of mental processing.

REPLICABILITY
Can the results be duplicated in other studies?

Psychologists have also studied the relation of intelligence to *reaction time,* or the speed of responding to a stimulus (Jensen, 2006). The results of numerous studies indicate that measured intelligence correlates negatively (about −.3 to −.4) with reaction times (Deary, Der, & Ford, 2001; Detterman, 1987): People with higher intelligence react more quickly (have a shorter reaction time) than other people.

Finally, intelligence bears an intimate connection to memory capacity. Many researchers have examined the relation of tasks that assess "working memory" to intelligence. As we learned in Chapter 6, this type of memory is closely related to short-term memory. Scores on working memory tasks (like repeating back a string of numbers) are moderately correlated (about .5) with scores on intelligence tests (Ackerman, Beier, & Boyle, 2005; Engle, 2002; Kane, Hambrick, & Conway, 2005).

So where in the brain is intelligence located? It's unlikely that a specific region of the brain is entirely responsible for intelligence. Yet intelligence is more localized to certain areas of the cortex than others. One group of investigators administered a number of reasoning tasks that are highly "*g*-loaded," meaning they're substantially related to general intelligence (see **Figure 7.10**). They found that these tasks all activated the same area: the prefrontal cortex (Duncan et al., 2000). As we saw in Chapter 3, the prefrontal cortex is intimately involved in planning and impulse control, as well as in short-term memory.

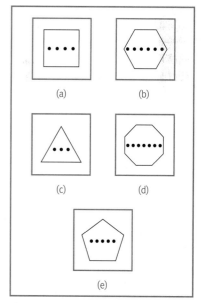

Figure 7.10 Sample Task (a Highly *g*-Loaded Item). This sample item is similar to items that researchers have identified as highly "*g*-loaded," meaning that it's a good predictor of general intelligence. In this item, one of the five choices differs from the others. Can you figure out which one it is? (The answer is printed upside down on the next page)

Pulling It All Together. How can we make sense of all of these findings? If there's one central theme, it's that intelligence is related to efficiency or speed of information processing (Vernon, 1987). So common sense may be partly correct: People who are quick thinkers tend to be especially intelligent. Still, the associations are far less than a perfect correlation of 1.0, which tells us that intelligence is more than quickness of thinking.

Answer to Figure 7.9: d

QUIZ

1 Almost all items on modern intelligence tests tend to be positively correlated with each other. **TRUE** **FALSE**

2 Highly creative people display highly divergent thinking and little convergent thinking. **TRUE** **FALSE**

3 Within humans, brain size tends to be moderately positively correlated with measured intelligence. **TRUE** **FALSE**

4 Intelligence is unrelated to reaction time. **TRUE** **FALSE**

Answers: (1) T (p. 240); (2) F (p. 242); (3) T (p. 243); (4) F (p. 243)

PEARSON
mypsychlab

▼ Can research on intelligence be conducted anywhere? Watch the video titled "Practical Intelligence: Robert Sternberg" at www.mypsychlab.com to find out.

Intelligence Testing: The Good, the Bad, and the Ugly

When Binet and Simon created the first intelligence test more than a century ago, they had no inkling that they'd alter the landscape of psychology. Yet their invention has changed how we select people for schools, jobs, and the military; it's changed schooling and social policies; and it's changed how we think about ourselves. The history of intelligence testing begins where Binet and Simon left off.

TWO MORE CONTROVERSIAL LETTERS: *IQ*

Shortly before World War I, German psychologist Wilhelm Stern (1912) invented the formula for the **intelligence quotient,** which will forever be known by two letters: **IQ.** Stern's formula for computing IQ was simple: Divide *mental age* by *chronological age* and multiply the resulting number by 100. **Mental age** is the age corresponding to the average person's performance on an intelligence test. A girl who takes an IQ test and does as well as the average 6-year-old has a mental age of 6, regardless of her actual age. Her chronological age is nothing more than her actual age. So, if a 10-year-old child does as well on an IQ test as the average 8-year-old, his IQ according to Stern's formula would be 80 (a mental age of 8 divided by a chronological age of 10, multiplied by 100). Conversely, if an 8-year-old child does as well on an IQ test as the average 10-year-old, his IQ according to Stern's formula would be 125 (a mental age of 10 divided by a chronological age of 8 multiplied by 100).

For children and young adolescents, this formula does a respectable job of estimating intelligence. But Stern's formula contains a critical flaw. Mental age scores increase progressively in childhood, but start to level out at around age 16 (Eysenck, 1994). Once we hit 16 or so, our performance on IQ test items doesn't increase by much. Because our mental age levels off but our chronological age increases with time, Stern's formula would result in everyone's IQ getting lower and lower as he or she gets older. That's why almost all modern intelligence researchers rely on a statistic called **deviation IQ** when

Answer to Figure 7.10: d

GLOSSARY

intelligence quotient (IQ)
systematic means of quantifying differences among people in their intelligence

mental age
age corresponding to the average individual's performance on an intelligence test

deviation IQ
expression of a person's IQ relative to his or her same-aged peers

computing IQ for adults (Wechsler, 1939). Basically, the deviation IQ expresses each person's IQ relative to his or her same-aged peers. **[LEARNING OBJECTIVE 7.9]** An IQ of 100, which is average, means that a person's IQ is exactly typical of people of his age. An IQ of 80 is a standard amount below average for any age group, and an IQ of 120 is the same amount above. In this way, the deviation IQ gets rid of the problem posed by Stern's formula because it doesn't result in IQ decreasing after age 16.

THE EUGENICS MOVEMENT: MISUSES AND ABUSES OF IQ TESTING

Only a few years after Binet and Simon developed their intelligence test, IQ testing became a booming business in the United States. It was no longer merely a vehicle for targeting schoolchildren in need of special help but a means of identifying adults deemed intellectually inferior.

The IQ testing movement quickly spiraled out of control. Moreover, many psychologists adapted childhood tests for use in testing adults, without fully understanding how the IQ scores applied to adults (Kevles, 1985). As a consequence, legions of adults given these tests, including new immigrants to the United States, prison inmates, and delinquents, were inappropriately classified as having mental retardation. Alarm among American citizens regarding the reports of low IQs among many immigrants and even many Americans led to a social movement called **eugenics** (meaning "good genes"). Eugenics was the effort to improve a population's "genetic stock" by encouraging people with "good genes" to reproduce (*positive eugenics*) and by discouraging people with "bad genes" from reproducing (*negative eugenics*).

Eugenics was particularly popular in the United States from 1910 to 1930. Dozens of universities, among them Harvard, Cornell, Columbia, and Brown, offered courses in eugenics to approximately 20,000 undergraduates (Selden, 1999). Most high school and college biology texts presented eugenics as a scientific enterprise. Eugenics came to be associated with at least two disturbing practices. First, beginning in the 1920s, the U.S. Congress passed laws designed to restrict immigration from other countries supposedly marked by low intelligence, especially those in eastern and southern Europe (Gould, 1981). **[LEARNING OBJECTIVE 7.10]** Second, beginning in 1907, 33 U.S. states passed laws requiring the sterilization of low-IQ individuals. Some of the surgeons who performed these sterilizations tricked their patients into believing they were undergoing emergency appendectomies (removal of their appendices) (Leslie, 2000). The assumption behind mandatory sterilization was that IQ was genetically influenced, so preventing low-IQ individuals from reproducing would halt the supposed deterioration of the population's intelligence. When all was said and done, about 66,000 North Americans, many of them African Americans and other poor minorities, underwent forced sterilizations (Reynolds, 2003). Fortunately, the practice of sterilization slowed in the 1940s and had subsided almost completely by the early 1960s, although involuntary sterilization laws remained on the books in America for years. Virginia became the last state to repeal them in 1974.

Fact -OID The popularity of the eugenics movement of the early twentieth century contributed to the popularity of the name "Eugene," which became one of the most frequently used boys' names in the United States at that time.

Addie Lee Anderson, 87, shown August 8, 2006, at her home in Fayetteville, North Carolina, was involuntarily sterilized in 1950 by the Eugenics Board of North Carolina after the birth of her last child.

⌐**WHAT DO** *you* **THINK** *?*

Your friend says she doesn't want to have children. You think she should because her kids would be really smart, as she is. She accuses you of advocating a eugenics plan requiring IQ tests before people are permitted to have babies. How would you explain that your statement doesn't mean you want to prevent certain people from becoming parents?

GLOSSARY

eugenics
movement in the early twentieth century to improve a population's genetic stock by encouraging those with good genes to reproduce, preventing those with bad genes from reproducing, or both

IQ TESTING TODAY

Today, the IQ test stands as one of psychology's best-known, yet most controversial, accomplishments. In 1989, the American Academy for the Advancement of Science listed the IQ test as one of the 20 greatest scientific achievements of the twentieth century (Henshaw, 2006). Although psychologists have developed dozens of IQ tests, a mere handful have come to dominate the modern testing scene. We'll discuss these tests next.

Commonly Used Adult IQ Tests. The IQ test administered most widely to assess intelligence in adults is the **Wechsler Adult Intelligence Scale,** or **WAIS** (see **Figure 7.11** as an example) (Watkins, Campbell, Nieberding, et al., 1995), now in its third version (the WAIS-III; Wechsler, 1997). Ironically, David Wechsler, a psychologist who developed this test, was a Romanian immigrant to the United States who was among those classified as feebleminded by early, flawed IQ tests. The WAIS-III consists of 14 "subtests," or specific tasks, designed to assess mental abilities such as vocabulary, arithmetic, spatial ability, reasoning about proverbs, and general knowledge about the world. We can find sample items from 11 of the 14 subtests in Figure 7.11. The WAIS-III yields three major scores: (1) an overall IQ score, (2) a verbal IQ score, and (3) a performance (nonverbal) IQ score. Verbal IQ relates primarily to crystallized intelligence, and performance IQ relates primarily to fluid intelligence.

Commonly Used Childhood IQ Tests. Two widely used IQ tests for children are the Wechsler Intelligence Scale for Children (WISC) used with older children and adolescents and the Wechsler Primary and Preschool Scale of Intelligence (WPPSI; pronounced "WHIP-see"), used with children aged 2½ to 7 years, both also in their third editions. Both measures are versions of the WAIS adapted for children (Kaplan & Saccuzzo, 2005).

Shortly after Binet and Simon introduced their test to France, Lewis Terman of Stanford University developed a modified and translated version called the **Stanford-Binet IQ test,** which psychologists still use today. The Stanford-Binet consists of a wide variety of tasks like those Binet and Simon used, such as tests of children's vocabulary, memory for pictures, naming of familiar objects, repeating sentences, and following commands.

Culture-Fair IQ Tests. One major criticism of IQ tests is that they rely heavily on language. Test takers who aren't fluent in the native language may do poorly on IQ tests largely because they don't comprehend the test instructions or the questions themselves. Moreover, cultural factors can affect people's familiarity with test materials, and in turn their performance on intellectual tasks (Sonke et al., 2008; van de Vijver, 2008). In one study, a researcher asked schoolchildren in England and Zambia (a country in southern Africa) to reproduce a series of visual patterns using both paper and pencil—a medium with which British children tend to be familiar—and wire—a medium with which Zambian children tend to be more familiar. The British children did better than the Zambian children when using paper and pencil, but the Zambian children did better than the British children when using wire (Serpell, 1979).

Psychologists have developed a variety of **culture-fair IQ tests,** which consist of abstract reasoning items that don't depend on language (Cattell, 1949). Presumably these tests are less influenced by cultural differences than standard IQ tests are. Perhaps the best-known culture-fair test is Raven's Progressive Matrices, used widely in Great Britain as a measure of intelligence (Raven, Raven, & Court, 1998). As **Figure 7.12** shows, this test requires examinees to pick out the final geometrical pattern in a sequence (the matrices are "progressive" because they start off easy and become increasingly difficult). Raven's Progressive Matrices is an excellent measure of g (Neisser et al., 1996).

GLOSSARY

Wechsler Adult Intelligence Scale (WAIS)
most widely used intelligence test for adults today, consisting of 14 subtests to assess different types of mental abilities

Stanford-Binet IQ test
intelligence test based on the measure developed by Binet and Simon, adapted by Lewis Terman of Stanford University

culture-fair IQ tests
abstract reasoning items that don't depend on language and are often believed to be less influenced by cultural factors than other IQ tests

Wechsler Adult Intelligence Scale (WAIS) Sample Items*		
Test	**Description**	**Example**
Verbal Scale		
Information	Taps general range of information	On which continent is France?
Comprehension	Tests understanding of social conventions and ability to evaluate past experience	Why do people need birth certificates?
Arithmetic	Tests arithmetic reasoning through verbal problems	How many hours will it take to drive 150 miles at 50 miles per hour?
Similarities	Asks in what way certain objects or concepts are similar; measures abstract thinking	How are a calculator and a typewriter alike?
Digit span	Tests attention and rote memory by orally presenting series of digits to be repeated forward or backward	Repeat the following numbers backward: 2 4 3 5 1 8 6
Vocabulary	Tests ability to define increasingly difficult words	What does *repudiate* mean?
Performance Scale		
Digit symbol	Tests speed of learning through timed coding tasks in which numbers must be associated with marks of various shapes	Shown: / Fill in:
Picture completion	Tests visual alertness and visual memory through presentation of an incompletely drawn figure; the missing part must be discovered and named	Tell me what is missing:
Block design	Tests ability to perceive and analyze patterns presenting designs that must be copied with blocks	Assemble blocks to match this design:
Picture arrangement	Tests understanding of social situations through a series of comic-strip-type pictures that must be arranged in the right sequence to tell a story	Put these pictures in the right order:
Object assembly	Tests ability to deal with part/whole relationships by presenting puzzle pieces that must be assembled to form a complete object	Assemble the pieces into a complete object:

Figure 7.11 **Sample Items from WAIS.** Eleven of 14 subtests of the WAIS-III, along with items similar to those on the test.
Note: For copyright reasons, we can't present the items on the actual test. (*Source:* NCS Pearson, Inc.)

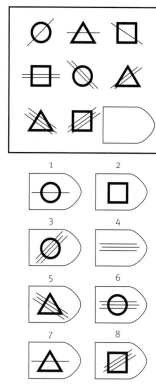

Figure 7.12 Item Similar to That on Raven's Progressive Matrices. An item similar to those in the *Raven's Progressive Matrices—Advanced Progressive Matrices.* The answer is positioned upside down at the bottom of this page. (*Source:* NCS Pearson, Inc., 1998)

RELIABILITY OF IQ SCORES: IS IQ FOREVER?

We often think of people's IQ scores in much the same way we think of their Social Security numbers: as sticking with them for life. Joe's a 116, Maria a 130, and Bill a 97. Yet IQ scores almost never remain exactly the same over time; in fact, they occasionally shift within the same person by as much as 10 points or more over a matter of months.

Still, IQ scores usually remain reasonably stable in adulthood. Even across long stretches of time, IQ scores tend to be reasonably stable (Deary et al., 2000). There's a key exception, though. Prior to age 2 or 3, IQ tests aren't stable over time. In fact, IQ mea-

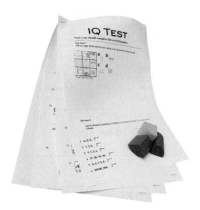

We can find dozens of informal "Test Yourself" IQ tests on the Internet, in magazines, or in self-help books. Most of these tests haven't been validated, so we shouldn't put much stock in the IQ scores they yield.

Reading Confusion Into Drug Warnings
When researchers asked consumers to interpret prescription warning stickers, these are among the responses they gave:

DO NOT CHEW OR CRUSH. SWALLOW WHOLE.
"Chew pill and crush before swallowing."
"Chew it up so it will dissolve, don't swallow whole or you might choke."

FOR EXTERNAL USE ONLY
"Use extreme caution in how you take it."
"Medicine will make you feel dizzy."
"Take only if you need it."

YOU SHOULD **AVOID** PROLONGED OR EXCESSIVE EXPOSURE TO DIRECT AND/OR ARTIFICIAL **SUNLIGHT** WHILE TAKING THIS MEDICATION.
"Don't take medicine if you've been in the sunlight too long."
"Don't leave medicine in the sun."

Low levels of health literacy, which are associated with IQ, can lead to dangerous misunderstandings of medication instructions (Davis et al., 2006). (*Source:* Franklin, 2005)

RULING OUT RIVAL HYPOTHESES
Have important alternative explanations for the findings been excluded?

GLOSSARY

bell curve
distribution of scores in which the bulk of the scores fall toward the middle, with progressively fewer scores toward the "tails" or extremes

sured in the first 6 months of life correlates just about zero with adult IQ (Brody, 1992). Nor do IQ scores obtained in the first few years of life do a good job of forecasting outcomes, unless they're extremely low, such as under 50; such scores tend to be predictive of later mental retardation.

VALIDITY OF IQ SCORES: PREDICTING LIFE OUTCOMES

Whatever we think of IQ tests, there's little question that they're valid for at least some purposes. As we learned in Chapter 2, *validity* refers to the extent to which a test measures what it purports to measure. One important indicator of a test's validity is its capacity to forecast future outcomes (or what psychologists call "predictive" validity).

IQ scores do a good job of predicting academic success; they correlate about .5 with grades in high school and college (Neisser et al., 1996). Still, because this correlation is considerably lower than 1.0, it tells us there's more to school success than IQ. Motivation, intellectual curiosity, and effort also play crucial roles.

IQ scores also predict performance across a wide variety of occupations, with the average correlation again being about .5 (Ones, Viswesvaran, & Dilchert, 2005). By comparison, the correlation between ratings of how well people do in job interviews and job performance is only about .15, which is ironic given that many employers place heavier weight on interviews than on IQ when selecting job applicants (Hunter & Hunter, 1984). The correlation between IQ and job performance is higher in more mentally demanding occupations, such as physician or lawyer, than in less mentally demanding occupations, like clerk or newspaper delivery person (Salgado et al., 2003).

IQ also predicts a variety of important real-world behaviors outside the classroom and workplace. For example, IQ is associated with health-related outcomes, including sickness and car accidents (Gottfredson, 2004; Lubinski & Humphreys, 1992). At least some of the negative correlation between IQ and illness may be attributable to *health literacy*, the ability to understand health-related information, such as instructions from doctors or on drug labels. People with low health literacy may have difficulty maintaining good health behaviors, such as getting enough exercise, eating the right foods, or taking the right dosage of their medications. IQ is also associated with criminal tendencies: The IQs of delinquent adolescents are about 7 points lower than those of other adolescents (Wilson & Herrnstein, 1985).

But there's a potential confound here (see Chapter 2). IQ is negatively associated with social-economic class, as poorer people tend to have lower IQs. So poverty, rather than IQ, may explain at least some of the associations we've discussed. Researchers have tried to address this rival hypothesis by determining whether the correlations hold up even when accounting for income level. In most cases, including health outcomes and crime, they do (Herrnstein & Murray, 1994; Neisser et al., 1996).

A TALE OF TWO TAILS: FROM MENTAL RETARDATION TO GENIUS

Within a population, IQ scores are distributed in a bell shape across the range of possible IQ scores. In a **bell curve** distribution, the bulk of the scores fall toward the middle, with progressively fewer scores toward the "tails" or extremes, forming the shape of a bell.

Figure 7.13 shows that the bell curve fits the distribution of IQ scores in the population fairly well. The bulk of scores fall in the broad middle of the distribution; about 95 percent of people have IQs between 70 and 130.

Let's now look at what we know about the small percentage of people who are in the two tails of the IQ score distribution: mental retardation and genius.

Mental Retardation.

Psychologists define **mental retardation** by three criteria, all of which must be present: (1) onset prior to adulthood, (2) IQ below approximately 70, and (3) inadequate adaptive functioning, as assessed by difficulties with dressing and feeding oneself, communicating with others, and other basic life skills (Greenspan & Switzky, 2003). The adaptive functioning criterion largely explains why about two-thirds of children with mental retardation lose this diagnosis in adulthood (Grossman, 1983); as individuals acquire life-functioning skills, they no longer qualify for this diagnosis.

About 1 percent of persons in the United States, most of them males, fulfill the criteria for mental retardation (American Psychiatric Association, 2000). The current system of psychiatric diagnosis classifies mental retardation into four categories: mild (once called "educable"), moderate (once called "trainable"), severe, and profound. Contrary to popular conception, most individuals with mental retardation—at least 85 percent—fall into the "mild" category. In most cases, children with mild retardation can be integrated or *mainstreamed* into classrooms along with typically developing individuals. Still, the term "mild mental retardation" is misleading, because individuals in this category still have significant deficits in adaptive functioning.

There are at least 200 different causes of mental retardation. Two of the most common genetic conditions associated with mental retardation are fragile X syndrome, which is produced by a mutation on the X chromosome; and Down syndrome, which is the result of an extra copy of chromosome 21. Most children with Down syndrome have either mild or moderate retardation.

Societal attitudes toward individuals with mental retardation have improved, and many with retardation are able to live productive and semi-independent lives. The Americans with Disabilities Act (ADA), passed in 1990, outlawed job and educational discrimination on the basis of mental and physical disabilities, and the Individuals with Disabilities Education Act (IDEA), passed in 1996, provided federal aid to states and local educational districts for accommodations to youth with mental and physical disabilities.

Genius and Exceptional Intelligence.

Let's now turn to the opposite tail of the bell curve, those with scores in the top few percent of the IQ range. A large proportion of individuals with IQs at or near this range populate certain occupations, such as doctors, lawyers, engineers, and college professors (Herrnstein & Murray, 1994). Yet we know relatively little about the psychological characteristics of individuals with high IQs. Several research studies offer tantalizing clues.

In the 1920s, Lewis Terman and his colleagues (Terman & Oden, 1959) initiated one of the classic studies of intellectually gifted individuals. He tracked these individuals, known affectionately as "Terman's Termites," for several decades. Although Terman's study was flawed, in part because he didn't recruit a control group of individuals with average or low IQs, it refuted three common misconceptions regarding people with high IQs, depicted in **Table 7.2** on page 250.

What's the recipe for creating a genius? Genetic factors probably play a significant role. Still, becoming a genius in one's chosen field takes many years of hard work. The best predictor of exceptional career success in violin, piano, ballet, chess, and sports is the sheer amount of time we spend in practice. For example, the most talented musicians practice twice as much as the less talented ones (Ericsson, Krampe, & Tesch-Römer, 1993). Of course, the causal arrow here isn't clear. Greater amounts of practice could be causing greater success, or greater levels of initial talent could be causing greater amounts of practice.

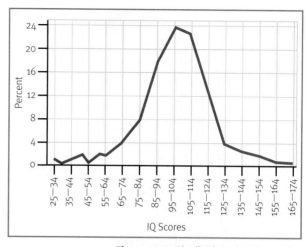

Figure 7.13 Distribution of IQ Scores in the General Population. The bell curve roughly approximates the distribution of IQ scores in the general population.

Most individuals with Down syndrome have mild or moderate mental retardation. Nevertheless, many have been successfully mainstreamed into traditional classrooms.

GLOSSARY

mental retardation
condition characterized by an onset prior to adulthood, an IQ below about 70, and an inability to engage in adequate daily functioning

CORRELATION vs. CAUSATION
Can we be sure that A causes B?

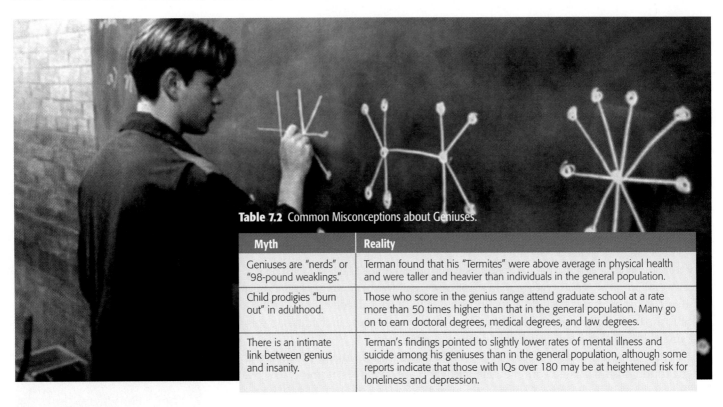

Table 7.2 Common Misconceptions about Geniuses.

Myth	Reality
Geniuses are "nerds" or "98-pound weaklings."	Terman found that his "Termites" were above average in physical health and were taller and heavier than individuals in the general population.
Child prodigies "burn out" in adulthood.	Those who score in the genius range attend graduate school at a rate more than 50 times higher than that in the general population. Many go on to earn doctoral degrees, medical degrees, and law degrees.
There is an intimate link between genius and insanity.	Terman's findings pointed to slightly lower rates of mental illness and suicide among his geniuses than in the general population, although some reports indicate that those with IQs over 180 may be at heightened risk for loneliness and depression.

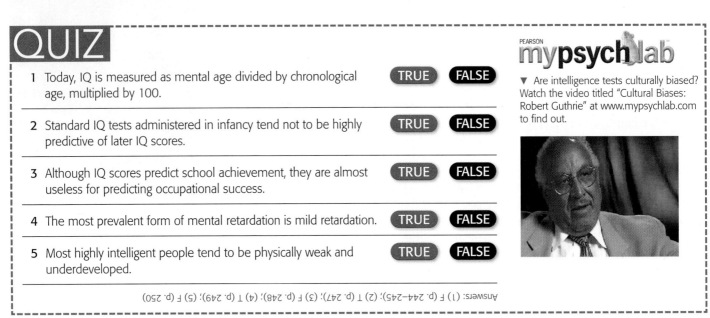

QUIZ

1 Today, IQ is measured as mental age divided by chronological age, multiplied by 100. **TRUE** **FALSE**

2 Standard IQ tests administered in infancy tend not to be highly predictive of later IQ scores. **TRUE** **FALSE**

3 Although IQ scores predict school achievement, they are almost useless for predicting occupational success. **TRUE** **FALSE**

4 The most prevalent form of mental retardation is mild retardation. **TRUE** **FALSE**

5 Most highly intelligent people tend to be physically weak and underdeveloped. **TRUE** **FALSE**

PEARSON
mypsychlab

▼ Are intelligence tests culturally biased? Watch the video titled "Cultural Biases: Robert Guthrie" at www.mypsychlab.com to find out.

Answers: (1) F (p. 244–245); (2) T (p. 247); (3) F (p. 248); (4) T (p. 249); (5) F (p. 250)

Individual and Group Differences in IQ

Up to this point, we've talked at length about what intelligence is and how we measure it. But we've said little about what factors contribute to differences in intelligence across individuals. Fortunately, over the past few decades, psychologists have obtained a much better handle on the factors that contribute to IQ. As we'll discover, however, significant flash points of controversy remain.

EXPLORING GENETIC AND ENVIRONMENTAL INFLUENCES ON IQ

Both genetic and environmental factors contribute to how individuals perform on IQ tests. **[LEARNING OBJECTIVE 7.11]** Evidence consistent with genetic influences comes from studies of the degree to which IQ runs in families. For example, the correlation of IQ for brothers and sisters raised in the same family is about .5, whereas for cousins it's about .15 (Bouchard & McGue, 1981). However, this type of study doesn't allow us to distinguish the effects of genes from those of the environment. That's because individuals in these families share both genes and environment. As a consequence, when a trait runs in families, we don't know whether it's for genetic reasons, environmental reasons, or both (see Chapter 3). Because family studies don't permit investigators to disentangle the effects of nature from those of nurture, they've turned to more informative research designs. These include *twin studies,* which compare correlations in a trait in two types of twins: identical (monozygotic) and fraternal (dizygotic).

Twin Studies of Intelligence.
Because identical twins share twice as many of their genes on average as fraternal twins, correlations among identical twins should be higher than among fraternal twins if genes are playing a strong role. In typical studies of IQ, identical twin correlations have been in the .7 to .8 range, whereas fraternal twin correlations have been in the .3 to .4 range. Nevertheless, in all studies of twins raised together, identical twin correlations have been lower than 1.0. The higher identical than fraternal twin correlations tell us that IQ is influenced by genetic factors.

These twin findings also provide convincing evidence for environmental influences on IQ. Why? Because the identical twin correlations for IQ are less than perfect. Given that identical twins share 100 percent of their genes, they would correlate 1.0 if genetic influences alone were operative (assuming the IQ tests are reliable). The fact that they correlate less than 1.0 tells us that environmental influences also play a role, although the studies don't tell us what these influences are.

Adoption Studies of Intelligence.
Studies of intact families are limited because they can't disentangle genetic from environmental influences. To address this shortcoming, psychologists have turned to *adoption studies* (Chapter 3), which examine the extent to which children adopted into new homes resemble their adoptive versus biological parents. Adoption studies have established a clear contribution of the environment in IQ. For example, adopted children who come from extremely deprived environments show an increase in IQ when adopted into homes that provide more enriched environments (Capron & Duyme, 1989). But do adopted children's IQs resemble their biological parents' IQs? The results of adoption studies indicate that the answer is yes. IQs of adopted children tend to be similar to the IQs of their biological parents, offering evidence of genetic influence.

What environmental factors influence IQ? Psychologists don't know for sure, although they've made significant inroads toward identifying promising candidates.

Educational Influences on IQ.
The number of years of schooling correlates between .5 and .6 with IQ scores (Neisser et al., 1996). Although some authors have interpreted this correlation as meaning that schooling leads to higher IQ, it's equally possible that the causal arrow is reversed. Indeed, there's evidence that individuals with high IQ scores enjoy taking classes more than individuals with low IQ scores (Rehberg & Rosenthal, 1978).

Can we boost IQ with early educational interventions? Some of the best evidence comes from studies of *Head Start,* a preschool program launched in the 1960s to give disadvantaged children a *jump start* by offering them an enriched educational experience.

Twin studies of intelligence compare the mental performance of identical (*top*) versus fraternal (*bottom*) twins raised together.

RULING OUT RIVAL HYPOTHESES
Have important alternative explanations for the findings been excluded?

CORRELATION vs. CAUSATION
Can we be sure that A causes B?

The federal Head Start program was launched in the 1960s to give disadvantaged preschoolers a jump start on their education. Studies show that Head Start programs typically produce short-term increases in IQ, but that these increases fade with time.

CORRELATION vs. CAUSATION
Can we be sure that A causes B?

The hope was that this program would allow them to catch up intellectually to other children. Dozens of studies of Head Start programs have yielded consistent results, and they've been largely disappointing. Although these programs produce short-term increases in IQ, these increases don't typically persist after the programs end (Caruso, Taylor, & Detterman, 1982; Royce, Darlington, & Murray, 1983).

Poverty and IQ: Socioeconomic and Nutritional Deprivation.

It's difficult to put a firm number on the effects of poverty, but there's reason to believe that social and economic deprivation can adversely affect IQ (Jensen, 1977) and that deprivation can have an increasing effect as children age (Willerman, 1979).

Along with poverty often comes inadequate diet. Studies from poor areas in Central America suggest that malnutrition in childhood, especially if prolonged, can lower IQ (Eysenck & Schoenthaler, 1997). Poor children are also especially likely to be exposed to lead as a result of drinking lead-contaminated water, breathing lead-contaminated dust, or eating lead paint chips. Such exposure is also associated with intellectual deficits (Bellinger & Needleman, 2003; Canfield et al., 2003; Ris, Dietrich, Succop, et al., 2004). Nevertheless, it's unclear how much of this correlation is due to the direct effects of lead itself as opposed to poverty or other factors, like malnutrition.

Getting Smarter All the Time: The Mysterious Flynn Effect.

In the 1980s, political scientist James Flynn noticed something very odd (Dickens & Flynn, 2001; Flynn, 1981, 1987). Over time, the average IQ score of the population was rising at a rate of about 3 points per decade, a phenomenon now known as the **Flynn effect** (Herrnstein & Murray, 1994). This mean that, on average, our IQs are a full 15 points higher than those of our grandparents. Most researchers agree that this effect is due to unidentified environmental influences because genetic influences would be unlikely to have such a rapid impact on IQ. Still, we don't fully understand the causes of the Flynn effect. Adding to the mystery, recent data suggests that the effect may actually be subsiding, or even reversing, at least in Europe (Sundet, Barlaug, & Torjussen, 2004). The causes of the apparent end to the Flynn effect are as puzzling as the causes of its beginning.

GROUP DIFFERENCES IN IQ: THE SCIENCE AND THE POLITICS

Thus far, we've focused almost entirely on the thorny question of *individual differences* in IQ: Why does measured intelligence differ among people within a population? If you think that what we've discussed so far is controversial, fasten your seat belts. The topic of *group differences* in IQ is perhaps the most bitterly disputed in all of psychology. Here we'll look at what the research says about two group differences in IQ: (1) differences between men and women and (2) differences among races. **[LEARNING OBJECTIVE 7.12]**

As we'll discover, the issues are as emotionally charged as they are scientifically complex. They've also become deeply entangled with politics (Hunt, 1999), with people on differing sides of these debates accusing each other of biases and bad intentions. When evaluating these issues, it's crucial that we try our best to be as objective as possible. That's not always easy, as it requires us to put aside our understandable emotional reactions to examine the scientific evidence.

GLOSSARY

Flynn effect
finding that average IQ scores have been rising at a rate of approximately 3 points per decade

Sex Differences in IQ and Mental Abilities.

In January 2005, then Harvard University President Lawrence Summers created a furor. Speaking at an informal meeting of university faculty from around the country, Summers wondered aloud why there were so few women in the "hard" sciences, like physics, chemistry, and biology (see

Figure 7.14). He tentatively proposed a few reasons, one involving discrimination against women and a second involving women's preference for raising families rather than for competing in grueling, cutthroat occupations. But it was Summers's third reason that really got people going. Summers conjectured that perhaps women enter the world with a genetic disadvantage in science and mathematics. A firestorm of controversy regarding sex differences in mental abilities followed on the heels of Summers's provocative statements. In this section, we'll do our best to take a scientifically balanced look at the evidence.

Sex Differences in IQ. Do men and women differ in overall IQ? A handful of researchers have recently reported that on average men have slightly higher IQs than women—perhaps between 3 and 5 points (Jackson & Rushton, 2006; Lynn & Irwing, 2004)—but these claims are controversial. Most researchers have found few or no average sex differences in IQ (Jensen, 1998). The best current scientific bet is that males and females are extremely similar, if not identical, in IQ.

Yet average differences don't tell the whole story. Numerous studies indicate that men are more *variable* in their overall IQ scores than women (Hedges & Nowell, 1995). So although men don't appear to have higher average IQs than women, there are more men at both the low and the high ends of IQ bell curve (see **Figure 7.15**). We don't know the reason for this difference; researchers have, not surprisingly, proposed both genetic and environmental explanations.

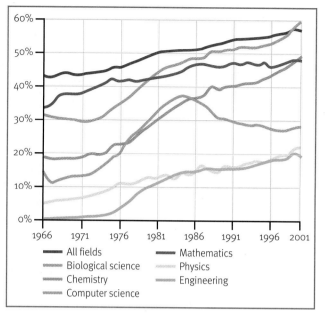

Figure 7.14 Bachelor's Degrees Earned by Women in Selected Fields, 1966–2001. Across a 35-year period, women have been underrepresented in most of the "hard" sciences, comprising only a minority of those graduating with a degree in these areas of study. (*Source:* Ivie & Ray, 2005)

WHAT DO *you* THINK?

Imagine you were working in the public relations office of Harvard University when former president Lawrence Summers made his controversial statement about women in science. How might you use your knowledge of relationships between gender and IQ to help diffuse the situation?

Sex Differences in Specific Mental Abilities. Even though there's little, if any, difference in overall IQ between men and women, the picture becomes more interesting—and more complicated—when we get to specific mental abilities. Men and women are quite similar when it comes to most intellectual abilities (Hyde, 2005; Maccoby & Jacklin, 1974), but a closer look reveals some consistent sex differences (Block, 1976; Halpern, 1992; Halpern et al., 2007; Pinker, 2005).

Women tend to do better than men on some verbal tasks, like spelling, writing, and pronouncing words (Feingold, 1988; Halpern et al., 2007; Kimura, 1999). This sex difference may have a hormonal component; even within women, verbal ability seems to ebb and flow along with the level of estrogen, a sex hormone that's more plentiful in women than men. On average, females also do better than males in arithmetic calculation, like adding or subtracting numbers, although this difference is present only in childhood (Hyde, Fennema, & Lamon, 1990). Finally, females tend to be better than males in detecting and recognizing emotional expressions in others, especially when they reach adulthood (Hall, 1978; McClure, 2000).

In contrast, men tend to do better than women on most tasks requiring spatial ability (Halpern et al., 2007). The largest difference emerges on *mental rotation* tasks, like the

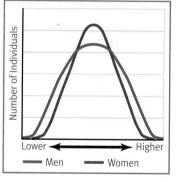

Figure 7.15 Distributions of Men and Women in IQ Tests. The IQ distribution of men is wider than the distribution of women. As a consequence, there are more men than women with both low and high IQ scores and more women with scores in the middle.

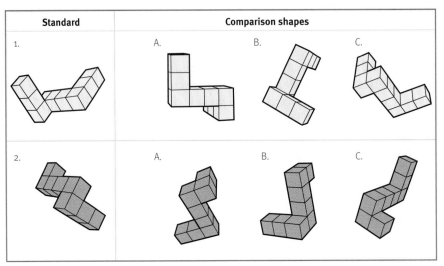

Figure 7.16 **Mental Rotation Task.** Men tend to do better than women on tests of mental rotation, which require subjects to figure out which "comparison" shape on the right matches the "standard" shape on the left. You may want to try your hand (or your mind, to be more exact) at these two items. Turn the book upside-down and see the bottom of this page for the answers. (*Source:* Metzler & Shepard, 1974)

Men and women tend to differ in how they solve spatial problems.

REPLICABILITY
Can the results be duplicated in other studies?

REPLICABILITY
Can the results be duplicated in other studies?

Answers to Figure 7.16: 1. A, 2. B

ones shown in **Figure 7.16,** which require subjects to determine which of a series of rotated blocks matches a target group of rotated blocks (Voyer, Voyer, & Bryden, 1995). Interestingly, one of the largest reported psychological sex differences is in geography, an area of study that relies heavily on spatial ability. Males also tend to do better than females on mathematics tasks that involve complicated reasoning, like deriving proofs in geometry (Benbow & Stanley, 1980). This difference doesn't emerge until adolescence (Hyde et al., 1990).

So what's the bottom line? On the one hand, it's possible that some sex differences in mental abilities, such as women's higher scores on certain verbal tasks and men's higher scores on spatial and complex math-solving tasks, are rooted in genes. Indeed, despite many changes in men's and women's roles over the past several decades, sex differences in spatial ability haven't decreased over time (Voyer et al., 1995). Moreover, some studies indicate that excess levels of prenatal testosterone, a hormone of which males have more than females, are associated with better spatial ability (Hampson, Rovet, & Altmann, 1998), although not all researchers have replicated this finding.

On the other hand, there's ample reason to suspect that some, perhaps even most, of the sex differences in science and math ability are environmental (Levine, Vasilyeva, Lourenco, et al., 2005). Sex differences may be due more to differences in problem-solving strategies than in inherent abilities. For example, when researchers have encouraged both men and women to solve math problems using spatial imagery (which men usually prefer) rather than verbal reasoning (which women usually prefer), the sex difference in math performance becomes noticeably smaller (Geary, 1996). Moreover, if we look back at the graph in Figure 7.14 on page 253, we can see something striking. From 1966 to 2001, the percentage of women entering the "hard" sciences has been increasing steadily. This finding suggests underrepresentation of women in the "hard" sciences is the result of societal factors, such as discrimination and society's expectations, rather than women's weaker science skills.

Racial Differences in IQ. Perhaps one of the most controversial and troubling findings in the study of intelligence is that average IQ scores differ among races. The differences vary in size but have been replicated multiple times (Loehlin, Lindzey, & Spuhler, 1977). On average, African Americans and Hispanic Americans score lower than Caucasians on standard IQ tests (Hunt & Carlson, 2007; Lynn, 2006; Neisser et al., 1996), and Asian Americans score higher than Caucasians (Lynn, 1996; Sue, 1993). Among Caucasians in the United States, the IQs of Jews are slightly higher than those of non-Jews (Lynn, 2003). The average IQ difference between Caucasians and African Americans, which some researchers have estimated to be as high as 15 points, has received the most attention. What do these differences tell us about the abilities and potential of individuals from different races, and why these differences exist?

Over the years, some sectors of society have attempted to use these findings in a misguided, and at times even malicious, attempt to argue that some races are innately superior to others. For instance, in 1994, Richard Herrnstein and Charles Murray touched off a bitter dispute when they published a book called *The Bell Curve*. In it, they argued that at least some of the IQ gap between races might be genetic in origin. There are several serious problems with this claim. The preponderance of evidence supports the idea that racial differences in IQ are largely or entirely *environmental* in origin. Most likely, these differences stem primarily from the different resources and opportunities available to individuals from different races. Furthermore, the IQ differences among races may be narrowing over recent decades (Dickens & Flynn, 2006; Hauser, 1998). Another important consideration is that the variability *within* any given race tends to be considerably larger than the variability *between* races (Nisbett, 1995). This finding means that the distributions of IQ scores for different races overlap substantially (see **Figure 7.17**). As a result, many African Americans and Hispanic Americans have higher IQs than many Caucasians and Asian Americans. The bottom line is clear: We can't use race as a basis for inferring any given person's IQ.

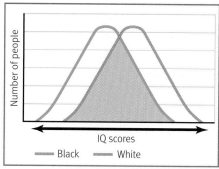

Figure 7.17 Diagram of African American and Caucasian Distributions for IQ. African American and Caucasian IQ distributions differ by as much as 15 IQ points—but they show substantial overlap, as indicated by the shaded area.

Reconciling Racial Differences. To see why racial differences in IQ don't necessarily imply genetic differences in intelligence or learning potential, let's look at the two groups of plants in the upper panel of **Figure 7.18** (Lewontin, 1970). As we can see, in this "thought experiment" the plants within each group differ in height. These differences in height reflect (at least in part) genetic influences on plants' tendencies to grow and flourish. Note, however, that at this point in the growth cycle, the plants in the two groups are, on average, roughly equal in height. Now let's imagine that we provide one of these groups of plants, in this case the one on the left, with plenty of water and light, but provide the other group with minimal water and light. We twiddle our thumbs and wait a few weeks, and then voilà: We now find that the plants on the left are, on average, taller than the plants on the right. Although the two groups each had equal potential to grow and flourish, environmental influences resulted in one group growing taller than the other.

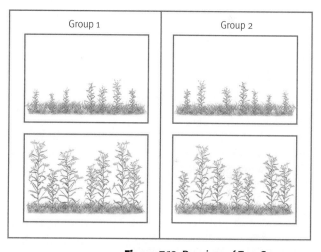

Figure 7.18 Drawings of Two Groups of Plants. These two groups of plants are well matched in height to start, but one outstrips the other over time due to different environmental conditions. This demonstrates how group differences in IQ could be "real" but completely environmentally determined. (*Source:* Based on Lewontin, 1970)

So what's the take-home message? The difference in height between these groups is *entirely environmental*—it's due to watering and light—so we can't explain the difference between the two groups in genetic terms. In other words, the between-group differences aren't at all heritable. We can easily imagine that different races begin life with no average genetic differences in IQ. But over time, the cumulative effects of factors such as social deprivation and prejudice may produce a notable difference in IQ between racial groups, one that's entirely environmental in origin.

It's also important to point out that although one group of plants in our example grew taller than the other, one or two individual plants in the shorter group actually grew taller than some plants from the taller group. This highlights the overlapping distributions of heights in the two groups, demonstrating that even within a relatively "deprived" group, some plants exceed the growth of some members of the more "privileged" group. This point reminds us that we can't use group differences in IQ to infer the IQ of any given person. Although this example demonstrates that racial differences in IQ *could* be entirely environmental in nature, it doesn't demonstrate that they *are*. We need to look at the scientific evidence for answers to that question.

Test Bias. One popular explanation for race differences in IQ is that the tests are biased against some groups and in favor of others. *Test bias* has a specific meaning for psychologists,

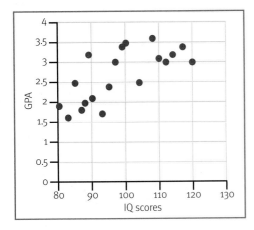

(a)

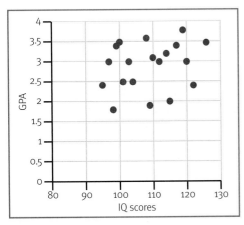

(b)

Figure 7.19 Two Scatterplots Representing Test Bias. These two scatterplots display a made-up example of test bias. In (a) IQ scores correlate highly with GPA for Caucasians (.7 correlation), whereas in (b) correlations between IQ scores and GPA are much lower for Asian Americans (.25). Even though Asian Americans display higher IQs on average in this example, the test is biased against them because it's a weaker predictor of GPA in that group.

GLOSSARY

test bias
tendency of a test to predict outcomes better in one group than another

within-group heritability
extent to which the variability of a trait within a group is genetically influenced

between-group heritability
extent to which differences in a trait between groups is genetically influenced

which differs from the popular use of the term. In scientific terms, a test isn't biased merely because some groups perform better on it than others. Psychologists don't regard a tape measure as biased, even though men obtain higher average scores than women when we use it to measure height. When psychologists refer to **test bias,** they mean that a test predicts outcomes—such as grades or occupational success—better in one group than in another (Anastasi & Urbina, 1996). Putting it a bit differently, a biased test is one that means different things in one group than in another. Let's suppose that the correlation between IQ scores and college grade point average (GPA) in Caucasians was .7, as shown in **Figure 7.19a,** but only .25 for Asian Americans, as shown in **Figure 7.19b.** This finding would imply that IQ was a better predictor of GPA in Caucasians than in Asian Americans. In this case, the IQ test would be biased *against* Asian Americans, even though the average IQ scores for that group were higher than those of Caucasians. Thus, average differences between groups *do not* necessarily indicate test bias.

So are IQ tests racially biased? The answer seems to be no (Brody, 1992; Neisser et al., 1996). In almost all studies, researchers have found that the correlations between IQ tests and both academic and occupational achievement are about equal across races (Brody, 1992; Herrnstein & Murray, 1994; Hunter, Schmidt, & Hunter, 1979). This finding leads to the conclusion that IQ differences among races go hand-in-hand with differences in average *achievement* among races. Unfortunately, in U.S. society some races tend to do better in school and have higher-ranking and higher-paying jobs than others. According to some psychologists, the most likely explanation for why both IQ and achievement vary across races is that *society,* not IQ tests themselves, is biased, leading both to differences in IQ test performance and to differences in grades and career achievement among races.

So Why Aren't Racial Differences in IQ Genetic? The finding that IQ tests aren't biased means we can't blame the tests for the race gap in IQ, but it doesn't address the question of what's producing these gaps. Some researchers have pointed out that IQ is heritable and have argued from this finding that racial differences must be due at least partly to genetic influences. However, this is a faulty conclusion based on a misunderstanding of how the heritability of a trait among individuals *within* a group relates to the heritability of this trait *between* groups.

Within-group heritability is the extent to which a trait, like IQ, is heritable within groups, such as Asian Americans or women. **Between-group heritability** is the extent to which the difference in this trait between groups, such as between Asian Americans and Caucasians or between men and women, is heritable. It's critical to keep in mind that *within-group heritability doesn't necessarily imply between-group heritability.* That is, just because IQ is heritable within groups doesn't imply that the difference between these groups has anything to do with their genes. Some researchers have confused within-group and between-group heritability, assuming mistakenly that because IQ is heritable within any group such as a race or gender, racial differences in IQ must themselves be heritable (Lilienfeld & Waldman, 2000; Nisbett, 1995). To return to our plant analogy, we must remember that within each group, some plants grew taller than others. These differences were caused by differences in the heartiness of the genetic strain of the individual plants within each group. Nevertheless, the differences between the two groups of plants were due entirely to environmental factors, even though within-group differences were due entirely to genes.

So what's the evidence that racial differences in IQ result from environmental and *not* genetic factors? Most of this research comes from analyses of differences between African Americans and Caucasians, and it largely points away from a genetic explanation of racial IQ gaps.

One study conducted in Germany shortly after World War II compared the IQ scores of children of African American soldiers and Caucasian German mothers with the children of

Caucasian American soldiers and Caucasian German mothers. In both groups, mothers raised the children, so the societal environment was approximately the same. The IQs of these two groups of children didn't differ (Eyferth, 1961). Thus, the differing race-related genes appeared to have no bearing on children's IQ when environment was roughly equated.

Another study examined the effect of cross-racial adoption on IQ. This study showed that the IQs of African American children adopted by middle-class Caucasian parents were higher at age 7 than those of either the average African American or Caucasian child (Scarr & Weinberg, 1976). This finding suggests that what appears to be a race-related effect may actually be more related to socioeconomic status, because a much higher percentage of African and Hispanic Americans than Caucasians and Asian Americans are living in poverty. A follow-up of these children revealed that their IQs declined over a 10-year period (Weinberg, Scarr, & Waldman, 1992), which may mean that the effects of socioeconomic status are short lived. Or it may mean that the negative effects (such as discrimination) of being a member of an ethnic minority group in a predominantly Caucasian community gradually counteracts the effects of a changed environment.

Stereotype Threat. One other environmental factor that may affect how individuals perform and achieve is **stereotype threat.** Stereotype threat refers to the fear that we may confirm a negative group stereotype, such as a stereotype of our group as less intelligent or less athletic than others. Stereotype threat creates a self-fulfilling prophecy, in which those who are anxious about confirming a negative stereotype actually increase their likelihood of doing so (Steele & Aronson, 1995). According to Claude Steele, stereotype threat can impair individuals' performance on IQ tests and standardized tests, like the SAT. Here's his reasoning: If we're members of a group that has a reputation for doing poorly on IQ tests, the mere thought that we're taking an IQ test will arouse stereotype threat. We think, "I'm supposed to do really badly on this test." This belief, Steele (1997) contends, can itself influence behavior, leading some people who would otherwise do well to display reduced performance.

Our discussion leads us to the unsettling conclusion that broader societal differences in resources, opportunities, attitudes, and experiences are probably responsible for much, if not all, of the racial differences in IQ. The encouraging news, however, is that nothing in the research literature implies that racial differences in IQ are unchangeable. If environmental disadvantages can contribute to IQ differences, then eliminating the disadvantages may eliminate these differences.

Research suggests that stereotype threat can lead African American students to perform worse on tests on which they believe members of their race tend to do poorly.

GLOSSARY

stereotype threat
fear that we may confirm a negative group stereotype

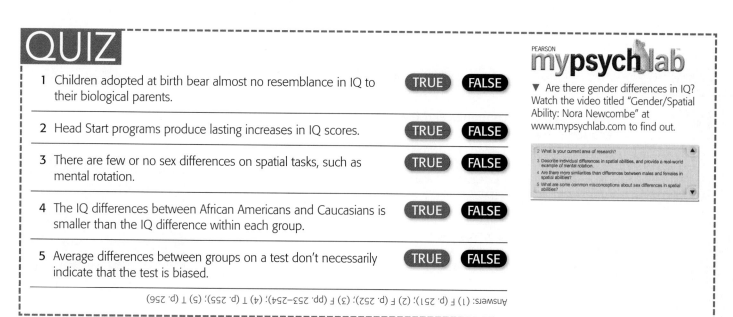

QUIZ

1 Children adopted at birth bear almost no resemblance in IQ to their biological parents.   TRUE   FALSE

2 Head Start programs produce lasting increases in IQ scores.   TRUE   FALSE

3 There are few or no sex differences on spatial tasks, such as mental rotation.   TRUE   FALSE

4 The IQ differences between African Americans and Caucasians is smaller than the IQ difference within each group.   TRUE   FALSE

5 Average differences between groups on a test don't necessarily indicate that the test is biased.   TRUE   FALSE

PEARSON
mypsychlab

▼ Are there gender differences in IQ? Watch the video titled "Gender/Spatial Ability: Nora Newcombe" at www.mypsychlab.com to find out.

2 What is your current area of research?

3 Describe individual differences in spatial abilities, and provide a real-world example of mental rotation.

4 Are there more similarities than differences between males and females in spatial abilities?

5 What are some common misconceptions about sex differences in spatial abilities?

Answers: (1) F (p. 251); (2) F (p. 252); (3) F (pp. 253–254); (4) T (p. 255); (5) T (p. 256)

HOW DOES LANGUAGE WORK? (pp. 226–234)

7.1 **Describe the process by which children learn language and explain how the process is influenced by deafness or bilingualism**

Infants' babbling becomes more sophisticated over the course of their first year, as control over their vocal tracts increases. They also fine-tune their perception of phonemes over the course of the first year of listening to their native language. Children's word and syntax comprehension precedes their production of language. Sign languages possess the same linguistic features and complexity as spoken languages. Bilingual individuals typically have one dominant language. Learning two languages slows some aspects of the acquisition process but ultimately results in stronger linguistic skills.

1. By what month of pregnancy are fetuses' ears developed enough for them to detect sounds and how much do they learn about their mothers' languages and voices in utero? (p. 227)

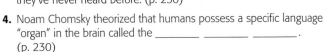

2. Children (can/can't) learn to recognize and interpret words before they can pronounce them. (p. 228)

3. Even very young children use language in _____ ways, producing sentences or combinations of words they've never heard before. (p. 230)

4. Noam Chomsky theorized that humans possess a specific language "organ" in the brain called the _____ _____ _____. (p. 230)

5. Sign languages (exhibit/do not exhibit) the same features as spoken languages, such as generativity and a complex set of syntactic rules. (p. 231)

7.2 **Distinguish human language from nonhuman animal communication**

Most nonhuman animal communication systems involve aggression and mating displays, but little else. Attempts to teach language to nonhuman animals have been only modestly successful. Chimpanzees and African gray parrots can learn the basics of linguistic communication but learn very differently from humans. Bonobos seem to learn more like humans do but fail to exceed the proficiency level of about a 2½-year-old human.

6. Unlike chimpanzees, _____ have a learning pathway that more closely resembles human learning. (p. 232)

7.3 **Identify the ways in which our language may influence our thinking**

The notion that language completely determines our thinking (linguistic determinism) has little or no scientific support. However, evidence supports the idea that language can influence some aspects of our thinking (linguistic relativity).

7. The view that all thought is represented linguistically is called _____ _____. (p. 233)

8. Recent neuroimaging studies suggest that thought (can/can't) occur without language. (p. 233)

9. The fact that the Dani of New Guinea can perceive different color categories, despite not having terms for colors in their language, presents a challenge to what hypothesis? (p. 233)

10. When researchers identify language-related differences in thought, it (is/isn't) easy to disentangle the influences of language from culture. (p. 234)

succeed with mypsychlab

1. **SIMULATION** Be a participant in a study that illustrates how errors in language occur.
   Lexical Bias in Slips of the Tongue

2. **SIMULATION** Participate in a replication of a classic study to see how powerful language can be when we form first impressions of others.
   Power of Words

3. **WATCH** Watch children interact in a bilingual classroom and discover the effects on learning.
   Bilingual Education

THINKING AND REASONING (pp. 234–238)

7.4 **Identify types of cognitive economies and the pros and cons of economizing**

Cognitive economy is a necessary and valuable aspect of our cognitive functioning. We would be unable to function effectively without some way of streamlining our information processing. Categorization and using heuristics in decision making are examples of cognitive economy. There are downsides to cognitive economy, including the reasoning errors outlined in Chapters 1 and 2 as obstacles to critical thinking. Heuristics and biases are often useful, but can lead us to make costly mistakes. The scientific method is designed to guard against biased thinking.

11. We define _____ as any mental activity or processing of information. (p. 234)

12. _____ _____ allows us to simplify what we need to attend to and keep the information we need to make decisions to a manageable minimum. (p. 235)

13. What do cultural differences in prototypes tell us about how our categories are organized? (p. 235)

Answers are located at the end of the text.

14. Collections of objects, actions, characteristics, and other entities that share core properties are called _____ . (p. 235)

15. The _____ of flowers is the group of all individual items that can be classified as flowers, the _____ of flowers is the idea of colorful, scented blooms growing on plants. (p. 235)

16. What kind of effects can an interviewer's cognitive economy have on an interview? (p. 236)

7.5 **Describe the challenges that humans face when attempting to solve problems or make decisions**

Three hurdles to effective problem solving are the salience of surface similarities, mental set/functional fixedness, and context effects. The scientific method doesn't come naturally to us. Keeping in mind the principles of scientific thinking outlined in this text and our vulnerability to biased reasoning can help make us better consumers of information in everyday life.

17. When we generate a cognitive strategy to accomplish a specific goal, we are engaging in _____ _____ . (p. 236)

18. The phenomenon of becoming entrenched in a particular problem-solving strategy that inhibits generating alternative strategies is called a _____ _____ . (p. 237)

19. _____ _____ occurs when we experience difficulty conceptualizing that an object typically used for one purpose can be used for another. (p. 237)

20. Cognitive economizing comes much more naturally to us than _____ _____ . (p. 238)

succeed with mypsychlab

1. How many uses are there for everyday objects? Watch this illustration of a classic task that measures problem solving. **The Two-String Problem**

2. See how your timed responses on a computer task inform researchers how your brain organizes information. **The Mind's Organization of Conceptual Knowledge**

WHAT IS INTELLIGENCE? DEFINITIONAL CONFUSION (pp. 239–244)

7.6 **Identify different models and types of intelligences**

Sir Francis Galton proposed that intelligence stems from sensory capacity. Binet and Simon, who developed the first intelligence test, argued that intelligence consists of higher mental processes, such as reasoning, understanding, and judgment. Spearman invoked the existence of *g*, or general intelligence, but also posited the existence of *s*, or specific factors unique to particular mental tasks. Some psychologists have argued for the existence of multiple intelligences. According to them, there are many different ways of being smart. However, it's not clear whether these proposed intelligences are independent of each other or of a more general intelligence factor.

21. According to Galton's hypothesis about intelligence, someone who has excellent eyesight and hearing would have (high/low) intelligence. (p. 239)

22. Binet and Simon developed what is considered to be the first _____ _____, which served as a model for many intelligence researchers who followed in their footsteps. (p. 239)

23. In trying to define intelligence, early 20th century researchers agreed that it was related to _____ _____ . (p. 239)

24. The theory of _____ _____, developed by Charles Spearman, explains differences in intellect among people based on a single factor. (p. 240)

25. According to Spearman, someone's intelligence is not only dependent on his/her *g*, general intelligence, or but also on his/her _____ or _____ _____ . (p. 240)

26. When driving a vehicle you've never driven, you are relying on _____ _____, but when you answer a question on a history test, you are relying on _____ _____ . (p. 240)

27. Identify the three kinds of intelligences in Sternberg's Triarchic Model of Intelligence. (p. 240)

(a) (book smarts)
(b) (street smarts)
(c) (creativity)

7.7 **Evaluate scientific research on creativity and emotional intelligence**

Creativity is difficult to define, but psychologists agree that creative accomplishments are novel and successful. Psychologists measure creativity with tests of divergent thinking, although creativity also requires skill at convergent thinking. Emotional intelligence refers to the ability to understand our emotions and those of others and to apply this knowledge to our lives. It's not clear whether the concept of emotional intelligence provides psychological information not provided by personality traits, such as extraversion, or by general intelligence.

28. _____ _____ is the capacity to generate many different solutions to problems. (p. 242)

29. The ability to understand our emotions and those of others is called _____ _____ . (p. 242)

succeed with mypsychlab

Do You Know All of the Terms in This Chapter?

Find out by using the Flashcards. Want more practice? Take additional quizzes, try simulations, and watch video to be sure you are prepared for the test!

7.8 Describe the connection between our brains and intelligence

Brain size and intelligence are moderately correlated in humans. Some evidence suggests that people with high levels of intelligence possess especially efficient brains. Intelligence also seems to be related to faster reaction times, as well as working memory capacity, and probably stems in part from the activity of the prefrontal cortex.

succeed with mypsychlab

1. Test your knowledge of different types of intelligence.
   Gardner's Multiple Intelligences

2. Drag and click the appropriate terms from the Triarchic Theory of Intelligence with their definitions.
   Sternberg's Triarchic Theory of Intelligence

3. Play the role of researcher and evaluate case studies that illustrate an individual who excels in one area of multiple intelligence.
   Gardner's Theory of Intelligence

30. Which of these images displays a different pattern from the others? What underlying abilities might be required to enable someone to answer this *g*-loaded question correctly? (p. 243)

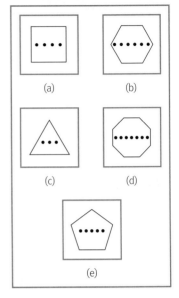

INTELLIGENCE TESTING: THE GOOD, THE BAD, AND THE UGLY (pp. 244–250)

7.9 Determine how psychologists calculate IQ

Stern defined the intelligence quotient (IQ) as mental age divided by chronological age multiplied by 100. This simple formula becomes problematic in adolescence and adulthood because mental age tends to level out at around age 16. As a consequence, most modern intelligence tests define IQ in terms of deviation IQ.

31. Using Wilhelm Stern's IQ formula, complete the equation and calculate IQ for the example provided. Next explain the central flaw in this formula when applying it to two adults with a mental age of 18, the first of whom is 18 years old, and the second of whom is 35 years old. (p. 244)

8	÷	10	=	_____	x	_____	=	_____
(mental age)		(chronological age)		(total)				(IQ)

32. _____ _____ is the age corresponding to the average person's performance on an intelligence test. (p. 244)

33. When computing IQ, modern researchers rely on a statistic called _____ _____ . (p. 244)

34. Psychologists have developed many different adult IQ tests, but the most commonly used is the _____ _____ _____ _____ . (p. 246)

35. Apply your knowledge of the WAIS by viewing each visual example and identifying its corresponding test and description. (p. 247)

Test	Description	Example
(a)		Shown: Fill in: 1 2 3 4 4 2 1 3 ○□△⊙ ⊙□○△
(b)		Tell me what is missing:
(c)		Assemble blocks to match this design:

36. The test-retest reliability of IQ tests in adults is (high/low), and the test-retest reliability of IQ tests in infancy is (high/low). (pp. 247–248)

37. The _____ of IQ tests indicates whether these tests accurately measure what they purport to measure. (p. 248)

38. IQ scores (do/don't do) a good job of predicting academic success. (p. 248)

7.10 Explain the history of misuse of intelligence tests in the United States

Eugenics was the effort to improve a population's "genetic stock" by encouraging people with "good genes" to reproduce, by discouraging people with "bad genes" from reproducing, or both. IQ tests became an important tool of the eugenics movement, because many proponents of eugenics wished to minimize the reproduction of individuals with low IQs. In part because of eugenics, some people today view IQ tests with skepticism.

39. Eugenics was particularly popular in the United States from _____ to _____ . (p. 245)

40. _____ _____ is one of the extremely disturbing practices that came about as a result of the eugenics movement. (p. 245)

succeed with mypsychlab

1. Watch as researcher Robert Guthrie discusses questions that should be raised about IQ tests.
   Are Intelligence Tests Valid?: Robert Guthrie

INDIVIDUAL AND GROUP DIFFERENCES IN IQ (pp. 250–257)

7.11 **Identify ways in which the environment and genetics affect IQ measures**

Twin and adoption studies show that at least some of the tendency for IQ to run in families is genetic, but the environment plays a role as well. Schooling is related to high IQ scores. Research suggests that both poverty and nutrition are causally related to IQ, although disentangling the effects of nutrition from other factors, such as social class, is challenging.

41. Twin studies tell us that IQ is influenced both by _____ and _____ factors. (p. 251)

42. _____ studies are a way for researchers to separate environmental effects from genetic effects. (p. 251)

43. If a child from a deprived environment is adopted into an enriched family environment, we would expect this child's IQ to (increase/decrease/stay the same). (p. 251)

44. If your IQ is higher than your grandparents' IQ, this may be attributable to the _____ _____. (p. 252)

7.12 **Evaluate the evidence concerning gender and racial differences in IQ**

Most research suggests little, if any, overall average sex differences in IQ between men and women. Nevertheless, men are more variable in their IQ scores than women. Women tend to do better than men on some verbal tasks, whereas men tend to do better than women on some spatial tasks. On average, African Americans score about 15 points lower than Caucasians on standard IQ tests. Asian Americans score about 5 points higher than Caucasians. Nevertheless, there is substantial overlap in the IQ distributions across races. Test bias does not appear to explain the IQ test gap between African Americans and Caucasians. Just because IQ scores are heritable within races does not mean that the IQ difference between races is heritable. Most research points toward an environmental explanation for the race IQ gap, with such factors as poverty, societal discrimination, and stereotype threat playing a role.

succeed with mypsychlab

1. Tune in to this discussion, as two psychologists explore the concept of stereotype threat as an explanation for gender and racial differences in intelligence.
Stereotype Threat

2. Can your diet affect intelligence? Explore what factors may improve or decrease your level of intelligence.
Factors Affecting Intelligence

3. Can you visualize the best route to get to campus? Test your spatial abilities in this experiment.
Mental Rotation

45. There is little evidence for sex differences in IQ overall, but research has shown that there are consistent differences between the sexes in some specific skills. Indicate below which sex (M/F) has scored higher on each of the skills listed. (pp. 253–254)

_____ Spelling

_____ Arithmetic calculation (in childhood)

_____ Complex mathematical tasks (in adolescence)

_____ Safe driving

_____ Geography

_____ Sociability

_____ Reading facial expression for emotion

_____ Spatial ability

46. Men tend to do better than women on some tasks requiring _____ ability, and women tend to do better than men on some tasks requiring _____ ability. (p. 253)

47. How can environmental influences explain how two sets of plants that started out at the same height can end up so different? What does this thought experiment tell us about potential environmental effects on IQ? (p. 255)

Group 1   Group 2

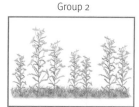

48. The authors of *The Bell Curve* revived a bitter public debate when they speculated that the IQ gap between races might be _____ in origin. (p. 255)

49. In order to demonstrate that there is no genetic explanation for the IQ gap between African Americans and Caucasian Americans; one needs to understand the difference between _____ heritability and _____ heritability. (p. 256)

50. If you are a member of a group that has a reputation for doing poorly on standardized tests, you may do poorly when you take one simply because of _____ _____. (p. 257)

SCIENTIFIC THINKING SKILLS
Questions and Summary

1 There is a widely held myth that highly stimulating early environments are critical for infant intellectual development. In reality, most normal environments provide adequate stimulation for infant development. While research does show a negative effect of deprived environments on intelligence, adding *more* stimulation to already normal environments is an exaggeration of the findings. Look for websites marketing "infant stimulation" products. How have these marketers misinterpreted the scientific research?

2 In your introductory psychology class, you are asked to present evidence and arguments in support of the idea that your own gender is *less* intelligent that the other gender. How would you overcome your own biases to fulfill your assignment?

RULING OUT RIVAL HYPOTHESES
pp. 230, 248, 251

CORRELATION VS. CAUSATION
pp. 233, 234, 243, 249, 251, 252

FALSIFIABILITY
pp. 230, 239, 240

REPLICABILITY
pp. 243, 254

EXTRAORDINARY CLAIMS
p. 238

OCCAM'S RAZOR
p. 243

Human
Development

Do infants have survival instincts? (p. 270)

What parenting styles help or hinder children's development? (p. 284)

CHAPTER 8

Are there gender differences in moral reasoning? (p. 286)

Can adolescents make mature decisions? (p. 290)

Is the aging process all downhill? (p. 295)

CORRELATION vs. CAUSATION

Can we be sure that A causes B?

Nora, Iris, Myra, and Hester Genain grew up together. They're in their 70s now. Yet advancing age isn't the first thing that strikes you when you meet them. After being introduced to them, you soon realize that something is very wrong. All of them are emotionally disturbed in some way that you can't quite put your finger on.

It turns out that these four women have two striking things in common. First, they are identical quadruplets, products of the same **zygote** (fertilized egg; see Chapter 3), and born within 17 minutes of each other. Second, Nora, Iris, Myra, and Hester all have schizophrenia.

The Genain quadruplets, as they're known in the psychological literature, offer a classic illustration of the interplay between nature and nurture over the course of development (Rosenthal, 1963). Both of their parents suffered from serious psychological problems. Given what we know about the genetics of schizophrenia—which as we'll learn in Chapter 13 is a severe disorder of thinking and emotion that usually results in a loss of contact with reality—it's likely that the Genain quadruplets inherited a predisposition toward this condition.

Yet the timing and expression of each quadruplet's disorder differed. This finding offers powerful evidence for the role of the environment in the manifestation of schizophrenia. That's because identical quadruplets, like identical twins, possess the same DNA; in effect they're genetic clones of one another (see Chapter 3). So any behavioral differences among the Genains must be due to differences in their environments.

Although three of the sisters—Nora, Iris, and Hester—were hospitalized for their disorder, one of them—Myra—wasn't. Indeed, Myra was clearly disturbed but better adjusted than the others. Unlike the other quadruplets, she'd once married and even held a job for many years. In contrast, Hester was the most seriously ill of the sisters; she was disoriented, confused, and almost completely incapable of caring for herself. Nora, although also disturbed, was healthier than Iris, who like Hester was frequently bewildered and out of touch with reality.

What environmental variables might account for these differences? From birth, the four sisters differed in weight. The two severely afflicted sisters—Hester and Iris—weighed less than Myra and Nora (Rosenthal, 1963). Moreover, their mother clearly favored Myra and Nora over Hester and Iris. In particular, she frequently punished Hester and Iris for what she perceived as inappropriate behavior (Bernheim & Lewine, 1979; Stierlin, 1972). Yet even today, the role that these environmental factors played in the development of the Genain quadruplets' schizophrenia remains a mystery.

The fascinating story of the Genain quadruplets underscores the enormous challenges that psychologists confront in disentangling nature from nurture throughout development. Was the mother's harsher treatment of Hester and Iris compared with Myra and Nora a *cause* of their more severe schizophrenia? It's certainly possible. But it's equally possible that their mother's harsher treatment of Hester and Iris was a *reaction* to their more severe symptoms in the first place. In these cases, harsher treatment from their parents may cause difficult children to become even more disturbed, resulting in even harsher treatment from parents, thereby creating a vicious cycle (Bell, 1968; Rutter, 1997). In the case of the Genain quadruplets, there's no way to distinguish whether chicken or egg came first. Yet, as we'll learn, psychologists have developed methods for figuring out whether environmental factors, like parenting, are causes or effects of children's behavior.

Special Considerations in Human Development

The story of the Genain quadruplets raises fascinating and complex questions regarding the interplay of nature and nurture in development.

Developmental psychology is the study of how behavior changes over time. Before we explore issues of how we develop, we need to come to grips with several challenges that often arise when investigating psychological development. Understanding these challenges, along with the scientific thinking principles we've relied on throughout this book, will provide us with the equipment we need to evaluate the causes of cognitive and social changes from childhood to old age.

POST HOC FALLACY

One critical consideration to bear in mind is that things that occur first don't necessarily cause things that come later. It's tempting to conclude, for example, that because nearly 100 percent of serial killers drank milk as children, milk drinking creates mass murderers. But, of course, drinking milk in infancy has nothing to do with *why* some people became serial (not cereal, that is) killers; it just happens to come beforehand. This logical error is called the **post hoc fallacy** (*post hoc* is Latin for "after this").

┌─ WHAT DO *you* THINK ?

You have introduced a new-fangled method of teaching mathematics in your first grade classroom. A year later, the school's standardized tests indicate that the students' math performance scores had improved. How could the post hoc fallacy lead us to conclude that this method is effective, even if it's not?

BIDIRECTIONAL INFLUENCES

Human development is almost always a two-way street. That is, developmental influences are bidirectional. Children's experiences influence their development, but their development also influences their experiences. For example, parents influence their children's behavior, which in turn feeds back to influence their parents, and so on (Bell, 1968; Collins, Sorocco, Haala, et al., 2000; O'Connor, Deater-Deckard, Fulker, et al., 1998). Children also change their environments by acting in ways that influence their parents, siblings, friends, and teachers to respond differently from how they might have otherwise (Plomin, DeFries, & Loehlin, 1977). Furthermore, as children grow older, they play an increasingly active role in altering and selecting their environments.

It's crucial to keep bidirectional influences in mind, because pop psychology is full of *unidirectional* explanations: those that attempt to explain development in terms of a one-headed arrow. Parents fight with each other → their children react negatively. Children witness violence at school → they become more aggressive. There's probably a kernel of truth in each of these explanations. Yet they typically tell only part of the story. That's why so many arrows in psychology contain two heads (↔), not one. In the study of human development, two "heads" are almost always better—or least more accurate—than one, at least as far as arrows are concerned.

Gangs of delinquent adolescents don't arise by chance. Research suggests that delinquent individuals typically seek out and find each other, in part because of their genetic propensities.

GLOSSARY

zygote
fertilized egg

developmental psychology
study of how behavior changes over time

post hoc fallacy
false assumption that because one event occurred before another event, it must have caused that event

KEEPING AN EYE ON COHORT EFFECTS

Imagine we conduct a study designed to examine how people's knowledge of computers changes with age. We enter our study armed with a reasonable hypothesis: People's knowledge of computers should increase steadily from adolescence until early adulthood, after which it should level off at about age 30. After about age 30, we predict, knowledge of computers should remain about the same or increase slightly. To test our hypothesis, we sample 100,000 people in the U.S. population, with a broad age range of 18 to 80. However, contrary to our hypothesis, we find that people's knowledge of computers declines dramatically with age, especially between the ages of 60 and 80. What did we do wrong?

It turns out that we forgot to consider an alternative explanation for our findings. We started out by asking a perfectly sensible question. But in science, we also must make sure that the design we select is the right one for answering it. In this case, it wasn't. **[LEARNING OBJECTIVE 8.1]** We used a **cross-sectional design**, a design in which researchers examine people of different ages at a single point in time (Achenbach, 1982; Raulin & Lilienfeld, 2008). In a cross-sectional design, we obtain a "snapshot" of each person at a single age; we assess some people when they're 24, some when they're 47, others when they're 63, and so on.

The major problem with cross-sectional designs is that they don't control for **cohort effects:** Effects due to the fact that sets of people who lived during one time period, called *cohorts,* can differ from other cohorts. In this study, cohort effects are a serious shortcoming, because before the late 1980s, few Americans used computers. So those over 60 years old may not be as computer savvy as younger folks. This has nothing to do with the effects of aging, but everything to do with the effects of the era in which they grew up.

A longitudinal design is the only sure way around this problem. In a **longitudinal design,** psychologists track the development of the same group of subjects over time (Shadish et al., 2002). Rather than obtaining a snapshot of each person at only one point in time, we obtain the equivalent of a series of home movies, taken at different ages. This design allows us to examine true *developmental* effects: changes over time as a consequence of growing older. Without longitudinal designs, we can be tricked into concluding that event A comes before result B even when it doesn't. For example, much of the pop psychology literature warns us that divorce leads to *externalizing behaviors*—behaviors such as breaking rules, defying authority figures, and committing crimes—in children (Wallerstein, 1989). Yet a longitudinal study that tracked a sample of boys over several decades revealed otherwise: Boys whose parents divorced exhibited externalizing behaviors *years before* the divorce even occurred (Block & Block, 2006; Block, Block, & Gjerde, 1986).

Although longitudinal designs are ideal for studying change over time, they can be costly and time-consuming. For example, our study of computer literacy would take about six decades to complete. We should also bear in mind that longitudinal designs aren't experimental designs (see Chapter 2), because we can't randomly assign people to groups in these studies. As a result, we can't use them to infer cause-and-effect relationships.

RULING OUT RIVAL HYPOTHESES
Have important alternative explanations for the findings been excluded?

The classic "Up Series" directed by Michael Apted traces the lives of 14 British people "longitudinally" over time, from age 7 all the way up through age 49. Here, three "stars" of the documentary, Jackie, Lynn, and Sue, now in their 40s, proudly display photographs of themselves at younger ages.

GLOSSARY

cross-sectional design
research design that examines people of different ages at a single point in time

cohort effects
effects observed in a sample of participants that result from individuals in the sample growing up at the same time

longitudinal design
research design that examines development in the same group of people on multiple occasions over time

THE INFLUENCE OF EARLY EXPERIENCE

There's no doubt that early life experiences can sometimes shape later development in powerful ways. Because many diverse influences on behavior operate throughout the life span, however, we shouldn't overestimate the impact of experiences in infancy on long-term development (Bruer, 1999; Clarke & Clarke, 1976; Kagan, 1998; Paris, 2000).

In particular, we must be careful to avoid two myths concerning development. The first is the myth of *infant determinism,* the widespread assumption that extremely early experiences—especially in the first three years of life—are almost always more influential than later experiences in shaping us as adults. For example, contrary to popular psychology sources there's no evidence that separating an infant from its mother during the first few hours after birth can produce lasting negative consequences for emotional adjustment (Klaus & Kennell, 1976). Later experiences in life can be as influential as those in early childhood (Greenough, 1997).

The second myth is that of *childhood fragility,* which holds that children are delicate little creatures who are easily damaged (Paris, 2000). Research shows most children are remarkably *resilient,* or capable of withstanding stress (see Chapter 10), and that most children emerge from potentially traumatic situations in surprisingly good shape (Bonanno, 2004; Garmezy, Masten, & Tellegen, 1984; Sommers & Satel, 2005).

DISTINGUISHING NATURE FROM NURTURE

Both *nature*—our genetic endowment—and *nurture*—the environments we encounter—play powerful roles in shaping development. Yet, as we'll soon see, disentangling their effects is far from simple.

In the mid-1990s, Betty Hart and Todd Risley (1995) conducted a 6-month longitudinal investigation that showed that parents who speak a lot to their children produce children with larger vocabularies than parents who don't. Hart and Risley's study provides evidence for a powerful environmental influence on children's vocabulary, right? Well, not so fast. In intact families, parents and children share not only an environment but also genes. To borrow a term we learned in Chapter 2, genes and environment are *confounded.* So there's an alternative explanation for Hart and Risley's findings: Perhaps they reflect the fact that parents who speak a lot to their children have higher vocabularies themselves. It turns out that vocabulary is partly influenced by genetic factors (Stromswold, 2005), so these parents may merely be passing on their genetic predisposition for better vocabularies to their children. Many studies of human development are subject to the same confound. **[LEARNING OBJECTIVE 8.2]**

What's more, nature and nurture often *interact* over the course of development, meaning that the effect of one depends on the contribution of the other. In 2002, Avshalom Caspi and his colleagues conducted a longitudinal study of children who possessed a gene for low levels of an enzyme called *monoamine oxidase* (MAO), which places them at elevated risk for committing violent crimes later in life (Moore, Scarpa, & Raine, 2002). However, not all children with low MAO activity became violent. Caspi and his colleagues discovered that whether this genetic risk factor is associated with violence depends on a specific environmental factor (see **Figure 8.1**). Specifically, children with *both* the low MAO gene *and* a history of maltreatment (such as physical abuse) were at heightened risk for antisocial behaviors, like stealing, assault, and rape. Children with the low MAO gene alone weren't at heightened risk (Caspi et al., 2002). This finding illustrates the phenomenon of **gene–environment interaction:** In many cases, the effects of genes depend on the environment, and vice versa (Rutter, 2008).

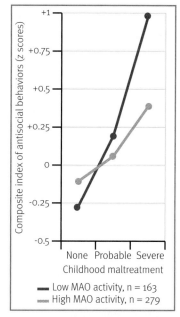

Figure 8.1 Gene–Environment Interactions. For adolescents with high MAO activity, maltreatment in childhood made no difference in their risk for later antisocial behavior. But for adolescents with low MAO activity, maltreatment in childhood resulted in increased risk for antisocial behavior. The effects of genes are sometimes dependent on the environment, and vice versa. (*Source:* Caspi et al., 2002)

RULING OUT RIVAL HYPOTHESES
Have important alternative explanations for the findings been excluded?

GLOSSARY

gene–environment interaction
situation in which the effects of genes depend on the environment in which they are expressed

QUIZ

1 Just because one event precedes a second event doesn't necessarily mean that it causes it. **TRUE** **FALSE**

2 Research shows that most children are passive recipients of their parents' influence. **TRUE** **FALSE**

3 Most children exposed to severe stressors or trauma end up with healthy patterns of psychological adjustment. **TRUE** **FALSE**

4 The effect of environmental experiences on a child's development can depend on the child's genes. **TRUE** **FALSE**

Answers: (1) T (p. 265); (2) F (p. 265); (3) T (p. 267); (4) T (p. 267)

PEARSON
mypsych lab

▼ Define and identify challenges associated with various research designs. Try the Explore titled "Cross-Sectional and Longitudinal Research Designs" on www.mypsychlab.com.

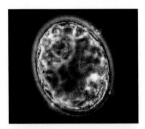

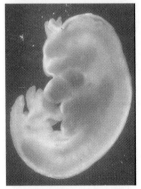

This series of photos depicts the transition from blastocyst (*top*) to embryo (*middle*) to fetus (*bottom*) during the first 3 months of pregnancy.

The Developing Body Before and After Birth: Physical and Motor Development

Child development begins long before birth. Learning, memory, and even preferences—for particular sounds or body positions, for example—are already well under way in unborn infants. Nevertheless, most of what develops in the **prenatal** (prior to birth) period is physical, including the form and structure of the body and, most important from a psychological standpoint, the brain.

CONCEPTION AND PRENATAL DEVELOPMENT: FROM ZYGOTE TO BABY

The greatest changes in prenatal development occur in the earliest stages of pregnancy. Following fertilization of an egg by a sperm cell, prenatal physical development unfolds in three basic stages. **[LEARNING OBJECTIVE 8.3]** First, the zygote begins to divide and double, forming a **blastocyst**—a ball of identical cells that haven't yet begun to take on any specific function in a body part. The blastocyst keeps growing as cells continue to divide for the first week and a half or so after fertilization. Around the middle of the second week, the cells begin to differentiate, taking on different roles as the organs of the body begin to develop.

Once different cells start to assume different functions, the blastocyst becomes an **embryo.** The embryonic stage continues from the second to the eighth week of development, during which limbs, facial features, and major organs of the body (including the heart, lungs, and brain) begin to take shape. By the ninth week, the major organs are established, and the heart—although it only has two chambers instead of the four we all have—has begun to beat. At this point, the embryo becomes a **fetus.** The fetus's job for the rest of the pregnancy is physical maturation. This phase is more about fleshing out the details of what's already there than establishing completely new structures. But the amount of change the basic structures undergo is substantial. The last third of pregnancy in particular is devoted largely to "bulking up."

Brain Development: 18 Days and Beyond.

The human brain begins to develop a mere 18 days after fertilization. Unlike most organs, which are completely formed by birth and continue to grow only in size, our brains continue to develop into adolescence and probably even early adulthood (Caviness, Kennedy, Bates, et al., 1996).

Between the eighteenth day of pregnancy and the end of the sixth month, neurons begin developing at an astronomical rate, a process called *proliferation*. Some estimates place the rate of neural development as high as an astonishing 250,000 brain cells per minute during peak times. The fetus ends up manufacturing many, many more neurons than it will need as an infant. In addition to producing all of these cells, the brain must organize them to perform coordinated functions. Starting in the fourth month and continuing throughout pregnancy, migration of cells begins to occur. Neurons start to sort themselves out, moving to their final positions in a specific structure of the brain, such as the visual system, cerebellum, and so on.

The final stage of prenatal brain development begins only late in pregnancy but continues well after birth. It includes three additional processes that help the brain work more efficiently—myelinization, synaptogenesis, and pruning (see Chapter 3)—all of which enhance transmission of information within the brain.

Obstacles to Normal Fetal Development.

Although most babies are born healthy and fully intact, fetal development can be disrupted in two ways: (1) by exposure to hazardous environmental influences and (2) by biological influences resulting from genetic disorders or errors in cell duplication during cell division.

Most women don't even realize they're pregnant until after the fetus's body and brain development are well under way. Unfortunately, this means that women often engage unknowingly in activities that are potentially harmful to the fetus. **Teratogens** are environmental factors that can exert a negative impact on prenatal development. They run the gamut from drugs and alcohol to chickenpox and X-rays. Even anxiety and depression in the mother are potential teratogens because they alter the fetus's chemical and physiological environment. Depending on the teratogen and when the embryo or fetus is exposed to it, some teratogens influence how specific parts of the brain develop, whereas others exert a more general impact on development. Because the brain has such a long period of maturation relative to most other organs, it's particularly vulnerable to teratogens.

Genetic disorders or random errors in cell division are a second adverse influence on prenatal development. Often, a single cell, including the egg or sperm cell prior to fertilization, or a family of cells, is copied with some error or break in the genetic material. Like a page with a smudge that keeps being photocopied with that smudge preserved, these cells go on to replicate with the error retained, resulting in impaired development of organs or organ systems. Any number of irregularities can result, some as minor as a birthmark and others as major as mental retardation, including Down syndrome.

Growth and Physical Development after Infancy.

Once born, our bodies continue to change dramatically through early childhood, adolescence, and adulthood. A variety of changes in our body's proportions take place as we mature. Careful inspection of a young infant reveals that he has no apparent neck, a head almost half the size of his torso, and arms that don't even reach the top of his head. Over the course of childhood, different

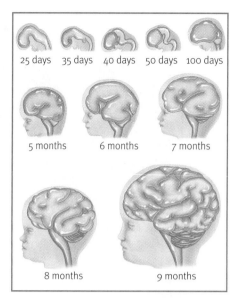

25 days   35 days   40 days   50 days   100 days

5 months   6 months   7 months

8 months   9 months

The fetal brain begins as a long tube that develops into a variety of different structures with the brain stem (which controls basic functions like breathing and digestion) developing first, followed by cortical structures later in pregnancy. (*Source:* Restak, 1984)

Exposure to alcohol during pregnancy can result in *fetal alcohol syndrome* which results in physical, cognitive, and behavioral impairment. (*Source:* Abel & Sokol, 1986).

GLOSSARY

prenatal
prior to birth

blastocyst
ball of identical cells early in pregnancy that haven't yet begun to take on any specific function in a body part

embryo
second to eighth week of prenatal development, during which limbs, facial features, and major organs of the body take form

fetus
period of prenatal development from the ninth week until birth after all major organs are established and physical maturation is the primary change

teratogens
environmental factors that can exert a negative impact on prenatal development

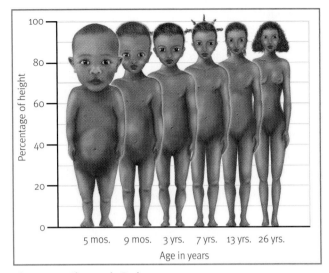

Figure 8.2 Changes in Body Proportions over Development. This figure displays the proportional size of the head, torso, and limbs across the life span when scaled to the same overall height. The size of the head relative to the body decreases dramatically over the course of development, whereas the relative length of the legs increases dramatically.

parts of the body grow at different rates, and the ultimate proportions of the body are quite different from the way they were at birth. For example, the absolute size of the head continues to increase with development, but it grows at a slower pace than the torso or legs. As a result, an adolescent or young adult has a smaller head-size-to-body-size ratio than an infant (**Figure 8.2**).

INFANT MOTOR DEVELOPMENT: HOW BABIES GET GOING

Starting at birth, infants begin to learn how to make use of their bodies through movement and to coordinate interactions with their environment. Some aspects of motor coordination are evident even at birth as a series of reflexes, whereas others develop gradually throughout infancy and early childhood.

Reflexes are automatic motor behaviors that are triggered by specific types of stimulation and fulfill important survival needs (Swaiman & Ashwal, 1999). For example, the *sucking reflex* is an automatic response to oral stimulation. If we put something in a baby's mouth (including a finger—try it sometime . . . with the parents' permission, of course!), she'll clamp down and begin sucking. Such reflexes help keep infants alive without having to take the time to learn them through trial and error.

Reflexes are a critical part of survival, but they get babies only so far. Infants must learn other types of motor behaviors through trial and error. **Motor behaviors** are bodily motions that occur as a result of self-initiated force that moves the bones and muscles. The age at which different children reach motor milestones varies enormously, although almost all acquire them in the same order (see **Figure 8.3**).

What factors influence how children build up strength and motor coordination? Physical maturation plays a key role in allowing children to become increasingly steady and flexible in their movements. There are several reasons to believe that experience also plays a crucial role in motor development (Thelen, 1995). **[LEARNING OBJECTIVE 8.4]** First, there's considerable variability across cultures in the timing of developmental milestones. Second, the fact that some children occasionally skip a stage suggests that there isn't an innate and inflexible motor program. Third, even among children who pass through all stages, there are large individual differences within cultures in the age at which children achieve motor milestones. These findings suggest that over time, children are training their brains and bodies to solve motor-based challenges, building up skills and control with practice.

Parenting styles and cultural practices also matter. Infants who spend most of their time on Mom's lap or in the crib have fewer opportunities to explore than do infants placed on their bellies on a blanket on the floor. In Peru and China, infants are tightly swaddled in blankets that provide warmth and a sense of security but prevent free movement of the limbs (Li et al., 2000), which slows down their motor development. In contrast, many African and West Indian mothers engage in a variety of stretching, massage, and strength-building exercises with their infants that speed up infants' motor development (Hopkins & Westra, 1988).

The practices of swaddling and stretching infants can seem extreme to many Americans, but these are our cultural perspectives. Although cultural variability in these practices influences the rate of motor development, none of these early physical experiences results in long-term impairments or advantages.

┌ **WHAT DO** *you* **THINK**❓

As a physician's assistant working for a pediatrician (children's doctor) you notice that babies who are heavier for their age achieve motor milestones at a slower rate than babies with lower weights. What's your hypothesis about why this might be?

GLOSSARY

motor behavior
bodily motion that occurs as result of self-initiated force that moves the bones and muscles

Figure 8.3 The Progression of Motor Development. Different children typically achieve major motor milestones in the same order, although each milestone requires an entirely new set of motor coordination skills. For example, cruising, walking, and running look similar but require very different muscle groups and shifts in weight to accomplish movement.

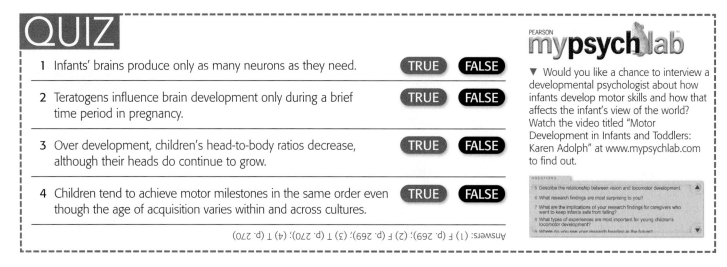

QUIZ

1 Infants' brains produce only as many neurons as they need. **TRUE** **FALSE**

2 Teratogens influence brain development only during a brief time period in pregnancy. **TRUE** **FALSE**

3 Over development, children's head-to-body ratios decrease, although their heads do continue to grow. **TRUE** **FALSE**

4 Children tend to achieve motor milestones in the same order even though the age of acquisition varies within and across cultures. **TRUE** **FALSE**

Answers: (1) F (p. 269); (2) F (p. 269); (3) T (p. 270); (4) T (p. 270).

PEARSON
mypsychlab

▼ Would you like a chance to interview a developmental psychologist about how infants develop motor skills and how that affects the infant's view of the world? Watch the video titled "Motor Development in Infants and Toddlers: Karen Adolph" at www.mypsychlab.com to find out.

QUESTIONS
5 Describe the relationship between vision and locomotor development.
6 What research findings are most surprising to you?
7 What are the implications of your research findings for caregivers who want to keep infants safe from falling?
8 What types of experiences are most important for young children's locomotor development?
9 Where do you see your research heading in the future?

Cognitive Development: Children's Learning about the World

Cognitive development—how children learn, think, reason, communicate, and remember—enables children to come to understand their worlds. Yet only relatively recently have psychologists constructed systematic theories of cognitive development.

PIAGET: HOW CHILDREN CONSTRUCT THEIR WORLDS

The pioneering Swiss psychologist Jean Piaget (1896–1980) was the first to present a comprehensive account of cognitive development. He attempted to identify the stages that children pass through on their way to adultlike cognitive abilities. Piaget's theory led to the formation of cognitive development as a distinct discipline, and for decades most research in this field focused on substantiating—or in more recent years refuting—his claims.

One of Piaget's greatest contributions was his insight that children aren't miniature adults. He showed that children's understanding of the world is fundamentally different from adults', but perfectly rational given the limited experience of children. For example, children often believe that their teachers live at school, a reasonable assumption, given that's the only place they've seen their teachers. Piaget also altered our view of children's learning by demonstrating that children are active learners who seek information and observe the consequences of their actions, rather than passive observers of the world. **[LEARNING OBJECTIVE 8.5]**

Piaget was a *stage theorist*. He believed that children's development is marked by radical reorganizations of thinking at specific points in development—stages—followed by prolonged periods during which their understanding of the world remains stable. Piaget also believed that the end point of cognitive development is achieving the ability to reason logically about hypothetical problems. As we'll soon see, each stage in Piaget's theory is characterized by a certain level of abstract reasoning capacity, with the ability to think beyond the here and now increasing at each stage.

Jean Piaget was the first and most influential scholar to propose a comprehensive account of cognitive development.

GLOSSARY

cognitive development
study of how children learn, think, reason, communicate, and remember

assimilation
Piagetian process of absorbing new experience into current knowledge structures

accommodation
Piagetian process of altering a belief to make it more compatible with experience

sensorimotor stage
stage in Piaget's theory characterized by a focus on the here and now without the ability to represent experiences mentally

Piaget believed that cognitive change is marked by *equilibration:* maintaining a balance between our experience in the world and our thoughts about it. He suggested that children use two "adjustment" processes—assimilation and accommodation—to keep their thinking about the world in balance with their experiences.

Assimilation.
The process of absorbing new experience into current knowledge structures is **assimilation.** If a child who believes the earth is flat is told that the earth is round, she might assimilate the fact that the earth is round into her knowledge bases by picturing a flat disk, shaped like a coin (see **Figure 8.4a & b**). This adjustment allows her to absorb this new fact without changing her belief that the earth is flat. Children use assimilation to acquire new knowledge within a stage. During assimilation, the child's underlying cognitive skills and worldviews remain unchanged, so she reinterprets new experiences to fit into what she already knows.

Accommodation.
The assimilation process can continue for only so long. Eventually, the child can no longer reconcile what she believes with what she experiences. A child confronted with a globe will have a difficult time assimilating this information into her belief that the earth is flat. When a child can no longer assimilate experiences into her existing knowledge structures, she's compelled to engage in *accommodation* (see **Figure 8.4c**).

Accommodation is the altering of the child's beliefs to make them more compatible with experience. Accommodation drives stage change by forcing children to enter a new way of looking at the world. This process of assimilating and accommodating ensures a state of harmony between the world and mind of the child—equilibration.

Piaget's Stages of Development.
Piaget identified four stages, each marked by a specific way of looking at the world and a set of cognitive limitations (see **Table 8.1**).

(a)

(b) Assimilation

(c) Accommodation

Figure 8.4 An Example of Assimilation and Accommodation in Action. A child's initial belief that the earth is flat (a) is adjusted through assimilation (b) when she learns the earth is round. Once her assimilated belief no longer fits with her experience, her belief undergoes accommodation (c).

Table 8.1 Descriptions of the Four Stages of Cognitive Development in Piaget's Theory.

Stage	Typical Ages	Description
Sensorimotor	Birth to 2 years	No thought beyond immediate physical experiences
Preoperational	2 to 7 years	Able to think beyond the here and now, but egocentric and unable to perform mental transformations
Concrete Operations	7 to 11 years	Able to perform mental transformations but only on concrete physical objects
Formal Operations	11 years to adulthood	Able to perform hypothetical and abstract reasoning

(1) *Sensorimotor stage:* From birth to about 2 years, the **sensorimotor stage** is marked by a focus on the here and now. Children's main sources of knowledge, thinking, and experience are their physical interactions with the world. They acquire all information through perceiving sensory information from the world and observing the physical consequences of their actions. The major milestone of this stage, which forces children to accommodate and enter a new stage, is *mental representation*—the ability to think about things that are absent from immediate surroundings, such as remembering previously encountered objects. Children in this stage lack **object permanence,** the understanding that objects continue to exist even when out of view. For them, it's "out of sight, out of mind."

(2) *Preoperational stage:* From 2 until about 7 years, children go through the **preoperational stage,** which is marked by an ability to construct mental representations of experience. Children in this stage can use such symbols as language, drawings, and objects as representations of ideas.

This child, who was just playing happily with these blocks, appears to have forgotten the blocks continue to exist after they've been hidden from view. That is, he fails to exhibit object permanence. In contrast, if the child attempted to move the partition or look behind it, this would reveal he understood the blocks continue to exist when out of view.

GLOSSARY

object permanence
the understanding that objects continue to exist even when out of view

preoperational stage
stage in Piaget's theory characterized by the ability to construct mental representations of experience, but not yet perform operations on them

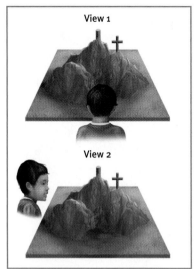

Figure 8.5 Piaget's Three Mountain Task. Piaget's three mountain task requires children to look at a display from one perspective (View 1) and infer what someone would see if viewing the mountains from a different perspective, such as View 2. Piaget argued that egocentric reasoning in the preoperational stage prevents children from succeeding at this task.

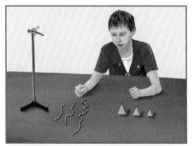

Figure 8.6 Pendulum Task. Piaget's pendulum task requires children to answer the question: "What makes a pendulum swing faster or slower?" Children have the opportunity to construct a pendulum using longer and shorter strings with heavier and lighter weights. Children in the formal operations stage can systematically manipulate various combinations of weights and lengths to observe how they influenced the speed of the swing.

REPLICABILITY
Can the results be duplicated in other studies?

GLOSSARY

egocentrism
inability to see the world from others' perspectives

conservation
Piagetian task requiring children to understand that despite a transformation in the physical presentation of an amount, the amount remains the same

When a child holds a banana and pretends it's a phone, he's displaying symbolic behavior. He has a mental representation that differs from his physical experience.

Although the preoperational stage witnesses the emergence of clear advances in thinking, Piaget believed children in this stage were hampered by **egocentrism**—an inability to see the world from others' perspectives (see **Figure 8.5**). The preoperational stage is called "preoperational" because of another limitation, the inability to perform mental operations. Although children in this stage have mental representations, they can't perform mental transformations on them. For example, they can generate a mental image of a vase sitting on a table even if the vase isn't there. But they can't imagine what would happen to the vase if they knocked it off the table. Piaget developed a set of **conservation** tasks to test children's ability to perform operations. These tasks ask children whether an amount wil be "conserved" (stay the same) after a physical transformation. For example, children might see a glass of water and then watch as the water is poured into a taller, thinner glass. The question is whether the child understands that the amount of water hasn't changed.

(3) *Concrete operational stage:* Children between 7 and 11 years old enter the **concrete operations stage,** characterized by the long-awaited ability to perform mental operations, but only for actual physical events. Children in this stage can now perform conservation tasks. They can also perform organizational tasks that require mental operations on physical objects, such as sorting coins by size or setting up a battle scene with toy soldiers. But they're still poor at performing mental operations in abstract or hypothetical situations. They need physical experience as an anchor to which they can link their mental operations.

(4) *Formal operations stage:* Piaget's fourth and final stage, which he believed didn't emerge until early adolescence, is the **formal operations stage.** It's then that children can perform what Piaget regarded as the most sophisticated type of thinking: hypothetical reasoning beyond the here and now, such as in the pendulum task in **Figure 8.6.** This task requires children to experiment systematically with hypotheses and explain outcomes. Children at this stage can understand logical concepts, such as if–then statements ("If I'm late for school, then I'll get sent to the principal's office.") and either–or statements ("Mom says I can either go to the game tonight or go to the sleepover tomorrow night.").

Pros and Cons of Piaget's Theory.

Piaget's theory was a significant landmark in psychology, as it helped us understand how children's thinking evolves into more adult-like thinking. Nevertheless, his theory turned out to be inaccurate in several ways. For example, much of development appears to be more gradual than stagelike (Flavell, 1992; Klahr & MacWhinney, 1998; Siegler, 1995).

Also, many of the phenomena Piaget observed appeared to be at least partly a product of task demands. He often relied on children's ability to reflect and report on their reasoning processes. As a result, he probably underestimated children's underlying competence. Investigators have found it difficult to replicate the developmental progression he observed using less language-dependent tasks.

Piaget's methodologies may have been culturally biased in that they elicited more sophisticated responses from children in Westernized societies with formal education than from those in non-Westernized societies. Yet non-Westernized children often reveal sophisticated insights when interviewed in a more culturally sensitive manner (Cole, 1990; Gellatly, 1987; Luria, 1976; Rogoff & Chavajay, 1995). Meanwhile, even in Western societies, a significant proportion of adolescents fail on some formal operational tasks (Byrnes, 1988; Kuhn, Garcia-Mila, Zohar, et al., 1995), indicating that Piaget may have been overly optimistic about the typical course of cognitive development. Perhaps Piaget based his conclusions on a particularly educated or scientifically sophisticated sample that skewed his estimates of the typical developmental trajectory. Piaget's observations themselves may also have been biased because many were based on tests of his own three children.

Despite these shortcomings, Piaget justifiably remains a towering figure in the field of cognitive development (Lourenco & Machado, 1996). As a result of his legacy, psychologists today have reconceptualized cognitive development by:

(1) viewing children as different in kind rather than degree from adults;

(2) characterizing learning as an active rather than passive process; and

(3) exploring general cognitive processes that may operate across multiple domains of knowledge, thereby accounting for cognitive development in terms of fewer—and more parsimonious—explanations.

OCCAM'S RAZOR
Does a simpler explanation fit the data just as well?

VYGOTSKY: SOCIAL AND CULTURAL INFLUENCES ON LEARNING

At around the same time that Piaget was constructing his theory, Russian researcher Lev Vygotsky (1896–1934) was developing a different but equally comprehensive theory of cognitive development that examined how social and cultural factors influence learning. Vygotsky adopted a different approach to cognitive development, because he was particularly interested in how social and cultural factors influence learning. He noted that parents and other caretakers tend to structure the learning environment for children in ways that guide them to behave as if they've learned something before they have. Vygostky referred to this process as **scaffolding,** a term he borrowed from building construction. Just as builders provide external scaffolds for support while a building is under construction, parents provide a structure to aid their children. Over time, parents gradually remove structure as children become better able to complete tasks on their own.

One of Vygotsky's most influential notions was the idea of developmental readiness for learning. He identified the **zone of proximal development** as the phase, or learning period, when children are receptive to learning a new skill but aren't yet successful at it. He suggested that for any given skill, children move from a phase when they can't learn a skill, even with assistance, to the zone of proximal development, during which they're ready to make use of scaffolding. In his view, children gradually learn to perform a task independently but require guidance when getting started. Vygotsky also believed that different children can acquire skills and master tasks at different rates. Unlike Piaget, he believed that change was gradual rather than stagelike.

Vygotsky, like Piaget, has left a lasting legacy. His work is particularly influential in educational settings, where guided learning and peer collaboration are common approaches. Vygotsky's influence also lives on in accounts of early learning in infancy and toddlerhood. Whereas Piaget emphasized physical interaction with the world as the primary source of learning, Vygotsky emphasized children's interactions with the social world.

Vygotsky used the term *scaffolding* to refer to the way parents structure the learning environment for children. Here, the father is instructing the child how to fit the shape onto a peg but allowing the child to insert the shape himself.

┌ **WHAT DO** *you* **THINK** *?*

Your child's dentist says it's time for your daughter to begin having her teeth brushed regularly. Using Vygotsky's theory of scaffolding, how would you help your child learn to brush her teeth by herself?

CONTEMPORARY THEORIES OF COGNITIVE DEVELOPMENT

Theoretical accounts today are much more diverse than when the field of cognitive development first got off the ground, and few researchers are strictly Piagetian or Vygotskian. Still, we can trace the roots of each theory to one of these two theorists.

GLOSSARY

concrete operations stage
stage in Piaget's theory characterized by the ability to perform mental operations on physical events only

formal operations stage
stage in Piaget's theory characterized by the ability to perform hypothetical reasoning beyond the here and now

scaffolding
Vygotskian learning process in which parents provide initial assistance in children's learning but gradually remove structure as children become more competent

zone of proximal development
phase of learning during which children can benefit from instruction

Several influential modern theories resemble Piaget's theories in that they emphasize general cognitive abilities, experience-based learning, and acquired rather than innate knowledge (Elman, 1993; McClelland, 1995; Plunkett, Karmiloff-Smith, Bates, et al., 1997; Thelen & Smith, 1994). General cognitive theorists share Piaget's commitment to general cognitive processes and experience-based learning. However, they differ from Piaget in that they tend to explain learning as gradual rather than stagelike.

Sociocultural theories emphasize the social context and the ways in which interactions with caretakers and other children guide children's understanding of the world (Rogoff, 1998; Tomasello, 1999). Some sociocultural theorists emphasize experience-based learning, whereas others emphasize innate knowledge. But, along with Vygotsky, they share a focus on the child's interaction with the social world as the primary source of development.

Modularity theories emphasize the idea of separate spheres of knowledge in different learning domains (Carey, 1985; Spelke, 1994; Wellman & Gelman, 1998). For example, the knowledge base for understanding language may be completely independent from the ability to reason about space, with no overlapping cognitive skills between them. Many modularity theorists developed their ideas in reaction to Piaget's theory and instead argued that children come into the world with innate knowledge about these different domains.

myth CONCEPTIONS CAN LISTENING TO MOZART CREATE "SUPERBABIES"?

Claims for the Mozart effect have contributed to a huge industry of products for babies and young children, yet the scientific evidence for this effect is surprisingly weak.

For years, parents have yearned for a quick and easy educational method to boost their infants' intelligence. After all, in today's cutthroat world, what parents wouldn't want to place their child at a competitive advantage? To get a jump start, of course, parents must begin early, ideally soon after birth. This seemingly far-fetched hope that parents can turn their babies into miniature geniuses turned into apparent reality in 1993 with the publication of an article in the prestigious journal *Nature*. That paper reported that college students who listened to about 10 minutes of a Mozart piano sonata showed a significant improvement on a spatial reasoning task compared with a group of students who listened to a relaxation tape (Rauscher, Shaw, & Ky, 1993). The *Mozart effect*—the supposed enhancement in intelligence after listening to classical music (Campbell, 1997)—was born.

The 1993 finding didn't say anything about long-term enhancement of spatial ability, let alone intelligence in general. It applied only to a task administered almost immediately after listening to Mozart's music. And the findings were based entirely on college students. But this didn't stop the popular press or toy companies from taking the Mozart effect ball and running with it. Companies soon marketed scores of Mozart effect CDs and cassettes targeted toward babies, featuring claims that listening to the music of Mozart and other composers boosts infant intelligence. In 1998, then Georgia Governor Zell Miller added $105,000 to the state budget to allow each newborn in Georgia to receive a free Mozart CD or cassette.

Miller's decision was premature. In fact, researchers had a devil of a time replicating the Mozart effect. Many couldn't find the effect at all, and those who did discovered that it was trivial in magnitude (2 IQ points or less) and of short duration (an hour or less; Chabris, 1999; Steele, Bass, & Crook, 1999). Zell Miller (1999) urged advocates of the Mozart effect to ignore these negative findings, imploring them not "to be misled or discouraged by some academics debunking other academics." But this is precisely how science works at its best: by trying to falsify claims made by other investigators.

REPLICABILITY
Can the results be duplicated in other studies?

FALSIFIABILITY
Can the claim be disproved?

Later researchers helped to nail down the source of the Mozart effect. The results of one study suggested that the effect may be due to the greater emotional arousal produced by listening to Mozart relative to either other composers or silence (Thompson, Schellenberg, & Husain, 2001). Another researcher found that listening to Mozart was no better for improving spatial ability than listening to a passage from a scary story. These findings suggest that a more parsimonious explanation for the Mozart effect is short-term arousal. Anything that boosts alertness is likely to increase performance on mentally demanding tasks, but it's unlikely to produce long-term effects on spatial ability or, for that matter, overall intelligence. Our advice: It's a wonderful idea to expose infants and children to great music. But don't expect it to turn babies into superbabies.

> **OCCAM'S RAZOR**
> Does a simpler explanation fit the data just as well?

COGNITIVE LANDMARKS OF EARLY DEVELOPMENT

We've already learned about some of the major cognitive accomplishments within the realms of memory (Chapter 6) and language (Chapter 7). But children must attain a variety of other cognitive skills to make sense of their worlds. Here, we'll review some of the highlights.

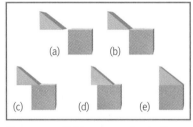

Figure 8.7 Children Learn Gradually That Unsupported Objects Will Fall. As early as 4½ months, infants expect objects that are completely unsupported, as in (a), to fall and objects that are completely supported, as in (e), not to fall. An understanding of how much support must be present to prevent an object from falling develops over time. Early on, infants expect that any contact with a support surface will prevent the object from falling, as in (b), (c), and (d). With experience, infants learn to expect that only those in (d) and (e), in which the majority of the weight is on the support surface, won't fall.

Physical Reasoning: Figuring out Which Way Is Up. To understand their physical worlds, children must learn to reason about them. They need to learn that objects are solid, that they fall when dropped, and that one object can disappear behind another and reappear on the other side. We adults take all of these concepts for granted, but they aren't obvious to novice experiencers of the world.

Infants possess a basic understanding of some aspects of how physical objects behave, a set of beliefs sometimes called *naive physics*. For example, they know that objects that are unsupported should fall (Spelke, 1994). However, this basic knowledge becomes more refined and sophisticated with experience **(Figure 8.7)** (Baillargeon & Hanko-Summers, 1990; Needham & Baillargeon, 1993). **[LEARNING OBJECTIVE 8.6]**

Self-Concept and the Concept of "Other": Who We Are and Who We Aren't. Developing a sense of self, as different from others, is critical for children's development. Their ability to understand themselves as possessing separate and unique identities unfolds gradually during the toddler and preschool years. But even by 3 months of age, infants possess some sense of self as distinct from others. Babies at this age who view a video of themselves side by side with a video of another baby prefer to look at the image of the other baby

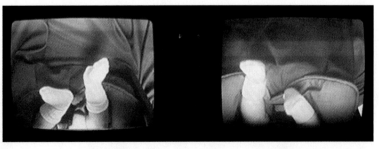

Infants who view a video image of their own legs side by side with a videotape of another infant's legs will look longer at the video of the other baby suggesting self-recognition (Bahrick & Watson, 1985).

(Bahrick, Moss, & Fadil, 1996; Rochat, 2001). Indeed, infants who see a live-action video of only their legs side by side with a recording of another infant's legs still prefer to watch the video of the other baby's legs, even if both sets of legs are dressed identically. This finding reveals that babies aren't just demonstrating a preference for the other baby's face because they've seen their own face before in the mirror or in photographs.

As early as their first birthdays, children can recognize their images in a mirror (Amsterdam, 1972; Priel & deSchonen, 1986; see Chapter 6). By 2 years, they can

> **RULING OUT RIVAL HYPOTHESES**
> Have important alternative explanations for the findings been excluded?

recognize pictures of themselves and refer to themselves by name (Lewis & Brooks-Gunn, 1979). These accomplishments appear to be tied to development in a specific brain region, the junction of the left temporal and parietal lobe (Lewis & Carmody, 2008).

A further milestone is children's ability to understand that others' perspectives can differ from theirs. An ability called **theory of mind** is a key component of perspective-taking (Premack & Woodruff, 1978). Theory of mind refers to children's ability to reason about what other people know or believe. (Note that according to Chapter 1 this "theory" isn't really a theory!) The big challenge for children on this front is to realize that "other people may not know what I know."

A classic test of theory of mind is the *false-belief task* (Birch & Bloom, 2007; Wimmer & Perner, 1983) (see **Figure 8.8**), which tests children's ability to understand that someone else believes something they know to be wrong. Children typically don't succeed at this task until around age 4 or 5. Yet how early children succeed on false-belief tasks varies enormously depending on the task (Wellman, Cross, & Watson, 2001; Onishi & Baillargeon, 2005). If researchers arrange the false-belief task so that it's more of a real-world situation and less of a story, most children can pass it. Also, if researchers tell children the reason for the change was to "trick" someone, they're more successful at an earlier age. Thus, children's failure on the classic false-belief task before age 4 may be due to aspects of the task rather than their inadequate understanding of others' knowledge. Nonetheless, it's clear that the ability to understand others' perspectives increases with age.

RULING OUT RIVAL HYPOTHESES
Have important alternative explanations
for the findings been excluded?

Numbers and Mathematics: What Counts.
Counting and math are relatively recent cognitive achievements in human history. Humans developed the first counting system only a few thousand years ago. Unlike many cognitive skills that children acquire, counting and mathematics don't always develop. In fact, there are a few remaining nonindustrialized cultures such as the Pirahã, a tribe in Brazil, in which conventional counting and mathematics appear not to exist (Gordon, 2004).

GLOSSARY

theory of mind
ability to reason about what other people
know or believe

(a)   (b)   (c)   (d)

Figure 8.8 **The False-Belief Task.** In the false-belief task, the child participant knows something about which someone else is unaware. In this scenario, the child learns that Joey in the story believes the candy bar is in the cabinet. But because she's heard the whole story, the child knows the candy bar is really in the refrigerator. When asked where Joey thinks the candy is, will the child respond with her own knowledge of the true location, or will she realize that Joey is unaware of this change?

Learning to count is a lot more complex than it seems. Of course, many children learn to "count to ten" at a very early age, reciting "1-2-3-4-5-6-7-8-9-10" in rapid succession and waiting for applause to follow. But children must also learn that (1) numbers are about amount and (2) number words refer to specific quantities (and not just "a bunch" or "a few"). After that, children must grasp many subtle aspects of number concepts before they can count accurately (Gelman & Gallistel, 1978). One of the most challenging concepts for children to master is the idea that two elephants is the same number as two grains of rice—that the *size* of entities isn't relevant to quantity (Mix, 1999; Mix, Huttenlocher, & Levine, 1996).

Counting and other mathematical skills in preschool- and school-aged children develop at different rates across cultures. Cross-cultural differences in how parents and teachers introduce counting to children seem to account, at least in part, for these differences (Miller, Smith, Zhu, et al., 1995).

Fact-OID Not all cultures count to 10 on their fingers; many have much more elaborate systems of tracking amounts on their fingers, hands, arms, heads, and other body parts. Some systems have specific body locations assigned for numbers from 1 to as high at 74!

QUIZ

1 Piaget argued that development was gradual. **TRUE** **FALSE**

2 Vygotsky's theory proposes that individual children vary in the age at which they achieve developmental readiness for particular cognitive abilities. **TRUE** **FALSE**

3 Children fail to display evidence of theory of mind before age 4. **TRUE** **FALSE**

4 The ability to count precise quantities is absent in some cultures. **TRUE** **FALSE**

Answers: (1) F (p. 272); (2) T (p. 275); (3) F (p. 278); (4) T (p. 278)

PEARSON mypsychlab

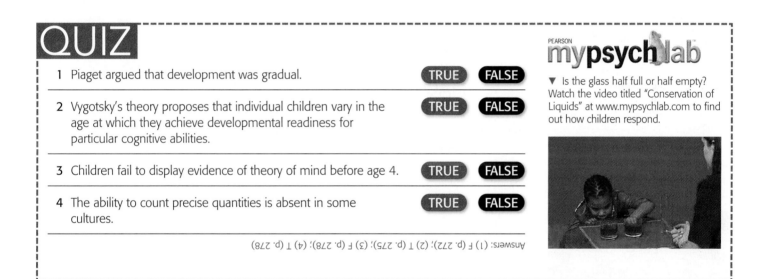

▼ Is the glass half full or half empty? Watch the video titled "Conservation of Liquids" at www.mypsychlab.com to find out how children respond.

Social and Moral Development: Children's Relations with Others

Although infants are largely in their own little worlds, almost immediately after birth, they soon begin to take a keen interest in others. Infants prefer looking at faces over just about all other visual information. In fact, as early as 4 days after birth, infants show a marked preference for Mommy's face compared with that of other women (Pascalis, de Schonen, Morton, et al., 1995). Infants are profoundly interested in other people, and this is a good thing because people (particularly familiar people, like their parents) are a valuable source of information and provide the love and support they need to flourish.

STRANGER ANXIETY: THE SUDDEN CHANGE AT 8 MONTHS

As sociable as infants are, something changes dramatically over the course of only a few months. The same infant who was giggling on the floor with a perfect stranger at 6 months may scream in terror if approached by that same stranger only a few months later. This phenomenon is known as **stranger anxiety.** Known also as *8 months anxiety,* this behavior manifests itself in a fear of strangers beginning at about 8 or 9 months of age (Greenberg, Hillman, & Grice, 1973; Konner, 1990) (see **Figure 8.9**). It generally increases up until about 12 to 15 months of age, and then declines steadily. Interestingly, the onset of stranger anxiety appears to be virtually identical in all cultures (Kagan, 1976). Eight months anxiety makes good evolutionary sense, because it's at about this age that most infants begin to crawl around on their own. As a result, it's the age at which infants can—and usually do—find a way to get themselves into trouble. So this anxiety may be an adaptive mechanism for keeping infants away from unknown adults who could pose a danger to them.

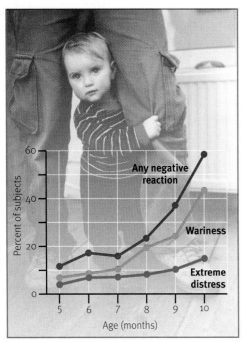

Figure 8.9 Stranger Anxiety. As we can see in this graph from one published study, infants' anxiety and negative reactions when confronted with a stranger first begin at around 8 or 9 months and continue to increase. Typically, they won't begin to decline until about 12 or 15 months. (*Source:* Waters, Matas, & Sroufe, 1975)

ATTACHMENT: ESTABLISHING BONDS

Stranger anxiety is merely one manifestation of a broader phenomenon of **attachment,** the emotional connection we share with those to whom we are closest. With rare exceptions, such as autism (see Chapters 2 and 13), all infants forge close emotional bonds with important adults, usually their parents. Again, there may be a good evolutionary reason for the attachment bond. It ensures that infants and children don't stray too far from the powerful others who feed and protect them (Bowlby, 1973). To understand the origins of attachment, we need to begin with the story of an Austrian zoologist and his birds.

Imprinting. In the 1930s, Konrad Lorenz—who went on to win a Nobel Prize for the work we're about to describe—was observing the behaviors of geese. By sheer accident, he discovered that goslings (young geese) displayed a remarkable behavior shortly following birth. Specifically, goslings seemed to follow around the first large, moving object they saw after hatching. Although Lorenz (1937) referred to this phenomenon as "stamping in" in German, it's come to be known in English as **imprinting.**

Of course, 99 percent or more of the time, the first large, moving object that a gosling sees after emerging from the egg is none other than Mother Goose. But Lorenz showed that goslings will cheerfully imprint onto whatever large, moving object they see following birth—including Lorenz himself. Newborn goslings will even imprint onto inanimate objects, such as large white bouncing balls and boxes on wheels if they have nothing better to choose from (Johnson, 1992).

As Nobel Prize–winning biologist Konrad Lorenz goes for a swim, he's followed by three geese who imprinted on him almost immediately after they hatched.

Critical Periods. Lorenz discovered that imprinting occurs only during a *critical period* (Almli & Finger, 1987): a specific window of time during which an event must occur. In the case of Lorenz's goslings, this critical period was about 36 hours. If the goslings didn't see their mothers until after that window closed, they never imprinted to her, or to anything else for that matter. Once the critical period passes, it's difficult for goslings to establish bonds with their mother or other attachment figures.

In reality, most critical periods don't end as abruptly as Lorenz believed (Bruer, 1999). That's especially true of intelligent mammals, like cats, dogs, and humans, whose behav-

GLOSSARY

stranger anxiety
a fear of strangers developing at 8 or 9 months of age

attachment
the strong emotional connection we share with those to whom we feel closest

imprinting
phenomenon observed in which baby birds begin to follow around and attach themselves to any large moving object they see in the hours immediately after hatching

iors are more flexible than those of geese. That's why most psychologists now use the term *sensitive period* to refer to developmental windows in humans.

Do humans also have sensitive periods for social bonding? This question is controversial. When it comes to attachment, there's some indication that early separation from attachment figures can produce detrimental effects. Some of the best evidence comes from a longitudinal study of Romanian infants adopted from orphanages. Sir Michael Rutter and his colleagues found that although infants adopted before 6 months of age fared well later, those older than 6 months of age when adopted often exhibited what appeared to be negative effects of their early environment, including low IQs and serious emotional problems, such as inattention and hyperactivity (Kreppner, O'Connor, & Rutter, 2001; O'Connor & Rutter, 2000). Nevertheless, there may be another explanation for these findings: The children who were adopted later may have had more emotional difficulties to begin with. As a consequence, they may have been more difficult to place in adoptive families. The finding that early institutionalization is associated with later emotional problems has been replicated in numerous studies using different methodologies (Ames, 1997; Kreppner et al., 2001).

> **RULING OUT RIVAL HYPOTHESES**
> Have important alternative explanations for the findings been excluded?

> **REPLICABILITY**
> Can the results be duplicated in other studies?

Contact Comfort: The Healing Touch.

Given that human infants don't imprint onto attachment figures, on what basis do they bond to their parents? For decades, psychologists assumed that the primary basis for the attachment bond is the nourishment supplied by mothers. Children bond to those who provide them with milk and food, and in most cases this happens to be Mommy. This view is consistent with the assumptions of behaviorism (see Chapter 5), which posited that reinforcement is the primary influence on our preferences.

Harry Harlow overturned this assumption in the 1950s with his research on infant rhesus monkeys, which are close genetic relatives of humans (Blum, 2002). Harlow (1958) separated baby monkeys from their mothers only a few hours after birth. He then placed them in a cage with two "surrogate" mothers, both inanimate. One—the "wire mother"—consisted of an angular face and a cold, mangled mesh of uncomfortable metal wires. This wire mother did have one thing going for her, though: nourishment. She sported a little bottle of milk from which the baby monkey could drink. In sharp contrast, the second mother, the "terry cloth mother," was made of foam rubber, overlaid with a comfortable layer of terry cloth, and heated with a lightbulb. Harlow found that although baby monkeys routinely went to wire mothers for milk, they actually spent much more of their time with terry cloth mothers. In addition, when Harlow exposed monkeys to a scary stimulus, like a toy robot playing a drum, they were much more likely to run to the terry cloth mother and cling to her for reassurance. Harlow termed this phenomenon **contact comfort:** the positive emotions resulting from touch.

Attachment Styles: The Strange Situation.

As every professional baby sitter or day care worker knows, infants attach to their parents in radically different ways. Some are cuddly and affectionate, whereas others are distant and standoffish. Some are calm, whereas others are jittery.

Although these anecdotal observations offer useful insights, it wasn't until Mary Ainsworth and her colleagues developed the *Strange Situation* that psychologists settled on a systematic way of quantifying infants' attachment styles (Ainsworth et al., 1978). The Strange Situation is a laboratory procedure for examining 1-year-olds' reactions to separation from their mothers. Here's how it works. First, researchers place

When frightened by a novel object, Harlow's infant monkeys almost always preferred the terry cloth mother over the wire mother. Contact comfort prevails over nourishment.

GLOSSARY

contact comfort
positive emotions resulting from touch

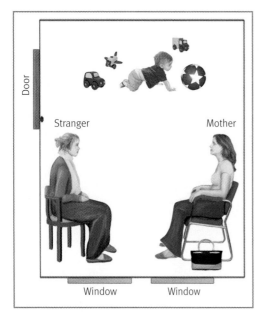

Figure 8.10 Physical Setup of the Strange Situation. In the Strange Situation, both the mother and a stranger are present before the mother leaves the child with the stranger. (*Source:* Ainsworth et al., 1978)

MYTH: Infants develop attachment relationships only with their mothers.

REALITY: Infants form attachment bonds with both mothers and fathers and with siblings, grandparents, and other caregivers. In two-parent households, a strong preference for the primary caregiver disappears around the age of 18 months.

the infant in an unfamiliar room with his or her mother. The room is loaded with all kinds of interesting toys, and the mother gives the infant the chance to play with them. Then a stranger enters. On two different occasions, the mother exits the room, leaving the infant alone with the stranger before reuniting with her infant. Researchers observe the infant's reactions to each departure and return. The Strange Situation takes advantage of infants' stranger anxiety, which as we've learned tends to peak at about 1 year. Today, most attachment researchers rely on the Strange Situation to measure infants' attachment styles **(Figure 8.10).**

Most researchers find that infants' behaviors fall into one of four categories: **[LEARNING OBJECTIVE 8.7]**

(1) *Secure attachment* (about 60 percent of U.S. infants). The infant reacts to mom's departure by becoming upset but greets her return with joy. In essence, the infant uses mom as a *secure base:* a rock-solid source of support to which to turn in times of trouble (Bowlby, 1990).

(2) *Insecure-avoidant attachment* (about 15 to 20 percent of U.S. infants). The infant reacts to mom's departure with indifference and shows little reaction on her return.

(3) *Insecure-anxious attachment* (about 15 to 20 percent of U.S. infants). The infant reacts to mom's departure with panic. He then shows a mixed emotional reaction on her return, simultaneously reaching for her yet squirming to get away after she picks him up (for this reason, some psychologists refer to this style as "anxious-ambivalent").

(4) *Disorganized attachment* (about 5 to 10 percent of U.S infants). This rarest of attachment styles wasn't included in the original classification, but was added later by Mary Main and her colleagues (Main & Cassidy, 1988). Children with this pattern react to mom's departure and return with an inconsistent and confused set of responses. They may appear dazed when reunited with her.

Note that we wrote "U.S. infants" in parentheses following each classification. That's because there are cultural differences in attachment style. For example, more infants in Japan than in the United States fall into the insecure-anxious category, whereas more infants in the United States than in Japan fall into the insecure-avoidant category (Rothbaum, Weisz, Pott, et al., 2000). The reasons for these differences aren't known, but they may stem in part from the fact that Japanese babies tend to experience fewer separations from mom in everyday life than American babies do. As a consequence, Japanese babies may find the Strange Situation to be even "stranger"—and more stressful—than do American babies (van Ijzendoorn & Sagi, 1999).

The attachment styles derived from the Strange Situation predict children's later behavior. Infants with a secure attachment style tend to grow up to be more well adjusted, helpful, and empathic than infants with other attachment styles (LaFreniere & Sroufe, 1985; Sroufe, 1983). In contrast, infants with an anxious attachment style are more likely to be disliked and mistreated by their peers later in childhood than infants with other attachment styles (Renken, Egeland, Marvinney, et al., 1989).

Still, the Strange Situation has its shortcomings. In particular, the Strange Situation isn't especially reliable. Children may be classified in different attachment categories at different points in development (Lamb, Thompson, Gardner, et al., 1984; Paris, 2000). Moreover, almost 40 percent of children display a different attachment style with their mother than with their father (van Ijzendoorn & De Wolff, 1997), suggesting that many children can't simply be pigeonholed into a single attachment classification.

┌─ WHAT DO *you* THINK?

While doing research for a class assignment, you come across an article (Fonagy, Steele, & Steele, 1991) reporting that infants' attachment styles can be predicted by interviewing the infants' mothers while they were still pregnant (in other words, before the babies were born). How might you explain this finding?

(a)

TEMPERAMENT AND SOCIAL DEVELOPMENT: OUR EMOTIONAL ENDOWMENT

Another factor that contributes to children's social and emotional development is **temperament.** Psychologists define *temperament* as comprising differences in people's basic emotional styles (Mervielde, De Clercq, De Fruyt, et al., 2005). They distinguish temperament from other general personality characteristics by two key features: Temperament is *early appearing* and *largely genetic* in origin. **[LEARNING OBJECTIVE 8.8]**

In their studies of 141 American children, Alexander Thomas and Stella Chess (1977) identified three major temperamental styles. *Easy* infants (about 40 percent of babies) are adaptable and relaxed; *difficult* infants (about 10 percent of babies) are fussy and easily frustrated; and *slow-to-warm-up* infants (about 15 percent of babies) are disturbed by new stimuli at first but gradually adjust to them. The remaining 35 percent of children, Thomas and Chess found, don't fit neatly into any of these three categories.

Based initially on research with cats, Jerome Kagan identified another temperament that he termed *behavioral inhibition* (Kagan, Snidman, Kahn, et al., 2007). Behaviorally inhibited human infants become frightened at the sight of novel or unexpected stimuli, like unfamiliar faces, loud tones, or little moving robots (Kagan, Reznick, & Snidman, 1988). According to Kagan and his colleagues, we find this temperamental style in about 10 percent of human children. Infants with high levels of behavioral inhibition are also at heightened risk for shyness and anxiety disorders in childhood or adolescence (Biederman et al., 2001; Turner, Beidel, & Wolff, 1996).

(b)

(c)

The majority of children fall into one of three temperament categories: (a) easy, (b) difficult, and (c) slow to warm up.

PARENTING: WHAT'S RIGHT AND WHAT'S WRONG?

Over the past century, self-proclaimed parenting experts have bombarded nervous mothers and fathers with contradictory advice about how to raise their children (Hulbert, 2003; Rankin, 2005). In the 1950s and 1960s, pediatrician Dr. Benjamin Spock became a major proponent of a *child-centered* or "soft" approach to parenting, in which parents should be highly responsive to their children's needs (Hulbert, 2003). Other experts have instead called for a *parent-centered* or "hard" approach to parenting, in which parents don't reinforce children's calls for excessive attention.

With all of this confusing and at times inconsistent advice, what are parents to do aside from shrugging their shoulders? We can find some helpful hints in the work of Diana Baumrind (1971, 1991). Based on her observations of Caucasian middle-class families, Baumrind concluded that parenting styles fall into three major categories:

GLOSSARY

temperament
basic emotional style that appears early in development and is largely genetic in origin

A host of newsstand magazines provides parents with advice about different parenting behaviors and styles. Psychological science can help them evaluate the validity of this advice.

CORRELATION vs. CAUSATION
Can we be sure that A causes B?

In collectivist cultures, where obedience to authority is highly valued, authoritarian parenting may be associated with better outcomes than authoritative parenting.

GLOSSARY

average expectable environment
environment that provides children with basic needs for affection and discipline

- *Permissive*. Permissive parents tend to be lenient with their children, allowing them considerable freedom inside and outside the household. They use discipline sparingly, if at all, and often shower their children with affection.
- *Authoritarian*. Authoritarian parents tend to be strict with their children, punishing them when they don't respond appropriately to their demands. They show little affection toward their children.
- *Authoritative*. Authoritative parents combine the best features of both permissive and authoritarian worlds. They're supportive of their children but set clear and firm limits with them.

Since Baumrind developed her initial threefold classification, some authors (Maccoby & Martin, 1983) identified a fourth style of parenting:

- *Uninvolved*. Neglectful parents tend to ignore their children, paying little attention to either their positive or negative behaviors.

Baumrind (1991) and other investigators (Weiss & Schwarz, 1996) found that children with *authoritative* parents tend to exhibit the best social and emotional adjustment and the lowest levels of behavior problems, at least among Caucasian middle-class American families. Children with uninvolved parents tend to fare the worst, and children with either permissive or authoritarian parents fall in between.

Superficially, these findings appear to suggest that parents should raise their children authoritatively. Yet Baumrind's findings are only correlational and therefore don't permit us to draw cause-and-effect inferences. In fact, the correlations that Baumrind reported could be largely or entirely genetic in origin. For example, permissive parents may tend to be impulsive and pass on genes predisposing to impulsivity to their children.

There's one more limitation to Baumrind's conclusions. Some researchers have found that her findings don't hold up as well in *collectivist* cultures, like China, as they do in *individualistic* cultures, like the United States. Collectivist cultures place a high premium on group harmony, whereas individualist cultures place a high premium on achievement and independence (Triandis & Suh, 2002). In particular, some data suggests that authoritarian parenting is associated with better outcomes in collectivist than in individualist societies (Sorkhabi, 2005; Steinberg, 2001).

So what's the bottom line on parenting styles? The bulk of the research suggests that specific parenting styles may not matter as much as experts had once thought. By and large, if parents provide their children with what Heinz Hartmann (1939) termed the **average expectable environment**—that is, an environment that provides children with basic needs for affection and appropriate discipline—most of their children will probably turn out just fine.

MORAL DEVELOPMENT: KNOWING RIGHT FROM WRONG

Children begin to develop ideas of right and wrong as toddlers and preschoolers. But *moral dilemmas*—situations in which there are no clear right or wrong answers—arise much more frequently in the teen and young adult years. Should I lie to my parents about where I've been so they don't worry about me? Should I avoid my nice but dorky friend so that my popular friends will like me better? The approach we adopt to these and other moral problems changes over the course of development.

Origins of Conscience.

There's good reason to believe that we can trace the roots of our conscience—that little voice inside our heads that tells us what is and isn't morally appropriate—to *fear*. We initially fear the punishment of our parents—and later our teachers—for misbehavior, so we learn not to do bad things to avoid their wrath. Over time, our fears become internalized. **[LEARNING OBJECTIVE 8.9]** We come to fear not merely the recriminations of our parents and teachers but the recriminations of our own moral sensibilities (Lykken, 1995). As Freud (1932) observed, we become afraid of ourselves.

Piaget and Morality.

Piaget believed that children's moral development is constrained by their stage of cognitive development (Loevinger, 1987). For example, he suggested that children in the concrete operational stage tend to evaluate people in terms of *objective responsibility*—how much harm they've done. As they approach formal operations, however, they tend to evaluate people in terms of *subjective responsibility*—their intentions to produce harm (Piaget, 1932).

If we ask a 6- or 7-year-old who's more to blame, (a) a child who accidentally knocks over 20 kitchen plates in his parents' cabinet or (b) a child who purposefully knocks over 10 kitchen plates because he was hopping mad at his parents, she's more likely to say (a), because it produced more damage. In contrast, a 12- or 13-year-old is more likely to say (b), because it was intentional. With age, children become better able to understand that there's more to personal responsibility than the sheer amount of damage one has wrought. Whether they mean to inflict damage also counts.

Early in development, children judge morality based on how much damage was done. Older children distinguish between accidental and intentional damage.

Kohlberg and Morality: Finding the Moral High Ground.

Lawrence Kohlberg extended Piaget's thinking to identify how morality unfolds over time. He studied how morality changes with development by exploring how participants wrestle with moral dilemmas. Because Kohlberg's moral dilemmas don't have clear right or wrong answers, he didn't score the answers that participants provided; he scored only the *reasoning processes* they used. For Kohlberg, what's crucial are the underlying principles that people invoke to solve moral problems.

We'll explain this point using one famous moral dilemma that Kohlberg used. Consider Heinz's dilemma and think about how you'd handle it.

Heinz and the Drug

In Europe, a woman was near death from a special kind of cancer. There was one drug that the doctors thought might save her. It was a form of radium that a druggist in the same town had recently discovered. The drug was expensive to make, but the druggist was charging ten times what the drug cost him to make. He paid $400 for the radium and charged $4,000 for a small dose of the drug. The sick woman's husband, Heinz, went to everyone he knew to borrow the money and tried every legal means, but he could only get together about $2,000, which is half of what it cost. He told the druggist that his wife was dying, and asked him to sell it cheaper or let him pay later. But the druggist said, "No, I discovered the drug and I'm going to make money from it." So, having tried every legal means, Heinz gets desperate and considers breaking into the man's store to steal the drug.
Question: Should Heinz steal the drug? Why or why not?

Imagine you've just learned that your long-time next-door neighbor, a kind and caring person, is wanted for an attempted murder committed three decades ago (this scenario describes Sara Jane Olson, ex-member of a violent revolutionary organization, shown here with her daughter). Would you turn her in to the police?

After testing many children, adolescents, and adults, Kohlberg (1976, 1981) concluded that the development of morality occurs in three major stages. We can see these stages, along with sample answers to the Heinz dilemma that go along with them, in **Table 8.2** on page 286. The first level, *preconventional morality,* is marked by a focus on punishment and reward. What's right is what we're rewarded for; what's wrong is what we're punished

Table 8.2 Kohlberg's Scheme of Moral Development and Sample Explanations. Kohlberg scored the reasoning processes underlying the answer to the Heinz dilemma, not the answers themselves.

Level	Heinz should steal the drug because . . .	Heinz should *not* steal the drug because . . .
Preconventional morality	He can get away with it	He might get caught
Conventional morality	Others will look down on him if he lets his wife die	It's against the law
Postconventional morality	The protection of human life is a higher moral principle that can overrule laws against stealing	Doing so violates a basic social contract needed to preserve civilization: Thou shalt not steal

for. The second level, *conventional morality,* is marked by a focus on societal values. What's right is what society approves of; what's wrong is what society disapproves of. The third level, *postconventional morality,* is marked by a focus on internal moral principles that transcend society. What's right is what accords with fundamental human rights and values; what's wrong is what contradicts these rights and values.

Criticisms of Kohlberg's Work.

Kohlberg's work has been enormously influential; his research has shed light on the development of morality, and it's informed educational efforts to enhance people's moral reasoning (Kohlberg & Turiel, 1971; Loevinger, 1987). Still, Kohlberg's findings have met with more than their share of criticism.

Some have argued that there is cultural or gender bias in Kohlberg's coding scheme (Gilligan, 1982; Schweder, Mahapatra, & Miller, 1990). Others have argued that his scheme has low external validity (see Chapter 2) because the correlations between scores on Kohlberg's scheme and measures of real-world moral behavior are only moderate in size (Blasi, 1980; Krebs & Denton, 2005). Another criticism involves Kohlberg's assumption that our moral reasoning precedes our emotional reaction to moral issues. Some have suggested that our reactions to moral situations occur almost instantaneously (Luo et al., 2006). Moral reasoning may sometimes come after, rather than before, our emotional reactions. Nonetheless, Kohlberg's insights have withstood the test of time and have made important contributions to our understanding of morality.

GENDER IDENTITY

One important aspect of children's social development that we haven't discussed yet is their developing understanding of their own and others' genders. Gender concepts are crucial to children's understanding of themselves as social beings. Before addressing how we develop a sense of ourselves as boys or girls, men or women, we need to sort through a bit of confusing terminology. Most psychologists distinguish sex from gender, with *sex* referring to individuals' biological status as male or female and *gender* referring to the psychological characteristics—behaviors, thoughts, and emotions—that tend to be associated with being male or female. But we're not done yet. **Gender identity** refers to people's sense of being male or female. As many as 1 out of every 1,000 babies born are actually *intersex*—possessing neither complete male nor complete female genitals resulting from chromosomal abnormalities. These individuals are typically assigned a gender at birth but sometimes have difficulty developing a normal gender identity due to the biological ambiguity of their sex. Other people with *gender identity disorder,* sometimes called *transsexualism* in adulthood, report feeling

According to Carol Gilligan, women's preference for a caring orientation affects their responses to moral dilemmas. Even so, women score just as highly as men on Kohlberg's moral development scheme, suggesting that their thinking about moral problems is equally sophisticated.

GLOSSARY

gender identity
individuals' sense of being male or female

"trapped" in the body of the opposite sex. They may be biologically male, yet feel like a woman, or vice versa. In contrast, **gender role** refers to the behaviors that tend to accompany being male or female. Gender identity and gender role don't always go together. An adolescent may see herself as quite feminine, yet engage in behaviors more consistent with masculine gender roles, like playing football and playing the role of class clown. How do gender identity and gender role arise?

A popular misconception is that gender differences don't emerge until socializing influences, like parenting practices, have had the opportunity to act on children. Yet some gender differences are evident in early infancy, making this explanation unlikely.

As early as 1 year of age or less, boys and girls prefer to play with different types of toys. Boys generally like balls, guns, and fire trucks; girls like dolls, stuffed animals, and cookware (Caldera, Huston, & O'Brien, 1989; Smith & Daglish, 1977). Remarkably, investigators have observed these preferences in nonhuman primates, including vervet monkeys. When placed in cages with toys, boy monkeys tend to choose trucks and balls, whereas girl monkeys tend to choose dolls and pots (Alexander & Hines, 2002). This finding suggests that toy preferences may reflect differences in biological predispositions, such as aggressiveness and nurturance, shared by many primates.

Although there are clear biological underpinnings, it's also clear that socialization experiences influence gender development. Parents tend to encourage children to engage in gender-stereotyped behaviors, such as achievement and independence among boys and dependence and nurturance among girls.

Teachers also tend to respond to boys and girls in accord with prevailing gender stereotypes. They give boys more attention when they exhibit aggression and girls more attention when they exhibit dependent or "needy" behaviors (Serbin & O'Leary, 1975). Even when boys and girls are equally assertive and equally verbal, teachers tend to lavish assertive boys and verbal girls with greater amounts of attention (Fagot, Hagan, Leinbach, et al., 1985; Beaman, Wheldall, & Kemp, 2006). In modern-day America, gender-role socialization tends to be stricter for boys than for girls. Parents tolerate cross-sex "tomboy" behavior in girls, like playing with both trucks and dolls, more than in boys, who tend to be stereotyped as "sissies" if they play with dolls (Langlois & Downs, 1980; Lytton & Romney, 1991).

Research suggests that parents tend to be more accepting of "tomboyish" behaviors among girls than "sissyish" behavior among boys.

Researchers have observed that when monkeys are given a choice of toys to play with, female monkeys (*left*) tend to prefer dolls, whereas male monkeys (*right*) tend to prefer trucks.

GLOSSARY

gender role
behaviors that tend to be associated with being male or female

QUIZ

1. There's strong evidence for abruptly ending critical periods in humans.   **TRUE** **FALSE**

2. Studies of contact comfort suggest that nourishment isn't the principal basis for attachment in primates.   **TRUE** **FALSE**

3. Children's attachment styles almost never change over time.   **TRUE** **FALSE**

4. When evaluating Kohlberg's moral dilemmas, the answers people give are more important than the reasoning processes they used to arrive at these answers.   **TRUE** **FALSE**

5. Gender differences don't emerge until parenting practices have the opportunity to influence children's behavior.   **TRUE** **FALSE**

Answers: (1) F (pp. 280–281); (2) T (p. 281); (3) F (p. 282); (4) F (p. 285); (5) F (p. 287)

PEARSON
mypsychlab

▼ Is it possible to avoid the notion that blue is for boys and pink is for girls? Watch the video titled "Early Gender Typing" at www.mypsychlab.com to find out.

Development Doesn't Stop: Changes in Adolescence and Adulthood

Although people tend to think of developmental psychology as focusing only on children, we don't emerge from elementary school as fully formed individuals. Substantial physical, cognitive, and social changes take place throughout adolescence, adulthood, and even old age.

ADOLESCENCE: A TIME OF DRAMATIC CHANGE

Common wisdom regards **adolescence**—the transition between childhood and adulthood commonly associated with the teenage years—as one of the most traumatic times in development, and it's certainly a time of dramatic changes in body, brain, and social activities. Yet the teenage years can also be a wonderful time of discovery, of opportunity to participate in adultlike activities, and of deep friendships. We might characterize adolescence in the words of Charles Dickens: "It was the best of times, it was the worst of times." There's plenty of turmoil, such as increased conflicts with parents (Laursen, Coy, & Collins, 1998), increased risk taking (Arnett, 1995), and heightened negative emotions (Larson & Richards, 1994) relative to younger children and adults. Yet most evidence suggests that the idea of adolescence as an intense roller coaster ride is a misconception (Arnett, 1999; Epstein, 2007). On balance, stress and unhappiness aren't that much more pronounced during adolescence than during other times of life. But perhaps because teenagers are less inhibited than adults, they're more likely to talk and complain about their ups and downs. When they're upset, we hear about it.

GLOSSARY

adolescence
the transition between childhood and adulthood commonly associated with the teenage years

Physical Maturation: The Power of Puberty. Many of the physical changes that adolescents undergo are hormonal. The pituitary gland stimulates physical growth, and the reproductive system releases the sex hormones estrogens and androgens (see Chapters 3 and 9) into the bloodstream, resulting in physical changes in addition to growth. **[LEARNING OBJECTIVE 8.10]** In boys, androgens promote increases in muscle tissue, growth of facial and body hair, and broadening of the shoulders. In girls, estrogens promote breast growth, uterus and vaginal maturation, hip broadening, and the onset of menstruation. Androgens in girls also induce physical growth and the growth of pubic hair (see **Figure 8.11**). Boys' muscle strength begins to exceed girls' in adolescence, and boys undergo a variety of changes in lung function and blood circulation. These changes result in greater average physical strength and endurance in boys than in girls, explaining the divergence between boys' and girls' athletic ability that emerges in adolescence (Beunen & Malina, 1996; Malina & Bouchard, 1991). Some unpleasant effects of these hormonal changes are increases in body odor, sweat, and oily skin, often leading to acne.

A crucial part of hormonal changes in adolescence is *sexual maturation*—the attainment of physical potential for reproduction. Maturation includes changes in **primary sex characteristics,** which include the reproductive organs and genitals. It also includes changes in **secondary sex characteristics,** which include sex-differentiating characteristics that don't relate directly to reproduction, such as breast enlargement in girls, deepening voices in boys, and pubic hair in both genders. In girls, **menarche**—the onset of menstruation—occurs. There's variability in when menstruation begins because girls reach physical maturity at different ages.

Spermarche, the first ejaculation, is the comparable milestone in boys. This event occurs on average at around 13 years of age, but it's also variable. In fact, boys often take a much longer time to mature than girls, which is why we'll often see sixth- and seventh-grade girls towering above their male counterparts.

The timing of puberty in boys and girls is genetically influenced; identical twins tend to begin menstruating within a month of each other, whereas fraternal twins average about a year's difference in onset (Tanner, 1990). However, a variety of environmental factors, some relating to physical health, affect when adolescents reach puberty. Adolescents from higher socioeconomic status households tend to have better nutrition and health care and reach puberty earlier as a result (Eveleth & Tanner, 1976). Girls from wealthier countries tend to begin menstruating earlier than those from poorer countries (Eveleth & Tanner, 1990).

These seventh-grade students vary in physical height, but the girl (on the right) is the tallest of the bunch. Girls tend to mature earlier and more rapidly than boys. The girl is probably close to reaching her adult height, whereas the boys still have lots of growing to do.

Fact -OID The age of menarche has decreased over the past 100 years, moving from around 15 to around 13 years of age on average. This change is probably due primarily to better nutrition and health care (Tanner, 1998).

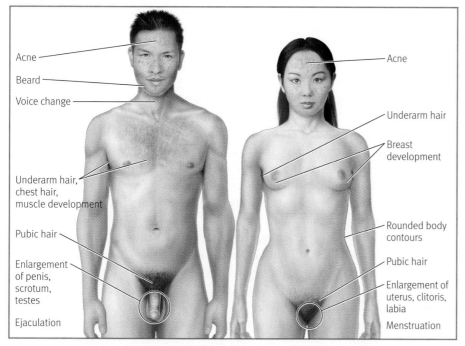

Acne

Beard

Voice change

Underarm hair, chest hair, muscle development

Pubic hair

Enlargement of penis, scrotum, testes

Ejaculation

Acne

Underarm hair

Breast development

Rounded body contours

Pubic hair

Enlargement of uterus, clitoris, labia

Menstruation

Figure 8.11 Physical and Sexual Maturation during the Preteen and Teenage Years. Hormones result in rapid growth to full adult height. They also trigger changes in the reproductive system and in secondary sex characteristics, such as increased breast size and broader hips in girls, and broader shoulders in boys.

GLOSSARY

primary sex characteristics
the reproductive organs and genitals that distinguish the sexes

secondary sex characteristics
sex-differentiating characteristics that don't relate directly to reproduction, such as breast enlargement in women and deepening voices in men

menarche
start of menstruation

spermarche
boys' first ejaculation

Lee Boyd Malvo participated in the Washington, DC, sniper killings in October 2002. He was 17 years old at the time of the crimes. Some (but not all) researchers argue that adolescents who commit crimes should be considered "less guilty by reason of adolescence" because their frontal lobes aren't fully mature (Steinberg & Scott, 2003).

RULING OUT RIVAL HYPOTHESES
Have important alternative explanations for the findings been excluded?

According to Erikson, adolescence is a time of exploring who we are. Trying on different identities by acting and dressing in particular ways is part of this process.

GLOSSARY

identity
our sense of who we are and our life goals and priorities

psychosocial crisis
dilemma concerning an individual's relations to other people

CORRELATION vs. CAUSATION
Can we be sure that A causes B?

Cognitive Changes in Adolescence: The Teen Brain. Although most brain maturation occurs prenatally and in the first few years of life, the frontal lobes don't mature fully until late adolescence or early adulthood (Casey, Giedd, & Thomas, 2000; Johnson, 1998). As we discovered in Chapter 3, the frontal lobes are responsible primarily for reasoning, planning, decision making, and impulse control. The fact that the frontal lobes are still maturing during adolescence may explain some of the impulsive behaviors, like skateboarding down a steep incline, for which teens are notorious (Weinberger, Elvevag, & Giedd, 2005). Even on the simplest of tasks, such as inhibiting the impulse to look at a flashing light, teens have a more difficult time and require more brain processing than do adults (Luna & Sweeney, 2004).

Adolescents routinely encounter new adultlike opportunities to engage in potentially harmful activities, but their brains aren't ready to make mature, well-reasoned decisions. For example, teens are often faced with making decisions such as whether to have sex, to try illegal drugs, or drive drunk. Adolescents must negotiate these choices without a "full deck" of decision-making cards. However, there's debate over whether we can blame teen behavioral problems entirely on the "teen brain." Some researchers have argued that these behaviors don't appear in non-Westernized cultures, suggesting that the causes of this phenomenon may be at least as cultural as they are biological (Epstein, 2007; Schlegel & Barry, 1991).

Building an Identity in Adolescence. Our personalities, priorities, interests, and, most important, self-perceptions all exert an important impact on our decisions. We've all asked ourselves "Who am I?" at some point. Indeed, one of the central challenges of adolescence is to get a firm handle on our **identity,** our sense of who we are, as well as our life goals and priorities. Most teenagers struggle mightily with this problem, "trying on different hats" in an effort to see which one fits best; psychologists call this process *role experimentation*. Even in college, we may juggle "nerdy," "cool," and "jock" friends at varying times, scope out different potential majors, and even explore alternative religious and philosophical beliefs. Our identities undergo a variety of changes over the course of adolescence and early adulthood as we fine-tune the fit between who we are and who we want to be.

Erik Erikson (1902–1994) developed the most comprehensive theory of how identity develops. Erikson (1963, 1970) coined the term *identity crisis* to describe the confusion that most adolescents experience regarding their sense of self.

In fact, Erikson's theoretical work went well beyond the topic of adolescence. He believed that personality growth continues throughout the life span. Erikson formulated an eight-stage model of human development from "womb to tomb," as psychologists like to say (see **Figure 8.12**). In each of his "Eight Ages," we confront a different **psychosocial crisis:** a dilemma concerning our relations to other people, whether they be parents, friends, teachers, or the larger society.

Erikson suggested that adolescents undergo a stage called "Identity versus Role Confusion" during which they grapple with fundamental questions about who they are. In most cases, they emerge from this crisis relatively unscathed. But if they don't, they may be at risk for later psychological conditions marked by confusion regarding identity (such as borderline personality disorder, which we'll encounter in Chapter 13).

Erikson's theorizing has been influential, but the research basis for many of his claims is slim. There's not much research on whether there are exactly eight stages or on whether we pass through them in the same order. There's evidence that individuals who don't successfully negotiate early stages of development, like identity versus role confusion, experience more difficulty with later stages than do other individuals (Vaillant & Milofsky, 1980). Although consistent with Erikson's model, these findings are only correlational and don't demonstrate that problems with early stages *produce* problems in later stages.

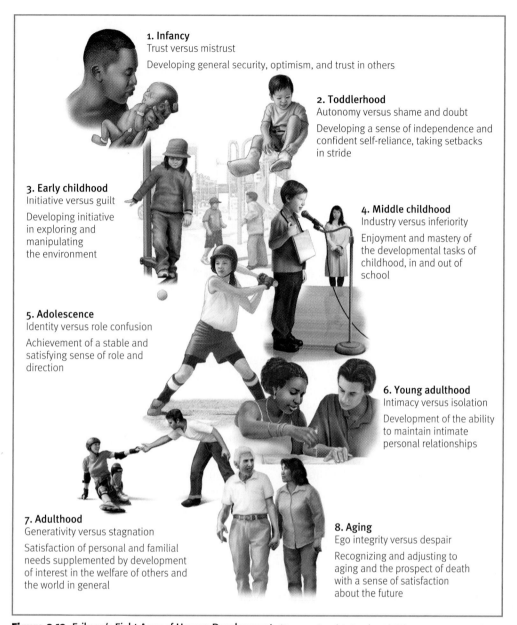

1. **Infancy**
Trust versus mistrust

Developing general security, optimism, and trust in others

2. **Toddlerhood**
Autonomy versus shame and doubt

Developing a sense of independence and confident self-reliance, taking setbacks in stride

3. **Early childhood**
Initiative versus guilt

Developing initiative in exploring and manipulating the environment

4. **Middle childhood**
Industry versus inferiority

Enjoyment and mastery of the developmental tasks of childhood, in and out of school

5. **Adolescence**
Identity versus role confusion

Achievement of a stable and satisfying sense of role and direction

6. **Young adulthood**
Intimacy versus isolation

Development of the ability to maintain intimate personal relationships

7. **Adulthood**
Generativity versus stagnation

Satisfaction of personal and familial needs supplemented by development of interest in the welfare of others and the world in general

8. **Aging**
Ego integrity versus despair

Recognizing and adjusting to aging and the prospect of death with a sense of satisfaction about the future

Figure 8.12 Erikson's Eight Ages of Human Development. (*Source:* Good & Brophy, 1995)

THE UPS AND DOWNS OF ADULTHOOD

As we transition from adolescence to adulthood, many aspects of our lives begin to stabilize, but others begin to change even more dramatically. After reaching full physical and sexual maturation during puberty, most of us reach our physical peak in our early twenties (Larsson, Grimby, & Karlsson, 1979; Lindle et al., 1997). Strength, coordination, speed of cognitive processing, and physical and mental flexibility are at their peak in early adulthood. And some of the most crucial milestones in social development typically occur in early to middle adulthood.

Life Transitions in Adulthood. Adults, like children, undergo a variety of changes. These changes tend to be associated with major transitions in lifestyle or societal status, such as shifting from student to wage earner, entering a serious relationship, or becoming a parent. Many of these transitions are wonderful experiences, but they can be stressful. **[LEARNING OBJECTIVE 8.11]** We tend to think of adults as following a predictable life trajectory: attending college, getting that first job, falling in love, getting married, having children, watching them grow up, and growing old gracefully. In reality, we vastly overestimate the number of individuals who adhere to this tidy stereotype of the road of life (Coontz, 1992). Many college students are in their late twenties, thirties, or forties, attending school while maintaining a job, and have families who are financially dependent on them. Many family units consist of single parents, same-sex parents, unmarried parents, second families following a divorce, and childless couples. Recent census reports (U.S. Census Bureau, 2005) indicate that fewer than 25 percent of adults live in conventional nuclear families (mom, dad, and children).

Careers. One of the biggest sources of anxiety for young adults graduating from college—particularly those who haven't served in the workforce—is what they're going to do for a living. Many recent graduates cast around a bit for a career path that matches their qualifications and interests. For some, this can be a beneficial strategy because they end up discovering unexpected careers that are good fits for their skills and passions. Although it was once the norm for people to work for one company or in one career for their entire lives, this is no longer the case. A longitudinal study conducted by the Bureau of Labor Statistics (2006) revealed that the average American worker changed jobs 10.5 times between the ages of 18 and 40. Although changes were more frequent in the teens and early twenties, people between 36 and 40 changed jobs at least once on average.

Love and Commitment. Falling in love and making a serious commitment to sharing a life with someone can be exciting, romantic, and fulfilling. Yet romantic relationships often call for a major shift in lifestyle. Even something as simple as integrating our music collections with our partners' can be an exceptionally stressful experience. Nevertheless, there may be benefits to sharing life with a significant other. Physical and emotional intimacy is associated with greater physical health and lower stress (Coombs, 1991). Overall, those in serious long-term relationships—both homosexual and heterosexual—report higher overall levels of happiness than those who are single (Gove, Hughes, & Style, 1983; Wayment & Peplau, 1995). Nevertheless, this finding is only correlational and could reflect a tendency for happier people to enter into stable relationships (see Chapter 9).

Although the average age of marriage in the United States is increasing, from 20 for women and 22 for men in 1960 to about 25 for women and 27 for men today, more than 50 percent of adults in the United States are married, and about 5 percent are cohabitating but unmarried. Approximately 11 percent of unmarried couples today are same-sex couples, almost evenly divided between male and female partner relationships (U.S. Census Bureau, 2000). The vast majority of people become part of a serious, long-term committed relationship at some point during adulthood.

Parenthood. Becoming a parent is probably the biggest transition that adults can undergo. Having a child involves a fundamental shift in lifestyle because, suddenly, adults are completely responsible for the well-being of someone other than themselves—someone who can't survive on his or her own. Although this experience is incredibly rewarding for most parents, it's also anxiety provoking, particularly because few first-time parents have spent much time caring for newborn babies. Becoming a parent requires a huge change in schedule, a reduction in sleep, and challenges associated with balancing competing demands of work and family. New parents are often unprepared for these changes, imagining that they'll just stick to their routine and bring baby along with them wherever they go—which

Although we usually think of college students as being in their late teens or early twenties and financially dependent on their parents, many "nontraditional" students enroll in college while working full-time and supporting families.

CORRELATION vs. CAUSATION
Can we be sure that A causes B?

Although the popular stereotype of a family includes a husband, wife, and several children, a surprisingly small number of families fit this mold. Single-parent families, same-sex parents, blended families following a second marriage, and childless couples are far more common than most people think.

almost never works the way they envision it. Research indicates that new parents who have the hardest time adjusting to parenthood are those whose expectations about the amount of change involved are the most unrealistic (Belsky & Kelly, 1994).

Midlife Transitions. Although becoming a parent tends to be the highest-impact life transition in adulthood, major adjustments also take place as adults reach middle age and begin to see the first signs of gray hairs and wrinkles. As adults begin to feel their age, they often confront new challenges, such as having their children leave home or caring for aging parents whose health is declining.

One popular conception about middle age is that most men, and some women, undergo a **midlife crisis,** marked by emotional distress about the aging process and an attempt to regain their youth. Although psychologists once viewed this period of transition as a normal part of adult development (Gould, 1978), more recent work has failed to replicate findings of an increase in emotional distress during middle age (Eisler & Ragsdale, 1992; Rosenberg, Rosenberg, & Farrell, 1999). The midlife crisis seems to be more myth than reality.

The parallel female version of the midlife crisis in popular psychology is the **empty-nest syndrome,** a supposed period of depression in mothers following the "flight" of their children from the house as they reach adulthood. The idea of the empty-nest syndrome, like the midlife crisis, seems to be overstated and may be specific to women who have more traditional gender roles.

Women who define themselves less exclusively in terms of their roles as parents, even those who aren't employed outside the home, are less vulnerable to empty-nest syndrome than those who have more traditional attitudes toward women's roles in society and the family (Harkins, 1978). Some researchers have even speculated that empty-nest syndrome is specific to Caucasian women who don't work outside the home. The social norms, lifestyles, and extended family demands of African American and Mexican American women, and of women of lower socioeconomic status who more commonly work outside the home, seem to buffer them against the feeling of being at loose ends once their children leave the nest (Borland, 1982; Woehrer, 1982). Fortunately, and contrary to popular belief, most empty nesters experience an *increase* in life satisfaction following their newfound flexibility and freedom (Black & Hill, 1984). Nonetheless, the shift in role, not to mention the sudden increase in free time, takes some adjustment (Walsh, 1999).

WHO IS OLD? DIFFERING CONCEPTS OF OLD AGE

In the early twenty-first century, people are living longer than ever. The life expectancy of the average American man is 75; for the American woman it's 80. Contrast those numbers with those only a century ago, when the average life span was 48 for men and 51 for women (National Center for Health Statistics, 2005). The elderly are our fastest-growing population, accounting for the increasing "graying" of America. Over the last 100 years, the total population of the United States has more than tripled to over 300 million today. But the number of people over 65 has increased more than seven times.

This shift in life expectancy means that there are millions more "elderly" people around than ever before. But how should we define "old age"? Chronological age conveys a variety of expectations. But chronological age doesn't necessarily predict or explain the behavioral or biological changes that accompany aging (Birren & Renner, 1977). An analogy may help: An iron railing on a house porch doesn't rust because it's grown old but because it's become oxidized over time. How rapidly the railing rusts depends on many factors, so two railings of the same age may contain very different amounts of rust.

Other ways of measuring age may do a better job of describing the impact of changes in later life (Birren & Renner, 1977). For example, we can use *biological age,* the estimate of a person's age in terms of the body's biological functioning, or *psychological age,* a person's mental attitudes and agility, and the capacity to deal with

REPLICABILITY
Can the results be duplicated in other studies?

Having a baby is a significant and wonderful life event, but becoming a new parent is also a significant source of stress.

For women who have worked throughout the years spent raising their children, the "empty-nest" transition tends to be easier than for stay-at-home mothers.

GLOSSARY

midlife crisis
supposed phase of adulthood characterized by emotional distress about the aging process and an attempt to regain youth

empty-nest syndrome
alleged period of depression in mothers following the departure of their grown children from the home

Every day, 96-year-old Mitchell Namy (the great-uncle of one of your book's authors) sends e-mails, web surfs, and trades stocks online. He drives himself to his weekly bridge games. Although his hearing and his knees have declined, his "functional age" is well below his chronological age.

the stresses of an ever-changing environment. Another useful way to conceptualize aging is in terms of *functional age,* a person's ability to function in given roles in society. Functional age may be a more appropriate basis for judging readiness to retire, replacing the arbitrary criterion of chronological age (for example, that people should retire at the age of 65 or 70).

Physical Decline and Aging.

Americans spend millions of dollars each year on products, techniques, and gimmicks marketed to make them look and feel younger as they attempt to stave off the inevitable effects of aging. However, some of the effects of age on physical appearance and physical functioning are inescapable facts of life.

One of the major milestones of physical aging in women is **menopause**—the termination of menstruation, signaling the end of a woman's reproductive potential. As women approach 50, their menstrual cycles may become increasingly irregular; ultimately, they stop. Some women find this time difficult because they're faced with evidence of their physical decline, with their youthful, reproductive years behind them. What's more, menopause is often accompanied by unpleasant side effects. Menopause is caused by a reduction in estrogen, which can result in sudden "hot flashes" marked by becoming incredibly hot, sweaty, and dry-mouthed. Many women report mood swings, sleep disruption, and temporary loss of sexual drive or pleasure. Interestingly, the prevalence of these effects varies across cultures. Although about 50 percent of American and Canadian women report hot flashes, fewer than 15 percent of Japanese women do (Lock, 1998).

Men experience nothing equivalent to menopause; they can continue to reproduce well into old age. Still, there's a gradual decline in sperm production and testosterone levels with age, and maintaining an erection and achieving ejaculation can become a challenge. Despite changes in the reproductive equipment of aging adults, most senior citizens—both men and women—experience healthy sex drives (see Chapter 9).

Changes in Agility and Physical Coordination with Age.

There are individual and task-specific differences in the effects of aging on motor coordination. **[LEARNING OBJECTIVE 8.12]** Complex tasks show greater effects of age than simpler ones (Luchies et al., 2002; Welford, 1977); simple motor tasks, such as tapping a finger to a beat, show relatively small age-related declines (Ruff & Parker, 1993). This finding suggests that some aspects of decline may be related to either decreasing sensory capacities, such as poor vision or hearing, or to attentional strategies used by older versus younger adults (Botwinick, 1966; Redfern et al., 2002). Elderly adults also become less flexible in their ability to learn new motor skills (Guan & Wade, 2000). This change creates a special challenge when vision and other senses decline and individuals must depend more on other senses, such as proprioception (the sense of how parts of the body are oriented in space relative to each other) and vestibular cues (balance information derived from the inner ear) to compensate (Chapter 4).

Research suggests that physical activity and strength training are valuable in minimizing age-related declines.

There are large individual differences in age-related decline. Strength training and increased physical activity may minimize some of these declines and increase life span (Fiatarone et al., 1990; Frontera, Meredith, O'Reilly, et al., 1988). Many of the changes we typically associate with aging are actually due to diseases that are correlated with age, like high blood pressure, heart disease, and arthritis. Although chronological age and physical health are correlated, the great variability in how people age refutes the popular notion that old age invariably produces physical decline.

Aging and Cognitive Decline.

There are minuses and pluses to getting older. On the downside, many aging adults complain they just can't remember things they used to. They're right: Many aspects of cognitive function *do* decline as people get older. In fact,

CORRELATION vs. CAUSATION
Can we be sure that A causes B?

GLOSSARY

menopause
the termination of menstruation, marking the end of a woman's reproductive potential

people's ability to recall information begins to decrease sharply after age 30. However, there's considerable variability in how much memory declines, with most people experiencing only modest decreases with age (Shimamura, Berry, Mangels, et al., 1995). Basic sensory processing such as vision, hearing, and even smell starts to decline when people reach their 60s or 70s (Doty et al., 1984). People's overall speed of processing also declines, which is why teenagers can regularly beat older adults at video games and other speed-sensitive tasks (Cerella, 1985; Salthouse, 2004).

On the upside, some aspects of cognitive function are spared from age-related decline, and others actually improve with age:

(1) Although free recall (being asked to generate items from memory; see Chapter 6) declines with age, cued recall or recognition remains intact (Schonfield & Robertson, 1966).

(2) Aging adults show relatively little decline when asked to remember material that's meaningful or pertinent to their everyday lives as opposed to the random lists of words that some memory researchers prefer (Graf, 1990; Perlmutter, 1983).

(3) Older adults perform better on analogy tests and vocabulary tests than do younger adults (Cattell, 1963). Crystallized intelligence (see Chapter 7), our accumulated knowledge and experience, gives older adults a greater database of information on which to draw when solving problems or interpreting new information (Baltes, Staudinger, & Lindenberger, 1999; Beier & Ackerman, 2001; Horn & Hofer, 1992). Here's a case in which common sense is true: Older *is* wiser!

When we consider that older adults have decades of accumulated knowledge and crystallized intelligence outstripping that of younger adults, we can see why many of the world's cultures honor and revere the elderly.

WHAT DO *you* THINK?

The elderly have good recognition memory but poor recall. As director of a nursing home, can you think of ways to improve residents' ability to remember important information using reminders?

QUIZ

1 Androgens cause changes in boys, but not girls, at puberty. **TRUE** **FALSE**

2 Adolescents may not always make mature decisions about engaging in risky behaviors because their frontal lobes aren't fully mature. **TRUE** **FALSE**

3 Marriage and becoming a parent both exert an overall positive impact on adults' stress levels. **TRUE** **FALSE**

4 Elderly people's hearing, sight, and other senses decline, but their reaction times are the same as those of younger adults. **TRUE** **FALSE**

5 Older adults perform worse on tests that require memory for random lists of words but perform better on tests of analogy and vocabulary. **TRUE** **FALSE**

PEARSON
mypsych lab

▼ Do our teenage years affect our adulthood? Watch the video titled "Adolescent Behavior: Health and Lifestyle Choices" at www.mypsychlab.com to find out.

Answers: (1) F (p. 289); (2) T (p. 290); (3) F (p. 292); (4) F (p. 295); (5) T (p. 295)

Your Complete Review System

8.1 Identify ways to think critically about developmental findings

In evaluating how and why children change, we must resist the temptation to assume that things that happened prior necessarily cause things that happen later and keep in mind that cause and effect is often a two-way street.

1. The study of how behavior changes over time is called _____ _____. (p. 265)

2. The _____ _____ fallacy is the assumption that because one event happened before another event, the two events are causally related. (p. 265)

3. How can bidirectional influences explain gangs of delinquent adolescents? (p. 265)

4. In a _____ design, researchers obtain a "snapshot" of people of different ages at a single point in time. (p. 266)

5. _____ _____ can be observed when a sample of participants grew up in the same time period. (p. 266)

6. How was the classic "Up Series" documentary set up similar to longitudinal designs in psychology? Can you identify a positive and negative aspect of utilizing longitudinal designs? (p. 266)

7. Research shows that most children (are/aren't) resilient and capable of withstanding stress. (p. 267)

8.2 Clarify how nature and nurture can contribute to development

Genes and environment intersect in complex ways, so we can't always conclude that one or the other is driving behavior. For example, as children develop, the effects of their genes often depend on their experiences.

8. Both _____, our genetic endowment, and _____, the environments we encounter, play powerful roles in shaping our development. (p. 267)

9. Many studies of human development are subject to a _____, meaning it is difficult to identify the relative effects of genes and environment. (p. 267)

10. Caspi and colleagues' longitudinal study of children with low levels of MAO illustrates the phenomenon of _____ _____, in which the effect of genes depends on environment, and vice versa. (p. 267)

succeed with mypsychlab

1. Practice comparing the benefits and challenges of different research designs.
   Cross-Sectional and Longitudinal Research Designs

2. How do developmental psychologists study individuals over time? Listen as two psychologists discuss the methods that developmental psychologists use and the implications that we can draw from them.
   Longitudinal and Cross-Sectional Research Designs

succeed with mypsychlab

Do You Know All of the Terms in This Chapter?

Find out by using the Flashcards. Want more practice? Take additional quizzes, try simulations, and watch video to be sure you are prepared for the test!

8.3 Describe the stages of prenatal development and identify obstacles to normal development

Many important aspects of fetal development occur early in pregnancy. The brain begins to develop 18 days after conception and continues to mature into adolescence. Teratogens such as drugs, alcohol, and even maternal stress can damage or slow fetal development.

11. Early in pregnancy, a ball of identical cells that hasn't yet taken on any specific function is called the _____. (p. 268)

12. The embryonic stage of prenatal development occurs from the _____ to the _____ week of pregnancy. (p. 268)

13. The embryo becomes a _____ once the major organs are established and the heart has begun to beat. (p. 268)

14. The _____ begins to develop 18 days after fertilization and unlike most other organs, keeps developing through adolescence and sometimes into early adulthood. (p. 269)

15. Environmental factors that can have a negative effect on prenatal development are called _____. (p. 269)

Answers are located at the end of the text.

8.4 Describe how infants learn to coordinate motion and achieve major motor milestones

Children tend to achieve motor milestones such as crawling and walking in roughly the same order, although the ages when they accomplish these milestones vary. Infants are born with reflexes that help them get started, but experience plays a critical role in building up children's muscles and motor coordination.

16. Infants are born with certain _____ that are triggered by specific types of stimulation and help them know how to survive in the world. (p. 270)

17. The _____ _____ is an automatic response to oral stimulation. (p. 270)

18. Plot the progression of development in the figure on the right by listing the age and major motor milestone depicted by each child. (p. 271)

(a) _____

(b) _____

(c) _____

(d) _____

(e) _____

(f) _____

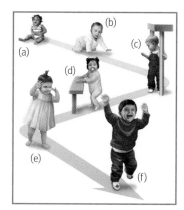

19. Children rely on _____ _____ as they learn how to coordinate their movements in order to reach or crawl. (p. 270)

20. How do child-rearing practices in other cultures (such as swaddling in Peru), compared with those in the United States affect children's short- and long-term motor development? (p. 270)

succeed with mypsychlab

1. Take a guided visual tour of the developing embryo. **The Embryonic Period**

2. How and when does a baby's brain develop? Watch the development before and after birth to see how quickly the brain changes. **Dendritic Spreading: Forming Interconnections in the Brain**

3. Role play a pediatrician as you try to determine environmental factors that may have affected a child's development. **Teratogens and Their Effects**

COGNITIVE DEVELOPMENT: CHILDREN'S LEARNING ABOUT THE WORLD (pp. 272–279)

8.5 Understand major theories of the mechanisms by which children learn

Piaget believed that development happens in four stages that influence all aspects of cognitive development. Vygotsky believed that different children develop skills in different domains at different rates and that social structuring on the part of the parent drives children's learning and development. Researchers continue to debate whether learning happens in more general or domain-specific ways, whether learning is gradual or stagelike, and how much innate cognitive knowledge children possess.

21. Piaget was a _____ _____. He believed that children's development is marked by radical reorganizations of thinking at specific points, followed by prolonged periods during which their understanding of the world remains stable. (p. 272)

22. According to Piaget, when children can no longer use _____ to absorb a new experience into their current knowledge structures, they will engage in _____ by altering an existing belief to make it more compatible with the new experience. (p. 273)

23. In the first of Piaget's four stages of development, the _____ stage (birth to 2 years), children focus on the here and now, and lack an understanding of object _____. (p. 273)

24. Children in Piaget's second stage, called the _____ stage, can't perform _____ tasks. (pp. 273–274)

25. Using the descriptions provided, complete the table to show Piaget's four stages of cognitive development. (p. 273)

Stage	Typical Ages	Description
(a) _____	_____	No thought beyond immediate physical experiences
(b) _____	_____	Able to think beyond the here and now, but egocentric and unable to perform mental transformations
(c) _____	_____	Able to perform mental transformations but only on concrete physical objects
(d) _____	_____	Able to perform hypothetical and abstract reasoning

26. What ability does Piaget's three mountains task (below) measure? In what stage can children pass this task? (p. 274)

View 1   View 2

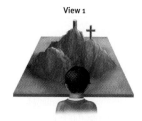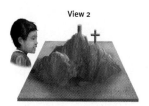

27. Whereas Piaget emphasized children's exploration of the physical world, Vygotsky believed that _____ and _____ factors were children's primary source of learning. (p. 275)

28. Vygotsky identified the zone of _____ _____ as the phase when a child is receptive to learning a new skill and can make use of _____, the structure provided by parents to aid the child's learning. (p. 275)

8.6 Explain the processes by which children acquire knowledge in important cognitive domains

Physical reasoning in infants involves both basic, apparently innate knowledge, and refinement of knowledge based on experience. Self-recognition becomes increasingly sophisticated as children move from understanding they are physically distinct entities to understanding that others have minds distinct from their own. Numerical development requires a complex understanding of counting rules and the nature of precise quantities. This ability develops slowly and is easily disrupted.

SOCIAL AND MORAL DEVELOPMENT: CHILDREN'S RELATIONS WITH OTHERS (pp. 279–288)

8.7 Describe how and when children establish emotional bonds with their caregivers

Although infants may recognize and react positively to their caregivers, they don't develop a specific attachment until around 8 months of age. The type of attachment that infants form with their caregivers varies depending on both parental style and the infant's temperament.

31. Usually starting at 8 or 9 months, babies can develop _____ _____, which may be an adaptive mechanism for keeping infants away from danger. (p. 280)

32. The strong emotional connection we share with those to whom we feel closest is called _____. (p. 280)

33. Lorenz showed that newborn goslings bonded to the first moving thing they see, a phenomenon called _____. (p. 280)

34. Harlow's experiment with rhesus monkeys demonstrated the phenomenon of _____ _____. (p. 281)

35. Define Harlow's notion of contact comfort and describe the role each "mother" played in helping meet the monkey's needs. (p. 281)

36. Complete the table by describing the four attachment styles identified in Ainsworth's Strange Situation research. (p. 282)

Attachment Style	Description/Child's Reaction
1. Secure attachment	
2. Insecure-avoidant attachment	
3. Insecure-anxious attachment	
4. Disorganized attachment	

8.8 Explain the environmental and genetic influences on social behavior and social style in children

Parenting style (permissive, authoritative, authoritarian, or uninvolved), as well as genetic aspects of children such as temperament, can affect children's long-term social development.

29. Infants (do/don't) have a basic understanding of the physics of an object's behavior. (p. 277)

30. A classic test of _____ _____ _____ is the false-belief task, which examines children's ability to reason about what other people know or believe. (p. 278)

succeed with mypsychlab

1. How do developmental psychologists measure a child's development? Review Piaget's theory of development.
Piaget's Stages of Cognitive Development

2. Are young children egocentric? Watch as children of different ages perform a task with an experimenter.
The Preschool Years: Egocentrism

37. A person's basic emotional style that appears early in development and is largely genetic is called _____. (p. 283)

38. Research suggests that specific parenting styles may not matter so much as whether the parent can provide the _____ _____ environment. (p. 284)

8.9 Determine how children's understanding of morality and important social concepts like gender develop

Children's initial concepts of morality are based largely on fear of punishment but over time become more sophisticated and based on intentions rather than consequences. Children's understanding of gender develops gradually over the first several years, but gender differences in behavior emerge early on and can't be accounted for entirely by gender socialization. Differences in how parents and teachers interact with boys and girls also play important roles in children's gender-typed behavior.

39. Kohlberg studied the development of _____ by scoring the _____ _____ people used as they wrestled with a moral dilemma. (p. 285)

40. An individual's sense of being male or female is called gender _____, and the behaviors that tend to accompany being male or female are called gender _____. (pp. 286–287)

succeed with mypsychlab

1. Play the role of a researcher and identify the attachment style of a child.
Attachment Classifications in the Strange Situation

2. How good is your understanding of morality? Test your knowledge with these case histories.
Kohlberg's Stages of Moral Reasoning

DEVELOPMENT DOESN'T STOP: CHANGES IN ADOLESCENCE AND ADULTHOOD (pp. 288–295)

8.10 **Determine the physical, emotional, and cognitive changes that take place during the transition from childhood to adulthood**

Sexual maturation and significant physical changes mark adolescence. Adolescents are also confronted with more adultlike opportunities and decisions that their brain's immature frontal lobes are not always prepared to handle.

41. The transition between childhood and adulthood commonly associated with the teenage years is called _____. (p. 288)

42. Sexual maturation includes changes in _____ _____ _____, such as the reproductive organs and genitals, and _____ _____ _____, such as breast enlargement in girls and deepening voices in boys. (p. 289)

43. One of the challenges during adolescence is to get a handle on our _____, our sense of who we are and how we fit in the world. (p. 290)

8.11 **Identify developmental changes during major life transitions in adults**

Major life transitions including career changes, finding a romantic partner, and having children can be stressful for adults. However, midlife crises are infrequent.

44. As the profiles of the traditional college student continue to evolve, so do changes in our beliefs about careers and job changes. According to the Bureau of Labor Statistics, how many job changes can the average American expect to make between the ages of 18 and 40? (p. 292)

45. One of the biggest transitions an adult can go through is becoming a _____. (p. 292)

8.12 **Summarize the nature of age-related decline in physical, social, and cognitive domains**

Chronological age isn't a perfect predictor of physical, social, or cognitive ability in the elderly. Some aspects of cognitive and physical functions begin to decline as early as age 30. However, other cognitive abilities increase with age; how much we slow down depends on a variety of factors, including our activity levels.

46. A 65-year-old person who is in excellent health and top physical condition may have a _____ _____ of 45 years old. (p. 293)

47. A major physical milestone of aging in women is _____. (p. 294)

48. Some aspects of physical decline may be related to decreasing _____ capacities. (p. 295)

49. (All/Not all) aspects of cognitive function decline as we age. (p. 295)

50. Describe how different cultures approach aging and identify some of the myths surrounding physical and cognitive declines in later years. (p. 295)

succeed with mypsych lab

1. At what age is toilet training important? Test your knowledge of a young child's development.
Erikson's First Four Stages of Psychosocial Development

2. Use this photomorphing activity to see how an individual's appearance changes over time.
Aging and Changes in Physical Appearance

3. Review changes in personal and physical development across the lifespan.
Major Changes in Important Domains of Adult Functioning

SCIENTIFIC THINKING SKILLS
Questions and Summary

1 As a social worker dealing with young children who have undergone extreme trauma, what would you do to educate others about the realities of childhood fragility and resilience?

2 Looking back at your own upbringing, how would you describe the parenting style used by your mother/father/caregiver? What would you do (or have you done) differently, if anything, when raising your own children?

RULING OUT RIVAL HYPOTHESES
pp. 266, 267, 277, 278, 281, 290

CORRELATION vs. CAUSATION
pp. 264, 284, 290, 292, 294

FALSIFIABILITY
p. 276

REPLICABILITY
pp. 274, 276, 281, 293

OCCAM'S RAZOR
pp. 275, 277

Emotion and Motivation

Are emotion and reason opposites of each other? (p. 302)

Are emotional expressions unique to different cultures? (p. 305)

CHAPTER 9

Is the polygraph test really a "lie detector"? (p. 310)

Do genes contribute to obesity? (p. 323)

Do opposites attract in romantic relationships? (p. 329)

Meet Elliott. He's a Caucasian male, 30 years of age. At first blush, Elliott looks and acts pretty much like everyone else. He's well dressed and socially appropriate, and his scores on tests of intelligence, memory, and language are boringly normal. On standard measures of personality, he's entirely unremarkable. Yet Elliott is different—very different—from the average person in two ways.

First, Elliott has recently recovered from brain surgery. Diagnosed with a frontal lobe tumor that had ballooned to the size of a small orange, Elliott underwent a radical operation to remove not only the tumor but also a sizable chunk of surrounding brain tissue. In many respects, Elliott is a contemporary version of Vermont railroad worker Phineas Gage, who, as we'll recall from Chapter 3, lost much of his frontal cortex in a catastrophic accident in 1848 (Damasio, 1994; Eslinger & Damasio, 1985).

Second, like Gage, Elliott behaves strikingly differently from the way he behaved before he lost a goodly portion of his brain. Before the operation, Elliott was a successful businessman with a happy and balanced home life. Yet Elliott is now different in one crucial way: He seems entirely devoid of emotion. As Antonio Damasio (1994), who studied Elliott in depth, remarked: "I never saw a tinge of emotion in my many hours of conversation with him: no sadness, no impatience, no frustration . . ." (p. 45). When Damasio's colleague Daniel Tranel showed Elliott a series of upsetting photographs, including pictures of gruesome injuries, buildings crumbling during earthquakes, and houses in flames, Elliott displayed virtually no emotional response, as measured by either his subjective report or his physiological reaction such as heart rate. Nor does Elliott express much joy when describing the wonderful moments of his life.

We might think that being devoid of emotion might make him better able to function because he can make rational decisions unhindered by emotional distraction. But in fact, Elliott's experience was very much the opposite. Following his surgery, Elliott's life, like that of Phineas Gage, is in utter shambles. Elliott has made foolish decisions in his personal life, investing all of his savings in a risky business venture and going bankrupt. He married a woman who was a poor match for him, resulting in an abrupt divorce. His on-the-job performance is no better.

The tragic case of Elliott imparts a valuable lesson: Emotion and reason aren't necessarily opposites. To the contrary, emotion seems to play an important role in decision making. Elliott married the wrong woman in part because he'd lost access to his "gut feelings" concerning his attraction to members of the opposite sex. He based his choice of a romantic partner largely on reason alone, which is typically a recipe for disaster (Gigerenzer, 2007).

Popular wisdom teaches us that many emotions, especially negative ones, are bad for us. Many pop psychology books encourage us not to feel angry, guilty, ashamed, or sad. Such emotions, the books inform us, are unhealthy, even "toxic." Pop psychologists are right to remind us that excessive anger, guilt, and the like can be self-destructive. "Everything in moderation," as our grandmother reminded us. But they're wrong to suggest we'd be better off without these feelings. As we'll discover, at least small doses of negative emotions are essential in certain situations.

Theories of Emotion:
What Causes Our Feelings?

Elliott aside, virtually all of us experience **emotions,** mental states or feelings associated with our evaluation of our experiences. Emotions often have physical and behavioral responses associated with them as well. Yet psychologists don't agree fully on what causes our emotions or even on what distinguishes our emotions from our thoughts. As we'll soon discover, however, they've made significant strides toward unraveling these enduring mysteries.

DISCRETE EMOTIONS THEORY: EMOTIONS AS EVOLVED EXPRESSIONS

According to **discrete emotions theory,** humans experience a small number of distinct emotions, even if they combine in complex ways (Ekman & Friesen, 1971; Griffiths, 1997; Izard, 1971, 1994; Tomkins, 1962). Advocates of this theory further propose that emotions have distinct biological roots and serve evolutionary functions. Each emotion, they suggest, is associated with a specific physiological response that is essentially the same in all people. **[LEARNING OBJECTIVE 9.1]**

Adaptive Value of Emotions. Consider the emotion of *disgust,* which derives from the Latin term for "bad taste." Imagine we asked you to swallow a piece of food that you find repulsive, like a dried-up cockroach (apologies to those of you reading this chapter over lunch or dinner). As you picture putting this less than delicious "delicacy" in your mouth, attend carefully to how you react. The odds are high you displayed at least some of these behaviors: wrinkling your nose, contracting your mouth, sticking out your tongue, turning your head slightly to one side, and closing your eyes, at least partly (Phillips et al., 1997).

Why did you do these things? Discrete emotions theorists would say that this disgust response evolved to make it less likely that a toxic substance will find its way into your body. When you wrinkle your nose and contract your mouth, you're reducing the chances you'll ingest this substance; by sticking out your tongue, you're increasing the chances you'll expel it; by turning your head, you're doing your best to avoid it; and by closing your eyes, you're limiting the damage that it can do to your visual system. Other emotions similarly prepare us for biologically important actions (Frijda, 1986). For example, our eyes open wide when we're afraid, allowing us to better spot potential dangers, like predators, lurking in our environment. When we're angry, our teeth and fists often become clenched, readying us to bite and fight.

Further evidence for an evolutionary role in emotional expression is the fact that some emotional expressions emerge in the first few months of life, presumably before parents have had much of an opportunity to shape them through socialization (Ekman & Oster, 1979). By about 6 weeks, babies start to smile whenever they see a favorite face (Plutchik, 2003). They also frown and cry when left alone. The fact that some emotional expressions emerge even without direct reinforcement suggests that they're innate (Freedman, 1964; Panksepp, 2007).

Emotions in Humans and Animals. Charles Darwin (1872) was among the first to point out that the emotional expressions of humans and nonhuman animals are often similar. For example, he observed that the smile of chimpanzees bears an uncanny resemblance to a human smile. He also noted that the angry snarl of dogs, marked by the baring of their fangs, is reminiscent of the dismissive sneer of humans. Our emotional systems and those of animals, he concluded, share the same evolutionary heritage. Jaak Panksepp

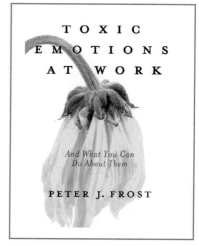

Pop psychology books often tell us that many emotions, especially in the extreme, are "toxic." Are they right?

People have recognized the facial reaction of disgust for centuries. This is a photograph from Charles Darwin's book on the expression of emotions, published in 1872.

GLOSSARY

emotion
mental, physical, and behavioral state associated with our evaluation of our experiences

discrete emotions theory
theory that humans experience a small number of distinct emotions

(2005) demonstrated another example of cross-species similarity. He found that rats emit a high-pitched chirp beyond the range of human hearing, perhaps similar to human laughter, when tickled. The high-pitched panting of dogs during play also seems similar in many ways to human laughter.

Of course, Darwin and Panksepp might have been wrong. The mere fact that two things are superficially similar doesn't prove that they share evolutionary origins. Birds and bats both have wings, but their wings evolved independently of each other. In the case of emotions, however, we know that all mammals share an evolutionary ancestor. For example, rats and humans appear to have split off from the same ancestor, a small shrewlike creature, about 75 million years ago. The fact that many mammals display similar emotional reactions during similar social behaviors, such as tickling and play, lends itself to a parsimonious hypothesis: Perhaps these reactions stem from the same evolutionary roots.

OCCAM'S RAZOR
Does a simpler explanation fit the data just as well?

Real versus Fake Emotions. We can use certain facial expressions to help us distinguish real from fake emotions. In genuine happiness, we see an upward turning of the corners of the mouth, along with a drooping of the eyelids and a crinkling of the corners of the eyes (Ekman, Davidson, & Friesen, 1990). Emotion theorists distinguish this genuine emotional expression, called the *Duchenne smile* after the neurologist who discovered it, from the fake or *Pan Am smile,* which is marked by a movement of the mouth but not the eyes. The term *Pan Am smile* derives from an old television commercial featuring the now defunct airline Pan Am, in which all of the flight attendants flashed obviously fake smiles. If you page through your family albums, you'll probably find an abundance of Pan Am smiles, especially in posed photographs. Interestingly, among subjects asked to produce facial expressions, only Duchenne smiles are associated with increased activity of the front region of the left hemisphere, which appears specialized for positive emotions (Ekman et al., 1990).

The Duchenne (genuine) smile is marked by a turning upward of the corners of the mouth and changes in the eyelids and corners of the eye.

Emotions and Physiology. In addition to differentiating emotions based on facial expressions, we can also differentiate at least some emotions by their patterns of physiological responding (Ax, 1953; Rainville, Bechara, Naqui, et al., 2006). The mere act of making a face associated with a specific emotion alters our bodily reactions in characteristic ways (Ekman, Levenson, & Friesen, 1983). Our heart rates tend to increase more when we make angry and fearful facial expressions than when we make happy or surprised facial expressions (Cacioppo, Berntson, Klein, et al., 1997), probably because the first two emotions are more closely linked to the emergency reactions we experience when threatened (see Chapters 3 and 10). Yet even fear and anger differ physiologically. When we're afraid, our digestive systems tend to slow down. In contrast, when we're angry, our digestive systems tend to speed up, which explains why our "stomachs churn" when we're furious (Carlson & Hatfield, 1992). How likely we are to experience a startle response to a loud noise also depends on our emotional state.

Brain imaging data also provide at least some evidence for distinct patterns for different emotions (Murphy, Nimmo-Smith, & Lawrence, 2003). For example, fear tends to activate the amygdala (see Chapter 3), whereas anger tends to activate a region of the frontal cortex.

Yet in many other cases we can't distinguish different emotions by means of their physiology (Cacioppo, Tassinary, & Berntson, 2000; Feldman Barrett, 2006; Feldman Barrett et al., 2007). Surprisingly, happiness and sadness aren't terribly different in their patterns of brain activation (Murphy et al., 2003). Moreover, it's clear that multiple brain regions participate in all emotions (Schienle et al., 2002).

David Matsumoto and Bob Willingham, former national judo competitors, examined the facial expressions of judo competition winners and losers at the 2004 Athens Olympics. Medalists and match winners from 35 countries displayed extremely similar facial reactions (Matsumoto & Willingham, 2006).

Culture and Emotion. One important way to evaluate claims that discrete emotions are a product of evolution is to investigate the *universality* of emotional expressions. If our species evolved to express emotions a certain way, we would expect expressions to carry the same meaning across different cultures.

Recognition of Emotions across Cultures. One telling piece of evidence for discrete emotions theory derives from research showing that people recognize and generate the same emotional expressions across cultures (Izard, 1971). Nevertheless, this research is vulnerable to a rival explanation: Because these people have all been exposed to Western culture, the similarities may be due to shared experiences rather than a shared evolutionary heritage.

To rule out this explanation, in the late 1960s American psychologist Paul Ekman traveled to the wilds of southeastern New Guinea to study a group of people who'd been essentially isolated from Western culture and still used Stone Age tools. With the aid of a translator, Ekman read them a brief story (for example, "His mother has died, and he feels very sad"), along with a display of photographs of Americans depicting various emotions, like happiness, sadness, and anger. Then Ekman asked them to select the photograph that matched the story.

Ekman (1994, 1999) and his colleagues (Ekman & Friesen, 1986) concluded that a small number of **primary emotions**—perhaps seven—are cross-culturally universal. Specifically, they found that the facial expressions associated with these emotions are recognized across most, if not all, cultures. Discrete emotions theorists call these emotions "primary" because they're presumably the biologically based emotions from which other emotions arise:

- Happiness
- Sadness
- Surprise
- Anger
- Disgust
- Fear
- Contempt

RULING OUT RIVAL HYPOTHESES
Have important alternative explanations for the findings been excluded?

Recent research suggests that pride may also be a cross-culturally universal emotion, although the evidence for this claim is preliminary (Tracy & Robins, 2007).

Secondary Emotions. Primary emotions don't tell the whole story of our feelings. We also experience an enormous array of *secondary emotions* that seem less likely to be cross-culturally universal. Examples include alarm, jealousy, and an emotion with no name in English that Germans call *schadenfreude,* pleasure we experience at witnessing the misfortune of others, especially those we see as arrogant (Ortony, Clore, & Collins, 1988).

Cultural Differences in Emotional Expression: Display Rules.

The finding that certain emotions exist across most or all cultures doesn't mean that cultures are identical in their emotional expressions. In part, that's because cultures differ in **display rules,** their societal guidelines for how and when to express emotions (Ekman & Friesen, 1975; Matsumoto, Yoo, Hirayama, et al., 2005). In Western culture, parents teach most boys not to cry, whereas they typically teach girls that crying is acceptable (Plutchik, 2003). Americans can be taken aback when a visitor from South America, the Middle East, or some European countries, like Russia, greets them with one or two kisses on their cheek.

In a study of display rules, Wallace Friesen (1972) used *covert observation* (see Chapter 2) to videotape Japanese and American college students without their knowledge. He asked both groups of students to watch two film clips, one of a neutral travel scene (the control condition) and one of an incredibly gory film depicting a ritual genital mutilation (the experimental condition). When these students were alone, their facial reactions to the films were similar: Both groups showed little emotional reaction to the neutral film but clear signs of fear, disgust, and distress to the gory film. Yet when an older experimenter entered the room, the role of culture became apparent. Although American students' reactions to the films didn't change, Japanese students typically smiled during the gory film, concealing

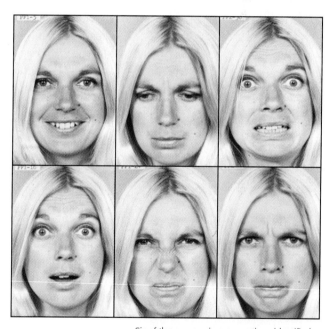

Six of the seven primary emotions identified by Paul Ekman and his colleagues. Can you match each face to the corresponding emotions of anger, disgust, fear, happiness, sadness, and surprise?

GLOSSARY

primary emotion
one of a small number (perhaps seven) of emotions believed by some theorists to be cross-culturally universal

display rule
one of the cultural guidelines for how and when to express emotions

In April 2007, American actor Richard Gere scandalized much of India by kissing Indian actress Shilpa Shetty's cheek on stage. Gere was apparently unaware of display rules in India that strictly forbid kissing in public.

their negative emotional reactions. In Japanese culture, deference to authority figures is the norm, so the students acted as though they were happy to see the films. So, in many cases, culture doesn't influence emotion itself; it influences its overt expression.

WHAT DO *you* THINK?

You are cramming to learn Turkish before your trip to Turkey, but you know you won't have it mastered by the time you leave. Using Ekman's research, what could you do to prepare yourself to read people's emotions even when you can't understand their words?

COGNITIVE THEORIES OF EMOTION: THINK FIRST, FEEL LATER

As we've seen, discrete emotions theorists emphasize the biological underpinnings of emotion. For them, emotions are largely innate. Advocates of **cognitive theories of emotion** disagree. For them, emotions are products of thinking. What we feel in response to a situation is determined by how we interpret it (Scherer, 1988). As we'll learn in Chapter 10, the way we appraise situations influences whether we find them stressful (Lazarus & Folkman, 1984). If we see an upcoming job interview as a potential catastrophe, we'll be hopelessly stressed out; if we see it as a healthy challenge, we'll be appropriately geared up for it. Moreover, for cognitive theorists, there is no discrete set of emotions, because the boundaries across emotions are fuzzy (Barrett & Russell, 1999; Ortony & Turner, 1990). They believe that there are as many different kinds of emotions as there are kinds of thoughts. There have been three prevalent cognitive theories of emotion that each emphasize a different connection between thinking and feeling. We'll review each one briefly.

James-Lange Theory of Emotion. Perhaps the oldest cognitive theory of emotion, and still one of the most influential, owes its origins to American psychologist William James (1890), whom we met in Chapter 1. Because Danish researcher Carl Lange (1885) advanced a similar version of this theory around the same time, psychologists refer to it as the **James-Lange theory of emotion.** According to the James-Lange theory, emotions result from our interpretations of our bodily reactions to stimuli.

To take James's famous example, let's imagine that, while hiking through the forest, we come upon a bear. What happens next? Common wisdom tells us that we first become scared and then run away. Yet as James recognized, the link between our fear and running away is only a correlation; this link doesn't demonstrate that our fear *causes* us to run away. Indeed, James and Lange argued that the causal arrow is reversed: *We're afraid because we run away.* That is, we observe our physiological and behavioral reactions to a stimulus, in this case our hearts pounding, our palms sweating, and our feet running, and then conclude that we must have been scared (see **Figure 9.1**).

In support of this theory, a researcher examined five groups of patients with injuries in different regions of their spinal cord (Hohmann, 1966). Patients with injuries high in their spinal cord had lost almost all of their bodily sensation, and those with lower injuries had lost only part of their bodily sensation. Just as James and Lange would have predicted, patients with higher spinal cord damage reported less emotion—fear and anger—than those with lower spinal cord damage. Presumably, patients with lower injuries could feel more of their bodies, which allowed them a greater range of emotional reactions. Still, some researchers have criticized these findings because of a possible experimenter bias effect (Chapter 2): The researcher knew which spinal cord patients were which when he assessed their emotions, and this knowledge could have biased the results (Prinz, 2004).

CORRELATION vs. CAUSATION
Can we be sure that A causes B?

GLOSSARY

cognitive theory of emotion
theory proposing that emotions are products of thinking

James-Lange theory of emotion
theory proposing that emotions result from our interpretations of our bodily reactions to stimuli

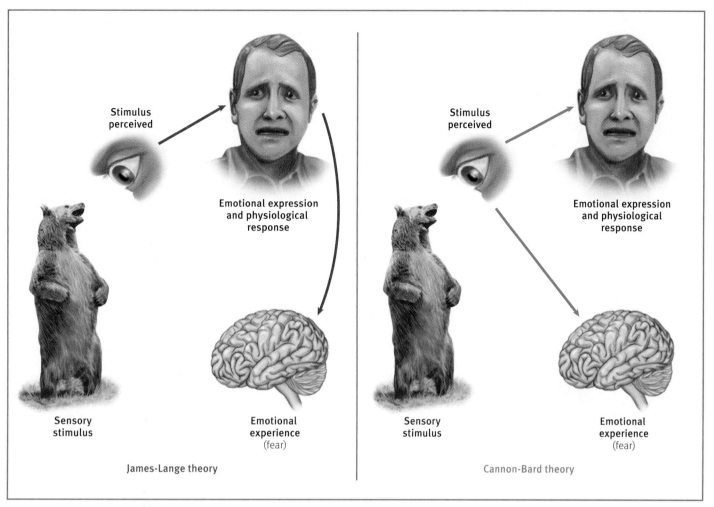

Figure 9.1 What Triggers Emotions? The James-Lange and Cannon-Bard theories differ in their views of how emotions are generated. (*Source:* Adapted from Cardoso)

REPLICABILITY
Can the results be duplicated in other studies?

Moreover, some investigators haven't replicated these findings: One research team found no differences in the happiness of patients with or without spinal cord injuries (Chwalisz, Diener, & Gallagher, 1988).

Cannon-Bard Theory of Emotion.
Walter Cannon (1929) and Philip Bard (1942) pointed out several flaws with James's and Lange's reasoning. They noted that most physiological changes occur too slowly—often taking at least a few seconds—to trigger emotional reactions, which happen almost instantaneously. Cannon and Bard also argued that we aren't aware of many of our bodily reactions, like the contractions of our stomach or liver. As a consequence, we can't use them to infer our emotions.

Cannon and Bard proposed a different model for the correlation between emotions and bodily reactions. According to the **Cannon-Bard theory of emotion,** an emotion-provoking event leads simultaneously to both an emotion and bodily reactions. To return to James's example, Cannon and Bard would say that when we see a bear while hiking in the forest, the sight of that bear triggers both fear (the emotion) and running (the reaction) at the same time (again refer to Figure 9.1).

Two-Factor Theory of Emotion.
Stanley Schachter and Jerome Singer (1962) argued that both the James-Lange and Cannon-Bard models of emotion were too simple. They agreed with James and Lange that our cognitive interpretations of our bodily reactions play a crucial role in emotions, but they disagreed with James and

GLOSSARY

Cannon-Bard theory of emotion
theory proposing that an emotion-provoking event leads simultaneously to an emotion and to bodily reactions

According to Schachter and Singer's two-factor theory of emotion, we first experience arousal after an emotion-provoking event, like a car accident, and then seek to interpret the cause of that arousal. The resulting label we attach to our arousal is the emotion.

Schachter and Singer showed that observing someone else's emotion can influence our own, but only when we are experiencing arousal.

REPLICABILITY
Can the results be duplicated in other studies?

GLOSSARY

two-factor theory
theory proposing that emotions are produced by an undifferentiated state of arousal along with an attribution (explanation) of that arousal

Lange that these bodily reactions are sufficient for emotion. According to their **two-factor theory of emotion** (Schachter & Singer, 1962), two psychological events are required to produce an emotion:

(1) After encountering an emotion-provoking event, we experience an undifferentiated state of arousal, that is, alertness. By "undifferentiated," Schachter and Singer meant that this experience of arousal is the same across emotions.

(2) As we try to explain the source of this autonomic arousal we examine the circumstances, either within us or in the external environment, that provoked the arousal. Once we figure out what's making us aroused, we "label" that arousal with a particular emotion that seems appropriate for the situation. This labeling process, Schachter and Singer proposed, typically occurs so rapidly that we're not even aware of it. According to this view, emotions are the explanations we attach to our arousal.

So, when we come upon a bear in the woods, we first become physiologically aroused, according to Schachter and Singer. Then, we try to figure out the source of that arousal. Because our arousal probably has something to do with the bear, we interpret this arousal as fear.

It sounds plausible, but do our emotions really work this way? In a classic study, Schachter and Singer (1962) decided to find out. As a "cover story," they informed subjects that they were testing the effectiveness of a new vitamin supplement—"Suproxin"—on vision. But in reality, they were testing the effects of *adrenaline,* a chemical that produces physiological arousal (see Chapter 3). Schachter and Singer randomly assigned some subjects to receive an injection of Suproxin (again, actually adrenaline) and others an injection of placebo. While the adrenaline was entering their systems, Schachter and Singer randomly assigned subjects to two additional conditions: one in which a confederate (an undercover research assistant) acted in a happy fashion while completing questionnaires, and a second in which a confederate acted in an angry fashion while completing questionnaires. The confederate was blind as to whether subjects had received an injection of adrenaline or the placebo. Finally, Schachter and Singer asked participants to describe how strongly they were experiencing different emotions.

Schachter and Singer found that the emotions of the subjects who'd received the placebo weren't influenced by the behavior of the confederate, but the emotions of the subjects who received adrenaline were. Subjects exposed to the happy confederate reported feeling happier, and those exposed to the angry confederate reported feeling angrier—but in both cases only if they'd received adrenaline. Emotion, Schachter and Singer concluded, requires *both* physiological arousal *and* an attribution of that arousal to an emotion-inducing event.

Support for two-factor theory has been mixed. Not all researchers have replicated Schachter and Singer's (1962) results (Marshall & Zimbardo, 1979; Maslach, 1979). Moreover, research suggests that although arousal often intensifies emotions, emotions can occur in the absence of arousal (Reisenzein, 1983). Contrary to what Schachter and Singer claimed, arousal isn't necessary for emotional experience.

Putting It All Together. So which of these theories should we believe? As is so often the case in psychology, there's probably a kernel of truth in several explanations. Discrete emotions theory is probably correct that our emotional reactions are shaped in part by natural selection and that these reactions serve crucial adaptive functions. It's also likely that our thinking influences our emotions in significant ways, as cognitive theorists propose. Indeed, the James-Lange theory is probably correct in assuming that our inferences concerning our bodily reactions can influence our emotional states. Finally, two-factor theory may also be right that physiological arousal plays a key role in the intensity of our emotional experiences, although it's unlikely to be the entire story.

UNCONSCIOUS INFLUENCES ON EMOTION

In recent decades, researchers have become especially interested in *unconscious influences on emotion:* Factors outside our awareness that can affect our feelings. One piece of evidence for unconscious influences on emotion comes from research on *automatic behaviors.*

Automatic Generation of Emotion. Research suggests that a good deal of our behavior is produced automatically, that is, with no voluntary influence on our part (Bargh & Ferguson, 2000). Yet we often perceive such behavior as intentional (Kirsch & Lynn, 1999; Wegner, 2002). The same may hold for our emotional reactions; many may be generated more or less automatically, like the knee-jerk reflex that our doctor elicits when she taps on our knees with a hammer. **[LEARNING OBJECTIVE 9.2]**

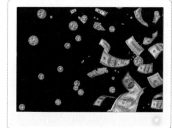

Stimuli can influence our emotional behavior even when we don't recognize them as the culprits. Watching a computer screensaver of floating currency (*left*) makes people put more physical distance between themselves and a stranger than does watching a screensaver of floating fish (*right*), presumably because thinking of money makes people more self-centered (Vohs, Mead, & Goode, 2006).

For example, two investigators visually presented some subjects with a set of words describing positive stimuli (like *friends* and *music*) and others with words describing negative stimuli (like *cancer* and *cockroach*). These stimuli appeared so quickly that they were *subliminal,* that is, below the threshold for awareness (see Chapter 4). Even though subjects couldn't identify what they saw at better than chance levels, those exposed to positive stimuli reported being in a better mood than those exposed to negative stimuli (Bargh & Chartrand, 1999).

Mere Exposure Effect.

Psychology: A Framework for Everyday Thinking
Psychology: A Framework for Everyday Thinking
Psychology: A Framework for Everyday Thinking
Psychology: A Framework for Everyday Thinking

After reading the four lines above, how do you feel about your textbook? Do you like it better than you did before?

Most people prefer their mirror image to their image as taken by a photographer, due to the mere exposure effect. We are more accustomed to a mirror view of ourselves.

Popular wisdom would say no. It tells us that "familiarity breeds contempt": The more often we've seen or heard something, the more we come to dislike it. There's surely some truth to this notion, as most of us have had the experience of hearing a jingle on the radio that grates on our nerves increasingly with each passing repetition. Yet research by Robert Zajonc and others on the **mere exposure effect** suggests that the opposite is actually more common: That is, familiarity breeds *comfort* (Zajonc, 1968). The mere exposure effect refers to the fact that repeated exposure to a stimulus makes us more likely to feel positive emotion toward it (Bornstein, 1989; Kunst-Wilson & Zajonc, 1980).

This correlation between exposure and liking could be due to the fact that we repeatedly expose ourselves to things we like. If we love ice cream, we're likely to spend more time seeking ice cream than are people who hate ice cream, assuming such human beings actually exist. So to find out whether mere exposure actually exerts an effect on preferences, we need to turn from correlational studies to experiments. Some of the best evidence for the mere exposure effect derives from experiments using meaningless material, for which individuals are unlikely to have any prior feelings. Experiments show that repeated exposure to various stimuli, such as nonsense syllables (like "zab" and "gar"), Chinese letters (to non-Chinese subjects), and new soft drink flavors results in greater liking toward these stimuli compared to those with little or no exposure. These effects have been replicated by multiple investigators using quite different stimuli, attesting to their generality.

CORRELATION vs. CAUSATION
Can we be sure that A causes B?

GLOSSARY

mere exposure effect
phenomenon in which repeated exposure to a stimulus makes us more likely to feel favorably toward it

REPLICABILITY
Can the results be duplicated in other studies?

Fact **-OID** The results of a small study suggest that the chemical *botox,* used to treat wrinkles by paralyzing the skin around them, may be helpful in treating depression (Finzi & Wasserman, 2006). Although this preliminary finding requires replication, it's consistent with the facial feedback hypothesis because *botox* may decrease the sad facial expressions of depressed people, in turn dampening their sad emotions.

RULING OUT RIVAL HYPOTHESES
Have important alternative explanations for the findings been excluded?

The modern polygraph test relies on the assumption that people exhibit physiological arousal when they lie. However, people can display arousal for a variety of reasons, and some people show no arousal response while lying.

GLOSSARY

facial feedback hypothesis
theory that blood vessels in the face feed back temperature information to the brain, altering our experience of emotions

nonverbal leakage
unconscious spillover of emotions into nonverbal behavior

Facial Feedback Hypothesis. If no one is near you, and you're not afraid of looking foolish, make a big smile and hold it for a while, maybe for 15 seconds. How do you feel (other than silly)? Next, make a big frown, and again hold it for a while. How do you feel now?

According to the **facial feedback hypothesis,** you're likely to feel emotions that correspond to your facial expressions—first happy, and then sad or angry (Adelmann & Zajonc, 1989; Niedenthal, 2007; Zajonc, Murphy, & Inglehart, 1989). This hypothesis originated with none other than Charles Darwin (1872), although Robert Zajonc revived it in the 1980s. Zajonc went beyond Darwin by proposing that changes in the blood vessels of the face "feed back" temperature information to the brain, altering our emotions in predictable ways. Like James and Lange, Zajonc argued that our emotions typically arise from our behaviors and physiological reactions. But unlike James and Lange, Zajonc viewed this process as purely biochemical and noncognitive, that is, as involving no thinking.

There's scientific support for the facial feedback hypothesis. In one study, researchers asked subjects to rate how funny they found various cartoons (Strack, Martin, & Stepper, 1988). They randomly assigned some subjects to watch cartoons while holding a pen with their teeth which forced their mouths into a smile and others to watch cartoons while holding a pen with their lips which forced their mouths into a frown. Subjects who held a pen with their teeth rated the cartoons as funnier than did other subjects.

Still, it's not clear that these effects work by means of facial feedback to the brain, as Zajonc claimed. An alternative hypothesis for these effects is classical conditioning (see Chapter 5). Over the course of our lives, we've experienced countless conditioning "trials" in which we smile while feeling happy and frown while feeling unhappy. Eventually, smiles become conditioned stimuli for happiness, frowns for unhappiness.

myth **CONCEPTIONS** **DO LIE DETECTORS LIE?**

The *polygraph,* or lie detector test, makes frequent appearances in television detective and courtroom dramas and features prominently in news stories about criminal suspects. Most recently, talk shows and reality shows have even begun using lie detector tests. Polygraph tests measure physiological signals such as blood pressure, breathing rate, and skin conductance, which is a measure of hand sweatiness as a result of arousal. These measures are presumed to detect anxiety associated with lying. But do they actually detect when a suspect is telling a falsehood? There is virtual universal agreement that the polygraph test usually does better than chance at detecting lies (Kircher, Horowitz, & Raskin, 1988) by comparing suspects' physiological response to questions about a crime with their responses to control questions unrelated to the crime under investigation. Yet research suggests that this test yields a high rate of *false positives*—innocent individuals whom the test labels incorrectly as guilty (Iacono & Patrick, 2006; Lykken, 1998; National Research Council, 2003). Why such a high rate of false positives? This poor predictability is probably due to the fact that being interrogated about a serious crime is extremely anxiety producing, even for those who are innocent. Many people display physiological arousal under interrogation for reasons other than lying, such as the fear of being convicted for a crime they didn't commit. Largely as a result of this high rate of false positives, polygraph test outcomes are not admissible in most U.S. courts (Saxe & Ben-Skakhar, 1999).

False positives aren't the only problem for the polygraph test because this test may also yield significant numbers of *false negatives,* cases where guilty individuals are incorrectly labeled by the test as innocent. If the polygraph is so flawed, why are polygraph examiners persuaded of its validity? The answer probably lies in the fact that the polygraph is often effective for eliciting confessions, especially when people fail the test (Lykken, 1998; Ruscio, 2005). As a result, polygraph examiners may come to believe the test works, because many people who fail the polygraph test will subsequently confess. However, there's good evidence that such confessions are often false and a result of interrogation pressure (Kassin & Gudjonsson, 2004).

MYTH: "Shifty eyes" are good indicators of lying.

REALITY: There's no evidence for this belief, which is held by about 70 percent of people (Bond, 2006). To the contrary, pathological liars (see Chapters 5 and 13) tend to stare their victims straight in the eye (Ekman, 2001). Still, because shifty eyes might give away *bad* liars, they may not be useless as emotional cues.

EMOTIONAL EXPRESSION THROUGH BODY LANGUAGE

Not only do our facial expressions frequently change when we experience a strong emotion, but so do our gestures and postures. What's more, our nonverbal behaviors are often more valid indicators of our emotions than our words, largely because we're better at disguising our verbal language than our gestures and tone of voice (DePaulo, 1992). As baseball Hall of Famer Yogi Berra (known for his funny words of wisdom) said, "You can observe a lot just by watching." **Nonverbal leakage**—an unconscious spillover of emotions into nonverbal behavior—is often a powerful cue that we're trying to hide an emotion. In sharp contrast to our verbal behaviors, we're frequently unaware of our nonverbal behaviors.

The types of gestures and movements we display—flamboyant arm waving, twitching at our clothes, biting our nails nervously, or jerky hand movements—can all convey something about our state of mind. Likewise, our postures can convey a lot about our emotional states (see **Figure 9.2**). Slumped posture can convey sadness and upright posture can convey happiness or excitement, although an upright posture involving a lot of body tension may also convey anger. This nonverbal leakage is largely unconscious. When interpreting the emotional states of others, we typically take both facial and body information into account.

Figure 9.2 Emotional Expression through Posture. Even in these stick figure drawings with no facial features, we can easily interpret their emotional states from their "body language."

QUIZ

1 Psychological research demonstrates that emotion and reason are direct opposites of each other.　TRUE　FALSE

2 Some emotions, like happiness, appear to be recognized by a substantial majority of people in all cultures.　TRUE　FALSE

3 According to the James-Lange theory, emotions follow from our bodily reactions.　TRUE　FALSE

4 Two-factor theory proposes that arousal is necessary for emotion.　TRUE　FALSE

5 The mere exposure effect refers to the finding that repeated presentations of a stimulus lead to less liking of that stimulus.　TRUE　FALSE

Answers: (1) F (p. 302); (2) T (p. 305); (3) T (p. 306); (4) T (p. 308); (5) F (p. 309)

▼ Are there gender differences in positive emotions? Watch the video titled "Positive Emotions: Michael Cohn" at www.mypsychlab.com to find out.

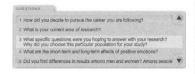

Happiness and Self-Esteem: Science Confronts Pop Psychology

Figure 9.3 Bhutan, Home of Gross National Happiness. In the Himalayan country of Bhutan, the king has made increasing his country's gross national happiness a major domestic policy goal.

GLOSSARY

positive psychology
discipline that has sought to emphasize human strengths

broaden and build theory
theory proposing that happiness predisposes us to think more openly

Happiness is the only completely positive primary emotion and can sometimes seem like the one we experience least often. The pursuit of happiness has long been considered a noble endeavor, but one of the hardest to achieve. The ruler of the tiny country of Bhutan, nestled in the Himalayan mountain range, recently had an unconventional idea (see **Figure 9.3**). Rather than focusing on increasing his nation's gross national product (GNP, a measure of economic success), the king decided to try to improve his nation's gross national happiness (GNH; Nettle, 2005). He hopes to boost Bhutan's GNH, as it's called, by preserving the beauty of its natural environment, promoting positive cultural values, and giving citizens more of a voice in government decisions. Until recently, almost all psychologists would have probably viewed the king as a naive idealist. Not anymore.

POSITIVE PSYCHOLOGY: PSYCHOLOGY'S FUTURE OR PSYCHOLOGY'S FAD?

Since about the turn of the twenty-first century, the emerging discipline of **positive psychology** has sought to emphasize human strengths, such as resilience, coping, life satisfaction, love, and happiness (Myers & Diener, 1996; Seligman, 1998; Seligman & Csikszentmihalyi, 2000). Some authors have argued that much of popular psychology has underestimated people's resilience in the face of stressful life events (Bonanno, Field, Kovacevic, et al., 2002; Garmezy, Masten, & Tellegen, 1984; see also Chapter 10). In this respect, the field of positive psychology has considerable potential, as it may help psychologists to pinpoint the traits that allow us to cope with adversity. **[LEARNING OBJECTIVE 9.3]**

Much of contemporary psychology has also focused on minimizing severe distress and on returning disturbed people to adequate levels of functioning. But it's done little to encourage adequately functioning people to achieve their full emotional potential—that is, to become "better than well" (Keyes & Haidt, 2003). To fill this void, Christopher Peterson and Martin Seligman (2004) outlined 24 "character strengths and virtues" they view as essential to positive psychology (see **Table 9.1**). Several of these traits, such as curiosity, love, and gratitude, are positively associated with people's long-term life satisfaction (Park, Peterson, & Seligman, 2004). Positive psychologists have begun to teach

Table 9.1 The Twenty-Four Character Strengths and Virtues Identified by Positive Psychologists.

Wisdom and Knowledge	Courage	Humanity	Justice	Temperance	Transcendence
• Creativity (originality, ingenuity) • Curiosity (interest, novelty-seeking, openness to experience) • Open-mindedness (judgment, critical thinking) • Love of learning • Perspective (wisdom)	• Bravery (valor) • Persistence (perseverance, industriousness) • Integrity (authenticity, honesty) • Vitality (zest, enthusiasm, vigor, energy)	• Love • Kindness (generosity, nurturance, care, compassion, altruistic love, "niceness") • Social intelligence (emotional intelligence, personal intelligence)	• Citizenship (social responsibility, loyalty, teamwork) • Fairness • Leadership	• Forgiveness and mercy • Humility/modesty • Prudence • Self-regulation (self-control)	• Appreciation of beauty and excellence (awe, wonder, elevation) • Gratitude • Hope (optimism, future-mindedness, future orientation) • Humor (playfulness) • Spirituality (religiousness, faith, purpose)

(*Source:* Park, Peterson, & Seligman, 2004)

students how to incorporate these strengths and virtues into their daily lives with the hope of boosting their happiness (Max, 2007).

WHAT HAPPINESS IS GOOD FOR

For most of the twentieth century, psychologists largely dismissed happiness as a "fluffy" topic better suited to self-help books and motivational seminars than to rigorous research. Yet over the past few decades, a growing body of research has suggested that happiness may produce enduring psychological and physical benefits (see **Figure 9.4**).

Happiness and Longevity.
Consider the results of a study that has tracked a group of 180 nuns in Wisconsin for six decades. These nuns had kept daily diaries starting in the 1930s, when they were in their early twenties. Nuns whose sentences featured many positive words—such as those dealing with love, joy, and hope—outlived other nuns by an average of almost 10 years (Danner, Snowdon, & Friesen, 2001). Of course, correlation doesn't imply causation, and the nuns who used more happy words may have differed in subtle ways from other nuns, such as in their exercise or health practices. Still, the findings are tantalizing.

Adaptive Value of Happiness.
Like all primary emotions, happiness may serve evolutionarily adaptive functions. According to Barbara Fredrickson's (2001, 2003) **broaden and build theory,** happiness predisposes us to think more openly, allowing us to see the "big picture" we might have otherwise overlooked. In turn, this broader thinking often permits us to find novel solutions to life's problems. When we're happy, we see more of the world and seek out more opportunities, like romantic partners we wouldn't have previously considered. Happiness breeds success in our work, family, and love lives, in turn breeding more happiness (Lyubomirsky, King, & Diener, 2005). As one test of the broaden and build theory, doctors who received a small bag of candy made more accurate diagnoses of liver disease than other doctors, apparently because being in a good mood allowed them to consider alternative diagnostic possibilities (Isen, Rosenzweig, & Young, 1991).

Moreover, all else being equal, life is easier for those of us who are optimists (see Chapter 10). Optimists tend to be happier in everyday life than pessimists (Seligman & Pawelski, 2003) and find it easier than pessimists to cope with life's rocky road (Watson & Clark, 1984). For example, when given threatening medical information (such as their risk for developing cancer), optimists tend to pay more attention to it and remember it better than pessimists (Aspinwall & Brunhart, 2000). This finding may partly explain why optimists tend to live longer than pessimists (Maruta, Colligan, Malinchoc, et al., 2000): They may be less likely to ignore risks to their health.

WHAT MAKES US HAPPY: THE MYTHS

We all ought to be veritable experts on happiness. Given that Americans spend about $750 million a year on self-help books designed to make them happy and another $1 billion a year on motivational speakers, we might assume that we have all of the advice about happiness we need. Yet as psychologist Daniel Gilbert observed, "People have a lot of bad theories about happiness" (Martin, 2006). So to understand happiness, we first need to burst some pop psychology bubbles. **[LEARNING OBJECTIVE 9.4]**

(1) **Misconception 1: *The prime determinant of happiness is what happens to us.*** Ed Diener and Martin Seligman screened more than 200 college students for their levels of happiness and compared the upper 10 percent with the middle and lowest 10 percent. The happiest students didn't experience any more positive life events than the other groups (Diener & Seligman, 2002). How we react to life events is more critical to our emotional well-being than the events themselves.

(2) **Misconception 2: *Money makes us happy.*** From what psychological research tells us, money can't buy long-term happiness (Wilson, 2002). Admittedly, when we're running short of it,

---

CORRELATION vs. CAUSATION
Can we be sure that A causes B?

Measure Your Happiness:
Take the Satisfaction with Life Scale

Below are five statements that you may agree or disagree with. Using the 1 to 7 scale below, indicate your agreement with each item by placing the appropriate number on the line preceding that item. Please be open and honest in your responding.

1	Strongly disagree	5	Slightly agree
2	Disagree	6	Agree
3	Slightly disagree	7	Strongly agree

4 — Neither agree nor disagree

_____ In most ways my life is close to my ideal.

_____ The conditions of my life are excellent.

_____ I am satisfied with my life.

_____ So far I have gotten the important things I want in life.

_____ If I could live my life over, I would change almost nothing.

Scoring:
• 31–35 Extremely satisfied
• 26–30 Satisfied
• 21–25 Slightly satisfied
• 20 Neutral
• 15–19 Slightly dissatisfied
• 10–14 Dissatisfied
• 5–9 Extremely dissatisfied

Figure 9.4 Satisfaction with Life Scale (SWLS). Do you wonder how happy you are? Take this quick test developed by psychologist Ed Diener and his colleagues to help you find out. (*Source:* Diener, Emmons, Larsen, et al., 1985)

money is a bit related to happiness. Below about $50,000, there's a modest association between how wealthy we are and how happy we are (Helliwell & Putnam, 2004) (see **Figure 9.5**). But the average life satisfaction among *Forbes* magazine's 400 richest Americans is 5.8 on a 7-point scale (Diener, Horwitz, & Emmons, 1985), precisely the same level as the Pennsylvania Amish, whose average annual income is a few billion (that's right—*billion*) dollars lower (Diener & Seligman, 2004).

(3) **Misconception 3: *Happiness declines in old age.*** We're all familiar with the widespread stereotype of the sad old man or woman, sitting all alone in a sparsely decorated room with no one to talk to. Yet this stereotype is misleading because happiness tends to increase with age, at least through the late sixties and perhaps seventies (Lacey, Smith, & Ubel, 2006; Mrozek & Kolarz, 1998). Only when people become quite old, typically in their eighties, does happiness decrease noticeably. Interestingly, happiness drops dramatically in the last year of life (Mrozek & Spiro, 2005). Although this correlation may reflect a causal effect of unhappiness on health, it may also reflect a causal effect of declining health on unhappiness.

(4) **Misconception 4: *People on the West Coast are the happiest.*** Beautiful beaches, sunshine, warm weather, great celebrity watching . . . who could ask for a better recipe for happiness? Even though non-Californians believe that Southern Californians are especially happy, Southern Californians are no happier than anyone else, including people in the chilly upper Midwest (Schkade & Kahneman, 1998). In this case, non-Californians are probably falling prey to the *availability heuristic* (see Chapter 2). When we think of the West Coast, we think of the great weather and the glamour. We forget about the high cost of living, traffic congestion, and all of the other things that often come with living in heavily populated areas.

CORRELATION vs. CAUSATION
Can we be sure that A causes B?

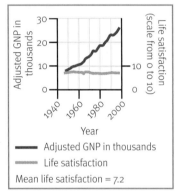

Figure 9.5 Does Wealth Bring Happiness? Over a 60-year span, the U.S. gross national product (a measure of economic prosperity) has increased dramatically. Yet Americans' average level of life satisfaction has stayed remarkably constant over the same time period. (*Source:* Diener & Seligman, 2004)

Married people are happier, on average, than unmarried people. Whether this correlational finding reflects a causal association is unclear.

GLOSSARY

affective forecasting
ability to predict our own and others' happiness

durability bias
belief that both our good and bad moods will last longer than they do

---

WHAT DO *you* THINK*?*

As the director of a nursing home facility, you decide to do some investigating into whether the correlation between depression and declining health in the elderly is causal. What kind of a study could you conduct with your residents to determine whether depression is a cause or a consequence of declining health?

WHAT MAKES US HAPPY: THE REALITIES

We've talked about four things that don't make us happy, but we haven't said much about what *does* make us happy. Fortunately, research offers some helpful clues. In particular, psychologists have found that the following variables are correlated with happiness (Martin, 2006; Myers, 1993b; Myers & Diener, 1996):

- *Marriage.* Married people tend to be happier than unmarried people (Mastekaasa, 1994).
- *Friendships.* People with many friends tend to be happier than people with few friends (Diener & Seligman, 2002).
- *College.* People who graduate from college tend to be happier than people who don't (Martin, 2006).
- *Religion.* People who are deeply religious tend to be happier than people who aren't (Myers, 1993b).
- *Political affiliation.* Republicans tend to be happier than Democrats, both of whom tend to be happier than Independents (Pew Research Center, 2006).

- *Exercise*. People who exercise regularly tend to be happier and less depressed than people who don't (Babyak et al., 2000; Stathopoulou, Powers, Berry, et al., 2006).

- *Gratitude*. Merely asking participants on a daily basis to list reasons why they should be grateful about their lives, like having good friends, intimate romantic partners, and a fulfilling job, can enhance short-term happiness (Emmons & McCullough, 2003; Sheldon & Lyubomirsky, 2006).

- *Flow*. Mihaly Csikszentmihalyi (pronounced "cheeks sent me high") has found that individuals in the midst of *flow,* a mental state in which we're completely immersed in what we are doing, tend to be especially happy (Csikszentmihalyi, 1990, 1997). Some of us experience flow while writing, others while reading, others while performing manual labor, and still others while playing sports, performing music, or creating works of art. During moments of flow, we're so intensely engaged in a rewarding activity that we screen out unpleasant distractions. We also feel a powerful sense of control over our actions.

We should bear two cautions in mind when interpreting these findings. First, the associations between these variables and happiness are typically modest in magnitude, and there are many exceptions to the trends. For example, although there's a slight tendency for married people to be happier than unmarried people, there are plenty of unhappy married people and happy unmarried people.

Second, most of these findings derive from correlational research alone, so the direction of the causal arrow is unclear. For example, although religious people tend to be happier than nonreligious people, happier people may find it easier than unhappy people to embrace a meaningful religious faith.

If psychological research tells us anything about how to find happiness, it's that consciously going out of our way to seek it out rarely works. As the concept of flow implies, happiness often emerges from the sheer act of enjoying what we do best, whether it's our work, hobbies, friends, or romantic partners. Happiness lies in the pursuit of the prize, not the prize itself.

FORECASTING HAPPINESS

We're remarkably poor at **affective forecasting:** predicting our own and others' happiness (Gilbert, 2006; Gilbert, Pinel, Wilson, et al., 1998; Wilson, 2002). We engage in affective forecasting whenever we make a life decision: picking a college, entering into a long-term relationship, or buying a car. We tell ourselves that each of our choices will boost our happiness, but we're typically no more accurate than a meteorologist who tries to forecast next week's weather by poking his head out the window.

Our affective forecasts aren't merely wrong; they're consistently wrong in one direction. Specifically, *we overestimate the long-term impact of events on our moods* (Gilbert, 2006; Sevdalis & Harvey, 2007). That is, we suffer from a **durability bias:** We believe that both our good and bad moods will last longer than they do (Frederick & Loewenstein, 1999; Gilbert et al., 1998; Wilson, 2002). Consider the following counterintuitive findings:

- Multimillion dollar lottery winners' happiness shoots up sky-high immediately after hitting the big jackpot. Yet within 2 months, their happiness is back to normal—and not much higher than anyone else's (Brickman, Coates, & Janoff-Bulman, 1978).

- Most people with paraplegia—paralysis from the waist down—have returned largely (although not entirely) to their baseline levels of happiness only a few months after their accidents (Brickman et al., 1978).

- Before taking an HIV test, people understandably predict that they'd be profoundly distressed were they to turn up HIV-positive. Yet only 5 weeks after discovering they're HIV positive, people are considerably happier than they expected to be. Moreover, people who discovered they were HIV negative are considerably less happy than they expected to be (Sieff, Dawes, & Loewenstein, 1999).

The state of "flow" is associated with high levels of satisfaction and subjective well-being. We can experience flow in many work situations and enjoyable pastimes.

CORRELATION vs. CAUSATION
Can we be sure that A causes B?

Fact-OID The world champions of happiness appear to be the Danes. For reasons that are unknown, people in Denmark report the highest level of satisfaction in the world, with the Swiss a close second. Americans come in at twenty-third (White, 2006).

Following accidents, those experiencing paralysis typically regain much of their preaccident levels of happiness. The upbeat attitude of actor Christopher Reeve, who died in 2004, 9 years after being paralyzed in a horse-riding accident, was both a surprise and an inspiration to many Americans.

What's going on here? We markedly underestimate how rapidly we adjust to our baseline levels of happiness or unhappiness (Brickman & Campbell, 1971). Our levels of happiness quickly adjust to our ongoing life situations. When something good happens to us, we feel better in the short term. Yet we soon adapt to our positive life circumstances, bringing us back to our emotional "default" setting (Helson, 1948). There's a life lesson lurking in all of this. Here popular wisdom is correct: The grass *is* greener on the other side. But once we make it over to the other side, we eventually realize that the grass is still greener on yet another lawn.

SELF-ESTEEM: IMPORTANT OR OVERHYPED?

Many pop psychology sources tie virtually all psychological difficulties to one, and only one, core problem: low self-esteem (Branden, 1994; Reasoner, 2000). Schools and social agencies have developed outreach and intervention programs designed to boost self-esteem. If you log onto Amazon.com, you'll find dozens of books, tapes, and other products devoted to boosting self-esteem. You can even find a self-esteem cereal bowl emblazoned with positive affirmations, like "I'm talented!" and "I'm good-looking!"

Happiness is influenced by social comparison. The 2008 U.S. Men's Olympic gymnastics team was overjoyed to receive an unexpected bronze medal whereas the Japanese team (not pictured) who had hoped to earn gold was disappointed with its silver medal.

The Great Myths of Self-Esteem.
There are two big problems with the widespread claim that low self-esteem is the root of all unhappiness. First, this assertion is a prime example of a *single-variable explanation,* which as we noted in Chapter 1 reduces complex psychological problems, like depression or aggression, to one cause. Although low self-esteem may play some causal role in these problems, it's unlikely to be the sole culprit.

Second, the evidence linking self-esteem to mental health and life success is feeble (Dawes, 1994; Sommers & Satel, 2005). For example, people with high self-esteem aren't much more likely than people with low self-esteem to have good social skills or to do well in school. They're also just about as likely to abuse alcohol and other drugs (Baumeister, Campbell, Krueger, et al., 2003).

When it comes to links between self-esteem and aggression, the story becomes more interesting. Most of the popular psychology literature links aggression to low self-esteem. There may be some truth to this view (Donnellen, Trzesniewski, Robins, et al., 2005). Yet most evidence suggests that a subset of people with *high* self-esteem is especially prone to aggression, especially when confronted with "ego threats": challenges to their self-worth (Bushman & Baumeister, 1998).

The Realities of Self-Esteem.
Still, research suggests that self-esteem affords two apparent benefits (Baumeister et al., 2003). First, high self-esteem is associated with greater initiative and persistence. Those with high self-esteem are more willing to attempt new challenges and to stick with them even when the going gets rough. Second, high self-esteem is related to happiness and resilience in the face of stress. Nevertheless, these findings are correlational and may not be causal.

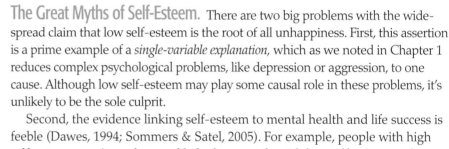

CORRELATION vs. **CAUSATION**
Can we be sure that A causes B?

Criticisms of Positive Psychology.
The field of positive psychology has heightened our appreciation for the full range of human experience. Yet some psychologists have condemned positive psychology as a "fad" (Lazarus, 2003) whose claims have outstripped the scientific evidence (Max, 2007).

Many positive psychology proponents have assumed that we'd all be better off if we could just eliminate our strong negative emotions. Yet this "always look on the bright side of life" approach may have its downside. As Julie Norem (2001) observed, **defensive pessimism** probably serves a valuable function for many anxious people. Defensive pessimism is the strategy of anticipating failure and then compensating for this expectation by mentally overpreparing for negative outcomes (see **Table 9.2**). Defensive pessimism

GLOSSARY

defensive pessimism
strategy of anticipating failure and then compensating for this expectation by mentally overpreparing for negative outcomes

helps certain people to improve their performance, probably because it encourages them to work harder (Norem & Cantor, 1986). Robbing defensive pessimists of their pessimism—say, by cheering them up—makes them perform worse (Norem & Chang, 2002).

Moreover, optimists' rose-colored glasses and tendency to gloss over their mistakes may sometimes prevent them from seeing reality clearly. For example, optimists tend to recall feedback about their social skills as better than it actually was (Norem, 2001), which could prevent them from learning from their interpersonal errors, such as inadvertently offending other people. Moreover, optimists sometimes display greater physiological responses to stressors, like bad health news, than do pessimists, perhaps because they don't spend enough time preparing themselves mentally for the worst (Segerstrom, 2005).

None of this takes away from the value of positive psychology for many people. But the problem of *individual differences* (see Chapter 1) reminds us to be wary of "one size fits all" solutions to life's multifaceted problems. Positive thinking is a key ingredient in many people's recipe for happiness, but it may not be for everyone.

Table 9.2 Defensive Pessimism Questionnaire. Do you use defensive pessimism as a coping strategy? Here are some questions to help you find out

Think of a situation where you want to do your best. It may be related to work, to your social life, or to any of your goals. When you answer the following questions, please think about how you prepare for that kind of situation. Rate how true each statement is for you then add up your answers—higher scores (out of 70) indicate high defensive pessimism.

Not True						True
1	2	3	4	5	6	7

_____ 1. I often start out expecting the worst, even though I will probably do OK.

_____ 2. I worry about how things will turn out.

_____ 3. I carefully consider all possible outcomes.

_____ 4. I often worry that I won't be able to carry through my intentions.

_____ 5. I spend lots of time imagining what could go wrong.

_____ 6. I imagine how I would feel if things went badly.

_____ 7. I try to picture how I could fix things if something went wrong.

_____ 8. I'm careful not to become overconfident in these situations.

_____ 9. In these situations, sometimes I worry more about looking like a fool than doing really well.

_____ 10. Considering what can go wrong helps me to prepare.

(*Source:* Norem, 2001)

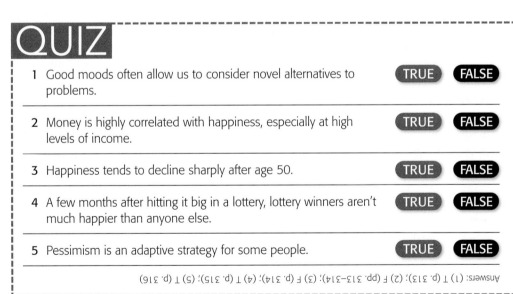

QUIZ

1 Good moods often allow us to consider novel alternatives to problems. TRUE FALSE

2 Money is highly correlated with happiness, especially at high levels of income. TRUE FALSE

3 Happiness tends to decline sharply after age 50. TRUE FALSE

4 A few months after hitting it big in a lottery, lottery winners aren't much happier than anyone else. TRUE FALSE

5 Pessimism is an adaptive strategy for some people. TRUE FALSE

Answers: (1) T (p. 313); (2) F (pp. 313–314); (3) F (p. 314); (4) T (p. 315); (5) T (p. 316)

▼ Do jokes have health benefits above just laughing? Watch the video titled "Humor and Brains" at www.mypsychlab.com to find out.

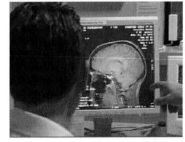

Motivation: Our Wants and Needs

Up to this point, we've discussed how and why we experience emotions. Yet to explain why we do things, we also need to understand the psychological forces that pull and push us in various, and sometimes opposing, directions. **Motivation** refers to the

GLOSSARY

motivation
psychological drives that propel us in a specific direction

Motivational speakers, like Anthony Robbins, are adept at persuading their audiences that they can accomplish just about anything with enough drive and effort. Nevertheless, there's no solid research evidence that such speakers produce long-term changes in people's behavior.

drives—especially wants and needs—that urge us in specific directions. When we're motivated to do something, like read an interesting book, talk to a friend, or avoid studying for an exam, we're driven to *move* toward or away from that act—both psychologically and physically. Most of us wish we could be more motivated to perform the tasks of life that we need to do but manage to put off, like pay our bills or begin work on that long-overdue term paper. **[LEARNING OBJECTIVE 9.5]**

So it's no surprise that the world of popular psychology is bursting at the seams with "motivational speakers" who line their pockets with cash from people hoping to receive inspiration in love or work. Although such speakers may get our adrenaline flowing and make us feel good in the short term, there's no evidence that they deliver long-term benefits (Wilson, 2003).

MOTIVATION: A BEGINNER'S GUIDE

Two of the most overpowering motivators in life are food and sex. We'll soon learn about the whys and the hows of these two great "facts of life." Before we do, we first need to learn about a few basic principles of motivation.

Drive Reduction Theory.

One of the most influential motivational concepts in psychology is **drive reduction theory,** formulated by Clark Hull (1943), Donald Hebb (1949), and others. According to this theory, certain *drives,* like hunger, thirst, and sexual frustration, motivate us to act to minimize aversive states (Dollard & Miller, 1950). Note that all of these drives are unpleasant, but that satisfaction of them is pleasurable. **[LEARNING OBJECTIVE 9.6]**

Some drives are more powerful than others. Thirst is more potent than hunger, and for good reason. Natural selection has probably ensured that our drive to quench our thirst is stronger than our drive to satisfy our hunger because most of us can survive only a few days without water but over a month without food.

Most drive reduction theories propose that we're motivated to maintain a given level of psychological **homeostasis,** that is, equilibrium. To understand homeostasis, think of how a thermostat works to control the temperature in your house or apartment. It's set to a given temperature, say 68 degrees Fahrenheit, and when the room temperature deviates up or down from that set point, the thermostat "tells" your cooling or heating system to restore the equilibrium. Similarly, when we're hungry, we're motivated to satisfy that drive by eating, but ideally not too much. If we eat too much, our brain signals to us that we've overdone things and doesn't allow us to become hungry again for a while.

Drives and Arousal: Not Getting Ahead of the Curve.

One factor that affects the strength of our drives is arousal. According to the **Yerkes-Dodson law** (Yerkes & Dodson, 1908), formulated about a century ago, there's an inverted U–shaped relation between arousal on the one hand and mood and performance on the other (although its developers actually referred to the strength of stimuli rather than the strength of arousal; Winton, 1987). As we can see in **Figure 9.6,** for each of us there's an optimal point of arousal, typically near the middle of the curve. If we're below that optimal point, we typically experience low motivation and don't perform well as a result. If we're above that optimal point, we typically feel too anxious or stimulated and likewise don't perform well. Only when we're moderately aroused do we experience the perfect balance of motivation and control to accomplish our goals. Our peak performance level also depends on the complexity of the task, with slightly lower arousal levels optimal for complex tasks than for simple ones.

The Yerkes-Dodson law is popular among sports psychologists. Think of a basketball player who's underaroused before a major game. She's unlikely to perform as well as she

GLOSSARY

drive reduction theory
theory proposing that certain drives, like hunger, thirst, and sexual frustration, motivate us to act in ways that minimize aversive states

homeostasis
equilibrium

Yerkes-Dodson law
inverted U–shaped relation between arousal on the one hand and performance on the other

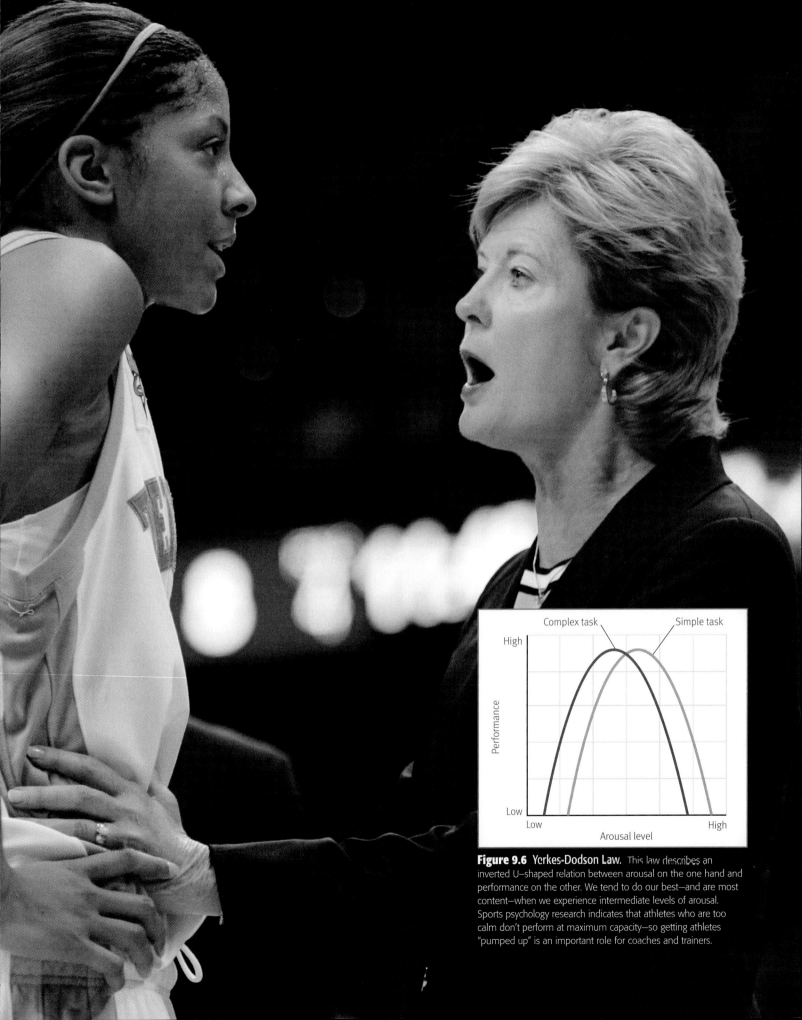

Figure 9.6 Yerkes-Dodson Law. This law describes an inverted U–shaped relation between arousal on the one hand and performance on the other. We tend to do our best—and are most content—when we experience intermediate levels of arousal. Sports psychology research indicates that athletes who are too calm don't perform at maximum capacity—so getting athletes "pumped up" is an important role for coaches and trainers.

could because she's not sufficiently motivated to do her best. So her coach or sports psychologist may try to get her into the "psyched up" range of the Yerkes-Dodson curve, where she's feeling just aroused enough to want to do well but not so aroused she can't concentrate (Anderson, Revelle, & Lynch, 1989).

Incentive Theories: Positive Motivation Valuable as drive reduction theories have been to psychology, they don't explain why we often engage in behaviors even when our drives are satisfied. For example, according to drive reduction theories, once Maya Angelou, Pablo Picasso, or Wolfgang Amadeus Mozart completed a masterpiece, their desire to generate another one would decrease because they would have quenched their creative thirsts. Yet the opposite often happens; creative success seems to encourage an even greater desire to create.

Children who are rewarded for their drawings are less motivated later to draw for fun. Can you think of examples from your own life where reward or compensation lowered your intrinsic motivation?

As a consequence, psychologists have come to recognize that drive reduction theories of motivation need to be supplemented by **incentive theories,** which propose that we're often motivated by positive goals, like the pleasure of creating a great painting or the glory of finishing first in a track meet. Many of these theories, in turn, distinguish *intrinsic motivation,* in which people are motivated by internal goals, from *extrinsic motivation,* in which people are motivated by external goals. If we're intrinsically motivated to do well in a psychology class, we're driven primarily by our desire to master the material; if we're extrinsically motivated to do well in this class, we're driven primarily by our desire to get a good grade or earn the professor's approval.

As we learned in Chapter 5, behaviorists define reinforcement as any outcome that makes the behavior that preceded it more likely. Yet there's evidence that certain reinforcements may *undermine* intrinsic motivation, rendering us less likely to perform behaviors we once enjoyed (Deci, 1971; Deci, Koestner, & Ryan, 1999). In a classic study, Mark Lepper and his colleagues (Lepper, Greene, & Nisbett, 1973) identified preschool children who were especially interested in drawing and either rewarded them for their work or didn't. Two weeks later, the experimenters again gave children the chance to draw pictures. Interestingly, children who'd received a reward showed significantly less interest in drawing than did children in the other condition. Many psychologists and some popular writers have interpreted these findings as implying that when we see ourselves performing a behavior to obtain an external goal, we conclude that we weren't all that interested in that behavior in the first place (Kohn, 1993). As a result, our intrinsic motivation for that behavior decreases.

REPLICABILITY
Can the results be duplicated in other studies?

RULING OUT RIVAL HYPOTHESES
Have important alternative explanations for the findings been excluded?

Not all psychologists accept this interpretation (Carton, 1996; Eisenberger & Cameron, 1996). For one thing, some researchers haven't replicated the undermining effect (Cameron & Pierce, 1994). Still others have offered rival explanations for these findings. One is a *contrast effect:* Once we receive reinforcement for performing a behavior, we anticipate that reinforcement again. If the reinforcement is suddenly withdrawn, we're less likely to perform the behavior.

OUR NEEDS: PHYSICAL AND PSYCHOLOGICAL URGES

We humans have a few basic biological needs; food, drink, and shelter are high on our shopping lists. Yet as Henry Murray (1938) noted, we have a wide variety of other

GLOSSARY

incentive theory
theory proposing that we're often motivated by positive goals

needs. Murray distinguished *primary* from *secondary* needs, with primary needs reflecting biological necessities, like hunger and thirst, and secondary needs reflecting psychological desires. Murray identified more than 20 secondary needs; one such need, the *need for achievement,* has received particular attention from psychologists (McClelland, Atkinson, Clark, et al., 1958). Researchers have found measures of this need to be useful in predicting individuals' academic performance (Spangler, 1992). David McClelland (1961) even demonstrated that, across countries, citizens' need for achievement levels forecast these countries' future economic growth, although this finding hasn't been entirely consistent (Mazur & Rosa, 1977).

Abraham Maslow (1954, 1971) argued that, in the grand scheme of life, some needs inevitably take priority over others. According to Maslow's **hierarchy of needs,** we must satisfy physiological needs and needs for safety and security before we can progress to more complex needs. These complex needs include desires for belongingness and love, self-esteem, and finally self-actualization, the drive to realize our full psychological potential (see Chapter 12). As we progress up Maslow's hierarchy, we move away from needs produced by drives, that is, by biological or psychological deficiencies, and toward needs produced by incentives, that is, by positive goals (see **Figure 9.7**).

Although Maslow's hierarchy is a helpful starting point, we shouldn't take it literally. Some needs are more crucial than others, but there's evidence that people who haven't achieved lower levels of his hierarchy can sometimes attain higher levels (Rowan, 1998; Soper, Milford, & Rosenthal, 1995). The numerous cases of starving artists, who continue to paint masterworks despite being hungry and poor, appear to falsify Maslow's claim of a fixed hierarchy of needs (Zautra, 2003).

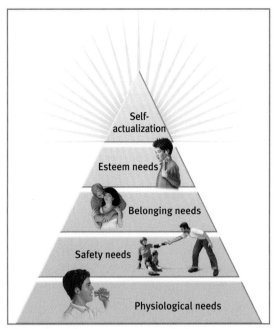

Figure 9.7 Maslow's Hierarchy of Needs. According to Abraham Maslow, our needs are arranged in a hierarchy or pyramid, with the most "basic" needs at the bottom. If our basic needs aren't satisfied, Maslow claimed, we can't progress up the hierarchy. Does research support this assertion?

FALSIFIABILITY
Can the claim be disproved?

HUNGER, EATING, AND EATING DISORDERS

If we're lucky, we don't experience the pangs of hunger very often or for very long and can refuel with a Big Mac, a veggie sandwich, or whatever satisfies our cravings. But, for billions of less privileged people, hunger is a fact of everyday life. As unpleasant as feelings of hunger can be, our very survival depends on it. We experience hunger and thirst to motivate us to acquire food and drink, which provide us with nutrients and energy needed to be active and alert and maintain a properly functioning immune system (Mattes, Hollis, Hayes, et al., 2005).

Hunger and Eating: Regulatory Processes. If food is available, we eat when we're hungry. And when we feel full (satiated), we stop eating. Simple, right? Not when we consider that inside our bodies, a complex series of events governing hunger and eating unfolds.

Although we usually refer to our stomachs when we're hungry, the brain is far more influential than the stomach as a command and control center for food cravings. Scientists began to get an inkling of this truth more than 50 years ago, when they learned that two areas of the hypothalamus play different roles in eating. Consider two rats in the same cage that couldn't look more different. Rat 1 is very large; some might say humongous. Rat 2 is scrawny to the point of requiring force-feeding to survive. Scientists supersized the first rat by electrically stimulating the lateral (side) parts of its hypothalamus (Delgado & Anand, 1952). The second rat became slimmer than a supermodel rodent

GLOSSARY

hierarchy of needs
model, developed by Abraham Maslow, proposing that we must satisfy physiological needs and needs for safety and security before progressing to more complex needs

The supersized rat on the left experienced damage to its ventromedial hypothalamus, resulting in massive overeating.

when researchers destroyed its lateral hypothalamus by making a small lesion in it (Anand & Brobeck, 1951; Hetherington & Ranson, 1940; Teitelbaum & Epstein, 1962). Based on these findings, scientists concluded that the lateral hypothalamus plays a key role in initiating eating. **[LEARNING OBJECTIVE 9.7]**

Something remarkable happens when researchers stimulate the *ventromedial* or lower middle part of rats' hypothalamus: The furry creatures eat very little or stop eating entirely (Olds, 1958). When researchers lesion the same part of the brain, the rats become so hefty they look like they're about to burst (Anand & Brobeck, 1951; Hetherington & Ranson, 1940; King, 2006). The ventromedial hypothalamus seems to let rats know when to stop eating.

Many psychology books have proclaimed that the lateral hypothalamus is a "feeding center" and the ventromedial hypothalamus a "satiety center," but this conclusion is too simple. In reality, a complex sequence of events mediated by different brain areas and body regions choreographs eating (Grill & Kaplan, 2002). For example, a distended or full stomach activates neurons in the hypothalamus, and in response we resist our impulses to reach for that second cookie (Anand & Pillai, 1967; Jordan, 1969; Smith, 1996; Stunkard, 1975).

The hypothalamus is also in tune with changing levels of glucose (blood sugar) produced by our bodies (Schwartz, Woods, Porte, et al., 2000; Woods, Seeley, Porte, et al., 1998). According to *glucostatic theory* (Campfield, Smith, Rosenbaum, et al., 1996; van Itallie, 1990), when our blood glucose levels drop, typically after we haven't eaten for some time, hunger creates a drive to eat to restore the proper level of glucose. In this way, we achieve homeostasis, the balance of energy we take in and expend. People gain weight when there's an imbalance, such that more energy is taken into the body than expended by way of exercise or the body's ability to "burn" excess calories through metabolic processes.

Weight Gain and Obesity: Biological and Psychological Influences. When we go "people watching" in the mall, we can't help but notice that adults and children come in more shapes and sizes than varieties of Campbell's soup. If that mall or supermarket is in the United States, we'll also observe that about two-thirds of the passersby are overweight or obese. Here we'll examine the physiology and psychology of eating and overeating.

As many as two-thirds of Americans are overweight.

Chemical Messengers and Eating. When we eat a candy bar, some of the glucose from the treat may get converted into fat, which stores energy for the long term. As energy is stored in fat cells, they produce a hormone called **leptin.** Leptin signals the hypothalamus and brain stem to reduce appetite and increase the amount of energy used (Grill et al., 2002). Researchers discovered a clue to the causes of obesity when they found that mice that lacked the gene for leptin become obese at an early age (Hamann & Matthaei, 1996). Interestingly, obese people seem resistant to the effects of leptin.

Obese individuals also find food difficult to resist because they think about food a lot and find the tasty qualities of food especially rewarding. The mere sight, taste, smell, and thought of plentiful food in our environment can trigger the release of neurotransmitters, including serotonin, that activate the brain's pleasure circuits (Ciarella, Ciarella, Graziani, et al., 1991; Lowe & Levine, 2005). Obese people also may overeat to provide comfort or distraction to counter negative emotions (Hoppa & Hallstrom, 1981; Stice, Presnell, Shaw, et al., 2005).

The Set Point. Another reason why the battle of the bulge isn't easy to win is that each of us may have a genetically programmed **set point,** a value—much like that on our car's fuel gauges—that establishes a range of body fat and muscle mass we tend to maintain (Mrosovsky & Powley, 1977; Nisbett, 1972). When we eat too little and drop below our set point, regulatory mechanisms kick in to increase our appetite or decrease our metabolism (Knecht, Ellger, & Levine, 2007). In this way, our bodies defend against weight loss.

GLOSSARY

leptin
hormone that signals the hypothalamus and brain stem to reduce appetite and increase the amount of energy used

set point
value that establishes a range of body and muscle mass we tend to maintain

When we eat too much, the opposite occurs. Without our ever realizing it, our bodies turn down our appetite and increase our metabolism.

According to the set point hypothesis, an obese person has a biological predisposition toward greater weight than does a thin person. No one knows for sure what "sets" the set point, but number of fat cells we're born with, metabolic rates at which our bodies burn calories, and sensitivity to leptin all likely play a role.

The Role of Genes in Obesity. Genes probably play a major role in our set points. Twin studies point to a genetic predisposition toward obesity. Researchers have found correlations for fat mass in the range of 0.7 to 0.9 for identical twins and a range of 0.35 to 0.45 for fraternal twins (Lee, 2009; Stunkard, Foch, & Hrubec, 1986). Because twins are raised in the same family and often share the same general diet and lifestyle, it's especially important for researchers to study identical twins raised in different families. When they've done so, they've found correlations of 0.4 to 0.7 for body mass (Maes, Neale, & Eaves, 1997). Adoption studies lend further support for the role of genes. People's body mass is correlated with their biological, but not adoptive, parents' body mass (Allison et al., 1996).

Sensitivity to Cues and Expectations. Genes don't completely determine whether a person will be shaped more like a pear than a stick. External cues and expectations also play a prominent role in food consumption.

Stanley Schachter proposed the **internal–external theory,** which holds that obese people are motivated to eat more by such external cues as the taste, smell, and appearance of food than by such internal cues as a growling stomach or feelings of fullness (Canetti, Bachar, & Berry, 2002; Nisbett, 1968; Schachter, 1968). According to this theory, individuals are at risk for obesity when they continue to eat even after being full and base their food choices on the appealing qualities of food, time of day, or social circumstances. In the laboratory, obese people eat more than nonobese people after researchers manipulate the clocks in the room to fool participants into thinking it's dinner time (Schachter & Gross, 1968). However, another possibility, which research favors, is that the oversensitivity to external cues is a consequence rather than a cause of eating patterns (Nisbett, 1972).

Eating Disorders: Bulimia and Anorexia.
People who try to lose a lot of weight over a short period of time are especially prone to binge eating (Lowe, Gleaves, & Murphy-Eberenz, 1998). Individuals with the eating disorder of *bulimia nervosa,* or bulimia, for short, engage in recurrent binge eating (twice a week or more for 3 months), followed by efforts to minimize weight gain (see Chapter 13). During a binge, some people gorge themselves with food equaling more than 10,000 calories in a 2-hour period and, across a number of studies, average about 3,500 calories per binge. That amounts to about six Big Macs without cheese (Walsh, 1993; Walsh, Hadigan, Kissileff, et al., 1992). Frequently, their answer to this problem is to *purge,* which typically takes the form of self-induced vomiting, but some abuse laxatives or diet pills or exercise excessively (Williamson et al., 2002). **[LEARNING OBJECTIVE 9.8]**

Bingeing and purging set up a vicious cycle. Purging is rewarding because it relieves anxious feelings after overeating and sidesteps weight gain. But it sets the stage for bouts of overeating. For example, vomiting allows individuals with bulimia to "undo" the binge, and to rationalize later bouts of overeating ("I can always get rid of the ice cream"). When their eating spirals out of control, self-esteem plummets, increasing their concerns about dieting and the likelihood of a binge. This completes the self-destructive circle (Fairburn, Cooper, & Shafran, 2003; Lynn & Kirsch, 2006). This binge-purge cycle can be physically hazardous, resulting in heart problems (which can be fatal), tears to the esophagus, and wearing away of tooth enamel from frequent exposure to stomach acids (Mehler, 2003).

People differ in their genetic tendency toward obesity, so differences in food consumption and weight may be apparent at an early age.

RULING OUT RIVAL HYPOTHESES
Have important alternative explanations for the findings been excluded?

The sight of tasty desserts, displayed in an attractive manner, can provide strong "external" cues for eating, even when we aren't particularly hungry. Upscale restaurants have discovered this principle, which is why they bring dessert trays over to our table after our main meal.

GLOSSARY

internal–external theory
theory holding that obese people are motivated to eat more by external cues than internal cues

Anorexia isn't limited to women, although it's comparatively rare among men. It's associated with body image distortion, which contributes to a fear of being fat despite being severely underweight.

Bulimia is the most common eating disorder, afflicting 1 to 3 percent of the population (Craighead, 2002; Keski-Rahkonen et al., 2008). About 95 percent of people with this diagnosis are women. An additional 8 to 16 percent of young women, including many in college, fall short of a diagnosis of bulimia, but show signs of disordered eating, such as repeated bingeing. Many women with bulimia are perfectionists and have an especially strong need for approval from others (Friedman & Wishman, 1998; Joiner, Heatherton, Rudd, et al., 1997).

Anorexia nervosa, or anorexia, usually begins in adolescence, is much more common in girls than boys, and is fueled by sociocultural pressures to be thin (see also Chapter 13). Although anorexia is less common than bulimia, it is much more life threatening. Whereas those with bulimia tend to be in the normal weight range, those with anorexia become emaciated in their relentless pursuit of thinness (Mitchell & Peterson, 2007). Along with a "fear of fatness," anorexia—like bulimia—is associated with a distorted perception of body size. Even those with bones showing through their skin may describe themselves as fat. Psychologists diagnose anorexia when individuals display a refusal to maintain body weight at or above a minimally normal weight for age and height (specifically, when their body weight is less than 85 percent of that expected). Individuals with anorexia often lose between 25 and 50 percent of their body weight.

Maintaining such a low weight is extremely dangerous, causing a loss of menstrual periods, hair loss, heart problems, life-threatening electrolyte imbalances, and fragile bones (Gottdiener, Gross, Henry, et al., 1978; Katzman, 2005). Some researchers put the mortality rate for anorexia at 5 to 10 percent, making it one of the most life-threatening of all psychiatric conditions (Birmingham, Su, Hlynsky, et al., 2005; Sullivan, 1995).

SEXUAL MOTIVATION

Sexual desire—called *libido*—is a wish or craving for sexual activity and sexual pleasure (Regan & Berscheid, 1999). Sexual desire is deeply rooted in our genes and biology; but, as we'll see, it's also influenced by social and cultural factors.

Sexual Desire and Its Determinants.
The sex hormone testosterone can enhance sexual interest (see Chapter 3), but other biological influences also are at play. Researchers recently discovered that variations in a gene that produces DRD4, a protein related to dopamine transmission, are correlated with students' reports of sexual desire and arousal (Zion et al., 2006). The scientists estimated that approximately 20 percent of the population possesses the mutation for increased sexual desire, whereas another 70 percent possesses a variant of the gene that depresses sexual desire.

Many people believe that men have a stronger desire for sex than women have. This stereotype may hold a kernel of truth. Compared with women, men desire sex more frequently, experience more sexual arousal (Hiller, 2005; Klusmann, 2002; Knoth, Boyd, & Singer, 1988), have a greater number and variety of sexual fantasies (Laumann, Gagnon, Michael, et al., 1994; Leitenberg & Henning, 1995), masturbate more frequently (Oliver & Hyde, 1993), want to have more sexual partners (Buss & Schmitt, 1993), and desire sex earlier in a relationship (Sprecher, Barbee, & Schwartz, 1995). These differences may be due in part to the fact that men produce more testosterone than women. Of course, these findings don't necessarily apply to any individual man or woman, and there's tremendous variability in sexual interest among men and women.

Socialization provides another explanation for why men and women appear to differ in sexual desire. Women are socialized to be less assertive and aggressive in many spheres of life, including expressing their sexual desires. So perhaps women and men actually experience comparable sexual drives, but women don't express their desires as much. Although the evidence tilts toward the conclusion that men have an inherently stronger sex drive than women, the evidence isn't definitive.

MYTH: The average man thinks about sex every 7 seconds.

REALITY: Although this claim and others very much like it (you may have heard "every 8 seconds," or "every 15 seconds") are widespread, there's no research evidence for them. Some survey data indicate that 54 percent of men say they think about sex at least once a day or more (www.kinseyinstitute.org/resources/FAQ.html), but offer no support for the "every 7 seconds" claim (www.snopes.com/science/stats/thinksex.asp).

RULING OUT RIVAL HYPOTHESES
Have important alternative explanations for the findings been excluded?

The Physiology of the Human Sexual Response.

In 1954, the husband and wife team of William Masters and Virginia Johnson launched their pioneering investigations of sexual desire and the human sexual response. Their observations included sexual behaviors under virtually every imaginable condition, and some virtually unimaginable. Masters and Johnson (1966) reported that the basic sexual arousal cycle was the same for men and women. Based on their research and other observations (Kaplan, 1977), scientists define the sexual response cycle in terms of four phases: (1) desire, (2) excitement, (3) orgasm, and (4) resolution (see **Figure 9.8**). **[LEARNING OBJECTIVE 9.9]**

The **desire phase** is initiated by whatever prompts sexual interest. People often experience little sexual desire when they're tired, distracted, stressed out, in pain, or ill. Lack of attraction to a partner, depression, anxiety, and resentment can also inhibit sexual desire. In the **excitement phase,** people experience sexual pleasure and start to notice physiological changes, such as penile erection in men and vaginal swelling and lubrication in women. During the **orgasm (climax) phase,** sexual pleasure and physical changes peak, there are involuntary rhythmic contractions in the muscles of the genitals in men and women, and men ejaculate. Brain scans reveal that when individuals achieve orgasm, the areas that control fear in the amygdala become less active than when people aren't sexually aroused (Georgiadis et al., 2006). This finding may explain why in the **resolution phase,** after orgasm, people report relaxation and a sense of well-being as the body returns to its unstimulated state (Belliveau & Richter, 1970; Resnick & Ithman, 2009).

Masters and Johnson's groundbreaking efforts didn't capture a crucial fact: People's sexuality is deeply embedded in their relationships and feelings for one another. People experience more frequent and consistent orgasms when they love their partner and feel loved in return (Birnbaum, Glaubman, & Mikulincer, 2001) and feel satisfied in their relationship (Young, Denny, Young, et al., 2000). But we can question the causal direction between relationship quality and the frequency and consistency of orgasms. Frequent orgasms may not merely reflect healthy relationships but contribute to them too.

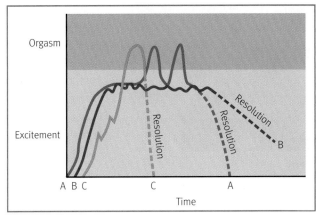

Figure 9.8 Variations in Female Sexual Response Cycle. This figure depicts the sexual arousal cycle for three different women, each represented by a different color. Two of the three women experienced at least one orgasm. The woman whose response is traced by the red line experienced excitement but no orgasm. (*Source:* Rathus, Nevid, & Fichner-Rathus, 2000)

CORRELATION vs. CAUSATION
Can we be sure that A causes B?

Sexuality and Culture.

The way people express sexual desires is shaped by social norms and culture. Clellan Ford and Frank Beach's (1951) fascinating observations reveal how cultural norms influence people's ideas of what's sexually appropriate or inappropriate. When members of the Tsonga tribe in Africa first saw Europeans kissing, they laughed and remarked, "Look at them—they eat each other's saliva and dirt" (Ford & Beach, 1951). Admittedly, they have a point. Members of the Apinaly society in Brazil don't kiss, but women of the tribe may bite off their lovers' eyebrows and noisily spit them to one side. Women of the island Turk customarily poke a finger into the man's ear when they're sexually excited.

David Buss (1989) found that residents of non-Western societies, including India, Iran, and China, place a much greater value on chastity in a potential partner than do individuals in Western European countries, including Sweden, the Netherlands, and France. Americans are divided on whether they generally approve (59 percent) or disapprove (41 percent) of premarital sex (Widmer, Treas, & Newcomb, 1998). This latter percentage stands at odds with the prevalence of premarital sex in the United States, with men reporting rates of 85 percent and women reporting rates of 80 percent (Laumann et al., 1994).

Sexual Orientation: Science and Politics.

Same-sex romantic relationships develop in virtually all cultures and have done so since the dawn of recorded history.

GLOSSARY

desire phase
phase in human sexual response triggered by whatever prompts sexual interest

excitement phase
phase in human sexual response in which people experience sexual pleasure and notice physiological changes associated with it

orgasm (climax) phase
phase in human sexual response marked by involuntary rhythmic contractions in the muscles of genitals in both men and women

resolution phase
phase in human sexual response following orgasm, in which people report relaxation and a sense of well-being

Research indicates that homosexual people are as likely as heterosexual people to provide supportive environments for children.

Canadian identical twin singers and songwriters, Tegan and Sara Quin, are openly gay, consistent with research on concordance rates.

Moreover, biologists have documented homosexual behaviors in some 450 species (Bagemihl, 1999). Since pioneering sex researcher Alfred Kinsey reported in the 1940s and 1950s (in what became known as the "Kinsey Report") that homosexuality was far more widespread than believed, scientists have pondered the question of what percentage of people engage in homosexual activities. The Kinsey Report indicated that 10 percent of the sample was almost exclusively gay for at least three years between the ages of 16 and 55 (Kinsey, Pomeroy, & Martin, 1948; Kinsey, Pomeroy, & Martin, et al., 1953). More recent research with larger and more representative samples suggests that about 2.8 percent of males and 1.4 percent of females 18 or older identify themselves as gay, lesbian, or bisexual (Laumann et al., 1994; National Opinion Research Center, 2003). Nevertheless, even the best estimates may not represent the general population because researchers often conduct surveys in prisons, college dorms, military barracks, or under the sponsorship of gay organizations, which may result in sampling bias.

Kinsey discovered that people he classified as homosexual reported widely varying amounts of homosexual experience. Some were exclusively gay, whereas others experienced only a single homosexual contact in early adolescence. People also differ in how they think and feel about their homosexuality. Many people who engage in occasional homosexual activities don't view themselves as gay. Some of the men Kinsey studied were married and identified themselves as heterosexual, even though they reported several homosexual experiences.

Since Kinsey's groundbreaking research, scientists have acquired a better understanding of homosexuality and challenged common misconceptions about homosexuals. Contrary to the stereotype that one person in a gay relationship adopts a masculine role, whereas the other adopts a feminine role, less than a fourth of gay men and women fit neatly into these categories (Jay & Young, 1979; Lever, 1995). A good deal of media coverage also implies that gay individuals recruit others to become homosexual or are especially likely to sexually abuse children and adolescents. Yet scientific evidence supports neither view (Freund, Watson, & Rienzo, 1989; Jenny, Roesler, & Poyer, 1994). Another widespread myth is that gay individuals are unfit to be parents. In fact, homosexual and heterosexual adults don't differ in their approach to parenting (Bos, van Balen, & van den Boom, 2004, 2007; Patterson, 1992) and are equally likely to provide supportive environments for their children (Patterson & Chan, 1996; Weston, 1991).

WHAT DO *you* THINK ?

For your senior project, you are interested in replicating some of Kinsey's research on human sexuality. Why might you want to avoid using the same volunteer-based recruitment strategy that he used?

Most scientists find clear indications of inborn differences between homosexual and heterosexual individuals, suggesting that biological tendencies toward a particular sexual orientation are sometimes present even before birth. Michael Bailey and Richard Pillard (1991) found that sexual orientation has a concordance rate of 52 percent in identical twins, in contrast with a concordance rate of 22 percent in fraternal twins (*concordance* refers to the proportion of cotwins who exhibit a characteristic, in this case, sexual orientation, when the other twin also exhibits this characteristic). But the fact that a substantial percentage of identical twins aren't concordant tells us that environmental influences play an important role in sexual orientation although it doesn't tell us what these influences are. **[LEARNING OBJECTIVE 9.10]**

Sex Hormones and Sexual Orientation. To trace the biological roots of homosexuality, researchers have looked to the prenatal environment. When the fetus develops, sex hormones called androgens (see Chapter 3) determine whether the brain sets the child on a path toward more masculine than feminine characteristics or vice versa. According to one theory, girls exposed to excessive testosterone in the womb develop masculinized brains, and boys exposed to too little testosterone develop feminized brains (Ellis & Ames, 1987). These hormonal influences affect temperament and set the stage for deviation from traditional gender roles and a homosexual orientation in later life (Bem, 1996).

Sexual Orientation: Brain Differences. In 1981, Simon LeVay created a stir among scientists and laypersons alike by reporting that a small cluster of neurons in the hypothalamus, no larger than a millimeter, was less than half the size in gay men compared with nongay men. The study is open to several criticisms: LeVay studied men's brains at autopsy after they died, and the gay men died from AIDS-related complications. However, it's unlikely that the differences LeVay uncovered are due entirely to AIDS because a number of the nongay men also died of AIDS-related complications. The differences LeVay observed in the hypothalamus might also have been the result rather than the cause of homosexuality. Yet another limitation was that LeVay's sample of gay men with AIDS wasn't necessarily representative of all gay men, so replicating his results is especially important.

Some of the concerns about LeVay's research are tempered by a recent brain imaging study (Savic, Berglund, & Lindstrom, 2005) in which investigators exposed gay men and nongay men and women to substances believed to be *pheromones* (see Chapter 4). When nongay men smelled chemicals released in women's urine, their hypothalamuses became active. When nongay women smelled a substance derived from testosterone produced in men's sweat, the same thing happened. The most intriguing finding was that gay men's brains responded like women's when they smelled the substance derived from male sweat. These results are consistent with LeVay's finding that the hypothalamus is related to sexual orientation. Once again, though, we must be careful not to assume that the differences in brain activity cause homosexuality because the pattern of brain activity could be a consequence of sexual orientation.

Psychologists still don't fully grasp how biological and environmental factors work together in the development of sexual orientation. In all likelihood, social and cultural influences that remain to be understood play a substantial role in shaping people's sexual orientation.

Fact
-OID

In males, having older brothers increases the odds of homosexuality by 33 percent for each older brother, which amounts to an increase in the rate of homosexuality from about 3 percent to 5 percent (Blanchard & Bogaert, 1996). The reason for this phenomenon remains unknown.

CORRELATION vs. CAUSATION
Can we be sure that A causes B?

RULING OUT RIVAL HYPOTHESES
Have important alternative explanations for the findings been excluded?

CORRELATION vs. CAUSATION
Can we be sure that A causes B?

QUIZ

1 According to the Yerkes-Dodson law, we generally do best when we're at our highest levels of arousal.	TRUE	FALSE
2 Obese individuals seem resistant to the effects of leptin.	TRUE	FALSE
3 Women's sexual arousal cycles are completely different from men's.	TRUE	FALSE
4 Sexual orientation has a strong genetic component.	TRUE	FALSE

Answers: (1) F (p. 318); (2) T (p. 322); (3) F (p. 325); (4) T (pp. 326–327)

PEARSON
mypsychlab

▼ Does your brain react to your favorite foods like the brains of drug addicts? Watch the video titled "Your Brain on Food" at www.mypsychlab.com to find out.

Attraction, Love, and Hate: The Greatest Mysteries of Them All

The origins of love are remarkably old, even ancient. In 2007, archeologists unearthed these skeletons of a male and female couple in Italy (ironically, only 25 miles from Verona, the site of Shakespeare's legendary *Romeo and Juliet*), frozen in an embrace over 5,000 years ago.

In 1975, psychologists Ellen Berscheid and Elaine Hatfield received a dubious distinction (Benson, 2006). They became the first individuals to receive the Golden Fleece Award, an "honor" (actually, a dishonor) bestowed on them by then Wisconsin Senator William Proxmire. Proxmire had cooked up this award as a way of drawing public attention to projects that he regarded as colossal wastes of taxpayer money. Berscheid and Hatfield, it so happens, had won this award for their government-funded research on the psychological determinants of attraction and love (look for their names in the section you're about to read). Proxmire had found the very idea of studying these topics scientifically to be absurd:

> "I'm strongly against this," he said, "not only because no one—not even the National Science Foundation—can argue that falling in love is a science; not only because I am sure that even if they spend 84 million or 84 billion they wouldn't get an answer that anyone would believe. I'm also against it because I don't *want* to know the answer!" (Hatfield & Walster, 1978, viii)

Of course, Proxmire was entitled not to know the answer. Yet more than three decades of research have since shown that Proxmire was woefully wrong in one critical respect: Psychologists *can* study love scientifically. None of this takes away from the profound mysteries of falling in love, but it suggests that love may not be quite as unfathomable as we—or the thousands of poets who've written about love across the centuries—might believe.

SOCIAL INFLUENCES ON INTERPERSONAL ATTRACTION

How can two people meet and become lovers in a world teeming with over six and a half billion people? Of course, attraction is only the initial stage in a relationship, but we need to feel a twinkle of chemistry with someone before deciding whether we're compatible enough with him or her in our core values and attitudes toward relationships before proceeding any further (Murstein, 1977). We might ascribe finding our true love to the fickle finger of destiny, but scientists suggest that friendship, dating, and mate choices aren't random. Three major principles guide attraction and relationship formation: proximity, similarity, and reciprocity (Berscheid & Reis, 1998; Fehr, 1996; Luo & Klohnen, 2005; Sprecher, 1998). **[LEARNING OBJECTIVE 9.11]**

Psychological research shows that physical proximity, such as being seated next to each other in a classroom, can set the stage for later attraction.

Proximity: When Near Becomes Dear. A simple truth of human relationships is that our closest friends often live, study, work, or play closest to us. Many years after high school, the second author of your textbook married the woman who sat in front of him in numerous classes. Because their last names started with the letter L, the fact that the seats were arranged alphabetically ensured they'd have an opportunity to become acquainted. After their 30-year high school reunion brought them together again, they fell in love and married.

This example illustrates how physical nearness—or **proximity**—affords the opportunity for relationship formation. Like reunited schoolmates, people in classrooms with alphabetically assigned seats tend to have friends with last names that start with the same letter or a letter close in the alphabet (Segal, 1974). We're most likely to be attracted to and befriend people nearby, whom we see on a regular basis (Nahemow & Lawton, 1975).

GLOSSARY

proximity
physical nearness, a predictor of attraction

Leon Festinger, Stanley Schachter, and Kurt Back (1950) asked individuals living in apartments for married students at the Massachusetts Institute of Technology to name three of their closest friends. Of these friends, 65 percent lived in the same building, and 41 percent lived next door. The effects of mere exposure we encountered earlier in the chapter may at least partially explain why seeing someone on a frequent basis, whether in the supermarket or workout room, heightens attraction and liking.

Similarity: Like Attracts Like.

Proximity is also critical in establishing relationships because we are likely to live and work near people who share our interests, so we have a lot to talk about when we meet. This point brings us to our next principle: **similarity,** the extent to which we have things in common with others. Consider this question: Would you rather be stranded on a desert island with someone very much like yourself or very different? Would you prefer a virtual clone of yourself or someone with vastly different tastes in music, books, and food? Perhaps if you like Mozart and your island mate prefers Metallica, you'd have a lot to talk or at least debate about. Yet with little in common, you might find it difficult to establish a personal connection.

Scientists have found that there's much more truth to the adage "Birds of a feather flock together" than the equally well-worn proverb "Opposites attract." Whether it's art, music, food preferences, educational level, physical attractiveness, or values, we're attracted to people we perceive as similar to us (Byrne, 1971; Montoya, Horton, & Kirchner, 2008; Newcomb, 1961; Swann & Pelham, 2002). We're also more likely to befriend, date, and marry compatible people (Curran & Lippold, 1975; Knox et al., 1997).

Online dating services have caught on to the fact that similarity breeds liking (Hill, Rubin, & Peplau, 1976). These services try to match prospective partners on the basis of personality similarity.

-WHAT DO *you* THINK?-

You are hired as a consultant to an online dating service. Drawing on the literature on romantic attraction and relationship formation, what advice would you have for matching prospective clients?

Reciprocity: All Give and No Take Does Not a Good Relationship Make.

For a relationship to move to deeper levels, the third principle of attraction—**reciprocity,** or the rule of give and take—is often crucial. Across cultures, there's a norm of reciprocity (Gouldner, 1960) that begins to kick into motion as early as 11 years of age (Rotenberg & Mann, 1986). That is, we tend to feel obligated to give what we get and maintain equity in a relationship (Walster, Berscheid, & Walster, 1973). Liking results in being liked, and revealing personal information encourages disclosure. When we believe people like us, we're inclined to feel attracted to them (Brehm, Miller, Perlman, et al., 2002; Carlson & Rose, 2007). When we believe that our partner finds us attractive or likable, we generally act more likable in response to this ego-boosting information (Curtis & Miller, 1986). Talking about meaningful things is a vital element of most friendships. In particular, disclosure about intimate topics often brings about intimacy. In contrast, when one person talks about superficial topics or discusses intimate topics in a superficial way, low levels of reciprocal disclosure from the other person often result (Lynn, 1978).

Physical Attraction: Like It or Not, We Do Judge Books by Their Covers.

As we saw in Chapter 5, some important scientific discoveries arise from *serendipity,* that is, sheer luck. So it was with a study that Elaine Hatfield and her colleagues conducted over 40 years ago (Hatfield, Aronson, Abrahams, et al., 1966). They administered a large battery of

GLOSSARY

similarity
extent to which we have things in common with others, a predictor of attraction

reciprocity
rule of give and take, a predictor of attraction

When students were randomly paired at a dance, the only factor that determined whether the students wanted a second date was the attractiveness of their partners (Hatfield et al., 1966).

personality, attitude, and interest measures to 725 incoming college men and women during freshman "Welcome Week." Hatfield and her coworkers paired these students randomly for a leisurely date and dance lasting two and a half hours, giving them the chance to get acquainted. Which variables, the researchers wondered, would predict whether the partners were interested in a second date? Much to their surprise, the only variable that significantly predicted attraction was one the researchers had included only as an afterthought (Gangestad & Scheyd, 2005): people's level of physical attractiveness as rated by their partners (Hatfield et al., 1966).

If psychologists have learned anything about physical attractiveness, it's that it matters in everyday life. Physically attractive people tend to be more popular than physically unattractive people (Dion, Berscheid, & Walster, 1972; Fehr, 2008). Yet what makes us find others physically attractive? Is it all merely a matter of "chemistry," an inexplicable process that lies beyond the grasp of science, as Senator Proxmire would have had us believe? Or is there a science to "love at first sight," or at least attraction at first sight?

Sex Differences in What We Find Attractive: Nature or Nurture?

Although physical attractiveness is important to both sexes when it comes to choosing our romantic partners, it's especially important to men (Buss & Schmitt, 1993; Buunk, Dijkstra, Fetchenhauer, et al., 2002; Feingold, 1992). David Buss (1989) conducted a comprehensive survey of mate preferences among heterosexuals in 37 cultures across six continents, with countries as diverse as Canada, Spain, Finland, Greece, Bulgaria, Venezuela, Iran, Japan, and South Africa. Although he found that the importance people attach to physical attractiveness varies across cultures, men consistently place more weight on looks in women than women do in men. Men also prefer women who are somewhat younger than they are. Conversely, Buss found that women tend to place more emphasis than do men on having a partner with a high level of financial resources. In contrast to men, women prefer partners who are somewhat older than they are. Still, men and women value many of the same things. Both sexes put a premium on having a partner who's intelligent, dependable, and a nice person (Buss, 1994).

Although standards of beauty differ somewhat within and across cultures, research suggests that both most African American men and most Caucasian men agree on which African American women (such as Halle Berry, *left*) and Caucasian women (such as Jennifer Aniston, *right*) are physically attractive.

Evolutionary Models of Attraction. Putting aside these commonalities, how can we make sense of sex differences in mate preferences? Evolutionary theorists point out that men typically pursue a mating strategy that maximizes the chances that at least one of the approximately 300 million sperm released during each ejaculation will find a receptive egg at the end of its long journey (Symons, 1979). As a consequence, evolutionary psychologists contend, men are on the lookout for cues of potential health and fertility, such as physical attractiveness and youth. Women, in contrast, typically produce only one egg per month, so they must be choosy. Therefore, they typically pursue a mating strategy that maximizes the chances that the man with whom they mate will provide well for their offspring; hence women's preference for men who are older, well off monetarily, and a bit more experienced in the ways of life (Buunk et al., 2002).

RULING OUT RIVAL HYPOTHESES
Have important alternative explanations for the findings been excluded?

Social Role Theory. Still, some researchers have offered plausible alternatives to evolutionary models of attraction. According to Alice Eagly and Wendy Wood's (1999) social role theory, biological variables play a role in men's and women's preferences but not in the way that evolutionary psychologists contend. Instead, biological factors constrain the roles that men and women adopt (Eagly, Wood, & Johannesen-Schmidt, 2004). Because men tend to be bigger and stronger than women, they've more often ended up playing the roles of hunter, food provider, and warrior. Moreover, because men don't bear children, they have considerable opportunities to pursue high-status positions. In contrast, because women bear children, they've more often ended up playing the role of child care provider and have been more limited in pursuing high-status positions.

Some of these differences in traditional roles may help to explain men's and women's differing mate preferences. For example, because women have typically held fewer high-status positions than men, they may have preferred men who are dependable financial providers (Eagly et al., 2004). Consistent with social role theory, men and women have become more similar in their mate preferences over the past half century (Buss et al., 2001), perhaps reflecting the increasing social opportunities for women across that time period.

Is Beauty in the Eye of the Beholder? Popular wisdom tells us that "beauty is in the eye of the beholder." To some extent that saying is true. Yet it's also an oversimplification. People tend to agree at considerably higher than chance levels about who is, and isn't, physically attractive (Burns & Farina, 1992). This is the case not only within a race but across races; for example, Caucasian and African American men tend to agree on which women are attractive, as do Caucasian and Asian American men (Cunningham et al., 1995). Even across vastly different cultures, both men and women tend to agree on whom they find physically attractive (Langlois et al., 2000).

Still, there are important differences in physical preferences within and across cultures. For example, men from African American and Caribbean cultures often find women with a large body size more physically attractive than do men of European cultures (Rosenblum & Lewis, 1999). Furthermore, preferences toward thinness have frequently shifted over historical time, as even a casual inspection of paintings of nude women over time reveals.

When Being "Just Average" Is Just Fine. Which person are we more likely to find attractive: (a) someone who's exotic, unusual, or distinctive in some way or (b) someone who's just plain average? If you're like most people, you'd choose (a). Indeed, we sometimes insult people's appearance by calling women "plain Janes," and men "average Joes."

Yet as Judith Langlois and Lori Roggman (1990) showed, being average has its pluses. By using a computer to digitize the faces of students and then combine them progressively, they found that people generally prefer faces that are the most average. In their study, people preferred average faces a whopping 96 percent of the time (see **Figure 9.9;** to try your hand at averaging faces, see a demonstration at www.faceresearch.org/tech/demos/average). Although some psychologists found these results difficult to believe, many investigators have since replicated them for European faces as well as Japanese and Chinese faces (Gangestad & Scheyd, 2005; Rhodes, Halberstadt, & Brajkovich, 2001). Averaged faces are also more symmetrical than nonaveraged faces, so our preferences for average faces might be due to their greater symmetry. Yet studies show that even when faces are symmetrical, people still prefer faces that are more average (Valentine, Darling, & Donnelly, 2004).

Evolutionary psychologists have speculated that "averageness" in a face tends to reflect an absence of genetic mutations, serious diseases, and other abnormalities. As a consequence, we could be drawn to people with such faces, as they're often better "genetic catches." Maybe. But there's a fly in the ointment. Studies also show that people prefer not merely averaged faces, but averaged animals, like birds and fish, and even averaged objects, like cars and watches (Halberstadt & Rhodes, 2003). So our preference for averaged faces may be due to an alternative mechanism, namely, a more general preference for anything that's average. Perhaps we find average stimuli to be more familiar and easier to process mentally because they reflect stimuli we've seen before many times (Gangestad & Scheyd, 2005).

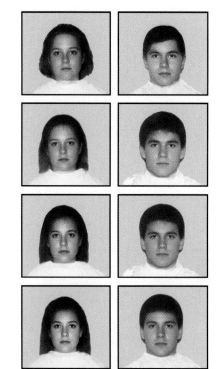

Figure 9.9 Which Face Is Most Attractive? The two columns depict faces that have been averaged with other faces (from *top* to *bottom*) 4, 8, 16, and 32 times. Most people find the faces on the bottom, which are the most "average," to be the most attractive (Langlois & Roggman, 1990). Remarkably, Sir Francis Galton (1878), whom we met in Chapter 7, anticipated these findings well over a century ago. (*Source:* Langlois & Roggman, 1990)

REPLICABILITY
Can the results be duplicated in other studies?

RULING OUT RIVAL HYPOTHESES
Have important alternative explanations for the findings been excluded?

RULING OUT RIVAL HYPOTHESES
Have important alternative explanations for the findings been excluded?

LOVE: SCIENCE CONFRONTS THE MYSTERIOUS

Elizabeth Barrett Browning wrote famously: "How do I love thee? Let me count the ways." According to some psychologists, we may not need to count all that high. We'll explain.

Psychologists are no different from the rest of us. They've tried to understand the myriad varieties of love, with some concluding that there's only one type of love and others that love comes in many shapes and sizes. According to Elaine Hatfield and Richard Rapson (1996), there are two major types of love: passionate and companionate. Robert Sternberg, as we'll soon see, puts the number at seven.

According to Hatfield and Rapson, **passionate love** is marked by a powerful, even overwhelming, longing for one's partner. It's a strange mix of delirious happiness when we're around the object of our desire and utter misery when we're not. **[LEARNING OBJECTIVE 9.12]** It's the stuff of which Hollywood movies are made. As Romeo and Juliet knew all too well, passionate love is fueled when obstacles, such as seemingly insurmountable physical distance or the strenuous objection of parents, are placed in the way of romance (Driscoll, Davis, & Lipetz, 1972). Such obstacles may heighten arousal, thereby intensifying passion, as Schachter and Singer's two-factor theory would predict (Kenrick, Neuberg, & Cialdini, 2005).

In contrast, **companionate love** is marked by a sense of deep friendship and fondness for one's partner. Romantic relationships tend to progress over time from passionate to companionate love (Wojciszke, 2002), although most healthy relationships retain at least a spark of passion. In older couples, companionate love may be the overriding emotion in the relationship.

There's growing evidence that companionate and passionate love are psychologically independent. Studies indicate that people can "fall in love" with partners in the sense of caring deeply about them, yet experience little or no sexual desire toward them (Diamond, 2004). In addition, these two forms of love may be associated with differing brain systems (Diamond, 2003; Gonzaga, Turner, Keltner, et al., 2006). Animal research suggests that emotional attachment to others is influenced largely by hormones such as oxytocin, which as we noted in Chapter 3 plays a key role in pair bonding and interpersonal trust. In contrast, sexual desire is influenced by sex hormones, such as testosterone and estrogen.

Robert Sternberg believes that the "two types of love" model is too simple. In his *triangular theory of love,* Sternberg (1986, 1988a) proposes the existence of three major elements of love: (1) intimacy ("I feel really close to this person"); (2) passion ("I'm crazy about this person"); and (3) commitment ("I really want to stay with this person"). These three elements combine to form seven varieties of love (see **Figure 9.10**). Sternberg's model is more of a description of love types than an explanation of why people fall in love, but as a road map it's a helpful starting point toward understanding one of life's great mysteries.

HATE: A NEGLECTED TOPIC

Until recently, psychologists didn't want to have much to do with the topic of hate. Most introductory psychology textbooks don't even list the word *hate* in their indexes. Yet with the horrific events of September 11, 2001, and the burgeoning problem of terrorism around the globe, it's clear that psychologists can no longer turn a blind eye to the question of why some people despise others, at times to the point of wanting to destroy them (Sternberg, 2004b).

Using his triangular theory of love as a starting point, Robert Sternberg (2004b) developed a theory of hate, with hatred consisting of three elements:

(1) negation of intimacy ("I would never want to get close to these people");

(2) passion ("I absolutely and positively despise these people"); and

(3) commitment ("I'm determined to stop or harm these people").

As in his theory of love, differing forms of hate arise from combinations of these three elements, with "burning hate"—the most severe—reflecting high scores on all three. For

Companionate love is often the primary form of love among the elderly. It can be a powerful emotional bond between couples across the life span.

GLOSSARY

passionate love
love marked by powerful, even overwhelming, longing for one's partner

companionate love
love marked by a sense of deep friendship and fondness for one's partner

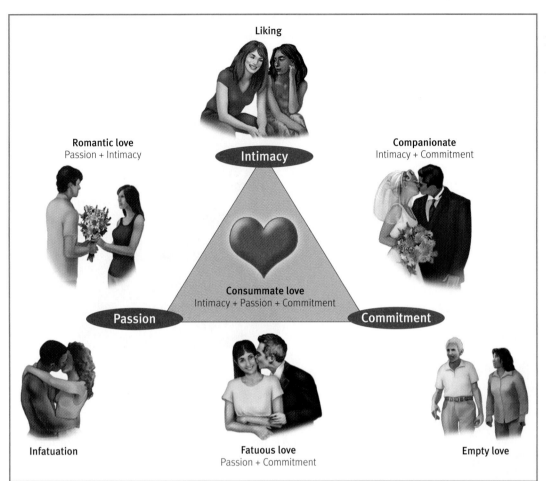

Figure 9.10 What Is Love?
According to Sternberg's triangular theory of love, intimacy, passion, and commitment combine to form seven varieties of love, with "consummate love" being the ultimate form of love marked by high levels of all three components.

Sternberg, the key to fueling hate is propaganda. Groups and governments that "teach" hatred of other groups are experts at portraying these groups as evil and worthy of disdain (Keen, 1986; Sternberg, 2003a).

The good news is that if we can learn hate, we can probably unlearn it. Teaching individuals to overcome their confirmation bias (Chapter 2) toward perceiving only the negative attributes of individuals or groups they dislike may be an essential first step (Harrington, 2004). Recognizing that "there's good and bad in everyone," as the saying goes, may help us combat our deep-seated animosity toward our enemies.

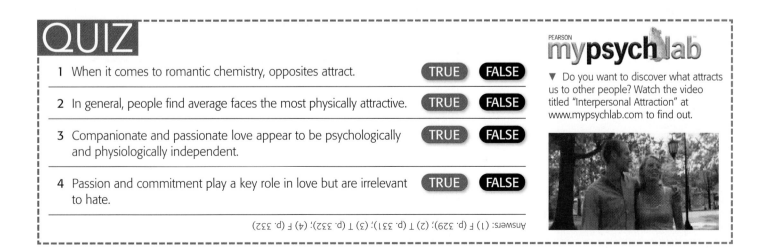

QUIZ

1 When it comes to romantic chemistry, opposites attract. **TRUE** **FALSE**

2 In general, people find average faces the most physically attractive. **TRUE** **FALSE**

3 Companionate and passionate love appear to be psychologically and physiologically independent. **TRUE** **FALSE**

4 Passion and commitment play a key role in love but are irrelevant to hate. **TRUE** **FALSE**

Answers: (1) F (p. 329); (2) T (p. 331); (3) T (p. 332); (4) F (p. 332)

PEARSON
mypsychlab

▼ Do you want to discover what attracts us to other people? Watch the video titled "Interpersonal Attraction" at www.mypsychlab.com to find out.

THEORIES OF EMOTION: WHAT CAUSES OUR FEELINGS? (pp. 303–311)

9.1 Describe the major theories of emotion

According to discrete emotions theory, people experience a small number (perhaps seven) of distinct biologically determined emotions and combinations of these emotions called secondary emotions. According to cognitive theories, emotions result from our interpretation of situations. The James-Lange theory proposes that emotions result from our bodily reactions to stimuli. According to the Cannon-Bard theory, emotion-provoking events lead to emotions and bodily reactions. Schachter and Singer's two-factor theory states that emotions are the explanations we attach to our general state of arousal following an emotion-provoking event.

1. According to _____ _____ theory, humans experience a small number of distinct emotions that combine in complex ways. (p. 303)

2. One of the first researchers to study how emotional expressions of humans and nonhumans are similar, _____ observed that the smile of a chimpanzee bears a resemblance to a human smile. (p. 303)

3. What kind of smile, marked by the turning upward of the corners of the mouth and changes in the eyelids and corners of the eye, is the woman in this photo displaying? (p. 304)

4. According to the _____ theories of emotion, emotions are products of thinking. (p. 306)

5. Emotions result from our interpretations of our bodily reactions to stimuli according to the _____ theory of emotion. (p. 306)

6. According to the Cannon-Bard theory, an emotion-provoking event leads _____ to both an emotion and to bodily reactions. (p. 307)

7. Describe how we experience emotions during an event like a car accident, according to Schachter and Singer's two-factor theory of emotion. (p. 308)

9.2 Identify unconscious influences on emotion

Many emotions are generated automatically and operate unconsciously, as illustrated by the mere exposure effect and the facial feedback hypothesis.

8. According to the mere exposure effect, repeated exposure to a stimulus makes us (more/less) likely to feel favorably toward it. (p. 309)

9. According to the facial feedback hypothesis, you're likely to feel emotions that correspond to your _____ _____. (p. 310)

10. An alternative hypothesis for the facial feedback effects is _____ _____. (p. 310)

succeed with mypsychlab

1. Does being exposed to an advertisement multiple times contribute to our preference for the product? Participate in this study and evaluate the evidence.
   Mere Exposure

2. Participate in this study to see how sounds in movies affect our emotional state.
   Transfer of Emotions

3. How well do you read others' emotions? See if you can identify looks of fear or surprise on others.
   Recognizing Facial Expressions of Emotions

Answers are located at the end of the text.

HAPPINESS AND SELF-ESTEEM: SCIENCE CONFRONTS POP PSYCHOLOGY (pp. 312–317)

9.3 **Describe the emerging discipline of positive psychology**

Positive psychology emphasizes strengths, love, and happiness. Happiness is adaptive; it allows us to build on strengths and opportunities.

11. Explain how the King of Bhutan plans to increase the gross national happiness of his country and why this initiative may be beneficial to all. (p. 312)

12. Peterson and Seligman identified 24 _____ _____ and _____ as essential to positive psychology. (p. 312)

9.4 **Identify common myths and realities about happiness and self-esteem**

Myths: The prime determinant of happiness is what happens to us; money makes us happy; happiness declines in old age; happiness and negative emotions are opposites; and people on the West Coast are the happiest. Realities: Happiness is associated with marriage, college education, and religious beliefs; voting Republican; exercise; gratitude; and immersion in what we're doing ("flow"). We tend to overestimate the long-term impact of events on our happiness. Self-esteem is less related to happiness than commonly believed.

succeed with PEARSON **mypsych lab**

Do You Know All of the Terms in This Chapter?

 Find out by using the Flashcards. Want more practice? Take additional quizzes, try simulations, and watch video to be sure you are prepared for the test!

13. According to Fredrickson's _____ _____ _____ theory, happiness predisposes us to think more openly. (p. 313)

14. According to psychological research, money (can/can't) buy long-term happiness. (p. 313)

15. Individuals who are extremely engaged in a rewarding activity experience _____, which is highly related to happiness. (p. 315)

16. The ability to predict our own and others' happiness is called _____ _____. (p. 315)

17. When we believe that both our good and bad moods will last longer than they do, we are suffering from a _____ _____. (p. 315)

18. The evidence linking self-esteem to mental health and life success is (strong/weak). (p. 316)

19. Why do second-place finishers tend to be less happy than third-place finishers? (p. 316)

20. _____ _____ is a strategy of anticipating failures and compensating for this expectation by mentally overpreparing for negative outcomes. (p. 316)

succeed with PEARSON **mypsych lab**

1. Do jokes have health benefits above just laughing? Watch this video and evaluate the evidence.
Humor and Brains

2. How happy are you? Take this survey and find out.
Survey on Happiness

MOTIVATION: OUR WANTS AND NEEDS (pp. 317–327)

9.5 Define motivation

Motivation refers to the drives—especially our wants and needs—that propel us in a specific direction.

21. Is there any research evidence that motivational speakers, like Anthony Robbins, produce long-term changes in people's behavior? (p. 318)

9.6 Explain the basic principles and theories of motivation

Drive reduction theory states that drives (hunger, thirst) pull us to act in certain ways. According to the Yerkes-Dodson law, there's an inverted U–shaped relation between arousal and performance. According to incentive theories, positive goals are motivators. These motivators include primary (biological) and secondary (psychological desires) needs.

22. Most drive reduction theories propose that we're motivated to maintain a given level of psychological _____. (p. 318)

23. The _____ law describes an inverted U–shaped relation between arousal on the one hand and performance on the other. (p. 318)

24. _____ theories propose that we're often motivated by positive goals. (p. 320)

25. Using Maslow's hierarchy of needs, insert the appropriate need at each level of the pyramid in the path to achieving self-actualization. (p. 321)

9.7 Describe the determinants of hunger, weight gain, and obesity

The lateral hypothalamus has been called a feeding center and the ventromedial hypothalamus a satiety center. However, hunger is also associated with hormones, low glucose levels, neurotransmitters (leptin, serotonin), a genetically programmed set point, specific genes, and sensitivity to food cues and expectations.

26. According to _____ theory, when our blood glucose levels drop, hunger creates a drive to eat to restore the proper level of glucose. (p. 322)

27. Each of us may have a genetically programmed _____ _____ that establishes a range of body and muscle mass we tend to maintain. (p. 322)

9.8 Identify the symptoms of bulimia and anorexia

Bulimia is marked by recurrent binge eating, followed by attempts to minimize weight gain. Anorexia occurs when refusal to eat results in body weight less than 85 percent of that expected for age and height.

28. _____ is the most common eating disorder, and 95 percent of the people with this diagnosis are women. (p. 324)

9.9 Describe the human sexual response cycle and factors that influence sexual activity

Masters and Johnson described four stages: desire, excitement, orgasm, and resolution. Social norms and culture shape expression of sexual desire.

29. Masters and Johnson reported in their pioneering investigation that the basic sexual arousal cycle was (the same/different) for men and women. (p. 325)

9.10 Describe potential influences on sexual orientation

Potential influences on sexual orientation are an inherited tendency toward childhood gender nonconformity, sex hormones, prenatal influences, and brain differences.

30. According to one theory of influences on sexual orientation, girls exposed to excessive testosterone in the womb develop _____ brains, and boys exposed to too little testosterone develop _____ brains. (p. 327)

succeed with mypsychlab

1. Test your understanding of theories of motivation and how motivation applies to your job performance.
Theories of Motivation and Job Performance

2. Can an animal continue to overeat until it dies? Explore what brain structure regulates eating behavior.
The Effects of the Hypothalamus on Eating Behavior

3. Listen as two psychologists discuss how you decide whether to study for an exam or go to a party on Friday night.
Psychological Conflict

ATTRACTION, LOVE, AND HATE: THE GREATEST MYSTERIES OF THEM ALL (pp. 328–333)

9.11 Identify the principles and factors that guide attraction and relationship formation

Factors guiding attraction and relationship formation are proximity, similarity, and reciprocity. Physical attractiveness, evolutionary influence, social roles, and preference for "average" faces also influence attractiveness.

31. Physical nearness, or _____, affords the opportunity for relationship formation. (p. 328)

32. We're often attracted to people with whom we have high levels of _____, or things in common. (p. 329)

33. In order for a relationship to move to deeper levels, the rule of give and take, or _____, is often crucial. (p. 329)

34. According to Buss, across cultures, which gender attaches more importance to physical attractiveness? (p. 330)

35. Across vastly different cultures, men and women tend to (agree/disagree) on whom they find physically attractive. (p. 330)

36. Average faces are rated as (less/more) attractive than distinctive or exotic faces. (p. 331)

9.12 Describe the major types of love and the elements of love and hate

The major love types are passionate and companionate. The major love elements are intimacy, passion, and commitment. The major hate elements are negation of intimacy, passion, and commitment.

37. _____ love can be a mix of delirious happiness when we're near the object of our desire, and misery when separated from it. (p. 332)

38. A relationship marked by a sense of deep friendship and fondness for our partner is called _____ _____. (p. 332)

39. Using Sternberg's triangular theory of love, complete this figure by identifying the three major elements of love (forming the points of the triangle) illustrated here. According to Sternberg, which is the ultimate form of love (box d)? (p. 333)

40. Teaching individuals to overcome their _____ _____ toward perceiving only negative attributions of groups they dislike may be an essential first step in unlearning hate. (p. 333)

succeed with mypsychlab

1. What determines physical attraction? Does it vary across cultures and gender? Find out in this activity.
   Perceptions of Attractiveness

2. How passionate are you about your significant other?
   Passionate Love Scale

3. Can you meet someone on the Internet? How do you know who they really are?
   Online Dating

SCIENTIFIC THINKING SKILLS
Questions and Summary

1. Your parents disagree with your decision to become a psychology major, arguing that it is a field devoted to disorders. How would you educate them about positive psychology's impact on people's lives?

2. According to Maslow's hierarchy of needs, what life changes would you make to achieve self-actualization?

RULING OUT RIVAL HYPOTHESES
pp. 305, 310, 320, 323, 324, 327, 330, 331

CORRELATION vs. CAUSATION
pp. 306, 309, 313, 314, 315, 316, 325, 327

FALSIFIABILITY
p. 321

REPLICABILITY
pp. 307, 308, 309, 320, 331

OCCAM'S RAZOR
p. 304

Stress, Health, and Sleep

Do most people who encounter highly aversive events develop posttraumatic stress disorder? (pp. 347–348)

Is there one best way to cope with stressful events? (pp. 352–353)

CHAPTER 10

Are crash diets that promise quick and enduring weight loss effective? (p. 362)

Are acupuncture and other alternative medical treatments more effective than traditional medical procedures? (pp. 362–364)

Is it dangerous to wake up sleepwalkers? (p. 371)

Tuesday, September 11, 2001, is a day that few Americans will forget. Across the country, people were glued to their television sets, watching in horror as two loaded passenger planes flew into the Twin Towers of the World Trade Center (WTC) in New York City. In the worst terrorist attack in American history, more than 2,700 people were killed at the WTC alone. Hundreds more were killed when terrorists crashed two other planes into the Pentagon and a field in rural Pennsylvania, where passengers had attempted to regain control of the plane.

In the aftermath of this tragedy, inspiring stories emerged of courageous first responders—firefighters, paramedics, police, and emergency service workers—who risked their lives to save others. Nearly 400 people who participated in rescue operations died on 9/11. Many others survived to tell their stories. The following accounts by first responders at the WTC (McNally, 2003) are a sample of reactions to some of the most stressful circumstances imaginable—and some unimaginable:

- Juana Lomi, a paramedic, raced to the WTC and survived the collapse of the towers. "It was an overwhelming feeling of fear, horror—and not being able to do more. There were hundreds of people that needed to be treated. I was at risk of losing my life, but I had to stay and help other people."

- Louie Cacchioli, a firefighter, saved the lives of many people. "I stepped outside after bringing about 40 or 50 people down a stairway. I looked around. It was crazy. Somebody yelled, 'Look out! The tower's coming down!' I started running. I tossed my air mask away to make myself lighter. Next thing I know, there's a big black ball of smoke. I threw myself on my knees, and I'm crying. I said to myself, 'Oh, my God, I'm going to die.' I was crawling. Then—the biggest miracle thing in the world. My hands came onto an air mask. It still had air. Another 15 seconds, I wouldn't have made it."

- Mike Hanson, a member of the Emergency Services Unit of the New York Police Department, used a torch to cut through steel to rescue people. "Emotionally, it's taken a toll. Just like I work in small sectors of massive destruction, I have to take it in little pieces mentally. That's the only way I can manage it."

These stories raise fascinating questions that are crucial to the study of stress and coping. What happens after we experience a traumatic event? How do people like Louie Cacchioli fare following a close brush with death? Do the effects reverberate long afterward, producing lasting psychological or physical illnesses? Or can many people instead manage to cope, even thrive, in the aftermath of harrowing circumstances?

In this chapter, we'll explore the various ways in which people cope with stressful circumstances, ranging from the annoyance of a computer crash to the terror of surviving a plane crash. We'll also examine the complex interplay between stress and physical health. Ronald Kessler and his colleagues (Kessler, Sonnega, Bromet, et al., 1995) studied nearly 6,000 men and women in the general population and found that the majority (60 percent to 90 percent) had experienced at least one potentially traumatic event, such as a sexual or physical assault or car accident. So it's actually the unusual person who doesn't experience severe stress in his or her lifetime (Ozer, Best, Lipsey, et al., 2003). Finally, we'll explore some ways to promote good health and discover the importance of sleep to our physical and mental well-being.

What Is Stress?

Fortunately, exposure to events like the 9/11 terrorist attacks, Hurricane Katrina, and frontline combat in Iraq doesn't guarantee that people will be traumatized for life. Here is another case in which scientific research contradicts popular psychology. Many self-help books inform us that most people require psychological help from grief counselors or other therapists in the face of stressful circumstances (Sommers & Satel, 2005). Yet research shows that even in the face of horrific circumstances, like shootings and natural disasters, most of us are surprisingly resilient (Bonanno, 2004). Even most victims of child sexual abuse turn out to be psychologically healthy adults, although there are certainly exceptions (Rind, Tromovitch, & Bauserman, 1998).

How do we explain how and why the impact of such traumatic events varies across individuals? Before discussing why some people thrive and others nosedive in the face of stressful events, we'll first discuss different views about what stress is. Many ways of thinking about stress have evolved over the years (Cooper & Dewe, 2004). Stress and trauma aren't synonymous. **Stress** consists of the tension, discomfort, or physical symptoms that arise when a situation, which we'll refer to as a *stressor*, strains our ability to cope effectively. In contrast, a *traumatic* event is so severe that it has the potential to produce long-term psychological or health consequences.

Before the 1940s, scientists rarely used the term *stress* outside of the engineering profession (Hayward, 1960, p. 185), where it referred to stresses on materials and building structures. A building was said to withstand stress if it didn't collapse under intense pressure. It wasn't until 1944 that the term *stress* found its way into the psychological literature (Jones & Bright, 2001). But just as two buildings can withstand differing amounts of stress before weakening and collapsing, people differ widely in their personal resources, the meaning and significance they attach to stressful events, and their ability to grapple with them.

In 2007, grief counselors arrived at the scene to help traumatized college students deal with the horrific shootings at Virginia Tech.

STRESS IN THE EYE OF THE BEHOLDER: THREE APPROACHES

Researchers have approached the study of stress in three different, yet interrelated, ways (Kessler, Price, & Wortman, 1985). Each approach has yielded valuable insights, illuminating the big and small events that generate distress and the ways we perceive and respond to stressful situations.

Stressors as Stimuli.
When asked to think about stressful life events, some people conjure up catastrophic images of earthquakes, combat, terrorist attacks, and hurricanes. Others think of rape, job loss, physical assault, and car accidents or the typical role alterations that can occur in the unfolding of life: parenthood, retirement, and caring for family members who need special assistance (Pearlin & Lieberman, 1979; see Chapter 8). **[LEARNING OBJECTIVE 10.1]**

The stressors as stimuli approach focuses on identifying different types of stressful events. This approach has succeeded in pinpointing categories of events that most people find dangerous and unpredictable, as well as the people who are most susceptible to stress following different events (Collins et al., 2003; Costa & McCrae, 1990). For

The stress of unemployment includes not only the frustration and despair of looking for a new job, but the economic hardship of living on a sharply reduced income.

GLOSSARY

stress
the tension, discomfort, or physical symptoms that arise when a situation strains our ability to cope effectively

Hurricane Katrina devastated much of New Orleans in 2005, forcing many displaced residents to relocate as far away as Michigan and California.

example, college freshmen show a greater response to such negative life events as the breakup of a relationship than do older men or women (Jackson & Finney, 2002). When people are retired, the combination of low income and physical disability can make matters worse, suggesting that stressful situations can produce cumulative effects (Smith, Langa, Kabeto, et al., 2005).

Stress as a Transaction.
Stress is a highly subjective experience. Some people are devastated by the breakup of a meaningful relationship, whereas others are optimistic about the opportunity to start afresh. People's varied reactions to the same event suggest that we can view stress as a transaction or exchange between people and their environments (Coyne & Holroyd, 1982; Lazarus, 1999; Lazarus & Folkman, 1984). Researchers who study stress as a transaction examine how people interpret and cope with stressful events. This means that the same event can be incredibly stressful for one person and a minor annoyance for another. Richard Lazarus and his coworkers contended that a critical factor determining whether we experience an event as stressful is our appraisal, that is, evaluation, of the event. When we encounter a potentially threatening event, we initially engage in *primary appraisal*. That is, we first decide whether the event is harmful and then make a *secondary appraisal* about how well we can cope with it (Lazarus & Folkman, 1984).

When we believe we can't cope, we're more likely to experience a full-blown stress reaction than when we believe we can (Lazarus, 1999). When we're optimistic and think we can achieve our goals, we're more likely to engage in **problem-focused coping,** a coping strategy in which we tackle life's challenges head-on, generating specific ideas about ways to fix the situation or alter the environment (Baker & Berenbaum, 2008; Carver & Scheier, 1999; Lazarus & Folkman, 1984). When situations arise that we can't avoid or control, we're more likely to adopt **emotion-focused coping,** a coping strategy in which we try to place a positive spin on our feelings or predicaments and engage in behaviors to reduce painful emotions (Carver, Scheier, & Weintraub, 1989; Lazarus & Folkman, 1984). For example, after the breakup of a relationship, we may make a concerted effort to socialize and meet potential partners (problem-focused coping) or remind ourselves that we were unhappy months before the breakup occurred (emotion-focused coping).

Emotion-focused coping may encourage people who've divorced to begin dating again.

WHAT DO *you* THINK?

Your cousin and her husband just became guardians of their close friend's 3-year-old daughter after their friend was killed in a car accident. Your cousin feels completely overwhelmed by her friend's death and her new responsibilities as a guardian. Her husband feels she needs to just relax and not let it all get to her. What approaches to stress do each of their perspectives reflect?

GLOSSARY

problem-focused coping
coping strategy by which we tackle life's challenges head-on

emotion-focused coping
coping strategy that features a positive outlook on feelings or situations accompanied by behaviors that reduce painful emotions

Stress as a Response.
Stress researchers also study stress as a response—that is, they assess people's psychological and physical reactions to stressful circumstances. Typically, scientists expose subjects to independent variables like stress-producing stimuli; in other cases, they study people who've encountered real-life stressors. Then they measure a host of dependent variables: stress-related feelings such as depression, hopelessness, and hostility, physiological responses such as heart rate, blood pressure, and the release

of stress hormones called **corticosteroids.** These hormones activate the body and prepare us for stressful circumstances.

NO TWO STRESSES ARE CREATED EQUAL: MEASURING STRESS

Measuring stress is a tricky business, largely because what's exceedingly stressful for one person, like an argument with a boss, may be no big deal for another. Two scales—the Social Readjustment Rating Scale and the Hassles Scale—endeavor to gauge the nature and impact of differing stressful events. **[LEARNING OBJECTIVE 10.2]**

Major Life Events.

Adopting the view that stressors are stimuli, David Holmes and his colleagues developed the Social Readjustment Rating Scale (SRRS) based on 43 life events ranked in terms of how stressful participants rated them (Holmes & Rahe, 1967; Miller & Rahe, 1997). The first of many efforts to measure life events systematically, the SRRS assigns a stress score to each event and then derives a total score indicating overall stress levels (see **Figure 10.1** on page 344).

Studies using the SRRS and related measures indicate that the number of stressful events people report over the previous year or so is associated with a variety of physical disorders (Dohrenwend & Dohrenwend, 1974; Holmes & Masuda, 1974) and psychological disorders, like depression (Coyne, 1992; Holahan & Moos, 1991; Schmidt, Murphy, Haq, et al., 2004). Nevertheless, the sheer number of stressful life events is far from a perfect predictor of who'll become physically or psychologically ill (Coyne & Racioppo, 2000). That's because this approach to measuring stressors doesn't take into consideration other crucial factors, including people's interpretation of events, their coping behaviors and resources, and their problems in recalling events accurately (Coyne & Racioppo, 2000; Lazarus, 1999). In addition, it neglects to take into account some of the more "chronic" ongoing stressors that many individuals experience. Experiencing even subtle forms of discrimination or differential treatment based on race, gender, sexual orientation, or religion, for example, can be a significant source of stress even if there is no single stressful event that we can check off from a list. It also neglects the fact that some stressful life events, like divorce or troubles with bosses, can be *consequences* rather than *causes* of people's psychological problems (Depue & Monroe, 1986).

Hassles: Sweating the Small Stuff.

We've all had days when just about everything goes wrong and everybody seems to get on our nerves: Our daily lives are often loaded with **hassles,** minor annoyances or nuisances that strain our ability to cope. Traffic, deadlines, and misunderstandings with friends can all contribute to our overall stress levels. But can lots of hassles add up to be as taxing as the monumental events that shake the foundations of our world? Both major life events and hassles are associated with poor general health. Nevertheless, the frequency and perceived severity of hassles are actually better predictors of physical health, depression, and anxiety than are major life events (Fernandez & Sheffield, 1996; Kanner, Coyne, Schaefer, et al., 1981). Still, it's possible that major stressful events are the real culprits because they set us off when we already feel hassled, or create hassles with which we then need to cope. To test this alternative hypothesis, researchers have used statistical procedures to show that even when the influence of major life events is subtracted from the mix, hassles still predict psychological adjustment (Forshaw, 2002; Kanner et al., 1981).

Getting stuck in traffic is one of many "hassles" we encounter in our daily lives. Research suggests that such hassles can be quite stressful over the long haul.

CORRELATION vs. CAUSATION
Can we be sure that A causes B?

GLOSSARY

corticosteroids
stress hormones that activate the body and prepare us to respond to stressful circumstances

hassle
minor annoyance or nuisance that strains our ability to cope

RULING OUT RIVAL HYPOTHESES
Have important alternative explanations for the findings been excluded?

1. Death of a spouse 100

2. Divorce 73
3. Marital separation 65
4. Jail term 63

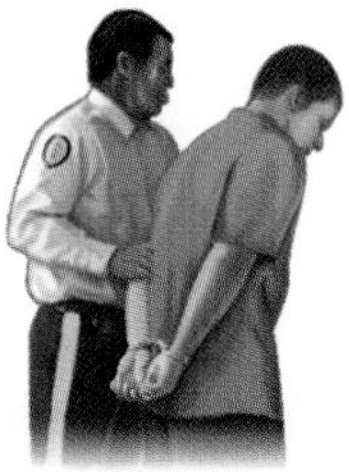

5. Death of a close family member 63
6. Personal injury or illness 53
7. Marriage 50

8. Fired at work 47
9. Marital reconciliation 45
10. Retirement 45

11. Change in health of family member 44

12. Pregnancy 40

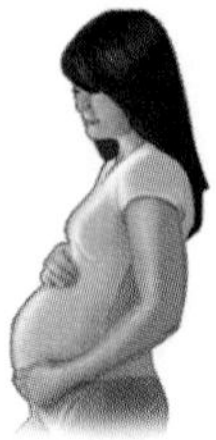

13. Sex difficulties 39
14. Gain of a new family member 39

15. Business readjustments 39
16. Change in financial state 38
17. Death of a close friend 37
18. Change to different line of work 36
19. Change in number of arguments with spouse 35
20. Mortgage over $50,000 31

21. Foreclosure of mortgage 30
22. Change in responsibilities at work 29
23. Son or daughter leaving home 29
24. Trouble with in-laws 29
25. Outstanding personal achievements 28

26. Spouse begins or stops work 26
27. Begin or end school 26
28. Change in living conditions 25
29. Revision of personal habits 24
30. Trouble with boss 23

31. Change in work hours or conditions 20
32. Change in residence 20
33. Change in school 20
34. Change in recreation 19
35. Change in religious activities 19
36. Change in social activities 18
37. Loan less than $50,000 17
38. Change in sleeping habits 16

39. Change in number of family get-togethers 15
40. Change in eating habits 15

41. Vacation 13
42. Holidays 12
43. Minor violation of laws 11

Figure 10.1 **Forty-Three Stressful Life Events from the Social Readjustment Rating Scale.** Scoring: Each event should be considered if it's taken place in the past 12 months. Add values to the right of each item to obtain the total score. Your susceptibility to illness and mental health problems: Low < 149; Mild = 150–200; Moderate = 200–299; Major > 300. (*Source:* Holmes & Rahe, 1967)

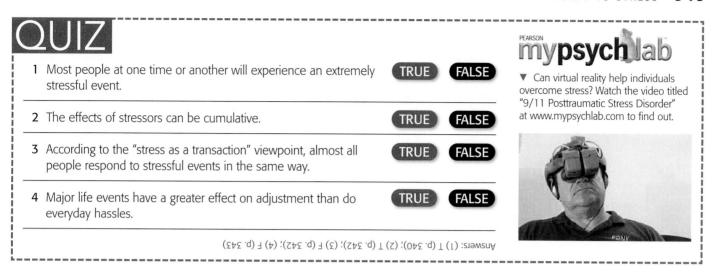

QUIZ

1. Most people at one time or another will experience an extremely stressful event. **TRUE** **FALSE**

2. The effects of stressors can be cumulative. **TRUE** **FALSE**

3. According to the "stress as a transaction" viewpoint, almost all people respond to stressful events in the same way. **TRUE** **FALSE**

4. Major life events have a greater effect on adjustment than do everyday hassles. **TRUE** **FALSE**

Answers: (1) T (p. 340); (2) T (p. 342); (3) F (p. 342); (4) F (p. 343)

PEARSON
mypsychlab

▼ Can virtual reality help individuals overcome stress? Watch the video titled "9/11 Posttraumatic Stress Disorder" at www.mypsychlab.com to find out.

How We Adapt to Stress:
Change and Challenge

As any of us who's had to confront a harrowing event—like a car accident or high-pressure interview for a big job—knows, adapting to stress isn't easy. Yet natural selection has provided us with a set of responses for coping with anxiety-provoking circumstances.

THE MECHANICS OF STRESS: SELYE'S GENERAL ADAPTATION SYNDROME

In 1956, Canadian physician Hans Selye ignited the field of modern-day stress research by publishing *The Stress of Life,* a landmark book that unveiled his decades of study on the effects of prolonged stress on the body. Selye believed that too much stress leads to breakdowns. He argued that we're equipped with a sensitive physiology that responds to stressful circumstances by kicking us into high gear. He called the pattern of responding to stress the **general adaptation syndrome (GAS).** According to Selye, all prolonged stressors take us through three stages of adaptation: *alarm, resistance,* and *exhaustion* (see **Figure 10.2**). **[LEARNING OBJECTIVE 10.3]**

To illustrate key aspects of the GAS and the extent to which our appraisals determine our reactions to stress, let's consider the experience of someone who's afraid of flying. We'll call him Mark and hone in on what he experienced during a flight.

The Alarm Reaction. Selye's first stage, the *alarm reaction,* involves excitation of the autonomic nervous system, the discharge of the stress hormone adrenaline, and physical symptoms of anxiety. Joseph LeDoux (1996) and others have identified the seat of anxiety within a region of the midbrain—dubbed the *emotional brain*—that consists of the amygdala, hypothalamus, and hippocampus (see Chapter 3). Once in flight, our flyer, Mark, feels some slight turbulence and experiences a swift emotional reaction controlled largely by the amygdala, where vital emotional memories are stored (see Chapters 6 and 9), creating gut feelings of a possible crash.

This emotional response signals the body to release a flood of hormones, including adrenaline. Blood pressure rises as adrenaline readies Mark for the **fight-or-flight response** that Walter Cannon first described in 1915. This response is a set of physiological

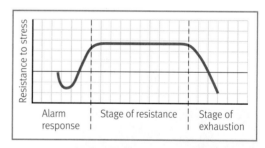

Figure 10.2 Selye's General Adaptation Syndrome. According to Selye's general adaptation syndrome, our level of resistance to stress drops during the alarm phase, increases during the resistance phase, and drops again during the exhaustion phase. (*Source:* Selye, 1956)

GLOSSARY

general adaptation syndrome (GAS)
stress-response pattern proposed by Hans Selye that consists of three stages: alarm, resistance, and exhaustion

fight-or-flight response
physical and psychological reaction that mobilizes people and animals to either defend themselves (fight) or escape (flee) a threatening situation

or psychological reactions that mobilize us to either confront or leave a threatening situation. Cannon noted that people and animals have evolved to respond to threats to their safety with one of two options: *fight* (actively attack the threat or cope in the immediate situation) or *flee* (escape). Of course, Mark can't flee. So his fear escalates, with his hippocampus retrieving terrifying images from news stories of planes going down in flames.

Resistance. After the initial rush of adrenaline, Mark enters Selye's second stage of the GAS: *resistance*. He adapts to the stressor and finds ways to cope with it. The instant Mark's hippocampus detected danger from the first apparent jolt of rough air, it opened up a gateway to portions of his cerebral cortex, which LeDoux (1996) called the "thinking brain." Confronted with a stressful situation, we examine each new development as it unfolds, consider alternative solutions, and direct our efforts toward constructing a coping plan. Mark slowly but surely gets a handle on his fears. He reminds himself that flying is statistically much safer than driving and that he's flown through choppy air in the past without being injured. He looks around and observes that most of the passengers look calm. He reminds himself to breathe slowly, and with each breath his relaxation replaces tension.

Exhaustion. Mark calmed down, and was able to complete his flight. But what happens when a stressor, such as wartime combat lasting months, is more prolonged and uncontrollable? Here's when the third stage of Selye's GAS—*exhaustion*—sets in. If our personal resources are limited and we lack good coping measures, our resistance may ultimately break down, causing our levels of activation to bottom out. The results can range from damage to an organ system, to depression and anxiety, to a breakdown in the immune system (which we'll discuss later in the chapter).

THE DIVERSITY OF STRESS RESPONSES

Not all of us react to stressors with a fight-or-flight response. Our reactions vary from one stressor to another, and these reactions may be shaped by gender.

Fight or Flight or Tend and Befriend? Shelley Taylor and her colleagues coined the catchy phrase **tend and befriend** to describe a common pattern of reacting to stress among women (Taylor et al., 2000), although some men display it too. Taylor observed that in times of stress, women generally rely on their social contacts and nurturing abilities— they *tend* to those around them and to themselves—more than men do. When stressed out, women also typically *befriend*, or turn to others for support. **[LEARNING OBJECTIVE 10.4]**

That's not to say that women lack a self-preservation instinct. They don't shirk from defending themselves and their children or from attempting to escape when physically threatened. However, compared with men, women generally have more to lose—especially when they're pregnant, nursing, or caring for children—if they're injured or killed fighting or fleeing. Therefore, over the course of evolutionary history, they've developed a tend-and-befriend rather than a fight-or-flight pattern of reacting to stressful circumstances to boost the odds of their and their offsprings' survival.

Long-Lasting Stress Reactions. Bad things happen to all of us. For most of us, life goes on. But others experience long-lasting psychological repercussions including stress disorders, anxiety, and depression (Comijs, Beekman, Smit, Bremmer, Tilburg, & Deeg, 2008; Meichenbaum, 1994; Yehuda, Resnick, Kahana, et al., 1993).

Anxiety and Depression. Anxiety and depression can arise in the wake of stressful events. In dire straits, we're likely to feel overwhelmed by seemingly unresolvable situations and unsolvable problems (Mellinger & Lynn, 2003). When we interpret events as threatening, dangerous, and uncontrollable, we're especially vulnerable to anxiety (Gibb & Coles, 2005).

MYTH: All stress is "bad" and can never be advantageous.

REALITY: Selye coined the term *eustress*, based on the Greek word "eu" meaning "good," to distinguish it from *distress*, or "bad" stress. Events that are challenging yet not overwhelming, such as competing in an athletic event or giving a speech, are examples of "positive stress" that provide opportunities for personal growth.

In stressful times, women often rely on friendships for support and comfort, a pattern that psychologist Shelley Taylor called "tend and befriend."

GLOSSARY

tend and befriend
reaction that mobilizes people to nurture (tend) or seek social support (befriend) under stress

The longer we feel we lack control over our lives, and the longer we feel helpless or responsible for our failures, the greater the likelihood that our anxiety will transform into depression (Chorpita & Barlow, 1998; see also Chapter 13). People with depression are 2.5 times more likely than nondepressed people to have experienced one or more events that involve loss, like the death of a loved one (Mazure, 1998; Shrout et al., 1989).

When Stress Is Too Much: Posttraumatic Stress Disorder. On April 16, 2007, 23-year-old Cho Seung-Hui, a student at Virginia Tech, went on a shooting rampage, killing 31 classmates and professors before taking his own life. When Marjorie Lindholm, 24, heard the news of the massacre, she immediately relived the terror she experienced as a student at Columbine High School on April 20, 1999. On that day, two students, Eric Harris and Dylan Klebold, shot 12 of her classmates and a teacher before turning the guns on themselves. In a television interview she said, "I started crying, then shaking. I remembered everything I saw at Columbine. I got physically ill. There is no way I'm going to forget that day" (Stepp, 2007).

Combat along with sexual assault are the two events producing the highest risk for PTSD.

Marjorie displays some of the hallmark symptoms of *posttraumatic stress disorder* (PTSD), a condition that sometimes follows extremely stressful life events. Its telltale symptoms include vivid memories, feelings, and images of traumatic experiences, known commonly as *flashbacks*. Other symptoms of PTSD, which we'll consider in greater depth in Chapter 13, include efforts to avoid reminders of the trauma, feeling detached or estranged from others, and symptoms of increased arousal, such as difficulty sleeping and startling easily. The lifetime prevalence of PTSD is 5 percent in men and 10 percent in women (Kessler et al., 1995). The severity, duration, and nearness to the stressor all affect people's likelihood of developing PTSD (American Psychiatric Association, 2000).

myth CONCEPTIONS ARE WE ALL TRAUMATIZED BY HIGHLY AVERSIVE EVENTS?

A widespread view in popular psychology is that most people exposed to trauma develop PTSD or other serious psychological disorders. Immediately following the 9/11 attacks, for example, many mental health professionals predicted an epidemic of PTSD across the United States (Sommers & Satel, 2005). Were they right?

George Bonanno and his colleagues conducted a study that underscores the remarkable resilience of survivors of extremely aversive events (Bonanno, Galea, Bucciarelli, et al., 2006). Using a random-digit dialing procedure, researchers sampled 2,752 adults in the New York City area about 6 months after the 9/11 attacks. They conducted their assessments using a computer-assisted telephone interview system. People were judged to be resilient if they reported 0 or 1 PTSD symptom during the first 6 months after the attack. Bonanno's results offered surprising evidence for psychological adjustment; 65.1 percent of the sample was resilient. A quarter of the people who were in the World Trade Center at the time of the attack had probable PTSD, although more than half of the people in this category were resilient. Other research indicates that although most Americans were profoundly upset for several days following the 9/11 attacks, nearly all quickly regained their equilibrium and returned to their previous level of functioning (McNally, 2003). So when it comes to responses to trauma, resilience is the rule rather than the exception.

Table 10.1 Percentages of People Who Develop Posttraumatic Conditions as a Function of the Event.

Percentage of People Who Develop PTSD	
Bombing	34%
Plane crash into hotel	29%
Mass shooting	28%
Natural disaster	4%–5%

People who cope well in the aftermath of a serious stressor tend to display relatively high levels of functioning before the event (Bonanno, Moskowitz, Papa, et al., 2005). Yet resilience isn't limited to a few particularly well-adjusted, brave, or tough-minded people nor to a single type or class of events. Instead, it's actually the most common response to traumatic events. Most people who take care of a partner dying of AIDS, suffer the death of a spouse, or survive a physical or sexual assault report few long-term psychological symptoms (Bonanno, 2004). **Table 10.1** presents the rates of PTSD associated with a number of other disturbing events. As we can see, only a minority of people who contend with such events develop PTSD.

THE BRAIN–BODY REACTION TO STRESS

In 1962, two Japanese physicians, Y. Ikemi and S. Nakagawa, conducted a study demonstrating the intimate connection between brain and body. Their study, which researchers today might find difficult to carry out for ethical reasons, showed how suggestions from a respected authority figure can produce dramatic skin reactions. The researchers selected 13 boys who contracted a red, itchy skin reaction when touched with the leaves of a tree similar to poison ivy. A respected physician told all the boys that he was touching them with the leaves of the poison ivy–type tree, when in fact he was touching them with leaves from a harmless tree. In the second phase, Ikemi and Nakagawa reversed the conditions: They rubbed the boys' arms with the poison–ivy type leaves but told them the leaves were harmless.

The reactions were remarkable. In the first phase, all subjects showed significant skin disturbance as a result of believing they were touched by the poison ivy–type leaves. In the second phase only two subjects showed any skin reactions to the leaves, even though all had developed skin reactions to the leaves prior to the study (Ikemi & Nakagawa, 1962).

This study demonstrates how psychological factors, in this case the stressful idea of contracting an itchy rash, can influence physical processes. Indeed, much of what we call a "psychological" response to events manifests itself in physiological reactions. Stress can spill over into multiple domains of life, creating physical difficulties that disrupt our sleep and sexual functioning. **[LEARNING OBJECTIVE 10.5]** But can stress seep into our cells and weaken our body's defenses against infections? A number of fascinating studies tell us that the answer is yes.

People from all walks of life can contract the HIV virus and develop AIDS.

The Immune System. Ordinarily (and thankfully!), we never have to think about the billions of viruses, fungi, protozoa, and bacteria that share our environment or inhabit our body. That's because our **immune system** neutralizes or destroys them. The immune system is our body's defense against invading bacteria, viruses, and other potentially illness-producing organisms and substances. Our first shield from these foreign invaders, called *antigens,* is the skin, which blocks the entry of many disease-producing organisms, called *pathogens*. When we cough or sneeze, the lungs expel harmful bacteria and viruses. Saliva, urine, tears, perspiration, and stomach acid also rid our body of pathogens.

Some viruses or bacteria penetrate these defenses, but the immune system is wily and has other means of safeguarding us. Under ordinary circumstances, the immune system is remarkably effective. But it's not a perfect barrier against infection. For example, some cancer cells can suppress an effective immune response, multiply, and

GLOSSARY

immune system
our body's defense system against invading bacteria, viruses, and other potentially illness-producing organisms and substances

wreak havoc in the body. Serious disorders of the immune system, such as **acquired immune deficiency syndrome (AIDS),** are life threatening. AIDS is an incurable yet often treatable condition in which the human immunodeficiency virus (HIV) attacks and damages the immune system. When the immune system is overactive, it can launch an attack on various organs of the body, causing *autoimmune diseases* like arthritis, in which the immune system causes swelling and pain at the joints, and multiple sclerosis, in which the immune system attacks the protective myelin sheath surrounding neurons (see Chapter 3).

The study of the relationship between the immune system and central nervous system—the seat of our emotions and reactions to the environment (Chapter 3)—goes by a mouthful of a name: **psychoneuroimmunology** (Cohen & Herbert, 1996). When evaluating psychoneuroimmunology we must be careful not to fall prey to exaggerated claims. Illnesses aren't the result of negative thinking, nor can positive thinking reverse serious illnesses like cancer (Hines, 2003)—despite assertions by immensely popular alternative medical practitioners like Andrew Weil (2000) and Deepak Chopra (1989). Nor, despite early and widely publicized claims (Fawzy et al., 1993; Spiegel, Bloom, Kramer, et al., 1989), does psychotherapy appear to prolong the survival of people diagnosed with cancer (Coyne, Stefanek, & Palmer, 2007). Nevertheless, researchers using rigorous designs have discovered at least some fascinating links between our life circumstances and our ability to fend off illnesses.

Dr. Andrew Weil and Dr. Deepak Chopra have popularized the idea that the "mind" can cure serious illnesses. Yet most of their optimistic claims aren't supported by scientific evidence.

Stress and Colds. Many people believe they're more likely to get a cold when they're really stressed out—and they're right. Sheldon Cohen and his associates placed cold viruses into volunteers' nasal passages (Cohen, Tyrell, & Smith, 1991). Other volunteers, in a placebo condition, didn't receive the virus, but instead received nasal drops with a saline solution. Stressful life events in the year preceding the study predicted the number of colds people developed when exposed to the virus. Exposure to the virus was also important. People in the placebo condition didn't develop as many colds, even when they experienced stressful events in the year before the study. The researchers (Cohen et al., 1998) later discovered that significant stressors, such as unemployment and interpersonal difficulties lasting at least a month, were the best predictors of who developed a cold. But a network of friends and relatives and close ties to the community provided protection against colds (Cohen, Doyle, Skoner, et al., 1997; Cohen, Doyle, Turner, et al., 2003).

Caretakers of people with Alzheimer's disease experience high levels of stress, are at heightened risk of developing depression, and even show decreases in their blood's ability to clot (associated with having a stroke) in response to stressful life events (von Känel, Dimsdale, Patterson, et al., 2003).

Stress and Immune Function: Beyond the Common Cold. Janice Kiecolt-Glaser and her associates are pioneers in the study of the connection between stressors and the immune system. Caring for a family member with Alzheimer's disease, a severe form of dementia (see Chapter 3), can be exceedingly stressful and cause long-term disruption of the immune system. Kiecolt-Glaser demonstrated that a small wound (standardized for size across people) took 24 percent longer to heal in Alzheimer's caregivers compared with a group of people who weren't taking care of a relative with Alzheimer's (Kiecolt-Glaser, Marucha, Malarkey, et al., 1995). To demonstrate the generalizability of this finding, research has shown that the following stressors can lead to disruptions in the immune system (Kiecolt-Glaser, McGuire, Robles, et al., 2002):

- taking an important test
- the death of a spouse
- unemployment
- marital conflict
- living near a damaged nuclear reactor
- natural disasters

GLOSSARY

acquired immune deficiency syndrome (AIDS)
a life-threatening, incurable, yet treatable condition in which the human immunodeficiency virus (HIV) attacks and damages the immune system

psychoneuroimmunology
study of the relationship between the immune system and central nervous system

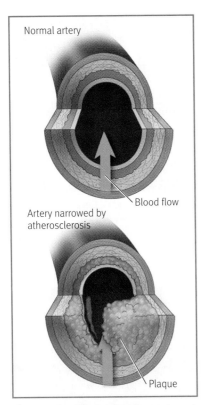

Figure 10.3 Atherosclerosis. Cholesterol deposits in the large arteries form plaque, restricting the flow of blood. This condition, called *atherosclerosis,* can result in stroke, heart attack, and serious chest pain.

MYTH: Stress and spicy foods cause ulcers.

REALITY: Ulcers are caused by a bacterium called *Helicobacter pylori.* However, only a subset of people with this bacteria develop ulcers, so it's likely that stress and other general health factors play an indirect role.

GLOSSARY

psychophysiological
illnesses such as asthma and ulcers in which emotions and stress contribute to, maintain, or aggravate the physical condition

biopsychosocial perspective
the view that an illness or medical condition is the product of the interplay of biological, psychological, and social factors

The good news is that positive emotions and social support, which we'll consider later in the chapter, can fortify our immune systems (Esterling, Kiecolt-Glaser, & Glaser, 1996; Kennedy, Kiecolt-Glaser, & Glaser, 1990).

Stress-Related Illnesses: A Biopsychosocial View.
We've all heard the expression that an illness is "all in your head." Today that's just a polite way of saying "Quit worrying." But not long ago a common myth of popular psychology was that beliefs and mental states were the root causes of many physical ailments. Certain illnesses or disorders were once called *psychosomatic,* because psychologists believed that psychological conflicts and emotional reactions were the culprits. Today, psychologists use the term **psychophysiological** to describe illnesses like asthma and ulcers in which emotions and stress contribute to, maintain, or aggravate physical conditions.

Today, psychologists widely acknowledge that emotions and stress are associated with physical disorders, including coronary heart disease and AIDS. Most scientists have adopted a **biopsychosocial perspective,** which proposes that most medical conditions are neither all physical nor all psychological. Numerous physical illnesses depend on the interplay of genes, lifestyle, immunity, social support, everyday stressors, and self-perceptions (Engel, 1977; Fava & Sonino, 2008; Turk, 1996).

Stress and Coronary Heart Disease.
Scientists have learned that psychological factors, including stress and personality traits, are key risk factors for **coronary heart disease (CHD).** CHD is the complete or partial blockage of the arteries that provide oxygen to the heart and is the number one cause of death and disability in the United States (Kung, Hoyert, Xu, & Murphy, 2008). It accounts for an astonishing 1 in every 2.5 deaths, and almost a million deaths every year (Gatchel & Oordt, 2003). CHD develops when deposits of *cholesterol*—a waxy, fatty substance that travels in the bloodstream—collect in the walls of arteries, narrowing and blocking the coronary arteries, creating a condition called *atherosclerosis* (see **Figure 10.3**).

A host of factors is associated with CHD. Advanced age, diabetes, high blood pressure, and a family history of the disease are high on the list of risk factors. As we mentioned earlier, stress is also associated with CHD risk. Stressful life events predict recurrences of heart attacks, high blood pressure, increased glucose levels, and enlargement of the heart associated with CHD (Repetti, Taylor, & Seeman, 2002; Schnall et al., 1990; Troxel, Matthews, Bromberger, et al., 2003). Although only correlational, these data suggest that stressors may sometimes produce negative physiological effects.

The ABCs of Personality in CHD.
In addition to stress, researchers have suggested that long-standing behavior patterns or traits contribute to risk for CHD. When we picture someone at risk for a heart attack, certain personality characteristics come to mind: competitive, hard-driving, ambitious, and impatient. The media have widely popularized the so-called **Type A personality** (as opposed to the calmer and mellower *Type B personality*) who fits this description.

Two cardiologists, Meyer Friedman and Ray Rosenman (1959), coined this term to describe a curious behavior pattern they observed among CHD patients. They noticed that the chairs in their hospital waiting room were rapidly becoming worn out around the edges. Many of their CHD patients were literally sitting and bouncing on the edges of their seats because of restlessness. Later, Friedman and Rosenman (1974) identified additional characteristics that clustered under the Type A description: perfectionistic, prone to hostility, stubborn, opinionated, cynical, and controlling.

Rosenman and Friedman launched the Western Collaborative Group Study (Rosenman et al., 1964, 1975) of 3,500 males to determine whether Type A personality traits predict CHD risk over an 8½-year period. They found that even when they took other risk factors, like smoking and diet, into account, Type A traits were still associated with later heart disease risk. Of all Type A traits, hostility appears to be the most predictive of heart disease (Matthews, Gump, Harris, et al., 2004; Myrtek, 2001; Smith & Gallo, 2001).

Health, Everyday Experiences, and Socioeconomic Factors. Hostility, depression, and hopelessness don't always arise from enduring personality traits. These negative emotions can stem from the many pressures and demands we confront in our fast-paced, competitive society. Let's consider three sources of support for the claim that everyday experiences set the stage for many physical problems, including heart disease. First, people who experience even one significant drop in their income over a 5-year period face a 30 percent increase in their risk of dying from any cause. Two such drops in income jack up the risk to a whopping 70 percent (Duncan, 1996). Second, African American women who experience discrimination and unfair treatment, and who report high stress levels, have more narrowing and blockage of their arteries than other African American women (Troxel et al., 2003). Third, CHD is associated with substantial job stress and dissatisfaction (Quick, Quick, Nelson, et al., 1997). Although job stress is correlated with CHD, it may not cause it in all circumstances. An interesting possibility that has yet to be fully explored is that the causal arrow is reversed: perhaps CHD causes job stress in some people.

Researchers have also established a strong correlation between poverty and poor health (Antonovsky, 1967; Repetti et al., 2002). Life can prove immensely challenging for people who have little education, struggle in a bad job with a nasty supervisor, and barely make enough money to pay the bills. People from low-income backgrounds who regularly encounter these circumstances experience a powerful drain on their personal and interpersonal resources. This state of affairs decreases their ability to cope with future stressors and with depression, hopelessness, and hostility, which, as we've seen, increase the risk of poor health and CHD. To make matters worse, negative thoughts and feelings can promote unhealthy habits like smoking, drinking, and lack of exercise, which further increase the risk of physical problems (Gallo & Matthews, 2003).

Can chronic anger be bad for our health? Research indicates that the anger component of the Type A personality can be deadly, increasing our risk for coronary heart disease.

CORRELATION vs. CAUSATION
Can we be sure that A causes B?

WHAT DO *you* THINK?

You're conducting research on the potential effects of stressful life events, such as losing a job or marital conflict, on people's health. How might you determine whether some of the stress associated with these events could have been generated by people's own behaviors, such as their tendency to argue with others?

Illness Can Create Stress. We've seen that stress can contribute to physical disorders, such as CHD. But of course, physical disorders can also create stress. Not surprisingly, being diagnosed with a potentially fatal illness that has an uncertain outcome, like cancer, can be unimaginably stressful and pose innumerable challenges. People who suffer from cancer often endure chronic pain and wonder whether even a slight increase in pain signals a downward, perhaps fatal, turn in the progression of their illness. Irritability, anger, and frustration can also be by-products of prolonged periods of pain-related sleeplessness and the fatigue that result from it (Kreitler & Merimsky, 2006; Moffitt, Kalvey, Kalvey, et al., 1991).

GLOSSARY

coronary heart disease (CHD)
damage to the heart from the complete or partial blockage of the arteries that provide oxygen to the heart

Type A personality
personality type that describes people who are competitive, driven, hostile, and ambitious

QUIZ

1 People's first reaction to an extreme stressor involves activation of the autonomic nervous system. **TRUE** **FALSE**

2 Few people are resilient in the face of extreme stress. **TRUE** **FALSE**

3 Physical illness can be a reaction to a prolonged stressor. **TRUE** **FALSE**

4 Psychologists once termed diseases psychophysiological because they believed them to be caused by psychological conflicts and emotional reactions. **TRUE** **FALSE**

5 Socioeconomic factors are largely or entirely unrelated to risk for physical diseases. **TRUE** **FALSE**

Answers: (1) T (p. 345); (2) F (p. 348); (3) T (p. 349); (4) F (p. 350); (5) F (p. 351)

PEARSON
mypsychlab

▼ Do men or women have more stress? Watch the video titled "Gender Differences in Stress Vulnerability" at www.mypsychlab.com to find out.

HOW TO RELIEVE STRESS
- RELAX 15 MINUTES A DAY
- DEEP BREATHING
- PRAYER
- CLOSING YOUR EYES

Coping with Stress

Clearly, some of us adapt better in the face of challenge and change than others. Why is this so, and what can we do to reduce stress, manage our lives, and stay healthy? We'll next take stock of how we can use social support and coping strategies to surmount stressful circumstances.

SOCIAL SUPPORT

When we ask our students how they cope with stress many say the support of family, friends, neighbors, teachers, coworkers, and clergy is invaluable. **Social support** encompasses social relations with people, groups, and the larger community. Social support can provide us with emotional comfort, financial assistance, and information to make decisions, solve problems, and contend with stressful situations (Schaefer, Coyne, & Lazarus, 1981; Stroebe, 2000; Wills & Fegan, 2001). **[LEARNING OBJECTIVE 10.6]**

Lisa Berkman and Leonard Syme (1979) conducted a landmark study of the hypothesis that social support protects against the adverse effects of stress on health. They found a strong relationship between the number of social connections and the likelihood that the participants would die during the 9-year period. James House, Cynthia Robbins, and Helen Metzner (1982) replicated Berkman and Syme's (1979) findings: Even when they took initial health status into account, people with less social support had higher mortality rates.

Fortunately, the positive influence of social support isn't limited to health outcomes. Supportive and caring relationships can help us cope with short-term crises and life transitions. A happy marriage, for example, is protective against depression, even when people encounter major stressors (Alloway & Bebbington, 1987; Gotlib & Hammen, 1992). But the breakup of close relationships through separation, divorce, discrimination, or bereavement ranks among the most stressful events we can experience (Gardner, Gabriel, & Deikman, 2000). Moreover, lonely and socially isolated people have higher mortality rates than other people and are more likely than other people to smoke and drink, get little exercise, and sleep poorly (Cacioppo et al., 2000; Hawkley & Cacioppo, 2007).

Support and comfort from others can buffer us from the effects of highly aversive situations.

REPLICABILITY
Can the results be duplicated in other studies?

GLOSSARY

social support
relationships with people and groups that can provide us with emotional comfort and personal and financial resources

GAINING CONTROL

We can also relieve stress by acquiring control of situations. Next, we'll discuss five types of control we can use in different situations (Bonanno, 2004; Cohen, Evans, Stokols, et al., 1986; Higgins & Endler, 1995; Lazarus & Folkman, 1984; Sarafino, 2006). Each of these approaches can contribute to a reduction in stress.

- **Behavioral Control.** Behavioral control is the ability to step up and do something to reduce the impact of a stressful situation.

- **Cognitive Control.** Cognitive control is the ability to *cognitively restructure* or think differently about negative emotions that arise in response to stress-provoking events (Higgins & Endler, 1995; Lazarus & Folkman, 1984; Skinner, Edge, Altman, et al., 2003).

- **Decisional Control.** Decisional control is the ability to choose among alternative courses of action (Sarafino, 2006).

- **Informational Control.** Informational control is the ability to acquire information about a stressful event.

- **Emotional Control.** Emotional control is the ability to suppress and express emotions. Communication can strengthen social bonds, enhance problem solving, and regulate emotions (Bonanno, 2004; Ekman & Davidson, 1993).

"Howl at an ambulance or fire siren every chance you get. Run around the room in circles with a sock in your mouth. Eat a messy meal without using your hands or utensils. Ask a friend to scratch your belly..."

(Copyright 2003 by Randy Glasbergen. www.glasbergen.com)

Is Catharsis a Good Thing? Contrary to the popular notion that expressing what we feel is always beneficial, disclosing painful feelings, called *catharsis,* is a double-edged sword. When it involves problem solving and constructive efforts to make troubling situations "right," it can be beneficial. But when catharsis reinforces a sense of helplessness, as when we stew endlessly about something we can't or won't change, catharsis can actually be harmful (Littrell, 1998). This finding is worrisome, because a slew of popular psychotherapies rely on catharsis, encouraging clients to "get it out of your system," "get things off your chest," or "let it all hang out." Some of these therapies instruct clients to yell, punch pillows, or throw balls against walls when they become upset (Lewis & Bucher, 1992; Lohr, Olatunji, Baumeister, et al., 2007). Yet research shows that these activities rarely reduce our long-term stress, although they may make us feel slightly better for a few moments. In other cases, they actually seem to heighten our anger or anxiety in the long run (Tavris, 1989).

GRE preparation classes can be useful sources of informational control.

┌─ **WHAT DO** *you* **THINK?** ───────

A close friend is clearly under stress and feels his life is out of control. He talks through his sources of stress every time he sees you, but doesn't seem able to reduce his stress as a result. How might you help him regain a sense of control?

Does Crisis Debriefing Help? Some therapists—especially those employed by fire, police, or other emergency services—administer a popular treatment called *crisis debriefing,* which is designed to ward off PTSD among people exposed to trauma. Crisis debriefing is a single-session procedure, typically conducted in groups, that usually lasts 3 to 4 hours. Most often, therapists conduct this procedure within a few days of a traumatic event, such as a terrible accident. It proceeds according to standardized steps, including strongly encouraging group members to discuss and "process" their negative emotions,

Crisis debriefing sessions, in which people discuss their reactions to a traumatic event in a group, may actually increase PTSD risk.

listing the posttraumatic symptoms that group members are likely to experience, and discouraging group members from discontinuing participation once the session has started.

Yet, recent studies indicate that crisis debriefing isn't effective for trauma reactions. What's worse, several studies suggest that it may actually increase the risk of PTSD among people exposed to trauma, perhaps because it gets in the way of people's natural coping strategies (Lilienfeld, 2007; Litz, Gray, Bryant, et al., 2002; McNally, Bryant, & Ehlers, 2003).

Nor is there much evidence that merely talking about our problems when we're upset is helpful. A review of 61 studies (Meads & Nouwen, 2005) revealed no overall benefits for emotional disclosure (compared with nondisclosure) on a variety of measures of physical and psychological health. None of this implies that we should never discuss our feelings with others when we're upset. But it does mean that doing so is most likely to be beneficial when it allows us to think about and work through our problems in a more constructive light.

INDIVIDUAL DIFFERENCES IN COPING: ATTITUDES, BELIEFS, AND PERSONALITY

Some people survive almost unimaginably horrific circumstances with few or no visible psychological scars, whereas others view the world through the dark lens of pessimism and crumble when the little things in life don't go their way. Our attitudes, personality, and socialization shape our reactions—for better and worse—to potential stressors.

Hardiness: Challenge, Commitment, and Control.
About three decades ago, Salvatore Maddi and his colleagues (Kobasa, Hilker, & Maddi, 1979) initiated a study of the qualities of stress-resistant people. They determined that resilient people possess a set of attitudes they called **hardiness.** Hardy people view change as a challenge rather than a threat, are committed to their life and work, and believe they can control events. Hardy individuals have the courage and motivation to confront stressors and engage in problem solving to contend with them (Maddi, 2004). **[LEARNING OBJECTIVE 10.7]**

Suzanne Kobasa and Maddi asked 670 managers at a public utility to report their stressful experiences on a checklist. Then they selected executives who scored high on both stress and illness and another group who scored equally high on stress but reported below-average levels of illness. Managers who showed high stress but low levels of illness were more motivated by challenges, scored higher in their sense of control over events, and felt a deep sense of involvement in their work and social lives.

CORRELATION VS. CAUSATION
Can we be sure that A causes B?

When we're physically ill, we don't usually feel especially hardy. So we can appreciate the fact that another explanation for Kobasa and Maddi's findings is that illness creates negative attitudes, rather than the other way around. To address the question of causal direction, Maddi and Kobasa (1984) conducted a longitudinal study (see Chapter 8) that examined changes in health and attitudes over time. At the end of 2 years, people whose attitudes toward life reflected high levels of control, commitment, and challenge remained healthier than those whose attitudes didn't. Hardiness also can boost stress resistance among nurses in hospice settings, immigrants adjusting to life in the United States, and military personnel who survive life-threatening stressors (Atri, Sharma, & Cottrell, 2006; Bartone, 1999; Maddi, 2002).

Optimism.
Optimistic people have a rosy outlook and don't dwell on the dark side of life. Even on a cloudy day, we can bask in their sunshine. As we learned in Chapter 9,

GLOSSARY

hardiness
set of attitudes marked by a sense of control over events, commitment to life and work, and courage and motivation to confront stressful events

there are some distinct advantages to being optimistic. Optimistic people are more productive, focused, persistent, and better at handling frustration than pessimists (Peterson, 2000; Seligman, 1990). Optimism is also associated with a lower mortality rate (Stern, Dhanda, & Hazuda, et al., 2001), a more vigorous immune response (Segerstrom, Taylor, Kemeny, et al., 1998), lower distress in infertile women trying to have a child (Abbey, Halman, & Andrews, 1992), better surgical outcomes (Scheier et al., 1989), and fewer physical complaints (Scheier & Carver, 1992).

Spirituality and Religious Involvement.

Spirituality is a search for the sacred, which may or may not extend to belief in God. Spiritual and religious beliefs play vital roles in many of our lives. Compared with nonreligious people, religious people have lower mortality rates, improved immune system functioning, lower blood pressure, and a greater ability to recover from illnesses (Koenig, McCullough, & Larson, 2001; Levin, 2001; Matthews, Larson, & Barry, 1993). One explanation for these findings is that religious involvements activate a healing energy that scientists can't measure (Ellison & Levin, 1998). This is an intriguing hypothesis. Nevertheless, explanations that depend on an undetectable force or energy can't be falsified and therefore lie outside the boundaries of science (see Chapter 1).

The correlation between religiosity and physical health isn't easy to interpret. Some authors have measured religiosity by counting how often people attend church or other religious services and found that such attendance is associated with better physical health. But this correlation is potentially attributable to a confound: People who are sick are less likely to attend religious services, so the causal arrow may be reversed (Sloan, Bagiella, & Powell, 1999).

Research on the links between spirituality and religious involvement, on the one hand, and health, on the other, is limited. But until more definitive evidence is available, let's consider several potential reasons why spirituality and religious involvements may be a boon to many people:

(1) Many religions prohibit health risk behaviors, including alcohol, drugs, and unsafe sexual practices.

(2) Religious engagement, such as attendance at services, often boosts social support.

(3) A sense of meaning and purpose, control over life, positive emotions, and positive appraisals of stressful situations associated with prayer and religious activities may enhance coping (Potts, 2004).

Optimists—who proverbially see the glass as "half full" rather than "half empty"—are more likely than pessimists to view change as a challenge.

FALSIFIABILITY
Can the claim be disproved?

CORRELATION vs. **CAUSATION**
Can we be sure that A causes B?

GLOSSARY

spirituality
search for the sacred, which may or may not extend to belief in God

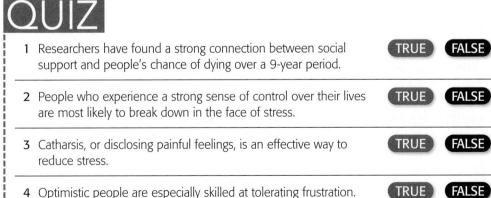

QUIZ

1 Researchers have found a strong connection between social support and people's chance of dying over a 9-year period.   TRUE FALSE

2 People who experience a strong sense of control over their lives are most likely to break down in the face of stress.   TRUE FALSE

3 Catharsis, or disclosing painful feelings, is an effective way to reduce stress.   TRUE FALSE

4 Optimistic people are especially skilled at tolerating frustration.   TRUE FALSE

Answers: (1) T (p. 352); (2) F (p. 353); (3) F (p. 353); (4) T (p. 355)

PEARSON
mypsychlab

▼ What are the symptoms of stress and how should we cope? Watch the video titled 'Coping with Stress' at www.mypsychlab.com to find out.

Promoting Good Health— and Less Stress!

If we could all reduce or eliminate stress in our lives, the public health consequences would be enormous. Stress is a risk factor for many behaviors, such as smoking and alcohol, which are themselves risk factors for many illnesses. What can we do to decrease stress-related diseases? How can we modify health-destructive habits and help people stricken with a serious illness? **Table 10.2** describes three keys to good health, as well as some consequences of not practicing these behaviors.

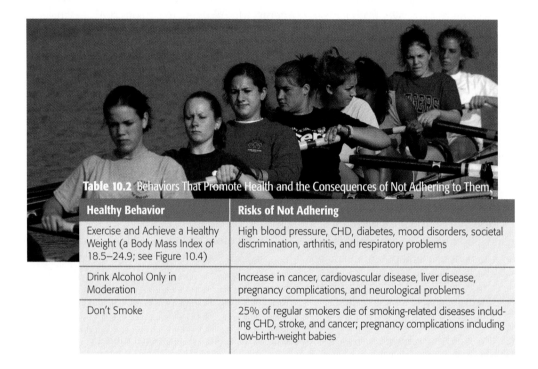

Table 10.2 Behaviors That Promote Health and the Consequences of Not Adhering to Them.

Healthy Behavior	Risks of Not Adhering
Exercise and Achieve a Healthy Weight (a Body Mass Index of 18.5–24.9; see Figure 10.4)	High blood pressure, CHD, diabetes, mood disorders, societal discrimination, arthritis, and respiratory problems
Drink Alcohol Only in Moderation	Increase in cancer, cardiovascular disease, liver disease, pregnancy complications, and neurological problems
Don't Smoke	25% of regular smokers die of smoking-related diseases including CHD, stroke, and cancer; pregnancy complications including low-birth-weight babies

ACHIEVING A HEALTHY WEIGHT

The statistics tell the grim story. As of 2006, two-thirds of adult Americans are overweight, and in turn about a third (34%) of these Americans are obese, as indicated by a statistic known as the *body mass index* (*BMI*) (see **Figure 10.4**) (Ogden, Karroll, McDowell & Flegel, 2007). The number of obese children and adolescents has tripled over the past decade or so, signaling an ominous trend (Ogden et al., 2006). According to some researchers, our society faces an "obesity epidemic" of enormous proportions, due in large measure to decreases in our physical activity (Heini & Weinsier, 1997; Wing & Polley, 2001).

The obese are at greater risk of heart disease, stroke, high blood pressure, arthritis, some types of cancer, respiratory problems, and diabetes (Klein et al., 2004; Kurth et al., 2003). Those of us who carry our weight around our abdomens (so-called spare tires) are at even greater risk for health problems, including CHD (Yusuf et al., 2004). Exercise is one of the best means of shedding that annoying fat around the belly and of losing weight over the long haul (Pronk & Wing, 1994).

If an obese person, say a 300-pound man, sheds even 10 percent of his weight, his health will improve (Wing & Polley, 2001). Losing weight reduces blood pressure, cholesterol, and the risk of diabetes (Kanders & Blackburn, 1992), and often has the added benefit of reducing anxiety and improving mood (Wadden & Stunkard, 1993).

Overweight individuals suffer from a variety of social and emotional problems as well. Teasing in childhood, and stereotyping and discrimination in adulthood are common (Crandall, 1994; Schwartz, Vartanian, Nosek, et al., 2006). Obese individuals are more likely to suffer from anxiety and depression (Simon et al., 2006). And those who are overweight tend to be less wealthy, fail to progress as far in their school and professional life, and less likely to be married than those of healthy weights (Gortmaker, Must, Perrin, et al., 1993). Here's some basic advice to follow for controlling our weight and eating a healthy diet:

(1) Exercise regularly.

(2) Monitor total calories and body weight (Wing & Hill, 2001).

(3) Eat foods with "good fats," such as olive oil and fish oil, which exert protective effects on health.

(4) Get lots of help from your social network to support your efforts to lose weight (Wing & Jeffrey, 1999).

(5) Control portion size. By all means, don't make a habit of "supersizing" your cheeseburgers and fries.

DRUG USE AND ABUSE

One type of behavior that can have serious negative implications for our health is drug use. Virtually every culture has discovered that certain plant substances can alter our mental experiences, often dramatically. These **psychoactive drugs** contain chemicals similar to those found naturally in our brains. These molecules alter experience by changing chemical processes in neurons. The precise psychological and physical effects depend on the type of drug and dosage.

Some psychoactive drugs are used to treat physical and mental illness, but others are used almost exclusively for recreational purposes. As we'll see, the effects of drugs depend on far more than their chemical properties or dosages. *Mental set*—beliefs and expectancies about the effects of drugs—and the setting in which people take these drugs also account for people's responses to them. People's reactions to drugs are also rooted in their cultural heritage and genetic endowment.

Substance Abuse and Dependence.

Drugs are substances that change the way we think, feel, or act. It's easy to forget that alcohol, caffeine, and the nicotine in tobacco are drugs, because they're commonplace and legal. Still, the misuse of both legal and illegal drugs is a serious societal problem. According to a national survey (Johnston, O'Malley, Bachman, et al., 2008), 65 percent of adults (ages 29–30) reported having tried marijuana, and 43 percent reported having tried other illegal drugs, like cocaine, heroin, and hallucinogens.

Abuse versus Dependence: A Fine Line. There's often a fine line between drug use and abuse. What starts out as experimentation with drugs to "get high" and be sociable with friends can become a pattern of intensified use and lead to substance abuse and dependence. Generally speaking, people qualify for a diagnosis of *substance abuse* when they experience recurrent problems associated with the drug (American Psychiatric Association, 2000). Problems often surface in the family, with friends, on the job, in fulfilling life responsibilities, and with the law.

Substance dependence is associated with symptoms of tolerance and withdrawal. Tolerance means that over time a user requires more and more of a drug to experience the

Calculate BMI by dividing weight in pounds (lbs) by height in inches (in) squared and multiplying by a conversion factor of 703.

Example: Weight = 155 lbs, height = 5'9" (69")
Calculation: [155 ÷ (69)²] × 703 = 22.89

BMI	Weight Status
Below 18.5	Underweight
18.5 to 24.9	Normal
25.0 to 29.9	Overweight
30.0 and above	Obese

Height	Weight Range	BMI	Weight Status
5'9"	124 lbs or less	Below 18.5	Underweight
	125 lbs to 168 lbs	18.5 to 24.9	Normal
	169 lbs to 202 lbs	25.0 to 29.9	Overweight
	203 lbs or more	30 or higher	Obese

Figure 10.4 Body Mass Index (BMI) and Weight Status.
(*Source:* Centers for Disease Control and Prevention, 2007, Division of Nutrition and Physical Activity National Center for Chronic Disease Prevention and Health Promotion)

GLOSSARY

psychoactive drugs
chemicals similar to those found naturally in our brains that alter consciousness by changing chemical processes in neurons

In France and other "vinocultural" societies, drinking alcohol is viewed as a healthy part of life.

same "high." Withdrawal refers to physical symptoms resulting from failing to continue to use the drug. Symptoms of withdrawal can be as mild as a headache but can in some cases be fatal. According to one survey (Knight et al., 2002), within a 12-month period, 6 percent of college students met the criteria for a diagnosis of alcohol dependence and 31 percent for the diagnosis of alcohol abuse. Still, most people don't neatly fall into categories of substance abuse versus dependence and vary a good deal in the severity of their symptoms (Harford & Muthen, 2001; Sher, Grekin, & Williams, 2005).

Sociocultural Influences. Cultures or groups in which drinking is strictly prohibited, such as Muslims or Mormons, exhibit low rates of alcoholism (Chentsova-Dutton & Tsai, 2006). In Egypt, the annual rate of alcohol dependence is only 0.2 percent (World Health Organization, 2004). The situation differs markedly in some so-called vinocultural or "wet" societies, which view drinking as a healthy part of daily life (*vino* refers to wine in many languages). For example, in Poland, a "wet" country, the annual rate of alcohol dependence among adults is 11.2 percent. Some researchers attribute these differences to cultural differences in attitudes toward alcohol and its abuse. Nevertheless, these differences could also be due in part to genetic influences, and the cultural attitudes themselves may reflect these differences.

CORRELATION vs. CAUSATION
Can we be sure that A causes B?

WHAT DO *you* THINK?

You are a dorm counselor for a group of college students who are engaging in heavy drinking. What information could you provide to alter their attitudes about alcohol consumption?

Fict-OID

MYTH: Switching among different types of alcohol—like beer, wine, and hard liquor—is more likely to lead to drunkenness than sticking with one type of alcohol.

REALITY: The level of intoxication is determined entirely by the blood alcohol level, not by the type of alcohol a person drinks. Different types of alcohol produce the same subjective effects.

Is There an Addictive Personality? Sociocultural factors don't account for individual variations within cultures. We can find alcoholics in societies with strong sanctions against drinking and teetotalers in societies in which drinking is widespread. To explain these facts, popular and scientific psychologists alike have long wondered whether certain people have an "addictive personality" that predisposes them to abuse alcohol and other drugs (Shaffer, 2000). On the one hand, research suggests that there's no single addictive personality (Rozin & Stoess, 1993). On the other hand, researchers have found that certain personality traits predispose us to alcohol and drug abuse. In particular, studies have tied substance abuse to impulsivity (Baker & Yardley, 2002; Kanzler & Rosenthal, 2003; Kollins, 2003), sociability (Wennberg, 2002), and a predisposition toward negative emotions, like anxiety and hostility (Jackson & Sher, 2003). But some of these traits may result from, rather than cause, substance misuse.

CORRELATION vs. CAUSATION
Can we be sure that A causes B?

RULING OUT RIVAL HYPOTHESES
Have important alternative explanations for the findings been excluded?

Genetic Influences. Alcoholism and drug addiction tend to run in families (Sher, Grekin, & Williams, 2005). But this evidence doesn't tell us whether this finding is due to genes, shared environment, or both. Twin and adoption studies have resolved the issue: They show that genetic factors play a key role in the vulnerability to alcoholism (McGue, 1999). Multiple genes are probably involved (National Institute on Alcohol Abuse and Alcoholism, 2000), but what's inherited? No one knows for sure, but researchers have uncovered some promising leads. One inherited trait is our physiological response to alcohol or other drugs. Those who have an adverse physical reaction to alcohol are less likely to become addicted. Interestingly, people who have a *weak* reaction to alcohol are significantly more likely to become alcoholics, perhaps in part because they must drink significantly more alcohol to experience the same effect as the average person (Schuckit, 1998).

Types of Drugs. Different drug types produce different physical and psychological effects based on their chemical composition and how they interact with the brain and body (see **Table 10.3**). Alcohol and sedative-hypnotics (barbiturates and benzodi-azepines) are depressant drugs, so-called because they depress the effects of the central nervous system. In contrast, stimulant drugs, like nicotine and cocaine, rev up our central nervous system. [**LEARNING OBJECTIVE 10.8**]

Table 10.3 Major Drug Types and Their Effects.

Drug Type	Examples	Effect on Behavior
Depressants	Alcohol, barbiturates, Quaaludes, Valium	Decreased activity of the central nervous system (initial high followed by sleepiness, slower thinking, and impaired concentration)
Stimulants	Tobacco, cocaine, ampheta-mines, methamphetamine	Increased activity of the central nervous system (sense of alertness, well being, energy)
Opiates	Heroin, morphine, codeine	Sense of euphoria, decreased pain
Psychedelics	Marijuana, LSD, Ecstasy	Dramatically altered perception, mood, and thoughts

The Depressant Drugs: Alcohol and the Sedative-Hypnotics. Depressants typically influence the body as **sedatives** that calm us and **hypnotics** that make us sleepy. Although many people believe that alcohol is a stimulant, physiologically it's primarily a depressant. Alcohol only behaves as an emotional and physiological stimulant at relatively low doses because it depresses areas of the brain that inhibit emotion and behavior (Pohorecky, 1977; Tucker, Vucinich, & Sobell, 1982). Small amounts of alcohol can promote feelings of relaxation, elevate mood, increase talkativeness and activity, and lower inhibitions and impair judgment. At higher doses, when the blood alcohol content (BAC)—the concentration of alcohol in the blood—reaches 0.05 to 0.10, the sedating and depressant effects of alcohol generally become more apparent. Brain centers become depressed, slowing thinking and impairing concentration, walking, and muscular coordination (Erblich, Earlywine, Erblich et al., 2003). At higher doses, users sometimes experience a mixture of stimulating and sedating effects (King, Houle, de Wit et al., 2002).

A variety of additional depressant drugs have similar psychological and physical effects to alcohol. Researchers usually group sedative-hypnotics into three categories: *barbiturates* (for example, Seconal, Nembutal, and Tuinal); *nonbarbiturates* (for example, Sopor and methaqualone, better known as Quaalude); and *benzodiazepines*. Benzodiazepines, including Valium, are widely used to relieve anxiety. Barbiturates have the greatest abuse potential, which is troubling because the consequences of overdose are often fatal. Barbiturates produce a state of intoxication very similar to that of alcohol.

The Stimulant Drugs: Tobacco, Cocaine, and Amphetamines. Tobacco, cocaine, and amphetamines are **stimulants** because they rev up our central nervous system. In contrast to depressants, they increase heart rate, respiration, and blood pressure. Yet each of these drugs produces distinctive physiological and subjective effects.

As cigarette companies have long known but were reluctant to admit, the nicotine in tobacco is a potent and addictive drug. Nicotine activates receptors sensitive to the neurotransmitter acetylcholine, and smokers often report feelings of stimulation as well as relaxation and alertness.

Cocaine is the most powerful natural stimulant. Cocaine users commonly report euphoria, enhanced mental and physical capacity, stimulation, a decrease in hunger, indifference to pain, and a sense of well-being accompanied by diminished fatigue. These effects peak quickly and usually fade within a half hour.

Cocaine users can inject it intravenously. But they more commonly inhale or "snort" it through the nose, where the nasal mucous membranes absorb it. *Crack cocaine* is a highly concentrated dose of cocaine produced by dissolving cocaine in an alkaline (basic) solution and boiling it until a whitish lump, or "rock," remains that can be smoked. Crack's popularity

For years, cigarette companies published advertisements claiming that smoking is good for people's health, as in this 1946 ad boasting of Camel's popularity among physicians.

GLOSSARY

sedative
drug that exerts a calming effect

hypnotic
drug that exerts a sleep-inducing effect

stimulant
drug that increases activity in the central nervous system, including heart rate, respiration, and blood pressure

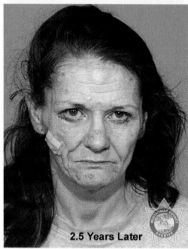

2.5 Years Later

The photo of 42-year-old Theresa Baxter on the top was taken before she became a methamphetamine addict. The photo on the bottom was taken 2 ½ years later, after she was arrested for fraud and identity theft to support her addiction.

GLOSSARY

narcotic
drug that relieves pain and induces sleep

hallucinogenic
causing dramatic alterations of perception, mood, and thought

is attributable to the intense euphoria it generates and its relative affordability. But the "high" is short-lived and followed by unpleasant feelings, which can lead to consuming cocaine whenever available to regain the high (Gottheil & Weinstein, 1983).

Amphetamines illustrate how different patterns of use can produce different subjective effects. The first pattern involves occasional use of small doses of oral amphetamines to postpone fatigue, elevate mood while performing an unpleasant task, cram for a test, or experience well-being. In the second pattern, users obtain amphetamines from a doctor, but use them on a regular basis for euphoria-producing effects rather than for the prescribed purpose. The third pattern is associated with street users—"speed freaks"—who inject large doses of amphetamines intravenously to achieve the "rush" of pleasure immediately following the injection. These users are likely to be restless, talkative, and excited and to inject amphetamines repeatedly to prolong euphoria.

In recent years, *methamphetamine,* a drug closely related chemically to amphetamines, has emerged as a widely used drug of abuse. As many as 1 in 20 high school students report having used methamphetamine (Johnston et al., 2008). In its crystalline and highly addictive form, it's known as *crystal meth* or simply "meth." Users experience intense exhilaration when they smoke it, followed by a feeling of euphoria that can last 12 to 16 hours. Crystal meth is stronger than amphetamines, generally has a higher purity level, and carries a high risk of overdose and dependence.

The Opiate Narcotic Drugs: Heroin, Morphine, and Codeine. The opiate drugs heroin, morphine, and codeine are derived from the opium poppy, a plant found in abundance in Asia. Morphine is the major ingredient in opium. The action of heroin is virtually identical to that of morphine, but heroin is about three times as powerful and now accounts for 90 percent of opiate abuse. The opiates often are called **narcotics** because they relieve pain and induce sleep.

At first glance, heroin's psychological effects might appear mostly pleasurable. Users often experience a sense of the euphoria that opiate users may experience. But the pleasurable effects of heroin are limited to the 3 or 4 hours that the usual dose lasts. If people addicted to heroin don't take another dose within 4 to 6 hours, they experience *heroin withdrawal syndrome,* with symptoms like abdominal cramps, vomiting, craving for the drug, yawning, runny nose, sweating, and chills. With continued heroin use, the drug's euphoric effect gradually diminishes. The addict may continue using heroin as much to avoid withdrawal symptoms as to experience the intense high of the first few injections (Hutcheson, Everitt, Robbins, et al., 2001; Julien, 2004).

The Psychedelic Drugs: Marijuana, LSD, and Ecstasy. Scientists describe such drugs as LSD, mescaline, PCP, and ecstasy as **hallucinogenic,** or *psychedelic,* because their primary effects are dramatic alterations in perception, mood, and thought. Because the effects of marijuana aren't as "mind bending" as those of LSD, some researchers don't classify marijuana as a hallucinogen. In contrast, other researchers describe it as a "mild hallucinogen." Interestingly, marijuana may also have sedative or hypnotic qualities.

Known in popular culture as pot, grass, herb, Mary Jane, 420, and weed, marijuana comes from the leaves and flowering part of the hemp plant (*Cannabis sativa*). The subjective effects of marijuana are produced by its primary ingredient, THC (delta-9-tetrahydrocannabinol). People experience a "high" feeling within a few minutes, which peaks within a half hour. Hashish, manufactured from the buds and flowers of female plants, contains much greater concentrations of THC than does marijuana and is more potent.

Whether marijuana is smoked or, less frequently, eaten or consumed in tea, users report short-term effects, including a sense of time slowing down, enhanced sensations of touch, increased appreciation for sounds, hunger ("the munchies"), feelings of well-being, and a tendency to giggle and laugh. Later, they may become quiet, introspective, and sleepy. At higher doses, users may experience disturbances in short-term memory, exaggerated emotions, and an altered sense of self. The intoxicating effects of marijuana can last for 2 or 3 hours.

Scientists have debated the long-term psychological and physical effects of marijuana. Mounting evidence suggests that marijuana use may trigger schizophrenia, a serious disorder of thinking we'll encounter in Chapter 13, among young adults who have either a personal or family history of the disorder (Degenhardt & Hall, 2006). In addition, some researchers have argued that marijuana is a "gateway" drug that predisposes users to try more serious drugs, like heroin and cocaine (Kandel, Yamaguchi, & Chen, 1992). In a study of identical twin pairs in which one twin tried marijuana in adolescence but the other didn't, the twin who tried marijuana was later at heightened risk for abusing alcohol and other drugs (Lynskey et al., 2003). Nevertheless, evaluating whether marijuana is a gateway drug isn't easy. Merely because one event precedes another doesn't mean it causes it (see Chapter 8).

In 1938, Swiss chemist Albert Hofman synthesized a chemical compound, d-lysergic acid diethylamide-25 (LSD), from chemicals found in a fungus that grows on rye. The psychedelic effects of LSD may stem from its interference with the action of the neurotransmitter serotonin (see Chapter 3) at the synapse. The effects of LSD are also associated with areas of the brain rich in receptors for the neurotransmitter dopamine. Some users report astonishingly clear thoughts and fascinating changes in sensations and perceptions, including synesthesia (the blending of senses—for example, the "smelling of noises"; see Chapter 4). Some users also report mystical experiences (Pahnke, Kurland, Unger, et al., 1970). But LSD and other hallucinogens can also produce panic, paranoid delusions, confusion, depression, and bodily discomfort. Occasionally, psychotic reactions persist long after a psychedelic experience, most often in people with a history of psychological problems (Abraham & Aldridge, 1993). *Flashbacks*—recurrences of a psychedelic experience—occur occasionally. Curiously, there's no known pharmacological basis for their occurrence. One explanation is that they're triggered by something in the environment or an emotional state associated with a past psychedelic experience.

Unlike LSD, Ecstasy has both stimulant and hallucinogenic properties. It produces cascades of the neurotransmitter serotonin in the brain, which increases self-confidence and well-being and produces powerful feelings of empathy for others. But its use has a serious downside: Its side effects can include high blood pressure, depression, nausea, blurred vision, liver problems, and possibly memory loss and damage to neurons that use serotonin (Kish, 2002; Soar, Parrott, & Fox, 2004).

The ground-up leaves of the hemp plant are the source of marijuana.

All-night dance parties termed *raves,* in which Ecstasy and other psychedelic drugs are widely available, became popular in the mid-1990s in the United States.

STRATEGIES FOR POSITIVE CHANGE

Why do we have difficulty changing our lifestyles, even when we know that bad habits can endanger our health?

- **Personal Inertia.** One reason is that it's difficult to overcome personal inertia—to try something new. Many self-destructive habits relieve stress and don't create an imminent health threat, so it's easy for us to "let things be." Eating a heaping portion of ice cream doesn't seem terribly dangerous when we view heart disease as a distant and uncertain catastrophe.

- **Misestimating Risk.** Another reason we maintain the status quo is that we underestimate certain risks to our health and overestimate others. For example, which causes more deaths each year, all types of accidents or strokes? The answer is strokes, but we usually overestimate the frequency of fatal accidents because of the availability heuristic (see Chapter 2). Because the news media provide far more coverage of dramatic accidents than stroke, we overestimate the probability of accidents and underestimate the probability of many diseases.

- **Feeling Powerless.** Still others of us feel powerless to change, perhaps because our habits are so deeply ingrained. Consider a person who has smoked a pack of cigarettes a day for 15 years. She's inhaled cigarette smoke more than a million times. It's no wonder if she feels helpless to change her habits.

Diet crazes, like the *grapefruit diet,* come into and go out of fashion. Because the reported success of most fad diets comes from personal anecdotes rather than from scientific research, we should be skeptical of them.

Despite its popularity, the DARE program isn't effective for preventing substance abuse or enhancing self-esteem.

Despite these challenges, there are a variety of research-supported strategies that can help people implement healthy changes. One of the most compelling ways to eliminate unhealthy behaviors is to educate ourselves about the risks associated with those behaviors. Also, one of the behind-the-scene consequences of stress is that it increases our tendency to engage in unhealthy behaviors, so managing life stress is important. Identifying and avoiding situations that elicit an urge to engage in a problematic behavior such as smoking, overeating, or drinking to excess is also important. For example, recreational drug users often find that visiting particular locations in which they've engaged in drug use in the past can re-activate cravings.

Some of the best things we can do for ourselves are to follow doctors' advice and to avoid trendy "cures" such as the grapefruit diet or subliminal smoking cessation tapes (see Chapter 4) that advertise dramatic results but don't have any demonstrated long-term benefits. Social support for exercising, moderating eating or drinking habits, or quitting smoking also can go a long way toward helping us to change.

Because modifying such well-ingrained behaviors can be so difficult, we're best off not developing them in the first place. Prevention efforts should begin by adolescence, if not earlier, because the earlier in life we develop unhealthy habits, the more likely they'll create problems, like alcohol abuse, for us later in life (Hingson, Heeren, & Winter, 2006). Particularly important is educating young people about the benefits of healthy living and stress management, as well as the risks and negative consequences of unhealthy behavior and the benefits of positive health behaviors. Exposing young people to positive role models can also be extremely influential.

But not all prevention efforts are successful. The Drug Abuse Resistance Education, or DARE, program, used in schools nationwide, attempts to convince students to stay "clean" by providing information about the potentially catastrophic effects of getting into drugs, gangs, and violent activities (Ringwalt & Greene, 1993). Programs that focus on coping skills and managing stress generally show better treatment and prevention outcomes than those attempting to scare people into avoiding negative behaviors (MacKillop, Lisman, Weinstein, et al., 2003). These findings remind us that we need to evaluate programs carefully before they're widely promoted based on their intuitive appeal alone.

HEALTH PSYCHOLOGY AND BEHAVIORAL MEDICINE

Health psychologists use a variety of educational and behavioral interventions to promote and maintain health, and assist people in coping with serious illnesses.

Health psychology, also called *behavioral medicine,* is a rapidly growing field that's contributed to our understanding of the influences of stress and biological, social, and behavioral factors on physical disorders and their treatment. Health psychologists integrate behavioral sciences with the practice of medicine. They also combine educational, research, and psychological interventions to promote and maintain health and prevent and treat illness (Gatchel & Baum, 1983; Leventhal, Weinman, Leventhal & Phillips, 2006; Matarazzo, 1980). Health psychologists are employed in hospitals, rehabilitation centers, medical schools, industry, government agencies, and academic and research settings. Interventions developed within health psychology include teaching patients stress management skills and pain reduction techniques and helping them to mobilize social support, comply with medical regimens, and pursue healthy lifestyles. With the number of elderly citizens increasing each year, we can anticipate that the need for health psychologists who treat chronic conditions such as arthritis, CHD, cancer, and Alzheimer's disease will increase rapidly in coming years.

GLOSSARY

health psychology
field of psychology that integrates the behavioral sciences with the practice of medicine

ALTERNATIVE AND COMPLEMENTARY MEDICINE

Americans shell out more than $22 billion each year for herbal treatments of uncertain effectiveness (Gupta, 2007; Walach & Kirsch, 2003). Yet many herbal and natural preparations that some once viewed as promising have generally proved to be no more effective than a placebo (see Chapter 2). For example, negative findings have challenged still-popular beliefs that:

- The herb St. John's-wort can alleviate the symptoms of moderate to severe depression (Davidson et al., 2002).

- An extract from the saw palmetto plant can relieve prostate problems (Kane et al., 2006).

- Shark cartilage can cure some cancers (Loprinzi et al., 2005).

These are all examples of alternative and complementary medicine. **Alternative medicine** refers to health care practices and products used *in place of* conventional medicine. **Complementary medicine,** in contrast, refers to products and practices that are used *along with* conventional medicine (National Center for Complementary and Alternative Medicine, 2002). Although many of these alternative and complementary approaches can be harmless, many others are potentially dangerous. **[LEARNING OBJECTIVE 10.9]**

The U.S. Food and Drug Administration (FDA) carefully regulates most medicines. But because of federal legislation passed in 1999, it doesn't monitor the safety, purity, or effectiveness of herbs, vitamins, or dietary supplements. So if we go to our local drugstore and purchase a bottle of St. John's-wort or gingko we're gambling with our safety. Some impure herbal preparations contain dangerous amounts of lead and even the poison arsenic (Ernst, 2002). Still other supplements, such as kava (extracted from a shrub and used for anxiety and insomnia), prompted the FDA to issue a warning about liver damage (Saper et al., 2004). Finally, some natural products can interfere with the actions of conventional medicines. For example, St. John's-wort can block the effectiveness of drugs used to combat AIDS and blood clots (Gupta, 2007). Just because something is natural doesn't mean that it's necessarily safe or healthy for us.

Energy Medicine: The Example of Acupuncture.
Energy medicines are based on the idea that disruptions in our body's energy field can be mapped and treated. Chinese physicians first developed and practiced **acupuncture** at least 2,000 years ago. In acupuncture, practitioners insert thin needles into specific points in the body. More than 4 percent of Americans (Barnes, Powell-Griner, McFann, et al., 2004) have consulted acupuncturists. These practitioners place the needles on specific spots called *meridians,* which they believe channel a subtle energy or life force called *qi* (pronounced "chee"). Acupuncturists claim to relieve blockages of qi by applying needles or electrical, laser, or heat stimulation, to one or more of 2,000 points on the body.

Acupuncture by itself can help to relieve nausea following surgical operations and treat pain-related conditions (Berman & Straus, 2004). Still, there's no reason to believe that any of its beneficial effects are due to energy changes (Posner & Sampson, 1999). The acupuncture points were mapped long before the rise of modern science. Even today, scientists haven't been able to measure, much less identify, the energy associated with specific illnesses. As a result, the concept of *qi* isn't falsifiable.

Meditation.
One form of complementary medicine that plays a critical role in many people's stress management is meditation. **Meditation** refers to a variety of practices that train attention and awareness (Shapiro & Walsh, 2003).

Meditative practices are embedded in many world religions and are integrated into the lives of people of all races and creeds. In Western countries, people typically practice meditation to achieve stress reduction, whereas in non-Western countries people typically practice meditation to achieve insight and spiritual growth.

For centuries, meditation fell well outside the scientific mainstream. Yet in the 1960s, scientists began to take a serious look at its possible benefits. Since then, they've identified a wide range of positive effects. These effects include heightened creativity, empathy, alertness,

MYTH: Magnets, such as those embedded in shoe insoles, can reduce pain.

REALITY: Most controlled studies show that magnets are useless in alleviating pain, including foot pain, when compared with fake (placebo) magnets (Winemiller et al., 2003).

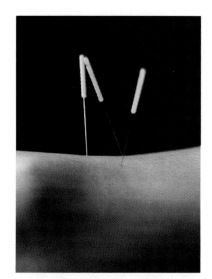

Acupuncture needles are thin and can be inserted virtually any place on the skin of the body.

GLOSSARY

alternative medicine
health care practices and products used in place of conventional medicine

FALSIFIABILITY
Can the claim be disproved?

complementary medicine
health care practices and products used along with conventional medicine

acupuncture
ancient Chinese practice of inserting thin needles into more than 2,000 points in the body to alter energy forces believed to run through the body

meditation
set of ritualized practices that train attention and awareness

These meditators are focusing on their breathing.

Since the late 1700s, physicians have known that digitalis, a drug that comes from the purple foxglove plant (*top*), can control heart rate and treat heart disease. More recently, taxol (*bottom*), which comes from the Pacific yew tree, was identified as an anticancer drug. Some, but by no means all, natural plants are effective medicines.

and self-esteem (Haimerl & Valentine, 2001; So & Orme-Johnson, 2001), along with decreases in anxiety, interpersonal problems (Tloczynski & Tantriella, 1998), and recurrences of depression (Segal, Williams, & Teasdale, 2002). Clinicians have added meditative techniques to a variety of psychotherapies and used them with some success in treating pain and numerous medical conditions (Baer, 2003; Kabat-Zinn, 2003). Meditation can also enhance blood flow in the brain (Newberg et al., 2001) and immune function (Davidson et al., 2003).

Many people seem to benefit from meditation, although it's not clear why: Its positive effects may derive from a greater acceptance of our troubling thoughts and feelings (Kabat-Zinn, 2003; Lynn et al., 2006b). They may also derive not from meditation itself but from sitting quietly, resting, and relaxing with eyes closed (Farthing, 1992; Holmes, 1987). People's positive attitudes, beliefs, and expectancies about meditation may also account for why it's beneficial.

Alternative Treatments: To Use or Not to Use, That Is the Question.

Should we conclude that all alternative treatments are worthless? Not at all. It's essential that we keep an open mind and not simply dismiss new and potentially useful treatments out of hand. Many drugs derive from plant and natural products, and many effective medicines surely remain to be discovered. Every year, drug companies screen thousands of natural products for disease-fighting properties, and a few prove worthy of further testing. For example, *taxol,* derived from the Pacific yew tree, has been shown to be effective as an anticancer drug. Although St. John's-wort doesn't appear especially effective for severe depression, it may be somewhat helpful for mild depression (Wallach & Kirsch, 2003). These and other herbal medicines may become part of mainstream treatment if they turn out to be safe and effective.

The same is true of psychological practices. Meditation, once regarded as an alternative approach, now appears to be an effective means of reducing stress and has increasingly blended into the spectrum of conventional approaches.

Barry Beyerstein (1997) recommended that we ask the following two questions before trying an alternative approach:

(1) Does it lack a scientific rationale or contradict well-accepted scientific laws or principles?

(2) Do carefully done studies show that the product or treatment is less effective than conventional approaches?

If the answer to both questions is "yes," we should be especially skeptical. When in doubt, it's wise to consult a physician about an alternative or complementary treatment. Doing so will give us confidence that the treatment we select, regardless of whether it's conventional, is genuinely a "good alternative."

QUIZ

1   Alcohol is primarily a central nervous system depressant.   **TRUE**   **FALSE**

2   Tobacco is the most potent natural stimulant drug.   **TRUE**   **FALSE**

3   The fact that a health product is "natural" means it's likely to be safe.   **TRUE**   **FALSE**

4   The effects of acupuncture appear to be due to the redistribution of energy in the body.   **TRUE**   **FALSE**

Answers: (1) T (p. 359); (2) F (p. 359); (3) F (p. 363); (4) F (p. 363)

PEARSON
mypsych lab

▼ How do you respond to one drink of alcohol? Watch the video titled "Alcoholism" at www.mypsychlab.com to find out.

To Sleep, Perchance
to Dream

One of the most important aspects of our daily lives that contribute to our overall health and daily function is sleep. The average adult needs about 7 to 10 hours of sleep per night, but as many as 60 percent of adults get less than that. Sleep deprivation is associated with a variety of adverse health outcomes: weight gain (we burn off a lot of calories just by sleeping); increased risk for high blood pressure, diabetes, and heart problems; and a less vigorous immune response (Dement & Vaughan, 1999; Motivala & Irwin, 2007). What function does sleep serve, and how does it work?

Although it is clear that sleep is of central importance to our health and daily functioning, why we sleep is not well understood. Some theories suggest that sleep plays a critical role in memory consolidation (see Chapter 6), others suggest that it's critical for neural development and neural connectivity more generally (see Chapter 3). Some evolutionary theories have proposed that sleep contributes to our survival by taking us out of circulation at times when we might be most vulnerable to unseen predators. But of course, this doesn't explain why we feel the need to "catch up" on lost sleep if we got less than our usual hours of zzz's the night before or why sleep deprivation can lead to slower reaction times in situations that require quick thinking (such as driving in traffic). We may not know much about why we sleep, but researchers now know an awful lot about how sleep works.

THE CIRCADIAN RHYTHM: THE CYCLE OF EVERYDAY LIFE

Long before scientists began to probe the secrets of sleep in the laboratory, primitive hunters were keenly aware of daily cycles of sleep and wakefulness. The circadian rhythm controls our feelings of sleepiness and drowsiness. **Circadian rhythm** is a fancy term (it's Latin for "around a day") for changes that occur on a roughly 24-hour basis in many of our biological processes, including hormone release, brain waves, body temperature, and drowsiness. Popularly known as the brain's **biological clock,** the meager 20,000 neurons located in the *suprachiasmatic nucleus* (SCN) in the hypothalamus (see Chapter 3) make us feel drowsy at different times of the day and night. Many of us have noticed that we feel like taking a nap at around 3 or 4 in the afternoon. Indeed, in many European and Latin American countries, a midafternoon nap (a "siesta" in Spanish) is part of the daily ritual. This sense of fatigue is triggered by our biological clocks. The urge to snooze comes over us at night as well because levels of the hormone *melatonin,* which triggers feelings of sleepiness, increase after dark.

Although we need an average of 7 to 10 hours of sleep per night, the amount of sleep we require varies with age. Newborns are gluttons for sleep and need about 16 hours over the course of a day. College students may need as many as 9 hours of sleep a night to be fully alert the next day. The elderly seem to require less sleep.

Ordinarily, there don't seem to be many negative consequences of losing one night's sleep other than feeling edgy, irritable, and unable to concentrate well the next day. Yet after a few nights of sleep deprivation, we feel more "out of it" and begin to accumulate a balance of "sleep debt." If we don't settle that balance, sleep deprivation

Sleep deprivation can lead to extreme fatigue the next day. Most college students need 9 hours of sleep to be fully alert the next day but typically only get an average of 6 hours.

GLOSSARY

circadian rhythm
cyclical changes that occur on a roughly 24-hour basis in many biological processes

biological clock
term for the suprachiasmatic nucleus (SCN) in the hypothalamus that's responsible for controlling our levels of alertness

Jet lag, which can create sleep problems, occurs when travelers cross time zones.

will catch up with us. People deprived of multiple nights of sleep often experience depression and difficulties in learning new information. After more than 4 days of severe sleep deprivation, we may even experience brief hallucinations, such as hearing voices or seeing things (Wolfe & Pruitt, 2003).

If you've ever taken a long flight across time zones, you'll be no stranger to *jet lag,* the result of a disruption of our body's circadian rhythms. Our biological clocks can also be disrupted when we work late shifts, which can result in sleeping problems, including drowsiness during work and insomnia when we try to fall asleep. Numerous famous catastrophes, including airplane crashes, have probably resulted largely from sleep deprivation.

STAGES OF SLEEP AND DREAMING

Sixty years ago, most people believed there was something like a switch in our brains that turned consciousness on when we were awake and off when we were asleep. But one night in 1951 in Nathaniel Kleitman's sleep laboratory at the University of Chicago, Eugene Aserinsky, Kleitman's graduate student, monitored his son Armond's eye movements and brain waves while he slept. Aserinsky was astonished to observe that Armond's eyes danced periodically back and forth under his closed lids. Whenever the eye movements occurred, Armond's brain pulsed with electrical activity, as measured by an electroencephalogram (EEG; see Chapter 3), much as it did when Armond was awake (Aserinsky, 1996).

The fledgling scientist had the good sense to know that he was onto something of immense importance. The slumbering brain wasn't an inert tangle of neurons; rather, it was abuzz with activity, at least at various intervals. Aserinsky further suspected that Armond's eye movements signaled episodes of dreaming. Aserinsky and Kleitman (1953) confirmed this hunch when they awakened subjects while they were displaying **rapid**

Electrical recording devices make it possible to study the relations among brain activity, eye movements, and physical relaxation.

eye movements (REM). In almost all cases, these subjects reported vivid dreams. In contrast, subjects were much less likely to report experiencing vivid dreams when researchers awakened them from **non-REM (NREM) sleep,** although later research showed that vivid dreams sometimes happened during NREM sleep too.

Kleitman and William Dement (Dement & Kleitman, 1957) went on to discover that during sleep we pass through five distinct stages. Using all-night recording devices, they found that we travel through repeated cycles of these five stages every night. Each cycle lasts about 90 minutes, and each stage of sleep is clearly distinguishable from awake states, as shown in **Figure 10.5.** **[LEARNING OBJECTIVE 10.10]**

Stage 1 Sleep. Has someone ever nudged you to wake up, and you weren't even sure whether you were awake or asleep? If so, you were probably in stage 1 sleep. In this light stage of sleep, which lasts for 5 to 10 minutes, our brain activity powers down by 50 percent or more, producing waves occurring 4 to 7 times per second known as *theta* waves. These waves are slower than the *beta* waves of 13 or more times per second produced during active alert states, and the *alpha* waves of 8 to 12 times per second when we're quiet and relaxed.

Stage 2 Sleep. In stage 2 sleep, our brain waves slow down even more. Sudden intense bursts of electrical activity called *sleep spindles* of about 12 to 14 cycles a second, and occasional sudden sharply rising and falling waves known as *K-complexes,* first appear in the EEG (Aldrich, 1999). K-complexes appear only when we're asleep. As our brain activity decelerates, our heart rate slows, our body temperature decreases, our muscles relax even

GLOSSARY

rapid eye movements (REM)
darting of the eyes underneath the closed eyelids during sleep

non-REM (NREM) sleep
stages 1 through 4 of the sleep cycle, during which eye movements do not occur and dreaming is less frequent and vivid

more, and our eye movements cease. We spend as much as 65 percent of our sleep in stage 2.

Stages 3 and 4 Sleep. After about 10 to 30 minutes, light sleep gives way to much deeper slow-wave sleep, in which we can observe *delta waves,* which are as slow as one to two cycles a second, in the EEG. In stage 3, delta waves appear 20 to 50 percent of the time, and in stage 4, they appear more than half the time. To feel fully rested in the morning, we need to experience these deeper stages of sleep throughout the night. Children are famously good sleepers because they spend as much as 40 percent of their sleep time in deep sleep, when they may appear "dead to the world" and are difficult to awaken. In contrast, adults spend only about one-quarter of their sleep "sleeping like a baby," in deep sleep.

Stage 5: Paradoxical or REM Sleep. After 15 to 30 minutes, we return to stage 2 before our brains shift dramatically into high gear, with wakelike high-frequency, low-amplitude waves. We've entered stage 5, known commonly as *paradoxical* or **REM sleep.** It's called paradoxical sleep because the brain is active at the same time that the body is inactive. As we've seen, it's during this stage that most vivid dreaming occurs.

Our hyped brain waves during REM sleep are accompanied by increased heart rate and blood pressure and rapid and irregular breathing, a state that occupies about 20 to 25 percent of our night's sleep. After 10 to 20 minutes of REM sleep, the cycle starts up again, as we glide back to the early stages of sleep and then back into deeper sleep. The amount of time spent in REM sleep increases with each cycle. By the morning, we may spend as much as an hour in REM sleep, compared with the 10 to 20 minutes we spend in REM after falling asleep. Each night, we circle back to REM sleep five or six times.

REM sleep is biologically important, probably even essential. Depriving rats of REM sleep typically leads to their death within a few weeks (National Institute on Alcohol Abuse and Alcoholism, 1998), although rats die even sooner from total sleep deprivation (Rechtschaffen, 1998). When we humans are deprived of REM for a few nights, we experience a phenomenon known as *REM rebound:* The amount and intensity of REM sleep increase, suggesting that REM serves a critical biological function (Ocampo-Garces, Molina, Rodriguez, et al., 2000). Many of us have observed REM rebound in our night lives when we haven't slept much for a few nights in a row. When we finally get a good night's sleep, we often experience much more intense dreams, even nightmares, reflecting a powerful bounce-back of REM sleep. Yet scientists are still debating the biological functions of REM sleep.

THEORIES AND PSYCHOLOGY OF DREAMS

We can trace the quest to decipher the meaning of dreams to thousands of years ago. The Babylonians believed that dreams were sent by the gods, the Assyrians thought that dreams contained signs or omens, the Greeks built dream temples in which visitors awaited prophecies sent by the gods during dreams, and North American Indians believed that dreams revealed hidden wishes and desires (Van de Castle, 1994).

Freud and Wish Fulfillment: The Dream Protection Theory.
Sigmund Freud sided with the Native Americans. His landmark book, *The Interpretation of Dreams* (1900), shaped how people thought of dreams for decades before rigorous laboratory research. According to Freud, dreams are the guardians or protectors of sleep. During sleep, the ego (see

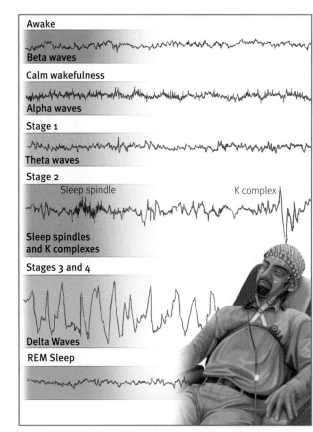

Figure 10.5 The Stages of Sleep. The EEG allows scientists to distinguish among the major stages of sleep, along with two levels of wakefulness. As we can see, brain activity during REM sleep is similar to that when we're awake and alert, because our brains during REM are typically engaged in vivid dreaming.

Fict-OID

MYTH: Dreams occur in only a few seconds, although they take much longer to recount later.

REALITY: This belief, held by Sigmund Freud and others, is wrong. In fact, our later REM periods toward the early morning typically last for half an hour or more. So if it seems as if one of your dreams has lasted for 45 minutes, that's often because it has.

GLOSSARY

REM sleep
stage of sleep during which the brain is most active and during which vivid dreaming most often occurs

Chapter 12), which acts as a sort of mental censor, is less able than when awake to keep sexual and aggressive instincts at bay by repressing them. If not for dreams, these instincts would bubble up, disturbing sleep. The *dream-work* disguises and contains the pesky sexual and aggressive impulses by transforming them into symbols that represent *wish fulfillment*—how we wish things could be (see also Chapter 12). **[LEARNING OBJECTIVE 10.11]**

According to Freud, dreams don't give up their secrets easily—they require interpretation to reverse the dream-work and reveal their true meaning. He distinguished between the details of the dream itself, which he called the *manifest content,* and the true, hidden meaning, which he called the *latent content*. For example, a dream about getting a flat tire (manifest content) might signify anxiety about the loss of status at your job (latent content).

Most scientists have rejected the dream protection and wish fulfillment theories of dreams (Domhoff, 2001a). If, as Freud claimed, "wish fulfillment is the meaning of each and every dream" (Freud, 1900, p. 106), we'd expect dream content to be mostly positive. Yet although most of us have occasional dreams of flying, winning the lottery, or being with the object of our wildest fantasies, these themes are less frequent than dreams of misfortune. In addition, many dreams don't appear to be disguised, as Freud contended. As many as 90 percent of dream reports are straightforward descriptions of everyday activities and problems (see **Table 10.4**) (Domhoff, 2003; Dorus, Dorus, & Rechtschaffen, 1971).

Activation–Synthesis Theory.

Starting in the 1960s and 1970s, Alan Hobson and Robert McCarley developed a theory that links dreams to brain activity. According to their **activation–synthesis theory** (Hobson & McCarley, 1977; Hobson, Pace-Schott, & Stickgold, 2000), dreams reflect brain activation in sleep, rather than a repressed unconscious wish, as Freud claimed. Far from having deep, universal meaning, Hobson and McCarley maintained that dreams reflect the activated brain's attempt to make sense of random and internally generated neural signals during REM sleep.

Throughout the day and night, the balance of neurotransmitters in the brain shifts continually. REM is turned on by surges of the neurotransmitter acetylcholine. Acetylcholine activates nerve cells in the pons, located at the base of the brain (see Chapter 3). The activated pons sends incomplete signals to the lateral geniculate nucleus of the thalamus, a relay for sensory information to the language and visual areas of the cortex, as shown in **Figure 10.6** (see Chapter 3). The cortex does its best to piece together the signals it receives into a meaningful story. Nevertheless, the bits of information it receives are random and chaotic, so the narrative is rarely coherent or logical. The amygdala is also ramped up, adding the emotional colors of fear, anxiety, anger, sadness, and elation to the mix (see Chapters 3 and 9). According to activation–synthesis theory, the net result of these complex brain changes is what we experience as a dream.

Neurocognitive Perspectives on Dreaming: Information Processing and Development.

Scientists who've advanced a *neurocognitive* view of dreaming argue that explaining dreams only in terms of neurotransmitters and random neural impulses doesn't tell the full story. Instead, they contend, we must also consider our cognitive capacities, which shape what we dream about. For example, children under the age of 7 or 8 recall dreaming on only 20 to 30 percent of occasions when awakened from REM sleep compared with 80 to 90 percent of adults (Foulkes, 1982, 1999). Until they reach the age of 9 or 10, children's dreams tend to be simple, lacking in movement, and less emotional and bizarre than adult dreams (Domhoff, 1996). According to the neurocognitive perspective, complex dreams are "cognitive achievements" that parallel the gradual development of visual imagination and other advanced cognitive abilities. We begin to dream like adults when our brains develop the "wiring" to do so (Domhoff, 2001b).

Content analyses of tens of thousands of dreams (Hall & Van de Castle, 1966) reveal that many are associated with emotional concerns and everyday preoccupations, and that dream content is surprisingly stable over long time periods (Domhoff, 1996; Hall &

FALSIFIABILITY
Can the claim be disproved?

Table 10.4 Most Frequent Dream Themes.

(1) Being chased or pursued
(2) Being lost, late, or trapped
(3) Falling
(4) Flying
(5) Losing valuable possessions
(6) Sexual dreams
(7) Experiencing great natural beauty
(8) Being naked or dressed oddly
(9) Injury or illness
(*Source:* Domhoff, 2003)

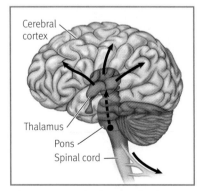

Figure 10.6 Activation–Synthesis Theory. According to activation–synthesis theory, the pons transmits random signals to the thalamus, which relays information to the cerebral cortex. The cortex in turn attempts to create a story from the incomplete information it receives.

Nordby, 1972; Smith & Hall, 1964). Whether we're researchers in Timbuktu or New York City, we'll find cross-culturally consistent patterns in dreaming. Virtually all of us experience dreams that contain more aggression than friendliness, more negative than positive emotions, and more misfortune than good fortune. The dreams of older adults resemble those of college students, but with age, negative emotions and physical aggression may decrease (Hall & Domhoff, 1963; Lortie-Lussier, Cote, & Vachon, 2000). Women's dreams are likely to contain more emotion than men's dreams, and their dream characters are about evenly divided between men and women. In contrast, men are more likely to dream about men by a 2:1 ratio (Hall, 1984). At least a few differences in dreams depend on cultural factors. For example, the dreams of people in more technologically advanced societies feature fewer animals than those in small, traditional societies (Domhoff, 1996, 2001). The bottom line? Although dreams are sometimes bizarre, they're more consistent over time than we'd expect if they reflected only random neural impulses generated by the brain stem (Domhoff, 2001b; Foulkes, 1985; Revonsuo, 2000; Strauch & Meier, 1996).

What's the Function of Dreams? Scientists still don't know for sure why we dream. But evidence from a variety of sources suggests that dreams are involved in (a) processing emotional memories (Maquet & Franck, 1997); (b) integrating new experiences with established memories to make sense of the world (Stickgold, James, & Hobson, 2002); (c) learning new strategies and ways of doing things, like swinging a golf club (Walker, Brakefield, Morgan et al., 2002); (d) simulating threatening events so we can better cope with them in everyday life (Revonsuo, 2000); and (e) reorganizing and consolidating memories (Capellini, McNamara, Preston et al., 2009; Crick & Mitchison, 1986). Still, the function of dreams remains a puzzle because research evidence concerning the role of learning and memory in dreams is controversial and mixed.

DISORDERS OF SLEEP

Nearly all of us have trouble falling asleep or staying asleep from time to time. When sleep problems recur, interfere with our ability to function at work or school, or affect our health, they can exact a dear price. The cost of sleep disorders in terms of health and lost work productivity amounts to as much as $35 billion per year (Althius, Fredman, Langenberg et al., 1998). We can also gauge the cost in human lives, with an estimated 1,500 Americans who fall asleep at the wheel killed each year (Fenton, 2007). These grim statistics are understandable given that 30 to 50 percent of people report some sort of sleep problem (Althius et al., 1998).

Insomnia. The most common sleep disturbance is **insomnia.** Insomnia can take the following forms: (a) having trouble falling asleep (regularly taking more than 30 minutes to doze off), (b) waking too early in the morning, and (c) waking up during the night and having trouble returning to sleep. An estimated 15 percent of people report severe or longstanding problems with insomnia (Ancoli-Israel & Roth, 1999; Hauri, 1998).

People who suffer from depression, pain, or a variety of medical conditions report especially high rates of insomnia (Ford & Kamerow, 1989; Katz & McHorney, 2002; Smith & Haythornthwaite, 2004). Brief bouts of insomnia are often due to stress and relationship problems, medications and illness, working late or variable shifts, jet lag, drinking caffeine, and napping during the day. **[LEARNING OBJECTIVE 10.12]** Insomnia can become recurrent if we become frustrated and anxious when we can't fall asleep right away. Many people don't know that even most "good sleepers" take 15 to 20 minutes to fall asleep. James Maas (1999) recommends hiding clocks to avoid becoming preoccupied with the inability to fall asleep quickly. **Table 10.5** displays some additional tips to combat insomnia.

Table 10.5 How to Get a Good Night's Sleep.

(1)	Don't do anything stressful and relax as much as possible before bedtime.
(2)	Sleep and wake up at regular times.
(3)	Sleep in a cool room.
(4)	Avoid consuming caffeine (especially after 2 P.M.), taking naps longer than 20 minutes, or watching television and surfing the web right before bedtime.
(5)	Try to sleep only when you're tired.
(6)	Get out of bed if you're having a hard time sleeping and go back to bed when you're tired so that your bed becomes a classically conditioned stimulus (see Chapter 5) for sleep.

GLOSSARY

activation–synthesis theory
theory that dreams reflect inputs from brain activation originating in the pons, which the cortex then attempts to weave into a story

insomnia
difficulty falling or staying asleep

Short-term psychotherapy can effectively treat most cases of general insomnia (Morin et al., 1999). Another common approach to treating insomnia is sleeping pills. Although sleeping pills can be effective, researchers have discovered that brief psychotherapy is more effective than Ambien, a popular sleeping pill (Jacobs, Pace-Schott, Stickgold, et al., 2004). Moreover, longstanding use of many sleeping pills can make it more difficult to sleep once people stop taking them, a phenomenon called *rebound insomnia*. When people try sleeping pills, they should use them for short periods of time and with caution, as there's a risk of dependency.

WHAT DO *you* THINK?

Your senior thesis defense is in 2 days but you are battling insomnia. What research-supported steps can you take to ensure that you are well rested and able to perform at your best on the day of your defense?

Narcolepsy. **Narcolepsy** can appear as almost the opposite of insomnia. In narcolepsy, the most prominent symptom is the rapid and often unexpected onset of sleep. People with narcolepsy can experience episodes of sudden sleep lasting anywhere from a few seconds to several minutes and, less frequently, as long as an hour. The overwhelming urge to sleep can strike at any moment. Surprise, elation, or other strong emotions—even those associated with laughing at a joke or engaging in sexual intercourse—can lead people with narcolepsy to experience *cataplexy*, a complete loss of muscle tone. During cataplexy, people can fall because their muscles become limp as a rag doll. Cataplexy occurs in healthy people during REM sleep. But, in narcolepsy, people experiencing cataplexy remain alert the whole time, even though they can't move. Ordinarily, sleepers don't enter REM sleep for more than an hour after they fall asleep. But when people who experience an episode of narcolepsy doze off, they plummet into REM sleep immediately, suggesting that it results from a sleep–wake cycle that's badly off-kilter. Fortunately, people with narcolepsy can be helped by taking short naps, taking antidepressant and stimulant medication, and avoiding alcohol and caffeine.

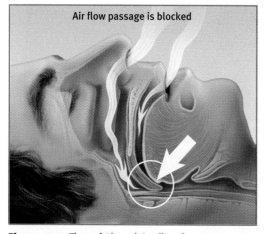

Figure 10.7 Flow of Air and Quality of Sleep. When the flow of air is blocked, as in sleep apnea, the quality of sleep can be seriously disrupted.

Sleep Apnea. Being tired during the day and falling asleep during class or on the job is rarely due to narcolepsy. Many more people with these problems suffer from **sleep apnea**, which afflicts between 2 and 20 percent of the general population, depending on how broadly or narrowly it's defined (Shamsuzzaman, Gersh, & Somers, 2003; Strohl & Redline, 1996). Apnea is caused by a blockage of the airway during sleep, as shown in **Figure 10.7.** This problem causes people with apnea to snore loudly, gasp, and sometimes stop breathing for more than 20 seconds. Struggling to breathe rouses the person many times—often several hundred times—during the night and interferes with sleep, causing fatigue the next day. Yet most people with sleep apnea have no awareness of these multiple awakenings. A lack of oxygen and the buildup of carbon dioxide can lead to many problems, including night sweats, weight gain, fatigue, and an irregular heartbeat. Because apnea is associated with being overweight, doctors typically recommend weight loss as a first option. Many people benefit from wearing a face mask attached to a machine that blows air into their nasal passages, forcing the

GLOSSARY

narcolepsy
disorder characterized by the rapid and often unexpected onset of sleep

sleep apnea
disorder caused by a blockage of the airway during sleep, resulting in daytime fatigue

airway to remain open. Nevertheless, adjusting to this machine can be challenging (Wolfe & Pruitt, 2003).

Night Terrors.
Night terrors are often more disturbing to onlookers than to sleepers. Parents who witness a child's night terrors can hardly believe that the child has no recollection of what occurred. Screaming, perspiring, confused, and wide-eyed, the child may even thrash about before falling back into a deep sleep. Such episodes usually last for only a few minutes. Despite their dramatic nature, **night terrors** are typically harmless events that take place during deep non-REM sleep (stages 3 and 4). They occur almost exclusively in children, who spend more time than adults in deep stages of sleep (Wolfe & Pruitt, 2003). Night terrors are often confused with nightmares, which typically occur only during REM sleep (American Psychiatric Association, 2000). Parents often learn not to overreact and even to ignore the episodes if the child isn't in physical danger. Night terrors occasionally occur in adults, especially when they're under intense stress.

Sleepwalking.
The popular image of a "somnambulist," or sleepwalker, is a person with eyes closed, arms outstretched, and both hands at shoulder height, walking like a zombie. In actuality, a sleepwalking person often acts like any fully awake person, although a sleepwalker may be somewhat clumsier. **Sleepwalking** (walking while fully asleep) often involves relatively little activity, but sleepwalkers have been known to drive cars, turn on computers, or fire guns.

For most people, sleepwalking is harmless, and sleepwalkers rarely remember their actions on awakening. But for children and adults who engage in potentially dangerous activities (such as climbing out an open window) while sleepwalking, doors and windows can be wired with alarms to alert others to direct them back to bed. If someone is sleepwalking, it's perfectly safe to wake him or her up, despite what we may have seen in movies (Wolfe & Pruitt, 2003).

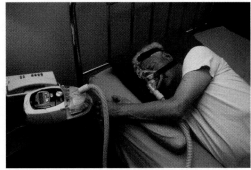
Person using a device to combat sleep apnea at home.

Fact-OID We can fall asleep with our eyes open. In a 1960 study, an investigator taped the eyes of three volunteers—one of them severely sleep-deprived—wide open while flashing bright lights at them, blasting loud music into their ears, and administering periodic electric shocks to their legs. They fell sound asleep within 12 minutes (Boese, 2007).

GLOSSARY

night terrors
sudden waking episodes characterized by screaming, perspiring, and confusion followed by a return to a deep sleep

sleepwalking
walking while fully asleep

QUIZ

1 People move slowly through the first four stages of sleep but then spend the rest of the night in REM sleep. TRUE FALSE

2 When we dream, our brains are much less active than when awake TRUE FALSE

3 Activation-synthesis theory proposes that dreams result from incomplete neural signals being generated by the pons. TRUE FALSE

4 Night terrors are different from nightmares. TRUE FALSE

Answers: (1) F (pp. 366–367); (2) F (p. 367); (3) T (p. 368); (4) T (p. 371)

PEARSON mypsychlab

▼ Can you control your own dreams? Watch the video titled "Lucid Dreaming" at www.mypsychlab.com to find out.

Your Complete Review System

WHAT IS STRESS? (pp. 341–345)

10.1 Explain how stress is defined and approached in different ways

Stress is a part of daily life. Most people experience one or more extremely stressful events in their lifetime. People experience stress when they feel physically threatened, unsafe, or unable to meet the perceived demands of life. Stress can be viewed as a stimulus, a response, or a transaction with the environment. Stressful events and their consequences are important in studying the response aspects of stress, whereas identifying specific categories of stressful events (unemployment, natural disasters) is the focus of stressors as stimuli view of stress. The stress as a transaction view holds that the experience of stress depends on both primary appraisal (the decision regarding whether the event is harmful) and secondary appraisal (perceptions of our ability to cope with the event) of the potentially stressful event.

1. The tension, discomfort, or physical symptoms that arise when a situation strains our ability to cope is called _____ . (p. 341)

2. Survivors of Hurricane Katrina might be of particular interest to researchers who study stress from which viewpoint? (pp. 341–342)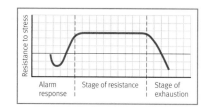

3. People's varied reactions to the same event suggest that we can view stress as a _____ between people and their environments. (p. 342)

4. When we encounter a potentially threatening event, we initially engage in _____ _____ to decide whether the event is harmful. (p. 342)

5. We make a _____ _____ to determine how well we can cope with a harmful event. (p. 342)

6. _____ _____ is a coping strategy people use to tackle life's challenges head-on. (p. 342)

7. When we try to put a positive spin on our feelings or predicaments and engage in behaviors to reduce painful emotions, we are engaging in _____ _____ . (p. 342)

10.2 Identify different approaches to measuring stress

Psychologists often assess life events that require major adaptations and adjustments, such as illness and unemployment. They also assess hassles—annoying, frustrating daily events, which may be more related to adverse psychological and health outcomes than major stressors.

8. The _____ _____ _____ Scale is based on forty-three life events ranked in terms of how stressful participants rated them. (p. 343)

9. How can daily hassles such as traffic, a difficult relationship with a boss, or getting the wrong order at a drive-through restaurant affect our health? (p. 343)

10. The frequency and perceived severity of hassles are (better/worse) predictors of physical health than are major life events. (p. 343)

succeed with mypsychlab

1. Take the Undergraduate Stress Questionnaire and find out how stressed you are.
   How Stressed Are You?

2. How would you react if your instructor announced a pop quiz? Look at how your thoughts affect how you cope with this stressor.
   The Effect of Cognitive Appraisal on Responses to Stressors

HOW WE ADAPT TO STRESS: CHANGE AND CHALLENGE (pp. 345–352)

10.3 Describe Selye's general adaptation syndrome

The GAS consists of three stages: (1) Alarm: The autonomic nervous system is activated; (2) Resistance: Adaptation and coping occurs; (3) Exhaustion: Resources and coping abilities are depleted, which can damage organs and engender depression and posttraumatic stress disorder (PTSD).

11. Identify the brain and body components activated in the alarm reaction of Selye's GAS, depicted here. (p. 345)

12. The _____ response is a set of physiological or psychological reactions that mobilize us to either confront or escape a threatening situation. (pp. 345–346)

13. During the second stage of the GAS, _____, we adapt to the stressor and try to find a way to cope with it. (p. 346)

14. During the _____ stage of the GAS, resources and coping abilities are limited, and stress can damage organs and engender depression and posttraumatic stress disorder. (p. 346)

10.4 Describe the diversity of stress responses, including PTSD, anxiety, and depression

About 5 percent (men) to 10 percent (women) of people experience PTSD in the face of a potentially traumatic stressor. Yet as many as two-thirds of people are resilient in the face of stressors. The longer we feel we lack control over our lives, and the longer we feel helpless or responsible for our failures, the greater the likelihood that our anxiety will transform into depression.

Answers are located at the end of the text.

15. What are the similarities and differences between Shelley Taylor's tend and befriend response and the flight-or-fight response? (p. 346)

16. People with depression are (more/not more) likely than nondepressed people to have experienced one or more events that involve loss, like the death of a loved one. (p. 347)

17. The severity, duration, and nearness to the stressor affect people's likelihood of developing _____ _____ _____. (p. 347)

succeed with mypsychlab

1. Watch your physiological and behavioral responses when stress occurs.
Selye's General Adaptation Syndrome

2. How do you maintain your body after experiencing stress? Listen as two psychologists discuss three important stages of adaptation to stress.
General Adaptation Syndrome

3. Can virtual reality help individuals overcome stress? Watch this video of a firefighter who survived the collapse of the World Trade Center.
9/11 Posttraumatic Stress Disorder

10.5 Describe the relation between stress and physical health

Stress can decrease resistance to illness, delay healing, and impair the immune system. Psychophysiological disorders are influenced by stress and emotional factors. According to the biopsychosocial model, illnesses depend on the interplay of genes, lifestyles, immunity, stress, social support, and self-perceptions.

18. Research has shown that stress (can/can't) decrease resistance to the cold virus. (p. 349)

19. Scientists have learned that psychological factors, including stress and personality traits, are key risk factors for _____ _____ _____. (p. 350)

20. Of all Type A personality traits, _____ appears to be the most predictive of heart disease. (p. 351)

succeed with mypsychlab

Do You Know All of the Terms in This Chapter?
Find out by using the Flashcards. Want more practice? Take additional quizzes, try simulations, and watch video to be sure you are prepared for the test!

COPING WITH STRESS (pp. 352–355)

10.6 Describe the role of social support and different types of control in coping with stress

Social support and the following types of stress control are important: (1) behavioral control (taking action to reduce stress), (2) cognitive control (reappraising stressful events that can't be avoided), (3) decisional control (choosing between alternatives), (4) informational control (acquiring information about a stressor), and (5) emotional control (suppressing and expressing emotions at will).

21. _____ _____ encompasses our relationships with people and groups that provide emotional and financial assistance as we contend with important decisions or stressful situations. (p. 352)

22. What are the benefits of a strong social network when an individual is undergoing stressful or challenging life events? (p. 352)

23. The ability to step up and take action to reduce the impact of a stressful situation is an example of _____ _____. (p. 353)

24. _____ _____ is the ability to think differently about negative emotions that arise in response to stress-provoking events. (p. 353)

25. When you can suppress or express emotions at will, you are exhibiting _____ _____. (p. 353)

26. According to researchers, catharsis, or expressing what we feel, (is/is not) always beneficial. (p. 353)

27. What is crisis debriefing and how effective is it for people who have experienced a traumatic event? (pp. 353–354)

10.7 Explain how hardiness, optimism, and spirituality may influence responses to stress

Hardy people view change as a challenge, have a deep sense of commitment to their life and work, and believe they can control events. Optimism and spirituality also boost stress resistance.

28. _____ is a set of attitudes, marked by a sense of control over events, commitment to life and work, and motivation and courage to confront stressful events. (p. 354)

29. Optimistic people are (better/worse) at handling frustration than pessimists. (p. 355)

30. _____ is the search for the sacred, which may or may not extend to belief in God. (p. 355)

succeed with

1. What are some passive and active coping strategies?
   Coping Strategies and Their Effects

2. What are the symptoms of stress and how should we cope?
   Coping with Stress

3. Learn about the importance of optimism during times of intense stress.
   Optimism and Resilience

PROMOTING GOOD HEALTH — AND LESS STRESS! (pp. 356–364)

10.8 Distinguish different types of drugs and their effects

The effects of drugs are associated with the dose of the drug, as well as with users' expectancies, personalities, and culture. Stimulants, such as tobacco and cocaine, increase activity of the central nervous system. In contrast, depressants, such as alcohol, decrease activity of the central nervous system. Opiates, such as heroin and morphine, are responsible for a sense of euphoria, decreased pain, and sleep. Psychedelic drugs, such as marijuana and Ecstasy, dramatically alter perception, mood, and thoughts.

31. Psychoactive drugs are chemicals that (are/are not) similar to those found in our brains that alter experience by changing chemical processes in _____. (p. 357)

32. People qualify for a diagnosis of _____ _____ when they experience recurrent problems related to the drug. (p. 357)

33. Substance dependence is associated with symptoms of _____ and _____. (p. 357)

34. Cultures in which drinking is strictly prohibited exhibit (low/high) rates of alcoholism. (p. 358)

35. Twin and adoption studies show that _____ factors play a key role in the vulnerability to alcoholism. (p. 358)

36. Complete the table by adding examples of and the effects for each drug type listed. (p. 359)

Drug Type	Examples	Effect on Behavior
Depressants		
Stimulants		
Opiates		
Psychedelics		

37. _____ is the most powerful natural stimulant. (p. 359)

10.9 Describe different alternative medical approaches and compare their effectiveness with placebos

Alternative medical approaches include therapies using vitamins, herbs, and food supplements, as well as energy medicine (acupuncture), and meditation. Many alternative approaches are no more effective than placebos. Alternative medical products and procedures can become part of conventional medicine when demonstrated to be safe and effective.

38. _____ _____ refers to health care practices and products that are used in place of conventional medicine. (p. 363)

39. Herbs, vitamins, and dietary supplements (are/are not) regulated by the FDA for safety, purity, and effectiveness. (p. 363)

40. List some of the positive effects of meditation and possible explanations for each. (p. 364)

succeed with

1. Take a quiz to find out how your lifestyle choices affect your health.
   How Healthy Are You?

2. How do you respond to one drink of alcohol? Researchers argue that your reactions can tell us your likelihood of becoming an alcoholic.
   Alcoholism

3. Evaluate the evidence of the effects of smoking damage to your health.
   Smoking Damage

TO SLEEP, PERCHANCE TO DREAM (pp. 365–371)

10.10 Identify the different stages of sleep and the neural activity and dreaming that occur in each

Sleep and wakefulness vary in response to a circadian rhythm that regulates many bodily processes over a 24-hour period. The "biological clock" is located in the suprachiasmatic nucleus in the hypothalamus. There are five stages of sleep. As we progress through the first four stages, our brain waves slow down, heart rate slows, body temperature decreases, and muscles relax. In stage 5, rapid eye movement, or REM sleep, the brain is activated much as it is during waking life.

41. The changes that occur in many of our biological processes during a 24-hour period are referred to as the _____ _____. (p. 365)

42. As a college student you may like to sleep late in the morning because your _____ _____ is set that way. (p. 365)

43. Label the types of brain waves displayed at each sleep stage. (p. 367)

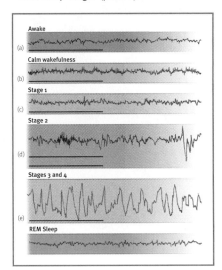

Awake

(a)

Calm wakefulness

(b)

Stage 1

(c)

Stage 2

(d)

Stages 3 and 4

(e)

REM Sleep

44. During the _____ stage of sleep, also called the _____ stage, the activity in our brains is similar to when we are awake because we are typically engaged in vivid dreaming. (p. 367)

10.11 Explain how different theories attempt to account for dreaming

Freud theorized that dreams represent disguised wishes. However, many dreams involve unpleasant or undesirable experiences, and many involve uninteresting reviews of routine daily events. According to activation synthesis theory, the forebrain attempts to interpret nonsensical signals. Neurocognitive theories hold that our dreams depend in large part on who we are, so that dreams vary depending on our cognitive and visuospatial abilities.

45. According to Freud's _____ _____ theory, our dreams represent how we wish things would be. (pp. 367–368)

46. Label the brain components that the activation–synthesis theory suggests are involved in dreaming. (p. 368)

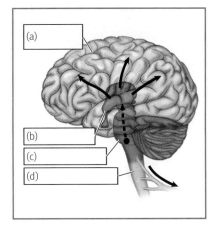

(a)

(b)

(c)

(d)

47. Children's dreams tend to be (more/less) bizarre than adults' dreams. (p. 368)

48. Scientists agree that dreams (are/are not) involved in processing emotional memories and integrating new experiences with established memories to make sense of the world. (p. 369)

10.12 Identify the features and causes of sleep disorders

Insomnia (problems falling asleep, waking in the night, or waking early) is the most common sleep disorder. Episodes of narcolepsy, which can last as long as an hour, are marked by the rapid onset of sleep. Sleep apnea is caused by a blockage of the airways during sleep. Night terrors and sleepwalking, are typically harmless.

49. People who have _____ fall asleep suddenly and at inopportune times, like while driving a car. (p. 370)

50. During a _____ _____, a child can experience a dramatic episode of crying or thrashing during non-REM sleep and won't remember it in the morning. (p. 371)

SCIENTIFIC THINKING SKILLS
Questions and Summary

1 As the college application season approaches, you are asked to help students to identify, appraise, and cope with the stress involved in acceptance and rejection. What coping skills would you teach them?

2 In your health psychology course, you are asked to make a presentation on the link between stress and the immune system. What would you do to make this link clear using the common cold as an example?

succeed with mypsychlab

1. Can you control your own dreams? Watch this video and evaluate the evidence. **Lucid Dreaming**

2. Watch an interview with somone who has experienced insomnia for years and learn how it has affected her life. **Roberta: Insomnia**

3. Watch the brain wave activity of individuals as they enter different stages of sleep. **REM versus NREM Sleep**

RULING OUT RIVAL HYPOTHESES
pp. 343, 358

CORRELATION vs. CAUSATION
pp. 343, 351, 354, 355, 358

FALSIFIABILITY
pp. 355, 363, 368

REPLICABILITY
p. 352

Social Psychology

What causes mass hysteria
over rumors about things
like Martian landings?
(pp. 381–382)

How do cults
persuade people
to become fanatics? (p. 388)

How can a woman be stabbed to death in plain view of many people who don't come to her aid? (p. 394)

Does how we act reflect what we believe, or is it the other way around? (p. 401)

Are stereotypes always a bad thing? (p. 408)

On October 30, 1938—a few hours before Halloween—much of the United States temporarily lost its grip on reality. That night, 6 million Americans tuned in to a popular radio show hosted by 23-year-old Hollywood sensation Orson Welles. The program featured an adaptation of H.G. Wells's science fiction classic *The War of the Worlds,* which vividly describes the invasion of Earth by a race of enormous Martians. (In 2005, Steven Spielberg made this book into a movie starring Tom Cruise.) To make *The War of the Worlds* more entertaining—and to play a good-natured pre-Halloween trick on his listeners—Welles presented the story in the form of a phony news broadcast. Anyone listening carefully to the program would have known that it was a clever hoax, as Welles informed his audience no fewer than four times that the show was merely an adaptation of a science fiction story.

As the broadcast unfolded over the next hour, a newscaster periodically interrupted live orchestral music with increasingly alarming news bulletins that first reported a series of explosions on the surface of Mars and later the landing of a mysterious metal capsule on a farm in Grover's Mill, New Jersey, some 50 miles from New York City. Against the backdrop of screaming witnesses, a terrified reporter described a large alien with tentacles emerging from a hatch in the capsule. By the program's end, the newscaster informed listeners that an army of giant Martians was launching a full-scale invasion of New York City.

The War of the Worlds triggered a mass panic (Bartholomew, 1998). Hundreds of frightened listeners fled into the streets, while others hid in their basements. Still others called the police or loaded their guns. Some even wrapped their heads in towels in preparation for a Martian chemical attack (Cantril, 1947). Although most listeners didn't panic, at least tens of thousands did (Bainbridge, 1987). Surprisingly, many listeners apparently never bothered to consider alternative explanations for the program or to seek out evidence that could have falsified claims of a massive alien invasion. Had they tuned their radios to a different station, they would have heard no coverage of this presumably momentous event in human history. That surely would have tipped them off that Welles's program was a huge practical joke. Instead, many listeners fell prey to confirmation bias (see Chapter 1), focusing on only one hypothesis—that the news bulletins were real—at the expense of all others.

Welles had pulled off the most successful Halloween prank of all time. How did he do it? One thing's for certain: Welles had never taken an introductory psychology course, so he didn't rely on scientific research. Yet he understood the power of social influence, although even he was caught off guard by just how potent it was.

What Is Social Psychology?

Social psychology helps us to understand not only why *The War of the Worlds* hoax succeeded, but why many forms of social influence are so powerful. **Social psychology** is the study of how people influence others' behavior, beliefs, and attitudes—for both good and bad (Lewin, 1951). Social psychology helps us to understand not only why we sometimes act helpfully and even heroically in the presence of others, but also why we occasionally show our worst sides, caving in to group pressure or standing by idly while others suffer. It also helps us to understand why we're prone to blindly accept irrational, even pseudoscientific, beliefs.

In this chapter, we'll begin by examining the power of social interactions and how and why we often underestimate the impact of social influence on others' behavior. We'll move on to examine two especially potent social influences: conformity and obedience, and then address the question of why we help other people at some times and harm them at others. Then we'll discuss our attitudes and how social pressure shapes them. We'll end by exploring the troubling question of how prejudice toward others arises and, more optimistically, how we can combat it.

In the 2000 film *Cast Away*, actor Tom Hanks (portraying a Federal Express worker stranded on a remote desert island) strikes up an unusual companionship with a volleyball. The character's social motives are so powerful that when deprived of interpersonal contact, he found a way to re-create it.

HUMANS AS A SOCIAL SPECIES

Social psychology is important for one reason: We humans are a highly social species. Most evidence suggests that humans evolved hundreds of thousands of years ago, in relatively small and tight social groups (Barchas, 1986). Even as modern-day humans, most of us naturally gravitate to small groups. In forming cliques, or groups that include some people, we exclude others by extension.

The Need to Belong: Why We Form Groups. When we're deprived of social contact for a considerable length of time, we usually become lonely. According to Roy Baumeister and Mark Leary's (1995) *need to belong theory*, we humans have a biologically based need for interpersonal connections. We seek out social bonds when we can and suffer negative psychological and physical consequences when we can't.

Moreover, the threat of social isolation can lead us to behave in self-destructive ways and even impair our mental functioning. For example, feeling lonely can lead us to engage in unhealthy behaviors, like eating a fattening snack or procrastinating on an assignment (Twenge, Catanese, & Baumeister, 2002). It can even impair students' performance on IQ tests (Baumeister, Twenge, & Nuss, 2002).

Brain imaging research goes a step further, shedding light on the commonplace observation that being cut off from social contact "hurts," literally and figuratively. Using a virtual game similar to the popular television show *Survivor*, Kip Williams and his collaborators created a scenario where the subjects were seemingly "rejected" by fictitious co-participants. Upon experiencing the sting of social rejection, participants displayed pronounced activation in a region of the cingulate cortex (see Chapter 3) that also becomes active during physical pain. So that "ouch" we feel after being thrown out of a group may bear more than a metaphorical similarity to the ouch we feel after stubbing our toe (Eisenberger, Lieberman, & Williams, 2003).

Orderly evacuation of a building in an emergency highlights how conformity and obedience can be constructive.

How We Came to Be This Way: Evolution and Social Behavior. Because we'll soon be examining many unhealthy forms of social influence, such as how unquestioning acceptance of authority figures can lead us to do foolish things, we might be tempted to conclude that almost all social influence is negative. That would be a serious mistake. Virtually all of the social influence processes we'll discuss are adaptive under most circumstances and help to regulate cultural practices. **[LEARNING OBJECTIVE 11.1]** From the perspective of an evolutionary approach to social behavior, many social influence processes have served us well over the course of evolution (Buss & Kenrick, 1998). *Conformity, obedience, and many other forms of social influence become maladaptive only when they're blind or unquestioning.* From this standpoint, irrational group behavior—like the disastrous obedience of thousands of German citizens during the Nazi regime of the 1930s and 1940s and the massive genocide in Rwanda in the 1990s—are by-products of adaptive processes that have gone wildly wrong because people accepted social influence without evaluating it critically.

GLOSSARY

social psychology
study of how people influence others' behavior, beliefs, and attitudes

The presence of others enhances our performance on simple or familiar tasks. These cyclists will likely ride faster together than either would alone.

Social Facilitation: From Bicyclists to Cockroaches.
Because we're social creatures, being surrounded by others can make us perform better. Research shows that the mere presence of others can enhance our performance in certain situations, a phenomenon that Robert Zajonc called **social facilitation.** In the world's first social psychological study, Norman Triplett (1897) found that bicycle racers obtained faster speeds (32.6 miles per hour on average) when racing along with other bicyclists than when racing against only the clock (24 miles per hour on average). Zajonc (1965) found that social facilitation applies to birds, fish, and even insects. In what's surely one of the most creative studies in the history of psychology, Zajonc and two colleagues randomly assigned cockroaches to two conditions: one in which they ran a maze alone and another in which they ran a maze while being observed by an audience of fellow cockroaches from a "spectator box." Compared with the lone cockroaches, cockroaches in the second condition ran the maze significantly faster and committed fewer errors (Zajonc, Heingartner, & Herman, 1969).

Yet the impact of others on our behavior isn't always positive (Bond & Titus, 1983). Social facilitation occurs only on tasks we find easy, whereas *social disruption*—a worsening of performance in the presence of others—occurs on tasks we find difficult. You've probably discovered this principle if you've ever "choked" in the company of others while singing a difficult song or telling a lengthy joke with a complicated punch line. One team of five researchers watched people playing pool (Michaels, Blommel, Brocato, et al., 1982). The experienced pool players did better in the presence of others, but the inexperienced pool players did worse. The effects of social influence can be either positive or negative depending on the situation.

THE GREAT LESSON OF SOCIAL PSYCHOLOGY

When we try to figure out why other people—or indeed, we ourselves—did something, we're forming **attributions,** or assigning causes to behavior. We make attributions every day. Some attributions are internal (inside the person), such as when we conclude that Joe Smith robbed a bank because he's impulsive. Other attributions are external (outside the person), such as when we conclude that Bill Jones robbed a bank because his family was broke. We can explain a great deal of our everyday behavior by situational factors, like peer pressure, that are external to us.

The Fundamental Attribution Error.
When we read about the frenzied behavior of some Americans during *The War of the Worlds,* we shake our heads in amazement and pat ourselves on the back with the confident reassurance that we'd never have behaved this way. Yet if the field of social psychology imparts one lesson that we should take with us for the rest of our lives (Myers, 1993a), it's the **fundamental attribution error.** Coined by Lee Ross (1977), this term refers to the tendency to overestimate the impact of *dispositional influences* on others' behavior. By dispositional influences, we mean enduring characteristics, such as personality traits, attitudes, and intelligence. Because of this error, we attribute too much of people's behavior to who they are and too little of their behavior to what's going on around them. **[LEARNING OBJECTIVE 11.2]** We may assume incorrectly that a boss in a failing company who fired several of his loyal employees to save money must be callous, when in fact he was under enormous pressure to rescue his company—and spare the jobs of hundreds of other loyal employees. Incidentally, the fundamental attribution error applies only to explaining *other* people's behavior; when explaining the causes of our *own* behavior, we typically invoke situational influences (Jones & Nisbett, 1972).

Evidence for the Fundamental Attribution Error. Edward E. Jones and Victor Harris (1967) conducted the first study to demonstrate the fundamental attribution error. They asked undergraduates to serve as "debaters" in a discussion of U.S. attitudes toward

GLOSSARY

social facilitation
enhancement of performance brought about by the presence of others

attribution
process of assigning causes to behavior

fundamental attribution error
tendency to overestimate the impact of dispositional influences on *other* people's behavior

Cuba and its controversial leader, Fidel Castro. In full view of the other debaters, they randomly assigned students to read aloud debate speeches that adopted either a pro-Castro or an anti-Castro position.

After hearing these speeches, the researchers asked the other debaters to evaluate each debater's *true* attitudes toward Castro. That is, putting aside the speech he or she read, what do you think each debater *really* believes about Castro? Students fell prey to the fundamental attribution error; they inferred that what debaters said reflected their true position regarding Castro *even when they knew that the assignment to conditions was entirely random* **(Figure 11.1).** They forgot to take the situation—namely, the random assignment of subjects to the experimental condition—into account when evaluating debaters' attitudes (Ross, Amabile, & Steinmetz, 1977).

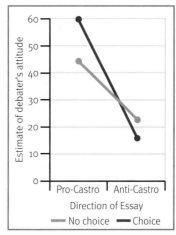

Figure 11.1 Subjects' Performance in Jones & Harris's (1967) Castro Study. Subjects inferred that debaters' pro- or anti-Castro positions reflected their actual attitudes even though debaters couldn't choose which position to adopt—an example of the fundamental attribution error. (*Source:* Jones & Harris, 1967)

WHAT DO *you* THINK?

Your uncle argues that people living in poverty have no one to blame but themselves—if they really wanted to, they'd set their mind to it and start making some money. How might you explain his perspective in terms of the fundamental attribution error?

The Fundamental Attribution Error: Cultural Influences. Interestingly, the severity of the fundamental attribution error varies by culture. For example, Japanese and Chinese people seem less prone to this error (Nisbett, 2003). That may be because they're more likely than those in Western cultures to attribute behaviors to context. As a result, they may be more prone to take situational influences into account. For example, after reading newspaper descriptions of mass murderers, Chinese subjects are considerably less likely to invoke dispositional explanations for their behavior ("He must be an evil person") and more likely to invoke situational explanations ("He must have been under terrible stress in his life"). In contrast, U.S. subjects tend to show the opposite pattern (Morris & Peng, 1994).

SOCIAL COMPARISON: PERSON SEE, PERSON DO

The War of the Worlds hoax was successful for one reason: We're inherently social creatures. When a situation is unclear, we look to others for guidance about what to believe and how to act. According to Leon Festinger's (1954) **social comparison theory,** we evaluate our beliefs, abilities, and reactions by comparing them with those of others. Doing so helps us to understand ourselves and our social worlds better. For example, if you want to find out whether you're a good psychology student, it's only natural to compare your exam performance with that of your classmates.

Yet we can take social comparison too far. Although we can often learn valuable information from others' reactions, it's another thing to base our actions solely on their behavior. After all, what if other people are behaving unreasonably? *The War of the Worlds* might seem like an isolated case of human irrationality, but that's far from the truth. *The War of the Worlds* is merely one example of a broad class of events called *mass hysteria.*

Mass Hysteria: Irrationality at a Group Level. **Mass hysteria** is a contagious outbreak of irrational behavior that spreads much like a flu epidemic. Because we tend to engage in social comparison when a situation is ambiguous, most of us are prone to mass hysteria under the right circumstances. In some cases, episodes of mass hysteria

GLOSSARY

social comparison theory
theory that we seek to evaluate our beliefs, attitudes, and abilities by comparing our reactions with others'

mass hysteria
outbreak of irrational behavior that is spread by social contagion

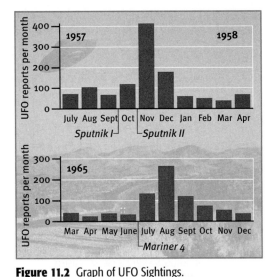

Figure 11.2 Graph of UFO Sightings.
In the 1950s and 1960s, the number of UFO sightings shot up dramatically following the launches of *Sputnik I* and *II* (the Russian satellites that were the first objects launched into space) and following the U.S. launch of the space probe *Mariner 4*. Although these data don't permit definite cause-and-effect conclusions, they're consistent with the possibility that UFO sightings are of social origin. (*Source:* Hartmann, 1992)

can lead to *collective delusions,* in which many people simultaneously come to be convinced of bizarre things that are false. Consider how the frequency of unidentified flying objects (UFOs) sightings shot up at times when societal consciousness of space travel was heightened, as shown in **Figure 11.2.**

This fad started on June 24, 1947, when pilot Kenneth Arnold spotted nine mysterious shiny objects while flying over the ocean near Mount Rainier in Washington State that he said "skipped over the water like saucers." Within days, the phrase "flying saucers" appeared in over 150 newspapers across the United States (Bartholomew & Goode, 2000). Even more interestingly, within only a few years thousands of people were claiming to see saucer-shaped objects in the sky that they believed were alien spaceships.

Another example of collective delusions took place in the spring of 1954, when the city of Seattle, Washington experienced an epidemic of "windshield pitting." Thousands of residents noticed tiny indentations, or pits, in their car windshields that they suspected were the result of a secret nuclear test performed by the federal government. Their concerns spun so out of control that Seattle's mayor eventually sought emergency help from President Eisenhower (Bartholomew & Goode, 2000). Although the residents of Seattle hadn't realized it, the windshield pits had been there all along, as they are on most cars.

Urban Legends. One of the simplest demonstrations of the power of social influence comes from the study of *urban legends;* false stories repeated so many times that people believe them to be true (Brunvand, 1999). Have you heard any of the urban legends in **Figure 11.3?**

Each of the false stories in Figure 11.3 is too bizarre to be true, yet people consistently believe them, and spread the stories to others. Urban legends are convincing in part because they fit our preconceptions (Gilovich, 1991). Urban legends also make good stories because they tug on our emotions, especially negative ones (Rosnow, 2002). Research shows that the most popular urban legends contain a heavy dose of material relevant to the emotion of disgust, probably because they arouse our perverse sense of curiosity. As a result, they often spread like wildfire. It's probably not coincidental that many feature rats and other animals that we don't exactly find appealing (Heath, Bell, & Sternberg, 2001).

A woman heated her poodle in a microwave oven in a well-meaning attempt to dry it off following a rainstorm. It exploded.	While still alive, Walt Disney arranged to have his body frozen after his death so that it could be unfrozen at a future date when advanced technology will permit him to live again.	Outside her home, a woman found a stray Chihuahua. She cared for the pet for several weeks and eventually brought it to a veterinarian, who informed her that her cute little "dog" was actually a giant rat.	Many gang members drive around late at night without their car lights on and then shoot people who flash their lights at them.	A woman on a transatlantic flight was trapped in the bathroom for over 2 hours after flushing the toilet created a vacuum, binding her to the seat.

Figure 11.3 Urban Legend? These popular urban legends are all widely known, yet all are false. Check out the high-quality web site www.snopes.com for information on the accuracy of these and other urban legends.

QUIZ

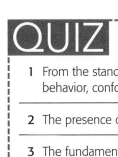

1 From the standpoint of an evolutionary approach to social behavior, conformity and obedience are inherently maladaptive. **TRUE** **FALSE**

2 The presence of other people always enhances our performance. **TRUE** **FALSE**

3 The fundamental attribution error reminds us that we tend to attribute others' behavior primarily to their personality traits and attitudes. **TRUE** **FALSE**

4 We're especially likely to engage in social comparison when a situation is clear-cut. **TRUE** **FALSE**

Answers: (1) F (p. 379); (2) F (p. 380); (3) T (p. 380); (4) F (p. 381)

PEARSON
mypsych lab

▼ Can social psychologists manipulate your behavior? Watch the video titled "Introduction to Social Psychology" at www.mypsychlab.com to find out.

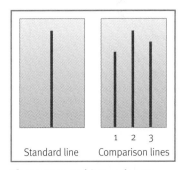

Social Influence: Conformity and Obedience

Think of an organization or group to which you've belonged, like a club, school committee, fraternity, or sorority. Have you ever just gone along with one of the group's ideas even though you knew that it was bad, perhaps even unethical? If you have, don't feel ashamed, because you're in good company. **Conformity** refers to the tendency of people to alter their behavior as a result of group pressure (Kiesler & Kiesler, 1969). We all conform to social pressure from time to time. Yet, as we'll see, we occasionally take this tendency too far.

CONFORMITY: THE ASCH PARADIGM

Solomon Asch conducted the classic study of conformity in the 1950s. Asch's (1955) research design was as straightforward as it was elegant. In some social psychological studies, such as Asch's, participants are lured in by a cover story that doesn't reveal the study's true goal. Often, other "participants" in the study are actually *confederates,* or undercover agents of the researcher. But the actual subjects are unaware of that.

In this chapter, we'll ask you to imagine yourself as a subject in several classic social psychological studies. Let's begin with Asch's.

The Setup: Asch invites subjects to participate in a "study of perceptual judgments" that asks eight subjects—including you—to compare a standard line with three comparison lines: 1, 2, and 3. Unbeknownst to you, the other "subjects" are actually Asch's confederates. A researcher explains that your job is to say out loud which of three comparison lines matches the standard line. The researcher starts with a person across the table, so you're always the fifth or sixth to be called.

The Study: On the first trial, the correct answer is clearly "1." You listen intently as the first few subjects call out their answers. Subject 1: "1." Subject 2: "1." Subject 3: "1." Subject 4: "1." As Subject 5, you simply follow, and say "1." The three subjects following you give the same answer: 1. "This study is going to be a breeze," you say to yourself.

The second trial displays a similar problem, just as easy to answer, in which the correct answer is clearly "2" (see **Figure 11.4**). Again, you listen while the subjects call out their answers. Subject 1: "3." Subject 2: "3." Subject 3: "3." Subject 4: "3."

Figure 11.4 Asch's Experiments.
Which of the "comparison lines" is the same length as the "standard line"? If several other participants said it was line #3, would you go along with them?

Standard line   Comparison lines
1 2 3

GLOSSARY

conformity
tendency of people to alter their behavior as a result of group pressure

In this photo from the Asch experiment, we see the lone actual subject (*middle*), barely believing his eyes, straining to look at the stimulus cards after the confederates gave the wrong answer.

You can hardly believe your eyes. It seems obvious that "2" is the correct answer, but everyone is calling "3." What on Earth is going on? Are your eyes deceiving you? Or did you perhaps misunderstand the instructions? What are you going to do?

The Results: If you're like 75 percent of subjects in the original Asch study, you'd conform to the incorrect norm on at least one of 12 trials. Across all 12 trials in the Asch study, subjects conformed to the wrong answer 37 percent of the time. Some subjects conformed even when the comparison line differed from the standard line by more than 6 inches! Understandably, subjects reported being confused and even distressed because they experienced a sharp conflict between their perceptions and what they believed to be others' perceptions.

Dissecting Social Influences on Conformity. Asch (1955) and later researchers went on to pinpoint some of the social factors that influenced how likely we are to conform. **[LEARNING OBJECTIVE 11.3]** Researchers concluded that conformity was influenced by the following independent variables:

- **Unanimity:** If all confederates gave the same wrong answer, the subject was more likely to conform. However, if one confederate gave the correct response, the level of conformity dropped by three-fourths.

- **Giving a different wrong answer:** Knowing that someone else in the group differed from the majority—even if that person held a different view from the subject—makes the subject less likely to conform.

- **Size:** The size of the majority made a difference, but only up to about five or six subjects. People were no more likely to conform in a group of ten subjects than in a group of five subjects (see **Figure 11.5**).

RULING OUT RIVAL HYPOTHESES
Have important alternative explanations for the findings been excluded?

Asch also tried to rule out alternative hypotheses for his findings. To determine whether group norms affected subjects' *perceptions* of the lines, he replicated his original study but asked subjects to write, rather than call out, their responses. In this condition, subjects' answers were right more than 99 percent of the time.

Individual and Cultural Differences in Conformity. People's responses to social pressure are associated with individual differences. For example, people with low self-esteem are especially prone to conformity (Hardy, 1957). Cultural differences in conformity also exist. Asians are also more likely to conform than Americans (Bond & Smith, 1996), probably because, as discussed in Chapter 8, many Asian cultures are more collectivist than American culture (Oyserman, Coon, Kemmelmeier, et al., 2002). This greater collectivism probably leads many Asians to be more concerned about group opinion than Americans. In addition, people in individualistic cultures, like the United States, generally prefer to stand out from the crowd, whereas people in collectivist cultures prefer to blend in. In one study, researchers presented American and Asian subjects with a bunch of orange and green pens that had a majority of one color and a minority of the other. Americans tended to pick the minority-colored pens, whereas Asians tended to pick the majority-colored pens (Kim & Markus, 1999).

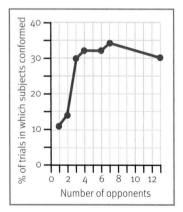

Figure 11.5 The Effect of the Number of Opponents on Conformity In Asch's studies, conformity increased as the size of the majority increased—but only up to about five or six subjects. (*Source:* Asch, 1955)

GLOSSARY

deindividuation
tendency of people to engage in uncharacteristic behavior when they are stripped of their usual identities

DEINDIVIDUATION: LOSING OUR TYPICAL IDENTITIES

One process that can make us more vulnerable to conformity is **deindividuation:** the tendency of people to engage in atypical behavior when stripped of their usual identities (Festinger, Pepitone, & Newcomb, 1952). Several factors contribute to deindividuation, but the most prominent are a feeling of anonymity and a lack of individual responsibility (Dipboye, 1977; Postmes & Spears, 1998). When we're deindividuated, we become more vulnerable to social influences, including the impact of social roles.

Every day, we play multiple social roles: student or teacher, son or daughter, sister or brother, roommate, athlete, social-club member, and employee, to name but a few. What happens when we temporarily lose our typical social identities and are forced to adopt different identities?

Stanford Prison Study: Chaos in Palo Alto.
Philip Zimbardo and his colleagues first approached this question over three decades ago (Haney, Banks, & Zimbardo, 1973). Zimbardo knew about the dehumanizing conditions in many prisons, and he wondered whether they stemmed from peoples' personalities or from the roles they're required to adopt. The roles of prisoner and guard, which are inherently opposed, may carry such powerful expectations that they generate self-fulfilling prophecies. What would happen if ordinary people played the roles of prisoner and guard? Would they begin to assume the identities assigned to them?

The Setup: Zimbardo and his colleagues advertised for volunteers for a 2-week "psychological study of prison life" (see **Figure 11.6**). Using a coin toss, he randomly assigned 24 male undergraduates, prescreened for normal adjustment using personality tests, to be either prisoners or guards.

The Study: Zimbardo transformed the basement of the Stanford psychology department in Palo Alto, California, into a simulated prison, complete with jail cells. To add to the realism, actual Palo Alto police officers arrested the would-be prisoners at their homes and transported them to the simulated prison. The prisoners and guards were forced to dress in clothes reflecting their assigned roles. Zimbardo, who acted as the prison "superintendent," instructed guards to refer to prisoners only by numbers, not by names.

The Results: The first day passed without incident, but soon something went horribly wrong. Guards began to treat prisoners cruelly and subject them to harsh punishments. Guards forced prisoners to perform humiliating lineups, do push-ups, sing, strip naked, and clean filthy toilets with their bare hands. In some cases, they even placed bags over prisoners' heads.

By day two, the prisoners mounted a rebellion, which the guards quickly quashed. Things went steadily downhill from there. The guards became increasingly cruel, using fire extinguishers on the prisoners and forcing them to simulate sexual acts. Soon, many prisoners began to display signs of emotional disturbance, including depression, hopelessness, and anger. Zimbardo released two prisoners from the study because they appeared to be on the verge of a psychological breakdown. One prisoner went on a hunger strike in protest.

At day six, Zimbardo—after some prodding from one of his former graduate students, Christina Maslach—ended the study 8 days early. Although the prisoners were relieved at the news, some guards were disappointed (Haney et al., 1973).

Perhaps Zimbardo was right; once prisoners and guards had been assigned roles that deemphasized their individuality, they adopted their designated roles more easily than anyone might have imagined. Although the results of this study are striking, Zimbardo's study wasn't carefully controlled: In many respects, it was more of a demonstration than an experiment. In particular, his prisoners and guards may have experienced demand characteristics (see Chapter 2) to behave in accord with their assigned roles. For example, they may have assumed that the investigators wanted them to play the parts of prisoners and guards, and they obliged. Moreover, at least one attempt to replicate the Stanford prison study was unsuccessful, suggesting that the effects of deindividuation may not be inevitable (Reicher & Haslam, 2006).

The Real World: Chaos in Abu Ghraib.
The Stanford prison study wasn't an isolated event (Zimbardo, 2007). In 2004 the world witnessed disturbingly similar images in the now-infamous Iraqi prison of Abu Ghraib. There, we saw guards—this time, actual U.S. soldiers—placing bags over Iraqi prisoners' heads, leading them around with dog leashes,

Male college students needed for psychological study of prison life. $15 per day for 1-2 weeks beginning Aug. 14. For further information & application come to Room 218, Jordan Hall, Stanford U.

Figure 11.6 Newspaper Ad for Zimbardo's Prison Study. A facsimile of the newspaper advertisement for Zimbardo's Stanford prison study, 1972. (*Source:* Zimbardo, 1972)

Psychologist Phil Zimbardo, shown at home with masks on his wall. Zimbardo is fond of masks, as research suggests that they can produce deindividuation.

REPLICABILITY
Can the results be duplicated in other studies?

Stanford Prison Experiment (1973)

Abu Ghraib (2004)

To some observers, some of the behaviors documented at Abu Ghraib prison in Iraq in 2004 (photos at *right*) are eerily similar to those of Zimbardo's prison study in 1972 (photos at left). Were the same processes of deindividuation at work?

pointing mockingly at their exposed genitals, and arranging them in human pyramids for their amusement. These similarities weren't lost on Zimbardo (2004b, 2007), who maintained that the Abu Ghraib fiasco was a product of situational forces. According to Zimbardo, the dehumanization of prisoners and prison guards made it likely they'd lose themselves in the social roles to which their superiors assigned them.

That said, the overwhelming majority of U.S. prison guards during the Iraqi War haven't engaged in abuse, so the reasons for such abuse don't lie entirely in the situation. As research using Asch's paradigm reminds us, individual differences in personality play a key role in conformity. Indeed, several guards who perpetrated the Abu Ghraib abuses had a history of irresponsible behavior (Saletan, 2004).

Furthermore, deindividuation doesn't necessarily make us behave badly; it makes us more likely to conform to whatever norms are present in the situation (Postmes & Spears, 1998). Some researchers have found that a loss of identity actually makes people more likely to engage in prosocial, or helping, behavior when others are helping out (Johnson & Downing, 1979). For good or bad, deindividuation makes us behave more like a member of the group and less like an individual.

WHAT DO *you* THINK?

For your historical anthropology class, you are reading about battle preparations throughout history and across cultures. You notice that common soldier preparations include wearing similar uniforms, painting their faces, and wearing masks or facial armor. How might these factors contribute to soldiers' ability to engage in violent acts against other people?

Crowds *sometimes* engage in irrational, even violent, behavior. But research suggests that crowds aren't necessarily more violent than individuals.

Deindividuation helps explain why crowd behavior is so unpredictable: The actions of people in crowds depend largely on whether others are acting prosocially or antisocially (against others). A myth that's endured for centuries is that crowds are always more aggressive than individuals. In some cases, crowds do become aggressive. Yet in other cases, crowds are less aggressive than individuals (de Waal, 1989b; de Waal, Aurelli, & Judge, 2000). Moreover, people in crowds typically limit their social interactions to minimize conflict (Baum, 1987). For example, people on crowded buses and elevators generally avoid staring at one another, instead preferring to stare at the road or the floor. This behavior is probably adaptive because people are less likely to say or do something that could offend others.

GROUPTHINK

Closely related to conformity is a phenomenon that Irving Janis (1972) termed **groupthink:** an emphasis on group unanimity at the expense of critical thinking. Groups sometimes become so intent on ensuring that everyone agrees with everyone else that they give up their capacity to evaluate issues objectively. **[LEARNING OBJECTIVE 11.4]**

Janis arrived at the concept of groupthink after studying the reasoning processes behind the failed 1961 invasion of the Bay of Pigs in Cuba. Following lengthy discussions with cabinet members, President John F. Kennedy recruited 1,400 Cuban immigrants to invade Cuba and overthrow its dictator, Fidel Castro. But Castro found out about the invasion in advance and nearly all the invaders were captured or killed. After the failed invasion, Kennedy asked, "How could I have been so stupid?" (Dallek, 2003). Janis had a simple answer: Kennedy and his cabinet fell prey to groupthink. They became convinced that their plan was a good one because they all agreed to it, and they failed to ask themselves the tough questions that could have averted the disaster.

The Bay of Pigs invasion wasn't the last time that groupthink led intelligent people to make catastrophic decisions. In 1986, the space shuttle *Challenger* exploded, killing the seven astronauts aboard a mere 73 seconds after takeoff. Project managers of the *Challenger* agreed to launch it after a series of bitterly cold days in January, despite warnings from NASA engineers that the shuttle might explode because rubber rings on the rocket booster could fail in freezing temperatures.

Table 11.1 depicts some of the characteristics or "symptoms" identified by Janis (1972) that render groups vulnerable to groupthink. Not all psychologists accept Janis's description of groupthink. For one thing, groupthink doesn't always lead to bad decisions, just overconfident ones (Tyson, 1987). Moreover, seeking group consensus isn't always a bad idea, although doing so before all of the evidence is available is (Longley & Pruitt, 1980).

NASA groupthink may have contributed to the destruction of the space shuttle *Columbia* in February 2003 which, like the 1986 *Challenger* disaster, killed its crew of seven astronauts (shown here). Project managers ignored warnings about potential hazards posed by debris hitting the shuttle's wings during liftoff—resulting in the disintegration of the shuttle upon reentry into the atmosphere. (*Source:* Ferraris & Carveth, 2003)

Table 11.1 Symptoms of Groupthink.

Symptom	Example
An illusion of the group's invulnerability	"We can't possibly fail!"
An illusion of the group's unanimity	"Obviously, we all agree."
An unquestioned belief in the group's moral correctness	"We know we're on the right side."
Conformity pressure—pressure on group members to go along with everyone else	"Don't rock the boat!"
Stereotyping of the out-group—a caricaturing of the enemy	"They're all morons."
Self-censorship—the tendency of group members to keep their mouths shut even when they have doubts	"I suspect the group leader's idea is stupid, but I'd better not say anything."
Mindguards—self-appointed individuals whose job it is to stifle disagreement	"Oh, you think you know better than the rest of us?"

GLOSSARY

groupthink
emphasis on group unanimity at the expense of critical thinking and sound decision making

As a psychological condition, groupthink is often treatable. Janis (1972) noted that the best way to avoid groupthink is to encourage active dissent within an organization. He recommended that all groups appoint a "devil's advocate"—a person whose role is to voice doubts about the wisdom of the group's decisions. In addition, he suggested having independent experts on hand to evaluate whether the group's decisions make sense. Finally, it can be useful to hold a follow-up meeting to evaluate whether the decision reached in the first meeting still seems reasonable.

Cults and Brainwashing.

In extreme forms, groupthink can lead to **cults:** groups of individuals who exhibit intense and unquestioning devotion to a single cause. In many cases, they're devoted to one charismatic individual.

Cults can occasionally have disastrous consequences. Consider Heaven's Gate, a southern California–based group founded by Marshall Applewhite, a former psychiatric patient. Heaven's Gate members believed that Applewhite was a reincarnated version of Jesus Christ. Applewhite, they were convinced, would take them to a starship in their afterlives. In 1997, a major comet approached Earth, and several false reports circulated in the media that a spaceship was tailing it. The Heaven's Gate members apparently believed this was their calling. Virtually all of the cult members—39 of them—committed suicide by drinking a poisoned cocktail.

Because cults are secretive and difficult to study, psychologists know relatively little about them. But evidence suggests that cults promote groupthink in four major ways (Lalich, 2004): having a persuasive leader who fosters loyalty; disconnecting group members from the outside world; discouraging questioning of the group's or leader's assumptions; and establishing training practices that gradually indoctrinate members (Galanter, 1980).

Misconceptions about cults abound. One is that cult members are usually emotionally disturbed. Studies show that most cult members are psychologically normal (Aronoff, Lynn, & Malinowski, 2000; Lalich, 2004), although many cult leaders probably suffer from serious mental illness. This erroneous belief probably stems from the fundamental attribution error: In trying to explain why people join cults, we overestimate the role of personality traits and underestimate the role of social influences.

A second misconception is that all cult members are *brainwashed*, or transformed by group leaders into unthinking zombies. Although some psychologists have argued that many cults use brainwashing techniques (Singer, 1979), there's considerable scientific controversy about the existence of brainwashing. For one thing, there's not much evidence that brainwashing permanently alters victims' beliefs (Melton, 1999). Moreover, there's not much evidence that brainwashing is a unique means of changing people's behavior. Instead, the persuasive techniques of brainwashing probably aren't all that different from those used by effective political leaders and salespeople (Zimbardo, 1997). We'll have more to say about these techniques later in the chapter.

How can we best resist the indoctrination that leads to cults? Here, the social psychological research is clear, although counterintuitive: First expose people to information consistent with cult beliefs and then debunk it. In his work on the **inoculation effect,** William McGuire (1964) demonstrated that the best way of immunizing people against an undesirable belief is to gently introduce them to reasons why this belief seems to be correct and then refute those reasons. This approach works much like a vaccine, which inoculates people against a virus by presenting them with a small dose of it, thereby activating the body's defenses (McGuire, 1964; McGuire & Papageorgis, 1961). For example, if we want to persuade someone that sleep learning doesn't work (see Chapter 5), we might point out that it is true that the brain remains very active during sleep (see Chapter 10) so it's possible that learning could take place. This inocu-

Cult membership involves following the cult's practices without question. Rev. Sun Yung Moon of the Unification Church has united thousands of total strangers in mass wedding ceremonies. The couples are determined by pairing photos of prospective brides and grooms.

GLOSSARY

cult
group of individuals who exhibit intense and unquestioning devotion to a single cause

inoculation effect
approach to convincing people to change their minds about something by first introducing reasons why the perspective might be correct and then debunking it

lation makes people more receptive to then learning that there is no evidence to support the idea that we can learn in our sleep.

Two sides of the coin of obedience: Lt. William Calley (*left*) was charged with murder by the Army for ordering his platoon to massacre unarmed civilians in the My Lai massacre in 1968. Hugh Thompson (*right*), landed his helicopter between the Army platoon and civilians in an effort to save the lives of the unarmed villagers.

OBEDIENCE: THE PSYCHOLOGY OF FOLLOWING ORDERS

In the case of conformity, we go along to get along. The transmission is "horizontal"—the group influence originates from our peers. In the case of **obedience,** we take our marching orders from people who are above us in the hierarchy of authority, such as a teacher, parent, or boss. Here the transmission is "vertical"—the group influence springs not from our peers but from our leaders (Loevinger, 1987). Many groups, such as cults, acquire their influence from a powerful combination of both conformity and obedience.

Obedience: A Double-Edged Sword. Obedience is a necessary, even essential, ingredient in our daily lives. Without it, society couldn't run smoothly. You're reading this book in part because your professor told you to, and you'll obey the traffic lights and stop signs on your next trip to school or work (we hope!) because you know you're expected to. Yet like conformity, obedience can produce troubling consequences when people stop asking questions about *why* they're behaving as others want them to.

During the Vietnam War, U.S. Lieutenant William Calley commanded a platoon of a division named Charlie Company that had encountered heavy arms fire for weeks. Understandably, the members of Charlie Company were on edge during the morning of March 16, 1968, as they entered the village of My Lai (pronounced "Me Lie"), expecting to find a hideout for North Vietnamese soldiers. Although the platoon located no enemy soldiers in My Lai, Calley ordered the soldiers in Charlie Company to open fire on the villagers, none of whom had initiated combat. They bludgeoned several old men to death with the butts of their rifles and shot praying children and women in the head. When all was said and done, the American platoon had brutally slaughtered about 500 innocent Vietnamese ranging in age from 1 to 82 years.

Afterward Calley insisted that he was merely taking orders from his superiors and bore no direct responsibility for the massacre. In turn, the soldiers in Calley's platoon claimed they were merely taking orders from Calley.

In sharp contrast to Calley's behavior, Officer Hugh Thompson Jr. attempted to halt the massacre by landing his U.S. Army helicopter between Calley's troops and the innocent villagers. Risking their lives, Thompson and his two crewmen ordered the troops to stop shooting and evacuated the village, saving scores of innocent lives.

The My Lai massacre may seem inexplicable to us. Yet it's only one instance of the perils of unthinking obedience. How can we make sense of this behavior? And how can we predict when someone will obey or disobey orders?

Stanley Milgram: Sources of Destructive Obedience. Stanley Milgram wanted to understand the principles underlying irrational group behavior. The child of Jewish parents who grew up during World War II, Milgram became preoccupied with the profoundly troubling question of how the Holocaust could have occurred. The prevailing wisdom in the late 1940s and 1950s was that the Holocaust was primarily the product of twisted minds that had perpetuated dastardly deeds. Yet Milgram suspected that the atrocities

GLOSSARY

obedience
adherence to instructions from those of higher authority

committed by the Nazis during the Holocaust were a result of commonplace social influences taken to an extreme and that any of us might have done the same under similar circumstances.

The Milgram Paradigm. In the early 1960s, Milgram began to tinker with a laboratory paradigm (a model experiment) that could provide a window into the causes of obedience (Blass, 2004). The paradigm he developed was a powerful one that would become one of the most influential in the history of psychology (Cialdini & Goldstein, 2004; Slater, 2004):

The Setup: You spot an advertisement in a local New Haven, Connecticut, newspaper, asking for volunteers for a study of memory. The ad notes that participants will be paid $4.50, which in the 1960s was a hefty chunk of change. You arrive at the laboratory at Yale University, where a tall and imposing man in a white lab coat, Mr. Williams, greets you. You also meet another friendly, middle-aged subject, Mr. Wallace, who unbeknownst to you is actually a confederate. The cover story is that you and Mr. Wallace will be participating in a study of the effects of "punishment on learning," with one of you being the teacher and the other the learner. You draw lots to see who'll play which role, and you get the piece of paper that says "teacher" (the lots are rigged). From here on in, Mr. Williams refers to you as the "teacher" and to Mr. Wallace as the "learner."

As the teacher, Mr. Williams explains, you'll present Mr. Wallace with what psychologists call a *paired-associate task*. In this task, you'll read a long list of word pairs, like strong–arm and black–curtain. Then you'll present the learner with the first word in each pair (such as "strong") and ask him to select the second word ("arm") from a list of four alternative words. Now here's the surprise: To evaluate the effects of punishment on learning, you'll be delivering a series of painful electric shocks to the learner. With each wrong answer, you'll move up one step on a shock generator. The shocks range from 15 volts up to 450 volts and are accompanied by labels ranging from "Slight Shock" and "Moderate Shock," to "Danger: Severe Shock," and finally, and most ominously, "XXX."

The Study: You watch as Mr. Williams brings the learner into a room and straps his arm to a shock plate. The learner, Mr. Williams explains, will push a button corresponding to his answer to the first word in each pair. His answer will light up in an adjoining room where you sit. For a correct answer, you do nothing. But for an incorrect answer, you'll give the learner an electric shock, with the intensity increasing with each mistake. At this point, the learner mentions to Mr. Williams that he has "a slight heart condition" and asks anxiously how powerful the shocks will be. Mr. Williams responds curtly that although the shocks will be painful, they "will cause no permanent tissue damage."

You're led into the adjoining room and seated in front of the shock generator. Following Milgram's plan, the learner makes a few correct responses but soon begins to make errors. If, at any time, you turn to Mr. Williams to ask if you should continue, he responds with a set of prearranged sentences that urge you to go on ("Please go on," "The experiment requires that you continue," "You have no other choice; you *must* go on"). Milgram standardized the verbal statements of the learner, which, also unbeknownst to you, have been prerecorded on audiotape (Milgram, 1974). At 75 volts, the learner grunts "Ugh!" and by 330 volts, he frantically yells "Let me out of here!" repeatedly and complains of chest pain. From 345 volts onward, there's nothing—only silence. The learner stops responding to your items, and Mr. Williams instructs you to treat these nonresponses as incorrect answers and to keep administering increasingly intense shocks.

The Results: When Milgram first designed this study, he asked 40 psychiatrists at Yale University to forecast the outcome. Their predictions? According to them, most subjects would break

Scenes from Milgram's obedience experiment:

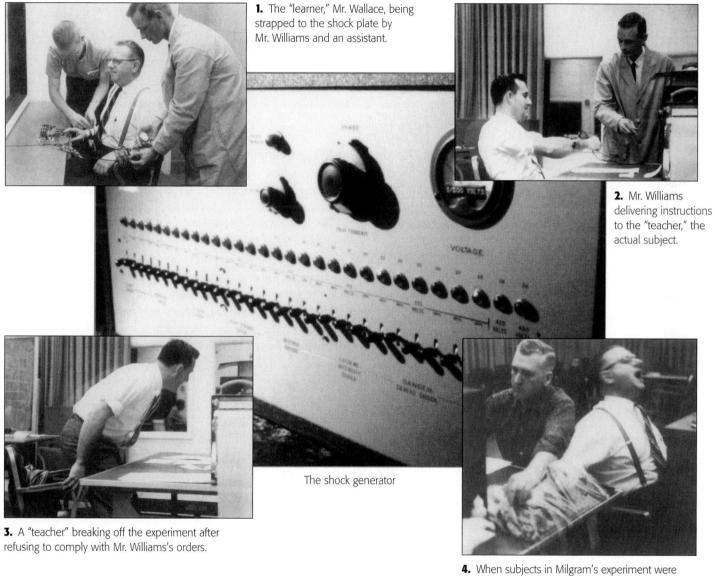

1. The "learner," Mr. Wallace, being strapped to the shock plate by Mr. Williams and an assistant.

2. Mr. Williams delivering instructions to the "teacher," the actual subject.

The shock generator

3. A "teacher" breaking off the experiment after refusing to comply with Mr. Williams's orders.

4. When subjects in Milgram's experiment were forced to hold the "learner's" hand on a shock plate, the level of obedience plummeted. Decreasing the psychological distance between teacher and learner leads to decreased obedience.

off at 150 volts and only 0.1 percent (that's 1 in 1,000), representing a "pathological fringe" (Milgram, 1974), would go all the way to 450 volts. They were wrong. In fact, in the original Milgram study, all subjects administered at least some shocks. Most went up to at least 150 volts, and a remarkable 62 percent of subjects displayed complete compliance, going all the way up 450 volts.

These results were, well, shocking. Milgram himself was startled by them (Blass, 2004). Before Milgram's study, most psychologists assumed that the overwhelming majority of normal subjects would disobey what were obviously cruel and outrageous orders. But like the Yale psychiatrists, they committed the fundamental attribution error: They underestimated the impact of the situation on subjects' behaviors.

There were other surprises. Many subjects showed uncontrollable tics and fits of nervous laughter. Yet few appeared to be sadistic. Even those who complied to the bitter end seemed reluctant to deliver shocks, asking or even begging the experimenter to allow them to stop. Yet most subjects still followed Mr. Williams's orders despite these pleas, often assuming no responsibility for their actions. For example, one subject's response was, "I stopped, but he [the experimenter] made me go on" (Milgram, 1974).

The Milgram Paradigm: Themes and Variations. Milgram conducted a variety of studies to pinpoint the situational factors that increased or decreased obedience and to rule out alternative explanations for his findings. **[LEARNING OBJECTIVE 11.5]** They also afford a powerful test of the replicability of Milgram's paradigm and its generalizability across different situations.

RULING OUT RIVAL HYPOTHESES
Have important alternative explanations for the findings been excluded?

The level of subjects' obedience varied substantially depending on the circumstances, including the amount of feedback from the learner, proximity of the learner to the teacher, and the physical proximity and prestige of the experimenter. Though there were numerous variations on the paradigm, two key themes emerge. First, the greater the "psychological distance" between teacher (the actual participant) and experimenter, the *less* the obedience. When the experimenter became more psychologically distant, as when he gave instructions by telephone, compliance plummeted. Second, the greater the psychological distance between teacher and learner, the *more* the obedience. Most striking was the level of compliance when Milgram increased the psychological distance between teacher and learner by having the teacher direct someone else to administer the shocks. Here the level of complete compliance shot up to 93 percent. Like Lieutenant Calley, whose defense during the My Lai massacre was that he was "just taking orders," subjects in this condition probably felt relieved of personal responsibility. Many Nazis, like Adolph Eichmann, offered similar excuses for their orders to kill thousands of Jews: They were just following instructions from their superiors (Aronson, 1998). When people do immoral things, they often look to pass the responsibility on to somebody else.

The Milgram Paradigm: Individual, Gender, and Cultural Differences. When evaluating Milgram's findings, it's only natural to focus on the sizable proportion of subjects who followed orders. Yet many of his subjects didn't go along with the experimenter's commands despite intense pressure to do so. So despite powerful situational pressures, some people disobey authority figures who give unethical orders. Who are they?

Researchers have identified a few consistent predictors of disobedience in Milgram's paradigm. Lawrence Kohlberg found that the level of moral development using his interview-based scheme (see Chapter 8) was negatively correlated with compliance; more morally advanced subjects were more willing to defy the experimenter (Kohlberg, 1965; Milgram, 1974). Another researcher found that people with high levels of a personality trait called *authoritarianism* are more likely to comply with the experimenters' demands (Elms, 1972). People with high levels of authoritarianism see the world as a big hierarchy of power. For them, authority figures such as the experimenter are to be respected, not questioned (Adorno, Frenkel-Brunswik, Levinson, et al., 1950; Dillehay, 1978).

Milgram found no consistent sex differences in obedience; this finding has held up in later studies using his paradigm (Blass, 1999). Milgram's findings have also been replicated in different countries. The overall rates of obedience among Americans don't differ significantly from those of non-Americans (Blass, 2004), including people in Italy (Ancona & Pareyson, 1968), South Africa (Edwards, Franks, Friedgood, et al., 1969), Spain (Miranda, Caballero, Gomez, et al., 1981), Germany (Mantell, 1971), Australia (Kilham & Mann, 1974), and Jordan (Shanab & Yahya, 1977).

REPLICABILITY
Can the results be duplicated in other studies?

Milgram's Studies: Lessons. Psychologists have learned a great deal from Milgram's work. They've learned that the power of authority figures is greater than almost anyone had imagined. They've learned that obedience doesn't typically result from cruelty; most of Milgram's subjects wanted to stop but kept going out of deference to authority. Milgram's research also reminds us of the potency of the fundamental attribution error: Most people, even psychiatrists, underestimate situational influences on behavior (Bierbrauer, 1973).

Psychologists continue to debate whether Milgram's study offers an adequate model of what happened during the Holocaust and at My Lai. Milgram's critics correctly note that, in contrast to Milgram's subjects, some concentration camp guards actively enjoyed torturing innocent people (Cialdini & Goldstein, 2004). These critics further argue that destructive obedience on a grand scale probably requires not only an authority figure bearing an official stamp of approval, but also a core group of genuinely wicked people. They may well be right. Another important criticism relates to the ethics of Milgram's studies. Subjects were asked to perform a task that many found quite distressing, and the potential for psychological harm in learning the true purpose of the study was high. Such a study could not be performed today due to current ethical guidelines. These controversies aside, Stanley Milgram made us more aware of the fact that good people can do bad things and that rational people can behave irrationally (Aronson, 1998). By warning us of these perils, Milgram may have helped us prevent them.

Rosa Parks (1913–2005) became a role model for "civil disobedience" during the 1950s and 1960s when she refused to give up her seat on a bus to a white man as was required by law. Morality, for her, overrode law.

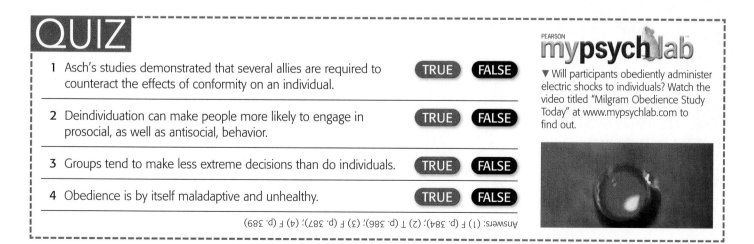

QUIZ

1 Asch's studies demonstrated that several allies are required to counteract the effects of conformity on an individual. **TRUE** **FALSE**

2 Deindividuation can make people more likely to engage in prosocial, as well as antisocial, behavior. **TRUE** **FALSE**

3 Groups tend to make less extreme decisions than do individuals. **TRUE** **FALSE**

4 Obedience is by itself maladaptive and unhealthy. **TRUE** **FALSE**

Answers: (1) F (p. 384); (2) T (p. 386); (3) F (p. 387); (4) F (p. 389)

PEARSON
mypsychlab

▼ Will participants obediently administer electric shocks to individuals? Watch the video titled "Milgram Obedience Study Today" at www.mypsychlab.com to find out.

This remarkable photo by primate researcher Frans de Waal shows a male chimpanzee (*left*) extending a hand of appeasement to another chimpanzee after a fight. Many psychologists have argued that our tendency toward prosocial behavior has deep roots in our primate heritage.

Figure 11.7 The Murder of Kitty Genovese. Place in Kew Gardens, New York, where Kitty Genovese was murdered on March 13, 1964, at 3:20 A.M. She drove into the parking lot at the Kew Gardens train station and parked her car at spot **1**. Noticing a man in the lot, she became nervous and headed toward a police telephone box. The man caught her and attacked her with a knife at spot **2**. She managed to get away, but he attacked her again at spot **3** and again at spot **4**.

Helping and Harming Others: Prosocial Behavior and Aggression

For centuries, philosophers have debated the question of whether human nature is good or bad. Yet scientific truth rarely falls neatly into one of two extremes. Indeed, mounting evidence suggests that human nature is a blend of both socially constructive and destructive tendencies. Primate researcher Frans de Waal (1982, 1996) argues that our two closest animal relatives, the bonobo (pygmy chimpanzee) and the chimpanzee, display the seeds of both prosocial and antisocial behavior. Because we share more than 98 percent of our DNA with both species, they offer a slightly fuzzy evolutionary window onto our own nature. Although these species overlap in their social behaviors, the bonobo is more of a model for *prosocial behavior*—that is, behavior intended to help others—and the chimpanzee is more of a model for antisocial behavior, including aggressive acts. Chimpanzees engage in prosocial behavior too, like making up after fights.

To which species are we more similar, the peace-loving bonobo or the belligerent chimpanzee? In reality, we're a bit of both. De Waal (2006) is fond of calling the human species "the bipolar ape," because our social behavior is a blend of that of our closest ape relatives.

In this next section, we'll examine the psychological roots of prosocial and antisocial actions, with a particular emphasis on situational factors that contribute to both behaviors. We'll begin by examining why we fail to help in some situations, but why we do help in others. We'll then explore why we occasionally act aggressively toward fellow members of our species.

SAFETY IN NUMBERS OR DANGER IN NUMBERS? BYSTANDER NONINTERVENTION

You've probably heard the saying, "There's safety in numbers." Popular wisdom teaches us that when we find ourselves in danger, it's best to be in the company of others. Is that true? Let's look at two real-life examples.

Two Tragic Stories of Bystander Nonintervention

- On March 13, 1964, at 3 A.M., 28-year-old Catherine (Kitty) Genovese was returning to her apartment in New York City, having just gotten off work. Suddenly, a man appeared and began stabbing her. He came and left no fewer than three times over a 35-minute time span. Kitty repeatedly screamed and pleaded for help as the lights from nearby apartments flipped on. Although the precise facts remain in dispute (Manning, Levine, & Collins, 2007), most of the evidence suggests that at least half a dozen—and perhaps many more—of her 30 or so neighbors heard the events but failed to come to her aid. Most didn't even bother to call the police. By the end of the gruesome attack, Kitty Genovese was dead (see **Figure 11.7**).

- On the morning of August 19, 1995, 33-year-old Deletha Word was driving across a bridge in Detroit, Michigan, when she accidentally hit the fender of a car driven by Martell Welsh. Welsh and the two boys with him jumped out of their car, stripped Deletha down to her underwear and beat her repeatedly with a tire jack. At one point, Welsh even held Deletha up in the air and asked bystanders whether anyone "wanted a piece" of her. About 40 people drove by in their cars, but none intervened or even called the police. In a desperate attempt to escape her attackers, Deletha jumped off the bridge into the river below. She drowned.

Causes of Bystander Nonintervention: Why We Don't Help.

Like most anecdotes, these real-world stories are useful for illustrating concepts, but they don't allow for scientific generalizations. For years, many psychologists assumed that the nonresponsiveness of bystanders was due simply to a lack of caring. But psychologists John Darley and Bibb Latané suspected that the *bystander effect* was less a consequence of apathy than of "psychological paralysis." According to Darley and Latané (1968a), bystanders in emergencies typically want to intervene but often find themselves frozen, seemingly powerless to help. Darley and Latané also suspected that popular psychology was wrong—that there's actually danger rather than safety in numbers. Bucking conventional wisdom, they hypothesized that the presence of others makes people less, not more, likely to help in emergencies. Why?

Deletha Word was a tragic victim of bystander nonintervention. After her death, loved ones gathered to mourn on the bridge where she was attacked.

Pluralistic Ignorance: It Must Just Be Me. Darley and Latané maintained that two major factors explain bystander nonintervention. The first is **pluralistic ignorance:** the error of assuming that no one in the group perceives things as we do. **[LEARNING OBJECTIVE 11.6]** To intervene in an emergency, we first need to recognize that the situation is in fact an emergency. Imagine that on your way to class tomorrow you see a student in dirty clothing slumped across a bench. As you stroll by, thoughts whiz through your mind: Is he asleep? Is he drunk? Could he be seriously ill, even dead? Could my psychology professor be conducting a study to examine my responses to emergencies? Here's where pluralistic ignorance comes into play. We look around, notice that nobody else is responding, and assume—perhaps mistakenly—that the situation isn't an emergency. We assume we're the only one who thinks the situation might be an emergency. Reassured that the coast is clear and that there's nothing to worry about, we continue on our way to class.

So pluralistic ignorance is relevant when we're trying to figure out whether an ambiguous situation is really an emergency. But pluralistic ignorance doesn't fully explain the behavior of bystanders in the Kitty Genovese or Deletha Word tragedies, because those situations were clearly emergencies. Even once we've recognized that the situation is an emergency, the presence of others still tends to inhibit helping.

Diffusion of Responsibility: Passing the Buck. A second step is required for us to intervene in an emergency. We need to feel a burden of responsibility for the consequences of *not* intervening. Here's the rub: The more people present at an emergency, *the less each person feels responsible for the negative consequences of not helping.* Darley and Latané called this phenomenon **diffusion of responsibility:** The presence of others makes each person feel less responsible for the outcome. If you don't assist someone who's having a heart attack and that person later dies, you can always say to yourself, "Well, that's a terrible tragedy, but it wasn't really *my* fault. After all, plenty of other people could have helped too."

So we can experience pluralistic ignorance, which prevents us from interpreting a situation as an emergency, *and* we can experience diffusion of responsibility, which discourages us from offering assistance in an emergency. From this perspective, it's actually surprising that any of us helps in emergencies, because the obstacles to intervening are considerable.

Even when a situation appears to be an emergency, we still may not offer assistance. The social psychological principle of diffusion of responsibility helps to explain why.

Studies of Bystander Nonintervention. To get at the psychological roots of the bystander effect in tragedies like the Kitty Genovese story, Darley, Latané, and their colleagues tested the effect of bystanders on subjects' willingness to (1) report that smoke was filling a room (Darley & Latané, 1968b); (2) react to what sounded like a woman falling off a ladder and injuring herself (Latané & Rodin, 1969); and (3) respond to what sounded like

GLOSSARY

pluralistic ignorance
error of assuming that no one in a group perceives things as we do

diffusion of responsibility
reduction in feelings of personal responsibility in the presence of others

another student experiencing an epileptic seizure (Darley & Latané, 1968a). In all of these studies, participants were significantly more likely to seek or offer help when they were alone than in a group (see **Figure 11.8**).

Researchers have replicated these findings many times using slightly different designs. In an analysis of almost 50 studies of bystander intervention involving almost 6,000 participants, Latané and Nida (1981) found that participants were more likely to help when alone than in groups about 90 percent of the time. That's an impressive degree of replicability. Even *thinking* about being in a large group makes us less likely to help in an emergency (Garcia, Weaver, Moskowitz, et al., 2002).

REPLICABILITY
Can the results be duplicated in other studies?

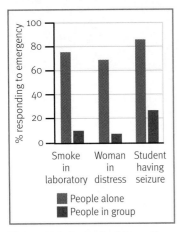

Figure 11.8 Bystander Intervention. Across three classic experiments of bystander intervention, the percentage of people helping when in groups was markedly lower than the percentage of people helping when alone.

WHAT DO *you* THINK?

Imagine you found yourself attacked by a mugger in a crowd while leaving a concert. How could you handle the situation to maximize the chances that you'd receive help from onlookers?

SOCIAL LOAFING: WITH A LITTLE TOO MUCH HELP FROM MY FRIENDS

Have you ever been a member of a group that got virtually nothing accomplished? If so, you may have been a victim of **social loafing,** the phenomenon in which people slack off in groups (Latané, Williams, & Harkins, 1979; North, Linley, & Hargreaves, 2000).

Some psychologists believe that social loafing is a variant of bystander nonintervention. That's because social loafing appears to be due in part to diffusion of responsibility: People working in groups typically feel less personally responsible for the outcome of a project than they do when working alone. As a result, they don't invest as much effort.

Psychologists have demonstrated social loafing in numerous experiments. In one, a researcher placed blindfolds and headphones on six participants and asked them to clap or yell as loudly as possible. When participants thought they were making noises as part of a group, they were less loud than when they thought they were making noises alone (Harkins, 1981). Investigators have also identified social loafing effects in studies of rope pulling (the "tug-of-war" game), navigating mazes, identifying radar signals, and evaluating job candidates (Karau & Williams, 1995).

One of the best ways to prevent social loafing is to ensure that each person in the group is identifiable, for example, by guaranteeing that managers and bosses can evaluate each individual's performance. By doing so, we can help "diffuse" the diffusion of responsibility that often arises in groups.

Studies of social loafing demonstrate that in large groups, individuals often work (or in this case, pull) less hard than they do when alone.

myth CONCEPTIONS | IS BRAINSTORMING IN GROUPS A GOOD WAY TO GENERATE IDEAS?

Imagine that you've been hired by an advertising firm to cook up a new marketing campaign for Mrs. Yummy's Chicken Noodle Soup. The soup hasn't been selling well of late, and your job is to come up with an advertising jingle that will instill in every American an uncontrollable urge to reach for the nearest cup of chicken noodle soup.

Although you initially plan to come up with possible slogans on your own, your boss walks into your cubicle and informs you that you'll be participating in a "group brainstorming"

GLOSSARY

social loafing
phenomenon whereby individuals become less productive in groups

meeting later that afternoon in the executive suite. There, you and twelve other firm members will let your imaginations run wild, saying whatever comes to mind in the hopes of hitting on a winning chicken noodle soup advertising formula. Companies across the world regularly use group brainstorming as a means of generating novel ideas. They assume that several heads that generate a flurry of ideas are better than one. In a book titled *Applied Imagination,* which influenced many companies to adopt brainstorming, Osborn (1957) argued that "the average person can think up twice as many ideas when working with a group than when working alone" (p. 229).

Although the idea behind group brainstorming is intuitively appealing, it turns out to be wrong. Numerous studies demonstrate that group brainstorming is actually less effective than individual brainstorming (Brown & Paulus, 2002; Diehl & Stroebe, 1987). When brainstorming, groups tend to come up with fewer ideas, and often fewer good ones, than individuals (Paulus, 2004). Group brainstorming generally also results in ideas that are less creative than those generated by individual brainstorming. Making matters worse, groups often overestimate how successful they are at producing new ideas, which may help to explain brainstorming's popularity (Paulus, Larey, & Ortega, 1995).

There are at least two reasons why group brainstorming is less effective than individual brainstorming. One is that group members may be anxious about being evaluated by others, leading them to hold back potentially good ideas. The second is social loafing. When brainstorming in groups, people frequently engage in what's called "free riding": They sit back and let others do the hard work (Diehl & Stroebe, 1987). Whatever the reason, research suggests that when it comes to brainstorming, one brain may be better than two—or many more—at least when the brains can communicate with each other.

PROSOCIAL BEHAVIOR AND ALTRUISM

Even though there's usually danger rather than safety in numbers when it comes to others helping us, many of us do help in emergencies even when others are around (Fischer et al., 2006). In the Deletha Word tragedy, two men jumped into the water in an unsuccessful attempt to save her from drowning. Indeed, there's good evidence that many of us engage in **altruism,** that is, helping others for unselfish reasons (Batson, 1987; Dovidio, Piliavin, Schroeder, et al., 2006; Penner, Dovidio, Schroeder, et al., 2005).

Altruism: Helping Selflessly.
Over the years, some scientists have argued that we help others entirely for egoistic (self-centered) reasons, like relieving our own distress or experiencing the joy of others we've helped (Hoffman, 1981). From this perspective, we help others only to make ourselves feel better. Yet in a series of experiments, Daniel Batson and his colleagues have shown that we sometimes engage in genuine altruism. That is, in some cases we help others in discomfort primarily because we feel empathic toward them (Batson et al., 1991; Batson & Shaw, 1991; Fischer, Greitemeyer, Pollozek, et al., 2006). In some studies, they exposed participants to a female victim (actually a confederate) who was receiving painful electric shocks and gave them the option of either (a) taking her place and receiving the shocks themselves or (b) turning away and not watching her receive shocks. When participants were made to feel empathic toward the victim (for example, by being informed that their values and interests were similar to hers), they generally offered to take her place and receive shocks rather than turn away (Batson et al., 1981). So in some cases we seem to help not only to relieve our distress but to relieve the distress of others.

Along with empathy, a number of psychological variables increase the odds of helping. Let's look at some of the most crucial ones.

Psychological research suggests that we sometimes engage in genuine altruism, helping largely out of empathy.

GLOSSARY

altruism
helping others for unselfish reasons

Helping: Situational Influences. People are more likely to help in some situations than in others. They're more likely to help others when they can't easily escape the situation by running away, driving away, or as in the case of the Kitty Genovese murder, turning off their lights and drifting back to sleep. For example, individuals are more likely to help someone who collapses on a crowded subway than on the sidewalk. Characteristics of the victim also affect the likelihood of helping. In one study, bystanders helped a person with a cane 95 percent of the time but helped an obviously drunk person only 50 percent of the time (Piliavin, Rodin, & Piliavin, 1969). Being in a good mood also makes us more likely to help (Isen, Clark, & Schwartz, 1976). So does exposure to role models who help others (Bryan & Test, 1967; Rushton & Campbell, 1977).

There's a silver lining to the gray cloud of bystander nonintervention. Research suggests that exposure to research on bystander effects increases the chances of intervening in emergencies. In one study, students who had heard a lecture on the bystander effect were significantly more likely than students who hadn't heard the lecture to help someone in distress they encountered 2 weeks later (Beaman, Barnes, Klentz, et al., 1978). This study worked probably because it imparted new knowledge about bystander intervention and perhaps also because it made people more aware of the importance of helping. So the very act of reading this chapter may have made you more likely to become a responsive bystander.

Helping: Individual Differences. Individual differences in personality can also influence the likelihood of helping. Participants who are less concerned about social approval and less traditional are more likely to go against the grain and intervene in emergencies even when others are present (Latané & Darley, 1970). Extraverted people are also more prone to help others than introverted people (Krueger, Hicks, McGue, et al., 2001). In addition, people with lifesaving skills, such as trained medical workers, are more likely to offer assistance to others in emergencies than other people are, even when they're off duty (Huston, Ruggiero, Conner, et al., 1981). Some people may not help on certain occasions simply because they don't know what to do.

Both interpersonal provocation and frustration from being stuck in traffic likely contribute to "road rage."

AGGRESSION: WHY WE HURT OTHERS

Like our primate cousins, the chimpanzees, we occasionally engage in violent behavior toward others. And like them, we're a war-waging species; as we write this chapter, there are at least 15 full-scale wars raging across the globe. Psychologists define **aggression** as behavior intended to harm others, either verbally or physically. To account for aggressive behavior on both large and small scales, we need to examine the role of situational factors, both short-term and long-term, and dispositional factors.

Aggression: Situational Influences. Using both laboratory and naturalistic designs, psychologists have pinpointed a host of situational influences on human aggression. **[LEARNING OBJECTIVE 11.7]** Next, we'll review some of the best-replicated findings.

REPLICABILITY
Can the results be duplicated in other studies?

- **Interpersonal Provocation:** Not surprisingly, we're especially likely to strike out aggressively against those who have provoked us, say, by insulting, threatening, or hitting us (Geen, 2001).

- **Frustration:** We're especially likely to behave aggressively when we're frustrated, that is, thwarted from reaching a goal (Anderson & Bushman, 2002a; Berkowitz, 1989).

- **Media Influences:** Watching media violence increases the odds of violence through observational learning (C.A. Anderson et al., 2003; Bandura, 1973). Laboratory experiments show that playing violent video games also boosts the odds of real-world violence (Gentile & Anderson, 2003).

GLOSSARY

aggression
behavior intended to harm others, either verbally or physically

- **Aggressive Cues:** External cues associated with violence, such as guns and knives, can serve as discriminant stimuli (see Chapter 5) for aggression, making us more likely to act violently in response to provocation (Carlson, Marcus-Newhall, & Miller, 1990).

- **Arousal:** When our autonomic nervous systems (see Chapter 3) are hyped up, we may mistakenly attribute this arousal to anger, leading us to act aggressively (Zillman, 1988).

- **Alcohol and Other Drugs:** Certain substances can disinhibit our brain's prefrontal cortex (see Chapter 3), lowering our inhibitions toward behaving violently (Kelly, Cherek, Steinberg, et al., 1988).

- **Temperature:** Rates of violent crime in different regions of the United States mirror the average temperatures in these regions (Anderson, et al., 1997). Because warm temperatures increase irritability, they may make people more likely to lose their tempers when provoked or frustrated (Anderson & Bushman, 2002b). See **Figure 11.9.**

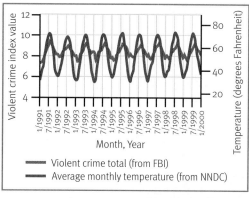

Violent crime total (from FBI)
Average monthly temperature (from NNDC)

Figure 11.9 Monthly Violent Crime versus Average Temperature, 1991–1999. Research demonstrates that violent crime rates coincide with outdoor temperatures. How might we determine whether this correlation indicates a causal effect? (*Source:* Nienberg)

Aggression: Individual, Gender, and Cultural Differences.

On a typical day in the United States, there are between 40 and 45 murders; that's one about every half hour. There are also about 230 reported rapes, or one about every 5 or 6 minutes (Federal Bureau of Investigation, 2005). These statistics paint a grim picture. Yet the substantial majority of people are generally law-abiding citizens, and only a tiny percentage ever engage in serious physical aggression toward others. Across a wide swath of societies that scientists have studied, only a small percentage of people— perhaps 5 or 6 percent—account for more than half of all crimes, including violent crimes (Wilson & Herrnstein, 1985). What makes these individuals so much more aggressive than the rest of us?

Personality Traits. When confronted with the same situation, like an insult, people differ in their tendencies to behave aggressively. Certain personality traits can combine to create a dangerous cocktail of aggression-proneness. People with high levels of negative emotions (such as irritability and mistrust), impulsivity, and a lack of closeness to others are especially prone to violence (Krueger et al., 1994).

Sex Differences. One of the best replicated sex differences in humans, and across the animal kingdom for that matter, is the higher level of physical aggressiveness among males than females (Eagly & Steffen, 1986; Maccoby & Jacklin, 1980; Storch, Bagner, Gefken, et al., 2004). In conjunction with biological sex, age plays a role: The rates of crime, including violent crime, would drop by two-thirds if all males between the ages of 12 and 28 were magically placed into a state of temporary hibernation (Lykken, 1995).

The reasons for the sex difference in aggression are controversial. Some researchers have traced it to the higher levels of the hormone testosterone in males (Dabbs, 2001). Social factors almost surely play a role too, at least in humans: Parents and teachers tend to pay more attention to boys when they engage in aggression and to girls when they engage in dependent behaviors, like clinginess (Serbin & O'Leary, 1975).

Yet the well-replicated male predominance in aggression may apply only to physical violence, not indirect aggression. Nicki Crick (1995) discovered that girls tend to be higher than boys in **relational aggression,** a form of indirect aggression marked by spreading rumors, gossiping, social exclusion, and nonverbal putdowns (like giving other girls "the silent treatment") for the purposes of social manipulation.

Cultural Differences. Culture may also shape aggression. For example, physical aggression and violent crime tend to be less prevalent among Asian individuals, such as Japanese and Chinese, than among Americans or Europeans (Wilson & Herrnstein, 1985;

Research suggests although males tend to be more physically aggressive than females, girls are more likely than boys to engage in relational aggression, which includes gossiping and making fun of others behind their backs.

GLOSSARY

relational aggression
form of indirect aggression, prevalent in girls, involving spreading rumors, gossiping, and nonverbal putdowns for the purpose of social manipulation

Zhang & Snowden, 1999). Richard Nisbett, Dov Cohen, and their colleagues have also found that people from the southern regions of the United States are more likely than people from other regions of the country to adhere to a *culture of honor*, that is, a social norm of defending one's reputation in the face of perceived insults (Nisbett & Cohen, 1996). The culture of honor may help to explain why the rates of violence are higher in the South than in other parts of the United States. Interestingly, these rates are higher only for violence that arises in the context of disputes, not in robberies, burglaries, or other crimes (Cohen & Nisbett, 1994).

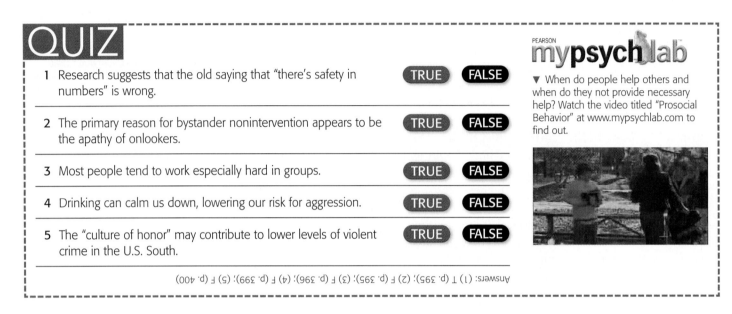

QUIZ

1 Research suggests that the old saying that "there's safety in numbers" is wrong. TRUE FALSE

2 The primary reason for bystander nonintervention appears to be the apathy of onlookers. TRUE FALSE

3 Most people tend to work especially hard in groups. TRUE FALSE

4 Drinking can calm us down, lowering our risk for aggression. TRUE FALSE

5 The "culture of honor" may contribute to lower levels of violent crime in the U.S. South. TRUE FALSE

Answers: (1) T (p. 395); (2) F (p. 395); (3) F (p. 396); (4) F (p. 399); (5) F (p. 400)

PEARSON mypsychlab

▼ When do people help others and when do they not provide necessary help? Watch the video titled "Prosocial Behavior" at www.mypsychlab.com to find out.

Attitudes and Persuasion: Changing Minds

First, answer the following question: Do you think that the death penalty is effective in discouraging people from committing murder? Second, answer this question: How do you feel about the death penalty?

Now that you've gone through this exercise, you can grasp the difference between beliefs and attitudes. The first question assessed your *beliefs* about the death penalty, the second question your *attitudes* toward the death penalty. A **belief** is a conclusion regarding factual evidence; in contrast, an **attitude** is a belief that includes an emotional component. An attitude reflects how you feel about an issue or person. Attitudes are an important part of our social world because they're shaped in significant ways by the people around us.

ATTITUDES AND BEHAVIOR

A prevalent misconception is that attitudes are good predictors of behavior. For example, most people believe that how we feel about a political candidate predicts with a high level of certainty whether we'll vote for or against that candidate. It makes sense, doesn't it? But it's wrong (Wicker, 1969). In part, this finding explains why even carefully conducted political polls are rarely foolproof: We don't always act on our stated preferences.
[LEARNING OBJECTIVE 11.8]

GLOSSARY

belief
conclusion regarding factual evidence

attitude
belief that includes an emotional component

When Attitudes Don't Predict Behavior. In a study conducted over 70 years ago, Robert LaPiere asked 128 hotel and restaurant owners whether they'd be willing to serve guests who were Chinese, who at the time were widely discriminated against. Over 90 percent of LaPiere's subjects said no. Yet when LaPiere had previously toured the country with a Chinese couple, 127 of 128 of the same owners had served them (LaPiere, 1934). Indeed, a review of 88 studies revealed that the average correlation between attitudes and behavior is about 0.38 (Kraus, 1995), which is only a moderate association. So although attitudes forecast behavior at better than chance levels, they're far from guaranteed predictors. This finding probably reflects the fact that our behaviors are the outcome of many factors, only one of which is our attitudes. For example, LaPiere's prejudiced subjects may not have been especially fond of the idea of serving Chinese guests. Yet when they met these guests in person, they may have found them more likable than they expected. Or when push came to shove, they may have been reluctant to pass up the chance for good business.

When Attitudes Do Predict Behavior. Occasionally, though, our attitudes predict our behaviors reasonably well. Attitudes that are highly *accessible*—those that come to mind easily—tend to be strongly predictive of our behavior (Fazio, 1995). Imagine that we asked you two questions: (1) How do you feel about the idea of purchasing a new brand of yogurt that's been scientifically demonstrated to produce a 2 percent decrease in the levels of low-density cholesterol over a 5-year period? and (2) How do you feel about the idea of purchasing chocolate ice cream? If you're like most people, you'll find question 2 much easier to answer than question 1, because you've thought more about it. If so, your attitude toward chocolate ice cream is more likely to predict your purchasing behavior than is your attitude toward the new-fangled yogurt.

Attitudes also predict behavior well for a group of people known as low self-monitors (Kraus, 1995). **Self-monitoring** is a trait that assesses the extent to which people's behaviors reflect their true feelings and attitudes (Snyder, 1974; Snyder & Gangestad, 1986). Low self-monitors tend to be straight shooters, whereas high self-monitors tend to be social chameleons. Not surprisingly, we can usually trust low self-monitors' actions to mirror their attitudes.

Still, the attitude–behavior correlation is, after all, just a correlation. The fact that attitudes are correlated with behaviors doesn't mean they cause them. Other explanations are possible; for example, our behaviors may sometimes cause our attitudes. Imagine that we start out with a negative attitude toward homeless persons. If a friend persuades us to volunteer to help the homeless for 3 hours a week and we end up enjoying this type of work, our attitudes toward homeless people may improve.

ORIGINS OF ATTITUDES

Our attitudes stem from a variety of sources. Among them are our prior experience, our ability to relate to messengers who provide information, and our personalities.

Recognition. Our experiences shape our attitudes. The *recognition heuristic* makes us more likely to believe something we've heard many times (Arkes, 1993). Like most heuristics (mental shortcuts or rules of thumb; see Chapter 2), the recognition heuristic generally serves us well because things we hear many times from many different people often *are* true. Moreover, this heuristic can help us to make snap judgments that are surprisingly accurate. To test this possibility, two researchers asked a group of students in Chicago and in Munich, Germany, the following question: *Which city has a larger population: San Diego, California, or San Antonio, Texas?* Unexpectedly, only 62 percent of American students got the correct answer (San Diego), whereas 100 percent of German students did (Goldstein & Gigerenzer,

People's expressed voting preferences to pollsters don't always predict their actual voting behavior.

CORRELATION vs. CAUSATION
Can we be sure that A causes B?

GLOSSARY

self-monitoring
personality trait that assesses the extent to which people's behavior reflects their true feelings and attitudes

1999). The German students didn't get it right more often than the Americans because they had more knowledge of U.S. cities; in fact, they got it right because they had *less* knowledge of U.S. cities. Most of the German students had never heard of San Antonio, so they simply relied on the recognition heuristic ("The city I've heard of probably has more people in it"). In contrast, the American students had heard of both cities and then tried to guess which one had a larger population. In this case, the recognition heuristic worked.

But when a story is persuasive or interesting, the recognition heuristic can get us into trouble. It can lead us to fall for stories that are too good to be true, like some urban legends, or to buy products that seem familiar just because we've heard their names repeated many times.

Characteristics of the Messenger.
Our attitudes are shaped not only by the message but by the messenger. Research demonstrates that we're more likely to swallow a persuasive message if famous or attractive people deliver it—whether or not they would logically know something about the product they're hawking. Fortunately, we can safeguard ourselves against *maladaptive gullibility*—falling for messages delivered by phony authority figures—by monitoring and distinguishing legitimate from illegitimate authorities (Cialdini & Sagarin, 2005).

Researchers have also reported an *implicit egotism* effect—the finding that we're more positively disposed toward people, places, or things that resemble us—across many domains including even shared birthdays or first names (Finch & Cialdini, 1989; Pelham, Carvallo, & Jones, 2005).

Attitudes and Personality.
Our attitudes are associated in important ways with our personality traits. Although we may persuade ourselves that our political attitudes derive from completely objective analyses of social issues, these attitudes are often affected by our personalities. In an article that stirred up more than its share of controversy, one team of researchers (Jost, Glaser, Sulloway, et al., 2003) reported that across many studies, political conservatives tend to be more fearful, more sensitive to threat, and less tolerant of uncertainty than political liberals. They suggested that these personality traits are the "psychological glue" that binds together conservatives' political attitudes toward the death penalty, abortion, gun control, school prayer, national defense, and a host of other seemingly unrelated issues. Nevertheless, some researchers criticized these authors for not considering an alternative hypothesis: namely, that these personality traits predict political extremism in general rather than right-wing conservatism specifically (Greenberg & Jonas, 2003). According to these critics, left-wing extremists are just as likely to be fearful, dogmatic, and the like, as right-wing extremists are. Because there are few studies of left-wing extremists, we don't know who's right.

COGNITIVE DISSONANCE AND ATTITUDE CHANGE

Many of us are surprised to discover that our attitudes on many topics, like the death penalty and abortion, change over the years. We tend to perceive ourselves as more consistent over time in our attitudes than we really are (Bem & McConnell, 1970; Goethals & Reckman, 1973; Ross, 1989), perhaps in part because we don't like to think of ourselves as weak-willed flip-floppers. Yet this point raises a question that psychologists have long struggled to answer: What makes us change our attitudes?

Cognitive Dissonance Theory.
In the 1950s, Leon Festinger developed *cognitive dissonance theory,* an influential model of why our attitudes change. According to this theory, we alter our attitudes when we experience an unpleasant state of tension—**cognitive dissonance**—between two or more conflicting thoughts (cognitions). Because we dislike

Endorsements from attractive celebrities, like Hilary Duff, can lead us to prefer some products over others for irrational reasons.

RULING OUT RIVAL HYPOTHESES
Have important alternative explanations for the findings been excluded?

GLOSSARY

cognitive dissonance
unpleasant mental experience of tension resulting from two conflicting thoughts or beliefs

this state of tension, we're motivated to reduce or eliminate it. **[LEARNING OBJECTIVE 11.9]** If we hold an attitude or belief (cognition A) that's inconsistent with another attitude or belief (cognition B), we can reduce the anxiety resulting from this inconsistency in three major ways: change cognition A, change cognition B, or introduce a new cognition, C, that resolves the inconsistency between A and B (see **Figure 11.10**).

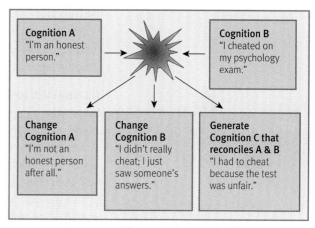

Figure 11.10 Cognitive Dissonance Theory. According to cognitive dissonance theory, we can reduce the conflicts between two cognitions (beliefs) in the multiple ways shown above.

Let's move from As, Bs, and Cs to a real-world example. Imagine that you believe that your new friend, Sandy, is a nice person. You learn from another friend, Chris, that Sandy recently stole a wallet from a fellow classmate. According to Festinger, this news should produce cognitive dissonance, because it creates a conflict between cognition A (Sandy is a nice person) and cognition B (Sandy stole money from someone and therefore isn't such a nice person after all). To resolve this nagging sense of tension, you can change cognition A and decide that Sandy isn't really a nice person after all. Or you can change cognition B, perhaps by deciding that the news that Sandy stole money must be a false rumor spread by her enemies. Or you can instead introduce a new thought, cognition C, that resolves the discrepancy between cognitions A and B. For example, you could persuade yourself that Sandy is still a nice person but that she took her classmate's wallet because she was starving and in desperate need of a short-term infusion of cash ("I'm sure she'll return the wallet and all of the money in a day or two once she's grabbed something to eat," you reassure yourself).

We all experience a form of cognitive dissonance at some time or other when trying to make a decision between two or more things (shirts, desserts, even colleges or apartments). This type of dissonance, called *post-decision dissonance,* occurs when our positive feelings toward one option decrease immediately after we decide to go with the other option. By decreasing our liking of what we didn't select, we reduce our cognitive dissonance regarding difficult choices.

Festinger, along with J. Merrill Carlsmith, conducted the first systematic test of cognitive dissonance theory in the late 1950s (Festinger & Carlsmith, 1959):

The Setup: You sign up for a 2-hour study of "Measures of Performance." At the lab, an experimenter provides you with instructions for some manual tasks—all mind-numbingly boring, like inserting 12 spools into a tray, emptying the tray, refilling the tray, and so on, for half an hour. Now here's the twist: The experimenter explains that a research assistant normally informs the next subject waiting in the hallway about the study and, to help recruit this subject, he says how interesting and enjoyable the study was. Unfortunately, the research assistant couldn't make it into the lab today. So, the experimenter wonders, would you be kind enough to substitute for him?

The Study: Festinger and Carlsmith randomly assigned some subjects to receive $1 to perform this favor and others to receive $20. Afterward, they asked subjects how much they enjoyed performing the tasks. From the perspective of learning theory, especially operant conditioning (Chapter 5), we might expect subjects paid $20 to say they enjoyed the task more. Yet cognitive dissonance theory makes a counterintuitive prediction: Subjects paid $1 should say they enjoyed the task more. Why? Because all subjects should experience cognitive dissonance: They performed an incredibly boring task but told the next subject it was fun. Yet subjects given $20 had a good *external justification* for telling this little fib, namely, that the experimenter bribed them to do it. In contrast, subjects given $1 had almost no external justification. As a result, the only easy way to resolve their cognitive dissonance was to persuade themselves that they must have enjoyed the task after all. They deceive themselves.

The Results: The results supported this surprising prediction. Subjects given less money reported enjoying the task more, presumably because they needed to justify their lies to themselves.

Fact-OID In one of the most creative demonstrations of cognitive dissonance theory, four researchers asked subjects to taste fried grasshoppers (Zimbardo, Weisenberg, Firestone, et al., 1965). They randomly assigned some subjects to receive this bizarre request from a friendly person and others to receive it from an unfriendly person. Consistent with cognitive dissonance theory, the latter subjects reported liking the fried grasshoppers more than the former subjects did. Subjects who tasted the grasshoppers at the request of the friendly person had a good external justification ("I did it to help out a nice person"), but the other subjects didn't. So the latter subjects resolved their dissonance by changing their attitudes—mmm, those little critters were delicious.

This study not only supported cognitive dissonance theory but also made a bigger point. It seems logical that our attitudes might influence our behaviors (although as we discussed earlier, this isn't always the case). But this study demonstrated the much less intuitive opposite conclusion. Their *behaviors* had changed their *attitudes*.

Alternatives to Cognitive Dissonance Theory. Since Festinger and Carlsmith's study, hundreds of experiments have yielded results consistent with cognitive dissonance theory (Harmon-Jones & Mills, 1999). Yet researchers continue to debate whether alternative processes account for attitude change. Some scholars contend that it's not dissonance itself that's responsible for shifting our attitudes but rather threats to our self-concepts (Aronson, 1992; Wood, 2000). In Festinger and Carlsmith's (1959) study, perhaps what motivated subjects in the $1 condition to change their attitudes was a discrepancy between who they believed they were (a decent person) and what they did (lie to another subject). From this perspective, only certain conflicts between attitudes produce cognitive dissonance, namely, those that challenge our views of who we are.

Another explanation, **impression management theory** (Goffman, 1959), proposes that we don't really change our attitudes in cognitive dissonance studies; we only tell the experimenters we have. We do so because we don't want to appear inconsistent (Tedeschi, Schlenker, & Bonoma, 1971). According to this model, Festinger and Carlsmith's subjects in the $1 condition didn't want to look like hypocrites. So they told the experimenter they enjoyed the task even though they didn't. As is often the case in psychology, there may be some truth to each of these explanations. Some subjects may exhibit attitude change because of cognitive dissonance, others because of self-perception, and still others because of impression management (Bem & Funder, 1978).

PERSUASION: HUMANS AS SALESPEOPLE

Whether or not we realize it, we encounter attempts at persuasion every day. If you're like the average student entering college, you've already watched 360,000 commercials; that number will reach a staggering 2 million by the time you turn 65. Each time you walk into a store or supermarket, you see hundreds of products that marketers have crafted carefully to make you more likely to purchase them.

Routes to Persuasion.
According to *dual process models* of persuasion, there are two alternative pathways to persuading others (Petty & Cacioppo, 1986). One, the *central* route, leads us to evaluate the merits of persuasive arguments carefully and thoughtfully. The other, the *peripheral* route, leads us to respond to persuasive arguments on the basis of snap judgments. The danger of persuasive messages that travel through the peripheral route is that we can be easily fooled by superficial factors, such as how physically attractive, famous, or likable the communicator is or how many times we've heard the message (Hemsley & Doob, 1978; Hovland, Janis, & Kelly, 1953; Kenrick et al., 2005).

Persuasion Techniques.
Drawing on the research literature concerning attitudes and attitude change, psychologists have identified a host of effective techniques for persuading others. **[LEARNING OBJECTIVE 11.10]** Many of these methods operate by means of the peripheral persuasion route, largely bypassing our reasoning capacities. Interestingly, successful businesspeople have used many of these techniques for decades (Cialdini, 2001). Let's look at three of them.

REPLICABILITY
Can the results be duplicated in other studies?

RULING OUT RIVAL HYPOTHESES
Have important alternative explanations for the findings been excluded?

GLOSSARY

impression management theory
theory that we don't really change our attitudes, but report that we have so that our behaviors appear consistent with them

- **Foot-in-the-door technique:** Following on the heels of cognitive dissonance theory (Freedman & Fraser, 1966; Gorassini & Olson, 1995), the **foot-in-the-door technique** suggests that we start with a small request before making a bigger one. If we want to get our classmate to volunteer 5 hours a week for the "Helping a Starving Psychologist" charity organization, we can first ask her to volunteer 1 hour a week. Once we've gotten her to agree to that request, we have our "foot in the door," because, from the perspective of cognitive dissonance theory she'll feel a need to justify her initial commitment. As a consequence, she'll probably end up with a positive attitude toward the organization, making it easier to get her to volunteer even more of her time later.

- **Door-in-the-face technique:** Alternatively, we can start with a large request, like asking for a $100 donation to our charity, before asking for a small one, like a $10 donation (Cialdini et al., 1975; O'Keefe & Hale, 2001). One reason the **door-in-the-face technique** works may be that refusing the initial large request often induces guilt in recipients (O'Keefe & Figge, 1997). But if the initial request is so outrageous that it appears insincere or unreasonable, this method often backfires (Cialdini & Goldstein, 2004). The foot-in-the-door and door-in-the-face techniques appear to work about equally well (Pascual & Guéguen, 2005).

- **Low-ball technique:** In the **low-ball technique,** the seller of a product starts by quoting a price well below the actual sales price (Burger & Petty, 1981; Cialdini, 2001). Once the buyer agrees to purchase the product, the seller mentions all of the desirable or necessary "add-ons" that come along with the product. By the time the deal is done, the buyer may end up paying twice as much as he'd initially agreed to pay. We can even use this technique to obtain favors from friends. In one study, a confederate asked strangers to look after his dog while he visited a friend in the hospital. In some cases, he first got the stranger to agree to the request and only then told him he'd be gone for half an hour; in other cases, he told the stranger up front he'd be gone for half an hour. The first tactic worked better (Guéguen, Pascual, & Dagot, 2002).

Studies of the foot-in-the-door technique suggest that once a person agrees to place a small political sign in her yard, she'll be more likely to later agree to place an even larger sign in her yard.

Using the low-ball technique, a used car salesperson may begin the deal by quoting a low base price and then mention all the extra features that cost more once the person has agreed to purchase the car.

WHAT DO *you* THINK?

You have just been hired to advertise a new pillow that helps to align the spine during sleep. Although many studies have demonstrated the benefits of this pillow, you know that an ad explaining the research isn't going to be particularly persuasive. What persuasion techniques might you use to design an effective ad?

The Marketing of Pseudoscience. Many proponents of pseudoscience make good use of persuasion tactics, although they may sometimes do so with the best of intentions. The appeal of these tactics helps to explain why so many intelligent people fall prey to pseudoscientific claims. To resist these tactics, we first must be able to recognize them. Anthony Pratkanis (1995) identified a variety of persuasion tactics to watch out for when evaluating unsubstantiated claims. **Table 11.2** on page 406 lists seven of them; we should bear in mind that people can use most of these tactics to persuade us of a wide variety of claims of both the pseudoscientific and everyday variety. As we can see, several of these tactics make use of heuristics; that is, mental shortcuts (Chapter 2) that are appealing and seductive, but misleading. Several also take the peripheral route to persuasion, making it less likely that we'll evaluate these claims critically.

GLOSSARY

foot-in-the-door technique
persuasive technique involving making a small request before making a bigger one

door-in-the-face technique
persuasive technique involving making an unreasonably large request before making the small request we're hoping to have granted

low-ball technique
persuasive technique in which the seller of a product starts by quoting a low sales price and then mentions all of the "add-on" costs once the customer has agreed to purchase the product

Table 11.2 Pseudoscience Marketing Techniques.

Pseudoscience Tactic	Concept	Example	Problem
Creation of a "phantom" goal	Capitalize on desire to accomplish unrealistic objectives.	"Master the complete works of Shakespeare while sleeping!"	Extreme claims are usually impossible to achieve.
Vivid testimonials	Learning about someone else's personal experience.	"Sandra Sadness was severely depressed for 5 years until she underwent rebirthing therapy!"	A single person's perspective is virtually worthless as scientific evidence but can be extremely persuasive (see Chapter 2).
Manufacturing source credibility	We're more likely to believe sources that we judge to be trustworthy or legitimate.	"Dr. Jonathan Nobel from Princeton endorses this subliminal tape to build self-esteem."	Advertisers may present the source in a deceptive fashion (such as appearing to have more prestigious credentials than is actually the case).
Scarcity heuristic	Something that's rare must be especially valuable.	"Call before midnight to get your copy of Dr. Genius's Improvement Program; it's going to sell out fast!"	Scarcity may be false or a result of low production because of low anticipated demand.
Consensus heuristic	If most people believe that something works, it must work.	"Thousands of people have tried the Atkins diet, so it must be effective."	Common "knowledge" is often wrong (see Chapter 1).
The natural commonplace	A widely held belief that things that are natural are good.	"Mrs. Candy Cure's new over-the-counter antianxiety medication is made from all-natural ingredients!"	*Natural* doesn't mean healthy—just look at poisonous mushrooms (see Chapter 10).
The goddess within	A widely held belief that we all possess a hidden mystical side that traditional Western science neglects or denies.	"The Magical Mind ESP Enhancement program allows you to get in touch with your unrecognized psychic potential!"	Carefully controlled tests fail to support supernatural ability or potential (see Chapter 4).

QUIZ

1 People's attitudes often don't predict their behaviors especially well. **TRUE** **FALSE**

2 We're less likely to believe something we've heard many times. **TRUE** **FALSE**

3 The best way to change people's minds on an issue is to pay them a large sum of money for doing so. **TRUE** **FALSE**

4 Using the door-in-the-face technique, we begin with a small request before making a larger one. **TRUE** **FALSE**

Answers: (1) T (p. 401); (2) F (p. 401); (3) F (p. 403); (4) F (p. 405)

▼ Can a psychologist predict your car buying behavior? Watch the video titled "Car Salesman Example: Robert Cialdini" at www.mypsychlab.com to find out.

Prejudice and Discrimination

The term **prejudice** means to prejudge—to arrive at a conclusion before we've evaluated all of the evidence. If we're prejudiced toward a specific class of persons, whether they be women, African Americans, Norwegians, or hair stylists, it means we've jumped to a premature conclusion about them.

GLOSSARY

prejudice
drawing conclusions about a person, group of people, or situation prior to evaluating the evidence

THE NATURE OF PREJUDICE

It's safe to say that we all harbor at least some prejudices against certain groups of people (Aronson, 1998). Some have argued that a tendency toward prejudice is deeply rooted in human evolution. From the standpoint of natural selection, organisms benefit from forging close alliances with insiders and mistrusting outsiders (Cottrell & Neuberg, 2005). Indeed, members of one race learn to associate fear-relevant stimuli—a snake and a spider, with faces of a different race more easily than with faces of their own race. This effect was not found for fear-irrelevant stimuli such as a butterfly (Olsson, Ebert, Banaji, et al., 2005). We quite easily, and perhaps quite naturally, associate people from other races with scary things.

Still, notice that we used the term *tendency* in the previous paragraph. Even if there's an evolutionary predisposition toward fearing or mistrusting outsiders, that doesn't mean that prejudice is inevitable. Two major biases are associated with our tendency to forge alliances with people like ourselves.

In-group bias is the tendency to favor individuals inside our group relative to members outside our group. If you've ever watched a sporting event, you've observed in-group bias: thousands of screaming fans (the term *fan*, incidentally, is short for *fanatic*) cheering their home team wildly and booing the visiting team with equal gusto, even though most of these fans have no financial stake in the game's outcome. Yet the home team is their "tribe," and they'll happily spend several hours out of their day to cheer them on against their mortal enemy.

The second bias is **out-group homogeneity,** the tendency to view all people outside of our group as highly similar (Park & Rothbart, 1982). Out-group homogeneity makes it easy for us to dismiss all members of other groups in one fell swoop because we can simply tell ourselves that they all share at least one undesirable characteristic. In this way, we don't need to bother getting to know them.

Demonizing an outgroup (such as immigrants) is a frequent manifestation of in-group bias.

DISCRIMINATION

Prejudice can also lead to discrimination, a term with which it's often confused. **Discrimination** is the act of treating members of out-groups differently from members of in-groups. Whereas prejudice refers to *attitudes* toward others, discrimination refers to *behaviors* toward others. We can be prejudiced against people without discriminating against them. **[LEARNING OBJECTIVE 11.11]**

Consequences of Discrimination. Discrimination has significant real-world consequences. For example, far fewer women than men are members of major American orchestras. To investigate this issue, one research team examined how music judges evaluated female musicians during auditions. In some cases, judges could see the musicians; in others, the musicians played behind a screen. When judges were blind to the musicians' sex, women were 50 percent more likely to pass auditions (Goldin & Rouse, 2000). For this reason, most major American orchestras today use blind auditions (Gladwell, 2005).

Most U.S. orchestras now use blind auditions as a safeguard against sex bias and discrimination.

WHAT DO *you* THINK?

You are chairing the selection committee for your school paper's next editor. What steps can you take to ensure that bias doesn't influence the committee's evaluation of the application materials?

Creating Discrimination: Don't Try This at Home. Iowa schoolteacher Jane Elliott demonstrated how easily discrimination can arise on the day after civil rights leader Reverend Martin Luther King, Jr. was assassinated in 1969. She divided her third-grade class into favored and disfavored groups based solely on their eye color (Monteith & Winters, 2002). Informing her pupils that brown-eyed children are superior because of excess melanin in their eyes, Elliott deprived blue-eyed children of basic privileges,

GLOSSARY

in-group bias
tendency to favor individuals within our group over those from outside our group

out-group homogeneity
tendency to view all individuals outside our group as highly similar

discrimination
negative behavior toward members of out-groups

such as second helpings at lunch or drinking from the water fountain. She also insulted blue-eyed children, calling them lazy, dumb, and dishonest. According to Elliott, the results were dramatic; most brown-eyed children quickly became arrogant and condescending, and most blue-eyed children became submissive and insecure.

Teachers across the United States used the now-famous blue eyes–brown eyes demonstration in the late 1960s and 1970s to teach students about the dangers of discrimination (the first author of your textbook was a subject in one of these demonstrations as an elementary school student in New York City). One follow-up study investigating the effects of this demonstration suggests that Caucasian students who go through it report less prejudice toward minorities than do Caucasian students in a control group (Stewart, LaDuke, Bracht, et al., 2003). Nevertheless, because students who underwent this demonstration may have felt demand characteristics to report less prejudice, additional studies are needed to rule out this alternative explanation.

STEREOTYPES

Prejudice results in part from stereotyping. A **stereotype** is a belief—positive or negative—about a group's characteristics that we apply to most members of that group. Like many mental shortcuts, stereotypes typically stem from adaptive psychological processes. As we learned in Chapter 2, we humans are *cognitive misers*—we strive to save mental energy by simplifying reality. By lumping enormous numbers of people who share a single characteristic into a single category, stereotypes help us to make sense of our often confusing social worlds (Macrae & Bodenhausen, 2000). In this regard, they're like other schemas (see Chapter 6) in that they help us to process information.

Yet stereotypes can mislead us, as when we assume that *all* members of a group share a given characteristic. They can also mislead us when we cling to them too rigidly and are unwilling to modify them in light of disconfirming evidence.

Once we've learned them, stereotypes come to us naturally. Research suggests that overcoming stereotypes takes hard mental work. The key difference between prejudiced and nonprejudiced people isn't that the former have stereotypes and the latter don't, because both groups harbor such stereotypes. Instead, it's that prejudiced people don't try hard to resist their stereotypes, but nonprejudiced people do (Devine, 1989; Devine, Montieth, Zuwerink, et al., 1991).

Stereotypes "Behind the Scenes."
Surveys demonstrate that interracial prejudice has declined substantially in the United States over the past four to five decades (Schuman, Steeh, Bobo, et al., 1997). Nevertheless, some scholars contend that much prejudice, particularly that of Caucasians toward African Americans, has merely "gone underground"—that is, become subtler (Fiske, 2002; Hackney, 2005; Sue et al., 2007). An alternative approach to studying subtle prejudice is to measure implicit (unconscious) prejudice (Fazio & Olson, 2003; Vanman, Paul, Ito, et al., 1997; Vanman, Saltz, Nathan, et al., 2004). **Implicit stereotypes** are those of which we're unaware, and **explicit stereotypes** are those of which we're aware.

An implicit prejudice technique that's received a great deal of attention in recent years is the Implicit Association Test (IAT) developed by Anthony Greenwald and Mahzarin Banaji. As shown in **Figure 11.11,** researchers might ask a participant to press a key on the computer keyboard with his left hand if he sees either a photograph of an African American or a positive word (like *joy*) and to press a different key with his right hand if he sees a photograph of a Caucasian or a negative word (like *bad*). After performing this task for a number of trials, researchers ask participants to

RULING OUT RIVAL HYPOTHESES
Have important alternative explanations for the findings been excluded?

Jane Elliott's classic blue eyes–brown eyes demonstration highlighted the negative interpersonal effects of discrimination.

GLOSSARY

stereotype
a belief, positive or negative, about the characteristics of members of a group that is applied generally to most members of the group

implicit and **explicit stereotype**
belief about the characteristics of an out-group about which we're either unaware (implicit) or aware (explicit)

again press the left and right keys, but this time for the reverse pairing (that is, to press the left key for a photograph of either an African American or a negative word, and the right key for a photograph of either a Caucasian or a positive word) (Greenwald, McGhee, & Schwartz, 1998). The results of numerous studies demonstrate that most Caucasian participants respond more quickly to pairings in which African American faces are paired with negative words and Caucasian faces are paired with positive words (Banaji, 2001). Investigators have recently expanded the IAT to test a variety of forms of prejudice, including racism, sexism, homophobia, religious discrimination, and ageism (prejudice against older individuals). Many authors argue that the results of the IAT reflect unconscious prejudice (Gladwell, 2005; Greenwald & Nosek, 2001). If you want to try out the IAT, check out the website https://implicit.harvard.edu/implicit/demo.

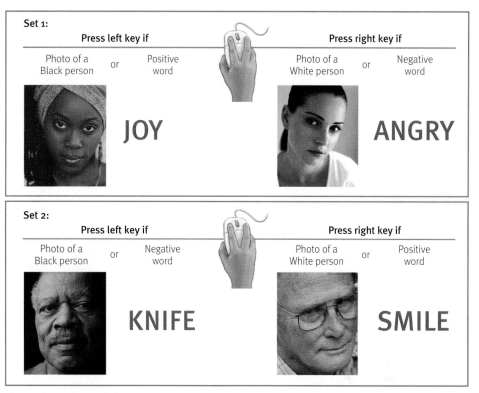

Figure 11.11 The Implicit Association Test. The Implicit Association Test (IAT) is the most widely researched measure of implicit or unconscious prejudice using examples like this one. Many people (across races) associate negative words more readily with African American than Causasian faces. But does the test really measure unconscious prejudice, or does it measure something else?

Nevertheless, things may not be quite that simple. For one thing, the IAT rarely correlates significantly with explicit measures of prejudice, such as questionnaire measures of racist attitudes (Arkes & Tetlock, 2004). Proponents of the IAT argue that this absence of a correlation actually supports the IAT's validity, because the IAT supposedly measures unconscious rather than conscious racial attitudes. Yet this reasoning raises questions regarding the falsifiability of the IAT because IAT proponents could presumably interpret either a positive or a zero correlation as evidence for the IAT's validity. Moreover, it's not clear whether the IAT measures prejudice as much as awareness of stereotypes. That is, unprejudiced persons may correctly perceive that much of mainstream American society links Muslims, for example, with many negative characteristics and Christians with many positive characteristics, yet they may personally reject these associations as biased (Arkes & Tetlock, 2004; Redding, 2004). The true meaning of scores on the IAT and other implicit prejudice measures remains controversial (Gawronski, LeBel, & Peters, 2007).

FALSIFIABILITY
Can the claim be disproved?

Ultimate Attribution Error.

Stereotypes can also result in what Thomas Pettigrew (1979) called the **ultimate attribution error:** the mistake of attributing the behavior of entire groups—like women, Christians, or African Americans—to their dispositions. Like the fundamental attribution error, after which it's named, this error leads us to underestimate the impact of situational factors on people's behavior. For example, Caucasian students are more likely to interpret a shove as intentionally aggressive, as opposed to accidental, when it originates from an African American than from another Caucasian (B. Duncan, 1976).

GLOSSARY

ultimate attribution error
assumption that behaviors among individual members of a group are due to their internal dispositions

ROOTS OF PREJUDICE: A TANGLED WEB

The roots of prejudice are complex and multifaceted. Nevertheless, psychologists have honed in on several crucial factors that contribute to prejudice. **[LEARNING OBJECTIVE 11.12]** We'll examine a few of them: scapegoating, the just-world hypothesis, and conformity.

Scapegoat Hypothesis.
According to the **scapegoat hypothesis,** prejudice arises from a need to blame other groups for our misfortunes. Between 1882 and 1930, for instance, the number of lynchings of African Americans in the U.S. South rose when the price of cotton went down (Tolnay & Beck, 1995). This finding suggests that some Caucasians may have blamed African Americans for the bad prices, although we don't know this for certain. For example, it's possible that lower cotton prices were associated with greater violence toward all members of society, not just African Americans. Nevertheless, there's more direct research support for the scapegoat hypothesis. In an experiment disguised as a study of learning, Caucasian students administered more intense electric shocks to an African American student than to a Caucasian student, but only when the African American student was unfriendly (Rogers & Prentice-Dunn, 1981). This finding suggests that frustration can produce aggression, which people then displace onto minority groups. This may be simply because they are members of an out-group or, more likely, because they have lower power and status in society and seem safer to target as a result.

Just-World Hypothesis.
Melvin Lerner's (1980) **just-world hypothesis** implies that many of us have a deep-seated need to perceive the world as fair—to believe that all things happen for a reason. Ironically, this need for a sense of fair play, especially if powerful, may lead to prejudice. That's because it can lead us to place blame on groups who are already in a one-down position. People with a strong belief in a just world are especially likely to believe that victims of serious illnesses, including cancer and AIDS, are responsible for their woes (Hafer & Begue, 2005). Sociologists and psychologists have referred to this phenomenon as "blaming the victim" (Ryan, 1976).

Conformity.
Some prejudiced attitudes and behaviors probably stem from conformity to social norms. Such conformity may originate from a need for social approval or acceptance. In a study of college fraternities and sororities, researchers found that established members of Greek organizations were about equally likely to express negative views of out-groups (other fraternities and sororities) regardless of whether their opinions were public or private. In contrast, new pledges to these organizations were more likely to express negative views of out-groups when their opinions were public (Noel, Wann, & Branscombe, 1995). Presumably, the pledges wanted to be liked by in-group members and went out of their way to voice their dislike of the "outsiders."

COMBATING PREJUDICE: SOME REMEDIES

Having covered some depressing ground—blind conformity, destructive obedience, bystander nonintervention, social loafing, and now prejudice—we're pleased to close our chapter with a piece of good news: We can overcome prejudice, at least to some extent. How?

Robbers Cave Study.
We can find some clues in a study that Muzafer Sherif and his colleagues conducted in Robbers Cave, Oklahoma (so named because robbers once used these caves to hide from law enforcement authorities). Sherif split 22 well-adjusted fifth-grade boys into two groups, the Eagles and the Rattlers, and sent them packing to summer camp.

RULING OUT RIVAL HYPOTHESES
Have important alternative explanations for the findings been excluded?

Fact-OID The term *scapegoat* originates from biblical times, when rabbis engaged in an unusual practice for eliminating sin on the Jewish holy day of Yom Kippur. They brought forth two goats, one of which they sacrificed to God. The other goat lucked out. The rabbis grabbed the lucky goat's head while recounting all of the sins of the people, symbolically transferring these sins onto it. They then released the escaping goat—the *scapegoat*—into the woods, where it carried away the burden of society's moral errors.

GLOSSARY

scapegoat hypothesis
claim that prejudice arises from a need to blame other groups for our misfortunes

just-world hypothesis
claim that our attributions and behaviors are shaped by a deep-seated assumption that the world is fair and all things happen for a reason

jigsaw classroom
educational approach designed to minimize prejudice by requiring all children to make independent contributions to a shared project

After giving the boys within each group the chance to form strong bonds, Sherif introduced the groups to each other and engaged them in a 4-day sports and games tournament. When he did, pandemonium ensued. The Eagles and Rattlers displayed intense animosity toward one another, eventually manifesting in name calling, food throwing, and fistfights.

Sherif next wanted to find out whether he could "cure" the prejudice he'd helped to create. His treatment was simple: engaging the groups in activities that required them to cooperate to achieve an overarching goal. For example, he rigged a series of mishaps, such as a breakdown of a truck carrying food supplies, that forced the Eagles and the Rattlers to work together. Sure enough, such cooperation toward a shared goal produced a dramatic decrease in hostility between the groups (Sherif, Harvey, White, et al., 1961).

In jigsaw classrooms, children cooperate on a multipart project, with each child assuming a small but essential role.

Jigsaw Classrooms.
Elliott Aronson (Aronson, Blaney, Stephan, et al., 1978) incorporated the lessons of the Robbers Cave research into his educational work on **jigsaw classrooms,** in which teachers assign children separate tasks that all need to be fitted together to complete a project. A teacher might give each student in a class a different piece of history to investigate regarding the U.S. Civil War. One might present on Virginia's role, another on New York's, another on Georgia's, and so on. The students then cooperate to assemble the pieces into an integrated lesson. Numerous studies reveal that jigsaw classrooms result in significant decreases in racial prejudice (Aronson, 2004; Slavin & Cooper, 1999).

The Robbers Cave study and Aronson's work on jigsaw classrooms underscore a lesson confirmed by many other social psychology studies: *Increased contact between racial groups is rarely sufficient to reduce prejudice.* Indeed, during the early Civil Rights era in the United States, many attempts to reduce prejudice by means of desegregation backfired, resulting in increases in racial tension (Stephan, 1978). The advocates of these well-intended efforts assumed mistakenly that contact by itself could heal the deep wounds of prejudice. We now know that interventions are most likely to reduce prejudice only if they satisfy several conditions (see **Table 11.3**). These conditions lead to an optimistic conclusion: Prejudice is neither inevitable nor irreversible.

Table 11.3 Ideal Conditions for Reducing Prejudice.

• The groups should cooperate toward shared goals.
• The contact between groups should be enjoyable.
• The groups should be of roughly equal status.
• Group members should disconfirm the other group's negative stereotypes.
• Group members should have the potential to become friends.

(*Source:* Kenrick et al., 2005; Pettigrew, 1998)

QUIZ

1 Prejudice refers to negative behavior against out-group members.   TRUE FALSE

2 Research demonstrates that nonprejudiced people lack stereotypes of other groups.   TRUE FALSE

3 Cooperation toward shared goals is a key ingredient in reducing prejudice.   TRUE FALSE

4 Research suggests that increased contact between groups is sufficient to reduce prejudice.   TRUE FALSE

Answers: (1) F (p. 406); (2) F (p. 408); (3) T (p. 411); (4) F (p. 411)

PEARSON
mypsych lab

▼ What would you do if someone expressed prejudiced beliefs? Watch the video titled "Prejudice" at www.mypsychlab.com to find out.

Your Complete Review System

WHAT IS SOCIAL PSYCHOLOGY? (pp. 378–383)

11.1 Identify the ways in which social situations influence the behavior of individuals

The need to belong theory proposes that humans have a biological need for interpersonal connections. Social facilitation refers to the presence of others enhancing our performance in certain situations. According to social comparison theory, we're motivated to evaluate our beliefs, attitudes, and reactions by comparing them with the beliefs, attitudes, and reactions of others. Mass hysteria is an outbreak of irrational behavior spread by social contagion.

1. Social psychologists study how people influence others' _____, _____, and _____, for both good and bad. (p. 378)

2. The idea that we have a biologically based need for interpersonal connections is known as the _____ _____ _____ theory. (p. 379)

3. A worsened performance in the presence of others is explained by _____ _____. (p. 380)

4. Researchers have found that our performance in front of others is determined by our level of _____ in that particular performance area. (p. 380)

5. According to Festinger's _____ _____ theory, when a situation is unclear, we look to others for guidance about what to believe and how to act. (p. 381)

6. The flying saucer craze is arguably one of the most widespread cases of what phenomenon? (pp. 381–382)

7. What factors contribute to the rise and spread of urban legends? (p. 382)

While still alive, Walt Disney arranged to have his body frozen after his death so that it could be unfrozen at a future date when advanced technology will permit him to live again.

11.2 Explain how the fundamental attribution error can cause us to misjudge others' behaviors

Attributions refer to our efforts to explain behavior; some attributions are internal, others external. The great lesson of social psychology is the fundamental attribution error—the tendency to overestimate the impact of dispositions on others' behavior.

8. We tend to form _____ in our desire to assign causes to other people's behavior. (p. 380)

9. The tendency to overestimate the impact of _____ _____ on others' behavior is called the fundamental attribution error. (p. 380)

10. The fundamental attribution error (does/doesn't) apply to people's attributions about themselves. (p. 380)

succeed with mypsychlab

1. Will you shoot a better game of pool if people are watching you? Examine how the mere presence of others affects our behavior.
   Social Facilitation

2. How accurate are our perceptions of celebrities? Explore how psychologists explain the judgments we make about actors.
   Fundamental Attribution Error

3. Are there really alligators living in the New York sewer system? Explore psychological explanations of urban legends.
   Urban Legends

SOCIAL INFLUENCE: CONFORMITY AND OBEDIENCE (pp. 383–393)

11.3 Determine the factors that influence when we conform to others

Conformity refers to the tendency of people to change their behavior as a result of group pressure. Asch's conformity studies underscore the power of social pressure, although there are individual and cultural differences in conformity. Deindividuation refers to the tendency of people to engage in atypical behavior when stripped of their usual identities. The Stanford prison study is regarded as a powerful demonstration of the effects of deindividuation on behavior.

11. Changing your personal style, habits, or behavior in order to fit into a social or peer group is an example of _____. (p. 383)

Answers are located at the end of the text.

12. Under what circumstances discussed in the text would you identify line 3 as equal in length to the standard line? (pp. 383–384)

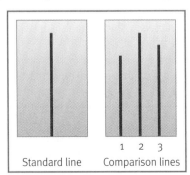

Standard line   Comparison lines
1 2 3

13. People's responses to social pressure (are/are not) associated with individual and cultural differences. (p. 384)

14. People with (high/low) self-esteem are especially prone to conformity. (p. 384)

15. Researchers like Phil Zimbardo found that the two prominent factors that contribute to deindividuation are a feeling of _____ and a lack of _____ _____. (p. 384)

16. The Stanford prison study results have been recently compared with the prison guard atrocities at _____ _____ in Iraq. (p. 385)

11.4 Recognize the dangers of group decision making and identify ways to avoid mistakes common in group decisions

Groupthink is a preoccupation with group unanimity that impairs critical thinking. It can be treated by interventions that encourage dissent within the group. Cults are groups of individuals who exhibit extreme groupthink, marked by intense and unquestioning devotion to a single individual.

17. NASA's decision to launch the 1986 *Challenger* shuttle despite warnings of potential problems from engineers may have resulted from _____. (p. 387)

18. The best way to resist the indoctrination that leads to cults is through the _____ _____, which involves exposing people to information consistent with cult beliefs, and then debunking it. (pp. 388–389)

11.5 Identify the contexts that maximize or minimize obedience to authority

Milgram's classic work on authority demonstrates the power of destructive obedience to authority and helps to clarify the situational factors that both foster and impede obedience.

19. Milgram's experiment testing the effects of "punishment on learning" was, in reality, an experiment designed to measure _____. (pp. 390–391)

20. What factors in the Milgram study increased the likelihood that subjects would refuse to comply with orders to shock the "learner"? (p. 392)

succeed with mypsychlab

1. Can only boys wear blue and play with trucks? Watch this video that explores gender conformity and other influences that groups have on our behavior. **Conformity and Influence in Groups**

2. Students are arrested and imprisoned as part of an experiment. Watch the original footage of this controversial study. **The Stanford Prison Experiment**

3. The power of situations: Watch Dr. Zimbardo explain his experiment, the Stanford prison experiment, and hear first hand how the study was run. **Stanford Prison Experiment: Phil Zimbardo**

HELPING AND HARMING OTHERS: PROSOCIAL BEHAVIOR AND AGGRESSION (pp. 394–400)

11.6 Explain which aspects of a situation increase or decrease the likelihood of bystanders helping others, and why

Although common wisdom suggests that there's "safety in numbers," psychological research suggests otherwise. Bystander nonintervention results from two major factors: pluralistic ignorance and diffusion of responsibility. The first affects whether we recognize ambiguous situations as emergencies, and the second affects how we respond once we've identified situations as emergencies. People are more likely to help when they're unable to escape from a situation, have adequate time to intervene, are in a good mood, and have been exposed to research on bystander intervention.

21. What phenomenon did primate researcher Frans de Waal capture in this photo of two chimpanzees? (p. 394)

22. The presence of others makes people (less/more) likely to help someone in need. (p. 395)

23. What steps could you take to improve your chances of getting help if you were badly hurt or seriously ill in a public place? (p. 395)

24. The phenomenon in which people exert less effort on a task when in a group than when alone is known as _____ _____. (p. 396)

25. Group brainstorming proves to be (more/less) effective than individual brainstorming. (p. 397)

26. Prior exposure to psychological research (can/can't) change an individual's real-world behavior for the better. (p. 398)

27. Extraverted people are (more/less) prone to help others than introverted people. (p. 398)

succeed with mypsychlab

Do You Know All of the Terms in This Chapter?

 Find out by using the Flashcards. Want more practice? Take additional quizzes, try simulations, and watch video to be sure you are prepared for the test!

11.7 **Describe the social and individual difference variables that contribute to human aggression**

A variety of situational variables, including provocation, frustration, aggressive cues, media influences, arousal, and temperature, increase the likelihood of aggression. Men tend to be more physically aggressive than women, although girls are more relationally aggressive than boys; the Southern "culture of honor" may help to explain why murder rates are higher in the southern United States.

28. Aggressive behavior, both at the individual and group levels, is influenced by _____ and _____ factors. (p. 398)

29. Because warm temperatures increase _____, they may make people more likely to lose their tempers when provoked or frustrated. (p. 399)

30. _____ aggression is a form of indirect aggression that involves spreading rumors, gossiping, and nonverbal putdowns for the purpose of social manipulation. (p. 399)

succeed with mypsychlab

1. What do social psychological studies on helping tell us about your likelihood of being helped when you have an emergency? Review some classic research on helping behaviors in the lab.
Bystander Intervention

2. Why do people not provide help? Review some classic studies and see if you can help to determine when and why people will provide assistance.
Helping a Stranger

3. Is there really safety in numbers? Listen as two psychologists discuss why people do not help and how we can increase the chances that people will help.
Bystander Apathy

ATTITUDES AND PERSUASION: CHANGING MINDS (pp. 400–406)

11.8 **Describe how attitudes relate to behavior**

Attitudes aren't typically good predictors of behavior, although attitudes predict behavior relatively well when they're highly accessible.

31. The major distinction between a belief and an attitude is that an attitude involves an _____ component. (p. 400)

32. LaPiere's research showed that people's stated attitudes (did/didn't) accurately predict their situational behavior. (p. 401)

33. The behavior of someone who is a (low/high) self-monitor is likely to reflect his/her true feelings and attitudes. (p. 401)

34. The _____ _____, which makes us more likely to believe something we've heard many times, generally reflects accurate information. (p. 401)

35. Messages are especially persuasive if the messenger seems (similar to/different from) us. (p. 402)

36. Why do advertisers use celebrity endorsers like Hilary Duff? (p. 402)

11.9 **Evaluate theoretical accounts of how and when we alter our attitudes**

According to cognitive dissonance theory, a discrepancy between two beliefs leads to an unpleasant state of tension that we're motivated to reduce. In some cases, we reduce this state by altering our attitudes. An alternative view is impression management theory, which proposes that we don't really change our attitudes but report that we have so that our behaviors appear consistent with our attitudes.

37. Using your knowledge of cognitive dissonance, complete the bottom set of boxes with statements geared toward resolving the stated conflict. (p. 403)

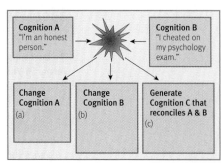

38. In Festinger and Carlsmith's test of cognitive dissonance theory, subjects given less money reported enjoying the task (more/less). (p. 403)

11.10 **Identify common and effective persuasion techniques and how they're exploited by pseudoscientists**

According to dual process models of persuasion, there are two routes to persuasion: a central route that involves careful evaluation of arguments and a peripheral route that relies on superficial cues. Effective persuasion techniques include the foot-in-the-door technique, the door-in-the-face technique, and the low-ball technique.

39. Once a friend has agreed to help you select paint colors for your dorm room, asking her to help you actually paint the room is an example of the _____ technique. (p. 405)

40. The _____ technique is often practiced by retail stores when they advertise a limited offer price on an item, failing to mention until after you've agreed to the purchase that there are several separately priced items highly desired or essential to making the item purchased complete. (p. 405)

succeed with mypsychlab

1. Will you like an experimental task more if you are paid $1 or $20? Explore how money can change an individual's perception of a boring task.
Cognitive Dissonance and Attitude Change

2. From quitting smoking to changing our attitudes about hybrid cars, how does the theory of cognitive dissonance help us understand attitude change?
Cognitive Dissonance

3. Watch as people on the streets explain why they engage in negative behaviors.
The Need to Justify Our Actions

PREJUDICE AND DISCRIMINATION (pp. 406–411)

11.11 **Distinguish prejudice and stereotypes as beliefs from discrimination as a behavior**

Prejudice is coming to a conclusion before we've evaluated all the evidence. Prejudice is accompanied by several other biases, including in-group bias and out-group homogeneity. Discrimination is the act of treating outgroup members differently from in-group members. Stereotypes are beliefs about a group's characteristics that we apply to most members of that group. They can be either positive or negative.

41. Concluding that all Americans are loud, materialistic, and arrogant without ever having spent time with any of them is an example of _____. (p. 406)

42. Our tendency to view all people outside of our group as highly similar is known as _____ _____. (p. 407)

43. Believing—without first-hand knowledge—that teens with nose piercings who frequent the local mall are troublemakers is a form of _____, and refusing to serve them in your mall restaurant is a form of _____. (p. 407)

44. A belief that all cheerleaders are ditzy, flirty, and interested only in dating is a _____. (p. 408)

45. How did one school teacher use her pupils' eye color to demonstrate how discrimination occurs? (pp. 407–408)

11.12 **Identify the factors that contribute to prejudice and describe methods for combating it**

There's evidence for various social explanations of prejudice, including scapegoating, belief in a just world, and conformity. One of the most effective means of combating prejudice is to make members of different groups work together toward achieving shared overarching goals.

46. According to the _____ _____, prejudice arises from a need to blame other groups for our misfortunes. (p. 410)

47. The idea that our behaviors and attributions are based on the assumption that all things happen for a reason supports the _____ hypothesis. (p. 410)

48. Sherif's Robber's Cave study, which initially separated two groups of competing fifth graders, used activities requiring _____ across groups to overcome developed prejudices. (p. 411)

49. How do Aronson's jigsaw classrooms work to reduce prejudice? (p. 411)

50. One condition for reducing prejudice is to (encourage/discourage) group members in becoming friends. (p. 411)

SCIENTIFIC THINKING SKILLS
Questions and Summary

1 You are standing in a crowded elevator when suddenly all of the other riders turn to the right. How likely would you be to follow suit?

2 Imagine that starting today, anyone wearing jeans is considered more important than anyone who wears dress pants. If you were a jeans wearer, would you act any differently now that you have this knowledge?

RULING OUT RIVAL HYPOTHESES
pp. 384, 392, 402, 404, 408, 410

CORRELATION vs. CAUSATION
p. 401

FALSIFIABILITY
p. 409

REPLICABILITY
pp. 385, 393, 396, 398, 404

succeed with mypsychlab

1. How would you react if your taxi driver started making racially insensitive jokes? Watch how customers behave as they are videotaped in a taxi.
Prejudice

2. Explore some sources of prejudice and think about how discrimination can be reduced.
Origins of Prejudice

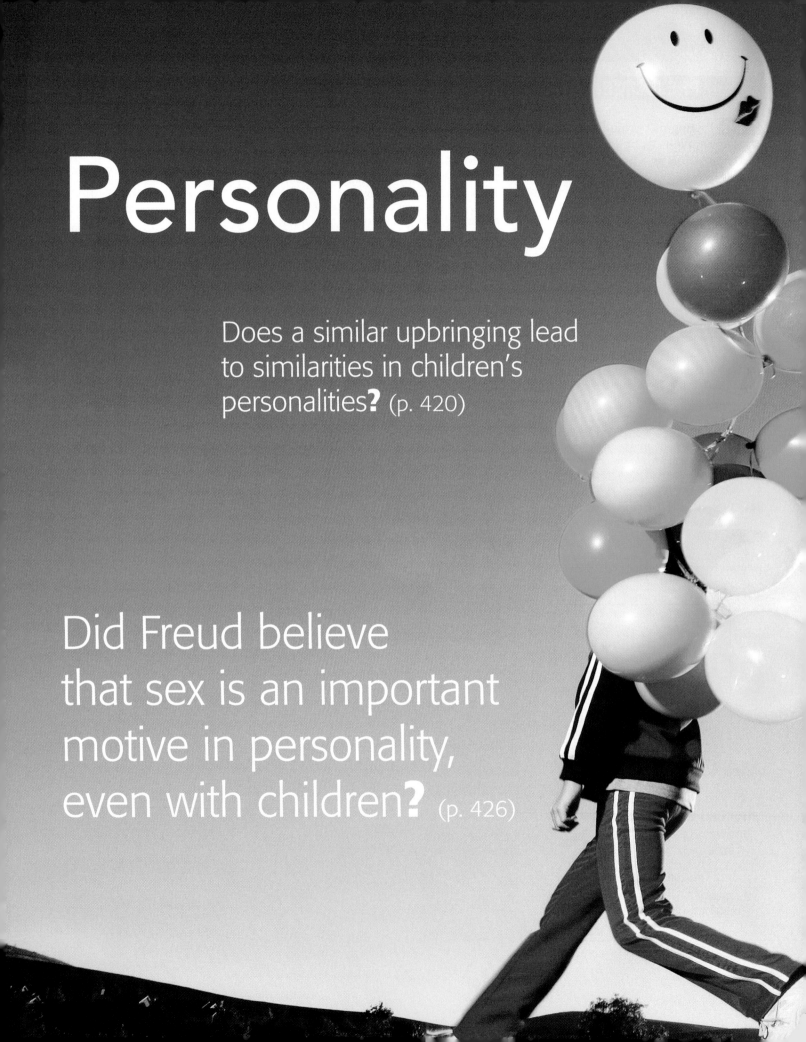

Personality

Does a similar upbringing lead to similarities in children's personalities? (p. 420)

Did Freud believe that sex is an important motive in personality, even with children? (p. 426)

How consistent are we in our
behavior across situations? (p. 437)

Can we use responses to inkblots to infer people's personality traits? (p. 443)

Is criminal profiling
scientific? (pp. 445–446)

Born in 1933, Jack and Oskar are alike in two crucial ways. The first is obvious when you meet them: They're identical twins, genetic clones of each other. In contrast to most identical twins, though, they didn't grow up together. Instead, along with several dozen twin pairs studied by Thomas Bouchard and his colleagues at the University of Minnesota during the 1980s and 1990s, Jack and Oskar were separated almost immediately after birth and reunited decades later (Begley & Kasindorf, 1979). There's another similarity: Despite not having known each other for 40 years (they met once only briefly in 1954), Jack and Oskar have nearly identical personalities. Their scores on the Minnesota Multiphasic Personality Inventory, a personality questionnaire we'll discuss later in the chapter, are just about as similar as that of the same person taking the test twice.

That's where the similarities end. Jack was raised by a Jewish family in the Caribbean until age 17, when he moved to Israel. Oskar was raised by his maternal grandmother in a region of the former Czechoslovakia that was under Adolph Hitler's control during World War II. Although Jack's and Oskar's underlying personalities are similar, their political attitudes are as different as night and day. Jack was a deeply religious Jew who enjoyed war movies that portrayed Germans in a bad light. While in Israel, he worked with others to help build the Jewish state. In stark contrast, Oskar was an ardent Nazi and anti-Semite who became a dedicated member of the Hitler Youth movement as World War II drew to a close. So although Jack and Oskar had similar personalities—intense, loyal, and politically engaged—they manifested them in dramatically different ways.

The case of Jack and Oskar is just that—a case. As we learned in Chapter 2, case studies have their limitations. For one thing, it's hard to know how far we can generalize Jack and Oskar's case to other twin pairs, let alone to all other people. Yet Jack and Oskar's story raises a host of fascinating questions that psychologists can go on to examine using rigorous research designs. Why were Jack and Oskar so similar in personality despite having had no contact with each other for decades? What motivated both of them to pursue political causes? How can two people with such similar personalities end up with such dissimilar political attitudes? How did environmental influences shape the expression of their personalities?

The answers to these questions, as we'll soon discover, aren't simple. We might conclude that someone committed murder because he had an unhappy childhood or that someone overeats because she has low self-esteem. Intuitively appealing as these explanations are, we must beware of *single-cause explanations* of human behavior. When trying to uncover the root causes of people's actions, we must keep in mind that personality is multiply determined. Indeed, personality is the unimaginably complicated outcome of dozens of causal influences: genetic, prenatal, parenting, peer influences, life stressors, and plain old luck, both good and bad.

Personality: What Is It, and How Can We Study It?

In Chapter 11, we learned how social context can influence our behavior in profound ways. There, we also met up with the *fundamental attribution error,* the tendency to attribute too much of others' behavior to their personalities and not enough to the situations they confront.

With this critical caution in mind, most psychologists agree that we do have individual differences in tendencies that can affect how we respond to our environments. In other words, there *is* such a thing as **personality;** we aren't exclusively a product of the social influences impinging on us at any given moment. Most also agree with the American psychologist Gordon Allport (1966) that personality consists of **traits:** relatively enduring predispositions that influence our behavior across many situations (Funder, 1991; Tellegen, 1991). Personality traits—such as introversion, aggressiveness, and conscientiousness—account in part for consistencies in our behavior, across both time and situations.

How do personality traits originate? We'll first approach this question from the vantage point of behavior-genetic studies of personality and move on to various theories of personality, including Freudian and behavioral models, that offer competing answers to this question. As we'll discover, all of these theories strive to explain *both commonalities and differences* among people in their personality traits. For example, they try to account for not only how we develop a conscience, but also why some of us have a stronger conscience than others.

Psychologists use behavior-genetic methods to disentangle three broad influences on behavior:

- *genetic* factors

- *shared environmental* factors—experiences that make individuals within the same family more alike

- *nonshared environmental* factors—experiences that make individuals within the same family less alike, such as a parent treating one child more affectionately than another resulting in the favored child having higher self-esteem

Oskar Stohr and Jack Yufe, identical twins reared apart, obtained extremely similar scores on personality tests. But the outward expressions of their personality traits were remarkably different. Why?

RESEARCHING THE CAUSES OF PERSONALITY: OVERVIEW OF TWIN AND ADOPTION STUDIES

To differentiate among the three influences, behavior geneticists have applied twin studies and adoption studies (see Chapter 3) to the study of personality. Because identical (monozygotic) twins are more similar genetically than fraternal (dizygotic) twins and most twins (identical and fraternal) are likely to experience many shared environmental factors, a higher correlation of a trait among identical than fraternal twins suggests a genetic influence. In contrast, identical twin correlations that are equal to or less than fraternal twin correlations suggest the absence of a genetic component, and instead point to shared environmental influences. **[LEARNING OBJECTIVE 12.1]**

Reared-Together Twins: Genes or Environment? From the findings of one major twin study of personality, we can see that numerous personality traits—including anxiety proneness and impulse control—are influenced substantially by genetic factors (see the left side of **Table 12.1** on page 420). This study examined identical twin pairs who were raised together and fraternal twins who were either both male or both female (Tellegen et al., 1988). A number of researchers have replicated these findings in other twin samples from intact families (Loehlin, 1992; Plomin, 2004).

Yet the results in Table 12.1 impart another lesson. What do the identical twin correlations have in common? The answer is so self-evident that we can easily overlook it: All of these correlations are substantially less than 1.0. This finding demonstrates that nonshared environment plays an important role in personality (Plomin & Daniels, 1987; Turkheimer, 2000). If heritability were 1.0 (that is, 100 percent), the identical twin correlations would also be 1.0. Because they're considerably less than 1.0, nonshared environmental influences that affect the two twins in each pair differently must play a key role in personality. Regrettably, these twin findings don't tell us what these nonshared environmental influences are.

REPLICABILITY
Can the results be duplicated in other studies?

GLOSSARY

personality
stable tendencies within individuals that influence how they respond to their environments

trait
relatively enduring predisposition that influences our behavior across many situations

Table 12.1 Comparison of Correlations of Twins Reared Together and Apart for Selected Personality Traits.

	Twins Reared Together		Twins Reared Apart	
	Identical twin correlation	Fraternal twin correlation	Identical twin correlation	Fraternal twin correlation
Anxiety proneness	.52	.24	.61	.27
Aggression	.43	.14	.46	.06
Alienation	.55	.38	.55	.38
Impulse control	.41	.06	.50	.03
Emotional well-being	.58	.23	.48	.18
Traditionalism	.50	.47	.53	.39
Achievement orientation	.36	.07	.36	.07

(*Source:* Tellegen et al., 1988)

RULING OUT RIVAL HYPOTHESES
Have important alternative explanations for the findings been excluded?

These twin brothers, Gerald Levey and Mark Newman, separated at birth, both became firefighters (one in New Jersey and the other in Queens, New York).

REPLICABILITY
Can the results be duplicated in other studies?

Table 12.2 Correlations among Various Relatives in an Adoption Study of the Personality Trait of Neuroticism.

Correlation	
Mother and biological child	.21
Mother and adopted child	.12
Biologically related children	.28
Adoptively related children	.05

(*Source:* Scarr et al., 1981)

Reared-Apart Twins: Shining a Spotlight on Genes. Table 12.1 may tempt us to conclude that the similarities between identical twins are primarily a result of their similar upbringing rather than their shared genes. But this explanation is refuted by studies of identical and fraternal twins raised apart.

In an extraordinary investigation, researchers at the University of Minnesota spent more than two decades accumulating a large sample of identical and fraternal twins—about 130 in total—who were reared apart, sometimes in different countries (Bouchard, Lykken, McGue, et al., 1990). Many had been separated almost immediately after birth and reunited for the first time decades later in the Minneapolis–St. Paul airport. Jack and Oskar, whom we met at the outset of this chapter, were among those in the "Minnesota Twins" study, as it came to be known.

Before psychologists conducted these studies, some prominent social scientists predicted confidently that identical twins reared apart would barely resemble one another in personality.

Were they right? The right side of Table 12.1 displays some of the principal findings from the Minnesota Twin Study. Two findings in the right side of this table stand out. First, identical twins reared apart tend to be strikingly similar in their personality traits. They're also far more similar than fraternal twins reared apart (Tellegen et al., 1988). A more convincing case for the role of genetic influences on personality would be hard to come by. Second, when comparing the results in the left and right sides of Table 12.1, it's evident that identical twins reared apart are about as similar as identical twins reared together! This amazing finding suggests that *shared environment plays little or no role in the causes of adult personality.* Behavior-genetic researchers have replicated this surprising result in other twin samples (Loehlin, 1992; Pedersen, Plomin, McClearn, et al., 1988).

Adoption Studies: Further Separating Genes and Environment. *Adoption studies* (see Chapter 3) permit investigators to separate the effects of genes and environment by comparing adopted children's similarities to their adopted versus their biological parents.

In one adoption study, Sandra Scarr and her colleagues examined the personality trait of neuroticism (Scarr, Webber, Weinberg, et al., 1981). As we'll discover later in this chapter, people with high levels of neuroticism tend to be tense and high-strung, whereas those with low levels of neuroticism tend to be mellow and calm. As we can see in **Table 12.2,** the correlations between biological parents (in this case, mothers) and their adopted-away children are actually slightly higher than the correlations between adoptive parents and their adopted children *even though the biological parents had essentially no environmental contact with their children after birth* (Scarr et al., 1981). These findings have been replicated by other investigators and for other personality traits (Loehlin, 1992). Moreover, Table 12.2 reveals that, unlike biological siblings raised in the same household, adoptive siblings raised in the same household exhibit almost no similarity in personality. This finding further undermines the hypothesis that shared environment is influential in adult personality: Being brought up together doesn't make brothers and sisters more alike.

REPLICABILITY
Can the results be duplicated in other studies?

BEHAVIOR-GENETIC STUDIES: A NOTE OF CAUTION

Researchers using twin studies have found that genes influence a variety of behaviors often associated with personality traits. These behaviors include divorce (McGue & Lykken, 1992), religiosity (Waller, Kojetin, Bouchard, et al., 1990), and even the tendency to watch television (Plomin, Corley, DeFries, et al., 1990). Many social attitudes, including those concerning the death penalty and nudist colonies, are also moderately heritable (Martin et al., 1986). For each of these characteristics, identical twin correlations are considerably higher than fraternal twin correlations.

Do these findings mean, as the popular press often implies, that there are specific genes for divorce, religiosity, death penalty attitudes, and the like? Don't bet on it. Genes code for proteins, not specific behaviors or attitudes. It's far more likely that genes influence behaviors and attitudes in a highly indirect fashion (Block, 1995). As we learned from Jack and Oskar, genes probably influence certain personality traits—like deep emotions—but how these traits play out in our lives, such as becoming either an observant Jew or a passionate anti-Semite, are influenced by our environments. The pathways from genes to behavior are often lengthy and circuitous. So when we hear media reports of a "gay gene" or a "divorce gene," we should be skeptical. The truth is bound to be considerably more complex, regardless of how heritable a trait is.

Twin studies demonstrate that religiosity has a substantial genetic component. But does that finding mean there are specific genes for religiosity?

WHAT DO *you* THINK?

A friend from a devout Catholic family has stopped attending Mass since he started college. His explanation is, "What can I say? I obviously didn't inherit the religious gene!" How would you try to convince him that the story isn't that simple?

QUIZ

1 Traits are predispositions to behave in particular ways across a variety of different environments. **TRUE FALSE**

2 Identical twins reared together tend to be about as similar in their personality traits as identical twins reared apart. **TRUE FALSE**

3 Environmental factors shared among members of the same family play an important role in the causes of most personality traits in adulthood. **TRUE FALSE**

▼ Can strangers turn out to be identical twins? Watch the video titled "Twins Separated at Birth, Reunited" at www.mypsychlab.com to find out.

Answers: (1) T (p. 419); (2) T (p. 420); (3) F (pp. 420–421)

Psychoanalytic Theory: The Controversial Legacy of Sigmund Freud and His Followers

Long before researchers stepped in to conduct controlled studies of the causes of personality, psychologists, psychiatrists, and many other thinkers had generated theoretical models that sought to explain the development and workings of personality. These models addressed three key questions:

(1) How do our personalities develop?

(2) What are the core driving forces in our personalities or, more informally, what makes us tick?

(3) What accounts for individual differences in personality?

We'll examine and evaluate four influential models of personality, starting with the granddaddy of them all: Sigmund Freud's psychoanalytic theory.

To most nonpsychologists, psychoanalytic theory is virtually synonymous with the writings of a Viennese physician (contrary to popular belief, he was not a psychologist or psychiatrist) named Sigmund Freud (1856–1939). Although psychoanalytic theory has been extremely controversial, even Freud's most vocal detractors acknowledge that he was an ingenious thinker. In fact, one major challenge in evaluating psychoanalytic theory lies in separating the brilliance of Freud the theorist from the scientific soundness of Freud's theory. Freudian theory has been enormously influential in the thinking of psychologists, literary critics, and laypersons, and for that reason alone his ideas merit a careful and balanced look (Kramer, 2007).

Table 12.3 Examples of "Freudian Slips" from Notes by Freud.

"A member of the House of Commons referred to another as the honorable member for Central Hell instead of Central Hull."
"A soldier said to a friend that 'I wish there were a thousand men mortified on that hill' instead of 'fortified on that hill.'"
"A lady, attempting to compliment another, says that 'I am sure that you must have thrown this delightful hat together' instead of 'sewn it together,' thereby betraying her thought that the hat was poorly made."
"A lady states that few gentlemen know how to value the 'ineffectual' qualities in a woman, as opposed to 'intellectual.'"
(*Source:* Freud, 1901)

GLOSSARY

psychic determinism
the assumption that all psychological events have a cause

THE PSYCHOANALYTIC THEORY OF PERSONALITY

Psychoanalytic theory rests on three core assumptions (Brenner, 1973; Loevinger, 1987). These assumptions, especially the second and third, set this theory apart from most other personality theories. **[LEARNING OBJECTIVE 12.2]**

- *Psychic Determinism.* Freudians believe in **psychic determinism:** the assumption that all psychological events have a cause. Psychic determinism is a specific case of determinism as a general concept (see Chapter 1), which states that all events in general have a cause. We aren't free to choose our actions, Freudians claim, because we're at the mercy of powerful forces that lie outside of our awareness. Dreams, neurotic symptoms, and "Freudian slips" of the tongue are all reflections of deep psychological conflict bubbling up to the surface (see **Table 12.3**).

- *Symbolic Meaning.* For Freudians, no action, no matter how seemingly trivial, is meaningless. If, while teaching a class, your male professor manages to crack a long piece of chalk in two, some might be inclined to disregard this action as uninteresting. Rest assured, however, that most Freudians would find an explanation for it. Specifically, they'd be likely to argue that this piece of chalk is *symbolic* of something else; perhaps something sexual in nature.

- *Unconscious Motivation.* Freudians argue for the crucial importance of *unconscious motivation.* According to Freud (1933), we rarely understand why we do what we do, although we quite readily cook up explanations for our actions after the fact. Some authors have likened the Freudian view of the mind (Freud, 1923) to an iceberg, with the unconscious being the vast and largely uncharted area of the psyche submerged entirely underwater (see **Figure 12.1**). The conscious component of the mind is merely the "tip of the iceberg," barely visible above the water's surface. For Freud, the unconscious is of immensely greater importance in the causes of our personality than the conscious.

The Id, Ego, and Superego: The Structure of Personality.

Freud (1933, 1935) hypothesized that the human psyche consists of three agencies or components: id, ego, and superego. For Freud, the interplay among these three agencies gives rise to our personalities, and differences in the strength of these agencies help to account for individual differences in personality.

The Id: Basic Instincts. The **id,** according to Freud, is the reservoir of our most primitive impulses, a seething cauldron of passions and desires that provides the impetus for much of our behavior. The id is entirely unconscious; it's the part of the iceberg completely submerged underwater. It contains a variety of drives, particularly the sexual drive or *libido* (see Chapter 9) and the aggressive drive. Freud believed that the desire to fulfill sexual and aggressive impulses plays a significant role in shaping personality.

The Ego: The Boss. The **ego** is the boss of the personality, its principal decision maker. The ego's primary tasks are interacting with the real world and finding ways to resolve the competing demands of the other two psychic agencies. We shouldn't confuse the Freudian ego with the ego, or inflated sense of self-worth, that's crept into everyday language. Unlike the id, the ego strives to delay gratification until it can find an appropriate or socially acceptable outlet for our drives.

The Superego: Moral Standards. The **superego** is our sense of morality. The term literally means "above ego," and Freud conceptualized this agency much like a judgmental parent looking down on the ego. This psychic agency contains the sense of right and wrong we've internalized from our interactions with society, particularly our parents.

How the Psychic Agencies Interact. According to Freud, a constant struggle to maintain balance among the three psychic agencies is occurring within all of us, all the time. Much of the time the id, ego, and superego interact harmoniously, much like a chamber music trio playing in perfect synchrony. Yet the agendas of these agencies sometimes collide. If you're attracted to your best friend's partner, your id is at odds with your ego and (hopefully!) your superego. You might fantasize about a romantic fling with this person (id), but feel both frightened about what would happen to you (ego) and stricken with pangs of guilt about hurting your friend's feelings (superego) if you were foolish enough to act on your impulses. Freud (1935) hypothesized that psychological distress results from conflict among these three agencies.

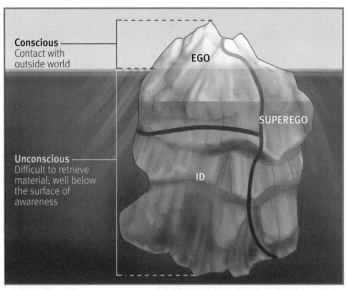

Figure 12.1 Freud's Model of Personality Structure. According to some authors, Freud's conception of personality is analogous to an iceberg, with the conscious mind being the tip barely visible above the surface and the unconscious being the vast submerged area entirely underwater. Nevertheless, we shouldn't take the iceberg metaphor too literally (indeed, Freud himself apparently never used it) because, according to Freud, different aspects of personality are in constant interaction.

WHAT DO *you* THINK?

In a mock courtroom exercise, you must defend a client who killed her husband in the heat of passion after finding him with another woman. Using Freud's three agencies of personality, how would you attempt to lessen your client's sentence?

GLOSSARY

id
reservoir of our most primitive impulses, including sex and aggression

ego
psyche's executive and principal decision maker

superego
our sense of morality

Most dream dictionaries available in bookstores imply that there are universal meanings for dream symbols. Even most psychoanalysts reject this claim.

Freud became famous for his interest in dream interpretation because he believed that dreams give us insight into the internal struggles among psychic agencies. According to Freud, all dreams are *wish fulfillments,* that is, expressions of the id's impulses. The bizarre images and "plot twists" that sometimes happen in dreams, Freud argued, are our super-egos' attempts to disguise our wishes with symbols.

Popular psychology offers intriguing methods for interpreting dream symbols based on Freudian theory. According to one dream-symbol dictionary (Schoenewolf, 1997) a duck, icicle, spear, umbrella, or tie symbolizes the penis; a pocket, tunnel, jug, or gate symbolizes the vagina; and a kangaroo symbolizes sexual vitality (please don't ask us to explain this one). Books of dream symbols (Ackroyd, 1993) vastly oversimplify Freudian theory, because Freudians believe that symbols often mean different things to different dreamers, and there is pretty slim evidence that any of the interesting imagery in dreams has a deeper symbolic meaning.

Anxiety and the Defense Mechanisms.
A principal function of the ego, according to Freud, is to contend with threats from the outside world. When danger is present, the ego experiences anxiety, signaling it to undertake corrective actions. Sometimes these actions are straightforward, such as jumping out of the way of an oncoming car. In other cases, we can't do much to correct the situation, so we must change our perception of it.

In these cases, the ego engages in **defense mechanisms:** unconscious maneuvers intended to minimize anxiety. The concept of defense mechanisms has crept into our everyday language ("Stop being so defensive"). Contrary to popular belief, Freud held that defense mechanisms are essential for psychological health. Indeed, the person lacking any defense mechanisms would be at the mercy of uncontrollable anxiety. Nonetheless, an excessive reliance on one or two defense mechanisms, Freud insisted, is pathological. Freud and his daughter, Anna, who became a prominent psychoanalyst in her own right, outlined the principal defense mechanisms (A. Freud, 1937). We'll present a brief tour of some of them here (see **Table 12.4**).

What evidence is there that these defense mechanisms actually influence our behavior? Many Freudians believe that **repression,** forgetting of threatening memories, explains *infantile amnesia* (Chapter 6), the inability to remember anything prior to about age 3 (Fivush & Hudson, 1990). According to Freud, we repress unhappy childhood memories to avoid the pain they engender. We now know this explanation is unlikely, largely because investigators have identified infantile amnesia in other animals, including mice and rats (Berk, Vigorito, & Miller, 1979; Richardson, Riccio, & Axiotis, 1986). A committed Freudian could presumably argue that mice and other rodents also repress traumatic memories of early childhood, but Occam's razor renders this explanation unlikely. However, other defense mechanisms are more plausible.

We sometimes experience **denial,** the motivated forgetting of distressing external experiences, when we are undergoing extreme stress. It's not uncommon, for example, for the relatives of individuals who have recently died in a tragic accident to insist that their loved ones must somehow, somewhere, be alive. **Regression,** the act of returning psychologically to a younger age, also occurs occasionally when people are under duress. Older children who've long since stopped sucking their thumbs sometimes suddenly resume thumb sucking under stress.

OCCAM'S RAZOR
Does a simpler explanation fit the data just as well?

GLOSSARY

defense mechanism
unconscious maneuver intended to minimize anxiety

repression
motivated forgetting of emotionally threatening memories or impulses

denial
motivated forgetting of distressing external experiences

regression
the act of returning psychologically to a younger, and typically simpler and safer, age

PSYCHOSEXUAL STAGES OF DEVELOPMENT

No aspect of Freud's theory is more controversial than his model of personality development. Nor has any aspect of his theory been more widely criticized as pseudoscientific

Table 12.4 Some of the Major Freudian Defense Mechanisms and an Example of Each.

Defense Mechanism	Definition	Example
Repression	Motivated forgetting of emotionally threatening memories or impulses	A person who witnesses a traumatic combat scene finds himself unable to remember it.
Denial	Motivated forgetting of distressing experiences	A mother who loses a child in a car accident insists her child is alive.
Regression	Returning psychologically to a younger and safer time	A college student starts sucking his thumb during a difficult exam.
Reaction-formation	Transforming an anxiety-producing experience into its opposite	A married woman who's sexually attracted to a coworker experiences hatred and revulsion toward him.
Projection	Unconscious attribution of our negative qualities onto others	A married man with powerful unconscious sexual impulses toward females complains that other women are always "after him."
Displacement	Directing an impulse from a socially unacceptable target onto a more acceptable one	A golfer throws his club into the woods after his partner's cell phone rings, distracting him during his putt.
Rationalization	Providing reasonable-sounding explanations for unreasonable behaviors or failures	A political candidate who loses an election convinces herself that she didn't really want the position after all.

(Cioffi, 1998). According to Freud, personality development proceeds through a series of stages. He termed these stages *psychosexual* because each focuses on an erogenous, or sexually arousing, zone of the body (see **Table 12.5**). Although we're accustomed to thinking of our genitals as our primary sexual organs, Freud contended that other bodily areas are sources of sexual gratification in early development. Contrary to prevailing wisdom at the time, Freud insisted that sexuality begins in infancy. He further maintained that the extent to which we resolve each stage successfully bears crucial implications for later personality development. He believed that individuals can become *fixated* or "stuck" in an early stage of development. This can occur either because they were deprived of sexual gratification that was supposed to take place during that stage or because they became excessively gratified during that stage and had difficulty moving on to the next stage. We'll next examine the five psychosexual stages as Freud conceptualized them, bearing in mind that many modern critics don't share his views.

Table 12.5 Freud's Stages of Psychosexual Development.

Stage	Approximate Age	Primary Source of Sexual Pleasure
Oral	Birth to 12–18 months	Sucking and drinking
Anal	18 months to 3 years	Alleviating tension by expelling feces
Phallic*	3 years to 6 years	Genitals (penis or clitoris)
Latency	6 years to 12 years	Dormant sexual stage
Genital	12 years and beyond	Renewed sexual impulses; emergence of mature romantic relationships

*Oedipus and Electra complexes.

The Oral Stage. The first stage of psychosexual development, the **oral stage,** which generally lasts from birth to 12 to 18 months, focuses on the mouth. During this stage, infants obtain sexual pleasure primarily by sucking and drinking. Freud believed that adults who are orally fixated tend to react to stress by becoming intensely dependent on others for reassurance, just as infants depend on their mother's breast as a source of satisfaction.

The Anal Stage. At the second stage, the **anal stage,** which lasts from about 18 months to 3 years, children first come face to face with psychological conflict. During this stage, children want to alleviate tension and experience pleasure by moving their bowels but soon discover that they can't do so whenever nature calls. Instead, they must learn to inhibit their urges and wait to move their bowels in a socially appropriate place—ideally, the toilet. Freudians believe that anally fixated individuals—*anal personalities*—are prone to excessive neatness, stinginess, and stubbornness in adulthood.

The Phallic Stage. The **phallic stage,** which lasts from approximately age 3 years to 6 years, is of paramount importance to Freudians in explaining personality. During this stage, the penis (for boys) and clitoris (for girls) become the primary erogenous zones for sexual pleasure. Simultaneously, children develop a powerful attraction for the opposite-sex parent as well as a desire to eliminate the same-sex parent as a rival.

In boys, the phallic stage is termed the **Oedipus complex,** after the Greek character who unknowingly killed his father and married his mother. The boy, who wants Mommy all for himself, wants to kill or at least rid himself of Daddy. The boy comes to

GLOSSARY

oral stage
psychosexual stage that focuses on the mouth

anal stage
psychosexual stage that focuses on toilet training

phallic stage
psychosexual stage that focuses on the genitals

Oedipus complex
conflict during the phallic stage in which boys supposedly love their mothers romantically and want to eliminate their fathers as rivals

believe that his father perceives him as a rival for his mother's affection and fears that his father will castrate him as a result. Ultimately, these castration anxieties and the impossibility of ever attaining his mother as a love object lead the boy to abandon this love. He then identifies with the aggressor, in this case his father, and adopts his personality characteristics. If children don't resolve this complex, claimed Freud, the stage is set for psychological problems later in life.

In girls, in contrast, the phallic stage is often termed the **Electra complex** after the Greek character who avenged her father's murder by killing her mother. Girls, like boys, desire the affections of the opposite-sex parent and fantasize about doing away with the same-sex parent. In girls, however, the phallic stage takes the form of *penis envy,* in which the girl desires to possess a penis, just like Daddy has. Penis envy is probably Freud's most ridiculed concept, and with good reason, largely because there's no research support for it.

In the classic Greek tragedy by Sophocles, Oedipus blinds himself soon after discovering that he'd unknowingly murdered his father and married his mother. Freud was so influenced by this play that he referred to the supposed love of all boys for their mothers as the Oedipus complex.

The Latency Stage.

The fourth psychosexual stage, the **latency stage,** is a period of calm following the stormy phallic stage. In latency, which lasts from about age 6 years to 12 years, Freud believed that sexual impulses are submerged into the unconscious. Consistent with this belief, most boys and girls during this stage find members of the opposite sex to be "yucky" and utterly unappealing.

The Genital Stage.

During the fifth and final psychosexual stage, the **genital stage**—which generally begins at around age 12—sexual impulses reawaken. If development up to this point has proceeded without major glitches, this stage witnesses the emergence of mature romantic relationships. In contrast, if serious problems weren't resolved at earlier stages, difficulties with establishing intimate love attachments are likely.

PSYCHOANALYTIC THEORY EVALUATED CRITICALLY

Freud has probably exerted a greater impact on the public's understanding of personality than any other thinker. His insights into the importance of developmental experiences, the unconscious, and the roles of sex and guilt as motivators have continued to influence modern thought. Nevertheless, researchers have raised a number of troubling questions concerning the scientific status of psychoanalytic theory. Here we'll examine four major criticisms. **[LEARNING OBJECTIVE 12.3]**

(1) Unfalsifiability. Critics have noted that many features of Freudian theory are unfalsifiable. For example, suppose we found that contrary to the Oedipus complex, most 5-year-old boys report being sexually repulsed by their mothers. Freudians could maintain that these boys are engaging in reaction-formation and are attracted to their mothers at an unconscious level.

(2) Failed Predictions. Although much of Freudian theory is difficult to falsify, those portions of the theory that can be falsified often have been (Grunbaum, 1984). For example, Freud claimed that children exposed to overly harsh toilet training would grow up to be rigid and perfectionistic. Yet most investigators have found no association between toilet training practices and adult personality (Fisher & Greenberg, 1996). Similarly, there's little scientific support for many Freudian defense mechanisms. For example, laboratory studies have failed to yield strong evidence for the

FALSIFIABILITY
Can the claim be disproved?

GLOSSARY

Electra complex
conflict during the phallic stage in which girls supposedly love their fathers romantically and want to eliminate their mothers as rivals

latency stage
psychosexual stage in which sexual impulses are submerged into the unconscious

genital stage
psychosexual stage in which sexual impulses awaken and typically begin to mature into romantic attraction toward others

One of Freud's best-known patients, known as "Anna O.," was Bertha Pappenheim, who later became the founder of social work in Germany. Because many of Freud's patients, like Pappenheim, were relatively wealthy Viennese women, critics have questioned the generalizability of his conclusions.

existence of repression. In particular, people are no more likely to forget negative life experiences than equally arousing, but positive, life experiences (Holmes, 1974, 1990).

(3) Questionable Conception of the Unconscious. There's increasing reason to doubt the existence of the unconscious as Freud conceived of it. It's true that we're often unaware of why we do things, and our thinking can be influenced by subliminal information (Bargh & Chartrand, 1999; Nisbett & Wilson, 1977). Yet there's no clear evidence for *the* unconscious: a massive reservoir of impulses and memories submerged beneath awareness (Wilson, 2002). Freud viewed the unconscious as a "place" where sexual and aggressive energies, along with repressed memories, are housed. Nevertheless, research doesn't support the existence of this place, let alone tell us where it's located (Kihlstrom, 1987).

(4) Reliance on Unrepresentative Samples. Many critics have charged that Freud based his theories on atypical samples and generalized them to the rest of humanity. Most of Freud's patients were upper-class, neurotic Viennese women, a far cry from the average Nigerian man or Malaysian woman. Freud's theories may therefore possess limited external validity, that is, generalizability (see Chapter 2), for people from other cultural backgrounds.

FREUD'S FOLLOWERS: THE NEO-FREUDIANS

Largely in reaction to criticisms of Freudian theory, a number of psychiatrists and psychologists—many of them Freud's own students—broke from their mentor to forge their own models of personality. Because these thinkers modified Freud's views in significant ways, their approaches are typically called neo-Freudian theories.

Neo-Freudian Theories: Core Features.
Most neo-Freudian theories share with Freudian theory an emphasis on (a) unconscious influences on behavior and (b) the importance of early experience in shaping personality. Nevertheless, **neo-Freudian theories** differ from Freudian theory in two key ways: [LEARNING OBJECTIVE 12.4]

(1) Neo-Freudian theories place less emphasis than does Freudian theory on sexuality as a driving force in personality and more emphasis on social drives, such as the need for approval.

(2) Most neo-Freudian theories are more optimistic than Freudian theory concerning the prospects for personality growth throughout the life span. Freud was notoriously pessimistic about the possibility of personality change after childhood; he once wrote that the goal of psychoanalysis was to turn neurotic misery into ordinary, everyday unhappiness (Breuer & Freud, 1895).

Alfred Adler: The Striving for Superiority.
The first major follower of Freud to defect was Viennese psychiatrist Alfred Adler (1870–1937). According to Adler (1931), the principal motive in human personality is not sex or aggression, but the *striving for superiority.* Our overriding goal in life, said Adler, is to be better than others. We aim to accomplish this goal by crafting our distinctive *style of life,* or long-standing pattern of achieving superiority. People may try to satisfy their superiority strivings by becoming famous entertainers, great athletes, or outstanding parents.

According to Adler (1922), those who were pampered or neglected by their parents are prone to later developing an **inferiority complex,** a popular term inspired by Adler. People with an inferiority complex are prone to low self-esteem and tend to overcompensate for this feeling. As a result, they often attempt to demonstrate their superiority to others at all costs, even if it means dominating them.

Adler's hypotheses, like Freud's, are difficult to falsify (Popper, 1965). For example, Adler argued that a person's decision to become a homeless alcoholic could be used

GLOSSARY

neo-Freudian theories
theories derived from Freud's model but that place less emphasis on sexuality as a driving force in personality and are more optimistic regarding the prospects for long-term personality growth

inferiority complex
feelings of low self-esteem that can lead to overcompensation for such feelings

FALSIFIABILITY
Can the claim be disproved?

to support his theory that people always try to attain superiority over others, because making excuses is one way to protect ourselves from feelings of inferiority. In effect, we can tell ourselves, "If only I didn't drink, I would have become successful." As we can see, with a little creativity, we can cook up an Adlerian explanation for almost any behavior.

Carl Jung: The Collective Unconscious.

Another pupil of Freud who parted ways with his mentor was Swiss psychiatrist Carl Gustav Jung (1875–1961). Jung became disenchanted with Freud's emphasis on sexuality. His views have become enormously influential in popular psychology, and he is something of a cult figure in New Age circles.

Jung (1936) actually believed that Freud didn't take the idea of the unconscious far enough. He argued that in addition to Freud's version of the unconscious—which Jung termed the *personal unconscious*—there's also a **collective unconscious.** For Jung, the collective unconscious comprises all of the memories that ancestors have passed down to us across the generations. It's our shared storehouse of ancestral memories and accounts for cultural similarities in myths and legends. We recognize our mothers immediately after birth, Jung argued, because the memories of thousands of generations of individuals who've seen their mothers after birth have been passed down to us genetically.

Jung believed that the collective unconscious contains numerous **archetypes,** or cross-culturally universal emotional symbols, which explain the similarities across people in their emotional reactions to many features of the world. Archetypes include the mother, the goddess, the hero, and the mandala (circle), which Jung believed symbolized a desire for wholeness or unity (Campbell, 1988; Jung, 1950). Jung (1958) speculated that the modern epidemic of flying saucer reports stems from an unconscious desire to achieve a sense of unity with the universe because flying saucers are shaped like mandalas.

Provocative as it is, Jung's theory suffers from some of the same shortcomings as those of Freud and Adler. It's difficult to falsify because it generates few clear-cut predictions (Gallo, 1994; Monte, 1995). For example, how could we try to falsify Jung's claim that flying saucer sightings stem from an underlying wish for wholeness with the universe? It's difficult to imagine what evidence could refute this claim. In addition, although Jung hypothesized that archetypes are wired into us by evolution, he may not have sufficiently considered a rival explanation for their origins. Perhaps archetypes are cross-culturally universal because they represent crucial elements of the social and physical environment—mothers, wise elders, the sun, and moon (which are, after all, shaped like mandalas)—that people across all cultures experience. Shared experiences rather than a collective unconscious may account for commonalities in archetypes across the world.

Karen Horney: Feminist Psychology.

Karen Horney (1885–1952), a German physician, was the first major feminist personality theorist. Although not departing drastically from Freud's core assumptions, Horney (1939) took aim at those aspects of his theory that she saw as gender biased. She viewed Freud's concept of penis envy as especially misguided. Horney maintained that women's sense of inferiority stems not from their anatomy but their excessive dependency on men, which parents and society have ingrained in them from an early age. She similarly objected to the Oedipus complex on

(© ScienceCartoonPlus.com)

A mandala symbol similar to one drawn by one of Jung's patients.

FALSIFIABILITY
Can the claim be disproved?

RULING OUT RIVAL HYPOTHESES
Have important alternative explanations for the findings been excluded?

GLOSSARY

collective unconscious
according to Jung, our shared storehouse of memories that ancestors have passed down to us across generations

archetypes
cross-culturally universal emotional symbols

the grounds that it's neither inevitable nor universal. This complex, she maintained, is a *symptom* rather than a cause of psychological problems, because it arises only when the opposite-sex parent is overly protective and the same-sex parent overly critical.

Freud's Followers Evaluated Critically.
Many neo-Freudian theorists tempered some of the excesses of Freudian theory. They pointed out that anatomy isn't always destiny when it comes to the psychological differences between the sexes and argued that social influences must be reckoned with in the development of personality. Nevertheless, as we've seen, falsifiability remains a serious concern for neo-Freudian theories, especially those of Adler and Jung.

FALSIFIABILITY
Can the claim be disproved?

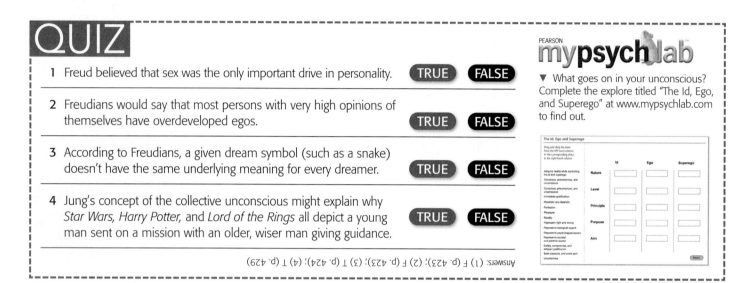

QUIZ

1 Freud believed that sex was the only important drive in personality. **TRUE** **FALSE**

2 Freudians would say that most persons with very high opinions of themselves have overdeveloped egos. **TRUE** **FALSE**

3 According to Freudians, a given dream symbol (such as a snake) doesn't have the same underlying meaning for every dreamer. **TRUE** **FALSE**

4 Jung's concept of the collective unconscious might explain why *Star Wars, Harry Potter,* and *Lord of the Rings* all depict a young man sent on a mission with an older, wiser man giving guidance. **TRUE** **FALSE**

Answers: (1) F (p. 423); (2) F (p. 423); (3) T (p. 424); (4) T (p. 429)

PEARSON
mypsychlab

▼ What goes on in your unconscious? Complete the explore titled "The Id, Ego, and Superego" at www.mypsychlab.com to find out.

Behavioral, Social Learning, and Humanistic Theories of Personality

Psychoanalytic theories were highly influential, but there are other theories of the origins and determinants of personality. These theories focus more on our experiences, emotions, social interactions, and *conscious* motivations to explain our personalities. We'll discuss three of these theories here: behavioral, social learning, and humanistic theories.

BEHAVIORAL VIEWS OF THE CAUSES OF PERSONALITY

We've already encountered behaviorism as an account of learning in Chapter 5. So why are we again crossing paths with behaviorism? After all, behaviorism is a theory of learning rather than a theory of personality, isn't it?

Actually, behaviorism is both. Radical behaviorists, like B. F. Skinner (see Chapter 5), believe that differences in our personalities stem largely from differences in our learning histories. Unlike Freudians, radical behaviorists reject the notion that the first few years of life are especially critical in personality development. Childhood certainly matters, but learning continues to mold our personalities throughout the life span.

For radical behaviorists, our personalities are bundles of habits acquired by classical and operant conditioning. In contrast to other personality theorists, radical behaviorists don't believe that personality plays a role in *causing* behavior. For them, personality *consists of* behaviors. These behaviors are both overt (observable) and covert (unobservable), such as thoughts and feelings. A radical behaviorist wouldn't have much trouble accepting the idea that some people are extraverted or that extraverted people tend to have many friends and attend many parties. But radical behaviorists would disagree that certain people have many friends and attend many parties *because* they're extraverted.

Radical behaviorists view personality as under the control of two major influences: (a) genetic factors and (b) *contingencies* in the environment, that is, reinforcers and punishers (see Chapter 5). Together, these influences explain why our personalities differ. [LEARNING OBJECTIVE 12.5]

Behavioral Views of Determinism.
Like psychoanalysts, radical behaviorists are strict determinists: They believe all of our actions are products of preexisting causal influences. This is one of the precious few issues on which Freud and Skinner would probably have agreed. For radical behaviorists, free will is an illusion. We may believe we're free to either continue reading this sentence or to instead stop to grab a bowl of ice cream, but we're fooling ourselves. We're convinced that we're free to select our behaviors only because we're usually oblivious to how situational factors elicit those behaviors.

Behavioral Views of Unconscious Processing.
The belief in unconscious processing is another point of consensus between Freudians and Skinnerians (Overskeid, 2007), although their views of this processing differ sharply. For Skinner, we're unconscious of many things because we're often unaware of immediate influences on our behavior (Skinner, 1974). We may have had the experience of suddenly humming a song to ourselves and wondering why we were doing so, until we realized that this song had been playing softly on a distant radio. According to Skinner, we were initially unconscious of the reasons for our behavior because we were unaware of the environmental cause of this behavior, in this case, the song in the distant background.

Such unconscious processing is a far cry from the Freudian unconscious, which is a vast storehouse of inaccessible thoughts, memories, and impulses. For radical behaviorists, there's no such storehouse because the unconscious influences that play a role in causing behavior are external, not inside our heads.

Behavioral Views Evaluated Critically.
Radical behaviorism placed the field of psychology on firmer, less speculative scientific footing than Freud did. However, many critics charged that radical behaviorists went too far in their exclusion of any causal role for thinking. Indeed, the claim that thoughts play no causal role in behavior strikes most modern thinkers as implausible from an evolutionary perspective. Natural selection has endowed us with an enormous cerebral cortex (see Chapter 3), which is specialized for problem solving, planning, reasoning, and other high-level cognitive processes. It seems difficult to comprehend why our huge cortexes would have evolved if our thoughts were merely by-products of learned associations.

SOCIAL LEARNING THEORIES OF PERSONALITY: THE CAUSAL ROLE OF THINKING RESURRECTED

Although influenced by radical behaviorists, **social learning theorists** believed that Skinner had gone too far in his wholesale rejection of the influence of thoughts on behavior. Spurred on by Edward Chase Tolman and others who believed that learning relies on our plans and goals (see Chapter 5), these theorists emphasized thinking as a cause of personality. How we interpret our environments affects how we react to them; if we tend to perceive others as threatening, we'll typically display hostile and suspicious

Although this person may perceive her decision to either eat or not eat a piece of candy as under her control, radical behaviorists would regard her perception as an illusion.

GLOSSARY

social learning theorists
theorists who emphasized thinking as a cause of personality

In observational learning, parents, teachers, and other adults play significant roles in shaping children's personalities: Children learn good and bad habits by watching and later emulating adults. This child may learn early that charitable giving is a worthy endeavor.

personality in return. As we acquire information in classical and operant conditioning, we're actively thinking about and interpreting what it means. **[LEARNING OBJECTIVE 12.6]**

Observational Learning and Personality.
Social learning theorists proposed that much of learning occurs by watching others. As we learned in Chapter 5, *observational learning* appears to be a key form of learning neglected by traditional behaviorists (Bandura, 1965). Observational learning expands greatly the range of stimuli from which we can benefit. It also means that our parents and teachers can play significant roles in shaping our personalities, because we acquire both good and bad habits by watching and, later, emulating them. For example, through observational learning, we can learn to behave altruistically by seeing our parents donate money to charities.

Sense of Perceived Control.
Social learning theorists emphasized individuals' sense of control over life events. Julian Rotter (1966) introduced the concept of **locus of control** to describe the extent to which people believe that reinforcers and punishers lie inside or outside of their control. People with an internal locus of control ("internals") believe that life events are due largely to their own efforts and personal characteristics. In contrast, people with an external locus of control ("externals") believe that life events are largely a product of chance and fate (see **Table 12.6**).

Table 12.6 Sample Items from a Measure of Locus of Control.

	True or False
(1) Many people live miserable lives because of their parents.	True/False
(2) If you set realistic goals, you can succeed no matter what.	True/False
(3) One can climb the professional ladder just by being around at the right time.	True/False
(4) If I study hard enough, I can pass any exam.	True/False

For items 1 and 3, a "True" response is scored in the direction of an external locus of control, and a "False" response is scored in the direction of an internal locus of control. Items 2 and 4 are scored in the opposite fashion. (*Source:* Reprinted with permission of Psychtests.com)

Rotter hypothesized that internals are less prone than externals to emotional upset following life stressors because they're more likely to believe they can remedy problems on their own. Indeed, almost all forms of psychological distress, including depression and anxiety, are associated with an external locus of control (Benassi, Sweeney, & Dufour, 1988; Carton & Nowicki, 1996). It's not clear, though, whether these correlational findings reflect a causal relationship between external locus of control and mental disorders, as Rotter believed. Perhaps once people develop depression or anxiety, they begin to feel their lives are spiraling out of control. Or perhaps people who doubt their abilities are prone to both an external locus of control, on the one hand, and depression and anxiety, on the other.

CORRELATION vs. CAUSATION
Can we be sure that A causes B?

⌐ **WHAT DO** *you* **THINK** ⁂

As a hospital social worker, you are responsible for communicating important medical information to patients. How might you adapt the way you explain the recovery process following surgery for those with internal versus external locus of control?

GLOSSARY

locus of control
extent to which people believe that reinforcers and punishers lie inside or outside of their control

Social Learning Theories Evaluated Critically.
Social learning theorists rekindled psychologists' interests in thinking and argued that observational learning is a crucial

form of learning in addition to classical and operant conditioning. Nevertheless, social learning theory isn't immune to criticism. In particular, the claim that observational learning exerts a powerful influence over our personalities implies an important causal role of shared environment. After all, if we learn largely by modeling the behaviors of our parents and other relatives, we should become like them. Yet behavior-genetic studies have shown that the effects of shared environment on adult personality are weak or nonexistent.

HUMANISTIC MODELS OF PERSONALITY: THE THIRD FORCE

Psychoanalytic theory, along with behavioral and social learning models, dominated personality psychology throughout the first half of the twentieth century. In the 1950s and 1960s, however, *humanistic models* emerged as a powerful "third force" in personality psychology. Humanistic psychologists rejected the determinism of psychoanalysts and behaviorists and embraced the notion of free will. We're perfectly free, they maintained, to choose either socially constructive or destructive paths in life.

Most humanistic psychologists propose that the core motive in personality is **self-actualization:** the drive to develop our innate potential to the fullest possible extent. Freudians would say that self-actualization would be disastrous for society because our innate drives, housed in the id, are selfish and destructive. Humanistic theorists, in contrast, view human nature as inherently constructive, so they see self-actualization as a worthy goal. **[LEARNING OBJECTIVE 12.7]**

Rogers and Maslow: Self-Actualization Realized and Unrealized. The best-known humanistic theorist was Carl Rogers (1902–1987), who, as we'll learn in Chapter 14, used his personality theory as a point of departure for an influential form of psychotherapy. Ever the optimist, Rogers believed that we could all achieve our full potential for emotional fulfillment if only society allowed it.

Rogers's Model of Personality. According to Rogers (1947), our personalities consist of three major components: organism, self, and conditions of worth:

(1) The *organism* is our innate genetic blueprint. In this regard it's like the Freudian id, except that Rogers viewed the organism as inherently positive and helpful toward others.

(2) The *self* is our self-concept, the set of beliefs about who we are.

(3) **Conditions of worth** are the expectations we place on ourselves for appropriate and inappropriate behavior. They emanate from our parents and society, and eventually we internalize them. Conditions of worth arise when others make their acceptance of us conditional—dependent—only on certain behaviors but not others. As a result, we only accept ourselves if we act in specific ways. A child who enjoys writing poetry may develop conditions of worth if taunted by peers. "When I'm teased for writing poetry, I'm not worthwhile. When I stop, I'm not teased so I become worthwhile."

For Rogers, individual differences in personality stem largely from differences in the conditions of worth that others impose on us. Conditions of worth result in *incongruence* between self and organism. Incongruence means that our personalities are inconsistent with our innate dispositions: We're not our true selves.

Maslow: The Characteristics of Self-Actualized People. Whereas Rogers focused largely on pathological individuals whose tendencies toward self-actualization were thwarted, Abraham Maslow (1908–1970) focused on individuals who were self-actualized, especially historical figures. Among those whom Maslow considered self-actualized were Thomas Jefferson, Abraham Lincoln, Martin Luther King, Jr., Helen Keller, and Mahatma Gandhi.

How much of the daughter's personality and mannerisms are due to social learning from the mother? The scientific verdict is still out.

Carl Rogers, pioneer of humanistic psychology, held an optimistic view of human nature, although some critics have accused him of being naive in minimizing the dark side of human nature.

GLOSSARY

self-actualization
drive to develop our innate potential to the fullest possible extent

conditions of worth
according to Rogers, expectations we place on ourselves for appropriate and inappropriate behavior

Mahatma Gandhi and Mother Teresa: According to Maslow's theorizing, what do these two people have in common? Can you think of any people in today's society who would be considered self-actualized in Maslow's view?

Our basic personality and dispositions may share a common basis with other primates.

FALSIFIABILITY
Can the claim be disproved?

According to Maslow (1971), self-actualized people tend to be creative, spontaneous, and accepting of themselves and others. They're self-confident but not self-centered. They focus on real-world and intellectual problems and have a few deep friendships rather than many superficial ones. Self-actualized individuals typically crave privacy and can come off as introverted, aloof, or even difficult to deal with because they've outgrown the need to be popular. As a consequence, they're not afraid to "rock the boat" when necessary or express unpopular opinions. They're also prone to *peak experiences*—transcendent moments of intense excitement and tranquility marked by a profound sense of connection to the world.

Humanistic Models Evaluated Critically. Humanistic models of personality boldly proclaimed the importance of free will and the inherent drive for self-actualization. Yet investigators in *comparative psychology,* the branch of psychology that compares behavior across species, have challenged Rogers's claim that human nature is entirely positive. Their research suggests that the capacity for aggression is inherent in our closest primate cousins, the chimpanzees (Goodall & van Lawick, 1971; see also Chapter 11). There's also evidence from twin studies that aggression is probably part of humans' genetic heritage (Krueger et al., 2001). Therefore, actualization of our full genetic potential is unlikely to bring about the state of bliss that Rogers imagined. At the same time, research suggests that the capacity for altruism is intrinsic to both human and nonhuman primates (de Waal, 1990; Wilson, 1993). Human nature, it seems, is a complex mix of selfish and selfless motives.

Maslow's work is problematic on methodological grounds. His assumption that self-actualized individuals tend to be creative and spontaneous may have led him to limit his search to historical figures who displayed these traits. As such, Maslow may have fallen prey to confirmation bias: Because he wasn't blind to his hypothesis concerning the personality features of self-actualized individuals, he had no easy way of guarding against this bias.

Humanistic models are also difficult to falsify. If a study of the general population showed that many people were self-actualized, humanistic psychologists could interpret this finding as evidence that self-actualization is an important influence on personality. But if this study showed that virtually no one was self-actualized, humanistic psychologists could explain away this finding by saying that most individuals' drives toward self-actualization had been stifled.

QUIZ

1 Radical behaviorists argue that we're sometimes "unconscious" of the true causes of our behavior.   `TRUE` `FALSE`

2 According to social learning theorists, individuals with an internal locus of control—who are more likely to blame themselves for mistakes—are more prone to depression than individuals with an external locus of control.   `TRUE` `FALSE`

3 According to Rogers, human nature is inherently positive.   `TRUE` `FALSE`

4 Maslow claimed that almost all self-actualized individuals are sociable and easy to get along with.   `TRUE` `FALSE`

5 Many claims of humanistic models are difficult to falsify.   `TRUE` `FALSE`

PEARSON
mypsychlab

▼ What type of theorist would argue that personality is developed by watching our peers? Complete the explore titled "Behavioral versus Social Learning Theories of Personality" at www.mypsychlab.com to find out.

Answers: (1) T (p. 431); (2) F (p. 432); (3) T (p. 433); (4) F (p. 434); (5) T (p. 434)

Trait Models of Personality: Consistencies in Our Behavior

In contrast to most of the personality theorists we've reviewed, proponents of trait models are interested primarily in describing and understanding the *structure* of personality. Much like early chemists who strove to identify the elements of the periodic table, trait theorists aim to pinpoint the major elements that combine in different amounts to explain differences in our personalities. **[LEARNING OBJECTIVE 12.8]**

TRAIT MODELS: KEY CHALLENGES

Invoking personality traits as causes of behavior has its challenges. To start with, we must avoid *circular reasoning*. We might conclude that a child who kicks others on the playground is aggressive. But in asking how we know that this child is aggressive, we might respond "because he kicks other children on the playground." To avoid this logical trap, we need to demonstrate that personality traits predict behaviors in novel situations or correlate with biological or laboratory measures.

From there, we need to narrow down the pool of possible traits. There are over 17,000 terms in the English language referring to personality traits: shy, stubborn, impulsive, greedy, cheerful, and so on (Allport & Odbert, 1936). To reduce this diversity of traits to perhaps as few as three or five underlying traits, trait theorists use a statistical technique called **factor analysis.** This technique analyzes the correlations among responses on personality inventories and other measures and tries to identify the underlying "factors" that give rise to these correlations.

For example, **Table 12.7** on page 436 displays the results of a study examining which of four traits (popularity, liveliness, sensation seeking, and impulsivity) are correlated with two other traits, sociability and risk taking. We can see that two of the four variables (popularity and liveliness) are correlated with sociability but not with risk taking. The other two traits, sensation seeking and impulsivity, are correlated with risk taking but not sociability. Also, we see that sociability and risk taking are uncorrelated. This pattern suggests two distinct groups of traits, two separate factors identified through factor analysis. One of these factors (the one that includes sociability, liveliness, and popularity) might be called "extraversion" and the other (the one that includes risk taking, sensation seeking, and impulsivity) might be called "fearlessness."

PERSONALITY TRAITS UNDER SIEGE: WALTER MISCHEL'S CRITIQUE

Trait theory was highly influential through the early and mid-twentieth century. Then in a stunning 1968 book, *Personality and Assessment,* Walter Mischel called the very notion of personality traits into question, embroiling the field of trait psychology in heated controversy for over a decade.

Mischel's Argument: Behavioral Inconsistency.

As we noted earlier, psychologists had long assumed that traits influence behavior across many situations. But in his review of the literature, Mischel found low correlations among different behaviors believed to reflect the same trait. For example, he cited a study by Hugh Hartschorne and Mark May (1928) that had examined the correlations among various behavioral indicators of honesty among children. Hartschorne and May concocted situations that allowed children to

Claiming that a child is "aggressive" merely because he engages in aggressive behavior gives us no new information and is an example of circular reasoning. To be meaningful, personality traits must do more than merely describe behaviors we've already observed.

People who are dishonest in one setting (such as cheating on a test) aren't necessarily dishonest in other situations.

GLOSSARY

factor analysis
statistical technique that analyzes the correlations among responses on personality inventories and other measures

Table 12.7 Example of Factor Analysis. The fact that groups of traits correlate with each other enables us to identify factors. An examination of what the different traits within a factor have in common allows us to characterize what types of attitudes and behaviors are represented by the factor.

Trait	Popularity	Liveliness	Sensation Seeking	Impulsivity
Sociability	.78	.82	.07	.03
Risk Taking	.08	.05	.69	.85

*Correlation between sociability and risk taking is .12.

REPLICABILITY
Can the results be duplicated in other studies?

behave either honestly or dishonestly, giving them the opportunity to steal a dime, change answers on an exam, and lie. Surprisingly, the correlations among children's behavior across these situations were low, with none exceeding 0.30. So children who steal in one situation, for example, aren't much more likely than other children to cheat in a different situation. Numerous researchers have reported similar findings in adults for such traits as dependency, friendliness, and conscientiousness (Bem & Allen, 1974; Mischel, 1968). People, it seems, aren't nearly as consistent across situations as most of us believe, a message we already encountered in Chapter 11 when discussing the fundamental attribution error. Mischel concluded that measures of personality aren't especially helpful for what they were designed to do—forecast behavior.

Personality Traits Reborn: Psychologists Respond to Mischel. Were Mischel's criticisms valid? Yes and no. As Seymour Epstein (1979) noted, Mischel was correct that personality traits aren't highly predictive of isolated behaviors, such as lying or cheating in a single situation. **[LEARNING OBJECTIVE 12.9]** Nevertheless, in several studies Epstein showed that personality traits are often highly predictive of *aggregated* behaviors, that is, composites of behavior averaged across many situations. If we use a measure of extraversion to predict whether our friend will attend a party next Saturday night, we'll probably do only slightly better than chance. In contrast, if we use this measure to predict our friend's behavior across an average of many situations—attendance at parties, friendliness in small classes, and willingness to engage in conversations with strangers in the grocery checkout line—we'll probably do rather well. Contrary to Mischel's conclusions, personality traits can be useful for predicting overall behavioral trends (Rushton, Brainerd, & Presley, 1983). Still, Mischel performed a valuable service by pointing out that traits are rarely useful for predicting people's behavior in any given situation (Kenrick & Funder, 1988).

MODELS OF PERSONALITY STRUCTURE: THE BIG FIVE

Although there's no complete consensus among trait theorists regarding the ideal number of factors that comprehensively explains personality structure, one model has received considerable research support. This model, the **Big Five,** consists of five traits that have surfaced repeatedly in factor analyses of personality measures.

REPLICABILITY
Can the results be duplicated in other studies?

The Big Five emerged from factor analyses of trait terms in dictionaries and works of literature. According to Paul Costa, Robert McCrae, and their collaborators (Costa & McCrae, 1992; Widiger, 2001), these five dimensions are:

- *Openness to Experience,* sometimes just called "Openness"—open people tend to be intellectually curious and unconventional
- *Conscientiousness*—conscientious people tend to be careful and responsible
- *Extraversion*—extraverted people tend to be social and lively
- *Agreeableness*—agreeable people tend to be friendly and easy to get along with
- *Neuroticism*—neurotic people tend to be tense and moody

We can use either of two waterlogged acronyms—OCEAN or CANOE—as a handy mnemonic for remembering the Big Five. According to Big Five advocates, we can use these factors to describe all people, including those with psychological disorders. Individuals can be high, moderate, or low on each trait. A severely depressed person, for example, may be low in Extraversion, high in Neuroticism, and about average on the other three dimensions.

The Big Five appear in people's ratings of personality even when researchers ask participants to describe people they've only seen, not met (Passini & Norman, 1966). The popular dating website eHarmony.com uses the Big Five to match prospective partners, although the research evidence for its success is minimal (see also Chapter 9).

 Fact -OID Individuals' handshakes can tell us something about their Big Five personality traits. Research demonstrates that people with firm handshakes tend to be somewhat higher in extraversion and openness to experience, and lower in neuroticism, than people with limp handshakes (Chaplin, Phillips, Brown, et al., 2000).

WHAT DO *you* THINK?

You are working for a new computer dating service that is trying to compete with eHarmony.com. Can you think of some additional personality characteristics besides the Big Five to add to your profiles to improve the matching process?

The Big Five and Behavior. The Big Five predict many interesting real-world behaviors. For example, high Conscientiousness, low Neuroticism, and perhaps high Agreeableness are correlated with successful job performance (Barrick & Mount, 1991; Tett, Jackson, & Rothstein, 1991). Three researchers (Rubenzer, Faschingbauer, & Ones, 2000) asked presidential biographers to rate the U.S. presidents from George Washington through Bill

GLOSSARY

Big Five
five traits that have surfaced repeatedly in factor analyses of personality measures

His biographers have ranked Harry ("Give 'em hell") Truman (*right*) as low in Big Five Agreeableness, but most presidential historians rank him as among America's best presidents.

Clinton. Scores on Openness to Experience were correlated positively with independently assessed ratings of presidents' historical greatness. Interestingly, Agreeableness was correlated *negatively* with historical greatness, suggesting that the best presidents often aren't always the easiest to get along with.

Longitudinal studies (see Chapter 8) show that personality traits are fairly stable over time, especially in adults. With a few exceptions (Srivastava, Gosling, & Potter et al., 2003), the levels of most personality traits don't change much after age 30 and change even less after about age 50 (McCrae & Costa, 1994; Roberts & Del Vecchio, 2000).

Personality traits don't tell us everything about why we differ from each other. The story of Jack and Oskar underscores the distinction between *basic tendencies* and *characteristic adaptations* (Harkness & Lilienfeld, 1997; McCrae & Costa, 1995). Basic tendencies are underlying personality traits, whereas characteristic adaptations are their behavioral manifestations. The key point here is that people can express their personality traits in very different ways. In Jack and Oskar's case, the same basic tendencies—intense loyalty and devotion to social causes—were expressed in two drastically different characteristic adaptations: Jack's Judaism and profound dislike of Germans and Oskar's Nazism and profound dislike of Jews.

The Big Five Evaluated Critically. Despite the usefulness of the Big Five, there's reason to be cautious about concluding that these traits capture the whole range of human personalities. For example, there's no Big Five factor corresponding to morality (Loevinger, 1993), despite the centrality of this variable to many theories of personality, including those of Freud and his followers. Still other psychologists, like Hans Eysenck (1991) and Auke Tellegen (1982), have maintained that three dimensions rather than five offer the most accurate model of personality structure. According to them, the Big Five dimensions of Agreeableness, Conscientiousness, and (low) Openness to Experience combine to form one larger dimension of impulse control along with the dimensions of Extraversion and Neuroticism. The "Big Three" model of personality structure is a worthy alternative to the Big Five (Tellegen & Waller, in press).

CULTURAL INFLUENCES ON PERSONALITY

A unique personality characteristic in Chinese culture called "Chinese tradition" emphasizes group harmony.

Researchers have discovered that the Big Five are identifiable in China, Japan, Italy, Hungary, and Turkey (De Raad, Perugini, Herbickova et al., 1998; McCrae & Costa, 1997; Triandis & Suh, 2002). Nevertheless, there may be limits to the Big Five's cross-cultural universality. Openness to experience doesn't emerge clearly in all cultures (De Raad & Perugini et al., 2002) and some investigators have found dimensions in addition to the Big Five. For example, personality studies in China have revealed an additional "Chinese tradition" factor that encompasses aspects of personality distinctive to Chinese culture, including an emphasis on group harmony and on saving face to avoid embarrassment (Cheung & Leung, 1998). Moreover, studies in Germany, Finland, and several other countries suggest the presence of a factor reflecting honesty and humility in addition to the Big Five (Lee & Ashton, 2004).

Cross-cultural researchers have devoted considerable attention to a key dimension relevant to personality we first encountered in Chapter 8: *Individualism–collectivism.* People from largely individualistic cultures, like the United States, tend to focus on themselves and their personal goals, whereas people from largely collectivist cultures, primarily in Asia, tend to focus on their relations with others (Triandis, 1989). People from individualistic cultures tend to report higher self-esteem than do those from collectivist cultures (Heine, Lehman, Markus et al., 1999). In addition, personality traits may be less predictive of behavior in collectivist than individualistic cultures, probably because people's behavior in collectivist cultures is more influenced by social norms (Church & Katigbak, 2002).

Yet we shouldn't oversimplify the distinction between individualistic and collectivist cultures. Only about 60 percent of people in individualist cultures possess individualistic personalities, and only about 60 percent of people in collectivist cultures possess collectivist personalities (Triandis & Suh, 2002). Furthermore, Asian countries differ markedly in their levels of collectivism, reminding us of the perils of stereotyping and overgeneralization (see Chapter 11). For example, although Chinese are generally more collectivist than Americans, Japanese and Koreans aren't (Oyserman, Coon, & Kemmelmeier, 2002).

TRAIT MODELS EVALUATED CRITICALLY

Challenges by Mischel (1968) to the contrary, personality traits can be useful predictors of real-world behaviors, but only when they're aggregated (averaged) across different situations. Trait models have proved helpful to therapists, clinicians in prison settings, and psychologists who hope to predict long-term behavioral trends. In contrast to other personality theories we've reviewed, trait models are primarily efforts to *describe* individual differences in personality rather than to *explain* their causes. This emphasis on description is both a strength and a weakness. On the one hand, these models have advanced our understanding of personality structure and helped psychologists to predict performance in jobs. On the other hand, trait models don't necessarily provide much insight into the causes of personality. For example, although the Big Five do a decent job of capturing personality differences among people, they don't shed much light on the origins of these differences.

Some researchers, like Hans Eysenck, have tried to remedy this shortcoming. For example, according to Eysenck (1973), the personality dimension of extraversion–introversion is produced by differences in the threshold of arousal of the reticular activating system (RAS). The RAS controls alertness and is responsible for keeping us awake. Although the following hypothesis is paradoxical, Eysenck argued that extraverts have an *underactive* RAS: They're habitually underaroused and bored. So they seek out stimulation, including other people, to jack up their arousal. In contrast, introverts tend to have an overactive RAS: They're habitually overaroused and overwhelmed and try to minimize or shut out stimulation, again including other people. Interestingly, extraverts like loud music more than do introverts (Kageyama, 1999). Although the evidence for Eysenck's hypothesis isn't entirely consistent (Gray, 1981), his theorizing demonstrates that trait theories can generate fruitful hypotheses concerning the relations between personality traits and biological variables.

Eysenck's model of personality proposes that introverts tend to be overaroused and extraverts underaroused. As a result, Eysenck argued, introverts try to shut out stimulation, whereas extraverts try to seek it out.

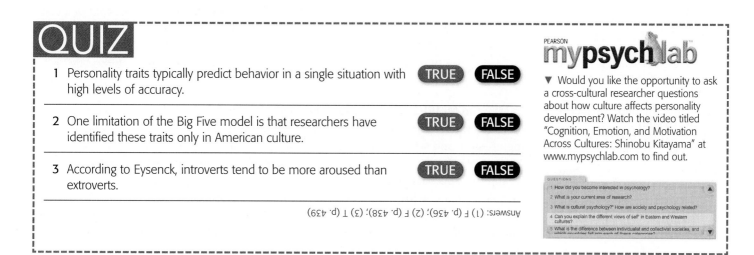

QUIZ

1 Personality traits typically predict behavior in a single situation with high levels of accuracy. TRUE FALSE

2 One limitation of the Big Five model is that researchers have identified these traits only in American culture. TRUE FALSE

3 According to Eysenck, introverts tend to be more aroused than extroverts. TRUE FALSE

Answers: (1) F (p. 436); (2) F (p. 438); (3) T (p. 439)

PEARSON
mypsychlab

▼ Would you like the opportunity to ask a cross-cultural researcher questions about how culture affects personality development? Watch the video titled "Cognition, Emotion, and Motivation Across Cultures: Shinobu Kitayama" at www.mypsychlab.com to find out.

QUESTIONS
1 How did you become interested in psychology?
2 What is your current area of research?
3 What is cultural psychology? How are society and psychology related?
4 Can you explain the different views of self in Eastern and Western cultures?
5 What is the difference between individualist and collectivist societies, and which countries fall into each of these categories?

Personality Assessment: Measuring and Mismeasuring the Psyche

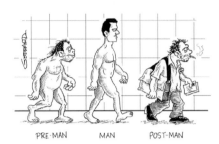

PRE-MAN   MAN   POST-MAN

Traditional beliefs persist that those with protruding foreheads and low brow lines are less intelligent or cultured.
(© Clive Goddard/www.CartoonStock.com)

FALSIFIABILITY
Can the claim be disproved?

Personality wouldn't be useful to psychologists if they had no way of measuring it. That's where personality assessment enters into the picture: It offers us the promise of detecting individual differences in personality in a rigorous fashion. But developing accurate tools to measure personality is easier said than done. Indeed, personality psychology has long been plagued by questionable assessment methods. Phrenology, which we encountered in Chapter 3, purported to detect people's personality traits by measuring the patterns of bumps on their heads. Related to phrenology was *physiognomy,* popular in the eighteenth and nineteenth centuries, which claimed to detect people's personality traits from their facial characteristics (Collins, 1999). The term *lowbrow,* which today refers to someone who's uncultured, derives from the old belief that most nonintellectual people have protruding foreheads and a low brow line. This claim, like virtually all other claims of physiognomy, has been falsified.

With these errors of the past in mind, how can we distinguish good from bad personality assessment methods? Two key criteria for evaluating all tests, including personality tests, are reliability and validity (see Chapter 2). *Reliability* refers to consistency of measurement and *validity* to the extent to which a test measures what it purports to measure. We'll keep these dual criteria in mind as we examine the two major types of personality tests: structured and projective.

STRUCTURED PERSONALITY TESTS

The best-known personality instruments are **structured personality tests.** These are typically paper-and-pencil tests consisting of questions that respondents answer in one of a few fixed ways. By fixed ways, we mean choosing between true and false answers, or by selecting options on a scale with, for example, 1 being "always true," 2 being "somewhat true," and so on, until 5, which is "always false." These numerical scales are called *Likert* formats.

MMPI and MMPI-2: Detecting Abnormal Personality.
The **Minnesota Multiphasic Personality Inventory,** or **MMPI** (Hathaway & McKinley, 1940), is the most extensively researched of all structured personality tests. Psychologists across the world use the MMPI to detect symptoms of mental disorders. **[LEARNING OBJECTIVE 12.10]** Developed in the early 1940s by psychologist Starke Hathaway and neurologist J. Charnley McKinley of the University of Minnesota, the MMPI was revised in the 1980s by James Butcher and his colleagues (Butcher, Dahlstrom, Graham, et al., 1989). This revised test, the MMPI-2, consists of 567 true/false items.

MMPI and MMPI-2: Construction and Content.
The MMPI-2, like its predecessor, consists of ten *basic* scales, most of which assess mental disorders, such as paranoia, depression, and schizophrenia (see Chapter 13). Hathaway and McKinley developed these scales by means of an **empirical** (or data-based) **method of test construction.** Using this approach, researchers begin with two or more criterion groups, such as people with and without a specific psychological disorder, and examine which items best distinguish them. For example, the items on the MMPI depression scale are those that best differentiate patients with clinical depression from nondepressed people.

GLOSSARY

structured personality test
paper-and-pencil test consisting of questions that respondents answer in one of a few fixed ways

Minnesota Multiphasic Personality Inventory (MMPI)
widely used structured test designed to assess symptoms of mental disorders

empirical (or data-based) **method of test construction**
approach to building tests in which researchers begin with two or more criterion groups and examine which items best distinguish them

One consequence of the empirical method of test construction is that many MMPI and MMPI-2 items possess low **face validity.** Face validity refers to the extent to which respondents can tell what the items are measuring. In a face valid test, we can take the items on "face value": They assess what they appear to assess. Because Hathaway and McKinley were concerned only with *whether,* but not *why,* the MMPI items differentiated among criterion groups, they ended up with some items that bear little obvious connection with the disorder they supposedly assess. To take an example of an item with low face validity from another structured personality test, can you guess what personality trait the following item assesses: "I think newborn babies look very much like little monkeys"? The answer is nurturance, that is, a tendency to care for others—with a "True" answer reflecting low nurturance and a "False" answer reflecting high nurturance—although few people who take the test can figure that out (Jackson, 1971, p. 238).

The MMPI-2 contains 3 major *validity* scales. These scales detect various *response sets,* which are tendencies to distort reponses to items. Response sets, which can compromise the validity of psychological tests, include *impression management*—making ourselves look better than we really are—and *malingering*—making ourselves appear psychologically disturbed. For example, people who respond "false" to the statement "I occasionally become angry" are probably engaging in impression management.

As we can see in **Figure 12.2,** psychologists plot the ten basic scales of the MMPI-2 in profile form, which displays the pattern of each person's scale scores. Although many clinicians enjoy interpreting MMPI-2 profiles by "eyeballing," research demonstrates that simple statistical formulas yield interpretations that are equally, if not more, valid than those of experienced clinicians (Garb, 1998; Goldberg, 1969).

 There are now more MMPI scales than MMPI items. Researchers have derived hundreds of empirically constructed scales (in addition to the ten basic scales) from the MMPI and MMPI-2 item pools. Among the strangest of these scales are the "Success in Baseball" scale, constructed by comparing major with minor league baseball players and the "Tired Homemaker" scale, constructed by comparing happy with unhappy homemakers (Dahlstrom, Welsh, & Dahlstrom, 1975; Graham, 2006). Obviously, this inventory is sensitive to differences along a variety of dimensions. Nevertheless, the scientific support for many of these scales is weak.

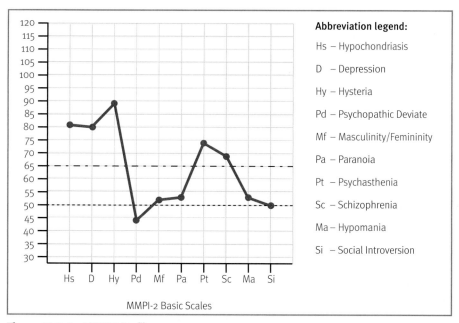

Figure 12.2 An MMPI-2 Profile. MMPI scores of 50 are average, and scores of 65 or above are abnormally high. This individual received elevated scores on several MMPI-2 clinical scales, including Hs (Hypochondriasis), D (Depression), Hy (Hysteria), Pt (Psychasthenia–Anxiety), and Sc (Schizophrenia).
(*Source:* Adapted from the *MMPI®-2 (Minnesota Multiphasic Personality Inventory®-2) Manual for Administration, Scoring, and Interpretation,* Revised Edition. Copyright © 2001 by the Regents of the University of Minnesota. Used by permission of the University of Minnesota Press. All rights reserved. "MMPI-2" and "Minnesota Multiphasic Personality Inventory-2" are trademarks owned by the Regents of the University of Minnesota.)

GLOSSARY

face validity
extent to which respondents can tell what the items are measuring

The MMPI and MMPI-2 Evaluated Critically. Extensive research supports the reliability of most MMPI-2 scales, as well as their validity for differentiating among mental disorders (Graham, 2006; Greene, 2000). For example, the MMPI-2 schizophrenia scale distinguishes patients with schizophrenia from patients with other severe psychological disorders, like clinical depression (Walters & Greene, 1988). Nevertheless, the MMPI-2 is problematic; because many of its scales are correlated highly, they're largely redundant with each other (Helmes & Reddon, 1993). As a result, it is difficult to differentiate personality traits and, in particular, different personality disorders, using these ten scales.

We can find variants of the Myers-Brigg Type Indicator on the Internet—personality inventories that claim to tell us which characters from books, TV shows, and movies we most closely resemble.

Rationally/Theoretically Constructed Tests. Psychologists have also developed many structured personality measures using a **rational/theoretical method of test construction.** In contrast to an empirical approach, this approach requires test developers to begin with a clear-cut conceptualization of a trait and then write items to assess that conceptualization. Auke Tellegen (1982) adopted a rational/theoretical approach in constructing the Multidimensional Personality Questionnaire (MPQ) and later used factor analyses to select the best items for this test. The MPQ assesses three major self-reported personality traits related to (1) positive emotions (such as happiness and social intimacy), (2) negative emotions (such as anxiety and anger), and (3) impulse control (Tellegen et al., 1988). Studies show that the MPQ validly assesses these personality traits; scores on its scales correlate highly with ratings of the same traits by peers (Harkness, Tellegen, & Waller, 1995).

But not all rational/theoretical tests boast a strong track record of validity. The Myers-Briggs Type Indicator (MBTI) is perhaps the most widely administered personality test in the world. Given several million times a year, it's used by thousands of companies in the United States alone, including 89 of the Fortune 100 (Paul, 2004). Even Harry Potter was placed in his mythical school based on a variant of the MBTI (Rowling, 1998). Based loosely on Jung's theory of personality, the MBTI sorts respondents into one of two categories on each of four dimensions—introversion–extraversion, sensing–intuiting, thinking–feeling, and judging–perceiving—yielding a total of 16 personality types. Although some claim that the MBTI is helpful for predicting job performance and satisfaction, research raises doubts about its reliability and validity. Most respondents don't obtain the same MBTI personality type on retesting only a few months later, and MBTI scores don't relate in consistent ways to either the Big Five or measures of job preferences (Costa & McCrae, 1998; Hunsley, Lee, & Wood, 2003).

PROJECTIVE TESTS

Projective tests consist of ambiguous stimuli, such as inkblots, drawings of social situations, or incomplete sentences, that examinees must interpret or make sense of. If you've ever looked for shapes in clouds in the sky, you have a sense of what it's like to take a projective test.

These techniques rest on a crucial premise: the **projective hypothesis** (Frank, 1948). This hypothesis assumes that in the process of interpreting ambiguous stimuli, people inevitably project aspects of their personality onto the stimulus. Test interpreters can then work in reverse by examining people's answers for clues concerning their personality

GLOSSARY

rational/theoretical method of test construction
approach to building tests that requires test developers to begin with a clear-cut conceptualization of a trait and then write items to assess that conceptualization

projective test
test consisting of ambiguous stimuli that examinees must interpret or make sense of

projective hypothesis
hypothesis that, in the process of interpreting ambiguous stimuli, examinees project aspects of their personality onto the stimulus

traits. In contrast to structured personality measures, projective techniques permit respondents considerable latitude in their answers. **[LEARNING OBJECTIVE 12.11]** The projective hypothesis corresponds to the Freudian concept of projection as a defense mechanism, imposing our thoughts and feelings onto others.

Proponents of projective tests view them as the "stealth weapons" of the psychologist's arsenal, circumventing respondents' defense mechanisms (Dosajh, 1966). Projective tests are among the most controversial of all psychological instruments, largely because their reliability and validity remain in dispute (Hunsley & Bailey, 1999; Lilienfeld, 1999b; Lilienfeld, Wood, & Garb, 2001). Why, then, are they still widely used? Very likely this is due, at least in part, to psychologists falling prey to confirmation bias (see Chapter 1). The tests "feel" valid, regardless of whether they are.

Rorschach Inkblot Test: What Might This Be?

The best-known projective measure is the **Rorschach Inkblot Test,** developed by Swiss psychiatrist Hermann Rorschach in the early 1920s. The Rorschach, as it's commonly known, consists of ten symmetrical inkblots, five in black-and-white and five containing color. The Rorschach is one of the most commonly used of all personality measures (Watkins et al., 1995): It's administered about 6 million times every year (Sutherland, 1992; Wood, Lilienfeld, Garb, et al., 2000).

Rorschach examiners ask respondents to look at each inkblot and say what it resembles. Examiners then score their answers for numerous characteristics supposedly associated with personality traits. Examples of these kinds of associations are listed in **Table 12.8.**

The Rorschach Evaluated Critically. Despite its widespread use, the Rorschach is scientifically controversial. The test-retest reliabilities of many of its scores are unknown, and their interrater reliabilities (see Chapter 2) are often problematic (Lilienfeld et al., 2001; Sultan et al., 2006; Wood & Lilienfeld, 1999). Moreover, although psychologists commonly use the Rorschach to assist in making psychiatric diagnoses (Weiner, 1997), there's little evidence that it validly detects the features of most mental disorders (Wood et al., 2000). Specifically, with the exception of schizophrenia and other conditions marked by abnormal thinking (see Chapter 13), there are few replicated associations between Rorschach scores and mental illnesses. Nor are there consistent associations between Rorschach scores and most personality traits (Wood, Nezworski, & Stejskal, 1996).

Many investigators and social workers allow children to play freely with anatomically detailed dolls. They try to infer whether the children had been sexually abused based on their play. Unfortunately, this projective test has led to numerous false accusations. (*Source:* Hunsley, Lee, & Wood, 2003)

GLOSSARY

Rorschach Inkblot Test
projective test consisting of ten symmetrical inkblots

REPLICABILITY
Can the results be duplicated in other studies?

Table 12.8 Sample Rorschach Responses and Their Interpretations.
Look at the inkblot to the right. What do you see? This table describes how responses might be scored and interpreted.

Rorschach Score	Sample Response	Typical Interpretation
Pair response	"The top middle part looks like a pair of lungs."	Self-centeredness
Unusual detail response	"I see a tiny spot, like a speck of dust, to the left of the blot."	Obsessive-compulsive tendencies
Space response	"That white area in the lower middle looks like an upside-down bat."	Rebelliousness, anger
Human movement response	"The sides of the blot look like a person raising his hands."	Impulse control, inhibition

Figure 12.3 Thematic Apperception Test (TAT) Sample Item. One of the 31 cards of the TAT. Note that the sex of the figure in the foreground is ambiguous (although Murray apparently intended this person to be male), as is the emotional expression of the woman in the background. (*Source:* Murray, 1971)

Fict-OID

MYTH: A popular projective test, the Luscher Color Test, predicts respondents' personality traits, such as need for tranquility or need to impress others based on their color preferences (Luscher & Scott, 1969).

REALITY: Research suggests that this test is essentially worthless for assessing personality (Holmes, Wurtz, Waln, et al., 1984).

GLOSSARY

Thematic Apperception Test (TAT) projective test requiring examinees to tell a story in response to ambiguous pictures

TAT: Tell a Tale.
The second most frequently administered projective test is the **Thematic Apperception Test (TAT),** developed by Henry Murray and his student Christiana Morgan (Morgan & Murray, 1935). The TAT consists of 31 cards depicting ambiguous situations, most of them interpersonal in nature **(Figure 12.3).** One of these cards represents the ultimate ambiguity: It's entirely blank. We can think of the TAT as the "Tell a Tale" test because examinees construct a story based on each card. Most clinicians interpret the TAT on an "impressionistic" basis, meaning that they inspect the content of the examinee's stories and analyze them using clinical intuition alone (Vane, 1981).

Although some researchers disagree (Karon, 2000), there's little evidence that impressionistic TAT interpretations generate scores with adequate reliability or validity (Ryan, 1985). Scores derived from the TAT have often failed to distinguish psychiatric patients, such as people with clinical depression, from nonpatients, or to correlate in predicted directions with personality traits (Lilienfeld, 1999b).

One promising scoring system for the TAT uses cards similar to those on the TAT to assess needs for achievement (McClelland, Atkinson, Clark, et al., 1953). Using this system, psychologists score responses to the cards based on the extent to which respondents' stories emphasize achievement-oriented themes, such as academic or career success. In contrast to most TAT scoring schemes, TAT measures of achievement possess at least some validity: They correlate positively with occupational success and income, although these associations are low in magnitude (Spangler, 1992).

Human Figure Drawings.
Another popular group of projective tests is *human figure drawings,* such as the Draw-A-Person test (DAP; Machover, 1949), which requires respondents to draw a person (or persons) in any way they wish. Many clinicians who administer these measures interpret them on the basis of specific drawing "signs" (Chapman & Chapman, 1967; Smith & Dumont, 1995). For example, large eyes in drawings presumably reflect suspiciousness, while large genitalia in drawings presumably reflect concerns about sexuality.

Nevertheless, the correlations between human figure drawing signs and personality traits are low to nonexistent (Kahill, 1984; Motta, Little, & Tobin, 1993; Swenson, 1968). Moreover, because people often produce markedly different drawing characteristics on different occasions, the test-retest reliabilities of these signs are frequently poor (Kahill, 1984). Perhaps most problematically, scores derived from human figure drawings are confounded with artistic ability: Research suggests that people may be diagnosed as psychologically disturbed merely because they draw poorly (Cressen, 1975; Kahill, 1984).

COMMON PITFALLS IN PERSONALITY ASSESSMENT

Imagine that as part of a research requirement for your introductory psychology class you've just completed a structured personality test, like the MMPI-2. You look on with anxious anticipation as the research assistant inputs your data into a computer, which spits out the following personality description:

> Some of your hopes and dreams are pretty unrealistic. You have a great deal of unused potential that you have not yet turned to your advantage. Although you sometimes enjoy being around others, you value your privacy. You prize your independence and dislike being hemmed in by rules and restrictions. You are an independent thinker and do not accept others' opinions without strong evidence. You sometimes have serious doubts about whether you have made the right decision or done the right thing. Despite these doubts, you are a strong person whom others can count on in times of trouble.

After reading this description, you turn to the research assistant with a mixture of amazement and awe, and exclaim, "This description fits me perfectly. You've hit the nail on the head!"

But there's a catch. This description, the research assistant informs you, wasn't based on your test results at all. Instead, this description is identical to one that all 100 previous participants have received. You've been the victim of a devilish hoax. This example illustrates what Paul Meehl (1956) termed the *P.T. Barnum effect,* after the circus entrepreneur who said, "I try to give a little something to everyone."

The P.T. Barnum Effect: The Perils of Personal Validation.

The P.T. Barnum effect is the tendency of people to accept high base rate descriptions—descriptions that apply to almost everyone—as accurate. We may be convinced that the results of a personality test fit us to a T, but that doesn't mean the test is valid. The P.T. Barnum effect helps to explain the popularity of astrological horoscopes, palmistry, and crystal ball, tea leaf, and tarot card readings. These assessment methods generate highly generalized descriptions that apply to just about everyone. Despite their widespread use, there's no evidence for their validity (Hines, 2003; Park, 1982).

The popularity of tarot card reading, crystal ball reading, palmistry, and many similar techniques probably stems largely from the P.T. Barnum effect.

WHAT DO *you* THINK?

You've received a small research grant from your school to investigate the P.T. Barnum effect by testing whether fortune tellers and tarot card readers alter their predictions for different clients or use similar general fortune themes for everyone. How would you design your study?

Fact -OID The word *disaster*, which means "bad star" in Latin, originates from astrology. Many ancient people believed that catastrophic events often resulted from unfortunate configurations of stars in the night sky.

One illustration of the P. T. Barnum effect is that people can't pick out their horoscope from others at better than chance levels (Dean, 1987). Nevertheless, when people read their horoscope in the newspaper they're often certain it applies to them. One probable reason for this curious discrepancy is that people tend to read only the horoscope for their own sign, but not others. If they bothered to read all 12 horoscopes, they'd probably realize that most or even all of these horoscopes fit them equally well. Although astrology makes extraordinary claims, namely, that it can divine people's personality traits with nearly perfect accuracy, the evidence for these claims is virtually nonexistent.

EXTRAORDINARY CLAIMS
Is the evidence as convincing as the claim?

myth CONCEPTIONS | IS CRIMINAL PROFILING VALID?

Another practice whose popularity may derive in part from the P.T. Barnum effect is *criminal profiling,* a technique depicted in the Academy Award–winning 1991 movie *The Silence of the Lambs,* starring Jodie Foster. Criminal profilers at the FBI and other law enforcement agencies claim to draw detailed inferences about perpetrators' personality traits and motives from the pattern of crimes committed.

It's true that we can often guess certain characteristics of criminals at better than chance levels. If we're investigating a homicide, we'll do better than flipping a coin by guessing that the murderer was a male (most murders are committed by men) between the ages of 15 and 25 (most murders are committed by adolescents and young adults) who suffers from psychological problems (most murderers suffer from psychological problems). But criminal profilers purport to go considerably beyond such widely available statistics. They typically claim to possess unique expertise and to be able to harness their years of accumulated experience to outperform statistical formulas.

Nevertheless, their assessments sometimes echo P.T. Barnum. In the fall of 2002, when the Washington, DC, area was paralyzed by random sniper shootings at gas stations and in parking lots, one former FBI profiler predicted that the sniper would turn out to be someone who is "self-centered" and "angry" at others—both fairly obvious guesses that most laypeople could make.

Hit shows such as *CSI: New York* have stimulated Americans' interest in criminal profiling. Nevertheless, research suggests that criminal profiling is more art than science.

Indeed, research demonstrates that police officers can't distinguish genuine criminal profiles from bogus criminal profiles consisting of vague and general personality characteristics (such as "he has deep-seated problems with hostility"). This finding suggests the parsimonious hypothesis that profilers often base their conclusions about criminals on little more than P.T. Barnum statements (Alison, Smith, & Morgan, 2003; Gladwell, 2007). Moreover, although some researchers have found that profilers sometimes perform better than untrained individuals in identifying criminal suspects, others have found that professional profilers are no more accurate in gauging the personality features of murderers than are college students with no training in criminology (Homant & Kennedy, 1998; Snook, Cullen, Bennell, et al., 2008). Perhaps most important, there's no persuasive evidence that criminal profilers outperform statistical formulas that take into account the psychological traits of known murderers.

Criminal profiling may thus be more of an urban legend than a scientifically demonstrated ability. Yet tradition dies hard, and the FBI and other crime organizations remain in the full-time business of training criminal profilers.

Fict-OID

MYTH: A practitioner's number of years of experience with using a personality test, like the MMPI-2 or Rorschach, is positively correlated with the accuracy of his or her clinical judgments using that test.

REALITY: For most personality measures, including the MMPI-2 and Rorschach, there's essentially no correlation between experience with using a test and clinical accuracy once a person has been trained in how to administer and interpret the measure (Garb, 1998; Levenberg, 1975).

Personality Assessment Evaluated Critically. Personality assessment has contributed to psychologists' ability to detect personality traits, both normal and abnormal, and has helped them to predict significant real-world behaviors. Moreover, psychologists have succeeded in developing a number of personality measures, especially structured personality tests, with adequate reliability and validity. Given the scientific progress that psychologists have made in assessing personality, it's troubling that many continue to use measures with weak scientific support. In particular, some clinicians still rely on scores derived from the Myers-Briggs and projective tests, like the Rorschach, TAT, and human figure drawings, that are of questionable reliability and validity.

Still, research indicates that some projective techniques can achieve satisfactory reliability and validity. Certain *sentence completion tests,* which ask respondents to complete a sentence stem (for example, "My father was . . ."), are predictive of delinquency, moral development, and other important characteristics (Loevinger, 1998). Ironically, many of these well-supported projective tests are used less widely than projective tests whose validity is weak (Lilienfeld et al., 2001).

To understand why psychologists continue to use questionable psychological tests, we must remember that they're prone to the same errors in judgment that afflict the rest of us (Lilienfeld, et al., 2001). In particular, they are vulnerable to the phenomenon of illusory correlation, the perception of a nonexistent statistical association between variables (see Chapter 2), a theme we've underscored throughout this book. Personal experience, although enormously useful in generating hypotheses, can be misleading when it comes to testing them. Only scientific methods, which are essential safeguards against human error, allow us to determine whether we should trust our personal experience or disregard it in favor of evidence to the contrary.

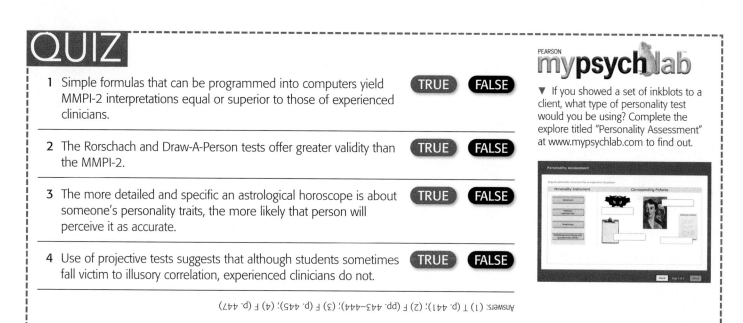

QUIZ

1 Simple formulas that can be programmed into computers yield MMPI-2 interpretations equal or superior to those of experienced clinicians. **TRUE   FALSE**

2 The Rorschach and Draw-A-Person tests offer greater validity than the MMPI-2. **TRUE   FALSE**

3 The more detailed and specific an astrological horoscope is about someone's personality traits, the more likely that person will perceive it as accurate. **TRUE   FALSE**

4 Use of projective tests suggests that although students sometimes fall victim to illusory correlation, experienced clinicians do not. **TRUE   FALSE**

Answers: (1) T (p. 441); (2) F (pp. 443–444); (3) F (p. 445); (4) F (p. 447)

PEARSON
mypsychlab

▼ If you showed a set of inkblots to a client, what type of personality test would you be using? Complete the explore titled "Personality Assessment" at www.mypsychlab.com to find out.

PERSONALITY: WHAT IS IT, AND HOW CAN WE STUDY IT? (pp. 418–421)

12.1 Describe how twin and adoption studies shed light on genetic and environmental influences on personality

Twin and adoption studies suggest that many personality traits are heritable and point to a key role for nonshared environment but not shared environment.

1. Name the major influences (factors) on personality discussed by behavior geneticists. (p. 419)

   1. _____

   2. _____

   3. _____

2. _____ _____ influences make individuals within the same family less alike. (p. 419)

3. To distinguish the effects of genes from the effects of environment, behavior geneticists have conducted _____ studies and _____ studies of personality. (p. 419)

4. If the heritability of personality were 1.0 (that is, 100 percent) then correlations of personality traits in identical twins would be _____. (p. 419)

5. The Minnesota Twins study found that identical twins reared apart tend to be strikingly (similar/dissimilar) in their personality traits. (p. 420)

6. According to the Minnesota Twins study, _____ environment plays little to no role in adult personality. (p. 420)

7. Adoption studies permit investigators to separate the effects of _____ and _____ by comparing adopted children's similarities to their adopted versus their biological parents. (p. 420)

8. In Scarr's adoption study of neuroticism, the correlations between biological parents and their adopted-away children are slightly (lower/higher) than the correlations between adoptive parents and their adopted children. (pp. 420–421)

9. The pathways from genes to behavior are (circuitous/straightforward). (p. 421)

10. How would you challenge the notion that a specific gene exists for divorce, religiosity, or political attitudes? (p. 421)

succeed with **mypsychlab**

1. Can strangers turn out to be identical twins? Watch these twins as they reunite in adulthood.
   Twins Separated at Birth, Reunited

2. How similar are twins' personalities when they are raised apart? Explore how geneticists investigate nature versus nurture.
   Twin Studies

PSYCHOANALYTIC THEORY: THE CONTROVERSIAL LEGACY OF SIGMUND FREUD AND HIS FOLLOWERS (pp. 422–430)

12.2 Describe the core assumptions of psychoanalytic theory

Freud's psychoanalytic theory rests on three core assumptions: psychic determinism, symbolic meaning, and unconscious motivation. Freud's five psychosexual stages included oral, anal, phallic, latency, and genital. According to Freud, personality results from the interactions among id, ego, and superego. The ego copes with threat by deploying defense mechanisms.

11. Freudians believe in _____ _____, the assumption that all psychological events have a cause. (p. 422)

12. The _____, according to Freud, is the reservoir of our most primitive impulses (like sex and aggression), while the _____ is the psyche's executive and principal decision maker. (p. 423)

13. Freud hypothesized that _____ _____ results from conflicts among the id, ego, and superego. (p. 423)

14. Freud believed that the ego maintained psychological health by engaging in _____ _____, unconscious maneuvers intended to minimize anxiety. (p. 424)

15. Complete this table by indicating the approximate age ranges for each of Freud's psychosexual stages of development. (pp. 426)

Stage	Approximate Age
Oral	
Anal	
Phallic*	
Latency	
Genital	

*Oedipus and Electra complexes.

16. The conflict during Freud's phallic stage in which boys supposedly love their mothers romantically and want to eliminate their fathers as rivals is termed the _____ _____. (p. 426)

12.3 **Describe key criticisms of psychoanalytic theory**

Psychoanalytic theory has been criticized for unfalsifiability, failed predictions, a questionable conception of the unconscious and reliance on unrepresentative samples.

17. Recent research has shown that many aspects of Freud's psychoanalytic theory (are/aren't) supported when scientific standards, such as falsifiability, are applied. (p. 427)

18. There's increasing reason to doubt the existence of the _____ as Freud conceived it, as a "place" where sexual and aggressive energies, along with repressed memories, are housed. (p. 428)

12.4 **Identify the central features of neo-Freudian theories**

Neo-Freudians shared with Freud an emphasis on unconscious influences and the importance of early experience, but put less emphasis on sexuality as a driving force in personality.

19. According to Alfred Adler, the principal motive in human personality is not sex or aggression but the _____ _____ _____. (p. 428)

20. Describe Jung's theory of archetypes and the collective unconscious and identify a possible shortcoming in this theory. (p. 429)

succeed with my**psych**lab

1. What would Freud say about a child who puts objects in his or her mouth? Test your knowledge of Freud's psychosexual stages.
   Freud's Five Psychosexual Stages of Personality Development

2. How well do you understand Freud's concept of the unconscious? Test your knowledge.
   The Id, Ego, and Superego

BEHAVIORAL, SOCIAL LEARNING, AND HUMANISTIC THEORIES OF PERSONALITY (pp. 430–434)

12.5 **Identify the core assumptions and key criticisms of behavioral views of personality**

Radical behaviorists view personality as under the control of two major influences: genetic factors and contingencies in the environment. Radical behaviorists, like psychoanalysts, are determinists and believe in unconscious processing, but they deny the existence of "the" unconscious. Critics have accused radical behaviorists of going too far in their exclusion of thinking in the causes of personality.

21. Radical behaviorists like Skinner believe that our personalities stem largely from differences in our learning _____. (p. 430)

22. Radical behaviorists believe that personality (causes/consists of) behaviors. (p. 431)

23. One of the few things that Freud and Skinner would have agreed on is the concept of _____, the belief that all our actions are products of preexisting causal influences. (p. 431)

12.6 **Identify the core assumptions and key criticisms of social learning theories of personality**

In contrast to radical behaviorists, social learning theorists support a central role for thinking in the causes of personality, and argue that observational learning and a sense of personal control play key roles in personality. The social learning theory claim that observational learning plays a crucial role in personality runs counter to findings that shared environmental influence on adult personality is minimal.

24. Unlike Skinner, social learning theorists emphasize _____ as a cause of personality. (p. 431)

25. Summarize the role of observational learning in shaping children's personalities. (p. 432)

26. Rotter introduced the concept of _____ _____ _____ to describe the extent to which individuals believe that the reinforcers and punishers lie inside or outside of their control. (p. 432)

27. Someone with an internal locus of control is (more/less) prone than someone with an external locus of control to emotional upset following life stressors. (p. 432)

28. Social learning theorists' claim that observational learning plays a powerful role in personality is subject to criticism because it implies that _____ _____ plays a causal role. (p. 433)

12.7 **Identify the core assumptions and key criticisms of humanistic views of personality**

Most humanistic psychologists argue that the core motive in personality is self-actualization. According to Carl Rogers, unhealthy behavior results from the imposition of conditions of worth, which block drives toward self-actualization. According to Maslow, self-actualized individuals are creative, spontaneous, accepting, and prone to peak experiences. Critics have attacked humanistic models for being naive about human nature and for advancing theories that are difficult to falsify.

succeed with mypsych**lab**

Do You Know All of the Terms in This Chapter?

  Find out by using the Flashcards. Want more practice? Take additional quizzes, try simulations, and watch video to be sure you are prepared for the test!

29. Followers of Maslow would probably argue that both Mother Teresa and Mahatma Gandhi were self-actualized people. Name three to five traits of self-actualized people. (p. 434)

30. Maslow may have fallen prey to _____ _____ because he may have limited his study to individuals who displayed the traits he hypothesized were associated with self-actualized people. (p. 434)

succeed with mypsychlab

1. Is personality determined by our peers or the environment? Test your knowledge of different theories.
   Behavioral versus Social Learning Theories of Personality

2. Which approach do you prefer? Test your understanding of the different theories of personality.
   Psychodynamic, Behavioral, Trait and Type, Humanistic, and Cognitive Approaches to Personality

---

TRAIT MODELS OF PERSONALITY: CONSISTENCIES IN OUR BEHAVIOR (pp. 435–439)

12.8 Identify the core assumptions and key criticisms of trait models

Trait theories use factor analysis to identify groups of personality features that tend to correlate. These groups often correspond to broader traits such as extroversion or agreeableness. Some models of personality structure, including the Big Five, are more descriptive than explanatory. Trait theorists must be careful to avoid circular reasoning.

31. Claiming that a child is "aggressive" merely because he engages in aggressive behavior gives us no new information and is an example of circular reasoning. What must personality traits do to be meaningful? (p. 435)

32. Trait theorists are interested primarily in describing and understanding the _____ of personality. (p. 435)

33. A statistical technique called _____ _____ analyzes the correlations among responses on personality inventories. (p. 435)

34. Mischel's review suggested that people's behaviors (are/aren't) very consistent across different situations. (p. 436)

35. A group of traits that have surfaced repeatedly in factor analyses of personality measures is known as the _____ _____. (p. 437)

36. Using the acronym OCEAN as a mnemonic device, these traits include: _____ _____ _____, _____, _____, _____, and _____. (p. 437)

37. Match the appropriate personality trait and description with the Big Five trait. (p. 437)

___ Extraversion	a. tend to be careful and responsible
___ Neuroticism	b. tend to be intellectually curious and unconventional
___ Conscientiousness	c. tend to be friendly and easy to get along with
___ Agreeableness	d. tend to be social and lively
___ Openness to Experience	e. tend to be tense and moody

38. In studying cultural influences on personality, researchers have found that _____ _____ _____ doesn't emerge clearly in all cultures. (p. 438)

12.9 Explain what personality traits can and can't predict

Personality traits rarely predict isolated behaviors but are helpful for predicting long-term behavioral trends. They can predict job performance and even historical greatness of presidents. But they don't predict how basic tendencies will be adapted within a particular individual's life circumstances.

39. Personality traits can be useful predictors of real-world behaviors, but only when they're _____ across different situations. (p. 439)

40. According to Eysenck, extraverts seek out stimulation because they have an (underactive/overactive) reticular activating system (RAS). (p. 439)

succeed with mypsychlab

1. What are extraversion and introversion? Test your knowledge of the five factor model of personality.
   The Five Factor Model

2. What is the difference between personal values and personal beliefs? Test your understanding of Mischel's theory of personality.
   Mischel's Theory of Personality

3. Choose questions to ask cross-cultural researcher Dr. Shinobu Kitayama, and hear his answers about the influence of culture on individuals.
   Cognition, Emotion, and Motivation across Cultures: Shinobu Kitayama

PERSONALITY ASSESSMENT: MEASURING AND MISMEASURING THE PSYCHE (pp. 440–447)

12.10 **Describe structured personality tests, particularly the MMPI-2, and their methods of construction**

Structured personality tests consist of questions that people can answer in only one of a few fixed ways. Some are developed empirically, others rationally/theoretically.

41. The _____ _____ _____ _____ is widely used to assess mental disorders and consists of ten basic scales. (p. 440)

42. Hathaway and McKinley developed these scales using an _____ method of test construction. (p. 440)

43. Many MMPI and MMPI-2 items possess low _____ _____, which refers to the extent to which respondents can tell what the items are measuring. (p. 441)

44. _____ _____ is making ourselves look better than we are and _____ is making ourselves appear psychologically disturbed. (p. 441)

45. Extensive research (supports/doesn't support) the reliability of most MMPI-2 scales, as well as their validity for differentiating among mental disorders. (p. 442)

46. The _____ method of test construction requires test developers to begin with a clear-cut conceptualization of a trait and then write items to assess that conceptualization. (p. 442)

12.11 **Describe projective tests and their strengths and weaknesses**

Projective tests consist of ambiguous stimuli that the examinee must interpret. Many of these tests lack reliability and validity.

47. The _____ hypothesis assumes that in the process of interpreting ambiguous stimuli, examinees inevitably project aspects of their personality onto the stimulus. (p. 442)

succeed with mypsychlab

1. If you asked a client to describe an inkblot, would you be using a personality test? Test your knowledge of the different personality assessment tools.
Personality Assessment

48. In what situations might investigators or social workers use these dolls? What are the downfalls of this technique? (p. 443)

49. The widely used _____ _____ test consists of ten symmetrical inkblots and remains scientifically controversial. (p. 443)

50. From which projective test of personality does this item derive? (p. 444)

SCIENTIFIC THINKING SKILLS
Questions and Summary

1 The argument against trait approaches–that behaviors are inconsistent across situations–is tempered by the finding that traits do predict behavior averaged across many situations. Consider two traits of your own and note situations in which you behaved *in*consistently. Would you agree that on average, across a wide range of situations, your behavior is consistent? Why or why not?

2 Imagine you are ordered by a judge to undergo a psychological assessment. The court appointed psychologist plans to base his entire assessment on the Rorschach Inkblot Test. What would you tell your attorney to convince him to ask the judge for a different psychologist?

RULING OUT RIVAL HYPOTHESES
pp. 420, 429

CORRELATION vs. CAUSATION
p. 432

FALSIFIABILITY
pp. 427, 428, 429, 430, 434, 440

REPLICABILITY
pp. 419, 420, 421, 436, 437, 443

EXTRAORDINARY CLAIMS
p. 445

OCCAM'S RAZOR
p. 424

Psychological Disorders

Are psychiatric diagnoses meaningful, or are they just labels for undesirable behaviors? (p. 458)

What is mental illness, and how should we define it? (p. 455)

CHAPTER 13

Are all persons with psychopathic personality violent? (p. 475)

Is it possible for one body to house more than 100 personalities? (p. 477)

Is schizophrenia the same as split personality? (p. 479)

B elow are descriptions of five actual patients (with their names changed to safeguard their identities). Read each description and ask yourself what these five people have in common.

- Ida, 43 years old, was strolling around a shopping mall by herself. Suddenly and out of the blue, she experienced a burst of incredibly intense anxiety that left her feeling terrified, faint, and nauseated. She thought she was having a heart attack and took a taxi to the nearest hospital emergency room. The doctors found nothing wrong with her heart and told her the problem was "all in her head." Since then, Ida has refused to leave her house or go anywhere without her husband. She's scared to drive or take buses or trains. Ida's diagnosis: *panic disorder (with agoraphobia)*.

- Bill, 45 years old, hasn't shaved or showered in over 10 years. His beard is several feet long. Bill doesn't want to shave or shower because he's terrified that tiny "metal slivers" from the water will find their way into his skin. As much as possible, Bill avoids talking on the telephone or walking through doorways because he's petrified of acquiring germs. Bill recognizes these behaviors as irrational but hasn't been able to change them despite about 15 years of treatment. Bill's diagnosis: *obsessive-compulsive disorder*.

- A few days after having a baby at age 30, Ann became incredibly giddy. She felt on top of the world, barely needed any sleep, and soon began sleeping with men she'd just met. Ann also became convinced she'd turned into a clown—literally, complete with a bright red round nose. Ann's diagnosis: *bipolar disorder (manic depression)*.

- Terrell, 28 years old, has just been released from the intensive care unit of a city hospital. He had shot himself in the stomach after becoming convinced that fish were swimming there. He suspects these fish are part of a government conspiracy to make him physically ill. Terrell's diagnosis: *schizophrenia*.

- Johnny is 13 years old. He's charming and articulate yet furious that his parents have helped commit him to the inpatient unit of a psychiatric hospital, after he began engaging in behaviors like cursing at teachers, holding live cats underwater until they drown, beating up other children, and attempting to blow up his junior high school with stolen dynamite. He sees nothing especially wrong with these behaviors and admits that he's never felt guilty about anything. Johnny's diagnosis: *conduct disorder (with probable psychopathic personality)*.

These brief sketches don't do justice to the extraordinarily rich and complex lives of these five people, but they give us some sense of the broad scope of *psychopathology,* or mental illness.

Conceptions of Mental Illness: Yesterday and Today

In almost all mental disorders, we witness a failure of adaptation to the environment. In one way or another, people with mental disorders aren't adjusting well to the demands of daily life. In extreme cases such as these, it seems relatively easy to agree that disordered behavior is present. But defining precisely what distinguishes normal from disordered thinking is challenging. Moreover, standards in what is considered disordered can change across time and cultures.

So what do Ida, Bill, Ann, Terrell, and Johnny have in common? Putting it differently, what distinguishes psychological abnormality from normality?

WHAT IS MENTAL ILLNESS? A DECEPTIVELY COMPLEX QUESTION

Psychologists and psychiatrists have proposed a host of criteria over the years for defining *mental disorder*; we'll review five of them here. **[LEARNING OBJECTIVE 13.1]** Each criterion captures something important about mental disorder, but each has its shortcomings (Gorenstein, 1984; Wakefield, 1992).

- *Statistical rarity:* Many mental disorders, like schizophrenia, are uncommon in the population. Yet we can't rely on statistical rarity to define mental disorder because not all rare conditions—such as extraordinary creativity—are pathological, and many mental illnesses—such as mild depression—are quite common (Kendell, 1975).

- *Subjective distress:* Most mental disorders, including mood and anxiety disorders, produce emotional pain for individuals afflicted with them. But not all psychological disorders generate distress. For example, during the manic phases of bipolar disorder, which Ann experienced, people frequently feel better than normal and perceive nothing wrong with their behaviors.

- *Impairment:* Most mental disorders interfere with people's ability to function in everyday life. These disorders may destroy marriages, friendships, jobs, and in extreme cases, threaten the well-being of the self and others. Although the degree of impairment associated with mental illness can be severe, the presence of impairment by itself can't define mental illness. This is because some conditions, like laziness, can also produce impairment but aren't mental disorders.

- *Societal disapproval:* Nearly 50 years ago, psychiatrist Thomas Szasz (1960) argued famously that "mental illness is a myth" and that "mental disorders" are nothing more than conditions that society dislikes. He even proposed that psychologists and psychiatrists use diagnoses as weapons of control, attaching negative labels to people whose behaviors they find objectionable. Szasz was both right and wrong. He was right that our negative attitudes toward those with serious mental illnesses are often deep seated and widespread. Szasz was also right that societal attitudes shape our views of abnormality. For example, only a few decades ago, most psychologists regarded homosexuality as a mental illness; the official diagnostic manual listed it as a "sexual deviation." This designation was reversed in 1973. But Szasz was wrong that society regards all disapproved conditions as mental disorders (Wakefield, 1992). To take just one example, racism is justifiably deplored by society but isn't considered a mental disorder by either laypersons or mental health professionals (Yamey & Shaw, 2002).

- *Biological dysfunction:* Many mental disorders probably result from breakdowns or failures of physiological systems. For example, we'll learn that schizophrenia is often marked by an underactivity in the brain's frontal lobes. In contrast, some mental disorders, like specific *phobias* (intense and irrational fears of objects, places, or situations; see Chapter 5), appear to be acquired largely through learning experiences and may require only a weak genetic predisposition to trigger them.

In fact, it's unlikely that any single criterion distinguishes mental disorders from normality. As a consequence, some authors have argued for a *family resemblance view* of mental disorder (Kirmayer & Young, 1999; Lilienfeld & Marino, 1995; Rosenhan & Seligman, 1989). According to this perspective, mental disorders don't all have one thing in common. Just as brothers and sisters within a family look similar but don't all possess exactly the same eyes, ears, or noses, mental disorders share a loose set of features. These features include those we've described—statistical rarity, subjective distress, impairment, societal disapproval, and biological dysfunction—as well as others, such as a need for treatment, irrationality, and loss of control over one's behavior (Bergner, 1997).

Brothers and sisters share a family resemblance; they look like each other but don't all have any one feature in common. The broad category of "mental disorders" may be similar.

WHAT DO *you* **THINK** *?*

You are a lawyer whose client believes he was fired due to discrimination after he was diagnosed with schizophrenia. How might you determine whether the diagnosis or the erratic behaviors that led to the diagnosis were the reason he was fired?

HISTORICAL CONCEPTIONS OF MENTAL ILLNESS: MOVING BEYOND THE DEMONS WITHIN

Throughout history, people have recognized certain behaviors as abnormal. Yet their explanations and treatments for these behaviors have shifted in tune with prevailing cultural conceptions. **[LEARNING OBJECTIVE 13.2]** During the Middle Ages, many people in Europe and later in America believed behaviors associated with mental illnesses, such as hearing voices, talking to oneself, and other odd behaviors were due to evil spirits infesting the body (Hunter & Macalpine, 1963). The often bizarre "treatments" of the day, including exorcisms, flowed directly from this belief. Even today, thousands of exorcisms are still performed in Italy, Mexico, and other countries (Harrington, 2005).

As the Middle Ages faded and the Renaissance took hold, views of those with mental illnesses became more enlightened. Over time, more people came to perceive mental illness primarily as a physical disorder, requiring medical treatment, a view that some scholars refer to as the **medical model.** Beginning in the fifteenth century and especially in later centuries, European governments began to house psychologically troubled individuals in asylums—institutions for those with mental illnesses (Gottesman, 1991).

Unfortunately, the medical treatments of that era were scarcely more scientific than those of the Middle Ages, and several were equally barbaric. One gruesome treatment was "bloodletting," which was based on the mistaken notion that excessive blood causes mental illness. In still other cases, staff workers tried to frighten patients "out of their diseases" by tossing them into a pit of snakes, hence the term *snake pit* as a synonym for an insane asylum (Szasz, 2006).

Fortunately, reform was on the way. Thanks to the heroic efforts of Phillippe Pinel (1748–1826) in France and Dorothea Dix (1802–1887) in America, an approach called *moral treatment* gained a foothold in Europe and America. Advocates of moral treatment insisted that those with mental illnesses be treated with dignity, kindness, and respect. Still, effective treatments for mental illnesses were virtually nonexistent, so many people continued to suffer for years with no hope of relief.

It wasn't until the early 1950s that a dramatic change in society's treatment of those with mental illnesses arrived on the scene. It was then that psychiatrists introduced a medication imported from France called *chlorpromazine* (its brand name is Thorazine) into mental hospitals. Chlorpromazine wasn't a miracle cure, but it offered a modestly effective treatment for some symptoms of schizophrenia and other disorders marked by a loss of contact with reality. For the first time, patients with these conditions often became able to function independently, and some returned to their families. Others held jobs for the first time in years, even decades.

By the 1960s and 1970s, the government developed a policy called **deinstitutionalization.** Deinstitutionalization featured two major components: releasing hospitalized psychiatric patients into the community and closing mental hospitals (Torrey, 1997). But deinstitutionalization was a decidedly mixed blessing. Some patients returned to a semblance of a regular life, but tens of thousands of others spilled into cities and rural areas

The "tranquilizing chair," designed by psychiatrist Benjamin Rush (1745–1813), founder of American psychiatry, supposedly slowed the flow of blood to the brain to help treat mental disturbances. In fact, this treatment probably accomplished little other than to physically restrain agitated patients.

GLOSSARY

medical model
view that regards mental illness as due to a physical disorder requiring medical treatment

deinstitutionalization
1960s and 1970s governmental policy that focused on releasing hospitalized psychiatric patients into the community and closing mental hospitals

without adequate follow-up care. Many went off their medications and wandered the streets aimlessly. Some of the homeless people we can see today on the streets of major American cities are a tragic legacy of deinstitutionalization (Leeper, 1988).

Thankfully, our understanding of mental illness and its treatment today is considerably more sophisticated than it was centuries ago. Still, few of today's treatments are genuine cures.

PSYCHIATRIC DIAGNOSIS ACROSS CULTURES: CULTURE-BOUND SYNDROMES

Psychiatric diagnoses are shaped not only by history, but by culture (Chentsova-Dutton & Tsai, 2006). Psychologists have increasingly recognized that certain conditions are *culture-bound,* that is, specific to one or more societies, although many of these conditions remain poorly researched (Kleinman, 1988; Simons & Hughes, 1986). For example, some parts of Malaysia and several other Asian countries, including China and India, have witnessed periodic outbreaks of a strange and unexplained condition known as *koro.* The victims of koro, most of whom are male, typically believe that their penis and testicles are disappearing and receding into their abdomen (female victims of koro sometimes believe that their breasts are disappearing; American Psychiatric Association, 2000).

"Mal de ojo," or the "evil eye," is a culture-bound syndrome common in many Mediterranean and Latin countries. Believed by its victims to be brought on by the glance of a malicious person, mal de ojo is marked by insomnia, nervousness, crying for no reason, and vomiting. Here, a customer in Egypt selects pendants for warding off the evil eye.

Another example of a culture-specific diagnosis is bulimia nervosa, which is largely unique to the United States and Europe. **Bulimia nervosa** (better known simply as *bulimia*) is associated with a pattern of *bingeing*—eating large amounts of highly caloric foods in brief periods of time—followed by *purging* (vomiting) or other means of drastic weight loss, like frantic exercise or extreme dieting. There are good reasons to believe that bulimia, although influenced substantially by genetic factors (Bulik, Sullivan, & Kendler, 1998), is triggered by sociocultural expectations concerning the ideal body image, particularly those images depicted in the media.

In contrast to bulimia, **anorexia nervosa** (better known simply as *anorexia*) appears to be present not only in Western countries but also in regions that have had little exposure to Western media, including some Middle Eastern nations and parts of India (Keel & Klump, 2003; Lynn, Matthews, Williams, et al., 2007). Anorexia is marked by excessive weight loss (15 percent or more of one's original body weight) and the irrational perception of being overweight.

Jane Murphy (1976) conducted a classic study investigating the culture-specificity of mental illness. She studied two isolated societies—a group of Yorubas in Nigeria and a group of Inuit Eskimos near the Bering Strait—that had experienced essentially no contact with Western culture. These cultures possessed terms for disorders that are strikingly similar to schizophrenia, alcoholism, and *psychopathic personality,* a condition marked by dishonesty, manipulativeness, and an absence of guilt and empathy. So, despite the existence of cultural differences, we shouldn't exaggerate the cultural relativity of mental disorders. Many mental disorders appear to exist in most, perhaps all, cultures.

A woman with anorexia. In contrast to bulimia, anorexia may be present in many, even most, cultures.

SPECIAL CONSIDERATIONS IN PSYCHIATRIC CLASSIFICATION AND DIAGNOSIS

Because there are so many ways in which psychological adaptation can go awry, we'd be hopelessly lost without some system of diagnostic classification. Psychiatric diagnoses serve at least two crucial functions. *First,* they help us to pinpoint the psychological problem a person is experiencing. Once we've identified this problem, it's often easier to select a treatment. *Second,* psychiatric diagnoses make it easier for mental health

GLOSSARY

bulimia nervosa
eating disorder associated with a pattern of bingeing and purging in an effort to lose or maintain weight

anorexia nervosa
eating disorder associated with excessive weight loss and the irrational perception that one is overweight

professionals to communicate with each other. When a psychologist diagnoses a patient with schizophrenia, she can be reasonably certain that other psychologists know his or her principal symptoms. So diagnoses operate as forms of mental shorthand, simplifying complex descriptions of problematic behaviors into convenient summary phrases.

Still, there are a host of misconceptions regarding psychiatric diagnosis. Before turning to our present system of psychiatric classification, we'll examine the four most prevalent misconceptions. **[LEARNING OBJECTIVE 13.3]**

Misconception 1. *Psychiatric diagnosis is nothing more than pigeonholing, that is, sorting people into different "boxes."* To the contrary, a diagnosis implies only that all people with that diagnosis are alike in at least *one* important respect (Lilienfeld & Landfield, 2008). Psychologists recognize that even within a diagnostic category, like schizophrenia or bipolar disorder, people differ dramatically in their cultural background, personality traits, interests, cognitive skills, and other psychological difficulties. People are far more than their disorders.

Misconception 2. *Psychiatric diagnoses are unreliable.* As we learned in Chapter 2, *reliability* refers to consistency of measurement. In the case of psychiatric diagnoses, the form of reliability that matters most is *interrater reliability:* the extent to which different raters (such as different psychologists) agree on patients' diagnoses. Many laypersons believe that psychiatric diagnosis is unreliable. This perception is probably fueled by high-profile media coverage of "dueling expert witnesses" in criminal trials, in which one expert witness diagnoses a defendant as schizophrenic and another diagnoses him as normal.

In fact, for major mental disorders, like schizophrenia, mood disorders, anxiety disorders, and alcoholism, interrater reliabilities are typically quite high—correlations between raters of 0.8 or above (Matarazzo, 1983). Still, the picture isn't entirely rosy. For many personality disorders, a class of disorders we'll discuss later, interrater reliabilities tend to be considerably lower (Zimmerman, 1994).

Misconception 3. *Psychiatric diagnoses are invalid.* Some critics argue that psychiatric diagnoses are largely useless because they don't provide us with much, if any, new information (Szasz, 1960). They're merely descriptive labels for behaviors we don't like. But there's now considerable evidence that many psychiatric diagnoses *do* tell us something new about the person. In a classic paper, psychiatrists Eli Robins and Samuel Guze (1970) outlined several criteria for determining whether a psychiatric diagnosis is valid. These criteria include whether the diagnosis correlates with personality and brain measures, is predicted by family history of psychiatric disorders, and predicts the individual's response to treatment. There's good evidence that many mental disorders fulfill Robins and Guze's criteria for validity.

Misconception 4. *Psychiatric diagnoses stigmatize people.* According to a group of scholars called **labeling theorists,** psychiatric diagnoses exert powerful negative effects on people's perceptions and behaviors (Scheff, 1984; Slater, 2004). Labeling theorists argue that once a psychologist or psychiatrist gives us a diagnosis, others come to perceive us differently. This diagnosis leads others to treat us differently, perhaps leading us in turn to behave in pathological ways. The diagnosis thereby becomes a self-fulfilling prophecy.

In a sensational study, David Rosenhan (1973) got eight individuals with no symptoms of mental illness (himself included) to pose as fake patients in 12 psychiatric hospitals. These "pseudopatients," as Rosenhan called them, presented themselves to the admitting psychiatrists with a single complaint: They were hearing a voice saying "empty, hollow, and thud." In all 12 cases, the psychiatrists admitted these pseudopatients to the

RULING OUT RIVAL HYPOTHESES
Have important alternative explanations for the findings been excluded?

Trials involving dueling "expert witnesses" may contribute to the erroneous public perception that psychologists can't agree on the diagnoses of individuals with suspected mental disorders.

GLOSSARY

labeling theorist
scholar who argues that psychiatric diagnoses exert powerful negative effects on people's perceptions and behaviors

hospital, almost always with diagnoses of schizophrenia (one received a diagnosis of manic depression). Remarkably, the pseudopatients were kept in the hospital for an average of 3 weeks despite displaying no further symptoms of mental illness. The diagnosis of schizophrenia, Rosenhan concluded, became a self-fulfilling prophecy, leading doctors and nursing staff to view these individuals as disturbed.

It's true that there's still considerable stigma attached to some psychiatric diagnoses. If someone tells us that a person has schizophrenia, for instance, we may be wary of him at first or misinterpret his behaviors as consistent with this diagnosis. Yet the negative effects of labels last only so long. Even in Rosenhan's study, all pseudopatients were released from hospitals with diagnoses of either schizophrenia or manic depression "in remission" ("in remission" means without any symptoms) (Spitzer, 1975). These discharge diagnoses tell us that the psychiatrists eventually recognized that these individuals were behaving normally. Overall there's not much evidence that psychiatric diagnoses themselves generate long-term negative effects above and beyond the effects of the disordered behaviors themselves (Ruscio, 2003).

myth CONCEPTIONS | IS THERE AN AUTISM EPIDEMIC?

One in 150.

That's the widely proclaimed proportion of individuals with autism in the population whom you may have seen on television commercials or read about in magazines. Although this proportion may not seem all that high, it's remarkably high compared with the figure of one in 2,000 to 2,500, which researchers had, until recently, accepted for many years (Wing & Potter, 2002). Across a mere 10-year period—from 1993 to 2003—statistics from the U.S. Department of Education revealed a 657 percent increase in the rates of autism (technically called infantile autism) across the country. In Wisconsin, the increase was a staggering 15,117 percent (Rust, 2006). These dramatic upsurges in the prevalence of autism have led many researchers and educators, and even some politicians, to speak of an autism "epidemic" (Kippes & Garrison, 2006). But is the epidemic real?

As we learned in Chapter 2, individuals with autism are marked by severe deficits in language, social bonding, and imagination, usually accompanied by mental retardation (American Psychiatric Association, 2000). The causes of autism remain mysterious, although twin studies suggest that genetic influences play a prominent role (Rutter, 2000). Still, genetic influences alone can't easily account for an astronomical rise in a disorder's prevalence over the span of a decade. It's therefore not surprising that researchers have looked to environmental variables to explain this bewildering increase. In particular, some investigators have pointed their fingers squarely at one potential culprit: vaccines (Rimland, 2004).

Much of the hype surrounding the vaccine–autism link was fueled by a study of only 12 children in the late 1990s (Wakefield et al., 1998) demonstrating an apparent linkage between autistic symptoms and the MMR vaccine, the vaccine for mumps, measles, and rubella (German measles). The symptoms of autism usually become most apparent shortly after the age of 2, not long after infants have received MMR and other vaccinations for a host of diseases. Indeed, tens of thousands of parents have insisted that their children developed autism following the MMR vaccine or following vaccines containing a preservative known as *thimerosol*, which is present in many mercury-bearing vaccines. Nevertheless, studies in the United States, Europe, and Japan failed to replicate the association between the

Many parents remain convinced that vaccines trigger autism, despite scientific evidence to the contrary.

REPLICABILITY
Can the results be duplicated in other studies?

MMR vaccine and autism, strongly suggesting that the seeming correlation between vaccinations and autism was a mirage (Herbert, Sharp, & Gaudiano, 2002; Honda, Shimizu, & Rutter, 2005). Moreover, even after the Danish government stopped administering thimerosol-containing vaccines, the prevalence of autism still skyrocketed (Madsen et al., 2002).

Many parents of children with autism probably fell prey to *illusory correlation* (Chapter 2); they'd "seen" a statistical association that didn't exist. Their error was entirely understandable. Given that their children had received vaccines and developed autistic symptoms at around the same time, it was only natural to perceive an association between the two events.

Most evidence suggests that more liberal diagnostic criteria rather than vaccines can account for most, if not all, of the reported autism epidemic (Gernsbacher, Dawson, & Goldsmith, 2005; Lilienfeld & Arkowitz, 2007). Of course, at least a small part of the epidemic might be genuine, and some still unidentified environmental cause could account for the increase. But in evaluating the evidence, we should ask ourselves a critical question. Which is more parsimonious as an explanation of a 657 percent increase within one decade, a vaccine that's yet to be shown to produce any increase in the symptoms of autism or a simple change in diagnostic practices?

OCCAM'S RAZOR
Does a simpler explanation fit the data just as well?

PSYCHIATRIC DIAGNOSIS TODAY: THE DSM-IV

The official system for classifying individuals with mental disorders is the **Diagnostic and Statistical Manual of Mental Disorders (DSM),** which originated in 1952 and is now in its fourth edition, called DSM-IV (American Psychiatric Association, 2000). The next edition, DSM-V, is due out in about 2012. **Table 13.1** lists the 17 different classes of disorders in the DSM-IV. We'll be discussing several of these classes in the pages to come.

DSM-IV is the standard manual around the world for diagnosing mental disorders. The "text revision" (DSM-IV-TR), shown here, was published in 2000. DSM-IV-TR is a minor modification of DSM-IV, the most recent version of the manual.

Table 13.1 The 17 Major Classes of Disorders in DSM-IV.

(1) Disorders Usually First Diagnosed in Infancy, Childhood, or Adolescence—mental retardation, attention deficit and disruptive behavior disorders, tic disorders	(9) Factitious Disorders
	(10) Dissociative Disorders Not Elsewhere Classified
	(11) Sexual and Gender Identity Disorders
(2) Delirium, Dementia, and Amnestic and Other Cognitive Disorders–dementia due to Alzheimer's disease and Parkinson disease	(12) Eating Disorders
	(13) Sleep Disorders
(3) Mental Disorders Due to a General Medical Condition	(14) Impulse-Control Disorders Not Elsewhere Classified
(4) Substance-Related Disorders	(15) Adjustment Disorders
(5) Schizophrenia and Other Psychotic Disorders	(16) Personality Disorders
(6) Mood Disorders	(17) Other Conditions That May Be a Focus of Clinical Attention—problems related to abuse or neglect, personality traits that affect coping style, or medical conditions
(7) Anxiety Disorders	
(8) Somatoform Disorders	

(*Source:* From *Diagnostic and Statistical Manual of Mental Disorders,* 4th ed., American Psychiatric Association, 2000)

GLOSSARY

Diagnostic and Statistical Manual of Mental Disorders (DSM)
diagnostic system containing the American Psychiatric Association (APA) criteria for mental disorders

Diagnostic Criteria and Decision Rules. Psychiatric classification has come a long way over the past several centuries. The DSM-IV provides psychologists and psychiatrists with a list of diagnostic criteria for each condition and a set of decision rules for deciding how many of these criteria need to be met. For example, in **Table 13.2,** we'll find the DSM-IV criteria for the diagnosis of *major depression,* a condition we'll encounter later in the chapter. As we can see in Criterion A, to diagnose a person with major depression,

Table 13.2 The DSM-IV Criteria for Major Depressive Disorder.

(A) Five (or more) of the following (must include one of the symptoms [1] or [2])

    (1) depressed mood most of the day

    (2) markedly diminished interest or pleasure in all, or almost all, activities

    (3) significant weight loss when not dieting or weight gain (more or less than 5% per month)

    (4) insomnia or hypersomnia (excessive sleep) nearly every day

    (5) psychomotor agitation or retardation (slowing) nearly every day

    (6) fatigue or loss of energy nearly every day

    (7) feelings of worthlessness or excessive or inappropriate guilt nearly every day

    (8) diminished ability to think or concentrate, or indecisiveness, nearly every day

    (9) recurrent thoughts of death (not just fear of dying), recurrent suicidal ideation

(B) Symptoms do not meet criteria for a mixed episode (simultaneous depression and mania)

(C) Symptoms cause clinically significant distress or impairment in social, occupational, or other important areas of functioning

(D) Symptoms are not due to the physiological effects of a substance or a medical condition

(E) Symptoms are not better accounted for by bereavement (loss of a loved one); that is, after a loss, symptoms persist for longer than 2 months or are characterized by marked functional impairment, morbid preoccupation with worthlessness, suicidal ideation, psychotic symptoms, or psychomotor retardation

(*Source:* From *Diagnostic and Statistical Manual of Mental Disorders,* 4th ed., American Psychiatric Association, 2000)

DSM-IV requires this person to exhibit at least five of nine symptoms over a 2-week period, with the requirement that at least one of the first two symptoms (depressed mood and diminished interest or pleasure) be present. DSM-IV also reminds clinicians, in Criterion D, to rule out medical or drug-related diagnoses that may cause symptoms similar to depression.

The DSM-IV: Other Features. DSM-IV is more than a tool for diagnosing mental disorders; it's a valuable source of information concerning the characteristics, such as the **prevalence,** of many mental disorders. *Prevalence* refers to the percentage of people in the population with a disorder.

DSM-IV also recognizes that there's more to people than their disorders. Accordingly, it asks psychologists and psychiatrists to assess patients along multiple **axes,** or dimensions of functioning. DSM-IV contains axes not only for mental disorders but also for associated medical conditions, life stressors, and overall level of daily functioning. In this respect, DSM-IV adopts a *biopsychosocial approach* (see Chapter 10), one that acknowledges the interplay of biological (like hormonal abnormalities), psychological (like irrational thoughts), and social (interpersonal interactions) influences. We'll be emphasizing these three factors throughout our discussion of specific disorders.

Finally, DSM-IV acknowledges that we live in a culturally diverse world filled with people from vastly different ethnic, socioeconomic, and cultural backgrounds. Some of them embrace unconventional beliefs, sexual identities, and behaviors that are "abnormal" from the viewpoint of our contemporary society. DSM-IV provides information about how differing cultural backgrounds can affect the content and expression of symptoms and how people respond to distress. This information is vital to ensuring that diagnosticians can distinguish normal from abnormal behavior.

The DSM-IV: Criticisms. There's little dispute that DSM-IV is a helpful system for slicing up the enormous pie of psychopathology into more meaningful and manageable

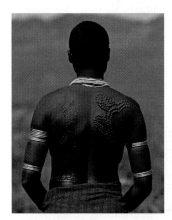

A clinical psychologist would probably perceive cutting oneself as pathological, but the DSM-IV reminds clinicians that in some cultures, such practices are used to produce tribal scars and should be regarded as normal.

GLOSSARY

prevalence
percentage of people within a population who have a specific mental disorder

axes
dimensions of functioning

pieces. Yet DSM-IV has received more than its share of criticism, and sometimes for good reason (Widiger & Clark, 2000).

There are well over 350 diagnoses in DSM-IV, not all of which meet Robins and Guze's criteria for validity. To take only one example, the DSM-IV diagnosis of "Mathematics Disorder" describes little more than difficulties with performing arithmetic or math reasoning problems. It seems to be more of a label for learning problems than a diagnosis that tells us something new about the person. In addition, although the diagnostic criteria and decision rules for many DSM-IV disorders are based primarily on scientific findings, others are based largely on subjective committee decisions. Another problem with DSM-IV is the high level of **comorbidity** among many of its diagnoses (Angold, 1999; Lilienfeld, Waldman, & Israel, 1994), meaning that individuals with one diagnosis frequently have one or more diagnoses. For example, it's extremely common for people with a major depression diagnosis to meet criteria for one or more anxiety disorders. This extensive comorbidity raises the troubling question of whether DSM-IV is diagnosing genuinely independent conditions as opposed to slightly different variations of a single underlying condition.

QUIZ

PEARSON
mypsychlab

1. According to a family resemblance view, no one criterion distinguishes mental disorder from normality. **TRUE** **FALSE**

▼ Why is "going crazy" not an applicable term for mental illness? Find out by watching the video titled "Going Crazy: Sue Mineka" at www.mypsychlab.com to find out.

2. Once the medical model began to take hold in the Renaissance, treatments for mental disorders came to be based on strong scientific evidence. **TRUE** **FALSE**

3. Some mental disorders appear to be present in most, if not all, cultures. **TRUE** **FALSE**

4. Virtually all psychiatric diagnoses are unreliable. **TRUE** **FALSE**

Answers: (1) T (p. 455); (2) F (p. 456); (3) T (p. 457); (4) F (p. 458)

Many anxiety disorders, including phobias, frequently have an initial onset in childhood.

GLOSSARY

comorbidity
cooccurrence of two or more diagnoses within the same person

Anxiety Disorders: The Many Faces of Worry and Fear

We'll begin our tour of psychological disorders with problems stemming from anxiety. Fortunately, most everyday anxieties generally don't last long or feel especially uncomfortable. Anxiety in small doses can even be adaptive. It can permit a lightning-quick response to danger, steer us away from harmful behaviors, and inspire us to solve festering problems. Yet sometimes anxiety spirals out of control, and it can become excessive and inappropriate. It may even feel life-threatening (Mendelowicz & Stein, 2000).

[LEARNING OBJECTIVE 13.4]

Anxiety disorders are among the most prevalent of all mental disorders; 29 percent of us will meet the diagnostic criteria for one or more anxiety disorders at some point in our lives (Kessler, Berglund, Demlen, et al., 2005). We tend to develop anxiety disorders earlier in development than most other disorders. The average age of onset for anxiety disorders is 11 years (Kessler et al., 2005).

PANIC DISORDER: TERROR THAT COMES OUT OF THE BLUE

A prevalent form of anxiety disorder is one that results in **panic attacks,** which occur when nervous feelings gather momentum and escalate into intense bouts of fear, even terror. Panic attacks peak in less than 10 minutes and can include sweating, dizziness, faintness, light-headedness, a racing or pounding heart, shortness of breath, feelings of unreality, and fears of going crazy or dying. Because many patients experiencing their initial panic attacks believe they're having heart attacks, many first go to emergency rooms, only to be sent home and—like Ida, whom we met at the outset of the chapter—told "it's all in their heads."

WHAT DO *you* THINK?

An acquaintance mistakenly uses the phrase "I keep having panic attacks" to describe becoming stressed out over homework and conflicts with friends. What information could you give her to help her to become more accurate in her self-description?

Some panic attacks are associated with specific situations, such as riding in elevators or shopping in supermarkets, but others come entirely out of the blue, that is, without warning. Not surprisingly, panic attacks often generate fears of the situations in which they occur. Panic can occur in every anxiety disorder, as well as in mood and eating disorders. Even high-functioning people can experience panic attacks in anticipation of stressful events (Cox & Taylor, 1999): About 20 to 25 percent of college students report at least one panic attack in a 1-year period, with about half that number reporting unexpected attacks (Lilienfeld, 1997).

Panic attacks can occur only rarely or on a daily basis for weeks, months, or even years at a time. People suffer from **panic disorder** when they experience panic attacks that are repeated and unexpected, and when they either experience persistent concerns about panicking or change their behavior (for example, change jobs) as a result of the attacks (American Psychiatric Association, 2000).

GENERALIZED ANXIETY DISORDER: PERPETUAL WORRY

We all get caught up with worry from time to time. Yet for the 3 percent of the population who have **generalized anxiety disorder (GAD),** worry is a way of life. They spend an average of 60 percent of each day worrying, compared with 18 percent for the rest of the general population (Craske, Rapee, Jackel, et al., 1989). Many describe themselves as "worry warts." They tend to think anxious thoughts, feel irritable and on edge, have trouble sleeping, and experience a great deal of bodily tension (Barlow, Chorpita, & Turovsky, 1996; Wittchen, 2002). Often they worry too much about the small things in life, like an upcoming meeting at work or a social event (Hazlett-Stevens, Pruitt, & Collins, 2008).

PHOBIAS: IRRATIONAL FEARS

A **phobia** is an intense fear of an object or situation that's greatly out of proportion to its actual threat. Many of us have mild fears—of things like spiders and snakes—that aren't severe enough to be phobias. For a fear to be diagnosed as a phobia, it must restrict our lives, create considerable distress, or both.

Phobias are the most common of all anxiety disorders. One in nine of us has a phobia of an animal, blood or injury, or a situation like a thunderstorm. Social fears are just as

First Person Account: Panic Disorder
"For me, a panic attack is almost a violent experience. I feel disconnected from reality. I feel like I'm losing control in a very extreme way. My heart pounds really hard, I feel like I can't get my breath, and there's an overwhelming feeling that things are crashing in on me." (Dickey, 1994)

Symptoms of a panic attack include a pounding or racing heart, shortness of breath, and faintness or dizziness. This can lead people to believe they are having a heart attack.

GLOSSARY

panic attack
brief, intense episode of extreme fear characterized by sweating, dizziness, light-headedness, racing heartbeat, and feelings of impending death or going crazy

panic disorder
repeated and unexpected panic attacks, along with either persistent concerns about future attacks or a change in personal behavior in an attempt to avoid them

generalized anxiety disorder (GAD)
continual feelings of worry, anxiety, physical tension, and irritability across many areas of life functioning

phobia
intense fear of an object or situation that's greatly out of proportion to its actual threat

First Person Account: Social Phobia
"When I would walk into a room full of people, I'd turn red and it would feel like everybody's eyes were on me. I was embarrassed to stand off in a corner by myself, but I couldn't think of anything to say to anybody. It was humiliating. I felt so clumsy, I couldn't wait to get out." (Dickey, 1994)

Posttraumatic stress disorder involves a cluster of symptoms that can be quite debilitating. Combat veterans are at high risk for developing this disorder.

GLOSSARY

agoraphobia
fear of being in a place or situation from which escape is difficult or embarrassing, or in which help is unavailable in the event of a panic attack

social phobia
marked fear of public appearances in which embarrassment or humiliation is possible

posttraumatic stress disorder (PTSD)
marked emotional disturbance after experiencing or witnessing a severely stressful event

RULING OUT RIVAL HYPOTHESES
Have important alternative explanations for the findings been excluded?

common (Kessler et al., 1994). Phobias of objects, places, or situations—called *specific phobias*—commonly arise in response to animals, insects, thunderstorms, heights, water, elevators, and darkness. Many of these fears, especially of animals, are widespread in childhood but disappear with age (American Psychiatric Association, 2000). Agoraphobia, which we'll examine next, is the most disruptive of the phobias, and occurs in about 1 in 25 of us (Keller & Craske, 2008; Kessler, Chiu, Jin, et al., 2006).

Agoraphobia. Some 2,700 years ago in the city-states of ancient Greece, agoraphobia acquired its name as a condition in which certain fearful citizens couldn't pass through the central city's open-air markets (*agoras*). A common misconception is that agoraphobia is a fear of crowds or public places. But **agoraphobia** actually refers to a fear of being in a place or situation in which escape is difficult or embarrassing, or in which help is unavailable in the event of a panic attack (American Psychiatric Association, 2000).

Most fears originate in childhood, but agoraphobia emerges in the midteens when individuals become apprehensive in a host of settings, such as malls, crowded movie theaters, tunnels, bridges, or wide-open spaces. The manifestation of agoraphobia seems to differ across cultures. For example, some Eskimos in Greenland suffer from a condition called "kayak angst," marked by a pronounced fear of going out to sea by oneself in a kayak (Barlow, 2000; Gusow, 1963). Fortunately, as we'll learn in Chapter 14, many cases of agoraphobia and other anxiety disorders are quite treatable.

Social Phobia. Surveys show that most people rank public speaking as a greater fear than dying (Wallechinsky, Wallace, & Wallace, 1977). Given that statistic, imagine how people with **social phobia** must feel. People with this condition—a marked fear of public appearances in which embarrassment or humiliation seems likely—experience anxiety well beyond the stage fright that most of us feel occasionally (Heimberg & Juster, 1995). People with social phobia are often deathly afraid of speaking, eating, or performing in public and are alert to the slightest hint of disapproval from others.

POSTTRAUMATIC STRESS DISORDER: THE ENDURING EFFECTS OF EXPERIENCING HORROR

When people experience or witness a traumatic event, such as front-line combat, an earthquake, or sexual assault, they may develop **posttraumatic stress disorder (PTSD)**. To qualify for a diagnosis of PTSD, the event must be physically dangerous or life-threatening, either to oneself or someone else. The person's response must also involve intense fear, helplessness, or horror (American Psychiatric Association, 2000).

Flashbacks are among the hallmarks of PTSD. The terror of war can return decades after the original trauma and be reactivated by everyday stressful experiences (Foa & Kozak, 1986). Other symptoms include efforts to avoid thoughts, feelings, places, and conversations associated with the trauma; recurrent dreams of the trauma; and increased arousal, such as sleep difficulties and startling easily (American Psychiatric Association, 2000). Reminders of the incident can trigger full-blown panic attacks, as in the case of a Vietnam veteran who hid under his bed whenever he heard a city helicopter in the distance—well over 20 years after the war ended (Baum, Cohen, & Hall, 1993; Foa & Rothbaum, 1998; Jones & Barlow, 1990). PTSD isn't easy to diagnose. Some of its symptoms, such as anxiety and difficulty sleeping, may have been present *before* the stressful event. Moreover, some people *malinger* (fake) PTSD to obtain government benefits, so diagnosticians must rule out this possibility (Rosen, 2006).

OBSESSIVE-COMPULSIVE DISORDER: TRAPPED IN ONE'S THOUGHTS

Just about all of us have had a thought or even a silly song jingle that we just couldn't get out of our heads. Patients with **obsessive-compulsive disorder (OCD)** know all too well what this experience is like, except that their symptoms are much more severe. They typically suffer from **obsessions:** persistent ideas, thoughts, or impulses that are unwanted and inappropriate and cause marked distress. But, unlike typical worries, obsessions aren't extreme responses to everyday stressors. They usually center on "unacceptable" thoughts about such topics as contamination, sex, aggression, or religion. For example, individuals with OCD may be consumed with fears of being dirty or thoughts of killing others. Despite their best efforts, people with OCD can't find a way to make these thoughts stop.

Most patients with OCD also experience symptoms linked closely to obsessions, namely, **compulsions:** repetitive behaviors or mental acts that they initiate to reduce or prevent anxiety. In most cases, patients feel driven to perform the action that accompanies an obsession, prevent some dreaded event, or "make things right." Common OCD-type rituals include:

- Repeatedly checking door locks, windows, electronic controls, and ovens
- Performing tasks in set ways, like putting on one's shoes in a fixed pattern
- Counting the number of dots on a wall or touching or tapping objects
- Repeatedly arranging and rearranging objects
- Washing and cleaning repeatedly and unnecessarily
- Saying a prayer or specific phrase every time an obsession comes to mind
- Hoarding newspapers, books, letters, soda cans, or other objects

By definition, people diagnosed with OCD spend at least an hour a day immersed in obsessions, compulsions, or both; one patient spent 15 to 18 hours per day washing his hands, showering, getting dressed, and cleaning money. Still, many people with OCD lead remarkably successful lives. Charles Darwin, the "father of evolution," and Florence Nightingale, the "mother of nursing," both suffered from OCD (OCD-UK, 2005). Howard Hughes, the billionaire industrialist, struggled for years with severe, untreated symptoms of OCD. More recently, celebrities like Cameron Diaz, Billy Bob Thornton, and David Beckham have spoken publicly about their battles with the disorder.

EXPLANATIONS FOR ANXIETY DISORDERS: THE ROOTS OF PATHOLOGICAL WORRY AND FEAR

How do anxiety disorders come about? Differing theories propose explanations focusing on the environment, catastrophic thinking, and biological influences. **[LEARNING OBJECTIVE 13.5]**

Learning Models of Anxiety: Anxious Responses as Acquired Habits. According to learning theories, fears are—you guessed it—learned. Watson and Raynor's (1920) famous demonstration of classical conditioning of the fear of a small furry animal (remember poor Little Albert from Chapter 5?) powerfully conveys how people learn fears.

Operant conditioning, which relies on reinforcements and punishments (see Chapter 5), offers another account of how fears are maintained. If a socially awkward girl repeatedly experiences rejection when she asks boys to go to the movies, she may become shy around them. If this pattern of rejection continues, she could develop a full-blown social phobia. Paradoxically, her avoidance of boys provides negative reinforcement because it allows her to escape the unpleasant consequences of social interaction. This sense of relief reinforces her avoidance and ultimately perpetuates her anxiety.

Howard Hughes, the billionaire industrialist, suffered from debilitating obsessive-compulsive disorder later in his life.

**First Person Account:
Obsessive-Compulsive Disorder**
"I couldn't do anything without rituals. They transcended every aspect of my life. Counting was big for me. When I set my alarm at night, I had to set it to a number that wouldn't add up to a 'bad' number. I would wash my hair three times as opposed to once because three was a good luck number and one wasn't. It took me longer to read because I'd count the lines in a paragraph. If I was writing a term paper, I couldn't have a certain number of words on a line if it added up to a bad number. I was always worried that if I didn't do something, my parents were going to die." (Dickey, 1994)

GLOSSARY

obsessive-compulsive disorder (OCD)
condition marked by repeated and lengthy (at least 1 hour per day) immersion in obsessions, compulsions, or both

obsession
persistent idea, thought, or impulse that is unwanted and inappropriate, causing marked distress

compulsion
repetitive behavior or mental act performed to reduce or prevent anxiety

Learning theorists (Rachman, 1977) believe that fears can arise in two additional ways. First, we can acquire fears by observing others engage in fearful behaviors (Mineka & Cook, 1993). A father's fear of dogs might instill the same in his child. Second, fears can stem from information or misinformation from others. If a mother tells her children that riding in elevators is dangerous, they may end up taking the stairs.

Catastrophizing and Anxiety Sensitivity.

People with social phobias predict that many social encounters will be interpersonal disasters, and some people with fears of storms are so fearful that they seek the shelter of a basement when mild thunderstorms are detected on radar 50 miles away (Voncken, Bogels, & deVries, 2003). As these examples illustrate, *catastrophizing* is a core feature of anxious thinking (Beck, 1976; Brown, Dowd, & Freeman (in press); Ellis, 1962). People catastrophize when they predict terrible events—such as contracting a life-threatening illness from touching a door-knob—despite their low probability (Beck, 1964; Beck, 1995).

People with anxiety tend to interpret ambiguous situations such as the words shown in **Table 13.3** in a negative light (Matthews & MacLeod, 2005). Many people with anxiety disorders harbor high levels of anxiety or concern about anxiety-related sensations (Reiss & McNally, 1985; Stein, Jang, & Livesley, 1999). Think of the times your muscles felt tight, you felt a bit dizzy when you stood up quickly, or your heart raced after climbing a flight of stairs. You may have dismissed these physical symptoms as harmless. Yet people with high anxiety tend to misinterpret them as dangerous—perhaps as early signs of a heart attack or stroke—and react with intense worry (Clark, 1986; Lilienfeld, 1997; McNally & Eke, 1996). As a result, their barely noticeable physical sensations or minor anxiety can spiral into full-blown panic attacks.

Anxiety: Genetic and Biological Influences.

Numerous twin studies show that many anxiety disorders, including panic disorder and phobias, are genetically influenced (Andrews, Stewart, Morris-Yates, et al., 1990; Roy, McNeale, Pedersen, et al., 1995). In particular, genes affect whether we inherit high levels of neuroticism—a tendency to be high strung and irritable (see Chapter 12)—which can set the stage for excessive worry (Anderson, Taylor, & McLean, 1996; Zinbarg & Barlow, 1996). Family studies show that people with OCD are twice as likely as people without OCD to inherit a specific overactive gene. This gene is related to the transport of the neurotransmitter serotonin (Goldman, Hu, Kennedy, et al., 2006). The obsession-compulsive response in the brain is distinctive. It involves a malfunction of the caudate nucleus, a portion of the basal ganglia (see Chapter 3), which initiates and controls body movement (Hansen, Hasselbach, Law, et al., 2002; Pigott, Myers, & Williams, 1996). Brain scans also reveal increased activity in portions of the frontal lobes where information is filtered, prioritized, and organized. Under these circumstances, people can't seem to get troubling thoughts out of their minds or inhibit repeated rituals.

Table 13.3 Anxiety and Interpretation of Ambiguity. Anxiety leads us to interpret ambiguous stimuli negatively. Compared with nonanxious subjects, subjects with anxiety are more likely to interpret an ambiguous word (such as the homophones—same-sounding words—listed here) as a negative or threatening word rather than a neutral one. (*Source:* Blanchette & Richards, 2003; Mathews, Richards, & Eysenck, 1989)

Selected Homophones	
Threatening Meaning/ Spelling	**Nonthreatening Meaning/ Spelling**
Bury	Berry
Die	Dye
Patients	Patience
Bruise	Brews
Flu	Flew
Sword	Soared

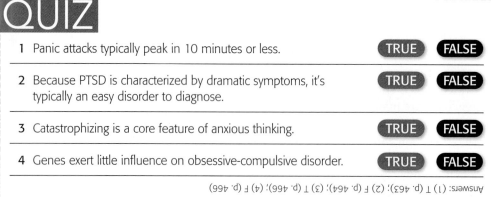

QUIZ

1 Panic attacks typically peak in 10 minutes or less.   TRUE FALSE

2 Because PTSD is characterized by dramatic symptoms, it's typically an easy disorder to diagnose.   TRUE FALSE

3 Catastrophizing is a core feature of anxious thinking.   TRUE FALSE

4 Genes exert little influence on obsessive-compulsive disorder.   TRUE FALSE

Answers: (1) T (p. 463); (2) F (p. 464); (3) T (p. 466); (4) F (p. 466)

PEARSON
mypsychlab

▼ What is it really like to live with OCD? Watch the video titled "Margo: Obsessive-Compulsive Disorder" at www.mypsychlab.com to find out.

Mood Disorders

Imagine we're therapists interviewing someone who's come to us for help. As the client begins to talk about his life, it becomes clear that even the simplest activities, like dressing or driving to work, have become enormous acts of will. He reports difficulty sleeping and unaccountably wakes up before dawn each day. He refuses to answer the telephone. He lies listlessly for hours staring at the television set. His mood is downcast, and occasionally tears well up in his eyes. He's recently lost a fair amount of weight. His world is gray, a void. Toward the end of the interview, he tells us he's begun to contemplate suicide.

We've just interviewed a person who suffers from a *mood disorder,* so called because his difficulties center on his bleak mood, which colors all aspects of his existence. When we check his symptoms against those in Table 13.2 (refer back to p. 461), we can see that he meets the criteria for a **major depressive episode.** We'll soon encounter another mood disorder, *bipolar disorder,* in which people's mood is often the mirror image of depression. **Table 13.4** on p. 468 outlines the range of mood disorders in DSM-IV. **[LEARNING OBJECTIVE 13.6]**

MAJOR DEPRESSIVE DISORDER: COMMON, BUT NOT THE COMMON COLD

Over the course of a lifetime, more than 20 percent of us will experience a mood disorder. Major depression alone darkens the lives of more than 16 percent of Americans (Kessler et al., 2005). Depressive disorders can begin at any age but are most likely to strike people in their 30s. Women are about twice as likely to be depressed as men. This difference may be associated with differences between men and women in economic power, sex hormones, social support, and history of physical or sexual abuse (Howland & Thase, 1998). The sex difference in depression is widespread but not universal. In some cultures, such as certain Mediterranean populations, Orthodox Jews, and the Amish, this sex difference is largely absent (Piccinelli & Wilkinson, 2000).

In most cultures, women are generally at greater risk for developing depression than men. Nevertheless, the reasons for this difference aren't fully understood.

The symptoms of depression may develop gradually over days or weeks; in other cases, they may surface rather suddenly. Depression, like the common cold, is recurrent. The average person with major depression experiences five or six episodes over the course of a lifetime. Most of these episodes last from 6 months to a year. But in as many as a fifth of cases, depression is *chronic,* that is, present for decades with no relief (Ingram, Scott, & Siegle, 1999). Depression produces severe impairment. In extreme cases, people may fail to feed or clothe themselves or take care of basic health needs, like brushing their teeth or showering.

EXPLANATIONS FOR MAJOR DEPRESSIVE DISORDER: A TANGLED WEB

The multifaceted phenomenon of depression illustrates the biopsychosocial approach, underscoring how physical and social factors can combine to produce psychological symptoms. Let's reconsider the man we imagined interviewing at the beginning of this section. From his father who has depression and mother who has anxiety, he may have inherited a tendency to respond to stressful situations with doubt and negative emotions (neuroticism). He felt that a competitive colleague continually tried to undermine his

GLOSSARY

major depressive episode
state in which a person experiences a lingering depressed mood or diminished interest in pleasurable activities, along with symptoms that include weight loss and sleep difficulties

Table 13.4 Mood Disorders and Conditions.

Disorder	Symptoms
Major Depressive Disorder	Chronic or recurrent state in which a person experiences a lingering depressed mood or diminished interest in pleasurable activities, along with symptoms that include weight loss or sleep difficulties
Manic Episode	Markedly inflated self-esteem or grandiosity, greatly decreased need for sleep, much more talkative than usual, racing thoughts, distractibility, increased activity level or agitation, and excessive involvement in pleasurable activities that can cause problems (like unprotected sex, excessive spending, reckless driving)
Bipolar Disorder I	Presence of one or more manic episodes
Dysthymic Disorder	Low-level depression of at least 2 years' duration; feelings of inadequacy, sadness, low energy, poor appetite, decreased pleasure and productivity, and hopelessness
Hypomanic Episode	A less intense and disruptive version of a manic episode; feelings of elation, grouchiness or irritability, distractability, and talkativeness
Bipolar Disorder II	Patients must experience at least one episode of major depression and one hypomanic episode.
Cyclothymia	Moods alternate between numerous periods of hypomanic symptoms and numerous periods of depressive symptoms. To remember cyclothymia, think of "cycles" of up and down moods. Cyclothymia increases the risk of developing bipolar disorder.
Postpartum Depression	A depressive episode that occurs within a month after childbirth. As many as 15 percent of women develop postpartum depression. A much more serious condition, postpartum psychosis, occurs in about 1 or 2 per 1,000 childbirths, with psychotic symptoms, including command hallucinations to kill the infant or delusions that the infant is possessed by an evil spirit (Beck & Gable, 2001).
Seasonal Affective Disorder	Depressive episodes that display a seasonal pattern, most commonly beginning in fall or winter and improving in spring. There must be 2 consecutive years in which the episode appears on a seasonal basis. Symptoms often include weight gain, lack of energy, carbohydrate craving, and excessive sleep.

(*Source:* Data from DSM-IV, APA, 2000)

authority as a television producer. In response, he felt insecure and began to second-guess his every decision. Each day he wasted hours worrying about losing his job. The quality of his work nose-dived. He withdrew socially and began to refuse invitations to go golfing with his buddies. His friends tried to cheer him up, but the black cloud that hung over his head wouldn't budge. Feeling rebuffed, his friends stopped inviting him to do anything. His once-bright social world became a black void, and he moped around doing virtually nothing. He felt helpless. Eventually, his dark thoughts turned to suicide.

This example highlights a key point. To fully understand depression, we must appreciate the complex interplay of inborn tendencies, stressful events, interpersonal relationships, the loss of reinforcers in everyday life, negative thoughts, and feelings of helplessness (Akiskal & McKinney, 1973; Ilardi & Feldman, 2001). **[LEARNING OBJECTIVE 13.7]**

Depression and Life Events. Stressful life events that represent loss or threat of separation are especially tied to depression (Brugha, 1995; Mazure, 1998; Paykel, 2003). But the loss created by a blow to our sense of self-worth can sting every bit as much as the

loss of a close relationship (Finlay-Jones & Brown, 1981). A crucial determinant of whether we'll become depressed is whether we've lost or are about to lose something we value dearly, like someone we love, social support, financial support, or self-esteem (Beck, 1963; Blatt, 1974; Prince, Harwood, Blizard, et al., 1997; Zuroff, Mongrain, & Santor, 2004).

WHAT DO *you* THINK?

Your sister has just ended her relationship with her long-time partner. Although she is showing symptoms of depression, she insists that she isn't depressed because her symptoms are due to a major life change. How could you convince her that she may still have depression?

Interpersonal Model: Depression as a Social Disorder.

James Coyne (1976; Joiner & Coyne, 1999; Rudolph, et al., 2006) hypothesized that depression creates interpersonal problems. When people become depressed, he argued, they seek excessive reassurance, which in turn leads others to dislike and reject them. Coyne (1976) asked undergraduates to talk on the telephone for 20 minutes with patients with depression, patients without depression, or nonpatients drawn from the community. He didn't inform students they'd be interacting with patients with depression. Yet following the interaction, students who spoke with these patients became more depressed, anxious, and hostile than those who interacted with individuals without depression. Moreover, subjects were more rejecting of patients with depression and expressed much less interest in interacting with them in the future. For Coyne, depression is a vicious cycle. People with depression often elicit hostility and rejection from others, which in turn maintains or worsens their depression.

Many, but not all, studies have replicated Coyne's findings that people with depression tend to stir up negative feelings in others (Joiner & Coyne, 1999; McNeil, Arkowitz, & Pritchard, 1987; Starr & Davila, 2008). Other research suggests that constant worrying, mistrust, and socially inappropriate behaviors can also be a social turn off to many people (Zborowski & Garske, 1993).

According to James Coyne's interpersonal model of depression, depression can trigger rejection from others, in turn contributing to further depression.

REPLICABILITY
Can the results be duplicated in other studies?

Behavioral Model: Depression as a Loss of Reinforcement.

Peter Lewinsohn's (1974) *behavioral model* assumes that depression results from a low rate of response-contingent positive reinforcement. Put in simpler terms, when people with depression try different things and receive no payoff for them, they eventually give up. They stop participating in many pleasant activities, leaving them little opportunity to obtain reinforcement from other people. In time, their personal and social worlds shrink, as depression seeps into virtually every nook and cranny of their lives. Lewinsohn later observed that people with depression sometimes lack social skills (Segrin, 2000; Youngren & Lewinsohn, 1980), making it even harder for them to obtain reinforcement from others. To make matters worse, if people respond to individuals with depression with sympathy and concern, they may reinforce and maintain these individuals' withdrawal. This view implies a straightforward recipe for breaking the grip of depression: pushing ourselves to engage in pleasant activities. Sometimes merely getting out of bed can be the first step toward conquering depression (Gortner, Gollan, Dobson, et al., 1998).

Cognitive Model: Depression as a Disorder of Thinking.

In contrast, Aaron Beck's influential **cognitive model of depression** holds that depression is caused by negative beliefs and expectations (Beck, 1987). Beck focused on three components of depressed thinking: negative views of oneself, one's experiences, and the future. These habitual

GLOSSARY

cognitive model of depression
theory that depression is caused by negative beliefs and expectations

Most people have an illusion of control; for example, they mistakenly believe that they're more likely to win a gamble if they toss the dice than if someone else does. Interestingly, people who have mild or modest depression tend not to fall prey to this thinking error (Golin, Terrell, & Johnson, 1977), suggesting they may actually be more realistic than nondepressed people under certain circumstances.

Men may be more likely than women to play sports, which often decreases the tendency to ruminate when stressed out.

GLOSSARY

learned helplessness
tendency to feel helpless in the face of events we can't control

thought patterns, called *negative schemas,* presumably originate in early experiences of loss, failure, and rejection. Activated by stressful events in later life, these schemas reinforce people with depression's negative experiences (Scher, Ingram, & Segal, 2005).

People with depression's view of the world is bleak because they put a decidedly negative mental spin on their experiences. They also suffer from *cognitive distortions,* that is, skewed ways of thinking. For example, after receiving a parking ticket, a woman might conclude she's worthless and that nothing will ever go right for her. A man might single out a trivial error he made in a softball game and blame himself completely for the loss of the game. It's as though these people wear glasses that filter out all of life's positive experiences and bring all of life's negative experiences into sharper focus.

There's considerable support for Beck's idea that people with depression hold negative views of themselves, the future, and the world (Haaga, Dyck, & Ernst, 1991; Ingram, 2003). But the evidence for the role of cognitive distortions in nonhospitalized individuals, or those without severe depression, isn't as strong (Haack, Metalsky, Dykman, et al., 1996). In fact, some research suggests that, compared with people without depression, people with mild depression actually have a *more* accurate view of circumstances, a phenomenon called *depressive realism* (Alloy & Abramson, 1979, 1988; Msetfi, Murphy, Simpson, et al., 2005).

Rumination: Recycling the Mental Garbage.
Susan Nolen-Hoeksema (1987) suggested that recycling negative events in our minds can lead us to become depressed. More specifically, some of us spend a great deal of time *ruminating—* focusing on how bad we feel and endlessly analyzing the causes and consequences of our problems.

Nolen-Hoeksema (2000, 2003) contended that women have much higher rates and more frequent bouts of depression than men because they tend to ruminate more than men. In contrast, when stressed out, men are more likely to focus on pleasurable or distracting activities such as work, watching football games, or drinking copious amounts of alcohol (which we don't recommend). They also adopt a more direct approach to solving their problems than do women (Nolen-Hoeksema, 2002, 2003). Early socialization may, in part, pave the way for these differing reactions (Nolen-Hoeksema & Girgus, 1994). Although parents encourage girls to analyze and talk about their problems, they often actively discourage boys from expressing their feelings and instead encourage them to take action or tough it out. Still, men and women alike can benefit from cutting down on rumination and confronting their problems head-on.

Learned Helplessness: Depression as a Consequence of Uncontrollable Events.
Martin Seligman (1975; Seligman & Maier, 1967) accidentally stumbled across some unusual findings related to depression in his work with dogs. He was testing dogs in a shuttle box, depicted in **Figure 13.1;** one side of the box was electrified and the other side, separated by a barrier, wasn't. Ordinarily, dogs avoid painful shocks by jumping over the barrier to the nonelectrified side of the box. Yet Seligman found something surprising. Dogs first restrained in a hammock and exposed to shocks they couldn't escape later often made no attempt to escape shocks in the shuttle box, even when they could easily get away from them. Some of the dogs just sat there, whimpering and crying, passively accepting the shocks as though they were inescapable. They'd learned to become helpless.

Bruce Overmier and Seligman (1967) described **learned helplessness** as the tendency to feel helpless in the face of events we can't control, and argued that it offers an animal model of depression. They noted striking parallels between the effects of learned helplessness and depressive symptoms: passivity, appetite and weight loss, and difficulty learning that one can change circumstances for the better. But we must be cautious in drawing conclusions from animal studies because many psychological conditions, including depression, may differ in animals and humans (Raulin & Lilienfeld, 2008).

Seligman and his colleagues (Abramson, Seligman, & Teasdale, 1978) argued that persons prone to depression attribute negative outcomes to *internal* as opposed to external factors and positive outcomes to *external* as opposed to internal factors. A person with depression might blame a poor test grade on a lack of ability, an internal factor, and a good score on the ease of the exam, an external factor.

Depression: The Role of Biology.

Twin studies indicate that genes exert a moderate effect on the risk of developing major depression (Kendler, Neale, Kressler, et al., 1993). Depression is often associated with low levels of the neurotransmitter serotonin (Robinson, 2007). Specific variations in the serotonin transporter gene (which affects the rate of reuptake; see Chapter 3) seem to play a role in depression, especially in conjunction with life experiences. People who inherit two copies of this stress-sensitive gene are two and a half times more likely to develop depression following four stressful events than people with another version of the gene that isn't sensitive to stress (Caspi et al., 2003). The stress-sensitive gene probably affects people's ability to dampen negative emotions in the face of stress (Kendler, Gardner, & Prescott, 2003). It's not clear whether these genetic irregularities are specific to depression; they may be associated with anxiety too (Hariri et al., 2002).

Depression also appears linked to low levels of the neurotransmitter norepinephrine (Leonard, 1997; Robinson, 2007) and to problems in the brain's reward and stress-response systems (Depue & Iacono, 1989; Forbes, Shaw, & Dahl, 2007). Many patients with depression have decreased levels of dopamine, the neurotransmitter most closely tied to reward (Martinot et al., 2001). This finding may help to explain why depression is often associated with an inability to experience pleasure.

BIPOLAR DISORDER: WHEN MOOD GOES TO EXTREMES

Ann, the giddy patient with bipolar disorder we met at the beginning of the chapter, experienced many of the classic symptoms of a **manic episode.** These episodes are typically marked by dramatically elevated mood (feeling "on top of the world"), decreased need for sleep, greatly heightened energy, inflated self-esteem, increased talkativeness, and irresponsible behavior. People in a manic episode often display "pressured speech," as though they can't get their words out quickly enough, and are difficult to interrupt (Goodwin & Jamison, 1990). Their ideas often race through their heads quickly, which may account for the heightened rate of creative accomplishments in some individuals with bipolar disorder. These and other symptoms, (refer back to Table 13.4 on page 468), typically begin with a rapid increase over only a few days. People usually experience their first manic episode after their early twenties (Kessler et al., 2005).

Bipolar disorder, formerly called manic-depressive disorder, is diagnosed when there's a history of at least one manic episode (American Psychiatric Association, 2000). In contrast to major depression, bipolar disorder is equally common in men and women. In the great majority of cases—upward of 90 percent (Alda, 1997)—people who've had one manic episode experience at least one more. Some have episodes separated by many years and then have a series of episodes, one rapidly following the other. More than half

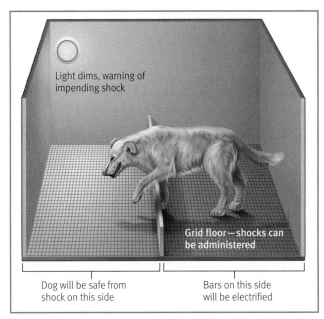

Light dims, warning of impending shock

Grid floor—shocks can be administered

Dog will be safe from shock on this side

Bars on this side will be electrified

Figure 13.1 The Shuttle Box. Using an apparatus like this, Martin Seligman found that dogs who were first prevented from escaping the shock gave up trying to escape electric shocks even when they were free to do so. He called this phenomenon "learned helplessness."

People in the midst of manic episodes frequently go on uncontrolled spending sprees and may "max out" multiple credit cards in the process.

GLOSSARY

manic episode
state marked by dramatically elevated mood, decreased need for sleep, increased energy, inflated self-esteem, increased talkativeness, and irresponsible behavior

bipolar disorder
condition marked by a history of at least one manic episode

First Person Account:
Bipolar Disorder

"When I start going into a high, I no longer feel like an ordinary [home-maker]. Instead I feel organized and accomplished and I begin to feel I am my most creative self. I can write poetry easily . . . melodies without effort . . . paint . . . I feel a sense of euphoria or elation. . . . I don't seem to need much sleep . . . I've just bought six new dresses . . . I feel sexy and men stare at me. Maybe I'll have an affair, or perhaps several. . . . However, when I go beyond this state, I become manic. . . . I begin to see things in my mind that aren't real. . . . One night I created an entire movie. . . . I also experienced complete terror . . . when I knew that an assassination scene was about to take place. . . . I went into a manic psychosis at that point. My screams awakened my husband. . . . I was admitted to the hospital the next day." (Fieve, 1975)

CORRELATION vs. CAUSATION
Can we be sure that A causes B?

MYTH: Suicide rates increase around the Christmas holidays, largely because people without close family members feel especially lonely.

REALITY: There's little support for this view; in fact, several studies suggest a slight decrease in suicides and attempted suicide around Christmas (Ajdacic-Gross et al., 2003; Phillips & Wills, 1987).

the time, a major depressive episode precedes or follows a manic episode (American Psychiatric Association, 2000).

Manic episodes often produce serious problems in social and occupational functioning, such as substance abuse and unrestrained sexual behavior. Because their judgment is so impaired, people in the midst of manic episodes may go on wild spending sprees, sleep with many partners in a short period of time, or drive while intoxicated. One patient passed himself off to a financial company as his own father, gained access to his father's savings for retirement, and gambled away his entire family fortune. Another frittered away most of his life's savings by purchasing more than a hundred bowling balls, none of which he needed. The negative effects of a manic episode, including loss of employment, family conflicts, and divorce, can persist for many years (Coryell et al., 1993).

Bipolar disorder is among the most genetically influenced of all mental disorders (Miklowitz & Johnson, 2006). Twin studies suggest that its heritability may be as high as 85 percent (Alda, 1997; McGuffin et al., 2003). Scientists believe that genes that increase the sensitivity of the dopamine receptors (Willner, 1995) and decrease the sensitivity of serotonin receptors may boost the risk of bipolar disorder (Ogden et al., 2004).

Brain imaging studies suggest that people with bipolar disorder experience increased activity in structures related to emotion, including the amygdala (Chang, Wagner, Garrett, et al., 2008; Yurgelun-Todd et al., 2000), and decreased activity in structures associated with planning, such as the prefrontal cortex (Kruger, Seminowicz, Goldapple, et al., 2003). Still, the cause–effect relationship between these physiological findings and mood disorders isn't entirely clear. For example, differences in brain activity observed in people with bipolar disorder may be an effect rather than a cause of the disorder (Thase, Jindal, & Howland, 2002).

Our discussion might seem to imply that bipolar disorder is determined entirely by biological factors. Not so. Stressful life events are associated with an increased risk of manic episodes, more frequent relapse, and a longer recovery from manic episodes (Johnson & Miller, 1997). Interestingly, some manic episodes appear to be triggered by *positive* life events associated with achieving goals, such as job promotions (Johnson et al., 2000).

SUICIDE: FACTS AND FICTIONS

Major depression and bipolar disorder are associated with a higher risk of suicide than most other disorders (Miklowitz & Johnson, 2006; Wolfsdorf, Freeman, D'Eramo, et al., 2003). Estimates suggest that the suicide rate of people with bipolar disorder is about 15 times higher than that of the general population (Harris & Barraclough, 1997). Some anxiety disorders, like panic disorder and social phobia, and substance abuse are also associated with heightened suicide risk (Spirito & Esposito-Smythers, 2006). But suicide itself isn't a psychological disorder, and its deadly reach extends far beyond any one condition. In 2001, scientists ranked suicide as the eleventh leading cause of death in the United States (National Institute of Mental Health, 2004), and the third leading cause of death for children, adolescents, and young adults (Kochanek, Murphy, Anderson, et al., 2004).

Typically, more than 30,000 people commit suicide in the United States each year, a number that surely underestimates the problem because relatives report many suicides as accidents. For each completed suicide, there are an estimated 8 to 25 attempts. In **Table 13.5** we present a number of common myths and misconceptions about suicide. **[LEARNING OBJECTIVE 13.8]**

The good news is that research has taught us a great deal about risk factors for suicide. The single best predictor of suicide is a previous attempt, because 30 to 40 percent of all people who kill themselves have made at least one prior attempt (Maris, 1992;

Pelkonen & Marttunen, 2003). Interestingly, hopelessness may be an even better predictor of suicide than depression (Beck, Brown, Berchick, et al., 1990; Goldston et al., 2001) because people are most likely to try to kill themselves when they see no escape from their pain. Intense agitation is also a powerful predictor of suicide risk (Fawcett, 1997).

Table 13.5 Common Myths and Misconceptions about Suicide.

Myth	Reality
Talking to persons with depression about suicide often makes them more likely to commit the act.	Talking to persons with depression about suicide makes them more likely to obtain help.
Suicide is almost always completed with no warning.	Many or most individuals who commit suicide communicate their intent to others, which gives us an opportunity to seek help for a suicidal person.
As a severe depression lifts, people's suicide risk decreases.	As a severe depression lifts, the risk of suicide may actually increase, in part because individuals possess more energy to attempt the act.
Most people who threaten suicide are seeking attention.	Although attention seeking motivates some suicidal behaviors, most suicidal acts stem from severe depression and hopelessness.
People who talk a lot about suicide almost never commit it.	Talking about suicide is associated with a considerably greater risk of suicide.

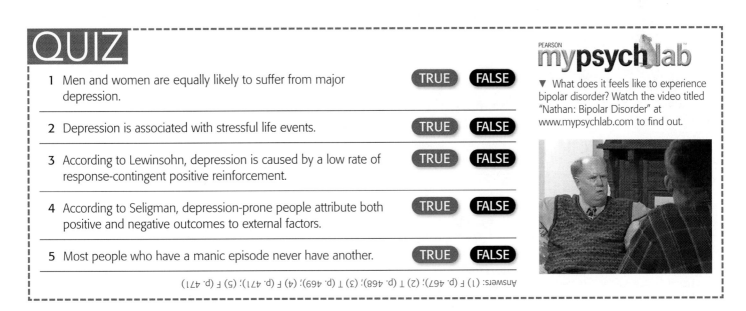

QUIZ

1 Men and women are equally likely to suffer from major depression.   **TRUE** **FALSE**

2 Depression is associated with stressful life events.   **TRUE** **FALSE**

3 According to Lewinsohn, depression is caused by a low rate of response-contingent positive reinforcement.   **TRUE** **FALSE**

4 According to Seligman, depression-prone people attribute both positive and negative outcomes to external factors.   **TRUE** **FALSE**

5 Most people who have a manic episode never have another.   **TRUE** **FALSE**

Answers: (1) F (p. 467); (2) T (p. 468); (3) T (p. 469); (4) F (p. 471); (5) F (p. 471)

PEARSON mypsychlab

▼ What does it feels like to experience bipolar disorder? Watch the video titled "Nathan: Bipolar Disorder" at www.mypsychlab.com to find out.

Personality and Dissociative Disorders: The Disrupted and Divided Self

Most of us are accustomed to thinking of ourselves as one coherent unified identity. But some unfortunate individuals experience a serious disruption of their thoughts or behaviors that prevents them from experiencing a healthy, consistent identity. Distinguishing normal variations in personality and sense of self from personality and identity disorders isn't easy because we all have our personal quirks.

The homicidal and unstable character in the movie *Fatal Attraction*, would probably qualify for a diagnosis of borderline personality disorder, although most people with this diagnosis aren't violent.

PERSONALITY DISORDERS

Of all psychiatric conditions, personality disorders are historically the least reliably diagnosed (Fowler, O'Donohue, & Lilienfeld, 2007; Perry, 1992; Zimmerman, 1994). DSM-IV states that we should diagnose a **personality disorder** only when personality traits first appear by adolescence; are inflexible, stable, and expressed in a wide variety of situations; and lead to distress or impairment (American Psychiatric Association, 2000, p. 685). But more than most patterns of behavior we've described, whether we perceive someone with a personality disorder as abnormal depends heavily on the context in which his or her behavior occurs (Price & Bouffard, 1974). **[LEARNING OBJECTIVE 13.9]** For example, the suspiciousness of a person with a paranoid personality disorder may be a liability in a cooperative work group, but an asset in a private investigator.

In **Table 13.6** we list the major personality disorders in DSM-IV. DSM-IV groups these disorders into three clusters—odd or eccentric; dramatic, emotional or erratic; and anxious or fearful. We'll consider in detail two major and extensively researched personality disorders—borderline personality disorder and psychopathic personality.

Table 13.6 The DSM-IV Classification of Major Personality Disorders.

Paranoid Personality Disorder	**Odd, Eccentric Cluster**	
	Paranoid personality disorder	Distrust, suspiciousness, oversensitivity
	Schizotypal personality disorder	Intense discomfort in social situations; odd thinking, perception, communication, behaviors
	Schizoid personality disorder	Detachment from social relationships, bland or limited expression of emotion
Narcissistic Personality Disorder	**Dramatic, Emotional, Erratic Cluster**	
	Histrionic personality disorder	Attention seeking, overemotional, dramatic, shallow, seductive, suggestible
	Narcissistic personality disorder	Grandiose sense of self-importance or uniqueness, need for constant attention and admiration, lacks empathy, preoccupation with fantasies of unlimited success or power
	Antisocial personality disorder	Antisocial behavior, violates or disregards rights of others, lying, stealing, irresponsibility, lack of remorse
	Borderline personality disorder	Instability in various areas of life, tense and unstable relationships, recurrent suicide attempts, efforts to avoid being abandoned, unstable self-image/identity disturbance
Obsessive-Compulsive Personality Disorder	**Anxious, Fearful Cluster**	
	Avoidant personality disorder	Unwilling to enter into relationships unless guarantee of uncritical acceptance; social withdrawal; fear of social criticism or rejection; reluctant to take risks or try new things that may bring about embarrassment
	Dependent personality disorder	Difficulty making everyday decisions; excessive reliance on and need for reassurance, support, nurturance from others; feels helpless when alone
	Obsessive-compulsive personality disorder	Preoccupied with order, organization, rules, small details; perfectionistic; rigid and stubborn; overinvolved in work; inflexible

(*Source:* From *Diagnostic and Statistical Manual of Mental Disorders*, 4th ed., American Psychiatric Association, 2000)

Borderline Personality Disorder: Stable Instability.

About 1-2 percent of adults, most of them women (Lieb, Zanarini, Schmahl, Linehan, & Bohus, 2008), develop **borderline personality disorder,** a condition marked by instability in mood, identity, and impulse control. Individuals with borderline personality tend to be extremely impulsive and unpredictable, although many are married and hold down good jobs. **[LEARNING OBJECTIVE 13.10]** Their relationships frequently alternate from extremes of worshipping partners one day to hating them the next.

Persons with borderline personality disorder's impulsivity and rapidly fluctuating emotions often have a self-destructive quality: Many engage in drug abuse, sexual promiscuity, overeating, and even self-mutilation, like cutting themselves when upset. They may threaten suicide to manipulate others, reflecting the chaotic nature of their relationships. Because many of them experience intense feelings of abandonment when alone, they may jump frantically from one unhealthy relationship to another.

According to Marsha Linehan's (1993) sociobiological model, individuals with borderline personality disorder inherit a tendency to overreact to stress and experience lifelong difficulties with regulating their emotions. Twin studies suggest that borderline personality traits are substantially heritable (Torgersen et al., 2000). Difficulties in controlling emotions may be responsible for the rejection many individuals with borderline personality disorder encounter, as well as their concerns about being accepted. Linehan suggests the following recipe for creating a borderline personality: Expose a child to a great deal of trauma and stress, don't legitimize the child's feelings, and don't provide the child with skills to cope with stress. Needless to say, we don't recommend that you follow this prescription with your children.

Psychopathic Personality: Don't Judge a Book by Its Cover.

We don't intend to alarm you. Yet the odds are high that in your life you've met—perhaps even dated—at least one person whom psychologists describe as having a **psychopathic personality,** known more informally as a *psychopath* or *sociopath*. Psychopathic personality overlaps with the DSM-IV diagnosis of **antisocial personality disorder (ASPD),** although it differs from it in important ways. In contrast to ASPD, which is marked by a lengthy history of illegal and irresponsible actions, psychopathic personality is marked by a distinctive set of personality traits (Lilienfeld, 1994). If those with borderline personality disorder are moody and impulsive, psychopathic personality is almost the opposite.

Those with psychopathic personality are guiltless, dishonest, manipulative, callous, and self-centered (Cleckley, 1941/1988; Lykken, 1995). Because of these distinctly unpleasant personality traits, one might assume we'd all go out of our way to avoid individuals with this disorder—and we'd probably be better off if we did. However, many of us seek out people with psychopathic disorder as friends and even romantic partners because they tend to be charming, personable, and engaging (Hare, 1993). Many have a history of *conduct disorder,* marked by lying, cheating, and stealing in childhood and adolescence. For unknown reasons, psychopathic personality is more common in men than women (Vitale & Newman, 2001).

Despite popular conception, most people with psychopathic disorder aren't physically aggressive. Nevertheless, they are at heightened risk for crime compared with the average person, and a handful—probably a few percent—are habitually violent. Mass murderer Ted Bundy almost certainly had a psychopathic personality. About 25 percent of prison inmates have psychopathic personalities (Hare, 2003). Also, despite scores of movie portrayals of crazed serial killers, people with psychopathic personalities typically aren't psychotic. To the contrary, most are entirely rational. They know full well that their irresponsible actions are morally wrong; they just don't care.

**First Person Account:
Borderline Personality Disorder**

"*I can act perfectly fine one minute, see or hear something and turn into an absolute monster. I turn into a monster when people raise their voices. Television shows can trigger intense feelings of hate, anger, and sometimes psychosis. Arguing, shouting, and abusive scenes send raging emotions through my body and mind. . . . My anger is intense and sudden. . . . I don't care if I am hurt, I don't care who I hurt. Once that switch is thrown, I turn into a short-term terrorist. I hope I'm never holding a knife or gun when this anger attacks. This doesn't happen frequently, and is usually confined to within the family.*"
http://www.angelfire.com/biz/BPD

**First Person Account:
Psychopathic Personality**

"*[Whatever] I've done in the past, you know—the emotions of omissions or commissions—doesn't bother me. . . . Guilt? It's this mechanism we use to control people. It's an illusion. It does terrible things to our bodies. And there are much better ways to control our behavior than that rather extraordinary use of guilt.*" [Excerpt from interview with serial killer Ted Bundy shortly before his execution (Hare, 1993)]

GLOSSARY

personality disorder
condition in which personality traits, appearing first in adolescence, are inflexible, stable, expressed in a wide variety of situations, and lead to distress or impairment

borderline personality disorder
condition marked by extreme instability in mood, identity, and impulse control

psychopathic personality
condition marked by superficial charm, dishonesty, manipulativeness, self-centeredness, and risk taking

antisocial personality disorder (ASPD)
condition marked by a lengthy history of irresponsible and/or illegal actions

There's reason to suspect that psychopathic personality characterizes not only much of the criminal justice system but also positions of leadership in corporations and politics (Babiak & Hare, 2006). Many psychopathic traits, such as interpersonal skills, superficial likability, ruthlessness, and risk taking, may give them a leg up for getting ahead of the rest of the pack. Still, there's surprisingly little research on "successful psychopaths," people with high levels of psychopathic traits who function well in society (Hall & Benning, 2006; Widom, 1977).

Despite over five decades of research, the causes of psychopathic personality remain mysterious. Those with this disorder don't show much classical conditioning to unpleasant unconditioned stimuli, like electric shocks. Similarly, when asked to sit patiently in a chair for an impending electric shock or loud blast of noise, their levels of skin conductance—an indicator of arousal—increase only about one-fifth as much as that of people without psychopathic personality (Hare, 1978; Lorber 2004). These abnormalities probably stem from a deficit in fear, which may give rise to many of the other features of the disorder (Lykken, 1995; Patrick, 2006). Perhaps as a consequence of this lack of fear, those with psychopathic personality aren't motivated to learn from punishment and tend to make the same mistakes in life over and over again (Newman & Kosson, 1986).

An alternative explanation is that those with psychopathic personality are underaroused. As we learned in Chapter 9, the *Yerkes-Dodson law* describes a well-established psychological principle: an inverted U–shaped relationship between arousal, on the one hand, and mood and performance, on the other. People who are habitually underaroused may seek out excitement. The underarousal hypothesis may help to explain why psychopathic personality is associated with risk taking (Zuckerman, 1989).

DISSOCIATIVE DISORDERS

When speaking about ourselves, we use the words *me* and *I* without giving it a second thought. That's not the case in most **dissociative disorders,** which involve disruptions in consciousness, memory, identity, or perception (American Psychiatric Association, 2000). Nadean Cool, whom we met in Chapter 6, was diagnosed with dissociative identity disorder (DID), the best known of dissociative disorders. Before Nadean came to question her diagnosis, she was convinced that her body housed more than 130 distinct personalities. The idea that one person can have more than one identity, let alone more than a hundred, is an extraordinary claim. So it's no wonder that DID is one of the most controversial of all diagnoses. Before we consider the debate that swirls around this condition, we'll consider several other dissociative disorders.

Dissociative Amnesia. In **dissociative amnesia,** people can't recall important personal information—most often following a stressful experience—that isn't due to normal forgetting. Their memory loss is extensive, and can include suicide attempts or violent outbursts (American Psychiatric Association, 2000; Sar et al., 2007). More commonly, psychologists diagnose dissociative amnesia when adults report gaps in their memories for child abuse. **[LEARNING OBJECTIVE 13.11]**

This diagnosis has proven controversial for several reasons. First, memory gaps regarding nontraumatic events are common in healthy individuals and aren't necessarily either stress-related or indicative of dissociation (Belli, Winkielman, Read, et al., 1998). Second, most people may not be especially motivated to recall child abuse or other upsetting events. As Richard McNally (2003) pointed out, not thinking about something isn't the same as

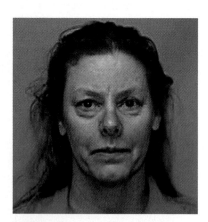

In rare cases, women with psychopathic personalities turn violent (Arrigo & Griffin, 2004). Aileen Wuomos (pictured *above*), a serial killer called the Damsel of Death, was executed for the murders of six men she lured to their death by posing as a stranded driver. Charlize Theron won an Academy Award for her portrayal of Wuomos in the movie *Monster*.

EXTRAORDINARY CLAIMS
Is the evidence as convincing as the claim?

GLOSSARY

dissociative disorder
condition involving disruptions in consciousness, memory, identity, or perception

dissociative amnesia
inability to recall important personal information—most often related to a stressful experience—that can't be explained by ordinary forgetfulness

being *unable* to remember it, which is amnesia. Third, careful studies have turned up no convincing cases of amnesia that can't be explained by other factors, like brain injury, normal forgetting, or an unwillingness to think about disturbing events (Kihlstrom, 2005; Pope et al., 2007).

RULING OUT RIVAL HYPOTHESES
Have important alternative explanations for the findings been excluded?

Dissociative Fugue. At times, we've all felt like running away from our troubles. In **dissociative fugue,** people not only forget significant events in their lives but also flee their stressful circumstances (*fugue* is Latin for "flight"). In some cases, they move to another city or even another country, assuming a new identity. Fugues can last for hours or, in unusual cases, years. Dissociative fugue is rare, occurring in about 2 of every 1,000 people (American Psychiatric Association, 2000), with more prolonged fugue states even rarer (Karlin & Orne, 1996).

In 2006, a 57-year-old husband, father, and Boy Scout leader from New York was found living under a new name in a homeless shelter in Chicago, after he left his garage near his office and disappeared. When a tip to *America's Most Wanted* uncovered his true identity 6 months later, his family contacted him, but he had no memory of who they were (Brody, 2007).

In this and other fugue cases, it's essential to find out whether the fugue resulted from a head injury, stroke, or other neurological cause. Moreover, some people merely claim amnesia to avoid responsibilities or stressful circumstances, relocate to a different area, and get a fresh start in life.

Jeffrey Ingram, age 40, experienced a dissociative fugue in which he claimed for over a month that he couldn't remember anything about his life. He was reunited with his fiancée in 2006 only after he appeared on television shows asking the public to identify him.

Dissociative Identity Disorder: Multiple Personalities, Multiple Controversies.
According to DSM-IV (American Psychiatric Association, 2000), **dissociative identity disorder (DID)** is characterized by the presence of two or more distinct identities or personality states, which are more temporary patterns of behavior (see Chapter 6). The identities or personality states alternately assume control over the person's behavior. These alternate identities or "alters," as they're called, are often very different from the primary or "host" personality and may be of different names, ages, genders, and races. In some cases, these features are the opposite of those exhibited by the host personality. For example, if the host personality is shy and retiring, one or more alters may be outgoing or flamboyant. Psychologists have reported the number of alters to range from one (the so-called split personality) to hundreds or even thousands, with one reported case of 4,500 personalities (Acocella, 1999). Women are more likely to receive a DID diagnosis and report more alters than men (American Psychiatric Association, 2000).

Researchers have identified intriguing differences among alters in their respiration rates (Bahnson & Smith, 1975), brain wave activity (EEG; Ludwig, Brandsma, Wilbur, et al., 1972), eyeglass prescriptions (Miller, 1989), handedness (Savitz et al., 2004), skin conductance responses (Brende, 1984), voice patterns, and handwriting (Lilienfeld & Lynn, 2003). Fascinating as these findings are, they don't provide conclusive evidence for the existence of different alters. These differences could arise from changes in mood or thoughts over time or to bodily changes, such as muscle tension, that people can produce on a voluntary basis (Allen & Movius, 2000; Merckelbach, Devilly, & Rassin, 2002). The primary controversy surrounding DID revolves around one question: Is DID a response to early trauma, or is it a consequence of social and cultural factors (Merskey, 1992)? There are two competing models of why DID occurs.

GLOSSARY

dissociative fugue
sudden, unexpected travel away from home or the workplace, accompanied by amnesia for significant life events

dissociative identity disorder (DID)
condition characterized by the presence of two or more distinct identities or personality states that recurrently take control of the person's behavior

RULING OUT RIVAL HYPOTHESES
Have important alternative explanations for the findings been excluded?

Posttrauma Explanations. According to the *posttraumatic model* (Gleaves, 1996; Gleaves, May, & Cardeña, 2001; Ross, 1997), DID arises from a history of severe abuse—physical,

"I HAVE 25 PATIENTS IN MY COUNSELING GROUP—MRS. SHERMAN, MR. MARTIN, AND MR. MARTIN'S 23 OTHER PERSONALITIES."

(Dan Rosandich, www.CartoonStock.com)

sexual, or both—during childhood. This abuse leads individuals to "compartmentalize" their identity into alters as a means of coping with intense emotional pain. In this way, the person can feel as though the abuse happened to someone else.

Advocates of the posttraumatic model claim that 90 percent or more of individuals with DID were severely abused in childhood (Gleaves, 1996). Nevertheless, many of the studies that reported this association didn't check the accuracy of abuse claims against objective information, such as court records of abuse (Coons, Bowman, & Milstein, 1988). Moreover, researchers haven't shown that early abuse is specific to DID, as it's present in many other disorders (Giesbrecht, Lynn, Lilienfeld, & Merckelbach, 2008; Pope & Hudson, 1992). These considerations don't exclude a role for early trauma in DID, but they suggest that researchers must conduct further controlled studies before drawing strong conclusions (Gleaves, 1996; Gleaves et al., 2001).

EXTRAORDINARY CLAIMS
Is the evidence as convincing as the claim?

Sociocognitive Explanations. According to advocates of the competing *sociocognitive model,* the claim that some people have hundreds of personalities is extraordinary, and the evidence for it is unconvincing (Lilienfeld et al., 1999; Lynn & Pintar, 1997; McHugh, 1993; Merskey, 1992; Spanos, 1994, 1996). According to this model, people's expectancies and beliefs—shaped by certain psychotherapeutic procedures and cultural influences, rather than early traumas—account for the origin and maintenance of DID. Advocates of this model claim that some therapists, like Nadean Cool's, use procedures, like hypnosis and repeated prompting of alters, that suggest to patients that their puzzling symptoms are the products of alternative identities (Lilienfeld & Lynn, 2003; Lilienfeld et al., 1999). This hypothesis is supported by the fact that reports of alters and an increase in the number of alters are much more likely to occur after therapists begin using these techniques (Kluft, 1984; Piper, 1997).

As of 1970, there were 79 documented cases of DID in the world literature. As of 1986, the number of DID cases had mushroomed to approximately 6,000 (Lilienfeld et al., 1999), and some estimates in the early twenty-first century are in the hundreds of thousands. The sociocognitive model holds that the popular media have played a pivotal role in the DID epidemic (Elzinga, van Dyck, & Spinhoven, 1998). Over the past two decades, media coverage of DID has skyrocketed (Showalter, 1997; Spanos, 1996; Wilson, 2003). DID is now diagnosed with considerable frequency in some countries (such as Holland) in which it's recently received more publicity. In summary, there's considerable support for the sociocognitive model and the claim that therapists, along with the media, are creating alters rather than discovering them.

WHAT DO *you* THINK?

For a journalism class, you are asked to write an article on a widely publicized case of dissociative identity disorder. In your reporting, how would you characterize the range of possible causes of this condition?

QUIZ

1 Personality disorders are almost always reliably diagnosed. TRUE FALSE

2 Borderline personality is characterized by extreme and consistent lack of stability in mood and behavior. TRUE FALSE

3 Most people with psychopathic personality are not habitually violent. TRUE FALSE

4 Child abuse clearly causes DID. TRUE FALSE

5 Most DID patients show few signs of the disorder before they begin therapy. TRUE FALSE

Answers: (1) F (p. 474); (2) T (p. 475); (3) T (p. 475); (4) F (p. 478); (5) T (p. 478)

PEARSON
mypsychlab

▼ How do individuals deal with borderline personality disorders? Watch the video titled "Janna: Borderline Personality Disorder" at www.mypsychlab.com to find out.

The Enigma of Schizophrenia

Psychiatrist Daniel Weinberger has called **schizophrenia** the "cancer" of mental illness: It's perhaps the most severe of all mental disorders and the most mysterious (Levy-Reiner, 1996). As we'll discover, it's a devastating disorder of thought and emotion associated with a loss of contact with reality (American Psychiatric Association, 2000).

SYMPTOMS OF SCHIZOPHRENIA: THE SHATTERED MIND

Even today, many people confuse schizophrenia with DID (Wahl, 1997). The term *schizophrenia* literally means "split mind," which no doubt contributed to the popular myth that the symptoms of schizophrenia stem from a split personality. You may have even heard people refer to a "schizophrenic attitude" when explaining that they're "of two minds" regarding an issue. Don't be misled. The difficulties of individuals with schizophrenia arise from disturbances in thinking, language, emotion, and relationships with others. In contrast to DID, which is supposedly characterized by multiple intact personalities, schizophrenia is characterized by one personality that's shattered.

Schizophrenia causes most of its sufferers' levels of functioning to plunge. More than half suffer from serious disabilities, such as the inability to hold a job and maintain close relationships (Harvey, Reichenberg, & Bowie, 2006). Indeed, a large proportion of homeless people would receive diagnoses of schizophrenia (Cornblatt, Green, & Walker, 1999). Some people diagnosed with schizophrenia display *positive symptoms* that involve excess or distortion of normal behavior such as hearing voices. Others display *negative symptoms* reflecting a decrease in normal functioning such as social withdrawal. Many experience a combination of positive and negative symptoms. **[LEARNING OBJECTIVE 13.12]**

Individuals who experience schizophrenia comprise less than 1 percent of the population, with estimates ranging from 0.4 to 0.7 percent (Saha, Chant, & Welham, et al., 2005). Yet they make up half of the approximately 100,000 patients in state and county

Contrary to popular belief, the symptoms of schizophrenia are not produced by a "split mind" or personality.

GLOSSARY

schizophrenia
severe disorder of thought and emotion associated with a loss of contact with reality

First Person Account: Schizophrenia

"The reflection in the store window—it's me, isn't it? I know it is, but it's hard to tell. Glassy shadows, polished pastels, a jigsaw puzzle of my body, face, and clothes, with pieces disappearing whenever I move. . . . Schizophrenia is painful, and it is craziness when I hear voices, when I believe people are following me, wanting to snatch my very soul. I am frightened too when every whisper, every laugh is about me; when newspapers suddenly contain cures, four-letter words shouting at me; when sparkles of light are demon eyes." (McGrath, 1984)

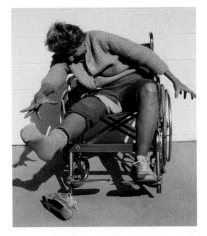

Catatonic individuals, like the one shown here, may permit their limbs to be moved to any position, and maintain this posture for lengthy periods of time, a condition called *waxy flexibility.*

GLOSSARY

delusion
strongly held, fixed belief that has no basis in reality

psychotic symptom
psychological problem reflecting serious distortions in reality

hallucination
sensory perception that occurs in the absence of an external stimulus

catatonic symptom
motor problem, including extreme resistance to complying with simple suggestions, holding the body in bizarre or rigid postures, or curling up in a fetal position

mental institutions in the United States (Grob, 1997). But there's some good news. Today, more than ever, people who have schizophrenia can function in society, even though they may need to return periodically to hospitals for treatment (Harding, Zubin, & Strauss, 1992; Lamb & Bachrach, 2001; Mueser & McGurk, 2004).

The typical onset of schizophrenia is in the midtwenties for men and the late twenties for women, but schizophrenia can also strike after age 45 (American Psychiatric Association, 2000). As many as one-half to two-thirds of people with schizophrenia improve significantly, although not completely, and a small percentage recover completely after a single episode (Robinson, Woerner, McMeniman, et al., 2004).

Delusions: Fixed False Beliefs.

Among the hallmark symptoms of schizophrenia are **delusions**—strongly held fixed beliefs that have no basis in reality. Delusions are called **psychotic symptoms** because they represent a serious distortion of reality. Terrell, whom we met at the beginning of the chapter, experienced delusions that led to a suicide attempt.

Delusions commonly involve themes of persecution. For example, a person with schizophrenia might believe that coworkers tapped his phone and conspired to get him fired. One patient was convinced that a helicopter in the distance beamed the Beatles song "All You Need Is Love" into his head to make him feel jealous and inadequate. Patients may also report delusions of grandeur (greatness), such as believing they've discovered the cure for cancer even though they had no medical training. Other delusions center on the body and may include a firm belief that one is infested with brain parasites.

Hallucinations: False Perceptions.

Among the other serious symptoms of schizophrenia are **hallucinations:** sensory perceptions that occur in the absence of an external stimulus. They can be auditory (involving hearing), olfactory (involving smell), gustatory (involving taste), tactile (involving the sense of feeling), or visual. Most hallucinations in schizophrenia are auditory, usually consisting of voices. In some patients, hallucinated voices express disapproval or carry on a running commentary about the person's thoughts or actions. *Command hallucinations,* which tell patients what to do ("Go over to that man and tell him to shut up!") may be associated with a heightened risk of violence toward others (McNiel, Eisner, & Binder, 2000). Visual hallucinations in the absence of auditory hallucinations are usually signs of an organic (medical) disorder or substance abuse rather than schizophrenia (Shea, 1998).

Disorganized Speech.

Consider a 39-year-old patient with schizophrenia's reply to the question of whether he felt that people imitated him. "Yes . . . I don't quite gather. I know one right and one left use both hands but I can't follow the system that's working. The idea is meant in a kind way, but it's not the way I understand life. It seems to be people taking sides. If certain people agree with me they speak, and if not, they don't. Everybody seems to be the doctor and Mr. H. [his own name] in turn" (Mayer-Gross, Slater, & Roth, 1969, p. 177).

We can see that his language skips from topic to topic in a disjointed way. Most researchers believe that this peculiar language is associated with thought disorder (Meehl, 1962; Strik, Dierks, Hubl, & Horn, 2008). In severe forms, the resulting speech is so jumbled that it's almost impossible to understand, leading psychologists to describe it as *word salad.*

Grossly Disorganized Behavior or Catatonia.

When people develop schizophrenia, self-care, personal hygiene, and motivation often deteriorate. These individuals may avoid conversation; laugh, cry, or swear inappropriately; or wear a warm coat on a sweltering summer day.

Catatonic symptoms involve motor (movement) problems, such as extreme resistance to complying with even simple suggestions, holding the body in bizarre or rigid postures, or curling up in a fetal position. Catatonic individuals' withdrawal can be so severe that they refuse to speak and move, or they may pace aimlessly. They may also repeat a phrase in conversation in a parrotlike manner, a symptom called *echolalia*. At the opposite extreme, they may occasionally engage in bouts of frenzied, purposeless motor activity.

EXPLANATIONS FOR SCHIZOPHRENIA: THE ROOTS OF A SHATTERED MIND

Today, virtually all scientists believe that psychosocial factors play some role in schizophrenia. Nevertheless, they also agree that these factors probably trigger the disorder only in people with a genetic vulnerability. **[LEARNING OBJECTIVE 13.13]**

The Family and Expressed Emotion.
Early theories of schizophrenia mistakenly laid the blame for the condition on mothers, with so-called *schizophrenogenic* (schizophrenia-producing) mothers being the culprits. Based on informal observations of families of children with schizophrenia, some authors described such mothers as overprotective, smothering, insensitive, rejecting, and controlling (Arieti, 1959; Lidz, 1973). Other theorists pointed the finger of blame at the interactions among all family members (Dolnick, 1998).

It's now widely acknowledged that parents and family members don't "cause" schizophrenia (Gottesman, 1991; Walker, Kestler, Bollini, et al., 2004). Instead, their behaviors are in response to the experience of living with a seriously disturbed person. Still, families may play a role in determining whether schizophrenia patients relapse. After leaving hospitals, patients experience more than twice the likelihood of relapse (50 percent to 60 percent) when their relatives display high *expressed emotion* (EE)—that is, criticism, hostility, and overinvolvement (Brown, Monck, Carstairs, et al., 1962; Butzlaff & Hooley, 1998). But the effects of EE appear to vary across ethnic groups (Chentsova-Dutton & Tsai, 2006). Caucasian American patients' relapse rate is positively correlated with EE, but Mexican American patients' relapse rate is uncorrelated with EE (Lopez et al., 2004). And among African Americans, EE is negatively correlated with relapse, meaning that those who encounter EE are less likely to relapse (Rosenfarb, Bellack, & Aziz, 2006).

Schizophrenia: Brain, Biochemical, and Genetic Findings.
Research using a variety of technologies has uncovered intriguing biological clues to the causes of schizophrenia. We'll focus on three such clues: brain abnormalities, neurotransmitter differences, and genetic findings.

Brain Abnormalities. Research indicates that one or more of four fluid-filled structures called *ventricles* (see Chapter 3), which cushion and nourish the brain, are typically enlarged in individuals with schizophrenia. This finding is important for two reasons. First, these brain areas frequently expand when others shrink (Barta, Pearlson, Powers, et al., 1990; Raz & Raz, 1990). Second, deterioration in these areas is associated with thought disorder (Vita et al., 1995).

Other brain abnormalities in schizophrenia include increases in the size of the *sulci*, or spaces between the ridges of the brain (Cannon, Mednick, & Parnas, 1989), and decreases in activation of the amygdala and hippocampus (Hempel, Hempel, Schöknecht, et al., 2003) and in the symmetry of the brain's hemispheres (Luchins, Weinberger, & Wyatt, 1982; Zivotofsky, Edelman, Green, et al., 2007). Functional brain imaging studies show that the frontal lobes of people with schizophrenia are less active than those of nonpatients, especially when engaged in demanding mental tasks (Andreasen et al., 1992; Knyazeva, Jalili, Meuli, Hasler, Feo, & Do, 2008), a phenomenon called *hypofrontality*. Still, it's not clear whether these findings are causes or consequences of the disorder. For

MYTH: Many non-Western cultures regard people with schizophrenia and other severe mental illnesses as "shamans," or medicine men, and often worship them as possessing divine powers.

REALITY: Jane Murphy's (1976) work suggests that the Yorubas of Nigeria and other cultures distinguish people with mental illnesses from shamans. The Yorubas, for example, referred to a man with mental illness living on an abandoned anthill as "out of mind and crazy." In contrast, they referred to a shaman during a healing session as "out of mind but not crazy," meaning that he was in a temporary trance state.

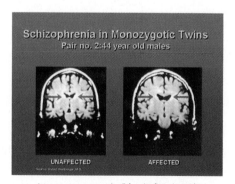

In one monozygotic (identical) twin with schizophrenia, the fluid-filled ventricles of the brain (*see red arrows*) are enlarged relative to his co-twin without schizophrenia.

CORRELATION vs. CAUSATION
Can we be sure that A causes B?

RULING OUT RIVAL HYPOTHESES
Have important alternative explanations
for the findings been excluded?

example, hypofrontality could be due to the tendency of patients with schizophrenia to concentrate less on tasks compared with other individuals. Researchers also need to rule out alternative explanations for brain underactivity that could arise from patients' diet, drinking and smoking habits, and medication use (Hanson & Gottesman, 2005).

Neurotransmitter Differences. The biochemistry of the brain is one of the keys to unlocking the mystery of schizophrenia. One early explanation was the *dopamine hypothesis* (Carlsson, 1995; Keith, Gunderson, Reifman, et al., 1976; Nicol & Gottesman, 1983). The evidence for the role of dopamine in schizophrenia is mostly indirect. First, most antischizophrenic drugs block dopamine receptor sites. To put it crudely, they "slow down" nerve impulses by partially blocking the action of dopamine. Second, amphetamine, a stimulant drug that blocks the reuptake of dopamine, tends to make the symptoms of schizophrenia worse (Lieberman & Koreen, 1993; Snyder, 1975). Nevertheless, a better supported rival hypothesis is that abnormalities in dopamine *receptors* produce these symptoms.

RULING OUT RIVAL HYPOTHESES
Have important alternative explanations
for the findings been excluded?

Genetic Influences. The seeds of schizophrenia are planted partly in individuals' genetic endowment. As we can see in **Figure 13.2,** being the offspring of someone diagnosed with schizophrenia greatly increases one's odds of developing the disorder. If we have a sibling with schizophrenia, we have about a 1 in 10 chance of developing the disorder; these odds are about 10 times higher than those of the average person. As genetic similarity increases, so does the risk of schizophrenia.

Still, it's possible the environment accounts for these findings because siblings not only share genes but also grow up in the same family. To eliminate this ambiguity, researchers have conducted twin studies (see Chapter 3). These studies provide convincing support for a genetic influence on schizophrenia. If we have an identical twin with schizophrenia, our risk rises to about 50 percent. An identical twin of a person with schizophrenia is about three times as likely as a fraternal twin of a person with schizophrenia to develop the disorder and about 50 times as likely as an average person (Gottesman & Shields, 1972; Kendler & Diehl, 1993; Meehl, 1962). Adoption data also point to a genetic influence. Even when children who have a biological parent with schizophrenia are adopted by parents with no hint of the disorder, their risk of schizophrenia is greater than that of a person with no biological relative with schizophrenia (Gottesman, 1991).

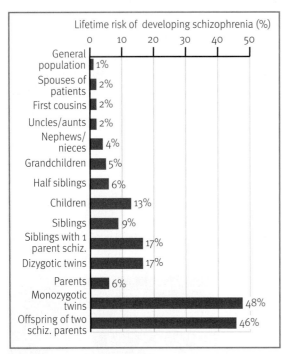

Figure 13.2 Schizophrenia Risk and the Family. The lifetime risk of developing schizophrenia is largely a function of how closely an individual is genetically related to a person with schizophrenia. (*Source:* Feldman, 1991)

Vulnerability to Schizophrenia: Diathesis-Stress Models. **Diathesis-stress models** incorporate much of what we know about schizophrenia. Such models propose that schizophrenia, along with many other mental disorders, is a joint product of a genetic vulnerability, called a *diathesis,* and stressors that trigger this vulnerability (Meehl, 1962; Walker & DiForio, 1997; Zubin & Spring, 1977).

Paul Meehl (1990) suggested that approximately 10 percent of the population has a genetic predisposition to schizophrenia. What are people with this predisposition like? During adolescence and adulthood, they may strike us as "odd ducks." They may seem socially uncomfortable, and their speech, thought processes, and perceptions may impress us as unusual. Such individuals display symptoms of psychosis-proneness or *schizotypal personality disorder* (refer back to Table 13.6 on page 474). Most people with schizotypal personality disorder don't develop full-blown schizophrenia,

GLOSSARY

diathesis-stress model
perspective proposing that mental disorders are a joint product of a genetic vulnerability, called a *diathesis,* and stressors that trigger this vulnerability

perhaps because they have a weaker genetic vulnerability or because they've experienced fewer stressors.

Whether someone with genetic vulnerability to schizophrenia ends up with the disorder depends on the impact of events that interfere with normal development. Children of women who had the flu during their second trimester of pregnancy (Brown et al., 2004; Mednick, Machon, Huttunen et al., 1988), suffered starvation early in pregnancy (Susser & Lin, 1992), or experienced complications during birth (Weinberger, 1987) are at a somewhat heightened risk of schizophrenia. Viral infections in the uterus may also play a key role in triggering certain cases of schizophrenia (Walker & DiForio, 1997). But the great majority of people exposed to infection or trauma before birth never show signs of schizophrenia. So these events probably create problems only for people who are genetically vulnerable to begin with (Cornblatt et al., 1999; Verdoux, 2004).

Fact -OID

Data show that more people with schizophrenia are born in the winter and spring than at other times of the year (Davies, Welham, Chant et al., 2003; Torrey, Miller, Rawlings et al., 1997). The reason for this strange finding doesn't appear to lie in astrology: Certain viral infections that affect pregnant women and that may trigger schizophrenia in vulnerable fetuses are most common in the winter months.

WHAT DO *you* THINK ?

A friend whose mother and sister both have schizophrenia is considering adopting a baby rather than having one herself because she's afraid that a biological child of hers would have schizophrenia too. What issues regarding both biological and environmental risk factors would you advise her to consider?

Complications during pregnancy or birth may trigger schizophrenia in those with a genetic predisposition for the disorder.

QUIZ

1 Delusions are rare in schizophrenia.	TRUE	FALSE
2 Most hallucinations in schizophrenia are visual.	TRUE	FALSE
3 Schizophrenogenic mothers often cause schizophrenia.	TRUE	FALSE
4 The evidence for the dopamine hypothesis is mostly indirect.	TRUE	FALSE
5 There's little support for the genetic transmission of schizophrenia.	TRUE	FALSE

Answers: (1) F (p. 480); (2) F (p. 480); (3) F (p. 481); (4) T (p. 482); (5) F (p. 482)

PEARSON
my**psych**lab

▼ Can animals help us understand the causes of schizophrenia in human beings? Watch the video titled "Genetic Schizophrenia" at www.mypsychlab.com to find out.

Eight-arm radial maze

Your Complete Review System

CONCEPTIONS OF MENTAL ILLNESS: YESTERDAY AND TODAY (pp. 454–462)

13.1 Identify criteria for defining mental disorders

Criteria for defining mental disorders include statistical rarity, subjective distress, impairment, societal disapproval, and biological dysfunction. No individual criterion is fulfilled by all cases of mental disorders.

1. Describe the family resemblance view of mental disorder. (p. 455)

13.2 Describe conceptions of mental illness across history and cultures

The belief that mental illness was caused by evil spirits was followed by the medical model of the Renaissance. In the early 1950s, medications to treat schizophrenia led to deinstitutionalization. Some psychological conditions are culture-specific. Still, many mental disorders can be found in most cultures.

2. During the Middle Ages, _____ was often used to treat mental illness. (p. 456)

3. Institutions for the mentally ill created in the fifteenth century were known as _____ . (p. 456)

4. In America in the nineteenth century, Dorothea Dix advocated for _____ _____ , an approach calling for dignity, kindness, and respect for those with mental illnesses. (p. 456)

5. In the early 1950s, medications that treated schizophrenia, like chlorpromazine, led to a government policy called _____ . (p. 456)

6. Bulimia is an example of a _____ disorder specific to Western cultures. (p. 457)

13.3 Identify common misconceptions about psychiatric diagnoses and the strengths and limitations of the current diagnostic system

Misconceptions include the ideas that a diagnosis is nothing more than pigeonholing and that diagnoses are unreliable, invalid, and stigmatizing. The *Diagnostic and Statistical Manual of Mental Disorders* (DSM-IV) is a valuable tool that contains separate axes for psychiatric diagnoses, medical conditions, life stressors, and overall life functioning. Its limitations include high levels of comorbidity.

7. What misconception regarding psychiatric diagnosis is fueled by high-profile media coverage of "dueling expert witnesses" in criminal trials? (p. 458)

8. The DSM-IV asks psychologists and psychiatrists to assess patients along multiple _____ , or dimensions, of functioning. (p. 461)

9. The diagnostic criteria used to classify individuals with mental disorders in the DSM-IV (are/are not) based completely on scientific evidence. (p. 462)

10. One of the problems with the DSM-IV is the high level of _____ among many of its diagnoses. (p. 462)

succeed with mypsychlab

1. If you were a clinician, how would you diagnose disorders? Become familiar with the different tools that are used in diagnoses.
   Overview of Clinical Assessment Tools

2. Role play being a clinician and see if you can identify the different axes of the DSM.
   The Axes of the DSM

3. Can you tell what psychological approach a clinician is using? Test your knowledge of the different clinical approaches.
   Overview of Clinical Assessment Methods

ANXIETY DISORDERS: THE MANY FACES OF WORRY AND FEAR (pp. 462–466)

13.4 Describe the many ways people experience anxiety

Panic involves intense yet brief rushes of fear that are out of proportion to the actual threat. People with generalized anxiety disorder spend much of their day worrying. Fears are highly focused in phobias. In posttraumatic stress disorder, highly aversive events produce enduring anxiety. People with obsessive-compulsive disorder experience intensely disturbing thoughts, senseless or irrational rituals, or both.

11. People suffer from _____ _____ when they experience panic attacks that are repeated and unexpected and when they change their behavior in an attempt to avoid panic attacks. (p. 463)

12. People with _____ _____ _____ spend an average of 60 percent of each day worrying. (p. 463)

13. A _____ is an intense fear of an object or a situation that's greatly out of proportion to its actual threat. (p. 463)

14. What are the symptoms of PTSD? Who is at high risk for developing this disorder? (p. 464)

Answers are located at the end of the text.

15. Persistent ideas, thoughts, or impulses that are unwanted and inappropriate and cause distress are called _____ . (p. 465)

16. Repetitive behaviors or mental acts initiated to reduce or prevent stress are called _____ . (p. 465)

17. What anxiety disorder did the billionaire industrialist Howard Hughes suffer from? Can you name some other well-known people who suffer from this disorder as well? (p. 465)

13.5 Identify three types of explanations for anxiety disorders

Learning theory proposes that fears can be learned via conditioning and observation. Anxious people tend to catastrophize or exaggerate the likelihood of negative events. Many anxiety disorders are genetically influenced.

18. People _____ when they predict terrible events, despite the low probability of their actual occurrence. (p. 466)

19. Anxious people tend to interpret ambiguous situations in a (negative/positive) light. (p. 466)

20. Genes affect whether we inherit high levels of _____ —a tendency to be high strung and irritable—which can set the stage for excessive worry. (p. 466)

succeed with mypsychlab

1. Take a test to measure your obsessive-compulsive thoughts. **The Obsessive-Compulsive Test**

2. All of us become nervous at some point in our lives, but when should we seek treatment? Listen as two psychologists discuss anxiety disorders. **Generalized Anxiety**

3. Choose interview questions and hear answers from researcher Dr. Edna Foa on the treatment of anxiety disorders. **Anxiety Treatment: Edna Foa**

MOOD DISORDERS (pp. 467–473)

13.6 Identify the characteristics of different mood disorders

The sad mood of major depression is the mirror image of the expansive mood associated with a manic episode, seen in bipolar disorder. Depression can be recurrent or sometimes chronic. Manic episodes are often preceded or followed by bouts of depression. Diagnosis of type of mood disorder depends in part on the intensity of the depressed or manic experience.

21. Over the course of a lifetime, more than _____ percent of us will experience a mood disorder. (p. 467)

22. The state in which a person experiences a lingering depressed mood or diminished interest in pleasurable activities is called a _____ _____ _____ . (p. 467)

13.7 Describe how life events can interact with characteristics of the individual to produce depression symptoms

Stressful life events are linked to depression. People with depression may face social rejection, which can amplify depression. According to Lewinsohn's behavioral model, when people with depression try different things and receive no payoff for them, they eventually give up. Aaron Beck's cognitive model holds that negative expectations play an important role in depression, whereas Martin Seligman's model emphasizes learned helplessness. Genes exert a moderate effect on the risk of developing depression.

23. Describe James Coyne's interpersonal model of depression. (p. 469)

24. Lewinsohn's behavioral model assumes that depression results from a (low/high) rate of response-contingent positive reinforcement. (p. 469)

25. Identify and describe the theory Martin Seligman proposed based on his shuttle box research. (pp. 470–471)

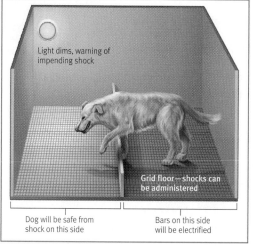

Light dims, warning of impending shock

Grid floor—shocks can be administered

Dog will be safe from shock on this side

Bars on this side will be electrified

26. Seligman's research indicated that people prone to depression attribute negative outcomes to (internal/external) factors. (p. 471)

27. Bipolar disorder is (equally common/more common) in women compared with men. (p. 471)

28. Twin studies suggest that the _____ of bipolar disorder may be as high as 85 percent. (p. 472)

13.8 **Identify common myths and misconceptions about suicide**

Myths about suicide include the misconception that talking to depressed people about suicide makes them more likely to commit the act, that suicide is almost always completed with no warning, that suicide risk decreases as a severe depression lifts, that most people who threaten suicide are seeking attention, and that people who talk a lot about suicide almost never commit it.

29. _____ _____ and _____ _____ are associated with a higher risk of suicide than most other disorders. (p. 472)

30. Many or most individuals who commit suicide (communicate/do not communicate) their intent to others. (p. 473)

succeed with **mypsychlab**

1. How well do you understand bipolar disorder? Take this interactive quiz to find out.
Bipolar Disorder

2. Watch as a woman explains her onset of major depression.
Helen: Major Depression

3. Choose questions to ask researcher Dr. Jutta Joorman about anxiety and depression and the role of an individual's thought processes.
Interaction of Cognition and Emotion: Jutta Joorman

PERSONALITY AND DISSOCIATIVE DISORDERS: THE DISRUPTED AND DIVIDED SELF (pp. 473–479)

13.9 **Distinguish between normal variations in personality and personality disorders**

Personality traits can become abnormal when they are stable and inflexible and lead to distress and impairment.

31. Of all psychiatric conditions, personality disorders are historically (least/most) reliably diagnosed. (p. 474)

13.10 **Identify the characteristics of borderline and psychopathic personality disorders**

Borderline personality disorder is marked by instability in mood, identity, and impulse control. People with psychopathic personality are guiltless, dishonest, callous, and self-centered.

32. Persons with borderline personality disorder's impulsivity and rapidly fluctuating emotions often have a _____ _____ . (p. 475)

33. A diagnosis of _____ personality disorder is characterized by a lengthy history of illegal and irresponsible actions. (p. 475)

34. Most people with psychopathic personality (are/are not) physically aggressive. (p. 475)

35. From a psychological perspective, what's rare about the case of serial killer Aileen Wuomos? (p. 476)

13.11 **Describe dissociative amnesia, fugue, and dissociative identity disorder**

Dissociative disorders involve disruptions in consciousness, memory, identity, or perception. In dissociative amnesia, people are unable to recall important personal information that isn't due to normal forgetting. In dissociative fugue, people forget significant events in their lives and flee their stressful circumstances. Dissociative identity disorder (DID) is characterized by the presence of two or more distinct identities or personality states.

36. What did this man experience when he disappeared for an extended length of time, only to be found without any memory of his previous life? (p. 477)

37. In DID, the alternate identities are often very (similar to/different from) the primary personality. (p. 477)

38. According to the _____ model, DID arises from a history of severe abuse during childhood. (pp. 477–478)

39. The _____ model argues that certain therapists, along with popular media, fuel the diagnosis of DID by creating alternative personalities rather than discovering them. (p. 478)

40. Some psychologists hold that the _____ _____ have played a pivotal role in the DID epidemic. (p. 478)

succeed with **mypsychlab**

1. Explore and test your understanding of individuals with dissociative identity disorder.
Dissociative Identity Disorder

THE ENIGMA OF SCHIZOPHRENIA (pp. 479–483)

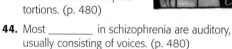

13.12 Recognize the characteristic symptoms of schizophrenia

The symptoms of schizophrenia include delusions, hallucinations, disorganized speech, and grossly disorganized behavior or catatonia.

41. From the perspective of what you've learned about schizophrenia, how does this art misrepresent the disorder? (p. 479)

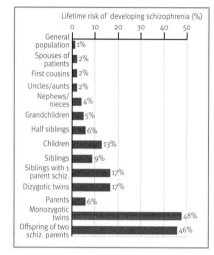

42. Strongly held, fixed beliefs that have no basis in reality are called _____ . (p. 480)

43. _____ symptoms represent serious reality distortions. (p. 480)

44. Most _____ in schizophrenia are auditory, usually consisting of voices. (p. 480)

45. People with schizophrenia can exhibit _____ _____ , in which their language skips from topic to topic in a disjointed way. (p. 480)

46. _____ symptoms involve motor problems, extreme resistance to complying with simple suggestions, holding the body in rigid postures, and refusing to speak or move. (pp. 480–481)

13.13 Explain how psychosocial, neural, biochemical, and genetic influences create the vulnerability to schizophrenia

Scientists have discovered brain abnormalities in patients with schizophrenia. Patients with schizophrenia are prone to relapse when their relatives display high expressed emotion (criticism, hostility, and overinvolvement).

47. It is widely acknowledged that parents and family members (cause/do not cause) schizophrenia. (p. 481)

48. Research indicates that one or more of four fluid-filled structures called ventricles, which cushion and nourish the brain, are typically (enlarged/diminished) in individuals with schizophrenia. (p. 481)

49. As illustrated in this figure, the lifetime risk of developing schizophrenia is largely a function of what? (p. 482)

Lifetime risk of developing schizophrenia (%)

General population	1%
Spouses of patients	2%
First cousins	2%
Uncles/aunts	2%
Nephews/nieces	4%
Grandchildren	5%
Half siblings	6%
Children	13%
Siblings	9%
Siblings with 1 parent schiz.	17%
Dizygotic twins	17%
Parents	6%
Monozygotic twins	48%
Offspring of two schiz. parents	46%

50. A _____ model proposes that schizophrenia, along with many other mental disorders, is a product of genetic vulnerability and stressors that trigger this vulnerability. (p. 482)

succeed with
mypsychlab

Do You Know All of the Terms in This Chapter?
Find out by using the Flashcards. Want more practice? Take additional quizzes, try simulations, and watch video to be sure you are prepared for the test!

succeed with **mypsychlab**

1. Review the types of schizophrenia and then watch and diagnose different case studies.
Schizophrenia Overview

2. How would you rate as a clinician? Test your knowledge of the different types of schizophrenia.
Types and Symptoms of Schizophrenia

3. Watch as an individual describes the development and treatment of his schizophrenia.
Rodney: Schizophrenia

SCIENTIFIC THINKING SKILLS
Questions and Summary

1. As you organize an orientation to prepare students to work in a mental health facility, how would you dispel misconceptions they might have about mental illness?

2. In preparing for a presentation to your psychology class, how would you make the audience aware of the myths about suicide and the realities that rebut each myth?

RULING OUT RIVAL HYPOTHESES
pp. 458, 464, 477, 482

CORRELATION vs. CAUSATION
pp. 472, 481

REPLICABILITY
pp. 459, 469

EXTRAORDINARY CLAIMS
pp. 476, 478

OCCAM'S RAZOR
p. 460

Psychological and Biological Treatments

Do all psychotherapies require patients to achieve insight to improve? (p. 498)

Is Alcoholics Anonymous better than other types of treatments for alcoholism? (p. 504)

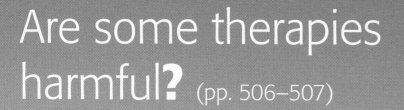

Are some therapies harmful? (pp. 506–507)

Is psychosurgery used primarily to control violent patients? (p. 517)

Does electroshock treatment produce long-term brain damage? (p. 516)

Picture a typical psychotherapy session. What's the patient doing? The therapist? What does the room look like? Perhaps your first thought was of a patient lying on a couch, with the therapist sitting behind her, pen and pad in hand, intent on unearthing long-forgotten memories, analyzing dreams, and encouraging the patient to vent painful feelings.

If this scenario came to mind, it's no wonder. From the early days of psychotherapy (often simply called "therapy"), these images have been etched into our cultural consciousness. But we'll discover that this picture doesn't begin to tell the story of the vast array of psychotherapeutic approaches that encompass individual therapy, treatments conducted in groups and with families, and even art, dance, and music therapy. Nor does the scenario capture the powerful biological treatments that have changed the lives of people with serious psychological disorders by targeting the brain's functioning. In this chapter, we'll examine a broad spectrum of therapies, both psychological and biological, that are designed to alleviate emotional suffering. Along the way, we'll offer critical thinking tools for distinguishing scientifically supported from unsupported treatments.

Like many concepts in psychology, *psychotherapy* isn't easy to define. For the purposes of this text, we can define **psychotherapy** as a psychological intervention designed to help people resolve emotional, behavioral, and interpersonal problems and improve the quality of their lives (Engler & Goleman, 1992, p. 15). Although the popular media often speak of therapy as though it were one thing, there are well over 500 "brands" of psychotherapy (Eisner, 2000). This number is about three times what it was in the 1970s. As we'll learn, research demonstrates that many of these therapies are effective, but many others have never been tested scientifically. Scientists have also developed biological treatments that include medications, electrical brain stimulation, and even brain surgery. We'll ponder fascinating scientific and ethical questions as we evaluate the application of these treatments.

Psychotherapy: Patients and Practitioners

We'll begin by considering several questions: Who seeks and benefits from psychotherapy? How is psychotherapy practiced? What makes a psychotherapist effective?

WHO SEEKS AND BENEFITS FROM TREATMENT?

A 2006 *Newsweek* poll found that about 20 percent of Americans have received psychological treatment at some point in their lives and that about 4 percent are currently in psychotherapy. **[LEARNING OBJECTIVE 14.1]** Therapists work with people of all ages and backgrounds as they confront challenges throughout the life cycle, including drug addiction, chronic pain, marital problems, and bouts of depression and anxiety. Patients (or *clients*) grapple with specific problems in psychotherapy, but they also contend frequently with feelings of helplessness, social isolation, and a sense of failure (Garfield, 1978; Lambert, 2003). Still other individuals turn to therapy to expand their self-awareness, learn better ways of relating to others, and consider lifestyle changes.

Entering Treatment: Gender, Ethnicity, and Culture.
Some people are more likely to enter treatment than others. Women are more likely to seek treatment than men (Addis & Mahalik, 2003; DuBrin & Zastowny, 1988), although both sexes benefit equally from psychotherapy (Petry, Tennen, & Affleck, 2000). Members of many racial and ethnic minority groups, particularly Asian Americans and Hispanic Americans, are less likely to seek mental health services than Caucasian Americans (Sue & Lam, 2002), perhaps because of the lingering stigma surrounding psychotherapy in these groups. There are also socio-economic factors that influence who seeks out therapy. Therapy can be very costly for those without health insurance or for those whose health plans don't include mental health coverage. Nevertheless, when individuals hailing from diverse cultural and ethnic backgrounds do obtain psychotherapy, they're likely to benefit from it (Navarro, 1993; Prochaska & Norcross, 2007).

Culturally sensitive psychotherapists tune their interventions to patients' cultural values and the difficulties they encounter in adapting to a dominant culture that, at times, is vastly different from their own (Sue & Sue, 2003; Whaley & Davis, 2007). Although ethnic minorities prefer therapists with a similar ethnic background (Coleman, Wampold, & Casali, 1995), there's no consistent evidence that therapy outcome is enhanced by patient–therapist ethnic matches (Shin et al., 2005) or gender matches (Bowman, Scogin, Floyd, et al., 2001). Still, when patients are relative newcomers to a particular culture and not well acquainted with its traditions, therapist–client ethnic match may play a greater role in therapy's effectiveness (Sue, 1998).

For many, the decision to enter therapy is difficult. In one study, over half of patients were aware of their problems long before they decided to seek help. Many waited for over 2 years (Strupp, Fox, & Lessler, 1969), a finding replicated by later researchers (DiClemente & Prochaska, 1985; Prochaska & DiClemente, 1984).

Reaping Benefits from Treatment.
People with problems of varying severity can all benefit from therapy. However, the effectiveness of therapy depends on the nature of the problems and of the individuals. For example, those who are better adjusted to begin with, who realize that they may be contributing to their own problems, and who are willing to work on those problems are most likely to benefit from therapy (Prochaska & DiClemente, 1982; Prochaska & Norcross, 2002). Research also shows that those with more temporary or situational problems such as relationship upheavals tend to have better outcomes from psychotherapy on average than those with longer standing and more pervasive problems (Gasperini, Scherillon, Manfredonia, et al., 1993; Steinmetz, Lewinsohn, & Antonuccio, 1983).

WHO PRACTICES PSYCHOTHERAPY?

As we learned in Chapter 1, clinical psychologists, psychiatrists, mental health counselors, and clinical social workers with professional degrees and licenses are the mainstays of the mental health profession (see **Table 14.1,** on the next page). But unlicensed religious, vocational, and rehabilitation counselors as well as art therapists, some with advanced degrees in fields other than psychology, also provide psychological services.

Contrary to the myth that all psychotherapists have advanced degrees in mental health, volunteers and **paraprofessionals,** helpers who work in the field with no formal professional training, often provide psychological services in such settings as crisis intervention centers and other social service agencies. **[LEARNING OBJECTIVE 14.2]** In most states, the term *therapist* isn't legally protected, so virtually anyone can offer psychological treatment. Many paraprofessionals obtain agency-specific training and attend workshops that enhance their general education backgrounds. Paraprofessionals may also be taught to recognize situa-

Popular portrayals of psychotherapy have a long history in the media. (Copyright © William M. Gaines, Agent, Inc. Used by permission)

REPLICABILITY
Can the results be duplicated in other studies?

(© The New Yorker Collection 1989 Danny Shanahan from CartoonBank.com. All Rights Reserved)

GLOSSARY

psychotherapy
a psychological intervention designed to help people resolve emotional, behavioral, and interpersonal problems and improve the quality of their lives

paraprofessional
person with no professional training who provides mental health services

Table 14.1 Occupations, Degrees, Roles, and Work Settings of Mental Health Professionals. Not all therapists are the same: Mental health consumers are often unaware of the substantial differences in education, training, and roles of different psychotherapists. This table provides some guidance.

Occupation	Degree/License	Role/Settings
Clinical Psychologist	PhD/PsyD, MA	Private practice, hospitals, schools, community agencies, medical settings, academic, other
Psychiatrist	MD or DO	Physicians, private practice, hospitals, medical centers, schools, academic, other
Counseling Psychologist	PhD, EdD, MA, MS, MC	University clinics, mental health centers; treat people with less severe psychological problems
School Psychologist	PhD, PsyD, EdD, EdS, MA, MS, MEd	In-school interventions, assessment, prevention programs, work with teachers, students, parents
Clinical Social Worker	Training varies widely; BSW, MSW, DSW, LCSW	Private practice following supervised experience, psychiatric facilities, hospitals/community agencies, schools, case managers; help with social and health problems
Mental Health Counselor	MSW, MS, MC	Private practice, community agencies, hospitals, other; career counseling, marriage issues, substance abuse
Psychiatric Nurse	Training varies widely; associate's degree, BSN, MSN, DNP, PhD	Hospitals, community health centers, primary care facilities, outpatient mental health clinics, manage medications; with advanced degrees can diagnose, treat mental patients
Pastoral Counselor	Training varies from bachelor's degree to more advanced degrees	Counseling, support in spiritual context, wellness programs; group, family, and couples therapy

Degree Key: BSN, bachelor of science in nursing; BSW, bachelor of social work; DNP, doctorate nurse practitioner; DO, doctor of osteopathy; DSW, doctor of social work; EdD, doctor of education; EdS, specialist in education; LCSW, licensed clinical social worker; MA, master of arts; MC, master of counseling; MD, doctor of medicine; MEd, master of education; MS, master of science; MSN, master of science in nursing; MSW, master of social work; PhD, doctor of philosophy; PsyD, doctor of psychology.

The ideal client? A 1964 study (Schofield, 1964) found that many therapists preferred to treat people who were relatively young, attractive, verbal, intelligent, and successful (YAVIS clients). Nevertheless, therapists have recently become more aware of the importance of assisting a broad clientele of all ages and cultural backgrounds.

RULING OUT RIVAL HYPOTHESES
Have important alternative explanations for the findings been excluded?

tions that require consultation with professionals with greater expertise. Paraprofessionals help to compensate for the sizable gap between the high demand for and meager supply of licensed practitioners (den Boer, Wiersma, Russo, et al., 2005).

Therapists don't actually need to be professionally trained or have many years of experience to be effective (Berman & Norton, 1985; Blatt, Sanislaw, Zuroff, et al., 1996; Christensen & Jacobson, 1994). Many researchers have found few or even no differences in effectiveness between more and less experienced therapists (Dawes, 1994; McFall, 2006). Why is this the case? Therapists who give patients hope, empathy, advice, support, and opportunities for new learning experiences can be effective regardless of their training background (Frank & Frank, 1991; Lambert & Ogles, 2004).

WHAT DOES IT TAKE TO BE AN EFFECTIVE PSYCHOTHERAPIST?

In 1995, *Consumer Reports* magazine surveyed 180,000 subscribers about their experiences with psychotherapy. Fully 90 percent of the 7,000 readers who responded to the mental health questions believed they were helped by psychotherapy. The strongest reported results were for those who consulted with a licensed professional for 6 months or longer (Seligman, 1995). Yet because the *Consumer Reports* study wasn't based on an experimental design (see Chapter 2), with patients randomly assigned to either treatment or no treatment, we need to be cautious in interpreting its results. Perhaps those who stayed in treatment for 6 months or more had already benefited at an earlier point in the process or were trying to justify the extra time they spent in therapy.

There are certain advantages to consulting with a professional. Professional helpers (1) understand how to operate effectively within the broader mental health system; (2) appreciate complex ethical, professional, and personal issues; and (3) can select treatments of demonstrated effectiveness (Garske & Anderson, 2003). Moreover, trained and experienced therapists may be more confident, less defensive, and better able to appreciate patients' worldview than paraprofessionals and inexperienced therapists (Teyber & McClure, 2000).

Type of training and years of experience aren't critical determinants of what makes a good therapist. So what is? Researchers are honing in on the answers. Effective therapists (Garske & Anderson, 2003) are likely to be warm and direct (Westerman, Foote, & Winston, 1995), establish a positive working relationship with patients (Kazdin, Marciano, & Whitley, 2005; Luborsky, McLellan, Diguer, et al., 1997), and tend not to contradict patients (Friedlander, 1984). **[LEARNING OBJECTIVE 14.3]** Effective therapists also select important topics to focus on in sessions (Goldfried, Raue, & Castonguay, 1998), and match their treatments to the needs and characteristics of patients (Beutler & Harwood, 2002). Differences among therapists in their abilities and characteristics may be so great that they overshadow differences in the types of therapies they provide (Ahn & Wampold, 2001; Luborsky et al., 1986). It is certainly important to consider how effective a particular therapeutic approach is for a particular problem or situation, but when it comes to the success of psychotherapy, the choice of *therapist* is every bit as important as the choice of *therapy* (Blow, Sprenkle, & Davis, 2007).

In **Table 14.2,** we present some tips for both selecting good therapists and avoiding bad ones.

WHAT DO *you* THINK?

You've decided to seek out therapy to help you cope with your social anxiety. The therapist at your student mental health facility is someone you "click" with and really feel good about talking to, but her specific therapy approach isn't the one you were looking for. What should you do?

In the television series *The Sopranos*, mobster Tony Soprano's therapist revealed private information about him at a dinner party and then abruptly dismissed him from therapy after becoming convinced he had an untreatable psychopathic personality. Breaking confidentiality and "abandonment" of a patient are serious—and fortunately rare—ethical violations on the part of psychotherapists.

Table 14.2 What Should I Look for in a Therapist, and What Type of Therapist Should I Avoid? Tens of thousands of people call themselves therapists, and it's often hard to know what kind of therapist to seek out or avoid. This checklist may help you, your friends, or your loved ones to select a good therapist—and to steer clear of a bad one.

If your answer is yes to most of the following statements, the therapist should be in a good position to help you:

(1) I can talk freely and openly with my therapist.

(2) My therapist listens carefully to what I say and understands my feelings.

(3) My therapist is warm and direct and provides useful feedback.

(4) My therapist explains up front what he or she will be doing and why and is willing to answer questions about his or her qualifications and training, my diagnosis, and our treatment plan.

(5) My therapist encourages me to confront challenges and solve problems.

(6) My therapist uses scientifically based approaches and discusses the pros and cons of other approaches.

(7) My therapist regularly monitors how I'm doing and is willing to change course when treatment isn't going well.

If your answer is yes to one or more of the following statements, the therapist may *not* be in a good position to help you, and may even be harmful:

(1) My therapist gets defensive and angry when challenged.

(2) My therapist has a "one size fits all" approach to all problems.

(3) My therapist spends considerable time each session making "small talk," telling me exactly what to do, and sharing personal anecdotes.

(4) My therapist isn't clear about what is expected of me in the treatment plan, and our discussions lack any focus and direction.

(5) My therapist doesn't seem willing to discuss the scientific support for what he or she is doing.

(6) There are no clear professional boundaries in my relationship with my therapist; for example, my therapist talks a lot about his or her personal life or asks me for personal favors.

QUIZ

1. Asian Americans are more likely to seek psychotherapy than Caucasians. **TRUE FALSE**

2. Most people who seek psychotherapy do so two years or more after they first notice they have psychological problems. **TRUE FALSE**

3. All people who practice therapy have advanced degrees in mental health. **TRUE FALSE**

4. Professional training is necessary to produce good therapy outcomes. **TRUE FALSE**

Answers: (1) F (p. 491); (2) T (p. 491); (3) F (p. 491); (4) F (p. 492)

PEARSON
mypsychlab

▼ How do psychologists treat disorders? Watch the video titled "Recent Trends in Treatments: Sue Mineka" at www.mypsychlab.com to find out.

Different "Flavors" of Therapy: A Review of Therapeutic Approaches

In much of the chapter that lies ahead, we'll examine some of the more prominent therapeutic approaches, describe their methods, and evaluate their scientific status. Some therapies focus on unconscious emotions, fears, and desires. Others deal primarily with changing our behaviors or our thinking and reasoning. Some therapies take place one-on-one and others with a family or couple together. Still others involve groups of unrelated people who share a problem or concern.

INSIGHT THERAPIES: ACQUIRING UNDERSTANDING

We'll begin our review of therapies with an overview of *psychodynamic therapists,* a term that refers to both Freudian therapists and those influenced by Freud's techniques. Psychodynamic therapies, and the humanistic therapies we'll also discuss, are often called **insight therapies,** as their goal is to cultivate insight, that is, expanded awareness.

Psychoanalytic and Psychodynamic Therapies: Freud's Legacy.
Psychodynamic therapists share the following five beliefs, which form the core of the psychodynamic approach (see Chapter 12): **[LEARNING OBJECTIVE 14.4]**

(1) Much of human behavior is motivated by unconscious conflicts, wishes, and impulses.

(2) Abnormal behaviors have meaningful causes that therapists can discover.

(3) People's present difficulties are rooted in their childhood experiences.

(4) Emotional expression and the opportunity to reexperience significant past events emotionally are critical aspects of therapy.

(5) When the patient achieves intellectual and emotional insight into previously unconscious material, the causes and the significance of symptoms become evident, often causing the symptoms to disappear.

Psychoanalysis: The First Therapy.
Freud's psychoanalysis was the first form of psychotherapy. According to Freud, the goal of psychoanalytic therapy is to *make the*

GLOSSARY

insight therapy
psychotherapy, including psychodynamic and humanistic approaches, with the goal of expanding awareness or insight

unconscious conscious. By that, he meant making the patient aware of previously repressed impulses, conflicts, and memories that generate psychological distress. Psychoanalytic therapy aims to clear away the emotional distortions bred by past experiences, guilt, and frustrations (Bornstein, 2001; Mellinger & Lynn, 2003). Psychoanalytic therapists, sometimes called "analysts," attempt to fill this tall order by using six primary approaches:

(1) **Free Association.** As patients lie on the couch in a comfortable, relaxed position, therapists instruct them to say whatever thoughts come to mind, no matter how meaningless or nonsensical they might seem. This process is called **free association** because patients are permitted to express themselves without censorship of any sort.

(2) **Interpretation.** From the patient's string of free associations, analysts form hypotheses regarding the origin of the patient's difficulties and share them with him or her as the therapy relationship develops. Therapists also formulate interpretations—that is, explanations—of the unconscious bases of a patient's dreams, emotions, and behaviors.

(3) **Dream Analysis.** According to Freud, dreams express unconscious themes that influence the patient's conscious life. The therapist's task is to interpret the relation of the dream to the patient's daytime experience and the dream's symbolic significance.

(4) **Resistance.** As treatment progresses and people become painfully aware of previously unconscious aspects of themselves, they often experience **resistance:** That is, they try to avoid further confrontation. Resistance helps patients sidestep the anxiety brought about by uncovering previously repressed thoughts, emotions, and impulses. Patients express resistance in many ways, including skipping therapy sessions or drawing a blank when the therapist asks a question about painful moments in their past, but all forms of resistance stall their progress. To minimize resistance, psychoanalysts attempt to make patients aware they're unconsciously obstructing therapeutic efforts and make it clear exactly *how* and *what* they're resisting (Anderson & Stewart, 1983; Reich, 1949).

(5) **Transference.** As analysis continues, patients begin to experience **transference:** They project intense, unrealistic feelings and expectations from their past onto the therapist. The ambiguous figure of the analyst supposedly becomes the focus of emotions once directed at significant persons from the patient's childhood. Research suggests that we indeed often react to people in our present lives in ways similar to people in our past (Berk & Andersen, 2000; Luborsky et al., 1985). These findings may suggest that Freud was right about transference; alternatively, they may mean that our stable personality traits (Chapter 12) lead us to react to people in similar ways over time. These lingering questions aside, therapists' interpretations of transference can be helpful for some patients (Ogrodniczuk & Piper, 1999).

(6) **Working Through.** In the final stage of psychoanalysis, therapists help patients **work through,** or process, their problems. The insight gained in treatment is a helpful starting point, but it's not sufficient. As a consequence, therapists must repeatedly address conflicts and resistance to achieving healthy behavior patterns and help patients to confront old and ineffective coping responses as they reemerge in everyday life (Menninger, 1958; Wachtel, 1997).

Developments in Psychoanalysis: The Neo-Freudian Tradition.
Freud's ideas spawned new schools and therapeutic approaches in the psychodynamic tradition (Ellis, Abrams, & Abrams, 2008). In contrast to Freudian therapists, neo-Freudian therapists are more concerned with conscious aspects of the patient's functioning. They also recognize the impact of cultural and interpersonal influences on behavior across the lifespan (Adler, 1938; Mitchell & Black, 1995). Beyond Freud's emphasis on sexuality and aggression, neo-Freudians acknowledge the impact of other powerful needs, including love, dependence, power, and status. They're also more optimistic than was Freud regarding people's prospects for achieving healthy psychological functioning (see Chapter 12).

One such neo-Freudian is Harry Stack Sullivan (1954), who argued that psychotherapy is a collaborative undertaking between patient and therapist. Sullivan contended that

The Freudian concept of free association is a bit like a magician pulling kerchiefs out of a hat, with one thought leading to the next, in turn leading to the next, and so on.

RULING OUT RIVAL HYPOTHESES
Have important alternative explanations for the findings been excluded?

GLOSSARY

free association
technique in which patients express themselves without censorship of any sort

resistance
attempts to avoid confrontation and anxiety associated with uncovering previously repressed thoughts, emotions, and impulses

transference
projecting intense, unrealistic feelings and expectations from the past onto the therapist

work through
confront and resolve problems, conflicts, and ineffective coping responses in everyday life

Interpersonal therapy aims to resolve interpersonal problems and conflicts and to teach people social skills.

REPLICABILITY
Can the results be duplicated in other studies?

FALSIFIABILITY
Can the claim be disproved?

RULING OUT RIVAL HYPOTHESES
Have important alternative explanations for the findings been excluded?

GLOSSARY

interpersonal therapy
treatment that strengthens social skills and targets interpersonal problems, conflicts, and life transitions

humanistic psychotherapy
therapy that shares an emphasis on the development of human potential and the belief that human nature is basically positive

the analyst's proper role is that of *participant observer*. Through her ongoing observation of the patient, the analyst discovers and communicates to the patient his unrealistic attitudes and behaviors in social situations and other arenas of everyday life.

Sullivan's work influenced the contemporary approach of **interpersonal therapy (IPT)**. Originally a treatment for depression (Klerman, Weisman, Rounsaville, et al., 1984; Santor & Kusumakar, 2001), IPT is a short-term (12 to 16 sessions) intervention designed to strengthen people's social skills and assist them in coping with interpersonal problems, conflicts (such as disputes with family members), and life transitions (such as childbirth and retirement). In addition to effectively treating depression (Klerman et al., 1984; Hinrichsen, 2008), IPT has demonstrated success in the treatment of substance abuse and eating disorders (Klerman & Weissman, 1993; Weissman, Markowitz, & Klerman, 2000).

Psychodynamic Therapies Evaluated Critically. Valuable as they've been, many psychodynamic therapies are questionable from a scientific standpoint. Freud based his therapeutic observations largely on small samples of wealthy, intelligent, and successful people, rendering their external validity (see Chapter 2) unclear. His clinical sessions weren't observed by others or conducted on a systematic basis that permitted examination and replication by others, as would be the case with rigorously controlled research. Moreover, Freud's patients relied on memories that stretched to the distant past. As we learned in Chapter 6, many early memories, especially those prompted by suggestive questions, are of questionable validity.

As we've seen, psychodynamic therapies rely heavily on insight. Many Hollywood films, like the 1999 movie *Analyze This*, reinforce the impression that insight—especially into the childhood origins of one's problems—is always the crucial ingredient in psychotherapeutic change. Yet extensive research demonstrates that understanding our emotional history, however deep and gratifying, isn't required to relieve psychological distress (Weisz, Weiss, Han, et al., 1995). To improve, patients typically need to practice new and more adaptive behaviors in everyday life (Wachtel, 1997).

Some psychodynamic concepts, including Freud's therapeutic interpretations, are difficult to falsify (see Chapter 12). How can we demonstrate that a person's dream of his father scowling at him, for example, points to repressed memories of child abuse, as a therapist might infer? A patient might respond, "Aha, that's it!" but this reaction could reflect transference or an attempt to please the therapist. If the patient improves, the therapist might conclude that the interpretation is accurate, but the timing could be coincidental (Grunbaum, 1984).

The failure to rule out rival hypotheses may lead both therapist and patient to mistakenly attribute progress to insight and interpretation when other influences are responsible (Meyer, 1981). The concerns we've raised aside, research indicates that brief versions of psychodynamic therapy are better than no treatment (Leichsenring, Rabung, & Liebing, 2004), at least for some problems.

Humanistic Psychotherapy: Achieving Our Potential.
Humanistic psychotherapy, logically enough, is rooted in the humanistic perspective (Chapter 12). In contrast to psychodynamic therapies, therapies within this orientation share an emphasis on the realization of human potential and the belief that human nature is basically positive (Maslow, 1954; Rogers, 1961; Shlien & Levant, 1984).

Humanistic therapists work to help people overcome the sense of alienation so prevalent in our culture; to develop their sensory and emotional awareness; and to express their creativity and help them become loving, responsible, and authentic. Humanistic psychotherapists stress the importance of assuming responsibility for decisions, not attributing our problems to the past, and living fully in the present.

Although sharing an emphasis on insight with psychoanalytic therapists, humanistic therapists reject their interpretive techniques. Instead, these therapists strive to understand the inner world of the patient through empathy and intuition. Therapists focus on the subjective phenomena (thoughts, feelings) patients experience in the present moment.

Person-Centered Therapy: Attaining Acceptance.

No therapist better exemplifies the practice of humanistic therapy than Carl Rogers (see Chapter 12). His therapy is nondirective because therapists don't define or diagnose patients' problems or try to get at the root cause of their difficulties. His approach is also called *person-centered therapy* because therapists don't tell patients how to solve their problems, and patients can use the therapy hour however they choose. Therapists assume that patients will reveal important emotional patterns as the therapist–patient dialogue unfolds (Rogers, 1942) (see **Table 14.3**). To ensure a positive outcome, the therapist must satisfy three conditions:

(1) The therapist must be an authentic, genuine person who reveals his or her own reactions to what the patient is communicating.

(2) The therapist must express *unconditional positive regard,* that is, a nonjudgmental acceptance of all feelings the patient expresses.

(3) The therapist must relate to patients with empathic understanding.

With increased awareness and heightened self-acceptance, people hopefully come to think more realistically, become more tolerant of others, and engage in more adaptive behaviors (Rogers, 1961).

Humanistic Therapies Evaluated Critically.

The core concepts of humanistic therapy, such as meaning and self-actualization, are difficult to measure and falsify. For example, at exactly what point can we say a person is self-aware and authentic?

According to Carl Rogers, when children receive unconditional positive regard from parents, they will develop unconditional self-regard, which promotes self-actualization.

FALSIFIABILITY
Can the claim be disproved?

Table 14.3 Simulated Conversation between Client and Computer Therapist, Eliza. Some researchers have developed computer programs that attempt to simulate Rogers's person-centered therapy. Here, we can read excerpts from a conversation between a patient and the computer therapist, Eliza, developed by computer scientist Joseph Weizenbaum. Would Eliza make a good therapist?

Client: Men are all alike.

Eliza: IN WHAT WAY?

Client: They're always bugging us about something or other.

Eliza: CAN YOU THINK OF A SPECIFIC EXAMPLE?

Client: Well, my boyfriend made me come here.

Eliza: YOUR BOYFRIEND MADE YOU COME HERE?

Client: He says I'm depressed much of the time.

Eliza: I AM SORRY TO HEAR YOU ARE DEPRESSED.

Client: It's true. I am unhappy.

Eliza: DO YOU THINK COMING HERE WILL HELP YOU NOT TO BE UNHAPPY?

Client: I need some help, that much seems certain.

Eliza: WHAT WOULD IT MEAN TO YOU IF YOU GOT SOME HELP?

Client: Perhaps I could learn to get along with my mother.

Eliza: TELL ME MORE ABOUT YOUR FAMILY.

Client: My mother takes care of me.

Eliza: WHO ELSE IN YOUR FAMILY TAKES CARE OF YOU?

Client: My father.

Eliza: YOUR FATHER?

Client: You are like my father in some ways.

Eliza: WHAT RESEMBLANCE DO YOU SEE?

(*Source:* http://i5.nyu.edu/~mm64/x52.9265/january1966.htm/; Weizenbaum)

Much to his credit, Rogers specified three key conditions for effective psychotherapy that could be falsified. Research has shown that he was largely on the mark when it comes to the therapeutic relationship. Establishing a strong alliance is extremely helpful to the ultimate success of therapy (Horvath & Bedi, 2002; Wampold, 2001). But Rogers was wrong in one key respect: The three core conditions he specified aren't the only way to achieve improvement (Bohart, 2003; Norcross & Beutler, 1997). In fact, we'll learn later in the chapter that some people can derive considerable benefits from self-help programs that don't even involve therapists (Gould & Clum, 1993), so the therapeutic relationship isn't necessary for improvement.

Person-centered therapy is more effective than no treatment (Greenberg, Elliott, & Lietaer, 1994) and is particularly popular in college counseling centers (Champney & Schultz, 1983). But findings concerning the effectiveness of person-centered therapy are inconsistent, with some suggesting it may not help much more than a placebo treatment, such as merely chatting for the same amount of time with a nonprofessional (Smith, Glass, & Miller, 1980). In contrast, other studies suggest that person-centered therapies and experiential approaches often result in substantial gains in many patients and may be comparable in effectiveness to the cognitive-behavioral therapies we'll encounter later (Elliott, 2002; Greenberg & Watson, 1998).

BEHAVIORAL APPROACHES: CHANGING MALADAPTIVE ACTIONS

In sharp contrast to psychotherapists who hold that insight is the key to improvement, **behavior therapists** are so named because they focus on the specific behaviors that lead the patient to seek therapy and the current variables that maintain problematic thoughts, feelings, and behaviors (Antony & Roemer, 2003). **[LEARNING OBJECTIVE 14.5]**

The results of behavior therapy are evaluated based on whether there is measurable improvement in target behaviors, like angry outbursts, compulsions (see Chapter 13), or suicide threats. Behavior therapists assume that behavior change, whether in the clinic, family, or school, results from the operation of basic principles of learning discovered in the laboratory, especially classical conditioning, operant conditioning, and observational learning (see Chapter 5). Behavior therapists use a wide variety of *behavioral assessment* techniques to pinpoint environmental causes of the person's problem, establish specific and measurable treatment goals, and devise therapeutic procedures. The emphasis is on current, rather than past, behaviors and on specific behaviors, rather than broad traits. Once the behavioral therapist has identified the problem, she may employ a variety of different treatment approaches.

Let's now examine the nuts and bolts of several behavioral approaches.

Systematic Desensitization and Exposure Therapies: Learning Principles in Action.
Systematic desensitization is an excellent example of how behavior therapists apply learning principles to treatment. Psychiatrist Joseph Wolpe developed systematic desensitization (SD) in 1958 to help patients manage phobias. Systematic desensitization gradually exposes patients to anxiety-producing situations through the use of imagined scenes. Systematic desensitization was the earliest **exposure therapy,** a term that refers to a class of procedures that confronts patients with what they fear, with the goal of reducing this fear.

How Desensitization Works: One Step at a Time. Systematic desensitization is based on the principle of *reciprocal inhibition,* which says that patients can't experience two conflicting responses simultaneously. We can't be anxious and relaxed at the same time. A therapist begins systematic desensitization by teaching the patient how to relax. She might imagine pleasant scenes, focus on breathing and maintaining a slow breathing

A behavior therapist performing an assessment of a bad habit, like nail-biting, would try to determine the situations in which nail-biting occurs, as well as the consequences of nail-biting for the person—such as short-term distraction from anxiety.

GLOSSARY

behavior therapist
therapist who focuses on specific problem behaviors and current variables that maintain problematic thoughts, feelings, and behaviors

systematic desensitization
patients are taught to relax as they are gradually exposed in a stepwise manner to what they fear

exposure therapy
therapy that confronts patients with what they fear, with the goal of reducing the fear

rate, and alternately tense and relax her muscles (Bernstein, Borkovec, & Hazlett-Stevens, 2000; Jacobson, 1938). Next, the therapist helps the patient to construct an *anxiety hierarchy*—a "ladder" of situations or scenes that climb from least to most anxiety provoking. We can find a hierarchy used to treat a person with height phobia in **Table 14.4.** The therapy proceeds in a stepwise manner. The therapist asks the patient to relax and imagine the first scene, and moves to the next, more anxiety-producing scene only after the patient reports feeling relaxed while imagining the first scene.

Table 14.4 A Systematic Desensitization Hierarchy of a Person with a Fear of Heights.

(1) You are beginning to climb the ladder leaning against the side of your house. You plan to work on the roof.

(2) You are driving with the family on a California coastal highway with a dropoff to the right.

(3) You are in a commercial airliner at the time of takeoff.

(4) You are in an airliner at an altitude of 30,000 feet experiencing considerable turbulence.

(5) You are on a California seaside cliff, approximately 2 feet (judged to be a safe distance) from the edge and looking down.

(6) You are climbing a water tower to assist in painting, about 10 feet from the ground.

(7) You are on the catwalk around the water tank, painting the tank.

(*Source:* Rimm & Masters, 1979)

If the patient reports anxiety at any point, the therapist interrupts the process and helps the patient relax again. Then, the therapist reintroduces the scene that preceded the one that caused anxiety. This process continues until the patient can confront the most frightening scenes without anxiety.

Desensitization can also occur *in vivo,* that is, in "real life." In vivo systematic desensitization involves real-life, gradual exposure to what the patient actually fears, rather than imagining the anxiety-provoking situation. Systematic desensitization is effective for a wide range of phobias, and can also help people to avoid anxiety that contributes to insomnia, speech disorders, asthma attacks, nightmares, and some cases of problem drinking (Spiegler & Guevremont, 2003).

Flooding and Virtual Reality Exposure. Flooding therapies provide a vivid contrast to systematic desensitization. Flooding therapists jump right to the top of the anxiety hierarchy and expose patients to images of the stimuli they fear the most for prolonged periods, ranging from 10 minutes to several hours. Flooding therapies are based on the idea that fears are maintained by avoidance. For example, because height phobics continually avoid high places, they never learn that the disastrous consequences they envision won't occur. Ironically, their avoidance only reinforces their fears by means of negative reinforcement (see Chapter 5). The flooding therapist provokes anxiety repeatedly in the absence of actual negative consequences, so that extinction of the fear can occur.

In vivo desensitization: Clients gradually approach and handle any fears, as these clients are doing as they overcome their fear of flying.

Like systematic desensitization, flooding can also be conducted in vivo (Chambless & Goldstein, 1980). During the very first session, a therapist who practices in vivo flooding might accompany a height phobic to the top of a skyscraper and look down for an hour or however long it takes for anxiety to dissipate. Remarkably, many people with specific phobias—including those who were in psychodynamic therapy for decades with no relief—have been essentially cured of their fears after only a single session (Antony & Barlow, 2002; Williams, Turner, & Peer, 1985). Therapists have used flooding with success in treating numerous anxiety disorders, including obsessive-compulsive disorder, social phobia, post-traumatic stress disorder, and agoraphobia.

A crucial component of flooding is *response prevention,* in which therapists prevent patients from performing their typical avoidance behaviors (Spiegler, 1983). A therapist may treat a person with a hand-washing compulsion by exposing her to dirt and preventing her from washing her hands (Franklin & Foa, 2002).

Exposure: Fringe and Fad Techniques. Traditionally, behavior therapists have been careful not to inflate claims of the effectiveness of exposure therapy or present it to the public as a cure-all. We can contrast this cautious approach with that of recent proponents of fringe therapeutic techniques who've made extraordinary claims that don't stack up well against the evidence.

EXTRAORDINARY CLAIMS
Is the evidence as convincing as the claim?

Roger Callahan, who developed *Thought Field Therapy* (TFT), claimed that his procedure can cure phobias in as little as 5 minutes (Callahan, 1995, 2001) and cure not only human fears but also fears in horses and dogs. In TFT, the patient thinks of a distressing problem while the therapist taps specific points on her body in a predetermined order. Meanwhile, the patient hums parts of "The Star Spangled Banner," rolls her eyes, or counts (how TFT therapists accomplish this feat with animals is unknown). These decidedly strange procedures supposedly remove invisible "energy blocks" associated with a specific fear. There's no research evidence for the extraordinary assertion that the technique cures anxiety by manipulating energy fields, which have never been shown to exist, or for the incredible claim of virtually instantaneous cures for the vast majority of phobia sufferers (Lohr et al., 2003). Because the "energy blocks" of TFT are not measurable, the theoretical claims of TFT are unfalsifiable.

FALSIFIABILITY
Can the claim be disproved?

Another unsupported therapy is *eye movement desensitization and reprocessing* (EMDR), which has been marketed widely as a "breakthrough" treatment for anxiety disorders (Shapiro, 1995; Shapiro & Forrest, 1997). As of 2007, more than 70,000 therapists had been trained in EMDR. EMDR proponents claim that patients' side-to-side eye movements, made while they imagine a past traumatic event, enhance their processing of painful memories. Yet research indicates that the eye movements of EMDR play no role in this treatment's effectiveness. Moreover, EMDR is no more effective than standard exposure treatments (Davidson & Parker, 2001; Lohr, Tolin, & Lilienfeld, 1998). A more parsimonious explanation is that the active ingredient of EMDR isn't the eye movements for which it's named but rather the exposure the technique provides.

OCCAM'S RAZOR
Does a simpler explanation fit the data just as well?

Modeling in Therapy: Learning by Watching.

Patients can learn many things by observing therapists model positive behaviors. Modeling is one form of *observational learning* (see Chapter 5). Albert Bandura (1971, 1977) has long advocated **participant modeling,** a technique in which the therapist first models a calm encounter with the patient's feared object or situation and then guides the patient through the steps of the encounter until she can cope unassisted. Modeling is also an important component of assertion and social skills training programs designed to help patients with social anxiety.

Behavioral rehearsal is used commonly in participant modeling techniques. In behavioral rehearsal, the patient engages in role-playing with a therapist to learn and practice new skills. The therapist plays the role of a relevant person such as a spouse, parent, or boss. The patient reacts to the character enacted by the therapist, and in return the therapist offers coaching and feedback. To give the patient an opportunity to model assertive behaviors, therapist and patient reverse roles, with the therapist playing the patient's role. To transfer what patients learn to everyday life, therapists encourage them to practice their newly found skills outside of therapy sessions. Modeling and social skills training can make valuable contributions to treating (although not curing) schizophrenia, depression, and social anxiety (Antony & Roemer, 2003; Dilk & Bond, 1996).

In EMDR, the patient focuses on the therapist's fingers as they move back and forth. Nevertheless, studies indicate that such eye movements play no useful role in EMDR's effectiveness.

Operant Procedures: Consequences Count.

As we learned in Chapter 5, token economy has been used as a form of operant conditioning in treatment programs in institutional and residential settings, as well as at home. As we'll recall, operant procedures modify behaviors based on their consequences. One of the essential features of token economies is that certain behaviors, like helping others, are consistently rewarded with tokens that patients can later exchange for more tangible rewards, whereas other behaviors, like screaming at hospital staff, are ignored or punished. In this way, token economy programs shape, maintain, or alter behaviors by the consistent application of operant conditioning principles (Kazdin, 1978). Token economies have proven successful in the classroom (Boniecki & Moore, 2003), in treating children with ADHD at home and at school (Mueser & Liberman, 1995), and in treating patients with schizophrenia in hospitals (Dickerson, Tenhula, & Green-Paden, 2005; McMonagle & Sultana, 2000; Paul & Lentz, 1977).

GLOSSARY

participant modeling
technique in which the therapist first models a problematic situation and then guides the patient through steps to cope with it unassisted

Aversion therapies use punishment to decrease the frequency of undesirable behaviors. Aversion therapies are aptly named. While a person engages in a problem behavior, therapists introduce a wide range of stimuli that most people experience as painful, distasteful, unpleasant, or even revolting. For example, therapists have used medications, such as disulfiram—better known as Antabuse—to make people vomit after drinking alcohol (Brewer, 1992), electric shocks to treat psychologically triggered recurrent sneezing (Kushner, 1968), and verbal descriptions of feeling nauseous while people imagine smoking cigarettes (Cautela, 1971).

Research provides at best mixed support for the effectiveness of aversive procedures (Spiegler & Guevremont, 2003). For example, alcohol abusers often prefer to stop taking Antabuse rather than stop drinking (MacKillop et al., 2003). In general, therapists attempt minimally unpleasant techniques before moving on to more aversive measures. The decision to implement aversion methods should be made only after carefully weighing the costs and benefits of these methods relative to alternative approaches.

Cognitive-Behavioral Therapies: Learning to Think Differently.
Advocates of **cognitive-behavioral therapies** hold that beliefs play the central role in our feelings and behaviors. For them, irrational thinking lies at the root of psychopathology. These therapies share the following core assumptions: (1) cognitions can be identified and measured, (2) cognitions are the key players in both healthy and unhealthy psychological functioning, and (3) irrational beliefs, such as "I'm worthless," can be replaced by more rational and adaptive cognitions.

The ABCs of Rational Emotive Behavior Therapy.
Beginning in the mid-1950s, pioneering therapist Albert Ellis (Ellis, 1958, 1962) advocated *rational emotive therapy* (RET), more recently renamed *rational emotive behavior therapy* (REBT). In many respects, REBT is a prime example of a cognitive-behavioral approach. It's cognitive in its emphasis on changing how we think (that's the "cognitive" part), but it also focuses on changing how we act (that's the "behavioral" part).

Ellis argued that we respond to an activating (internal or external) event (A) with a range of emotional and behavioral consequences (C). As we all know, people often respond very differently to the same objective event; some students respond to a C on an exam by celebrating, whereas others respond by berating themselves for not getting an A or B. The crucial differences in how we respond to the same objective events stem largely from differences in (B)—our belief systems (see **Figure 14.1** on page 502). The ABCs Ellis identified lie at the heart of most, if not all, cognitive-behavior therapies.

Some beliefs are rational: They're flexible, logical, and promote self-acceptance. In contrast, irrational beliefs are associated with unrealistic demands about the self ("I must be perfect"), other people ("I must become worried about other people's problems"), and life conditions ("I must be worried about things I can't control"). Ellis also maintained that psychologically unhealthy people frequently "awfulize," that is, engage in catastrophic thinking about their problems ("If I don't get this job, it would be the worst thing that ever happened to me"). We can find examples of 12 irrational beliefs outlined by Ellis in **Table 14.5** on page 502. According to Ellis, our vulnerability to psychological disturbance is a product of the frequency and strength of our irrational beliefs.

To his ABC scheme, Ellis added a (D) and an (E) component to describe how therapists treat patients. REBT therapists encourage patients to actively dispute (D) their irrational beliefs and adopt more effective (E) and rational beliefs to increase adaptive responses.

Other Cognitive-Behavioral Approaches.
Cognitive-behavioral therapists differ in the extent to which they incorporate behavioral methods. Aaron Beck's (Beck, Rush, Shaw, et al., 1979)

LOVE ME, LOVE ME, ONLY ME!

Love me, love me, only me
Or I'll die without you!
Make your love a guarantee,
So I can never doubt you!
Love me, love me totally
Really, really try dear.
But if you demand love, too,
I'll hate you till I die, dear!
Love me, love me all the time,
Thoroughly and wholly!
Life turns into slushy slime
Less you love me solely!
Love me with great tenderness,
With no ifs or buts dear.
If you love me somewhat less,
I'll really hate your guts, dear!

Albert Ellis wrote a number of humorous song lyrics to demonstrate REBT principles. This song, set to the tune of Yankee Doodle, pokes fun at the widespread but irrational belief that all romantic relationships should be characterized by promises of complete, unconditional, and never-ending love. (Adapted from "Love Me, Love Me, Only Me!" by Albert Ellis. Reprinted with permission of Albert Ellis Institute)

Two pioneers of cognitive-behavioral therapy, Aaron Beck (*left;* 1921–) and Albert Ellis (1913–2007).

GLOSSARY

aversion therapy
treatment that uses punishment to decrease the frequency of undesirable behaviors

cognitive-behavioral therapy
treatment that attempts to replace maladaptive or irrational cognitions and behaviors with more adaptive, rational ones

Figure 14.1 The ABCs of Rational Emotive Behavior Therapy. How someone feels about the consequences of an event is determined by his or her beliefs or opinions about the event.

Table 14.5 Irrational Beliefs: "The Dirty Dozen." Albert Ellis identified 12 irrational ideas ("The Dirty Dozen") that are widespread in our culture. You may find it interesting to see which of these beliefs you've entertained at some point in your life. Because these ideas are so much a part of many people's thinking, don't be surprised if you hold a number of them.

1 You must have sincere love and approval almost all the time from all the people you find significant.	7 You will find it easier to avoid facing many of life's difficulties and self-responsibilities than to undertake some rewarding forms of self-discipline.
2 You must prove yourself thoroughly competent, adequate, and achieving; or you must at least have real competence or talent at something important.	8 Your past remains all-important, and because something once strongly influenced your life, it has to keep determining your feelings and behavior today.
3 People who harm you or commit misdeeds rate as generally bad, wicked, or villainous individuals, and you should severely blame, damn, and punish them for their sins.	9 People and things should turn out better than they do, and you have to view it as awful and horrible if you do not quickly find good solutions to life's hassles.
4 Life proves awful, terrible, horrible, or catastrophic when things do not go the way you would like them to go.	10 You can achieve happiness by inaction or by passively and uncommitedly "enjoying yourself."
5 Emotional misery comes from external pressures, and you have little ability to control your feelings or rid yourself of depression and hostility.	11 You must have a high degree of order or certainty to feel comfortable.
6 If something seems dangerous or fearsome, you must become terribly occupied with and upset about it.	12 You give yourself a global rating as a human, and your general worth and self-acceptance depend on the goodness of your performance and the degree that people approve of you.

(*Source:* Ellis, 1977)

enormously popular *cognitive therapy,* which many credit as playing an instrumental role in creating the field of cognitive-behavioral therapy, emphasizes identifying and modifying distorted thoughts and long-held negative core beliefs ("I'm unlovable") (J.S. Beck, 1995). Nevertheless, cognitive therapy places somewhat greater weight on behavioral procedures than does Ellis's REBT (Stricker & Gold, 2003). Researchers have found Beck's approach helpful for people with depression and perhaps even bipolar disorder and schizophrenia (Beck, 2005; Hollon, Thase, & Markowitz, 2002).

The Effectiveness of CBT. Research allows us to draw the following conclusions about the effectiveness of behavioral and cognitive-behavioral therapies:

(1) They're more effective than no treatment or placebo treatment (Bowers & Clum, 1988; Smith, Glass, & Miller, 1980).

(2) They're at least as effective (Sloane, Staples, Cristol, et al., 1975; Smith & Glass, 1977), and in some cases more effective, than psychodynamic and person-centered therapies (Grawe, Donati, & Bernauer, 1998).

(3) Therapists can combine them effectively with other forms of treatment, such as drug therapy and couples counseling (Hahlweg & Markman, 1988; MTA Cooperative Group, 1999).

(4) They're at least as effective as drug therapies for depression (Elkin, 1994). In general, CBT and behavioral treatments are about equally effective for most problems (Feske & Chambless, 1995; Jacobson et al., 1996).

The Trend toward Eclecticism and Integration.

One of the current trends in psychotherapy is for therapists to create individually tailored, *eclectic* approaches—treatments that integrate techniques and theories from many existing therapy approaches (Garske & Anderson, 2003; Lazarus, 2006; Stricker & Gold, 2003). Nearly 30 percent of clinical and counseling psychologists and over 50 percent of psychiatrists characterize themselves as "eclectic" (Norcross, 2005; Prochaska & Norcross, 2007).

For example, Marsha Linehan's (Linehan, 1993; Lynch, Trost, Salsman, & Linehan, 2007) *dialectical behavior therapy,* used frequently in the treatment of borderline personality-disordered patients at risk for suicide, includes features from multiple therapeutic approaches. Steven Hayes's (Hayes, Strosahl, & Wilson, 1999) *acceptance and commitment therapy* also incorporates techniques from a wide variety of approaches. These approaches involve encouraging patients to accept their thoughts and feelings while making changes in their behaviors.

Although there's growing evidence that integrative approaches are effective (Linehan, Heard, & Armstrong, 1993; Norcross & Goldfried, 2005), psychologists know virtually nothing about the roles specific therapeutic components play in accounting for treatment success. The more ingredients tossed into the mix, the more challenging it becomes to dismantle integrative approaches and evaluate rival hypotheses regarding which ingredients matter.

There's at least some evidence that therapists' theoretical orientation is correlated with their personality traits. Several, although not all, studies suggest that compared with other therapists, psychoanalytic therapists tend to be especially insecure and serious, behavior therapists tend to be especially assertive and self-confident, and cognitive-behavioral therapists tend to be especially rational (Keinan, Almagor, & Ben-Porath, 1989; Walton, 1978).

RULING OUT RIVAL HYPOTHESES
Have important alternative explanations for the findings been excluded?

GROUP AND FAMILY SYSTEMS THERAPIES: THE MORE, THE MERRIER

Since the early 1920s, when Viennese psychiatrist Jacob Moreno introduced the term **group therapy,** helping professionals have appreciated the value of treating more than one person at a time. Group and family therapies are now well positioned in the mainstream of psychotherapeutic approaches.

Group Therapies.

Group therapies are efficient, time saving, and less costly than individual treatment methods and span all major schools of psychotherapy (Levine, 1979). In a safe group environment, participants can provide and receive support, exchange information and feedback, model effective behaviors and practice new skills, and recognize that adjustment problems are shared by many other people (Yalom, 1985). **[LEARNING OBJECTIVE 14.6]**

Group therapy reaches people of all races, ages, and economic levels, including people who are blind, divorced, experiencing marital problems, struggling with their gender identity, and suffering from alcoholism and eating disorders (Dies, 2003; Lynn & Frauman, 1985). The most recent trend is for self-help groups to form over the Internet, especially for people with illnesses and problems that may be embarrassing to

Group therapy procedures are efficient, time saving, and less costly than many individual treatment methods.

GLOSSARY

group therapy
therapy that treats more than one person at a time

Al-Anon is a support group organization designed to support the families of those with alcohol problems.

share in face-to-face encounters (Davison, Pennebaker, & Dickerson, 2000). Research suggests that many group procedures are effective for a wide range of problems and about as helpful as individual treatment methods (Davis, Olmstead, Rockert, et al., 1997; Fuhriman & Burlingame, 1994).

Alcoholics Anonymous. Self-help groups are composed of peers who share a similar problem. Over the past several decades, these groups, of which **Alcoholics Anonymous (AA)** is the best known, have become remarkably popular. AA was founded in 1935 and is now the largest organization for treating alcoholics, with more than 1.7 million members worldwide (Humphreys, 2000). At AA meetings, people share their struggles with alcohol, and new members are "sponsored" or mentored by more senior members who've often achieved years of sobriety. AA members encourage new participants to attend daily meetings for the first 3 months and regular meetings thereafter.

AA has inspired the creation of Al-Anon and Alateen, groups that help spouses and children of alcoholics cope with alcohol abuse. Groups based on the AA model have been established for drug users (Narcotics Anonymous), gamblers, overeaters, "shopaholics" (compulsive shoppers), sex addicts, and people experiencing problems with other types of impulse control.

Although AA appears to be helpful for some people, many of the claims regarding its success aren't supported by data. People who attend AA meetings fare about as well as, but no better than, people who receive other treatments, including cognitive-behavioral therapy (Brandsma, Maultsby, & Welsh, 1980; Ferri, Amoto, & Davoli, 2006; Project MATCH Research Group, 1997; Walsh et al., 1991). Moreover, people who participate in studies of AA may be atypical in certain respects. AA members who end up in studies are usually the most active participants and have received prior professional help. Also, as many as 68 percent of participants drop out within 3 months of joining AA (Emrick, 1987). Research is needed to clarify which alcoholics AA best serves (MacKillop et al., 2003).

WHAT DO *you* THINK?

You are interested in addiction treatments and have read about the effectiveness of AA and other group therapy programs, but you are concerned about the fact that many studies overlook the large proportion of participants who drop out early in the process. How might you design a longitudinal study (see Chapter 8) to get a more accurate sense of AA's success rate?

GLOSSARY

Alcoholics Anonymous
self-help program that provides social support for achieving sobriety

family therapy
therapy in which the focus of treatment is the family as a unit rather than an individual

Controlled Drinking and Relapse Prevention. Contrary to the AA belief that people are powerless to control their drinking and must remain totally abstinent from alcohol, the behavioral view assumes that excessive drinking is a learned behavior that therapists can modify and control without total abstinence (Marlatt, 1983). There's considerable evidence that treatment programs that encourage alcoholics to set limits, drink moderately, and reinforce their progress can be effective for many patients (MacKillop et al., 2003; Miller & Hester, 1980; Sobell & Sobell, 1973, 1976). Programs that teach people skills to cope with stressful life circumstances and tolerate negative emotions (Monti, Gulliver, & Myers, 1994) are at least as effective as programs such as AA (Project MATCH Research Group, 1997). Token economies (see Chapter 5) may also be effective in curbing substance use during addiction rehabilitation (Glosser, 1983).

Family Therapies: Treating The Dysfunctional Family System. Family therapists see most psychological problems as rooted in a dysfunctional family system. For them, treatment must focus on the family context out of which conflicts presumably arise. In **family therapy**, the "patient"—the focus of treatment—isn't one person but rather the family unit itself.

Strategic family interventions are designed to remove barriers to effective communication. **[LEARNING OBJECTIVE 14.7]** According to strategic therapists, families often scapegoat one family member as the problem even though the real source of difficulties lies in the dysfunctional ways in which family members communicate, solve problems, and relate to one another (see **Figure 14.2**) (Haley, 1976; Satir, 1964; Watzlawick, Weakland, & Fisch, 1974). Strategic therapists first identify the family's unhealthy communication patterns and its unsuccessful approaches to problem solving. Then, they invite family members to carry out planned tasks known as *directives.* Directives shift how family members solve problems and interact.

In *structural family therapy* (Minuchin, 1974), the therapist actively immerses herself in the everyday activities of the family to make changes in how they arrange and organize interactions. Salvatore Minuchin and his colleagues successfully treated a 14-year-old girl named Laura who obtained her father's attention by refusing to eat. Eventually, Laura could express in words the message that her refusal to eat conveyed indirectly, and she no longer refused to eat to attain affection (Aponte & Hoffman, 1973). Research indicates that family therapy is more effective than no treatment (Hazelrigg, Cooper, & Borduin, 1987; Vetere, 2001) and at least as effective as individual therapy (Foster & Gurman, 1985; Shadish, 1995).

Figure 14.2 Where's the Problem?
According to the strategic family therapy approach, families often single out one family member as "the problem" when the problem is actually rooted in the interactional patterns of all family members.

In structural family therapy, the therapist immerses herself in the family's everyday activities. Having observed what goes on in the family, the therapist can then advocate for changes in how the family arranges and organizes its interactions.

QUIZ

1 An important criticism of psychoanalytic therapy is that many of its key concepts aren't falsifiable.	TRUE	FALSE
2 Reflection is a central component of Rogers's therapy.	TRUE	FALSE
3 According to Albert Ellis, feelings create irrational beliefs.	TRUE	FALSE
4 Group psychotherapies are generally as effective as individual psychotherapies.	TRUE	FALSE
5 Family therapies focus on the one person in the family with the most problems.	TRUE	FALSE

Answers: (1) T (p. 496); (2) T (p. 497); (3) F (p. 501); (4) T (p. 503); (5) F (p. 505)

PEARSON
mypsychlab

▼ Would you like to experience what therapy is like? Watch the video titled "Family Therapist" at www.mypsychlab.com to find out.

Is Psychotherapy Effective?

In Lewis Carroll's book *Alice in Wonderland,* the dodo bird proclaimed after a race that "All have won, and all must have prizes." Seventy years ago, Saul Rosenzweig (1936) delivered the same verdict regarding the effectiveness of different psychotherapies. That is, all appear to be helpful but are roughly equivalent in terms of their outcomes (see **Figure 14.3**).

THE DODO BIRD VERDICT: ALIVE OR EXTINCT?

Today, some authors have concluded that the "dodo bird verdict" still holds. Some analyses suggest that a wide range of psychotherapies are about equal in their effects (Garske & Anderson, 2003; Grissom, 1996; Wampold et al., 1997, 2002). Studies with experienced therapists who've practiced behavioral, psychodynamic, and person-centered approaches have found that all are more successful in helping patients compared with no treatment but no different from each other in their effects (DiLoretto, 1971; Sloane et al., 1975). **[LEARNING OBJECTIVE 14.8]**

Other researchers aren't convinced. They contend that the dodo bird verdict, like the real dodo bird, is extinct. Although most forms of psychotherapy work well, and many are about equal in their effects, there are notable exceptions (Beutler, 2002; Hunsley & DiGuilio, 2002). For example, behavioral and cognitive-behavioral treatments are clearly more effective than other treatments for children and adolescents with behavior problems (Garske & Anderson, 2003; Weisz et al., 1995). Moreover, behavioral and cognitive-behavioral therapies consistently outperform most other therapies for anxiety disorders, including phobias, panic disorder, and obsessive-compulsive disorder (Addis et al., 2004; Chambless & Ollendick, 2001; Hunsley & DiGuilio, 2002).

Also calling into question the dodo bird verdict are findings that some psychotherapies can make people worse (Lilienfeld, 2007). Although we might assume that doing something is always better than doing nothing for psychological distress, research suggests otherwise. A nontrivial proportion of patients, perhaps 5 to 10 percent, tend to become worse following psychotherapy, and some of them may become worse *because of* psychotherapy (Lilienfeld, 2007; Rhule, 2005; Strupp, Hadley, & Gomez-Schwartz, 1978). For example, several researchers have found that crisis debriefing can sometimes increase the risk of posttraumatic stress symptoms in people exposed to trauma. The same may be true for certain grief therapies, especially among people who are experiencing relatively normal grief reactions to the death of loved ones (Neimeyer, 2000). We can see a number of other potentially harmful therapies in **Table 14.6.**

The bottom line? Many therapies are effective, and many do about equally well probably because most share certain features like empathetic listening and offer new ways of thinking and behaving. Yet there are clear-cut exceptions to the dodo bird verdict. Moreover, because at least some therapies appear to be harmful, we shouldn't assume that we'll always be safe picking a random therapist out of the telephone book.

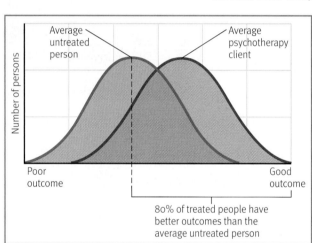

Figure 14.3 The Effectiveness of Psychotherapy. This graph shows two normal distributions (see Chapter 2) derived from nearly 500 studies of psychotherapy outcomes. The distribution on the left shows people who haven't received psychotherapy, and the distribution on the right shows people who've received psychotherapy. As we can see, across a variety of treatments and samples, 80 percent of people who receive therapy do better than the average untreated person (*Source:* Smith, Glass, and Miller, 1980)

EMPIRICALLY SUPPORTED TREATMENTS

With 500 or more therapies on the market, how are mental health consumers to tell which ones work better than others? Over the past decade or so, researchers have responded to this question by putting forth lists of **empirically supported therapies (ESTs)**—treatments for specific disorders that are backed by high-quality scientific evidence (Chambless et al., 1996).

GLOSSARY

empirically supported therapies treatments for specific disorders supported by high-quality scientific evidence

Table 14.6 List of Potentially Harmful Therapies.

Therapy	Intervention	Potential Harm
Facilitated Communication	A facilitator holds the hands of children with autism or other developmental disabilities as they type messages on a keyboard (Chapter 2).	False accusations of child abuse against family members
Scared Straight Programs	At-risk adolescents are exposed to the harsh realities of prison life to frighten them away from a life of future crime (shown here).	Worsening of conduct problems
Recovered-Memory Techniques	Therapists use methods to recover memories, including prompting of memories, leading questions, hypnosis, and guided imagery.	Production of false memories of trauma
Dissociative Identity Disorder (DID)–Oriented Psychotherapy	Therapists use techniques that imply to patients that they harbor "alter" personalities. Therapists attempt to summon and interact with alters.	Production of alters, creation of serious identity problems
Critical Incident Stress Debriefing	Shortly after a traumatic event, therapists urge group members to "process" their negative emotions, describe posttraumatic stress disorder symptoms that members are likely to experience, and discourage members from discontinuing participation.	Heightened risk for posttraumatic stress symptoms
DARE (Drug Abuse and Resistance Education) Programs	Police officers teach schoolchildren about the risks of drug use and social skills to resist peer pressure to try drugs (Chapter 10).	Increased intake of alcohol and other substances (such as cigarettes)
Coercive Restraint Therapies	Therapists physically restrain children who have difficulty forming attachments to their parents. These therapies include rebirthing (Chapter 1) and holding therapy, in which the therapist holds children down until they stop resisting or begin to show eye contact.	Physical injuries, suffocation, death

(*Source:* Lilienfeld, 2007)

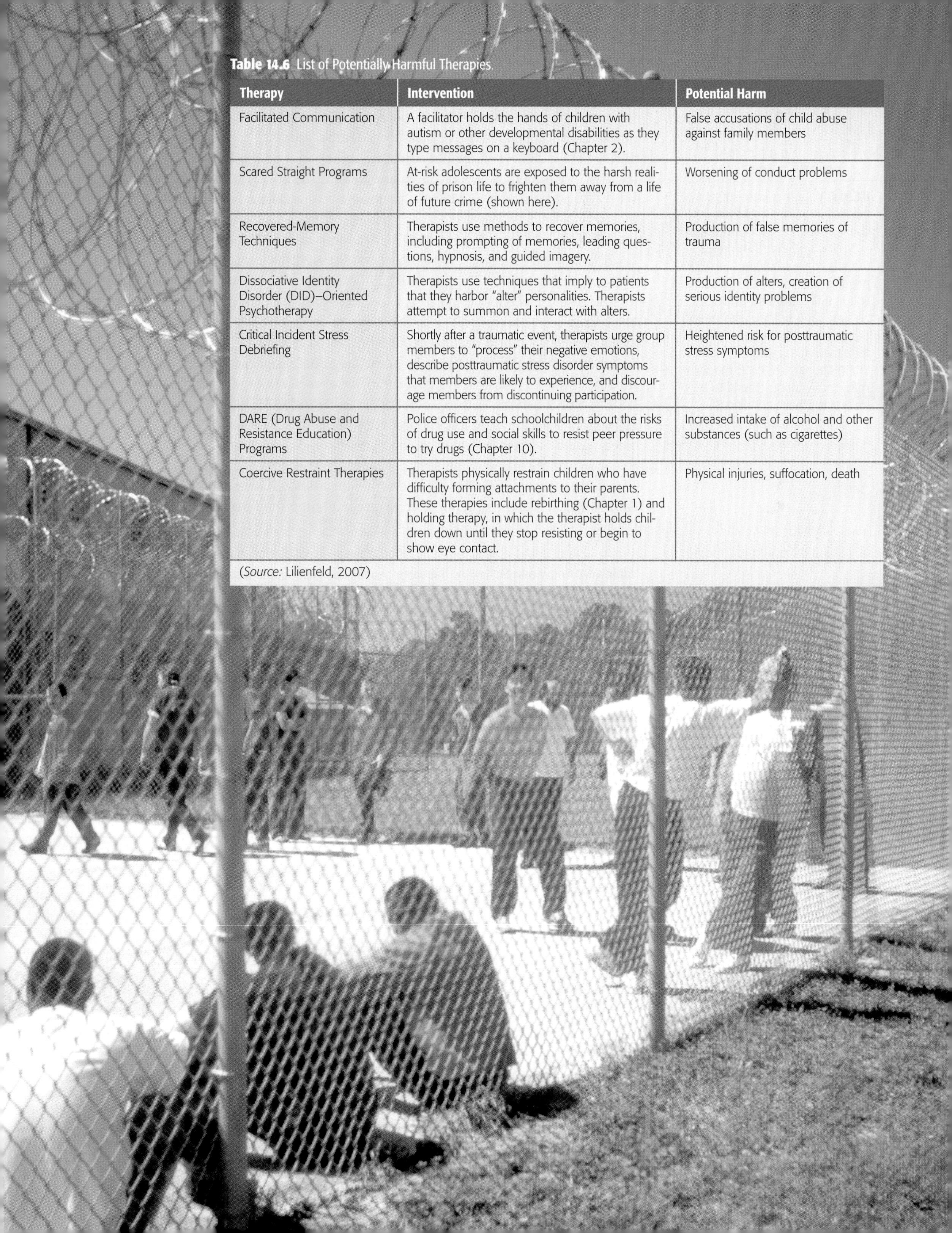

MYTH: Most psychotherapists use empirically supported therapies.

REALITY: Survey data suggest that only a minority of therapists use empirically supported therapies (Freiheit, Vye, Swan, et al., 2004). For example, a survey of practitioners who treat patients with eating disorders (especially anorexia and bulimia) indicated that most don't regularly administer either cognitive-behavioral or interpersonal therapies, the primary interventions found to be helpful for these conditions (Pederson Mussell et al., 2000).

Behavior therapy and cognitive-behavioral therapy have emerged as ESTs for depression, anxiety disorders, obesity, relationship problems, sexual dysfunction, and alcohol problems. Interpersonal therapy has considerable support for depression and bulimia. Still, we shouldn't conclude that a treatment that's not on the EST list isn't effective. The fact that a treatment isn't considered an EST may mean only that investigators haven't yet conducted research to demonstrate its effectiveness (Arkowitz & Lilienfeld, 2006).

The movement to develop lists of ESTs is controversial. Critics of this movement contend that the research literature isn't sufficiently well developed to conclude that certain treatments are clearly superior to others for certain disorders (Levant, 2004; Westen, Novotny, & Thompson-Brenner, 2004). For example, there may be cultural or individual differences in how effective particular therapies are to which research may not be sensitive. In response, proponents of this movement argue that the best scientific evidence available should inform clinical practice. Because current data suggest that at least some treatments are superior to others for some disorders, practitioners have an ethical obligation to rely on ESTs unless there's a compelling reason not to (Chambless & Ollendick, 2001; Crits-Christoph, Wilson, & Hollon, 2005; Hunsley & DiGuilio, 2002). The authors of your text find the latter argument more compelling. Naturally, it is important for researchers to undertake investigation of how individual and cultural differences affect the effectiveness of ESTs. But, if there's reasonable evidence that certain treatments are better than others for certain disorders, therapists should be guided by this evidence. In **Table 14.7,** we list and describe several research-supported treatments.

Good psychotherapists keep up with the current state of the research literature, staying informed about which therapies do and don't have strong scientific support.

Table 14.7 Empirically Supported Therapies. Selected therapies deemed "empirically supported" by the American Psychological Association Division 12 committee.

Therapy and Problem	Description of Therapy
Behavior Therapy for Depression	• Monitor and increase positive daily activities • Improve communication skills • Increase assertive behaviors • Increase positive reinforcement for nondepressed behaviors • Decrease life stresses
Cognitive-Behavior Therapy for Depression	• Teach patients to identify, reevaluate, and change negative thinking associated with depressed feelings • Conduct between-session experiments to test thoughts for accuracy • Monitor and increase daily activities
Interpersonal Therapy for Depression	• Help patients identify and resolve interpersonal difficulties associated with depression
Cognitive-Behavior Therapy for Bulimia	• Teach patients ways to prevent binge eating and create alternative behaviors • Develop a plan for a regular pattern of eating • Support skills to deal with high-risk situations for binge eating and purging • Modify attitudes toward eating and one's physical appearance
Cognitive-Behavior Therapy for Panic Disorder	• Produce panic attacks during sessions to help clients perceive them as less "dangerous" (to reassure them that they will not, for example, "go crazy" or die) • Introduce breathing retraining (slow deep breaths) to prevent hyperventilation • Control exposure to situations that trigger panic attacks

(*Source:* Arkowitz & Lilienfeld, 2006)

WHY DO INEFFECTIVE THERAPIES APPEAR TO BE HELPFUL? HOW WE CAN BE FOOLED

Some therapists have successfully marketed a wide variety of interventions that lack research support (Lilienfeld, Lynn, & Lohr, 2003; Norcross, Garofalo, & Koocher, 2006; Singer & Nievod, 2003). They include treatments as seemingly bizarre as dolphin therapy, laughter therapy, treatment for the trauma of abduction by aliens (Appelle, Lynn, & Newman, 2000) and even treatment for resolving problems due to traumas in a past life (Mills & Lynn, 2000).

Many of these treatments rest on questionable premises; for example, advocates of "primal scream therapy" (sometimes called *primal therapy*) believe that the only way to achieve relief from psychological pain is to release pent up rage in one's nervous system, including rage stemming from the trauma of birth. Yet there's virtually no research support for primal scream therapy (Singer & Lalich, 1996).

Some therapists claim that contact with dolphins can treat a variety of psychological problems, including autism. However, research does not support the idea that dolphin therapy is effective for any problem or disorder (Marino & Lilienfeld, 1998, 2007).

WHAT DO *you* THINK?

Your significant other convinces you that you have an anger management problem and proposes that you try out a therapy called *rage reduction therapy* (RRT), which involves getting the anger out of your system by yelling and punching inanimate objects. What questions would you want to ask the therapist before deciding whether this was a safe, effective, and empirically supported treatment?

How might patients and therapists alike come to believe that treatments that are ineffective are helpful? **[LEARNING OBJECTIVE 14.9]** The following five reasons can help us to understand why bogus therapies can gain a dedicated public following (Arkowitz & Lilienfeld, 2006; Beyerstein, 1997):

(1) ***Spontaneous remission.*** Many psychological problems are self-limiting or cyclical and improve without any intervention. A breakup with a significant other may depress us for a while, but most of us will improve even without professional help. This phenomenon is known as *spontaneous remission*. Only if people who are treated improve at a rate that exceeds that of untreated people, can we rule out the effects of spontaneous remission.

(2) ***The placebo effect.*** The pesky placebo effect (see Chapter 2) can lead to significant symptom relief. By instilling hope and the conviction that we can rise to life's challenges, virtually any credible treatment can be helpful in alleviating our demoralization.

(3) ***Self-serving biases.*** Even when they don't improve, patients who have invested time, money, and emotional effort in psychotherapy may convince themselves they've been helped. Because of this investment, there's often a strong psychological pull to find value in a treatment (Axsom & Cooper, 1985).

(4) ***Regression to the mean.*** It's a statistical fact of life that extreme scores tend to become less extreme on re-testing, a phenomenon known as *regression to the mean*. If you receive a zero on your first psychology exam, there's a silver lining to this gray cloud: You'll almost surely do better on your second exam! Conversely, if you receive a 100 on your first exam, odds are also high you won't do as well the second time around. Scores on measures of psychopathology are no different. If a patient comes into treatment extremely depressed, the chances are high she'll be less depressed in a few weeks. Regression to the mean can fool therapists and their

RULING OUT RIVAL HYPOTHESES
Have important alternative explanations for the findings been excluded?

Positive life events that occur outside therapy sessions, like major job promotions, can help to explain spontaneous remissions of some psychological problems, such as depression.

patients into believing that a useless treatment is effective. It's an especially tricky problem in evaluating whether psychotherapy is effective because most patients enter psychotherapy when their symptoms are most extreme.

(5) ***Retrospective rewriting of the past.*** In some cases, we may believe we've improved even when we haven't because we misremember our initial (pretreatment) level of adjustment as worse than it was. We *expect* to change after treatment and may adjust our memories to fit this expectation.

---

myth CONCEPTIONS — ARE SELF-HELP BOOKS ALWAYS HELPFUL?

Each year Americans can choose from about 3,500 newly published self-help books that promise everything from achieving everlasting bliss and expanded consciousness to freedom from virtually every human failing and foible imaginable. Self-help books are only one aspect of a self-improvement industry that extends to Internet sites, magazines, radio and television shows, CDs, DVDs, lectures, workshops, and advice columns. Americans spend $650 million a year on self-help books and at least 80 percent of therapists recommend them to their patients (Arkowitz & Lilienfeld, 2007).

The effects of reading self-help books and psychotherapy are often similar in treating depression, anxiety, and other problems (Gould & Clum, 1993). Still, we should keep

The "secret" to the 2007 best seller *The Secret* by Rhonda Byrne (*above*) is the so-called *law of attraction*—good thoughts attract good things and bad thoughts attract bad things. Yet there's no evidence that merely wishing for something good to happen without taking concrete steps to accomplish it is effective. We should be skeptical of self-help books that promise simple answers to complex problems.

three points in mind. First, we can't generalize the limited findings to all of the books on the shelf of our local bookstore because the overwhelming majority of self-help books remain untested (Rosen, Glasgow, & Moore, 2003). Second, people who volunteer for research on self-help books may be more motivated to read the entire book and benefit from it than the curious person who purchases the book under more casual circumstances. Third, many self-help books address relatively minor problems, like everyday worries and public speaking. When researchers (Menchola, Arkowitz, & Burke, 2007) have examined more serious problems, like major depression and panic disorder, psychotherapy has fared better than self-help books, although both do better than no treatment.

Some people don't respond at all to self-help books (Febbraro, Clum, Roodman, et al., 1999), and many self-help books promise far more than they can deliver. Readers who fall short of how the promotional materials on the cover assure them they'll respond may feel like failures and be less likely to seek professional help or make changes on their own initiative. Bearing this possibility in mind, Hal Arkowitz and Scott Lilienfeld (2007) offered the following recommendations about selecting self-help books:

- Use books that have research support and are based on valid psychological principles of change (Gambrill, 1992). Make sure the author refers to published research that supports the claims made. Some of the books that have shown positive effects in research studies include *Feeling Good* by David Burns, *Mind over Mood* by Dennis Greenberger and Christine Padesky, and *Coping with Panic* by George Clum.

- Evaluate the author's credentials. Does he or she have the professional training and expertise to write on the topic at hand?

- Be wary of books that make far-fetched promises, such as curing a phobia in 5 minutes. The 2007 blockbuster best seller *The Secret* (Byrne, 2007), popularized by Oprah Winfrey, informs readers that positive thinking alone can cure cancer, help one become a millionaire, or achieve just about any goal one wants. Yet there's not a shred of research evidence that this kind of wishful thinking is helpful (Smythe, 2007).

- Beware of books that rely on a "one size fits all" approach. A book that tells us to always express our anger to our relationship partner fails to take into account the complexity and specifics of the relationship.

- Serious problems like clinical depression, obsessive-compulsive disorder, or schizophrenia warrant professional help rather than self-help alone.

 QUIZ

1 Doing something about a psychological problem is not necessarily better than doing nothing. **TRUE** **FALSE**

2 Behavior therapy is inferior to most other therapeutic approaches. **TRUE** **FALSE**

3 Spontaneous remission of psychological problems is uncommon. **TRUE** **FALSE**

4 Psychotherapists generally shy away from recommending self-help books. **TRUE** **FALSE**

Answers: (1) T (p. 506); (2) F (p. 508); (3) F (p. 509); (4) F (p. 510)

PEARSON
mypsych lab

▼ How do you know it is your therapeutic treatment that resulted in a patient feeling better? Participate in the simulation titled "Ineffective Therapies" at www.mypsychlab.com to find out.

Biological Treatments: Drugs, Physical Stimulation, and Surgery

Biological treatments—including drugs, stimulation techniques, and brain surgery—directly alter the brain's chemistry or physiology. Just as the number of psychotherapy approaches has more than tripled since the 1970s, antidepressant prescriptions have tripled from 1988 to 1994 and from 1990 to 2000 (Smith, 2005). Many people are surprised to learn that about 10 percent of inpatients with major depression still receive electroconvulsive therapy (ECT)—informally called "shock therapy"—which delivers small electric shocks to people's brains to lift their mood (Olfson, Marcus, Sackeim, et al., 1998). By the 1950s, as many as 50,000 patients received psychosurgery, in which their frontal lobes or brain regions were damaged or removed in an effort to control serious psychological disorders (Tooth & Newton, 1961; Valenstein, 1973). Today, surgeons rarely perform such operations, reflecting the controversies surrounding psychosurgery and the fact that less risky treatments are available to treat many serious psychological conditions. As we consider the pros and cons of various biological treatments, we'll see that each approach has attracted its share of both critics and defenders.

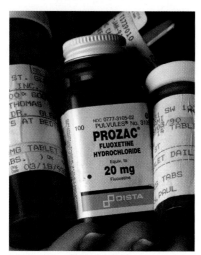

Prozac (fluoxetine) was the first of a new generation of SSRI drugs to treat depression and a variety of other psychological conditions.

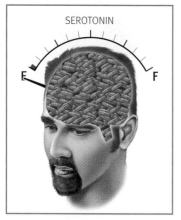

Despite what many drug company ads imply, there's no evidence that SSRIs or other medications work simply by correcting a "chemical imbalance" of serotonin (or other neurotransmitters) in the brain. These medications probably operate by means of more complex mechanisms.

GLOSSARY

pharmacotherapy
use of medications to treat psychological problems

PHARMACOTHERAPY: TARGETING BRAIN CHEMISTRY

We'll begin our tour of biological treatments with **pharmacotherapy**—the use of medications to treat psychological problems. For virtually every psychological disorder treated with psychotherapy, there's an available medication. In 1954, the widespread marketing of the drug Thorazine (chlorpromazine) ushered in the "pharmacological revolution" in the treatment of serious psychological disorders. For the first time, professionals could prescribe powerful medications to ease the symptoms of schizophrenia and related conditions (see Chapter 13). By 1970, it was unusual for any patient with schizophrenia not to be treated with Thorazine or another of the "major tranquilizers," as they came to be known.

Pharmaceutical companies soon sensed the promise of medicines to treat a broad spectrum of patients, and their efforts paid off handsomely. Researchers discovered that the emotional storms that plague people with bipolar disorder could be tamed with Lithium, Tegretol, and a new generation of mood stabilizer drugs. Drug treatments are now available for people who struggle with far more common conditions, ranging from anxiety about public speaking to the harsh realities of stressful circumstances. As of 2004, 10 percent of adult women and 4 percent of adult men were taking antidepressant medications (Smith, 2005). We can attribute the staggering number of prescriptions for depression largely to the phenomenal popularity of the selective serotonin reuptake inhibitor (SSRI) antidepressant drugs, including Prozac, Zoloft, and Paxil, which boost levels of the neurotransmitter serotonin.

In **Table 14.8,** we present commonly used drugs and their presumed mechanisms of action to treat anxiety disorders (anxiolytics or antianxiety drugs), depression (antidepressants), bipolar disorders (mood stabilizers), psychotic conditions (neuroleptics/antipsychotics or major tranquilizers), and attention problems (psychostimulants). **[LEARNING OBJECTIVE 14.10]** As we can see from this table, many of these medications ease the symptoms of multiple psychological conditions.

Nevertheless, when evaluating this table, we should bear in mind that we don't know for sure how most of these medications work. Although drug company advertisements, including those we've seen on television, often claim that medications—especially antidepressants—correct a "chemical imbalance" in the brain, this notion is almost surely oversimplified. For one thing, most medications probably work on multiple neurotransmitter systems. Moreover, there's no scientific evidence for an "optimal" level of serotonin or other neurotransmitters in the brain (Lacasse & Leo, 2005). Finally, many medications, including antidepressants, may exert their effects largely by affecting the sensitivity of receptors (see Chapter 3) rather than the levels of neurotransmitters.

Today, psychologists often refer patients to psychiatrists and other professionals who can prescribe medications and consult with prescribers to plan treatment. Until recently, only psychiatrists and a few other mental health professionals, like psychiatric nurse practitioners, could prescribe medications. But beginning in 1999, psychologists in the U.S. territory of Guam were granted legal permission to prescribe medications followed by two U.S. states (New Mexico in 2002 and Louisiana in 2004). Before being allowed to prescribe, these psychologists must first complete a curriculum of coursework on physiology, anatomy, and psychopharmacology (the study of medications that affect psychological functioning). Nevertheless, the growing movement to allow psychologists to prescribe medications has been exceedingly controversial, in part because many critics charge that psychologists don't possess sufficient knowledge of the anatomy and physiology of the human body to adequately evaluate the intended effects and side effects of medications (Stuart & Heiby, 2007).

Table 14.8 Commonly Used Medications for Psychological Disorders, Mechanisms of Action, and Other Uses.

	Medication	Examples	Action	Other Uses
Antianxiety Medications	Benzodiazepines	Diazepam (Valium), alprazolam (Xanax), clonazepam (Klonopin), lorazepam (Ativan)	Increase efficiency of GABA binding to receptor sites	Use with antipsychotic medications, treat medication side effects, alcohol detox
	Buspirone (Buspar)		Stabilizes serotonin levels	Depressive and anxiety states; sometimes used with antipsychotics; aggression in people with brain injuries and dementia
	Beta blockers	Atenolol (Tenormin), propranolol (Inderal)	Block norepinephrine receptor sites that control heart and muscle function; reduce rapid heartbeat, muscle tension	Control blood pressure, regulate heartbeat
Antidepressants	Monoamine oxidase (MAO) inhibitors	Isocarboxazid (Marplan), phenelzine (Nardil), tranylcypromine (Parnate)	Inhibit action of enzymes that metabolize norepinephrine and serotonin; inhibit dopamine	Panic and other anxiety disorders
	Cyclic antidepressants	Amitriptyline (Elavil), imipramine (Tofranil), desipramine (Norpramine), nortriptyline (Pamelor)	Inhibit reuptake of norepinephrine and serotonin	Panic and other anxiety disorders, pain relief
	SSRIs (selective serotonin reuptake inhibitors)	Fluoxetine (Prozac), citalopram (Celexa), sertraline (Zoloft)	Selectively inhibit reuptake of serotonin	Eating disorders (especially bulimia), obsessive-compulsive disorder, social phobia
Mood Stabilizers	Mineral salts	Lithium carbonate (Lithium)	Decrease noradrenaline, increase serotonin	
	Anticonvulsant medications	Carbamazepine (Tegretol), lamotrigine (Lamictal), valproic acid (Depakote)	Increase levels of neurotransmitter GABA, inhibit norepinephrine reuptake (Tegretol)	Bipolar disorder
Antipsychotics	Conventional antipsychotics	Chlorpromazine (Thorazine), haloperidol (Haldol)	Block postsynaptic dopamine receptors	Tourette syndrome (Haldol), bipolar disorder with the exception of Clozaril
	Serotonin-dopamine antagonists (atypical antipsychotics)	Clozapine (Clozaril), risperidone (Risperdal), olanzapine (Zyprexa), ziprasidone (Geodone), quetiapine (Seroquel)	Block activity of both serotonin and/or dopamine; also affect norepinephrine, acetylcholine	
Psychostimulants and Other Medications for Attentional Problems	Methylphenidate (Ritalin, Concerta), amphetamine (Adderall), dexmethylphenidate (Focalin)		Release norepinephrine, dopamine, serotonin in frontal regions of the brain, where attention and behavior are regulated	
	Atomoxetine (Strattera)		Selectively inhibit reuptake of norepinephrine	

WHAT DO *you* THINK?

A friend has been taking an SSRI for depression for several years and has discovered that the current drug and dosage no longer seem to be working for him. He's confused about how this can happen because he thought the drugs were just a matter of fixing a chemical imbalance in his brain. What might you say to help him understand that the explanation for his depression is more complex than a chemical imbalance?

Cautions to Consider: Dosage and Side Effects. Pharmacotherapy isn't a cure-all. Virtually all medications have side effects that practitioners must weigh against their potential benefits. **[LEARNING OBJECTIVE 14.11]** Most adverse reactions, including nausea, drowsiness, weakness, fatigue, and impaired sexual performance, are reversible when medications are discontinued or when their dosage is lowered. Nevertheless, this isn't the case with *tardive dyskinesia* (TD), a serious side effect of some antipsychotic medications, that is, medications used to treat schizophrenia and other psychoses. The symptoms of TD include grotesque involuntary movements of the facial muscles and mouth and twitching of the neck, arms, and legs. Most often, the disorder begins after several years of high-dosage treatment (*tardive*, like *tardy*, means late-appearing), but it occasionally begins after only a few months of therapy at low dosages (Simpson & Kline, 1976). Newer antipsychotic medicines, such as Risperdal, generally produce fewer serious adverse effects, but they're costly (Correll & Schenk, 2008).

One Dose Doesn't Fit All: Differences in Responses to Medication. Professionals who prescribe drugs must proceed with caution. People don't all respond equally to the same dose of medication. Weight, age, and even racial differences often affect drug response. African Americans tend to require lower doses of certain antianxiety and anti-depressant drugs and have a faster response than do Caucasians, and Asians metabolize (break down) these medications more slowly than do Caucasians (Baker & Bell, 1999; Campinha-Bacote, 2002; Strickland, Stein, Lin, et al., 1997). Because some people become physically and psychologically dependent on medications, such as the widely prescribed antianxiety medications Valium and Xanax (benzodiazepines), physicians try to determine the lowest dose possible to achieve positive results and minimize unpleasant side effects (Wigal et al., 2006). Discontinuation of certain drugs, such as those for anxiety and depression, should be performed gradually to minimize withdrawal reactions, including anxiety and agitation (Lejoyeux & Ades, 1997).

Medications on Trial: Harmful and Overprescribed? Some psychologists have raised serious questions about the effectiveness of SSRIs, especially among children and adolescents (Kendall, Pilling, & Whittington, 2005). There also are widely publicized indications that SSRIs increase the risk of suicidal thoughts in people younger than 18 years of age, although there's no clear evidence that they increase the risk of actually attempting suicide. For this reason, the U.S. Food and Drug Administration (FDA) now requires drug manufacturers to include warnings of possible suicide risk on the labels of SSRIs. Following these "black box" warnings (so called because they're enclosed in a box with black borders on the medication label), antidepressant prescriptions dropped by nearly 20 percent (Nemeroff et al., 2007).

Another area of public concern regarding drug treatments is overprescription. Parents, teachers, and helping professionals have expressed particular alarm that psychostimulants for ADHD such as Ritalin (methylphenidate) are overprescribed and may substitute for

Children with attention-deficit/hyperactivity disorder (ADHD) often benefit from stimulant medication. Nevertheless, critics contend that stimulants are often overprescribed, especially for children who are only slightly overactive, inattentive, or impulsive for their age.

effective coping strategies for focusing attention (LeFever, Arcona, & Antonuccio, 2003; Safer, 2000). Since the early 1990s, the number of prescriptions for ADHD has increased fourfold. Although little is known about the long-term safety of Ritalin with children under 6, the number of prescriptions for children ages 2(!) to 4 nearly tripled between 1991 and 1995 alone (Bentley & Walsh, 2006). Adverse effects include insomnia, irritability, heart-related complications, and stunted growth.

A final major area of concern is *polypharmacy:* prescribing many medications— sometimes five or more—at the same time. This practice can be hazardous if not carefully monitored, because certain medications may interfere with the effects of other medications or interact with them in dangerous ways. Polypharmacy is a particular problem among elderly individuals, who tend to be especially susceptible to drug side effects (Fulton & Allen, 2005).

To medicate or not medicate, that is the question. In many instances, psychotherapy, with no added medications, can successfully treat people with many disorders. CBT is at least as effective as antidepressants, even for severe depression, and perhaps more effective than antidepressants in preventing relapse (DeRubeis, Brotman, & Gibbons, 2005). Psychotherapy alone is also effective for a variety of anxiety disorders, dysthymia, bulimia, and insomnia (Otto, Smits, & Reese, 2005; Thase, 2000). Critics of pharmacotherapy claim that medications are of little value in helping patients learn social skills, modify self-defeating behaviors, or cope with conflict. Indeed, some patients relapse when they stop taking medications (Hollon, Haman, & Brown, 2002). For example, when patients with anxiety disorders discontinue their medications, half or more may relapse (Marks, Swinson, Basoglu, et al., 1993). Over the long haul, psychotherapy may be much less expensive than medications, so it often makes sense to try psychotherapy first (Arkowitz & Lilienfeld, 2007).

Still, there are often clear advantages of combining medication with psychotherapy (Thase, 2000). If people's symptoms interfere greatly with their functioning, or if psychotherapy alone hasn't worked for a 2-month period, adding medication is frequently justified. Generally, research suggests that combining medication with psychotherapy is warranted for treating schizophrenia, bipolar disorder, long-term major depression, and major depression with psychotic symptoms (Otto et al., 2005; Thase, 2000).

MYTH: One way of treating patients with ADHD effectively is by reducing the amount of sugar in their diets.

REALITY: There's no convincing evidence that reducing the amount of sugar in the diets of children with ADHD—or instituting other dietary changes (like eliminating artificial food coloring or flavors)—improves their symptoms (Waschbusch & Hill, 2003).

ELECTRICAL STIMULATION: CONCEPTIONS AND MISCONCEPTIONS

Consider the following account of **electroconvulsive therapy (ECT):**

> Strapped to a stretcher, you are wheeled into the ECT room. The electroshock machine is in clear view. The nurse places the electrodes on you. An injection is given. . . . You awaken in your hospital bed. You are confused to find it so difficult to recover memories. . . . You were scheduled to have ECT, but something must have happened. Perhaps it was postponed. But the nurse keeps asking, "How are you feeling?" You think to yourself: "It must have been given"; but you can't remember. You have forgotten, but something about it remains. (Taylor, 1975, p. 33)

Electroconvulsive Therapy: Fact and Fiction. What exactly happened here? Medical personnel first injected a muscle relaxant and then administered brief electrical pulses to the patient's brain to relieve severe depression that hadn't responded to other treatments. Physicians typically recommend ECT for individuals with serious depression, bipolar disorder, schizophrenia, and severe catatonia (see Chapter 13), and only then as a last resort when psychotherapy and pharmacotherapy have failed. A typical course of ECT is 6 to 10 treatments, given three times a week.

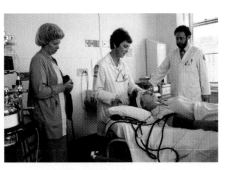

A team of professionals administer electroconvulsive therapy.

GLOSSARY

electroconvulsive therapy
patients receive brief electrical pulses to the brain that produce a seizure to treat serious psychological problems

MYTH: Patients who receive ECT display violent convulsions, sometimes leading to serious injuries.

REALITY: Although this was true decades ago and is still the case in some developing countries (Giles, 2002), muscle relaxant and anesthesia now administered along with ECT prevent violent convulsions. In Western countries today, ECT is no more physically dangerous than anesthesia itself.

RULING OUT RIVAL HYPOTHESES
Have important alternative explanations for the findings been excluded?

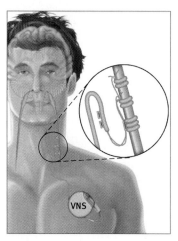

A small vagus nerve stimulator can be implanted under the breastbone in cases of serious treatment-resistant depression.

RULING OUT RIVAL HYPOTHESES
Have important alternative explanations for the findings been excluded?

GLOSSARY

psychosurgery
brain surgery to treat psychological problems

Misconceptions about ECT abound, including the erroneous beliefs that ECT is painful or dangerous and that it invariably produces long-term memory loss, personality changes, and even brain damage (Dowman, Patel, & Rajput, 2005; Malcom, 1989; Santa Maria, Baumeister, & Gouvier, 1999). **[LEARNING OBJECTIVE 14.12]** Not surprisingly, most Americans hold negative attitudes about ECT.

Nevertheless, the picture looks quite different when researchers interview individuals who've undergone ECT. In one study of 24 patients, 91 percent reported being happy to have received ECT (Goodman, Krahn, Smith, et al., 1999). In another study, 98 percent of patients said they would seek ECT again if their depression returned, and 62 percent said that the treatment was less frightening than a visit to the dentist (Pettinati, Taimburello, Ruetsch, et al., 1994). More important, researchers report improvement rates as high as 80 to 90 percent following ECT for severe depression (American Psychiatric Association, 2001), further suggesting that harsh public perceptions about ECT are unwarranted.

Although many patients report feeling better after ECT, they don't always show evidence of parallel changes on objective measures of depression and mental functioning (Scovern & Kilmann, 1980). ECT may be helpful because it increases the levels of serotonin in the brain (Rasmussen, Sampson, & Rummans, 2002). A rival hypothesis is that ECT induces strong expectations of improvement and serves as an "electrical placebo." But studies showing that ECT works better than "sham" (fake) ECT render this explanation less likely (Carney et al., 2003).

As the case we read suggested, ECT can create short-term confusion and cloud memory. In most cases, the memory loss is restricted to events that occur right before the treatment and generally subsides within a few weeks (Sackeim, 1986). However, in the first long-term study of patients in the community who received ECT, researchers found that memory and attention problems persist in some patients for 6 months after treatment (Sackeim et al., 2007). Before ECT is used, the physician, patient, and family must consider whether the therapeutic value outweighs the potential adverse effects.

Vagus Nerve Stimulation. In a recent development, surgeons can now implant a small electrical device under the skin near the breastbone to stimulate the *vagus nerve* to treat severe depression. The vagus nerve projects to many brain areas, and researchers believe that electrical pulses to this nerve stimulate serotonin and increase brain blood flow (George et al., 2000). The FDA has approved this procedure for depression that hasn't responded to other treatments, but well-controlled, large-scale studies are lacking. In one study, patients who received devices that weren't turned on performed as well as patients with working devices, suggesting that improvement may be due to placebo effects (Rush et al., 2005). Even if future studies show that vagus nerve stimulation is effective, the decision to try the treatment will need to be weighed against the potential side effects of headache, neck pain, cough, and voice changes.

PSYCHOSURGERY: AN ABSOLUTE LAST RESORT

Psychosurgery, or brain surgery to treat psychological disorders, is the most radical of all biological treatments. So it's no surprise that it's attracted a firestorm of controversy. Critics of psychosurgery have raised questions about the merits of destroying brain tissue to control behavior and emotion, the use of psychosurgery for social control, and the ethical issues surrounding such control.

To understand the controversy, we must understand its history. As is often the case with new treatments, psychosurgery was hailed as a promising innovation not long after it was introduced in the twentieth century. Psychosurgery remained popular until the mid-1950s, when the tide of enthusiasm receded in the face of reports of scores of "dehumanized zombies" and the availability of medicines as alternatives to surgery (Mashour, Walker, & Matuza, 2005; Valenstein, 1973). To most critics, the benefits of psychosurgery rarely, if ever, outweighed the costs of impairing memory, diminishing emotion and creativity, and the risks of brain surgery (Neville, 1978).

In the 1960s, surgeons ushered new forms of psychosurgery to the forefront. The procedures involved creating small lesions in the amygdala or in other parts of the limbic system, such as the cingulate cortex, which plays a key role in controlling emotions (see Chapter 3). Surgeons replaced primitive procedures with ultrasound, electricity, freezing of tissues, and implants of radioactive materials. With the advent of modern psychosurgical techniques, negative physical side effects became far less frequent.

Today, surgeons sometimes perform psychosurgery as an absolute last resort for patients with a handful of conditions, such as severe obsessive-compulsive disorder, major depression, and bipolar disorder. In a study using strict criteria for improvement, 25 to 30 percent of 33 patients with obsessive-compulsive disorder who'd failed to respond to all other treatments benefited substantially from psychosurgery (Jenike et al., 1991). Unfortunately, there are few well-controlled long-term studies of psychosurgery and an absence of data about which patients respond best. Even when psychosurgery appears successful, we can generate alternative explanations, including placebo effects and self-serving biases, to account for apparent treatment gains (Dawes, 1994).

Recognizing the need to protect patient interests, institutional review boards (IRBs; see Chapter 2) in hospitals where surgeons perform psychosurgery must approve each operation. IRBs help ensure that (a) there's a clear rationale for the operation, (b) the patient has received an appropriate preoperative and postoperative evaluation, (c) the patient has consented to the operation, and (d) the surgeon is competent to conduct the procedure (Mashour et al., 2005). Scientific research may eventually lead to more effective forms of psychosurgery, but the ethical controversies surrounding such surgery are likely to endure.

Public attitudes and beliefs about psychosurgery may have been influenced by Tennessee Williams's widely acclaimed 1944 play, *The Glass Menagerie*. Its leading character, Laura, is an echo of the playwright's sister Rose, who underwent a botched psychosurgery to combat her "madness" several years before Williams wrote the play.

RULING OUT RIVAL HYPOTHESES
Have important alternative explanations for the findings been excluded?

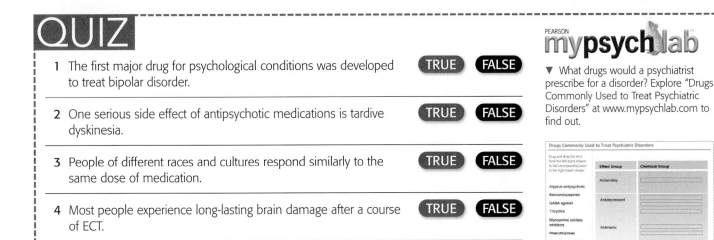

QUIZ

1 The first major drug for psychological conditions was developed to treat bipolar disorder. TRUE FALSE

2 One serious side effect of antipsychotic medications is tardive dyskinesia. TRUE FALSE

3 People of different races and cultures respond similarly to the same dose of medication. TRUE FALSE

4 Most people experience long-lasting brain damage after a course of ECT. TRUE FALSE

Answers: (1) F (p. 512); (2) T (p. 514); (3) F (p. 514); (4) F (p. 516)

PEARSON
mypsychlab

▼ What drugs would a psychiatrist prescribe for a disorder? Explore "Drugs Commonly Used to Treat Psychiatric Disorders" at www.mypsychlab.com to find out.

PSYCHOTHERAPY: PATIENTS AND PRACTITIONERS (pp. 490–494)

14.1 Describe who seeks treatment, who benefits from psychotherapy, and who practices psychotherapy

Therapists treat people of all ages and social, cultural, and ethnic backgrounds. Individuals with anxiety, and minor and temporary problems are likely to benefit from therapy. Socioeconomic status, gender, age, and ethnicity do not predict treatment outcome.

1. _____ can be defined as a psychological intervention designed to help people resolve emotional, behavioral, and interpersonal problems and improve the quality of their lives. (p. 490)

2. In general, (women/men) are more likely to seek psychotherapy. (p. 491)

3. Hispanic Americans are (less/more) likely than non-Hispanic Americans to seek mental health services. (p. 491)

4. Studies have shown that people often (wait/rush) to seek therapy for problems. (p. 491)

5. What was the ideal client like, according to a 1964 study of people in therapy? Has that view changed today? (p. 492)

14.2 Identify the training and effectiveness differences between professionals and paraprofessionals

Unlicensed paraprofessionals with no formal training, as well as licensed professionals, can be equally effective as therapists.

6. A person with no professional training who provides mental health services is called a _____. (p. 491)

7. In most states, the term *therapist* (is/isn't) legally protected. (p. 491)

14.3 Describe what it takes to be an effective therapist

Warmth, selecting important topics to discuss, not contradicting patients, and the ability to establish a positive relationship are the most important determinants of a therapist's effectiveness.

8. A therapist who talks a lot about his/her personal life is likely to be (effective/ineffective). (p. 493)

9. When it comes to the success of psychotherapy, the choice of _____ may often matter more than the choice of _____. (p. 493)

10. How ethical was the client–therapist relationship in the television drama series *The Sopranos*? (p. 493)

succeed with mypsych lab

1. What is the difference between a counselor and a psychiatrist? Test your knowledge of different practitioners.
Psychotherapy Practitioners and Their Activities

2. Learn about psychological and biological treatments for disorders.
Recent Trends in Treatment: Sue Mineka

Answers are located at the end of the text.

DIFFERENT "FLAVORS" OF THERAPY: A REVIEW OF THERAPEUTIC APPROACHES (pp. 494–505)

14.4 Describe the core beliefs and criticisms of psychodynamic and humanistic therapies

The core beliefs of psychodynamic therapies are the importance of the unconscious, childhood experiences, expressing emotions, reexperiencing past events, and acquiring insight. Evidence for psychodynamic therapies is based largely on small and highly select patient samples, anecdotal studies, and the questionable curative value of insight. Humanistic therapies hold that self-actualization is a universal human drive and adopt an experience-based approach in which patients work to fulfill their potential. Research suggests that genuineness, unconditional positive regard, and empathic understanding are necessary but not sufficient for improvement.

11. In the technique of _____ _____ patients are allowed to express themselves without censorship of any sort. (p. 495)

12. Neo-Freudians place (more/less) emphasis on the unconscious than did Freudians. (p. 495)

13. In Rogers's _____ therapy, the therapist uses reflection to communicate empathy to the patient. (p. 497)

14.5 Describe the features of behavioral and cognitive-behavioral therapies

Behavior therapy is grounded in the scientific method and based on learning principles. Cognitive-behavioral therapists modify irrational beliefs that play a key role in unhealthy feelings and behaviors.

14. A class of procedures that confronts patients with what they fear with the goal of reducing this fear is called _____ _____ . (p. 498)

15. What is in vivo exposure therapy and how can it help people with a fear of flying? (p. 499)

16. Patients are exposed right away to images of stimuli that they fear the most for prolonged periods during _____ . (p. 499)

17. What is EMDR therapy, and how effective is it in relieving symptoms of anxiety disorders? (p. 500)

18. Ellis's rational emotive-behavior therapy (REBT) emphasizes that our _____ systems play a key role in how we function psychologically. (p. 501)

14.6 List the advantages of group therapy approaches

Group methods span all schools of psychotherapy and are efficient, time saving, and less costly than individual methods. Participants learn from others' experiences, benefit from feedback and modeling others' behaviors, and discover that problems and suffering are widespread.

19. People who attend AA meetings fare (better than/about the same as) people who receive other treatments, including cognitive-behavioral therapy. (p. 504)

14.7 Identify different approaches to treating the dysfunctional family system

Family therapies treat problems in the family system. Strategic family therapists remove barriers to effective communication, whereas structural family therapists plan changes in the way family interactions are structured.

20. Research indicates that family therapy is (as effective as/not as effective as) individual therapy. (p. 505)

succeed with mypsychlab

1. What approach do you like best? Review and test your understanding of the different therapeutic approaches.
Key Components of Psychoanalytic, Humanistic, Behavioral, and Cognitive Therapies

2. Hear two psychologists discuss different psychological approaches to therapy and how they are applied.
Psychological Therapies

3. How is therapy applied? Watch this video and learn how psychologists apply CBT to persons with schizophrenia.
Cognitive Behavioral Therapy

IS PSYCHOTHERAPY EFFECTIVE? (pp. 506–511)

14.8 Evaluate the claim that all psychotherapies are equally effective

Many therapies are effective. Nevertheless, some therapies, including behavioral and cognitive-behavioral treatments, are more effective than other treatments for specific problems, such as anxiety disorders. Still other treatments appear to be harmful.

21. The dodo bird verdict suggests that all types of psychotherapies are equally _____ . (p. 506)

22. Among researchers there is (strong consensus/no consensus) that the dodo bird verdict is correct. (p. 506)

23. Research shows that behavioral and cognitive-behavioral therapies are (more/less) effective than other treatments for children and adolescents with behavioral problems. (p. 506)

24. Most studies show that (20 percent/80 percent) of people who receive psychotherapy do better than the average person who does not. (p. 506)

25. What does the research suggest about the effectiveness of Scared Straight programs? (p. 507)

26. _____ _____ _____ are treatments for specific disorders that are supported by high-quality scientific evidence. (p. 506)

14.9 Explain why ineffective therapies can appear to be effective

Ineffective therapies can appear to be helpful because of spontaneous remission, the placebo effect, self-serving biases, regression to the mean, and retrospective rewriting of the past.

27. What kind of effect can positive life events, like major job promotions, have on psychological problems? (p. 509)

28. Even when they don't improve, patients who have invested time, money, and emotional effort in psychotherapy may convince themselves they've been helped, a psychological phenomenon known as the _____ _____ . (p. 509)

29. According to the regression to the mean phenomenon, if a patient comes into treatment extremely depressed, the chances are (high/low) that she'll be less depressed in a few weeks. (p. 509)

30. Americans spend $650 million a year on _____ _____ that promise self-improvement. (p. 510)

succeed with PEARSON mypsych lab

1. How do psychologists test if their therapies are working? Test your knowledge and see if you can think like a scientist-practitioner.
Ineffective Therapies

succeed with PEARSON mypsych lab

Do You Know All of the Terms in This Chapter?

Find out by using the Flashcards. Want more practice? Take additional quizzes, try simulations, and watch video to be sure you are prepared for the test!

BIOLOGICAL TREATMENTS: DRUGS, PHYSICAL STIMULATION, AND SURGERY (pp. 511–517)

14.10 **Recognize different types of drugs associated with drug treatment**

Medications are available to treat psychotic conditions (neuroleptics/antispsychotics or major tranquilizers), bipolar disorder (mood stabilizers), depression (antidepressants), anxiety (anxiolytics), and attentional problems (psychostimulants).

31. The use of medications to treat psychological problems is called _____ . (p. 512)

32. The first major drug for a psychological disorder, Thorazine, was used to treat _____ . (p. 512)

33. Prozac and Zoloft are among the best known _____ _____ _____ inhibitors. (p. 512)

34. There (is/is not) scientific evidence for an "optimal level" of serotonin or other neurotransmitters in the brain. (p. 512)

14.11 **Outline key considerations in drug treatment**

People who prescribe drugs must be aware of side effects, not over prescribe medications, and carefully monitor the effects of multiple medications (polypharmacy).

35. People of different races and ages (do/do not) respond equally to the same dose of medication. (p. 514)

36. The safety and effectiveness of SSRIs when prescribed to _____ and _____ have been called into question because of increased risk of suicidal thoughts. (p. 514)

37. The drug Ritalin, used to treat ADHD, is an example of a medication that many feel has been _____ and may substitute for effective coping strategies for focusing attention. (pp. 514–515)

14.12 **Identify misconceptions about electrical stimulation**

Contrary to popular belief, electroconvulsive therapy (ECT) is not painful or dangerous and doesn't invariably produce memory loss, personality changes, or brain damage.

38. During _____ _____ , patients receive brief electrical pulses to the brain that produce a seizure to treat serious psychological problems. (p. 515)

39. How does vagus nerve stimulation work? Has research shown it to be an effective treatment? (p. 516)

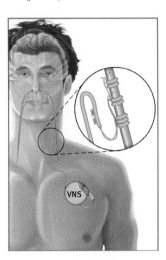

40. Define psychosurgery and explain the controversy surrounding this treatment, which was famously depicted in the play *The Glass Menagerie*. (pp. 516–517)

SCIENTIFIC THINKING SKILLS
Questions and Summary

1 Your parents are divorcing. Your father is struggling to adjust, yet is resisting your suggestion to speak to a therapist. How could you dispel his preconceived notions about who seeks and benefits from therapy?

2 A friend confesses that he buys many self-help books, but nothing works. What scientifically based guidelines could you give him to select more effective books?

RULING OUT RIVAL HYPOTHESES
pp. 492, 495, 496, 503, 509, 516, 517

FALSIFIABILITY
pp. 496, 497, 500

REPLICABILITY
pp. 491, 496

EXTRAORDINARY CLAIMS
p. 499

OCCAM'S RAZOR
p. 500

succeed with my**psych**lab

1. How well do you know your drugs? Test your knowledge of drugs commonly used to treat disorders.
Drugs Commonly Used to Treat Psychiatric Disorders

Glossary

absolute refractory period   time during which another action potential is impossible; limits maximal firing rate

absolute threshold   lowest level of a stimulus needed for the nervous system to detect a stimulus 50 percent of the time

abstract thinking   capacity to understand hypothetical concepts

accommodation   (Chapter 4) changing the shape of the lens to focus on objects near or far

accommodation   (Chapter 8) Piagetian process of altering a belief to make it more compatible with experience

acquired immune deficiency syndrome (AIDS)   a life-threatening, incurable, yet treatable condition in which the human immunodeficiency virus (HIV) attacks and damages the immune system

acquisition   learning phase during which a conditioned response is established

action potential   electrical impulse that travels down the axon triggering the release of neurotransmitters

activation–synthesis theory   theory that dreams reflect inputs from brain activation originating in the pons, which the cortex then attempts to weave into a story

acuity   sharpness of vision

acupuncture   ancient Chinese practice of inserting thin needles into more than 2,000 points in the body to alter energy forces believed to run through the body

adolescence   the transition between childhood and adulthood commonly associated with the teenage years

adoption study   analysis of how traits vary in individuals raised apart from their biological relatives

adrenal gland   tissue located on top of the kidneys that releases adrenaline and cortisol during states of emotional arousal

aggression   behavior intended to harm others, either verbally or physically

agoraphobia   fear of being in a place or situation from which escape is difficult or embarrassing, or in which help is unavailable in the event of a panic attack

Alcoholics Anonymous   self-help program that provides social support for achieving sobriety

alternative medicine   health care practices and products used in place of conventional medicine

altruism   helping others for unselfish reasons

amygdala   part of limbic system that plays key roles in fear, excitement, and arousal

anal stage   psychosexual stage that focuses on toilet training

anorexia nervosa   eating disorder associated with excessive weight loss and the irrational perception that one is overweight

anterograde amnesia   inability to encode new memories from our experiences

antisocial personality disorder (ASPD)   condition marked by a lengthy history of irresponsible and/or illegal actions

apophenia   tendency to perceive meaningful connections among unrelated phenomena

applied research   research examining how we can use basic research to solve real-world problems

archetypes   cross-culturally universal emotional symbols

assimilation   Piagetian process of absorbing new experience into current knowledge structures

association cortex   regions of the cerebral cortex that integrate simpler functions to perform more complex functions

attachment   the strong emotional connection we share with those to whom we feel closest

attitude   belief that includes an emotional component

attribution   process of assigning causes to behavior

audition   our sense of hearing

autonomic nervous system   part of the nervous system controlling the involuntary actions of our internal organs and glands, which (along with the limbic system) participates in emotion regulation

average expectable environment   environment that provides children with basic needs for affection and discipline

aversion therapy   treatment that uses punishment to decrease the frequency of undesirable behaviors

axes   dimensions of functioning

axon   portion of neuron that sends signals

babbling   intentional vocalization that lacks specific meaning

basal ganglia   structures in the forebrain that help to control movement

basic research   research examining how the mind works

basilar membrane   membrane supporting the organ of Corti and hair cells in the cochlea

behavior therapist   therapist who focuses on specific problem behaviors and current variables that maintain problematic thoughts, feelings, and behaviors

behaviorism   school of psychology that focuses on uncovering the general laws of learning by looking at observable behavior

belief   conclusion regarding factual evidence

belief perseverance   tendency to stick to our initial beliefs even when evidence contradicts them

bell curve   distribution of scores in which the bulk of the scores fall toward the middle, with progressively fewer scores toward the "tails" or extremes

between-group heritability   extent to which differences in a trait between groups is genetically influenced

Big Five   five traits that have surfaced repeatedly in factor analyses of personality measures

bilingual   proficient and fluent at speaking and comprehending two distinct languages

binocular depth cues   stimuli that enable us to judge depth using both eyes

biological clock   term for the suprachiasmatic nucleus (SCN) in the hypothalamus that's responsible for controlling our levels of alertness

biopsychosocial perspective   the view that an illness or medical condition is the product of the interplay of biological, psychological, and social factors

bipolar disorder   condition marked by a history of at least one manic episode

blastocyst   ball of identical cells early in pregnancy that haven't yet begun to take on any specific function in a body part

blind   unaware of whether one is in the experimental or control group

blind spot   part of the visual field we can't see, where the optic nerve connects to the retina

blood–brain barrier   glial cells forming a fatty coating that prevents certain substances from entering the brain

borderline personality disorder   condition marked by extreme instability in mood, identity, and impulse control

bottom-up processing   constructing a mental understanding of a stimulus by putting together the raw sensory information into a complete whole

brain stem   part of the brain between the spinal cord and cerebral cortex that contains the medulla, midbrain, pons, and cerebellum

brightness   intensity of reflected light that reaches our eyes

Broca's area   language area in the prefrontal cortex that helps to control speech production

bulimia nervosa   eating disorder associated with a pattern of bingeing and purging in an effort to lose or maintain weight

case study   research design that examines one person or a small number of people in depth, often over an extended time period

catatonic symptom   motor problem, including extreme resistance to complying with simple suggestions, holding the body in bizarre or rigid postures, or curling up in a fetal position

category   collection of real or imagined objects, actions, and characteristics that share core properties

central nervous system (CNS)   part of nervous system containing brain and spinal cord that controls the mind and behavior

central tendency   measure of the "central" scores in a data set, or where the group tends to cluster

cerebellum   brain structure responsible for our sense of balance

cerebral cortex   outermost part of forebrain, responsible for analyzing sensory processing and higher brain functions

cerebral hemispheres   two halves of the cerebral cortex, each of which serve distinct yet highly integrated functions

cerebral ventricles   pockets in the brain that contain cerebrospinal fluid (CSF), which provide the brain with nutrients and cushion against injury

chromosome   slender thread inside a cell's nucleus that carries genes

chunking   organizing information into meaningful groupings, allowing us to extend the span of short-term memory

circadian rhythm   cyclical changes that occur on a roughly 24-hour basis in many biological processes

classical (Pavlovian) conditioning   form of learning in which animals come to respond to a previously neutral stimulus that had been paired with another stimulus that elicits an automatic response

cochlea   bony, spiral-shaped sense organ used for hearing

cognition   mental processes involved in different aspects of thinking

cognitive development   study of how children learn, think, reason, communicate, and remember

cognitive dissonance   unpleasant mental experience of tension resulting from two conflicting thoughts or beliefs

cognitive map   mental representation of how a physical space is organized

cognitive model of depression   theory that depression is caused by negative beliefs and expectations

cognitive-behavioral therapy   treatment that attempts to replace maladaptive or irrational cognitions and behaviors with more adaptive, rational ones

cohort effects   effects observed in a sample of participants that result from individuals in the sample growing up at the same time

collective unconscious   according to Jung, our shared storehouse of memories that ancestors have passed down to us across generations

color blindness   inability to see some or all colors

comorbidity   cooccurrence of two or more diagnoses within the same person

complementary medicine   health care practices and products used along with conventional medicine

compulsion   repetitive behavior or mental act performed to reduce or prevent anxiety

computed tomography (CT)   a scanning technique using multiple x-rays to construct three-dimensional images

concept   the general ideas or thoughts associated with members of a category

concrete operations stage   stage in Piaget's theory characterized by the ability to perform mental operations on physical events only

conditioned response (CR)   response previously associated with a nonneutral stimulus that is elicited by a neutral stimulus through conditioning

conditioned stimulus (CS)   initially neutral stimulus that comes to elicit a response due to association with an unconditioned stimulus

conditions of worth   according to Rogers, expectations we place on ourselves for appropriate and inappropriate behavior

cones   receptor cells in the retina that allow us to see in color

confirmation bias   tendency to seek out evidence that supports our hypotheses and neglect or distort evidence that contradicts them

conformity   tendency of people to alter their behavior as a result of group pressure

confounding variable or **confound**   any difference between the experimental and control groups other than the independent variable

conservation   Piagetian task requiring children to understand that despite a transformation in the physical presentation of an amount, the amount remains the same

contact comfort   positive emotions resulting from touch

context-dependent learning   superior retrieval of memories when the external context of the original memories matches the retrieval context

continuous reinforcement   reinforcing a behavior every time it occurs, resulting in faster learning but faster extinction than only occasional reinforcement

control group   in an experiment, the group of participants that doesn't receive the manipulation

convergent thinking   capacity to generate the single best solution to a problem

cornea   part of the eye containing transparent cells that focus light on the retina

coronary heart disease (CHD)   damage to the heart from the complete or partial blockage of the arteries that provide oxygen to the heart

corpus callosum   large band of fibers connecting the two cerebral hemispheres

correlational design   research design that examines the extent to which two variables are associated

correlation–causation fallacy   error of assuming that because one thing is associated with another, it must cause the other

corticosteroids   stress hormones that activate the body and prepare us to respond to stressful circumstances

critical thinking   set of skills for evaluating all claims in an open-minded and careful fashion

cross-sectional design   research design that examines people of different ages at a single point in time

cryptophasia   secret language developed and understood only by a small number of people, typically twins

crystallized intelligence   accumulated knowledge of the world acquired over time

cult   group of individuals who exhibit intense and unquestioning devotion to a single cause

culture-fair IQ tests   abstract reasoning items that don't depend on language and are often believed to be less influenced by cultural factors than other IQ tests

decay   fading of information from memory

defense mechanism   unconscious maneuver intended to minimize anxiety

deindividuation   tendency of people to engage in uncharacteristic behavior when they are stripped of their usual identities

deinstitutionalization   1960s and 1970s governmental policy that focused on releasing hospitalized psychiatric patients into the community and closing mental hospitals

déjà vu   feeling of reliving an experience that's new

delusion   strongly held, fixed belief that has no basis in reality

demand characteristics   cues that participants pick up from a study that allow them to generate guesses regarding the researcher's hypotheses

dendrite   portion of neuron that receives signals

denial   motivated forgetting of distressing external experiences

dependent variable   variable that an experimenter measures to see whether the manipulation has an effect

depth perception   ability to judge distance and three-dimensional relations

descriptive statistics   numerical characterizations that describe data

developmental psychology study of how behavior changes over time

deviation IQ expression of a person's IQ relative to his or her same-aged peers

Diagnostic and Statistical Manual of Mental Disorders (DSM) diagnostic system containing the American Psychiatric Association (APA) criteria for mental disorders

diathesis-stress model perspective proposing that mental disorders are a joint product of a genetic vulnerability, called a diathesis, and stressors that trigger this vulnerability

diffusion of responsibility reduction in feelings of personal responsibility in the presence of others

discrimination negative behavior toward members of out-groups

discriminative stimulus stimulus associated with the presence of reinforcement

dispersion measure of how loosely or tightly bunched scores are

dissociative amnesia inability to recall important personal information—most often related to a stressful experience—that can't be explained by ordinary forgetfulness

dissociative disorder condition involving disruptions in consciousness, memory, identity, or perception

dissociative fugue sudden, unexpected travel away from home or the workplace, accompanied by amnesia for significant life events

dissociative identity disorder (DID) condition characterized by the presence of two or more distinct identities or personality states that recurrently take control of the person's behavior

distributed versus massed practice studying information in small increments over time (distributed) versus in large increments over a brief amount of time (massed)

divergent thinking capacity to generate many different solutions to a problem

dominant gene gene that masks other genes' effects

door-in-the-face technique persuasive technique involving making an unreasonably large request before making the small request we're hoping to have granted

double-blind when neither researchers nor participants are aware of who's in the experimental or control group

duration length of time for which a memory system can retain information

ego psyche's executive and principal decision maker

egocentrism inability to see the world from others' perspectives

elaborative rehearsal linking stimuli to each other in a meaningful way to improve retention of information in short-term memory

Electra complex conflict during the phallic stage in which girls supposedly love their fathers romantically and want to eliminate their mothers as rivals

electroconvulsive therapy patients receive brief electrical pulses to the brain that produce a seizure to treat serious psychological problems

electroencephalograph (EEG) recording of brain's electrical activity at the surface of the skull

embryo second to eighth week of prenatal development, during which limbs, facial features, and major organs of the body take form

emotional intelligence ability to understand our own emotions and those of others, and to apply this information to our daily lives

emotion-focused coping coping strategy that features a positive outlook on feelings or situations accompanied by behaviors that reduce painful emotions

empirical (or data-based) method of test construction approach to building tests in which researchers begin with two or more criterion groups and examine which items best distinguish them

empirically supported therapies treatments for specific disorders supported by high-quality scientific evidence

empty-nest syndrome alleged period of depression in mothers following the departure of their grown children from the home

encoding process of getting information into our memory banks

encoding specificity phenomenon of remembering something better when the conditions under which we retrieve information are similar to the conditions under which we encoded it

endocrine system system of glands and hormones that controls secretion of blood-borne chemical messengers

endorphin chemical in the brain that plays a specialized role in pain reduction

episodic memory recollection of events in our lives

equipotentiality assumption that any conditioned stimulus can be associated equally well with any unconditioned stimulus

eugenics movement in the early twentieth century to improve a population's genetic stock by encouraging those with good genes to reproduce, preventing those with bad genes from reproducing, or both

evolutionary psychology discipline that applies Darwin's theory of natural selection to human and animal behavior

existence proof demonstration that a given psychological phenomenon can occur

experiment research design characterized by random assignment of participants to conditions and manipulation of an independent variable

experimental group   in an experiment, the group of participants that receives the manipulation

experimenter bias effect   phenomenon in which researchers' hypotheses lead them to unintentionally bias the outcome of a study

explicit memory   memories we recall intentionally and of which we have conscious awareness

exposure therapy   therapy that confronts patients with what they fear, with the goal of reducing the fear

external validity   extent to which we can generalize findings to real-world settings

extinction   gradual reduction and eventual elimination of the conditioned response after the conditioned stimulus is presented repeatedly without the unconditioned stimulus

extrasensory perception (ESP)   perception of events outside the known channels of sensation

face validity   extent to which respondents can tell what the items are measuring

factor analysis   statistical technique that analyzes the correlations among responses on personality inventories and other measures

falsifiable   capable of being disproved

family study   analysis of how traits run in families

family therapy   therapy in which the focus of treatment is the family as a unit rather than an individual

fetus   period of prenatal development from the ninth week until birth after all major organs are established and physical maturation is the primary change

fight-or-flight response   physical and psychological reaction that mobilizes people and animals to either defend themselves (fight) or escape (flee) a threatening situation

fitness   organisms' capacity to pass on their genes

fixed interval (FI) schedule   pattern in which we provide reinforcement for producing the response at least once following a specified time interval

fixed ratio (FR) schedule   pattern in which we provide reinforcement following a regular number of responses

flashbulb memories   emotional memories that are thought to be extraordinarily vivid and detailed

fluid intelligence   capacity to learn new ways of solving problems

Flynn effect   finding that average IQ scores have been rising at a rate of approximately 3 points per decade

foot-in-the-door technique   persuasive technique involving making a small request before making a bigger one

forebrain (cerebrum)   forward part of the brain that allows advanced intellectual abilities

formal operations stage   stage in Piaget's theory characterized by the ability to perform hypothetical reasoning beyond the here and now

fovea   central portion of the retina

free association   technique in which patients express themselves without censorship of any sort

frontal lobe   forward part of cerebral cortex responsible for motor function, language, memory, and planning

functional fixedness   difficulty conceptualizing that an object typically used for one purpose can be used for another

functional MRI (fMRI)   technique that uses magnetic fields to visualize brain activity using the BOLD response

functionalism   school of psychology that aimed to understand the adaptive purposes of psychological characteristics

fundamental attribution error   tendency to overestimate the impact of dispositional influences on other people's behavior

g (general intelligence)   hypothetical factor that accounts for overall differences in intellect among people

gender identity   individuals' sense of being male or female

gender role   behaviors that tend to be associated with being male or female

gene   genetic material, composed of deoxyribonucleic acid (DNA)

gene–environment interaction   situation in which the effects of genes depend on the environment in which they are expressed

general adaptation syndrome (GAS)   stress-response pattern proposed by Hans Selye that consists of three stages: alarm, resistance, and exhaustion

generalized anxiety disorder (GAD)   continual feelings of worry, anxiety, physical tension, and irritability across many areas of life functioning

generative   allowing an infinite number of unique sentences to be created by combining words in novel ways

genital stage   psychosexual stage in which sexual impulses awaken and typically begin to mature into romantic attraction toward others

genotype   our genetic makeup

glial cell   support cell in nervous system that plays a role in the formation of myelin and blood–brain barrier, responds to injury, and removes debris

group therapy   therapy that treats more than one person at a time

groupthink   emphasis on group unanimity at the expense of critical thinking and sound decision making

gustation   our sense of taste

habituation   process of responding less strongly over time to repeated stimuli

hallucination   sensory perception that occurs in the absence of an external stimulus

hallucinogenic   causing dramatic alterations of perception, mood, and thought

hardiness   set of attitudes marked by a sense of control over events, commitment to life and work, and courage and motivation to confront stressful events

hassle   minor annoyance or nuisance that strains our ability to cope

health psychology   field of psychology that integrates the behavioral sciences with the practice of medicine

heritability   percentage of the variability in a trait across individuals that is due to genes

higher-order conditioning   developing a conditioned response to a conditioned stimulus by virtue of its association with another conditioned stimulus

hindsight bias   tendency to overestimate how well we could have successfully forecasted known outcomes

hippocampus   part of the brain that plays a role in spatial memory

homesign   system of signs invented by deaf children of hearing parents who receive no language input

hormone   chemical released into the bloodstream that influences particular organs and glands

hue   color of light

humanistic psychotherapy   therapy that shares an emphasis on the development of human potential and the belief that human nature is basically positive

hypnosis   set of techniques that provides people with suggestions for alterations in their perceptions, thoughts, feelings, and behaviors

hypnotic   drug that exerts a sleep-inducing effect

hypothalamus   part of the brain responsible for maintaining a constant internal state

hypothesis   testable prediction derived from a scientific theory

id   reservoir of our most primitive impulses, including sex and aggression

identity   our sense of who we are and our life goals and priorities

illusory correlation   perception of a statistical association between two variables where none exists

immune system   our body's defense system against invading bacteria, viruses, and other potentially illness-producing organisms and substances

implicit and explicit stereotype   belief about the characteristics of an out-group about which we're either unaware (implicit) or aware (explicit)

implicit memory   memories we don't deliberately remember or reflect on consciously

impression management theory   theory that we don't really change our attitudes, but report that we have so that our behaviors appear consistent with them

imprinting   phenomenon observed in which baby birds begin to follow around and attach themselves to any large moving object they see in the hours immediately after hatching

independent variable   treatment or intervention that the experimenter "manipulates" or varies

individual differences   variations among people in their thinking, emotion, and behavior

infantile amnesia   inability of adults to remember personal experiences that took place before an early age

inferential statistics   mathematical methods that allow us to determine whether we can generalize findings from our sample to the full population

inferiority complex   feelings of low self-esteem that can lead to overcompensation for such feelings

informed consent   informing research participants of what is involved in a study before asking them to participate

in-group bias   tendency to favor individuals within our group over those from outside our group

inoculation effect   approach to convincing people to change their minds about something by first introducing reasons why the perspective might be correct and then debunking it

insight   grasping the nature of a problem

insight therapy   psychotherapy, including psychodynamic and humanistic approaches, with the goal of expanding awareness or insight

insomnia   difficulty falling or staying asleep

instinctive drift   tendency for animals to return to innate behaviors following repeated reinforcement

intelligence quotient (IQ)   systematic means of quantifying differences among people in their intelligence

intelligence test   diagnostic tool designed to measure overall thinking ability

interference   loss of information from memory because of competition from additional incoming information

internal validity   extent to which we can draw cause-and-effect inferences from a study

interneuron   neuron that sends messages to other neurons nearby

interpersonal therapy   treatment that strengthens social skills and targets interpersonal problems, conflicts, and life transitions

introspection method by which trained observers carefully reflect and report on their mental experiences

jigsaw classroom educational approach designed to minimize prejudice by requiring all children to make independent contributions to a shared project

just noticeable difference (JND) the smallest change in the intensity of a stimulus that we can detect

just-world hypothesis claim that our attributions and behaviors are shaped by a deep-seated assumption that the world is fair and all things happen for a reason

labeling theorist scholar who argues that psychiatric diagnoses exert powerful negative effects on people's perceptions and behaviors

language a largely arbitrary system of communication that combines symbols (such as words or gestural signs) in rule-based ways to create meaning

latency stage psychosexual stage in which sexual impulses are submerged into the unconscious

latent learning learning that's not directly observable

lateralization cognitive function that relies more on one side of the brain than the other

law of effect principle asserting that if a stimulus followed by a behavior results in a reward, the stimulus is more likely to elicit the behavior in the future

learned helplessness tendency to feel helpless in the face of events we can't control

learning change in an organism's behavior or thought as a result of experience

learning style an individual's preferred or optimal method of acquiring new information

lens part of the eye that changes curvature to keep images in focus

lesion area of damage due to surgery, injury, or disease

levels of explanation rungs on a ladder of explanation, with lower levels tied most closely to biological influences and higher levels tied most closely to social influences

levels-of-processing model model stating that the more deeply we process information, the better we remember it

limbic system emotional center of brain that also plays roles in smell, motivation, and memory

linguistic determinism view that all thought is represented verbally and that, as a result, our language defines our thinking

linguistic relativity view that characteristics of language shape our thought processes

locus of control extent to which people believe that reinforcers and punishers lie inside or outside of their control

longitudinal design research design that examines development in the same group of people on multiple occasions over time

long-term memory sustained (from minutes to years) retention of information stored regarding facts, our experiences, and skills

long-term potentiation (LTP) gradual strengthening of the connections among neurons from repetitive stimulation

low-ball technique persuasive technique in which the seller of a product starts by quoting a low sales price and then mentions all of the "add-on" costs once the customer has agreed to purchase the product

Magic Number the span of short-term memory, according to George Miller: seven plus or minus two pieces of information

magnetic resonance imaging (MRI) technique that uses magnetic fields to indirectly visualize brain structure

magnetoencephalography (MEG) measure of brain activity that measures tiny magnetic fields generated by the brain

maintenance rehearsal repeating stimuli in their original form to retain them in short-term memory

major depressive episode state in which a person experiences a lingering depressed mood or diminished interest in pleasurable activities, along with symptoms that include weight loss and sleep difficulties

manic episode state marked by dramatically elevated mood, decreased need for sleep, increased energy, inflated self-esteem, increased talkativeness, and irresponsible behavior

mass hysteria outbreak of irrational behavior that is spread by social contagion

mean average; a measure of central tendency

median middle score in a data set; a measure of central tendency

medical model view that regards mental illness as due to a physical disorder requiring medical treatment

meditation set of ritualized practices that train attention and awareness

medulla part of brain stem involved in basic functions, such as heartbeat and breathing

memory retention of information over time

memory illusion false but subjectively compelling memory

menarche start of menstruation

menopause the termination of menstruation, marking the end of a woman's reproductive potential

mental age age corresponding to the average individual's performance on an intelligence test

mental retardation condition characterized by an onset prior to adulthood, an IQ below about 70, and an inability to engage in adequate daily functioning

mental set phenomenon of becoming stuck in a specific problem-solving strategy, inhibiting our ability to generate alternatives

metaphysical claims assertions about the world that are not testable

midbrain part of the brain stem that contributes to movement, tracking of visual stimuli, and reflexes triggered by sound

midlife crisis supposed phase of adulthood characterized by emotional distress about the aging process and an attempt to regain youth

Minnesota Multiphasic Personality Inventory (MMPI) widely used structured test designed to assess symptoms of mental disorders

misinformation effect creation of fictitious memories by providing misleading information about an event after it takes place

mnemonic a learning aid, strategy, or device that enhances recall

mode most frequent score in a data set; a measure of central tendency

monocular depth cues stimuli that enable us to judge depth using only one eye

motor behavior bodily motion that occurs as result of self-initiated force that moves the bones and muscles

motor cortex part of frontal lobe responsible for body movement

multiple intelligences idea that people vary in their ability levels across different domains of intellectual skill

multiply determined caused by many factors

myelin sheath glial cells wrapped around axons that act as insulators of the neuron's signal

naive realism belief that we see the world precisely as it is

narcolepsy disorder characterized by the rapid and often unexpected onset of sleep

narcotic drug that relieves pain and induces sleep

natural selection principle that organisms that possess adaptations survive and reproduce at a higher rate than other organisms

naturalistic observation watching behavior in real-world settings

negative reinforcement removal of a stimulus that strengthens the probability of the behavior

neo-Freudian theories theories derived from Freud's model but that place less emphasis on sexuality as a driving force in personality and are more optimistic regarding the prospects for long-term personality growth

neurogenesis creation of new neurons in the adult brain

neuron nerve cell specialized for communication

neurotransmitter chemical messenger specialized for communication from neuron to neuron

night terrors sudden waking episodes characterized by screaming, perspiring, and confusion followed by a return to a deep sleep

non-REM (NREM) sleep stages 1 through 4 of the sleep cycle, during which eye movements do not occur and dreaming is less frequent and vivid

obedience adherence to instructions from those of higher authority

object permanence the understanding that objects continue to exist even when out of view

observational learning learning by watching others

obsession persistent idea, thought, or impulse that is unwanted and inappropriate, causing marked distress

obsessive-compulsive disorder condition marked by repeated and lengthy (at least 1 hour per day) immersion in obsessions, compulsions, or both

occipital lobe back part of cerebral cortex specialized for vision

Oedipus complex conflict during the phallic stage in which boys supposedly love their mothers romantically and want to eliminate their fathers as rivals

olfaction our sense of smell

operant conditioning learning controlled by the consequences of the organism's behavior

operationalization specification of how a variable is being measured for the purposes of a particular study

oral stage psychosexual stage that focuses on the mouth

organ of Corti tissue containing the hair cells necessary for hearing

out-group homogeneity tendency to view all individuals outside our group as highly similar

overconfidence tendency to overestimate our ability to make correct predictions

panic attack brief, intense episode of extreme fear characterized by sweating, dizziness, light-headedness, racing heartbeat, and feelings of impending death or going crazy

panic disorder repeated and unexpected panic attacks, along with either persistent concerns about future attacks or a change in personal behavior in an attempt to avoid them

paraprofessional person with no professional training who provides mental health services

parasympathetic division part of autonomic nervous system that controls rest and digestion

parietal lobe upper middle part of the cerebral cortex lying behind the frontal lobe that is specialized for touch and perception

partial reinforcement only occasional reinforcement of a behavior, resulting in slower extinction than if the behavior had been reinforced continually

participant modeling technique in which the therapist first models a problematic situation and then guides the patient through steps to cope with it unassisted

past life regression therapy therapeutic approach that hypnotizes and supposedly age-regresses patients back to a previous life to identify the source of a present-day problem

peer review mechanism by which experts in a field carefully screen the work of their colleagues

perception the brain's interpretation of raw sensory inputs

perceptual constancy the process by which we perceive stimuli consistently across varied conditions

perceptual set the influence that expectations have on perception

peripheral nervous system (PNS) nerves in the body that extend outside the central nervous system (CNS)

personality stable tendencies within individuals that influence how they respond to their environments

personality disorder condition in which personality traits, appearing first in adolescence, are inflexible, stable, expressed in a wide variety of situations, and lead to distress or impairment

phallic stage psychosexual stage that focuses on the genitals

pharmacotherapy use of medications to treat psychological problems

phenotype our observable traits

pheromone odorless chemical that serves as a social signal to members of one's species

phobia intense fear of an object or situation that's greatly out of proportion to its actual threat

pituitary gland master gland that, under the control of the hypothalamus, directs the other glands of the body

placebo effect improvement resulting from the mere expectation of improvement

plasticity ability of the nervous system to change

pluralistic ignorance error of assuming that no one in a group perceives things as we do

pons part of the brain stem that connects the cortex with the cerebellum

positive reinforcement presentation of a stimulus that strengthens the probability of the behavior

positron emission tomography (PET) imaging technique that measures consumption of glucoselike molecules, yielding a picture of neural activity in different regions of the brain

post hoc fallacy false assumption that because one event occurred before another event, it must have caused that event

posttraumatic stress disorder (PTSD) marked emotional disturbance after experiencing or witnessing a severely stressful event

prefrontal cortex part of frontal lobe responsible for thinking, planning, and language

prejudice drawing conclusions about a person, group of people, or situation prior to evaluating the evidence

Premack principle principle that a less frequently performed behavior can be increased in frequency by reinforcing it with a more frequent behavior

prenatal prior to birth

preoperational stage stage in Piaget's theory characterized by the ability to construct mental representations of experience, but not yet perform operations on them

prepared learning evolutionary predisposition to learn some pairings of feared stimuli over others owing to their survival value

prevalence percentage of people within a population who have a specific mental disorder

primacy effect tendency to remember words at the beginning of a list especially well

primary reinforcer item or outcome that naturally increases target behavior

primary sensory cortex regions of the cerebral cortex that initially process information from the senses

primary sex characteristics the reproductive organs and genitals that distinguish the sexes

priming our ability to identify a stimulus more easily or more quickly after we've encountered similar stimuli

proactive interference interference with acquisition of new information due to previous learning of information

problem solving generating a cognitive strategy to accomplish a goal

problem-focused coping coping strategy by which we tackle life's challenges head-on

procedural memory memory for how to do things, including motor skills and habits

projective hypothesis hypothesis that, in the process of interpreting ambiguous stimuli, examinees project aspects of their personality onto the stimulus

projective test test consisting of ambiguous stimuli that examinees must interpret or make sense of

proprioception   our sense of body position

pseudoscience   set of claims that seems scientific but isn't

psychic determinism   the assumption that all psychological events have a cause

psychoactive drugs   chemicals similar to those found naturally in our brains that alter consciousness by changing chemical processes in neurons

psychoanalysis   school of psychology, founded by Sigmund Freud, that focuses on internal psychological processes of which we're unaware

psychology   the scientific study of the mind, brain, and behavior

psychoneuroimmunology   study of the relationship between the immune system and central nervous system

psychopathic personality   condition marked by superficial charm, dishonesty, manipulativeness, self-centeredness, and risk taking

psychophysiological   illnesses such as asthma and ulcers in which emotions and stress contribute to, maintain, or aggravate the physical condition

psychosocial crisis   dilemma concerning an individual's relations to other people

psychosurgery   brain surgery to treat psychological problems

psychotherapy   a psychological intervention designed to help people resolve emotional, behavioral, and interpersonal problems and improve the quality of their lives

psychotic symptom   psychological problem reflecting serious distortions in reality

punishment   outcome or consequence of a behavior that weakens the probability of the behavior

random assignment   randomly sorting participants into two groups

random selection   procedure that ensures every person in a population has an equal chance of being chosen to participate

range   difference between the highest and lowest scores; a measure of dispersion

rapid eye movements (REM)   darting of the eyes underneath the closed eyelids during sleep

rational/theoretical method of test construction   approach to building tests that requires test developers to begin with a clear-cut conceptualization of a trait and then write items to assess that conceptualization

recall   generating previously remembered information

recency effect   tendency to remember words at the end of a list especially well

receptor site   location that uniquely recognizes a neurotransmitter

recessive gene   gene that is expressed only in the absence of a dominant gene

recognition   selecting previously remembered information from an array of options

reflex   an automatic motor response to a sensory stimulus

regression   the act of returning psychologically to a younger, and typically simpler and safer, age

rehearsal   repeating information to extend the duration of retention in short-term memory

reinforcement   outcome or consequence of a behavior that strengthens the probability of the behavior

relational aggression   form of indirect aggression, prevalent in girls, involving spreading rumors, gossiping, and nonverbal putdowns for the purpose of social manipulation

relearning   reacquiring knowledge that we'd previously learned but largely forgotten over time

reliability   consistency of measurement

REM sleep   stage of sleep during which the brain is most active and during which vivid dreaming most often occurs

replicability   when a study's findings are able to be duplicated, ideally by independent investigators

repression   motivated forgetting of emotionally threatening memories or impulses

resistance   attempts to avoid confrontation and anxiety associated with uncovering previously repressed thoughts, emotions, and impulses

response sets   tendencies of research participants to distort their responses to questionnaire items

resting potential   electrical charge difference (–60 millivolts) across the neuronal membrane, when the neuron is not being stimulated or inhibited

retina   membrane at the back of the eye responsible for converting light into neural activity

retrieval   reactivation or reconstruction of experiences from our memory stores

retrieval cues   hints that make it easier for us to recall information

retroactive interference   interference with retention of old information due to acquisition of new information

retrograde amnesia   loss of memories from our past

reuptake   means of recycling neurotransmitters

rods   receptor cells in the retina allowing us to see in low levels of light

Rorschach Inkblot Test   projective test consisting of ten symmetrical inkblots

s (specific abilities)   particular ability levels in a narrow domain

scaffolding   Vygotskian learning process in which parents provide initial assistance in children's learning but gradually remove structure as children become more competent

scapegoat hypothesis   claim that prejudice arises from a need to blame other groups for our misfortunes

scatterplot   grouping of points on a two-dimensional graph in which each dot represents a single person's data

schedule of reinforcement   pattern of reinforcing a behavior

schema   organized knowledge structure or mental model that we've stored in memory

schizophrenia   severe disorder of thought and emotion associated with a loss of contact with reality

scientific skepticism   approach of evaluating all claims with an open mind but insisting on persuasive evidence before accepting them

scientific theory   explanation for a large number of findings in the natural world

secondary reinforcer   neutral object that becomes associated with a primary reinforcer

secondary sex characteristics   sex-differentiating characteristics that don't relate directly to reproduction, such as breast enlargement in women and deepening voices in men

sedative   drug that exerts a calming effect

selective attention   process of selecting one sensory channel and ignoring or minimizing others

self-actualization   drive to develop our innate potential to the fullest possible extent

self-monitoring   personality trait that assesses the extent to which people's behavior reflects their true feelings and attitudes

semantic memory   our knowledge of facts about the world

sensation   detection of physical energy by sense organs, which then send information to the brain

sense receptor   specialized cell responsible for converting external stimuli into neural activity for a specific sensory system

sensorimotor stage   stage in Piaget's theory characterized by a focus on the here and now without the ability to represent experiences mentally

sensory adaptation   a decline in activation within a sense receptor after initial activation

sensory memory   brief storage of perceptual information before it is passed to short-term memory

serial position curve   graph depicting the effect of both primacy and recency on people's ability to recall items on a list

shaping by successive approximations   conditioning a target behavior by progressively reinforcing behaviors that come closer and closer to the target

short-term memory   memory system that retains the information we are currently thinking about for limited durations

sign language   language developed by members of deaf communities that uses visual rather than auditory communication

single-variable explanations   explanations that try to account for complex behaviors in terms of only a single cause

Skinner box   small animal chamber constructed by Skinner to allow sustained periods of conditioning to be administered and behaviors to be recorded unsupervised

sleep apnea   disorder caused by a blockage of the airway during sleep, resulting in daytime fatigue

sleepwalking   walking while fully asleep

social comparison theory   theory that we seek to evaluate our beliefs, attitudes, and abilities by comparing our reactions with others'

social facilitation   enhancement of performance brought about by the presence of others

social learning theorists   theorists who emphasized thinking as a cause of personality

social loafing   phenomenon whereby individuals become less productive in groups

social phobia   marked fear of public appearances in which embarrassment or humiliation is possible

social psychology   study of how people influence others' behavior, beliefs, and attitudes

social support   relationships with people and groups that can provide us with emotional comfort and personal and financial resources

somatic nervous system   part of the nervous system that conveys information between the CNS and the body, controlling and coordinating voluntary movement

somatosensation   our sense of touch

source monitoring   ability to identify the origins of a memory

span   how much information a memory system can retain

spermarche   boys' first ejaculation

spinal cord   thick bundle of nerves that conveys signals between the brain and the body

spirituality   search for the sacred, which may or may not extend to belief in God

split-brain surgery   procedure that involves severing the corpus callosum to reduce the spread of epileptic seizures

spontaneous recovery   sudden reemergence of an extinct conditioned response after a delay in exposure to the conditioned stimulus

standard deviation   measure of dispersion that takes into account how far each data point is from the mean

Stanford-Binet IQ test   intelligence test based on the measure developed by Binet and Simon, adapted by Lewis Terman of Stanford University

state-dependent learning   superior retrieval of memories when the organism is in the same physiological or psychological state as it was during encoding

statistics   application of mathematics to describing and analyzing data

stereotype   a belief, positive or negative, about the characteristics of members of a group that is applied generally to most members of the group

stereotype threat   fear that we may confirm a negative group stereotype

stimulant   drug that increases activity in the central nervous system, including heart rate, respiration, and blood pressure

stimulus discrimination   displaying a less pronounced conditioned response to conditioned stimuli that differ from the original conditioned stimulus

stimulus generalization   process by which conditioned stimuli similar, but not identical to, the original conditioned stimulus elicit a conditioned response

storage   process of keeping information in memory

stranger anxiety   a fear of strangers developing at 8 or 9 months of age

stress   the tension, discomfort, or physical symptoms that arise when a situation strains our ability to cope effectively

structuralism   school of psychology that aimed to identify the basic elements of psychological experience

structured personality test   paper-and-pencil test consisting of questions that respondents answer in one of a few fixed ways

suggestive memory techniques   procedures that encourage patients to recall memories that may or may not have taken place

superego   our sense of morality

sympathetic division   part of the autonomic nervous system engaged during a crisis or after actions requiring fight or flight

synapse   space between two connecting neurons through which messages are transmitted chemically

synaptic vesicle   spherical sac containing neurotransmitters

systematic desensitization   patients are taught to relax as they are gradually exposed in a stepwise manner to what they fear

taste buds   sense receptors in the tongue that respond to sweet, salty, sour, bitter, umami, and perhaps fat

temperament   basic emotional style that appears early in development and is largely genetic in origin

temporal lobe   lower part of cerebral cortex that plays roles in hearing, understanding language, and memory

tend and befriend   reaction that mobilizes people to nurture (tend) or seek social support (befriend) under stress

teratogens   environmental factors that can exert a negative impact on prenatal development

test bias   tendency of a test to predict outcomes better in one group than another

thalamus   gateway from the sense organs to the primary sensory cortex

Thematic Apperception Test (TAT)   projective test requiring examinees to tell a story in response to ambiguous pictures

theory of mind   ability to reason about what other people know or believe

thinking   any mental activity or processing of information, including learning, remembering, perceiving, believing, and deciding

threshold   membrane potential necessary to trigger an action potential

top-down processing   constructing a mental understanding of a stimulus using our existing knowledge and expectations

trait   relatively enduring predisposition that influences our behavior across many situations

transcranial magnetic stimulation (TMS)   technique that applies strong and quickly changing magnetic fields to the surface of the skull that can either enhance or interrupt brain function

transduction   the process of converting an external energy or substance into neural activity

transference   projecting intense, unrealistic feelings and expectations from the past onto the therapist

triarchic model   model of intelligence proposed by Robert Sternberg positing three distinct types of intelligences: analytical, practical, and creative

trichromatic theory   idea that color vision is based on our sensitivity to three different colors

twin study   analysis of how traits differ in identical versus fraternal twins

Type A personality   personality type that describes people who are competitive, driven, hostile, and ambitious

ultimate attribution error   assumption that behaviors among individual members of a group are due to their internal dispositions

unconditioned response (UCR) automatic response to a nonneutral stimulus that does not need to be learned

unconditioned stimulus (UCS) stimulus that elicits an automatic response

validity extent to which a measure assesses what it claims to measure

variable anything that can vary

variable interval (VI) schedule pattern in which we provide reinforcement for producing the response at least once during an average time interval, with the interval varying randomly

variable ratio (VR) schedule pattern in which we provide reinforcement after a specific number of responses on average, with the number varying randomly

vestibular sense our sense of equilibrium or balance

Wechsler Adult Intelligence Scale (WAIS) most widely used intelligence test for adults today, consisting of 14 subtests to assess different types of mental abilities

Wernicke's area part of the temporal lobe involved in understanding speech

within-group heritability extent to which the variability of a trait within a group is genetically influenced

work through confront and resolve problems, conflicts, and ineffective coping responses in everyday life

zone of proximal development phase of learning during which children can benefit from instruction

zygote fertilized egg

Answer Key for Your
Complete Review System

1: PSYCHOLOGY AND SCIENTIFIC THINKING

What is Psychology? Common versus Uncommon Sense

1. believing is seeing
2. These tables are identical in size – one can be directly superimposed on top of the other. Even though our perceptions are often accurate, we can't always trust them to provide us with an error-free picture of the world.
3. isn't
4. approach
5. confirmation bias
6. belief perseverance
7. often
8. scientific theory
9. theories; hypotheses
10. 1: H; 2: T; 3: T; 4: H; 5: H

Psychological Pseudoscience: Imposters of Science

11. misinformation
12. 95
13. psychotherapy
14. widespread
15. 1b; 2c; 3e; 4g; 5d; 6a; 7f
16. unrelated
17. chance
18. testable
19. The tragic case of Candace Newmaker, who died of suffocation after undergoing a pseudoscientific rebirthing therapy, teaches us that pseudoscience can be harmful, and evenly deadly.
20. effective treatments

Scientific Thinking: Distinguishing Fact from Fiction

21. scientific skepticism
22. critical (or scientific) thinking
23. can
24. explanations
25. correlation-causation fallacy
26. falsifiable
27. replicability
28. parsimony
30. There are two explanations for crop circles— one supernatural and the other natural. According to Occam's Razor, we should select the simplest explanation.
30. 1d; 2a; 3b; 4e; 5f; 6c

Psychology's Past and Present: What a Long Strange Trip It's Been

31. introspection
32. William James
33. black box
34. interpretation
35. Freudian slips
36. don't need
37. different than
38. Developmental psychologists spend most of their time in the lab, collecting and analyzing data on children's behavior.
39. Evolutionary psychology
40. illusion

Applying Psychological Science and Thinking to Everyday Life

41. basic; applied
42. lime-yellow
43. three
44. 61
45. John Watson
46. Human faces better capture readers' attention on the left rather than on the right side of pages. Written text, in contrast, better captures readers' attention on the right side.
47. SAT; ACT
48. simultaneous
49. sequential
50. Kenneth and Marie Clark conducted studies that showed African American children preferred White to African American dolls, leading the U.S. Supreme Court to decide that school segregation exerted a negative impact on the self-esteem of African American children.

2: RESEARCH METHODS

The Beauty and Necessity of Good Research Design

1. research designs
2. Biklen fell prey to confirmation bias, as we all do sometimes. He believed that facilitated communication would unlock the mind of the child with autism and as a result, found what he expected to find. Only careful, unbiased research ruled out this interpretation of what was really going on.
3. heuristics
4. representativeness
5. base rate
6. availability
7. By relying on a mental shortcut or a heuristic based on the knowledge that California is on the West Coast, most people forget or don't know that a large chunk of CA is east of Nevada.
8. cognitive biases
9. hindsight bias
10. overconfidence

The Scientific Method: A Toolbox of Skills

11. case study, correlational design
12. up
13. Exceptions don't invalidate the existence of correlations. Unless the correlation is perfect (1.0 or -1.0), it is mathematically necessary that there will be some exceptions.
14. experiment
15. can; can't
16. control
17. reliability; validity
18. placebo; blind
19. experimenter bias
20. The pollsters got it wrong largely because they based their results on telephone surveys. Back in 1948, considerably more Republicans (who tended to be richer) owned telephones than Democrats, resulting in a biased sampling and a skewed preelection prediction.

Ethical Issues in Research Design

21. ethics
22. institutional review board
23. informed consent
24. deception
25. would not
26. All research with human subjects requires approval from an IRB before it can be conducted. IRBs evaluate the ethics of the study and require a procedure called informed consent: researchers must tell subjects what they're getting into before asking them to participate.
27. invasive
28. 7-8
29. Arguments for: some animal research has led to direct benefits to humans as well as immensely useful knowledge in its own right; many psychological treatments were derived from animal research that could not have been developed using human participants. Arguments against: the deaths of approximately 20 million lab animals a year aren't worth the benefits – critics argue that the knowledge gleaned from animal research is of such doubtful external validity to humans as to be virtually useless.
30. scientific gains

Statistics: The Currency of Psychological Research

31. statistics
32. descriptive; central tendency
33. Mode: 2; Mean: 3; Median: 1

34. mean
35. range
36. dispersion
37. a) negative skew; b) positive skew
38. standard deviation
39. inferential
40. truncated line graph

Becoming a Peer Reviewer of Psychological Research
41. peer reviewer
42. independent variable
43. control
44. placebo
45. experimenter bias

46. confound
47. are not
48. source
49. sharpening; leveling
50. pseudosymmetry

3: BIOLOGICAL PSYCHOLOGY

Nerve Cells: Communication Portals
1. cell body
2. dendrites
3. synapse
4. axons; send
5. myelin sheath
6. endorphins
7. resting potential
8. electric discharge
9.

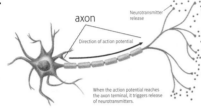

10. neurons

The Brain-Behavior Network
11. central nervous system
12. peripheral nervous
13. cortex
14. a) cortex; b) basal ganglia; c) limbic system; d) cerebellum; e) brain stem; f) spinal cord

15. a) generates signals responsible for voluntary movements; b) receives data about sensations in skin, muscles, and joints; c) analyzes visual data to form images; d) receives information from the optic nerve, transmitted through the visual thalamus; e) interprets spoken and written language; f) analyzes data about sound, so that we can recognize words or melodies; g) detects discrete qualities of sound, such as pitch and volume; h) vital for the formation of speech; i) influences various aspects of behavior, personality, planning, and reasoning
16. basal ganglia
17. sympathetic
18. respiration; perspiration
19. pituitary gland
20. do

Mapping the Mind: The Brain in Action
21. phrenology
22. electroencephalograph (EEG)
23. wouldn't
24. the change in blood oxygen level
25. aren't
26. split-brain
27. lateralization

28. The subject's right hemisphere recognizes the snow scene leading her to point with her left hand (controlled by the right hemisphere) to the shovel, but her left hemisphere recognizes the claw leading her to indicate verbally that the chicken is the matching object.
29. right; left
30. aren't

Nature and Nurture: Did Your Genes – Or Parents – Make You Do It?
31. chromosomes
32. Genes
33. phenotype; genotype
34. Dominant
35. 46; just 1 pair
36. natural selection
37. behavioral genetics
38. groups of people
39. No, because environmental manipulation is still possible and can result in substantial changes. In fact, heritability can actually change over time.
40. adoption studies

4: SENSATION AND PERCEPTION)

Two Sides of the Coin: Sensation and Perception
1. sensation
2. Perception
3. transduction
4. sense receptor
5. absolute threshold
6. just noticeable difference
7. bottom-up
8. top-down processing
9. selective attention
10. Information that we've supposedly filtered out of our attention is still being processed at some level.

Seeing: The Visual System
11. human visible
12. brightness
13. retina
14. lens
15. Rods; cones
16. a) fovea: part of the retina where light rays are most sharply focused; b) optic nerve: transmits impulses from the retina to the rest of the brain; c) retina: innermost layer of the eye, where incoming light is converted into nerve impulses; d) eye muscle: one of six surrounding muscles

that rotate the eye in all directions; e) lens: transparent disk that focuses light rays for near or distant vision; f) cornea: curved, transparent dome that bends incoming light; g) iris: colored area containing muscles that control the pupil; h) pupil: opening in the center of the iris that lets in light
17. visual cortex
18. a) proximity; b) closure
19. depth perception
20. perceptual constancy

Hearing: The Auditory System
21. pitch
22. amplitude
23. timbre
24. cochlea
25. hair cells
26. a) eardrum: membrane that vibrates in response to sound waves; b) semicircular canal: one of three fluid-filled structures that play a role in balance; c) cochlea: converts vibration into neural activity; d) pinna: flexible outer flap of the ear, which channels sound waves into the ear canal; e) ear canal: conducts sound waves to the eardrum

27. place
28. localize
29. When someone standing to our left speaks to us, the sound reaches our left ear slightly earlier than it reaches our right. Also the intensity detected by the left ear is greater than the intensity detected by the right ear, because the right ear lies in a sound shadow produced by the head and shoulders. The amount of discrepancy in timing and intensity enables us to determine where the sound originated.
30. binaural cues

Smell, Taste, and Touch: The Sensual Senses
31. taste buds
32. five; umami
33. orbitofrontal cortex
34. a) somatosensory cortex; b) thalamus; c) olfactory cortex; d) olfactory bulb; e) orbitofrontal cortex; f) pons; g) medulla oblongata
35. Pheromones
36. The skin contains many different types of receptors and free nerve endings that specialize

to detect mechanical pressure, stretching, and pain.
37. free nerve endings
38. quickly
39. proprioception
40. vestibular sense

Alterations in Sensation and Perception
41. extrasensory perception
42. hallucinations
43. out-of-body
44. near death
45. déjà vu

46. are
47. past life regression therapy
48. The Poggendorf Illusion
49. dissociation
50. has

5: LEARNING

Classical Conditioning
1. learning
2. classical conditioning
3. a) neutral stimulus; b) no salivation; c) UCS; d) UCR (salivation); e) neutral stimulus; f) UCS; g) UCR (salivation); h) previously neutral stimulus is now CS; i) CR (salivation)
4. conditioned; unconditioned
5. acquisition
6. extinction
7. spontaneous recovery
8. discrimination
9. higher-order conditioning
10. Little Albert liked small furry animals. Watson and Raynor first allowed Little Albert to play with a white rat. But only seconds afterward, Watson sneaked up behind Little Albert and struck a gong with a steel hammer, creating an earsplitting noise and startling him out of his wits. After 7 such pairings of CS (rat) and UCS (loud sound from gong), Little Albert displayed a CR (fear) to the rat alone. Because inducing a prolonged fear response in an infant raises a host of serious ethical questions, the study would never get past a modern IRB.

Operant Conditioning
11. operants
12.

	Classical Conditioning	Operant Conditioning
Target behavior is . . .	Elicited automatically	Emitted voluntarily
Reward is . . .	Provided unconditionally	Contingent on behavior
Behavior depends primarily on . . .	Autonomic nervous system	Skeletal muscles

13. increase
14. negative reinforcement
15. negative reinforcement; punishment
16. anxiety
17. slower

18. reinforcement schedules
19. variable ratio schedule
20. a) fixed ratio; b) fixed interval; c) variable ratio; d) variable interval

Cognitive Models of Learning
21. didn't believe
22. overt
23. thinking; emotion
24. S-O-R
25. S-O-R theorists believe that cognition is central to explaining learning and contend that people respond differently because they interpret the criticism in different ways. So managers need to take into account individual reactions when offering performance evaluations.
26. cognitive maps
27. observational
28. Albert Bandura
29. have not
30. Observational learning takes place by watching others. Children acquire a great deal of their behavior by observing and imitating the behaviors of adults, especially their parents.

Biological Influences on Learning
31. conditioned taste aversion
32. By using a scapegoat food, they can help minimize conditioned taste aversions to their favorite foods.

33. biological
34. taste
35. equipotentiality
36. adaptive
37. prepared learning
38. didn't acquire
39. unafraid
40. Instinctive drift is the tendency for animals to return to innate behaviors despite repeated reinforcement to perform a different behavior. Psychologists don't fully understand the reasons for such drift, but it does suggest that we can't fully understand learning without taking into account innate biological influences, since these influences place limits on what kind of behaviors we can train.

Learning Fads: Do They Work?
41. sleep-assisted learning
42. refuting
43. Proponents of sleep-assisted learning claim you can learn languages, or learn how to stop smoking, lose weight, or reduce stress while asleep. The problem with almost all of the studies showing positive effects of sleep-assisted learning is they didn't monitor subjects' EEGs to ensure they were actually asleep while listening to the tapes.
44. discovery learning
45. direct instruction
46. advanced; beginning
47. learning style
48. analytical; holistic
49. doesn't
50. Scientific research provides little evidence that tailoring teaching to individual learning styles enhances learning. For example, it is difficult to assess learning style reliably.

6: MEMORY

How Memory Operates: The Memory Assembly Line
1. memory illusion
2. reconstructive; reproductive
3. observer
4. span; duration
5. a) sensory memory; b) short-term memory; c) long-term memory
6. Sensory; short-term
7. chunking
8. primacy effect
9. Explicit; implicit
10. a) semantic; b) episodic; c) procedural; d) priming; e) conditioning; f) habituation

The Three Stages of Remembering
11. encoding; storage; retrieval
12. Encoding
13. mnemonic
14.

15. Relearning
16. distributed versus massed practicethe table to show the differences
17. tip-of-the-tongue
18. Encoding specificity
19. context-dependent learning
20. 1) distributed versus massed study; 2) elaborative rehearsal; 3) levels of processing; 4) mnemonic devices

The Biology of Memory
21. learning
22. hippocampus
23. retrograde
24. anterograde

25. gradually
26. hippocampus; hypothalamus; amygdala
27. Such messages rarely help people with antero-grade amnesia because they usually don't remember to look at the notes.
28. implicit memory
29. isn't
30. dementia

The Development of Memory: Acquiring a Personal History

31. metamemory
32. implicit memory
33. Rovee-Collier and others used mobiles to study infants' implicit memory. Infants were conditioned to kick in a particular setting in order to see a mobile move. Although infants can't tell you they remember the mobile when they later see it again, their kicking behavior gives us insight into whether they recall the mobile and for how long.
34. specific
35. Infantile amnesia
36. earlier
37. isn't
38. self
39. language skills
40. mirror self-recognition

When Good Memory Goes Bad: False Memories

41. Flashbulb memories
42. source monitoring
43. cryptomnesia
44. The misinformation effect is the creation of fictitious memories by providing misleading information about an event after it takes place.
45. By using powerful suggestions and fake photo-graphs, researchers have demonstrated that it's possible to create elaborate memories of events that never happened.
46. therapists
47. absentmindedness
48. blocking
49. typical
50. Suggestibility

7: LANGUAGE, THINKING, AND INTELLIGENCE

How Does Language Work?

1. Babies begin to hear inside the womb by the fifth month of pregnancy. They can learn to recognize their mother's voices and some characteristics of their mother's native lan-guage, and can even recognize specific songs or stories they've heard over and over again.
2. can
3. generative
4. language acquisition device
5. exhibit
6. bonobos
7. linguistic determinism
8. can
9. linguistic relativity
10. isn't

Thinking and Reasoning

11. thinking
12. cognitive economy
13. Cultural differences in our prototypes indicate that our category knowledge is influenced by our everyday experience.
14. categories
15. category; concept
16. Our cognitive economy can sometimes lead us to make incorrect snap judgments such as hiring the well dressed, socially skilled appli-cant over the one with the most talent and experience.
17. problem solving
18. mental set
19. Functional fixedness
20. scientific reasoning

What is Intelligence? Definitional Confusion

21. high
22. intelligence test
23. abstract thinking
24. general intelligence
25. s; specific abilities
26. fluid intelligence; crystallized intelligence
27. a) analytical; b) practical; c) creative
28. Divergent thinking
29. emotional intelligence
30. d. General abilities such as reasoning, short-term memory, and pattern recognition could explain people's ability to answer this question correctly.

Intelligence Testing: The Good, the Bad, and the Ugly

31. In the example provided, .8 x 100 = 80. If we apply this formula to an 18-year-old with a mental age of 18, we'd have the following: 18 (mental age)/18 (chronological age) = 1 x 100 = 100 (IQ). If we apply it to a 35-year-old who also has a mental age of 18, we'd have: 18 (mental age)/35 (chronological age) = .51 x 100 = 51 (IQ). Because our mental age lev-els off but our chronological age increases with time, Stern's formula would result in everyone's IQ getting lower and lower as they got older.
32. Mental age
33. deviation IQ
34. Wechsler Adult Intelligence Scale (WAIS)
35. a) Digit symbol: tests speed of learning through timed coding tasks in which numbers must be associated with marks of various shapes; b) Pic-ture completion: tests visual alertness and visual memory through presentation of an incom-pletely drawn figure; the missing part must be discovered and named; c) Block design: tests ability to perceive and analyze patterns present-ing designs that must be copied with blocks.
36. high; low
37. validity
38. do
39. 1910; 1930
40. Mandatory sterilization

Individual and Group Differences in IQ

41. genetic; environmental
42. Adoption
43. increase
44. Flynn effect
45. F: spelling; M: arithmetic calculation; M: com-plex mathematical tasks; M: safe driving, M: geography, F: sociability; F: reading facial expression in emotion; M: spatial ability
46. spatial; verbal
47. The two groups of plants started at the same height but were exposed to different environ-mental conditions. This demonstrates how group differences in IQ could be "real" but completely environmentally determined.
48. genetic
49. within-group; between-group
50. stereotype threat

8: HUMAN DEVELOPMENT

Special Considerations in Human Development

1. developmental psychology
2. post hoc
3. Individuals can certainly influence each other to behave in delinquent ways, but research also suggests that individuals with a tendency towards delinquency seek out and find each other, in part because of their genetic propen-sities.
4. cross-sectional
5. Cohort effects
6. Like a longitudinal design, the series traces the lives of the same four British people over time, from age 7 all the way up through age 49. Longitudinal design allows us to examine true developmental effects: changes over time as a consequence of growing older. However, this type of design is time consuming and is not experimental so it can't be used to infer cause-and-effect relationships.
7. are
8. nature; nurture
9. confound
10. gene-environment interaction

The Developing Body before and after Birth: Physical and Motor Development

11. blastocyst
12. second; eighth
13. fetus
14. brain
15. teratogens

16. reflexes
17. sucking reflex
18. a) sitting without support (6 months); b) crawling (9 months); c) standing (11 months); d) cruising (12 months); e) walking without assistance (13 months); f) running (18-24 months)
19. motor behaviors
20. Although cultural variability in practices such as swaddling or stretching influences the rate of motor development, none of these early physical experiences results in long-term advantages or impairments.

Cognitive Development: Children's Learning about the World

21. stage theorist
22. assimilation; accommodation
23. sensorimotor; permanence
24. preoperational; conservation
25. a) sensorimotor (birth to 2 years); b) preoperational (2 to 7 years); c) concrete operations (7 to 11 years); d) formal operations (11 years to adulthood)
26. The task measures egocentrism – the inability to see the world from others' perspectives. Children in the concrete operational stage can pass this task.

27. social; cultural
28. proximal development; scaffolding
29. do
30. theory of mind

Social and Moral Development: Children's Relations with Others

31. stranger anxiety
32. attachment
33. imprinting
34. contact comfort
35. Contact comfort refers to positive emotions afforded by touch. When frightened by a novel object, Harlow's infant monkeys almost always preferred the terry cloth mother over the wire mother even though the wire mother was the monkeys' source of food. Contact comfort prevails over nourishment.
36. 1) The infant becomes upset upon mom's departure but greets her return with joy; 2) The infant reacts with indifference to mom's departure and shows little reaction upon her return; 3) The infant reacts to mom's departure with panic and shows a mixed emotional reaction on her return; 4) The infant reacts to mom's departure and return with an inconsistent and confused set of responses. They may appear dazed when reunited with her.

37. temperament
38. average expectable
39. morality; reasoning processes
40. identity; roles

Development Doesn't Stop: Changes in Adolescence and Adulthood

41. adolescence
42. primary sex characteristics; secondary sex characteristics
43. identity
44. 10.5
45. parent
46. biological age
47. menopause
48. sensory
49. Not all
50. Many cultures honor and revere the elderly. Myths: physical aging is the same for everyone (there are in fact large individual differences); younger adults have better cognitive functioning across the board than older adults (decades of accumulated knowledge and crystallized intelligence means that older adults perform better on analogy tests and vocabulary tests)

9: EMOTION AND MOTIVATION

Theories of Emotion: What Causes Our Feelings?

1. discrete emotions
2. Darwin
3. The Duchenne smile
4. cognitive
5. James-Lange
6. simultaneously
7. We first experience arousal after an emotion-provoking event and then look to the situation to determine the cause of that arousal. The emotional label we attach to our arousal based on our interpretation of the situation is the emotion we then experience.
8. more
9. facial expressions
10. classical conditioning

Happiness and Self-Esteem: Science Confronts Pop Psychology

11. The King plans to boost GNH in Bhutan by preserving the beauty of its natural environment, promoting cultural values, and giving citizens more of a voice in government decisions. This is beneficial because happiness breeds both health and success in our work, family, and love lives.
12. character strengths; virtues
13. broaden and build
14. can't
15. flow
16. affective forecasting
17. durability bias
18. weak
19. Probably because silver medal winners compare their outcome with what "might have been."
20. Defensive pessimism

Motivation: Our Wants and Needs

21. No
22. homeostasis
23. Yerkes-Dodson
24. Incentive
25. a) physiological needs; b) safety needs; c) belonging needs; d) esteem needs

26. glucostatic
27. set point
28. Bulimia
29. the same
30. masculinized; feminized

Attraction, Love, and Hate: The Greatest Mysteries of Them All

31. proximity
32. similarity
33. reciprocity
34. men
35. agree
36. more
37. Passionate
38. companionate love
39. a) Intimacy; b) Passion; c) Commitment; d) Consummate love
40. confirmation bias

10: STRESS, HEALTH, AND SLEEP

What is Stress?

1. stress
2. stressors as stimuli approach
3. transaction
4. primary appraisal
5. secondary appraisal
6. Problem-focused coping
7. emotion-focused coping
8. Social Readjustment Rating
9. Daily hassles and minor annoyances can add up and strain our ability to cope.
10. better

How We Adapt to Stress: Change and Challenge

11. The alarm reaction involves the excitation of the autonomic nervous system, the discharge of the stress hormone adrenaline, and physical symptoms of anxiety.
12. fight-or-flight
13. resistance
14. exhaustion
15. Both responses refer to ways of coping with stressors. During the fight-or-flight responses, a person is physically and psychologically mobilized to either fight the enemy or flee from the situation. In contrast, during times of stress women often rely on their social supports and nurturing abilities (the tend and befriend response) to help them cope with stressful situations.

16. more
17. posttraumatic stress disorder (PTSD)
18. can

19. coronary heart disease
20. hostility

Coping with Stress
21. Social support
22. Social support can provide us with emotional comfort, financial assistance, and information to make decisions, solve problems, and contend with stressful situations.
23. behavioral control
24. Cognitive control
25. emotional control
26. is not
27. Crisis debriefing sessions, in which a facilitator structures a group discussion of people's reactions to a shared traumatic event, may actually increase PTSD risk.
28. Hardiness
29. better
30. Spirituality

**Promoting Good
Health – and Less Stress!**
31. are; neurons
32. substance abuse
33. tolerance; withdrawal
34. low
35. genetic

36.

Drug Type	Examples	Effect on Behavior
Depressants	alcohol, barbiturates, Quaaludes, Valium	decreased activity of the central nervous system (initial high followed by sleepiness, slower thinking and impaired concentration)
Stimulants	tobacco, cocaine, amphetamines, methamphetamine	increased activity of the central nervous system (sense of alertness, well being, energy)
Opiates	heroin, morphine, codeine	sense of euphoria, decreased pain
Psychedelics	marijuana, LSD, Ecstasy	dramatically altered perception, mood, and thoughts

37. Cocaine
38. Alternative medicine
39. are not
40. Positive effects include increases in creativity, empathy, alertness, and self-esteem, as well as decreases in anxiety, interpersonal problems, and recurrence of depression. It can also enhance blood flow in the brain and immune function. Its positive effects may derive from a greater acceptance of our troubling thoughts and feelings. The effects may not be due to meditation itself, but from sitting quietly, resting, and relaxing with eyes closed. Positive attitudes, beliefs, and expectancies about meditation may also account for why it is beneficial.

To Sleep, Perchance to Dream
41. circadian rhythm
42. biological clock
43. a) beta waves; b) alpha waves; c) theta waves; d) sleep spindles and K complexes; e) delta waves
44. 5th; paradoxical or REM
45. wish fulfillment
46. a) cerebral cortex; b) thalamus; c) pons; d) spinal cord
47. less
48. are
49. narcolepsy
50. night terror

11: SOCIAL PSYCHOLOGY

What is Social Psychology?
1. behavior; beliefs; attitudes
2. need to belong
3. social disruption
4. experience
5. social comparison
6. collective delusion
7. Urban legends are convincing in part because they fit our preconceptions. They make good stories because they tug on our emotions, especially negative ones.
8. attributions
9. dispositional influences
10. doesn't

Social Influence: Conformity and Obedience
11. conformity
12. If others responding before you all consistently supplied this same (obviously incorrect) answer, you would be extremely likely to provide the same wrong answer yourself.
13. are
14. low
15. anonymity; individual responsibility
16. Abu Ghraib
17. groupthink
18. inoculation effect
19. obedience
20. The greater the psychological distance between the teacher and experimenter, the less the obedience. For instance, compliance plummeted when the experimenter gave instructions by telephone. Compliance also varied depending on the psychological distance between the teacher and learner. For example, if the teacher was in the same room with the learner, compliance decreased, but if the teacher was instructed to have a third person administer the shock, compliance increased.

**Helping and Harming Others:
Prosocial Behavior and Aggression**
21. prosocial behavior
22. less
23. Address a specific person (i.e. "man in the blue shirt, help me!") to decrease the chances of bystander nonintervention.
24. social loafing
25. less
26. can
27. more
28. situational; dispositional
29. irritability
30. Relational

**Attitudes and Persuasion:
Changing Minds**
31. emotional
32. didn't
33. low
34. recognition heuristic
35. similar to
36. Because endorsements from attractive celebrities can lead us to prefer some products over others for irrational reasons.
37. a) "I'm not an honest person at all"; b) "I didn't really cheat; I just saw someone's answers"; c) "I had to cheat because the test was unfair"
38. more
39. foot-in-the-door
40. low-ball

Prejudice and Discrimination
41. prejudice
42. out-group homogeneity
43. prejudice; discrimination
44. stereotype
45. Jane Elliott divided her class into favored and disfavored groups based solely on their eye color, informing her students that children with brown eyes are superior because of excess melanin in their eyes. The results were dramatic – the brown-eyed children quickly become arrogant and condescending, and the blue-eyed children became submissive and insecure.
46. scapegoat hypothesis
47. just-world
48. cooperation
49. In jigsaw classrooms, children cooperate on a multipart project, with each child assuming a small but essential role.
50. encourage

12: PERSONALITY

Personality: What Is It and How Can We Study It?

1. 1) genetic factors; 2) shared environmental factors; 3) nonshared environmental factors
2. Nonshared environmental
3. twin; adoption
4. 1.0
5. similar
6. shared
7. genes; environment
8. higher
9. circuitous
10. Genes code for proteins, not specific behaviors or attitudes. It's far more likely that genes influence behaviors and attitudes in a highly indirect fashion.

Psychoanalytic Theory: The Controversial Legacy of Sigmund Freud

11. psychic determinism
12. id; ego
13. psychological distress
14. defense mechanisms
15. Oral: birth to 12-18 months; Anal: 18 months to 3 years; Phallic: 3 – 6 years; Latency: 6 – 12 years; Genital: 12 years and beyond
16. Oedipus complex
17. aren't
18. unconscious
19. striving for superiority
20. Jung argued that in addition to Freud's version of the unconscious, there's also a collective unconscious that comprises all of the memories that ancestors have passed down to us across the generations. Jung believed the collective unconscious contains numerous archetypes, or cross culturally universal emotional symbols, which explain the similarities across people in their emotional reactions to many features of the world. Jung's theory is difficult to falsify and does not rule out rival hypotheses.

Behavioral, Social Learning, and Humanistic Theories of Personality

21. histories
22. consists of
23. determinism
24. thinking
25. In observational learning, parents, teachers and others play significant roles in shaping children's personalities: Children learn good and bad habits by watching and later emulating adults. This child may learn early that charitable giving is a worthy endeavor.
26. locus of control
27. less
28. shared environment
29. Self-actualized people tend to be creative, spontaneous, and accepting of themselves and others. They're self-confident (but not self-centered) and focus on real-world and intellectual problems and have a few deep friendships rather than many superficial ones. They typically crave privacy and can come off as introverted or aloof.
30. confirmation bias

Trait Models of Personality: Consistencies in Our Behavior

31. Personality traits must do more than merely describe behaviors we've already observed – they must predict behaviors in novel situations or correlate with biological or laboratory measures.
32. structure
33. factor analysis
34. aren't
35. Big Five
36. openness to experience, conscientiousness, extraversion, agreeableness, neuroticism
37. d: Extraversion; e: Neuroticism; a: Conscientiousness: c: Agreeableness; b: Openness to Experience
38. openness to experience
39. aggregated
40. underactive

Personality Assessment: Measuring and Mismeasuring the Psyche

41. Minnesota Multiphasic Personality Inventory
42. empirical
43. face validity
44. Impression management; malingering
45. supports
46. rational/theoretical
47. projective
48. Investigators and social workers allow children to play freely with anatomically detailed dolls to try to infer whether the children have been sexually abused based on their play. This projective test have lead to numerous false accusations.
49. Rorschach Inkblot
50. The Thematic Apperception Test (TAT)

13: PSYCHOLOGICAL DISORDERS

Conceptions of Mental Illness: Yesterday and Today

1. Brothers and sisters share a family resemblance; they look like each other but don't have any one feature in common. The broad category of "mental disorders" may be similar. Different mental disorders aren't alike in the same exact way, but they share a number of features.
2. exorcism
3. asylums
4. moral treatment
5. deinstitutionalization
6. culture-bound
7. Trials involving dueling expert witnesses may contribute to the erroneous public perception that psychologists can't agree on the diagnoses of individuals with suspected mental disorders.
8. axes
9. are not
10. comorbidity

Anxiety Disorders: The Many Faces of Worry and Fear

11. panic disorder
12. generalized anxiety disorder
13. phobia
14. PTSD is marked by emotional disturbance after experiencing or witnessing a severely stressful event. Symptoms include flashbacks to the event; efforts to avoid thoughts, feelings, places and conversations associated with the trauma; recurrent dreams of the trauma; and increased arousal, such as sleep difficulties and startling easily. Combat veterans and those who have experienced a natural disaster or sexual assault are at high risk.
15. obsessions
16. compulsions
17. OCD; also Charles Darwin, Florence Nightingale, Cameron Diaz, Billy Bob Thornton, and David Beckham
18. catastrophize
19. negative
20. neuroticism

Mood Disorders

21. 20
22. major depressive episode
23. According to this model, depression can trigger rejection from others, in turn contributing to further depression.
24. low
25. Using the shuttle box, Seligman found that dogs who were first prevented from escaping the shock gave up trying to escape electric shocks even when they were free to do so. He called this phenomenon "learned helplessness" and hypothesized that this might be one way that depression develops in humans.
26. internal
27. equally common
28. heritability
29. Major depression; bipolar disorder
30. communicate

Personality and Dissociative Disorders: The Disrupted and Divided Self

31. least
32. self-destructive quality
33. antisocial
34. are not
35. She's a woman—those with psychopathic personality disorder are usually men.
36. dissociative fugue
37. different from
38. posttraumatic

39. sociocognitive

40. popular media

The Enigma of Schizophrenia

41. Contrary to popular belief, the symptoms of schizophrenia are not produced by a "split mind" or personality.

42. delusions

43. Psychotic

44. hallucinations

45. word salad

46. Catatonic

47. do not cause

48. enlarged

49. It is a function of how closely an individual is genetically related to a person with schizophrenia.

50. diathesis-stress

14: PSYCHOLOGICAL AND BIOLOGICAL TREATMENTS

Psychotherapy: Patients and Practitioners

1. Psychotherapy

2. women

3. less

4. wait

5. A 1964 study found that many therapists preferred to treat people who were relatively young, attractive, verbal, intelligent, and successful. Therapists have recently become more aware of the importance of assisting a broad clientele of all ages and cultural backgrounds.

6. paraprofessional

7. isn't

8. ineffective

9. therapist; therapy

10. In this show, Tony Soprano's therapist revealed private information about him at a dinner party and then abruptly dismissed him from therapy after becoming convinced he had an untreatable psychopathic personality. Breaking confidentiality and "abandonment" of a patient are serious (and rare) ethical violations on the part of psychotherapists.

Different "Flavors" of Therapy: A Review of Therapeutic Approaches

11. free association

12. less

13. person-centered

14. exposure therapy

15. Clients gradually approach and handle any fears, as these clients are doing as they overcome their fear of flying. In vivo desensitization involves real-life, gradual exposure to what the patient actually fears, rather than imagining the anxiety-provoking situation.

16. flooding

17. In EMDR, the patient focuses on the therapist's fingers as they move back and forth, while reliving a traumatic memory. Studies indicate that such eye movements play no useful role in EMDR's effectiveness.

18. belief

19. about the same as

20. as effective as

Is Psychotherapy Effective?

21. effective

22. no consensus

23. more

24. 80 percent

25. Scared Straight programs expose adolescents to prisoners and prison life in an effort to scare them away from criminal careers. Despite their popularity, research suggests that such programs are not merely ineffective, but can actually increase the rate of problem behaviors in teens.

26. Empirically supported therapies

27. Positive life events can help to explain spontaneous remission, the phenomenon of a psychological problem improving without any intervention.

28. self-serving bias

29. high

30. self-help books

Biological Treatments: Drugs, Physical Stimulation, and Surgery

31. pharmacotherapy

32. shizophrenia

33. selective serotonin reuptake

34. is not

35. do not

36. children; adolescents

37. overprescribed

38. electroconvulsive therapy

39. A small electrical device is implanted under the skin near the breastbone to stimulate the vagus nerve (which projects to many brain areas) and is believed to stimulate serotonin release. It is used to treat severe depression. Well-controlled, large-scale studies are lacking.

40. Psychosurgery is brain surgery used to treat psychological problems. Psychosurgery once involved destruction of significant portions of the brain, resulting in impaired memory, diminished emotion and creativity, and personality change. Psychosurgery today is much more sophisticated with significantly milder side effects. Nonetheless, the stigma surrounding psychosurgery remains.

References

A

Aarons, L. (1976). Sleep-assisted instruction. *Psychological Bulletin, 83*(1), 1–40.

Abbey, A., Halman, L., & Andrews, F. (1992). Psychosocial, treatment and demographic predictors of the stress associated with infertility. *Fertility and Sterility, 57,* 122–127.

Abel, E. L., & Sokol, R. J. (1986). Fetal alcohol syndrome is now leading cause of mental retardation. *Lancet, 2,* 1222.

Abraham, H. D., & Aldridge, A. M. (1993). Adverse consequences of lysergic acid diethylamide. *Addiction, 88,* 1327–1334.

Abramson, L.Y., Seligman, M.E.P., & Teasdale, J.D. (1978). Learned helplessness in humans: Critique and reformulation. *Journal of Abnormal Psychology, 87,* 49–74.

Achenbach, T. M. (1982). Research methods in developmental psychopathology. In P. C. Kendall & J. Butcher (Eds.), *Handbook of research methods in clinical psychology* (pp. 127–181). New York: Wiley.

Ackerman, P. L., Beier, M. E., & Boyle, M. O. (2005). Working memory and intelligence: The same or different constructs? *Psychological Bulletin, 131,* 30–60.

Ackroyd, E. (1993). *A dictionary of dream symbols.* London: Blanford.

Acocella, J. (1999). *Creating hysteria: Women and multiple personality disorder.* San Francisco: Jossey-Bass Publishers.

Acton, G. S., & Schroeder, D. H. (2001). Sensory discrimination as related to general intelligence. *Intelligence, 29*(3), 263–271.

Adachi, N., Akanu, N., Adachi, T., Takekawa, Y., Adachi, Y., Ito, M., & Ikeda, H. (2008). Déjà vu experiences are rarely associated with pathological dissociation. *The Journal of Nervous and Mental Disease, 196*(5), 417–419.

Addis, M. E., Hatgis, C., Krasnow, A. D., Jacob, K., Bourne, L., & Mansfield, A. (2004). Effectiveness of cognitive-behavioral treatment for panic disorder versus treatment as usual in a managed care setting. *Journal of Consulting and Clinical Psychology, 72,* 625–635.

Addis, M. E., & Mahalik, J. R. (2003). Men, masculinity, and the contexts of help seeking. *American Psychologist, 58,* 5–14.

Adelmann, P. K., & Zajonc, R. B. (1989). Facial efference and the experience of emotion. *Annual Review of Psychology, 40,* 249–280.

Adler, A. (1922). *Practice and theory of individual psychology.* London: Routledge and K. Paul.

Adler, A. (1931). *What life should mean to you.* Boston: Little Brown.

Adler, A. (1938). *Social interest: A challenge of mankind.* London: Faber & Faber.

Adolphs, R., Tranel, D., Damasio, H., & Damasio, A. (1994). Impaired recognition of emotion in facial expressions following bilateral damage to the human amygdala. *Nature, 372,* 669–672.

Adorno, T. W., Frenkel-Brunswik, E., Levinson, D., & Sanford, R. N. (1950). *The authoritarian personality.* New York: Harper & Row.

Ahn, H., & Wampold, B. E. (2001). Where oh where are the specific ingredients? A meta-analysis of component studies in counseling and psychotherapy. *Journal of Counseling Psychology, 48,* 251–257.

Aimone, J. B., Wiles, J., & Gage, F. H. (2006). Potential role for adult neurogenesis in the encoding of time in new memories. *Nature Neuroscience, 9,* 723–727.

Ainsworth, M. D. S., Blehar, M. C., Waters, E., & Wall, S. (1978). *Patterns of attachment: A psychological study of the Strange Situation.* Hillsdale, NJ: Erlbaum.

Ajdacic-Gross, V., Wang, J., Bopp, M., Eich, D., Rossler, W., & Gutzwiller, F. (2003). Are seasonalities in suicide dependent on suicide methods? A reappraisal. *Social Science and Medicine, 57,* 1173–1181.

Akins, C. K. (2004). The role of Pavlovian conditioning in sexual behavior: A comparative analysis of human and nonhuman animals. *International Journal of Comparative Psychology, 17*(2–3), 241–262.

Akiskal, H. S., & McKinney, W. T. (1973). Depressive disorders: Toward a unified hypothesis. *Science, 182,* 20–29.

Alcock, J. E. (1990). *Science and supernature: A critical appraisal of parapsychology.* Buffalo, NY: Prometheus Books.

Alcock, J. E. (1995). The belief engine. *Skeptical Inquirer, 19*(3), 14–18.

Alda, M. (1997). Bipolar disorder: From families to genes. *Canadian Journal of Psychiatry, 42*(4), 378–387.

Aldrich, M. S. (1999). *Sleep medicine.* New York: Oxford University Press.

Aleman, A., & Laroi, F. (2008). *Hallucinations: The science of idiosyncratic perception.* Washington, D.C.: The American Psychological Association.

Alexander, G. M., & Hines, M. (2002). Sex differences in response to children's toys in non-human primates (*cercopithecus aethiops sabaeus*). *Evolution and Human Behavior, 23,* 467–479.

Alferink, L. A. (2007). Educational practices, superstitious behavior, and mythed opportunities. *Scientific Review of Mental Health Practice, 5*(2), 21–30.

Alison, L. J., Smith, M. D., & Morgan, K. (2003). Interpreting the accuracy of offender profiles. *Psychology, Crime & Law, 9,* 185–195.

Al-Issa, I. (1995). The illusion of reality or the reality of illusion: Hallucinations and culture. *British Journal of Psychiatry, 166*(3), 368–373.

Allen, J. J. B., & Movius, H. L. (2000). The objective assessment of amnesia in dissociative identity disorder using event-related potentials. *International Journal of Psychophysiology, 38,* 21–41.

Allen, P., Laroi, F., McGuire, P. K., & Aleman, A. (2008). The hallucinating brain: A review of structural and functional neuroimaging studies of hallucinations. *Neuroscience & Biobehavioral Reviews, 32,* 175–191.

Allison, D. B., Kaprio, J., Korkeila, M., Koskenvuo, M., Neale, M. C., & Hayakawa, K. (1996). The heritability of body mass index among an international sample of monozygotic twins reared apart. *International Journal of Obesity and Related Disorders, 20,* 501–506.

Alloway, R., & Bebbington, P. (1987). The buffer theory of social support: A review of the literature. *Psychological Medicine, 17,* 91–108.

Alloy, L. B., & Abramson, L.Y. (1979). Judgment of contingency in depressed and nondepressed students: Sadder but wiser? *Journal of Experimental Psychology: General, 108,* 441–485.

Alloy, L. B., & Abramson, L.Y. (1988). Depressive realism: Four theoretical perspectives. In L. B. Alloy (Ed.), *Cognitive process in depression* (pp. 223–265). New York: Guilford.

Allport, G. W. (1966). Traits revisited. *American Psychologist, 21,* 1–10.

Allport, G. W., & Odbert, H. S. (1936). Trait names, a psycholexical study. *Psychological Monographs, 47* (1, Whole No. 211).

Allport, G. W., & Postman, L. J. (1956). The basic psychology of rumor. *Journal of Abnormal and Social Psychology, 53,* 27–33.

Almli, C. R., & Finger, S. (1987). Neural insult and critical period concepts. In M. H. Bornstein (Ed.), *Sensitive periods in development: Interdisciplinary perspectives* (pp. 123–143). Hillsdale, NJ: Lawrence Erlbaum.

Althius, M. D., Fredman, L., Langenberg, P. W., & Magaziner, J. (1998). The relationship between insomnia and mortality among community-dwelling older women. *Journal of the American Geriatric Society, 46,* 1270–1273.

Altmann, E. M., & Schunn, C. D. (2002). Integrating decay and interference: A new look at an old interaction. In the *Proceedings of the 24th Annual Conference of the Cognitive Science Society.* Mahwah, NJ: Erlbaum.

Alvarado, C. S. (2000). Out of body experiences. In E. Cardena, S. J. Lynn, & S. Krippner (Eds.), *The variety of anomalous experiences* (pp. 183–218). Washington, DC: American Psychological Association.

Alvarez, C. A., & Brown, S. W. (2001). *What people believe about memory despite the research evidence.* Paper presented at the Annual Convention of the American Psychological Association, San Francisco, CA.

Ambady, N., & Rosenthal, R. (1993). Half a minute: Predicting teacher evaluations from thin slices of nonverbal behavior and physical attractiveness. *Journal of Personality and Social Psychology, 64,* 431–441.

American Psychiatric Association. (2000). *Diagnostic and statistical manual of mental disorders: DSM-IV-TR* (4th ed.). Washington, DC: Author.

American Psychiatric Association Committee on Electroconvulsive Therapy. (2001). *The practice of electroconvulsive therapy: Recommendations for treatment, training and privileging* (2nd ed.). Washington, DC: American Psychiatric Association.

American Psychological Association. (2002). Ethical Principles of Psychologists and Code of Conduct. www.apa.org/ethics/code2002.html

American Psychological Association. (2003). Fire Trucks Are Supposed To Be Red, Right? Not If You Want To Reduce Accidents. Retrieved September 10, 2008, from www.psychologymatters.org/solomon.html

American Psychological Association. (2008). Animals used in psychological research vary. *Animal Research in Psychology.* Retrieved May 14, 2008, from www.apa.org/science/animal2.html

Ames, E. (1997). *The development of Romanian orphanage children adopted to Canada. Final report to National Welfare Grants Program: Human Resources Development, Canada.* Barnaby, British Columbia, Canada: Simon Fraser University.

Amsterdam, B. (1972). Mirror self-image reactions before the age of two. *Developmental Psychobiology, 5,* 297–305.

Anand, B. K., & Brobeck, J. R. (1951). Hypothalamic control of food intake in rats and cats. *Yale Journal of Biological Medicine, 24,* 123.

Anand, B. K., & Pillai, R. V. (1967). Activity of single neurons in the hypothalamic feeding centres: Effect of gastric distension. *Journal of Physiology, 192,* 63–77.

Anastasi, A., & Urbina, S. (1996). *Psychological testing.* New York: Prentice Hall.

Ancoli-Israel, S., & Roth T. (1999). Characteristics of insomnia in the United States: Results of the 1991 National Sleep Foundation Survey. *Sleep, 22,* 347–353.

Ancona, L., & Pareyson, R. (1968). Contributo allo studio della aggressione: La dinamica della obbedienza distruttiva [Contribution to the study of aggression: The dynamics of destructive obedience]. *Archivio di Psicologia, Neurologia, e Psichiatria, 29,* 340–372.

Anderson, A. K., Christoff, K., Stappen, I., Panitz, D., Ghahremani, D. G., Glover, G., et al. (2003). Dissociated neural representations of intensity and valence in human olfaction. *Nature Neuroscience, 6,* 196–202.

Anderson, C. A., Berkowitz, L., Donnerstein, E., Huesmann, L. R., Johnson, J. D., Linz, D., et al. (2003). The influence of media violence on youth. *Psychological Science in the Public Interest, 4,* 81–110.

Anderson, C. A., & Bushman, B. J. (2002a). The effects of media violence on society. *Science, 295,* 2377–2378.

Anderson, C. A., & Bushman, B. J. (2002b). Human aggression. *Annual Review of Psychology, 53,* 27–51.

Anderson, C. A., & Bushman, B. J. (2002c). Media violence and the American public revisited. *American Psychologist, 57,* 448–450.

Anderson, C. A., Bushman, B. J., & Groom, R. W. (1997). Hot years and serious and deadly assault: Empirical tests of the heat hypothesis. *Journal of Personality and Social Psychology, 73,* 1213–1223.

Anderson, C. A., Lindsay, J. J., & Bushman, B. J. (1999). Research in the psychological laboratory: Truth or triviality? *Current Directions in Psychological Science, 8,* 3–9.

Anderson, C. M., & Stewart, S. (1983). *Mastering resistance.* New York: Guilford Press.

Anderson, K. J., Revelle, W., & Lynch, M. J. (1989). Caffeine, impulsivity, and memory scanning: A comparison of two explanations for the Yerkes-Dodson effect. *Motivation and Emotion, 13,* 1–20.

Anderson, K. W., Taylor, S., & McLean, P. (1996). Panic disorder associated with blood-injury-reactivity: The necessity of establishing functional relationships among maladaptive behaviors. *Behavior Therapy, 27,* 463–472.

Andreasen, N. C., Rezai, K., Alliger, R., Swayze, V. W. II, Flaum, M., Kirchner, P., et al. (1992). Hypofrontality in neuroleptic-naive patients and in patients with chronic schizophrenia: Assessment with xenon 133 single-photon emission computed tomography and the Tower of London. *Archives of General Psychiatry, 49,* 943–958.

Andresen, G. V., Birch, L. L., & Johnson, P. A. (1990). The scapegoat effect on food aversions after chemotherapy. *Cancer, 66*(7), 1649–1653.

Andrews, G., Stewart, G., Morris-Yates, A., Holt, P., & Henderson, S. (1990). Evidence for a general neurotic syndrome. *The British Journal of Psychiatry, 157,* 6–12.

Angold, A. (1999). Comorbidity. *Journal of Child Psychology and Psychiatry, 40,* 57–87.

Antonovsky, A. (1967). Social class, life expectancy and overall mortality. *Milbank Memorial Fund Quarterly, 45,* 31–73.

Antony, M. A., & Barlow, D. H. (2002). Specific phobia. In D. H. Barlow (Ed.), *Anxiety and its disorders: The nature and treatment of anxiety and panic* (2nd ed., pp. 380–417). New York: Guilford Press.

Antony, M. A., & Roemer, L. (2003). Behavior therapy. In A. S. Gurman & S. B. Messer (Eds.), *Essential psychotherapies:* Theory and practice (2nd ed., pp. 182–223). New York: Guilford Press.

Aponte, H., & Hoffman, L. (1973). The open door: A structural approach to a family with an anorectic child. *Family Process, 12,* 1–44.

Appelle, S., Lynn, S. J., & Newman, L. (2000). The alien abduction experience: Theoretical and empirical issues. In E. Cardena, S. J. Lynn, & S. Krippner (Eds.), *The varieties of anomalous experience: Examining the scientific evidence.* Washington, DC: American Psychological Association.

Arieti, S. (1959). Manic-depressive psychosis. In S. Arieti (Ed.), *American handbook of psychiatry.* New York: Basic Books.

Arkes, H. R. (1993). Some practical judgement and decision-making research. In N. J. Castellan (Ed.), *Individual and Group Decision Making: Current Issues, Hillsdale, NJ: Lawrence Erlbaum Assoc Inc*

Arkes, H. R., & Tetlock, P. E. (2004). Attributions of implicit prejudice or "Would Jesse Jackson 'fail' the Implicit Association Test?" *Psychological Inquiry, 15,* 257–278.

Arkowitz, H., & Lilienfeld, S. O. (2006). Psychotherapy on trial. *Scientific American Mind, 3,* 42–49.

Arkowitz, H., & Lilienfeld, S. O. (2007). A pill to fix your ills? *Scientific American Mind, 18,* 80–81.

Arnett, J. J. (1995). The young and the reckless: Adolescent reckless behavior. *Current Directions in Psychological Science, 4,* 67–71.

Arnett, J. J. (1999). Adolescent storm and stress, reconsidered. *American Psychologist, 4,* 317–326.

Aronoff, J., Lynn, S. J., & Malinowski, P. (2000). Are cultic environments psychologically harmful? *Clinical Psychology Review, 20,* 91–111.

Aronson, E. (1992). *The social animal* (6th ed.). New York: W. H. Freeman.

Aronson, E. (1998). *The social animal* (8th ed.). New York: Worth.

Aronson, E. (2004). Reducing hostility and building compassion: Lessons from the jigsaw classroom. In A. G. Miller (Ed.), *The social psychology of good and evil* (pp. 469–488). New York: Guilford Press.

Aronson, E., Blaney, N., Stephan, C., Sikes, J., & Snapp, M. (1978). *The jigsaw classroom.* Beverly Hills, CA: Sage.

Arrigo, B., & Griffin, A. (2004). Serial murder and the case of Aileen Wuornos: Attachment theory, psychopathy, and predatory aggression. *Behavioral Sciences and the Law, 22,* 375–393.

Asch, S. E. (1955). Opinions and social pressure. *Scientific American, 193,* 31–35.

Ascher, L. M., Barber, T. X., & Spanos, N. P. (1972). Two attempts to replicate the Parrish-Lundy-Leibowitz experiment on hypnotic age regression. *American Journal of Clinical Hypnosis, 14*(3), 178–185.

Aserinsky, E. (1996). Memories of famous neuropsychologists: The discovery of REM sleep. *Journal of the History of the Neurosciences, 5,* 213–227.

Aserinsky, E., & Kleitman, N. (1953). Regularly occurring periods of ocular motility and concomitant phenomena during sleep. *Science, 118,* 361–375.

Aspinwall, L., & Brunhart, S. (2000). What I don't know won't hurt me. In J. Gillham (Ed.), *The science of optimism and hope: Research essays in honor of Martin E. P. Seligman* (pp. 163–200). Philadelphia: Templeton Foundation Press.

Atkinson, R. C., & Shiffrin, R. M. (1968). Human memory: A proposed system and its control processes. In K. W. Spence and J. T. Spence (Eds.), *The psychology of learning and motivation: Advances in research and theory* (Vol. 2, pp. 89–195). New York: Academic Press.

Atri, A., Sharma, M., & Cottrell, R. (2006). Role of social support, hardiness, and acculturation as predictors of mental health among international students of Asian Indian origin. *International Quarterly of Community Health Education, 27*(1), 59–73.

Ax, A. F. (1953). The physiological differentiation between fear and anger in humans. *Psychosomatic Medicine, 55,* 433–442.

Axsom, D., & Cooper, J. (1985). Cognitive dissonance and psychotherapy: The role of effort justification in inducing weight loss. *Journal of Experimental Social Psychology, 21,* 149–160.

Ayllon, T., & Milan, M. (2002). Token economy: Guidelines for operation. In M. Hersen & W. Sledge, *Encyclopedia of psychotherapy* (pp. 829–833). New York: Academic Press.

Azar, B. (1999, July/August). Destructive lab attack sends a wake-up call. *APA Monitor.* Retrieved October 22, 2007, from www.apa.org/monitor/julaug99/sc1.html.

Azrin, N. H., & Holz, W. C. (1966). Punishment. In W. K. Honig (Ed.), *Operant behavior: Areas of research and application* (pp. 380–447). New York: Appleton-Century-Crofts.

B

Babiak, P., & Hare, R. D. (2006). *Snakes in suits: When psychopaths go to work.* New York: Regan Books.

Babyak, M. A., Blumenthal, J. A., Herman, S., Khatri, P., Doraiswamy, P. M., Moore, K. A., et al. (2000). Exercise treatment for major depression: Maintenance of therapeutic benefit at 10 months. *Psychosomatic Medicine, 62,* 633–638.

Baddeley, A. D. (1993). *Your memory: A user's guide* (2nd ed.). London: Lifecycle Publications.

Baddeley, A. D., & Hitch, G. J. (1974). Working memory, In G. A. Bower (Ed.), *Recent advances in learning and motivation, Vol. 8* (pp. 47–90). New York: Academic Press.

Baer, R. A. (2003). Mindfulness training as a clinical intervention: A conceptual and an empirical review. *Clinical Psychology: Science and Practice, 10,* 125–143.

Bagemihl, B. (1999). *Biological exuberance, animal homosexuality and natural diversity.* London: Profile Books.

Bahnson, C. B., Smith, K. (1975). Autonomic changes in a multiple personality. *Psychosomatic Medicine, 37,* 85–86.

Bahrick, H. P. (1984). Semantic memory content in permastore: Fifty years of memory for Spanish learning in school. *Journal of Experimental Psychology: General, 113,* 1–29.

Bahrick, H. P., Bahrick, P. O., & Wittlinger, R. P. (1975). Fifty years of memory for names and faces: A cross-sectional approach. *Journal of Experimental Psychology: General, 104,* 54–75.

Bahrick, H. P., & Phelps, E. (1987). Retention of Spanish vocabulary over 8 years. *Journal of Experimental Psychology: Learning, Memory, & Cognition, 13,* 344–349.

Bahrick, L. E., Moss, L., & Fadil, C. (1996). The development of self recognition in infancy. *Ecological Psychology, 8,* 189–208.

Bahrick, L. E., & Watson, J. S. (1985). Detection of intermodal proprioceptive visual contingency as a potential basis of self perception in infancy. *Developmental Psychology, 21,* 963–973.

Bailenson, J. N., Shum, M. S., Atran, S., Medin, D. L., & Coley, J. D. (2002). A bird's eye view: Biological categorization and reasoning within and across cultures. *Cognition, 84,* 1–53.

Bailey, J. M., & Pillard, R. C. (1991). A genetic study of male sexual orientation. *Archives of General Psychiatry, 48,* 1089–1096.

Baillargeon, R., & Hanko-Summers, S. (1990). Is the top object adequately supported by the bottom object? Young infants' understanding of support relations. *Cognitive Development, 5,* 29–53.

Bainbridge, W. S. (1987). Collective behavior and social movements. In R. Stark (Ed.), *Sociology* (pp. 544–576). Belmont, CA: Wadsworth.

Baker, F. M., & Bell, C. C. (1999). Issues in the psychiatric treatment of African Americans. *Psychiatry Services, 50,* 362–368.

Baker, J. P., & Berenbaum, H. (2008). The efficacy of problem-focused and emotional approach intervention varies as a function of emotional processing style. *Cognitive Therapy and Research, 32,* 66–82.

Baker, J. R., & Yardley, J. K. (2002). Moderating effect of gender on the relationship between sensation-seeking impulsivity and substance use in adolescents. *Journal of Child and Adolescence Substance Abuse, 12,* 27–43.

Baldwin, D. A. (1993). Infants' ability to consult the speaker for clues to word reference. *Journal of Child Language, 20,* 395–418.

Baldwin, M. W., Carrell, S. E., & Lopez, D. F. (1990). Priming relationship schemas: My advisor and the Pope are watching me from the back of my mind. *Journal of Experimental Social Psychology, 26*(5), 435–454.

Baltes, P. B., Staudinger, U. M., & Lindenberger, U. (1999). Lifespan psychology: Theory and application to intellectual functioning. *Annual Review of Psychology, 50,* 471–507.

Banaji, M. R. (2001). Implicit attitudes can be measured. In H. D. Roediger III, J. S. Naime, I. Neath, & A. Surprenant (Eds.), *The nature of remembering: Essays in honor of Robert G. Crowder* (pp. 117–150). Washington, DC: American Psychological Association.

Bancaud, J., Brunet-Bourgin, F., Chauvel, P., & Halgren, E. (1994). Anatomical origin of déjà vu and vivid "memories" in human temporal lobe epilepsy. *Brain, 117,* 71–90.

Bancroft, J. (2005). The endocrinology of sexual arousal. *Journal of Endocrinology, 186,* 411–427.

Bandura, A. (1965). Vicarious processes: A case of no-trial learning. In L. Berkowitz (Ed.), *Advances in experimental social psychology* (Vol. 2, pp. 3–55). New York: Academic Press.

Bandura, A. (1971). *Psychological modeling.* Chicago: Aldine/Atherton.

Bandura, A. (1973). *Aggression: A social learning analysis.* Oxford, England: Prentice-Hall.

Bandura, A. (1977). Self-efficacy: Toward a unifying theory of behavioral change. *Psychological Review, 84,* 191–215.

Bandura, A., Ross, D., & Ross, S. A. (1961). Transmission of aggression through imitation of aggressive models. *Journal of Abnormal and Social Psychology, 63,* 575–582.

Bandura, A., Ross, D., & Ross, S. A. (1963). Imitation of film mediated aggressive models. *Journal of Abnormal and Social Psychology, 66,* 3–11.

Barber, T. X. (1969). *Hypnosis: A scientific approach.* New York: Van Nostrand Reinhold.

Barchas, P. (1986). A sociophysiological orientation to small groups. In E. Lawler (Ed.), *Advances in group processes* (Vol. 3, pp. 209–246). Greenwich, CT: JAI Press.

Bard, P. (1942). Neural mechanisms in emotional and sexual behavior. *Psychosomatic Medicine, 4,* 171–172.

Bargh, J. A. (1994). The four horsemen of automaticity: Awareness, efficiency, intention, and control in social cognition. In R. S. Wyer Jr. & T. K. Srull (Eds.), *Handbook of social cognition* (2nd ed., pp. 1–40). Hillsdale, NJ: Erlbaum.

Bargh, J. A., & Chartrand, T. L. (1999). The unbearable automaticity of being. *American Psychologist, 54,* 462–479.

Bargh, J. A., & Ferguson, M. L. (2000). Beyond behaviorism: On the automaticity of higher mental processes. *Psychological Bulletin, 126,* 925–945.

Bargh, J. A., & Pietromonaco, P. (1982). Automatic information processing and social perception: The influence of trait information presented outside of conscious awareness on impression formation. *Journal of Personality and Social Psychology, 43,* 437–449.

Barker, A. T., Jalinous, R., & Freeston, I. L. (1985). Non-invasive magnetic stimulation of human motor cortex. *Lancet, 1,* 1106–1107.

Barkow, J. H., Cosmides, L., & Tooby, J. (1992). *The adapted mind: Evolutionary psychology and the generation of culture.* New York: Oxford University Press.

Barlow, D. H. (2000). Unraveling the mysteries of anxiety and its disorders from the perspective of emotion theory. *American Psychologist, 55,* 1247–1263.

Barlow, D. H., Chorpita, B. F., & Turovsky, J. (1996). Fear, panic, anxiety, and disorders of emotion. In D. A. Hope (Ed.), *Perspectives on anxiety, panic, and fear* (The 43rd Annual Nebraska Symposium on Motivation) (pp. 251–328). Lincoln: University of Nebraska Press.

Barnes, P. M., Powell-Griner, E., McFann, K., & Nahin, R. L. (2004). *Complementary and alternative medicine use among adults: United States, 2002.* CDC Advance Data Report #343.

Baron-Cohen, S., Harrison, J., Goldstein, L. H., & Wyke, M. (1993). Coloured speech-perception: Is synaesthesia what happens when modularity breaks down? *Perception, 22*(4), 419–426.

Barrett, L. F., & Russell, J. A. (1999). Structure of current affect. *Current Directions in Psychological Science, 8,* 10–14.

Barrick, M. R., & Mount, M. K. (1991). The Big Five personality dimensions and job performance: A meta-analysis. *Personnel Psychology, 44,* 1–26.

Barta, P. E., Pearlson, G. D., Powers, R. E., Richards, S. S., & Tune, L. E. (1990). Auditory hallucinations and smaller superior temporal gyral volume in schizophrenia. *American Journal of Psychiatry, 147,* 1457–1462.

Bartels, A., & Zeki, S. (2006). The temporal order of binding visual attributes. *Vision Research, 46,* 2280–2286.

Bartholomew, R. E. (1998). The Martian panic sixty years later: What have we learned? *Skeptical Inquirer, 22*(6), 40–43.

Bartholomew, R. E., & Goode, E. (2000). Mass delusions and hysterias: Highlights from the past millennium. *Skeptical Inquirer, 24,* 20–28.

Bartone, P. T. (1999). Hardiness protects against war-related stress in army reserve forces. *Consulting Psychology Journal, 51,* 72–82.

Bartz, W. R. (2002, September/October). Teaching skepticism via the CRITIC acronym and the *Skeptical Inquirer. Skeptical Inquirer, 17,* 42–44.

Batson, C. D. (1987). Prosocial motivation: Is it ever truly altruistic? In L. Berkowitz (Ed.), *Advances in experimental social psychology* (Vol. 20, pp. 65–122). New York: Academic Press.

Batson, C. D., Batson, J., Singlsby, J., Harrell, K., Peekna, H., & Todd, R. (1991). Empathic joy and the empathy-altruism hypothesis. *Journal of Personality and Social Psychology, 61,* 413–426.

Batson, C. D., Duncan, B. D., Ackerman, P., Buckley, T., & Birch, K. (1981). Is empathic emotion a source of altruistic motivation? *Journal of Personality and Social Psychology, 40,* 290–302.

Batson, C. D., & Shaw, L. (1991). Evidence for altruism: Toward a pluralism of prosocial motives. *Psychological Inquiry, 2,* 107–122.

Bauer, P. J. (2006). Constructing a past in infancy: A neuro-developmental account. *Trends in Cognitive Sciences, 10*(4), 175–181.

Baum, A., Cohen, L., & Hall, M. (1993). Control and intrusive memories as possible determinants of chronic stress. *Psychosomatic Medicine, 55,* 274–286.

Baum, H. S. (1987). *The invisible bureaucracy.* Oxford, England: Oxford University Press.

Baumeister, R. F., Campbell, J. D., Krueger, J. I., & Vohs, K. D. (2003). Does high self-esteem cause better performance, interpersonal success, happiness, or healthier lifestyles? *Psychological Science in the Public Interest, 4,* 1–44.

Baumeister, R. F., & Leary, M. R. (1995). The need to belong: Desire for interpersonal attachments as a fundamental human motivation. *Psychological Bulletin, 117*(3), 497–529.

Baumeister, R. F., Twenge, J. M., & Nuss, C. (2002). Effects of social exclusion on cognitive processes: Anticipated aloneness reduces intelligent thought. *Journal of Personality and Social Psychology, 83*, 817–827.

Baumrind, D. (1971). Current patterns of parental authority. *Developmental Psychology Monographs, 4* (Pts. 1 & 2).

Baumrind, D. (1991). The influence of parenting style on adolescent competence and substance use. *Journal of Early Adolescence, 11*, 56–95.

Baxendale, S. (2004). Memories aren't made of this: Amnesia at the movies. *British Medical Journal, 18*, 1480–1483.

Beaman, A., Barnes, P., Klentz, B., & McQuirk, B. (1978). Increasing helping rates through information dissemination: Teaching pays. *Personality and Social Psychology Bulletin, 4*, 406–411.

Beaman, C. P., Bridges, A. M., & Scott, S. K. (2007). From dichotic listening to the irrelevant sound effect: A behavioural and neuroimaging analysis of the processing of unattended speech. *Cortex, 43*, 124–134.

Beaman, R., Wheldall, K., & Kemp, C. (2006). Differential teacher attention to boys and girls in the classroom. *Educational Review, 58*(3), 339–366.

Beatty, J. (1982). Task-evoked pupillary responses, processing load, and the structure of processing resources. *Psychological Bulletin, 91*(2), 276–292.

Beauregard, M., & Paquette, V. (2006). Neural correlates of a mystical experience in Carmelite nuns. *Neuroscience Letters, 405*, 186–190.

Beck, A. T. (1963). Thinking and depression. *Archives of General Psychiatry, 9*, 324–333.

Beck, A. T., (1964). Thinking and depression: 2. Theory and therapy. *Archives of General Psychiatry, 10*, 561–571.

Beck, A. T. (1976). *Cognitive therapy and the emotional disorders*. New York: International Universities Press.

Beck, A. T. (1987) Cognitive models of depression. *Journal of Cognitive Psychotherapy, 1*(1), 5–37.

Beck, A. T. (2005). The current state of cognitive therapy: A 40-year retrospective. *Archives of General Psychiatry, 62*, 953–959.

Beck, A. T., Brown, G., Berchick, R. J., Stewart, B. L., & Steer, R. A. (1990). Relationship between hopelessness and ultimate suicide: A replication with psychiatric outpatients. *American Journal of Psychiatry, 147*, 190–195.

Beck, A. T., Rush, A. J., Shaw, B. F., & Emery, G. (1979). *Cognitive therapy of depression*. New York: Guilford Press.

Beck, C. T., & Gable, R. K. (2001). Comparative analysis of the performance of the Postpartum Depression Screening Scale with two other depression instruments. *Nursing Research, 50*, 242–250.

Beck, J. S. (1995). *Cognitive therapy: Basics and beyond*. New York: Guilford Press.

Begley, S., & Kasindorf, M. (1979, December 3). Twins: Nazi and Jew. *Newsweek*, 139.

Beier, M. E., & Ackerman, P. L. (2001). Current events knowledge in adults: An investigation of age, intelligence and non-ability determinants. *Psychology and Aging, 16*, 615–628.

Bell, R. (1968). A reinterpretation of the direction of effects in studies of socialization. *Psychological Review, 75*, 81–95.

Belli, R. F., Winkielman, P., Read, J. D., Schwarz, N., & Lynn, S. J. (1998). Recalling more childhood events leads to judgments of poorer memory: Implications for the recovered/false memory debate. *Psychonomic Bulletin & Review, 5*, 318–323.

Bellinger, D. C., & Needleman, H. L. (2003). Intellectual impairment and blood lead levels. *New England Journal of Medicine, 349*, 500–502.

Belliveau, F., & Richter, L. (1970). *Understanding human sexual inadequacy*. New York: Bantam Books.

Belsky, J., & Kelly, J. (1994). *The transition to parenthood*. New York: Delacourte.

Bem, D. J. (1996). Exotic becomes erotic: A developmental theory of sexual orientation. *Psychological Review, 103*, 320–335.

Bem, D. J., & Allen, A. (1974). On predicting some of the people some of the time: The search for cross-situational consistencies in behavior. *Psychological Review, 81*, 506–520.

Bem, D. J., & Funder, D. C. (1978). Predicting more of the people more of the time: Assessing the personality of situations. *Psychological Review, 85*, 485–500.

Bem, D. J., & Honorton, C. (1994). Does psi exist? Replicable evidence for an anomalous process of information transfer. *Psychological Bulletin, 115*(1), 4–18.

Bem, D. J., & McConnell, H. K. (1970). Testing the self-perception explanation of dissonance phenomena: On the salience of premanipulation attitudes. *Journal of Personality and Social Psychology, 14*, 23–31.

Benassi, V. A., Sweeney, P. D., & Dufour, C. L. (1988). Is there a relation between locus of control orientation and depression? *Journal of Abnormal Psychology, 8*, 357–367.

Benbow, C. P., & Stanley, J. C. (1980). Sex differences in mathematical ability: Fact or artifact? *Science, 210*, 1262–1264.

Bennett, M. R. (1998). Monoaminergic synapses and schizophrenia: 45 years of neuroleptics. *Journal of Psychopharmacology, 12*, 289–304.

Benson, E. (2006, June). All that's gold doesn't glitter: How the Golden Fleece tarnished psychological science. *APS Observer*. Retrieved from www.psychologicalscience.org/observer/getArticle.cfm?id=1998.

Bentall, R. P. (2000). Hallucinatory experiences. In E. Cardena, S. J. Lynn, & S. Krippner (Eds.), *Varieties of anomalous experience: Examining the scientific evidence* (pp. 85–120). Washington, DC: American Psychological Association.

Bentley, K. J., & Walsh, J. (2006). *The social worker and psychotropic medication: Toward effective collaboration with mental health clients, families, and providers* (3rd ed.). Belmont, CA: Thompson.

Berger, H. (1929). Ueber das Elektroenkephalogramm des Menschen. *Archiv für Psychiatrie und Nervenkrankheiten, 87*, 527–570.

Bergner, R. M. (1997). What is psychopathology? And so what? *Clinical Psychology: Science and Practice, 4*, 235–248.

Berk, A. M., Vigorito, M., & Miller, R. R. (1979). Retroactive stimulus interference with conditioned emotional response retention in infant and adult rats: Implications for infantile amnesia. *Journal of Experimental Psychology: Animal Behavior Processes, 3*, 284–299.

Berk, M. S., & Andersen, S. M. (2000). The impact of past relationships on interpersonal behavior: Behavioral confirmation in the social-cognitive process of transference. *Journal of Personality and Social Psychology, 79*, 546–562.

Berkman, L. F., & Syme, S. L. (1979). Social networks, host resistance, and mortality: A nine year follow-up study of Alameda County residents. *American Journal of Epidemiology, 109*, 186–204.

Berkowitz, L. (1989). Frustration-aggression hypothesis: Examination and reformulation. *Psychological Bulletin, 106*, 59–73.

Berman, J. D., & Straus, S. E. (2004). Implementing a research agenda for complementary and alternative medicine. *Annual Review of Medicine, 55,* 239–254.

Berman, J. S., & Norton, N. C. (1985). Does professional training make a therapist more effective? *Psychological Bulletin, 98,* 401–406.

Bernheim, K. F., & Lewine, R. R. (1979). *Schizophrenia: symptoms, treatment, causes.* New York: Norton.

Bernstein, D. A., Borkovec, T. D., & Hazlett-Stevens, H. (2000). *New directions in progressive relaxation training: A guidebook for helping professionals.* Westport, CT: Praeger.

Bernstein, D. M., Laney, C., Morris, E. K., & Loftus, E. F. (2005). False memories about food can lead to food avoidance. *Social Cognition, 23,* 11–34.

Berscheid, E., & Reis, H. T. (1998). Attraction and close relationships. In D. Gilbert, S. Fiske, & G. Lindzey (Eds.), *The handbook of social psychology* (Vol. 2, 4th ed., pp. 193–281). New York: McGraw-Hill.

Beunen, G., & Malina, R. M. (1996). *The child and adolescent athlete.* Oxford, England: Blackwell.

Beutler, L. E. (2002). The dodo bird is extinct. *Clinical Psychology: Science and Practice, 9,* 30–34.

Beutler, L. E., & Harwood, T. M. (2002). What is and can be attributed to the therapeutic relationship. *Journal of Contemporary Psychotherapy, 32,* 25–33.

Beyerstein, B. L. (1997, September/October). Why bogus therapies seem to work. *Skeptical Inquirer, 21,* 29–34.

Beyerstein, B. L. (1999). Whence cometh the myth that we only use ten percent of our brains? In S. Della Sala (Ed.), *Mind myths: Exploring everyday mysteries of the mind and brain* (pp. 1–24). Chichester, England: John Wiley and Sons.

Bialystok, E. (1988). Levels of bilingualism and levels of linguistic awareness. *Developmental Psychology, 24,* 560–567.

Biasi, E., Silvotti, L., & Tirindelli, R. (2001). Pheromone detection in rodents. *Neuroreport, 12,* A81–A84.

Biederman, J., Hirshfeld-Becker, D. R., Rosenbaum, J. F., Herot, C., Friedman, D., Snidman, N., et al. (2001). Further evidence of association between behavioral inhibition and social anxiety in children. *American Journal of Psychiatry, 158,* 1673–1679.

Bierbrauer, G. (1973). *Effect of set, perspective, and temporal factors in attribution.* Unpublished doctoral dissertation, Stanford University, Palo Alto, CA.

Bikel, O. (Producer). (1995, April 11). *Frontline* [Television broadcast: "Divided Memories"]. New York: Public Broadcasting Service.

Biklen, D. (1990). Communication unbound: Autism and praxis. *Harvard Educational Review, 60,* 291–314.

Bink, M. L., & Marsh, R. L. (2000). Cognitive regularities in creative activity. *Review of General Psychology, 4,* 59–78.

Birch, S. A. J., & Bloom, P. (2007). The curse of knowledge in reasoning about false beliefs. *Psychological Science, 18*(5), 382–386.

Birmingham, C. L., Su, J., Hlynsky, J. A., Goldner, E. M., & Gao, M. (2005). The mortality rate from anorexia nervosa. *International Journal of Eating Disorders, 38,* 143–146.

Birnbaum, G., Glaubman, H., & Mikulincer, M. (2001). Women's experience of heterosexual intercourse—Scale construction, factor structure, and relations to orgasmic disorder. *Journal of Sex Research, 38,* 191–204.

Birren, J. E., & Renner, V. J. (1977). Research on the psychology of aging: Principles and experimentation. In J. E. Birren & K. W. Schaie (Eds.), *Handbook of the psychology of aging* (pp. 3–38). New York: Van Nostrand Reinhold.

Bishop, D. V. M., & Bishop, S. J. (1998). "Twin language": A risk factor for language impairment? *Journal of Speech, Language & Hearing Research, 41,* 150–160.

Bishop, G. F., Oldendick, R. W., & Tuchfarber, A. J. (1986). Opinions on fictitious issues: The pressure to answer survey questions. *Public Opinion Quarterly, 50,* 240–250.

Black, S. M., & Hill, C. E. (1984). The psychological well-being of women in their middle years. *Psychology of Women Quarterly, 8,* 282–292.

Blackmore, S. (1993). *Dying to live: Near-death experiences.* Buffalo, NY: Prometheus.

Blackmore, S. (1998). Abduction by aliens or sleep paralysis? *Skeptical Inquirer, 22,* 23–28.

Blackmore, S. (2004). *Consciousness: An introduction.* New York: Oxford University Press.

Blanchard, R., & Bogaert, A. F. (1996). Homosexuality in men and number of older brothers. *American Journal of Psychiatry, 153,* 27–31.

Blanchette, I., & Richards, A. (2003). Anxiety and the interpretation of ambiguous stimuli: Beyond the emotion-congruent effect. *Journal of Experimental Psychology: General, 13,* 294–309.

Blasi, A. (1980). Bridging moral cognition and moral action: A critical review of the literature. *Psychological Bulletin, 88,* 593–637.

Blass, T. (1999). The Milgram paradigm after 35 years. *Journal of Applied Social Psychology, 29,* 955–978.

Blass, T. (2004). *The man who shocked the world: The life and legacy of Stanley Milgram.* New York: Perseus.

Blatt, S. J. (1974). Levels of object representation in anaclitic and introjective depression. *Psychoanalytic Studies of the Child, 29,* 107–157.

Blatt, S. J., Sanislow, C. A., Zuroff, D. C., & Pilkonis, P. A. (1996). Characteristics of effective therapists: Further analyses of data from the NIMH. *TDCRP, Journal of Consulting and Clinical Psychology, 64,* 1276–1284.

Bliss, T., Collingridge, G., & Morris, R. (2004). *Long-term potentiation: Enhancing neuroscience for 30 years.* Oxford, England: Oxford University Press.

Block, J. (1976). Issues, problems and pitfalls in assessing sex differences: A critical review of "The Psychology of Sex Differences." *Merrill Palmer Quarterly, 22,* 283–340.

Block, J. (1995). A contrarian view of the five-factor approach to personality description. *Psychological Bulletin, 117,* 187–215.

Block, J. (2006). In whom should Americans trust? Jeff Block's personal idea fountain. Retrieved June 10, 2008, from http://jeffblock.wordpress.com/category/military/

Block, J., & Block, J. H. (2006). Venturing a 30-year longitudinal study. *American Psychologist, 61*(4), 315–327.

Block, J. H., Block, J., & Gjerde, P. F. (1986). The personality of children prior to divorce: A prospective study. *Child Development, 57,* 827–840.

Blodgett, H. C. (1929). The effect of the introduction of reward upon the maze performance of rats. *University of California Publications in Psychology, 4,* 113–134.

Blood, A. J., & Zatorre, R. J. (2001). Intensely pleasurable responses to music correlate with activity in brain regions implicated in reward and emotion. *Proceedings of the National Academy of Sciences, U. S. A., 98,* 11818–11823.

Blow, A. J., Sprenkle, D. H., & Davis, S. D. (2007). Is who delivers the treatment more important than the treatment itself? The role of the therapist in common factors. *Journal of Marital and Family Therapy, 33,* 298–317.

Blum, D. (2002). *Love at Goon Park: Harry Harlow and the science of affection.* Cambridge, MA: Perseus Publishing.

Boese, A. (2007, November 3). The whacko files. *New Scientist, 196,* 49–55.

Bohart, A. C. (2003). Person-centered psychotherapy and related experiential approaches. In A. S. Gurman & S. B. Messer (Eds.), *Essential psychotherapies: Theory and practice* (2nd ed., pp. 107–148). New York: Guilford Press.

Bolles, R. C. (1962). The difference between statistical hypotheses and scientific hypotheses. *Psychological Reports, 11,* 639–645.

Bonanno, G. A. (2004). Loss, trauma, and human resilience: Have we underestimated the human capacity to thrive after extremely aversive events? *American Psychologist, 59,* 20–28.

Bonanno, G. A., Field, N. P., Kovacevic, A., & Kaltman, S. (2002). Self-enhancement as a buffer against extreme adversity: Civil war in Bosnia and traumatic loss in the United States. *Personality and Social Psychology Bulletin, 28,* 184–196.

Bonanno, G. A., Galea, S., Bucciarelli, A., & Vlahov, D. (2006). Psychological resilience after disaster: New York City in the aftermath of the September 11th terrorist attack. *Psychological Science, 17,* 181–186.

Bonanno, G. A., Moskowitz, J. T., Papa, A., & Folkman, S. (2005). Resilience to loss in bereaved spouses, bereaved parents, and bereaved gay men. *Journal of Personality and Social Psychology, 88,* 827–843.

Bond, C. F. (2006). A world of lies. *Journal of Cross-Cultural Psychology, 30,* 60–74.

Bond, R., & Smith, R. P. (1996). Culture and conformity: A meta-analysis of studies using Asch's line judgment task. *Psychological Bulletin, 119,* 111–137.

Bond, R., & Titus, L. J. (1983). Social facilitation: A meta-analysis of 241 studies. *Psychological Bulletin, 94,* 265–292.

Bonham, V. L. (2001). Race, ethnicity, and pain treatment: Striving to understand the causes and solutions to the disparities in pain treatment. *Journal of Law & Medical Ethics, 29,* 52–68.

Boniecki, K. A., & Moore, S. (2003). Breaking the silence: Using a token economy to reinforce classroom participation. *Teaching of Psychology, 30,* 224–227.

Boring, E. G. (1923). Intelligence as the tests test it. *New Republic, 35,* 35–37.

Borland, D. C. (1982). A cohort analysis approach to the empty nest syndrome among three ethnic groups of women: A theoretical position. *Journal of Marriage and the Family, 44,* 117–129.

Bornstein, R. F. (1989). Exposure and affect: Overview and meta-analysis of research, 1968–1987. *Psychological Bulletin, 106*(2), 265–289.

Bornstein, R. F. (2001). The impending death of psychoanalysis. *Psychoanalytic Psychology, 18,* 3–20.

Bos, H. M. W., van Balen, F., & van den Boom, D. C. (2004). Experience of parenthood, couple relationship, social support, and child-rearing goals in planned lesbian mother families. *Journal of Child Psychology and Psychiatry, 45,* 755–764.

Bos, H. M. W., van Balen, F., & van den Boom, D. C. (2007). Child adjustment and parenting in planned lesbian-parent families. *American Journal of Orthopsychiatry, 77,* 38–48.

Bothwell, R. K., Deffenbacher, K. A., & Brigham, J. C. (1987). Correlation of eyewitness accuracy and confidence: Optimality hypothesis revisited. *Journal of Applied Psychology, 72,* 691–695.

Botwinick, J. (1966). Cautiousness in advanced age. *Journal of Gerontology, 21,* 347–353.

Bouchard, T. J. Jr. (2004). Genetic influence on human psychological traits. *Current Directions in Psychological Science, 4,* 148–151.

Bouchard, T. J., Lykken, D. T., McGue, M., Segal, N. L., & Tellegen, A. (1990, October 12). Sources of human psychological differences: The Minnesota study of twins reared apart. *Science, 250,* 223–228.

Bouchard, T. J., & McGue, M. (1981). Familial studies of intelligence: A review. *Science, 212,* 1055–1059.

Bourguignon, E. (1970). Hallucinations and trance: An anthropologist's perspective. In Keup, W. (Ed.), *Origins and mechanisms of hallucination* (pp. 183–190). New York: Plenum Press.

Bowers, T., & Clum, G. A. (1988). Specific and nonspecific treatment effects in controlled psychotherapy research. *Psychological Bulletin, 103,* 315–323.

Bowlby, J. (1973). *Attachment and loss. Vol. 2: Separation: Anxiety & anger.* London: Hogarth.

Bowlby, J. (1990). The study and reduction of group tensions in the family. In E. Trist, H. Murray, & B. Trist (Eds.), *The social engagement of social science: A Tavistock anthology, Vol. I: The socio-psychological perspective* (pp. 291–298). Philadelphia: University of Pennsylvania Press.

Bowman, D., Scogin, F., Floyd, M., & McKendree-Smith, N. (2001). Psychotherapy length of stay and outcome: A meta-analysis of the effect of therapist sex. *Psychotherapy, 38,* 142–150.

Bradbard, M. R., Martin, C. L., Endsley, R. C., & Halverson, C. F. (1986). Influence of sex stereotypes on children's exploration and memory: A competence versus performance distinction. *Developmental Psychology, 22*(4), 481–486.

Bradbury, E. J., & McMahon, S. B. (2006). Spinal cord repair strategies: Why do they work? *Nature Reviews Neuroscience, 7,* 644–653.

Bradbury, J. (2005). Molecular insights into human brain evolution. *PLoS Biology 3,* 50.

Braid, J. (1843). *Neurypnology or the rationale of nervous sleep considered in relation with animal magnetism illustrated by numerous cases of its successful application in the relief and cure of disease.* London: John Churchill.

Branden, N. (1994). *Six pillars of self-esteem.* New York: Bantam Books.

Brandsma, J. M., Maultsby, M. C., & Welsh, R. J. (1980). Alcoholics Anonymous: An empirical outcome study. *Addictive Behaviors, 5,* 359–370.

Brehm, S. S., Miller, R. S., Perlman, D., & Campbell, S. M. (2002). *Intimate relationships* (3rd ed.). New York: McGraw-Hill.

Breland, K., & Breland, M. (1961). The misbehavior of organisms. *American Psychologist, 16*(11), 681–684.

Brende, J. O. (1984). The psychophysiologic manifestations of dissociation: Electrodermal responses in a multiple personality patient. *Psychiatry Clinics of North America, 7,* 41–50.

Brennan, P. A., & Mednick, S. A. (1994). Learning theory approach to the deterrence of criminal recidivism. *Journal of Abnormal Psychology, 103,* 430–440.

Brenner, C. (1973). *An elementary textbook of psychoanalysis.* New York: International Universities Press.

Breuer, J., & Freud, S. (1895). *Studies on hysteria.* In Strachey, J. et al. (Trans. and ed.), *The standard edition of the Complete Psychological Works of Sigmund Freud (1953–74)* (Vol. 2). London: Hogarth.

Brewer, C. (1992). Controlled trials of Antabuse in alcoholism: The importance of supervision and adequate dosage. *Acta Psychiatrica Scandinavica, 86,* 51–58.

Brewer, W. F. (1974). There is no convincing evidence for operant or classical conditioning in adult humans. In W. B. Weimer & D. S. Palemo (Eds.), *Cognition and the symbolic processes* (pp. 1–42). Hillsdale, NJ: Erlbaum.

Brickman, P., & Campbell, D. T. (1971). Hedonic relativism and planning the good society. In M. H. Appley (Ed.), *Adaptation level theory: A symposium* (pp. 287–305). New York: Academic Press.

Brickman, P., Coates, D., & Janoff-Bulman, R. (1978). Lottery winners and accident victims: Is happiness relative? *Journal of Personality and Social Psychology, 36,* 917–927.

Broadbent, D. E. (1957). A mechanical model for human attention and immediate memory. *Psychological Review, 54,* 205–215.

Broca, P. P. (1861). Loss of speech, chronic softening and partial destruction of the anterior left lobe of the brain. *Bulletin de la Société Anthropologique, 2,* 235–238.

Brody, J. (2007, April 17). When a brain forgets where memory is. *New York Times.* Accessed August 2, 2007, from www.nytimes.com/2007/04/17/health/psychology/17brody.html.

Brody, N. (1992). *Intelligence* (2nd ed.). San Diego, CA: Academic Press.

Brown, A. S. (1991). A review of the tip of the tongue phenomenon. *Psychological Bulletin, 109,* 204–223.

Brown, A. S. (2003). A review of the déjà vu experience. *Psychological Bulletin, 129,* 394–413.

Brown, A. S. (2004a). *The déjà vu experience.* New York: Psychology Press.

Brown, A. S. (2004b). The déjà vu illusion. *Current Directions in Psychological Science, 13,* 256–259.

Brown, A. S., Begg, M. D., Gravenstein, S., Schaefer, C. A., Wyatt, W. J., Bresnahan, M., et al. (2004). Serologic evidence for prenatal influenza in the etiology of schizophrenia. *Archives of General Psychiatry, 61,* 774–780.

Brown, D., Scheflin, A. W., & Hammond, C. (1997). *Trauma, memory, treatment, and the law.* New York: W. W. Norton.

Brown, G. W., Monck, E. M., Carstairs, G. M., & Wing, J. K. (1962). Influence of family life on the course of schizophrenic illness. *British Journal of Preventive and Social Medicine, 16,* 55–68.

Brown, P. K., & Wald, G. (1964). Visual pigments in single rods and cones of the human retina. *Science, 144,* 45–52.

Brown, R., & Kulik, J. (1977). Flashbulb memories. *Cognition, 5,* 73–99.

Brown, V. R., & Paulus, P. B. (2002). Making group brainstorming more effective: Recommendations from an associative memory perspective. *Current Directions in Psychological Science, 11,* 208–212.

Browne, C., Dowd, T., & Freeman, A. (in press). Rational and irrational beliefs and psychopathology. In D. David, S. J. Lynn, & A. Ellis (Eds.), *Rational and irrational beliefs: Theory, research, and practice.* Oxford University Press.

Bruer, J. T. (1999). *The myth of the first three years: A new understanding of brain development and lifelong learning.* New York: Free Press.

Brugha, T. S. (Ed.). (1995). *Social support and psychiatric disorder research findings and guidelines for clinical practice.* Cambridge, England: Cambridge University Press.

Brunvand, J. H. (1999). *Too good to be true: The colossal book of urban legends.* New York: W. W. Norton.

Bryan, J. H., & Test, M. A. (1967). Models and helping: Naturalistic studies in aiding behavior. *Journal of Personality and Social Psychology, 6,* 400–407.

Buckalew, L. W., & Ross, S. (1981). Relationship of perceptual characteristics to efficacy of placebos. *Psychological Reports, 49,* 955–961.

Bulik, C. M., Sullivan, P. F., & Kendler, K. S. (1998). Heritability of binge-eating and broadly defined bulimia nervosa. *Biological Psychiatry, 44,* 1210–1218.

Bull, R., & Rumsey, N. (1988). *The social psychology of facial appearance.* New York: Springer-Verlag.

Bunge, M. (1998). *Philosophy of science: From problem to theory* (Vol. 1). Piscataway, NJ: Transaction Publishers.

Bureau of Labor Statistics. (2006). *Number of jobs held, labor market activity, and earnings growth among the youngest baby boomers: Results from a longitudinal survey.* Retrieved from www.bls.gov/news.release/nlsoy.nr0.htm.

Burger, J. M., & Petty, R. E. (1981). The low-ball compliance technique: Task or person commitment? *Journal of Personality and Social Psychology, 40,* 492–500.

Burns, G. L., & Farina, A. (1992). The role of physical attractiveness in adjustment. *Genetic, Social, and General Psychology Monographs, 118,* 157–194.

Bushman, B. J., & Anderson, C. A. (2001). Media violence and the American public: Scientific facts versus media misinformation. *American Psychologist, 56,* 477–489.

Buss, D. M. (1989). Sex differences in human mate preferences: Evolutionary hypotheses tested in 37 cultures. *Behavioral and Brain Sciences, 12,* 1–14.

Buss, D. M. (1994). *The evolution of desire: Strategies of human mating.* New York: Basic Books.

Buss, D. M. (1995). Evolutionary psychology: A new paradigm for psychological science. *Psychological Inquiry, 6,* 1–30.

Buss, D. M., & Kenrick, D. T. (1998). Evolutionary social psychology. In D. T. Gilbert, S. T. Fiske, & G. Lindzey (Eds.), *The handbook of social psychology* (4th ed., Vol. 1, pp. 982–1026). Boston: McGraw Hill.

Buss, D. M., & Schmitt, D. P. (1993). Sexual strategies theory: An evolutionary perspective on human mating. *Psychological Review, 100,* 204–232.

Buss, D. M., Shackelford, T. K., Kirkpatrick, L. A., & Larsen, R. J. (2001). A half-century of mate preferences: The cultural evolution of values. *Journal of Marriage and Families, 63,* 492–503.

Butcher, J. N., Dahlstrom, W. G., Graham, J. R., Tellegen, A., & Kaemmer, B. (1989). *MMPI-2: Manual for administration and scoring.* Minneapolis: University of Minnesota Press.

Butzlaff, R. L., & Hooley, J. M. (1998). Expressed emotion and psychiatric relapse: A meta-analysis. *Archives of General Psychiatry, 55,* 547–552.

Buunk, B. P., Dijkstra, P., Fetchenhauer, D., & Kenrick, D. (2002). Age and gender differences in mate selection criteria for various involvement levels. *Personal Relationships, 9,* 271–278.

Byrne, D. (1971). *The attraction paradigm.* New York: Academic Press.

Byrne, R. (2007). *The secret.* New York: Atria Books.

Byrnes, J. P. (1988). Formal operations: A systematic reformulation. *Developmental Review, 8,* 66–87.

C

Cabeza, R., & Nyberg, L. (1997). Imaging cognition: An empirical review of PET studies with normal subjects. *Journal of Cognitive Neuroscience, 9,* 1–26.

Cacioppo, J. T. (2004). Common sense, intuition, and theory in personality and social psychology. *Personality and Social Psychology Review, 8,* 114–122.

Cacioppo, J. T., Berntson, G. G., Klein, D. J., & Poehlmann, K. M. (1997). The psychophysiology of emotion across the lifespan. *Annual Review of Gerontology and Geriatrics, 17,* 27–74.

Cacioppo, J. T., Berntson, G. G., Sheridan, J. F., & McClintock, M. K. (2000). Multi-level integrative analyses of human behavior: Social neuroscience and the complementing nature of social and biological approaches. *Psychological Bulletin, 126,* 829–843.

Cacioppo, J. T., Tassinary, L. G., & Berntson, G. G. (2000). *Handbook of psychophysiology.* Cambridge, England: Cambridge University Press.

Calder, A. J., Keane, J., Manes, F., Antoun, N., & Young, A. W. (2000). Impaired recognition and experience of disgust following brain injury. *Nature Neuroscience, 3,* 1077–1078.

Caldera, Y. M., Huston, A. C., & O'Brien, M. (1989). Social interactions and play patterns of parents and toddlers with feminine, masculine and neutral toys. *Child Development, 60,* 70–76.

Callahan, R. J. (1995, August). *A thought field therapy (TFT) algorithm for trauma: A reproducible experiment in psychotherapy*. Paper presented at the 105th Annual Convention of the American Psychological Association, Chicago, IL.

Callahan, R. J. (2001). The impact of thought field therapy on heart rate variability (HRV). *Journal of Clinical Psychology, 57*, 1153–1170.

Calvin, W. H. (2004). *A brief history of the mind: From apes to intellect and beyond*. New York: Oxford University Press.

Cameron, J., & Pierce, W. D. (1994). Reinforcement, reward, and intrinsic motivation: A meta-analysis. *Review of Educational Research, 64*, 363–423.

Campbell, D. (1997). *The Mozart effect: Tapping the power of music to heal the body, strengthen the mind, and unlock the creative spirit*. New York: Avon Books.

Campbell, J. (1988). *The power of myth*. New York: Doubleday.

Campfield, L. A., Smith, F. J., Rosenbaum, M., & Hirsch, J. (1996). Human eating: Evidence for a physiological basis using a modified paradigm. *Neuroscience Biobehavioral Review, 20*, 133–137.

Campinha-Bacote, J. (2002). *Resources in transcultural care and mental health* (13th ed.). Wyoming, OH: Transcultural Care Associated.

Canetti, L., Bachar, E., & Berry, E. M. (2002). Food and emotion. *Behavioural Processes, 60*, 157–164.

Canfield, R. L., Henderson, C. R. Jr., Cory-Slechta, D. A., Cox, C., Jusko, T. A., & Lanphear, B. P. (2003). Intellectual impairment in children with blood lead concentrations below 10 microg per deciliter. *New England Journal of Medicine, 348*, 1517–1526.

Cannon, T. D., Mednick, S. A., & Parnas, J. (1989). Genetic and perinatal determinants of structural brain deficits in schizophrenia. *Archives of General Psychiatry, 46*, 883–889.

Cannon, W. B. (1915). *Bodily changes in pain, hunger, fear and rage: An account of recent researches into the functions of emotional excitement*. New York: Appleton.

Cannon, W. B. (1929). *Bodily changes in pain, hunger, fear and rage*. New York: D. Appleton.

Cantril, H. (1947). *The invasion from Mars*. Princeton, NJ: Princeton University Press.

Capellini, I., McNamara, P., Preston, B. T., Nunn, C. I., & Barton, R. A. (2009). Does sleep play a role in memory consolidation? A comparative test. *PloS One, 4*(4), e4609.

Capron, C., & Duyme, M. (1989). Assessment of effects of socioeconomic status on IQ in a full cross-fostering study. *Nature, 340*, 552–553.

Cardeña, E. (2005). The phenomenology of deep hypnosis: Quiescent and physically active. *International Journal of Clinical & Experimental Hypnosis, 53*, 37–59.

Cardón, L. A. (2005). *Popular psychology: An encyclopedia*. Westport, CT: Greenwood.

Carey, S. (1985). *Conceptual change in childhood*. Cambridge, MA: Bradford Books, MIT Press.

Carlson, J. G., & Hatfield, E. (1992). *Psychology of emotion*. New York: Harcourt, Brace, Jovanovich.

Carlson, M., Marcus-Newhall, A., & Miller, N. (1990). The effects of situational aggression cues: A quantitative review. *Journal of Personality and Social Psychology, 58*, 622–633.

Carlson, N. R., Heth, C. D., Miller, H. L., Donahoe, J. W., Buskist, W., & Martin, G. N. (2007). *Psychology: The Science of Behavior* (6th ed.). Boston: Allyn & Bacon.

Carlson, W., & Rose, A. J. (2007). The role of reciprocity in romantic relationships in middle childhood and early adolescence. *Merrill-Palmer Quarterly, 53*, 262–290.

Carlsson, A. (1995). Towards a new understanding of dopamine receptors. Symposium: Dopamine receptor subtypes in neurological and psychiatric diseases. *Clinical Neuropharmacology, 18*(Suppl.), 65–135.

Carney, S., Cowen, P., Geddes, J., Goodwin, G., Rogers, R., Dearness, K., Tomlin, A., Eastaugh, J., Freemantle, N., Lester, H., Harvey, A., & Scott, A. (2003). Efficacy and safety of electroconvulsive therapy in depressive disorders: A systematic review and meta-analysis. *Lancet, 361*(9360), 799–808.

Carr, J. E., Fraizer, T. J., & Roland, J. P. (2005). Token economy. In A. M. Gross & R. S. Drabman (Eds.) *Encyclopedia of behavior modification and cognitive behavior therapy—Volume 2: Child clinical applications* (pp. 1075–1079). Thousand Oaks, CA: Sage.

Carroll, R. T. (2003). *The skeptic's dictionary: A collection of strange beliefs, amusing deceptions, and dangerous delusions*. New York: Wiley.

Carton, J. S. (1996). The differential effects of tangible rewards and praise on intrinsic motivation: A comparison of cognitive evaluation theory and operant theory. *The Behavior Analyst, 19*, 237–255.

Carton, J. S., & Nowicki, S. Jr. (1996). Origins of generalized control expectancies: Reported child stress and observed maternal control and warmth. *Journal of Social Psychology, 136*(6), 753–760.

Cartwright, J. (2000). *Evolution and human behaviour*. London: Macmillan.

Caruso, D. R., Taylor, J., & Detterman, D. K. (1982). Intelligence research and intelligent policy. In D. K. Detterman & R. J. Sternberg (Eds.), *How and how much can intelligence be increased?* (pp. 45–65). Norwood, NJ: Ablex.

Carver, C. S., & Scheier, M. F. (1999). Themes and issues in the self-regulation of behavior. In R. S. Wyer Jr. (Ed.), *Advances in social cognition* (Vol. 12). Mahwah, NJ: Erlbaum.

Carver, C. S., Scheier, M. F., & Weintraub, J. K. (1989). Assessing coping strategies: A theoretically based approach. *Journal of Personality and Social Psychology, 56*, 267–283.

Casey, B., Giedd, J. N., & Thomas, K. M. (2000). Structural and functional brain development and its relation to cognitive development. *Biological Psychology, 54*, 241–257.

Caspi, A., McClay, J., Moffitt, T., Mill, J., Martin, J., Craig, I. W., et al. (2002). Role of genotype in the cycle of violence in maltreated children. *Science, 297*, 851–854.

Caspi, A., Sugden, K., Moffitt, T. E., Taylor, A., Craig, I., Harrington, H. L., et al. (2003). Influence of life stress on depression: Moderation by a polymorphism in the 5-HTT gene. *Science, 301*, 386–389.

Cassidy, K. L. (2004). The adult learner rediscovered: Psychiatry residents' push for cognitive-behavioral therapy training and a learner-driven model of educational change. *Academic Psychiatry, 28*(3), 215–220.

Cattell, R. B. (1949). *Culture Free Intelligence Test, Scale 1, Handbook*. Champaign, IL: Institute of Personality and Ability.

Cattell, R. B. (1963). Theory of fluid and crystallized intelligence: A critical experiment. *Journal of Educational Psychology, 54*, 1–22.

Cattell, R. B. (1971). *Abilities: Their structure, growth, and action*. Boston: Houghton-Mifflin.

Cautela, J. R. (1971). Covert conditioning. In A. Jacobs & L. B. Sachs (Eds.), *The psychology of private events: Perspectives on covert response systems*. New York: Academic Press.

Caviness, V. S. Jr., Kennedy, D. N., Bates, J. F., & Makris, N. (1996). The developing human brain: A morphometric profile. In R. W. Thatcher, G. R. Lyon, J. Rumsey, & N. Krasnegor (Eds.), *Developmental neuroimaging: Mapping the development of brain and behavior* (pp. 3–14). San Diego, CA: Academic Press.

Ceci, S. J., & Bruck, M. (1993). Suggestibility of the child witness: A historical review and synthesis. *Psychological Bulletin, 113*, 403–439.

Ceci, S. J., Crotteau-Huffman, M., Smith, E., & Loftus, E. W. (1994). Repeatedly thinking about non-events. *Consciousness & Cognition, 3,* 388–407.

Centers for Disease Control and Prevention. (2007). About BMI for adults. Retrieved January 31, 2008 from http://www.edc.gov/nccdphp/dnpa/bmi/adult_BMI/about_adult_BMI.htm

Cepeda, N. J., Pashler, H., Vul, E., Wixted, J. T., & Rohrer, D. (2006). Distributed practice in verbal recall tasks: A review and quantitative synthesis. *Psychological Bulletin, 132,* 354–380.

Cerella, J. (1985). Information processing rates in the elderly. *Psychological Bulletin, 98,* 67–83.

Chabris, C. F. (1999). Prelude or requiem for the "Mozart effect"? *Nature, 400,* 826–827.

Chambless, D. L., & Goldstein, A. (1980). The treatment of agoraphobia. In A. Goldstein & E. B. Foz (Eds.), *Handbook of behavioral interventions.* New York: John Wiley & Sons.

Chambless, D. L., & Ollendick, T. H. (2001). Empirically supported psychological interventions: Controversies and evidence. *Annual Review of Psychology, 52,* 685–716.

Chambless, D. L., Sanderson, W. C., Shoham, V., Bennett Johnson, S., Pope, K. S., Crits-Christoph, P., et al. (1996). An update on empirically validated therapies. *The Clinical Psychologist, 49,* 5–18.

Champney, T. F., & Schultz, E. M. (1983). *A reassessment of the effects of psychotherapy.* Paper presented at the 55th annual meeting of the Midwestern Psychological Association, Chicago, IL. (ERIC document ED 237895)

Chandrashekar, J., Hoon, M. A., Ryba, N. J., & Zuker, C. S. (2006). The receptors and cells for mammalian taste. *Nature, 444,* 288–294.

Chang, K. D., Wagner, C., Garrett, A., Howe, M., & Reiss, A. (2008). A preliminary functional magnetic resonance imaging study of prefrontal-amygdalar activation changes in adolescents with bipolar depression treated with lamotrigine. *Bipolar Disorders, 10*(3), 426–431.

Chaplin, W. F., Phillips, J. B., Brown, J. D., Clanton, N. R., & Stein, J. L. (2000). Handshaking, gender, personality, and first impressions. *Journal of Personality and Social Psychology, 79*(I), 110–117

Chapman, L. J., & Chapman, J. P. (1967). Genesis of popular but erroneous diagnostic observations. *Journal of Abnormal Psychology, 72,* 193–204.

Chapman, L. J., & Chapman, J. P. (1969). Illusory correlation as an obstacle to the use of valid psychodiagnostic signs. *Journal of Abnormal Psychology, 74,* 271–280.

Chase, W. G., & Simon, H. A. (1973). The mind's eye in chess. In W. G. Chase (Ed.), *Visual information processing* (pp. 215–281). New York: Academic Press.

Chayer, C., & Freedman, M. (2001). Frontal lobe functions. *Current Neurology & Neuroscience Reports, 1,* 547–552.

Cheesman, J., & Merikle, P. M. (1986). Distinguishing conscious from unconscious perceptual processes. *Canadian Journal of Psychology, 40,* 343–367.

Chentsova-Dutton, Y. E., & Tsai, J. L. (2006). Cultural factors influence the expression of psychopathology. In S. O. Lilienfeld & W. O'Donohue (Eds.), *The great ideas of clinical science: 17 principles that every mental health professional should understand.* New York: Brunner-Taylor, 375–396.

Cheung, F. M., & Leung, K. (1998). Indigenous personality measures: Chinese examples. *Journal of Cross-Cultural Psychology, 29,* 233–248.

Cheyne, J. A., & Girard, T. A. (2009). The body unbound: Vestibular-motor hallucinations and out of body experiences. *Cortex, 45,* 201–215.

Chomsky, N. (1972). *Language and mind.* New York: Harcourt Brace Jovanovich.

Chopra, D. (1989). *Quantum healing: Exploring the frontiers of mind/body medicine.* New York: Bantam.

Chorpita, B. F., & Barlow, D. H. (1998). The development of anxiety: The role of control in the early environment. *Psychological Bulletin, 124,* 3–21.

Christensen, A., & Jacobson, N. S. (1994). Who (or what) can do psychotherapy: The status and challenge of nonprofessional therapies. *Psychological Science, 5,* 8–14.

Chua, H. F., Boland, J. E., & Nisbett, R. E. (2005). Cultural variation in eye movements during scene perception. *Proceedings of the National Academy of Sciences, 102,* 12629–12633.

Church, A. T., & Katigbak, M. S. (2002). The five-factor model in the Philippines: Investigating trait structure and levels across cultures. In R. R. McCrae & J. Allik (Eds.), *The five-factor model across cultures* (pp. 129–154). New York: Kluwer Academic/Plenum Publishers.

Church, R. M. (1969). Response suppression. In B. Campbell & R. Church (Eds.), *Punishment and aversive behavior* (pp. 111–156). New York: Appleton-Century-Crofts.

Chwalisz, K., Diener, E., & Gallagher, D. (1988). Autonomic arousal feedback and emotional experience: Evidence from the spinal cord injured. *Journal of Personality and Social Psychology, 54,* 820–828.

Cialdini, R. B. (2001). *Influence: Science and practice* (4th ed.). Boston: Allyn & Bacon.

Cialdini, R. B., & Goldstein, N. J. (2004). Social influence: Compliance and conformity. *Annual Review of Psychology, 55,* 591–621.

Cialdini, R. B., & Sagarin, B. J. (2005). Interpersonal influence. In T. Brock & M. Green (Eds.), *Persuasion: Psychological insights and perspectives* (pp. 143–169). Newbury Park, CA: Sage Press.

Cialdini, R. B., Vincent, J. E., Lewis, S. K., Catalan, J., Wheeler, D., & Darby, B. L. (1975). Reciprocal concessions procedure for inducing compliance: The door-in-the-face technique. *Journal of Personality and Social Psychology, 31*(2), 206–215.

Ciarella, G., Ciarella, M., Graziani, P., & Mirante, M. (1991). Changes in food consumption of obese patients induced by dietary treatment combined with dexfenfluramine. *International Journal of Obesity, 15,* 69.

Cioffi, F. (1998). *Freud and the question of pseudoscience.* Chicago: Open Court.

Clancy, S. A. (2005). *Abducted: How people come to believe they were kidnapped by aliens.* Cambridge, MA: Harvard University Press.

Clark, D. M. (1986). A cognitive approach to panic. *Behaviour Research and Therapy, 24,* 156–163.

Clark, K. B. & Clark, M. P. (1950) Emotional Factors in Racial Identification and Preference in Negro Children. *Journal of Negro Education, 19,* 506–513.

Clark, M. (1997). *Reason to believe.* New York: Avon Books.

Clarke, A. M., & Clarke, A. D. B. (1976). *Early experience: Myth and evidence.* London: Open Books.

Clay, R. A. (2002). Advertising as science. *American Psychological Association Monitor, 33,* 38.

Cleckley, H. (1941/1988). *The mask of sanity.* St. Louis, MO: Mosby.

Coe, W. C., & Sarbin, T. R. (1991). Role theory: hypnosis from a dramaturgical and narrational perspective. In S. J. Lynn & J. W. Rhue (Eds.), *Theories of hypnosis: Current models and perspectives* (pp. 303–323). New York: Guilford Press.

Cohen, D., & Nisbett, R. E. (1994). Self-protection and the culture of honor: Explaining Southern violence. *Personality and Social Psychology Bulletin, 20,* 551–567.

Cohen, S., Doyle, W. J., Skoner, D. P., Rabin, B. S., & Gwaltney, J. M.

(1997). Social ties and susceptibility to the common cold. *Journal of the American Medical Association, 277*, 1940–1944.

Cohen, S., Doyle, W. J., Turner, R. B., Alper, C. M., & Skoner, D. P. (2003). Emotional style and susceptibility to the common cold. *Psychosomatic Medicine, 65*, 652–657.

Cohen, S., Evans, G. W., Stokols, D., & Krantz, D. S. (1986). *Behavior, health, and environmental stress.* New York: Plenum.

Cohen, S., Frank, E., Doyle, B. J., Skoner, D. P., Rabin, B. S. & Gwaltney, J. M. (1998). Types of stressors that increase susceptibility to the common cold. *Health Psychology, 17*, 214–223.

Cohen, S., & Herbert, T. B. (1996). Health psychology: Psychological factors and physical disease from the perspective of human psychoneuroimmunology. *Annual Review of Psychology, 47*, 113–142.

Cohen, S., Tyrell, D. A. J., & Smith, A. P. (1991). Psychological stress and susceptibility to the common cold. *New England Journal of Medicine, 325*, 606–612.

Cole, M. (1990). Cultural psychology: A once and future discipline? In J. J. Berman (Ed.), *Nebraska Symposium on Motivation, 1989: Cross-cultural perspectives* (pp. 279–335). Lincoln: University of Nebraska Press.

Coleman, H. L. K., Wampold, B. E., & Casali, S. L. (1995). Ethnic minorities' ratings of ethnically similar and European American counselors: A meta-analysis. *Journal of Counseling Psychology, 42*, 55–64.

College Board. (1976–1977). *Student descriptive questionnaire.* Princeton, NJ: Educational Testing Service.

Collins, A. F. (1999). The enduring appeal of physiognomy: Physical appearance as a sign of temperament, character, and intelligence. *History of Psychology, 2*, 251–276.

Collins, A. W., Maccoby, E. E., Steinberg, L., Hetherington, M. E., & Bornstein, M. H. (2000). Contemporary research on parenting. *American Psychologist, 55*, 218–232.

Collins, F. L., Sorocco, K. H., Haala, K. R., Miller, B. I., & Lovallo, W. R. (2003). Stress and health. In L. M. Cohen, D. E. McChargue, & F. L. Collins (Eds.), *The health psychology handbook: Practical issues for the behavioral medicine specialist* (pp. 169–186). London: Sage Publications.

Comijs, H., Beekman, A., Smits, F., Bremmer, M., Tilburg, T., & Deeg, D. (2008). Childhood adversity, recent life events, and depression in later life. *Journal of Affective Disorders, 103*, 243–246.

Conrad, R. (1964). Acoustic confusion and immediate memory. *British Journal of Psychology, 55*, 75–84.

Consumer Reports. (2006, November 1). *Flip up or flip out.* Retrieved May 26, 2008, from www.accessmylibrary.com/coms2/summary_0286-29406170_ITM

Conte, J. M. (2005). A review and critique of emotional intelligence measures. *Journal of Organizational Behavior, 26*, 433–440.

Coombs, R. H. (1991). Marital status and personal well-being: A literature review. *Family Relations: Journal of Applied Family and Child Studies, 40*, 17–102.

Coons, P. M., Bowman, E. S., & Milstein, V. (1988). Multiple personality disorder: A clinical investigation of 50 cases. *Journal of Nervous and Mental Disease, 176*, 519–527.

Coontz, S. (1992). *The way we never were: American families and the nostalgia trap.* New York: Basic Books.

Cooper, C. L., & Dewe, P. (2004). *Stress: A brief history.* Malden, MA: Blackwell Publishing.

Coover, J. E. & Angell, F. (1907). General practice effect of special exercise. *American Journal of Psychology, 18*, 328–340.

Corballis, M. C. (1999). Are we in our right minds? In S. Della Sala (Ed.), *Mind myths* (pp. 26–42). Chichester, England: John Wiley & Sons.

Coren, S. (1996). *Sleep thieves.* New York: Free Press.

Corkin, S. (1984). Lasting consequences of bilateral medial temporal lobectomy: Clinical course and experimental findings. In S. M. Kosslyn & R. A. Anderson (Eds.), *Frontiers in cognitive neuroscience* (pp. 516–526). London: The MIT Press.

Corkin, S., Amaral, D. G., Gonzalez, R. G., Johnson, K. A., & Hyman, B. T. (1997). H.M.'s medial temporal lobe lesion: Findings from magnetic resonance imaging. *Journal of Neuroscience, 17*, 3964–3979.

Cornblatt, B. A., Green, M. F., & Walker, E. F. (1999). Schizophrenia: Etiology and neurocognition. In T. Millon, P. H. Blaney, & R. D. Davis (Eds.), *Oxford textbook of psychopathology* (pp. 227–310). New York: Oxford University Press.

Cornell, E. H. (1980). Distributed study facilitates infants' delayed recognition memory. *Memory and Cognition, 8*, 539–542.

Cornell, E. H., & Bergstrom, L. I. (1983). Serial-position effects in infants' recognition memory. *Memory and Cognition, 11*, 494–499.

Correll, C. U., & Schenk, E. M. (2008). Tardive dyskinesia and new antipsychotics. *Current Opinion in Psychiatry, 21*, 151–156.

Coryell, W., Scheftner, W., Keller, M., Endicott, J., Maser, J., & Klerman, G. L. (1993). The enduring psychosocial consequences of mania and depression. *American Journal of Psychiatry, 150*(5), 720–727.

Costa, P. T. Jr., & McCrae, R. R. (1990). Personality disorders and the five-factor model of personality. *Journal of Personality Disorders, 4*, 362–371.

Costa, P. T., & McCrae, R. R. (1992). 4 ways 5 factors are basic. *Personality and Individual Differences, 13*(6), 653–665.

Costa, P. T., & McCrae, R. R. (1998). Trait theories of personality. In D. F. Barone, M. Hersen, & V. B. Van Hasselt (Eds.), *Advanced Personality* (pp. 103–121). New York: Plenum.

Cottrell, C. A., & Neuberg, S. L. (2005). Different emotional reactions to different groups: A sociofunctional threat-based approach to "prejudice." *Journal of Personality and Social Psychology, 88*, 770–789.

Cowan, N. (2001). The magical number 4 in short-term memory: A reconsideration of mental storage capacity. *Behavioral and Brain Sciences, 24*, 87–185.

Cowan, N., Lichty, W., & Grove, T. R. (1990). Properties of memory for unattended spoken syllables. *Journal of Experimental Psychology: Learning, Memory, & Cognition, 16*, 258–269.

Cox, B. J., & Taylor, S. (1999). Anxiety disorders: Panic and phobias. In T. Millon, P. H. Blaney, & R. D. Davis (Eds.), *Oxford textbook of psychopathology* (pp. 81–113). New York: Oxford University Press.

Coyne, J. C. (1976). Depression and the response of others. *Journal of Abnormal Psychology, 85*, 186–193.

Coyne, J. C. (1992). Cognition in depression: A paradigm in crisis. *Psychological Inquiry, 3*, 232–235.

Coyne, J. C., & Holroyd, K. (1982). Stress, coping, and illness: A transactional perspective. In T. Millon, C. Green, & R. Meachem (Eds.), *Handbook of clinical health psychology* (pp. 103–127). New York: Plenum Press.

Coyne, J. C., & Racioppo, M. W. (2000). Never the twain shall meet? Closing the gap between coping research and clinical intervention research. *American Psychologist, 55*, 655–664.

Coyne, J. C., Stefanek, M., & Palmer, S. C. (2007). Psychotherapy and survival in cancer: The conflict between hope and evidence. *Psychological Bulletin, 133*(3), 367–394.

Craighead, L. W. (2002). Obesity and eating disorders. In M. M. Antony & D. H. Barlow (Eds.), *A guide to treatments that work* (2nd ed., pp. 245–262). New York: Oxford.

Craik, F. I. M., & Lockhart, R. (1972). Levels of processing: A framework for memory research. *Journal of Verbal Learning & Verbal Behavior, 11*, 671–684.

Craik, F. I. M., & Tulving, E. (1975). Depth of processing and the retention of words in episodic memory. *Journal of Experimental Psychology: General, 104,* 268–294.

Crandall, C. S. (1994). Prejudice against fat people: Ideology and self-interest. *Journal of Personality and Social Psychology, 66,* 882–894.

Craske, M. G., Rapee, R. M., Jackel, L., & Barlow, D. H. (1989). Qualitative dimensions of worry in DSM-III-R generalized anxiety disorder subjects and nonanxious controls. *Behaviour Research and Therapy, 27,* 397–402.

Cressen, R. (1975). Artistic quality of drawings and judges' evaluations of the DAP. *Journal of Personality Assessment, 39*(2), 132–137.

Crews, F. (2005). Response to Holland. *Scientific Review of Alternative Medicine, 10,* 24–28.

Crick, F., & Mitchison, G. (1983). The function of dream sleep. *Nature, 304,* 111–114.

Crick, F., & Mitchison, G. (1986). REM sleep and neural nets. *Journal of Mind and Behavior, 7,* 229–250.

Crick, N. (1995). Relational aggression: The role of intent attributions, feelings of distress, and provocation type. *Development and Psychopathology, 7,* 313–322.

Crits-Christoph, P., Wilson, G. T., & Hollon, S. D. (2005). Empirically supported psychotherapies: Comment on Westen, Novotny, and Thompson-Brenner (2004). *Psychological Bulletin, 131,* 412–417.

Cromer, A. (1993). *Uncommon sense: The heretical nature of science.* New York: Oxford University Press.

Cross, P. (1977). Not can but will college teaching be improved? *New Directions for Higher Education, 17,* 1–15.

Csikszentmihalyi, M. (1990). *Flow, the psychology of optimal experience.* New York: Harper & Row.

Csikszentmihalyi, M. (1997). *Finding flow: The psychology of engagement with everyday life.* New York: Basic Books.

Culham, J. C., & Valyear, K. F. (2006). Human parietal cortex in action. *Current Opinion in Neurobiology, 16,* 205–212.

Culliton, B. J. (1989). The dismal state of scientific literacy. *Science, 243,* 600.

Cunningham, M. R., Roberts, A. R., Wu, H., Barbee, A. P., & Bruen, P. B. (1995). Their ideas of beauty are, on the whole, the same as ours: Consistency and variability in the cross-cultural perception of female physical attractiveness. *Journal of Personality and Social Psychology, 68,* 261–279.

Cunningham, P. F. (1993, October). *Can the use of animals in neuropsychological and psychopharmacological experiments continue to be justified?* Paper presented at the New England Psychological Association 33rd Annual Meeting, Goffstown, NH.

Curran, J. P., & Lippold, S. (1975). The effects of physical attraction and attitude similarity on attraction in dating dyads. *Journal of Personality, 43,* 528–539.

Curtis, R. C., & Miller, K. (1986). Believing another likes or dislikes you: Behavior making the beliefs come true. *Journal of Personality and Social Psychology, 51,* 284–290.

Cytowic, Richard E. (1993). *The man who tasted shapes: A bizarre medical mystery offers revolutionary insights into emotions, reasoning, and consciousness.* New York: G. P. Putnam's Sons.

D

Dabbs, J. B. (2001). *Heroes, rogues, and lovers: Testosterone and behavior.* New York: McGraw Hill.

Dahlstrom, W. G., Welsh, G. S., & Dahlstrom, L. E. (1975). *An MMPI handbook: A revised edition.* Minneapolis: University of Minnesota Press.

Dallek, R. (2003). *An unfinished life: John F. Kennedy, 1917–1963.* Boston: Little, Brown and Company.

Damasio, A. (1994). *Descartes' error.* New York: G. P. Putnam's Sons.

Damasio, H., Grabowski, T., Frank, R., Galaburda, A. M., & Damasio, A. R. (1994). The return of Phineas Gage: Clues about the brain from the skull of a famous patient. *Science, 264,* 1102–1105.

Danaher, B. C. (1974). Theoretical foundations and clinical applications of the Premack principle: Review and critique. *Behavior Therapy, 5*(3), 307–324.

Danner, D. D., Snowdon, D. A., & Friesen, W. V. (2001). Positive emotions in early life and longevity: Findings from the nun study. *Journal of Personality and Social Psychology, 80,* 804–813.

Darley, J. M., & Latané, B. (1968a). Bystander intervention in emergencies: Diffusion of responsibility. *Journal of Personality and Social Psychology, 8,* 377–383.

Darley, J. M., & Latané, B. (1968b). When will people help in a crisis? *Psychology Today, 2,* 54–57, 70–71.

Darwin, C. R. (1872). *The expression of the emotions in man and animals.* London: John Murray.

Davey, G. C. L. (1995). Rumination and the enhancement of fear: Some laboratory findings. *Behavioural and Cognitive Psychotherapy, 23*(3), 203–215.

Davidson, J. R., Gadde, K. M., Fairbank, J. A., Krishnan, R. R., Califf, R. M., Binanay, C., et al. (2002). Hypericum Depression Trial Study Group. Effect of *Hypericum perforatum* (St. John's wort) in major depressive disorder: A randomized, controlled trial. *Journal of the American Medical Association, 287,* 1807–1814.

Davidson, P. R., & Parker, K. C. (2001). Eye movement desensitization and reprocessing (EMDR): A meta-analysis. *Journal of Consulting and Clinical Psychology, 69,* 305–316.

Davidson, R. J., Kabat-Zinn, J., Schumacher, J., Rosenkranz, M., Muller, D., Santorelli, S. F., et al. (2003). Alternations in brain and immune function produced by mindfulness meditation. *Psychosomatic Medicine, 65*(4), 564–570.

Davies, G., Welham, J., Chant, D., Torrey, E. F., & McGrath, J. (2003). A systematic review and meta-analysis of northern hemisphere season of birth in schizophrenia. *Schizophrenia Research, 29,* 587–593.

Davis, R., Olmsted, M., Rockert, W., Marques, T., & Dolhanty, J. (1997). Group psychoeducation for bulimia nervosa with and without additional psychotherapy process sessions. *International Journal of Eating Disorders, 22,* 25–35.

Davis, S. R., Davison, S. L., Donath, S., & Bell, R. J. (2005). Circulating androgen levels and self-reported sexual function in women. *Journal of the American Medical Association, 294,* 91–96.

Davis, T. C., Wolf, M. S., Bass, P. F., Middlebrooks, M., Kennen, E., Baker, D. W., Bennett, C., Durazo-Arvizu, R., Bocchini, A., Savory, S., & Parker, R. (2006). Low literacy impairs comprehension of prescription drug warning labels. *Journal of General Internal Medicine, 21*(8), 847–851.

Davison, G. C., & Lazarus, A. A. (2007). Clinical case studies are important in the science and practice of psychotherapy. In S. O. Lilienfeld & W. T. O'Donohue (Eds.), *The great ideas of clinical science: 17 principles that every mental health professional should understand* (pp. 149–162). New York: Routledge.

Davison, K. P., Pennebaker, J. W., & Dickerson, S. S. (2000). Who talks? The social psychology of illness support groups. *American Psychologist, 55,* 205–217.

Dawes, R. M. (1994). *House of cards: Psychology and psychotherapy built on myth.* New York: Free Press.

Dawes, R. M. (1998, June). "Listening to Prozac but hearing placebo": Commentary on Kirsch and Sapirstein. *Prevention & Treatment, 1*(2).

De Raad, B., & Perugini, M. (2002). *Big Five assessment.* Ashland, OH: Hogrefe & Huber.

De Raad, B., Perugini, M., Hrebickova, M., & Szarota, P. (1998). The lingua franca of personality: Taxonomies and structure. *Journal of Cross Cultural Psychology, 29,* 212–232.

de Waal, F. B. M. (1982). *Chimpanzee politics: Power and sex among apes.* Baltimore: Johns Hopkins University Press.

de Waal, F. B. M. (1989). The myth of a simple relation between space and aggression in captive primates. *Zoo Biology, 8,* 141–148.

de Waal, F. B. M. (1990). *Peacemaking among primates.* Cambridge, MA: Harvard University Press.

de Waal, F. B. M. (1996). *Good natured: The origins of right and wrong in humans and other animals.* Cambridge, MA: Harvard University Press.

de Waal, F. B. M. (2002). Evolutionary psychology: The wheat and the chaff. *Current Directions in Psychological Science, 11,* 187–191.

de Waal, F. B. M. (2006). *Primates and philosophers: How morality evolved* (S. Macedo & J. Ober, Eds.). Princeton, NJ: Princeton University Press.

de Waal, F. B. M., Aureli, F., & Judge, P. G. (2000, May). Coping with crowding. *Scientific American, 282,* 76–81.

Dean, G. (1987). Does astrology need to be true? Part 2: The answer is no. *Skeptical Inquirer, 11,* 257–273.

Deary, I. J., Der, G., & Ford, G. (2001). Reaction time and intelligence differences: A population based cohort study. *Intelligence, 29,* 1–11.

Deary, I. J., Whalley, L. J., Lemmon, H., Crawford, J. R., & Starr, J. M. (2000). The stability of individual differences in mental ability from childhood to old age: Follow-up of the 1932 Scottish Mental Survey. *Intelligence, 28,* 49–55.

DeBreuil, S. C., Garry, M., & Loftus, E. F. (1998). Tales from the crib: Age regression and the creation of unlikely memories. In S. J. Lynn & K. M. McConkey (Eds.) *Truth in memory.* (pp. 137–160). New York: Guilford Press.

DeCasper, A. J., & Spence, M. J. (1988). Prenatal maternal speech influences newborns' perception of speech sounds. In S. Chess, A. Thomas, & M. Hertzig (Eds.), *Annual progress in child psychiatry and child development, 1987* (pp. 5–25). Philadelphia: Brunner/Mazel.

Deci, E. L. (1971). Effects of externally mediated rewards on intrinsic motivation. *Journal of Personality and Social Psychology, 18,* 105–115.

Deci, E. L., Koestner, R., & Ryan, R. M. (1999). A meta-analytic review of experiments examining the effects of extrinsic rewards on intrinsic motivation. *Psychological Bulletin, 125,* 627–668.

Deese, J. (1959). On the prediction of occurrence of particular verbal intrusions in immediate recall. *Journal of Experimental Psychology, 58,* 17–22.

Deffenbacher, K. A., Bornstein, B. H., Penrod, S. D., & McGorty, E. K. (2004). A meta-analytic review of the effects of high stress on eyewitness memory. *Law and Human Behavior, 28,* 687–706.

DeFries, J. C., & Plomin, R. (1978). Behavioral genetics. *Annual Review of Psychology, 29,* 473–515.

Degenhardt, L., & Hall, W. (2006). Is cannabis a contributory cause of psychosis? *Canadian Journal of Psychiatry, 51,* 556–565.

Dehue, T. (2000). From deception trials to control reagents. The introduction of the control group about a century ago. *American Psychologist, 55*(2), 264–269.

Delgado, J. M. R., & Anand, B. K. (1952). Increase of food intake induced by electrical stimulation of the lateral hypothalamus. *American Journal of Physiology, 172,* 162–168.

Dement, W. C., & Kleitman, N. (1957). The relation of eye movements during sleep to dream activity: An objective method for the study of dreaming. *Journal of Experimental Psychology, 53,* 339–346.

Dement, W. C., & Vaughan, C. (1999*). The promise of sleep: A pioneer in sleep medicine explores the vital connection between health, happiness, and a good night's sleep.* New York: Dell Trade Paperbacks.

den Boer, P. C. A. M., Wiersma, D., Russo, S. & van den Bosch, R. J. (2005). Paraprofessionals for anxiety and depressive disorders: A meta-analysis. *The Cochrane Database of Systematic Reviews,* Issue 2. Art No: CD004688.

Dennett, D. C. (1995). *Darwin's dangerous idea: Evolution and the meanings of life.* New York: Simon and Schuster.

Dennis, M., Sugar, J., & Whitaker, H. A. (1982). The acquisition of tag questions. *Child Development, 53,* 1254–1257.

DePaulo, B. (1992). Nonverbal behavior and self-presentation. *Psychological Bulletin, 111,* 203–243.

Depue, R. A., & Iacono, W. G. (1989). Neurobehavioral aspects of affective disorders. *Annual Review of Psychology, 40,* 457–492.

Depue, R. A., & Monroe, S. M. (1986). Conceptualization and measurement of human disorder in life stress research—The problem of chronic disturbance. *Psychological Bulletin, 99*(1), 36–51.

DeRubeis, R. J., Brotman, M. A., & Gibbons, C. J. (2005). A conceptual and methodological analysis of the nonspecifics argument. *Clinical Psychology: Science & Practice, 12,* 174–183.

Desmedt, E., & Valcke, M. (2004). Mapping the learning styles "jungle": An overview of the literature based on citation analysis. *Educational Psychology, 24*(4), 445–464.

Detterman, D. K. (1987). What does reaction time tell us about intelligence? In P. Vernon (Ed.), *Speed of information-processing and intelligence.* Norwood, NJ: Ablex.

Devine, P. G. (1989). Stereotypes and prejudice: Their automatic and controlled components. *Journal of Personality and Social Psychology, 56,* 5–18.

Devine, P. G., Monteith, M. J., Zuwerink, J. R., & Elliot, A. J. (1991). Prejudice with and without compunction. *Journal of Personality and Social Psychology, 60,* 817–830.

Diamond, L. M. (2003). What does sexual orientation orient? A biobehavioral model distinguishing romantic love and sexual desire. *Psychological Review, 110,* 173–192.

Diamond, L. M. (2004). Emerging perspectives on distinctions between romantic love and sexual desire. *Current Directions in Psychological Science, 13,* 116–119.

Dickens, W. T., & Flynn, J. R. (2001). Heritability estimates versus large environmental effects: The IQ paradox resolved. *Psychological Review, 108,* 346–369.

Dickens, W. T., & Flynn, J. R. (2006). Black Americans reduce the racial IQ gap: Evidence from standardization samples. *Psychological Science, 17,* 1101–1107.

Dickerson, F. B., Tenhula, W. N., & Green-Paden, L. D. (2005). The token economy for schizophrenia: Review of the literature and recommendations for future research. *Schizophrenia Research, 75,* 405–416.

Dickey, M. (1994). *Anxiety disorders.* National Institute of Mental Health. Washington, DC: U.S. Government Printing Office.

DiClemente, C. C., & Prochaska, J. O. (1985). Coping and competence in smoking behavior change. In S. Shiffman & T. A. Willis (Eds.), *Coping and substance abuse.* New York: Academic Press.

Didierjean, A., & Marmèche, E. (2005). Anticipatory representation of visual basketball scenes by novice and expert players. *Visual Cognition, 12,* 265–283.

Diehl, M., & Stroebe, W. (1987). Productivity loss in brainstorming groups: Toward the solution of a riddle. *Journal of Personality and Social Psychology, 53,* 497–509.

Diener, E., Emmons, R. A., Larsen, R. J., & Griffin, S. (1985). The satisfaction with life scale. *Journal of Personality Assessment, 49,* 71–75.

Diener, E., Horwitz, J., & Emmons, R. A. (1985). Happiness of the very wealthy. *Social Indicators Research, 16,* 263–274.

Diener, E., & Seligman, M. E. P. (2002). Very happy people. *Psychological Science, 13,* 81–84.

Diener, E., & Seligman, M. E. P. (2004). Beyond money: Toward an economy of well-being. *Psychological Science in the Public Interest, 5,* 1–31.

Dies, R. R. (2003). Group psychotherapies. In A. S. Gurman & S. B. Messer (Eds.), *Essential psychotherapies*: Theory and practice (2nd ed., pp. 515–550). New York: Guilford Press.

DiLalla, L. F., & Gottesman, I. I. (1991). Biological and genetic contributors to violence—Widom's untold tale. *Psychological Bulletin, 109,* 125–129.

Dilk, M. N., & Bond, G. R. (1996). Meta-analytic evaluation of skills training research for individuals with severe mental illness. *Journal of Consulting and Clinical Psychology, 64,* 1337–1346.

Dillehay, R. C. (1978). Authoritarianism. In H. London & J. E. Exner (Eds.), *Dimensions of personality* (pp. 85–127). New York: John Wiley & Sons.

DiLoretto, A. O. (1971). *Comparative psychotherapy: An experimental analysis.* Chicago: Aldine-Atherton.

Dion, K., Berscheid, E., & Walster, E. (1972). What is beautiful is good. *Journal of Personality and Social Psychology, 24,* 285–290.

Dipboye, R. L. (1977). Alternative approaches to deindividuation. *Psychological Bulletin, 85,* 1057–1075.

Dodd, B., & McEvoy, S. (1994). Twin language or phonological disorder? *Journal of Child Language, 21,* 273–289.

Dohrenwend, B. S., & Dohrenwend, B. P. (Eds.) (1974). *Stressful life events: Their nature and effects* (pp. 245–258). New York: Wiley.

Dollard, J., & Miller, N. (1950). *Personality and psychotherapy: An analysis in terms of learning, thinking and culture.* New York: McGraw-Hill.

Dolnick, E. (1998). *Madness on the couch: Blaming the victim in the heyday of psychoanalysis.* New York: Simon & Schuster.

Domhoff, G. W. (1996). *Finding meaning in dreams: A quantitative approach.* New York: Plenum.

Domhoff, G. W. (2001a). A new neurocognitive theory of dreams. *Dreaming, 11,* 13–33.

Domhoff, G. W. (2001b). Using content analysis to study dreams: Applications and implications for the humanities. In K. Bulkeley (Ed.), *Dreams: A reader on religious, cultural, and psychological dimensions of dreaming* (pp. 307–319). New York: Palgrave Macmillan.

Domhoff, G. W. (2003). Dreaming—An introduction to the science of sleep. *Science, 299*(5615), 1987–1988.

Domjan, M., & Purdy, J. E. (1995). Animal research in psychology. *American Psychologist, 50,* 496–503.

Donnellen, M. B., Trzesniewski, K. H., Robins, R. W., Moffitt, T. E., & Caspi, A. (2005). Exploring the link between self-esteem and externalizing behaviors: Low self-esteem is related to antisocial behavior, conduct disorder, and delinquency. *Psychological Science, 16,* 328–335.

Donovan, J. J., & Radosevich, D. R. (1999). A meta-analytic review of the distribution of practice effect: Now you see it, now you don't. *Journal of Applied Psychology, 84,* 795–805.

Dorus, E., Dorus, W., & Rechtschaffen, A. (1971). The incidence of novelty in dreams. *Archives of General Psychiatry, 25,* 364–368.

Dosajh, N. L. (1996). Projective techniques with particular reference to inkblot tests. *Journal of Projective Psychology and Mental Health, 3,* 59–68.

Doty, R. L., Shaman, P., Applebaum, S. L., Giberson, R., Siksorski, L.,

& Rosenberg, L. (1984). Smell identification ability: Changes with age. *Science, 226,* 1441–1443.

Dovidio, J., Piliavin, J., Schroeder, D., & Penner, L. (2006). *The social psychology of prosocial behavior.* Mahwah, NJ: Erlbaum.

Dowman, J., Patel, A., & Rajput, K. (2005). Electroconvulsive therapy: Attitudes and misconceptions. *The Journal of ECT, 21,* 84–87.

Driscoll, R., Davis, K. E., & Lipetz, M. E. (1972). Parental interference and romantic love: The Romeo and Juliet effect. *Journal of Personality and Social Structure, 24,* 1–10.

Druckman, D., & Bjork, R. A. (Eds.). (1994). *Learning, remembering, believing: Enhancing human performance.* Washington, DC: National Academy Press.

Druckman, D., & Swets, J. A. (Eds.). (1988). *Enhancing human performance: Issues, theories, and techniques.* Washington, DC: National Academy Press.

DuBrin, J. R., & Zastowny, T. R. (1988). Predicting early attrition from psychotherapy: An analysis of a large private practice cohort. *Psychotherapy, 25,* 393–498.

Dunbar, R. (1996). *Grooming, gossip, and the evolution of language.* London: Faber & Faber.

Dunbar, R. (2003). Psychology: Evolution of the social brain. *Science, 302,* 1160–1161.

Duncan, B. (1976). Differential social perception and attribution of intergroup violence. *Journal of Personality and Social Psychology, 34,* 590–598.

Duncan, G. (1996). Income dynamics and health. *International Journal of Health Services, 26,* 419–444.

Duncan, J., Seitz, R. J., Kolodny, J., Bor, D., Herzog, H., Ahmed, A., et al. (2000). A neural basis for general intelligence. *Science, 289,* 457–460.

Duncker, K. (1945). *On problem-solving.* Psychological Monographs (No. 270).

E

Eagly, A. H., & Steffen, V. J. (1986). Gender and aggressive behavior: A meta-analytic review of the social psychological literature. *Psychological Bulletin, 100,* 309–330.

Eagly, A. H., & Wood, W. (1999). The origins of sex differences in human behavior: Evolved dispositions versus social roles. *American Psychologist, 54,* 408–423.

Eagly, A. H., Wood, W., & Johannesen-Schmidt, M. C. (2004). Social role theory of sex differences and similarities: Implications for the partner preferences of women and men. In A. H. Eagly, A. Beall, & R. S. Sternberg (Eds.), *The psychology of gender* (2nd ed., pp. 269–295). New York: Guilford Press.

Ehrenwald, J. (1974). Out-of-the-body experiences and the denial of death. *Journal of Nervous and Mental Disease, 159,* 227–233.

Ehrsson, H. H. (2007). The experimental induction of out-of-body experiences. *Science, 317,* 1048.

Eich, E., & Hyman, R. (1991). Subliminal self help. In D. Druckman & R. A. Bjork (Eds.), *In the mind's eye: Enhancing human performance* (pp. 107–119). Washington, DC: National Academy Press.

Eimas, P. D., Siqueland, E. R., Jusczyk, P., & Vigorito, J. (1971). Speech perception in infants. *Science, 171,* 303–306.

Eisenberger, N. I., Lieberman, M. D., & Williams, K. D. (2003). Does rejection hurt? An fMRI study of social exclusion. *Science, 302,* 290–292.

Eisenberger, R., & Cameron, J. (1996). Detrimental effects of reward: Reality of or myth? *American Psychologist, 51,* 1153–1166.

Eisler, R. M., & Ragsdale, K. (1992). Masculine gender role and midlife transition in men. In V. B. Van Hasselt & M. Hersen (Eds.), *Handbook of social development: A lifespan perspective* (pp. 455–471). New York: Plenum Press.

Eisner, D. A. (2000). *The death of psychotherapy: From Freud to alien abductions.* Westport, CT: Praeger.

Ekman, P. (1994). Strong evidence for universals in facial expressions: A reply to Russell's mistaken critique. *Psychological Bulletin, 115,* 268–287.

Ekman, P. (1999). Facial expressions. In T. Dalgleish & M. J. Power (Eds.), *Handbook of cognition and emotion* (pp. 301–320). New York: John Wiley & Sons.

Ekman, P. (2001). *Telling lies: Clues to deceit in the marketplace, politics, and marriage.* New York: Norton.

Ekman, P., & Davidson, R. (1993). Voluntary smiling changes regional brain activity. *Psychological Science, 5,* 342–345.

Ekman, P., Davidson, R. J., & Friesen, W. V. (1990). Duchenne's smile: Emotional expression and brain physiology II. *Journal of Personality and Social Psychology, 58,* 342–353.

Ekman, P., & Friesen, W. V. (1971). Constants across cultures in the face and emotion. *Journal of Personality and Social Psychology, 17,* 124–129.

Ekman, P., & Friesen, W. V. (1975). *Unmasking the face: A guide to recognizing emotions from facial clues.* Englewood Cliffs, NJ: Prentice-Hall.

Ekman, P., & Friesen, W. V. (1986). A new pancultural facial expression of emotion. *Motivation and Emotion, 10,* 159–168.

Ekman, P., Levenson, R. W., & Friesen, W. V. (1983). Autonomic nervous system activity distinguishes between emotions. *Science, 221,* 1208–1210.

Ekman, P., & Oster, H. (1979). Facial expressions of emotion. *Annual Review of Psychology, 20,* 527–554.

Elkin, I. (1994). The NIMH Treatment of Depression Collaborative Research Program: Where we began and where we are now. In A. E. Bergin & S. L. Garfield (Eds.), *Handbook of psychotherapy and behavior change* (4th ed., pp. 114–135). New York: Wiley.

Elliott, R. (2002). The effectiveness of humanistic therapies: A meta-analysis. In D. J. Cain & J. Seeman (Eds.), *Humanistic psychotherapies: Handbook of research and practice* (pp. 57–81). Washington, DC: American Psychological Association.

Ellis, A. (1958). *Sex without guilt.* New York: Lyle Stuart.

Ellis, A. (1962). *Reason and emotion in psychotherapy.* New York: Lyle Stuart.

Ellis, A. (1977). The basic clinical theory of rational-emotive therapy. In A. Ellis & R. Grieger (Eds.), *Handbook of rational-emotive therapy* (pp. 3–34). New York: Springer.

Ellis, A., Abrams, M., & Abrams, L. D. (2008). *Personality theories: Critical perspectives.* New York: Sage.

Ellis, L., & Ames, M. A. (1987). Neurohormonal functioning and sexual orientation: A theory of homosexuality-heterosexuality. *Psychological Bulletin, 101,* 233–258.

Ellison, C. G., & Levin, S. L. (1998). The religion-health connection: Evidence, theory, and future directions. *Health Education and Behavior, 25,* 700–720.

Elman, J. (1993). Incremental learning, or the importance of starting small. *Cognition, 49,* 71–99.

Elms, A. C. (1972). *Social psychology and social relevance.* Boston: Little, Brown.

Elzinga, B. M., van Dyck, R., & Spinhoven, P. (1998). Three controversies about dissociative identity disorder. *Clinical Psychology and Psychotherapy, 5,* 13–23.

Emery, C., & Lilienfeld, S. O. (2004). The validity of child sexual abuse survivor checklists in the popular psychology literature: A Barnum effect? *Professional Psychology: Science and Practice, 35,* 268–274.

Emmons, R. A., & McCullough, M. E. (2003). Counting blessings versus burdens: An experimental investigation of gratitude and subjective well-being in daily life. *Journal of Personality and Social Psychology, 84*(2), 377–389.

Emrick, C. D. (1987). Alcoholics Anonymous: Affiliation processes and effectiveness as treatment. *Alcoholism: Clinical and Experimental Research, 11,* 416–423.

Engel, A. K., & Singer, W. (2001). Temporal binding and the neural correlates of sensory awareness. *Trends in Cognitive Science, 5,* 6–25.

Engel, G. L. (1977). The need for a new medical model: A challenge for biomedicine. *Science, 196,* 129–136.

Engle, R. W. (2002). Working memory capacity as executive attention. *Current Directions in Psychological Science, 11,* 19–23.

Engler, J., & Goleman, D. (1992). *A consumer's guide to psychotherapy.* New York: Simon & Schuster.

Epley, N., Savitsky, K., & Kachelski, R. A. (1999). What every skeptic should know about subliminal persuasion. *Skeptical Inquirer, 23,* 40–45, 58.

Epstein, R. (2007). Giving psychology away: A personal journey. *Perspectives on Psychological Science, 1,* 389–400.

Epstein, S. (1979). The stability of behavior: I. On predicting more of the people more of the time. *Journal of Personality and Social Psychology, 37,* 1097–1126.

Erblich, J., Earlywine, M., Erblich, B., & Bovjerg, D. H. (2003). Biphasic stimulant and sedative effects of ethanol: Are children of alcoholics really different? *Addictive Behaviors, 28,* 1129–1139.

Erdelyi, M. (1994). Hypnotic hypermnesia: The empty set of hypermnesia. *International Journal of Clinical and Experimental Hypnosis, 42,* 379–390.

Ericsson, K. A., Krampe, R. Th., & Tesch-Römer, C. (1993). The role of deliberate practice in the acquisition of expert performance. *Psychological Review, 100,* 363–406.

Erikson, E. H. (1963). *Childhood and society* (2nd ed.). New York: W. W. Norton.

Erikson, E. H. (1970). Reflections on the dissent of contemporary youth. *International Journal of Psychoanalysis, 51,* 11–22.

Ernst, E. (2002). Heavy metals in traditional Indian remedies. *European Journal of Clinical Pharmacology, 57,* 891–896.

Esch, T., & Stefano, G. B. (2005). The neurobiology of love. *Neuro Endocrinology Letters, 26,* 175–192.

Eslinger, P. J., & Damasio, A. R. (1985). Severe disturbance of higher cognition after bilateral frontal lobe ablation. Patient EVR. *Neurology, 35,* 1731–1741.

Esterling, B. A., Kiecolt-Glaser, J. K., & Glaser, R. (1996). Psychosocial modulation of cytokine-induced natural killer cell activity in older adults. *Psychosomatic Medicine, 58,* 264–272.

Esterson, A. (1993). *Seductive mirage: An exploration of the work of Sigmund Freud.* Chicago: Open court.

Evans, C. J. (2004). Secrets of the opium poppy revealed. *Neuropharmacology. 47*(Suppl. 1), 293–299.

Evans, R. B. (1972). Titchener and his lost system. *Journal of the History of the Behavioral Sciences, 8,* 168–180.

Eveleth, P. B., & Tanner, J. M. (1976). *Worldwide variation in human growth.* Cambridge, England: Cambridge University Press.

Eveleth, P. B., & Tanner, J. M. (1990). *Worldwide variation in human growth* (2nd ed.). Cambridge, England: Cambridge University Press.

Eyferth, K. (1961). Leistungen verschidener Gruppen von Besatzungskindern in Hamburg-Wechsler Intelligenztest fur Kinder (HAWIK) [Performance of different groups of occupation children on the Hamburg-Wechsler Intelligence Test for Children]. *Archhiv fur die gesamte Psychologie, 113,* 222–241.

Eysenck, H. J. (1973). *Eysenck on extraversion.* New York: Wiley.

Eysenck, H. J. (1991). Dimensions of personality: 16, 5, or 3?—Criteria for a taxonomic paradigm. *Personality and Individual Differences, 12*, 773–790.

Eysenck, H. J. (1994). *Test your IQ.* Toronto, Ontario, Canada: Penguin Books.

Eysenck, H. J., & Schoenthaler, S. J. (1997). Raising IQ level by vitamin and mineral supplementation. In R. Sternberg & E. Grigorenko (Eds.), *Intelligence, heredity, and environment* (pp. 363–392). Cambridge, England: Cambridge University Press.

F

Fagg, G. E., & Foster, A. C. (1983). Amino acid neurotransmitters and their pathways in the mammalian central nervous system. *Neuroscience, 9*, 701–719.

Fagot, B., Hagan, R., Leinbach, M., & Kronsberg, S. (1985). Differential reactions to assertive and communicative acts of toddler girls and boys. *Child Development, 56*, 1499–1505.

Fairburn, C. G., Cooper, Z., & Shafran, R. (2003). Cognitive behaviour therapy for eating disorders: A"transdiagnostic"theory and treatment. *Behavior Research and Therapy, 41*, 509–528.

Fang, X., & Corso, P. S. (2007). Child maltreatment, youth violence, and intimate partner violence: Developmental relationships. *American Journal of Preventive Medicine, 33*, 281–290.

Farthing, G. W. (1992). *The psychology of consciousness.* Englewood Cliffs, NJ: Prentice Hall.

Fava, G., & Sonino, N. (2008). The biopsychosocial model thirty years later. *Psychotherapy and Psychosomatics, 77*, 1–2.

Fawcett, J. (1997). The detection and consequences of anxiety in clinical depression. *Journal of Clinical Psychiatry, 58*, 35–40.

Fawzy, F. I., Fawzy, N. W., Hyun, C. S., Elashoff, R., Guthrie, D., Fahey, J. L., et al. (1993). Malignant melanoma. Effects of an early structured psychiatric intervention, coping, and affective state on recurrence and survival 6 years later. *Archives of General Psychiatry, 50*(9), 681–689.

Fazio, R. H. (1995). Attitudes as object-evaluation associations: Determinants, consequences, and correlates of attitude accessibility. In R. E. Petty & J. A. Krosnick (Eds.), *Attitude strength: Antecedents and consequences* (pp. 247–283). Mahwah, NJ: Erlbaum.

Fazio, R. H., & Olson, M. A. (2003). Implicit measures in social cognition: Their meaning and use. *Annual Review of Psychology, 54*, 297–327.

Febbraro, G. A. R., Clum, G. A., Roodman, A. A., & Wright, J. H. (1999). The limits of bibliotherapy: A study of the differential effectiveness of self-administered interventions in individuals with panic attacks. *Behavior Therapy, 30*, 209–222.

Federal Bureau of Investigation. (2005). *Crime in the United States.* Washington, DC: Author.

Fehr, B. (1996). *Friendship processes.* Thousand Oaks, CA: Sage.

Fehr, B. (2008). Friendship formation. In S. Sprecher, A. Wenzel, & J. Harvey (Eds.), *Handbook of relationship formation* (pp. 29–55). New York: Psychology Press.

Feingold, A. (1988). Cognitive gender differences are disappearing. *American Psychologist, 43*, 95–103.

Feingold, A. (1992). Good-looking people are not what we think. *Psychological Bulletin, 111*, 304–341.

Feldman Barrett, L. (2006). Are emotions natural kinds? *Perspectives on Psychological Science, 1*, 28–58.

Feldman, E. (1991). Identifying the genes for diabetes and schizophrenia. *British Medical Journal, 303*(6794), 124.

Feldman Barrett, L., Lindquist, K., Bliss-Moreau, E., Duncan, S., Gendron, M., Mize, J., & Brennan, L. (2007). Of mice and men:

Natural kinds of emotion in the mammalian brain? *Perspectives on Psychological Science, 2*, 297–312.

Fenson, L., Dale, P. S., Reznick, J. S., Bates, E., Thal, D. J., & Pethick, S. J. (1994). Variability in early communicative development. *Monographs of the Society for Research in Child Development, 59* (5, Serial No. 173).

Fenton, R. (2007, November 2). Drowsy driving is big killer in U.S. *ABC News.* Retrieved November 8, 2007, from http://abcnews .go.com/Health/wireStory?id=3811426.

Fernandez, E., & Sheffield, J. (1996). Relative contributions of life events versus daily hassles to the frequency and intensity of headaches. *Headache, 36*, 595–602.

Ferraris, C., & Carveth, R. (2003). NASA and the *Columbia* disaster: Decision-making by groupthink? *Proceedings of the 2003 Association for Business Communication Annual Convention.* Nacogdoches, TX: Association for Business Communication.

Ferri, M., Amoto, L., & Davoli, M. (2006). Alcoholics Anonymous and other 12-step programmes for alcohol dependence. The Cochrance Review. Art. No: CDOO5032.DOI: 10.1002/ 14651858. CD005032.pub2.

Ferris, C. F. (1996). The rage of innocents. *The Sciences, 36*, 22–26.

Feske, U., & Chambless, D. L. (1995). Cognitive behavioral versus exposure only treatment for social phobia: A meta-analysis. *Behavior Therapy, 26*, 695–720.

Festinger, L. (1954). A theory of social comparison processes. *Human Relations, 7*, 117–140.

Festinger, L., & Carlsmith, J. M. (1959). Cognitive consequences of forced compliance. *Journal of Abnormal and Social Psychology, 58*, 202–210.

Festinger, L., Pepitone, A., & Newcomb, T. (1952). Some consequences of deindividuation in a group. *Journal of Abnormal and Social Psychology, 47*, 382–389.

Festinger, L., Schachter, S., & Back, K. (1950). *Social pressures in informal groups.* New York: Harper.

Fiatarone, M. A., Marks, E. C., Ryan, N. D., Meredith, C. N., Lipsitz, L. A., & Evans, W. J. (1990). High-intensity strength training in nonagenarians. *Journal of the American Medical Association, 263*, 3029–3034.

Fidelman, U. (1993). Intelligence and the brain's consumption of energy: What is intelligence? *Personality and Individual Differences, 14*, 283–286.

Fields, R. D. (2007, February/March). Sex and the secret nerve. *Scientific American Mind*, 21–27.

Fieve, R.R. (1975). *Moodswing.* Bantum Books.

Finch, J. F., & Cialdini, R. B. (1989). Another indirect tactic of (self-) image management: Boosting. *Personality and Social Psychology Bulletin, 15*, 222–232.

Finger, S. (2000). *Minds behind the brain: A history of the pioneers and their discoveries.* New York: Oxford University Press.

Finlay-Jones, R. A., & Brown, G. W. (1981). Types of stressful life event and the onset of anxiety and depressive disorder. *Psychological Medicine, 11*, 803–815.

Finn, S. E., & Kamphuis, J. H. (1995). What a clinician needs to know about base rates. In J. N. Butcher (Ed.), *Clinical personality assessment: Practical approaches* (pp. 224–235). New York: Oxford University Press.

Finzi, E., & Wasserman, E. (2006). Treatment of depression with botulinum toxin A: A case series. *Dermatologic Surgery, 32*, 645–650.

Fischer, P., Greitemeyer, T., Pollozek, F., & Frey, D. (2006). The unresponsive bystander: Are bystanders more responsive in dangerous emergencies? *European Journal of Social Psychology, 36*, 267–278.

Fischoff, B. (1975). Hindsight does not equal foresight: The effect of outcome knowledge on judgment under uncertainty. *Journal of Experimental Psychology: Human Perception and Performance, 1,* 288–299.

Fisher, S., & Greenberg, R. (1996). *Freud scientifically appraised.* New York: Wiley.

Fiske, S. T. (2002). What we know about bias and intergroup conflict, problem of the century. *Current Directions in Psychological Science, 11,* 123–128.

Fiske, S. T., & Taylor, S. E. (1991). *Social cognition* (2nd ed.). New York: McGraw Hill.

Fivush, R. (1988). The functions of event memory: Some comments on Nelson and Barsalou. In U. Neisser & E. Winograd (Eds.), *Remembering reconsidered: Ecological and traditional approaches to the study of memory* (pp. 277–282). New York: Cambridge University Press.

Fivush, R., & Hudson, J. A. (Eds.). (1990). *Knowing and remembering in young children.* New York: Cambridge University Press.

Flavell, J. H. (1992). Cognitive development: Past, present and future. *Developmental Psychology, 28,* 998–1005.

Flavell, J. H., Beach, D. H., & Chinsky, J. M. (1966). Spontaneous verbal rehearsal in a memory test as a function of age. *Child Development, 37,* 283–299.

Flynn, J. R. (1981). The mean IQ of Americans: Massive gains 1932 to 1978. *Psychological Bulletin, 95,* 29–51.

Flynn, J. R. (1987). Massive IQ gains in 14 nations: What IQ tests really measure. *Psychological Bulletin, 101,* 171–191.

Foa, E. B., & Kozak, M. J. (1986). Emotional processing of fear: Exposure to corrective information. *Psychological Bulletin, 99,* 20–35.

Foa, E. B., & Rothbaum, B. O. (1998). *Treating the trauma of rape: Cognitive behavioral therapy for PTSD.* New York: Guilford Press.

Foer, J. (2007). Remember this. *National Geographic, 212,* 32–57.

Fonagy, P., Steele, H., & Steele, M. (1991). Maternal representations of attachment during pregnancy predict the organization of infant-mother attachment at one year of age. *Child Development, 62,* 891–905.

Forbes, E. E., Shaw, D. S., & Dahl, R. E. (2007). Alterations in reward-related decision making in boys with recent and future depression. *Biological Psychiatry, 61,* 633–639.

Ford, C. S., & Beach, F. (1951). *Patterns of sexual behavior.* New York: Harper and Row.

Ford, D. E., & Kamerow, D. B. (1989). Epidemiologic study of sleep disturbances and psychiatric disorders: An opportunity for prevention. *Journal of the American Medical Association, 263,* 1479–1484.

Forshaw, M. (2002). *Essential health psychology.* New York: Oxford University Press.

Foster, S., & Gurman, A. (1985). Family therapies. In S. Lynn & J. P. Garske (Eds.), *Contemporary psychotherapies: Models and methods* (pp. 377–418). Columbus, OH: Merrill Publishing.

Foulkes, D. (1982). *Children's dreams.* New York: Wiley.

Foulkes, D. (1985). *Dreaming: A cognitive-psychological analysis.* New York: Erlbaum.

Foulkes, D. (1999). *Children's dreaming and the development of consciousness.* Cambridge, MA: Harvard University Press.

Fowler, K. A., Lilienfeld, S. O., & Patrick, C. P. (2007, April). *Detecting psychopathic traits from thin slices of behavior.* Poster presented at the Society for the Scientific Study of Psychopathy Conference, St. Petersburg Beach, Florida.

Fowler, K. A., O'Donohue, W. T., & Lilienfeld, S. O. (2007). Personality disorders in perspective. In W. T. O'Donohue, K. A. Fowler, & S. O. Lilienfeld (Eds.), *Personality disorders: Toward the DSM-V* (pp. 1–19). Los Angeles, CA: Sage.

Frank, J. D., & Frank, J. B. (1991). *Persuasion and healing: A comparative study of psychotherapy* (3rd ed.). Baltimore: Johns Hopkins University Press.

Frank, L. K. (1948). *Projective methods.* Springfield, IL: Charles C Thomas.

Franklin, D. (2005, September 27). In heeding health warnings, memory can be tricky. *New York Times.* Retrieved November 12, 2007, from www.nytimes.com/2005/09/27/health/27cons.html?_r=1&oref=slogin

Franklin, M. E., & Foa, E. B. (2002). Cognitive behavioral treatment of obsessive-compulsive disorder. In P. Nathan & J. Gorman (Eds.), *A guide to treatments that work* (2nd ed., pp. 367–386). Oxford, England: Oxford University Press.

Frederick, S., & Loewenstein, G. (1999). Hedonic adaptation. In D. Kahneman, E. Diener, & N. Schwarz (Eds.), *Well-being: The foundations of hedonic psychology* (pp. 302–329). New York: Russell Sage Foundation.

Fredrickson, B. L. (2001). The role of positive emotions in positive psychology: The broaden-and-build theory of positive emotions. *American Psychologist, 56,* 218–226.

Fredrickson, B. L. (2003). The value of positive emotions. *American Scientist, 91,* 330–335.

Freedman, D. G. (1964). Smiling in blind infants and the issue of innate versus acquired. *Journal of Child Psychology and Psychiatry, 5,* 171–184.

Freedman, J. L. (1984). Effect of television violence on aggressiveness. *Psychological Bulletin, 96*(2), 227–246.

Freedman, J. L. (2002). *Media violence and its effects on aggression: Assessing the scientific evidence.* Toronto, Ontario, Canada: University of Toronto Press.

Freedman, J. L., & Fraser, S. C. (1966). Compliance without pressure: The foot-in-the-door technique. *Journal of Personality and Social Psychology, 4,* 195–203.

Freiheit, S. R., Vye, D., Swan, R., & Cady, M. (2004). Cognitive-behavioral therapy for anxiety: Is dissemination working? *The Behavior Therapist, 27,* 25–32.

Freud, A. (1937). *The ego and the mechanisms of defense.* London: Hogarth.

Freud, S. (1900). *The interpretation of dreams* (J. Crick, Trans.). London: Oxford University Press.

Freud, S. (1923). *The ego and the id. Standard Edition, 19,* 3–66.

Freud, S. (1932). *New introductory lectures in psychoanalysis.* New York: W. W. Norton.

Freud, S. (1933). *New introductory lectures on psychoanalysis.* New York: Carleton House.

Freud, S. (1935). *A general introduction to psychoanalysis.* New York: Washington Square Press.

Freund, K., Watson, R., & Rienzo, D. (1989). Heterosexuality, homosexuality, and erotic age preference. *The Journal of Sex Research, 26,* 107–117.

Friedlander, M. L. (1984). Psychotherapy talk as social control. *Psychotherapy, 21,* 335–341.

Friedman, M., & Rosenman, R. H. (1959). Association of a specific overt behavior pattern with increases in blood cholesterol, blood clotting time, incidence of arcus senilis and clinical coronary artery disease. *Journal of the American Medical Association, 169,* 1286–1296.

Friedman, M., & Rosenman, R. H. (1974). *Type A behavior and your heart.* New York: Alfred A. Knopf.

Friedman, M. A., & Wishman, M. A. (1998). Sociotropy, autonomy, and bulimic symptomatology. *International Journal of Eating Disorders, 23,* 439–442.

Friesen, W. V. (1972). *Cultural differences in facial expressions in a social situation: An experimental test of the concept of display rules.* Unpublished doctoral dissertation, University of California, San Francisco.

Frijda, N. H. (1986). *The emotions.* Cambridge, England: Cambridge University.

Fritsch, G. T., & Hitzig, E. (1870). Über die elektrische Erregbarkeit des Grosshirns. *Archivfur Anatomie, Physiologie und Wissenschaftliche Medizin*, 330–332.

Frontera, W. R., Meredith, C. N., O'Reilly, K. P., Knuttgen, H. H., & Evans, W. J. (1988). Strength conditioning in older men: Skeletal muscle hypertrophy and improved function. *Journal of Applied Physiology, 64,* 1038–1044.

Fu, K. M., Johnston, T. A., Shah, A. S., Arnold, L., Smiley, J., Hackett, T. A., et al. (2003). Auditory cortical neurons respond to somatosensory stimulation. *Journal of Neuroscience, 23,* 7510–7515.

Fuhriman, A., & Burlingame, G. M. (1994). Group psychotherapy: Research and practice. In A. Fuhriman & G. M. Burlingame (Eds.), *Handbook of group psychotherapy: An empirical and clinical synthesis* (pp. 3–40). New York: John Wiley & Sons.

Fulton, M. M., & Allen, E. R. (2005). Polypharmacy in the elderly: A literature review. *Journal of the American Academy of Nurse Practitioners, 17,* 123–132.

Funder, D. C. (1991). Global traits: A neo-Allportian approach to personality. *Psychological Science, 2,* 31–39.

Fuster, J. M. (2000). Executive frontal functions. *Experimental Brain Research, 133,* 66–70.

G

Gage, F. H. (2002). Neurogenesis in the adult brain. *Journal of Neuroscience, 22,* 612–613.

Galambos, S. J., & Hakuta, K. (1988). Subject-specific and task-specific characteristics of metalinguistic awareness in bilingual children. *Applied Psycholinguistics, 9,* 141–162.

Galanter, M. (1980). Psychological induction into the large group: Findings from a modern religious sect. *American Journal of Psychiatry, 137,* 1574–1579.

Gallo, E. (1994). Synchronicity and the archetypes: The imprecision of C. G. Jung's language and concepts. *Skeptical Inquirer, 18,* 376–403.

Gallo, L. C., & Matthews, K. A. (2003). Understanding the association between socioeconomic status and physical health: Do negative emotions play a role? *Psychological Bulletin, 129,* 10–51.

Gallup, G. G. Jr. (1979). Self-awareness in primates. *American Scientist, 67,* 417–421.

Gallup, G. G. Jr., & Suarez, S. D. (1985). Alternatives to the use of animals in psychological research. *American Psychologist, 40,* 1104–1111.

Galton, F. (1878). Composite portraits made by combining those of many different persons into a single resultant figure. *Journal of the Anthropological Institute of Great Britain and Ireland, 8,* 132.

Galton, F. (1880). Statistics of mental imagery. *Mind, 5,* 301–318.

Gambrill, E. D. (1992). Self-help books: Pseudoscience in the guise of science? *Skeptical Inquirer* 16(4), 389–399.

Gangestad, S., & Scheyd, G. J. (2005). The evolution of human physical attractiveness. *Annual Review of Anthropology, 34,* 523–548.

Garb, H. N. (1998). *Studying the clinician: Judgment, research, and psychological assessment.* Washington, DC: American Psychological Association.

Garcia, J., & Hankins, W. G. (1977). On the origin of food aversion paradigms. In L. M. Barker, M. R. Best, & M. Domjan (Eds.), *Learning mechanisms in food selection* (pp. 3–22). Houston, TX: Baylor University Press.

Garcia, S. M., Weaver, K., Moskowitz, G. B., & Darley, J. M. (2002). Crowded minds: The implicit bystander effect. *Journal of Personality and Social Psychology, 83,* 843–853.

Gardner, H. (1983). *Frames of mind: The theory of multiple intelligences.* New York: Basic Books.

Gardner, H. (1999). *Intelligence reframed: Multiple intelligences for the 21st century.* New York: Basic Books.

Gardner, M. (1958). *Fads and fallacies in the name of science.* New York: Dover.

Gardner, W. L., Gabriel, S., & Diekman, A. B. (2000). Interpersonal processes. In J. T. Cacioppo, L. G. Tassinary, & G. G. Berntson (Eds.), *Handbook of psychophysiology* (2nd ed., pp. 643–664). New York: Cambridge University Press.

Garfield, S. L. (1978). Research on client variables. In S. Garfield & A. Bergin (Eds.), *Handbook of psychotherapy and behavior change.* New York: John Wiley & Sons.

Garmezy, N., Masten, A. S., & Tellegen, A. (1984). The study of stress and competence in children: A building block for developmental psychopathology. *Child Development, 55,* 97–111.

Garske, J. P., & Anderson, T. (2003). Toward a science of psychotherapy research: Present status and evaluation. In S. O. Lilienfeld, S. J. Lynn, & J. M. Lohr (Eds.), *Science and pseudoscience in clinical psychology* (pp. 145–175). New York: Guilford Press.

Gasperini, M., Scherillo, P., Manfredonia, M. G., Franchini, L., & Smeraldi, E. (1993). A study of relapse in subjects with mood disorder on lithium treatment. *European Neuropsychopharmacology, 3,* 103–110.

Gatchel, R. J., & Baum, A. (1983). *An introduction to health psychology.* Reading, MA: Addison-Wesley.

Gatchel, R. J., & Oordt, M. S. (2003). *Clinical psychology and primary health care.* Washington, DC: American Psychological Association.

Gathercole, V. C. M. (2002a). Command of the mass/count distinction in bilingual and monolingual children: An English morphosyntactic distinction. In D. K. Oller & R. E. Eilers (Eds.), *Language and literacy in bilingual children* (pp. 175–206). Clevedon, England: Multilingual Matters.

Gathercole, V. C. M. (2002b). Grammatical gender in bilingual and monolingual children: A Spanish morphosyntactic distinction. In D. K. Oller & R. E. Eilers (Eds.), *Language and literacy in bilingual children* (pp. 207–219), Clevedon, England: Multilingual Matters.

Gawronski, B., LeBel, E. P., & Peters, K. R. (2007). What do implicit measures tell us? Scrutinizing the validity of three common assumptions. *Perspectives on Psychological Science, 2,* 181–193.

Gazzaniga, M. S. (2000). Cerebral specialization and interhemispheric communication: Does the corpus callosum enable the human condition? *Brain, 123,* 1293–1326.

Gazzaniga, M. S., Ivry, R., & Mangun, G. R. (2002). *Fundamentals of cognitive neuroscience* (2nd ed.). New York: W. W. Norton.

Geary, D. C. (1996). Sexual selection and sex differences in mathematical abilities. *Behavioral and Brain Sciences, 19,* 229–284.

Geen, R. G. (2001). *Human aggression* (2nd ed.). New York: Taylor & Francis.

Geiser, S. & Studley, R. (2002). UC and the SAT: Predictive validity and differential impact of the SAT I and SAT II at the University of California. *Educational Assessment, 8,* 1–26.

Gellatly, A. R. (1987). Acquisition of a concept of logical necessity. *Human Development, 30,* 32–47.

Gelman, R., & Gallistel, C. (1978). *The child's understanding of number.* Cambridge, MA: Harvard University Press.

Gentile, D. A., & Anderson, C. A. (2003). Violent video games: The newest media violence hazard. In D. A. Gentile (Ed.), *Media violence and children* (pp. 131–152). Westport, CT: Praeger Publishing.

George, M. S., Sackeim, H., Rush, A. J., Marangell, L. B., Nahas, Z., Husain, M. M., et al. (2000). Vagus nerve stimulation: A new tool for treatment-resistant depression. *Biological Psychiatry, 47,* 287–295.

Georgiadis, J. R., Kortekaas, R., Kuipers, R., Nieuwenburg, A., Pruim, J., Reinders, A. A., et al. (2006). Regional cerebral blood flow changes associated with clitorally induced orgasm in healthy women. *European Journal of Neuroscience, 24,* 3305–3316.

German, T. P., & Barrett, H. C. (2005). Functional fixedness in a technologically sparse culture. *Psychological Science, 16,* 1–5.

German, T. P., & Defeyter, M. A. (2000). Immunity to functional fixedness in young children. *Psychonomic Bulletin & Review, 7*(4), 707–712.

Gernsbacher, M. A., Dawson, M., & Goldsmith, H. H. (2005). Three reasons not to believe in an autism epidemic. *Current Directions in Psychological Science, 14,* 55–58.

Gershoff, E. T. (2002). Corporal punishment by parents and associated child behaviors and experiences: A meta-analytic and theoretical review. *Psychological Bulletin, 128*(4), 539–579.

Gewirtz, J. C., & Davis, M. (2000). Using Pavlovian "higher-order" conditioning paradigms to investigate the neural substrates of emotional learning and memory. *Learning and Memory, 7,* 257–266.

Gibb, B. E., & Coles, M. E. (2005). Cognitive vulnerability-stress models of psychopathology: A developmental perspective. In B. L. Hankin & J. R. Z. Abela (Eds.), *Development of psychopathology: A vulnerability-stress perspective* (pp. 104–135). Thousand Oaks, CA: Sage.

Gibson, B. (2008). Can evaluative conditioning change attitudes toward mature brands? New evidence from the Implicit Association Test. *Journal of Consumer Research, 35,* 178–188.

Gibson, E. J., (1991). *An odyssey in learning and perception.* Cambridge, MA: MIT Press.

Gibson, E. J., & Walk, R. D. (1960). The "visual cliff." *Scientific American, 202,* 64–71.

Giesbrecht, T., Lynn, S. J., Lilienfeld, S. O., & Merckelbach, H. (2008). Cognitive processes in dissociation: An analysis of core theoretical assumptions. *Psychological Bulletin, 134,* 617–647.

Gigerenzer, G. (2001). The adaptive toolbox. In G. Gigerenzer & R. Selten (Eds.), *Bounded rationality: The adaptive toolbox* (pp. 37–50). Cambridge, MA: MIT Press.

Gigerenzer, G. (2004). Dread risk, September 11, and fatal traffic accidents. *Psychological Science, 15,* 286–287.

Gigerenzer, G. (2007). *Gut feelings: The intelligence of the unconscious.* New York: Viking Press.

Gigerenzer, G., & Goldstein, D. G. (1996). Reasoning the fast and frugal way: Models of bounded rationality. *Psychological Review, 103,* 650–669.

Gilbert, D. T. (2006). *Stumbling on happiness.* New York: Knopf.

Gilbert, D. T., Pinel, E. C., Wilson, T. D., Blumberg, S. J., & Wheatley, T. (1998). Immune neglect: A source of durability bias in affective forecasting. *Journal of Personality and Social Psychology, 75,* 617–638.

Gilbertson, T. A., Fontenot D. T., Liu, L., Zhang, H., & Monroe, W. T. (1997). Fatty acid modulation of K⁺ channels in taste receptor cells: Gustatory cues for dietary fat. *American Journal of Physiology, 272*(4 Pt. 1), C1203–C1210.

Giles, J. (2002). Electroconvulsive therapy and the fear of deviance. *Journal for the Theory of Social Behaviour, 32,* 61–87.

Gilligan, C. (1982). *In a different voice: Psychological theory and women's development.* Cambridge, MA: Harvard University Press.

Gilovich, T. (1991). *How we know what isn't so: The fallibility of human reason in everyday life.* New York: Free Press.

Gladwell, M. (2005). *Blink: The power of thinking without thinking.* Boston: Little, Brown, & Company.

Gladwell, M. (2007, November 12). Dangerous minds: Criminal profiling made easy. *New Yorker.* Retrieved November 9, 2007, from www.newyorker.com/reporting/2007/11/12/071112fa_fact_gladwell.

Gleaves, D. H. (1996). The sociocognitive model of dissociative identity disorder: A reexamination of the evidence. *Psychological Bulletin, 120,* 42–59.

Gleaves, D. H., May, M. C., & Cardeña, E. (2001). An examination of the diagnostic validity of dissociative identity disorder. *Clinical Psychology Review, 21,* 577–608.

Glosser, D. S. (1983). The use of a token-economy to reduce illicit drug-use among methadone-maintenance clients. *Addictive Behaviors, 8*(2), 93–104.

Glynn, I. (1999). *An anatomy of thought: The origin and machinery of the mind.* New York: Oxford University Press.

Gobel, S. M., & Rushworth, M. F. (2004). Cognitive neuroscience: Acting on numbers. *Current Biology, 14,* R517–519.

Godden, D. R., & Baddeley, A. D. (1975). Context dependency in two natural environments: On land and underwater. *British Journal of Psychology, 91,* 99–104.

Goethals, G. R., & Reckman, R. F. (1973). The perception of consistency in attitudes. *Journal of Experimental Social Psychology, 9,* 491–501.

Goffman, E. (1959). *The presentation of self in everyday life.* London: Penguin.

Gold, P. E., Cahill, L., & Wenk, G. L. (2002). Gingko biloba: A cognitive enhancer? *Psychological Science in the Public Interest, 3,* 2–11.

Goldberg, L. R. (1969). The search for configural relationships in personality assessment: The diagnosis of psychosis vs. neurosis from the MMPI. *Multivariate Behavioral Research, 4,* 523–536.

Goldfield, B. A., & Reznick, J. S. (1990). Early lexical acquisition: Rate, content, and the vocabulary spurt. *Journal of Child Language, 23,* 241–246.

Goldfried, M. R., Raue, P. J., & Castonguay, L. G. (1998). The therapeutic focus in significant sessions of master therapists: A comparison of cognitive-behavioral and psychodynamic-interpersonal interventions. *Journal of Consulting and Clinical Psychology, 66,* 803–810.

Goldin, C., & Rouse, C. (2000). Orchestrating impartiality. *American Economic Review, 90,* 715–741.

Goldin-Meadow, S., & Mylander, C. (1998). Spontaneous sign systems created by deaf children in two cultures. *Nature, 391,* 279–281.

Goldman, D., Hu, X., Kennedy, J., & Murphy, D. (2006). Linkage of gain-of-function serotonin transporter alleles to obsessive compulsive disorder. *Biological Psychiatry, 59*(8), 99S–100S.

Goldstein, D. G., & Gigerenzer, G. (1999). The recognition heuristic: How ignorance makes us smart. In G. Gigerenzer, P. M. Todd, & the ABC Research Group (Eds.), *Simple heuristics that make us smart* (pp. 37–58). London: Oxford University Press.

Goldstein, M. H., & Schwade, J. A. (2008). Social feedback to infants' babbling facilitates rapid phonological learning. *Psychological Science, 19,* 515–523.

Goldston, D. B., Daniel, S. S., Reboussin, B., Reboussin, D., Frazier, P. H., & Harris, A. (2001). Cognitive risk factors and suicide attempts among formerly hospitalized adolescents: A prospective naturalistic study. *Journal of the American Academy of Child and Adolescent Psychiatry, 40,* 155–162.

Goleman, D. (1995). *Emotional Intelligence.* New York: Bantam Books.

Golin, S., Terrell, T., & Johnson, B. (1977). Depression and the illusion of control. *Journal of Abnormal Psychology, 86,* 440–442.

Gonzaga, G. C., Turner, R. A., Keltner, D., Campos, B., & Altemus, M. (2006). Romantic love and sexual desire in close relationships, *Emotion, 6*, 163–179.

Good, T. L., & Brophy, J. (1995). *Contemporary educational psychology.* Boston: Longman.

Goodall, J., & van Lawick, H. (1971). *In the shadow of man.* Boston: Houghton-Mifflin.

Goodman, J. A., Krahn, L. E., Smith, G. G., Rummans, T. A., & Pileggi, T. S. (1999). Patient satisfaction with electroconvulsive therapy. *Mayo Clinic Proceedings, 74*, 967–971.

Goodwin, D. W. (1995). Alcohol amnesia. *Addiction, 90*, 315–317.

Goodwin, D. W., Powell, B., Brenner, D., Hoine, H., & Sterne J. (1969). Alcohol and recall: State dependent effects in man. *Science, 163*, 1358–1360.

Goodwin, F. K., & Jamison K. R. (1990), *Manic-depressive illness.* New York: Oxford University Press.

Gorassini, D., & Olson, J. (1995). Does self-perception change explain the foot-in-the-door effect? *Journal of Personality and Social Psychology, 69*, 91–105.

Gordon, P. (2004). Numerical cognition without words: Evidence from Amazonia. *Science, 306*, 496–499.

Gorenstein, E. E. (1984). Debating mental illness: Implications for science, medicine, and social policy. *American Psychologist, 39*, 50–56.

Gorn, G. J. (1982). The effects of music in advertising on choice behavior: A classical conditioning approach. *Journal of Marketing, 46*, 94–101.

Gortmaker, S. L., Must, A., Perrin, J. M., Sobol, A. M., & Dietz, W. H. (1993). Social and economic consequences of overweight in adolescence and young adulthood. *New England Journal of Medicine, 329*, 1009–1012.

Gortner, E. T., Gollan, J. K., Dobson, K. S., & Jacobson, N. S. (1998). Cognitive-behavioral treatment for depression: Relapse prevention. *Journal of Consulting and Clinical Psychology, 66*, 377–384.

Gosling, S. D., Ko, S. J., Mannarelli, T., & Morris, M. E. (2002). A room with a cue: Personality judgments based on offices and bedrooms. *Journal of Personality & Social Psychology, 82*, 379–398.

Gotlib, I. H., & Hammen, C. (1992). *Psychological aspects of depression: Toward a cognitive-interpersonal integration.* New York: Wiley.

Gottdiener, J. S., Gross, H. A., Henry, W. L., Borer, J. S., & Ebert, M. H. (1978). Effects of self-induced starvation on cardiac size and function in anorexia nervosa. *Circulation, 58*, 425–433.

Gottesman, I. I. (1991). *Schizophrenia genesis: The origins of madness.* New York: W. H. Freeman.

Gottesman, I. I., & Shields, J. (1972). *Schizophrenia and genetics: A twin study vantage point.* New York: Academic Press.

Gottfredson, L. S. (1997). Why *g* matters: The complexity of everyday life. *Intelligence, 24*, 79–132.

Gottfredson, L. S. (2004). Intelligence: Is it the epidemiologists' elusive "fundamental cause" of social class inequalities in health? *Journal of Personality and Social Psychology, 86*, 174–199.

Gottheil, E., & Weinstein, S. O. (1983). Cocaine: An emerging problem. In S. Akhtar (Ed.), *New psychiatric syndromes; DSM III and beyond.* New York: Jason Aronson.

Gould, E., & Gross, C. G. (2002). Neurogenesis in adult mammals: Some progress and problems. *Journal of Neuroscience, 22*, 619–623.

Gould, R. (1978). *Transformations: Growth and change in adult life.* New York: Simon and Schuster.

Gould, R. A., & Clum, G. A. (1993). A meta-analysis of self-help treatment approaches. *Clinical Psychology Review, 13*, 169–186.

Gould, S. J. (1981). *The mismeasure of man.* New York: W. W. Norton.

Gould, S. J. (1997). Nonoverlapping magisteria. *Natural History, 106*, 16–22.

Gouldner, A. W. (1960). The norm of reciprocity: A preliminary statement. *American Sociological Review, 25*, 161–178.

Gove, W. R., Hughes, M., & Style, C. B. (1983). Does marriage have positive effects on the psychological well-being of the individual? *Journal of Health and Social Behavior, 24*, 122–131.

Graf, P. (1990). Life-span changes in implicit and explicit memory. *Bulletin of the Psychonomic Society, 28*, 353–358.

Graham, J. R. (2006). *MMPI-2: Assessing personality and psychopathology* (3rd ed.). New York: Oxford University Press.

Graham, S. J., Scaife, J. C., Langley, R. W., Bradshaw, C. M., Szabadi, E., Xi, L., et al. (2005). Effects of lorazepam on fear-potentiated startle responses in man. *Journal of Psychopharmacology, 19*, 249–258.

Grawe, K., Donati, R., & Bernauer, F. (1998). *Psychotherapy in transition.* Seattle, WA: Hogrefe & Huber.

Gray, J. (1981). A critique of Eysenck's theory of personality. In H. J. Eysenck (Ed.), *A model for personality* (pp. 246–276). New York: Springer.

Graybiel, A. M., Aosaki, T., Flaherty, A. W., & Kimura, M. (1994). The basal ganglia and adaptive motor control. *Science, 265*, 1826–1831.

Greeley, A. M. (1987). Mysticism goes mainstream. *American Health, 6*, 47–49.

Green, D. M., & Swets, J. A. (1966). *Signal detection theory and psychophysics.* New York: Wiley.

Greenberg, D. J., Hillman, D., & Grice, D. (1973). Infant and stranger variables related to stranger anxiety in the first year of life. *Development Psychology, 9*, 207–212.

Greenberg, J., & Jonas, E. (2003). Psychological motives and political orientation: The left, the right, and the rigid: Comment on Jost et al. (2003). *Psychological Bulletin, 129*, 376–382.

Greenberg, L. S., Elliot, R., & Lietaer, G. (1994). Research on humanistic and experiential psychotherapies. In A. E. Bergin & L. S. Garfield (Eds.), *Handbook of psychotherapy and behavior change* (4th ed., pp. 509–539). New York: Wiley.

Greenberg, L. S., & Watson, J. C. (1998). Experiential therapy of depression: Differential effects of client-centered relationship conditions and process experiential interventions. *Psychotherapy Research, 8*, 210–224.

Greene, R. L. (2000). *The MMPI-2: An interpretive manual* (2nd ed.). Boston: Allyn & Bacon.

Greenough, W. T. (1997). We can't just focus on the first three years. *American Psychological Association Monitor on Psychology, 28*, 19.

Greenspan, S., & Switzky, H. N. (Eds.). (2003). *What is mental retardation? Ideas for the new century.* Washington, DC: American Association on Mental Retardation.

Greenwald, A. G., McGhee, D. E., & Schwartz, J. L. K. (1998). Measuring individual differences in implicit cognition: The implicit association test. *Journal of Personality and Social Psychology, 74*, 1464–1480.

Greenwald, A. G., & Nosek, B. A. (2001). Health of the Implicit Association Test at age 3. *Zeitschrift für Experimentelle Psychologie, 48*, 85–93.

Gregory, R. J., Canning S. S., Lee, T. W., & Wise, J. (2004). Cognitive bibliotherapy for depression: A meta-analysis. *Professional Psychology: Research and Practice, 35*, 275–280.

Gresham, L. G., & Shimp, T. A. (1985). Attitude toward the advertisement and brand attitudes: A classical conditioning perspective. *Journal of Advertising, 14*, 10–17, 49.

Greyson, B. (2000). Near-death experiences. In E. Cardena, S. J. Lynn, & S. Krippner (Eds.), *Varieties of anomalous experiences* (pp. 315–352). Washington, DC: American Psychological Association.

Griffiths, P. E. (1997). *What emotions really are: The problem of psychological categories*. Chicago: Chicago University Press.

Grill, H. J., & Kaplan, J. M. (2002). The neuroanatomical axis for control of energy balance. *Frontiers in Neuroendocrinology, 21*, 2–40.

Grill, H. J., Schwartz, M. W., Kaplan, J. M., Foxhall, J. S., Breininger, J., & Baskin, D. G. (2002). Evidence that the caudal brainstem is a target for the inhibitory effect of leptin on food intake. *Endocrinology, 143*, 239–246.

Grings, W. W. (1973). Cognitive factors in electrodermal conditioning. *Psychological Bulletin, 79*(3), 200–210.

Grissom, R. J. (1996). The magical number, 7±2 meta-meta-analysis of the probability of superior outcome in comparisons involving therapy, placebo, and control. *Journal of Consulting and Clinical Psychology, 64*, 973–982.

Grob, G. N. (1997). Deinstitutionalization: The illusion of policy. *Journal of Policy History, 9*(1), 48–73.

Grossman, H. J. (Ed.). (1983). *Classification in mental retardation* (Rev. ed.). Washington, DC: American Association on Mental Deficiency.

Grunbaum, A. (1984). *The foundations of psychoanalysis: A philosophical critique*. Berkeley: University of California Press.

Guan, J. H., & Wade, M. G. (2000). The effect of aging on adaptive eye–hand coordination. *Journals of Gerontology Series B—Psychological Sciences and Social Sciences, 55*(3), P151–P162.

Guéguen, N., Pascual A., & Dagot L. (2002). The low-ball technique: An application in a field setting, *Psychological Reports, 91*, 81–84.

Guilford, J. P. (1967). *The nature of human intelligence*. New York: McGraw-Hill.

Gula, R. J. (2006). *Nonsense: A handbook of logical fallacies*. Mount Jackson, VA: Axios Press.

Gulya, M., Galluccio, L., Wilk, A., & Rovee-Collier, C. (2001). Infants' long-term memory for a serial list: Recognition and reactivation. *Developmental Psychobiology, 38*, 174–185.

Gupta, S. (2007, May 24). Herbal remedies' potential dangers. Time Inc. Retrieved from www.time.com/time/magazine/article/0,9171,1625175,00.html.

Gusow, W. (1963). A preliminary report of kayak-angst among the Eskimo of West Greenland: A study in sensory deprivation. *International Journal of Social Psychiatry, 9*, 18–26.

H

Haack, L. J., Metalsky, G. I., Dykman, B. M., & Abramson, L. Y. (1996). Use of current situational information and causal inference: Do dysphoric individuals make "unwarranted" causal inferences? *Cognitive Therapy and Research, 20*(4), 309–331.

Haaga, D. A., Dyck, M. J., & Ernst, D. (1991). Empirical status of cognitive theory of depression. *Psychological Bulletin, 110*, 215–236.

Hackney, A. (2005). Teaching students about stereotypes, prejudice, and discrimination: An interview with Susan Fiske. *Teaching of Psychology, 32*(3), 196–199.

Hafer, C. L., & Begue, L. (2005). Experimental research on just-world theory: Problems, developments, and future challenges. *Psychological Bulletin, 131*, 128–167.

Hahlweg, K., & Markman, H. J. (1988). Effectiveness of behavioral marital therapy: Empirical status of behavioral techniques in preventing and alleviating marital distress. *Journal of Consulting and Clinical Psychology, 56*, 440–447.

Haier, R. J., Siegel, B. V., MacLachlan, A., Soderling, E., Lottenberg, S., & Buchsbaum, M. S. (1992). Regional glucose metabolic changes after learning a complex visuospatial/motor task: A positron emission tomographic study. *Brain Research, 570*, 134–143.

Haimerl, C. J., & Valentine, E. (2001). The effect of contemplative practice on interpersonal, and transpersonal dimensions of the self-concept. *Journal of Transpersonal Psychology, 33*, 37–52.

Haist, F., Shimamura, A. P., & Squire, L. R. (1992). On the relationship between recall and recognition memory. *Journal of Experimental Psychology: Learning, Memory, and Cognition, 18*(4), 691–702.

Halberstadt, J., & Rhodes, G. (2003). It's not just the average face that's attractive: The attractiveness of averageness of computer-manipulated birds, fish, and automobiles. *Psychonomic Bulletin and Review, 10*, 149–156.

Haley, J. (1976*). Problem-solving therapy*. San Francisco: Jossey-Bass.

Hall, C. S., & Domhoff, G. W. (1963). Aggression in dreams. *International Journal of Social Psychiatry, 9*, 259–267.

Hall, C. S., & Nordby, V. J. (1972). *The individual and his dreams*. Winnipeg, Manitoba, Canada: New American Library.

Hall, C. S., & Van de Castle, R. (1966). *Content analysis of dreams*. New York: Appleton-Century-Crofts.

Hall, C. S. (1984). A ubiquitous sex difference in dreams, revisited. *Journal of Personality and Social Psychology, 46*, 1109–1117.

Hall, J. A. (1978). Gender effects in decoding nonverbal cues. *Psychological Bulletin, 85*, 845–857.

Hall, J. R., & Benning, S. D. (2006). The "successful" psychopath: Adaptive and subclinical manifestations of psychopathy in the general population. In C. J. Patrick (Ed.), *Handbook of psychopathy* (pp. 459–478). New York: Guilford Press.

Halpern, D. F. (1992). *Sex differences in cognitive abilities* (2nd ed.). Hillsdale, NJ: Erlbaum.

Halpern, D. F., Benbow, C. P., Geary, D. C., Gur, R. C., Hyde, J. S., & Gernsbacher, M. A. (2007). The science of sex differences in science and mathematics. *Psychological Science in the Public Interest, 8*, 1–51,

Hamann, A., & Matthaei, S. (1996). Regulation of energy balance by leptin. *Experimental Clinical Endocrinology Diabetes, 104*, 293–300.

Hampson, E., Rovet, J. F., & Altmann, D. (1998). Spatial reasoning in children with congenital adrenal hyperplasia due to 21-hydroxylase deficiency. *Developmental Neuropsychology, 14*, 299–320.

Haney, C., Banks, W. C., & Zimbardo, P. G. (1973). Interpersonal dynamics in a simulated prison. *International Journal of Criminology & Penology, 1*, 69–97.

Hansen, E. S., Hasselbalch, S., Law, J., & Bolwig, T. G. (2002). The caudate nucleus in obsessive-compulsive disorder. Reduced metabolism following treatment with paroxetine: A PET study. *International Journal of Neuropsychopharmacology, 5*, 1–10.

Hanson, D. R., & Gottesman, I. I. (2005). Theories of schizophrenia: A genetic-inflammatory-vascular synthesis. *Biomed Central Medical Genetics, 6*, Published online February 11, 2005. Doi: 10.1186/1471-2350-6-7.

Haraldsson, E., & Houtkooper, J. (1995). Meta-analysis of 10 experiments on perceptual defensiveness and ESP. *Journal of Parapsychology, 59*, 251–271.

Harding, C. M., Zubin, J., & Strauss, J. S. (1992). Chronicity in schizophrenia: Revisited. *British Journal of Psychiatry Supplement, 18*, 27–37.

Hardy, K. R. (1957). Determinants of conformity and attitude change. *Journal of Abnormal and Social Psychology, 4*, 289–294.

Hare, R. D. (1978). Electrodermal and cardiovascular correlates of psychopathy. In R. D. Hare & D. Schalling (Eds.), *Psychopathic behavior: Approaches to research* (pp. 107–144). Chichester, England: John Wiley & Sons.

Hare, R. D. (1993). *Without conscience: The disturbing world of the psychopaths among us.* New York: Simon & Schuster.

Hare, R. D. (2003). *The Hare Psychopathy Checklist—Revised.* Toronto, Ontario, Canada: Multi-Health Systems.

Harford, T., & Muthen, B. O. (2001). The dimensionality of alcohol abuse and dependence: A multivariate analysis of DSM-IV symptoms in the National Longitudinal Survey of Youth. *Journal of Studies in Alcohol, 62,* 150–157.

Hariri, A. R., Mattay, V. S., Tessitore, A., Kolachana, B., Fera, F., Goldman, D., et al. (2002). Serotonin transporter genetic variation and the response of the human amygdala. *Science, 297,* 400–403.

Harkins, E. B. (1978). Effects of empty nest transition on self-report of psychological and physical well-being. *Journal of Marriage and the Family, 40,* 549–556.

Harkness, A. R., & Lilienfeld, S. O. (1997). Individual differences science for treatment planning: Personality traits. *Psychological Assessment, 9,* 349–360.

Harkness, A. R., Tellegen, A., & Waller, N. G. (1995). Differential convergence of self-report and informant data for multi-dimensional personality questionnaire traits: Implications for the construct of negative emotionality. *Journal of Personality Assessment, 64,* 185–204.

Harlow, H. F. (1958). The nature of love. *American Psychologist, 13,* 673–685.

Harlow, J. M. (1848). Passage of an iron rod through the head. *Boston Medical and Surgical Journal, 39,* 389–393. (Republished in *Journal of Neuropsychiatry and Clinical Neuroscience, 1991, 11,* 281–283.)

Harmon-Jones, E., & Mills, J. (Eds.). (1999). *Cognitive dissonance: Progress on a pivotal theory in social psychology.* Washington, DC: American Psychological Association.

Harrington, E. R. (2004). The social psychology of hatred. *Journal of Hate Studies, 3,* 49–82.

Harrington, P. (2005, December). Exorcisms rise in Mexico, keeping Father Mendoza, healers busy. *Bloomberg News.* Retrieved June 2, 2008, from www.banderasnews.com/0512/nr-mexorcisms.htm

Harris, B. (1979). Whatever happened to Little Albert? *American Psychologist, 34*(2), 151–160.

Harris, E. C., & Barraclough, B. (1997). Suicide as an outcome for mental disorders—A meta-analysis. *British Journal of Psychiatry, 170,* 205–228.

Harris, J. L., & Qualls, C. D. (2000). The association of elaborative or maintenance rehearsal with age, reading comprehension, and verbal working memory performance. *Aphasiology, 14,* 515–526.

Harris, J. R. (2002). *The nurture assumption: Why children turn out the way they do.* New York: Free Press.

Hart, B., & Risley, T. R. (1995). *Meaningful differences in the everyday experience of young American children.* Baltimore: Paul H. Brookes.

Hartmann, H. (1939). *Ego psychology and the problem of adaptation.* New York: International Universities Press.

Hartmann, W. K. (1992). *Astronomy: The cosmic journey.* Belmont, CA: Wadsworth.

Hartschorne, H., & May, M. A. (1928). *Studies in the nature of character: Vol. 1. Studies in deceit.* New York: Macmillan.

Harvey, P. D., Reichenberg, A., & Bowie, C. R. (2006). Cognition and aging in psychopathology: Focus on schizophrenia and depression. In S. Nolen-Hoeksema, T. D. Cannon, & T. Widiger (Eds.), *Annual Review of Clinical Psychology* (Vol. 2 pp. 389–409). Palo Alto, CA: Annual Reviews.

Hatfield, E., Aronson, V., Abrahams, D., & Rottman, L. (1966). The importance of physical attractiveness in dating behavior. *Journal of Personality and Social Psychology, 4,* 508–516.

Hatfield, E., & Rapson, R. (1996). *Love and sex: Cross-cultural perspectives.* Boston: Allyn & Bacon.

Hatfield, E., & Walster, G. W. (1978). *A new look at love.* Reading, MA: Addison-Wesley.

Hathaway, S. R., & McKinley, J. C. (1940). A multiphasic personality schedule (Minnesota): I. Construction of the schedule. *Journal of Psychology, 14,* 73–84.

Hauri, P. J. (1998). Insomnia. *Clinical Chest Medicine, 19,* 157–168.

Hauser, R. M. (1998). Trends in black-white test score differences: I. Uses and misuses of NAEP/SAT data. In U. Neisser (Ed.), *The rising curve: Long-term gains in IQ and related measures* (pp. 219–249). Washington, DC: American Psychological Association.

Hawkley, L. C., & Cacioppo, J. T. (2007). Aging and loneliness: Downhill quickly? *Current Directions in Psychological Science, 16*(4), 187–191.

Hayes, S. C., Strosahl, K., & Wilson, K. G. (1999). *Acceptance and commitment therapy.* New York: Guilford Press.

Hayward, L. R. C. (1960). The subjective meaning of stress. *British Journal of Psychology, 33,* 185–194.

Hazelrigg, M. D., Cooper, H. M., & Borduin, C. M. (1987). Evaluating the effectiveness of family therapies: An integrative review and analysis. *Psychological Bulletin, 101,* 428–442.

Hazlett-Stevens, H., Pruitt, L. D., & Collins, A. (2008). Phenomenology of generalized anxiety disorder. In M. M. Anthony & M. B. Stein (Eds.), *Oxford handbook of anxiety and related disorders* (pp. 47–64). New York: Oxford University Press.

Heath, C. B., Bell, C., & Sternberg, E. (2001). Emotional selection in memes: The case of urban legends. *Journal of Personality and Social Psychology, 81*(6), 1028–1041.

Hebb, D. O. (1949). *The organization of behavior.* New York: John Wiley.

Hedges, L. V., & Nowell, A. (1995). Sex differences in mental test scores, variability, and numbers of high-scoring individuals. *Science, 269,* 41–45.

Heimberg, R. G., & Juster, H. R. (1995). Cognitive-behavioral treatments: Literature review. In R. G. Heimberg, M. R. Liebowitz, D. A. Hope, & F. R. Schneier (Eds.), *Social phobia: Diagnosis, assessment, and treatment.* New York: Guilford Press.

Heine, S. J., Lehman, D. R., Markus, H. R., & Kitayama, S. (1999). Is there a universal need for positive self-regard? *Psychological Review, 106,* 766–794.

Heini, A. F., & Weinsier, R. L. (1997). Divergent trends in obesity and fat intake patterns: The American paradox. *American Journal of Medicine, 102,* 259–264.

Helliwell, J. F., & Putnam, R. D. (2004). The social context of well-being. *Philosophical Transactions of the Royal Society (London) Series B, 359,* 1435–1446.

Helmes, E., & Reddon, J. R. (1993). A perspective on developments in assessing psychopathology: A critical review of the MMPI and MMPI-2. *Psychological Bulletin, 113,* 453–471.

Helmholtz, H. (1850). Ueber die Fortpflanzungsgeschwindigkeit der Nervenreizung. *Annalen der Physik, 155*(2), 329–330.

Helson, H. (1948). Adaptation-level as a basis for a quantitative theory of frames of reference. *Psychological Review, 55,* 297–313.

Helson, R., & Srivastava, S. (2002). Creativity and wisdom: Similarities, differences, and how they develop. *Personality and Social Psychology Bulletin, 28,* 1430–1440.

Hempel, A., Hempel, E., Schönknecht, P., Stippich, C., & Schröder, J. (2003). Impairment in basal limbic function in schizophrenia during affect recognition. *Psychiatry Research, 122,* 115–124.

Hemsley, G. D., & Doob, A. N. (1978). The effect of looking behavior on perceptions of a communicator's credibility. *Journal of Applied Social Psychology, 8*(2), 136–144.

Henriques, G. (2004). Psychology defined. *Journal of Clinical Psychology, 60,* 1207–1221.

Henshaw, J. M. (2006). *Does measurement measure up? How numbers reveal and conceal the truth.* Baltimore: Johns Hopkins University Press.

Herbert, J. D., Sharp, I. R., & Gaudiano, B. A. (2002). Separating fact from fiction in the etiology and treatment of autism: A scientific review of the evidence. *Scientific Review of Mental Health Practice, 1,* 25–45.

Hergenhahn, B. R. (2000). *An introduction to the history of psychology* (4th ed.). Pacific Grove, CA: Wadsworth.

Herrmann, C. S., & Friederici, A. D. (2001). Object processing in the infant brain. *Science, 292,* 163.

Herrmann, N. (1996). *The whole brain business book.* New York: McGraw-Hill.

Herrnstein, R. J., & Murray, C. (1994). *The bell curve: Intelligence and class structure in American life.* New York: Free Press.

Hess, E. H. (1965). Attitude and pupil size. *Scientific American, 212*(4), 46–54.

Hess, R. A. (2003). Estrogen in the adult male reproductive tract: A review. *Reproductive and Biological Endocrinology, 9,* 1–52.

Hetherington, A. W., & Ranson, S. W. (1940). Hypothalamic lesions and adiposity in the rat. *Anatomical Record, 78,* 149–158.

Higgins, J. E., & Endler, N. (1995). Coping, life stress, and psychological and somatic distress. *European Journal of Personality, 9,* 253–270.

Highstein, S. M., Fay, R. R., & Popper A. N. (2004). *The vestibular system.* Berlin, Germany: Springer-Verlag.

Hilgard, E. R. (1977). *Divided consciousness: Multiple controls in human thought and action.* New York: Wiley.

Hilgard, E. R. (1986). *Divided consciousness: Multiple controls in human thought and action* (expanded ed.). New York: Wiley.

Hilgard, E. R. (1994). Neodissociation theory. In S. J. Lynn & J. W. Rhue (Eds.), *Dissociation: Clinical, theoretical and research perspectives* (pp. 32–51). New York: Guilford Press.

Hiller, J. (2005). Gender differences in sexual motivation. *Journal of Men's Health and Gender, 2,* 339–345.

Hines, T. (1987). Left brain/right brain mythology and implications for management and training. *The Academy of Management Review, 12,* 600–606.

Hines, T. (2003). *Pseudoscience and the paranormal: A critical examination of the evidence* (2nd ed.). Buffalo, NY: Prometheus.

Hingson, R., Heeren, T., & Winter, M. R. (2006). Drinking onset and alcohol dependence: Age at onset, duration, and severity. *Archives of Pediatrics and Adolescent Medicine, 160,* 739–746.

Hinrichsen, G. A. (2008). Interpersonal psychotherapy for late life depression: Current status and new applications. *Journal of Rational-Emotive & Cognitive-Behavior Therapy, 26,* 263–275.

Hirsh-Pasek, K., & Golinkoff, R. (1996). *The origins of grammar.* Cambridge, MA: MIT Press.

Hite, S. (1987). *The Hite report on women and love: A cultural revolution in progress.* New York: Alfred A. Knopf.

Hobson, J. A., & McCarley, R. M. (1977). The brain as a dream state generator: An activation-synthesis hypothesis. *American Journal of Psychiatry, 134,* 1335–1348.

Hobson, J. A. Pace-Schott, E., & Stickgold, R. (2000). Dreaming and the brain: Towards a cognitive neuroscience of conscious states. *Behavioral and Brain Sciences, 23,* 793–842.

Hock, R. R. (2002). *Forty studies that changed psychology: Explorations into the history of psychological research* (4th ed.). Upper Saddle River, NJ: Prentice Hall.

Hoffman, M. B., & Morse, S. J. (2006, July 30). The insanity defense goes back on trial. Retrieved October 22, 2007, from www.nytimes.com/2006/07/30/opinion/30hoffman.html?_r=1&oref=slogin.

Hoffman, M. L. (1981). Is altruism part of human nature? *Journal of Personality and Social Psychology, 40*(1), 121–137.

Hoffrage, U. (2004). Overconfidence. In R. F. Pohl (Ed.), *Cognitive illusions: Fallacies and biases in thinking, judgment, and memory* (pp. 235–254). Hove, England: Psychology Press.

Hohmann, G. W. (1966). Some effects of spinal cord lesions on experienced emotional feelings. *Psychophysiology, 3,* 143–156.

Holahan, C., & Moos, R. H. (1991). Life stressors, personal and social resources and depression: A four-year structural model. *Journal of Abnormal Psychology, 100,* 31–38.

Holden, J. E., Jeong, Y., & Forrest, J. M. (2005). The endogenous opioid system and clinical pain management. *AACN Clinical Issues, 16,* 291–301.

Hollon, S. D., Haman, K. L., & Brown, L. L. (2002). Cognitive-behavioral treatment of depression. In I. H. Gotlib & C. L. Hammen (Eds.), *Handbook of depression* (pp. 383–403). New York: Guilford.

Hollon, S. D., Thase, M. E., & Markowitz, J. C. (2002). Treatment and prevention of depression. *Psychological Science in the Public Interest, 3,* 2002.

Holloway, R. L. (1983). Cerebral brain endocast pattern of *Australopithecus afarensis* hominid. *Nature, 303,* 420–422.

Holmes, C., Wurtz, P., Waln, R., Dungan, D., & Joseph, C. (1984). Relationship between the Luscher Color Test and the MMPI. *Journal of Clinical Psychology, 40,* 126–128.

Holmes, D. S. (1974). Investigation of repression: Differential recall of material experimentally or naturally associated with ego threat. *Psychological Bulletin, 81,* 632–653.

Holmes, D. S. (1987). The influence of meditation versus rest on physiological arousal. In M. West (Ed.), *The psychology of meditation* (pp. 81–103). Oxford, England: Clarendon Press.

Holmes, D. S. (1990). The evidence for repression: An examination of sixty years of research. In J. L. Singer (Ed.), *Repression and dissociation* (pp. 85–102). Chicago: University of Chicago Press.

Holmes, T. H., & Masuda, M. (1974). Life change and illness susceptibility. In B. S. Dohrenwend & P. P. Dohrenwend (Eds.), *Stressful life events: Their nature and effects* (pp. 45–72). New York: Wiley.

Holmes, T. H., & Rahe, R. H. (1967). The Social Readjustment Scale. *Journal of Psychosomatic Research, 11,* 213–218.

Homant, R. J., & Kennedy, D. B. (1998). Psychological aspects of crime scene profiling. *Criminal Justice and Behavior, 25,* 319–343.

Honda, H., Shimizu, Y., & Rutter, M. (2005). No effect of MMR withdrawal on the incidence of autism: A total population study. *Journal of Child Psychology and Psychiatry, 46,* 572–579.

Hopkins, B., & Westra, T. (1988). Maternal handling and motor development: An intracultural study. *Genetic, Social, and General Psychology Monographs, 114,* 377–408.

Hoppa, H., & Hallstrom, T. (1981). Weight gain in adulthood in relation to socioeconomic factors, mental illness, and personality traits: A prospective study of middle-aged men. *Journal of Psychosomatic Research, 25,* 83–89.

Horgan, J. (1999). *The undiscovered mind: How the human brain defies replication, medication, and explanation.* New York: Free Press.

Horn, J. L. (1994). The theory of fluid and crystallized intelligence. In R. J. Sternberg (Ed.), *The encyclopedia of intelligence* (pp. 443–451). New York: Macmillan.

Horn, J. L., & Hofer, S. M. (1992). Major abilities and development in the adult period. In R. J. Sternberg & C. A. Berg (Eds.), *Intellectual development* (pp. 44–99). New York: Cambridge University Press.

Horney, K. (1939). *New ways in psychoanalysis*. New York: Norton.

Horvath, A. O., & Bedi, R. P. (2002). The alliance. In J. C. Norcross (Ed.), *Psychotherapy relationships that work: Therapist contributions and responsiveness to patients* (pp. 37–69). New York: Oxford University Press.

Hounsfield, G. N. (1973). Computerized transverse axial scanning (tomography). 1. Description of system. *British Journal of Radiology, 46,* 1016–1022.

House, J. S., Robbins, C., & Metzner, H. L. (1982). The association of social relationships and activities with mortality: Prospective evidence from the Tecumseh Community Health Study. *American Journal of Epidemiology, 116,* 123–140.

Hovland, C. I., Janis, I. L., & Kelley, H. H. (1953). *Communication and persuasion: Psychological studies of opinion change*. New Haven, CT: Yale University Press.

Howe, M., & Courage, M. (1993). On resolving the enigma of infantile amnesia. *Psychological Bulletin, 113,* 305–326.

Howland, R. H., & Thase, M. E. (1998). Cyclothymic disorder. In T. A. Widiger (Ed.), *DSM-IV Sourcebook*. Washington, DC: American Psychiatric Association.

Hubel, D. H, & Wiesel, T. N. (1962). Receptive fields, binocular interaction and functional architecture in the cat's visual cortex. *Journal of Physiology, 160,* 106–154.

Hubel, D. H., & Wiesel, T. N. (1963). Shape and arrangement of columns in cat's striate cortex. *Journal of Physiology, 165,* 559–568.

Huesmann, L. R., Moise-Titus, J., Podolski, C., & Eron, L. D. (2003). Longitudinal relations between children's exposure to TV violence and their aggressive and violent behavior in young adulthood: 1977–1992. *Developmental Psychology, 39*(2), 201–221.

Huff, D. (1954). *How to lie with statistics*. New York: W. W. Norton.

Hulbert, A. (2003). *Raising America: Experts, parents, and a century of advice about children*. New York: Knopf.

Hull, C. L. (1943). *Principles of behavior*. New York: Appleton-Century-Crofts.

Humphreys, K. (2000). Community narratives and personal stories in Alcoholics Anonymous. *Journal of Community Psychology, 28*(5), 495–506.

Humphreys, L. G. (1939). Acquisition and extinction of verbal expectations in a situation analogous to conditioning. *Journal of Experimental Psychology, 25*(3), 294–301.

Hunsley, J., & Bailey, J. M. (1999). The clinical utility of the Rorschach: Unfulfilled promises and an uncertain future. *Psychological Assessment, 11,* 266–277.

Hunsley, J., & DiGuilio, G. (2002). Dodo bird, phoenix, or urban legend? *Scientific Review of Mental Health Practice, 1,* 11–22.

Hunsley, J., Lee, C. M., & Wood, J. (2003). Controversial and questionable assessment techniques. In S. O. Lilienfeld, J. M. Lohr, & S. J. Lynn (Eds.), *Science and pseudoscience in contemporary clinical psychology* (pp. 39–76). New York: Guilford.

Hunt, E. (1999). Intelligence and human resources: Past, present, and future. In P. L. Ackerman, P. C. Kyllonen, & R. D. Roberts (Eds.), *Learning and individual differences: Process, trait, and content determinants* (pp. 3–30). Washington, DC: American Psychological Association.

Hunt, E., & Carlson, J. (2007). Considerations relating to the study of group differences in intelligence. *Perspectives on Psychological Science, 2,* 194–213.

Hunt, M. (1993). *The story of psychology*. New York: Doubleday.

Hunter, J. E., & Hunter, R. F. (1984). Validity and utility of alternative predictors of job performance. *Psychological Bulletin, 96,* 72–98.

Hunter, J. E., Schmidt, F. L., & Hunter, R. (1979). Differential validity of employment tests by race: A comprehensive review and analysis. *Psychological Bulletin, 85,* 721–735.

Hunter, R. A., & Macalpine, I. (1963). *Three hundred years of psychiatry: 1535–1860*. London: Oxford University Press.

Huston, T. L., Ruggiero, M., Conner, R., & Geis, G. (1981). Bystander intervention into crime: A study based on naturally-occurring episodes. *Social Psychology Quarterly, 44,* 14–23.

Hutcheson, D. M., Everitt, B. J., Robbins, T. W., & Dickinson, A. (2001). The role of withdrawal in heroin addiction: Enhances reward or promotes avoidance? *Nature Neuroscience, 4,* 943–947.

Hyde, J. S. (2005). The gender similarities hypothesis. *American Psychologist, 60,* 581–592.

Hyde, J. S., Fennema, E., & Lamon, S. J. (1990). Gender differences in mathematics performance: A meta-analysis. *Psychological Bulletin, 107,* 139–155.

Hyman, I. E., Husband, T. H., & Billings, F. J. (1995). False memories of childhood experiences. *Applied Cognitive Psychology 9,* 181–197.

Hyman, R. (1977). Cold reading: How to convince strangers that you know all about them. *The Zetetic, 1*(2), 18–37.

Hyman, R. (1989). *The elusive quarry: A scientific appraisal of psychical research*. Buffalo, NY: Prometheus Books.

I

Iacono, W. G., & Patrick, C. J. (2006). Polygraph ("lie detector") testing: Current status and emerging trends. In I. B. Weiner & A. Hess (Eds.), *Handbook of forensic psychology* (3rd ed., pp. 552–588). New York: Wiley.

Ikemi, Y., & Nakagawa, S. (1962). A psychosomatic study of contagious dermatitis. *Kyushu Journal of Medical Science, 13,* 335–350.

Ilardi, S. S., & Feldman, D. (2001). The cognitive neuroscience paradigm: A unifying meta-theoretical framework for the science and practice of clinical psychology. *Journal of Clinical Psychology, 57,* 1067–1088.

Ilardi, S. S., Rand, K., & Karwoski, L. (2007). The cognitive neuroscience perspective allows us to understand abnormal behavior at multiple levels of complexity. In S. O. Lilienfeld & W. O. O'Donohue (Eds.), *The great ideas of clinical science: 17 principles that all mental health professionals should understand* (pp. 291–309). New York: Routledge.

Ingram, R. (2003). Origins of cognitive vulnerability to depression. *Cognitive Therapy and Research, 27,* 77–88.

Ingram, R. E., Scott, W., & Siegle, G. (1999). Depression: Social and cognitive aspects. In T. Millon, P. H. Blaney, & R. D. Davis (Eds.), *Oxford textbook of psychopathology* (pp. 203–226). New York: Oxford Press.

Intons-Peterson, M. J., & Fournier, J. (1986). External and internal memory aids: When and how often do we use them? *Journal of Experimental Psychology: General, 115,* 267–280.

Isen, A. M., Clark, M., & Schwartz, M. F. (1976). Duration of the effect of good mood on helping: Footprints in the sand of time. *Journal of Personality & Social Psychology, 34,* 385–393.

Isen, A. M., Rosenzweig, A. S., & Young, M. J. (1991). The influence of positive affect on clinical problem solving. *Medical Decision Making, 11,* 221–227.

Ivie, R., & Ray, K. N. (2005). *Women in physics and astronomy, 2005*. College Park, MD: American Institute of Physics.

Izard, C. E. (1971). *The face of emotion*. New York: Appleton-Century-Crofts.

Izard, C. E. (1994). Innate and universal facial expressions: Evidence from developmental and cross-country research. *Psychological Bulletin, 115*, 288–299.

J

Jackson, D. N. (1971). The dynamics of structured personality tests: 1971. *Psychological Review, 78*, 229–248.

Jackson, D. N., & Rushton, J. P. (2006). Males have greater *g*: Sex differences in general mental ability from 100,000 17- to 18-year-olds on the Scholastic Assessment Test. *Intelligence, 34*, 479–486.

Jackson, K. M., & Sher, K. J. (2003). Alcohol use disorders and psychological distress: A prospective state-trait analysis. *Journal of Abnormal Psychology, 112*, 599–613.

Jackson, P. B., & Finney, M. (2002). Negative life events and psychological distress among young adults. *Social Psychology Quarterly, 65*, 186–201.

Jacobs, G. D., Pace-Schott, E. F., Stickgold, R., & Otto, M. W. (2004). Cognitive behavior therapy and pharmacotherapy for insomnia: A randomized controlled trial and direct comparison. *Archives of Internal Medicine, 164*, 1888–1896.

Jacobson, E. (1938). *Progressive relaxation*. Chicago: University of Chicago Press.

Jacobson, J., Mulick, J., & Schwartz, A. (1995). A history of facilitated communication. *American Psychologist, 50*, 750–765.

Jacobson, N. S., Dobson, K. S., Truax, P. A., Addis, M. E., Koerner, K., Gollan, J. K., et al. (1996). A component analysis of cognitive-behavioral treatment for depression. *Journal of Consulting and Clinical Psychology, 64*, 295–304.

James, W. (1890). *The principles of psychology*. Cambridge, MA: Harvard University Press.

Jamieson, G. A., & Sheehan, P. W. (2004). An empirical test of Woody and Bowers's dissociated-control theory of hypnosis. *International Journal of Clinical and Experimental Hypnosis, 52*, 232–249.

Janis, I. L. (1972). *Victims of groupthink*. Boston: Houghton Mifflin.

Jansen, K. L. R. (1991). Transcendental explanations and the near-death experience. *Lancet, 337*, 207–243.

Jay, K., & Young, A. (1979). *Out of the closets: Voices of gay liberation*. New York: BJ Publishing Group.

Jenike, M. A., Baer, L., Ballantine, T., Martuza, R. L., Tynes, S., Giriunas, I., et al. (1991). Cingulotomy for refractory obsessive compulsive disorder. A long term follow-up of 33 patients. *Archives of General Psychiatry, 48*, 548–555.

Jenny, C., Roesler, T. A., & Poyer, K. L. (1994). Are children at risk for sexual abuse by homosexuals? *Pediatrics, 94*, 41–44.

Jensen, A. R. (1977). Cumulative deficit of blacks in the rural south. *Developmental Psychology, 13*, 184–191.

Jensen, A. R. (2006). *Clocking the mind: Mental chronometry and individual differences*. Oxford, England: Elsevier.

Jerison, H. J. (1983). The evolution of the mammalian brain as an information processing system. In J. F. Eisenberg and D. G. Kleiman (Eds.), Advances in the study of mammalian behavior. *America Society of Mammalogists Special Publication, 7*, 632–661.

John, O. P., & Robins, R. W. (1994). Accuracy and bias in self-perception: Individual differences in self-enhancement and the role of narcissism. *Journal of Personality and Social Psychology, 66*, 206–219.

Johnson, M. H. (1992). Imprinting and the development of face recognition: From chick to man. *Current Directions in Psychological Science, 1*, 52–55.

Johnson, M. H. (1998). The neural basis of cognitive development. In W. Damon (Ed.), *Handbook of child psychology: Vol. 2: Cognition, perception, and language* (pp. 1–49). Hoboken, NJ: Wiley.

Johnson, M. K., Hashtroudi, S., & Lindsay, D. S. (1993). Source monitoring. *Psychological Bulletin, 114*, 3–28.

Johnson, M. K., & Raye, C. L. (1981). Reality monitoring. *Psychological Review, 88*, 67–85.

Johnson, R. D., & Downing, L. L. (1979). Deindividuation and valence of cues: Effects on prosocial and anti-social behavior. *Journal of Personality and Social Psychology, 37*, 1532–1538.

Johnson, S. L., & Miller, I. (1997). Negative life events and time to recovery from episodes of bipolar disorder. *Journal of Abnormal Psychology, 106*(3), 449–457.

Johnson, S. L., Sandrow, D., Meyer, B., Winters, R., Miller, I., Solomon D., et al. (2000). Increases in manic symptoms after life events involving goal attainment. *Journal of Abnormal Psychology, 109*, 721–727.

Johnston, L. D., O'Malley, P. M., Bachman, J. G., & Schulenberg, J. E. (2008). *Monitoring the future national survey results on drug use. 1975–2007: Volume II, College students and adults ages 19–45*. National Institutes of Health, Bethesda, MD: National Institute on Drug Abuse.

Joiner, T. E., & Coyne, J. C. (1999). *The interactional nature of depression: Advances in interpersonal approaches*. Washington, DC: American Psychological Association.

Joiner, T. E., Heatherton, T. F., Rudd, M. D., & Schmidt, N. B. (1997). Perfectionism, perceived weight status, and bulimic symptoms: Two studies testing a diathesis stress model. *Journal of Abnormal Psychology, 106*, 145–153.

Jones, B. E. (2003). Arousal systems. *Frontiers in Bioscience, 8*, 438–451.

Jones, E. E., & Harris, V. A. (1967). The attribution of attitudes. *Journal of Experimental Social Psychology, 3*, 1–24.

Jones, E. E., & Nisbett, R. E. (1972). The actor and the observer: Divergent perceptions of the causes of the behavior. In E. E. Jones, D. E. Kanouse, H. H. Kelley, R. E. Nisbett, S. Valins & B. Weiner (Eds.), *Attribution: Perceiving the causes of behavior* (pp. 79–94). Morristown, NJ: General Learning Press.

Jones, F., & Bright, J. (2001). *Stress: Myth, theory, and research*. Harlow, England: Prentice Hall.

Jones, H. E. (1930). The retention of conditioned emotional reactions in infancy. *Pedagogical Seminary and Journal of Genetic Psychology, 37*(4), 485–498.

Jones, J. C., & Barlow, D. H. (1990). The etiology of posttraumatic stress disorder. *Clinical Psychology Review, 10*, 299–328.

Jones, L. L., Oudega, M., Bunge, M. B., & Tuszynski, M. H. (2001). Neurotrophic factors, cellular bridges and gene therapy for spinal cord injury. *Journal of Physiology, 15*, 83–89.

Jones, M. C. (1924). The elimination of children's fears. *Journal of Experimental Psychology, 7*, 382–390.

Jordan, H. A. (1969). Voluntary intragastric feeding: Oral and gastric contributions to food intake and hunger in man. *Journal of Comparative and Physiological Psychology, 68*, 498–506.

Joseph, R. (1988). Dual mental functioning in a split-brain patient. *Journal of Clinical Psychology, 44*, 770–779.

Jost, J. T., Glaser, J., Sulloway, F., & Kruglanski, A. W. (2003). Political conservatism as motivated social cognition. *Psychological Bulletin, 129*, 339–375.

Julien, R. M. (2004). *A primer of drug action* (10th ed.). San Francisco: W. H. Freeman.

Jung, C. G. (1936). *Archetypes and the collective unconscious*. Princeton, NJ: Princeton University Press.

Jung, C. G. (1950). On mandalas. In *The collected works of C. G. Jung* (Vol. 9ii). Princeton, NJ: Princeton University Press.

Jung, C. G. (1958). Flying saucers: A modern myth of things seen in the skies. In *The collected works of C. G. Jung* (Vol. 14). Princeton, NJ: Princeton University Press.

K

Kabat-Zinn, J. (2003). Mindfulness-based interventions in context: Past, present, and future. *Clinical Psychology: Science & Practice, 10,* 144–156.

Kagan, J. (1976). Emergent themes in human development. *American Scientist, 64,* 186–196.

Kagan, J. (1998). Biology and the child. In W. Damon & N. Eisenberg (Eds.), *Handbook of child psychology, Vol. 3: Social, emotional, and personality development* (5th ed., pp. 177–235). Hoboken, NJ: John Wiley.

Kagan, J., Reznick, J. S., & Snidman, N. (1988). Biological bases of childhood shyness. *Science, 240,* 167–171.

Kagan, J., Snidman, N., Kahn, V., & Towsley, S. (2007). The preservation of two infant temperaments into adolescence. *SRCD Monographs, 72*(2).

Kageyama, T. (1999). Loudness in listening to music with portable headphone stereos. *Perceptual and Motor Skills, 88,* 423.

Kahill, S. (1984). Human figure drawing in adults: An update of the empirical evidence, 1967–1982. *Canadian Psychology, 25,* 395–410.

Kahneman, D., Slovic, P., & Tversky, A. (Eds.). (1982). *Judgment under uncertainty: Heuristics and biases.* New York: Cambridge University Press.

Kalat, J. W. (2007). *Biological psychology* (9th ed.). Belmont, CA: Thomson Wadsworth.

Kamrin, M. A. (1988). *Toxicology: A primer on toxicology principles and applications.* Boca Raton, FL: Lewis Publishers.

Kandel, D., Yamaguchi, K., & Chen, K. (1992). Stages of progression in drug involvement from adolescence to adulthood: Further evidence of the Gateway theory. *Journal of Studies of Alcohol, 53,* 447–457.

Kanders, B. S., & Blackburn, G. L. (1992). Reducing primary risk factors by therapeutic weight loss. In T. A. Wadden & T. B. Van Itallie (Eds.), *Treatment of the seriously obese patient* (pp. 213–230). New York: Guilford Press.

Kane, B. S., Shinohara, K., Neuhaus, J., Hudes, E. S., Goldberg, H., & Avins, A. L. (2006). Saw palmetto for benign prostatic hyperplasia. *New England Journal of Medicine, 354,* 557–566.

Kane, M. J., Hambrick, D. Z., & Conway, A. R. A. (2005). Working memory capacity and fluid intelligence are strongly related constructs: Comment on Ackerman, Beier, and Boyle (2004). *Psychological Bulletin, 131,* 66–71.

Kanner, A. D., Coyne, J. C., Schaefer, C., & Lazarus, R. S. (1981). Comparison of two modes of stress measurement: Daily hassles and uplifts versus major life events. *Journal of Behavioral Medicine, 4,* 1–39.

Kanzler, H. R., & Rosenthal, R. N. (2003). Dual diagnosis: Alcoholism and co-morbid psychiatric disorders. *American Journal of Addiction, 12*(Suppl. 1), 21–40.

Kaplan, H. S. (1977). Hypoactive sexual desire. *Journal of Sex and Marital Therapy, 3,* 3–9.

Kaplan, R. M., & Saccuzzo, D. P. (2005). *Psychological testing: Principles, applications, and issues.* Belmont, CA: Thomson Wadsworth.

Karatekin, C. (2004). Development of attentional allocation in the dual task paradigm. *International Journal of Psychophysiology, 52*(1), 7–21.

Karau, S. J., & Williams, K. D. (1995). Social loafing—Research findings, implications, and future directions. *Current Directions in Psychological Science, 4*(5), 134–140.

Karlen, S. J., & Krubitzer, L. (2006). The evolution of the neocortex in mammals: Intrinsic and extrinsic contributions to the cortical phenotype. *Novartis Found Symposium 270,* 159–169.

Karlin, R. A., & Orne, M. T. (1996). Commentary on *Borawick v. Shay*: Hypnosis, social influence, incestuous child abuse, and satanic ritual abuse: The iatrogenic creation of horrific memories for the remote past. *Cultic Studies Journal, 13*(1), 42–94.

Karon, B. P. (2000). A clinical interpretation of the Thematic Apperception Test, Rorschach, and other clinical data: A reexamination of the statistical versus clinical prediction. *Professional Psychology: Research and Practice, 31,* 230–233.

Kassin, S. (2004). *Psychology* (4th ed.). Upper Saddle River, NJ: Prentice Hall.

Kassin, S. M., & Gudjonsson, G. H. (2004). The psychology of confession: A review of the literature and issues. *Psychological Science in the Public Interest, 5,* 33–67.

Kassin, S. M., Ellsworth, P. C., & Smith, V. L. (1989). The "general acceptance" of psychological research on eyewitness testimony: A survey of the experts. *American Psychologist, 44,* 1089–1098.

Kassin, S. M., Tubb, V. A., Hosch, H. M., & Memon, A. (2001). On the "general acceptance" of eyewitness testimony research. *American Psychologist, 56,* 405–416.

Katz, D. A., & McHorney, C. A. (2002). The relationship between insomnia and health-related quality of life in patients with chronic illness. *Journal of Family Practice, 51,* 229–235.

Katz, J. (1988). *Seductions of crime: Moral and sensual attractions in doing evil.* New York: Basic Books.

Katzman, D. K. (2005). Medical complications in adolescents with anorexia nervosa: A review of the literature. *International Journal of Eating Disorders, 37*(Suppl.), S52–S59.

Kavale, K. A., & Forness, S. R. (1987). Substance over style—Assessing the efficacy of modality testing and teaching. *Exceptional Children, 54*(3), 228–239.

Kazdin, A. E. (1978). The application of operant techniques in treatment, rehabilitation, and education. In S. L. Garfield & A. E. Bergin (Eds.), *Handbook of psychotherapy and behavior change* (2nd ed.). New York: John Wiley & Sons.

Kazdin, A. E. (1982). The token economy: A decade later. *Journal of Applied Behavior Analysis, 15*(3), 431–445.

Kazdin, A. E., Marciano, P. L., & Whitley, M. K. (2005). The therapeutic alliance in cognitive-behavioral treatment of children referred for oppositional, aggressive, and antisocial behavior. *Journal of Consulting and Clinical Psychology, 73,* 725–730.

Keel, P. K., & Klump, K. L. (2003). Are eating disorders culture-bound syndromes? Implications for conceptualizing their etiology. *Psychological Bulletin, 129,* 747–769.

Keen, S. (1986). *Faces of the enemy: Reflections of the hostile imagination.* San Francisco: Harper & Row.

Keinan, G., Almagor, M. & Ben-Porath, Y.S. (1989). A reevaluation of the relationships between psychotherapeutic orientation and perceived personality characteristics. *Psychotherapy, 26,* 218–226.

Keith, S. J., Gunderson, J. G., Reifman, A., Buchsbaum, S., & Mosher, L. R. (1976). Special report: Schizophrenia, 1976. *Schizophrenia Bulletin, 2,* 510–565.

Kellehear, A. (1993). Culture, biology, and the near-death experience: A reappraisal. *Journal of Nervous and Mental Disease, 181,* 148–156.

Keller, M. L., & Craske, M. G. (2008). Panic disorder and agoraphobia. In J. Hunsley & E. J. Mash (Eds.), *A guide to assessments that work* (pp. 229–253). New York: Oxford University Press.

Kelly, T. H., Cherek, D. R., Steinberg, J. L., & Robinson, D. (1988). Effects of provocation and alcohol on human aggressive behavior. *Drug and Alcohol Dependence, 21,* 105–112.

Kendall, T., Pilling, S., & Whittington, C. J. (2005). Are the SSRIs and atypical antidepressants safe and effective for children and adolescents? *Current Opinion in Psychiatry, 18,* 21–25.

Kendeigh, S. C. (1941). Territorial and mating behavior of the house wren. *Illinois Biographical Monographs, 18*(3) (Serial No. 120).

Kendell, R. E. (1975). The concept of disease and its implications for psychiatry. *British Journal of Psychiatry, 127,* 305–315.

Kendler, K. S. (2005). Toward a philosophical structure for psychiatry. *American Journal of Psychiatry, 162,* 433–440.

Kendler, K. S., & Diehl, S. R. (1993). The genetics of schizophrenia: A current, genetic-epidemiologic perspective. *Schizophrenia Bulletin, 19,* 261–285.

Kendler, K. S., Gardner, C. O., & Prescott, C. A. (2003). Personality and the experience of environmental adversity. *Psychological Medicine, 33,* 1193–1202.

Kendler, K. S., Neale, M. C., Kessler, R. C., Heath, A. C., & Eaves, L. J. (1993). A test of the equal-environment assumption in twin studies of psychiatric illness. *Behavior Genetics, 23,* 21–27.

Kenneally, C. (2006). The deepest cut—Radical neurosurgery and the brain's adaptability. *New Yorker, 82*(20), 36–42.

Kennedy, S., Kiecolt-Glaser, J. K., & Glaser, R. (1990). Social support, stress, and the immune system. In B. R. Sarason, I. G. Sarason, & G. R. Pierce (Eds.), *Social support: An interactional view* (pp. 253–266). New York: Wiley.

Kenrick, D. T., & Funder, D. C. (1988). Profiting from controversy: Lessons from the person-situation debate. *American Psychologist, 43,* 23–34.

Kenrick, D. T., Neuberg, S. L., & Cialdini, R. B. (2005). *Social psychology: Unraveling the mystery* (3rd ed.). Boston: Allyn & Bacon.

Kent, R. D., & Miolo, G. (1995). Phonetic abilities in the first year of life. In P. Flether & B. MacWhinney (Eds.), *The handbook of child language* (pp. 303–334). San Diego, CA: Academic Press.

Keski-Rahkonen, A., Hoek, H. W., Linna, M. S., Raevuori, A., Sihvola, E., Bulik, C. M., Rissanen, A., & Kaprio, J. (2008). Incidence and outcomes of bulimia nervosa: A nationwide population-based study. *Psychological Medicine, 8,* 1–9.

Kessler, R. C., Berglund, P., Demler, O., Jin, R., & Walters, E. E. (2005). Lifetime prevalence and age-of-onset distributions of DSM-IV disorders in the National Comorbidity Survey Replication. *Archives of General Psychiatry, 62,* 593–602.

Kessler, R. C., Chiu, W. T., Jin, R., Ruscio, A. M., Shear, K., & Walters, E. E. (2006). The epidemiology of panic attacks, panic disorder, and agoraphobia in the National Comorbidity Survey Replication. *Archives of General Psychiatry, 63,* 415–424.

Kessler, R. C., McGonagale, K. A., Zhao, S., Nelson, C. B., Hughes, M., Eshleman, S., et al. (1994). Lifetime and 12-month prevalence of DSM-III-R psychiatric disorders in the United States: Results from the National Comorbidity Survey. *Archives of General Psychiatry, 51,* 8–19.

Kessler, R. C., Price, R. H., & Wortman, C. B. (1985). Social factors in psychopathology: Stress, social support and coping processes. *Annual Review of Psychology, 36,* 351–372.

Kessler, R. C., Sonnega, A., Bromet, E., Hughes, M., & Nelson, C. B. (1995). Post-traumatic stress disorder in the National Comorbidity Survey. *Archives of General Psychiatry, 52,* 1048–1060.

Kevles, D. J. (1985). *In the name of eugenics: Genetics and the uses of human heredity.* New York: Knopf.

Key, W. B. (1973). *Subliminal seduction.* Englewood Cliffs, NJ: Signet.

Keyes, C. L. M., & Haidt, J. (Eds.). (2003). *Flourishing: Positive psychology and the life well lived.* Washington, DC: American Psychological Association.

Kiecolt-Glaser, J. K., Marucha, P. T., Malarkey, W. B., Mercado, A., M., & Glaser, R. (1995). Slowing of wound healing by psychological stress. *Lancet, 346,* 1194–1196.

Kiecolt-Glaser, J. K., McGuire, L., Robles, T. F., & Glaser, R. (2002). Psychoneuroimmunology: Psychological influences on immune function and health. *Journal of Consulting and Clinical Psychology, 70,* 537–547.

Kiesler, C. A., & Kiesler, S. B. (1969). *Conformity.* Menlo Park, CA: Addison-Wesley.

Kihlstrom, J. F. (1987). The cognitive unconscious. *Science, 237,* 1445–1452.

Kihlstrom, J. F. (1992). Hypnosis: A sesquicentennial essay. *International Journal of Clinical and Experimental Hypnosis, 40,* 301–314.

Kihlstrom, J. F. (1998). Dissociations and dissociation theory in hypnosis: Comment on Kirsch & Lynn (1998). *Psychological Bulletin, 123,* 186–191.

Kihlstrom, J. F. (2005). Dissociative disorders. In S. Nolen-Hoeksema, T. D. Cannon, & T. Widiger (Eds.), *Annual Review of Clinical Psychology, 1,* 227–254.

Kilham, W., & Mann, L. (1974). Level of destructive obedience as a function of transmitter and executant roles in the Milgram obedience paradigm. *Journal of Personality and Social Psychology, 29,* 696–702.

Kim, H., & Markus, H. R. (1999). Deviance or uniqueness, harmony or conformity? A cultural analysis. *Journal of Personality and Social Psychology, 77,* 785–800.

Kimura, D. (1999). *Sex and cognition.* Cambridge, MA: MIT Press.

King, A. C., Houle, T., de Wit, H., Holdstock, L., & Schuster, A. (2002). Biphasic alcohol response differs in heavy versus light drinkers. *Alcoholism: Clinical and Experimental Research, 26,* 827–835.

King, B. (2006). The rise, fall, and resurrection of the ventromedial hypothalamus in the regulation of feeding behavior and body weight. *Physiology & Behavior, 87,* 221–224.

Kinsey, A. C., Pomeroy, W. B., & Martin, C. E. (1948). *Sexual behavior in the human male.* Philadelphia: W. B. Saunders.

Kinsey, A. C., Pomeroy, W. B., Martin, C. E., & Gebhard, P. H. (1953). *Sexual behavior in the human female.* Philadelphia: W. B. Saunders.

Kippes, C., & Garrison, C. B. (2006). Are we in the midst of an autism epidemic? A review of prevalence data. *Missouri Medicine, 103*(1), 65–68.

Kircher, J. C., Horowitz, S. W., & Raskin, D. C. (1988). Meta-analysis of mock crime studies of the control question polygraph technique. *Law and Human Behavior, 12,* 79–90.

Kirmayer, L .J., & Young, A. (1999). Culture and context in the evolutionary concept of mental disorder. *Journal of Abnormal Psychology, 108,* 446–452.

Kirsch, I. (1999). *How expectancies shape experience.* Washington, DC: American Psychological Association.

Kirsch, I., & Lynn, S. J. (1995). The altered state of hypnosis: Changes in the theoretical landscape. *American Psychologist, 50,* 846–858.

Kirsch, I., & Lynn, S. J. (1998). Dissociation theories of hypnosis. *Psychological Bulletin, 123,* 100–115.

Kirsch, I., & Lynn, S. J. (1999). Automaticity in clinical psychology. *American Psychologist, 54,* 504–515.

Kirsch, I., Lynn, S. J., Vigorito, M., & Miller, R. R. (2004). The role of cognition in classical and operant conditioning. *Journal of Clinical Psychology, 60,* 369–392.

Kirsch, I., & Sapirstein, G. (1998). Listening to Prozac but hearing placebo: A meta-analysis of antidepressant medication. *Preven-*

tion & Treatment, 1, art. 0002a. Retrieved February 15, 2003, from journals.apa.org/prevention/volume1/pre0010002a.html.

Kirschner, P. A., Sweller, J., & Clark, R. E. (2006). Why minimal guidance during instruction does not work: An analysis of the failure of constructivist, discovery, problem-based, experiential, and inquiry-based teaching. *Educational Psychologist, 41,* 75–86.

Kish, S. J. (2002). How strong is the evidence that brain serotonin neurons are damaged in human users of ecstasy? *Pharmacology, Biochemistry, and Behavior, 71,* 845–855.

Kitcher, P. (1985). *Vaulting ambition: Sociobiology and the quest for human nature.* Cambridge, MA: MIT Press.

Klahr, D., & MacWhinney, B. (1998). Information processing. In W. Damon (Ed.), *Handbook of child psychology: Vol. 2: Cognition, perception, and language* (pp. 631–678). Hoboken, NJ: Wiley.

Klahr, D., & Nigam, M. (2004). The equivalence of learning paths in early science instruction: Effects of direct instruction and discovery learning. *Psychological Science, 15,* 661–667.

Klaus, M. H., & Kennell, J. H. (1976). *Maternal–infant bonding.* St. Louis, MO: Mosby.

Klein, D. F. (1998). Listening to meta-analysis but hearing bias. *Prevention & Treatment, 1,* art. 0006c. Retrieved May 12, 2006, from journals.apa.org/prevention/volume1/pre0010006c.html.

Klein, S., Burke, L. E., Bray, G. A., Blair, S., Allison, D. B., Pi-Sunyer, X., et al. (2004). AHA scientific statement: Clinical implications of obesity with specific focus on cardiovascular disease. *Circulation, 1110,* 2952–2967.

Kleinman, A. (1988). *Rethinking psychiatry: From cultural category to personal experience.* New York: Free Press.

Klerman, G. L., & Weissman, M. M. (Eds.). (1993). *New applications of interpersonal psychotherapy.* Washington, DC: American Psychiatric Press.

Klerman, G. L., Weissman, M. M., Rounsaville, B. J., & Chevron, E. S. (1984). *Interpersonal psychotherapy of depression.* New York: Basic Books.

Kluft, R. P. (1984). Multiple personality in childhood. *Psychiatric Clinics of North America, 7,* 121–134.

Kluger, A. N., & Tikochinsky, J. (2001). The error of accepting the "theoretical" null hypothesis: The rise, fall and resurrection of common sense hypotheses in psychology. *Psychological Bulletin, 127,* 408–423.

Klusmann, D. (2002). Sexual motivation and the duration of partnership. *Archives of Sexual Behavior, 31,* 275–287.

Knapp, T. J. (1976). Premack principle in human experimental and applied settings. *Behaviour Research and Therapy, 14*(2), 133–147.

Knecht, S., Ellger, T., & Levine, J. A. (2007). Obesity in neurobiology. *Progress in Neurobiology, 84,* 85–103.

Knight, J. R., Wechsler, H., Kuo, M., Seibring, M., Weitzman, E. R., & Schuckit, M. (2002). Alcohol abuse and dependence among U.S. college students. *Journal of Studies on Alcohol, 63,* 263–270.

Knoth, R., Boyd, K., & Singer, B. (1988). Empirical tests of sexual selection theory: Predictions of sex differences in onset, intensity, and time course of sexual arousal. *Journal of Sex Research, 24,* 73–89.

Knox, D., Zusman, M., & Nieves, W. (1997). College students' homogamous preferences for a date and mate. *College Student Journal, 31,* 445–448.

Knyazeva, M. G., Jalili, M. Meuli, R. Hasler, M. DeFeo, Ol, & Do, K. Q. (2008) Alpha rhythm and hypofrontality in schizophrenia. *Acta Psychiatrica Scandinavica, 118,* 188–199.

Kobasa, S. C., Hilker, R. R., & Maddi, S. R. (1979). Who stays healthy under stress? *Journal of Occupational Medicine, 21,* 595–598.

Koch, C. (1993). Computational approaches to cognition: The bottom-up view. *Current Opinion in Neurobiology, 3,* 203–208.

Kochanek, K. D., Murphy, S. L., Anderson, R. N., & Scott, C. (2004). Deaths: Final data for 2002. *National Vital Statistics Report, 53*(5), 1–116.

Koenig, H. G., McCullough, M. E., & Larson, D. B. (2001). *Handbook of religion and health.* New York: Oxford University Press.

Kohlberg, L. (1965, March 26). *Relationships between the development of moral judgment and moral conduct.* Paper presented at the Annual Meeting of the Society for Research in Child Development, Minneapolis, MN.

Kohlberg, L. (1976). Moral stages and moralization: The cognitive-developmental approach. In T. Lickona (Ed.), *Moral development and behavior: Theory, research and social issues* (pp. 31–53). New York: Holt, Rinehart and Winston.

Kohlberg, L. (1981). *The philosophy of moral development: Moral stages and the idea of justice.* San Francisco: Harper & Row.

Kohlberg, L., & Turiel, E. (1971). Moral development and moral education. In G. Lesser (Ed.), *Psychology and educational practice.* Chicago: Scott Foresman.

Kohn, A. (1993). *Punished by rewards: The trouble with gold stars, incentive plans, As, praise and other bribes.* Boston: Houghton Mifflin.

Köksal, F., Domjan, M., Kurt, A., Sertel, O., Orüng, S., Bowers, R., & Kumru, G. (2004). An animal model of fetishism. *Behaviour Research and Therapy, 42*(12), 1421–1434.

Kollins, S. H. (2003). Delay discounting is associated with substance use in college students. *Addictive Behaviors, 28,* 1167–1173.

Konner, M. (1990). *Why the reckless survive—And other secrets of human nature.* New York: Viking.

Kosfeld, M., Heinrichs, M., Zaks, P., Fischbacher, U., & Fehr, E. (2005). Oxytocin increases trust in humans. *Nature, 435,* 673–676.

Kounios, J., Frymiare, J. L., Bowden, E. M., Fleck, J. I., Subramaniam, K., Parrish, T. B., et al. (2006). The prepared mind: Neural activity prior to problem presentation predicts subsequent solution by sudden insight. *Psychological Science, 17,* 882–890.

Kozorovitskiy, Y., & Gould, E. (2003). Adult neurogenesis: A mechanism for brain repair? *Journal of Clinical & Experimental Neuropsychology, 25,* 721–732.

Krackow, E., Lynn, S. J., & Payne, D. (2005–2006). Death of Princess Diana: The effects of memory enhancement procedures on flashbulb memories. *Imagination, Cognition, and Personality, 25,* 197–220.

Kramer, P. (2007). *Freud: Inventor of the modern mind.* New York: HarperCollins.

Kratzig, G. P., & Arbuthnott, K. D. (2006). Perceptual learning style and learning proficiency: A test of the hypothesis. *Journal of Educational Psychology, 98,* 238–246.

Kraus, S. J. (1995). Attitudes and the prediction of behaviour: A meta-analysis of the empirical literature. *Personality and Social Psychology Bulletin, 21,* 58–75.

Krebs, D. L., & Denton, K. (2005). Toward a more pragmatic approach to morality: A critical evaluation of Kohlberg's model. *Psychological Review, 112,* 629–649.

Kreitler, S., & Merimsky, O. (2006). Pain and suffering in cancer. In S. Kreitler, D. Beltruitti, A. Lamberto, & D. Niv (Eds.). *Handbook of chronic pain* (pp. 533–546). Hauppage, NY: Nova Biomedical Books.

Kreppner, J. M., O'Connor, T. G., & Rutter, M. (2001). Can inattention/overactivity be an institutional deprivation syndrome? *Journal of Abnormal Child Psychology, 29*(6), 513–528.

Krubitzer, L., & Kaas, J. (2005). The evolution of the neocortex in mammals: How is phenotypic diversity generated? *Current Opinion in Neurobiology, 15,* 444–453.

Krueger, J. I., & Funder, D. C. (2004). Towards a balanced social psychology: Causes, consequences and cures for the problem-seeking approach to social behavior and cognition. *Behavioral and Brain Sciences 27*(3), 313–327.

Krueger, R. F., Hicks, B. M., & McGue, M. (2001). Altruism and antisocial behavior: Independent tendencies, unique personality correlates, distinct etiologies. *Psychological Science, 12,* 397–402.

Krueger, R. F., Schmutte, P. S., Caspi, A., Moffitt, T. E., Campbell, K., & Silva P. A. (1994). Personality traits are linked to crime among men and women: Evidence from a birth cohort. *Journal of Abnormal Psychology, 103,* 328–338.

Kruger, S., Seminowicz, D., Goldapple, K., Kennedy, S. H., & Mayberg, H. S. (2003). State and trait influences on mood regulation in bipolar disorder: Blood flow differences with an acute mood challenge. *Biological Psychiatry, 54*(11), 1274–1283.

Kuhn, D. (2007). Jumping to conclusions. *Scientific American Mind, 18*(1), 44–51.

Kuhn, D., & Dean, D. (2005). Is developing scientific thinking all about learning to control variables? *Psychological Science, 16,* 866–870.

Kuhn, D., Garcia-Mila, M., Zohar, A., & Andersen, C. (1995). Strategies of knowledge acquisition. *Monographs of the Society for Research in Child Development, 60,* Serial No. 4.

Kunda, Z. (1999). *Social cognition: Making sense of people.* Cambridge, MA: The MIT Press.

Kung, H. C., Hoyert, D. L., Xu, J., & Murphy, S. L. (2008). Deaths: Final data for 2005. *National Vital Statistics Reports, 56*(10), 1–120.

Kunst-Wilson, W. R., & Zajonc, R. B. (1980). Affective discrimination of stimuli that cannot be recognized. *Science, 207,* 557–558.

Kurth, T., Gaziano, J. M., Berger, K., Kase, C. S., Rexrode, K. M., Cook, N. R., et al. (2003). Body mass index and the risk of stroke in men. *Archives of Internal Medicine, 163,* 2557–2662.

Kurtus, R. (2000). I walked on fire and lived to tell about it. Retrieved May 24, 2007, from www.school-for-champions.com/excellence/firewalk.htm.

Kushner, M. (1968). The operant control of intractable sneezing. In C. D. Spielberger, R. Fox, & B. Masterson (Eds.), *Contributions to general psychology.* New York: Roland Press.

L

Lacasse, J. R., & Leo, J. (2005). Serotonin and depression: A disconnect between the advertisements and the scientific literature. *PLOS Medicine, 2,* 101–106.

Lacey, H. P., Smith, D. M., & Ubel, P. A. (2006). Hope I die before I get old: Mispredicting happiness across the adult lifespan. *Journal of Happiness Studies, 7,* 167–182.

LaFreniere, P. J., & Sroufe, L. A. (1985). Profiles of peer competence in the preschool: Interrelations among measures, influence of social ecology, and relation to attachment history. *Development Psychology, 21,* 56–69.

Lalich, J. (2004). *Bounded choice: True believers and charismatic cults.* Berkeley: University of California Press.

Lamb, H. R., & Bachrach, L. L. (2001). Some perspectives on deinstitutionalization. *Psychiatric Services, 52,* 1039–1045.

Lamb, M. E., Thompson, R. A., Gardner, W. P., Charnov, E. L., & Estes, D. (1984). Security of infantile attachment as assessed in the "strange situation": Its study and biological interpretation. *Behavioral and Brain Sciences, 7,* 127–171.

Lambert, M. J. (2003). *Bergin and Garfield's handbook of psychotherapy and behavior change.* New York: John Wiley.

Lambert, M. J., & Ogles, B. M. (2004). The efficacy and effectiveness of psychotherapy. In M. J. Lambert (Ed.), *Bergin and Garfield's handbook of psychotherapy and behavior change* (5th ed., pp. 139–193). New York: Wiley.

Lange, C. G. (1885). *Om sindsbevaegelser: et psyko-fysiologisk studie.* Kjbenhavn: Jacob Lunds. Reprinted in C. G. Lange and W. James (Eds.), *The emotions.* I. A. Haupt (Trans.). Baltimore: Williams & Wilkins.

Langlois, J. H., Kalakanis, L., Rubenstein, A. J., Larson, A., Hallam, M., & Smoot, M. (2000). Maxims or myths of beauty? A meta-analytic and theoretical review. *Psychological Bulletin, 126,* 390–423.

Langlois, J. H., & Downs, A. C. (1980). Mothers, fathers, and peers as socialization agents of sex-typed play behaviors in young children. *Child Development, 51,* 1237–1247.

Langlois, J. H., & Roggman, L. A. (1990). Attractive faces are only average. *Psychological Science, 1*(2), 115–121.

Lansford, J. E., Chang, L., Dodge, K. A., Malone, P. S., Oburu, P., Palmerus, K., et al. (2005). Physical discipline and children's adjustment: Cultural normativeness as a moderator. *Child Development, 76*(6), 1234–1246.

Lansford, J. E., Deater-Deckard, K., Dodge, K. A., Bates, J. E., & Pettit, G. S. (2004). Ethnic differences in the link between physical discipline and later adolescent externalizing behaviors. *Journal of Child Psychology and Psychiatry, 45*(4), 801–812.

LaPiere, R. T. (1934). Attitudes vs. action. *Social Forces, 13,* 230–237.

Larson, R., & Richards, M. (1994). *Divergent realities: The emotional lives of mothers, fathers, and adolescents.* New York: Basic Books.

Larsson, L. G., Grimby, G., & Karlsson, J. (1979). Muscle strength and speed of movement in relation to age and muscle morphology. *Journal of Applied Physiology, 46,* 451–456.

Lashley, K. S. (1929). *Brain mechanisms and intelligence.* Chicago: University of Chicago Press.

Latané, B., & Darley, J. M. (1970). *The unresponsive bystander: Why doesn't he help?* New York: Appleton-Century-Crofts.

Latané, B., & Nida, S. (1981). Ten years of research on group size and helping. *Psychological Bulletin, 89,* 308–324.

Latané, B., & Rodin, J. (1969). A lady in distress: Inhibiting effects of friends and strangers on bystander intervention. *Journal of Experimental Social Psychology, 5,* 189–302.

Latané, B., Williams, K., & Harkins, S. (1979). Many hands make light the work: The causes and consequences of social loafing. *Journal of Personality and Social Psychology, 37,* 822–832.

Laumann, E. O., Gagnon, J. H., Michael, R. T., & Michaels, S. (1994). *The social organization of sexuality: Sexual practices in the United States.* Chicago: University of Chicago Press.

Laurin, D., Verreault, R., Lindsay, J., MacPherson, K., & Rockwood, K. (2001). Physical activity and risk of cognitive impairment and dementia in elderly persons. *Archives of Neurology, 58,* 498–504.

Laursen, B., Coy, K. C., & Collins, W. (1998). Reconsidering changes in parent-child conflict across adolescence: A meta-analysis. *Child Development, 69,* 817–832.

Lauterbur, P. (1973). Image formation by induced local interaction; examples employing magnetic resonance. *Nature, 242,* 192.

Lazarus, A. A. (2006). *Brief but comprehensive psychotherapy: The multimodal way.* New York: Springer Publishing.

Lazarus, R. S. (1999). *Stress and emotion: A new synthesis.* New York: Springer Publishing.

Lazarus, R. S. (2003). Does the positive psychology movement have legs? *Psychological Inquiry, 14,* 93–109.

Lazarus, R. S., & Folkman, S. (1984). *Stress, appraisal, and coping.* New York: Springer.

Leahey, T. H., & Leahey, G. E. (1983). *Psychology's occult doubles: Psychology and the problem of pseudoscience*. Chicago: Nelson/Hall.

Leavy, J. (1992). Spooky presidential coincidences contest. *Skeptical Inquirer, 16,* 316–320.

LeDoux, J. (1996). *The emotional brain: The mysterious underpinnings of emotional life*. New York: Simon & Schuster.

LeDoux, J. E. (2000). Emotion circuits in the brain. *Annual Review of Neuroscience, 23,* 155–184.

Lee, K., & Ashton, M. C. (2004). Psychometric properties of the HEXACO personality inventory. *Multivariate Behavioral Research, 39,* 329–358.

Lee, Y. S. (2009). The role of genes in the obesity epidemic. *Annals of the Academy of Medicine Singapore, 38,* 45–47.

Leek, F. F. (1969). The problem of brain removal during embalming by the ancient Egyptians. *Journal of Egyptian Archeology, SS,* 112–116.

Leeper, P. (1988). Having a place to live is vital to good health. *NewsReport, 38,* 5–8.

LeFever, G. B., Arcona, A. P., & Antonuccio, D. O. (2003). ADHD among American schoolchildren: Evidence of overdiagnosis and overuse of medication. *Scientific Review of Mental Health Practice, 2*(1), 49–60.

Lehman, D. R., Chiu, C.-Y., & Schaller, M. (2004). Psychology and culture. *Annual Review of Psychology, 55,* 689–714.

Leichsenring, F., Rabung, S., & Leibing, E. (2004). The efficacy of short-term psychodynamic psychotherapy in specific psychiatric disorders. *Archives of General Psychiatry, 61,* 1208–1216.

Leitenberg, H., & Henning, K. (1995). Sexual fantasy. *Psychological Bulletin, 117,* 469–496.

Lejoyeux, M., & Ades, J. (1997). Antidepressant discontinuation: A review of the literature. *Journal of Clinical Psychiatry, 58*(Suppl. 7), 11–15.

Lenggenhager, B., Tadi, T., Metzinger, T., & Blanke, O. (2007). Video ergo sum: Manipulating bodily self-consciousness. *Science, 317*(5841), 1096–1099.

Lenneberg, E. (1967). *Biological foundations of language*. New York: Wiley.

Leonard, B. E. (1997). The role of noradrenaline in depression: A review. *Journal of Psychopharmacology, 11,* S39–47.

Lepper, M. R., Greene, D., & Nisbett, R. E. (1973). Undermining children's intrinsic interest with extrinsic rewards: A test of the "overjustification" hypothesis. *Journal of Personality and Social Psychology, 28,* 129–137.

Lerner, M. J. (1980). *The belief in a just world: A fundamental delusion*. New York: Plenum Press.

Leslie, M. (2000). The vexing legacy of Lewis Terman. Retrieved from www.stanfordalumni.org/news/magazine/2000/julaug/articles/terman.html.

Lett, J. (1990, Winter). A field guide to critical thinking. *Skeptical Inquirer, 14,* 153–160.

Levant, R. F. (2004). The empirically validated treatments movement: A practitioner/educator perspective. *Clinical Psychology: Science and Practice, 11,* 219–224.

Levenberg, S. B. (1975). Professional training, psychodiagnostic skill, and kinetic family drawings. *Journal of Personality Assessment, 39,* 389–393.

Leventhal, H., Weinman, J., Leventhal, E. A., & Phillips, L. A. (2006). Health psychology: The search for pathways between behavior and health. *Annual Review of Psychology, 59,* 477–505.

Lever, J. (1995, August 22). The 1995 Advocate survey of sexuality and relationship: The women. *Advocate,* 212–230.

Levin, J. (2001). *God, faith, and health: Exploring the spirituality-healing connection*. New York: John Wiley & Sons.

Levine, B. (1979). *Group psychotherapy: Practice and development*. Englewood Cliffs, NJ: Prentice-Hall.

Levine, S. C., Vasilyeva, M., Lourenco, S. F., Newcombe, N. S., & Huttenlocher, J. (2005). Research report: Socioeconomic status modifies the sex difference in spatial skill. *Psychological Science, 16,* 841–845.

Levy-Reiner, S. (1996). The decade of the brain: Library and NIMH hold symposia on mental illness. *Library of Congress Information Bulletin, 55*(15), 326–327.

Lewin, K. (1951). *Field theory in social science: Selected theoretical papers*. D. Cartwright (Ed.), New York: Harper & Row.

Lewinsohn, P. M. (1974). A behavioral approach to depression. In R. J. Friedman & M. M. Katz (Eds.), *Psychology of depression: Contemporary theory and research* (pp. 157–158). Oxford, England: John Wiley & Sons.

Lewis, M., & Brooks-Gunn, J. (1979). *Social cognition and the acquisition of self*. New York: Plenum.

Lewis, M., Brooks-Gunn, J., & Jaskir, J. J. (1985). Individual differences in visual self-recognition as a function of mother-infant attachment relationship. *Developmental Psychobiology, 21,* 1181–1187.

Lewis, M., & Carmody, D. P. (2008). Self-representation and brain development. *Developmental Psychology, 44,* 1329–1334.

Lewis, W. A., & Bucher, A. M. (1992). Anger, catharsis, the reformulated frustration-aggression hypothesis, and health consequences. *Psychotherapy, 29,* 385–392.

Lewontin, R. C. (1970). Further remarks on race and the genetics of intelligence. *Bulletin of the Atomic Scientists, 26,* 23–25.

Li, S. C., Jordanova, M., & Lindenberger, U. (1998). From good senses to good sense: A link between tactile information processing and intelligence. *Intelligence, 26*(2), 99–122.

Li, Y., Liu, J., Liu, F., Guo, G., Anme, T., & Ushijima, H. (2000). Maternal child-rearing behaviors and correlates in rural minority areas of Yunnan, China. *Journal of Developmental & Behavioral Pediatrics, 21,* 114–122.

Lidz, T. (1973). *The origin and treatment of schizophrenic disorders*. New York: Basic Books.

Lie, D. C., Song, H., Colamarino, S. A., Ming, G. L., & Gage, F. H. (2004). Neurogenesis in the adult brain: New strategies for central nervous system diseases. *Annual Review of Pharmacology & Toxicology, 44,* 399–421.

Lieb, K., Zanarini, M. C., Schmahl, C., Linehan, M. M., & Bohus, M. (2004). Borderline personality disorder. *Lancet, 364,* 453–461.

Lieberman, J. A., & Koreen, A. R. (1993). Neurochemistry and neuroendocrinology of schizophrenia: A selective review. *Schizophrenia Bulletin, 2,* 371–428.

Liem, E. B., Lin, C. M., Suleman, M. I., Doufas, A. G., Gregg, R. G., Veauthier, J. M., et al. (2004). Anesthetic requirement is increased in redheads. *Anesthesiology, 101,* 279–283.

Lilienfeld, S. O. (1994). Conceptual problems in the assessment of psychopathy. *Clinical Psychology Review, 14,* 17–38.

Lilienfeld, S. O. (1997). The relation of anxiety sensitivity to higher and lower order personality dimensions: Implications for the etiology of panic attacks. *Journal of Abnormal Psychology, 106*(4), 539–544.

Lilienfeld, S. O. (1999a, March/April). ABC's *20/20* features segment on "goggle therapy" for depression and anxiety. *Skeptical Inquirer, 23,* 8–9.

Lilienfeld, S. O. (1999b). Projective measures of personality and psychopathology: How well do they work? *Skeptical Inquirer, 23,* 32–39.

Lilienfeld, S. O. (1999c, November/December). New analyses raise doubts about replicability of ESP findings. *Skeptical Inquirer, 24,* 9–10.

Lilienfeld, S. O. (2007). Psychological treatments that can cause harm. *Perspectives on Psychological Science, 2*, 53–70.

Lilienfeld, S. O., & Arkowitz, H. (2007). Autism: An epidemic? *Scientific American Mind, 18*(2), 82–83.

Lilienfeld, S. O., & Landfield, K. (2008). Issues in diagnosis: Categorical vs. dimensional. In W. E. Craighead, D. J. Miklowitz, & L.W. Craighead (Eds.), *Psychopathology: History, diagnosis, and empirical foundations* (pp. 1–33). Hoboken, NJ: Wiley.

Lilienfeld, S. O., & Lynn, S. J. (2003). Dissociative identity disorder: Multiple personalities, multiple controversies. In S. O. Lilienfeld, S. J. Lynn, & J. M. Lohr (Eds.), *Science and pseudoscience in clinical psychology* (pp. 109–143). New York: Guilford Press.

Lilienfeld, S. O., Lynn, S. J., Kirsch, I., Chaves, J. F., Sarbin, T. R., Ganaway, G. K., et al. (1999). Dissociative identity disorder and the sociocognitive model: Recalling the lessons of the past. *Psychological Bulletin, 125*, 507–523.

Lilienfeld, S. O., Lynn, S. J., & Lohr, J. M. (2003). *Science and pseudoscience in clinical psychology*. New York: Guilford Press.

Lilienfeld, S. O., & Marino, L. (1995). Mental disorder as a Roschian concept: A critique of Wakefield's "harmful dysfunction" analysis. *Journal of Abnormal Psychology, 104*, 411–420.

Lilienfeld, S. O., Ruscio, J. P., & Lynn, S. J. 2008. *Navigating the mindfield: A user's guide to distinguishing science from pseudoscience in mental health*. Amherst, NY: Prometheus Books.

Lilienfeld, S. O., & Waldman, I. D. (2000, November 13). Race and IQ: What the science says. *Emory Report*, 3.

Lilienfeld, S. O., Waldman, I. D., & Israel, A. C. (1994). A critical examination of the use of the term "comorbidity" in psychopathology research. *Clinical Psychology: Science and Practice, 1*, 71–83.

Lilienfeld, S. O., Wood, J. M., & Garb, H. N. (2001). The scientific status of projective techniques. *Psychological Science in the Public Interest, 1*, 27–66.

Limb, C. J. (2006). Structural and functional neural correlates of music perception. *Anatomical Record, Part A, Discoveries in Molecular, Cellular, and Evolutionary Biology, 288*, 435–446.

Lindeman, M. (1998). Motivation, cognition and pseudoscience. *Scandinavian Journal of Psychology, 39*, 257–265.

Lindle, R. S., Metter, E. J., Lynch, N. A., Fleg, J. L., Fozard, J. L., Tobin, J., et al. (1997). Age and gender comparisons of muscle strength in 654 women and men aged 20–93 yr. *Journal of Applied Physiology, 83*, 1581–1587.

Lindsay, R. C. L., & Wells, G. L. (1985). Improving eyewitness identifications from lineups: Simultaneous versus sequential lineup presentation. *Journal of Applied Psychology, 70*(3), 556–564.

Linehan, M. M. (1993). *Cognitive behavioral treatment of borderline personality disorder*. New York: Guilford Press.

Linehan, M. M., Heard, H. L., & Armstrong, H. E. (1993). Naturalistic follow-up of a behavioral treatment for chronically parasuicidal borderline patients. *Archives of General Psychiatry, 50*, 971–974.

Lisman, J., & Raghavachari, S. (2006). A unified model of the presynaptic and postsynaptic changes during LTP at CA1 synapses. *Science STKE, 10*, 11.

Lisman, S. A. (1974). Alcohol "black-out": State dependent learning? *Archives of General Psychiatry, 30*, 46–53.

Littlewood, R. (2004). Unusual psychiatric syndromes: An introduction. *Psychiatry, 3*, 1–3.

Littrell, J. (1998). Is the experience of painful emotion therapeutic? *Clinical Psychology Review, 18*, 71–102.

Litz, B. T., Gray, M. J., Bryant, R., & Adler, A. B. (2002). Early intervention for trauma: Current status and future directions. *Clinical Psychology: Science and Practice, 9*, 112–134.

Lock, M. (1998). Menopause: Lessons from anthropology. *Psychosomatic Medicine, 60*, 410–419.

Locke, E. A. (2005). Why emotional intelligence is an invalid concept. *Journal of Organizational Behavior, 26*, 425–431.

Loehlin, J. C. (1992). *Genes and environment in personality development*. Newbury Park, CA: Sage.

Loehlin, J. C., Lindzey, G., & Spuhler, J. N. (1977). *Race differences in intelligence*. San Francisco: W. H. Freeman.

Loevinger, J. (1987). *Paradigms of personality*. New York: W. H. Freeman.

Loevinger, J. (1993). Conformity and conscientiousness: One factor or two stages? In D. C. Funder, R. D. Parke, C. Tomlinson-Keasey, & K. Widaman (Eds.), *Studying lives through time: Personality and development* (pp. 189–205). Washington, DC: American Psychological Association.

Loewenstein, J., Thompson, L., & Gentner, D. (1999). Analogical encoding facilitates knowledge transfer in negotiation. *Psychonomic Bulletin & Review, 6*, 586–597.

Loftus, E. F. (1979). *Eyewitness testimony*. Cambridge, MA: Harvard University Press.

Loftus, E. F. (1993). The reality of repressed memories. *American Psychologist, 48*, 518–537.

Loftus, E. F., Coan, J. A., & Pickrell, J. E. (1996). Manufacturing false memories using bits of reality. In L. M. Reder (Ed.), *Implicit memory and metacognition* (pp. 195–220). Mahwah, NJ: Lawrence Erlbaum Associates.

Loftus, E. F., Miller, D. G., & Burns, H. J. (1978). Semantic integration of verbal information into a visual memory. *Human Learning and Memory, 4*, 19–31.

Loftus E. F., & Palmer, J. C. (1974). Reconstruction of automobile destruction: An example of the interaction between language and memory. *Journal of Learning and Verbal Behavior, 13*, 585–589.

Loftus, E. F., & Pickrell, J. E. (1995). The formation of false memories. *Psychiatric Annals, 25*, 720–725.

Lohr, J. M., Hooke, W., Gist, R., & Tolin, D. F. (2003). Novel and controversial treatments for trauma-related disorders. In S. O. Lilienfeld, S. J. Lynn, & J. M. Lohr (Eds.), *Science and pseudoscience in clinical psychology* (pp. 243–272). New York: Guilford Press.

Lohr, J. M., Olatunji, B. O., Baumeister, R. F., & Bushman, B. J. (2007). The pseudopsychology of anger venting and empirically supported alternatives that do no harm. *Scientific Review of Mental Health Practice 5*, 54–65.

Lohr, J. M., Tolin, D. F., & Lilienfeld, S. O. (1998). Efficacy of eye movement desensitization and reprocessing. *Behavior Therapy, 29*, 123–156.

Longley, J., & Pruitt, D. G. (1980). Groupthink: A critique of Janis's theory. In L. Wheeler (Ed.), *Review of personality and social psychology* (Vol. I, pp. 74–93). Beverly Hills, CA: Sage.

Lopez, S. R., Nelson Hipke, K., Polo, A. J., Jenkins, J. H., Karno, M., Vaughn, C., et al. (2004). Ethnicity, expressed emotion, attributions, and course of schizophrenia: Family warmth matters. *Journal of Abnormal Psychology, 113*, 428–439.

Loprinzi, C. L., Levitt, R., Barton, E. L., Sloan, J. A., Atherton, P. J., Smith, D. J., et al. (2005). Evaluation of shark cartilage in patients with advanced cancer: A North Central Center Cancer Treatment Group trial. *Cancer, 104*, 176–182.

Lorber, M. F. (2004). Autonomic psychophysiology of aggression, psychopathy, and conduct problems: A meta-analysis. *Psychological Bulletin, 130*, 531–552.

Lorenz, K. (1937). The nature of instinct. In C. H. Schiller (Ed.), *Instinctive behavior: The development of a modern concept*. New York: International Universities Press.

Lortie-Lussier, M., Cote, L., & Vachon, J. (2000). The consistency and continuity hypotheses revisited through the dreams of women at two periods of their lives. *Dreaming, 10*, 67–76.

Lourenco, O., & Machado, A. (1996). In defense of Piaget's theory: A reply to 10 common criticisms. *Psychological Review, 103*, 143–164.

Lowe, M. R., Gleaves, D. H., & Murphy-Eberenz, K. P. (1998). On the relation of dieting and bingeing in bulimia nervosa. *Journal of Abnormal Psychology, 107*, 263–271.

Lowe, M. R., & Levine, A. S. (2005). Eating motives and the controversy over dieting: Eating less than needed versus less than wanted. *Obesity Research, 13*, 797–806.

Lubinski, D. (2000). Scientific and social significance of assessing individual differences: Sinking shafts at a few critical points. In S. T. Fiske (Ed.), *Annual Review of Psychology, 51*, 404–444.

Lubinski, D., & Humphreys, L. G. (1992). Some bodily and medical correlates of mathematical giftedness and commensurate levels of socioeconomic status. *Intelligence, 16*, 99–115.

Luborsky, L., Crits-Christoph, P., McLellan, T., Woody, G., Piper, W., Imber, S., et al. (1986). Do therapists vary much in their success? Findings from four outcome studies. *American Journal of Orthopsychiatry, 56*, 501–512.

Luborsky, L., McLellan, A. T., Diguer, L., Woody, G., & Seligman, D. A. (1997). The psychotherapist matters: Comparison of outcomes across twenty-two therapists and seven patient samples. *Clinical Psychology: Science and Practice, 4*, 53–65.

Luborsky, L., Mellon, J., van Ravenswaay, P., Childress, A. R., Colen, K., Hole, A., et al. (1985). A verification of Freud's grandest clinical hypothesis: The transference. *Clinical Psychology Review, 5*, 231–246.

Luchies, C. W., Schiffman, J., Richards, L. G., Thompson, M. R., Bazuin, D., & DeYoung, A. J. (2002). Effects of age, step direction, and reaction condition on the ability to step quickly. *Journals of Gerontology: Series A: Biological Sciences and Medical Sciences, 57A*, M246–M249.

Luchins, A. S. (1946). Classroom experiments on mental set. *American Journal of Psychology, 59*, 295–298.

Luchins, D. J., Weinberger, D. R., & Wyatt, R. J. (1982). Schizophrenia and cerebral asymmetry detected by computed tomography. *American Journal of Psychiatry, 139*, 753–757.

Ludwig, A. M., Brandsma, J. M., Wilbur, C. B., Bendfeldt, F., & Jameson, D. H. (1972). The objective study of a multiple personality: Or, are four heads better than one? *Archives of General Psychiatry, 26*, 298–310.

Luna, B., & Sweeney, J. A. (2004). The emergence of collaborative brain function: fMRI studies of the development of response inhibition. In R. E. Dahl & L. P. Spear (Eds.), *Adolescent brain development: Vulnerabilities and opportunities* (pp. 296–309). New York: New York Academy of Sciences.

Luo, Q., Nakic, M., Wheatley, T., Richell, R., Martin, A., & Blair, R. J. R. (2006). The neural basis of implicit moral attitude—An IAT study using event-related fMRI. *NeuroImage, 30*(4), 1449–1457.

Luo, S., & Klohnen, E. C. (2005). Assortative mating and marital quality in newlyweds: A couple-centered approach. *Journal of Personality and Social Psychology, 88*, 304–325.

Luria, A. (1976). *Cognitive development: Its cultural and social foundations*. (M. Lopez-Morillas & L. Solotaroff, Trans.). Cambridge, MA: Harvard University Press.

Luscher, M., & Scott, I. (1969) *The Luscher Color Test*. New York: Random House.

Lykken, D. T. (1995). *The antisocial personalities*. Mahwah, NJ: Lawrence Erlbaum.

Lykken, D. T. (1998). *A tremor in the blood: Uses and abuses of the lie detector* (2nd ed.). Reading, MA: Perseus.

Lynch, T. R., Trost, W. T., Salsman, N., & Linehan, M. M. (2007). Dialectical behavior therapy for borderline personality disorder. *Annual Review of Clinical Psychology, 3*, 181–205.

Lynn, R. (1996) *Dysgenics: Genetic deterioration in modern populations*. Westport, CT: Praeger.

Lynn, R. (2003). The intelligence of American Jews. *Personality and Individual Differences, 36*(1), 201–206.

Lynn, R. (2006). *Race differences in intelligence: An evolutionary analysis*. Augusta, GA: Washington Summit Books.

Lynn, R., & Irwing, P. (2004). Sex differences on the Progressive Matrices: A meta-analysis. *Intelligence, 32*, 481–498.

Lynn, S. J. (1978). Three theories of self-disclosure exchange. *Journal of Experimental Social Psychology, 14*, 466–479.

Lynn, S. J., & Frauman, D. (1985). Group psychotherapy. In S. J. Lynn, & J. P. Garske (Eds.), *Contemporary psychotherapies: Models and methods* (pp. 419–458). Columbus, OH: Merrill Publishing.

Lynn, S. J., & Kirsch, I. (2006). *Essentials of clinical hypnosis: An evidence-based approach*. Washington, DC: American Psychological Association.

Lynn, S. J., Kirsch, I., Crowley, M., & Campion, A. (2006a). Eating disorders and obesity with Maryellen Crowley and Anna Campion. In S. J. Lynn & I. Kirsch (Eds.), *Essentials of clinical hypnosis: An evidence-based approach* (pp. 99–120). Washington, DC: American Psychological Association.

Lynn, S. J., Kirsch, I., & Hallquist, M. (2008). Social cognitive theories of hypnosis. In M. R. Nash & A. M. Barnier (Eds.), *Oxford handbook of hypnosis*. New York: Oxford Press.

Lynn, S. J., Lock, T., Loftus, E. F., Krackow, E., & Lilienfeld, S. O. (2003a). The remembrance of things past: Problematic memory recovery techniques in psychotherapy. In S. O. Lilienfeld, S. J. Lynn, & J. Lohr (Eds.), *Science and pseudoscience in clinical psychology* (pp. 205–239). New York: Guilford Press.

Lynn, S. J., Matthews, A., Williams, J. C., Hallquist, M. N., & Lilienfeld, S. O. (2007). Some forms of psychopathology are partly socially constructed. In S. O. Lilienfeld & W. T. O'Donohue (Eds.), *The great ideas of clinical science: 17 principles that every mental health professional should know*. New York: Routledge.

Lynn, S. J., Nash, M. R., Rhue, J. W., Frauman, D. C., & Sweeney, C. A. (1984). Nonvolition, expectancies, and hypnotic rapport. *Journal of Abnormal Psychology, 93*, 295–303.

Lynn, S. J., & Pintar, J. (1997). A social narrative model of dissociative identity disorder. *Australian Journal of Clinical and Experimental Hypnosis, 25*, 1–7.

Lynn, S. J., Pintar, J., Sandberg, D., Fite, R. F., Ecklund, K., & Stafford, J. (2003b). Towards a social narrative model of revictimization. In L. Koenig, A. O'Leary, L. Doll, & W. Pequenat (Eds.), *From child sexual assault to adult sexual risk: Trauma, revictimization, and intervention*. Washington, DC: American Psychological Association.

Lynn, S. J., & Rhue, J. W. (1991). An integrative model of hypnosis. In S. J. Lynn & J. W. Rhue (Eds.), *Theories of hypnosis: Current models and perspectives* (pp. 397–438). New York: Guilford Press.

Lynn, S. J., Surya Das, L., Hallquist, M. N., & Williams, J. C. (2006b). Mindfulness, acceptance, and hypnosis: Cognitive and clinical perspectives. *International Journal of Clinical and Experimental Hypnosis, 54*, 143–166.

Lynn, S. J., Weekes, J. R., & Milano, M. (1989). Reality versus suggestion: Pseudomemory in hypnotizable and simulating subjects. *Journal of Abnormal Psychology, 98*, 75–79.

Lynskey, M. T., Heath, A. C., Bucholz, K. K., Slutske, W. S., Madden, P. A. F., Nelson, E. C., et al. (2003). Escalation of drug use in early-onset cannabis users vs. co-twin controls. *Journal of the American Medical Association, 289,* 427–433.

Lytton, H., & Romney, D. M. (1991). Parents' differential socialization of boys and girls: A meta-analysis. *Psychological Bulletin, 109,* 267–296.

Lyubomirsky, S., King, L. A., & Diener, E. (2005). The benefits of frequent positive affect: Does happiness lead to success? *Psychological Bulletin, 131,* 803–855.

M

Maas, J. B. (1999). *Power sleep: The revolutionary program that prepares your mind for peak performance.* New York: Collins.

Maccoby, E. E., & Jacklin, C. N. (1974). *Psychology of sex differences.* Stanford, CA: Stanford University Press.

Maccoby, E. E., & Jacklin, C. N. (1980). Sex differences in aggression: A rejoinder. *Child Development, 51,* 964–980.

Maccoby, E. E., & Martin, J. A. (1983). Socialization in the context of the family: Parent–child interaction. In P. H. Mussen (Ed.) & E. M. Hetherington (Vol. Ed.), *Handbook of child psychology: Vol. 4. Socialization, personality, and social development* (4th ed., pp. 1–101). New York: Wiley.

Machover, K. (1949). *Personality projection in the drawing of the human figure.* Springfield, IL: Charles C Thomas.

MacKillop, J., Lisman, S. A., Weinstein, A., & Rosenbaum, D. (2003). Controversial treatments for alcoholism. In S. O. Lilienfeld, S. J. Lynn, & J. W. Lohr (Eds.), *Science and pseudoscience in clinical psychology* (pp. 273–306). New York: Guilford.

MacKillop, J., Lynn, S. J., & Meyer, E. (2004). The impact of stage hypnosis on audience members and participants. *International Journal of Clinical and Experimental Hypnosis, 52,* 313–329.

Macmillan, M. (2000). Restoring Phineas Gage: A 150th retrospective. *Journal of the History of Neuroscience, 9,* 46–66.

Macrae, C. N., & Bodenhausen, G. V. (2000). Social cognition: Thinking categorically about others. *Annual Review of Psychology, 51,* 93–120.

Madden, G. J., Ewan, E. E., & Lagorio, C. H. (2007). Toward an animal model of gambling: Delay discounting and the allure of unpredicatable outcomes. *Journal of Gambling Studies, 23,* 63–83.

Maddi, S. R. (2002). The story of hardiness: Twenty years of theorizing, research, and practice. *Consulting Psychology Journal, 54,* 173–185.

Maddi, S. R. (2004). On hardiness and other pathways to resilience. *American Psychologist, 60,* 261–262.

Maddi, S. R., & Kobasa, S. C. (1984). *The hardy executive: Health under stress.* Homewood, IL: Dow Jones-Irwin.

Madsen, K. M., Hviid, A., Vestergaard, M., Schendel, D., Wohlfart, J., Thorsen, P., et al. (2002). A population-based study of measles, mumps and rubella vaccination and autism. *New England Journal of Medicine, 347,* 1477–1482.

Maes, H. M., Neale, M. C., & Eaves, L. J. (1997). Genetic and environmental factors in relative body weight and human adiposity. *Behavior Genetics, 27,* 325–351.

Maguire, E. A., Gadian, D. G., Johnsrude, I. S., Good, C. D., Ashburner, J., Frackowiak, R. S., et al. (2000). Navigation-related structural change in the hippocampi of taxi drivers. *Proceedings of the National Academy of Sciences U.S.A., 97,* 4398–4403.

Maier, I. C., & Schwab, M. E. (2006). Sprouting, regeneration and circuit formation in the injured spinal cord: Factors and activity. *Philosophical Transactions of the Royal Society London B Biological Sciences, 361,* 1611–1634.

Main, M., & Cassidy, J. (1988). Categories of response to reunion with the parent at age 6: Predictable from infant attachment classifications and stable over a 1-month period. *Developmental Psychology, 24,* 415–426.

Malcom, K. (1989). Patients' perceptions and knowledge of electroconvulsive therapy. *Psychiatric Bulletin, 13,* 161–165.

Malina, R. M., & Bouchard, C. (1991). *Growth, maturation, and physical activity.* Champaign, IL: Human Kinetics.

Malinoski, P., Lynn, S. J., & Sivec, H. (1998). The assessment, validity, and determinants of early memory reports: A critical review. In S. J. Lynn & K. McConkey (Eds.), *Truth in memory* (pp. 109–136). New York: Guilford.

Mandiyan, V. S., Coats. J. K., & Shah, N. M. (2005). Deficits in sexual and aggressive behaviors in Cnga2 mutant mice. *Nature Neuroscience, 8,* 1660–1662.

Manning, R., Levine, M. & Collins, A. (2007). The Kitty Genovese murder and the social psychology of helping: The parable of the 38 witnesses. *American Psychologist, 62,* 555–562.

Mantell, D. M. (1971). The potential for violence in Germany. *Journal of Social Issues, 27,* 101–112.

Maquet, P., & Franck, G. (1997). REM Sleep and the amygdala. *Molecular Psychiatry, 2,* 195–196.

Maren, S. (2005). Synaptic mechanisms of associative memory in the amygdala. *Neuron, 15,* 783–786.

Marian, V., & Neisser, U. (2000). Language-dependent recall of autobiographical memories. *Journal of Experimental Psychology: General, 129,* 361–368.

Marieb, E. N., & Hoehn, K. (2007). *Human anatomy and physiology* (7th ed.) San Francisco: Pearson.

Marino, L., & Lilienfeld, S. O. (1998). Dolphin-assisted therapy: Flawed data, flawed conclusions. *Anthrozoos, 11*(4), 194–200.

Marino, L., & Lilienfeld, S. O. (2007). Dolphin-assisted therapy: More flawed data and more flawed conclusions. *Anthrozoos, 20,* 239–249.

Marino, L., McShea, D. W., & Uhen, M. D. (2004). Origin and evolution of large brains in toothed whales. *Anatomical Record Part A: Discoveries in Molecular, Cellular, & Evolutionary Biology, 281,* 1247–1255.

Maris, R. W. (1992). The relationship of nonfatal suicide attempts to completed suicides. In R. W. Maris, A. L. Berman, J. T. Maltsberger, & R. I. Yufit (Eds.), *Assessment and prediction of suicide* (pp. 362–380). New York: Guilford Press.

Markman, A. B., & Gentner, D. (1993). Structural alignment during similarity comparisons. *Cognitive Psychology, 25,* 431–467.

Marks, R. P., Swinson, M., Basoglu, K., & Kuch, H. (1993). Alpraxolam and exposure alone and combined in panic disorder with agoraphobia. *British Journal of Psychiatry, 162,* 788–799.

Marlatt, G. A. (1983). The controlled-drinking controversy: A commentary. *American Psychologist, 10,* 1097–1110.

Marshall, G. D., & Zimbardo, P. G. (1979). Affective consequences of inadequately explained arousal. *Journal of Personality and Social Psychology, 37,* 970–988.

Marshall, J. (1969). *Law and psychology in conflict.* New York: Anchor Books.

Martin, D. (2006, November 20). *The truth about happiness may surprise you.* Retrieved from www.cnn.com/2006/HEALTH/conditions/11/10/happiness.overview/index.html

Martin, N. G., Eaves, L. J., Heath, A. C., Jardine, R., Feingold, L. M., & Eysenck, H. J. (1986). Transmission of social attitudes. *Proceedings of the National Academy of Sciences, 83,* 4364–4368.

Martino, S. C., Collins, R. L., Elliott, M. C., Strachman, A., Kanouse, D. E., & Berry, S. H. (2006). Exposure to degrading versus non-degrading music lyrics and sexual behavior among youth. *Pediatrics, 118,* 430–441.

Martinot, M.-L., Bragulat, V., Artiges, E., Dolle, F., Hinnen, F., Jouvent, R., et al. (2001). Decreased presynaptic dopamine function in the left caudate of depressed patients with affective flattening and psychomotor retardation. *American Journal of Psychiatry, 158,* 314–316.

Maruta, T., Colligan, R. C., Malinchoc, M., & Offord, K. P. (2000). Optimists vs pessimists: Survival rate among medical patients over a 30-year period. *Mayo Clinic Proceedings, 75,* 140–143.

Mashour, G. A., Walker, E. E. & Martuza, R. L. (2005). Psychosurgery: Past, present, and future. Brain Research Reviews, 48, 409–419.

Maslach, C. (1979). Negative and emotional biasing of unexplained arousal. *Journal of Personality and Social Psychology, 37,* 953–969.

Maslow, A. H. (1954). *Motivation and personality.* New York: Harper and Row.

Maslow, A. H. (1971). *The farther reaches of human nature.* New York: Viking Press.

Mastekaasa, A. (1994). The subjective well-being of the previously married: The importance of unmarried cohabitation and time since widowhood or divorce. *Social Forces, 73,* 665–692.

Masters, W. H., & Johnson, V. E. (1966). *Human sexual response.* Boston: Little, Brown.

Matarazzo, J. D. (1980). Behavioral health and behavioral medicine: Frontiers for a new health psychology. *American Psychologist, 35,* 807–817.

Matarazzo, J. D. (1983). The reliability of psychiatric and psychological diagnosis. *Clinical Psychology Review, 3,* 103–145.

Mathews, A., Richards, A., & Eysenck, M. W. (1989). Interpretation of homophones related to threat in anxiety states. *Journal of Abnormal Psychology, 98,* 31–34.

Mathews, V., Wang, Y., Kalnin, A. J., Mosier, K. M., Dunn, D. W., & Kronenberger, W. G. (2006). *Short-term effects of violent video game playing: An fMRI study.* Annual Meeting of the Radiological Society of North America, Chicago, IL.

Matsumoto, D., & Willingham, B. (2006). The thrill of victory and the agony of defeat: Spontaneous expressions of medal winners of the 2004 Athens Olympic Games. *Journal of Personality and Social Psychology, 91,* 568–581.

Matsumoto, D., Yoo, S. H., Hirayama, S., & Petrova, G. (2005). Development and validation of a measure of display rule knowledge: The Display Rule Assessment Inventory. *Emotion, 5,* 23–40.

Mattes, R. D., Hollis, J., Hayes, D., & Stunkard, A. J. (2005). Appetite measurement and manipulation misgivings. *Journal of the American Dietetic Association, 105,* 87–97.

Matthews, A., & MacLeod, C. (2005). Cognitive vulnerability to emotional disorders. In S. Nolen-Hoeksema, T. D. Cannon, & T. Widiger (Eds.), *Annual Review of Clinical Psychology* (Vol. 1, pp. 167–196). Palo Alto, CA: Annual Reviews.

Matthews, D. A., Larson, D. B., & Barry, C. P. (1993). *The faith factor: An annotated bibliography of clinical research on spiritual subjects* (Vol. 1). Rockville, MD: National Institute for Mental Healthcare Research.

Matthews, G., Zeidner, M., & Roberts, R. (2002). *Emotional intelligence: Science and myth.* London: MIT Press.

Matthews, K. A., Gump, B. B., Harris, K. F., Haney, T. L., & Barefoot, J. C. (2004). Hostile behaviors predict cardiovascular mortality among men enrolled in the Multiple Risk Factor Intervention Trial. *Circulation, 109,* 66–70.

Max, D. T. (2007, January 7). Happiness 101. *New York Times.*

Retrieved from www.nytimes.com/2007/01/07/magazine/07happiness.t.html?ex=1183608000&en=946a9bb65d8be3b7&ei=5070.

Mayer-Gross, W., Slater, E., & Roth, M. (1969). *Clinical psychiatry* (3rd ed.). Baltimore: Williams & Wilkins. Revised and reprinted 1977, Balliere, Tindall, London.

Mayo, E. (1933). *The human problems of an industrial civilization.* New York: Macmillan.

Mazur, A., & Rosa, E. (1977). An empirical test of McClelland's "achieving society" theory. *Social Forces, 55,* 769–774.

Mazure, C. M. (1998). Life stressors as risk factors in depression. *Clinical Psychology: Science and Practice, 5,* 291–313.

Mazzoni, G. A. L., Loftus, E. F., & Kirsch, I. (2001). Changing beliefs about implausible autobiographical events: A little plausibility goes a long way. *Journal of Experimental Psychology: Applied, 7,* 31–39.

McCabe, D. P., & Castel, A. D. (2008). Seeing is believing: The effect of brain images on judgements of scientific reasoning. *Cognition.*

McClelland, D. C. (1961). *The achieving society.* Princeton, NJ: Van Nostrand.

McClelland, D. C., Atkinson, J. W., Clark, R. A., & Lowell, E. L. (1953). *The achievement motive.* New York: Appleton-Century-Crofts.

McClelland, D. C., Atkinson, J. W., Clark, R. A., & Lowell, E. L. (1958). A scoring manual for the achievement motive. In J. W. Atkinson (Ed.), *Motives in fantasy, action, and society* (pp. 179–204). Princeton, NJ: Van Nostrand.

McClelland, J. L. (1995). A connectionist perspective on knowledge and development. In T. J. Simon & G. S. Halford (Eds.), *Developing cognitive competence: New approaches to process modeling* (pp. 157–204). Hillsdale, NJ: Erlbaum.

McClelland, J. L., & Plaut, D. C. (1993). Computational approaches to cognition: Top-down approaches. *Current Opinion in Neurobiology, 3,* 209–216.

McCloskey, M., Wible, C. G., & Cohen, N. J. (1988). Is there a special flashbulb-memory mechanism? *Journal of Experimental Psychology: General, 117,* 171–181.

McClure, E. B. (2000). A meta-analytic review of sex differences in facial expression processing and their development in infants, children, and adolescents. *Psychological Bulletin, 126,* 424–453.

McConnell, J. V. (1962). Memory transfer through cannibalism in planarians. *Journal of Neuropsychiatry, 3* (Suppl. 1), 542–548.

McCord, J. (2006). Punishments and alternate routes to crime prevention. In A. K. Hess & I. B. Weiner, (Eds.), *The handbook of forensic psychology* (3rd ed., pp. 701–721). Hoboken, NJ: John Wiley & Sons.

McCrae, R. R., & Costa, P. T. (1994). The stability of personality: Observation and evaluations. *Current Directions in Psychological Science, 3,* 173–175.

McCrae, R. R., & Costa, P. T. (1995). Trait explanations in personality psychology. *European Journal of Personality, 9,* 231–252.

McCrae, R. R., & Costa, P. T. (1997). Personality trait structure as a human universal. *American Psychologist, 52,* 509–516.

McDaniel, M. A. (2005) Big-brained people are smarter: A meta-analysis of the relationship between in vivo brain volume and intelligence. *Intelligence, 33,* 337–346.

McDaniel, M. A., Maier, S. F., & Einstein, G. O. (2002). "Brain-specific" nutrients: A memory cure? *Psychological Science in the Public Interest, 3,* 12–38.

McFall, R. M. (2006). Doctoral training in clinical psychology. *Annual Review of Clinical Psychology, 2,* 21–49.

McGilly, K., & Siegler, R. S. (1989). How children choose among serial recall strategies. *Child Development, 60,* 172–182.

McGrath, J. (1991). Ordering thoughts on thought disorder. *British Journal of Psychiatry, 158,* 307–316.

McGrath, M. E. (1984). 1st-person account—Where did I go? *Schizophrenia Bulletin, 10*(4), 638–640.

McGue, M. (1999). The behavioral genetics of alcoholism. *Current Directions in Psychological Science, 8,* 109–115.

McGue, M., & Lykken, D. T. (1992). Genetic influence on risk of divorce. *Psychological Science, 3,* 368–373.

McGuffin, P., Rijsdijk, F., Andrew, M., Sham, P., Katz, R., & Cardino, A. (2003). The heritability of bipolar affective disorder and the genetic relationship to unipolar depression. *Archives of General Psychiatry, 60*(5), 497–502.

McGuire, W. J. (1964). Inducing resistance to persuasion: Some contemporary approaches. In L. Berkowitz (Ed.), *Advances in experimental social psychology* (Vol. 1, pp. 191–229). San Diego, CA: Academic Press.

McGuire, W. J., & Papageorgis, D. (1961). The relative efficacy of various types of prior belief-defense in producing immunity against persuasion. *Journal of Abnormal and Social Psychology, 62,* 327–337.

McGurk, H., & MacDonald, J. (1976). Hearing lips and seeing voices. *Nature, 264,* 746–748.

McHugh, P. R. (1993). Multiple personality disorder. *Harvard Mental Health Newsletter, 10*(3), 4–6.

McKinney, M., & Jacksonville, M. C. (2005). Brain cholinergic vulnerability: Relevance to behavior and disease. *Biochemical Pharmacology, 70,* 1115–1124.

McMonagle, T., & Sultana, A. (2000). Token economy for schizophrenia. *Cochrane Database of Systematic Reviews*, Issue 3. Art. No.: CD001473. DOI: 10.1002/14651858.CD001473.

McNally, R. J. (1987). Preparedness and phobias—A review. *Psychological Bulletin, 101*(2), 283–303.

McNally, R. J. (2003). *Remembering trauma.* Cambridge, MA: Belknap Press.

McNally, R. J., Bryant, R. A., & Ehlers, A. (2003). Does early psychological intervention promote recovery from posttraumatic stress? *Psychological Science in the Public Interest, 4,* 45–79.

McNally, R. M., & Eke, M. (1996). Anxiety sensitivity, suffocation fear, and breath-holding duration as predictors of response to carbon dioxide challenge. *Journal of Abnormal Psychology, 105,* 146–149.

McNamara, H. J., Long, J. B., & Wike, E. L. (1956). Learning without response under two conditions of external cues. *Journal of Comparative and Physiological Psychology, 49*(5), 477–480.

McNeil, D. E., Arkowitz, H., & Pritchard, B. E. (1987). The response of others to face-to-face interaction with depressed patients. *Journal of Abnormal Psychology, 96,* 341–344.

McNiel, D. E., Eisner, J. P., & Binder, R. L. (2000). The relationship between command hallucinations and violence. *Psychiatric Services, 51,* 1288–1292.

McQuiston-Surrett, D., Malpass, R. S., & Tredoux, C. G. (2006). Sequential vs. simultaneous lineups: A review of methods, data, and theory. *Psychology, Public Policy and Law, 12*(2), 137–169.

Meads, C., & Nouwen, A. (2005). Does emotional disclosure have any effects? A systematic review of the literature with meta-analyses. *International Journal of Technology Assessment in Health Care, 21,* 153–164.

Mednick, S. A., Machon, R. A., Huttunen, M. O., & Bonett, D. (1988). Adult schizophrenia following prenatal exposure to an influenza epidemic. *Archives of General Psychiatry, 45,* 189–192.

Meehl, P. E. (1956). Wanted: A good cookbook. *American Psychologist, 11,* 263–272.

Meehl, P. E. (1962). Schizotaxia, schizotypy, and schizophrenia. *American Psychologist, 17,* 827–838.

Meehl, P. E. (1967). Theory-testing in psychology and physics: A methodological paradox. *Philosophy of Science, 34,* 103–115.

Meehl, P. E. (1972). Reactions, reflections, projections. In J. N. Butcher (Ed.), *Objective personality assessment: Changing perspectives* (pp. 131–189). New York: Academic Press.

Meehl, P. E., & Rosen, A. (1955). Antecedent probability and the efficiency of psychometric signs, patterns, or cutting scores. *Psychological Bulletin, 52,* 194–216.

Mehler, P. S. (2003). Bulimia nervosa. *New England Journal of Medicine, 349,* 875–881.

Meichenbaum, D. (1994). A clinical handbook/practical therapist manual for assessing and treating adults with post-traumatic stress disorder (PTSD). Clearwater, FL: Institute Press.

Meissner, C. A., & Brigham, J. C. (2001). Thirty years of investigating the own-race bias in memory for faces: A meta-analytic review. *Psychology, Public Policy, and Law, 7,* 3–35.

Mellinger, D. M., & Lynn, S. J. (2003). *The monster in the cave: How to face your fear and anxiety and live your life.* New York: Berkeley.

Melton, G. J. (1999). *Brainwashing and the cults: The rise and fall of a theory.* Retrieved October 29, 2007, from www.cesnur.org/testi/melton.htm.

Memon, A., Hope, L., & Bull, R. (2003). Exposure duration: Effects on eyewitness accuracy and confidence. *British Journal of Psychology, 94,* 339–354.

Menchola, B. L., Arkowitz, H., & Burke, B. L. (2007). Efficacy of self-administered treatments for depression and anxiety: A meta-analysis. *Professional Psychology: Research and Practice, 38,* 421–429.

Mendel, G. (1866). Versuche über Pflanzen-Hybriden. *Verhandlungen des naturforschenden Vereines in Brünn [Proceedings of the Natural History Society of Brünn], 4,* 1–47.

Mendelowicz, M.V., & Stein, M. B. (2000). Quality of life in individuals with anxiety disorders. *American Journal of Psychiatry, 157,* 669–682.

Menini, A., Picco, C., & Firestein, S. (1995). Quantal-like current fluctuations induced by odorants in olfactory receptor cells. *Nature, 373,* 435–437.

Menninger, K. (1958). *Theory of psychoanalytic technique.* New York: Basic Books.

Merckelbach, H., Devilly, G., & Rassin, E. (2002). Alters in dissociative identity disorder: Metaphors or genuine entities? *Clinical Psychology Review, 22,* 481–497.

Merskey, H. (1992). The manufacture of personalities: The production of multiple personality disorder. *British Journal of Psychiatry, 160,* 327–340.

Mervielde, I., De Clercq, B., De Fruyt, F., & Van Leeuwen, K. (2005). Temperament, personality, and developmental psychopathology as childhood antecedents of personality disorders. *Journal of Personality Disorders, 19*(2), 171–201.

Messick, S. (1992). Multiple intelligence or multilevel intelligence? Selective emphasis on distinctive properties of hierarchy: On Gardner's *Frames of Mind* and Sternberg's *Beyond IQ* in the context of theory and research on the structure of human abilities. *Psychological Inquiry, 3,* 365–384.

Metzler, J., & Shepard, R. N. (1974). Transformational studies of the internal representation of three-dimensional objects. In R. Solso (Ed.), *Theories in cognitive psychology: The Loyola Symposium* (pp. 147–201). Potomac, MD: Erlbaum.

Meyer, A. (Ed.). (1981). The Hamburg Short Psychotherapy Comparison Experiment. *Psychotherapy and Psycho-somatics, 35,* 81–207.

Michaels, J. W., Blommel, J. W., Brocato, R. M., Linkous, R. A., & Rowe, J. S. (1982). Social facilitation and inhibition in a natural setting. *Replications in Social Psychology, 2*, 21–24.

Miklowitz, D. J., & Johnson, S. L. (2006). The psychopathology and treatment of bipolar disorder. *Annual Review of Clinical Psychology, 2*, 199–235.

Milgram, S. (1963). Behavioral study of obedience. *Journal of Abnormal and Social Psychology, 67*, 371–378.

Milgram, S. (1964). Issues in the study of obedience: A reply to Baumrind. *American Psychologist, 19*, 848–852.

Milgram, S. (1974). *Obedience to authority: An experimental view.* New York: Harper & Row.

Miller, G. A. (1956). The magical number seven, plus or minus two: Some limits on our capacity for processing information. *Psychological Review, 63*, 81–97.

Miller, K. F., Smith, C. M., Zhu, J., & Zhang, H. (1995). Preschool origins of cross-national differences in mathematical competence: The role of number-naming systems. *Psychological Science, 6*, 56–60.

Miller, M. A., & Rahe, R. H. (1997). Life changes scaling for the 1990s. *Journal of Psychosomatic Research, 43*, 279–292.

Miller, S. D. (1989). Optical differences in cases of multiple personality disorder. *Journal of Nervous and Mental Disease, 177*, 480–486.

Miller, W. R., & Hester, R. K. (1980). Treating the problem drinker: Modern approaches. In W. R. Miller (Ed.), *The addictive behaviors: Treatment of alcoholism, drug abuse, smoking, and obesity* (pp. 11–141). Oxford, England: Pergamon Press.

Miller, Z. (1999, August 31). Music fertilizes the mind. *Atlanta Journal Constitution*, A17.

Mills, A., & Lynn, S. J. (2000). Past-life experiences. In E. Cardena, S. J. Lynn, & S. Krippner (Eds.), *The varieties of anomalous experience.* New York: Guilford.

Milner, B. (1964) Some effects of frontal lobectomy in man. In J. M. Warren & K. Akert (Eds.), *The frontal granular cortex and behavior.* New York: McGraw-Hill.

Milner, B. (1965) Visually guided maze learning in man: Effects of bilateral hippocampal, bilateral frontal and unilateral cerebral lesions. *Neuropsychologia, 3*, 317–338.

Milner, B. (1972). Disorders of learning and memory after temporal lobe lesions in man. *Clinical Neurosurgery, 19*, 421–446.

Milton, J., & Wiseman, R. (1999). Does psi exist? Lack of replication of an anomalous process of information transfer. *Psychological Bulletin, 125*(4), 387–391.

Mineka, S., & Cook, M. (1993). Mechanisms involved in the observational conditioning of fear. *Journal of Experimental Psychology: General, 122*, 23–38.

Minuchin, S. (1974). *Families and family therapy.* Cambridge, MA: Harvard University Press.

Miranda, F. S. B., Caballero, R. B., Gomez, M. N. G., & Zamorano, M. A. M. (1981). Obediencia a la authoridad [Obedience to authority]. *Psiquis, 2*, 212–221.

Mischel, W. (1968). *Personality and assessment.* New York: Wiley.

Mischel, W. (1973). Toward a cognitive social learning reconceptualization of personality. *Psychological Review, 80*, 252–283.

Mishkin, M., Malamut, B., & Bachevalier, J. (1984). Memories and habits: Two neural systems. In G. Lynch, J. McGaugh, & N. Weinberger (Eds.), *Neurobiology of Learning and Memory* (pp. 65–77). New York: Guilford.

Mitchell, D. B. (2006). Nonconscious priming after 17 years—Invulnerable implicit memory? *Psychological Science, 17*(11), 925–929.

Mitchell, J. E., & Peterson, C. B. (2007). *Assessment of eating disorders.* New York: Guilford Press.

Mitchell, S. A., & Black, M. J. (1995). *Freud and beyond: A history of modern psychoanalytic thought.* New York: Basic Books.

Mix, K. S. (1999). Similarity and numerical equivalence appearances count. *Cognitive Development, 14*, 269–297.

Mix, K. S., Huttenlocher, J., & Levine, S. C. (1996). Do preschool children recognize auditory-visual numerical correspondences? *Child Development, 67*, 1592–1608.

Moffitt, P. F., Kalucy, E. C., Kalucy, R. S., Baum, F. E., & Cooke, R. D. (1991). Sleep difficulties, pain, and other correlates. *Journal of Internal Medicine, 230*, 245–249.

Moffitt, T. E. (1983). The learning theory model of punishment: Implications for delinquency deterrence. *Criminal Justice and Behavior, 10*, 131–158.

Monte, C. F. (1995). *Beneath the mask: An introduction to theories of personality.* Fort Worth, TX: Harcourt Brace.

Monteith, M., & Winters, J. (2002). Why we hate. *Psychology Today, 35*(3), 44–52.

Monti, P. M., Gulliver, S. B., & Myers, M. G. (1994). Social skills training for alcoholics: Assessment and treatment. *Alcohol and Alcoholism, 29*, 627–637.

Montoya, R. M., Horton, R. S., & Kirchner, J. (2008). Is actual similarity necessary for attraction? A meta-analysis of actual and perceived similarity. *Journal of Social and Personal Relationships, 25*, 889–992.

Moody, R. A. (1975). *Life after life.* Covington, GA: Mockingbird Books.

Moody, R. A. (1977). *Reflections on life after life.* St. Simon's Island, GA: Mockingbird Books.

Mook, D. (1983). In defense of external invalidity. *American Psychologist, 38*, 379–387.

Moore, B., & Fine, B. (Eds.). (1995). *Psychoanalysis: The major concepts.* New Haven, CT: Yale University Press.

Moore, D. W. (2005, June 16). Three in four Americans believe in paranormal. *Gallup Poll News Service.* Retrieved February 20, 2007, from www.gallup.com/poll/content/default.aspx?ci=16915.

Moore, T., Rodman, H. R., Repp, A. B., Gross, C. G. (1995). Localization of visual stimuli after striate cortex damage in monkeys: parallels with human blindsight. *Proceedings of the National Academy of Sciences, 92*, 8215–8218.

Moore, T. E. (1992). Subliminal perception: Facts and fallacies. *Skeptical Inquirer, 16*, 273–281.

Moore, T. M., Scarpa, A., & Raine, A. (2002). A meta-analysis of serotonin metabolite 5-HIAA and antisocial behavior. *Aggressive Behavior, 28*, 299–316.

Morgan, C. D., & Murray, H. A. (1935). A method for investigating fantasies. *Archives of Neurology and Psychiatry, 34*, 289–304.

Morin, C. M., Hauri, P. J., Espic, C. A., Spielman, A. J., Buyesse, D. J., & Bootzin, R. R. (1999). Nonpharmacologic treatment of chronic insomnia. *Sleep, 22*, 1134–1155.

Morokuma, S., Fukushima, K., Kawai, N., Tomonaga, M., Satoh, S., & Nakano, H. (2004). Fetal habituation correlates with functional brain development. *Behavioural Brain Research, 153*(2), 459–463.

Morris, M. W., & Peng, K. (1994). Culture and cause: American and Chinese attributions for social and physical events. *Journal of Personality and Social Psychology, 67*, 949–971.

Morse, W. H., & Skinner, B. F. (1957). A second type of superstition in the pigeon. *American Journal of Psychology, 70*(2), 308–311.

Moscovitch, M., Rosenbaum, R. S., Gilboa, A., Addis, D. R., Westmacott, R., Grady, C., et al. (2005). Functional neuroanatomy of remote episodic, semantic and spatial memory: A unified account based on multiple trace theory. *Journal of Anatomy, 207*, 35–66.

Motivala, S., & Irwin, M. R. (2007). Sleep and immunity: Cytokine pathways linking sleep and health outcomes. *Psychological Science, 16*, 21–25.

Motta, R. W., Little, S. G., & Tobin, M. I. (1993). The use and abuse of human figure drawings. *School Psychology Quarterly, 8,* 162–169.

Moulton, S. T. , & Kosslyn, S. M. (2008). Using neuroimaging to resolve the Psi debate. *Journal of Cognitive Neuroscience, 20,* 182–192.

Mowrer, O. H. (1947). On the dual nature of learning—A re-interpretation of "conditioning" and "problem-solving." *Harvard Educational Review, 17,* 102–148.

Mrosovsky, N., & Powley, T. L. (1977). Set points for body weight and fat. *Behavioral Biology, 20,* 205–223.

Mrozek, D. K., & Kolarz, C. M. (1998). The effect of age on positive and negative affect: A developmental perspective on happiness. *Journal of Personality and Social Psychology, 75,* 1333–1349.

Mrozek, D. K., & Spiro, A. (2005). Change in life satisfaction during adulthood: Findings from the Veteran Affairs normative aging study. *Journal of Personality and Social Psychology, 88,* 189–192.

Msetfi, R. M., Murphy, R. A., Simpson, J., & Kornbrot, D. E. (2005). Depressive realism and outcome density bias in contingency judgments: The effect of the context and inter-trial interval. *Journal of Experimental Psychology: General, 134,* 10–22.

MTA Cooperative Group. (1999). Moderators and mediators of treatment response for children with attention-deficit/hyperactivity disorder. *Archives of General Psychiatry, 56,* 1088–1096.

Mueser, K. T., & Liberman, R. P. (1995). Behavior therapy in practice. In B. Bongar & L. E. Beutler (Eds.), *Comprehensive textbook of psychotherapy: Theory and practice* (pp. 84–110). New York: Oxford University Press.

Mueser, K. T., & McGurk, S. R. (2004). Schizophrenia. *Lancet, 363,* 2063–2072.

Murphy, F. C., Nimmo-Smith, I., & Lawrence, A. D. (2003). Functional neuroanatomy of emotion: A meta-analysis. *Cognitive, Affective, & Behavioral Neuroscience, 3,* 207–233.

Murphy, J. B. (1976). Psychiatric labeling in cross-cultural perspective: Similar kinds of disturbed behavior appear to be labeled abnormal in diverse cultures. *Science, 191,* 1019–1028.

Murray, H. A. (1938). *Explorations in personality.* New York: Oxford University Press.

Murray, H. A. (1971). *Thematic apperception test: Manual.* Cambridge, MA: Harvard University Press. (Original work published 1943).

Murstein, B. I. (1977). The stimulus-value-role (SVR) theory of dyadic relationship. In S. Duck (Ed.), *Theory and practice in interpersonal attraction* (pp. 105–127). New York: Academic Press.

Muscarella, F., & Cunningham, M. R. (1996). The evolutionary significance and social perception of male pattern baldness and facial hair. *Ethology and Sociobiology, 17,* 99–117.

Musella, D. P. (2005, September/October). Gallup poll shows that Americans' belief in the paranormal persists. *Skeptical Inquirer, 29,* 5.

Myers, D. G. (1993a). *Social psychology.* New York: McGraw Hill.

Myers, D. G. (1993b). *The pursuit of happiness.* London: Aquarian.

Myers, D. G. (2002). *Intuition: Its powers and perils.* New Haven, CT: Yale University Press.

Myers, D. G., & Diener, E. (1996). The pursuit of happiness. *Scientific American,* 70–72.

Myrtek, M. (2001). Meta-analyses of prospective studies on coronary heart disease, type A personality, and hostility. *International Journal of Cardiology, 79,* 245–251.

N

Nachev, P., & Husain, M. (2006). Disorders of visual attention and the posterior parietal cortex. *Cortex, 42,* 766–773.

Nahemow, L., & Lawton, M. P. (1975). Similarity and propinquity in friendship formation. *Journal of Personality and Social Psychology, 32,* 205–213.

Naito, E. (2004). Sensing limb movements in the motor cortex: How humans sense limb movement. *Neuroscientist, 10,* 73–82.

Namy, L. L., & Waxman, S. R. (2000). Naming and exclaiming: Infants' sensitivity to naming contexts. *Journal of Cognition and Development, 1,* 405–428.

Nash, M. R. (1987). What, if anything, is regressed about hypnotic age regression? A review of the empirical literature. *Psychological Bulletin, 102,* 42–52.

Nash, M. R., & Barnier, A. (Eds.). (2008). *The Oxford handbook of hypnosis.* New York: Oxford Press.

National Center for Complementary and Alternative Medicine. (2002). *What is complementary and alternative medicine?* (publication no. D156). Gaithersburg, MD: NCCAM.

National Center for Health Statistics. (2005). *Life expectancy at birth, 65 and 85 years of age, United States, selected years 1900–2004.* Retrieved from http://209.217.72.34/aging/TableViewer/tableView.aspx?ReportId=438.

National Institute of Mental Health. (2004). Suicide facts and statistics, U.S., 2001. U.S. Department of Health and Human Services. Posted April 9, 2004, at www.nimh.nih.gov/tools/helpusing.cfm.

National Institute on Alcohol Abuse and Alcoholism. (1998, July). *Alcohol and sleep,* no. 41. http://pubs.niaaa.nih.gov/publications/aa41.htm.

National Institute on Alcohol Abuse and Alcoholism. (2000, July). *Alcohol alert. From genes to geography: The cutting edge of alcohol research.* No 48. http://pubs.niaaa.nih.gov/publications/aa48.htm

National Opinion Research Center. (2003). *General social surveys, 1972–2002: Cumulative codebook.* Chicago: Author.

National Research Council. (2003). *The polygraph and lie detection.* Committee to review the scientific evidence on the polygraph. Washington, DC: National Academic Press.

National Science Foundation. (2003). Table C-2: Employed U.S. scientists and engineers, by level and field of highest degree attained, sex, and employment sector: 1999. Retrieved, 14 September 14, 2008, from http://www.nsf.gov/statistics/us-workforce/1999/dst1999.htm

Navarro, A. M. (1993). Effectiveness of psychotherapy with Latinos in the United States: A revised meta-analysis. *Interamerican Journal of Psychology, 27,* 131–146.

Neath, I., & Surprenant, A. M. (2003). *Human memory* (2nd ed.). Pacific Grove, CA: Wadsworth.

Needham, A., & Baillargeon, R. (1993). Intuitions about support in 4.5-month-old infants. *Cognition, 47,* 121–148.

Neely, J. (1976) Semantic priming and retrieval from lexical memory: Evidence for facilitory and inhibitory processes. *Memory and Cognition, 4,* 648–654.

Neimeyer, R. (2000). Searching for the meaning of meaning: Grief therapy and the process of reconstruction. *Death Studies, 24,* 541–558.

Neisser, U. (1967). *Cognitive psychology.* New York: Appleton-Century-Crofts.

Neisser, U., Boodoo, G., Bouchard, T. J. Jr., Boykin, A. W., Brody, N., Ceci, S. J., et al. (1996). Intelligence: Knowns and unknowns. *American Psychologist, 51,* 77–101.

Neisser, U., & Harsch, N. (1992). Phantom flashbulbs: False recollections of hearing the news about *Challenger.* In E. Winograd & U. Neisser (Eds.), *Affect and accuracy in recall: Studies of flashbulb memories* (pp. 9–31). Cambridge, England: Cambridge University.

Neisser, U., & Hyman, I. (Eds.). (1999). *Memory observed: Remembering in natural contexts.* New York: Worth Publishers.

Nemeroff, C. B., Kalali, A., Keller, M. B., Charney, D. S., Lenderts, S. E., Cascade, E. F., et al. (2007). Impact of publicity concerning pediatric suicidality data on physician practice patterns in the United States. *Archives of General Psychiatry, 64,* 397.

Nettle, D. (2005). *Happiness: The science behind your smile*. Oxford, England: Oxford University Press.

Neville, R. (1978). Psychosurgery. In W. Reich (Ed.), *Encyclopedia of bioethics* (Vol. 3). New York: Free Press.

Newberg, A., Alavi, A., Baime, M., Pourdehnad, M., Santanna, J., & d'Aquili, E. (2001). The measurement of regional cerebral blood flow during the complex cognitive task of meditation: A preliminary psychiatry research study. *Neuroimaging, 106*, 113–122.

Newcomb, T. M. (1961). *The acquaintance process*. New York: Holt, Rinehart and Winston.

Newman, J. P., & Kosson, D. S. (1986). Passive avoidance learning in psychopathic and nonpsychopathic offenders. *Journal of Abnormal Psychology, 95*, 252–256.

Newport, E. L., & Meier, R. (1985). The acquisition of American Sign Language. In D. Slobin (Ed.), *The cross-linguistic study of language acquisition, Vol. 1* (pp. 881–938). Hillsdale, NJ: Erlbaum.

Ngandu, T., von Strauss, E., Helkala, E.-L., Winblad, B., Nissinen, A., Tuomilehto, J., et al. (2007). Education and dementia: What lies behind the association? *Neurology, 69*, 1442–1450.

Nickerson, R. S. (1998). Confirmation bias: A ubiquitous phenomenon in many guises. *Review of General Psychology, 2*, 175–220.

Nickerson, R. S., & Adams, J. J. (1979). Long-term memory for a common object. *Cognitive Psychology, 11*, 287–307.

Nicol, S. E., & Gottesman, I. I. (1983). Clues to the genetics and neurobiology of schizophrenia. *American Scientist, 71*, 398–404.

Niedenthal, P. M. (2007). Embodying emotion. *Science, 316*, 1002–1005.

Nigro, G., & Neisser, N. (1983). Point of view in personal memories. *Cognitive Psychology, 15*, 467–482.

Nisbett, R. E. (1968). Determinants of food intake in human obesity. *Science, 159*, 1254–1255.

Nisbett, R. E. (1972). Hunger, obesity, and the ventromedial hypothalamus. *Psychological Review, 79*, 433–453.

Nisbett, R. E. (1995). Race, IQ and scientism. In S. Fraser (Ed.), *The bell curve wars* (pp. 36–57). New York: HarperCollins.

Nisbett, R. E. (2003). *The geography of thought: How Asians and Westerners think differently…and why*. New York: Free Press.

Nisbett, R. E., & Cohen, D. (1996). *Culture of honor: The psychology of violence in the South*. Boulder, CO: Westview.

Nisbett, R. E., & Wilson, T. D. (1977). Telling more than we can know: Verbal reports on mental processes. *Psychological Review, 84*, 231–259.

Noel, J. G., Wann, D. L., & Branscombe, N. R. (1995). Peripheral ingroup membership status and public negativity toward outgroups. *Journal of Personality and Social Psychology, 68*, 127–137.

Noelle-Neumann, E. (1970). Wanted: Rules for wording structured questionnaires. *Public Opinion Quarterly, 34*, 191–201.

Nolen-Hoeksema, S., & Girgus, J. S. (1994). The emergence of gender differences in depression during adolescence. *Psychological Bulletin, 115*, 424–443.

Norcross, J. C. (2005). A primer on psychotherapy integration. In J. C. Norcross & M. R. Goldfried (Eds.), *Handbook of psychotherapy integration* (2nd ed., pp. 3–23). New York: Oxford University Press.

Norcross, J. C., & Beutler, L. (1997). Determining the relationship of choice in brief therapy. In J. N. Butcher (Ed.), *Personality assessment in managed health care* (pp. 42–60). New York: Oxford University Press.

Norcross, J. C., Garofalo, A., & Koocher, G. (2006). Discredited psychological treatments and tests: A Delphi poll. *Professional Psychology: Research and Practice, 137*, 515–522.

Norcross, J. C., & Goldfried, M. R. (2005). *Handbook of psychotherapy integration* (2nd ed.). New York: Oxford University Press.

Norem, J. K. (2001). *The positive power of negative thinking*. New York: Basic Books.

Norem, J. K., & Cantor, N. (1986). Defensive pessimism: "Harnessing" anxiety as motivation. *Journal of Personality and Social Psychology, 52*, 1208–1217.

Norem, J. K., & Chang, E. C. (2002). The positive psychology of negative thinking. *Journal of Clinical Psychology, 37*, 1204–1238.

North, A. C., Linley, P. A., & Hargreaves, D. J. (2000). Social loafing in a co-operative classroom task. *Educational Psychology, 20*, 389–392.

Noyes, R., & Kletti, R. (1976). Depersonalization in the face of life-threatening danger: An interpretation. *Omega, 7*, 103–114.

O

O'Connor, T. G., Deater-Deckard, K., Fulker, D., Rutter, M., & Plomin, R. (1998). Genotype-environment correlations in late childhood and early adolescence: Antisocial behavioral problems and coercive parenting. *Developmental Psychology, 34*, 970–981.

O'Connor, T. G., & Rutter, M. (2000). Attachment disorder behavior following early severe deprivation: Extension and longitudinal follow-up. *Journal of the American Academy of Child and Adolescent Psychiatry, 39*(6), 703–712.

O'Keefe, D. J., & Figge, M. (1997). A guilt-based explanation of the door-in-the-face influence strategy. *Human Communication Research, 24*, 64–81.

O'Keefe, D. J., & Hale, S. L. (2001). An odds-ratio-based meta-analysis of research on the door-in-the-face influence strategy. *Communication Reports, 14*, 31–38.

Ocampo-Garces, A., Molina, E., Rodriguez, A., & Vivaldi, E. A. (2000). Homeostasis of REM sleep after total and selective sleep deprivation in the rat. *Journal of Neurophysiology, 84*(5), 2699–2702.

OCD-UK (2005). What is obsessive-compulsive disorder? Retrieved March 17, 2007, from www.ocduk.org/1/ocd.htm.

Ogawa, S., Lee, T. M., Kay, A. R., & Tank, D. W. (1990). Brain magnetic resonance imaging with contrast dependent on blood oxygenation. *Proceedings of the National Academy of Sciences, U.S.A., 87*, 9868–9872.

Ogden, C. A., Rich, M. E., Schork, N. J., Paulus, M. P., Geyer, M. A., Lohr, J. B., et al. (2004). Candidate genes, pathways and mechanisms for bipolar (manic–depressive) and related disorders: An expanded convergent functional genomics approach. *Molecular Psychiatry, 9*, 1007–1029.

Ogden, C. L., Carroll, M. D., McDowell, M. A., & Flegal, K. M. (2007). Obesity among adults in the United States—no change since 2003–2004. *NCHS data brief no. 1* Hyattesville, MD: National Center for Health Statistics.

Ogrodniczuk, J. S., & Piper, W. E. (1999). Use of transference interpretations in dynamically oriented individual psychotherapy for patients with personality disorders. *Journal of Personality Disorders, 13*, 297–311.

Ohayon, M. M. (2000). Prevalence of hallucinations and their pathological associations in the general population. *Psychiatry Research, 97*(2–3), 153–164.

Ohman, A., & Mineka, S. (2001). Fears, phobias, and preparedness: Toward an evolved module of fear and fear learning. *Psychological Review, 108*(3), 483–522.

Ohman, A., & Mineka, S. (2003). The malicious serpent: Snakes as a prototypical stimulus for an evolved module of fear. *Current Directions in Psychological Science, 12*(1), 5–9.

Olds, J. (1958). Satiation effects in self-stimulation of the brain. *Journal of Comparative and Physiological Psychology, 51*, 675–678.

Olfson, M., Marcus, S., Sackheim, H. A., Thompson, J., & Pincus, H. A. (1998). Use of ECT for the inpatient treatment of recurrent major depression. *American Journal of Psychiatry, 155*, 22–29.

Oliver, M. B., & Hyde, J. S. (1993). Gender differences in sexuality: A meta-analysis. *Psychological Bulletin, 114*, 29–51.

Olsson, A., Ebert, J. P., Banaji, M. R., & Phelps, E. A. (2005). The role of social groups in the persistence of learned fear. *Science, 309*, 785–787.

Ondeck, D. M. (2003). Impact of culture on pain. *Home Health Care Management Practice, 15*, 255–257.

Ones, D. S., Viswesvaran, C., & Dilchert, S. (2005). Personality at work: Raising awareness and correcting misconceptions. *Human Performance, 18*, 389–404.

Onishi, K. H., & Baillargeon, R. (2005). Do 15-month-old infants understand false beliefs? *Science, 308*, 255–258.

Oppenheim, R. W. (1991). Cell death during development of the nervous system. *Annual Review of Neuroscience, 14*, 453–501.

Orlanksy, M. D., & Bonvillian, J. D. (1984). The role of iconicity in early sign language acquisition. *Journal of Speech and Hearing Disorders, 49*, 287–292.

Orne, M. T. (1962). On the social psychology of the psychological experiment: With particular reference to demand characteristics and their implications. *American Psychologist, 17*, 776–783.

Ornstein, R. E. (1997). *The right mind: Making sense of the hemispheres.* Orlando, FL: Harcourt Brace.

Ortony, A., Clore, G. L., & Collins, A. (1988). *The cognitive structure of emotions.* New York: Cambridge University Press.

Ortony, A., & Turner, T. J. (1990). What's basic about basic emotions? *Psychological Review, 97*, 315–331.

Osborn, A. F. (1957). Applied imagination: Principles and procedures of creative problem solving (Rev ed.). New York: Charles Scribner's Sons.

Ott, R. (1995). The natural wrongs about animal rights and animal liberation. *Journal of the American Veterinary Medical Association, 207*, 1023–1030.

Otto, M. W., Smits, J. A. J., & Reese, H. E. (2005). Combined psychotherapy and pharmacotherapy for mood and anxiety disorders in adults: Review and analysis. *Clinical Psychology: Science & Practice, 12*, 72–86.

Overmier, J. B., & Seligman, M. E. P. (1967). Effects of inescapable shock upon subsequent escape and avoidance responding. *Journal of Comparative and Physiological Psychology, 63*, 28–33.

Overskeid, G. (2007). Looking for Skinner and finding Freud. *American Psychologist, 65*, 590–595.

Oyserman, D., Coon, H. M., & Kemmelmeier, M. (2002). Rethinking individualism and collectivism: Evaluation of theoretical assumptions and meta-analyses. *Psychological Bulletin, 128*, 3–72.

Ozer, E., Best, S., & Lipsey, T., & Weiss, D. L. (2003). Predictors of posttraumatic stress disorder symptoms in adults: A meta-analysis. *Psychological Bulletin, 129*, 52–73.

P

Pahnke, W. N., Kurland, A. A., Unger, S., Savage, C., & Grof, S. (1970). Experimental use of psychedelic (LSD) psychotherapy. *Journal of the American Medical Association, 212*(11), 1856.

Paivio, A. (1969). Mental imagery in associative learning and memory. *Psychological Review, 76*, 341–363.

Panksepp, J. (2005). Beyond a joke: From animal laughter to human joy? *Science, 208*, 62–63.

Panksepp, J. (2007). Neurologizing the psychology of affects: How appraisal-based constructivism and basic emotion theory can coexist. *Perspectives in Psychological Science, 2*, 281–296.

Panksepp, J., & Panksepp, J. B. (2000). The seven sins of evolutionary psychology. *Evolution and Cognition, 6*, 108–131.

Paris, J. (2000). *Myths of childhood.* New York: Brunner/Mazel.

Park, B., & Rothbart, M. (1982). Perception of out-group homogeneity and levels of social categorization: Memory for the subordinate attributes of in-group and out-group members. *Journal of Personality and Social Psychology, 42*, 1051–1068.

Park, D. C., Smith, A. D., & Cavanaugh, J. C. (1990). Metamemories of memory researchers. *Memory and Cognition, 18*, 321–327.

Park, M. A. (1982). Palmistry: Science or hand jive? *Skeptical Inquirer, 5*, 198–208.

Park, N., Peterson, C., & Seligman, M. E. P. (2004). Strengths of character and well-being. *Journal of Social and Clinical Psychology, 23*, 603–619.

Park, R. (2000). *Voodoo science: The road from foolishness to fraud.* New York: Oxford University Press.

Parker, E. S., Cahill, L., & McGaugh, J. L. (2006). A case of unusual autobiographical remembering. *Neurocase, 12*, 35–49.

Pascalis, O., de Schonen, S., Morton, J., Deruelle, C., & Fabre-Grenet, M. (1995). Mother's face recognition by neonates: A replication and an extension. *Infant Behavior and Development, 18*, 79–85.

Pascual, A., & Guéguen, N. (2005). Foot-in-the-door and door-in-the-face: A comparative meta-analytic study. *Psychological Reports, 96*, 122–128.

Pascual-Leone, J. (1989). An organismic process model of Witkin's field dependence-independence. In T. Globerson and T. Zelniker (Eds.), *Cognitive style and cognitive development* (pp. 36–70). Norwood, NJ: Ablex.

Passini, F. T., & Norman, W. T. (1966). A universal conception of personality structure? *Journal of Personality and Social Psychology, 4*, 44–49.

Patel, G. A., & Sathian, K. (2000). Visual search: Bottom-up or top-down? *Frontiers in Bioscience, 5*, D169–193.

Patrick, C. J. (Ed.). (2006). *Handbook of psychopathy.* New York: Guilford Press.

Patterson, C. J. (1992). Children of lesbian and gay parents. *Child Development, 63*, 1025–1042.

Patterson, C. J., & Chan, R. W. (1996). Gay fathers and their children. In R. P. Cabaj and T. S. Stein (Eds.), *Textbook of homosexuality and mental health* (pp. 371–393). Washington, DC: American Psychiatric Press.

Paul, A. M. (2004). *The cult of personality: How personality tests are leading us to miseducate our children, mismanage our companies, and misunderstand ourselves.* New York: Free Press.

Paul, G., & Lentz, R. J. (1977). *Psychosocial treatment of chronic mental patients: Milieu versus social-learning programs.* Cambridge, MA: Harvard University Press.

Paulus, P. B., Larey, T. S., & Ortega, A. H. (1995). Performance and perceptions of brainstormers in an organizational setting. *Basic and Applied Social Psychology, 17*, 249–265.

Paulus, T. M. (2004). Collaboration or cooperation? Small group interactions in a synchronous educational environment. In T. S. Roberts (Ed.), *Computer-supported collaborative learning in higher education* (pp. 100–124). Hershey, PA: Idea Group.

Pavlov, I. P. (1927). *Conditioned reflexes.* Oxford, England: Oxford University Press.

Paykel, E. S. (2003). Life events and affective disorders. *Acta Psychiatrica Scandinavia Supplement, 108*, 61–66.

Pearce, J. M. (2004). Sir Charles Scott Sherrington (1857–1952) and the synapse. *Journal of Neurology, Neurosurgery, and Psychiatry, 74*(4), 544.

Pearlin, L. I., & Lieberman, M. A. (1979). Social sources of emotional distress. In J. Simmons (Ed.), *Research in community and mental health* (pp. 217–248). Greenwich, CT: JAI Press.

Pearson, B. Z., & Fernàndez, S. C. (1994). Patterns of interaction in the lexical growth in two languages of bilingual infants and toddlers. *Language Learning, 44*, 617–653.

Pearson, B. Z., Fernàndez, S. C., & Oller, D. K. (1993). Lexical development in bilingual infants and toddlers: Comparison to monolingual norms. *Language Learning, 43*, 93–120.

Pearson, H. (2006). Mouse data hint at human pheromones. *Nature, 442*, 495.

Pedersen, N. L., Plomin, R., McClearn, G. E., & Friberg, L. (1988). Neuroticism, extraversion, and related traits in adult twins reared apart and reared together. *Journal of Personality and Social Psychology, 55*, 950–957.

Pederson Mussell, M., Crosby, R. D., Crow, S. J., Knopke, A. J., Peterson, C. B., Wonderlich, S. A., et al. (2000). Utilization of empirically supported psychotherapy treatments for individuals with eating disorders: A survey of psychologists. *International Journal of Eating Disorders, 27*, 230–237.

Pelham, B. W., Carvallo, M., & Jones, J. T. (2005). Implicit egotism. *Current Directions in Psychological Science, 14*, 106–110.

Pelkonen, M., & Marttunen, M. (2003). Child and adolescent suicide: Epidemiology, risk factors, and approaches to prevention. *Psychiatric Drugs, 5*, 243–265.

Penfield, W. (1958). *The excitable cortex in conscious man.* Liverpool, England: Liverpool University Press.

Penner, L. A., Dovidio, J. F., Schroeder, D. A., & Piliavin, J. A. (2005). Prosocial behavior: Multilevel perspectives. *Annual Review of Psychology, 56*, 365–392.

Pepperberg, I. M. (1999). *The Alex studies: Cognitive and communicative abilities of grey parrots.* Cambridge, MA: Harvard University Press.

Perlmutter, M. (1983). Learning and memory through adulthood. In M. W. Riley, B. B. Hess, & K. Bond (Eds.), *Aging in society: Selected reviews of recent research.* Hillsdale, NJ: Erlbaum.

Perry, J. C. (1992). Problems and considerations in the valid assessment of personality disorders. *American Journal of Psychiatry, 149*(12), 1645–1653.

Persinger, M. A. (1994). Near-death experiences: Determining the neuroanatomical pathways by experiential patterns and simulation in experimental settings. In L. Besette (Ed.), *Healing: Beyond suffering or death* (pp. 277–286). Chabanel, Quebec, Canada: MNH.

Peterson, C. (2000). The future of optimism. *American Psychologist, 55*, 44–55.

Peterson, C., & Seligman, M. E. P. (2004). *Character strengths and virtues: A handbook and classification.* New York: Oxford University Press.

Peterson, L. R., & Peterson, M. J. (1959). Short-term retention of individual verbal items. *Journal of Experimental Psychology, 58*, 193–198.

Petitto, L. A., & Marentette, P. F. (1991). Babbling in the manual mode: Evidence for the ontogeny of language. *Science, 251*, 1493–1496.

Petry, N. M., Tennen, H., & Affleck, G. (2000). Stalking the elusive client variable in psychotherapy research. In C. R. Snyder & R. Ingram (Eds.), *Handbook of psychological change* (pp. 88–108). New York: John Wiley & Sons.

Pettigrew, T. F. (1979). The ultimate attribution error: Extending Allport's cognitive analysis of prejudice. *Personality and Social Psychology Bulletin, 5*, 461–476.

Pettigrew, T. F. (1998). Intergroup contact theory. *Annual Review of Psychology, 49*, 65–85.

Pettinati, H. M., Tamburello, T. A., Ruetsch, C. R., & Kaplan, F. N. (1994). Patient attitudes toward electroconvulsive therapy. *Psychopharmacological Bulletin, 30*, 471–475.

Petty, R. E., & Cacioppo, J. T. (1986). *Communication and persuasion: Central and peripheral routes to attitude change.* New York: Springer Verlag.

Pew Research Center. (2006, February 13). Are we happy yet? Retrieved from http://pewresearch.org/pubs/301/are-we-happy-yet.

Pezdek, K., Blandon-Gitlin, I., & Moore, C. (2003). Children's face recognition memory: More evidence for the cross-race effect. *Journal of Applied Psychology, 88*, 760–763.

Phillips, D. P., & Wills, J. S. (1987). A drop in suicides around major national holidays. *Suicide and Life Threatening Behavior, 17*, 1–12.

Phillips, M. L., Young, A. W., Senior, C., Brammer, M., Andrew, A. J., Calder, J., et al. (1997). A specific neural substrate for perceiving facial expressions of disgust. *Nature, 389*, 495–498.

Piaget, J. (1932). *The moral judgment of the child.* London: Kegan Paul.

Piatelli-Palmarini, M. (1994). *Inevitable illusions: How mistakes of reason rule our minds.* New York: John Wiley & Sons.

Piccinelli, M., & Wilkinson, G. (2000). Gender differences in depression—Critical review. *British Journal of Psychiatry, 177*, 486–492.

Pigott, T. A., Myers, K. R., & Williams, D. A. (1996). Obsessive-compulsive disorder: A neuropsychiatric perspective. In R. M. Rapee (Ed.), *Current controversies in the anxiety disorders* (pp. 134–160). New York: Guilford.

Piliavin, I. M., Rodin, J., & Piliavin, J. A. (1969). Good samaritanism: An underground phenomenon? *Journal of Personality and Social Psychology, 13*, 289–299.

Pillemer, D. B. (1984). Flashbulb memories of the assassination attempt on President Reagan. *Cognition, 16*, 63–80.

Pinker, S. (1997). *How the mind works.* New York: Norton.

Pinker, S. (2002). *The blank slate: The modern denial of human nature.* New York: Penguin.

Pinker, S. (2005, February 14). The science of difference: Sex ed. *The New Republic, 232*, 15–17.

Pinto, A. C. (1992). Medidas de categorizacao: Frequencia de producao e de tipicidade. *Jornal de Psicologia, 10*, 10–15.

Piper, A. (1997). *Hoax and reality: The bizarre world of multiple personality disorder.* Northvale, NJ: Jason Aronson.

Platt, J. R. (1964). Strong inference. *Science, 146*, 347–353.

Plomin, R. (2004). Genetics and developmental psychology. *Merrill-Palmer Quarterly Journal of Developmental Psychology, 50*(3), 341–352.

Plomin, R., Corley, R., DeFries, J. C., & Fulker, D. W. (1990). Individual differences in television viewing in early childhood: Nature as well as nurture. *Psychological Science, 1*, 371–377.

Plomin, R., & Daniels, D. (1987). Why are children in the same family so different from one another? *Behavioral and Brain Sciences, 10*, 1–16.

Plomin, R., DeFries, J. C., & Loehlin, J. C. (1977). Genotype-environment interaction and correlation in the analysis of human behavior. *Psychological Bulletin, 84*, 309–322.

Plotkin, H. (2004). *Evolutionary thought in psychology: A brief history.* Oxford, England: Blackwell.

Plunkett, K., Karmiloff-Smith, A., Bates, E., Elman, J. L., & Johnson, M. H. (1997). Connectionism and developmental psychology. *Journal of Child Psychology and Psychiatry, 38*, 53–80.

Plutchik, R. (2003). *Emotions and life: Perspectives from psychology, biology, and evolution.* Washington, DC: American Psychological Association.

Pohorecky, L. (1977). Biphasic action of ethanol. *Biobehavioral Review, 1*, 231–240.

Poizner, H., Klima, E. S., & Bellugi, U. (1987). *What the hands reveal about the brain*. Cambridge, MA: MIT Press.

Pollard, K. S., Salama, S. R., King, B., Kern, A. D., Dreszer, T., Katzman, S., et al. (2006, October 13). Forces shaping the fastest evolving regions in the human genome. *PLoS Genetics, 2*(10), 168.

Polusny, M. A., & Follette, V. M. (1996). Remembering childhood sexual abuse: A national survey of psychologists' clinical practices, beliefs, and personal experiences. *Professional Psychology: Research and Practice, 27*, 41–52.

Poole, D. A., Lindsay, D. S., Memon, A., & Bull, R. (1995). Psychotherapists' opinions, practices, and experiences with recovery of memories of incestuous abuse. *Journal of Consulting and Clinical Psychology, 68*, 426–437.

Pope, H. G., & Hudson, J. I. (1992). Is childhood sexual abuse a risk factor for bulimia nervosa? *American Journal of Psychiatry, 149*, 455–463.

Pope, H. G. Jr., Poliakoff, M. B., Parker, M. P., Boynes, M., & Hudson, J. I. (2007). Is dissociative amnesia a culture-bound syndrome? Findings from a survey of historical literature. *Psychological Medicine, 37*, 225–233.

Popper, K. R. (1965). *The logic of scientific discovery*. New York: Harper.

Porter, S., Yuille, J. C., & Lehman, D. R. (1999). The nature of real, implanted, and fabricated memories for emotional childhood events: Implications for the recovered memory debate. *Law and Human Behavior, 23*, 517–538.

Posey, T. B., & Losch, M. E. (1983). Auditory hallucinations of hearing voices in 375 normal subjects. *Imagination, Cognition and Personality, 3*(2), 99–113.

Posner, G. P., & Sampson, W. (1999, Fall/Winter). Chinese acupuncture for heart surgery anesthesia. *The Scientific Review of Alternative Medicine, 3*(2), 15–19.

Posner, M. I., & Snyder, C. R. R. (1975). Facilitation and inhibition in the processing of signals. In P. M. A. Rabbitt & S. Dornic (Eds.), *Attention and performance* (pp. 669–682). New York: Academic Press.

Postmes, T., & Spears, R. (1998). Deindividuation and antinormative behavior: A meta-analysis. *Psychological Bulletin, 123*, 238–259.

Potts, R. G. (2004). Spirituality, religion, and the experience of illness. In P. Camic & S. Knight (Eds.), *Clinical handbook of health psychology: A practical guide to effective interventions* (pp. 297–314). Cambridge, MA: Hogrefe & Huber.

Powell, R. W., & Curley, M. (1984). Analysis of instinctive drift. 2. The development and control of species-specific responses in appetitive conditioning. *Psychological Record, 34*(3), 363–379.

Pratkanis, A. R. (1992). The cargo-cult science of subliminal persuasion. *Skeptical Inquirer, 16*, 260–272.

Pratkanis, A. R. (1995, July/August). How to sell a pseudoscience. *Skeptical Inquirer, 19*, 19–25.

Premack, D. (1965). Reinforcement theory. In D. Levine (Ed.), *Nebraska Symposium on Motivation* (pp. 123–180). Lincoln, NE: University of Nebraska Press.

Premack, D., & Woodruff, G. (1978). Does the chimpanzee have a theory of mind? *Behavioral and Brain Sciences, 1*, 515–526.

Price, R. H., & Bouffard, D. L. (1974). Behavioral appropriateness and situational constraint as dimensions of social behavior. *Journal of Personality and Social Psychology, 30*, 579–586.

Priel, B., & de Schonen, S. (1986). Self-recognition: A study of a population without mirrors. *Journal of Experimental Child Psychology, 41*, 237–250.

Prince, M. J., Harwood, R. H., Blizard, R. A., Thomas, A., & Mann, A. H. (1997). Social support deficits, loneliness and life events as risk factors for depression in old age. The Gospel Oak Project VI. *Psychological Medicine, 27*, 323–332.

Prinz, J. J. (2004). *Gut reactions: A perceptual theory of emotion*. New York: Oxford University Press.

Prochaska, J. O., & DiClemente, C. C. (1982). Transtheoretical therapy: Toward a more integrative model of change. *Psychotherapy: Theory, Research, and Practice, 20*, 161–173.

Prochaska, J. O., & DiClemente, C. C. (1984). *The transtheoretical approach: Crossing the traditional boundaries of therapy*. Homewood, IL: Dow Jones-Irwin.

Prochaska, J. O., & Norcross, J. C. (2002). Stages of change. In J. C. Norcross (Ed.), *Psychotherapy relationships that work*. New York: Oxford University Press.

Prochaska, J. O., & Norcross, J. C. (2007). *Systems of psychotherapy: A transtheoretical approach* (6th ed.). Pacific Grove, CA: Brooks/Cole.

Project MATCH Research Group. (1997). Matching alcoholism treatments to client heterogeneity: Project MATCH posttreatment drinking outcomes. *Journal of Studies on Alcohol, 58*, 7–29.

Pronin, E., Gilovich, T., & Ross, L. (2004). Objectivity in the eye of the beholder: Divergent perceptions of bias in self versus others. *Psychological Review, 3*, 781–799.

Pronk, N. P., & Wing, R. R. (1994). Physical activity and long-term maintenance of weight loss. *Obesity Research, 2*, 587–599.

Proske, U. (2006). Kinesthesia: The role of muscle receptors. *Muscle Nerve, 34*, 545–558.

Provine, R. R. (1996). Laughter. *American Scientist, 84*, 38–45.

Provine, R. R. (2000). *Laughter: A scientific investigation*. New York: Viking.

Pyszczynski, T., Greenberg, J., & Solomon, S. (2003). *In the wake of 9/11: The psychology of terror*. Washington, D.C.: American Psychological Association.

Q

Quick, D. C. (1999, March/April). Joint pain and weather. *Skeptical Inquirer, 23*, 49–51.

Quick, J. C., Quick, J. D., Nelson, D. L., & Hurrell, J. J. (1997). *Preventive stress management in organizations*. Washington, DC: American Psychological Association.

Quiroga, R. Q., Reddy, L., Kreiman, G., Koch, C., & Fried, I. (2005). Invariant visual representation by single neurons in the human brain. *Nature, 435*, 1102–1107.

R

Rachid, F., & Bertschy, G. (2006). Safety and efficacy of repetitive transcranial magnetic stimulation in the treatment of depression: A critical appraisal of the last 10 years. *Neurophysiologie Clinique, 36*, 157–183.

Rachlin, H., & Logue, A. W. (1991). Learning. In M. Hersen, A. E. Kazdin, & A. S. Bellack (Eds.), *The clinical psychology handbook* (2nd ed.) (pp. 170–184). Elmsford, NY, US: Pergamon Press.

Rachman, S. (1977). The conditioning theory of fear-acquisition: A critical examination. *Behaviour Research and Therapy, 15*, 375–387.

Rachman, S., & Hodgson, R. J. (1968). Experimentally induced "sexual fetishism": Replication and development. *Psychological Record, 18*, 25–27.

Rader, C. M., & Tellegen, A. (1987). An investigation of synesthesia. *Journal of Personality and Social Psychology, 52*(5) 981–987.

Rainville, P., Bechara, A., Naqvi, N., & Damasio, A. R. (2006). Basic emotions are associated with distinct patterns of cardiorespiratory activity. *International Journal of Psychophysiology, 61*, 5–18.

Ramachandran, V. S., & Hubbard, E. M. (2001). Synaesthesia: A window into perception, thought and language. *Journal of Consciousness Studies, 8,* 33–34.

Rankin, J. L. (2005). *Parenting experts: Their advice, the research, and getting it right.* Westport, CT: Praeger.

Rasmussen, K., Sampson, S. M., & Rummans, T. A. (2002). Electroconvulsive therapy and newer modalities for the treatment of medication-refractory mental illness. *Mayo Clinic Proceedings, 77,* 552–556.

Rassin, E., Merckelbach, H., & Spaan, V. (2001). When dreams become a royal road to confusion: Realistic dreams, dissociation, and fantasy proneness. *Journal of Nervous and Mental Disease, 189,* 478–481.

Rathus, S. A., Nevid, J. S., & Fichner-Rathus, L. (2000). *Human sexuality in a world of diversity.* Boston: Allyn & Bacon.

Raulin, M. L. (2003). *Abnormal psychology.* Boston: Allyn & Bacon.

Raulin, M. L., & Lilienfeld, S. O. (2008). Research paradigms in the study of psychopathology. In P. H. Blaney & T. Milton (Eds.), *Oxford textbook of psychopathology.* (2nd ed.) (pp. 86–115). New York: Oxford University Press.

Rauscher, F. H., Shaw, G. L., & Ky, K. N. (1993). Music and spatial task performance. *Nature, 365,* 611.

Raven, J., Raven, J. C., & Court, J. H. (1998). *Manual for Raven's Advanced Progressive Matrices.* Oxford, England: Oxford Psychologists Press.

Raz, S., & Raz, N. (1990). Structural brain abnormalities in the major psychoses: A quantitative review of the evidence from computerized imaging. *Psychological Bulletin, 108,* 93–108.

Razoumnikova, O. (2000). Functional organization of different brain areas during convergent and divergent thinking: An EEG investigation. *Cognitive Brain Research, 10,* 11–18.

Reasoner, R. (2000). *Self-esteem and youth: What research has to say about it.* Port Ludlow, WA: International Council for Self-Esteem.

Rechtschaffen, A. (1998). Current perspectives on the function of sleep. *Perspectives in Biology and Medicine, 41*(3), 359–390.

Redding, R. E. (1998). How common-sense psychology can inform law and psycholegal research. *University of Chicago Law School Roundtable, 5,* 107–142.

Redding, R. E. (2004). Bias or prejudice? The politics of research on racial prejudice. *Psychological Inquiry, 15*(4), 289–293.

Redfern, M. S., Muller, M. L., Jennings, J. R., & Furman, J. M. (2002). Attentional dynamics in postural control during perturbations in young and older adults. *Journals of Gerontology: Series A: Biological Sciences and Medical Sciences, 57A,* B298–B303.

Regan, P. C., & Berscheid, E. (1999). *Lust: What we know about human sexual desire.* Thousand Oaks, CA: Sage.

Regan, T. (2004). *Empty Cages: Facing the Challenge of Animal Rights.* Lanham, Maryland: Rowman and Littlefield.

Rehberg, R. A., & Rosenthal, E. R. (1978). *Class and merit in the American high school.* New York: Longman.

Reich, W. (1949). *Character analysis.* New York: Orgone Institute Press.

Reicher, S. D., & Haslam, S. A. (2006). Rethinking the social psychology of tyranny: The BBC Prison Study. *British Journal of Social Psychology, 45,* 1–40.

Reilly, S. & Schachtman, T. R. (2009). *Conditioned taste aversion: Behavioral and neural processes.* New York: Oxford University Press.

Reisenzein, R. (1983). The Schachter theory of emotion: Two decades later. *Psychological Bulletin, 94,* 239–264.

Reiss, D., & Marino, L. (2001). Mirror self-recognition in the bottlenose dolphin: A case of cognitive convergence. *Proceedings of the National Academy of Sciences, 98,* 5937–5942.

Reiss, S., & McNally, R. J. (1985). The expectancy model of fear. In S. Reiss & R. R. Bootzin (Eds.), *Theoretical issues in behavior therapy* (pp. 107–121). New York: Academic Press.

Reivich, M., Kuhl, D., Wolf, A., Greenberg, J., Phelps, M., Ido, T., et al. (1979). The [18F]fluorodeoxyglucose method for the measurement of local cerebral glucose utilization in man. *Circulation Research, 44,* 127–137.

Renken, B., Egeland, B., Marvinney, D., Mangelsdorf, S., & Sroufe, L. A. (1989). Early childhood antecedents of aggression and passive-withdrawal in early elementary school. *Journal of Personality, 57,* 257–281.

Repetti, R., Taylor, S., & Seeman, T. (2002). Risky families: Family social environments and the mental and physical health of offspring. *Psychological Bulletin 128,* 330–366.

Resnick, A. G., & Ithman, M. H. (2009). The human sexual response cycle: Psychotropic side effects and treatment strategies. *Psychiatric Annals, 38,* 267–280.

Restak, R. (1984). *The brain.* New York: Bantam Books.

Revonsuo, A. (2000). The reinterpretation of dreams: An evolutionary hypothesis of the function of dreaming. *Behavioral and Brain Sciences, 23,* 877–901.

Reynolds, D. (2003, April 25). Panel recommends counseling for sterilization survivors. *Inclusion Daily Express.* Retrieved from www.inclusiondaily.com/news/institutions/nc/eugenics.htm#04 2503.

Rhine, J. B.. (1934). *Extrasensory perception.* Oxford, England: Society for Psychic Research.

Rhodes, G., Halberstadt, J., & Brajkovich, G. (2001). Generalization of mere exposure effects to averaged composite faces. *Social Cognition, 19,* 57–70.

Rhule, D. M. (2005). Take care to do no harm: Harmful interventions for youth problem behavior. *Professional Psychology: Research and Practice, 36,* 618–625.

Ricciardelli, L. A. (1992). Bilingualism and cognitive development in relation to threshold theory. *Journal of Psycholinguistic Research, 21,* 301–316.

Richardson, R., Riccio, C., & Axiotis, R. (1986). Alleviation of infantile amnesia in rats by internal and external contextual cues. *Developmental Psychobiology, 19,* 453–462.

Rickels, K., Hesbacher, P. T., Weise, C. C., Gray, B., & Feldman, H. S. (1970). Pills and improvement: A study of placebo response in psychoneurotic outpatients. *Psychopharmacologia, 16*(4), 318–328.

Rilling, M. (1996). The mystery of the vanished citations: James McConnell's forgotten 1960s quest for planarian learning, a biochemical engram, and celebrity. *American Psychologist, 51*(1), 1039.

Rimland, B. (2004). Association between thimerosol-containing vaccine and autism. *Journal of the American Medical Association, 291,* 180.

Rimm, D., & Masters, J. C. (1979). *Behavior therapy: Techniques and empirical findings* (2nd ed.). New York: Academic Press.

Rind, B., Tromovitch, P., & Bauserman, R. (1998). A meta-analytic examination of assumed properties of child sexual abuse using college samples. *Psychological Bulletin, 124,* 22–53.

Ring, K. (1984). *Healing toward omega: In search of the meaning of the near-death experience.* New York: Morrow.

Ringwalt, C. L., & Greene, J. M. (1993, March). *Results of school districts' drug prevention coordinators survey.* Paper presented at the Alcohol, Tobacco, and Other Drugs Conference on Evaluating School-Linked Prevention Strategies, San Diego, CA.

Ris, M. D., Dietrich, K. N., Succop, P. A., Berger, O. G., & Bornschein, R. L. (2004). Early exposure to lead and neuropsychological outcome in adolescence. *Journal of the International Neuropsychological Society, 10,* 261–270.

Risen, J., & Gilovich, T. (2007). Informal logical fallacies. In R. J. Sternberg, H. L. Roediger, & D. F. Halpern (Eds.), *Critical thinking in psychology* (pp. 110–130). New York: Cambridge University Press.

Robbins, T. W., & Everitt, B. J. (1999). Interaction of the dopaminergic system with mechanisms of associative learning and cognition: Implications for drug abuse. *Psychological Science, 10*(3), 199–202.

Robbins, T. W., Granon, S., Muir, J. L., Durantou, F., Harrison, A., & Everitt, B. J. (1998). Neural systems underlying arousal and attention. Implications for drug abuse. In J. A. Harvey & B. E. Kosofsky (Eds.), *Cocaine: Effects on the developing brain* (pp. 222–237). New York, NY: New York Academy of Sciences.

Roberts, B. W., & DelVecchio, W. F. (2000). The rank-order consistency of personality traits from childhood to old age: Review of longitudinal studies. *Psychological Bulletin, 126,* 3–25.

Roberts, W. M., Howard, J., & Hudspeth, A. J. (1988). Hair cells: Transduction, tuning, and transmission in the inner ear. *Annual Review of Cell Biology, 4,* 63–92.

Robins, E., & Guze, S. B. (1970). Establishment of diagnostic validity in psychiatric illness: Its application to schizophrenia. *American Journal of Psychiatry, 126,* 983–987.

Robinson, D. G., Woerner, M. G., McMeniman, M., Mendelowitz, A., & Bilder, R. M. (2004). Systematic and functional recovery from a first episode of schizophrenia or schizoaffective disorder. *American Journal of Psychiatry, 161,* 473–479.

Robinson, D. S. (2007). The role of dopamine and norepinephrine in depression. *Primary Psychiatry, 14,* 21–23.

Rochat, P. (2001). *The infant's world.* Cambridge, MA: Harvard University Press.

Rodman, H. R. (2006). Behavioral and neural alterations following V1 damage in immature primates. In S. G. Lomber & J. J. Eggermont (Eds.), *Reprogramming the cerebral cortex: Plasticity following central and peripheral lesions* (pp. 91–113). New York, Oxford University Press.

Roediger, H. L., & McDermott, K. B. (1995). Creating false memories: Remembering words not presented in lists. *Journal of Experimental Psychology: Learning, Memory, and Cognition, 21,* 803–814.

Roediger, H. L., & McDermott, K. B. (1999). False alarms and false memories. *Psychological Review, 106,* 406–410.

Rogers, C. R. (1942). *Counseling and psychotherapy.* New York: Houghton Mifflin.

Rogers, C. R. (1947). Some observations on the organization of personality. *American Psychologist, 2,* 358–368.

Rogers, C. R. (1961). *On becoming a person.* Boston: Houghton Mifflin.

Rogers, M., & Smith, K. H. (1993). Public perceptions of subliminal advertising. *Journal of Advertising Research, 33,* 10–18.

Rogers, R. W., & Prentice-Dunn, S. (1981). Deindividuation and anger-mediated interracial aggression: Unmasking regressive racism. *Journal of Personality and Social Psychology, 41,* 63–73.

Rogoff, B. (1998). Cognition as a collaborative process. In D. Kuhn & R. S. Seigler (Eds.), *Handbook of child psychology, Vol. 2: Cognition, perception, & language* (5th ed., pp. 679–744). New York: Wiley.

Rogoff, B., & Chavajay, P. (1995). What's become of research on the cultural basis of cognitive development? *American Psychologist, 50,* 859–877.

Rolls, E. T. (2004). The functions of the orbitofrontal cortex. *Brain & Cognition, 55,* 11–29.

Romanczyk, R. G., Arnstein, L., Soorya, L. V., & Gillis, J. (2003). The myriad of controversial treatments for autism: A critical evaluation of efficacy. In S. O. Lilienfeld, S. J. Lynn, & J. M. Lohr (Eds.), *Science and pseudoscience in clinical psychology* (pp. 363–395). New York: Guilford.

Rosch, E. (1973). Natural categories. *Cognitive Psychology, 4,* 328–350.

Rosen, G. M. (1993). Self-help or hype? Comments on psychology's failure to advance self-care. *Professional Psychology: Research and Practice, 24,* 340–345.

Rosen, G. M. (2006). DSM's cautionary guideline to rule out malingering can protect the PTSD data base. *Journal of Anxiety Disorders, 20,* 530–535.

Rosen, G. M., Glasgow, R. E., & Moore, T. E. (2003). Self-help therapy: The science and business of giving psychology away. In S. O. Lilienfeld, S. J. Lynn, & J. M. Lohr (Eds.), *Science and pseudoscience in clinical psychology* (pp. 399–424). New York: Guilford.

Rosenberg, S. D., Rosenberg, H. J., & Farrell, M. P. (1999). The midlife crisis revisited. *Journal of Personality and Social Psychology, 77,* 415–427.

Rosenblum, D., & Lewis, M. (1999). The relations among body image, physical attractiveness, and body mass in adolescence. *Child Development, 70,* 50–64.

Rosenfarb, I. S., Bellack, A. S., & Aziz, N. (2006). Family interactions and the course of schizophrenia in African-American and white patients. *Journal of Abnormal Psychology, 115,* 112–120.

Rosenhan, D. L. (1973). On being sane in insane places. *Science, 179,* 250–258.

Rosenhan, D. L., & Seligman, M. E. P. (1989). *Abnormal psychology.* New York: W. W. Norton.

Rosenman, R. H., Brand, R. J., Jenkins, C. D., Friedman, M., Straus, R., & Wurm, M. (1975). Coronary heart disease in the Western Collaborative Group Study: Final follow-up experience of 81/2 years. *Journal of the American Medical Association, 233,* 872–877.

Rosenman, R. H., Friedman, M., Straus, R., Wurm, M., Kositchek, R., Hahn, W., et al. (1964). A predictive study of coronary heart disease: The Western Collaborative Group Study. *Journal of the American Medical Association, 189,* 15–22.

Rosenthal, D. (1963). *The Genain quadruplets.* New York: Basic Books.

Rosenthal, R., & Fode, K. L. (1963). Psychology of the scientist: V. Three experiments in experimenter bias. *Psychological Reports, 12,* 491–511.

Rosenzweig, S. (1936). Some implicit common factors in diverse methods in psychotherapy. *American Journal of Orthopsychiatry, 6,* 412–415.

Rosnow, R. L. (2002). The nature and role of demand characteristics in scientific inquiry. *Prevention and Treatment, 5*(1). Retrieved March 10, 2005, from http://content.apa.org/journals/pre/5/1/37.

Ross, C. A. (1997). *Dissociative identity disorder: Diagnosis, clinical features, and treatment of multiple personality.* New York: John Wiley & Sons.

Ross, H., & Plug, C. (2002). *The mystery of the moon illusion.* Oxford, England: Oxford University Press.

Ross, L. (1977). The intuitive psychologist and his shortcomings: Distortions in the attribution process. In L. Berkowitz (Ed.), *Advances in experimental social psychology* (Vol. 10, pp. 174–221). New York: Academic Press.

Ross, L., Amabile, T. M., & Steinmetz, J. L. (1977). Social roles, social control and biases in social perception. *Journal of Personality and Social Psychology, 35,* 485–494.

Ross, L., & Ward, A. (1996). Naive realism: Implications for social conflict and misunderstanding. In T. Brown, E. Reed, & E. Turiel (Eds.), *Values and knowledge* (pp. 103–135). Hillsdale, NJ: Lawrence Erlbaum Associates.

Ross, M. (1989). Relation of implicit theories to the construction of personal histories. *Psychological Review, 96,* 803–814.

Rotenberg, K. J., & Mann, L. (1986). The development of the norm of the reciprocity of self-disclosure and its function in children's attraction to peers. *Child Development, 57,* 1349–1357.

Rothbaum, R., Weisz, J., Pott, M., Miyake, K., & Morelli, G. (2000). Attachment and culture: Security in Japan and the U.S. *American Psychologist, 55,* 1093–1104.

Rotter, J. B. (1966). Generalized expectancies for internal versus external control of reinforcement. *Psychological Monographs* (1, Whole No. 609).

Rotton, J., & Kelly, I. W. (1985). Much ado about the full moon: A meta-analysis of lunar-lunacy research. *Psychological Bulletin, 97,* 286–306.

Rovee-Collier, C. (1993). The capacity for long-term memory in infancy. *Current Directions in Psychological Science, 2,* 130–135.

Rowan, J. (1998). Maslow amended. *Journal of Humanistic Psychology, 38,* 81–93.

Rowland, I. (2001). *The full facts on cold reading* (2nd ed.). London, England: Author.

Rowling, J. K. (1998). (Illustrations by Mary GrandPré.) *Harry Potter and the sorcerer's stone.* New York: Arthur A. Levine Books.

Roy, M., McNeale, M. C., Pedersen, N. L., Mathe, A. A., & Kendler, K. S. (1995). A twin study of generalized anxiety disorder and major depression. *Psychological Medicine, 25,* 1037–1049.

Roy-Byrne, P. P. (2005). The GABA-benzodiazepine receptor complex: Structure, function, and role in anxiety. *Journal of Clinical Psychiatry, 66* (Suppl. 2), 14–20.

Royce, J., Darlington, R., & Murray, H. (1983). Pooled analyses: Findings across studies. In The Consortium for Longitudinal Studies (Ed.), *As the twig is bent: Lasting effects of preschool programs* (pp. 411–459). Hillsdale, NJ: Erlbaum.

Rozin, P., & Stoess, C. (1993). Is there a general tendency to become addicted? *Addictive Behaviors, 18,* 81–87.

Rubenzer, S. J., Faschingbauer, T. R., & Ones, D. S. (2000, August). *Assessing the U.S. presidents using the Revised NEO Personality Inventory.* Paper presented at the Annual Convention of the American Psychological Association, Washington, DC.

Rudolph, K. D., Hammen, C., Burge, D., Lindberg, N., Herzberg, D., & Daley, S. E. (2000). Toward an interpersonal life-stress model of depression: The developmental context of stress generation. *Development and Psychopathology, 12,* 215–234.

Ruff, R. M., & Parker, S. B. (1993). Gender- and age-specific changes in motor speed and eye-hand coordination in adults: Normative values for the Finger Tapping and Grooved Pegboard tests. *Perceptual and Motor Skills, 76,* 1219–1230.

Rumelhart, D. E., & McClelland, J. L. (1986). *Parallel distributed processing* (Vol. 1). Cambridge, MA: MIT Press.

Ruscio, J. (2003). Diagnoses and the behaviors they denote: A critical evaluation of the labeling theory of mental illness. *Scientific Review of Mental Health Practice, 3,* 5–22.

Ruscio, J. (2005). Exploring controversies in the art and science of polygraph testing. *Skeptical Inquirer, 29*(1), 34–39.

Rush, A. J., Marangell, L. B., Sackeim, H. A., George, M. S., Brannan, S. K., Davis, S. M., et al. (2005). Vagus nerve stimulation for treatment-resistant depression: A randomized, controlled acute phase trial. *Biological Psychiatry, 58,* 347–354.

Rushton, J. P., Brainerd, C. J., & Presley, M. (1983). Behavioral development and construct validity: The principle of aggregation. *Psychological Bulletin, 94,* 18–38.

Rushton, J. P., & Campbell, A. C. (1977). Modelling, vicarious reinforcement, and extraversion on blood donating in adults: Immediate and long term effects. *European Journal of Social Psychology, 7,* 297–306.

Rust, S. (2006, April 3). Autism epidemic doubted. *Milwaukee Sentinel.* Retrieved April 16, 2006, from www.jsonline.com/story/index.aspx?id=412874.

Rutter, M. (2000). Genetic studies of autism: From the 1970s into the millennium. *Journal of Abnormal Child Psychology, 28,* 3–14.

Rutter, M. (2008). Biological implications of gene-environment interaction. *Journal of Abnormal Child Psychology, 36,* 969–975.

Rutter, M. L. (1997). Nature-nurture integration: The example of anti-social behavior. *American Psychologist 52,* 390–398.

Ryan, R. (1976). *Blaming the victim.* New York: Vintage Books.

Ryan, R. M. (1985). Thematic Apperception Test. In D. J. Keyser & R. C. Swetland (Eds.), *Test critiques* (Vol. 2, pp. 799–814). Kansas City, MO: Test Corporation of America.

S

Saba, G., Schurhoff, F., & Leboyer, M. (2006). Therapeutic and neurophysiologic aspects of transcranial magnetic stimulation in schizophrenia. *Neurophysiologie Clinique, 36,* 185–194.

Sabom, M. (1982). *Recollections of death: A medical investigation.* New York: Harper & Row.

Sackeim, H. A. (1986). The efficacy of electroconvulsive therapy. *Annals of the New York Academy of Sciences, 462,* 70–75.

Sackeim, H. A., Prudic, J., Fuller, R., Keilp, J., Lavori, P. W., & Olfson, M. (2007). The cognitive effects of electroconvulsive therapy in community settings. *Neuropsychopharmacology, 32,* 244–254.

Sacks, O. (1985). *The man who mistook his wife for a hat: And other clinical tales.* New York: Touchstone.

Sadler, P., & Woody, E. (2006). Does the more vivid imagery of high hypnotizables depend on greater cognitive effort? A test of dissociation and social-cognitive theories of hypnosis. *International Journal of Clinical and Experimental Hypnosis.*

Safer, D. J. (2000). Are stimulants overprescribed for youths with ADHD? *Annals of Clinical Psychiatry, 12,* 55–62.

Sagan, C. (1995). *The demon-haunted world: Science as a candle in the dark.* New York: Random House.

Saha, S., Chant, D., Welham, J., & McGrath, J. (2005). *PLoS Medicine, 2,* e141doi:10.1371/journal.pmed.0020141.

Saletan, W. (2004, May 12). The Stanford Prison Experiment doesn't explain Abu Ghraib. *Slate.* Retrieved December 2, 2004, from http://slate.msn.com/id/2100419/.

Salgado, J. F., Anderson, N., Mocsoso, S., Bertua, C., deFruyt, F., & Rolland, J. P. (2003). A meta-analytic study of general mental ability validity for different occupations in the European community. *Journal of Applied Psychology, 88,* 1068–1081.

Salovey, P., & Mayer, J. D. (1990). Emotional intelligence. *Imagination, Cognition, and Personality, 9,* 185–211.

Salthouse, T. A. (2004). Localizing age-related individual differences in a hierarchical structure. *Intelligence, 32,* 541–561.

Salzinger, K. (2002). Science directions: Gugelhupf. *APA Monitor on Psychology.* Retrieved May 14, 2008, from http://www.apa.org/monitor/jun02/sd.html

Samuelson, L. K., & Smith, L. B. (1998). Memory and attention make smart word learning: An alternative account of Akhtar, Carpenter, and Tomasello. *Child Development, 69,* 94–104.

Sanchez-Andres, J.V., Olds, J. L., & Alkon, D. L. (1993). Gated informational transfer within the mammalian hippocampus: A new hypothesis. *Behavioral Brain Research, 54,* 111–106.

Sanderson, W. C., & Barlow, D. H. (1990). A description of patients diagnosed with DSM-III-R generalized anxiety disorder. *Journal of Nervous and Mental Disease, 178,* 588–591.

Santa Maria, M. P., Baumeister, A. A., & Gouvier, W. D. (1999). Public knowledge and misconceptions about electroconvulsive therapy: A demographically stratified investigation. *International Journal of Rehabilitation and Health, 4,* 111–116.

Santor, D. A., & Kusumakar, V. (2001). Open trial of interpersonal therapy in adolescents with moderate to severe major depression: Effectiveness of novice IPT therapists. *Journal of the American Academy of Child and Adolescent Psychiatry, 40,* 236–240.

Saper, R. B., Kales, S. N., Paquin, J., Burns, M. J., Eisenberg, D. M., Davis, R. B., et al. (2004). Heavy metal content of Ayurvedic herbal medicine products. *Journal of the American Medical Association, 292,* 2868–2873.

Sapir, E. (1929). The status of linguistics as a science. *Language, 5,* 209.

Sar, V., Koyuncu, A., Ozturk, E, Yargic, L., Kundakci, T., Yazici, A., et al. (2007). Dissociative disorders in the psychiatric emergency ward. *General Hospital Psychiatry, 29,* 45–50.

Sarafino, E. P. (2006). *Health psychology: Biopsychosocial interactions* (5th ed.). Hoboken, NJ: John Wiley & Sons.

Satir, V. (1964). *Conjoint family therapy.* New York: Science and Behavior Books.

Saufley, W. H., Otaka, S. R., & Bavaresco, J. L. (1985). Context effects: Classroom tests and context independence. *Memory & Cognition, 13,* 522–528.

Savage-Rumbaugh, E. S. (1986). *Ape language: From conditioned response to symbol.* New York: Columbia University Press.

Savic, I., Berglund, H., & Lindstrom, P. (2005). Brain response to putative pheromones in homosexual men. *Proceedings of the National Academy of Sciences, U.S.A., 17,* 7356–7361.

Savitz, J., Solms, M., Pietersen, E., Ramesar, R., & Flor-Henry, P. (2004). Dissociative identity disorder associated with mania and change in handedness. *Cognitive and Behavioral Neurology, 17,* 233–237.

Saxe, L., & Ben-Shakhar, G. (1999). Admissibility of polygraph tests: The application of scientific standards post-Daubert. *Psychology, Public Policy and Law, 5,* 203–223.

Scarr, S. (1985). An author's frame of mind (Review of *Frames of mind: The theory of multiple intelligences*). *New Ideas in Psychology, 3,* 95–100.

Scarr, S., Webber, P. L., Weinberg, R. A., & Wittig, M. A. (1981). Personality resemblance among adolescents and their parents in biologically related and adoptive families. *Journal of Personality and Social Psychology, 40,* 885–898.

Scarr, S., & Weinberg, R. A. (1976). IQ test performance of black children adopted by white families. *American Psychologist, 31,* 726–739.

Schachter, S., & Gross, L. (1968). Manipulated time and eating behavior. *Journal of Personality and Social Psychology, 10,* 98–106.

Schachter, S., & Singer, J. E. (1962). Cognitive, social and physiological determinants of emotional state. *Psychological Review, 69,* 379–399.

Schacter, D. L. (1996). *Searching for memory: The brain, the mind, and the past.* New York: Basic Books.

Schacter, D. L. (2001). *The seven sins of memory.* Boston: Houghton-Mifflin.

Schacter, D. L., & Moscovitch, M. (1984). Infants, amnesics, and dissociable memory systems. In M. Moscovitch (Ed.), *Infant memory* (pp. 173–216). New York: Plenum.

Schaefer, C., Coyne, J. C., & Lazarus R. S. (1981). The health-related functions of social support. *Journal of Behavioral Medicine, 4,* 381–406.

Schank, R. C., & Abelson, R. (1977). *Scripts, plans, goals, and understanding.* Hillsdale, NJ: Erlbaum.

Schatzberg, A. F. (1998). Noradrenergic versus serotonergic antidepressants: Predictors of treatment response. *Journal of Clinical Psychiatry, 59* (Suppl. 14), 15–18.

Scheck, B., Neufeld, P., & Dwyer, J. (2000). *Actual innocence.* New York: Random House.

Scheff, S. W., Price, D. A., Schmitt, F. A., DeKosky, S. T., & Mufson, E. J. (2007). Synaptic alterations in CA1 in mild Alzheimer disease and mild cognitive impairment. *Neurology, 68,* 1501–1508.

Scheff, T. J. (1984). *Being mentally ill: A sociological theory.* New York: Aldine.

Scheier, M. F., & Carver, C. S. (1992). Effects of optimism on psychological and physical well-being: Theoretical overview and empirical update. *Cognitive Therapy and Research, 16,* 201–228.

Scheier, M. F., Matthews, K. A., Owens, J. F., Magovern, G. J., Lefebvre, R. C., Abbott, R. A., et al. (1989). Dispositional optimism and recovery from coronary artery bypass surgery: The beneficial effects on physical and psychological well-being. *Journal of Personality and Social Psychology, 57*(6), 1024–1040.

Scher, C. D., Ingram, R. E., & Segal, Z. V. (2005). Cognitive reactivity and vulnerability: Empirical evaluation of construct activation and cognitive diatheses in unipolar depression. *Clinical Psychology Review, 25,* 487–510.

Scherer, K. R. (1988). Criteria for emotion-antecedent appraisal: A review. In V. Hamilton, G. H. Bower, & N. H. Frijda (Eds.), *Cognitive perspectives on emotion and motivation* (pp. 89–126). Dordrecht: Nijhoff.

Schienle, A., Stark, R., Walter, B., Blecker, C., Ott, U., Kirsch, P., et al. (2002). The insula is not specifically involved in disgust processing: An fMRI study. *Neuroreport, 13,* 2023–2026.

Schkade, D. A., & Kahneman, D. (1998). Does living in California make people happy? A focusing illusion in judgments of life satisfaction. *Psychological Science, 9,* 340–346.

Schlegel, A., & Barry, H. III. (1991). *Adolescence: An anthropological inquiry.* New York: Free Press.

Schmahmann, J. D. (2004). Disorders of the cerebellum: Ataxia, dysmetria of thought, and the cerebellar cognitive affective syndrome. *Journal of Neuropsychiatry & Clinical Neurosciences, 16,* 367–378.

Schmidt, P. J., Murphy, J. H., Haq, N., Rubinow, D. R., & Danaceau, M. A. (2004). Stressful life events, personal losses, and perimenopause-related depression. *Archives of Women's Mental Health, 7,* 19–26.

Schmolk, H., Buffalo, E. A., & Squire, L. R. (2000). Memory distortions develop over time. Recollections of the O. J. Simpson trial verdict after 15 and 32 months. *Psychological Science, 11,* 39–45.

Schnall, P. L., Pieper, C., Schwartz, J. E., Karasek, R. A., Schlussel, Y., Devereux, R. B., et al. (1990). The relationship between "job strain," workplace diastolic blood pressure, and left ventricular mass index: Results of a case-control study. *Journal of the American Medical Association, 263,* 1929–1935.

Schneider, W., & Bjorklund, D. F. (1998). Memory. In W. Damon, R. S. Siegler, & D. Kuhn (Eds.), *Handbook of child psychology, Vol. 2.* (pp. 467–521). New York: Wiley.

Schoenewolf, G. (1997). *The dictionary of dream interpretation, including a glossary of dream symbols.* Northvale, NJ: Jason Aronson.

Schofield, W. (1964). *Psychotherapy: The purchase of friendship.* Englewood Cliffs, NJ: Prentice-Hall.

Schonfield, D., & Robertson, B. A. (1966). Memory storage and aging. *Canadian Journal of Psychology, 20,* 228–236.

Schuckit, M. A. (1998). Biological, psychological, and environmental predictors of the alcoholism risk: A longitudinal study. *Journal of Studies on Alcohol, 59,* 485–494.

Schuman, H., Steeh, C., Bobo, L., & Krysan, M. (1997). *Racial attitudes in America: Trends and interpretations* (Rev. ed.). Cambridge, MA: Harvard University Press.

Schwartz, B. L. (1999). Sparkling at the end of the tongue: The etiology of the tip-of-the-tongue phenomenology. *Psychonomic Bulletin & Review, 6*(3), 379–393.

Schwartz, M. B., Vartanian, L. R., Nosek, B. A., & Brownell, K. D. (2006). The influence of one's own body weight on implicit and explicit anti-fat bias. *Obesity, 14,* 440–447.

Schwartz, N. W., Woods, S. C., Porte, D., Seeley, R. J., & Baskin, D. G. (2000). Central nervous system control of food intake. *Nature, 404,* 661–671.

Schwarz, N. (1999). Self-reports: How the questions shape the answers. *American Psychologist, 54,* 93–105.

Schweder, R., Mahapatra, M., & Miller, J. (1990). Culture and moral development. In J. Kagan & S. Lamb (Eds.), *The emergence of morality in young children* (pp. 1–83). Chicago: University of Chicago Press.

Scoboria, A., Mazzoni, G., Kirsch, I., & Milling, L. S. (2002). Immediate and persistent effect of misleading questions and hypnosis on memory reports. *Journal of Experimental Psychology: Applied, 8,* 26–32.

Scovern, A. W., & Kilmann, P. R. (1980). Status of electroconvulsive therapy: Review of the outcome literature. *Psychological Bulletin, 87,* 260–295.

Scoville, W. B., & Milner, B. (1957). Loss of recent memory after bilateral hippocampal lesions. *Journal of Neurology, Neurosurgery, and Psychiatry, 20,* 11–21.

Sears, D. O. (1986). College sophomores in the laboratory: Influences of a narrow data base on social-psychology's view of human nature. *Journal of Personality and Social Psychology, 51,* 515–530.

Segal, M. W. (1974). Alphabet and attraction: An unobtrusive measure of the effect of propinquity in a field setting. *Journal of Personality and Social Psychology, 30,* 654–657.

Segal, Z. V., Williams, S., & Teasdale, J. (2002). *Mindfulness-based cognitive therapy for depression: A new approach to preventing relapse.* New York: Guilford.

Segall, M. H., Campbell, D. T., & Herskovits, M. J. (1966). *The influence of culture on visual perception.* Indianapolis, IN: Bobbs-Merrill.

Segerstrom, S. C. (2005). Optimism and immunity: Do positive thoughts always lead to positive effects? *Brain, Behavior, and Immunity, 19,* 195–200.

Segerstrom, S. C., Taylor, S. E., Kemeny, M. E., & Fahey, J. L. (1998). Optimism is associated with mood, coping, and immune change in response to stress. *Journal of Personality and Social Psychology, 74,* 1646–1655.

Segrin, C. (2000). Social skill deficits associated with depression. *Clinical Psychology Review, 20,* 379–403.

Seitz, A. R., & Watanabe, T. (2003). Psychophysics: Is subliminal learning really passive? *Nature, 422,* 36.

Selden, S. (1999). *Inheriting shame: The story of eugenics and racism in America.* New York: Teachers College Press.

Seligman, M. E. P. (1971). Phobias and preparedness. *Behavior Therapy, 2,* 307–320.

Seligman, M. E. P. (1975). *Helplessness: On depression, development, and death.* San Francisco: Freeman.

Seligman, M. E. P. (1990). *Learned optimism.* New York: Knopf.

Seligman, M. E. P. (1995). The effectiveness of psychotherapy: The *Consumer Reports* survey. *American Psychologist, 50,* 965–974.

Seligman, M. E. P. (1998). *Learned optimism* (2nd ed.). New York: Pocket Books.

Seligman, M. E. P., & Csikszentmihalyi, M. (2000). Positive psychology: An introduction. *American Psychologist, 55,* 5–14.

Seligman, M. E. P., & Hager, J. L. (1972). Sauce-bearnaise syndrome. *Psychology Today, 6*(3), 59.

Seligman, M. E. P., & Maier, S. F. (1967). Failure to escape traumatic shock. *Journal of Experimental Psychology, 74,* 1–9.

Seligman, M. E. P., & Pawelski, J. O. (2003). Positive psychology: FAQs. *Psychological Inquiry, 14,* 159–163.

Selye, H. (1956). *The stress of life.* New York: McGraw Hill.

Serbin, L. A., & O'Leary, K. D. (1975). How nursery schools teach girls to shut up. *Psychology Today, 9*(7), 56–58.

Serpell, R. (1979). How specific are perceptual skills? *British Journal of Psychology, 70,* 365–380.

Sevdalis, N., & Harvey, N. (2007) Biased forecasting of postdecisional affect. *Psychological Science 18*(8), 678–681.

Shadish, W. R. (1995). The logic of generalization: Five principles common to experiments and ethnographies. *American Journal of Community Psychology, 23*(3), 419–428.

Shadish, W. R., Cook, T. D., & Campbell, D. T. (2002). *Experimental and quasi-experimental designs for generalized causal inference.* Boston, MA: Houghton Mifflin.

Shaffer, H. J. (2000). Addictive personality. In A. E. Kazdin (Ed.), *Encyclopedia of psychology* (Vol. 1, pp. 35–36). Washington, DC: American Psychological Association and Oxford University Press.

Shamsuzzaman, A. S., Gersh, B. J., & Somers, V. K. (2003). Obstructive sleep apnea: Implications for cardiac and vascular disease. *Journal of the American Medical Association, 290,* 1906–1914.

Shanab, M. E., & Yahya, K. A. (1977). A behavioral study of obedience in children. *Journal of Personality and Social Psychology, 35,* 530–536.

Shapiro, F. (1989). Eye movement desensitization: A new treatment for post-traumatic stress disorder. *Journal of Behavior Therapy and Experimental Psychiatry, 20,* 211–217.

Shapiro, F. (1995). *Eye movement desensitization and reprocessing: Basic principles, protocols, and procedures.* New York: Guilford Press.

Shapiro, F., & Forrest, M. S. (1997). *EMDR: The breakthrough therapy for overcoming anxiety, stress, and trauma.* New York: Basic Books.

Shapiro, S. L., & Walsh, R. (2003). An analysis of recent meditation research and suggestions for future directions. *The Humanistic Psychologist, 31,* 86–113.

Shaw, P., Greenstein, D., Lerch, J., Clasen, L., Lenroot, R., Gogtay, N., et al. (2006). Intellectual ability and cortical development in children and adolescents. *Nature, 440,* 676–679.

Shea, S. C. (1998). *Psychiatric interviewing: The art of understanding* (2nd ed). Philadelphia: W. B. Saunders.

Sheldon, K. M., & Lyubomirsky, S. (2006). How to increase and sustain positive emotion: The effects of expressing gratitude and visualizing best possible selves. *The Journal of Positive Psychology, 1,* 73–82.

Shepard, R. N. (1990). *Mind sights: Original visual illusions, ambiguities, and other anomalies.* New York: W. H. Freeman.

Shepperd, J. A., & Koch, E. J. (2005). Pitfalls in teaching judgment heuristics. *Teaching of Psychology, 32,* 43–46.

Sher, K. J., Grekin, E. R., & Williams, N. A. (2005). The development of alcohol use disorders. In S. Nolen-Hoeksema, T. D. Cannon, & T. Widiger (Eds.), *Annual Review of Clinical Psychology, 1,* 493–524.

Sherif, M., Harvey, O. J., White, B. J., Hood, W. R., & Sherif, C. W. (1961). *The Robbers Cave experiment: Intergroup conflict and cooperation.* Middletown, CT: Wesleyan University Press.

Shermer, M. (2002). *Why people believe weird things: Pseudoscience, superstition, and other confusions of our time* (2nd ed.). New York: W. H. Freeman.

Sherrington, C. S. (1906). *The integrative action of the nervous system.* New York: Charles Scribner's Sons.

Shimamura, A. P. (1992). Organic amnesia. In L. Squire (Ed.), *Encyclopedia of learning and memory* (pp. 30–35). New York: Macmillan.

Shimamura, A. P., Berry, J. M., Mangels, J. A., Rusting, C. L., & Jurica, P. J. (1995). Memory and cognitive abilities in university professors: Evidence for successful aging. *Psychological Science, 6,* 271–277.

Shin, S. M., Chow, C., Camacho-Gonsalves, T., Levy, R. J., Allen, E., & Leff, S. H. (2005). A meta-analytic review of racial-ethnic matching for African American and Caucasian American clients and clinicians. *Journal of Counseling Psychology, 52,* 45–56.

Shlien, J., & Levant, R. (1984). Introduction. In R. Levant & J. Shlien, (Eds.), *Client-centered therapy and the person-centered approach: New directions in theory, research and practice* (pp. 1–16). New York: Praeger.

Shomstein, S., & Yantis, S. (2006). Parietal cortex mediates voluntary control of spatial and nonspatial auditory attention. *Journal of Neuroscience, 26,* 435–439.

Shors, T. J., & Matzel, L. D. (1999). Long-term potentiation: What's learning got to do with it? *Behavioral and Brain Sciences, 20,* 597–655.

Showalter, E. (1997). *Hystories: Hysterical epidemics and modern culture.* New York: Columbia University Press.

Shrout, P. E., Link, B. G., Dohrenwend, B. P., Skodol, A. E., Stueve, A., & Mirotznik, J. (1989). Characterizing life events as risk factors for depression: The role of fateful loss events. *Journal of Abnormal Psychology, 98,* 460–467.

Sidgwick, H. (1894). Report on the Census of Hallucinations. *Proc. Soc. for Psych. Res. X, Part XXXVI,* 25–422. [Ps. R. II, 69–75.].

Sieff, E. M., Dawes, R. M., & Loewenstein, G. (1999). Anticipated versus actual reaction to HIV test results. *American Journal of Psychology, 112,* 297–311.

Siegler, R. S. (1992). The other Alfred Binet. *Developmental Psychology, 28,* 179–190.

Siegler, R. S. (1995). Children's thinking: How does change occur? In F. E. Weinert & W. Schneider (Eds.), *Memory performance and competencies: Issues in growth and development* (pp. 405–430). Hillsdale, NJ: Erlbaum.

Sigurdsson, T., Doyere, V., Cain, C. K., & LeDoux, J. E. (2007). Long-term potentiation in the amygdala: A cellular mechanism of fear learning and memory. *Neuropharmacology, 52,* 215–227.

Silventoinen, K., Sammalisto, S., Perola, M., Boomsma, D. I., Cornes, B. K., Davis, C., et al. (2003). Heritability of adult body height: A comparative study of twin cohorts in eight countries. *Twin Research, 6,* 399–408.

Simon, C. W., & Emmons, W. H. (1955). Learning during sleep? *Psychological Bulletin, 52*(4), 328–342.

Simon, G., von Kopff, M., Saunders, K., Miglioretti, D. L., Crane, K., Van Belle, K., et al. (2006). Association between obesity and psychiatric disorders in the U.S. population. *Archives of General Psychiatry, 63,* 824–830.

Simon, M. J., & Salzberg, H. C. (1985). The effect of manipulated expectancies on posthypnotic amnesia. *International Journal of Clinical and Experimental Hypnosis, 33,* 40–51.

Simons, R. C., & Hughes, C. C. (1986). *The culture-bound syndromes: Folk illnesses of psychiatric and anthropological interest.* Boston: D. Reidel.

Simpson, G. M., & Kline, N. S. (1976). Tardive dyskinesias: Manifestations, etiology, and treatment. In M. D. Yahr (Ed.), *The basal ganglia* (pp. 167–183). New York: Raven Press.

Singer, M. (1979, January). Coming out of the cults. *Psychology Today,* 72–82.

Singer, M. T., & Lalich, J. (1996). *Crazy therapies.* Baltimore: Jossey-Bass.

Singer, M. T., & Nievod, A. (2003). New age therapies. In S. O. Lilienfeld, S. J. Lynn, & J. M. Lohr (Eds.), *Science and pseudoscience in clinical psychology* (pp. 176–204). New York: Guilford.

Skinner, B. F. (1938). *The behavior of organisms: An experimental analysis.* New York: Appleton-Century-Crofts.

Skinner, B. F. (1948). Superstition in the pigeon. *Journal of Experimental Psychology, 38,* 168–172.

Skinner, B. F. (1953). *Science and human behavior.* New York: Macmillan.

Skinner, B. F. (1969). *Contingencies of reinforcement.* East Norwalk, CT: Appleton-Century-Crofts.

Skinner, B. F. (1971). *Beyond freedom and dignity.* New York: Knopf.

Skinner, B. F. (1974). *About behaviorism.* New York: Vintage Books.

Skinner, E., Edge, K., Altman, J., & Sherwood, H. (2003). Searching for the structure of coping: A review and critique of category systems for classifying ways of coping. *Psychological Bulletin, 129,* 216–219.

Slater, L. (2004). *Opening Skinner's box: Great psychological experiments of the 20th century.* New York: W. W. Norton.

Slavin, R. E., & Cooper, R. (1999). Improving intergroup relations: Lessons learned from cooperative learning programs. *Journal of Social Issues, 55,* 647–663.

Sloan, R. P., Bagiella, E., & Powell, T. (1999). Religion, spirituality, and medicine. *Lancet, 353,* 644–647.

Sloane, R. B., Staples, F., Cristol, A., Yorkston, N., & Whipple, K. (1975). *Psycho-therapy versus behavior therapy.* Cambridge, MA: Harvard University Press.

Slovic, P., & Peters, E. (2006). Risk perception and affect. *Current Directions in Psychological Science, 15,* 322–325.

Smith, D., & Dumont, F. (1995). A cautionary study: Unwarranted interpretations of the Draw-A-Person Test. *Professional Psychology: Research and Practice, 26,* 298–303.

Smith, D. M., Langa, K. M., Kabeto, M. U., & Ubel, P. A. (2005). Health, wealth, and happiness: Financial resources buffer subjective well-being after the onset of a disability. *Psychological Science, 16,* 663–666.

Smith, E. E., Shoben, E. J., & Rips, L. J. (1974). Structure and process in semantic memory: A featural model for semantic decision. *Psychological Review, 81,* 214–241.

Smith, G. P. (1996). The direct and indirect controls of meal size. *Neuroscience Biobehavioral Review, 20,* 40–46.

Smith, J. D., & Dumont, F. (2002). Confidence in psychodiagnosis: What makes us so sure? *Clinical Psychology and Psychotherapy, 9,* 292–298.

Smith, M., & Hall, C. S. (1964). An investigation of regression in a long dream series. *Journal of Gerontology, 19,* 66–71.

Smith, M. L., & Glass, G. V. (1977). Meta-analysis of psychotherapy outcome studies. *American Psychologist, 32,* 752–760.

Smith, M. L., Glass, G. V., & Miller, T. I. (1980). *The benefits of psychotherapy.* Baltimore: Johns Hopkins University Press.

Smith, M. T., & Haythornthwaite, J. A. (2004). How do sleep disturbance and chronic pain inter-relate? Insights from the longitudinal and cognitive-behavioral clinical trials literature. *Sleep Medicine Review, 8,* 119–132.

Smith, P. K., & Daglish, L. (1977). Sex differences in parent and infant behavior in the home. *Child Development, 48,* 1250–1254.

Smith, R. A. (2001). *Challenging your preconceptions: Thinking critically about psychology.* Pacific Grove, CA: Wadsworth.

Smith, S. L., Gerhardt, K. J., Griffiths, S. K., Huang, X., & Abrams, R. M. (2003). Intelligibility of sentences recorded from the uterus of a pregnant ewe and from the fetal inner ear. *Audiology & Neuro-otology, 8,* 347–353.

Smith, S. M. (1979). Remembering in and out of context. *Journal of Experimental Psychology: Human Learning and Memory, 5,* 460–471.

Smith, S. M., Lindsay, R. C. L., Pryke, S., & Dysart, J. E. (2001). Postdictors of eyewitness errors: Can false identifications be diagnosed in the cross race situation? *Psychology, Public Policy, and Law, 7,* 153–169.

Smith, S. S. (2005). NCHS Dataline. *Public Health Reports, 120,* 353–354.

Smith, T. (2008). Empirically supported and unsupported treatments for autism spectrum disorders. *Scientific Review of Mental Health Practice, 6*(1), 3-20.

Smith, T. W., & Gallo, L. C. (2001). Personality traits as risk factors for physical illness. In A. Baum, T. A. Revenson, & J. Singer (Eds.), *Handbook of health psychology* (pp. 139–173). Mahwah, NJ: Erlbaum.

Smythe, I. H. (2007). The secret behind "The Secret": What is attracting millions to the "Law of Attraction"? *Skeptic, 13*(2), 8–11.

Snider, V. E. (1992). Learning styles and learning to read: A critique. *RASE: Remedial & Special Education, 13*(1), 6–18.

Snook, B., Cullen, R. M., Bennell, C., Taylor, P. J., & Gendreau, P. (2008). The criminal profiling illusion: What's behind the smoke and mirrors? *Criminal Justice and Behavior, 35*(10), 1257–1276.

Snyder, M. (1974). Self monitoring of expressive behavior. *Journal of Personality and Social Psychology, 30,* 526–537.

Snyder, M., & Gangestad, S. (1986). On the nature of self-monitoring: Matters of assessment, matters of validity. *Journal of Personality and Social Psychology, 51*(1), 125–139.

Snyder, S. H. (1975). *Madness and the brain.* New York: McGraw-Hill.

So, K., & Orme-Johnson, D. (2001). Three randomized experiments on the longitudinal effects of the transcendental meditation technique on cognition. *Intelligence, 29,* 419–440.

Soar, K., Parrott, A. C., & Fox, H. C. (2004). Persistent neuropsychological problems after 7 years of abstinence from recreational ecstasy (MDMA): A case study. *Psychological Reports, 95,* 192–196.

Sobell, M. B., & Sobell, L. C. (1973). Alcoholics treated by individualized behavior therapy: One year treatment outcome. *Behaviour Research and Therapy, 11,* 599–618.

Sobell, M. B., & Sobell, L. C. (1976). Second year treatment outcome of alcoholics treated by individualized behavior therapy: Results. *Behaviour Research and Therapy, 14,* 195–215.

Solomon, P. R., Adams, F., Silver, A., Zimmer, J., & DeVeaux, R. (2002). Ginkgo for memory enhancement: A randomized controlled trial. *Journal of the American Medical Association, 288,* 835–840.

Solomon, R. (2002). *That takes ovaries! Bold females and their brazen acts.* New York: Three Rivers Press.

Solomon, S. S., & King, J. G. (1995). Influence of color on fire vehicle accidents. *Journal of Safety Research, 26,* 41–48.

Sommers, C. H., & Satel, S. (2005). *One nation under therapy: How the helping culture is eroding self-reliance.* New York: St. Martin's Press.

Sonke, C. J., van Boxtel, G. J. M., Griesel, R. D., & Poortinga, Y. H. (2008). Brain wave concomitants of cross-cultural differences in scores on simple cognitive tasks. *Journal of Cross-Cultural Psychology, 39,* 37–54.

Soper, B., Milford, G., & Rosenthal, G. (1995). Belief when evidence does not support theory. *Psychology & Marketing, 12,* 415–422.

Sorace, A. (2007). The more, the merrier: Facts and beliefs about the bilingual mind. In S. Della Sala (Ed.), *Tall tales about the mind and the brain: Separating fact from fiction* (pp. 193–203). Oxford, England: Oxford University Press.

Sorkhabi, N. (2005). Applicability of Baumrind's parent typology to collective cultures: Analysis of cultural explanations of parent socialization effects. *International Journal of Behavioral Development, 29,* 552–563.

Spangler, W. D. (1992). Validity of questionnaire and TAT measures of need for achievement: Two meta-analyses. *Psychological Bulletin, 112,* 140–154.

Spanos, N. P. (1986). Hypnotic behavior: A social-psychological interpretation of amnesia, analgesia, and "trance logic." *The Behavioral and Brain Sciences, 9,* 499–502.

Spanos, N. P. (1994). Multiple identity enactments and multiple personality disorder: A sociocognitive perspective. *Psychological Bulletin, 116,* 143–165.

Spanos, N. P. (1996). *Multiple identities and false memories: A sociocognitive perspective.* Washington, DC: American Psychological Association.

Spanos, N. P., Cobb, P. C., & Gorassini, D. (1985). Failing to resist hypnotic test suggestions: A strategy for self-presenting as deeply hypnotized. *Psychiatry, 48,* 282–292.

Spanos, N. P., Menary, E., Gabora, M. J., DuBreuil, S. C., & Dewhirst, B. (1991). Secondary identity enactments during hypnotic past-life regression: A sociocognitive perspective. *Journal of Personality and Social Psychology, 61,* 308–320.

Spearman, C. (1927). *The abilities of man.* New York: Macmillan.

Spelke, E. S. (1994). Initial knowledge: Six suggestions. *Cognition, 50,* 431–445.

Spelke, E. S. (2005). Sex differences in intrinsic aptitude for mathematics and science: A critical review. *American Psychologist, 60,* 950–958.

Sperling, G. (1960). The information available in brief visual presentations. *Psychological Monographs: General and Applied, 74*(11, Whole No. 498), 1–29.

Sperry, R. W. (1974). Lateral specialization in the surgically separated hemispheres. In F. Schmitt & F. Worden (Eds.), *Neurosciences third study program* (pp. 5–19). Cambridge, MA: MIT Press.

Spiegel, D., Bloom, J. R., Kramer, H. C., & Gottheil, E. (1989). Effect of psychosocial treatment on survival of patients with metastatic breast cancer. *Lancet, 2,* 888–891.

Spiegler, M. (1983). *Contemporary behavior therapy.* Palo Alto, CA: Mayfield.

Spiegler, M. D., & Guevremont, D. C. (2003). *Contemporary behavior therapy* (4th ed). Belmont, CA: Wadsworth/Thompson Learning.

Spirito, A., & Esposito-Smythers, C. (2006). Attempted and completed suicide in adolescence. *Annual Review of Clinical Psychology, 2,* 237–266.

Spitzer, R. L. (1975). On pseudoscience, science, logic in remission, and psychiatric diagnosis: A critique of Rosenhan's "On being sane in insane places." *Journal of Abnormal Psychology, 84,* 442–452.

Sprecher, S. (1998). Insider's perspectives on reasons for attraction to a close other. *Social Psychology Quarterly, 61,* 287–300.

Sprecher, S., Barbee, A., & Schwartz, P. (1995). "Was it good for you, too?": Gender differences in first sexual experiences. *Journal of Sex Research, 32,* 3–15.

Squire, L. R. (1987). *Memory and brain,* New York: Oxford University Press.

Srivastava, S., John, O. P., Gosling, S. D., & Potter, J. (2003). Development of personality in early and middle adulthood: Set like plaster or persistent change? *Journal of Personality and Social Psychology, 84*(5), 1041–1053.

Sroufe, L. A. (1983). Infant-caregiver attachment and patterns of adaptations in preschool: The roots of maladaptations and competence. In M. Perlmutter (Ed.), *Minnesota Symposium on Child Psychology* (Vol. 16, pp. 41–81). Hillsdale, NJ: Erlbaum.

Staddon, J. E. R., (2007). Is animal learning optimal? In A. Bejan and G. W. Merkx (Eds.), *Constructal theory of social dynamics* (pp. 161–167). New York: Springer.

Staddon, J. E. R., & Simmelhag, V. L. (1971). Superstition experiment—A reexamination of its implications for principles of adaptive behavior. *Psychological Review, 78*(1), 3.

Stahl, S. (1999). Different strokes for different folks? A critique of learning styles. *American Educator, 23,* 27–31.

Standing, L., Conezio, J., & Haber, R. N. (1970). Perception and memory for pictures: Single-trial learning of 2500 visual stimuli. *Psychonomic Science 19*(2), 73–74.

Stanovich, K. (2006). *How to think straight about psychology* (8th ed.). Boston: Allyn & Bacon.

Stanovich, K. E., & West, R. F. (2000). Advancing the rationality debate. *Behavioral and Brain Sciences, 23*(5), 701–726.

Starr, L. R., & Davila, J. (2008). Excessive reassurance seeking, depression, and interpersonal rejection: A meta-analytic review. *Journal of Abnormal Psychology, 117,* 762–765.

Stathopoulou, G., Powers, M. B., Berry, A. C., Smits, J. A. J., & Otto, M. W. (2006). Exercise interventions for mental health: A quantitative and qualitative review. *Clinical Psychology: Science and Practice 13,* 179–193.

Steblay, N. M., & Bothwell, R. K. (1994). Evidence for hypnotically refreshed testimony: The view from the laboratory. *Law and Human Behavior, 18*(6), 635–651.

Steblay, N. M., Dysart, J., Fulero, S., & Lindsay, R. C. L. (2001). Eyewitness accuracy rates in sequential and simultaneous lineup presentations: A meta-analytic comparison. *Law and Human Behavior, 25,* 459–474.

Steblay, N. M., Dysart, J. E., Fulero, S., & Lindsay, R. C. L. (2003). Eyewitness accuracy rates in police showup and lineup presentations: A meta-analytic comparison. *Law and Human Behavior, 27,* 523–540.

Steele, C. M. (1997). A threat in the air: How stereotypes shape intellectual identity and performance. *American Psychologist, 52*(6), 613–629.

Steele, C. M., & Aronson, J. (1995). Stereotype threat and the intellectual test-performance of African-Americans. *Journal of Personality and Social Psychology, 69*(5), 797–811.

Steele, K. M., Bass, K. E., & Crook, M. D. (1999). The mystery of the Mozart effect: Failure to replicate. *Psychological Science, 10*(4), 366–369.

Stein, M. B., Jang, K. L., & Livesley, W. J. (1999). Heritability of anxiety sensitivity: A twin study. *American Journal of Psychiatry, 156*(2), 246–251.

Steinberg, L. (2001). We know some things: Adolescent-parent relationships in retrospect and prospect. *Journal of Research in Adolescence, 11,* 1–20.

Steinberg, L., & Scott, E. S. (2003). Less guilty by reason of adolescence—Developmental immaturity, diminished responsibility, and the juvenile death penalty. *American Psychologist, 58*(12), 1009–1018.

Steinmetz, J. L., Lewinsohn, P. M., & Antonuccio, D. O. (1983). Prediction of individual outcome in a group intervention for depression. *Journal of Consulting and Clinical Psychology, 51*(3), 331–337.

Stephan, W. G. (1978). School desegregation: An evaluation of predictions made in *Brown v. Board of Education. Psychological Bulletin, 85,* 217–238.

Stepp, L. S. (2007, April 24). For Virginia Tech survivors, memories will be powerful. Washingtonpost.com. Retrieved June 18, 2007, from www.washingtonpost.com/wp-dyn/content/2007/article/04/20/AR2007042001790_pf.html.

Stern, S. L., Dhanda, R., & Hazuda, H. P. (2001). Hopelessness predicts mortality in older Mexican and European Americans. *Psychosomatic Medicine, 63,* 344–351.

Stern, W. (1912). *The psychological methods of intelligence testing* (G. Whipple, Trans.). Baltimore: Warwick and York.

Sternberg, R. J. (1983). Components of human intelligence. *Cognition, 15,* 1–48.

Sternberg, R. J. (1986). A triangular theory of love. *Psychological Review, 93,* 119–135.

Sternberg, R. J. (1988a). Triangulating love. In R. J. Sternberg & M. L. Barnes (Eds.), *The psychology of love* (pp. 119–138). London: Yale University Press.

Sternberg, R. J. (1988b). *The triarchic mind: A new theory of human intelligence.* New York: Penguin Books.

Sternberg, R. J. (2002). Smart people are not stupid, but they sure can be foolish: The imbalance theory of foolishness. In R. J. Sternberg (Ed.), *Why smart people can be so stupid.* New Haven, CT: Yale University Press.

Sternberg, R. J. (2003a). A duplex theory of hate: Development and application to terrorism, massacres, and genocide. *Review of General Psychology, 7,* 299–328.

Sternberg, R. J. (2003b). Intelligence. In I. B. Weiner & D. K. Freedheim (Eds.), *Comprehensive handbook of psychology, Vol. 1* (pp. 135–156). New York: Wiley.

Sternberg, R. J. (2004a). *Psychology* (4th ed.). Belmont, CA: Wadsworth.

Sternberg, R. J., & Detterman, D. K. (Eds.). (1986). *What is intelligence? Contemporary viewpoints on its nature and definition.* Norwood, NJ: Ablex.

Sternberg, R. J., & Wagner, R. K. (1993). *Thinking styles inventory.* Unpublished instrument.

Sternberg, R. J., Wagner, R. K., Williams, W. M., & Horvath, J. A. (1995). Testing common sense. *American Psychologist, 50,* 912–927.

Stevenson, I. (1960). The evidence for survival from claimed memories of former incarnations. Part I: Review of the data. *Journal of the American Society for Psychical Research, 54,* 51–71.

Stevenson, I. (1974). *Twenty cases suggestive of reincarnation* (2nd rev. ed.), Charlottesville, VA: University Press of Virginia.

Stewart, N. (2009). The cost of anchoring on credit-card minimum repayments. *Psychological Science, 20,* 39–41.

Stewart, T. L., LaDuke, J. R., Bracht, C., Sweet, B. A. M., & Gamarel, K. E. (2003). Do the "eyes" have it? A program evaluation of Jane Elliott's "Blue-Eyes/Brown-Eyes" diversity training exercise. *Journal of Applied Social Psychology, 33,* 1898–1921.

Stice, E., Presnell, K., Shaw, H., & Rhode, P. (2005). Psychological and behavioral risk factors for obesity onset in adolescent girls: A prospective study. *Journal of Consulting and Clinical Psychology, 73,* 195–202.

Stickgold, R., James, L., & Hobson, J. A. (2002). Visual discrimination learning requires sleep after training. *Nature Neuroscience, 3,* 1235–1236.

Stierlin, H. (1972). *Conflict and reconciliation: A study in human relations and schizophrenia* (2nd ed.). New York: Science House.

Stoerig, P., & Cowey, A. (1997). Blindsight in man and monkey. *Brain, 120,* 535–559.

Stokoe, W. C., Casterline, D. C., & Croneberg, C. G. (1976). *A dictionary of American Sign Language on linguistic principles.* Silver Spring, MD: Linstok.

Stone, A. A. (1982). The insanity defense on trial. *Hospital and Community Psychiatry, 33,* 636–640.

Storch, E., Bagner, D., Geffken, G., & Baumeister, A. (2004). Association between overt and relational aggression and psychosocial adjustment in undergraduate college students. *Violence and Victims, 19,* 689–700.

Strack, F., Martin, L., & Stepper, S. (1988). Inhibiting and facilitating conditions of the human smile: A nonobtrusive test of the facial feedback hypothesis. *Journal of Personality and Social Psychology, 54*, 768–777.

Strauch, I., & Meier, B. (1996). *In search of dreams: Results of experimental dream research.* Albany: SUNY Press.

Straus, M. A., (1996) Corporal punishment in America and its effect on children. *Journal of Child Centered Practice, 3,* 57–77.

Straus, M. A., & McCord, J. (1998). Do physically punished children become violent adults? In S. Nolen-Hoeksema (Ed.), *Clashing views on abnormal psychology: A Taking Sides custom reader* (pp. 130–155). Guilford, CT: Dushkin/McGraw-Hill.

Straus, M. A., Sugarman, D. B., & Giles-Sims, J. (1997). Spanking by parents and subsequent antisocial behavior of children. *Archives of Pediatrics and Adolescent Medicine, 151*(8), 761–767.

Strayer, D. L., Drews, F. A., & Johnston, W. A. (2003). Cell phone-induced failures of visual attention during simulated driving. *Journal of Experimental Psychology: Applied, 9,* 23–32.

Stricker, G., & Gold, J. (2003). Integrative approaches to psychotherapy. In A. S. Gurman & S. B. Messer (Eds.), *Essential psychotherapies: Theory and practic* (2nd ed., pp. 317–349). New York: Guilford.

Strickland, T. L., Stein, R., Lin, K. M., Risby, E., & Fong, R. (1997). The pharmacologic treatment of anxiety and depression in African Americans: Considerations for the general practitioner. *Archives of Family Medicine, 6,* 371–375.

Strik, W., Dierks, T., Hubl, D., & Horn, H. (2008). Hallucinations, thought disorders, and the language domain in schizophrenia. *Clinical EEG Neuroscience, 39*(2), 91–94.

Stroebe, W. (2000). *Social psychology and health* (2nd ed.). Buckingham, England: Open University Press.

Strohl, K. P., & Redline, S. (1996). Recognition of obstructive sleep apnea. *American Journal of Respiratory and Critical Care Medicine, 154,* 279–289.

Stromswold, K. (2005). Genetic specificity of linguistic heritability. In A. Cutler (Ed.), *Twenty-first century psycholinguistics: Four cornerstones* (pp. 121–139). Mahwah, NJ: Lawrence Erlbaum.

Strupp, H. H., Fox, R. E., & Lessler, K. (1969). *Patients view their therapy.* Baltimore: Johns Hopkins University Press.

Strupp, H. H., Hadley, S. W., & Gomez-Schwartz, B. (1978). *Psychotherapy for better or worse: An analysis of the problem of negative effects.* New York: Jason Aronson.

Stuart, E. W., Shimp, T. A., & Engle, R. W. (1987). Classical conditioning of consumer attitudes: Four experiments in an advertising context. *Journal of Consumer Research, 14,* 334–349.

Stuart, R. B., & Heiby, E. M. (2007). To prescribe or not prescribe: Eleven exploratory questions. *The Scientific Review of Mental Health Practice, 5,* 4–32.

Stunkard, A. (1975). Satiety is a conditioned reflex. *Journal of Psychosomatic Medicine, 37,* 383–387.

Stunkard, A. J., Foch, T. T., & Hrubec, Z. (1986). A twin study of human obesity. *Journal of the American Medical Association, 256,* 51–54.

Sue, D. W., Capodilupo, C. M., Torino, G. C., Bucceri, J. M., Holder, A. M. B., Nadal, K. L., et al. (2007). Racial microaggressions in everyday life: Implications for clinical practice. *American Psychologist, 62*(4), 271–286.

Sue, D. W., & Sue, D. (2003). *Counseling the culturally diverse: Theory and practice* (4th ed.). New York: Wiley.

Sue, S. (1993, November). *Measurement, testing, and ethnic bias: Can solutions be found?* Keynote Address at the Ninth Buros-Nebraska Symposium on Measurement and Testing, Lincoln, NE, September.

Sue, S. (1998). In search of cultural competence in psychotherapy and counseling. *American Psychologist, 53,* 440–448.

Sue, S., & Lam, A. G. (2002). Cultural and demographic diversity. In J. C. Norcross (Ed.), *Psychotherapy relationships that work* (pp. 401–421). New York: Oxford University Press.

Sullivan, H. S. (1954). *The psychiatric interview.* New York: W. W. Norton.

Sullivan, P. F. (1995). Mortality of anorexia nervosa. *American Journal of Psychiatry, 152,* 1073–1074.

Sultan, S., Andronikof, A., Reveillere, C., & Lemmel, G. (2006). A Rorschach stability study in a nonpatient adult sample. *Journal of Personality Assessment, 87,* 330–348.

Sundet, J. M., Barlaug, D. G., & Torjussen, T. M. (2004). The end of the Flynn effect? A study of secular trends in mean intelligence test scores of Norwegian conscripts during half a century. *Intelligence, 32,* 349–362.

Susser, E. S., & Lin, S. P. (1992). Schizophrenia after prenatal exposure to the Dutch Hunger Winter of 1944–1945. *Archives of General Psychiatry, 49,* 983–988.

Sutherland, S. (1992). *Irrationality: Why we don't think straight!* New Brunswick, NJ: Rutgers University Press.

Swaiman, K. F., & Ashwal, S. (1999). *Pediatric neurology: Principles and practice* (3rd ed.). St. Louis, MO: Mosby.

Swann, W. B. Jr., & Pelham, B. W. (2002). Who wants out when the going gets good? Psychological investment and preference for self-verifying college roommates. *Journal of Self and Identity, 1,* 219–233.

Swenson, C. (1968). Empirical evaluations of human figure drawings: 1957–1966. *Psychological Bulletin, 70,* 20–44.

Symons, D. (1979). *The evolution of human sexuality.* New York: Oxford University Press.

Szasz, T. S. (1960). The myth of mental illness. *American Psychologist, 15,* 113–118.

Szasz, T. S. (2006). *Mental illness as a brain disease: A brief history lesson.* Cybercenter for Liberty and Responsibility. Retrieved December 22, 2006, from www.szasz.com/freeman13.html.

T

Taiminen, T., & Jääskeläinen, S. K. (2001). Intense and recurrent déjà vu experiences related to amantadine and phenylpropanolamine in a healthy male. *Journal of Clinical Neuroscience, 8,* 460–462.

Talbott, S. (2002). *The cortisol connection diet: The breakthrough program to control stress and lose weight.* Alameda, CA: Hunter House.

Tang, Y., Nyengaard, J. R., De Groot, D. M., & Gundersen, H. J. (2001). Total regional and global number of synapses in the human brain neocortex. *Synapse, 41,* 258–273.

Tanner, J. M. (1990). *Fetus into man: Physical growth from conception to maturity* (Rev. ed.). Cambridge, MA: Harvard University Press.

Tanner, J. M. (1998). Sequence, tempo, and individual variation in growth and development of boys and girls aged twelve to sixteen. In R. E. Muuss & H. D. Porton (Eds.), *Adolescent behavior and society: A book of readings* (5th ed., pp. 34–46). New York: McGraw-Hill.

Tanner, L. (2006, August 6). Sexual lyrics prompt teens to have sex. *Associated Press.* Retrieved August 6, 2006, from www.sfgate.com/cgibin/article.cgi?f=/n/a/2006/08/06/national/a215010D94.DTL.

Tarver, S. G., & Dawson, M. M. (1978). Modality preference and teaching of reading: Review. *Journal of Learning Disabilities, 11*(1), 5–17.

Tavris, C. (1989). *Anger: The misunderstood emotion.* New York: Touchstone.

Tavris, C., & Aronson, E. (2007). *Mistakes were made (but not by me): How we justify foolish beliefs, bad decisions, and hurtful acts.* New York: Harcourt.

Taylor, R. (1975, May/June). Electroconvulsive treatment (ECT): The control of therapeutic power. *Exchange, 32*–37.

Taylor, S. E., Klein, L. C., Lewis, B. P., Gruenewald, T. L., Gurung, R. A. R., & Updegraff, J. A. (2000). Biobehavioral responses to stress in females: Tend-and-befriend, not fight-or-flight. *Psychological Review, 107,* 411–429.

Tedeschi, J. T., Schlenker, B. R., & Bonoma, T. V. (1971). Cognitive dissonance: Private ratiocination or public spectacle? *American Psychologist, 26,* 680–695.

Tellegen, A. (1982). *Brief manual for the Multidimensional Personality Questionnaire.* Unpublished manuscript, University of Minnesota. (Original work created 1978.)

Tellegen, A. (1991). Personality traits: Issues of definition, evidence, and assessment. In D. Cicchetti & W. M. Grove (Eds.), *Thinking clearly about psychology: Essays in honor of Paul Everett Meehl* (pp. 10–35). Minneapolis: University of Minnesota Press.

Tellegen, A., Lykken, D. T., Bouchard, T. J., Wilcox, K. J., Segal, N. L., & Rich, S. (1988). Personality similarity in twins reared apart and together. *Journal of Personality and Social Psychology, 54,* 1031–1039.

Tellegen, A., & Waller, N. G. (in press). Exploring personality through test construction: Development of the multidimensional personality questionnaire. In S. Briggs & J. Cheek (Eds.), *Personality measures: Development and evaluation, vol. 1.* Greenwich, CT: JAI Press.

Terman, L. M., & Oden, M. H. (1959). *Genetic studies of genius: Vol. 5. The gifted group at mid-life.* Stanford, CA: Stanford University Press.

Tett, R. P., Jackson, D. N., & Rothstein, M. (1991). Personality measures as predictors of job performance: A meta-analytic review. Personnel Psychology, 44, 703–742.

Teyber, E., & McClure, E. T. (2000). Therapist variables. In C. R. Snyder & R. E. Ingram (Eds.), *Handbook of psychological change* (pp. 62–87). New York: Wiley & Sons.

Thase, M. E. (2000). Psychopharmacology in conjunction with psychotherapy. In C. R. Snyder & R. E. Ingram (Eds.), *Handbook of psychological change* (pp. 474–498). New York: Wiley & Sons.

Thase, M. E., Jindal, R., & Howland, R. H. (2002). Biological aspects of depression. In I. H. Gotlib & C. L. Hammen (Eds.), *Handbook of depression* (pp. 192–218). New York: Guilford Press.

Thelen, E. (1995). Time-scale dynamics and the development of an embodied cognition. In R. F. Port & T. van Gelder (Eds.), *Mind as motion: Explorations in the dynamics of cognition* (pp. 69–100). Cambridge, MA: MIT Press.

Thelen, E., & Smith, L. B. (1994). *A dynamic systems approach to the development of cognition and action.* Cambridge, MA: MIT Press.

Thomas, A., & Chess, S. (1977). *Temperament and development.* New York: Brunner/Mazel.

Thompson, R., & McConnell, J. (1955). Classical conditioning in the planarian, *Dugesia dorotocephala. Journal of Comparative and Physiological Psychology, 48*(1), 65–68.

Thompson, R., Emmorey, K., & Gollan, T. (2005). Tip-of-the-fingers experiences by ASL signers: Insights into the organization of a sign-based lexicon. *Psychological Science, 16,* 856–860.

Thompson, W. F., Schellenberg, E. G., & Husain, G. (2001). Arousal, mood, and the Mozart effect. *Psychological Science, 12,* 248–251.

Thorndike, E. L. (1898). *Animal intelligence: An experimental study of the associative processes in animals.* New York: Macmillan.

Thorpe, K., Greenwood, R., Eivers, A., & Rutter, M. (2001). Prevalence and developmental course of "secret language." *International Journal of Language & Communication Disorders, 36,* 43–62.

Thurstone, L. L. (1938). *Primary mental abilities.* Chicago: University of Chicago Press.

Tice, D. M., & Baumeister, R. F. (1997). Longitudinal study of procrastination, performance, stress, and health: The costs and benefits of dawdling. *Psychological Science, 8*(6), 454–458.

Tien, A. Y. (1991). Distributions of hallucinations in the population. *Social Psychiatry and Psychiatric Epidemiology, 26*(6), 287–292.

Timberlake, W. (2006). Evolution-based learning mechanisms can contribute to both adaptive and problematic behavior. In S. O. Lilienfeld & W. T. O'Donohue (Eds.), *The great ideas of clinical science: 17 principles that every mental health professional should understand* (pp. 187–218). New York: Routledge.

Tloczynski, J., & Tantriella, M. (1998). A comparison of the effects of Zen breath meditation or relaxation on college adjustment. *Psychologia: An International Journal of Psychology in the Orient, 41,* 32–43.

Tolman, E. C. (1932). *Purposive behavior in animals and men.* Oxford, England: Appleton-Century.

Tolman, E. C. (1948). Cognitive maps in rats and men. *Psychological Review, 55,* 189–208.

Tolman, E. C., & Honzik, C. H. (1930). Introduction and removal of reward, and maze performance in rats. *University of California Publications in Psychology, 4,* 257–275.

Tolnay, S. E., & Beck, E. M. (1995). *A festival of violence: An analysis of Southern lynchings, 1882–1930.* Urbana: University of Illinois Press.

Tomasello, M. (1999). *The cultural origins of human cognition.* Cambridge, MA: Harvard University Press.

Tombs, S., & Silverman, I. (2004). Pupillometry—A sexual selection approach. *Evolution and Human Behavior, 25*(4), 221–228.

Tomkins, S. S. (1962). *Affect, imagery, consciousness: Vol. 1: The positive affects.* New York: Springer.

Tomlinson, N., Hicks, R. A., & Pellegrini R. J. (1978). Attributions of female college students to variations in pupil size. *Bulletin of the Psychonomic Society, 12*(6), 477–478.

Tooby, J., & Cosmides, L. (1989). Evolutionary psychology and the generation of culture: I. Theoretical considerations. *Ethology & Sociobiology, 10*(1–3), 29–49.

Tooth, G. C., & Newton, M. P. (1961). *Leukotomy in England and Wales 1942–1954.* London, England: Her Majesty's Stationary Office.

Torgersen, S., Lygren, S., Oien, P. A., Skre, I., Onstad, S., Edvardsen, J., et al. (2000). A twin study of personality disorders. *Comprehensive Psychiatry, 41,* 416–425.

Torrey, E. F. (1997). *Out of the shadows: Confronting America's mental illness crisis.* New York: John Wiley.

Torrey, E. G., Miller, J., Rawlings, R., & Yolken, R. H. (1997). Seasonality of births in schizophrenia and bipolar disorder: A review of the literature. *Schizophrenia Research, 28,* 1–38.

Tracy, J. L., & Robins, R. W. (2007). Emerging insights into the nature and function of pride. *Current Directions in Psychological Science, 16,* 147–150.

Treisman, A. (1960). Contextual cues in selective listening. *Quarterly Journal of Experimental Psychology, 12,* 242–248.

Triandis, H. C. (1989). The self and social behavior in differing cultural contexts. *Psychological Review, 96,* 506–520.

Triandis, H. C., & Suh, E. M. (2002). Cultural influences on personality. *Annual Review of Psychology, 53,* 133–160.

Triplett, N. (1897). The dynamogenic factors in pacemaking and competition. *American Journal of Psychology, 9,* 507–533.

Troxel, W. M., Matthews, K. A., Bromberger, J. T., & Sutton-Tyrell, K. (2003). Chronic stress burden, discrimination, and subclinical carotid artery disease in African American and Caucasian women. *Health Psychology, 22,* 300–309.

Truzzi, M. (1978). On the extraordinary: An attempt at clarification. *Zetetic Scholar, 1,* 11–22.

Tschirgi, J. E. (1980). Sensible reasoning: A hypothesis about hypotheses. *Child Development, 51,* 1–10.

Tucker, J. A., Vucinich, R., & Sobell, M. (1982). Alcohol's effects on human emotions. *International Journal of the Addictions, 17,* 155–180.

Tulving, E. (1972). Episodic and semantic memory. In E. Tulving & W. Donaldson (Eds.), *Organization of memory* (pp. 378–402). New York: Academic Press.

Tulving, E. (1982). Synergistic ecphory in recall and recognition. *Canadian Journal of Psychology, 36,* 130–147.

Tulving, E., & Thomson, D. M. (1973). Encoding specificity and retrieval processes in episodic memory. *Psychological Review, 80,* 352–373.

Turk, D. C. (1996). Psychological aspects of pain and disability. *Journal of Musculoskeletal Pain, 4,* 145–154.

Turkheimer, E. (2000). Three laws of behavior genetics and what they mean. *Current Directions in Psychological Science, 9,* 160–163.

Turner, S. M., Beidel, D. C., & Wolff, P. L. (1996). Is behavioral inhibition related to the anxiety disorders? *Clinical Psychology Review, 16,* 57–172.

Tversky, A., & Kahneman, D. (1974). Judgment under uncertainty: Heuristics and biases. *Science, 185,* 1124–1131.

Twemlow, S. W., & Bennett, T. (2008). Psychic plasticity, resilience, and reactions to media violence. What is the right question? *American Behavioral Scientist, 21,* 1155–1183.

Twenge, J. M., Catanese, K. R., & Baumeister, R. F. (2002). Social exclusion causes self-defeating behavior. *Journal of Personality and Social Psychology, 83,* 606–615.

Tyson, G. A. (1987). *Introduction to psychology.* Johannesburg, South Africa: Westro Educational Books.

U

U.S. Census Bureau (2000). *Married-couple and unmarried-partner households: 2000.* Retrieved from http://www.census.gov/prod/2003pubs/censr-5.pdf.

Ullman, M., Krippner, S., & Vaughan, A. (1973). *Dream telepathy.* New York: Macmillan.

Ulrich, R. E. (1991). Animal rights, animal wrongs and the question of balance. *Psychological Science, 2,* 197–201.

Underwood, B. J. (1957) Interference and forgetting. *Psychological Review, 64,* 49–60.

Uttal, W. R. (2001). *The new phrenology: The limits of localizing cognitive processes in the brain.* Cambridge, MA: Bradford Books/MIT Press.

Uttal, W. R. (2003). *Psychomythics: Sources of artifacts and misconceptions in scientific psychology.* Mahwah, NJ: Lawrence Erlbaum.

V

Vaillant, G. E., & Milofsky, E. S. (1980). Natural history of male psychological health IX: Empirical evidence for Erikson's model of the life cycle. *American Journal of Psychiatry, 137,* 1348–1359.

Vaillant, G. E., & Milofsky, E. S. (1982). Natural history of male alcoholism IV: Paths to recovery. *Archives of General Psychiatry, 39,* 127–133.

Vaitl, D., & Lipp, O. V. (1997). Latent inhibition and autonomic responses: A psychophysiological approach. *Behavioural Brain Research, 88*(1), 85–93.

Valenstein, E. S. (1973). *Brain control.* New York: John Wiley & Sons.

Valentine, T., Darling, S., & Donnelly, M. (2004). Why are average faces attractive? The effect of view and averageness on the attractiveness of female faces. *Psychonomic Bulletin & Review, 11,* 482–487.

Van de Castle, R. (1994). *Our dreaming mind.* New York: Ballantine Books.

Van de Vijver, F. J. R. (2008). On the meaning of cross-cultural differences in simple cognitive measures. *Educational Research and Evaluation, 14,* 215–234.

van der Kolk, B., Britz, R., Burr, W., Sherry, S., & Hartmann, E. (1984). Nightmares and trauma: A comparison of nightmares after combat with lifelong nightmares in veterans. *American Journal of Psychiatry, 141,* 187–190.

van Hecke, M. L. (2007). *Blind spots: Why smart people do dumb things.* Amherst, NY: Prometheus Books.

van Ijzendoorn, M. H., & De Wolff, M. S. (1997). In search of the absent father: Meta-analyses on infant–father attachment. *Child Development, 68,* 604–609.

van Ijzendoorn, M. H., & Sagi, A. (1999). Cross-cultural patterns of attachment: Universal and cultural dimensions. In J. Cassidy & P. R. Shaver (Eds.), *Handbook of attachment: Theory, research, and clinical applications* (pp. 713–734). New York: Guilford.

van Itallie, T. B. (1990). The glucostatic theory 1953–1988: Roots and branches. *International Journal of Obesity, 14,* 1–10.

Van Lommel, P., van Wees, R., Meyers, V., & Elfferich, I. (2001). Near-death experiences in survivors of cardiac arrest: A prospective study in the Netherlands. *Lancet, 358,* 2039–2045.

Van Rooy, D. L., & Viswesvaran, C. (2004). Emotional intelligence: A meta-analytic investigation of predictive validity and nomological net. *Journal of Vocational Behavior, 65,* 71–95.

Vane, J. R. (1981). The Thematic Apperception Test: A review. *Clinical Psychology Review, 1,* 319–336.

Vanman, E. J., Paul, B. Y., Ito, T. A., & Miller, N. (1997). The modern face of prejudice and structural features that moderate the effect of cooperation on affect. *Journal of Personality and Social Psychology, 73,* 941–959.

Vanman, E. J., Saltz, J. L., Nathan, L. R., & Warren, J. A. (2004). Racial discrimination by low-prejudiced whites: Facial movements as implicit measures of attitudes related to behavior. *Psychological Science, 15,* 711–714.

Veit, R., Flor, H., Erb, M., Hermann, C., Lotze, M., Grodd, W., et al. (2002). Brain circuits involved in emotional learning in antisocial behavior and social phobia in humans. *Neuroscience Letters, 328*(3), 233–236.

Verdoux, H. (2004). Perinatal risk factors for schizophrenia: How specific are they? *Current Psychiatry Reports, 6,* 162–167.

Vernon, P. A. (1987). *Speed of information processing and intelligence.* Norwood, NJ: Ablex.

Vetere, A. (2001). Structural family therapy. *Child Psychology and Psychiatry Review, 6,* 133–139.

Vita, A., Dieci, G., Giobbio, A., Caputo, L., Ghrinighelli, M., & Comazzi, M., et al. (1995). Language and thought disorder in schizophrenia: Brain morphological correlates. *Schizophrenia Research, 15,* 243–251.

Vitale, J. E., & Newman, J. P. (2001). Using the Psychopathy Checklist-Revised with female samples: Reliability, validity, and implications for clinical utility. *Clinical Psychology: Science and Practice, 8,* 117–132.

Vitello, P. (2006, June 12). A ringtone meant to fall on deaf ears. *New York Times.* Retrieved from www.nytimes.com/2006/06/12/technology/12ring.html?_r=1&emc=eta1&oref=slogi.

Voevodsky, J. (1974). Evaluation of a deceleration warning light for reducing rear-end automobile collisions. *Journal of Applied Psychology, 59,* 270–273.

Vohs, K. D., Mead, N. L., & Goode, M. R. (2006). The psychological consequences of money. *Science, 314*(5802), 1154–1156.

von Känel, R., Dimsdale, J. E., Patterson, T. L., & Grant, I. (2003). Association of negative life event stress with coagulation activity in elderly Alzheimer caregivers. *Psychosomatic Medicine,* *65*(1), 145–150.

Voncken, M. J., Bogels, S. M., & deVries, K. (2003). Interpretation and judgmental biases in social phobias. *Behavior Research and Therapy, 41,* 1481–1488.

Voyer, D., Voyer, S., & Bryden, M. P. (1995). Magnitude of sex differences in spatial abilities: A meta-analysis and consideration of critical variables. *Psychological Bulletin, 117,* 250–270.

Vyse, S. A. (1997). *Believing in magic: The psychology of superstition.* New York: Oxford University Press.

W

Wachtel, P. L. (1997). *Psychoanalysis, behavior therapy, and the relational world.* Washington, DC: American Psychological Association.

Wadden, T. A., & Stunkard, A. J. (1993). Psychosocial consequence of obesity and dieting: Research and clinical findings. In A. J. Stunkard & T. A. Wadden (Eds.), *Obesity: Theory and therapy* (pp. 163–177). New York: Raven.

Wade, K. A., Garry, M., Read, J. D., & Lindsay, D. S. (2002). A picture is worth a thousand lies: Using false photographs to create false childhood memories. *Psychonomic Bulletin & Review, 9,* 597–603.

Wagner, G. A., & Morris, E. K. (1987). Superstitious behavior in children. *Psychological Record, 37*(4), 471–488.

Wagner, M. W., & Monnet, M. (1979). Attitudes of college professors toward extra-sensory perception. *Zetetic Scholar, 5,* 7–16.

Wagstaff, G. (2008). Hypnosis and the law. *Criminal Justice and Behavior, 35,* 1277–1294.

Wahl, O. (1997). *Consumer experience with stigma: Results of a national survey.* Alexandria, VA: NAMI.

Wakefield, A. J., Murch, S., Anthony, A., Linnell, J., Casson, D. M., Casson, M., et al. (1998). Ileal lymphoid nodular hyperplasia, non-specific colitis, and regressive developmental disorder in children. *Lancet, 351,* 637–641.

Wakefield, J. C. (1992). The concept of mental disorder: On the boundary between biological facts and social values. *American Psychologist, 47,* 373–388.

Walach, H., & Kirsch, I. (2003). Herbal treatments and antidepressant medication: Similar data, divergent conclusions. In S. O. Lilienfeld, S. J. Lynn, & J. M. Lohr (Eds.), *Science and pseudoscience in clinical psychology* (pp. 306–330). New York: Guilford.

Waldman, I. D. (2005). Statistical approaches to complex phenotypes: Evaluating neuropsychological endophenotypes for attention-deficit/hyperactivity disorder. *Biological Psychiatry, 57,* 1347–1356.

Walker, E. F., & DiForio, D. (1997). Schizophrenia: A neural-diathesis stress model. *Psychological Review, 104,* 1–19.

Walker, E., Kestler, L., Bollini, A., & Hochman, K. (2004). Schizophrenia: Etiology and course. *Annual Review of Psychology, 55,* 401–430.

Walker, M. P., Brakefield, A., Morgan, J., Hobson, J. A., & Stickgold, R. (2002). Practice, with sleep, makes perfect. *Neuron, 35,* 205–211.

Wallach, H., & Kirsch, I. (2003). Herbal treatments and antidepressant medication: Similar data, divergent conclusions. In S. O. Lilienfeld, S. J. Lynn, & J. M. Lohr (Eds.), *Science and pseudoscience in clinical psychology* (pp. 306–332). New York: Guilford.

Wallechinsky, D., Wallace, D., & Wallace, H. (1977). *The book of lists.* New York: Bantam Books.

Waller, N. G., Kojetin, B. A., Bouchard, T. J., Lykken, D. T., & Tellegen, A. (1990). Genetic and environmental influences on religious interests, attitudes, and values: A study of twins reared apart and together. *Psychological Science, 1,* 1–5.

Wallerstein, J. S. (1989, January 22). Children after divorce: Wounds that don't heal. *New York Times Magazine, 19,* 42.

Walonick, D. S. (1994). *Do researchers influence survey results with their question wording choices?* Retrieved May 5, 2006, from www.statpac.com/research-papers/researcher-bias.doc.

Walsh, B. T. (1993). Binge eating in bulimia nervosa. In C. G. Fairburn & G. T. Wilson (Eds.), *Binge eating: Nature, assessment, and treatment* (pp. 37–49). New York: Guilford.

Walsh, B. T., Hadigan, C. M., Kissileff, H. R., & LaChaussee, J. L. (1992). Bulimia nervosa: A syndrome of feast and famine. In G. H. Anderson & S. H. Kennedy (Eds.), *The biology of feast and famine.* New York: Academic Press.

Walsh, D. C., Hingson, R. W., Merrigan, D. M., Levenson, S. M., Cupples, L. A., Heeren, T., et al. (1991). A randomized trial of treatment options for alcohol abusing workers. *New England Journal of Medicine, 325,* 775–782.

Walsh, F. (1999). Families in later life: Challenges and opportunities. In B. Carter & M. McGoldrick (Eds.), *The expanded family life cycle: Individual, family and social perspectives* (3rd ed., pp. 307–326). Boston: Allyn & Bacon.

Walster, E., Berscheid, E., & Walster, G. W. (1973). New directions in equity theory and research. *Journal of Personality and Social Psychology, 25,* 151–176.

Walters, G. D., & Greene, R. L. (1988). Differentiating between schizophrenia and manic inpatients by means of the MMPI. *Journal of Personality Assessment, 52,* 91–95.

Walton, D. E. (1978). An exploratory study: Personality factors and theoretical orientations of therapists. *Psychotherapy: Theory, Research, and Practice, 15,* 390–395.

Wampold, B. E. (2001). *The great psychotherapy debate: Models, methods, and findings.* Mahwah, NJ: Lawrence Erlbaum.

Wampold, B. E., Minami, T., Baskin, T. W., & Tierney, S. C. (2002). A meta-(re)analysis of the effects of cognitive therapy versus "other therapies" for depression. *Journal of Affective Disorders, 68,* 159–165.

Wampold, B. E., Monding, W., Moody, M., Stich, I., Benson, K., & Ahn, H. (1997). A meta-analysis of outcome studies comparing bona fide psychotherapies: Empirically "all must have prizes." *Psychological Bulletin, 122,* 203–215.

Wang, Q. (2006). Culture and the development of self-knowledge. *Current Directions in Psychological Science, 15,* 182–187.

Waschbusch, D. A., & Hill, G. P. (2003). Empirically supported, promising, and unsupported treatments for children with attention-deficit/hyperactivity disorder. In S. O. Lilienfeld, S. J. Lynn, & J. M. Lohr (Eds.), *Science and pseudoscience in clinical psychology* (pp. 333–362). New York: Guilford.

Wason, P. C. (1966). Reasoning. In B. M. Foss (Ed.), *New horizons in psychology* (pp. 135–151). Harmondsworth, England: Penguin.

Watanabe, S., Sakamoto, J., & Wakita, M. (1995). Pigeons' discrimination of paintings by Monet and Picasso. *Journal of the Experimental Analysis of Behavior, 63,* 65–174.

Waters, E., Matas, L., & Sroufe, L. A. (1975). Infants' reactions to an approaching stranger: Description, validation, and functional significance of wariness. *Child Development 46*(2), 348–356.

Watkins, C. E., Campbell, V. L., Nieberding, R., & Hallmark, R. (1995). Contemporary practice of psychological assessment by clinical psychologists. *Professional Psychology: Science and Practice, 26,* 54–60.

Watson, D., & Clark, L. A. (1984). Negative affectivity: The disposition to experience negative emotional states. *Psychological Bulletin, 96,* 465–490.

Watson, J. B. (1913). Psychology as the behaviorist views it. *Psychological Review, 20,* 158–177.

Watson, J. B., & Rayner, R. (1920). Conditioned emotional reactions. *Journal of Experimental Psychology, 3,* 1–14.

Watzlawick, P., Weakland, J. H., & Fisch, R. (1974). *Change: Principles of problem formation and problem resolution.* New York: Norton.

Waugh, N. C., & Norman, D. A. (1965). Primary memory. *Psychological Review, 72,* 89–104.

Wayment, H. A., & Peplau, L. A. (1995). Social support and well-being among lesbian and heterosexual women: A structural modeling approach. *Personality and Social Psychology Bulletin, 21,* 1189–1199.

Wechsler, D. (1939). *The measurement of adult intelligence.* Baltimore: Williams & Wilkins.

Wechsler, D. (1997). *The Wechsler Adult Intelligence Scale—Third edition (WAIS-III).* San Antonio, TX: Harcourt Assessment.

Wegner, D. M. (2002). *The illusion of conscious will.* Cambridge, MA: MIT Press.

Weiek, A. I., Schupp, H. T., & Hamm, A. O. (2007). Fear acquisition requires awareness in trace but not delay conditioning. *Psychophysiology, 44,* 170–180.

Weil, A. (2000). *Spontaneous healing: How to discover and embrace your body's natural ability to maintain and heal itself.* New York: Ballantine Books.

Weinberg, M. S., Williams, C. J., & Calhan, C. (1995). If the shoe fits … Exploring male-homosexual foot fetishism. *Journal of Sex Research, 31*(1), 17–27.

Weinberg, R. A., Scarr, S., & Waldman, I. D. (1992). The Minnesota Transracial Adoption Study: A follow-up of IQ test performance at adolescence. *Intelligence, 16,* 117–135.

Weinberger, D. R. (1987). Implications of normal brain development for the pathogenesis of schizophrenia. *Archives of General Psychiatry, 44,* 660–669.

Weinberger, D. R., Elvevag, B., & Giedd, J. N., (2005). *The adolescent brain: A work in progress, The National Campaign to Prevent Teen Pregnancy.* Retrieved from www.teenpregnancy.org/resources/reading/pdf/BRAIN.pdf.

Weinberger, J., & Hardaway, R. (1990). Separating science from myth in subliminal psychodynamic activation. *Clinical Psychology Review, 10,* 727–756.

Weiner, I. B. (1997). Current status of the Rorschach Inkblot Method. *Journal of Personality Assessment, 68,* 5–19.

Weinert, F. (1989). The impact of schooling on cognitive development: One hypothetical assumption, some empirical results, and many theoretical implications. *EARLI News, 8,* 3–7.

Weisberg, D. S., Keil, F. C., Goodstein, J., Rawson, E., & Gray, J. R. (2008). The seductive allure of neuroscience explanations. *Journal of Cognitive Neuroscience, 20*(3), 470–477.

Weiskrantz, L. (1986). *Blindsight: A case study and its implications.* Oxford, England: Oxford University Press.

Weiss, B. L. (1988). *Many lives, many masters.* New York: Simon & Schuster.

Weiss, L. H., & Schwarz, J. C. (1996). The relationship between parenting types and older adolescents' personality, academic achievement, adjustment, and substance use. *Child Development, 67,* 2101–2114.

Weissman, M. M., Markowitz, J. C., & Klerman, G. L. (2000). *Comprehensive guide to interpersonal psychotherapy.* New York: Basic Books.

Weisz, J. R., Weiss, B., Han, S. S., Granger, D. A., & Morton, T. (1995). Effects of psychotherapy with children and adolescents revisited: A meta-analysis of treatment outcome studies. *Psychological Bulletin, 117,* 450–468.

Welford, A. (1977). Mental workload as a function of demand, capacity, strategy and skill: Synthesis report. *Travail Humain, 40,* 283–304.

Wellman, H. M., Cross, D., & Watson, J. (2001). Meta-analysis of theory-of-mind development: The truth about false belief. *Child Development, 72,* 655–684.

Wellman, H. M., & Gelman, S. A. (1998). Knowledge acquisition in foundational domains. In W. Damon (Ed.), *Handbook of child psychology: Vol. 2: Cognition, perception, and language* (pp. 523–573). Hoboken, NJ: Wiley.

Wells, G. L., & Bradford, A. L. (1998)."Good, you identified the suspect": Feedback to eyewitnesses distorts their reports of the witnessing experience. *Journal of Applied Psychology, 83,* 360–376.

Wells, G. L., & Loftus, E. F. (Eds.). (1984). *Eyewitness testimony: Psychological perspectives.* New York: Cambridge University Press.

Wells, G. L., Memon, A., & Penrod, S. D. (2006). Eyewitness evidence: Improving its probative value. *Psychological Science in the Public Interest, 7*(2), 45–75.

Wells, G. L., & Olson, E. (2003). Eyewitness identification. *Annual Review of Psychology, 54,* 277–295.

Wennberg, P. (2002). The development of alcohol habits in a Swedish male birth cohort. In S. P. Shohov (Ed.), *Advances in psychology research, vol. 15* (pp. 121–155). Hauppauge, NY: Nova Science Publishers.

Werker, J. F., Gilbert, J. H.V., Humphrey, K., & Tees, R. C. (1981). Developmental aspects of cross-language speech perception. *Child Development, 52,* 349–355.

Werker, J. F., & Tees, R. C. (1984). Cross-language speech perception: Evidence for perceptual reorganization during the first year of life. *Infant Behavior and Development, 7,* 49–63.

West, D. J. (1948). A mass observation questionnaire on hallucinations. *Journal of the Society for Psychical Research, 34,* 187–196.

West, T. A., & Bauer, P. J. (1999). Assumptions of infantile amnesia: Are there differences between early and later memories? *Memory, 7*(3), 257–278.

Westen, D. (1998). The scientific legacy of Sigmund Freud: Toward a psychodynamically informed psychological science. *Psychological Bulletin, 124,* 333–371.

Westen, D., Kilts, C., Blagov, P., Harenski, K., & Hamann, S. (2006). The neural basis of motivated reasoning: An fMRI study of emotional constraints on political judgment during the U.S. presidential election of 2004. *Journal of Cognitive Neuroscience, 18,* 1947–1958.

Westen, D., Novotny, C. M., & Thompson-Brenner, H. (2004). The empirical status of empirically supported psychotherapies: Assumptions, findings, and reporting in controlled clinical trials. *Psychological Bulletin, 130,* 631–663.

Westerman, M. A., Foote, J. P., & Winston, A. (1995). Change in coordination across phases of psychotherapy and outcome: Two mechanisms for the role played by patients' contribution to the alliance. *Journal of Consulting and Clinical Psychology, 63,* 672–675.

Weston, K. (1991). *Families we choose: Lesbians, gays, kinship.* New York: Columbia University Press.

Wetzler, S. E., & Sweeney, J. A. (1986). Childhood amnesia: An empirical demonstration. In D. C. Rubin (Ed.), *Autobiographical memory* (pp. 191–201). New York: Cambridge University Press.

Whaley, A. L., & Davis, K. E. (2007). Cultural competence and evidence-based practice in mental health services: A complementary perspective. *American Psychologist, 62,* 563–574.

Whinnery, J. E. (1997). Psychophysiologic correlates of unconsciousness and near-death experiences. *Journal of Near-Death Studies, 15,* 231–258.

Whorf, B. L. (1956). *Language, thought, and reality: Selected writings of Benjamin Lee Whorf* (J. B. Carroll, Ed.). Cambridge, MA: MIT Press.

Wickelgren, W. A. (1965). Acoustic similarity and retroactive interference in short-term memory. *Journal of Verbal Learning and Verbal Behavior, 4*, 53–61.

Wicker, A. W. (1969). Attitudes versus actions: The relationship of verbal and overt behavioral responses to attitude objects. *Journal of Social Issues, 25*, 41–78.

Wicker, B., Keysers, C., Plailly, J., Royet, J. P., Gallese, V., & Rizzolatti, G. (2003). Both of us disgusted in my insula: The common neural basis of seeing and feeling disgust. *Neuron, 40*, 655–664.

Widiger, T. A. (2001). The best and the worst of us? *Clinical Psychology: Science and Practice, 8*, 374–377.

Widiger, T. A., & Clark, L. A. (2000). Toward DSM-V and the classification of psychopathology. *Psychological Bulletin, 126*, 946–963.

Widmer, E. D., Treas, J., & Newcomb, R. (1998). Attitudes toward nonmarital sex in 24 countries. *Journal of Sex Research, 35*, 349–357.

Widom, C. S. (1977). A methodology for studying noninstitutionalized psychopaths. *Journal of Consulting and Clinical Psychology, 45*, 674–683.

Wigal, T., Greenhill, L. , Chuang, S., McGough, J., Vitiello, B., Skrobala, A., et al. (2006). Safety and tolerability of methylphenidate in preschool children with ADHD. *Journal of the American Academy of Adolescent Psychiatry, 45*, 1294.

Willerman, L. (1979). *The psychology of individual and group differences.* San Francisco: Freedman.

Willerman, R., Schultz, J. N., Rutledge, J. N., & Bigler, D. D. (1991). In vivo brain size and intelligence, *Intelligence, 15*, 223–228.

Williams, K., Harkins, S. G., & Latane, B. (1981). Identifiability as a deterrant to social loafing: Two cheering experiments. *Journal of Personality and Social Psychology, 40*(2), 303–311.

Williams, S. L., Turner, S. M., & Peer, D. F. (1985). Guided mastery and performance desensitization treatments for severe acrophobia. *Journal of Consulting and Clinical Psychology, 53*(2), 234–247.

Williams, T. M. (Ed.). (1986). *The impact of television: A naturalistic study in three communities.* Orlando, FL: Academic Press.

Williamson, D. A., Womble, L. G., Smeets, M. A. M., Netemeyer, R. G., Thaw, J. M., Kutlesic, V., et al. (2002). Latent structure of eating disorder symptoms: A factor analytic and taxometric investigation. *American Journal of Psychiatry, 159*, 412–418.

Willingham, D. T. (2002). *Allocating student study time: "Massed" versus "distributed" practice.* Retrieved May 22, 2006, from www.aft.org/american_educator/summer2002/askcognitivescientist.html.

Willingham, D. T. (2007, Summer). Why is critical thinking so hard to teach? *American Educator, 31*(2), 8–19.

Willner, P. (1995). Animal models of depression—Validity and applications. *Depression and Mania, 49*, 19–41.

Wills, T. A., & Fegan, M. F. (2001). Social networks and social support. In A. S. Baum, T. A. Revenson, J. E. Singer (Eds.), *Handbook of Health Psychology* (pp. 209–234). Mahwah, NJ: Erlbaum.

Wilson, J. Q. (1993). *The moral sense.* New York: Free Press.

Wilson, J. Q., & Herrnstein, R. J. (1985). *Crime and human nature: The definitive study of the causes of crime.* New York: Simon & Schuster.

Wilson, N. (2003). Commercializing mental health issues: Entertainment, advertising, and psychological advice. In S. O. Lilienfeld, S. J. Lynn, & J. M. Lohr (Eds.), *Science and pseudoscience in clinical psychology* (pp. 425–459). New York: Guilford.

Wilson, R. S., Scherr, P. A., Schneider, J. A., Tang, Y. & Bennett, D. A. (2007). Relation of cognitive activity to risk of developing Alzheimer disease. *Neurology, 69*, 1911–1920.

Wilson, T. D. (2002). *Strangers to ourselves: Discovering the adaptive unconscious.* Cambridge, MA: Harvard University Press.

Wimmer, H., & Perner, J. (1983). Beliefs about beliefs: Representation and constraining function of wrong beliefs in young children's understanding of deception. *Cognition, 13*, 103–128.

Winemiller, M. H., Billow, R. G., Laskwoski, E. R., & Harmsen, W. S. (2003). Effect of magnetic vs. sham-magnetic insoles on plantar heel pain. *Journal of the American Medical Association, 290*, 1474–1478.

Wing, L., & Potter, D. (2002). The epidemiology of autistic spectrum disorders: Is the prevalence rising? *Mental Retardation and Developmental Disabilities Research Reviews, 8*, 151–161.

Wing, R. R., & Hill, J. O. (2001). Successful weight loss maintenance. *Annual Review of Nutrition, 21*, 323–341.

Wing, R. R., & Jeffrey, R. W. (1999). Benefit of recruiting participants with friends and increasing social support for weight loss and maintenance. *Journal of Consulting and Clinical Psychology, 67*, 132–138.

Wing, R. R., & Polley, B. A. (2001). Obesity. In A. Baum, T. A. Revenson, & J. E. Singer (Eds.), *Handbook of health psychology* (pp. 263–279). Mahwah, NJ: Erlbaum.

Winograd, E., & Killinger, W. A. Jr. (1983). Relating age at encoding in early childhood to adult recall: Development of flashbulb memories. *Journal of Experimental Psychology: General, 112*, 413–422.

Winton, W. M. (1987). Do introductory textbooks present the Yerkes-Dodson law correctly? *American Psychologist, 42*, 202–203.

Witt, M., & Wozniak, W. (2006). Structure and function of the vomeronasal organ. *Advances in Otorhinolaryngology, 63*, 70–83.

Wittchen, H. U. (2002). Generalized anxiety disorder: Prevalence, burden, and cost to society. *Depression and Anxiety, 16*, 162–171.

Woehrer, C. E. (1982). The influence of ethnic families on intergenerational relationships and later life transitions. In F. M. Berardo (Ed.), *The Annals of the American Academy of Political and Social Science* (pp. 65–78). Beverly Hills, CA: Sage.

Wojciszke, B. (2002). From the first sight to the last breath: A six-stage model of love. *Polish Psychological Bulletin, 33*, 15–25.

Wolfe, V. A., & Pruitt, S. D. (2003). Insomnia and sleep disorders. In L. M. Cohen, D. E. McChargue, & F. L. Collins (Eds.), *The health psychology handbook* (pp. 425–440). Thousand Oaks, CA: Sage.

Wolfsdorf, B. A., Freeman, J., D'Eramo, K., Overholser, J., & Spirito, A. (2003). Mood states: Depression, anger, and anxiety. In A. Spirito & J. Overholser (Eds.), *Evaluating and treating adolescent suicide attempters: From research to practice* (pp. 53–88). New York: Academic Press.

Wolpe, J. (1990). *The practice of behavior therapy* (4th ed.). Elmsford, NY: Pergamon Press.

Wolpert, L. (1993). *The unnatural nature of science.* Cambridge, MA: Harvard University Press.

Wood, J. M., & Lilienfeld, S. O. (1999). The Rorschach Inkblot Test: A case of overstatement? *Assessment, 6*, 341–351.

Wood, J. M., Lilienfeld, S. O., Garb, H. N., & Nezworski, M. T. (2000). The Rorschach test in clinical diagnosis: A critical review, with a backward look at Garfield (1947). *Journal of Clinical Psychology, 56*, 395–430.

Wood, J. M., Nezworski, M. T., & Stejskal, W. J. (1996). The comprehensive system for the Rorschach: A critical examination. *Psychological Science, 7*, 3–10.

Wood, W. (2000). Attitude change: Persuasion and social influence. *Annual Review of Psychology, 51*, 539–570.

Woods, S. C., Seeley, R. J., Porte, D., & Schwartz, N. W. (1998). Signals that regulate food intake and energy homeostasis. *Science, 280*, 1378–1383.

Woody, E. Z., & Sadler, P. (2008). Dissociation theories of hypnosis. In M. R. Nash & A. Barnier (Eds.), *The Oxford Handbook of Hypnosis* (pp. 81–110). New York: Oxford University Press.

Woodworth, R. S. (1929). *Psychology* (Rev. ed.). Oxford, England: Holt.

Woolf, N. J. (1991). Cholinergic systems in mammalian brain and spinal cord. *Progress in Neurobiology, 37,* 475–524.

World Health Organization (WHO). (2004). *Global status report on alcohol 2004.* Geneva, Switzerland: WHO, Department of Mental Health and Substance Abuse.

Wysocki, C. J., & Preti, G. (2004). Facts, fallacies, fears, and frustrations with human pheromones. *Anatomical Record. A: Discoveries in Molecular, Cellular, & Evolutionary Biology, 281,* 1201–1211.

Y

Yalom, I. (1985). *The theory and practice of group psychotherapy.* New York: Basic Books.

Yamaguchi, S., & Ninomiya, K. (2000). Umami and food palatability. *Journal of Nutrition, 130*(4S Suppl.), 921S–926S.

Yamey, G., & Shaw, P. (2002). Is extreme racism a mental illness? No. *Western Journal of Medicine, 176,* 5.

Yehuda, R., Resnick, H., Kahana, B., & Giller, E. L. (1993). Long-lasting hormonal alterations to extreme stress in humans: Normative or maladaptive? *Psychosomatic Medicine, 55,* 287–297.

Yerkes, R. M., & Dodson, J. D. (1908). The relation of strength of stimulus to rapidity of habit-formation. *Journal of Comparative Neurology and Psychology, 18,* 459–482.

Young, J., & Cooper, L. M. (1972). Hypnotic recall amnesia as a function of manipulated expectancy. *Proceedings of the 80th Annual Convention of the American Psychological Association, 7,* 857–858.

Young, M., Denny, G., Young, T., & Luquis, R. (2000). Sexual satisfaction among married women. *American Journal of Health Studies, 16,* 73–84.

Young, T. (1802). On the theory of light and colours. *Philosophical Transactions of the Royal Society of London, 92,* 12–48.

Youngren, M. A., & Lewinsohn, P. M. (1980). The functional relationship between depressed and problematic interpersonal behavior. *Journal of Abnormal Psychology, 89,* 333–341.

Yurgelun-Todd, D. A., Gruber, S. A., Kanayama, G., Killgore, W. D. S., Baird, A. A., & Young, A. D. (2000). fMRI during affect discrimination in bipolar affective disorder. *Bipolar Disorders, 2*(3), 237–248.

Yusuf, S., Hawken, S., Ounpuu, S., Dans, T., Avezum, A., Lanas, F., et al. (2004). Effect of potentially modifiable risk factors associated with myocardial infarction in 52 countries (the INTERHEART study): Case-control study. *Lancet, 364,* 937–952.

Z

Zabrucky, K., & Ratner, H. H. (1986). Children's comprehension monitoring and recall of inconsistent stories. *Child Development, 57,* 1401–1418.

Zaidel, D. W. (1994). A view of the world from a split brain perspective. In E. M. R. Critchley (Ed.), *The neurological boundaries of reality* (pp. 161–174). London: Farrand Press.

Zajonc, R. B. (1965). Social facilitation. *Science, 149,* 169–274.

Zajonc, R. B. (1968). Attitudinal effects of mere exposure. *Journal of Personality and Social Psychology Monographs, 9,* 1–27.

Zajonc, R. B., Heingartner, A., & Herman, E. M. (1969). Social enhancement and impairment of performance in the cockroach. *Journal of Personality and Social Psychology, 13,* 83–92.

Zajonc, R. B., Murphy, S. T., & Inglehart, M. (1989). Feeling and facial efference: Implications for the vascular theory of emotion. *Psychological Review, 96,* 395–416.

Zautra, A. J. (2003). *Emotions, stress, and health.* New York: Oxford University Press.

Zborowski, M. J., & Garske, J. P. (1993). Interpersonal deviance and consequent social impact in hypothetically schizophrenia-prone men. *Journal of Abnormal Psychology, 102,* 482–489.

Zeinah, M. M., Engel, S. A., Thompson, P. M., & Bookheimer, S.Y. (2003). Dynamics of the hippocampus during encoding and retrieval of face-name pairs. *Science, 299,* 577–580.

Zhang, A.Y., & Snowden, L. R. (1999). Ethnic characteristics of mental disorders in five U.S. communities. *Cultural Diversity and Ethnic Minority Psychology, 5,* 134–136.

Zillmann, D. (1988). Cognition-excitation interdependencies in aggressive behavior. *Aggressive Behavior, 14,* 51–64.

Zimbardo, P. G. (1972). Pathology of imprisonment. *Society, 9*(6), 4–8.

Zimbardo, P. G. (1997, May). What messages are behind today's cults? *American Psychological Association Monitor, 28*(5), 14.

Zimbardo, P. G. (2004a). Does psychology make a significant difference in our lives? *American Psychologist, 59,* 339–351.

Zimbardo, P. G. (2004b, May 9). Power turns good soldiers into "bad apples." *Boston Globe.* Retrieved May 15, 2005, from www.boston.com/news/globe/editorial_opinion/oped/articles/2004/05/09/power_turns_good_soldiers_into_bad_apples/.

Zimbardo, P. G. (2007). *The Lucifer effect: How good people turn evil.* New York: Random House.

Zimbardo, P. G., Weisenberg, M., Firestone, I., & Levy, M. (1965). Communicator effectiveness in producing public conformity and private attitude change. *Journal of Personality, 33,* 233–255.

Zimmerman, M. (1994). Diagnosing personality disorders: A review of issues and research methods. *Archives of General Psychiatry, 51,* 225–245.

Zinbarg, R. E., & Barlow, D. H. (1996). The structure of anxiety and the anxiety disorders: A hierarchical model. *Journal of Abnormal Psychology, 105,* 81–193.

Zion, I. B., Tessler, R., Cohen, L., Lerer, E., Raz, Y., Bachner-Melman, R., et al. (2006). Polymorphisms in the dopamine D4 receptor gene (DRD4) contribute to individual differences in human sexual behavior: Desire, arousal and sexual function. *Journal for Molecular Psychiatry, 11,* 782–786.

Zivotofsky, A. Z., Edelman, S., Green, T., Fostick, L., & Strous, R. D. (2007). Hemisphere asymmetry in schizophrenia as revealed through line bisection, line trisection, and letter cancellation. *Brain Research, 1142,* 70–79.

Zubin, J., & Spring, B. (1977). Vulnerability: A new view of schizophrenia. *Journal of Abnormal Psychology, 86,* 103–126.

Zuckerman, M. (1989). Personality in the third dimension: A psychobiological approach. *Personality and Individual Differences, 10,* 391–418.

Zuroff, D. C., Mongrain, M., & Santor, D. A. (2004). Investing in the personality vulnerability research program: Current dividends and future growth: Rejoinder to Coyne, Thompson, and Whiffen. *Psychological Bulletin, 130,* 518–522.

Name Index

Subject Index

Note: Boldface terms and page numbers are key terms; page numbers followed by *f* indicate figures; those followed by *t* indicate tables.

Credits

TEXT AND ART

Chapter 1

Figure 1.1, p. 5: Adapted and modified from "The cognitive neuroscience perspective allows us to understand abnormal behavior at multiple levels of complexity," by S. S. Hardi, K. Rand & L. Karwoski as appeared in *The Great Ideas of Clinical Science: 17 Principles That Every Mental Health Professional Should Understand*, edited by S. O. Lilienfeld and W. O. O'Donohue. Copyright 2007 by Taylor & Francis Group LLC–Books. Reproduced with permission of Taylor & Francis Group LLC–Books in the format Textbook via Copyright Clearance Center.

Figure 1.2, p. 7: Table: "Naive Realism Can Fool Us," from *Mind Sights* by Roger N. Shepard. Copyright © 1990 by Roger N. Shepard. Reprinted by permission of Henry Holt and Company, LLC.

Learning Objective 1.3, p. 13, Used by permission of the *Skeptical Inquirer*, www.csicop.org.

Figure 1.6, p. 29: Adapted from Amy Cynkar (2007), "The changing gender composition of psychology," *Monitor on Psychology*, Volume 38, No. 6, June 2007, p. 47. Copyright © 2007 by the American Psychological Association. Reproduced with permission.

Chapter 2

Figure 2.5, p. 53: Used with permission from Jon Mueller.

Figure 2.6, p. 60: From C. A. Anderson, J. J. Lindsay, & B. J. Bushman, 1999. "Research in the psychological laboratory: Truth or triviality? *Current Directions in Psychological Science*, 8, pp. 3–9. Reprinted with permission of Blackwell Publishing Ltd.

Chapter 3

Figure 3.1, p. 81: *Combustion* © Dorling Kindersley. Adapted by permission.

Table 3.1, p. 84: Adapted from *Psychology: The Science of Behavior* by Carlson et al., Fig. 4.2, p. 101, © 2007. Reproduced by permission of Pearson Education, Inc.

Figure 3.5, p. 85: From Sternberg, R. J. (2004) *Psychology*, 4th Ed., Belmont, CA: Wadsworth (pp. 72–73). Adapted with permission from the author.

Figure 3.6, p. 88: © Dorling Kindersley. Adapted by permission.

Figure 3.9, p. 90: Adapted from *Human Anatomy & Physiology*, 7th ed. by Elaine N. Marieb and Katja Hoehn, Fig. 12.9, p. 438. Copyright © 2007 by Pearson Education, Inc. Reprinted by permission.

Figure 3.11, p. 92: (left) © Dorling Kindersley. Adapted by permission; (right) From Kalat, *Biological Psychology w/ CD + INFOTRAC, 9E*. © 2007 Wadsworth, a part of Cengage Learning, Inc. Reproduced by permission. www.cengage.com/permissions.

Chapter 4

Figure 4.1, p. 114: From *An Anatomy of Thought* by Ian Glynn. Published by Oxford University Press, 1999.

Figure 4.3, p. 117: Reprinted with permission from Imprint Academic.

Figure 4.8, p. 121: © Dorling Kindersley. Adapted by permission.

Figure 4.9, p. 122: Reprinted with permission from St. Luke's Cataract & Laser Institute of Tarpon Springs, FL.

Figure 4.12, p. 124: From Herrmann & Friederici. (2001). "Object Processing in the Infant Brain." *Science*, 292, p. 163, Figure 1C. Reprinted with permission from AAAS.

Figure 4.14, p. 125: From www.coolopticalillusions.com. Reprinted by permission of Scott Henderson.

Figure 4.19, p. 131: © Dorling Kindersley. Adapted by permission.

Table 4.3, p. 141: Adapted from B. Greyson (2000). "Near death experiences," in *Varieties of Anomalous Experiences: Examining the Scientific Evidence*, edited by Etzel Cardena, Ph.D.; Steven Jay Lynn, Ph.D.; and Stanley Krippner, Ph.D. Copyright © 2000 by the American Psychological Association. Reproduced with permission.

Chapter 5

Figure 5.9, p. 174: From L. R. Huesmann, J. Moise, C. P. Podolski, & L. D. Eron (2003), "Longitudinal relations between childhood exposure to media violence and adult agression and violence: 1977–1992." *Developmental Psychology*. Copyright © 2003 by the American Psychological Association. Reproduced with permission.

Chapter 6

Figure 6.2, p. 190: Adapted from *Cognitive Psychology*, Vol. 11, R. S. Nickerson and J. J. Adams, "Long-term memory for a common object," pp. 287–307, Copyright 1979, with permission from Elsevier.

Figure 6.3, p. 191: Figure taken from "Human Memory: A Proposed System and Its Control Processes." This article was published in *The Psychology of Learning and Motivation: Advances in Research and Theory*, Vol. 2, edited by K. W. Spence and J. T. Spence, pp. 89–195, New York: Academic Press. Copyright Elsevier (1968). Reprinted by permission.

Figure 6.8, p. 196: From Harry P. Bahrick (1984), "Semantic memory content in a permastore: Fifty years of memory for Spanish learned in school," *Journal of Experimental Psychology: General*, 113–129. Copyright © 1984 by the American Psychological Association. Reproduced with permission.

Figure 6.15, p. 207: (on-page credit), Reprinted by permission from Macmillan Publishers Ltd.: *Nature*, Quiroga et al. (2005), "Invariant visual representation by single neurons in the human brain." *Nature*, 435, 1102–1107, copyright 2005.

Chapter 7

Figure 7.1, p. 228: Adapted from Fenson, Dale, Reznick et al., 1994. "Variability in early communicative development," *Monographs of the Society for Research in Child Development*, 59 (5, Serial No. 173) Reproduced with permission of Blackwell Publishing Ltd.

Figure 7.11, p. 247: Sample items similar to those in the *Weschler Adult Intelligence Scale—Third Edition (WAIS-III)*. Copyright © 1997 by NCS Pearson, Inc. Reproduced with permission. All rights reserved. "Wechsler Adult Intelligence Scale" and "WAIS" are trademarks, in the US and/or other countries, of Pearson Education, Inc. or its affiliates(s).

Figure 7.12, p. 247: Simulated item similar to those in the *Raven's Progressive Matrices—Advanced Progressive Matrices*. Copyright 1998 by NCS Pearson, Inc. Reproduced with permission. All rights reserved. "Raven's Progressive Matrices and Vocabulary Scales" is a trademark, in the US and/or other countries of Pearson Education, Inc. or its affiliates(s).

Unnumbered figure, p. 248: (on-page credit), From "And Now, A Warning About Drug Labels" by Deborah Franklin, *The New York Times*, October 25, 2005. Copyright © 2005 by The New York Times. Reprinted by permission.

Figure 7.14, p. 253: Used with permission from the American Institute of Physics and Rachel Ivie.

Figure 7.16, p. 254: From "Transformational studies of the internal representation of 3-dimensional objects," by J. Metzler & R. N. Shepard. In R. L. Solso, ed., *Theories of cognitive psychology: The Loyola Symposium*. Potomac, MD. Published by Lawrence Erlbaum Associates, 1974.

Chapter 8

Figure 8.1, p. 267: From A. Caspi, J. McClay, T. E. Moffitt, J. Mill, J. Martin, I. W. Craig, A. Taylor, and R. Poulton. (2002). "The Role of Genotype in the Cycle of Violence in Maltreated Children." *Science*, 297, pp. 851–854, Figure 1. Reprinted with permission from AAAS.

Figure 8.9, p. 280: From E. Waters, L. Matas, and L. A. Sroufe. 1975. "Infants' reactions to an approaching stranger: Description, validation, and functional significance of wariness," *Child Development*, 46, pp. 348–356. Reprinted with permission of Blackwell Publishing Ltd.

Figure 8.10, p. 282: Copyright 1978 from *Patterns of Attachment* by M. D. S. Ainsworth, et al. Reproduced by permission of Lawrence Erlbaum Associates, Inc., a division of Taylor & Francis Group.

Figure 8.12 p. 291: (on-page credit), From Thomas L. Good & Jere Brophy, *Contemporary Educational Psychology, 5/e.* Published by Allyn & Bacon, Boston, MA. Copyright © 1995 by Pearson Education. Adapted by permission of the publisher.

Chapter 9

Figure 9.1, p. 307: Reproduced by permission of Dr. Silvia Helena Cardoso, www.cerebromente.org.br.

Table 9.1, p. 312: "VIA Classification," http://www.viastrengths.org. Copyright © Values in Action Institute (VIA Institute on Character) 2003. Reprinted by permission.

Figure 9.5, p. 314: From "Beyond money: Toward an economy of well-being," by E. Diener & M. E. P. Seligman in *Psychological Science in the Public Interest,* Vol. 5, No. 1, p. 3. Copyright © 2004 Blackwell Publishing Ltd. Reproduced with permission of Blackwell Publishing Ltd.

Table 9.2, p. 317: Pessimism Questionnaire by Dr. Julie Norem, www.wellesley.edu. © Julie K. Norem. Used by permission of the author.

Figure 9.8, p. 325: From *Human Sexuality in a World of Diversity* by Rathus et al., Fig. 5.2, p. 149, © 2008. Reproduced by permission of Pearson Education, Inc.

Chapter 10

Figure 10.1, p. 344: Reprinted from *Journal of Psychosomatic Research,* Vol. 11, Issue 2, T. H. Holmes & R. H. Rahe, "The Social Readjustment Scale," p. 214, Copyright 1967, with permission from Elsevier.

Figure 10.2, p. 345: "General Adaptation Syndrome" from *Stress Without Distress* by Hans Selye, M.D. Copyright © 1974 by Hans Selye, M.D. Reprinted by permission of HarperCollins Publishers.

Chapter 11

Figure 11.1, p. 381: Reprinted from *Journal of Experimental Social Psychology,* Vol. 3, Issue 1, E. E. Jones & V. A. Hanson, "The attribution of attitudes," pp. 1–24, Copyright 1967, with permission from Elsevier.

Figure 11.2, p. 382: Reprinted with permission from William K. Hartmann.

Figure 11.4, p. 383: From "Opinions and Social Pressure" by S. E. Asch. Published in *Scientific American,* 193, 31–35, 1955.

Figure 11.5, p. 384: From "Opinions and Social Pressure" by S. E. Asch. Published in *Scientific American,* 193, 31–35, 1955.

Figure 11.6, p. 385: Reprinted with permission from Philip Zimbardo, Ph.D., Professor Emeritus, Stanford University.

Figure 11.9, p. 399: From http://www-personal.umich.edu. Reprinted by permission of Troy Nienberg.

Chapter 12

Table 12.1, p. 420: Tellegen, Lykken, Bouchard, Wilcox, Segal, and Rich (1988), "Personality similar in twins reared apart and together." *Journal of Personality and Social Psychology.* Copyright © 1988 by the American Psychological Association. Reproduced with permission.

Table 12.2, p. 420: Scarr et al. (1981), "Personality resemblance among adolescents and their parents in biologically related and adoptive families." *Journal of Personality and Social Psychology.* Copyright © 1981 by the American Psychological Association. Reproduced with permission.

Figure 12.2, p. 441: An MMPI-2 Clinical Scales Profile. Scores of 50 are average, and scores of 65 or above are abnormally high. This individual received elevated scores on several MMPI-2 clinical scales, including Hs (Hypochondriasis), D (Depression), Hy (Hysteria), Pt (Pychasthenia), and Sc (Schizophrenia). Source: Adapted from the *MMPI®-2 (Minnesota Multiphasic Personality Inventory®-2) Manual for Administration, Scoring, and Interpretation,* Revised Edition. Copyright © 2001 by the Regents of the University of Minnesota. Used by permission of the University of Minnesota Press. All rights reserved. "MMPI-2" and "Minnesota Multiphasic Personality Inventory-2" are trademarks owned by the Regents of the University of Minnesota.

Figure 12.3, p. 444: Reprinted by permission of the publishers from Henry A. Murray, *Thematic Apperception Test,* Card 12F, Cambridge, Mass.: Harvard University Press, Copyright © 1943 by the President and Fellows of Harvard College, Copyright © 1971 by Henry A Murray.

Chapter 13

Table 13.1, p. 460: Reprinted with permission from the *Diagnostic and Statistical Manual of Mental Disorders, Text Revision,* Fourth Edition (Copyright 2000). American Psychiatric Association.

Table 13.2, p. 461: Reprinted with permission from the *Diagnostic and Statistical Manual of Mental Disorders, Text Revision,* Fourth Edition (Copyright 2000). American Psychiatric Association.

Figure 13.2, p. 482: From *Principles of Neuropsychopharmacology* by Robert S. Feldman. Reprinted by permission of Sinauer Associates, Inc.

Chapter 14

Table 14.3, p. 497: "Simulated conversation between client and computer, Eliza" by Joseph Weizenbaum as appeared in *Communications of the ACM,* Vol. 9, No. 1, January 1966: 36. Used by permission of Joseph Weizenbaum.

Table 14.4, p. 499: From Rimm, D. & Masters, J. C. (1979). *Behavior therapy; Techniques and Empirical Findings,* 2E.

Unnumbered Figure, p. 501: Adapted from "Love Me, Love Me, Only Me!" by Albert Ellis. Reprinted with permission of Albert Ellis Institute.

Table 14.5, p. 502: From Ellis, A. (1977), "The basic clinical theory of rational-emotive therapy" in A. Ellis and R. Grieger (Eds.), *Handbook of Rational-Emotive Therapy,* New York: Springer, p. 10. Reprinted with permission of Albert Ellis Institute.

Figure 14.3, p. 506: From "Defining rational prescribing of psychoactive drugs" by E. M. Sellers, M.D., Ph.D., *British Journal of Addiction,* 83, pp. 21–34. Reprinted by permission of Wiley-Blackwell Publishing Ltd.

Table 14.7, p. 508: From "Psychotherapy on trial" by Hal Arkowitz and Scott O. Lilienfeld, *Scientific American,* April/May 2006. Copyright © 2006 by Scientific American. All rights reserved. Reprinted by permission.

PHOTO CREDITS

Page xiv, photo of Steven Lynn, by Fern Pritkin Lynn

Chapter 1

pp. 2–3: © plainpicture GMBH & Co. KG/Alamy; p. 6: Courtesy of Hannah Faye Chua; p. 7: AP Images/Stuart Ramson; p. 9: Reproduced by permission, The John Rylands University Library of Manchester, and provided through the courtesy of Roger J. Wood, Faculty of Life Sciences, University of Manchester; p. 10: JIM BOURG/AFP/Getty Images; p. 12: Dion Ogust/The Image Works; p. 15: Stewart Cohen/Getty Images Royalty Free; p. 16, *top* (both): Corbis; pp. 17 & 37: AP Images/HO; p. 21: Danny Feld/© NBC/ Courtesy Everett Collection; p. 22, *top:* Design Pics Inc./Alamy Royalty Free; p. 22, *bottom:* Mary Evans Picture Library/The Image Works; pp. 23 & 38: Topham/The Image Works; p. 24: Archives of the History of American Psychology—The University of Akron; p. 26 (James): Library of Congress; p. 26 (Piaget): Bettmann/CORBIS; p. 26 (Skinner): Omikron/Photo Researchers, Inc.; p. 26 (Tichener): Archives of the History of American Psychology—The University of Akron; p. 26 (Freud): Library of Congress # LOT 11831-A; p. 27, *top:* Photo Researchers, Inc.; p. 27, *bottom:* Archives of the History of American Psychology—The University of Akron; pp. 29 & 38: Freud Museum Photo Library; p. 33: Courtesy of MikeL-911 via Flickr; pp. 34, *top* & 39: Dennis MacDonald/PhotoEdit, Inc.; p. 34, *middle:* Fat Chance Productions/ Corbis; pp. 34, *bottom* & 39: Photo of Kenneth & Mamie Clark used with Permission of the University Archives, Columbia University in the city of New York.

Chapter 2

pp. 40–41: Masterfile; p. 43, *left:* Alan Carey/The Image Works; p. 43, *right:* G.L. Booker/Kansas City Star/Newscom; p. 45: AP Images/Jonas Ekstromer/Pool; p. 46: John Birdsall/The Image Works; p. 47: AP Images /Ann Heisenfelt; p. 48: Penelope Breese/Liaison/Getty Images; p. 49: Michael Newman/PhotoEdit, Inc.; pp. 51 & 74: Alaska Stock LLC/Alamy; p. 52, left: Frank Siteman/PhotoEdit, Inc.; p. 52, right: Topham/ The Image Works; p. 56: Topham/The Image Works; p. 57: David M. Dennis/Animals Animals/Earth Scenes; pp. 59 & 75: Popperfoto/Alamy; pp. 61 & 75: Sygma/Corbis; pp. 63 & 76: William West/AFP/Getty Images; p. 66: moodboard/Alamy Royalty Free; p. 68: Brand X/Corbis Royalty Free; pp. 71, *top* & 77: Zigy Kaluzny/Stone/Getty Images; pp. 71, *bottom* & 77: Splash News/Newscom.

Chapter 3

pp. 78–79: © Syracuse Newspapers/Suzanne Dunn/The Image Works; p. 82: Dennis Kunkel/Phototake; pp. 84 & 108: Troy Wayrynen/NewSport/Corbis; p. 86: Courtesy of Simon Lovestone of the MRC Centre for Neurodegeneration Research at KCL; p. 92: John A. L. Cooke/Animals Animals/Earth Sciences; p. 96: DigitalVision/Alamy Royalty Free; p. 97: The Image Works Archive; p. 99, top: ER Productions/Corbis; pp. 99, middle & 110: Courtesy of Matthew Kirschen, Stanford University School of Medicine; p. 101: NOAH SEELAM/AFP/Getty Images; p. 105, top: Dornsife Neuroscience Imaging Center and Brain and Creativity Institute, University of Southern California; p. 105, middle: Denis Scott/ Corbis; pp. 106 & 111: Ragnar Schmuck/Getty Images Royalty Free; p. 107: Jamie Bakin/The Medical File/Peter Arnold, Inc.

Chapter 4

pp. 112–113: © Kazuyoshi Nomachi/Corbis; p. 127, top: Watercolour by John W Johnston, Northampton, UK. www.JWJarts.com; p. 127, bottom: Mark Richards/PhotoEdit, Inc.; p. 128: Jan Csernoch/Alamy; p. 129: JLP/Jose Luis Pelaez/zefa/Corbis; p. 133: AP Images/Stephen Morton; p. 136: AP Images/ Nikos Giakoumidis; p. 137: David R. Frazier Photolibrary, Inc./Alamy; p. 138: Fortean/Hart-Davis/Topham/The Image Works; p. 139: Patrick Blake/Alamy; p. 140: Adri Berger/Stone/Getty Images; p. 141: Hans Neleman/zefa/Corbis; p. 143: Syracuse Newspapers/Brian Phillips/The Image Works.

Chapter 5

pp. 150–151: Masterfile; p. 153: Elena Rooraid/PhotoEdit, Inc.; p. 154: PA/Topham/The Image Works; p. 157, top: Rob Wilkinson/Alamy; p. 157, middle: Bill Aron/PhotoEdit, Inc.; pp. 158 & 182: Benjamin Harris, Ph.D.; p. 159, top: Carvalho/FilmMagic/Getty Images; p. 159, bottom: Lester V. Bergman/Corbis; p. 160, middle: Erich Lessing/Art Resource; p. 160, bottom: Erich Lessing/Art Resource. © 2008 Estate of Pablo Picasso/Artists Rights Society (ARS), New York; p. 164, top: Elizabeth Crews Photography; p. 164, middle: Hugh Sitton/Stone/Getty Images; p. 165, middle: Design Pics Inc./ Alamy Royalty Free; p. 165, bottom: Pete Saloutos/Corbis; p. 167: Randy Faris/Corbis Royalty Free; p. 168: AP Images/Ed Andrieski; p. 169: Brooks Kraft/Sygma/Corbis; p. 170, top: Pressnet/Topham/The Image Works; p. 170, bottom: Medioimages/Photodisc/Getty Images Royalty Free; pp. 172 & 183: Stockbyte/Getty Images Royalty Free; pp. 173, bottom & 184, top: Elizabeth Crews/The Image Works; pp. 176, middle & 184, bottom left: Kevin Laubacher/ Taxi/Getty Images; p. 176, bottom: Stuart R. Ellins Ph.D.; p. 177: mediablitzimages (uk) Limited/Alamy; pp. 179, top & 184: Steven David Miller/Animals Animals; pp. 179, bottom & 185: Myrleen Ferguson Cate/PhotoEdit, Inc.; pp. 181 & 185: Corbis Royalty Free.

Chapter 6

pp. 186–187: © Gari Wyn Williams/Alamy; p. 189: Topham/The Image Works. © 2009 Salvador Dali, Gala-Salvador Foundation/Artists Rights Society (ARS), New York; p. 191: Jupiter Images/Brand X/Alamy Royalty Free; p. 196: Anne-Marie Palmer/Alamy Royalty Free; p. 198: Radius Images/Alamy Royalty Free; p. 200: Bob Daemmrich/PhotoEdit, Inc.; p. 201: Joe Raedle/Getty Images; p. 206: Will & Deni McIntyre/Photo Researchers, Inc.; p. 207 #1: Frank Trapper/Corbis; p. 207 #2: Doane Gregory/Warner Bros./Bureau L.A. Collection/Corbis; p. 207 #4: Mathur/ Reuters/Corbis; p. 207 #5: Carlo Allegri/ Getty Images; p. 207 #6: Phil Han/ZUMA/Corbis; pp. 208 & 221: Newmarket Releasing/Courtesy Everett Collection; p. 209: Index Open/PhotosToGo; pp. 211 & 222: Courtesy of Carolyn Rovee-Collier; p. 212, top: Denise Rego Bass/The Image Works; pp. 212, bottom & 222: Ann Brown/SuperStock; p. 213: Reuters NewMedia Inc./Shannon Stapleton/Corbis; p. 214: Daniel Acker/ Bloomberg News/Landov; pp. 215 & 223: Courtesy of Elizabeth Loftus, University of California, Irvine; pp. 216 & 223: Jeff Greenberg/PhotoEdit, Inc.; p. 217: AP Images/HO/Burlington Police Department; p. 218: AP Images/Al Francis; p. 219: Reuters/Jeff Christensen/Landov.

Chapter 7

pp. 224–225: Masterfile; p. 227, top: Jack Hollingsworth/Photodisc/Getty Images Royalty Free; pp. 227, bottom & 258: Michael Newman/PhotoEdit, Inc.; p. 228: Katrina Wittkamp/Riser/Getty Images; p. 230, top: Peter Parks/AFP/ Getty Images; p. 230, bottom: Ingram Publishing/INGRAM Publishing; p. 231: Ellen Senisi/The Image Works; p. 232, top: Bob Daemmrich/PhotoEdit, Inc.;

p. 232, middle: Photograph provided courtesy of Georgia State University; p. 232, bottom: Photo by Jenny Pegg/The Alex Foundation; p. 233, top: James Balog/ Stone/Getty Images; pp. 233, bottom & 258: Anders Ryman/Corbis; pp. 235 & 258: Bob Krist/Corbis; p. 236, top: David Grossman/The Image Works; pp. 236, middle & 259: Artiga Photo/Corbis; p. 241 (King): Bettmann/Corbis; p. 241 (McLachlan): Contographer/Corbis; p. 241 (Wiliams): Elsa/Getty Images; p. 241 (Hawking): Chris Davies/ArenaPAL/Topham/The Image Works; p. 241 (Earheart): Scherl/SV-Bilderdienst/The Image Works; p. 241 (Amanpour): UPI Photo/Robin Platzer/Landov; p. 241 (Dalai Lama): PASCAL ROSSIGNOL/ Reuters/Landov; p. 241 (Irwin): WILL BURGESS/ Reuters/Landov; p. 242: Richard A. Cooke/Corbis; p. 245: Sara D. Davis/ Chicago Tribune/MCT/ Newscom; p. 248: Stockdisc Classic/Alamy Royalty Free; p. 249: Grabowsky U./SV-Bilderdienst/The Image Works; p. 250: Miramax/Courtesy Everett Collection; p. 251, top: Brad Wilson/Stone/Getty Images; p. 251, bottom: MP Imagery/Alamy; p. 252: Nancy Sheehan Photography; p. 254: Ian Shaw/Alamy; p. 257: Malcolm Case-Green/Alamy.

Chapter 8

pp. 262–263: Oppenheim Bernhard/Getty Images; p. 265, top: Monte S. Buchsbaum, M.D., Mount Sinai School of Medicine, New York, N.Y.; pp. 265, bottom & 296: Peter Beavis/Taxi/Getty Images; pp. 266 & 296: Bureau L.A. Collection/Corbis; p. 268, top: RBM Online/epa/Corbis; p. 268, middle: Petit Format/Photo Researchers, Inc.; p. 268, bottom: Ace Stock Limited/Alamy; p. 269: David H. Wells/Corbis; pp. 270 & 297: Keren Su/Corbis; p. 272: Bill Anderson/Photo Researchers, Inc.; p. 273: Laura Dwight/PhotoEdit, Inc.; p. 275: James Shaffer/PhotoEdit, Inc.; p. 277: Courtesy of Lorraine E. Bahrick, Professor, Director, Infant Development Research Center, Florida International University Department of Psychology; p. 280, top: Kayoco/zefa/ Corbis; pp. 280, bottom, 281 & 298: Nina Leen/Time Life Pictures/Getty Images; p. 283, top: Elizabeth Crews/The Image Works; p. 283, middle: Matt Gray/Digital Vision/Getty Images Royalty Free; p. 283, bottom: Michael Newman/PhotoEdit, Inc.; p. 284, top: Courtesy of Annie Pickert; p. 284, bottom: Kenzaburo Fukuhara/Corbis; p. 285, top: Randy Faris/Corbis; p. 285, middle: Eric Miller/St. Paul Pioneer Press/Newscom; p. 286: Polka Dot Images/Jupiter Images Royalty Free; p. 287, top: Mira/Alamy; p. 287, bottom: Courtesy of Melissa Hines. Reprinted from Evolution and Human Behavior, November 2002, Alexander, Gerianne M. and Hines, Melissa, Sex differences in response to children's toys in nonhuman primates (Cercopithecus aethiops sabaeus), Pages 467–479, Copyright 2002, with permission from Elsevier; p. 289: Mary Kate Denny/PhotoEdit, Inc.; p. 290, top: Davis Turner/CNP/Corbis; p. 290, middle: Ei Katsumata/Alamy; p. 292, top & 299: Ariel Skelley/Blend Images/Getty Images Royalty Free; p. 292, bottom left: Rachel Epstein/The Image Works; p. 292, bottom right: Tony Freeman/PhotoEdit, Inc.; p. 293, middle: David Young-Wolff/PhotoEdit, Inc.; p. 293, bottom: Peter Hvizdak/The Image Works; p. 294, top: Courtesy of Nancy Law & Laura Namy; p. 294, bottom: Robert Michael/Corbis Royalty Free; pp. 295 & 299: Malie Rich-Griffith/Infocuspictures.com/Alamy.

Chapter 9

pp. 300–301: © Blend Images/Superstock; p. 303, top: Reprinted by permission of Harvard Business School Press. From Toxic Emotions at Work And What You Can do About Them by Peter J. Frost. Boston, MA 2007. Cover. Copyright © 2007 by the Harvard Business School Publishing Corporation; All rights reserved; p. 303, middle: NMPFT/SSPL/The Image Works; pp. 304, top & 334: Richard Lord/The Image Works; p. 304, middle: Issei Kato/Reuters/ Corbis; p. 305: PAUL EKMAN GROUP, LLC.; p. 306: AP Images/Gurinder Osan; p. 308: David Stuart/Photographer's Choice RF/Getty Images Royalty Free; p. 309: VStock LLC/Index Open/PhotosToGo; p. 310: Robert E Daemmrich/ Stone/Getty Images; pp. 312 & 335: David Shaw/Alamy; p. 314: Greg Hinsdale/Corbis; p. 315, top: Michael J. Doolittle/The Image Works; p. 315, bottom: Tim Wimborne/Reuters/Corbis; pp. 316 & 335: Tom Fox/Dallas Morning News/MCT/Newscom; pp. 318 & 336: Bill Greenblatt/UPI/ Newscom; p. 319: AP Images/Tony Dejak, file; p. 320: Network Productions/ The Image Works; p. 322, top: PHOTOTAKE Inc./Alamy; p. 322, bottom: AP Images/Matt Houston; p. 323, top: Mark Richards/PhotoEdit, Inc.; p. 323, bottom: Rita Maas/StockFood Creative/Getty Images; p. 324: Spots Illustration/Jupiterimages Royalty Free; p. 326, top: AP Images/Zack Seckler

326, *middle:* AP Images/Hermann J. Knippertz; p. 328, *top:* Reuters/Corbis; p. 329: Alex Segre/Alamy; p. 330, *top:* AP Images; ...dle left & 337: Lisa O'Connor/ZUMA/Corbis; p. 330, *middle right:* ...nnor/ ZUMA/Corbis; p. 331: Courtesy of Judith Langlois; p. 332: ...L. Pelaez/Corbis.

...er 10

...–339: Shuji Kobayashi/Getty Images; p. 341, *top:* Joshua ...Bloomberg News/Landov; p. 341, *bottom:* Viviane Moos/Corbis; pp. 342, ...& 372: Mario Tama/Getty Images; p. 342, *middle:* Kristy-Anne Glubish/ ...sign Pics/Corbis Royalty Free; pp. 343 & 372: CoverSpot/Alamy; pp. 346 & ...73: Randy Faris/Corbis Royalty Free; p. 347: Ali Abbas/epa/Corbis; p. 348, *top left:* John Birdsall/The Image Works; p. 348, *top center:* LLC, Vstock/Index Open/PhotosToGo; p. 348, *top right:* John Birdsall/The Image Works; p. 348, *middle left:* Gavin Hellier/JAI/Corbis; p. 348, *center:* Dennis MacDonald/ PhotoEdit, Inc.; p. 348, *middle right:* Jed Share and Kaoru/Corbis; p. 348, bottom left: Design Pics, Inc./Index Open/PhotosToGo; p. 348, *bottom center:* Bill Aron/PhotoEdit, Inc.; p. 348, *bottom right:* Stockbyte/Alamy Royalty Free; p. 349, *top left:* Evan Agostini/ImageDirect/Getty Images; p. 349, *top right:* Bill Olive/Getty Images; p. 349, *middle:* Bill Aron/PhotoEdit, Inc.; p. 351: Noel Hendrickson/Digital Vision/Getty Images Royalty Free; pp. 352 & 373: Zoriah/The Image Works; p. 353: Bill Aron/PhotoEdit, Inc.; p. 355: Emely/zefa/ Corbis; p. 356: Peter Hvizdak/The Image Works; p. 358: VCL/Taxi/Getty Images; p. 359: The Granger Collection; p. 360: Faces of Meth/Multnomah County Sheriff's Office; p. 361, top: Doug Menuez/ Photodisc/Getty Images Royalty Free; p. 361, middle: Gebhard Krewitt/VISUM/The Image Works; p. 362, *top:* Stockbyte/Alamy Royalty Free; p. 362, *middle:* Tony Freeman/ PhotoEdit, Inc.; p. 362, *bottom:* Dana White/PhotoEdit, Inc.; p. 363: VStock/ Alamy Royalty Free; pp. 364, *top* & 374: AP Images/ Sakchai Lalit; p. 364, *middle:* David J. Green/Alamy; p. 364, bottom: Topham/ The Image Works; p. 365: moodboard/Corbis Royalty Free; p. 366, *top:* Alan Oddie/PhotoEdit, Inc.; p. 366, *bottom:* Christian O. Bruch/VISUM/The Image Works; p. 369: Envision/ Corbis; p. 371: Phototake, Inc./Alamy.

Chapter 11

pp. 376–377: Linda Rich/ArenaPAL/The Image Works; p. 379, *top:* The Kobal Collection/20th Century Fox/Dreamworks; p. 379, *bottom:* Tony Freeman/ PhotoEdit, Inc.; p. 380: BlueMoon Stock/Alamy; p. 384: Dr. Solomon Asch; p. 385: Courtesy of PG Zimbardo, Inc.; pp. 386, *top left* & 386, *bottom left:* PG Zimbardo, Inc.; p. 386, *top right:* AP Images; p. 386, *bottom right:* Courtesy Wikipedia.com/Zuma Press; p. 386, *bottom:* AP Images/Daniel Luna; p. 387: NASA/Getty Images; p. 388: AP Images/Ahn Young-joon; p. 389, *left:* AP Images/Joe Holloway Jr., Files; p. 389, *right:* AP Images/File; p. 391, center: Archives of the History of American Psychology—The University of Akron; pp. 391, surrounding & 413: From the film *Obedience* © Stanley Milgram, by permission of Alexandra Milgram; p. 393: William Philpott/Reuters/Corbis; pp. 394, *top* & 413: Photograph by Frans de Waal; p. 394, *middle:* The New York Times/Redux; p. 394, *bottom:* AP Images; p. 395, *top:* AP Images/Detroit Free Press, Steven R. Nickerson; pp. 395, *bottom* & 413: Justin Guariglia/National Geographic/Getty Images; p. 396: David Young-Wolff/PhotoEdit, Inc.; p. 397: Keith Brofsky/Digital Vision/Getty Images Royalty Free; p. 398: Bob Daemmrich/The Image Works; p. 399: BananaStock/ Jupiterimages Royalty Free; p. 401: Bob Daemmrich/PhotoEdit, Inc.; pp. 402 & 414: Peter Kramer/ Getty Images; p. 405, *top:* Kateland Photo; p. 405, *middle:* Barry Austin Photography/Photodisc/Getty Images Royalty Free; p. 407, *top:* AP Images/ Mannie Garcia; p. 409, all: Index Open/PhotosToGo; pp. 411 & 415: Bob Daemmrich.

Chapter 12

pp. 416–417: Taxi/Getty Images; p. 412: Joe McBride/Stone/Getty Images; p. 419: Julia Eisenberg/Lichtfilm GmbH; p. 420: Thomas Wanstall/The Image Works; pp. 421 & 448: P Deliss/Godong/Corbis; p. 424: Spencer Grant/ PhotoEdit, Inc.; p. 425: Library of Congress # LOT 11831-A; p. 427: Universal/The Kobal Collection; p. 428: Mary Evans/Sigmund Freud Copyrights/The Image Works; pp. 429 & 449: Ian Woodcock/Illustration Works/Getty Images; p. 431: Fancy/Veer/Corbis Royalty Free; pp. 432 & 449: Spencer Grant/PhotoEdit, Inc.; p. 433, top: John Birdsall/The Image Works; p. 433, bottom: Carl Rogers Memorial Library; pp. 434, top left & 450: Hulton-Deutsch Collection/CORBIS; pp. 434, top right & 450: JP Laffont/Sygma/Corbis; p. 434, bottom: Michael Nichols/National Geographic/Getty Images; pp. 435, top & 450: Sally and Richard Greenhill/Alamy; p. 435, bottom: H&S Produktion/CORBIS; p. 436: AP Images/Reed Saxon; p. 438, top: Bettmann/ Corbis; p. 438, bottom: Adrian Bradshaw/epa/Corbis; p. 439: Ausloeser/ zefa/CORBIS; p. 442: Courtesy of http://www.matthewbarr.co.uk/harrypotter; pp. 443, top & 451: Amamanta Family Anatomically Correct Dolls, www.amamantafamily.com; p. 443, bottom: Hulton Archive/Getty Images; p. 445: Mark Harwood/Alamy; p. 446: Eric Liebowitz/© CBS/Courtesy Everett Collection.

Chapter 13

pp. 452–453: © Theo Allofs/zefa/Corbis; pp. 455 & 484: ColorBlind Images/Blend Images/Corbis Royalty Free; p. 456: Corbis; p. 457, *top:* Aladin Abdel Naby/Reuters; p. 457, *middle:* Ed Quinn/Corbis; pp. 458 & 484: AP Images/Tony Dejak; p. 459: Janine Wiedel Photolibrary/Alamy; p. 460: American Psychiatric Association; p. 461: Getty Images; p. 463: Michael Newman/PhotoEdit, Inc.; p. 464, *top:* Purestock/Alamy Royalty Free; pp. 464, *middle* & 484: Photographer's Mate First Class Alan D. Monyelle/US Navy/ Reuters/Corbis; pp. 465 & 485: Bettmann/CORBIS; p. 467: Rosanne Olson/ Digital Vision/Getty Images Royalty Free; p. 470, *top:* Rob Melnychuk/ Digital Vision/Getty Images Royalty Free; p. 470, *middle:* Journal-Courier/ Steve Warmowski/The Image Works; p. 471: Steven Puetzer/Photographer's Choice/ Getty Images; p. 474: Paramount/Courtesy Everett Collection; pp. 476 & 486: AP Images/Florida Department of Corrections; pp. 477 & 486: AP Images/ The Denver Post, Karl Gehring; pp. 479 & 487: Phillip Dvorak/ Images.com; p. 480: Grunnitus Studio/Photo Researchers, Inc.; p. 481: Courtesy NIH— Dr. Daniel Weinberger, Clinical Brain Disorders Branch; p. 483: PHANIE/Photo Researchers, Inc.

Chapter 14

pp. 488–489: Martin Barraud/Getty Images; pp. 492 & 518: Formcourt (Form Advertising)/Alamy Royalty Free; pp. 493 & 518: HBO/Courtesy Everett Collection; p. 496: Richard Hutchings/PhotoEdit, Inc.; p. 497, *top:* Bill Aron/ PhotoEdit, Inc.; p. 497, *bottom:* Colin Young-Wolff/PhotoEdit, Inc.; p. 498: Amanda Rohde/iStockphoto; p. 499, top: Bill Aron/PhotoEdit, Inc.; pp. 499, *middle* & 519: Rainer Jensen/dpa/Corbis; p. 501: © Michael Fenichel; p. 503: Manchan/Digital Vision/Getty Images Royalty Free; p. 504: Mary Kate Denny/ PhotoEdit, Inc.; p. 505: Burke/Triolo Productions/Brand X/ Jupiterimages Royalty Free; pp. 507 & 520: Joel Gordon; p. 509, top: INSADCO Photography/Alamy Royalty Free; pp. 509, *bottom* & 520: John Foxx/Stockbyte/ Getty Images Royalty Free; p. 510: Robert Pitts/Landov; p. 512: Tom McCarthy/ PhotoEdit, Inc.; p. 513: Marcelo Wain/iStockphoto; p. 514: Steve Liss/Time & Life Pictures/Getty Images; p. 515: Will & Deni McIntyre/ Photo Researchers, Inc.; pp. 517 & 521: Ray Fisher/ Time & Life Pictures/Getty Images.

Chapter 3

pp. 78-79: © Syracuse Newspapers/Suzanne Dunn/The Image Works; p. 82: Dennis Kunkel/Phototake; pp. 84 & 108: Troy Wayrynen/NewSport/Corbis; p. 86: Courtesy of Simon Lovestone of the MRC Centre for Neurodegeneration Research at KCL; p. 92: John A. L. Cooke/Animals Animals/Earth Sciences; p. 96: DigitalVision/Alamy Royalty Free; p. 97: The Image Works Archive; p. 99, top: ER Productions/Corbis; pp. 99, middle & 110: Courtesy of Matthew Kirschen, Stanford University School of Medicine; p. 101: NOAH SEELAM/AFP/Getty Images; p. 105, top: Dornsife Neuroscience Imaging Center and Brain and Creativity Institute, University of Southern California; p. 105, middle: Denis Scott/ Corbis; pp. 106 & 111: Ragnar Schmuck/Getty Images Royalty Free; p. 107: Jamie Bakin/The Medical File/Peter Arnold, Inc.

Chapter 4

pp. 112–113: © Kazuyoshi Nomachi/Corbis; p. 127, top: Watercolour by John W Johnston, Northampton, UK. www.JWJarts.com; p. 127, bottom: Mark Richards/PhotoEdit, Inc.; p. 128: Jan Csernoch/Alamy; p. 129: JLP/Jose Luis Pelaez/zefa/Corbis; p. 133: AP Images/Stephen Morton; p. 136: AP Images/ Nikos Giakoumidis; p. 137: David R. Frazier Photolibrary, Inc./Alamy; p. 138: Fortean/Hart-Davis/Topham/The Image Works; p. 139: Patrick Blake/Alamy; p. 140: Adri Berger/Stone/Getty Images; p. 141: Hans Neleman/zefa/Corbis; p. 143: Syracuse Newspapers/Brian Phillips/The Image Works.

Chapter 5

pp. 150–151: Masterfile; p. 153: Elena Rooraid/PhotoEdit, Inc.; p. 154: PA/Topham/The Image Works; p. 157, top: Rob Wilkinson/Alamy; p. 157, middle: Bill Aron/PhotoEdit, Inc.; pp. 158 & 182: Benjamin Harris, Ph.D.; p. 159, top: Carvalho/FilmMagic/Getty Images; p. 159, bottom: Lester V. Bergman/Corbis; p. 160, middle: Erich Lessing/Art Resource; p. 160, bottom: Erich Lessing/Art Resource. © 2008 Estate of Pablo Picasso/Artists Rights Society (ARS), New York; p. 164, top: Elizabeth Crews Photography; p. 164, middle: Hugh Sitton/Stone/Getty Images; p. 165, middle: Design Pics Inc./ Alamy Royalty Free; p. 165, bottom: Pete Saloutos/Corbis; p. 167: Randy Faris/Corbis Royalty Free; p. 168: AP Images/Ed Andrieski; p. 169: Brooks Kraft/Sygma/Corbis; p. 170, top: Pressnet/Topham/The Image Works; p. 170, bottom: Medioimages/Photodisc/Getty Images Royalty Free; pp. 172 & 183: Stockbyte/Getty Images Royalty Free; pp. 173, bottom & 184, top: Elizabeth Crews/The Image Works; pp. 176, middle & 184, bottom left: Kevin Laubacher/ Taxi/Getty Images; p. 176, bottom: Stuart R. Ellins Ph.D.; p. 177: mediablitzimages (uk) Limited/Alamy; pp. 179, top & 184: Steven David Miller/Animals Animals; pp. 179, bottom & 185: Myrleen Ferguson Cate/PhotoEdit, Inc.; pp. 181 & 185: Corbis Royalty Free.

Chapter 6

pp. 186–187: © Gari Wyn Williams/Alamy; p. 189: Topham/The Image Works. © 2009 Salvador Dali, Gala-Salvador Foundation/Artists Rights Society (ARS), New York; p. 191: Jupiter Images/Brand X/Alamy Royalty Free; p. 196: Anne-Marie Palmer/Alamy Royalty Free; p. 198: Radius Images/Alamy Royalty Free; p. 200: Bob Daemmrich/PhotoEdit, Inc.; p. 201: Joe Raedle/Getty Images; p. 206: Will & Deni McIntyre/Photo Researchers, Inc.; p. 207 #1: Frank Trapper/Corbis; p. 207 #2: Doane Gregory/Warner Bros./Bureau L.A. Collection/Corbis; p. 207 #4: Mathur/ Reuters/Corbis; p. 207 #5: Carlo Allegri/ Getty Images; p. 207 #6: Phil Han/ZUMA/Corbis; pp. 208 & 221: Newmarket Releasing/Courtesy Everett Collection; p. 209: Index Open/PhotosToGo; pp. 211 & 222: Courtesy of Carolyn Rovee-Collier; p. 212, top: Denise Rego Bass/The Image Works; pp. 212, bottom & 222: Ann Brown/SuperStock; p. 213: Reuters NewMedia Inc./Shannon Stapleton/Corbis; p. 214: Daniel Acker/ Bloomberg News/Landov; pp. 215 & 223: Courtesy of Elizabeth Loftus, University of California, Irvine; pp. 216 & 223: Jeff Greenberg/PhotoEdit, Inc.; p. 217: AP Images/HO/Burlington Police Department; p. 218: AP Images/Al Francis; p. 219: Reuters/Jeff Christensen/Landov.

Chapter 7

pp. 224–225: Masterfile; p. 227, top: Jack Hollingsworth/Photodisc/Getty Images Royalty Free; pp. 227, bottom & 258: Michael Newman/PhotoEdit, Inc.; p. 228: Katrina Wittkamp/Riser/Getty Images; p. 230, top: Peter Parks/AFP/ Getty Images; p. 230, bottom: Ingram Publishing/INGRAM Publishing; p. 231: Ellen Senisi/The Image Works; p. 232, top: Bob Daemmrich/PhotoEdit, Inc.;

p. 232, middle: Photograph provided courtesy of Georgia State University; p. 232, bottom: Photo by Jenny Pegg/The Alex Foundation; p. 233, top: James Balog/ Stone/Getty Images; pp. 233, bottom & 258: Anders Ryman/Corbis; pp. 235 & 258: Bob Krist/Corbis; p. 236, top: David Grossman/The Image Works; pp. 236, middle & 259: Artiga Photo/Corbis; p. 241 (King): Bettmann/Corbis; p. 241 (McLachlan): Contographer/Corbis; p. 241 (Wiliams): Elsa/Getty Images; p. 241 (Hawking): Chris Davies/ArenaPAL/Topham/The Image Works; p. 241 (Earheart): Scherl/SV-Bilderdienst/The Image Works; p. 241 (Amanpour): UPI Photo/Robin Platzer/Landov; p. 241 (Dalai Lama): PASCAL ROSSIGNOL/ Reuters/Landov; p. 241 (Irwin): WILL BURGESS/ Reuters/Landov; p. 242: Richard A. Cooke/Corbis; p. 245: Sara D. Davis/ Chicago Tribune/MCT/ Newscom; p. 248: Stockdisc Classic/Alamy Royalty Free; p. 249: Grabowsky U./SV-Bilderdienst/The Image Works; p. 250: Miramax/Courtesy Everett Collection; p. 251, top: Brad Wilson/Stone/Getty Images; p. 251, bottom: MP Imagery/Alamy; p. 252: Nancy Sheehan Photography; p. 254: Ian Shaw/Alamy; p. 257: Malcolm Case-Green/Alamy.

Chapter 8

pp. 262–263: Oppenheim Bernhard/Getty Images; p. 265, top: Monte S. Buchsbaum, M.D., Mount Sinai School of Medicine, New York, N.Y.; pp. 265, bottom & 296: Peter Beavis/Taxi/Getty Images; pp. 266 & 296: Bureau L.A. Collection/Corbis; p. 268, top: RBM Online/epa/Corbis; p. 268, middle: Petit Format/Photo Researchers, Inc.; p. 268, bottom: Ace Stock Limited/Alamy; p. 269: David H. Wells/Corbis; p. 270 & 297: Keren Su/Corbis; p. 272: Bill Anderson/Photo Researchers, Inc.; p. 273: Laura Dwight/PhotoEdit, Inc.; p. 275: James Shaffer/PhotoEdit, Inc.; p. 277: Courtesy of Lorraine E. Bahrick, Professor, Director, Infant Development Research Center, Florida International University Department of Psychology; p. 280, top: Kayoco/zefa/ Corbis; pp. 280, bottom, 281 & 298: Nina Leen/Time Life Pictures/Getty Images; p. 283, top: Elizabeth Crews/The Image Works; p. 283, middle: Matt Gray/Digital Vision/Getty Images Royalty Free; p. 283, bottom: Michael Newman/PhotoEdit, Inc.; p. 284, top: Courtesy of Annie Pickert; p. 284, bottom: Kenzaburo Fukuhara/Corbis; p. 285, top: Randy Faris/Corbis; p. 285, middle: Eric Miller/St. Paul Pioneer Press/Newscom; p. 286: Polka Dot Images/Jupiter Images Royalty Free; p. 287, top: Mira/Alamy; p. 287, bottom: Courtesy of Melissa Hines. Reprinted from Evolution and Human Behavior, November 2002, Alexander, Gerianne M. and Hines, Melissa, Sex differences in response to children's toys in nonhuman primates (Cercopithecus aethiops sabaeus), Pages 467–479, Copyright 2002, with permission from Elsevier; p. 289: Mary Kate Denny/PhotoEdit, Inc.; p. 290, top: Davis Turner/CNP/Corbis; p. 290, middle: Ei Katsumata/Alamy; pp. 292, top & 299: Ariel Skelley/Blend Images/Getty Images Royalty Free; p. 292, bottom left: Rachel Epstein/The Image Works; p. 292, bottom right: Tony Freeman/PhotoEdit, Inc.; p. 293, middle: David Young-Wolff/PhotoEdit, Inc.; p. 293, bottom: Peter Hvizdak/The Image Works; p. 294, top: Courtesy of Nancy Law & Laura Namy; p. 294, bottom: Robert Michael/Corbis Royalty Free; pp. 295 & 299: Malie Rich-Griffith/Infocuspictures.com/Alamy.

Chapter 9

pp. 300–301: © Blend Images/Superstock; p. 303, top: Reprinted by permission of Harvard Business School Press. From *Toxic Emotions at Work And What You Can do About Them* by Peter J. Frost. Boston, MA 2007. Cover. Copyright © 2007 by the Harvard Business School Publishing Corporation; All rights reserved; p. 303, middle: NMPFT/SSPL/The Image Works; pp. 304, top & 334: Richard Lord/The Image Works; p. 304, middle: Issei Kato/Reuters/ Corbis; p. 305: PAUL EKMAN GROUP, LLC.; p. 306: AP Images/Gurinder Osan; p. 308: David Stuart/Photographer's Choice RF/Getty Images Royalty Free; p. 309: VStock LLC/Index Open/PhotosToGo; p. 310: Robert E Daemmrich/ Stone/Getty Images; pp. 312 & 335: David Shaw/Alamy; p. 314: Greg Hinsdale/Corbis; p. 315, top: Michael J. Doolittle/The Image Works; p. 315, bottom: Tim Wimborne/Reuters/Corbis; pp. 316 & 335: Tom Fox/Dallas Morning News/MCT/Newscom; pp. 318 & 336: Bill Greenblatt/UPI/ Newscom; p. 319: AP Images/Tony Dejak, file; p. 320: Network Productions/ The Image Works; p. 322, top: PHOTOTAKE Inc./Alamy; p. 322, bottom: AP Images/Matt Houston; p. 323, top: Mark Richards/PhotoEdit, Inc.; p. 323, bottom: Rita Maas/StockFood Creative/Getty Images; p. 324: Spots Illustration/Jupiterimages Royalty Free; p. 326, top: AP Images/Zack Seckler

AP Images/p. 326, *middle*: AP Images/Hermann J. Knippertz; p. 328, *top*: Reuters TV/ Reuters/Corbis; p. 329: Alex Segre/Alamy; p. 330, *top*: AP Images; pp. 330, *middle* left & 337: Lisa O'Connor/ZUMA/Corbis; p. 330, *middle right*: Lisa O'Connor/ ZUMA/Corbis; p. 331: Courtesy of Judith Langlois; p. 332: JLP/Jose L. Pelaez/Corbis.

Chapter 10

pp. 338–339: Shuji Kobayashi/Getty Images; p. 341, *top*: Joshua Lott/Bloomberg News/Landov; p. 341, *bottom*: Viviane Moos/Corbis; pp. 342, *top* & 372: Mario Tama/Getty Images; p. 342, *middle*: Kristy-Anne Glubish/ Design Pics/Corbis Royalty Free; pp. 343 & 372: CoverSpot/Alamy; pp. 346 & 373: Randy Faris/Corbis Royalty Free; p. 347: Ali Abbas/epa/Corbis; p. 348, *top left*: John Birdsall/The Image Works; p. 348, *top center*: LLC, Vstock/Index Open/PhotosToGo; p. 348, *top right*: John Birdsall/The Image Works; p. 348, *middle left*: Gavin Hellier/JAI/Corbis; p. 348, *center*: Dennis MacDonald/ PhotoEdit, Inc.; p. 348, *middle right*: Jed Share and Kaoru/Corbis; p. 348, bottom left: Design Pics, Inc./Index Open/PhotosToGo; p. 348, *bottom center*: Bill Aron/PhotoEdit, Inc.; p. 348, *bottom right*: Stockbyte/Alamy Royalty Free; p. 349, *top left*: Evan Agostini/ImageDirect/Getty Images; p. 349, *top right*: Bill Olive/Getty Images; p. 349, *middle*: Bill Aron/PhotoEdit, Inc.; p. 351: Noel Hendrickson/Digital Vision/Getty Images Royalty Free; pp. 352 & 373: Zoriah/The Image Works; p. 353: Bill Aron/PhotoEdit, Inc.; p. 355: Emely/zefa/ Corbis; p. 356: Peter Hvizdak/The Image Works; p. 358: VCL/Taxi/Getty Images; p. 359: The Granger Collection; p. 360: Faces of Meth/Multnomah County Sheriff's Office; p. 361, top: Doug Menuez/ Photodisc/Getty Images Royalty Free; p. 361, middle: Gebhard Krewitt/ VISUM/The Image Works; p. 362, *top*: Stockbyte/Alamy Royalty Free; p. 362, *middle*: Tony Freeman/ PhotoEdit, Inc.; p. 362, *bottom*: Dana White/PhotoEdit, Inc.; p. 363: VStock/ Alamy Royalty Free; pp. 364, *top* & 374: AP Images/ Sakchai Lalit; p. 364, *middle*: David J. Green/Alamy; p. 364, bottom: Topham/ The Image Works; p. 365: moodboard/Corbis Royalty Free; p. 366, *top*: Alan Oddie/PhotoEdit, Inc.; p. 366, *bottom*: Christian O. Bruch/VISUM/The Image Works; p. 369: Envision/ Corbis; p. 371: Phototake, Inc./Alamy.

Chapter 11

pp. 376–377: Linda Rich/ArenaPAL/The Image Works; p. 379, *top*: The Kobal Collection/20th Century Fox/Dreamworks; p. 379, *bottom*: Tony Freeman/ PhotoEdit, Inc.; p. 380: BlueMoon Stock/Alamy; p. 384: Dr. Solomon Asch; p. 385: Courtesy of PG Zimbardo, Inc.; pp. 386, *top left* & 386, *bottom left*: PG Zimbardo, Inc.; p. 386, *top right*: AP Images; p. 386, *bottom right*: Courtesy Wikepedia.com/Zuma Press; p. 386, *bottom*: AP Images/Daniel Luna; p. 387: NASA/Getty Images; p. 388: AP Images/Ahn Young-joon; p. 389, *left*: AP Images/Joe Holloway Jr., Files; p. 389, *right*: AP Images/File; p. 391, center: Archives of the History of American Psychology—The University of Akron; pp. 391, surrounding & 413: From the film *Obedience* © Stanley Milgram, by permission of Alexandra Milgram; p. 393: William Philpott/Reuters/Corbis; pp. 394, *top* & 413: Photograph by Frans de Waal; p. 394, *middle*: The New York Times/Redux; p. 394, *bottom*: AP Images; p. 395, *top*: AP Images/Detroit Free Press, Steven R. Nickerson; pp. 395, *bottom* & 413: Justin Guariglia/National Geographic/Getty Images; p. 396: David Young-Wolff/PhotoEdit, Inc.; p. 397: Keith Brofsky/Digital Vision/Getty Images Royalty Free; p. 398: Bob Daemmrich/The Image Works; p. 399: BananaStock/ Jupiterimages Royalty Free; p. 401: Bob Daemmrich/PhotoEdit, Inc.; pp. 402 & 414: Peter Kramer/ Getty Images; p. 405, *top*: Kateland Photo; p. 405, *middle*: Barry Austin Photography/Photodisc/Getty Images Royalty Free; p. 407, *top*: AP Images/ Mannie Garcia; p. 409, all: Index Open/PhotosToGo; pp. 411 & 415: Bob Daemmrich.

Chapter 12

pp. 416–417: Taxi/Getty Images; p. 412: Joe McBride/Stone/Getty Images; p. 419: Julia Eisenberg/Lichtfilm GmbH; p. 420: Thomas Wanstall/The Image Works; pp. 421 & 448: P Deliss/Godong/Corbis; p. 424: Spencer Grant/ PhotoEdit, Inc.; p. 425: Library of Congress # LOT 11831-A; p. 427: Universal/The Kobal Collection; p. 428: Mary Evans/Sigmund Freud Copyrights/The Image Works; pp. 429 & 449: Ian Woodcock/Illustration Works/Getty Images; p. 431: Fancy/Veer/Corbis Royalty Free; pp. 432 & 449: Spencer Grant/PhotoEdit, Inc.; p. 433, top: John Birdsall/The Image Works; p. 433, bottom: Carl Rogers Memorial Library; pp. 434, top left & 450: Hulton-Deutsch Collection/CORBIS; pp. 434, top right & 450: JP Laffont/Sygma/Corbis; p. 434, bottom: Michael Nichols/National Geographic/Getty Images; pp. 435, top & 450: Sally and Richard Greenhill/Alamy; p. 435, bottom: H&S Produktion/CORBIS; p. 436: AP Images/Reed Saxon; p. 438, top: Bettmann/ Corbis; p. 438, bottom: Adrian Bradshaw/epa/Corbis; p. 439: Ausloeser/ zefa/CORBIS; p. 442: Courtesy of http://www.matthewbarr.co.uk/harrypotter; pp. 443, top & 451: Amamanta Family Anatomically Correct Dolls, www.amamantafamily.com; p. 443, bottom: Hulton Archive/Getty Images; p. 445: Mark Harwood/Alamy; p. 446: Eric Liebowitz/© CBS/Courtesy Everett Collection.

Chapter 13

pp. 452–453: © Theo Allofs/zefa/Corbis; pp. 455 & 484: ColorBlind Images/Blend Images/Corbis Royalty Free; p. 456: Corbis; p. 457, *top*: Aladin Abdel Naby/Reuters; p. 457, *middle*: Ed Quinn/Corbis; pp. 458 & 484: AP Images/Tony Dejak; p. 459: Janine Wiedel Photolibrary/Alamy; p. 460: American Psychiatric Association; p. 461: Getty Images; p. 463: Michael Newman/PhotoEdit, Inc.; p. 464, *top*: Purestock/Alamy Royalty Free; pp. 464, *middle* & 484: Photographer's Mate First Class Alan D. Monyelle/US Navy/ Reuters/Corbis; pp. 465 & 485: Bettmann/CORBIS; p. 467: Rosanne Olson/ Digital Vision/Getty Images Royalty Free; p. 470, *top*: Rob Melnychuk/ Digital Vision/Getty Images Royalty Free; p. 470, *middle*: Journal-Courier/ Steve Warmowski/The Image Works; p. 471: Steven Puetzer/Photographer's Choice/ Getty Images; p. 474: Paramount/Courtesy Everett Collection; pp. 476 & 486: AP Images/Florida Department of Corrections; pp. 477 & 486: AP Images/ The Denver Post, Karl Gehring; pp. 479 & 487: Phillip Dvorak/ Images.com; p. 480: Grunnitus Studio/Photo Researchers, Inc.; p. 481: Courtesy NIH— Dr. Daniel Weinberger, Clinical Brain Disorders Branch; p. 483: PHANIE/Photo Researchers, Inc.

Chapter 14

pp. 488–489: Martin Barraud/Getty Images; pp. 492 & 518: Formcourt (Form Advertising)/Alamy Royalty Free; pp. 493 & 518: HBO/Courtesy Everett Collection; p. 496: Richard Hutchings/PhotoEdit, Inc.; p. 497, *top*: Bill Aron/ PhotoEdit, Inc.; p. 497, *bottom*: Colin Young-Wolff/PhotoEdit, Inc.; p. 498: Amanda Rohde/iStockphoto; p. 499, top: Bill Aron/PhotoEdit, Inc.; pp. 499, *middle* & 519: Rainer Jensen/dpa/Corbis; p. 501: © Michael Fenichel; p. 503: Manchan/Digital Vision/Getty Images Royalty Free; p. 504: Mary Kate Denny/ PhotoEdit, Inc.; p. 505: Burke/Triolo Productions/Brand X/ Jupiterimages Royalty Free; pp. 507 & 520: Joel Gordon; p. 509, *top*: INSADCO Photography/Alamy Royalty Free; pp. 509, *bottom* & 520: John Foxx/Stockbyte/ Getty Images Royalty Free; p. 510: Robert Pitts/Landov; p. 512: Tom McCarthy/ PhotoEdit, Inc.; p. 513: Marcelo Wain/iStockphoto; p. 514: Steve Liss/Time & Life Pictures/Getty Images; p. 515: Will & Deni McIntyre/ Photo Researchers, Inc.; pp. 517 & 521: Ray Fisher/ Time & Life Pictures/Getty Images.